Hellenic Studies 79

Particles in Ancient Greek Discourse

Recent Titles in the Hellenic Studies Series

Agamemnon, the Pathetic Despot
Reading Characterization in Homer

Singer of Tales
Third Edition

One Man Show
The Dynamics of Performance in the Iliad *and* Odyssey

The Tears of Achilles

Equine Poetics

The Art of Reading
From Homer to Paul Celan

Masterpieces of Metonymy
From Ancient Greek Times to Now

The Aethiopis
Neo-Neoanalysis Reanalyzed

Kinyras
The Divine Lyre

The Theban Epics

Literary History in the Parian Marble

Plato's Four Muses
The Phaedrus *and the Poetics of Philosophy*

Plato's Wayward Path
Literary Form and the Republic

Dialoguing in Late Antiquity

Between Thucydides and Polybius
The Golden Age of Greek Historiography

Poetry as Initiation
The Center for Hellenic Studies Symposium on the Derveni Papyrus

Divine Yet Human Epics
Reflections of Poetic Rulers from Ancient Greece and India

The Web of Athenaeus

Eusebius of Caesarea
Tradition and Innovations

The Theology of Arithmetic
Number Symbolism in Platonism and Early Christianity

PARTICLES IN ANCIENT GREEK DISCOURSE

EXPLORING PARTICLE USE ACROSS GENRES

by
Anna Bonifazi, Annemieke Drummen,
and Mark de Kreij

CENTER FOR HELLENIC STUDIES
Trustees for Harvard University
Washington, DC
Distributed by Harvard University Press
Cambridge, Massachusetts, and London, England
2021

Particles in Ancient Greek Discourse: Exploring Particle Use across Genres
By Anna Bonifazi, Annemieke Drummen, and Mark de Kreij

Published by Center for Hellenic Studies, Trustees for Harvard University, Washington, D.C.
Distributed by Harvard University Press, Cambridge, Massachusetts and London, England
Printed by Maple Press, York, PA
Cover Design: Joni Godlove
Production: Kristin Murphy Romano

ISBN: 978-0-674-27129-6

Library of Congress Control Number (LCCN): 2021941954

Contents

Preface

Particles in Ancient Greek Discourse (*PAGD*) is the product of a collaborative project (2010-2015) funded by the German Research Foundation (DFG). Thanks to the support of the Center for Hellenic Studies, a freely-accessible online edition was published in March 2016 (http://nrs.harvard.edu/urn-3:hul.ebook:CHS_BonifaziA_DrummenA_deKreijM.Particles_in_Ancient_Greek_Discourse.2016). The 2016 acknowledgments outline the most important moments and interactions that accompanied the earlier years of the project. Since 2016, the authors have updated the research chapters and completed the online-only part of the work, the *Online Repository of Particle Studies* (ORPS). This preface will clarify how the two editions differ and what they have in common, and suggest ways to consult the work.

The initial title of the online version was *Particles in Ancient Greek Discourse: Five Volumes Exploring Particle Use Across Genres*. The print version encompasses all the research chapters from that online version (here called 'Parts' I to IV, formerly 'Volumes' I to IV) in this one tome. ORPS (Part V) is—and will continue to be—available only online (http://nrs.harvard.edu/URN-3:HLNC:CHS.Online_Repository_of_Particle_Studies), and is completely searchable. Since their size would have made it impossible for a single print volume to encompass all parts, the distribution and frequency graphs (I.5) appear exclusively online as well. A further difference is that only the print edition contains the Index of Subjects, conceived as a repertoire of recurring descriptions and linguistics topics that have informed and oriented our research. The online edition compensates for that by allowing readers to search for any term within the entire text.

At the time of printing, the body texts of the online and print editions are identical. Importantly, the numbering of parts, chapters, and paragraphs completely coincides, for ease of reference. Both editions include the bibliography, which incorporates all the full references, including those of ORPS, and—albeit partially—publications on ancient Greek particles published after 2016. The bibliography appears under I.6 in the online version, whereas in this print version you will find it at the beginning of the end matter, following the end of Part IV, Chapter 5. Likewise, both editions include the Particle Index (I.7 in the online version) and the Index Locorum. The Particle Index (p. 981) represents a guide not only to the actual items that are analyzed, but also to the terminology adopted to talk about their discourse functions. A glance at it may therefore be a good starting point for readers who want to get a quick illustration of the pragmatic and cognitive perspectives we employ in our chapters.

The present book can be consulted in many ways, by ancient author or by linguistic terms, by specific discourse perspectives (whole chapters), or by individual particles or particle combinations. At the same time, the different parts of the work build upon one another to produce a coherent analysis of the different kinds of discourse under discussion, and the reader will gain much from reading the research chapters in order. Unlike a lexicographical compilation, our analyses connect with the ancient idea that 'combiners' (σύνδεσμοι) co-signify (συσσημαίνουσι) together with the surrounding words.

In fact, through the discussion of ancient Greek instances, the book can also be seen as a contribution to general topics in discourse analysis and pragmatics such as anaphoric comprehension, dialogic syntax, discourse acts and moves, Conversation Analysis, stance-taking, segmentation, and coordination—besides, of course, discourse particles.

The tome includes the analysis of 461 Greek passages, consistently accompanied by English translations. The comments offer plenty of grammatical explanations, and often challenge traditional readings and labels. This is meant to draw the attention of philologists, commentators, teachers, and scholars of ancient Greek to the ways in which language phenomena can illuminate literary meanings.

Over the past few years, the study of ancient Greek particles has increased remarkably. The authors hope that this work and the research behind it will be received as one of the steps in the current reshaping of the knowledge of particles and, more generally, of the ancient Greek language.

How to Cite the Print Edition

Please refer to *PAGD* as "Bonifazi, Drummen, de Kreij 2021." The volume reflects the team research done by the authors; yet not every part is co-authored. To cite individually-authored chapters from the work, please refer to I.2 and all the chapters in Part II (pp. 99-325) as De Kreij 2021; I.3 and all the chapters in Part III (pp. 327-564) as Drummen 2021; and all the chapters in Part IV (pp. 565-879) as Bonifazi 2021.

In order to make consultations flexible and simple to reference in either online or print format, please use section and/or paragraph numbers—with or without page numbers—in your citations.

2021 Acknowledgments

We would like to warmly thank additional scholars who, since 2016, have shared their wisdom with us and offered comments on individual chapters: Rutger Allan, Ronald Blankenborg, David Goldstein, Alex Hollmann, Elizabeth Minchin, Lars Nordgren, and Gerry Wakker. Our gratefulness extends to the numerous colleagues who in the last years have given us feedback on *PAGD*, and on what *PAGD* means to them. Finally, we sincerely thank Martin Wewers for his multiple editorial checks across the editions, and Pinelopi Ioannidou for later checks.

We are now even more indebted to the whole editorial board of the CHS for its very generous efforts and the continuous support. In particular, we cannot thank enough Lenny Muellner for his insights in all the important moments of the journey towards the print volume, and Noel Spencer for his unfailing assistance with the online updates throughout. Our heartfelt thanks especially to Jill Curry Robbins, who shepherded the whole book production ingeniously, and Kristin Murphy Romano for her meticulous work on the book design.

Finally, special thanks to our families, growing and expanding, for their warm presence. They remain a source of inspiration.

Anna Bonifazi
Annemieke Drummen
Mark de Kreij
June 2021

PART I

FOUNDATIONS

I.1

General Introduction

§1. The study of ancient Greek particles has been an integral part of the study of the Greek language from its earliest beginnings. Among the first parts of speech to be distinguished in Greek scholarship were the σύνδεσμοι ("combiners"), which include the later category of particles.[1] In the Renaissance, Matthaeus Devarius—a Greek scholar working in Rome—published a monograph on particles only sixteen years after Estienne's *Thesaurus Linguae Graecae*,[2] and in the nineteenth century many great German philologists devoted considerable attention to particles and their forms, functions, and meanings.[3] In the second half of the twentieth century Greek particles have returned to scholarly attention, partly as a result of the developments in contemporary linguistics. In the Emmy-Noether project "The Pragmatic Functions and Meanings of Ancient Greek Particles," carried out in the Classics department of the University of Heidelberg (2010-2014), we have traced more than two millennia of research on Greek particles, and taken stock of current work on particles, both within and beyond ancient Greek. Building on the foundations of this scholarship, in this monograph we undertake an analysis of particle use across five genres of ancient Greek discourse: epic, lyric, tragedy, comedy, and historiography.

1.1 The Extent of the Project

§2. The genres listed above are represented by the following works: for epic, Homer's *Iliad* and *Odyssey*;[4] for lyric, Pindar's *Victory Odes*; for tragedy, Aeschylus' *Agamemnon*, *Libation Bearers*, and *Persians*, Sophocles' *Ajax*, *Antigone*, and *Oedipus King*, and Euripides' *Bacchae*, *Hippolytus*, and *Medea*; for comedy, Aristophanes' *Birds*, *Frogs*, and *Lysistrata*; and for historiography, the *Histories* of Herodotus and Thucydides.[5] The selected corpus entails

1 Aristotle, *Poetics* 1456b20-21, see I.2.4 for the earliest scholarship on σύνδεσμοι.

2 Estienne 1572a-d and Devarius 1588.

3 E.g. Gottfried Hermann, August Immanuel Bekker, and Karl Brugmann.

4 For some quantitative analyses we have limited ourselves to a selection of four books of the *Iliad* and four books of the *Odyssey*.

5 For some quantitative analyses we have limited ourselves to a selection of the first two books of Herodotus' *Histories* and the first two books of Thucydides' *Histories*.

limitation: on the one hand it does not represent any of the genres completely, while on the other hand it excludes important genres of the Archaic and Classical periods, such as iambos, philosophical discourse, and oratory. Even so, the range of authors and texts we focus on represents complete and well-studied examples of five genres, it includes both poetry and prose, and it covers Greek literature from the earliest source (Homer) to the middle of the Classical period (Aristophanes). Thus, our corpus gives a representative cross-section of early Greek discourse, while at the same time comprising texts of each genre that are large enough to better understand the influence of genre on particle use.

§3. In practice, we are concerned especially with the particles that occur most frequently in our corpus. We consider particles both on their own and as components of different combinations, some of which have come to serve a new function (clusters).[6] Our analyses range from global, such as frequency patterns in different genres and discourse situations, to local, in the form of close readings of individual passages. The local and global dimensions of our research complement and inform one another. Finally, where relevant we address questions of textual criticism and diachronic development. However, our focus throughout is on the synchronic functions of a certain particle or particle combinations, across different genres, authors, contexts, and co-texts.

1.2 Goals

§4. Particles are pervasive in Greek literature, and the attentive reader knows how important they are for interpretation. In this work we offer new tools for making sense of these words. The readings we propose point to multiple phenomena that impact the force[7] of particles and particle combinations.

§5. This work has the following metascientific, theoretical, and analytic goals. Metascientifically, we aim to reveal the wealth of particle studies up to the present. No fewer than fourteen monographs on Greek particles have appeared between 1588 and 1995,[8] not to mention the hundreds of insights in dedicated articles as well as entries in grammars, thesauruses, and lexica.

§6. On the theoretical level, we aim to raise awareness of dimensions of language besides the syntactic organization of texts and the semantics of their content. We pursue this goal by paying attention to a wider range of parameters than is usual when segmenting and interpreting classical texts, for example the communicative strategies, cognitive processes, and interactional dynamics of language production.

6 See below, §19.

7 See below, §16.

8 Devarius 1588, Hoogeveen 1769, Hartung 1832-33, Stephens 1837, Bäumlein 1861, Paley 1881, Des Places 1929, Denniston 1950 [1934], Labéy 1950, Thrall 1962, Blomqvist 1969, Thyresson 1977, Van Ophuijsen and Sicking 1993, and Redondo Moyano 1995.

§7. Analytically, we believe that it is important to take a holistic view of particles and particle combinations. By this we mean that in our analyses we intend to study particles *in situ*, within their co-text (co-occurring verbal features) and context, in order to identify and explain patterns of particle use. By context we mean the extralinguistic factors that influence the discourse in question, such as the occasion, the historical background, the explicit and implicit participants, and the speaker or writer's attitudes towards the subject. In particular, we explore how the particles relate to the most global contextual factor of genre: their use can be connected to the overarching goals and formal conventions of epic, lyric, tragedy, comedy, and historiography.

1.3 The Term "Particle"

§8. The term "particle" is potentially infelicitous, but we have chosen to employ it nonetheless. In the current section we first outline the problems of the term, and then explain our reasons for keeping it. Cross-linguistically, the lexical category "particles" is ill-defined.[9] It is insufficient to say that particles are indeclinable, since many adverbs and prepositions are too.[10] The fact that many particles are monosyllabic is likewise not a defining quality: there are disyllabic particles, and many other kinds of words can be monosyllabic. Attempting to define them functionally would be an improvement, as by saying that particles do not contribute propositional meaning—they do not add content. However, particles can contribute to propositional meaning, and other words can work non-propositionally (e.g. sentence adverbs). As a result, the boundaries of the category we call particles are fuzzy.

§9. In the study of ancient Greek, a group of words has formed the core of the group of "particles" from the earliest scholarship, at which point all such function words, mainly including adverbs and conjunctions, were known as "combiners" (σύνδεσμοι).[11] Renaissance scholars retrieved the notion of σύνδεσμοι, and progressively refined and delimited it, by producing a more or less fixed list of *particulae* that we have inherited.[12]

§10. We have decided to retain the word "particle" instead of choosing some other term for the following reasons. First, "particle" is neutral with respect to the notions "conjunctions" and "adverbs." We want to explore the relationship between the connective and adverbial functions of particles in a pragmatic perspective (as the next section clarifies), instead of regarding their syntactic role as either conjunctions or adverbs their

9 See I.3 for a more elaborate discussion of the problems in definition in contemporary linguistics.

10 For example, in Indo-European linguistics the term covers all indeclinable parts of language, such as affixes, suffixes, and prepositions.

11 A recent team project carried out in Spain on ancient Greek has given the title "Conjunctive Adverbs" to its research (see Crespo 2009). Their idea that there is something between adverbs and conjunctions harmonizes with the ancient unifying notion of "combiners."

12 The particles discussed by Bäumlein 1861 and Denniston 1934 (first edition of *The Greek Particles*) represent the core of the group of words currently regarded as particles.

raison d'être. Second, "particle" does not require *a priori* distinctions between words that have a propositional meaning and those that are only used non-propositionally.[13] On the one hand, the same lexical item can be used both propositionally and non-propositionally depending on genre or context. On the other hand, words can come to have a non-propositional value over time (e.g. τοι, ἰδού, λοιπόν).[14] Third, on a metascientific level it makes sense to retain a term that has survived centuries of scholarship, even if problems and unresolved questions continue to exist.

§11. Rather than working on a closed group of lexical items, we focus on particles in terms of a core and a periphery. The core consists of the list inherited from earlier scholarship, of which we have selected those that are most frequent in our corpus. The periphery potentially includes all other words or phrases that work non-propositionally in our corpus. By extension, discussions of other adverbials, connectives, and phrases used as metalanguage are mostly subsidiary, and our analyses primarily concern the "core" particles, such as δή and τε.

1.4 The Discourse Approach: Key Concepts

§12. Central to our monograph is the concept of discourse. This concept is anchored by the following key ideas: discourse is always situated, because it coincides with real utterances produced by people;[15] discourse is a process rather than an object, because it involves the negotiation of meaning;[16] discourse is often multimodal, an interaction between verbal and nonverbal media.[17] In line with these ideas, we regard discourse as a comprehensive concept. Additionally, we regard it as a superordinate concept: with respect to questions that are familiar to classical philologists and literary critics, "discourse" encompasses varieties in literary genre, in register, and in the level of textualization of works,[18] as well as poetry-prose distinctions.

§13. In our research, then, we apply Discourse Analysis, which in the words of Brown and Yule (1983:1), is "the analysis of language in use." This kind of analysis does not restrict itself to formal properties of language: it considers language's functions and manners in an effort to integrate the many ways in which utterances encode meanings.[19]

13 It is primarily for this reason that we do not view particles as fully coinciding with "discourse markers": as I.3 illustrates, discourse markers are typically defined on the basis of their non-propositional value.

14 See Cavallin 1941 for an analysis of (τὸ) λοιπόν as a word with non-propositional value.

15 This is the approach favored by Schiffrin in her 1994 monograph (*Approaches to Discourse*).

16 See Widdowson 1995:164.

17 "Multimodal discourse" appears first in Kress and Van Leeuwen 2001.

18 In Ong's terms (1984:5) textualization starts "when someone devises a way of putting the words of a language into a script."

19 Lakoff 2003 claims that Discourse Analysis has to rest on an interdisciplinary theory and method, from fields such as cognitive studies and socio-linguistics, as well as syntax and semantics.

A distinctive characteristic of Discourse Analysis is the consideration of language above the sentence level, that is, consideration of continuous blocks of texts on a larger scale.[20]

§14. The general perspective that informs Discourse Analysis is the pragmatic perspective on language. Pragmatics is "a general cognitive, social, and cultural perspective on linguistic phenomena in relation to their usage in forms of behaviour" (Verschueren 1999:7). Pragmatic analyses pay particular attention to two general phenomena: the ways in which the nonverbal context influences the syntactic and semantic choices of speakers, and the ways in which things are meant without being explicitly said. In other words, a pragmatic perspective illuminates the "how" rather than the "what" of messages.[21]

§15. The how of messages can be conveyed through something called metalanguage: in contrast to language, whose objects of reference are unrestricted, metalanguage is confined to communication about language itself, "about the process of using language" (Maschler 2009:1). A common conjunction like "and" can achieve a metalinguistic goal, in certain contexts:

(t1)

1. Yesterday we went to the movies *and* afterwards we went to the pub for a beer.

2. Why didn't Peter show up? *And*, where were you that night?

Van Dijk 1979:450

While in 1. "and" connects states of affairs (going to the movies and going to the pub), in 2. "and" connects the actions of the speaker (hence the metalinguistic value). Those actions consist in asking two questions that appear to have a joint purpose. Ancient Greek particles and particle combinations prototypically encode metalinguistic functions and meanings. Our chapters shed light on how particles signal, for instance, how the discourse is going to proceed, how traditional content is recalled, how accounts are segmented into manageable pieces, and how internal speakers exploit metalanguage. All these considerations illustrate the "doing of saying," to recall Austin's famous claim:[22] particles reflect metalinguistic action by marking, for example, narrative expansions and closings, or the insertion of evaluative or emotional comments.

20 Discourse Analysis shares this attention to blocks of discourse with narratology, a method that has been ever more prevalent in the study of ancient texts (e.g. De Jong 1987, 2001, (ed.) 2007, (ed.) 2012; Grethlein and Rengakos (eds) 2009).

21 An aspect of the "how" of messages concerns the Topic and the Focus relations between words, which has been explored in several works on ancient Greek sentences (e.g. Dik 1995 and 2007; Scheppers 2011).

22 *How to do things with words*, Austin 1962.

§16. Discourse Analysis and pragmatics are particularly well-suited to the study of particles, as particles tend to be syntactically irrelevant and semantically unstable. Ancient Greek grammarians speak of the δύναμις ("force") of combiners, rendered in later Latin works as the *vis* and *potestas* of particles. These terms convey the intangible quality of the discursive contribution of particles—what we regard as their elusive power to imply things left unsaid, as well as speakers' ability of doing by saying.

§17. The pragmatic perspective is relevant to any type of text, including those that were meant to be read silently. Literary texts undoubtedly are actual language, not an abstract and atemporal set of linguistic forms. All texts reveal a complex interlacing between verbal and nonverbal elements that encode meanings. The pragmatic approach is especially useful for studying texts designed for performance, because of the prominence of nonverbal meanings, and the fact that performed language is embodied.

1.5 A Discourse Approach to Ancient Greek Particles

§18. From a discourse perspective, the ill-defined nature of the term "particle" may yield theoretical advances. Language use is not black and white: categories usually have fuzzy boundaries. The interface between the non-propositional and propositional values of the individual items indicates multifunctionality, and points to the essential fact that they work together with other words to signify (συσσημαίνειν).[23] Our approach is therefore the opposite of a lexicographic one, which attaches specific meanings to individual lexical items. On the contrary, particles can only express specific meanings in constructions together with other linguistic or situational features: particles in isolation are not "explanatory," "indignant," "progressive," or the like. Moreover, a lexicographic approach would be limiting from the outset, because it is based on classifications that do not hold up in actual discourse.

§19. One important situation to consider is when a particle's co-text includes another particle, in which case we speak of particle combinations. Whenever the function of a particle combination cannot be explained as a sum of its component parts' functions, we call it a cluster. In these cases the different particles have a joint pragmatic function. An example is καὶ δὴ καί in several instances in Herodotus. In other cases, adjacent particles each have separate functions, as with καὶ γάρ in Homeric poetry.

§20. One of the features of the co-text that are essential for a particle's interpretation is its position. The reason is that the position of a particle may be linked to its scope. By scope we mean the extent of discourse over which a particle's contribution has effect.[24] When a particle is found in its first possible position—i.e. at the very start

23 The term συσσημαίνειν ("co-signifying") is used by Apollonius Dyscolus and by Heliodorus when discussing σύνδεσμοι; see I.2 §§61, 64n131, and 83.

24 We discuss the scope of all particles according to this broad definition of "scope." Other scholars call a specific group of particles "scope particles"; see, e.g., Van Emde Boas *et al.* 2019:692-694;

for prepositives such as ἀλλά, ἦ, or καί, or in peninitial position for postpositives such as γε, δέ, or μέν—it tends to have scope over its host unit.[25] Some particles (for example γε, δή, and καί) can also have smaller scope, over only an adjacent word or phrase; this is the most likely reading when those particles occur in a later position in a clause. In combination with other features, particles may also mark major transitions, or project large discourse units. Examples are γάρ marking the start of a new section in Thucydides, or οὖν marking a preliminary question in dramatic dialogue.

§21. The effect of a particle with small scope may have been partly prosodic, lending emphasis to the adjacent word. In fact, although particles are a verbal component of the ancient Greek language, several of their functions coincide with functions that in modern languages are fulfilled through paralinguistic means. That is, some of their functions may be best rendered in spoken English by intonation, while in written language they may be represented in the form of punctuation.

1.6 Guiding Questions

§22. The following questions exemplify the key concepts, methodology, and approach that we have outlined in this introduction. These are questions we have asked ourselves individually and as a group, benefiting from an ongoing dialectic, which in turn has led us to further questions. Each time we have encountered a particle or particle combination in a new passage, and each time we have examined a stretch of text containing multiple particles, our primary question has been, what is going on in the discourse? This ranges from the level of the co-text to that of the context, and also to the overarching issues of genre.

- Which linguistic features co-occur? In particular, are other pragmatically relevant elements, such as tense or anaphoric markers, co-present?[26] What does the whole co-signify?
- What communicative goal lies behind the current stretch of discourse?
- What is the scope of the particle(s)?
- Who is involved in the current piece of communication (speaking 'I', addressees, interlocutors, co-present characters)?

Sicking 1986:125, 135, 138; Wakker 1994:307-342, 363-364.

25 Chapter II.2 shows that the host unit need not be a syntactic clause, but can also be a phrase.

26 The discourse sensitivity of tense is explored, for example, in Bakker 2007 and in Adema 2008; that of anaphoric choices is explored, for example, in Kroon 2009 and in Bonifazi 2012. In general, our approach subscribes Bakker's (2010b) claim that the pragmatic dimension of ancient Greek texts is crucial—he points out in particular the importance of phenomena such as deixis, the anaphoric use of pronouns, and tense.

- Does the passage in question resonate with a preceding or following excerpt (not necessarily contiguous)? If so, what are the similarities and differences?
- Does the current stretch of discourse have an expected or projected place in some large-scale pattern, such as a conversational sequence, a script, an argumentative scheme, or a generic *topos*?
- To which macro-genre and to which sub-genre (if any) does the current discourse belong?
- How is this communicative place realized in other works or in other parts of the same work?
- Are there any linguistic patterns that recur in parallel examples? Can patterns and parallel examples illuminate *ad hoc* philological issues?
- How do the same particles make sense in different genres?

It is through continual discussion and comparison of evidence that we have approached the effort to answer our overriding question: "what is *here* the discourse function of particle X?"

1.7 Outline of the Work

§23. The monograph consists of five parts: I. Foundations; II. Particle Use in Homer and Pindar; III. Particle Use in Aeschylus, Sophocles, Euripides, and Aristophanes; IV. Particle Use in Herodotus and Thucydides; V. Online Repository of Particle Studies (ORPS). The first part includes this general introduction, a chapter on particle studies from ancient scholarship to the Renaissance, a chapter on current approaches to particles and discourse markers, and the general conclusions. The second, third, and fourth parts explore co-textual and contextual phenomena associated with particles in epic and lyric, in tragedy and comedy, and in historiography. The final part (V) gathers summaries of the modern (post-1500) research on twelve particles, and is meant to be a searchable database.

1.7.1 Part I

§24. Soon after the classical period, many of the particles used in Homeric and Classical poetry had ceased to be current and begged explanation. Starting with the scholia to the *Iliad*, chapter I.2 (*From* σύνδεσμος *to* Particula, by Mark de Kreij) tracks the history of the study of particles through early grammars, rhetorical works, and lexica, ranging from the third century BCE to the late Middle Ages. Although these early authors often employed different terms, or eschewed technical terminology altogether, many salient observations in modern literature can in fact be traced far back in time.

§25. Modern languages contain many lexical items that function similarly to Greek particles. These items—variously designated by terms such as "discourse markers," "pragmatic markers," and "discourse particles"—have been extensively studied in different theoretical frameworks. Our understanding of what writers and (represented) speakers do with Greek particles greatly profits from these studies, as they draw attention to different aspects of communication. Chapter I.3 (*Approaches to Particles and Discourse Markers*, by Annemieke Drummen) discusses selected approaches and their application i the study of ancient Greek particles.

1.7.2 Part II

§26. In this part, particles are considered from the perspective of performance of epic and lyric. Chapters II.2 (*Discourse Acts*) and II.3 (*Moves*) are devoted to the segmentation of discourse on a local and global level. Discourse proceeds in small steps, discourse acts, which are a crucial domain of particle analysis (II.2). Acts are equally important for understanding the hexameter verses of epic and the flow of lyric song. When groups of acts share a center of interest, they form larger segments of discourse called moves. These moves can take the form of embedded narratives or episodes within stories, but also include Pindaric *gnômai* and other metanarrative comments. Particles form an important part of the metalinguistic tools at the performer's disposal when negotiating transitions between such moves in the discourse (II.3).

§27. Performer and audience are participants in an interaction, and parts of a larger culture and tradition. It is the performer's task to maintain the body of inherited knowledge shared with the listener that reaches beyond the current discourse: the Homeric and Pindaric performances are always moments in the continuum of tradition. Existing and emergent assumptions about this shared knowledge, or discourse memory, are reflected in particle use (II.4: *Discourse Memory*). One aspect of the negotiation of shared knowledge is the process of referent tracking, the cognitive activity of the audience to keep track of the characters in a discourse. A performer of epic and lyric employs multiple forms of anaphoric reference along with different particles to guide the listener in this process (II.5: *Particles and Anaphoric Reference*).

1.7.3 Part III

§28. The communication represented in dramatic texts provides a unique opportunity to investigate dialogic features of language use. Visible in the texts are linguistic reflections of the live interaction that occurred among different speakers co-present on stage. At the same time, each play consists of various parts that are situationally as well as linguistically quite diverse. These play-internal differences are explored in chapter III.2 (*Varying One's Speech: Discourse Patterns*). For particle interpretation it is essential to know in which communicative situation a particle is usually found, and which features tend to co-occur.

§29. Chapters III.3 (*Reusing Others' Words: Resonance*) and III.4 (*Speaking in Turns: Conversation Analysis*) focus on the plays' dialogic parts, applying different pragmatic frameworks that were originally developed for the analysis of modern spoken language. The process of resonance (III.3) concerns how playwrights and characters reuse verbal elements for specific pragmatic goals. Particles may indicate how such echoes are intended, or they may be echoed themselves. *Conversation Analysis* (III.4) investigates the structures and rules of dialogic interaction—essential determinants for understanding particles in drama. For example, the interpretation of particles depends on their position in a turn of speaking, in a pair of initiating and reacting turns, and in a series of such pairs. Finally, chapter III.5 (*Reflecting Emotional States of Mind: Calmness Versus Agitation*) discusses how particle use, together with other linguistic features, reflects a character's calm or agitated state of mind.

1.7.4 Part IV

§30. The shaping of the historiographical texts of Herodotus and Thucydides does not depend on meter, music, and the physical presence of actors on stage. In order to articulate discourse, the two historiographers rely on resources that are more closely bound to the verbal level of communication. Still, there is the possibility that Herodotus' *Histories* were publicly delivered; in that case several linguistic features would facilitate the aural processing of discourse. However minor the degree of performativeness may be, particles in Herodotean and Thucydidean discourse are hinges between content and its presentation. Some of their functions can be compared to those of paralinguistic marking, and often encode metalanguage.

§31. Chapter IV.2 (*Multifunctionality of δέ, τε, and καί*) discusses a major device for narrative progress in historiography: *and*-connectives. When observed in situ, δέ, τε, and καί in each work reveal a range of functions that is wider and subtler than what is commonly assumed. The syntactic dichotomy between conjunctions and adverbs can be overcome by the idea of a continuum from propositional to pragmatically enriched meanings. Chapter IV.3 (*Discourse Segmentation*) sets forth first the relationship between prosody and punctuation, and the main differences between ancient and modern punctuation of ancient Greek texts. It also recalls ancient views on *kôla* and *kómmata*, together with the contemporary revival of the notion of prose colometry. The second part of the chapter focuses on the crucial role of particles and other linguistic features in identifying potential discourse acts and moves. Chapter IV.4 (*Tracking Voice and Stance*) analyzes occurrences of particles that mark one or more components of stance, that is, positioning, evaluating, and aligning. Ironic and polyphonic readings are investigated, as well as the contribution of particles to authorial assessments. Finally, chapter IV.5 offers a close reading of four excerpts (a narrative section and a speech for each author); it combines attention to segmentation, to voice and stance, and to *and*-coordination.

1.7.5 Part V (available online)

§32. The body of literature on particles before and after Denniston 1934 is much larger than most recent literature seems to be aware of. Notes on particles in modern commentaries tend to refer to Denniston first and foremost, and rarely to older or even to more recent works. A reason for this unduly limited focus may well be the lack of accessibility of the older studies on particles. Our online guides to particle scholarship were conceived with a view toward filling this gap in collective knowledge. They include all the discussions that we have been able to trace, from early modern scholarship to the most recent publications, concerning twelve of the most frequent or opaque particles in our corpus (ἀλλά, ἄρα/ἆρα, γάρ, γε, δέ, δή, ἦ, καί, μέν, μήν (μέν/μάν), οὖν (ὦν), τε) along with their combinations.

§33. The repository is ordered chronologically per particle and completely searchable. This organization allows for diachronic research (studies on a certain particle through time), synchronic research (studies on different particles by the same scholar), and associative research (study of a certain term, author, or combination within the scholarship on one particle or multiple particles).

I.2

From σύνδεσμοι to *Particulae*

Mark de Kreij

2.1 Introduction

§1. The group of lexical items generally called particles has never been clearly defined. Despite many attempts, no one has yet succeeded in isolating them based either on their form or their function.[1] The ancient grammarians had the same problem, barring the fact that they did not have to wrestle with the term particles, as it was not defined as a single word group yet. From the fourth century BCE onward, the lexical items under consideration were gathered among the conjunctions and in some cases the adverbs. Establishing the history of the scholarship on particles is complicated by the fact that our knowledge of the early study of grammar is sketchy at best. Therefore, the genesis of grammar as a field of study needs to be outlined, before we will attempt to reconstruct the ancient views on particles.

§2. In the following, I briefly outline the history of ancient Greek grammar in antiquity, first presenting in broad terms the vexed nature of our evidence, then focusing on the discussion surrounding the *Téchnē Grammatikê* attributed to Dionysius Thrax. I then turn to descriptions of particles themselves, starting from Aristotle's and Diogenes of Babylon's reported descriptions of the σύνδεσμος, the ancient word group closest to the modern notion of particle. A considerable section is devoted to σύνδεσμοι in the scholia, followed by the few extant discussions of the topic in the ancient grammarians up to Apollonius Dyscolus. Apollonius Dyscolus' *Περὶ συνδέσμων*, the only extant monograph on the word group from antiquity, then receives ample attention, before turning to the

1 As implicitly acknowledged, but summarily put to one side, by Sicking 1986:25-26, Schenkeveld 1988:81, and Duhoux 2006:520-523. Denniston 1934:xxxvii claims that he will attempt a definition, but what follows is a forty-five page description of those words that he regards as particles, not anything that qualifies as a true definition. See also Pinkster 1972:135n2 for problems with the term particle in general and I.3 for an overview of the discussion on particles and discourse markers in contemporary linguistics.

ancient grammarians after Apollonius Dyscolus through late antiquity and the medieval period, and finally early modern works on particles.

§3. Since it is my purpose to cover discussions of particles spanning almost two millennia, the chapter is necessarily selective. I have, however, tried to represent every kind of relevant source, offering closer analysis wherever the content warranted it. Finally, this chapter is meant as a background for the "Online Repository of Particle Studies" (part V) and the research presented in the individual parts. As such, it aims to offer both an idea of the starting point for early modern researchers, as well as a broader perspective on the degree of innovation—or lack of it—portrayed by later authors.

2.2 Early Study of Grammar

§4. It is now broadly agreed that the Stoic philosophers played a crucial role in developing thought on language and in defining the parts of speech.[2] In the third and second centuries BCE, the Alexandrian librarians Aristophanes of Byzantium and Aristarchus adopted the terms coined by the Stoics in their commentaries on ancient texts. Since direct sources for the Stoic philosophers are lacking, these Alexandrian commentaries form an important source for this early period. However, these commentaries did not survive directly, but eventually ended up as separate notes in the margin of manuscripts of literary texts. As a result, there is little certainty if the terminology found in these *scholia* can actually be traced back to the third- and second-century BCE.[3]

§5. In an important work on the grammatical thought of Aristarchus, Matthaios argues that the Alexandrian librarian already distinguished the eight parts of speech that would become standard later.[4] This claim notwithstanding, the several layers through which the notes of the Alexandrian commentators are filtered keep us from establishing firmly how far they had progressed to an actual theory of grammar and/or syntax. In fact, the evidence from contemporary and later sources suggests that grammar was not yet established as an independent field of study in the third and second century BCE,

2 Their activities are generally not regarded as linguistics, however, since if their starting point was always language as a reflection of the thinkable, i.e. the sayable, instead of instantiations of language, that is, actual texts or speech. Pagani 2011:23n27 gives the most relevant references regarding the Stoics and their influence on the study of linguistics.

3 See Matthaios 1999:193-198 with notes for an exposition of the problems.

4 See Matthaios 2002:163-169, the eight categories are: ὄνομα (noun), ῥῆμα (verb), μετοχή (participle), ἄρθρον (article), ἀντωνυμία (pronoun), πρόθεσις (preposition), ἐπίρρημα (adverb), σύνδεσμος (combiner). From the first grammars onward there appears to have been a constant discussion of the number of grammatical word categories, most grammarians arguing for eight or nine categories. See for instance Matthaios 2002:171 for a schema of the different grammarians and their particular system, and 171-213 for a discussion of the possible development. As far as Aristarchus is concerned, De Jonge and Van Ophuijsen 2010:496 take it from Matthaios and regard it as the *communis opinio* that Aristarchus already used a system of eight word categories.

neither as a theoretical exercise in philosophy nor as an *ad hoc* terminology in service of philology.[5]

§6. The scarcity of material between the Alexandrian commentators and the fully developed study of grammar by Apollonius Dyscolus in the second century CE (roughly four hundred years later), makes it practically impossible to know when exactly the decisive step to grammar as an autonomous field was taken. The evidence we do have has led scholars to posit an important shift in attitude in the first century BCE.[6] Taylor claims that Varro's *Lingua Latina*, composed in this period, is the first work to clearly show an application of the Stoic ideas in an independent study of grammar. But as we have lost all of the books on syntax, the part of his work that might best have substantiated or contradicted this claim, it is hard to agree or disagree with Taylor, even if his argument is persuasive.[7]

§7. The material from the second century CE shows that the study of grammar had been established by this point at the latest. The two crucial bodies of evidence from the first two centuries of our era are the grammatical papyri and the works of Apollonius Dyscolus.[8] The papyri contain basic short textbooks on grammar, often referred to as "school grammars." Although they differ from each other in form and content, they are all clearly part of a certain genre. The work of Apollonius Dyscolus stands at the other end of a methodological spectrum. Rather than little handbooks, his treatises are scholarly discussions of different aspects of grammar into the very details.[9]

§8. Current scholarship generally posits a roughly linear development from the pragmatic textual notes by third century BCE commentators to the full-fledged grammatical analysis in Apollonius Dyscolus. However, this hypothesis has two significant problems: the first is that it is based upon scanty evidence, and the second is that the evidence we do have is hard to date. Central to both issues is the *Téchnē Grammatikê* attributed to Dionysius Thrax. If this treatise is indeed accepted as the work of the second century BCE grammarian, it is proof of the early systematic study of language, but recently numerous scholars have challenged its authenticity, dating at least part of the *Téchnē* to after Apollonius Dyscolus. The question of the authenticity of this text is therefore a crucial point in any discussion of the development of the study of grammar.

5 Ax 1991:288 describes Aristarchus' approach to grammar as a "*Grammatik im Kopf*," a grammar in the mind.

6 Di Benedetto 1958:196-206, 1959:118, and 1973; Pinborg 1975:110-114; Siebenborn 1976:13; Fehling 1979:489; Taylor 1987:11; cf. Schmidhauser 2010:508. Schenkeveld 1994:287 adds the rise of *hellenismos* as a factor in the development of grammar in the first century BCE.

7 Varro, *Lingua Latina*, edited by Traglia 1974; of the originally twenty-five books, only Books 5-10 are partially extant. Taylor makes his argument in 1987:14-16.

8 See Di Benedetto 1958:185-196 for discussions, Wouters 1979 for additional editions, and also Wouters 1995 for discussions of the grammatical papyri.

9 Apart from his *Syntax*, treatises on adverbs, σύνδεσμοι (on which more below), and pronouns are (partially) extant.

In the following section we discuss the most important primary and secondary material pertaining to the issue.

2.3 The *Téchnē* Attributed to Dionysius Thrax

§9. Dionysius Thrax was a student of Aristarchus and worked from the second to first century BCE. Several works are attributed to him, but not a single treatise has survived in its entirety, except for the *Téchnē Grammatikê*, transmitted in multiple manuscripts and some papyri.[10] The *Téchnē* is a grammatical treatise that consists of twenty chapters: the first provides a definition of grammar, the second to fourth discuss prosody, the fifth traces the history and etymology of rhapsody, and the remainder of the work provides an overview of word classes and their forms and functions. In the second century CE, Sextus Empiricus quotes from the first four chapters of the treatise, attributing a definition of grammar directly to Dionysius Thrax. Since the quotation comes within a discussion of different definitions of grammar, proceeding diachronically, this has been adduced to prove that Dionysius Thrax did indeed write at least this part of the *Téchnē*. There is no such direct or indirect evidence for the rest of the treatise.[11]

§10. The *Téchnē's* authenticity was doubted in antiquity, but these doubts were laid to rest in the nineteenth century.[12] The problem was not picked up again until the second half of the twentieth century. The current discussion is roughly divided into two camps, with several scholars attempting—with differing degrees of success—to reconcile the two. On one side are the scholars who rekindled the discussion of the *Téchnē's* authenticity, led by Di Benedetto and including Pinborg, Siebenborn, and Fehling.[13] They argue that the *Téchnē* as we have it cannot have been a second century BCE composition. Instead, they believe that it obtained its current form only in the third or fourth century CE. Most strongly opposed to the idea that the *Téchnē* is a compilation, with different parts authored at different times, are Pfeiffer, Erbse, and more recently, Wouters.[14] Wouters bases his conclusions on grammatical papyri dating back to as early as the first century

10 The earliest papyri date from the fifth or sixth centuries CE: Pap. Hal. 55 a and PSI I 18, see Di Benedetto 1973:801-802.

11 Sextus Empiricus quotes Thrax's definition of grammar in *Against the Mathematicians* I 57, with only a slight variation compared to the manuscripts of the *Téchnē*. A discussion of the variation can be found in Pagani 2011:18, with further bibliography in notes 6 and 7.

12 Taylor 1987:8. The most recent editions are Kemp 1987, Lallot 1998, and Callipo 2011.

13 Di Benedetto 1958-1959, 1973, and 1990, Pinborg 1975:103-106, Siebenborn 1976:12-13, and Fehling 1979:488-489. For a discussion of the most important discrepancies in the tradition, see Di Benedetto 1958:171-178, Pagani 2011:33, and the scholia to the *Téchnē*, Hilgard 1901:160.24-161.18.

14 Pfeiffer 1968:267-272, Erbse 1980:244-258, and Wouters 1995:95-97. Frede 1977:52-54 believes in the *Téchnē*'s authenticity, though he does not argue for it, but he says (52) that it is generally accepted as genuine.

CE.[15] Schenkeveld, with help from Wouters' grammatical papyri, follows a middle road that has come to be the *communis opinio*.[16]

§11. Schenkeveld pays particular attention to the problems of the *Téchnē*'s internal coherence and concludes that a large part of the treatise (chapters 6-20) is more likely to have been the product of third century CE scholarship than the work of Dionysius Thrax.[17] On the other hand, he regards it as beyond doubt that Thrax wrote a work on grammar that "was of a systematic character."[18] In his view, the first four chapters of the *Téchnē* formed part of this work, but the rest of the *Téchnē* in its current form cannot be regarded as authentic. Robins has proposed that exactly because it was an actual grammar textbook the *Téchnē* developed and changed continuously.[19] He points out that modern-day textbooks are likewise constantly updated, while generally retaining the name of the original author; he uses this analogy to explain the discrepancies between the ideas expressed in the *Téchnē* and the time in which Thrax lived. Against Robins' hypothesis, one might argue that one would expect continual development to grant more internal coherence to the work, especially between the first parts and the rest.

§12. In spite of remaining doubts, the most prudent conclusion appears to be that only the first four chapters of the *Téchnē* can be attributed to Dionysius Thrax with any certainty,[20] and the other parts are later additions or redactions. As Pagani notes, this is not a completely negative conclusion. If we accept part of the work as authentic, this means that Thrax did write a work on grammar in the second century BCE, albeit one that has largely been lost to us.[21] The existence of this grammatical work by Thrax reflects a growing interest in the theoretical aspects of language and linguistics, an interest that would continue to develop in the following centuries, and culminate in Apollonius Dyscolus' works.[22]

§13. To conclude, language and its components steadily became more of an object of study from the third century BCE onwards. However, the establishment of grammar as an object of study *per se* appears to have been a development of the first century BCE, leading eventually to Apollonius Dyscolus' seminal work.[23] The following material on the

15 See Wouters 1995:99, "the kernel of the *Téchnē* must have undergone clear changes between the moments of its composition and the copying in the first medieval manuscripts."

16 Taylor 1987:8-9 and Schenkeveld 1994:266-269, who refers to Wouters 1979.

17 Schenkeveld 1994:269 and 1995:50-52; see Di Benedetto 1973:802. In a recent handbook, Schmidhauser 2010:508 cites this view as the *communis opinio*.

18 Schenkeveld 1995:42.

19 Robins 1995:18-24.

20 Although it is likely that chapter 5 was moved to its current position in the *Téchnē* from elsewhere.

21 Pagani 2011:36.

22 Pagani 2011 gives a neat summary of the development on 60-62.

23 See Taylor 1987:11 and Schenkeveld 1994:267-269 and 1995:42-44. A similarly problematic work is the *Téchnē* that is signed *Tryphonos technê grammatikê* on a third century CE papyrus (P.Lond. 126, see §50n95 below). The extant part of the text gives the last four of the eight parts of speech

study of particles will reinforce the argument that Thrax's *Téchnē*, whatever its original form, was an important stage in the development of grammatical studies but not its culmination.

2.4 Early Definitions of σύνδεσμοι

§14. The very first authors who wrote about the parts of speech referred to most of the words that we consider particles as σύνδεσμοι. Grammarians writing in Latin later rendered the term as *coniunctio*. However, despite the formal likeness this is not the equivalent of the English "conjunction." After all, in English grammar the word conjunction has very specific connotations that in many cases do not apply to the words that the Greeks and Romans gathered respectively under the terms σύνδεσμος and *coniunctio*. Instead, it is more productive to use Swiggers and Wouters' translation "combiner," since this term reflects the neutral nature of σύνδεσμος, something that "binds together."[24]

§15. Initially σύνδεσμος was used to cover anything from conjunctions to prepositions to interjections to noun phrases, in addition to the words we call particles. The term had such a wide application because it appears to have been coined to cover the words that were neither noun/adjective (ὄνομα), verb (ῥῆμα), nor adverb (ἐπίρρημα/μεσότης). The σύνδεσμος was probably the fourth lexical category to be introduced, just before or at the same time as the ἄρθρον ("joint"), the category that would later become the article. Aristotle is the first we know of to distinguish the σύνδεσμος and ἄρθρον in addition to the noun/adjective, verb, and adverb.[25] As the following definition shows, σύνδεσμος was by no means clearly defined—at least grammatically—at this point:[26]

(t1)

> σύνδεσμος δὲ ἐστιν φωνὴ ἄσημος ἣ οὔτε κωλύει οὔτε ποιεῖ φωνὴν μίαν σημαντικὴν ἐκ πλειόνων φωνῶν πεφυκυῖαν συντίτεσθαι καὶ ἐπὶ τῶν ἄκρων καὶ ἐπὶ τοῦ μέσου ἣν μὴ ἁρμόττει ἐν ἀρχῇ λόγου τιθέναι καθ' ἁυτόν, οἷον μέν ἤτοι δέ. ἢ φωνὴ ἄσημος ἣ ἐκ πλειόνων μὲν φωνῶν μιᾶς σημαντικῶν δὲ ποιεῖν πέφυκεν μίαν σημαντικὴν φώνην.
>
> *Poetics* XX, 6, 1456b38-1457a6

as listed in the *Téchnē* attributed to Thrax, which suggests that the two works are part of a similar tradition.

24 Swiggers and Wouters 2002:102n7.

25 *Poetics* 1456b20-21.

26 Van Bennekom 1975:408 takes it one step further, referring to Simplicius (*Commentary in Aristotle's Categories* 10), who mentions that Theophrastus (fourth century BCE) "and his associates" had already dealt with the question of whether to include ἄρθρα and σύνδεσμοι among the parts of speech.

> A combiner is a non-significant sound which neither precludes, nor brings about, the production of a single significant sound that by nature is composed of several sounds [i.e. an uttered sequence], and which can be used at either end and in the middle, but which it is not appropriate to place at the beginning of an utterance on its own,[27] e.g. μέν, ἤτοι, δέ. Or a non-significant sound, which by nature produces, as a result of [uniting together] several sounds that are significant, a single significant sound.
>
> Swiggers and Wouters 2002:108

The passage is broadly regarded as corrupt and highly opaque,[28] but what we may roughly deduce is that Aristotle here presents the σύνδεσμος as a word that can combine other significant (signifying) sounds into a significant whole. As is clear from the context, he is not discussing parts of speech (μέρη τοῦ λόγου) here, but parts of the lexis (μέρη τῆς λέξεως)—"diction" in Swiggers and Wouters' translation—one of the six components of (good) tragedy. As such his focus is not to offer "a systematic treatment of word-classes, but [to offer] us a list of definitions of elements constitutive of the λέξις, (oral) poetic expression."[29] A definition of ἄρθρον follows this passage; like the definition of σύνδεσμος it too shows that ἄρθρον is not yet conceived as denoting only the article. In view of the opaque nature of the passage, as well as Aristotle's non-grammatical concerns here, it is unclear which words fall in the category σύνδεσμος.[30] Swiggers and Wouters conclude tentatively that the connective and disjunctive particles would be covered by the term σύνδεσμος, whereas expletive particles would fall under ἄρθρον.

§16. The next extant definition of σύνδεσμος appears to go back to Diogenes of Babylon, a Stoic philosopher who lived in the third and second centuries BCE. In his *Lives of the Philosophers*, the third century CE biographer Diogenes Laertius reports that the Stoics Chrysippus (third century BCE) [31] and Diogenes of Babylon distinguished five parts of speech: ὄνομα (proper name), ῥῆμα (verb), προσηγορία (apellative), ἄρθρον (joint), and

27 Swiggers and Wouters take καθ' αὑτόν to refer to λόγου, but I believe it must here be taken to refer back to σύνδεσμος (even though one might have expected a female form here, as φωνή is the actual antecedent. In this case the first Latin translation (Moerbeke, 13th century) might be adduced, as it translates *ipsam*, to refer back to *vox*. This was followed by Kassel who emends αὑτήν 1965:32, which was then, wrongly I believe, thought by Swiggers and Wouters 2002:107 to refer back to ἀρχή, when it must also in Kassel be meant to refer back to φωνή), to mean: 'on its own' i.e. alone. After all, Aristotle has already said it can be found at the beginning, but not on its own. This would explain why he includes ἤτοι, which occurs only at the beginning of clauses, but of course always followed by another word.

28 For full discussions, see Dupont-Roc 1980:321-328, Laspia 1997:79-116, and a summary of the main points in Swiggers and Wouters 2002:107-112.

29 Swiggers and Wouters 2002:110.

30 Swiggers and Wouters 2002:112. Van Bennekom 1975:406 lists μέν, δέ, ἤτοι (possibly corrupt), τε, καί, ἐπεί and γάρ as words expressly regarded by Aristotle as σύνδεσμοι.

31 Schmidhauser discusses Chrysippus, the "first philosopher of language" in 2010:502-507.

σύνδεσμος (combiner); the μεσότης (adverb) was added by Diogenes of Babylon's student Antipater of Tarsus.[32] Diogenes Laertius then goes on to give definitions, introducing the first one as follows: Ἔστι δὲ προσηγορία μὲν κατὰ τὸν Διογένην ("the προσηγορία, according to Diogenes [of Babylon], is:"). The explicit attribution of this definition suggests that the subsequent definitions have their origin with Diogenes of Babylon as well. The definition of σύνδεσμος is as follows:

(t2)

σύνδεσμος δέ ἐστι μέρος λόγου ἄπτωτον, συνδοῦν τὰ μέρη τοῦ λόγου

Diogenes Laertius *Lives of the Philosophers* 7.58[33]

a combiner is an indeclinable part of speech, to bind together the parts of speech

Clearly, the category has been redefined, and a crucial step has been taken from Aristotle's philosophical comments on what the lexical category is to Diogenes' attempt to describe the morphology (ἄπτωτον) and function of its members. The description provided in the text, "indeclinable" (ἄπτωτον), is a characteristic of particles that seems natural to the modern reader, but barring the Stoic tradition the feature was, in fact, not a requisite part of the category's definition in antiquity until Priscian (sixth century CE).[34]

§17. Apart from the definition transmitted by Diogenes Laertius, the sources from the period between Aristotle and Apollonius Dyscolus (second century CE) cannot be securely assigned to an author or even a certain period. There are two bodies of evidence to draw from: (1) the Homeric scholia, and (2) grammatical handbooks, such as the *Téchnē* and some grammatical papyri, authored before Apollonius Dyscolus' work. In the following sections we first discuss the scholia, then the grammatical handbooks; because of the problems of dating the material, it cannot be presented in a strictly chronological way.

32 Diogenes Laertius *Lives of the Philosophers* 7.57: τοῦ δὲ λόγου ἐστὶ μέρη πέντε, ὥς φησι Διογένης τ' ἐν τῷ Περὶ φωνῆς καὶ Χρύσιππος, ὄνομα, προσηγορία, ῥῆμα, σύνδεσμος, ἄρθρον· ὁ δ' Ἀντίπατρος καὶ τὴν μεσότητα τίθησιν ἐν τοῖς Περὶ λέξεως καὶ τῶν λεγομένων.

33 This definition is part of Diogenes of Babylon, fr. 22 in Von Arnim 1923:213-214.

34 The one exception of a definition including the concept of indeclinability is that of the fourth-fifth century grammarian Theodosius of Alexandria, whose definition of σύνδεσμοι is based almost fully on the one by Diogenes: σύνδεσμός ἐστι μέρος λόγου ἄπτωτον συνδοῦν τὰ μέρη τὰ λοιπὰ τοῦ λόγου (*Grammar* 17.21-23). See also §83 below, on a definition (with ἄκλιτον) found in Heliodorus, but attributed to Apollonius Dyscolus by Pecorella.

2.5 The Scholia

2.5.1 Terminology

§18. The term σύνδεσμος is the closest thing to an equivalent of the modern "particle." However, particle comes from the Latin *particula*, whereas σύνδεσμος became *coniunctio* in Latin. There is, then, a mismatch of terminology, and this led Schenkeveld to investigate the use of the ancient Greek equivalent of *particula*: μόριον. After examining the use of the term in early Greek works about language, he concludes that μόριον was in fact never used as *particula* would be.[35]

§19. The scholia to the *Iliad* may be adduced to illustrate this. The word μόριον, when applied to language, almost without exception denotes an affix or suffix, such as the alpha privans,[36] νη privans,[37] the suffix -θεν, and several other morphemes at the beginning and end of words. Single words called μόρια include ὡς,[38] ἔτι,[39] εὖ,[40] articles or pronouns,[41] τῶς,[42] and μα.[43] The only case where μόριον is used in a description of a word that we consider a particle is in the scholion to A 210:

(t3)

A 210 ἀλλ' ἄγε.

ἀλλὰ φέρε. ἔστι δὲ ἐπίρρημα παρακελεύσεως, ἢ ἐπιρρηματικὸν μόριον.

[this means] "but come", and it is an exhortative adverb, or an adverbial μόριον.

This scholion hints at valuable insights, but the scholiast is not very helpful. First of all, it is not clear if his comment explains only ἀλλά or the whole construction ἀλλ' ἄγε. The paraphrase ἀλλὰ φέρε suggests the latter, but it seems completely superfluous: surely ἄγε would be as natural as φέρε to the audience in later antiquity, if not more so. More problematic is the following description of "exhortative adverb." Its sense is clear enough, but it is not entirely clear how ἐπίρρημα can be used to describe the combination ἀλλ' ἄγε. ἀλλά on its own might be regarded as an adverb or "adverbial" in the sense

35 Schenkeveld 1988:83.

36 5.341; in the hypotheseis to the following verses: 1.214, 3.267, 3.444, 4.489, 4.824, 5.402, 6.83, 10.570, and 16.57.

37 In the hypotheseis to the following verses: 4.439, 17.317, 19.498.

38 1.512b, 2.139b, 2.463b, 3.31b.

39 4.539a.

40 Hypothesis to 17.28.

41 19.63b.

42 2.330.

43 1.234 (where it is read as the negation μή).

that it co-occurs with a verb form (the imperative ἄγε). By extension the comment "or it is an adverbial μόριον" would refer just to ἀλλά, making this instance the only one in the scholia where μόριον describes a particle.[44] The weight of the evidence in the scholia, then, suggests that in early linguistic discussions σύνδεσμος was the normal term to refer to the words we would call particles. Note however, that although most particles were called σύνδεσμοι, not all σύνδεσμοι were what we would call particles.

2.5.2 σύνδεσμοι in the scholia

§20. The *Iliad* scholia, marginal notes found in several manuscripts, display a wealth of insights on σύνδεσμοι.[45] These marginalia contain textual commentaries by Aristarchus, Aristophanes of Byzantium, and Zenodotus—among many named or anonymous others. These librarians of the great *Mouseion* in Alexandria edited the most important archaic and classical Greek texts in the third and second centuries BCE. They worked in the same period as the Stoic philosophers, by whom they seem to have been influenced.[46] As a source, the scholia are problematic for two reasons: first, only a small number of scholia can be traced back confidently to a specific author, and second, even if the author is established we have no way of knowing beyond doubt that the wording of the note is original. These issues make it hard to determine the date of the terminology used, which is an especially pertinent question in the current attempt to sketch the development of the study of σύνδεσμοι.

§21. It will be useful at the outset to analyze a single scholion in detail to give a general sense of the kind of discussions we find in the scholia. Consider the scholion to *Iliad* 1.219a.

(t4)

[ἦ καὶ ἐπ' ἀργυρέῃ] τοῦτο τὸ ἦ ψιλῶς λεγόμενον καὶ περισπωμένως δηλοῖ *σύνδεσμον* παραπληρωματικὸν τὸν ἤτοι, ἴσον τῷ δή, οἷον „ἐπειῆ πολὺ φέρτερόν ἐστι“ (1.169), καὶ παραλλήλως „ἦ δὴ λοίγια ἔργα“ (1.518). δηλοῖ δὲ καὶ ἀπορρηματικὸν *σύνδεσμον*· „ἦ οὐχ Ἑλένης ἕνεκ' ἠϋκόμοιο; / ἦ μοῦνοι φιλέουσ' ἀλόχους μερόπων ἀνθρώπων / Ἀτρεῖδαι;“ (9.339–41). δηλοῖ δὲ καὶ τὸ ἔφη· „ἦ καὶ κυανέῃσιν“ (1.528). |

44 However, note the problematic use of μόριον in Trypho's definition of the redundant combiners, §§50-51 below.

45 The Homeric scholia to the *Iliad* form the source for most of the material in this paragraph. The scholia *vetera* to Pindar were also studied, and follow the same pattern. They will be referred to mainly in the footnotes, referenced in the main text only where they offer insights absent from the Homeric scholia.

46 See Matthaios 2002:163-169 for a well-annotated argument that the Alexandrians already distinguished and used the eight word groups established by the stoics.

καὶ σεσημείωται *Ἀρίσταρχος* ὅτι ὁ μὲν Ὅμηρος ἀεὶ ἐπὶ προειρημένοις λόγοις ἐπιφέρει τὸ δηλοῦν τὸ ἔφη, ὡς ἐπὶ τοῦ προκειμένου, ὁ δὲ Πλάτων μετ' αὐτὸ ἐπιφέρει τὸν λόγον. | ψιλούμενον δὲ καὶ βαρυτονούμενον δηλοῖ *σύνδεσμον* διαζευκτικόν· „ἦ εὖ ἠὲ κακῶς“ (2.253). ἔστι δὲ ὅτε καὶ ἀντὶ συναπτικοῦ τοῦ εἴ τίθεται, οἷον „οὐδ' ἀφαμαρτοεπής, ἦ καὶ γένει ὕστερος ἦεν“ (3.215). ποτὲ δὲ παρέλκει· „ἀλλὰ τίη με ταῦτα παρεξερέεσθαι ἕκαστα;“ (10.432).[47] δασυνόμενον δὲ καὶ ὀξυτονούμενον ἄρθρον προτακτικὸν δηλοῖ· „ἡ δ' ἑτέρη θέρεϊ προρρέει εἰκυῖα χαλάζῃ“ (22.151). δηλοῖ δὲ καὶ ἄρθρον ὑποτακτικόν, οἷον „ἣ μυρί' Ἀχαιοῖς“ (1.2). δηλοῖ δὲ καὶ ἀναφορικὴν ἀντωνυμίαν· „ὣς ἥ γ' ἀμφιπόλοισι μετέπρεπεν“ (6.109). δηλοῖ δὲ καὶ τὴν σύναρθρον ἀντωνυμίαν τρίτου προσώπου, συζυγοῦσαν τῇ ἐμή, σή. ὑποδείγματα δὲ ταύτης παρ' Ὁμήρῳ οὐχ εὑρίσκεται, ἐκ δὲ τοῦ ἀναλόγου νοεῖται· αἱ γὰρ πλάγιοι πᾶσαι δι' αὐτῆς παρ' Ὁμήρῳ σώζονται.

[ἦ καὶ ἐπ' ἀργυρέῃ] this unaspirated ἦ and with the circumflex is the filling *combiner* ἤτοι, similar to δή, as in "ἐπειὴ πολὺ φέρτερόν ἐστι" (1.169), and elsewhere "ἦ δὴ λοίγια ἔργα" (1.518). It is also the interrogative *combiner*: "ἦ οὐχ Ἑλένης ἕνεκ' ἠϋκόμοιο; / ἦ μοῦνοι φιλέουσ' ἀλόχους μερόπων ἀνθρώπων / Ἀτρεῖδαι;" (9.339–41). And it also means ἔφη: "ἦ καὶ κυανέῃσιν" (1.528). | And *Aristarchus* noted that Homer always uses it to mean ἔφη after the words have been spoken, as in the current example, while Plato starts the speech after it [sc. ἦ]. | Unaspirated and with the grave accent, it is the disjunctive *combiner*: "ἦ εὖ ἠὲ κακῶς." (2.253) And it happens that it is even placed instead of hypothetical εἰ, as in: "οὐδ' ἀφαμαρτοεπής, ἦ καὶ γένει ὕστερος ἦεν" (3.215). And sometimes it is redundant:

[47] Note that the text in the scholion diverges from the vulgate and is metrically unsound; read: ἀλλὰ τί ἦ ἐμὲ ταῦτα διεξερέεσθε ἕκαστα.

> “ἀλλὰ τίη με ταῦτα παρεξερέεσθαι ἕκαστα;” (10.432). Aspirated and with the acute accent, it is the prepositive article: “ἣ δ’ ἑτέρη θέρεϊ προρρέει εἰκυῖα χαλάζῃ” (22.151). It is also the postpositive article, as in: “ἣ μυρί’ Ἀχαιοῖς” (1.2). And it is also the anaphoric pronoun: “ὣς ἥ γ’ ἀμφιπόλοισι μετέπρεπεν” (6.109). It is also the possessive pronoun of the third person, to be added to ἐμή, σή. Signs of this are not found in Homer, but from analogy it may be reasoned, since all the oblique cases maintain that paradigm in Homer.

This long discussion of η (ἥ, ἤ, ἦ) is found as a whole in the Venetus A manuscript, but that does not mean it was conceived in its entirety by one person. It is typical of the scholia in containing an explicit references to a specific scholar, in this case Aristarchus (second century BCE). The embedded reference to a named scholar indicates that this scholion is probably a composite, that is, authored by someone who includes information from Aristarchus while adding other information drawn either from his own experience or, more likely, from other sources.[48]

§22. If the form of the scholion is typical, its content is not. As an exception among many literary and short linguistic notes, this scholion devotes a long discussion to a word that we would call a particle.[49] The reason for this inclusion illustrates a problem that is relevant to our work. As opposed to most other particles, η is inherently ambiguous. Although small words were probably always vulnerable in the process of transmission, η is a particularly unstable lexical item, because its possible force and function depend entirely on accentuation and breathings. In performance the audience must have had no problem distinguishing between ἥ, ἦ, and ἤ, but in the transition to written versions, this disambiguation was lost. Moreover, there seems to have been a significant period where nothing was done to resolve this problem.[50] It was not until the fourth or third century BCE that we find some accentuation added in papyri. Disambiguation to aid in reading seems to have been the main reason for the first diacritical signs and accents.[51] It was not until the third or second century BCE that Zenodotus or Aristophanes of Byzantium introduced a comprehensive system to provide literary texts with accentuation throughout.

48 Erbse attributes the scholion in its current form to Didymus or Aristonicus, who worked in the first century BCE and CE, respectively.

49 See ἦ in ORPS (our online database) for modern literature on ἦ.

50 This is a clear reflection of how written versions and oral performance must still have gone hand in hand.

51 For early accentuation, see Probert 2006:48-50.

In any case, there must have been a period of unaccented written versions of the Homer epics.

§23. Eventually, fully accented editions of most canonical texts—naturally including the Homeric corpus—circulated in antiquity, but that is not the end of the story. In the transition from papyrus roll to codex, a certain font, the so-called Biblical Uncial, became generally used, from around the fourth or fifth century CE. This type of writing, all in capitals, was not well-suited to accents, so accents fell out in many cases, until writing in minuscule around the ninth century CE brought back accentuation. Around this period it appears that accentuation was added to entire texts, following the Byzantine system.[52]

§24. At two separate moments, then, a decision had to be made about the accentuation of the texts: first when the Alexandrian scholars produced the first fully accented editions, and later when the Mediaeval copyists made the transition from capital to minuscule. This means that we read the instances of η at a double remove, through the interpretations of at least two post-Homeric scholars. The problems with η are of course not unique, but they serve as a concrete illustration of the challenges that the process of transmission posed, not only in the mediaeval and modern era, but even for scholars in antiquity.

§25. The scholion to A 219 shows that scholars in antiquity were aware of these ambiguities, and consciously made a decision to accentuate in a certain way, based on an analysis of the passage. For other particles these decisions are less problematic; exceptions are ταρ, δαί, and elided particles that are ambiguous, like τ' for τε, τοι, or the article τά. A large part of the scholia that concern σύνδεσμοι discuss exactly these questions of form.

§26. In two other respects, this scholion on ἤ is representative of the scholiasts' approach to particles. First, note that the word παραπληρωματικός occurs in line 2: the LSJ renders it as "expletive," working as a "filler." A typical way of describing σύνδεσμοι in antiquity, especially in the scholia, the term was used where the σύνδεσμος in question seemed redundant; we discuss the use of this term in greater detail below. Second, the scholiast of A 219 explains ἤ through analogy, comparing it to ἤτοι (l. 2) and δή (l. 2-3). Lacking a shared terminology, and probably also lacking any reason to offer in-depth analysis, giving a paraphrase or analogy is the scholiasts' preferred method to explain σύνδεσμοι.

§27. Before outlining the general tenor of discussions of particles in the scholia, we turn to the oldest traceable literary scholar in the scholia: Aristarchus. To keep up the attempt to present the material roughly chronologically, we first discuss the notes on σύνδεσμοι that Matthaios ascribes to him.[53]

52 See Probert 2006:49-50. In this second development, the possibility that the ninth-century scribes were in possession of an earlier, fully accented papyrus must not be discounted. However, this will certainly not have been the case for every text.

53 The fragments are gathered in Matthaios 1999:162-168, with an analysis in 566-585.

2.5.3 Aristarchus on σύνδεσμοι

§28. From the limited number of scholia attributed to Aristarchus, Matthaios tries to establish the Homeric scholar's methods and terminology. His analysis of the complete corpus of Aristarchus' fragments allows him to establish better whether Aristarchus, and by extension the other librarians, study grammar for grammar's sake, or if he only uses it as a philological and exegetical tool. For the purpose of tracing the history of scholarship on particles, we focus only on his discussions of σύνδεσμοι.

§29. First there is the question of terminology. Praxiphanes, a fourth century BCE Peripatetic philosopher, reportedly already discussed redundant conjunctions,[54] but the term παραπληρωματικός probably does not go quite so far back. Similarly, when we find the term in Aristarchus' scholia, we cannot know if the scholia represent only his thoughts or actually his *ipsissima verba*. The same problem applies to Aristarchus' use of the term συμπλέκειν (schol. *Il.* 16.636a) and συμπλεκτικός (copulative), which would later become another fixed category of σύνδεσμοι.[55]

§30. As regards the content of Aristarchus' scholia, his treatment of σύνδεσμοι is typical for the kind of comments we find in the scholia at large: they discuss σύνδεσμοι (1) as redundant or (2) in terms of interchangeability.[56] Although scholia commonly mark particles as redundant,[57] Matthaios argues that it cannot be established that Aristarchus regards the παραπληρωματικοὶ σύνδεσμοι as a word category.[58] He solves other troublesome instances of particles by positing that one particle is used for another, like περ used instead of δή or γε, in the scholion to *Iliad* 131. Elsewhere, Aristarchus is reported as regarding δαί as an equivalent of δέ and as a connective (συμπλεκτικός).[59] More remarkable is his note that in Homer a γάρ clause often comes first in causal constructions, commonly called anticipatory γάρ.[60] This argument may go back to his teacher and predecessor as head of the *Mouseion*, Aristophanes of Byzantium.[61] In a similar vein, Apollonius Dyscolus reports that Aristarchus chooses the reading δαί over δ'αἱ (elided δέ +

54 Demetrius, *Style* 55 = Praxiphanes fr. 13 in Wehrli.

55 Matthaios 1999:573 does not assume that Aristarchus already used the term συμπλεκτικός for copulative conjunctions.

56 It is open to discussion whether this means that (1) many of the anonymous comments in the scholia should also be ascribed to Aristarchus, or that (2) Aristarchus' notes functioned as a model for later scholiasts.

57 See Friedländer 1853:34; Aristarchus already discusses so-called apodotic δέ, see Matthaios 1999:571.

58 For a discussion of the history of the category of σύνδεσμοι παραπληρωματικοί, see Sluiter 1997:234-245.

59 In the scholion to *Iliad* 10.408, Matthaios 1999:123, fragment 99:42-43, with commentary on pages 581-582.

60 See Matthaios 1999:165 fr. 173 and the scholia in the notes for the relevant places, and page 574 for Aristarchus on γάρ. Also noted in Ax 1982:102-104 and Pagani 2011:43.

61 Matthaios 1999:575, see Cobet's comment in the footnote to schol. Eur. *Phoen*. 886, in Dindorf 1863, vol. 3, p. 244-245.

feminine nominative plural article αἱ), because Homer was wont to use δαί after question words.[62]

§31. Matthaios concludes that Aristarchus and the other Alexandrian scholars did contribute to the development of a study of grammar, but that they never practiced it as a goal in and of itself.[63] The representative selection of scholia discussed below corroborates this view, at least as far as particles are concerned. We present a range of examples concerning redundancy (2.5.4) and interchangeability (2.5.5). Then follows a brief overview of scholiasts' views on the difference between ἄν and κεν (2.5.6). Finally, we turn to glimpses of deeper insight hidden among the many paraphrases and dismissals (2.5.7).

2.5.4 Redundancy

§32. By far the most frequent kind of comment on σύνδεσμοι in the scholia takes the form "X is redundant."[64] Several words may be used to describe the function of many combiners as superfluous, or as a filler. In many scholia we find the term σύνδεσμος παραπληρωματικός, a "filling combiner." The adjective παραπληρωματικός is also the term that would become the standard in grammar treatises to describe a certain group of σύνδεσμοι that appears (to the ancient grammarians before Apollonius Dyscolus) to have no clear function. In the scholia, other words commonly used to describe redundant particles are περισσός (or -ττ-), forms of περισσεύω (or -ττ-), παρέλκω, πλεονάζωμ παραπληρόω, and the phrase ἐκ πλήρους. Although the words clearly do not mean exactly the same thing, they appear to be used rather interchangeably. Particles that get the predicate 'redundant' or 'filler' most often are: κε,[65] δέ,[66] περ,[67] πω/που,[68] and τε.[69]

2.5.5 Interchangeability

§33. In his work on the scholia by Aristonicus, Friedländer remarks about a note on περ used for δή: *Praeter illam particulae περ cum δή commutationem paucissimas conjunctionum*

[62] Apollonius Dyscolus, *Syntax* I.6, I.127; see Matthaios 1999:581. A similar note may be found in the scholion to *Iliad* 10.408. The scholia to the *Téchnē* repeat the observation; see Hilgard 1901:106 and 441.

[63] Matthaios 1999:625 and 2001:90.

[64] As Friedländer noted too in his work on Aristonicus. Almost all his notes on *coniunctiones* found in the scholia concern redundancy: Friedländer 1853:33-35.

[65] For a list, see Erbse VI 1983:181. The listings given here and below are as complete as possible. The indices offered by Erbse are invaluable and in combination with the *TLG* give unheard-of access to the scholia, but even so some relevant notes will be missed. There is therefore no claim that the material is exhaustive, but we are confident that the themes and instances presented here at least form a good representation of the discussions of σύνδεσμοι in the scholia.

[66] For a list, see Erbse VI 1983:154.

[67] Erbse does not give a separate list, but see at least the following: schol. *Il.* 1.352b, 13.317, 14.1e, 15.372-4, 20.21c, 21.189 (where the scholiast compares *Odyssey* 13.46), 22.416c, and 24.750.

[68] For a list, see Erbse VI 1983:213 for πω and schol. *Il.* 643a for που (παραπληρωματικός).

[69] For a list, see Erbse VI 1983:219.

enallagas notatas invenimus ("Apart from this exchange of περ for δή, we have found very few exchanges of combiners noted").[70] It is unclear if he is restricting himself only to scholia attributed to Aristonicus in this statement, but in any case offering a paraphrase in the form of another particle is a reasonably standard method in the scholia.

§34. The most frequent example of this type of comment is δὲ ἀντὶ τοῦ γάρ, δέ used instead of γάρ, as in the scholion to *Odyssey* 2.6: ἔστι δ' ὅτε καὶ ἀντὶ τοῦ γάρ αἰτιολογικῶς λαμβάνεται [sc. δέ] ("It also happens that [δέ] is used instead of γάρ, with a causal sense").[71] The terminology in this scholion is probably late, not Aristarchus or Aristonicus.[72] Similar is ἠδέ for καί (schol. *Il.* 6.149a, 9.134a), and the other way around in schol. *Il.* 15.670.

§35. In line with the discussions of δ', which could stand for δέ or δή, δέ is at times equated with δή.[73] In general, δή seems to have been a stable reference point in the centuries just before and after the beginning of the Common Era. In the scholion to *Iliad* 5.258, γε is paraphrased as δή. In schol. *Il.* 1.131a, περ is said to be used instead of γε or δή. ἄρ' (or τ'ἄρ) is also equated with δή, in 18.6b. Likewise, ἄρα is simply rendered δή in the D scholion to *Iliad* 1.308,[74] which may be compared to the many glosses of the form: ἦ μάν (or ἦ μέν, or ἦ ῥα, or ἦ που, or ἦ μάλα, or ἦ θήν): ὄντως δή.[75] δή clearly had some kind of emphatic force at this time, and was thought to render the different nuances contained in this list of words. ἤτοι, ἄρα, ἔπειτα, δέ, μάν, μέν, γε, περ, and τ'ἄρ are all at one point or another paraphrased as δή.

§36. In the same way that the scholiasts substitute δή for a host of difficult particles, ἄρα is often noted as having an alternative reading in other manuscripts. In the scholion to *Iliad* 18.151 we find [οὐδέ κε] ἐν ἄλλῳ "οὐδ' ἄρα"; and likewise: 19.96a: [ἀλλ' ἄρα καὶ τόν] παρὰ Ἀριστοφάνει "ἀλλά νυ καὶ τόν" and 23.362 [ἄρα] γράφεται, {οἱ δ'} "ἅμα." Finally, a scholiast observes that εἰ may be used as an equivalent of interrogative ἆρα (*Iliad* 21.567a).

§37. The scholion to *Iliad* 7.89d (and 13.622b, 23.311c, 24.488a, 24.732a) explains an utterance-initial μέν thus: τὸ μέν ἀντὶ τοῦ μήν. A scholion to the same verse (*Iliad* 7.89c) makes it a bit more complicated and argues that μέν is used instead of δέ, and that this hypothetical δέ would have the force of δή here, i.e. μέν - δή here.

70 Friedländer 1853:35.

71 See Erbse VI 1983:154 for an apparently exhaustive list of instances. To this may be added the list of *Odyssey* scholia in Matthaios 1999:164n1, and the scholia to Pindar: *Ol.* 2.106a[64] (quoted on the same page), *Ol.* 4.34b+c[22], *Ol.* 6.4b+c[3], *Ol.* 10.36-46[30], *Ol.* 10.47-50[39], *Ol.* 12.6-18[5-12], *Ol.* 13.83[60], *P.* 5.132[98], *P.* 6.38[38], *P.* 10.2-3[2], *N.* 4.95b[59].

72 Matthaios 1999:573n43.

73 For a list, see Erbse VI 1983:154, see also the scholia to Pindar, *Ol.* 2.102a[62] (δέ = δή), *Ol.* 9.33[21] (δέ τοι = δὴ οὖν), *Ol.* 10.63b[51] (δέ = δή), *Ol.* 13.69a[49] (δέ = δὴ οὖν).

74 Note also the following scholia to Pindar *Ol.* 8.61-70[46], Ol. 10.51b[43] (ἄρα = δή), P. 4.337[189] (ῥα = δή),

75 1.77, 10.322 (ἦ μέν), 3.43 (ἦ που), 3.204, 8.102 (ἦ μάλα), 13.354 (ἦ μάν), 13.813 (ἦ θήν), 20.347 (ἦ ῥα).

§38. Another common interchange is found in the scholia to Pindar, which argue that ἀλλά is used instead of δέ: *Ol.* 3.40[23], *P.* 4.270a[152], *N.* 1.59[39], *N.* 2.32b[20], *I.* 6.47e[35]. One scholiast (to *P.* 8.20[15]) reverses the interchange: δέ for ἀλλά.

2.5.6 ἄν and κε(ν)

§39. Two other particles that often led to discussion are κε and ἄν. In their interpretation of these words, the scholia are far from consistent. There is little doubt that the different scholiasts regarded κε and ἄν as words with different functions and possibilities, but it is unclear what these differences might have been, or if they would even have agreed on what distinguished the two. What the scholiasts appear to agree on is that κε is often redundant;[76] by contrast, they say this much less often of ἄν. This tendency may well be a result of the obscure nature of κε, a word extremely rare in Greek literature outside of Homer and Hesiod, except in instances of allusive imitation. The confusion over the particle κε emerges from the scholia to *Iliad* 1.175a and 5.212:

(t5)

1.175 οἵ κε με τιμήσουσι
ὅτι περισσὸς ὁ κέ σύνδεσμος, ἢ τὸ τιμήσουσιν ἀντὶ τοῦ τιμήσειαν.

[the sign] because the combiner κε is redundant, or τιμήσουσιν instead of τιμήσειαν.

5.212 εἰ δέ κε νοστήσω
ἀντὶ τοῦ νοστήσαιμι, ὡς "πληθὺν δ' οὐκ ἂν ἐγὼ ὀνομήνω" (2.488). περιττεύει δὲ καὶ ὁ κέ σύνδεσμος.

[νοστήσω] instead of νοστήσαιμι, like "I could not name the multitude" (*Iliad* 2.488). Also, the combiner κε is redundant.

The authors of these scholia are rightly confused about the forms in these two constructions, arguing in both cases that the verb form should be replaced by an optative. In the first case the argument is understandable: "either κε is redundant, *or* the verb form should be optative." The second, however, is confused: "[νοστήσω] instead of νοστήσαιμι, and κε is redundant." Clearly, the scholia do not regard κε as an equivalent of ἄν, but it remains unclear what kind of function they attributed to the Homeric particle κε.[77]

[76] In scholia ὅτι goes back to a construction like [ἡ διπλῆ] ὅτι (as preserved in example t8), explaining the critical sign in the edition; see Dickey 2007:122.

[77] Erbse VI 1969:141, s.v. περισσὸς ὁ ἄν.

§40. Consider further schol. *Il.* 9.262a:

(t6)

9.262 ἐγὼ δέ κέ τοι καταλέξω
ἡ διπλῆ δὲ πρὸς τὸ σχῆμα, ὅτι ἀντὶ τοῦ ἐγὼ δ'ἄν σοι καταλέξαιμι, ἢ περισσὸς ὁ κέ.

the diplê placed at this construction, because [this construction] is instead of ἐγὼ δ'ἄν σοι καταλέξαιμι, or κε is redundant.

Either the construction is a variant for ἄν plus the optative, or it is a future, and κε is simply superfluous. The only thing that appears to trigger the scholiast's belief that this construction should be a potential optative is the presence of κε, which he replaces with ἄν in his paraphrase. There is some awareness, then, that κε could fulfill—or used to fulfill—a function similar to that of ἄν. However, they seem to have believed that κε could be used simply as a filler too, without any bearing on the reading of the verb. The few notes on redundant ἄν (see note 27 below) fall in the same group, but the longer discussions suggest that the scholiasts had more trouble accepting a redundant instance of ἄν than of κε.[78]

2.5.7 Noteworthy readings of σύνδεσμοι

§41. Now that we have listed some of the most common discussions of σύνδεσμοι in the scholia, it is worthwhile to highlight some less common, and especially insightful comments. A selection of scholia reveal a nascent awareness of the possible polyfunctionality of some σύνδεσμοι. These few notes illustrate a broader interest in particles for which we have otherwise very little evidence outside of Apollonius Dyscolus' treatise.

§42. The quintessentially Homeric particle ἄρα clearly caused problems for the scholiasts, who knew the particle only in its classical "conclusive" sense; in most scholia the particle is simply ignored.[79] In the scholion to *Iliad* 16.147a, a scholiast paraphrases ἄρα as ὡς ἔοικεν, giving it the force of rendering a realization by the speaker. For comparison the scholiast adduces Hesiod *Works and Days* 11: "οὐκ ἄρα μοῦνον," adding that the realization marked by ἄρα may be contradictory to something previously stated or thought. Likewise, the scholion to *Iliad* 17.33 paraphrases οὐκ ἄρα σοί γε πατὴρ ἦν with οὐκ ἦν ὡς ἔοικέ σοι πατήρ. These readings of ἄρα may well be much more productive than the

78 See for Aristarchus on these particles Matthaios 1999:107-109, frr. 73-78 and pp. 363-373.

79 In the scholion to 13.521, for example, οὐδ' ἄρα πω is rendered οὐδέπω, eliminating ἄρα in the paraphrase.

explanations found in modern standard works, which regard marking "surprise" or "conclusion" as the main function of the particle.[80]

§43. The challenge of understanding ἄρα extends to the problematic particle or particle combination τ'ἄρ/ταρ.[81] Modern editors vacillate between spelling τ'ἄρ or τάρ, and this discussion goes back to the scholia. In the scholion to *Iliad* 1.93, τάρ is reported as one word (τέλειος), not from τε and ἄρ,[82] and the scholiast paraphrases the particle as δή. We see the same reading in schol. *Il.* 18.6b, where τί τ'ἄρ' αὖτε is paraphrased τί δὴ πάλιν. Another problem with τ'ἄρ/ταρ is the palaeographic similarity to γάρ—majuscule τ and γ are easily confused. In the scholion to *Iliad* 18.182, Didymus discusses the variants γάρ and τάρ, and decides in favour of the former (*contra* Aristarchus) on the basis that Homer was wont to start with γάρ.[83]

§44. Another recurring discussion in the scholia is the concept of μέν *solitarium*, μέν used without a corresponding particle in the following clause or sentence. The scholiast on *Iliad*. 4.301a finds a solitary μέν and asks simply: ποῦ ὁ δέ; "Where is the δέ?" This question is later integrated into the larger problem of the forms μέν (Ionic)—μήν (Attic, koinê)—μάν (Doric).[84] The scholion to *Iliad* 7.89d, mentioned above, explains an utterance-initial μέν as τὸ μέν ἀντὶ τοῦ μήν, but this comment reveals no awareness of the dialectal connection between the words. However, the scholion to *Iliad* 15.16a does remark that μάν is Doric. [85]

§45. Finally, the scholia contain some valuable notes on the position of σύνδεσμοι. Scholiasts, when confused about the sense of a passage, have recourse to rearranging the particles in the sequence, so that logical links between clauses are attained. Schol. *Il.* 1.211-212a, for example, explains the sequence: ὡς ἔσεταί περ, ὧδε γὰρ ἐξερέω with the paraphrase: ὥσπερ γὰρ ἔσται, οὕτω καὶ ἐρῶ. The scholiast speaks of a hyperbaton of γάρ, apparently to mean that γάρ is set far apart from its host clause.

§46. The comments selected above represent what we regard as the most remarkable discussions of σύνδεσμοι in the scholia. We have chosen them specifically because they anticipate a number of discussions about particles that still persist. The use of ἄρα in Homer still perplexes scholars, just as it confused the scholiasts, but their reading as

80 See ἄρα in ORPS (our online database), II.4.3.2, and II.4.4.

81 Katz 2007 argues that ταρ is one word, and that it might be a loanword from Luvian; see there for additional literature.

82 In 1.65a this is echoed: οὐ γάρ ἐστιν ὁ τέ σύνδεσμος; moreover, ταρ is described as a conclusive (ἐπιφερόμενος) enclitic combiner.

83 Elsewhere, in scholion 2.284a, Aristarchus himself argues for reading Ἀτρεΐδη, νῦν γάρ σε instead of Ἀτρεΐδη, νῦν δή σε (as most manuscripts), on the basis that in causal constructions Homer often starts with γάρ: ἔθος δὲ αὐτῷ (i.e. Ὁμήρῳ) ἀπὸ τοῦ γάρ ἄρχεσθαι; see Matthaios 1999:574-5 for a discussion. See II.3.2.2 and II.4.2 for more on γάρ beginning new parts of discourse in Homer and Pindar.

84 Apparently first in Eustathius, see §§87-89 below.

85 See also Haslam 2013:2-3 on a new scholion that reports Dionysius of Sidon preferring μήν over Aristarchus' μάν at *Iliad* 4.512.

"it appears" (ὡς ἔοικεν) may well be more helpful than the expression of a "lively feeling of interest" posited by Denniston.[86] The discussion surrounding τ'ἄρ/ταρ has recently revived because a particle "tar" has been found in Luwian. The word in Homer may thus be either a loanword or an inherited Indo-European word that has disappeared from later Greek. The scholia show that the possibility of a word ταρ was entertained even back then. The relation between μέν-μήν-μάν was discussed mostly in the nineteenth century, but our understanding of μέν in Homer still strongly depends on whether we assume a link with μήν or not.[87] Finally, the phrasing in the scholion to *Iliad* 1.211-212, "a hyperbaton of γάρ," reveals an awareness of the link between a particle and its host act, or more precisely of the scope of particles.[88] The accumulated intuitions of several generations of scholiasts have thus laid the foundations for centuries of particle research.

2.6 The *Téchnē* and Other Early Scholarship

§47. The particle καί may serve as an illustration of the development of the study of particles from the scholia to the early grammarians. The scholia appear to have given little attention to καί. Whenever the scholiasts find καί in an unexpected position (particularly when it is in second position and not copulative) they merely comment: "καί is redundant."[89] One possible exception is a comment in Eustathius (to *Iliad* 2.827), which Erbse believes might go back to a scholion: ἢ περιττὸς ὁ καί σύνδεσμος ἢ συμπλέκει καὶ ἕτερα θεόσδοτα τῷ τόξῳ ἀγαθά ("either the combiner καί is redundant, or it conjoins also other god-given goods to the bow").[90] The comment indicates that καί is read as "also". It is probable that in more cases "also" was a natural reading of καί, but we find this explanation only in one scholion.

§48. Even more exceptional is the scholion to *Iliad* 12.301. Its approach gives a glimpse into ways of describing more complicated uses of particles before Apollonius Dyscolus. The passage from the *Iliad* is as follows:

(t7)

βῆ ῥ' ἴμεν ὥς τε λέων ὀρεσίτροφος, ὅς τ' ἐπιδευὴς
δηρὸν ἔῃ κρειῶν, κέλεται δέ ἑ θυμὸς ἀγήνωρ
μήλων πειρήσοντα <u>καὶ</u> ἐς πυκινὸν δόμον ἐλθεῖν·

Iliad 12.299-301

86 Dennniston 1950²:33.
87 See II.2.4 for μέν in Homer and Pindar.
88 See I.1 for the concept of scope and its relevance to particle analysis; for an application, see II.3.3 on Homeric δή.
89 Erbse gives a list in part VI on page 179; Linke 1977:61 offers a few examples for the scholia to the *Odyssey*: 1.33, 8.154, 10.471, 11.453, 16.216.
90 The line is Πάνδαρος, ᾧ καὶ τόξον Ἀπόλλων αὐτὸς ἔδωκεν, the comment in Eustathius 354, 32.

> And so he went, like a mountain-born lion that was without
> meat for a long time, and whose proud spirit urges him
> to go and attack καί the closely built sheep-fold.

About καί in line 301 the scholion adduces the analysis and paraphrase of Dionysius Thrax:

(t8)

...καὶ ὅτι ὁ καί περισσός ἐστιν. ὁ δε Διονύσιος [Dionysius Thrax] ὅτι δύναται σημαίνειν τι πλέον, οὕτως ἐνδεὴς τροφῆς ὥστε καὶ ἐπι πεπυκνωμένον καὶ ἠσφαλισμένον δόμον ἐλθεῖν.

Scholion to 12.301[91]

... and because καί is redundant. Dionysius [Thrax], however, [argues] that it can signify something more: "so hungry for food that even to a fenced and secured fold he went."

The scholiast proposes that καί is redundant here, meaning it should not be translated: "to go and attack the closely built sheep-fold." Dionysius, conversely, proposes a paraphrase containing the construction οὕτως ... ὥστε (so hungry ... that) but without finding an adequate synonym for καί. We propose that this is an attempt by Dionysius to render what we now call the scalar function of καί with the addition of οὕτως ... ὥστε. With this paraphrase, then, Dionysius gives us a first attempt to express the force of καί as a scalar particle.[92]

§49. The scholion suggests that Dionysius' analysis was a departure from the ideas of his predecessors, and illustrates that he was devoting time and energy to σύνδεσμοι. In his readings, Dionysius was both innovative and traditional, but his work is still a few steps removed from the analyses of Apollonius Dyscolus. Unfortunately, nothing more of Dionysius Thrax' work on σύνδεσμοι is extant, so we will never know if he was an important precursor to Apollonius.

2.6.1 Trypho

§50. The first century BCE grammarian Trypho seems to have been a recognized authority in antiquity, as Apollonius Dyscolus refers to him most out of all his predecessors;[93]

91 The scholion is attributed to Aristonicus.

92 See IV.2.4.8 for a discussion of this function of καί.

93 Fifty-two instances, for the numbers see Lallot 1997:I.16-17.

twenty times to discuss issues regarding σύνδεσμοι.[94] Trypho's notes concern particles (43-46, 59-60) as well as words we now call conjunctions (ὅτι, τηνίκα, τοὔνεκα, διότι) or adverbs (ἕκητι, χάριν).[95]

§51. The observations on σύνδεσμοι that we find in these notes are very much in line with those found in the scholia. Trypho comments on the interchangeability of σύνδεσμοι, as in the following note on *Odyssey* 10.501-2: τὸν γάρ ἀντὶ τοῦ δέ καὶ τὸν δέ ἀντὶ τοῦ γάρ.[96] Likewise, in another fragment he claims that μὲν γάρ is to be regarded as one particle, with the value of δέ.[97] Trypho also uses analogy to show that ἦ and δή are not different forms of the same word.[98] Most valuable, however, is the (partial) definition of redundant σύνδεσμοι that Apollonius attributes to Trypho:[99]

(t9)

Ὁ γοῦν Τρύφων ἐν τῷ ὅρῳ βουλόμενος καὶ αὐτοὺς (sc. τοὺς παραπληρωματικούς) ἐμπεριλαβεῖν φησί: "...καὶ τὸ κεχηνὸς τῆς ἑρμηνείας ἔστιν ὅπου παραπληρῶν," ἀπείκασε δὲ καί τινας αὐτῶν ταῖς καλουμέναις στοιβαῖς: "ὃν γάρ," φησι, "τρόπον εἰς τὰς συνθέσεις τῶν ἀμφορέων εὐχρηστεῖ ἡ τῶν στοιβῶν παρένθεσις ὑπὲρ τοῦ μὴ καταθραύεσθαι τοὺς ἀμφορεῖς, τὸν αὐτὸν δὴ τρόπον ὑπὲρ τοῦ τὰ τῆς φράσεως μὴ τραχύνεσθαι ἥδε ἡ σύνταξις τῶν μορίων παραλαμβάνεται."

Apollonius Dyscolus, *Combiners* 247.23-29

Trypho, for example, wanting to incorporate them [sc. the σύνδεσμοι παραπληρωματικοί] in the definition too, says: "it also happens that they fill the gap(s) of the utterance," and moreover he compares some of them with what we call stuffings: "For," he says, "in the way it is helpful, when putting amphoras together, to put stuffings in between so that the amphoras are not

[94] Frr. 40-60, discussed in De Velsen 1853:34-45. De Velsen adds to Trypho's fragments on σύνδεσμοι one note (fr. 61) by an anonymous grammarian on Trypho's discussion of ὡς.

[95] Quite recently a *Téchnē* bearing the name of Trypho was found on a third century CE papyrus (P.Lond. 126). This text, like the one attributed to Dionysius Thrax, takes the form of a short (school) grammar. Towards the end of the extant part the section on conjunctions begins. The crucial first lines, containing a rough definition, are quite opaque, unfortunately. Whoever may have been the author of this papyrus, it is unlikely to have been the first century BCE grammarian.

[96] De Velsen 1853:40, fr. 52; the source is Apollonius Dyscolus, *Combiners* 240. In the same fragment, Trypho argues that γάρ can be redundant.

[97] De Velsen 1853:41, fr. 54 = Apollonius Dyscolus, *Combiners* 241.

[98] De Velsen 1853:44, fr. 59 = Apollonius Dyscolus, *Combiners* 257. Trypho notes that although the form of two words may be very similar, this does not mean anything for their meaning, adducing γαῖα - αἶα, μία - ἴα, and σῦς - ὗς.

[99] De Velsen 1853:35, fr. 41 = Apollonius Dyscolus, *Combiners* 247.23-29.

damaged, in just the same way, so that the constituents of the phrase do not become harsh, this combination of the μόρια[100] is used."

Here we find a definition of σύνδεσμοι παραπληρωματικοί that resonates strongly with the definition of σύνδεσμοι in the *Téchnē*, but with a focus on filling the gaps (παραπληρῶν, compare the variant reading πληροῦσα in the *Téchnē*). Trypho explains this with a metaphor of stuffing between amphoras: σύνδεσμοι παραπληρωματικοί serve to keep the other words from becoming "harsh." Trypho further argues that σύνδεσμοι should be regarded as words (as opposed to syllables). Elsewhere, Trypho has posited: "[if] they are [words] they must mean something."[101] If Trypho pursued this line of thought, his discussion is no longer extant. However, the combination of these two thoughts will form the basis of Apollonius Dyscolus' discussion of σύνδεσμοι παραπληρωματικοί.

2.6.2 Apollonius the Sophist

§52. The author of a first century CE *Homer Lexicon* appears to be of little significance in the development of the study of particles. However, his work has in places an overlap with the scholia, most notably with the scholion to *Iliad* 1.219 on η (quoted above in §21).[102] Apollonius the Sophist gives a shorter version of the same note—omitting the references to Aristarchus, for example—so it is more likely that he incorporated this note from an earlier commentary on the *Iliad* than that the entry in his *Lexicon* was later incorporated into the scholia.

§53. Apollonius the Sophist's work deserves some attention, however, because he notes diachronic development in the use of certain particles. In two instances he notes a difference in the use of a particle between Homer and "others," as well as his own time. ἄρα, for example, is used for δή throughout Homer, but is in fact a syllogistic, conclusive particle in other authors.[103] Likewise, ἤτοι stands for μέν in Homer, but is a disjunctive particle in other poets and in Sophistes' time.[104] It is of paramount importance to understand that particle use changes over time, and Apollonius the Sophist is one of the first sources to bring up the topic.

[100] See above, §§21-22 for a short note on μόρια. Its use here is not entirely clear, and thus difficult to translate.

[101] *Combiners* 249.9-10: [εἰ λέ]ξεις, ὀφείλουσί τι δηλοῦν.

[102] Apollonius Sophistes, *Lexicon Homericum* 81.27-82.8. The edition referred to is that by Bekker, published in 1833 and reproduced in 1967.

[103] Apollonius Sophistes, *Lexicon Homericum* 41.6, 43.13: ἄρα ἀντὶ τοῦ δὴ παρ' Ὁμήρῳ διὰ παντός, παρὰ δὲ τοῖς ἄλλοις ἐν τῷ βίῳ συλλογιστικὸς σύνδεσμος.

[104] Apollonius Sophistes, *Lexicon Homericum* 85.5-7 καθ' Ὅμηρον μὲν ἰσοδυναμεῖ τῷ μέν συνδέσμῳ, (...) παρὰ δὲ ἡμῖν καὶ ἄλλοις ποιηταῖς διαζευκτικὸς σύνδεσμος.

2.6.3 σύνδεσμοι in the *Téchnē*

§54. All of chapter 20 of the *Téchnē* is devoted to σύνδεσμοι. As we have discussed above, this part of the *Téchnē* probably does not go back to Dionysius Thrax, but looks like a later addition. Regardless of its exact date, perhaps somewhere between the first and third centuries CE, it is one of the few early discussions of σύνδεσμοι as a category. This systematic account of combiners begins with the following definition:

(t10)

Σύνδεσμός ἐστι λέξις συνδέουσα διάνοιαν μετὰ τάξεως καὶ τὸ τῆς ἑρμηνείας κεχηνὸς δηλοῦσα

Téchnē 20.1-2

A combiner is a word that conjoins the thought through order and clarifies the gap{s} of the expression.

This definition assigns two functions to a σύνδεσμος: on the one hand a σύνδεσμος knits together units of thought (διάνοια) in an utterance by imposing order, and on the other it has an effect on gap(s) in the expression.[105]

§55. The first part is clear enough, but the second requires more discussion; the difficulty lies in κεχηνὸς δηλοῦσα: how can anything "clarify a gap"? In antiquity Heliodorus, in his commentary on the *Téchnē*, explains it as referring specifically to the disjunctive (διαζευκτικοί) combiners.[106] Modern editors do not lean that way. Swiggers and Wouters argue that it is because σύνδεσμοι have no propositional content that they can be said to "show the void in linguistic symbolization" (ἑρμηνεία).[107] Lallot, likewise, translates: "... et qui révèle l'implicite de l'expression."[108] Kemp prefers the alternative reading πληροῦσα found in several manuscripts, a *lectio facilior* that allows him to translate: "... and fills up gaps in the expression." In our translation we have followed the Greek as closely as possible, and aligned with Lallot as to the interpretation of δηλοῦσα. However opaquely, it appears that the definition in the *Téchnē* states that σύνδεσμοι serves to clarify what is unexpressed in language, such as those things implied, or perhaps the

105 See Dickey 2007:239 for this translation of ἑρμενεία.

106 Commentary to Thrax *Téchnē*, attributed to Heliodorus, in Hilgard *Grammatici Graeci* 1.3:103 "Καὶ τὸ τῆς ἑρμηνείας κεχηνὸς δηλοῦσα." Τοῦτό φησι διὰ τοὺς διαζευκτικοὺς συνδέσμους· ἐκεῖνοι γὰρ τὸ τῆς ἑρμηνείας, ὅ ἐστι τὸ τῆς διανοίας, διεζευγμένον καὶ διεστηκὸς δηλοῦσι·

107 Swiggers and Wouters 1998:3.

108 See Lallot 1998:231-241 for an extensive discussion of the definition. His definition is attractive because it highlights the importance of combiners with respect to the implicit or the "unsaid" in interaction. On the other hand, I am not sure if we can read quite as much into the κεχηνὸς of the definition.

mode rather than the content of the utterance. Other definitions generally highlight the two functions of σύνδεσμοι to impose order, and show some force (δύναμις).[109] The *Téchnē* does not express it in those terms, but its author may have been thinking of the same thing.

§56. The *Téchnē* continues with enumerating eight or nine subcategories of σύνδεσμοι: (1) συμπλεκτικοί (copulative),[110] (2) διαζευκτικοί (disjunctive),[111] (3) συναπτικοί (hypothetical),[112] (4) παρασυναπτικοί (continuative),[113] (5) αἰτιολογικοί (causal),[114] (6) ἀπορηματικοί (dubitative),[115] (7) συλλογιστικοί (conclusive),[116] (8) παραπληρωματικοί (filling/redundant),[117] the ninth subcategory, ἐναντιωματικοί (concessive), is reported as accepted only by "some."[118]

§57. These subcategories, unfortunately, receive only cursory definitions, such as the following explanation of σύνδεσμοι παραπληρωματικοί:

(t11)

παραπληρωματικοὶ δέ εἰσιν ὅσοι μέτρου ἢ κόσμου ἕνεκεν παραλαμβάνονται

Téchnē 20.24-25

... and fillers are those that are employed for the sake of metre or beauty[119]

Beyond such brief definitions, the *Téchnē* only gives a few examples for each subcategory; i.e. καί is συμπλεκτικός, ἤ is διαζευκτικός, ἵνα is αἰτιολογικός *et cetera*. This discussion of σύνδεσμοι reveals none of the insight or interest found in Thrax' comment quoted in the scholion to *Iliad* 12.301, and may serve as another argument that it is unlikely that chapter 20 of the *Téchnē* can be attributed to Thrax.

109 The term δύναμις is already applied to particles in the Homeric scholia, especially in forms of the verb ἰσοδυναμέω, e.g. in the scholion to *Iliad* 9.134 τὸ δὲ ἠδέ ψιλωτέον· σύνδεσμος γάρ ἐστιν ἰσοδυναμῶν τῷ καί ("ἠδέ has a smooth breathing. For it is a combiner with the same force as καί").

110 The *Téchnē* lists: μέν, δέ, τε, καί, ἀλλά, ἠμέν, ἠδέ, ἰδέ, ἀτάρ, αὐτάρ, ἤτοι, κεν, ἄν.

111 ἤ, ἤτοι, ἠέ.

112 εἴ, εἴπερ, εἰδή, εἰδήπερ.

113 ἐπεί, ἐπείπερ, ἐπειδή, ἐπειδήπερ.

114 ἵνα, ὄφρα, ὅπως, ἕνεκα, οὕνεκα, διὅ, διὅτι, καθ' ὅ, καθ' ὅτι, καθ' ὅσον.

115 ἆρα, κᾶτα, μῶν.

116 ἄρα, ἀλλά, ἀλλαμήν, τοίνυν, τοιγάρτοι, τοιγαροῦν.

117 δή, ῥα, νυ, που, τοι, θήν, ἄρ, δῆτα, περ, πω, μήν, ἄν, αὖ, νῦν.

118 ἔμπης ὅμως.

119 Kemp 1987 and Lallot 1985 translate κόσμου with "embellishment" and "ornament", respectively; I have chosen a more neutral translation.

2.6.4 Demetrius' *Style*

§58. Before moving on to Apollonius Dyscolus I mention one more hard-to-date work, Περὶ Ἑρμενείας, a treatise on *Style* traditionally attributed to the fourth to third century BCE philosopher Demetrius of Phaleron but whose authenticity has been questioned.[120] This work—now believed to have been written anytime in a five-hundred year time span (between the third century BCE and the second century CE)—is innovative because it discusses σύνδεσμοι with style, rather than grammar, in mind. The author's interest in style is apparent in the following passage on σύνδεσμοι παραπληρωματικοί:

> (t12)
>
> λαμβάνεται δὲ κἀν παθητικοῖς πολλάκις ὁ σύνδεσμος οὗτος [sc. δή], ὥσπερ ἐπὶ τῆς Καλυψοῦς πρὸς τὸν Ὀδυσσέα
>
> Διογενὲς Λαερτιάδη πολυμήχαν' Ὀδυσσεῦ,
>
> οὕτω δὴ οἶκόνδε φίλην ἐς πατρίδα γαῖαν... (*Odyssey* 5.204)
>
> εἰ γοῦν τὸν σύνδεσμον ἐξέλοις, συνεξαιρήσεις καὶ τὸ πάθος.
>
> Pseudo-Demetrius, *Style* 57
>
> Also in emotional passages this combiner [sc. δή] is often used, as in the scene with Calypso in the *Odyssey*:
>
> Zeus-born Laertes' son, creative Odysseus,
>
> just like that, homeward to your beloved fatherland...
>
> so if you were to take out the combiner, you would also take out the πάθος.

This explicit discussion of the πάθος that a σύνδεσμος contributes is unparalleled in early sources, other than Apollonius Dyscolus' discussion of γε.[121]

§59. Demetrius discusses these combiners only in the context of how they contribute to the "grand style," he does not attempt to define them or categorize them. Perhaps

120 Schenkeveld 1964:135-148 presents the discussion with relevant literature, and argues that the work must have been written in the first century CE or later. Morpurgo-Tagliabue 1980:145 calls this a thesis born out of desperation. This is not the place to present the discussion, let alone join in, so I will focus only on the notes on σύνδεσμοι in the work.

121 See below, §75. Elsewhere (Demetrius, *Style* 56) Demetrius notes that δή is used to mark a new beginning (*Iliad* 21.1), and that if the combiner had not been used, you might have thought Homer was still talking about the same thing.

exactly because of that reason, his notes contain a philological angle that is suprisingly rare in the scholia and early grammars. Because it falls outside the scope of his work, the author of *Style* does not make generalizations about σύνδεσμοι—for these, we have to go on to Apollonius Dyscolus.[122]

2.7 Apollonius Dyscolus

§60. The grammatical work done by Apollonius Dyscolus forms a watershed in the study of language, as far as can be established from the extant literature. Among his works we discuss in the present section first his *Syntax*, since in this general work he presents some general ideas about σύνδεσμοι. Then we turn to Περὶ συνδέσμων, the oldest extant study devoted entirely to combiners.

§61. Early on in his seminal work on *Syntax*, Apollonius attempts to define the category of σύνδεσμοι. He finds that these words tend to work in two important ways: first, they conjoin two or more phrases such that an essential connection is lost without their presence; and second, like ἄρθρα (articles) and προθέσεις (prepositions), σύνδεσμοι can only co-signify (συσσημαίνειν): τὰ γὰρ τοιαῦτα τῶν μορίων ἀεὶ συσσημαίνει.[123] That is, prepositions, articles, and combiners obtain meaning only when used in combination with nouns, verbs, and/or adverbs. Combiners co-signify in the following way:

(t13)

οἵ τε σύνδεσμοι πρὸς τὰς τῶν λόγων τάξεις ἢ ἀκολουθίας τὰς ἰδίας δυνάμεις παρεμφαίνουσιν

Apollonius Dyscolus, *Syntax* I.14.4-6

and the σύνδεσμοι, with respect to the positions or constructions of the phrases,[124] show[125] their individual forces[126]

Several different elements in this cryptic passage require explication. Lallot interprets Apollonius to mean that σύνδεσμοι have their own force, but that context determines which specific σύνδεσμος should be used, as well as the particular force that the chosen σύνδεσμος acquires in the sentence.[127]

122 See IV.3.5 for Demetrius' discussion of *kôla* and *kómmata* in Greek prose.

123 Apollonius Dyscolus, *Syntax* I.11.3-7 and I.14.2. The edition used is Lallot 1997, vol. I.

124 On the difficult term λόγος in Apollonius Dyscolus, see Lallot 1997:II.10 and Dickey 2007:245.

125 Or "add," as Lallot 1997:II.18 argues. The difference in sense is minimal, so I chose the more literal translation.

126 Householder 1981:23 translates: "Conjunctions, too, may vary in force according to their position in the sentence or the context," which is a free translation amounting to the same thing.

127 Lallot 1997:II.18, chapter 227.

§62. The two aspects of context that allow the combiner to display its force are the τάξις and the ἀκολουθία of λόγοι. The meaning of τάξις here is clear: it refers to the order of phrases, as elsewhere in Apollonius.[128] Ἀκολουθία is more ambiguous. The term can be used to describe the succession of an argument, but this sense is unlikely given Apollonius' usage of the word: in general, ἀκολουθία in Apollonius refers either to agreement between words or to a pattern of regularity.[129] As an extension of this latter meaning we have translated ἀκολουθίας as "constructions": the relation between sequences of words and their specific meanings. Thus combiners co-signify not only with phrases, but also with the constructions that those phrases make up.[130]

§63. At first sight, Apollonius' definition of σύνδεσμοι may not appear to cover those combiners commonly gathered under the name σύνδεσμοι παραπληρωματικοί. Unlike his predecessors, however, Apollonius has concrete ideas about these "filling" combiners, and later in his *Syntax* he refers to the Περὶ Συνδέσμων, *Combiners*, the work in which he had developed these ideas more fully:

(t14)

οἵ γε μὴν καλούμενοι παραπληρωματικοὶ [sc. σύνδεσμοι] οὐκ ἀπὸ τοῦ δηλουμένου τὴν θέσιν ἔσχον. οὐ γὰρ ἀληθές ἐστιν, ὥς τινες ὑπέλαβον, μόνον αὐτοὺς ἀναπληροῦν τὸ κεχηνὸς τῆς ἑρμηνείας καὶ διὰ τοῦτο εἰρῆσθαι παραπληρωματικούς· ὅτι γὰρ ἕκαστος αὐτῶν [sc. συνδέσμων παραπληρωματικῶν] ἔχει τινὰ δύναμιν, παρεστήσαμεν ἐν τῷ Περὶ Συνδέσμων.

Apollonius Dyscolus, *Syntax* III.378.4-379.1

However, those called filling [sc. combiners] do not get their name from their meaning. For it is not true, as some have understood it, that those [sc. filling combiners] only fill in the gaps of the expression, and it is because of this that they are called filling. That every one of them has some force, we showed in the work *Combiners*.

128 Consider, for example, *Syntax* I.81.8-9 ἐν δευτέρᾳ τάξει "in second position."

129 See Dickey 2007:220; compare also the idiom ἐν ἀκολουθίᾳ in Apollonius Dyscolus, which means "regular" in the sense of regular versus irregular verbs or nouns.

130 This translation of ἀκολουθία would also work very well for Apollonius' discussion of the σύνδεσμοι παρασυναπτικοί in *Combiners* 82.13-16: ὁ καλούμενος παρασυνα<πτικός,> ἔχων καὶ ἐπαγγελίαν τὴν τοῦ συμπλεκτικοῦ, ἐν οἷς <συμπλέκει λόγους>, ἔχων δὲ καὶ τὴν τοῦ συναπτικοῦ, ἐν οἷς ἀκολουθίας ἐστὶ παραστατικός ("the [kind of combiner] called παρασυναπτικός, which has both the meaning of the connective [sc. combiner], in that it connects words, and that of the hypothetical [sc. combiner], in that it is indicative of a <hypothetical> construction").

And further down:

(t15)

...σχεδὸν γὰρ ἕκαστος αὐτῶν ἴδιόν τι ἐπηγγέλλετο

Apollonius Dyscolus, *Syntax* III.380.13-14

...for nearly each one of them signals something specific

These passages outline Apollonius' approach to those σύνδεσμοι he calls redundant, on which he expands in *Combiners*, the first and only work from antiquity known to be dedicated solely to σύνδεσμοι. The text of the treatise is damaged, apparently corrupt in places, and incomplete. Even so, it gives us more material on the subject than any other work. As Apollonius' definitions in the *Syntax* already suggest, his *Combiners* contains innovative insights about the workings of σύνδεσμοι in general and in specific instances.

§64. In *Combiners* 222.12, where he argues that negations are adverbs, not combiners,[131] Apollonius comes closest to defining combiners.[132] Later he argues that a combiner can be taken out and replaced with another, which is an important characteristic of words for Apollonius.[133]

§65. It is clear that Apollonius went much further than any of his predecessors in trying to grasp and define σύνδεσμοι. He gives many insightful discussions of individual σύνδεσμοι as a result. Apollonius discusses a number of words that we would consider conjunctions (ὅτι, ἕνεκα and cognates, διότι, ἵνα, ὅπως, ὄφρα) and the adverbially used χάριν. The individual particles discussed are (in alphabetic order): ἄρα, ἆρα, αὐτάρ, γάρ, γε, δή, ἦρα, ἤ, ἦ, ἤτοι, θήν, καίπερ, καίτοι, μέν, μέντοι, μών, νυ, οὐκοῦν, οὔκουν, οὖν, περ, που, τοίνυν, τοιγάρτοι, τοιγαροῦν, ὦν, as well as the combinations ἀλλὰ μήν, ἀλλὰ γάρ, ἆρα γε, δέ γε, καὶ μήν, μὲν γάρ. In the following subsections we first discuss Apollonius' notes on the subcategories of σύνδεσμοι that he identifies, and then we turn to his insights on individual σύνδεσμοι.

[131] The five differences (between οὐ and ἤ, in this case) are the following: first, the two cannot be interchanged indiscriminately: οὐ is not the same as ἤ, even if the one can sometimes be placed instead of the other. Second, combiners co-signify, whereas negations have a clear inherent meaning. Third, combiners cannot forxm an utterance on their own, whereas negations can. Fourth, negations can have derived forms (οὐ and οὐχί), while ἤ cannot. Fifth, a negation with a verb forms a complete predicate, whereas ἤ with a verb needs another form, a second verb in this case.

[132] Although the very first part of the treatise (*Combiners* 214.4-215.26) discusses the form of the words briefly, an actual definition of the category is missing. This is striking, but this first part is so lacunose that we may posit that a concise definition was lost in transmission.

[133] See, for instance, *Combiners* 249.12-16. See also §70 on how Apollonnius connects this with Trypho's thesis that "if they are words, they must mean something."

2.7.1 Subcategories

§66. As far as can be reconstructed from his damaged treatise, Apollonius uses roughly the same set of subcategories as can be found in the *Téchnē* although he adds a few and does not always use the same term. Unlike the *Téchnē*, he does not appear to discuss the subcategories one-by-one in a systematic order, but that lack of order may be a result of the state of the work. Probably for the same reason, not all of his definitions of the different subcategories are extant. For disjunctive, subdisjunctive, affirmative (Dalimier 2001:87 translates "manifestantes"), dubitative, syllogistic, and expletive conjunctions there are longer discussions; the other categories are mentioned only in passing.[134] Of most interest are Apollonius Dyscolus' definitions of the disjunctive, conclusive, and redundant combiners.

§67. Regarding disjunctive combiners, Apollonius makes a very pertinent observation. He asks the question: How can a word that combines, or *con*joins (σύνδεσμος), be *dis*junctive (διαζευκτικός)? Is this not contradictory? His answer is that a disjunctive combiner conjoins words by presenting a disjunction in the words referred to:

(t16)

εἴρηνται μὲν σύνδεσμοι ἕνεκα τοῦ συνδεῖν τὰς φράσεις (...) ἕνεκα δὲ τοῦ ἀπ' αὐτῶν δηλουμένου διαζευκτικοὶ ὠνομάσθησαν, ὅλης γὰρ τῆς φράσεως <...>[135] πράγματα διαζευγνύουσιν.

Apollonius Dyscolus, *Combiners* 216.2-6

They are called σύνδεσμοι because they join together the expressions (...) and because of what they clarify they are called disjunctive, for of the entire expression they disjoin the facts.[136]

[134] συμπλεκτικοί (copulative), διαζευκτικοί (disjunctive), παραδιαζευκτικοί (subdisjunctive), συναπτικοί (hypothetical), παρασυναπτικοί (continuative), διασαφητικοί (comparative), αἰτιολογικοί (causal), ἀποτελεστικός (resultative), διαπορητικοί (dubitative), συλλογιστικοί (conclusive), παραπληρωματικοί (redundant).

[135] There is a lacuna in the text after φράσεως, Dalimier 2001:71n1 gives Schneider's conjecture: ὅλης γὰρ τῆς φράσεως < ὄντες συνδετικοί, τὰ ἐν αὐτῇ > πράγματα διαζευγνύουσιν: "for, being conjoiners of the entire phrase, they disjoin the realities in them"; also giving a translation of Bekker's proposal. Neither seems convincing to me, as what is expected in this sentence is not a revisiting of both sides of the σύνδεσμοι διαζευκτικοί, but (ἕνεκα δὲ) an explanation of why they are called διαζευκτικοί. In that sense, the lacunose clause as it stands is clear enough: "they disjoin the realities of the entire utterance." Whatever is missing in the lacuna must be expected to only add clarity to the construction, no more.

[136] See De Kreij 2013 for a discussion of πρᾶγμα in the definitions given in the *Téchnē* and in Apollonius' *Combiners*; I follow Dalimier 2001:467, who reads πρᾶγμα as "*Réalité* pensée correspondant à un énoncé," which I paraphrase as "fact."

Apollonius' explanation bears a striking resemblance to the definition given in the *Téchnē*:

(t17)

διαζευκτικοὶ δέ εἰσιν ὅσοι τὴν μὲν φράσιν ἐπισυνδέουσιν, ἀπὸ δὲ πράγματος εἰς πρᾶγμα διιστᾶσιν.

Téchnē 20.10-11

Disjunctive are those [sc. combiners] that conjoin the expression, but set one fact apart from another.

The resonance of the terms φράσις, συνδεῖν and most of all πράγματα must be significant.[137] However the lacuna is resolved, the explanation in Apollonius is more extensive than the definition in the *Téchnē*, but its meaning is not as clear. Moreover, the term διιστᾶσιν in the *Téchnē's* definition seems more advanced than διαζευγνύουσιν, as it explains the category (διαζευκτικοί) without resorting to the same root. The definition in the *Téchnē* appears to be further developed than that given by Apollonius; yet another argument to regard this part of the *Téchnē* as composed later than Apollonius Dyscolus.

§68. Apollonius Dyscolus discusses conclusive (συλλογιστικοί) σύνδεσμοι several times, and mentions they used to be called ἐπιφορικοί by the Stoics.[138] If the *Téchnē* was indeed written by Dionysius Thrax, we may have perhaps expected to find this term, but this is not the case. Rather, like Apollonius, the *Téchnē* uses the word ἐπιφορά, "conclusion," in his definition, but never the adjective ἐπιφορικός.[139]

§69. Doubtlessly, Apollonius' most important contribution to the study of σύνδεσμοι is the contention that redundant combiners (σύνδεσμοι παραπληρωματικοί) are not only fillers. Recall that Trypho had compared σύνδεσμοι to pieces of cloth placed as buffers between amphorae.[140] Apollonius discusses the fact that some scholars say that σύνδεσμοι παραπληρωματικοί should not be called σύνδεσμοι, since they do not conjoin parts of the utterance as such.[141] While Apollonius concedes that not all σύνδεσμοι παραπληρωματικοί actually combine, he leans toward the views of one author (conjectured to be the Stoic

[137] Dalimier 2001:249n1+2notes the similarities with definitions in the scholia to Dionysius Thrax, but fails to discuss the similarities with the definition in the *Téchnē*.

[138] Apollonius Dyscolus, *Combiners* 251.28.

[139] See Dalimier 2001:411-412 for a discussion of the two definitions.

[140] See §51 for the text and the reference.

[141] *Combiners* 247.30-248.1 Ἔτι δὲ καί τινές φασιν οὐ δεόντως αὐτοὺς συνδέσμους εἰρῆσθαι, εἴγε συνδέσεως λόγων οὐκ εἰσὶν αἴτιοι, see §§53-54 above.

Chairemon)[142] who argues that since these words look like combiners formally (τύπῳ), they should be designated as such.[143]

§70. After reporting Trypho's discussion of σύνδεσμοι παραπληρωματικοί (see §51 above), Apollonius adds the following "for this we will plead too, having added something extra."[144] The "something extra" Apollonius actually deduces from a premise by Trypho quoted earlier in the work: "[if] they are [words] they must *mean* something."[145] What Apollonius is hinting at, and what he develops in his treatise *Combiners*, is that even expletive particles (can) contribute meaning to a sentence.[146] He argues that one characteristic of words is their interchangeability, the fact that they can be replaced by synonyms, such as αὐτάρ for δέ.[147] Moreover, even enclitics are actual words, as shown by the fact that they can bear the accent when placed next to each other. Thus, Apollonius concludes, if on formal grounds σύνδεσμοι may be regarded as words, they should mean something. Finally, he argues that just because a word is redundant in one utterance does not mean it ceases to be a word. He points out that an adjective λευκώλενος that is redundant in one passage is not redundant at all in another context.[148] Likewise, he argues, so-called fillers are not always redundant.

§71. Apollonius then moves on to another problem with the category. Unlike the copulative, disjunctive, or causal σύνδεσμοι, the παραπληρωματικοί cannot be said to all do roughly the same thing:[149]

(t18)

οἱ μέντοι παραπληρωματικοὶ οὐχ ἓν ἐπηγγέλλοντο κατὰ τὸ δηλούμενον. εἴγε ὁ μὲν δή περιγραφήν τινα ἐδήλου, ὁ δὲ πέρ ἐναντιότητά τινα μετ' αὐξήσεως, καὶ

142 On the conjecture <Χαιρήμων> (248.1) by Bekker, see Dalimier 2001:385-386. For the argument that Apollonius Dyscolus' work has much in common with the ideas of the Stoics, see Blank 1982.

143 After adducing the examples of patronymics that may not give a father's name, but are still called patronymics, and of masculine words that do not actually denote something masculine, but are still called masculine, he says οὕτω καὶ ἂν τύπῳ ᾖ ὁ παραπληρωματικὸς κεχορηγημένος συνδεσμικῷ, μὴ μὴν δηλουμένῳ, εἰρήσεται σύνδεσμος, in Apollonius Dyscolus, *Combiners* 248.8-9.

144 ᾧ καὶ συνηγορήσωμεν, ἔτι τινὰ προσθέντες. De Velsen [1853] 1965:44 also notes this addition by Apollonius.

145 *Combiners* 249.9-10: [εἰ λέ]ξεις, ὀφείλουσί τι δηλοῦν.

146 Regarding the argument that Apollonius Dyscolus is the first to claim this, see Wouters 1979:85n55 and Pecorella 1962:187-188.

147 Apollonius Dyscolus, *Combiners* 249.13.

148 Apollonius Dyscolus, *Combiners* 249.21-30; he compares λευκώλενος in *Iliad* 6.377 (πῇ ἔβη Ἀνδρομάχη λευκώλενος;) and *Iliad* 1.55 (λευκώλενος Ἥρη).

149 At the same time, some σύνδεσμοι παραπληρωματικοί have the same function and therefore need not be discussed separately: "It would be redundant to discuss ῥα after δή ... as we use them for the same thing [i.e. marking transitions]" (252.11-13).

ἔτι ὁ γέ μειότητα ἢ ἐπίτασιν θαυμασμοῦ, καὶ εἰ διάφοροι κατὰ τὸ δηλούμενον, πῶς ἦν δυνατὸν μίαν ὀνομασίαν ἀπὸ τοῦ δηλουμένου χωρίσαι;

Apollonius Dyscolus, *Combiners* 253.15-18

Still, the filling [combiners] do not say one thing as to their meaning. If δή signals a kind of conclusion,[150] περ indicates an opposition and amplification, and further γε signals limitation or underlines the amazement, and if they differ as to their meaning, how would it be possible to set them apart under one name [i.e. category] based on their meaning?

Apollonius answers this question by arguing that the majority of instances must have priority over the minority: copulative (συμπλεκτικοί) combiners often connect even if they are sometimes redundant—so they are rightly called copulative combiners. Similarly, σύνδεσμοι παραπληρωματικοί are filling in the majority of instances, hence their name.[151]

2.7.2 Important topics raised by Apollonius

§72. In the present section we focus on three discussions in the *Combiners* that coincide with three lines of research important to our monograph: (1) particles and prosody, (2) particles working above the sentence level, and (3) the polyfunctionality of particles.[152]

§73. First, on the issue of prosody, consider the following comment on καίπερ:

(t19)

ὑπεναντίωσιν γὰρ ἐδήλωσεν ὁ καί<περ>, καὶ δῆλον ὅτι διὰ τὸν πέρ, ὅπου γε καὶ κατ᾽ ἰδίαν ὁ πέρ ἐναντιωματικός ἐστι μετ᾽ αὐξήσεως.

Apollonius Dyscolus, *Combiners* 251.3.

καίπερ shows an opposition,[153] and it is clear that this is because of περ, as also on its own περ is concessive with amplification.

150 See the discussion in §74 below.

151 Apollonius Dyscolus, *Combiners* 252.22-28.

152 Notes on particles by Apollonius will be referenced in the relevant places in the monograph.

153 Dalimier translates "contrariété supposée," with a discussion on page 407, but a quick look at the other instances of this word in the TLG shows there is no reason to translate it as anything other than simply: opposition or contradiction. The question remains why Apollonius chooses ὑπεναντίωσιν over ἐναντίωσιν. It is tempting to regard the υπ- part as an indication that καίπερ shows an *implied* opposition. καίπερ signals that the clause it is in will in some way contradict the clause that follows after or comes before (such as: *Even though he was a good man, he died a horrible death*).

The combination καίπερ is described as getting its force from περ, as both combiners have the same function. The concessive force of περ is clear enough, and repeated in all later descriptions of the particle, but more notable is the comment on amplification (αὔξησις). When he talks of "amplification," Apollonius appears to be thinking of some form of emphasis: compare a similar comment in the *Syntax*, where Apollonius is more explicit: [σημαίνει] ἐναντιότητα ὁ πέρ μετ' αὐξήσεως ἐμφατικῆς ("περ [conveys] a concessive force, along with emphatic amplification").[154] What Apollonius has in mind by "amplification" is not self-evident, but we envision some kind of prosodic emphasis resulting from the addition of the enclitic περ.[155]

§74. Apollonius touches upon another important dimension of the function of σύνδεσμοι παραπληρωματικοί in his attempt to describe the function of δή, often called redundant. He argues that it can effect a transition in discourse, having an effect similar to that of a περιγραφή, a conclusion or summary, before one moves on to the next topic:

(t20)

Ἔτι ὁ δή ὡς μὲν παρέλκει, παντὶ προῦπτον· ὡς δὲ καὶ πολλάκις μετάβασιν λόγου ποιεῖται, σαφὲς ἐκ τῶν τοιούτων

οἱ μὲν δὴ παρ' ὄχεσφιν ἐρητύοντο μένοντες (*Iliad* 15.3)

καὶ τῶν παραπλησίων. νοοῦμεν γὰρ λόγου ἔκλειψιν καὶ ἀρχὴν ἑτέρου, ὡς εἰ καὶ ἐν περιγραφῇ κατελιμπάνετο ὁμοίως τῷ

ὣς οἱ μὲν Τρῶες φυλακὰς ἔχον (*Iliad* 9.1)

ὣς ὁ μὲν ἔνθ' ἠρᾶτο (*Odyssey* 7.1).

Apollonius Dyscolus, *Combiners* 251.19-26

Also for δή, that it is redundant is obvious, but that it also often effects a transition of discourse is clear from the following:

And they then were stopped around their chariots, waiting, (*Iliad* 15.3)

and similar [verses]. For we see a leaving off from [one part of] the discourse and the beginning of another, as if also leaving it with a conclusion, similar to:

154 Apollonius Dyscolus, *Syntax* III.380.16. Cf. Devine and Stephens 1994:345-347.

155 Out of the five instances of αὔξησις and cognates in Apollonius three are in the description of περ, the other two in descriptions of the inflections of cases. As a result, they are not much help in explaining what Apollonius means here.

Thus, the Trojans set up guards (*Iliad* 9.1)

Thus, he prayed there (*Odyssey* 7.1).

Apollonius compares the constructions οἱ μὲν δή and ὣς X μέν, both occurring often in transitional passages in Homer. Both constructions signal to the reader that one episode is left behind, and another begins.[156] Apollonius' analysis of δή in this context shows a crucial new step in the study of σύνδεσμοι. Rather than discussing the function of a σύνδεσμος only with respect to the surrounding words or the host clause, he shows how important it is to consider the place of a σύνδεσμος, or string of σύνδεσμοι, in the larger discourse. Here he has noted the common occurrence (καὶ τῶν παραπλησίων) of δή in such concluding verses just before a transition to a new episode.

§75. Finally, Apollonius shows a nascent awareness of the polyfunctionality of particles, that is, they can do different things depending on the context (remember his claim that combiners co-signify). When discussing σύνδεσμοι and the subcategories to which they are assigned, Apollonius often points out that categorization is not sacred: ἄρα, for example, though it generally has a conclusive force, can also be redundant, in clauses like ὣς ἄρα μιν εἰπόντα τέλος θανάτοιο κάλυψε ("so then, when he had spoken, the end of death enveloped him," *Iliad* 16.502).[157] Likewise, γε is often used as a filler, but that is not the case in constructions like καλῶς γε, where it intensifies the emotion (ἔκπληξις), nor in τοῦτό γέ μοι χάρισαι, "grant me just this one thing." He adds: ἔμφασις ἱκανὴ μειότητος καὶ τοῦ μηδὲν ἀποφαινομένου, "the suggestion[158] of limitation is sufficient, even if nothing expresses it explicitly."[159] That is to say, τοῦτό γέ μοι χάρισαι on its own is enough to convey "grant me just this one thing" rather than "grant me this one thing." Here, Apollonius is in fact contemplating the polyfunctionality of certain combiners. This reminds us of the brief definition he gives in the *Syntax*,[160] where he argues that combiners can have different forces depending on context. Even though the examples in the *Combiners* describe combiners that can either have a function or be redundant, he is the first to attempt explanation of this phenomenon.[161]

§76. Apollonius' *ad hoc* discussions of σύνδεσμοι contain several observations essential even for the modern student of particles. While his reading of περ may seem vague, it hints at an insight that is missing in all early and much of the modern literature. His observation that σύνδεσμοι may be connected to emphasis may be linked to prosody, an issue that we will pick up in several of the research chapters. His analysis of δή as a

156 For more literature on δή, see δή in ORPS (our online database).

157 Quoted in Apollonius Dyscolus, *Combiners* 254.22-25.

158 ἔμφασις can mean "suggestion (as opposed to expression)," Dickey 2007:237.

159 Apollonius Dyscolus, *Combiners* 250.6-10.

160 See §61 above.

161 Compare for example the *Téchnē*, which simply lists some particles under more than one category, without further explanation.

word that can effect transitions between larger stretches of narrative suggests that he thinks that σύνδεσμοι are relevant not only to the current and preceding clause, but also to larger subdivisions of discourse.[162] Finally, Apollonius reminds us throughout that σύνδεσμοι need not be limited to doing or meaning one thing, but can have multiple functions, depending on the context. Although he never comes to an all-encompassing description of redundant σύνδεσμοι that does justice to the combiners he collects under that term, the multiple angles from which he approaches these words must have made the ancient reader nod to the rhetorical question he asks:

(t21)

Πῶς οὖν ἔτι οὐδὲν πληροῦσιν οἱ παραπληρωματικοί;

Apollonius Dyscolus, *Conjunctions* 250.11-12.

How can we then still [say] that fillers add nothing?

2.8 After Apollonius Dyscolus

§77. Apollonius' work was not preserved by chance; his work on grammar remained the standard work on Greek grammar all through the middle ages. Still, some later scholars deserve mention: his son and pupil Aelius Herodianus, Nicanor "the punctuator," and Priscian, who wrote a Latin grammar in the fifth century CE heavily influenced by Apollonius' work. In between these figures come the majority of the extant grammatical papyri. To these scholars and works we now turn.

§78. Herodian, like his father, produced works on grammar himself, and these works include some notes on σύνδεσμοι.[163] The work's manner of organization enables us to establish what categories of σύνδεσμοι Herodian recognized.[164] Since most of his work is devoted to accents, however, his work does not yield any analyses of the function of σύνδεσμοι.[165] Nicanor's work cannot rightly be called grammatical, since he was first and foremost a scholar of Homer. He gained his nickname "the punctuator" (ὁ Στιγματίας) because he undertook to help the reader of the Homeric text by adding punctuation. In his system, particles play an important part in deciding what kind of punctuation he introduced: he linked different particles to pauses of different lengths (χρόνοι); his work is discussed at length in IV.3 §§31-36.

[162] See for this point II.3, III.4, IV.3, and IV.5 especially.

[163] Aelius Herodianus, *General Prosody* 515-520.

[164] συμπλεκτικοί, διαζευκτικοί, παραδιαζευκτικοί, συναπτικοί, παρασυναπτικοί, διασαφητικοί, αἰτιολογικοί, διαπορητικοί, συλλογιστικοί, παραπληρωματικοί.

[165] Many of his notes are also preserved in the scholia to the *Iliad*.

2.8.1 Early grammars

§79. The oldest substantial extant grammatical papyrus (*P.Yale* I 25, first century CE) discusses fewer subcategories of σύνδεσμοι than Apollonius and Herodian. The seven categories in the papyrus are, conversely, roughly the same as those listed in the *Téchnē* attributed to Thrax, though worded differently.[166] More importantly, the papyrus attempts a definition of σύνδεσμος:

(t22)

σύνδεσμος δ' ἐστὶν λέξις συνάπτουσα
τὰ μέρη τῆς ἑρμεν<ε>ίας.

P.Yale I 25, 54-55

and a combiner is a word that joins together
the parts of the expression.

The simplicity of the definition is striking, especially compared to all the other extant definitions.[167] Scholars have therefore concluded that it is a simple school grammar, designed with the practical aim of listing and describing lexical categories rather than providing a philosophical foundation of the workings of language. This conclusion may be extended to most of the papyri from this genre, dating from the second to the sixth century CE.[168]

§80. This brings us to the end of antiquity, and to a grammarian who flourished around 500 CE, Priscian. His *Institutions of Grammar* describes the Latin language and is strongly influenced by Appollonius. Perhaps as a result of his indebtedness, he calls the Latin equivalent of σύνδεσμοι *coniunctiones*, not *particulae*. In the book devoted to combiners (book XVI), Priscian gives one of the most comprehensive definitions of combiners in antiquity:[169]

166 παραλαμβάνεται (...) χάρις συνπλοκῆς, [χάρις] διαζεύξεως, [χάρις] ἀκολουθίας, [χάρις] αἰτίας, [χάρις] ἀπορίας, [χάρις] συλλογισμοῦ, [χάρις] τοῦ μὴ κεχηνέναι τὴν σύνθεσιν.

167 See I.3.2 for the similarity between this simple definition and modern attempts at defining particles and discourse markers.

168 See Di Benedetto 1958-1959 and Wouters 1979 and 1995; Wouters 1995:97 promises more papyri to be published in the Oxyrhynchus series, but as far as I have been able to establish, this has not happened yet.

169 The edition used is Keil 1859 *Grammatici Latini*, volumes II and III.

(t23)

Coniunctio est pars orationis indeclinabilis, coniunctiva aliarum partium orationis, quibus consignificat, vim vel ordinationem demonstrans

Priscian *Institutions of Grammar* XVI I.1-2 (Keil III.93.1-2)

A combiner is an indeclinable part of the expression, which connects the other parts of the expression, with which it co-signifies, signalling either a force [of its own] or the arrangement [of the parts of the utterance]

All separate aspects of Priscian's definition can be traced back to his predecessors, but this is the first time we find the elements combined. In book XVI of the *Institutions of Grammar*, Priscian discusses only a small selection of combiners, and often has recourse to Greek translations. The list of subcategories that Priscian identifies comes closest to that found in Herodian, but he has added a few categories not mentioned before. After listing all possible kinds of combiners,[170] Priscian devotes only a few lines to most kinds and none to some. Two apparent additions to the list, the *coniunctiones ablativae* and *praesumptivae*, remain undiscussed, which makes it hard to guess what he meant with the terms (hence the lack of translation) and which combiners he had in mind.

§81. In the centuries following Apollonius Dyscolus, grammars leaned heavily on his work, but there is little evidence for actual progress in the thinking about combiners. The genre of the school grammar emerged, and several examples are extant. For all these papyri their function is directly reflected in a focus on categorizing and exemplifying rather than analyzing combiners. Priscian wrote an entirely different kind of work, but as far as the study of combiners is concerned, he presents a synthesis of earlier ideas rather than innovative analyses.

2.8.2 Late antique scholia to the *Téchnē*

§82. By the fourth century CE, the *Téchnē* attributed to Dionysius Thrax appears to have become a common and often-copied work, and its manuscripts gathered a mass of scholia and commentaries over the centuries.[171] These scholia and commentaries are some of the few grammatical sources we can date with certainty, falling between the fifth and tenth centuries. Whatever additions they propose to the *Téchnē*'s analysis of σύνδεσμοι are taken directly from Apollonius Dyscolus or other sources we have already discussed.

[170] Copulativa, continuativa, subcontinuativa, adiunctiva, causalis, effectiva, approbativa, disiunctiva, subdisiunctiva, disertiva, ablativa, praesumptiva, adversativa, collectiva vel rationalis, dubitativa, confirmativa, completiva, see Keil III.93.13-16.

[171] Pecorella 1962:186-196.

§83. Heliodorus, one of these commentators,[172] offers a revised definition of σύνδεσμος. The definition adds several characteristics in comparison with the definition in the *Téchnē*,[173] and Pecorella believes that it was inspired by Apollonius' definition of σύνδεσμοι in a lost part of his *Syntax*. [174]

(t24)

> σύνδεσμος ἐστι μέρος λόγου ἄκλιτον, συνδετικὸν τῶν τοῦ λόγου μερῶν, οἷς καὶ συσσημαίνει, ἢ τάξιν ἢ δύναμιν <ἢ καὶ τάξιν καὶ δύναμιν> παριστῶν.
>
> Heliodorus *Commentary to Dionysius Thrax*[175]

> a combiner is an indeclinable part of speech, to bind together the parts of speech, with which it co-signifies, showing either order or force <or both order and force>.

Note the striking similarity with Priscian's definition, which we discuss above: "a combiner is an indeclinable part of the expression, which connects the other parts of the expression, with which it co-signifies, signalling either a force [of its own] or the arrangement [of the parts of the utterance]."[176] It is generally assumed, and may be observed in comparison, that Priscian based much of his *Institutions* on Apollonius Dyscolus' work, which supports Pecorella's hypothesis that this definition is in fact to be attributed to Apollonius. The definition combines different ideas in a way that fits well with our sense of Apollonius' approach to σύνδεσμοι. It is, in addition, more intricate than the definitions we find in the different *Téchnai*. Since a definition of σύνδεσμοι is extant in Apollonius' *Syntax*,[177] we find it more likely that the source both for Priscian and for Heliodorus was the definition of σύνδεσμοι in a lost part of Apollonius' *Combiners*.

§84. Apart from this definition, which is thus probably to be attributed to Apollonius, the scholia to the *Téchnē* cannot be said to offer new insights. Although the scholia expand upon their source text, the *Téchnē* attributed to Thrax, they do not form a body of innovative research when regarded in the broader scholarly context.

172 These commentators are hard to date, but Heliodorus is certainly later than the sixth century, as he excerpts the sixth century grammarian Choeroboscus. Schmidhauser 2010:509 dates him to the ninth century.

173 See §57 above.

174 Pecorella 1962:188 posits that it would have figured in one of the lost parts of the *Syntax* (strikingly, not in the *Combiners*).

175 The edition used is Hilgard 1901, with this passage on page 102. The words between <...> are an emendation by Hilgard, which I deem too bold, and have left untranslated.

176 Pecorella fails to mention this similarity in his commentary.

177 Apollonius Dyscolus, *Syntax* I.14.4-6, quoted and discussed in §61 above.

2.8.3 The medieval lexicographers

§85. Other more or less datable sources are Hesychius' *Lexicon*, the *Suidas*, and Eustathius' commentary to Homer. Hesychius' lexicon, as we would expect from the genre to which it belongs, rarely offers more than synonyms for σύνδεσμοι, which in turn usually have an analogue in the scholia. However, the lexicon's value lies in the fact that it was readily available to early modern researchers, as opposed to the scholia that were by that period attested in only a few manuscripts and thus were hardly accessible. The lexicon's popularity is probably why we find regular references to Hesychius in works from the fifteenth, sixteenth, and seventeenth century.

§86. The *Suidas* lexicon from the tenth century generally gives some more information per lemma than Hesychius, but like Hesychius the *Suidas* does not so much add new knowledge as compile older knowledge.

§87. Moderately more significant are Eustathius' commentaries on the *Iliad* and *Odyssey*, based in large part on the scholia. Indeed, Eustathius' explanations of σύνδεσμοι do not add much to the scholia. Although his classifications of individual σύνδεσμοι have a different focus than the scholia—he regards καί as redundant more often than δέ, for example—few of his comments on σύνδεσμοι are noteworthy, except for the following two on γάρ and μήν.

§88. On γάρ at *Iliad* 17.221, Eustathius remarks that it is either redundant, or gives the cause for something left out ("ἐλλείψεώς τινος"). The latter part of his comment adumbrates a whole tradition of positing ellipsis to explain the use of γάρ in problematic instances.[178] The topic of ellipsis returns in a discussion of γάρ in dialogue.[179] In this context implications and presuppositions are extremely relevant to particle use; as will become apparent, our approach acknowledges the value of these early views.

§89. On μήν, Eustathius is the first attested author to note its relation to μέν and μάν in other dialects, where μέν is Ionic, μάν Doric (which had already been noted in the scholia), and μήν is "most common," presumably in the Greek that he knew.[180] This realization would later lead to a reassessment of μέν as more than just one part of a μέν - δέ construction.[181]

2.9 A Renaissance of the Particle

§90. The incomplete material left to us strongly suggests that after Apollonius Dyscolus not much innovative work on σύνδεσμοι was done until the sixteenth century. This is

[178] See γάρ in ORPS (our online database) for literature.

[179] See III.3.3.1.5 for discussion.

[180] Eustathius, *Commentary* chapter 500.8-9.

[181] See μέν in ORPS (our online database) for more literature, and II.2.4 for an analysis of μέν in Homer and Pindar.

when Devarius wrote his *Liber de Graecae Linguae Particulis* (1588), a fully extant work on particles that would form the basis for all discussions of particles until well into the nineteenth century. He appears to be the first to use the Latin term *particula* rather than Priscian's *coniunctio*.[182] He set a new standard on form, quantity, and quality, yet his definition illustrates his strong dependence on the ancient scholarship:

(t25)

> *Constitui de Graecae linguae vocibus quibusdam agere, quae tametsi rem ipsae per se nullam fere significant; tamen in aliarum vocum constructione positae vim aliquam habent, efficacitatemque: seu emphasim aut certe qualitatem aliam sermoni tribuunt. (...) modique alicuius aut ordinis veluti signa sunt; continuandique aut transeundi, aut interrogandi, aut dubitandi, aut ratiocinandi, aut qualitatem aliam referendi vim habent.*
>
> Devarius 1588:1

> I have undertaken to discuss a number of Greek words, which, although they themselves signify almost nothing, still when put into constructions with other words have some force (*vis*) and power (*efficacitas*): they add either emphasis or some other quality to the utterance. (...) They are like signs of some mode or order, and have a continuative, transitional, interrogative, dubitative, or ratiocinative force, or a force that conveys some other quality.

Unlike Apollonius and his other predecessors, Devarius discussed the particles not in groups of functions, but rather per lexical item, roughly in alphabetical order.[183] This

[182] See Schenkeveld 1988:83.

[183] The extremely inclusive list of particles and combinations that Devarius discusses are, in order: ἀλλά, ἀλλὰ γάρ, ἀλλ' εἴπερ, ἀλλ' εἰ ἄρα, ἀλλ' ἤ, ἀλλ' ἦ, ἀλλὰ μή, ἀλλὰ μήν, ἀλλά νὴ Δία, ἄλλοτι, ἀλλ' ὅτι, ἄλλοτι ἤ, ἄλλοτι οὖν, ἄλλως τε καί, ἀμέλει, ἄν, ἄνθ' ὧν, ἄνθ' ὁτοῦ, ἄρα, ἀτάρ, αὐτάρ, ἄτινα, ἀτεχνῶς, αὖ, αὐτίκα, αὐτός, ἄχρι, μέχρι, γάρ, γε, γε δή, γέ τοι, γοῦν, δέ, δαί, δεῖνα, δή, δήπου, δῆθεν, δῆτα, Διά, δ' οὖν, ἐάν, εἰ, εἰ βούλει δέ, εἰ δὲ μή, εἰ καί, εἰ μή, εἴπερ, εἰς, εἶτα, ἐμοί, ἕνεκα ἐμοῦ, ἐπεί, ἐπειδή, ἔπειτα, ἐξ ὧν, ἀφ' ὧν, ἔξω, ἐς, ἔστε, ἔτι τοίνυν, ἐφ' ὅσον, ἐφ' ᾧ, ἐφ' οἷς, ἐφ' ὁ, ἕως, τέως, ἦ, ἤ, ἦ που, ἦ γάρ, ἦ γὰρ ἄν, ἤδη, ἦ μάλα δή, ἦ μήν, ἤπου, ἢ οὔ [sic], ἤτοι, ἵνα, καθό, καθ' ὅτι, καθ' ὅσον, καί, καὶ μήν, καὶ μέντοι, καὶ μὲν δή, καὶ τοίνυν, καίτοι, καὶ δή, κἄν, κοὐδ' οὖν, μά, μέν, μέντοι, μὲν οὖν, μέχρι, μέχρις, μή, μήν, μὴ γάρ, μὴ δῆτα, μὴ ὅτι, μὴ οὐ, μὴ οὐκ, μήποτε, μήτι, μήτις, μή τοι γε, μόνον οὐ, μόνον οὐκ, μῶν, ναί, νὴ δία, νῦν δέ, ὁ, ὅδε, ἥδε, τόδε, ὃ δήποτε, οἷος, οἷον, οἴμοι, ὅμως, ὅπη, ὅπου, ὁπόταν, ὅπως, ὅς, ὅσος, ὅση, ὅσον, τόσος, ὅτε, ὅτι, ὅτι μή, ὅτι τοίνυν, οὐ, οὐκ, οὐ γάρ, οὐ γὰρ δή, οὐ γὰρ ἄν που, οὐ γάρ που, οὐ γὰρ ἀλλά, οὐδ' εἰ, οὐδέν, οὐδέν τι μᾶλλον, οὐδὲ γὰρ οὐδέ, οὐδὲ μήν, οὐ δῆτα, οὐκοῦν, οὔκουν, οὐ μέν, οὐ μέντοι ἀλλά, οὐ μή, οὐ μήν, οὐ γὰρ ὅπως, οὕτως, οὐ μὴν οὐδέ, οὐ μὴν ἀλλά, οὐδέ, οὐ μήν πω, οὖν, οὔτι, οὔ τοι, οὐχ ὅτι, οὐχ ὅπως, οὐχ οἷον, οὐχ ὅσον, οὐ τοίνυν, πάνυ γε, πάνυ τοι, πάλιν, παρ' ὅ, παρ' ὅσον, περ, πῆ, πλήν, ποῦ, πρίν, προς, πῶς, σχολῇ, τὸ μέν, τὸ δέ, τὰ μέν, τὰ δέ, ταῦτα, προ τοῦ, ταύτῃ, ταχύ, τί, τί δέ...εἰ μή, τί δή, τί μήν, ποιός, τὸ καὶ τό, τὸ μέν τι, τὸ δέ τι, τοιοῦτος, τοῦτο μέν, τοῦτο δέ, τοι,

lexicographical organization made for a much more systematic work, and required Devarius (the first to do this as far as we know) to decide which specific lexical items to include and exclude from the category he defined as *particulae*.[184] As the list shows Devarius' selection is extremely diverse, ranging from single words to full phrases and including particles, conjunctions, interjections, pronominals, and verb forms.

§91. In later works on Greek particles the process of selection became central: from the long list of Devarius, Denniston only discusses thirty-two particles and their combinations.[185] There is hardly any agreement between the authors who worked from the sixteenth to the twenty-first century about the exact definition of the word "particle," or about the delineation of the group of words to be gathered under the term. Note, however, that it was not until the sixteenth century that delineation of the category was regarded as an actual problem.[186] Devarius' landmark work led to a new appreciation for particles and laid the foundations for the important scholarly works by Hoogeveen 1769, Hartung 1832-1833, Klotz 1842, Bäumlein 1861, and Denniston 1934.

τοίνυν, τοῦ, τῳ, ὑπέρ, ὑπὲρ ὧν, φεῦ, ῶ, ὦν, ὡς, ὥστε, ἄγε, φέρε, ἴθι, δεῦρο, ἴτε, ἔστιν ὅτε, ἔστιν οὗ, ἔστιν ὡς, ἐστί, τί δέ, τί οὖν, ἄπαγε, οὐαί, ὤ.

[184] Both Budé 1529 and Estienne 1572 already used the term, like the ancient Latin grammarians, but Devarius first treated it as an independent—if very diverse—group.

[185] ἀλλά, ἄρα, ἆρα, ἀτάρ, αὐτάρ, γάρ, γε, δέ, οὐδέ, μηδέ, δή, δαί, δῆθεν, δήπου, δήπουθεν, δῆτα, ἦ, θήν, καί, μάν (μέν/μήν), μέν, μέντοι, οὖν (ὦν), περ, που, τε, τοι, καίτοι, τοιγάρ, τοιγαροῦν, τοιγάρτοι, τοίνυν.

[186] This is not to say that there were no discussions about which grammatical category several lexical items belonged to, as we find these as early as in the Homeric scholia. However, no attempt was made at a normative definition of the category. As n. 1 shows, however, even in modern times there are more scholars who note the problem than those who attempt to tackle it.

I.3

Approaches to Particles and Discourse Markers

Annemieke Drummen

3.1 Introduction

§1. I.2 offers an overview of the scholarship on Greek particles up to the beginning of the Renaissance. The first authors in this period who paid considerable attention to the description of Greek words were Budaeus (Budé) in his *Commentarii Linguae Graecae* from 1529, and Stephanus (Estienne) in his 1572 *Thesaurus Linguae Graecae*. Devarius, a Greek scholar working in Rome, was the first modern scholar to devote an entire monograph to Greek particles in 1588.[1] Subsequently, Vigerus (Viger) with his 1627 *De Praecipuis Graecae Dictionis Idiotismis Liber* (a work not specifically on particles) and Hoogeveen with *Doctrina Particularum Linguae Graecae* (1769) made further major contributions to this scholarship. In the nineteenth century, the number of publications increased considerably; the main works were the monographs by Hartung 1832-1833 and Bäumlein 1861.[2] The twentieth century produced eight more particle monographs,[3] among many other studies.

§2. All these works are still available today and have been valuable to our research.[4] These studies, together with the ancients' descriptions of particles (see I.2), may be viewed as forming a diachronic, horizontal axis along which our work can be plotted—the gradually developing body of research on which we continue to build in this monograph.

1 See I.2 §§90-91 for more on Devarius' work, and the heterogeneous list of Greek words he regards as particles.

2 Other monographs on Greek particles from the nineteenth century are Stephens 1837 and Paley 1881. Other important works are Klotz's edition (1835) of and commentary (1842) on Devarius.

3 Des Places 1929, Denniston 1950 [1934], Labéy 1950, Thrall 1962, Blomqvist 1969, Thyresson 1977, Van Ophuijsen and Sicking 1993, and Redondo Moyano 1995. In the twenty-first century, the dissertations of Koier 2013 and Zakowski 2017 (see §73 below) have been added to this list.

4 The descriptions of a selection of particles found in these works are summarized in part V, our online repository of particle studies.

§3. The current chapter concerns the vertical axis of our research, which is formed by modern linguistic approaches to particles and functionally similar words in different languages. I (AD—see I.1 §25) will first describe the main theoretical issues that are important in this kind of research, and give an overview of several frameworks that are often applied. Subsequent sections will briefly discuss other relevant background from modern linguistic studies, as well as existing applications of the aforementioned approaches to Greek and Latin. The survey is intended, first and foremost, to provide a context for our research by familiarizing the reader with the cross-disciplinary antecedents to our work.[5] Secondarily, we aim, by providing this methodological overview, to suggest further avenues for application to the ancient languages.

§4. It is useful to be informed about general principles of verbal communication when investigating Greek particles, because ancient Greek, regardless of specific genres, was used for communication just like any language spoken and written today. Specifically, words functionally similar to Greek particles are found in languages around the world, and the research on these kinds of words has grown extraordinarily in the last few decades. Classicists can therefore profit from contemporary approaches to particles and discourse markers, in working to refine understanding of the communicative role of Greek particles.[6]

§5. For the overview four approaches have been selected that are employed especially frequently in discourse-marker studies or that have seemed particularly productive to us. First, coherence approaches, which cover a variety of pragmatic frameworks, aim to explain how particles and discourse markers help speakers and hearers construct relations in discourse. Second, Conversation Analysis explains how particles and discourse markers work within the regularities and social negotiations of talk-in-interaction. The third approach is Relevance Theory, which focuses on constraints imposed by particles and discourse markers on the hearer's inferential processes. Fourth and finally, Construction Grammar describes all linguistic knowledge as pairs of form

5 See §§7-10 below for discussion of terminology such as "discourse markers"; see I.1 §§12-13 on the general notion of discourse.

6 We have also profited from contemporary frameworks of a more general nature and their applications, that is, from research that does not (usually) deal with particles or discourse markers, but with general pragmatic and cognitive phenomena. Consider for example general analyses of narrative discourse, which illustrate that such discourse comes in many varieties, such as oral vs. written, and conversational vs. literary. The studies provide insight into e.g. the stories' internal structure and discourse transitions, their formulaic nature, and the cognitive processing of anaphoric expressions. Oral narrative, mainly in conversational settings, is the focus of e.g. Georgakopoulou 1997 and 2007; Norrick 2000; papers in Schiffrin, De Fina, and Nylund (eds.) 2010; and Rühlemann 2013 (this book includes remarks on the functions of *oh* and *well* in English conversational narrative). In contrast, Sanford and Emmott 2012, for instance, focus on written narrative, adopting a cognitive approach. Examples of other general frameworks besides narrative studies we have utilized in our chapters are the Birmingham and Geneva schools on discourse structure and segmentation (II.2, II.3, IV.3); cognitive linguistics (II.2, II.4, II.5); register studies (III.2); dialogic syntax (III.3); Du Bois' approach to stance (IV.4).

and meaning, and in this way makes it explicit which parts of the co-text are crucial for interpreting a particle or discourse marker. For each approach I will sketch its theoretical substance and provide a sample analysis. The descriptions will inevitably be selective, but are written in each case to capture a sense of the variety, in terms of the assumptions, questions, and methodologies used, that we have encountered. Before describing the four approaches, however, I will outline certain theoretical issues common to all of them.

3.2 Terminology, Definition, and Classification

§6. The same three related issues recur in many studies of particles and discourse markers across languages: terminology, definition, and classification.[7] They are inextricably linked, and will therefore be discussed together in this section (terminology in §§7-10, definition and classification in §§11-15). Each of these issues has troubled scholars working in this field, regardless of the selected language.

§7. First, how to call words that, rather than modifying propositional content, mainly have pragmatic functions? Many scholars point to this problem of terminology, noting that many different terms are used for roughly the same group of words in several languages. The term "discourse marker" is the most well-known and frequently used, but many other terms exist.[8] The four most frequent terms are "discourse marker,"[9]

[7] See also I.1 §§8-11; I.2 §1, §§14-17, §§54-55, §§61-65, §§90-91 on these problems concerning ancient Greek particles.

[8] Brinton 1996:29 cites the following other terms: "comment clause, connective, continuer, discourse connective, discourse-deictic item, discourse operator, discourse particle, discourse-shift marker, discourse word, filler, fumble, gambit, hedge, initiator, interjection, marker, marker of pragmatic structure, parenthetic phrase, (void) pragmatic connective, pragmatic expression, pragmatic particle, and reaction signal." Brinton is herself the first to use "pragmatic marker" instead. Taboada 2006:572 adds even more terms: "coherence discourse markers, (...) lexical discourse markers, (...) sentence connectives, cue phrases, clue words, discourse signalling devices".

[9] The term "discourse marker" is used by e.g. Schiffrin 1987, 2006; Brinton 1990; Redeker 1990, 2006; Jucker 1993, 1997; Fludernik 1995, 2000; Lenk 1997, 1998; Bell 1998; Jucker and Ziv 1998a, 1998b; Hansen 1998a; Risselada and Spooren 1998; Rouchota 1998; Fraser 1999; Schourup 1999; Bazzanella and Morra 2000; Archakis 2001; Norrick 2001; Waring 2003; Maschler 2003, 2009; Fleischman and Yaguello 2004; Onodera 2004; Bazzanella 2006; Bolden 2006, 2009; Fox Tree 2006; Stvan 2006; Taboada 2006; Yang 2006; Furman and Özyürek 2007; Cuenca and Marín 2009; Fairbanks 2009; Fuami 2009; Pons Bordería and Estellés Arguedas 2009; Christodoulidou 2011; Lee-Goldman 2011; Lewis 2011; Schourup 2011; Mazeland 2012; and Mišković-Luković and Dedaić 2012.

"pragmatic marker,"[10] "discourse particle,"[11] and "pragmatic particle."[12] The important terminological distinctions, then, are between "marker" and "particle," and between "discourse" and "pragmatic."

§8. Different scholars use "marker" and "particle" in different ways: they may refer to the same class of words, to two different, possibly overlapping classes, or to a class and its subclass.[13] For example, Jucker and Ziv (eds.) 1998b:2 see "discourse marker" as an umbrella term, comprising "discourse particles" as a subclass. Hölker 1990:81 and Andersen and Fretheim (eds.) 2000:1 also consider "marker" to be a broader term than "(pragmatic) particle." In contrast, Lenk claims that "discourse markers" are a subgroup of "particles" (1997:1; 1998:1, 37).[14] Schourup 1999:229 and Fischer 2006b:4, among others, argue that "particle" concerns the form and syntactic behavior of the words, whereas "marker" is a functional term. Particles are small, uninflected words that are only loosely integrated into the sentence structure, or not at all. Fischer adds that the term "particle" implies a contrast with clitics, full words, and bound morphemes, as well as with larger entities, such as phrasal idioms.

§9. As for the difference between "discourse" and "pragmatic," choosing one or the other often has theoretical and methodological implications.[15] Scholars who speak of "discourse markers" tend to consider these words as primarily playing a role in coherence,[16] whereas those who use the term "pragmatic markers" often focus on how they constrain a hearer's or reader's inferential processes in utterance interpretation.[17]

10 The term "pragmatic marker" is used by e.g. Brinton 1996, 2006; Andersen 1998, 2001; Andersen and Fretheim (eds.) 2000; Erman 2001; Aijmer and Simon-Vandenbergen 2004; González 2004; Aijmer, Foolen, and Simon-Vandenbergen 2006; Defour 2008; Norrick 2009a, 2009b; Feng 2010; Fischer 2010; and Aijmer 2013.

11 The term "discourse particle" is used by e.g. Schourup 1982; Abraham (ed.) 1991; Hansen 1998b; Hakulinen 1998, 2001; Fischer 2000, 2006a, 2006b; Aijmer 2002; Yılmaz 2004; Bolden 2008; Lam 2010; Briz and Estellés 2010; Mazeland and Plug 2010; and Mišković-Luković and Dedaić 2010.

12 The term "pragmatic particle" is used by e.g. Hölker 1990; Östman 1991, 1995; Foolen 1996; Kirsner and Van Heuven 1999; Fujii 2000; Beeching 2002; Fried and Östman 2005; Mišković-Luković 2009; and Denis 2015.
Note that Aijmer, Brinton, Fischer, Hansen, Mišković-Luković and Dedaić, Norrick, and Schourup use different terms in different publications: "discourse particle" in Schourup 1982, Hansen 1998b, Fischer 2000, 2006a, 2006b, Aijmer 2002, and Mišković-Luković and Dedaić 2010; "discourse marker" in Brinton 1990, Hansen 1998a, Schourup 1999, 2011, Norrick 2001, and Mišković-Luković and Dedaić 2012; "pragmatic marker" in Brinton 1996, 2006, Norrick 2009a, 2009b, Fischer 2010, and Aijmer 2013; "pragmatic particle" in Mišković-Luković 2009.

13 See Mišković-Luković and Dedaić 2010:4-5.

14 See also Degand, Cornillie, and Pietrandrea (eds.) 2013a, and the editors' introduction to that volume, for elaborate discussion of this problem of definition. The editors conclude that "DMs [discourse markers] and MPs [modal particles] are two subclasses of the general class of pragmatic markers." (2013b:15)

15 See e.g. Mišković-Luković and Dedaić 2010:2-3.

16 For example Schiffrin 1987, Lenk 1998, Taboada 2006. See also §§18-25 below on coherence-based approaches to discourse markers.

17 For example Andersen 2001.

Notably, Andersen and Fretheim 2000:2-3 claim that the term "discourse marker" implies that the words in question have textual functions only, and that the methodology is confined to corpus research.[18] As a result they adopt the term "pragmatic marker," which they consider more neutral. Lenk 1997:1 writes that studies of pragmatic markers focus more on interactional aspects between participants than studies of discourse markers, which tend to investigate the structural organization of discourse.

§10. It is evident, then, that although the four main terms (discourse vs. pragmatic, and marker vs. particle) refer to functionally comparable words, they are—consciously or unconsciously—associated with different perspectives. For economy, I will henceforth use "discourse marker," the most common term, as an umbrella term in this chapter, except when referring to specific studies that employ a different term.

§11. How to define discourse markers as a category is another issue. Different scholars often stipulate different criteria, even when they use the same terms.[19] This issue is closely intertwined with that of delineating the category. Regardless of the criteria chosen, all scholars consider some members of the class prototypical, that is, as satisfying all criteria, and others peripheral, satisfying only some.[20] It is therefore hard to decide which words should be included and which should not. If one takes a functional approach, there can be no finite and exclusive list of lexical items, since many words can be used both propositionally and as discourse markers. Often intuition seems to be involved, as researchers tend to be native speakers of the language under discussion. One classification strategy is to contrast discourse markers with other categories, such as conjunctions, but this dichotomy has been criticized.[21] In sum, while scholars disagree about which criteria to use, they tend to agree that the boundaries of the discourse-marker category are fuzzy: it is unclear where exactly the category, however defined, ends.

§12. One commonly-used criterion for discourse markers is the idea that they do not contribute to the propositional or truth-conditional content of their host utterance.[22]

18 See also Andersen 2001:40, who restates his restricted understanding of the term "discourse marker." We adopt a more comprehensive view of the term "discourse" in this monograph: see I.1 §§12-13.

19 See e.g. Schourup 1999 for an elaborate overview, and Taboada 2006:572 for a concise one.

20 Jucker and Ziv 1998b:2-3.

21 See IV.2 §4 and §§138-146 on this issue. See also e.g. Georgakopoulos and Goutsos 1998, and papers in Laury (ed.) 2008.

22 This criterion is used by e.g. Hölker 1990:78; Brinton 1996:6; Lenk 1997; Risselada and Spooren 1998:131; Schourup 1999:232; Imo 2013:159, 180. However, Andersen 2001:40 argues that "non-propositionality is only partly a valid criterion, because some pragmatic markers can be seen to have truth-conditional implications." Andersen's research concerns English, but his point also holds for several Greek particles: the same word may have propositional uses as well as non-propositional ones. We do not adopt non-propositionality as a defining criterion in this monograph, despite its centrality in many discourse-marker studies. Instead, we want to explore the different uses of these polyfunctional words without being potentially restricted by *a priori* distinctions. See I.1 and IV.2 for discussion of our view on this.

In addition to that characteristic, Hölker 1990:78-80 lists the following criteria to define what he calls "pragmatic particles" in French: they do not have a referential or denotative function; and they are very loosely integrated into the sentence, that is, they are syntactically flexible.[23] Brinton 1996:33-34 adds the following features as prototypical of what she calls "pragmatic markers" in English:[24] they are used more frequently in spoken than in written discourse; they have a high frequency in spoken discourse; they are negatively evaluated in written or formal discourse; they tend to be short items, often unstressed; they may form separate tone groups; they are often sentence-initial; they often have no clear grammatical function; they are syntactically optional; they are marginal in terms of word class; they are multifunctional; and they seem to be used more in women's than in men's speech. With Brinton, Onodera 2011:620-623 also stresses the criterion that discourse markers occur predominantly in initial position in units of talk. She compares the markers (cross-linguistically) to traffic signs that mark a speed limit at the entrance rather than the end of a street. However, Brinton 1996:33 notes that pragmatic markers actually occur in other positions as well.[25] In addition to these criteria, several discourse-marker analyses emphasize the importance of prosody: different prosodic realizations of the same lexical item may distinguish between the item's use as a propositional adverb and its use as a discourse marker, or between different discourse-marker uses.[26]

§13. Defining criteria are usually based on English discourse markers, and are not necessarily valid for functionally analogous words in other languages. For example, many particles in German and Dutch cannot occupy the first position of an utterance (e.g., in some of their uses, German *halt*, *ja*, *zwar*, and Dutch *even*, *maar*, *nou*).[27] More fundamentally, the English language and the cultural values attached to it are often mistakenly seen as the general human norm, as e.g. Wierzbicka 2006:11-13 discusses.[28]

23 The criterion of syntactic flexibility is also stated by e.g. Fischer 2006b:4; Lenk 1997:2; Schourup 1999:242; Imo 2013:180.

24 Beeching 2002 on French pragmatic particles follows Brinton's definition apart from the criterion of sentence-initial position.

25 See also Fischer 2000 on discourse particles (in her terminology) in different positions of a turn.

26 See e.g. Ferrara 1997 on the different prosodic profiles of *anyway* signaling different functions; Yang 2006 on the prosody of Chinese discourse markers; and Barth-Weingarten 2012 on *and*. Already Weydt 1969 offers insightful remarks on the prosodic realizations of German particles (e.g. on 39, 45-47, 55-58); however, he uses constructed examples.

27 See e.g. Weydt 1969 and Abraham (ed.) 1991 for early studies on German particles. For comparisons of cognate German and Dutch particles, see e.g. Foolen 2006 (*doch* vs. *toch*); Van Bergen, Van Gijn, Hogeweg, and Lestrade 2011 (*eigentlich* vs. *eigenlijk*).

28 Wierzbicka 1986b:519 even claims that the relative neglect of (in her terminology) particles in linguistic theory until at least 1986 was partly due to the focus on English, in which the role of particles is relatively limited. On the prevalence of discourse-marker studies on English, see also Schourup 1999:261 (this prevalence was even greater at the time than it is now).

However, studies have appeared on discourse markers in many other languages, among them several non-Indo-European ones.[29]

§14. Mišković-Luković and Dedaić 2010 summarize the definition issue as follows. After noting that there is little consensus about which words exactly should fall within categories such as "discourse particles," they add:

(t1)

> What seems uncontroversial, though, is the versatile nature of such linguistic phenomena—morphologically, syntactically, distributionally and functionally, they do not form a class. However, they do form a "class" in another important respect—these linguistic encoders facilitate the process of utterance understanding not as syntactically-integrated constituents of the proposition expressed by an utterance, but as pointers to the ways the basic proposition or message should be taken by the addressee.
>
> Mišković-Luković and Dedaić 2010:2

This perspective is close to the one taken by Andersen 2001:41, who considers the most central feature of pragmatic markers their ability to "guide the hearer in utterance interpretation and constrain the identification of the intended explicit and implicit meaning of an utterance."[30] Wierzbicka 1986b:524 makes the "pointing" or "guiding" metaphor explicit: some particles (in her terminology) may function as "road signs in conversational exchanges or in discourse structure."[31]

§15. In general, what connects words that are considered discourse markers is not their form, but their guiding function in utterance processing or in interaction. This general function can be subdivided: for example, Andersen 2001:26 describes the "main aspects of marker meaning" as subjective (referring to the speaker's attitude toward a proposition), interactional (concerning the hearer's relation, as perceived by the speaker, to a proposition), and textual (involving coherence relations). Others posit

[29] Examples of discourse-marker studies on non-Indo-European languages are R. Blass 1990 on Sissala (a language spoken in Ghana and Burkina Faso); Luke 1990 on Cantonese Chinese; Copeland 1997 on Tarahumara (a Mexican indigenous language); Fujii 2000 and Onodera 2004 on Japanese; Wouk 2001 on Indonesian; Walrod 2006 on Philippine languages; Yılmaz 2004, and Furman and Özyürek 2007 on Turkish; Keevallik 2008 and Valdmets 2013 on Estonian; Laury and Seppänen (eds.) 2008 on Finnish; Fairbanks 2009 on Ojibwe (an endangered North-American language); Maschler 2009 on Hebrew; Dér and Markó 2010 on Hungarian; Feng 2010 on Chinese; Chang and Su 2012 on Taiwanese; Masinyana 2013 on Xhosa (a South African language).

[30] See Lenk 1997 for a similar view.

[31] For this metaphor, see also Onodera 2011:620-623 (referred to in §12 above). Similarly, Rijksbaron 1997b:14 compares Greek particles to "policemen controlling the traffic," following Jespersen 1933:404, who compares particles and other small words to policemen that direct the other words to their proper place in the hearer's brain.

different subcategories.[32] What all discourse-marker studies share, however, is a focus on functions and meanings that transcend the transfer of referential information: they rather concern aspects such as those mentioned by Andersen. In order to get a grip on these kinds of functions and meanings, different approaches are available, to which we will now turn.

3.3 Different Approaches in Discourse-Marker Studies

§16. Different approaches to discourse markers illuminate their uses in different ways. This part of the chapter will introduce four: coherence approaches, Conversation Analysis, Relevance Theory, and Construction Grammar.[33] I will describe the theoretical substance of each approach, give a sample analysis, and discuss the advantages of each.

3.3.1 Coherence approaches

§17. Schiffrin's 1987 monograph on discourse markers inaugurated a productive line of research in this area. Although her work utilizes several other frameworks as well, she makes it clear that her main focus is on the role of discourse markers in coherence:

> (t2)
>
> The analysis of discourse markers is part of the more general analysis of discourse coherence—how speakers and hearers jointly integrate forms, meanings, and actions to make overall sense out of what is said (...).
>
> Schiffrin 1987:49

Schiffrin (9-10) builds on Halliday and Hasan 1976, who describe how certain linguistic forms work as cohesive devices. These forms indicate how different units of discourse relate to each other, but do not themselves create the relations. On the general concept of discourse coherence she (21-22) follows Gumperz (e.g. 1982), who argues that hearers infer speakers' intentions through situated interpretation: coherence depends

32 On the (functional) subclassification within the category of discourse markers, see e.g. Schiffrin 1987:e.g. 316-317; Brinton 1996:36-39; Fraser 1999; Louwerse and Mitchell 2003.

33 Aijmer 2002:7-8 mentions a different list of useful approaches to discourse particles, noting that only formal grammar seems to have less to say about such words. A formal, i.e. generative approach assumes that language users construct new utterances on the basis of subconscious rules, rather than from their knowledge of specific instances in context. Surprisingly (in view of the emphasis on non-propositional functions and context-dependence in discourse-marker studies), Urgelles-Coll 2010 does use a generative approach in her monograph on English *anyway*. See also e.g. Feng 2010:165-181 and Aijmer and Simon-Vandenbergen 2011 for elaborate overviews of discourse-marker approaches.

on the speaker's integration of verbal and nonverbal cues to situate a message, and the hearer's ability to interpret these cues as a totality.[34] Schiffrin describes the role of several discourse markers in establishing certain cohesive ties.

§18. According to Schiffrin, discourse markers "bracket units of talk. Sometimes those units are sentences, but sometimes they are prepositions, speech acts, tone units." (35) She defines discourse markers as verbal devices independent of sentential structure (32), "which provide contextual coordinates for ongoing talk" (41). Discourse markers, in other words, establish connections between discourse units and parts of their context. This functional definition encompasses items from different word classes, such as conjunctions, adverbs, and verb phrases (40).

§19. Schiffrin inspired many scholars to investigate discourse markers as connected to discourse coherence.[35] For example, Lenk 1998:1 considers the main function of discourse markers to be "to signal structural organization within discourse." According to Maschler 1998, 2003, and 2009, discourse markers have a "metalingual" function: they communicate about language use, that is, the text, the ongoing interaction, or the speaker's cognitive processes, rather than about some "extralingual" world.[36] This overarching metalingual function includes textual, interactional, and cognitive functions. Within a similar research framework, Aijmer, Foolen, and Simon-Vandenbergen 2006:105-110 list the following considerations as crucial for the understanding of what they term "pragmatic markers": how these words relate to the utterance, to the context, and to the hearer. That is, it is not only the verbal level of communication that is relevant in coherence approaches to discourse markers, but also the nonverbal level. Aijmer *et al.* assume that every pragmatic marker has a core meaning to which all "pragmatic meanings" can be related. For example, they argue that English *well* has acceptance as its core meaning.

§20. Though the precise definition and classification of discourse markers vary among the studies, all these scholars consider such words to contribute to the coherence or structure of discourse. Their aim is usually to describe the core meanings or functions of a certain discourse marker, and to identify contextual features (both verbal and nonverbal) that play a role in their interpretation. Methodologies include classifying

34 On Gumperz' notion of "contextualization cues" (coined in Cook-Gumperz and Gumperz 1976), see also III.4 §12. On the concepts of coherence and cohesion, see e.g. Drummen 2013b and 2013c, with further literature.

35 Other applications of a coherence-based approach include Redeker 1990 on a subclassification of discourse markers; Maschler 1998; 2003; 2009 on several Hebrew discourse markers; Risselada and Spooren 1998 on discourse markers and coherence relations; Bazzanella and Morra 2000 on translating English discourse markers into Italian; Norrick 2001 on discourse markers in English oral narrative; González 2004 on pragmatic markers in English and Catalan oral narrative; Aijmer, Foolen, and Simon-Vandenbergen 2006 on a methodological proposal concerning pragmatic markers in translation; Taboada 2006 on discourse markers and rhetorical relations; Fairbanks 2009 on discourse markers in Ojibwe; Pons Bordería and Estellés Arguedas 2009 on Spanish digressive markers; Aijmer 2013 on several English pragmatic markers.

36 See Maschler 2009:1-2.

functions across discourse domains or discourse types, and comparing different discourse markers, both within one language and cross-linguistically. Coherence approaches have been applied to the analysis of both spoken and written discourse.

§21. Let us have a look at a sample analysis: the description of English *well* by Aijmer 2013. The author builds on various pragmatic approaches, thereby extending the one of Schiffrin: Aijmer considers coherence to be just one of the factors playing a role in the functions of pragmatic markers (her term). In particular, she adopts the recently developed framework of variational pragmatics, an approach that studies language use as influenced by regional as well as social differences.[37] In her study of *well*, she investigates the marker in different communicative situations, such as face-to-face conversations, courtroom interviews, and radio discussions. Discourse markers such as *well*, she argues (148), have specific functions depending on the discourse type. Consider the following example:

(t3)

A: One's about human brain and language, and the other's about uh this guy called Chomsky who's uh, *well* one of the world's most important human beings if you happen to be interested in linguistics.

Fragment of a telephone conversation from
Aijmer 2013:32, transcript simplified[38]

Aijmer notes that this *well* is "lengthened and pronounced with a relatively high pitch and is accompanied by laughter."[39] The marker "reflects [the speaker's] ongoing cognitive process," in a use belonging to unplanned, spoken discourse. Aijmer interprets the marker here as connected to word search, one of the functions connected to coherence: *well* "signals that the speaker has found the right expression."

§22. She explains the instance in (t4) as a use of *well* that is typical for a broadcast discussion, specifically for the moderators of such a discussion. In this discourse type, moderators employ *well* for specialized functions such as introducing a controversial issue, achieving a shift of topics, or asking clarification questions. In this case the moderator invites a new speaker to take the floor:

[37] See Barron 2014 for a concise overview of variational pragmatics, and Schneider and Barron (eds.) 2008 for several papers using this approach.

[38] This example of *well* is also analyzed in Aijmer 2009:7.

[39] All quotations in this paragraph are from Aijmer 2013:32.

(t4)

A: *Well* Terence Hawkes as a professor, a university professor, you must disagree totally with (...)

Fragment of a broadcast discussion,
from Aijmer 2013:59

The moderator "selects a speaker by using *well* followed by the name of the nominated speaker" (59). Here the marker "signals both that the speaker is the moderator and that the transition is to a new stage in the broadcast discussion" (59).

§23. Aijmer points out that different discourse types lead to different interpretations of the same marker. Collocations play a role as well in selecting the intended interpretation; examples are "well I guess" for *well*'s function connected to word search (32), or "well here is" to introduce a new player in a radio sports commentary (69). Aijmer thus stresses that local and global contexts may simultaneously be relevant to the use of discourse markers.

§24. Investigations using a coherence-based approach provide analyses of a wide variety of discourse markers in many discourse types. In this way, they give insight into how different contexts influence the markers' uses. Scholars who adopt an approach along these lines pay attention to linguistic, paralinguistic, and extralinguistic features, such as the immediate co-text, the prosody or punctuation of an utterance, the speaker or writer's role in a situation, and her goal in communicating. More generally, coherence approaches show the fundamental relation of linguistic choices to language users within their environments.

3.3.2 Conversation Analysis

§25. Conversation Analysis (CA) looks at the regularities of talk-in-interaction.[40] It is concerned with the communicative actions performed by turns-at-talk, with the organization of turn-taking, the structuring of turns, the sequencing of actions, and the organization of turn sequences. The main focus of this approach is on the interaction between speaker and hearer.

§26. CA began with Sacks, Schegloff, and Jefferson 1974 on turn-taking practices.[41] These sociologists show that there is systematicity in conversation, even though it often seems otherwise. They identify certain general tendencies in turn-taking

[40] Helpful recent introductions to CA are Schegloff 2007 and Sidnell 2010, and in shorter form Gardner 2005 and Heritage 2010. See III.4 for elaborate discussion of CA and an application of this approach to the analysis of particle use in Greek tragedy and comedy.

[41] Prior to this publication, Sacks had given lectures on conversation (1964-1968), posthumously published as Sacks 1995; and Schegloff had analyzed conversational openings (1967, 1968).

practices, such as the general avoidance of overlap between turns by different speakers (1974:700-701). Following the seminal work of Sacks *et al.*, sociologists as well as linguists developed the theoretical framework that is now known as Conversation Analysis.[42]

§27. The main assumption within CA is that utterances are seen as vehicles for social action.[43] Examples of "actions" in CA are complaining, (dis)agreeing, evaluating, inviting, offering, requesting, summoning, and so on.[44] CA researchers find that for the accomplishment of such actions, the structural position of linguistic material within a turn and within a sequence or "pair" of turns is crucial.[45] Other contextual features, such as status differences between speaker and hearer, or the location of the interaction, are considered relevant whenever conversation participants show in their utterances or other behavior that they themselves take them into account.

§28. CA analyzes spoken language; written material is rarely used, and constructed examples never. CA scholars take into account not only linguistic, but also paralinguistic features (such as loudness and pauses) and extralinguistic features (such as laughter, and, if known, gestures, gaze, and movements). In their analyses of discourse markers they investigate, for example, for which actions a certain marker can be used, and what position it tends to occupy within the sequence and within the turn. Different positions are those in initiating versus reacting turns, and in turn-initial versus later positions.[46]

§29. Let us take the work of Heritage on English *oh* as an example. He distinguishes among the uses of this discourse marker in three different interactional environments. Consider the following example, in which speaker B receives a piece of news from speaker A.

(t5)

A: I was just ringing to say I'll be comin' down in a moment.

42 Examples of a CA approach to discourse markers are Jefferson 1983 on *yeah* and *mmhm*; Heritage 1984, 1998, 2002 on *oh*; Luke 1990 on several Cantonese Chinese particles; Hakulinen 1998 and 2001 on several Finnish particles; Mazeland and Huiskes 2001 on Dutch *maar*; Sorjonen 2001 on Finnish response particles; Waring 2003 on *also*; Raymond 2004 and Bolden 2006, 2009 on *so*; Bolden 2008 on Russian *-to*; Person 2009 on *oh* in Shakespeare; Mazeland and Plug 2010 on Dutch *hoor*; Christodoulidou 2011 on several Cypriot Greek discourse markers; Gaines 2011 on *okay*; Lee-Goldman 2011 on *no*; Mazeland 2012 on Dutch *nou*; Imo 2013 on German *ja* (combining CA with other frameworks).

43 See also the similar framework of Interactional Linguistics: e.g. Barth-Weingarten 2012; Ochs, Schegloff, and Thompson (eds.) 1996; Selting and Couper-Kuhlen (eds.) 2001. Couper-Kuhlen and Selting call Interactional Linguistics a research field "at the intersection of linguistics, conversation analysis and anthropology" (2001:1).

44 On actions in CA, see e.g. Schegloff 2006:73; 2007:xiv; Sidnell 2010:61; Sidnell and Enfield 2012:328; Enfield 2013:86-103. See also the discussion in III.4 §§19-22.

45 On the notion of "adjacency pair" in CA, see III.4 §§15-16.

46 See III.4 (passim) for the relevance of these positions for a number of Greek particles in drama.

B: *Oh* good.

Fragment of a telephone conversation,
from Heritage 1984:302

Heritage 1984 notes that turn-initial *oh* often occurs in responses to utterances that inform the hearer of something. Such *oh* receipts are often combined with assessments of the news, as in (t5). In this environment it signals that the new speaker has undergone a change in her current state of knowledge or awareness.

§30. However, in other interactional contexts, such as at the beginning of responses to questions (see Heritage 1998), *oh* works differently:

(t6)

A: Some of my students translated Eliot into Chinese. I think the very first.

B: Did you learn to speak Chinese?

A: *Oh* yes. You can't live in the country without speaking the language.

Fragment of a radio interview,
from Heritage 1998:294

Heritage interprets such *oh* as signaling that the preceding question was somehow inappropriate. In the interview in (t6), speaker A has already given information from which it can be inferred that he had learned Chinese; the interviewer's question is treated as problematic, because the answer is considered self-evident.

§31. In the third type of context, responses to assessments, Heritage finds that turn-initial *oh* can modify an expression of agreement or disagreement with the previous speaker (see Heritage 2002). In particular, *oh* may signal that the observation being evaluated had already been independently arrived at by the current speaker. This may suggest her greater expertise on the topic at hand. This is illustrated in "oh it's a great cat" in (t7).

(t7)

A: I acquired a Burmese. D'you know what that breed is?

B: Oh yes indeed, uh, we had a neighbour that had a couple of Burmese. They're nice.

A: *Oh* it's a great cat. It's the only cat I ever saw that chased dogs.

Fragment of a telephone conversation,
from Heritage 2002:207

Speaker A agrees with speaker B, yet at the same time "invokes his epistemic authority as a Burmese cat owner" by using turn-initial *oh*, as Heritage puts it. That is, A claims that he is in a better position than B to evaluate Burmese cats, since he owns one. Heritage finds that this implication of presenting oneself as a better judge than the addressee only arises when *oh* occurs at the start of a turn after an assessment.[47]

§32. In short, Heritage's analysis shows that a speaker's goal in speaking (receiving information, answering, agreeing), and the nature of the previous turn (news, question, assessment) are relevant to our interpretation of *oh*. This discourse marker, though apparently meaningless and random at first sight, turns out to be used according to clear patterns. The results serve as a reminder that when describing the functions of a discourse marker we should take into account its larger context and not just the individual sentence in which the marker appears. In particular, the action performed by the first turn in a sequence raises expectations about the form of the reacting turn. Finally, not only the utterances themselves, but everything that is happening during an interaction may play a role in utterance interpretation or understanding, e.g. what the speaker wants to accomplish in terms of negotiating the relationship with the hearer. CA sheds light on the interaction as a whole, not only on a specific linguistic item.

3.3.3 Relevance Theory

§33. Relevance Theory (RT) has been developed by Sperber and Wilson 1995 [1986], building especially on the ideas of Grice (e.g. 1961, 1989).[48] Grice argues that most communication involves the expression and recognition of intentions, and that not only the decoding of linguistic signs, but also inference, is crucial for successful communication. He claims that utterances automatically create expectations that guide the hearer toward the speaker's intended meaning. In particular, hearers expect speakers to be cooperative, that is, to produce utterances that are of proper length, truthful, relevant, and clear.[49]

§34. Although Sperber and Wilson criticize several aspects of Grice's claims, they follow him in that they too assume that utterances create expectations for hearers. More specifically, Sperber and Wilson start from the cognitive assumption that the human mind tends to be geared toward the maximization of relevance, that is, toward achieving as many cognitive effects as possible with a minimum of processing effort. Cognitive

[47] Note, incidentally, the other turn-initial *oh*, spoken by speaker B: this one is in an answer to a question, which implies, according to Heritage's analysis, that the question was somehow problematic.

[48] See e.g. Wilson and Sperber 2004 for a compact overview of Relevance Theory. See Wilson and Sperber 2012b for an elaborate, recently updated discussion of Relevance Theory; this collection of papers also includes previously published material by the two authors.

[49] See e.g. Grice 1989:26-27 on the corresponding "maxims" (as he calls them) that speakers are expected to conform to. These concepts have been highly influential in pragmatics.

effects can consist of producing a new assumption, strengthening an existing assumption, or deleting a previously held assumption. From this "cognitive principle of relevance" Sperber and Wilson develop a "communicative principle of relevance": "[e]very act of ostensive communication communicates a presumption of its own optimal relevance" (1995 [1986]:158). According to Sperber and Wilson, hearers approach all utterances with the presumption of optimal relevance in mind. This principle enables hearers to search for the intended context and the intended interpretation of an utterance.

§35. RT makes a fundamental distinction between conceptual meaning, which refers to something in the world spoken about, and procedural meaning, which restricts the ways in which a hearer can interpret an utterance. Some linguistic items have conceptual meaning, but discourse markers mainly have procedural meaning: they encode certain constraints on the inferential processes that are needed for utterance interpretation.[50]

§36. Works such as Blakemore 1987, 1992, 2002; Carston and Uchida 1998; Rouchota and Jucker (eds.)1998; Noh 2000; and Carston 2002 represent a few of the important developments made in RT.[51] Some scholars contrast RT with theories concerned with discourse and coherence. For example, Blakemore 2002:157 claims that hearers aim to construct representations of the speaker's thoughts, but not representations of relationships in discourse.[52] RT also differs from CA in that RT's primary focus is not on utterances as social actions, but on utterances as expressions of cognitive processes.[53]

§37. Another difference from CA is that RT researchers make use of constructed examples, usually in their native language, in addition to or instead of corpus data.[54] These constructed examples are analyzed, checked for acceptability, and compared to slightly different versions. For example, Wilson and Sperber 2012a:158 discuss the following constructed utterances:

50 See Andersen and Fretheim (eds.) 2000: 7: "From a relevance-theoretic point of view, pragmatic markers can be seen to facilitate inferential processes." See also Andersen 2001:33: pragmatic markers (in his terminology) "contribute to relevance by telling the hearer how an utterance is to be understood, thus reducing the processing effort that the hearer must employ in utterance comprehension."

51 Concerning discourse markers, RT has been elaborated upon by e.g. Blakemore 1987 (monograph); 2000; 2002 (monograph); R. Blass 1990 (monograph); Haegeman 1993; Jucker 1993; Andersen 2001 (monograph); Ifantidou 2001 (monograph); Mišković-Luković 2009; Fielder 2010; Schourup 2011; Mišković-Luković and Dedaić 2012; several contributions in Jucker and Ziv (eds.) 1998a (e.g. Rouchota on parenthetical discourse markers); Andersen and Fretheim 2000; and Dedaić and Mišković-Luković 2010; Schourup 2011.

52 See Blakemore 2002:149-185 for a full discussion. See also Schourup 2011:2110 on RT as different from discourse- or coherence-oriented approaches. Interestingly, Lenk 1998 combines a coherence-based and a relevance-theoretic approach in her study of "pragmatic markers".

53 See e.g. Blakemore 2002:155.

54 Exceptions are, for example, Zakowski 2017 on ancient Greek (see §73 below) and Fielder 2010, who applies RT to the connective *ama* in Bulgarian, which is not her native language. Both studies use only corpus material and no constructed examples.

(t8)

a. Peter's not stupid. He can find his own way home.

b. Peter's not stupid; *so* he can find his own way home.

c. Peter's not stupid; *after all*, he can find his own way home.

Example from Wilson and Sperber 2012a:158
(highlighting added)

The authors explain that the sentence "Peter's not stupid" is either interpreted as *evidence for the conclusion* "he can find his own way home," as represented in (t8b); or as a *conclusion derived from evidence* presented in the second sentence, as made explicit in (t8c). For (t8a) both interpretations are possible. Referring to Blakemore's account of procedural meaning (e.g. 1987, 2002), Wilson and Sperber argue that discourse connectives (in Blakemore's terminology) such as *so* and *after all* do not encode concepts, but instead constrain the hearer's inferential processes in different ways.

§38. An example of a relevance-theoretic discourse-marker study is found in Mišković-Luković 2010 on the Serbian "pragmatic particles" (her term) *baš* and *kao*. By using spoken, written, and constructed examples, the author describes both particles as semantic constraints on the explicit content of utterances. The two particles work in opposite directions: *baš* ("exactly," "really") makes an utterance stronger or more precise, whereas *kao* ("like," "or something," "kinda") makes it weaker or looser. I will discuss two *baš* examples in order to illustrate Mišković-Luković's analysis:

(t9)

A: *To je konzulat sakupljao. Ne znam zbog čega.*

B: *Konzulat u Štutgartu?*

A: *Da, <u>baš</u> konzulat.*

Fragment of spoken conversation, from
Mišković-Luković 2010:69 (her translation)

A: The consulate was collecting it [i.e. certain data]. I don't know what for.

B: The consulate in Stuttgart?

A: Yes, *baš* the consulate. ("That very consulate.")

Mišković-Luković points out that *baš* signals that the intended meaning of an utterance bears "literal resemblance" (75) to what is said. In RT the term "literal resemblance" is used to refer to a situation in which no conceptual adjustment is needed from the hearer. "Less-than-literal resemblance" is in fact much more common in everyday communication (74-75). In this case, the particle "serves to confirm the identity" between the concept of "consulate" that speaker A refers to in the first utterance, and the more specific consulate suggested in speaker B's question. That is, Mišković-Luković interprets *baš* as "a marker of non-loose use" of language (80). She argues that the particle helps the hearer in his "conceptual adjustment" (74-75): when *baš* is present, the concept that a speaker intends to communicate bears literal resemblance to the concept she puts into words.

§39. Mišković-Luković also offers one *baš* example from a newspaper article:

(t10)

Borislav Milošević slovi kao ključna figura u klanu. (...) Navodno je baš Borislav Milošević u Rusiji pohranio milionske sume, što sam osporava.

Newspaper fragment, from Mišković-Luković
2010:75-76n12 (her translation)

Borislav Milošević is considered to be a key figure in the clan. (...) Allegedly, it was *baš* Borislav Milošević who had deposited millions in Russia, which he himself denies.

At the time of publication of the newspaper, in 2003, the main referent in focus for the readers was not Borislav Milošević, but his brother Slobodan, the ex-president of Yugoslavia. According to Mišković-Luković, "*[b]aš* before the proper name is used to block this immediately accessible assumption [i.e. that Slobodan Milošević would be referred to] by reaffirming the identity of the referent [i.e. Borislav Milošević]" (76n12). In the processing of spoken or written *baš* utterances, the hearer or reader can exclude less-than-literal interpretations of the proposition as it is expressed, or of the part over which *baš* has scope.

§40. RT's strength lies in its use of a consistent explanation for every context and discourse type. It employs general cognitive principles to explain how different uses of a discourse marker are connected.[55] The distinction that it makes between procedural meaning and referential ("conceptual") meaning helps make it clear how discourse

[55] The prominent concept in RT of (minimizing) the hearer's processing effort also plays a role in cognitive analyses of, for example, anaphoric expressions; see e.g. II.5 on this topic.

markers, which have no referential meaning, can still provide a specific contribution to the communication.

3.3.4 Construction Grammar

§41. The research field of Construction Grammar (CxG) developed as one of the alternatives to generative linguistics.[56] A generative approach does not describe the use of language, but the knowledge of speakers about grammatical structures in a given language; speakers are said to "generate" sentences from a set of rules.[57] CxG, by contrast, is usage-based, and assumes that words and other linguistic structures are learned and interpreted in context. Langacker (e.g. 1987, 1990) has been especially influential in developing the framework of Cognitive Grammar, a field of research foundational to CxG.[58] He argues, for example, that the grammar of a language provides speakers with pairings of phonological and semantic units. All linguistic structures are based on general cognitive processes, according to Langacker.[59]

§42. CxG began with Fillmore, Kay, and O'Connor 1988 on the meaning of *let alone*. Based on the explanation of this idiomatic construction, these authors propose (501) that we view not rules, as in generative linguistics, but constructions, as the "proper units of grammar." CxG has been further developed by, among others, Goldberg 1995, 2006; Croft 2001; Verhagen 2005; Boas (ed.) 2010; and Traugott and Trousdale 2013.[60] Currently, numerous scholars are active in this field, including researchers of discourse markers.[61]

56 Other frameworks developed in the same vein are for example Functional Grammar (see e.g. Dik 1968; 1978; 1989), Cognitive Grammar (see below within §41, with note 58), and Emergent Grammar (see e.g. Hopper 1988; 2011; Bybee and Hopper [eds.] 2001).

57 The framework of generative linguistics originated in the work of Chomsky (e.g. 1965). Current overviews of generative linguistics are e.g. Philippi 2008; Ludlow 2011; Chomsky and McGilvray 2012; Den Dikken (ed.) 2013.

58 See Langacker 2008 and 2010 for recent overviews of Cognitive Grammar.

59 See also Bybee 2010 on general cognitive principles as an argument for a usage-based theory of grammar, such as CxG.

60 Östman and Fried 2004 give an overview of the historical and intellectual background of Construction Grammar. E.g. Traugott and Trousdale 2013:2-8 give a short overview of different constructional approaches to language. See e.g. the recent *Oxford Handbook of Construction Grammar* (Hoffmann and Trousdale [eds.] 2013) for a detailed overview of the theoretical substance, development, and sub-approaches within Construction Grammar.

61 Applications of Construction Grammar to discourse-marker studies include Fujii 2000 on Japanese *mono*; Fried and Östman 2005 on pragmatic particles in Czech and Solv (a Swedish dialect spoken in Finland); Imo 2005 on *I mean* (interestingly combining CxG and CA); Imo 2007 on several discourse markers developed from verbs in spoken German; Diewald 2008 on German *ruhig*; Imo 2008 on German *halt*; Fried 2009a on Czech *jestli;* Fischer 2010 on several pragmatic markers in spoken English; Masini and Pietrandrea 2010 on Italian *magari*; Lewis 2011 on the diachronic development of *instead* and *rather*; Fischer and Alm 2013 on German *also* and Swedish *alltså*; Van der Wouden and Foolen 2015 [2011] on several Dutch utterance-final particles; Koier 2013 on ancient Greek πoυ and Dutch *ergens*.

§43. Constructions are conventional and symbolic pairings of form and meaning. They are conventional because their use is shared among a group of speakers; and they are symbolic because they are signs, that is, potentially arbitrary associations of form and meaning.[62] Phonology, morphology, syntax, semantics, and pragmatics all work together in a construction: no one level of grammar is seen as autonomous in this approach.[63] This holistic view of grammar means, for example, that there is no sharp boundary between grammar and lexicon.[64] That is, individual words are considered constructions just as much as abstract syntactic structures that do not include specific lexical items, such as a transitive-verb-with-object construction.

§44. According to a CxG approach, words are not normally interpreted or learned in isolation. It is likely, therefore, that speakers and hearers use specific co-textual or contextual features to identify which forms (for speakers) or meanings (for hearers) they need. CxG does not assume specific communicative principles for this, as RT does, but assumes that speakers and hearers simply have knowledge about language use from their experience. The formal features of a construction can be morphemes, words, phrases, intonational patterns, syntactic structures, even whole text types, among others.[65] For a certain construction involving a discourse marker, the "form" pole would be the lexical item itself, but it possibly also includes information on co-occurring words or structures. A construction's description should thus specify which co-textual features, if any, are crucial for an interpretation of a word. On the "meaning" pole, not only semantic information, such as the reference to a certain concept, can be represented, but also pragmatic information, such as the expression of a specific stance of the speaker, and discourse-functional information, such as a connective function.

§45. CxG is informed by both monosemy and polysemy. On the one hand, each construction is monosemous, that is, it has only one meaning, though possibly a highly general or a highly complex one, involving semantic, pragmatic, and discourse-functional dimensions at the same time. On the other hand, many constructions are connected in a polysemous network.[66] If one specific grammatical or lexical form has several meanings, then it participates in several constructions. In such cases the meaning pole of a construction with *only* that one grammatical or lexical item as form pole will be highly general, and sometimes impossible to pin down. Specific constructions are

62 See e.g. Traugott and Trousdale 2013:1.

63 See e.g. Fried and Östman 2004:24; Traugott and Trousdale 2013:3.

64 Traugott and Trousdale 2013:31 note that outside of CxG the term "construction" has usually been associated with syntax only; however, in CxG it is explicitly extended to include lexicon as well.

65 See III.2 for examples and discussion of large-scale constructions, applied to the analysis of Greek drama.

66 On the relationship between CxG and both monosemy and polysemy, see e.g. Boogaart 2009; Drummen 2013a; Koier 2013. On networks and CxG, see e.g. Traugott and Trousdale 2013:8-11. For clarification about how the term "polysemy" has been used in CxG, see Traugott and Trousdale 2013:200-202.

called "daughter" constructions: they inherit all aspects of form and meaning from their more general "parent" constructions, but also have specific form features that lead to a slightly different interpretation. For example, the English construction *kick the bucket* is a daughter construction of the more general transitive-verb-with-object construction, but its idiomatic, metaphorical meaning ("to die") cannot be predicted from this parent construction; therefore it is considered a separate construction, that has to be learned independently from its parent constructions.[67] By specifying the particular features of form that make up the daughter construction, a constructional approach explains how hearers and readers arrive at a specific interpretation of a multifunctional item (that is, a word or phrase that participates in several constructions). Such a multifunctional word or phrase may form a parent construction for more specific daughter constructions.

§46. Questions concerning discourse markers within a constructional framework concern, for example, the different constructions in which a certain marker participates, and which other features exactly are relevant to the several constructions in which the marker is found. By analyzing how the interpretations of a linguistic expression change across many different contexts, CxG studies aim to map the features in the co-text and context that play a role in those changes. The data used is always drawn from actually spoken or written language; CxG does not use constructed examples.

§47. An example study is Koier 2013 on the Dutch "particle" (her term) *ergens*.[68] The author shows that readers use specific parts of the co-text when interpreting this multifunctional particle. *Ergens* can function as an adverb with a locative meaning ("somewhere," "anywhere") or one of several modal interpretations (e.g. "somehow," "from a certain point of view"). Koier asked a group of native speakers to choose one of eight interpretations of this form for a number of corpus instances.[69] The results enabled her to identify "triggers," that is, words in the co-text that are responsible for each specific interpretation (66).

§48. For instance, in (t11), *ergens* is generally interpreted as "in someone's feelings or thoughts."

(t11)

Ik zou dat <u>ergens</u> wel willen maar ja, we maken keuzes in het leven hè?

Fragment of a transcribed interview, from
Koier 2013:72 (her translation)

67 See Croft and Cruse 2004:263-264 for this example.

68 Koier also analyzes ancient Greek πoυ in the same monograph; see §73 below.

69 A similar online-survey method is used by e.g. Van Bergen, Van Gijn, Hogeweg, and Lestrade 2011 in their investigation of the Dutch discourse marker *eigenlijk*.

> I would *ergens* want [to do] that but well, we make choices in life, don't we?

Koier explains (72-74) that the interpretation "in someone's feelings or thoughts" is triggered by references to the first person, or by subjective forms such as the mental state predicate "want." Even informants who are presented with only the shorter word string "zou dat ergens wel willen" ("would *ergens* want that") tend to choose the same interpretation. In this case, one of the two triggers, namely "want," remains explicitly present in the version with a restricted co-text.

§49. In contrast, the interpretation of *ergens* in (t12) changes when the co-text is marginalized. *Ergens* is interpreted as "about," "around" when informants read the full co-text, but receives various other interpretations when only a restricted co-text is given.

(t12)

> *Stenen voorwerpen uit een periode die men het mesolithicum noemt. Dat is* <u>*ergens*</u> *ja pff laten we zeggen zesduizend, vijfduizend voor Christus.*
>
> Fragment of a transcribed interview, from Koier 2013:75 (her translation)
>
> Stone objects from a period that is called the mesolithicum. That is *ergens* yeah pff let's say six-thousand, five-thousand before Christ.

Koier points out (67) that numbers are a required co-textual trigger for the interpretation of *ergens* as "about," "around." Informants do not choose this interpretation when they only have access to "dat is ergens ja pff" ("that is *ergens* yeah pff"). The restricted version does not provide enough help on choosing an interpretation, and accordingly informants' answers vary widely (75).

§50. The important point to remember here is that the co-textual triggers of interpretations of *ergens* are not just co-occurring, but necessary for the interpretations—that is, they are part of the various constructions that *ergens* can appear in. For example, the specific construction that has the meaning pole "about," "around" does not only include the lexical item *ergens* in its form pole, but also "numbers" as a co-textual feature (see Koier 2013:67).

§51. A CxG approach, based on general cognitive principles, may explain how a hearer or reader interprets a multifunctional discourse marker, by specifying which co-textual elements are crucial for each interpretation. Since there is no distinction between grammar and lexicon in CxG, all kinds of linguistic information can be taken into account in the form pole.

3.4 Further Relevant Studies

§52. Modern studies on discourse markers do not only apply different approaches to language use, but also provide other useful background for investigating ancient Greek particles. Without claiming to be complete, I will in this section discuss four other areas of research that we have profited from.

§53. First, many discourse-marker studies are contrastive, that is, they compare markers across different languages, analyzing their functional similarities and differences. Weydt 1969 is an early example: he focuses mainly on differences in the particle systems of German and French, but he also briefly compares the German system to that of ancient Greek. Fleischman and Yaguello 2004 represents a more recent contrastive discourse-marker study.[70] These authors compare the uses and development of English *like* and French *genre*, two discourse markers that are functionally highly similar, although they developed from different lexical sources. For example, both words can be used as a hedge, as in (t13).

(t13)

Je me demandais si tu pourrais genre me donner un coup de main.

Fragment from conversation, from Fleischman and Yaguello 2004:134 (their translation)

I was wondering if you could *like* give me a hand?

Fleischman and Yaguello 2004 interpret this use of *genre* as related to the speaker's hesitation, to tentative suggestions, or to politeness. The authors see a functional correspondence to the English discourse marker *like* (see their translation of the French example). Such comparisons among formally and/or functionally similar words may clarify their multifunctionality. If the compared words have the same origin, such as German *doch* and Dutch *toch* analyzed by Foolen 2006, they may still differ in use. If the forms are not

[70] Other examples of cross-linguistic discourse-marker studies are Fraser and Malamud-Makowski 1996 on English and Spanish; Takahara 1998 on English and Japanese; Bazzanella and Morra 2000 on Italian and English; Aijmer and Simon-Vandenbergen 2003 on English, Swedish, and Dutch; González 2004 on English and Catalan; Foolen 2006 on Dutch and German; Bouma, Hendriks, and Hoeksema 2007 on Dutch, English, and German; Altenberg 2010 on English and Swedish; Sudhoff 2012 on German and Dutch; Bruijnen and Sudhoff 2013 on German and Dutch; Fischer and Alm 2013 on German and Swedish; Izutsu and Izutsu 2013 on German, French, Japanese, and English; Koier 2013 on Dutch and ancient Greek (see §73 below); Squartini 2013 on Italian and French.

etymologically related, as in Takahara's 1998 study of English and Japanese, their uses may show similarities because of similarities in context and development.[71]

§54. Second, diachronic studies on discourse markers describe their development from words or phrases with propositional content into items with mainly pragmatic functions. These studies cut across several of the approaches mentioned, and sometimes present the diachronic focus as a theoretical perspective in its own right.[72] Processes that play a role in the development of discourse markers are subjectification, intersubjectification, and grammaticalization.[73] These terms refer to the developments of meanings that are progressively more subjective (involving speaker reference or speaker perspective), more intersubjective (involving the speaker's attention to the addressee's "self"), or more grammatical than the original meanings of a form. For example, Margerie 2010 analyzes *kind of/kinda* from this perspective.[74] She shows that this construction originally had only a propositional meaning, as illustrated in (t14), and acquired additional intersubjective meanings, such as in (t15).

(t14)

They wanna look at the *kind of* college you're coming from.

Fragment of an American English conversation,
from Margerie 2010:317

(t15)

I was just *kinda* hoping you'd read over and say this has to be changed or you know whatever.

Fragment of an American English conversation,
from Margerie 2010:327

71 In this monograph we draw comparisons to English discourse markers in II.3 §26 and §72 (*because* and *for* compared to γάρ), II.5 §§53-56 (*of course* compared to ἄρα), III.4 (§§51-52 *okay* compared to καὶ δή and ἰδού, §55 *well* compared to μέν), IV.2 (*and* compared to δέ, τε, and καί).

72 Examples of diachronic discourse-marker studies (with or without a specific approach) are Traugott 1986 on *but* and *and*; Brinton 1990 and 2006 on English; Fludernik 1995 on Middle English *þo*; Jucker 1997 on *well;* Traugott and Dasher 2002:152-189; Onodera 2004 on Japanese; Diewald 2008 on German *ruhig*; Defour 2008 on *well* and *now*; Stvan 2006 on *why* and *say*; Visconti 2009 on Italian *mica*; Meurman-Solin 2012 on *and, for, but,* and *only*; Bolly and Degand 2013 on French discourse markers derived from *voir* ("to see"); Denis 2015 on general extenders (such as *and stuff*) and epistemic parentheticals (such as *I think*) in Canadian English; and papers in Davidse, Vandelanotte, and Cuyckens (eds.) 2010 and in Degand and Simon-Vandenbergen (eds.) 2011 on discourse markers in several languages. Heine 2013 discusses approaches to the genesis and development of discourse markers in general.

73 See e.g. Davidse, Vandelanotte, and Cuyckens 2010 on these three processes. See e.g. Traugott and Trousdale 2013 for elaborate discussion of several kinds of language change, including grammaticalization and pragmaticalization.

74 On the use of this marker, see also Mišković-Luković 2009.

Margerie explains that in (t14) *kind* is a noun and carries a propositional meaning. In contrast, in (t15) *kinda* has a hedging force: the speaker, an undergraduate student, tries to be polite in asking an older student for help in writing a paper. Margerie identifies intermediate examples, in which *kind of/kinda* has both a propositional and an expressive function. All these different uses, which developed separately, co-exist from a synchronic perspective. Considerations of a certain discourse marker's historical development are therefore illuminating for synchronic studies such as those represented in this monograph.[75]

§55. Third, several studies analyze discourse markers in historic corpora from a synchronic perspective. These scholars can obviously only use written language as their material, but they nevertheless pay attention to the interaction between a (explicit or implied) speaker and her addressees. Usually the corpus includes dramatic texts, such as Shakespeare, or narratives with direct speech. Consider the following example of Old English *hwæt*, from Brinton's 1996 monograph on "pragmatic markers" (her term) in Old and Middle English.[76] The cited passage, from the poem *Juliana* by Cynewulf, is spoken by a devil to the martyr Juliana, who had just asked who sent him.

(t16)

Hwæt, mec min fæder on þas fore to þe,/ hellwarena cyning, hider onsende (...)

Poem fragment (Old English, ca. ninth century), from Brinton 1996:188 (her translation)

What, my father, the king of the hell-dwellers, sent me hither on this journey to you (...)

Hwæt usually accompanies old (that is, shared) information, or the speaker at least pretends that the information is old. In this use, *hwæt* is similar to Modern English *you know*. The instance in (t16) can be considered "insulting": the information given by the devil is clearly new to Juliana, but he implies that she should have known it already, and conveys irritation at her "slowness in understanding" (188).

75 We refer to (suggestions about) particles' development in II.2 §§46-48 (μέν) and II.3 (§§40-42 ἦ, §57 δή).

76 Other examples of synchronic studies on historic corpora are Fludernik 1995 and 2000 on discourse markers in Middle English; Blake 1996 on *why* and *what* in Shakespeare; Fuami 2009 on *well* in Shakespeare; Person 2009 on *oh* in Shakespeare; Lutzky 2012 on three discourse markers in Early Modern English; Lutzky and Demmen 2013 on *pray* in Early Modern English; Jonker 2014 on several discourse markers in Jane Austen.

§56. Finally, studies of discourse markers in narrative discourse resemble our research.[77] Some of the works just mentioned that deal with older corpora inevitably discuss narrative, such as Fludernik 1995 and 2000, and Brinton 1996. Other analyses, however, describe the use of discourse markers in oral narrative, and therefore use modern, spoken corpora. An example is González 2004 on English and Catalan pragmatic markers.[78] Among other markers, she analyzes *so* as a "closing segment boundary marker": with it, a speaker "closes the last part of her story" (98).

§57. To sum up: beyond specific theoretical approaches, several general perspectives on discourse markers may inform our study of Greek particles. Cross-linguistic comparisons highlight differences and similarities across functionally or formally related markers in different languages. Diachronic studies illuminate how pragmatic meanings develop out of the lexical ones. Furthermore, synchronic research on discourse markers in historic corpora are close to our work. Whenever a narrative corpus is analyzed, finally, this may help us observe functions typical of such context. In fact many of the insights offered by these studies have already been applied to Greek and Latin. It is to an overview of this scholarship that I now turn.

3.5 Studies on Particles and Discourse Markers in Ancient Greek and Latin

§58. This section summarizes some recent analyses of ancient Greek and Latin particles and discourse markers that explicitly adopt an approach similar to the ones discussed above.[79] Let us first step back, however, in order to look at the general issues of terminology, definition, and classification discussed in §§6-15 from a Hellenist's perspective. These issues are relevant to the study of ancient Greek particles as well. Hellwig 1974, for example, observes that words which are sometimes called "particle" are at other times designated as "adverb," "interjection," or "conjunction."[80] Despite the problems surrounding the term "(Greek) particle,"[81] we adopt this term in the current monograph because it has been the common term in the long history of research on these words.[82]

77 In this monograph, these studies are especially relevant to the research on Homer and Pindar (part II) and Herodotus and Thucydides (part IV).

78 Other examples are Koike 1996 on Mexican Spanish *ya*; Fox Tree 2006 on *like*; Fairbanks 2009 on discourse markers in Ojibwe (an endangered North American language); Furman and Özyürek 2007 on Turkish discourse markers.

79 For studies on *Modern* Greek discourse markers, see e.g. Brewster 1992 on *lipon*; Georgakopoulos and Goutsos 1998 on the distinction between conjunctions and discourse markers; Ifantidou 2000 on *taha*; Archakis 2001 on *diladi*, *m ala loja*, *thelo na po*, and *i malon*; Christodoulidou 2011 on *lipón*, *ára*, and *oréa* in Cypriot Greek.

80 See also I.2 §1, §§14-15, §§18-19 on this issue.

81 See e.g. Revuelta Puigdollers 2006a:468-469; Bonifazi 2012:201.

82 See I.1 §§8-11.

§59. As for the issue of definition, Duhoux 1997a:16 posits that a defining feature of Greek particles is that they never form an utterance on their own, unlike adverbs.[83] This characteristic also makes them different from interjections, though Duhoux does not make this distinction explicit.[84] His 2006 article extends and clarifies the earlier discussion. He adds two other criteria to the provision that they never form an utterance on their own: they are morphologically invariant, and they have no referential meaning.[85]

§60. Bonifazi notes that Greek particles are mainly negatively defined, if at all, and proposes that we consider the pragmatic meaning of particles, that is, the interpersonal and/or procedural aspects of communication that they convey.[86] She argues that certain lexical items may function sometimes as adverbs, with propositional content, and sometimes as particles, without such content.[87] Koier 2013:28 also points out that particles form an ill-defined category, and chooses a working definition similar to Bonifazi's: "an uninflected form with no referential function that manages the speaker-hearer interaction on a textual or social level."[88]

§61. There is a clear similarity, then, between the way Greek particles are defined in modern scholarship and the way discourse markers are defined in discourse-marker studies: lack of propositional meaning is a standard criterion for both categories. Duhoux's criterion for Greek particles, however, the feature of not forming an utterance on their own, is not used to define discourse markers in modern languages.

§62. As for the issue of classification, the list of Greek lexical items considered to belong to the category of particles varies from study to study.[89] Many modern scholars take Denniston's 1950 [1934] list as their guideline, but some studies expand the range of

83 Duhoux 1997a: "Comme les adverbes, les particules sont invariables, mais elles diffèrent d'eux en ceci qu'elles ne peuvent pas être employées de façon autonome: elles doivent obligatoirement être utilisées avec d'autres mots, alors qu'un adverbe peut, à lui seul, constituer un énoncé (ainsi, Καλῶς, 'Bien')." He adds in a footnote that this is why he excludes οὐ and μή from his study on particles.

84 Hölker 1990 also mentions this criterion, concerning French, in order to distinguish connecting markers from interjectional markers: the former never occur as independent utterances, he claims.

85 Ancient scholars also used these criteria: see I.2 §16, §§54-55, §80, §83.

86 See Bonifazi 2008:36-37; 2009:30.

87 Bonifazi 2012:10, 186.

88 She here refers to the presentational and interactional levels of discourse as used by Kroon 1995 (see §64 below).

89 See e.g. Páez Martínez 2012 §4 on this issue.

words he includes.[90] Since the category is ill-defined, there can be no complete consensus about which words to include or exclude.[91]

§63. Studies on Greek particles adopt different approaches, just as discourse-marker studies do for the modern languages. Of the approaches described above, several Hellenists have applied insights from coherence approaches and Relevance Theory (see §§64-72 below). Construction Grammar is adopted in Koier 2013 on πού (see §73 below), and now in Drummen 2019 on καί, τε, and δέ. Conversation Analysis is used by Van Emde Boas 2017a.[92] More important, many classicists use a generally pragmatic approach. That is, they pay attention to the linguistic and extralinguistic context of a passage: they treat text as discourse, as language in use.[93] Therefore their descriptions of particles are not restricted to syntax or to the level of the sentence.[94]

§64. Apart from discourse-marker studies on modern languages, contemporary analyses of particles in Latin have clearly influenced the research on Greek particles. The most well-known Latinist in this field is Kroon, who has published numerous articles and a monograph on the topic.[95] In her 1995 monograph, the author develops a specific coherence-based approach to discourse particles in Latin, building in particular on Halliday and Hasan 1976, Roulet *et al.* 1985,[96] Mann and Thompson (e.g. 1987), Schiffrin

[90] See e.g. Blomqvist 1969 on several other particles in Hellenistic Greek; Muchnová 1993, 2000, 2003, 2006, 2009 and 2011 on ἐπεί; Sicking 1993:17-18 on εἶτα and ἔπειτα; Duhoux 1997a:16-17, who adds αὖ, ἤ, νυν, and ὅμως; e.g. Basset 1988 and Wathelet 1997 on ἄν and κε(ν) as particles; Muchnová 2004 on ὡς, and 2007 on ὅτι; Revuelta Puigdollers 2009b and Bonifazi 2012:185-292 on several αὖ-particles.

[91] On the (functional) subclassification *within* the category of ancient Greek particles, see e.g. Stephens 1837; Denniston 1950 [1934]; Blomqvist 1969; Hellwig 1974; Sicking 1986; George 2009; E. J. Bakker 2011.

[92] See III.4 for the application of CA to the study of particles in ancient Greek drama. See also Van Emde Boas 2017b for a CA approach to Greek tragedy; particles are however not his main focus here.

[93] See I.1 §§12-17 on the notions of discourse and pragmatics. On pragmatics in general, see e.g. Verschueren 1999; Grundy 2000; Mey 2001; Horn and Ward (eds.) 2006; Huang 2007; Cutting 2008. On applying a pragmatic approach to ancient Greek, see Collinge 1988; Bonifazi 2001, 2012; and E. J. Bakker 2010b.

[94] S. C. Dik's framework of Functional Grammar (see e.g. S. J. Dik 1978; 1989) has been highly influential and is sometimes even seen as equivalent to "pragmatics." Examples of Functional-Grammar applications to ancient Greek are Wakker 1994 (see §68 below), H. J. Dik 1995 (see note 112 below), Revuelta Puigdollers 2009a (see §69 below), and Polo Arrondo 2007; 2011. In this monograph we subscribe to a broader view of pragmatics, of which Functional Grammar is only one of several sub-branches.

[95] Kroon 1989 on *nam*, *enim*, *igitur*, and *ergo*; 1992 on several particles; 1994a on *at*; 1994b on Latin equivalents of Dutch *maar*; 1995 (monograph) on *nam*, *enim*, *autem*, *vero* and *at*; 1998 on a framework for Latin discourse markers; 2004, 2005, and 2009 on *quidem*; Kroon and Risselada 1998 and 2002 on *iam*.

[96] II.2 and II.3 are to a large extent informed by the work of Roulet and colleagues (the so-called "Geneva school").

1987, and Foolen 1993. Kroon establishes a definition of and distinction among the representational, presentational, and interactional levels of discourse.[97] The representational level concerns relations between states of affairs in a represented world. The presentational level involves the manner in which a language user organizes communicative units. The interactional level, finally, concerns the exchange and relationships between speaker and addressee within a particular communicative situation.

§65. Numerous other scholars have analyzed Latin particles using a pragmatic approach.[98] Particularly prolific scholars from the 1990s onwards include Orlandini,[99] Risselada,[100] and Rosén.[101] Recently, Schrickx has published several articles and a monograph on Latin particles.[102] In her 2011 book, this author points to problems of terminology and definition in the research on Latin particles, similar to the situation in studies of other languages. Schrickx mainly builds on Kroon 1995, and chooses Functional Discourse Grammar (see especially Hengeveld and Mackenzie 2008) as her approach.[103]

§66. Let us now turn to pragmatic analyses of Greek particles.[104] E. J. Bakker (in the other volumes referred to as Bakker; here to be distinguished from S. J. Bakker) has done important work in this area: from the 1980s onward he has published on several particles, primarily in Homer.[105] His approach is to a large extent based on the insights of the

97 This approach is explicitly adopted by e.g. Wakker 1997a on γε, δή, ἦ, and μήν in tragedy; 2009a on οὖν and τοίνυν in Lysias; Schrickx 2011 on Latin particles; Bonifazi 2012:185-291 on several discourse markers in Homer.

98 Examples are Revuelta Puigdollers 1998 on Latin "focusing particles"; Langslow 2000 on the diachronic development of several Latin particles, and the influence of genre differences; Moore 2006 on *videlicet*; Tarriño Ruiz 2009 on several Latin adverbs and particles; Molinelli 2010 on the pragmaticalization of certain Latin verb forms into discourse markers; Pinkster 2010 on *quia* and *quoniam*; Holmes 2011 on *nam*; Goldstein 2013a on *nedum*. See also the elaborate online bibliography on Latin particles at http://latinparticles.userweb.mwn.de (last accessed on 11 July, 2015), maintained by Josine Schrickx.

99 Her particle publications include Orlandini 1994 on *at;* 1995 on *atqui* and *immo*; 1999 on *autem* and *ceterum*; Orlandini and Poccetti 2007 and 2009 on several particles.

100 Her particle publications include Risselada 1994 on *modo* and *sane* in directives; 1996 on *nunc*; 1998a on *sane*; 1998b on *tandem* and *postremo*; 2005 on particles in questions; Kroon and Risselada 1998 and 2002 on *iam*.

101 Her particle publications include Rosén 1989 on several Latin particles; 1993 on *demum*; 2002 on several Latin particles as cohesive devices; 2003 on *immo*; 1999 on several Latin connecting particles; 2007 on *sed*; 2009 on several Latin particles.

102 Her particle publications include Schrickx 2009 on *nam* and *namque*; 2010 on *nempe*; 2011 (monograph) on *nempe*, *quippe*, *scilicet*, *videlicet* and *nimirum*; 2014 on *scilicet* and *videlicet*.

103 See II.2 and II.3 for discussion of ideas from Functional Discourse Grammar. See also note 6 above.

104 In the following overview, I will restrict myself to monographs on particles and scholars who have published repeatedly on this topic. The numerous other articles on Greek particles that adopt a modern linguistic approach are mentioned and summarized in part V, our database ORPS (Online Repository of Particle Studies).

105 See E. J. Bakker 1986, 1988, and 1993c on περ; 1993a on δέ; 1993b on ἄρα; 1997a on many aspects of the Homeric language, including the use of ἄρα, αὐτάρ, γάρ, δέ, δή, καί, μέν, and οὖν; 2005 on γάρ, γε, δέ, καί, περ, and τε; 2011 for a short overview of Homeric particles. See especially part II

cognitive linguist Chafe, who argues that spoken discourse represents the speaker's flow of consciousness.[106] Bakker approaches the Homeric poems in a similar way: he interprets the "intonation units" ("discourse acts" in our terminology[107]) that make up the discourse as reflecting the singer's focus of consciousness at a given moment. In other words, Bakker takes into account the wider discourse as well as the cognitive constraints on the speaker and listener.

§67. Sicking published several works on Greek particles in the 1980s and 1990s as well.[108] He implicitly adopts a pragmatic approach, as he emphasizes the general importance of analyzing segments larger than sentences, and of viewing language as a means for communication rather than merely a means for the expression of thoughts.[109] Sicking's 1993 study on particles in Lysias is published together with Van Ophuijsen 1993 on four particles in Plato.[110] Like Sicking, Van Ophuijsen takes a general pragmatic approach.

§68. Wakker adopts a pragmatic approach in her various studies of (primarily classical) Greek particles, published from the 1990s onwards.[111] In her 1994 monograph on conditional clauses in several Greek genres she uses the framework of Functional Grammar, mainly developed by S. J. Dik in 1978 and 1989.[112] Adopting the framework's distinction among several levels of a clause, Wakker divides the particles used in conditional clauses into two groups. The first group modifies conditional clauses as a whole and are labelled "scope particles"[113]; the second group modifies the proposition put forward in a conditional clause. Under the "scope particles" she includes γε, περ, and καί. The second group, "modal or attitudinal particles," marks the speaker's attitude to the proposition presented, and includes ἄρα, δή, που, and τοι. In later publications (1997a

of this monograph, on particle use in Homer and Pindar, for discussion of E. J. Bakker's particle analyses.

106 See e.g. Chafe (ed.) 1980, 1994. His research is discussed in II.2.

107 On discourse acts, see especially II.2 (with extensive discussion of E. J. Bakker's work) and IV.3.

108 See Sicking 1986 on classical Greek; 1993 on Lysias; 1996b and 1997 on Plato.

109 Sicking 1986:125-126, 138-139; 1993:7-8; 1997:157, 173-174. On 1986:136 and 1993:48 he cites the framework of Functional Grammar by S. J. Dik 1978 (see note 94 above).

110 Van Ophuijsen and Stork 1999 also pay considerable attention to particle use in their commentary on parts of book 7 of Herodotus' *Histories*.

111 See Wakker 1994 on ἄρα, γε, δή, καί, περ, που, and τοι in conditional clauses in several authors; 1995 on several particles in Sophocles; 1996 on μάν and μήν in Theocritus; 1997a on μήν in tragedy; 1997b on several particles in Herodotus and Thucydides; 2001 on μέν in Xenophon; 2002 on ἤδη in Xenophon; 2009a on οὖν and τοίνυν in Lysias; 2009b on several particles in several authors.

112 Similarly to Wakker, H. J. Dik uses Functional Grammar in her 1995 monograph on word order in Herodotus, and includes some observations on particle use. Polo Arrondo 2007 and 2011 on πλήν also uses the framework.

113 See I.1 §20 for a brief discussion of "scope" as used in this monograph; we do not adopt the term "scope particles."

on γε, δή, ἦ, and μήν in tragedy; 2009a on οὖν and τοίνυν in Lysias) Wakker adopts the discourse model developed by Kroon 1995 (see above, §64).

§69. Revuelta Puigdollers has investigated several Greek particles in the 1990s and 2000s.[114] He pays special attention to αὖ and αὖτε, and to πάλιν. In his 2006a article on πάλιν Revuelta Puigdollers uses, as Wakker does, ideas from Functional Grammar as well as from the discourse model developed by Kroon 1995. His 2009a and 2009b publications, which mainly analyze αὖ and αὖτε, explicitly apply Functional Grammar.

§70. The volume *New Approaches to Greek Particles* (1997) edited by Rijksbaron presents several applications of modern linguistic frameworks to the study of Greek particles. Apart from Wakker, also Basset 1997 on ἀλλά, Jacquinod 1997 on καίτοι, and Slings 1997a on adversative particles use specific approaches that fall under pragmatics.[115]

§71. Bonifazi 2008, 2009, and 2012 throw light on several particles and adverbs in Homeric Greek. The author analyzes αὖ, αὖτε, αὐτάρ, αὖτις, αὐτίκα, αὔτως, αὖθι/αὐτόθι, and αὐτοῦ from a pragmatic perspective, explicitly applying insights from coherence approaches to discourse markers in modern languages, as well as from Relevance Theory, in particular the concept of "procedural meaning."[116] She also builds on E. J. Bakker's work on particles and Homeric discourse, and on Kroon's 1995 research on Latin particles. In addition, Bonifazi pays attention to the role of memory constraints and the visual and narrative role of the lexical items under investigation.

§72. In 2009 S. J. Bakker and Wakker published *Discourse Cohesion in Ancient Greek*, a collection of papers on several cohesive devices, including particles. In this volume I myself analyze ἀλλά in drama; S. J. Bakker discusses γάρ and οὖν in Plato; Van Erp Taalman Kip writes about καὶ μήν, καὶ δή, and ἤδη in drama; Revuelta Puigdollers investigates αὖ and αὖτε in several genres; and Wakker delves into οὖν and τοίνυν in Lysias.[117] Each of these authors emphasizes different aspects of the broad framework of pragmatics.

§73. Other recent particle studies are the dissertations of Koier 2013 and Zakowski 2017, and several papers in Denizot and Spevak eds. 2017. Koier takes a Construction

[114] His particle research includes Revuelta Puigdollers 1996 (the author's unpublished dissertation) on αὖ, αὖτε, αὖθις, ἄψ, πάλιν and ὀπίσω; 2000 on focus particles; 2006a on πάλιν; 2006b is an overview (in Spanish) of Greek particles; 2009a and 2009b on αὖ, αὖτε, and other particles as topicalizing devices (2009b is a more elaborate version of 2009a); 2013 is an encyclopedia entry on Greek particles in general.

[115] Basset and Jacquinod mainly build on the ideas of Ducrot 1972, 1975, 1980, 1984; Slings on those of Polanyi and Scha 1983, and Roulet *et al.* 1985.

[116] Bonifazi 2012 drops "procedural meaning" in favor of the terms proposed by Kroon 1995 (see §64 above).

[117] R. J. Allan 2009 on narrative modes in Euripides in the same volume also provides many remarks on particles. Additionally, George 2009 in the same volume is highly relevant to the study of particles: he qualifies the findings of Duhoux 1997a; 1997b; 1998; 2006 on the distribution of particles across dialogic versus non-dialogic texts.

Grammar approach to πoυ in several genres.[118] The author identifies co-textual features that lead to a specific interpretation of this polyfunctional particle. In addition, she carries out a diachronic analysis in order to describe the functional development of πoυ from Homer to Isocrates.

§74. Several pragmatic approaches have been applied to the analysis of ancient Greek and Latin particles over the past few decades. The studies make it clear that we can understand particle use better than before if we pay attention to the larger co-text—that is, beyond the single sentence in which a particle occurs—and to communicatively relevant aspects of the extralinguistic context. These insights, taken over from research on modern languages, have led to a shift of attention, from a sentence-based view to a more discourse-based view, in the study of Greek and Latin particles. Zakowski uses Relevance Theory to analyze δέ, γάρ, and οὖν in several texts from the fourth century CE. He argues that it is more fruitful to describe these particles as procedural items, rather than as connected to coherence. δέ, γάρ, and οὖν help a hearer's interpretation process, each in their own specific way. In the 2017 volume edited by Denizot and Spevak, Allan analyzes Greek adversative particles as polysemous networks of semantic extensions, and Crespo gives a unitary description of καί. Other articles focus on Latin particles.

3.6 Conclusions

§75. In recent years much linguistic research has been carried out on words in various languages that are functionally similar to ancient Greek particles. These words are often called "discourse markers." Three related issues surrounding them recur: terminology, definition, and classification. Despite disagreements on these points, scholars of discourse markers have developed many theoretical insights and methodological tools.

§76. Different approaches are used in discourse-marker studies, with varying assumptions, questions, and methods. This chapter has discussed four of them: coherence approaches, Conversation Analysis (CA), Relevance Theory (RT), and Construction Grammar (CxG). Beyond these specific approaches, cross-linguistic, diachronic, synchronically historical, and narrative discourse-marker studies have also been useful to us. Finally, approaches similar to the ones described here have already been applied to the study of Greek and Latin particles by numerous classicists.

§77. The study of Greek particles can profit from taking into account both the findings of previous work on the particles themselves—this monograph's "horizontal axis"—and the theoretical and methodological insights of contemporary research on functionally similar words in other languages—our work's "vertical axis." This chapter is designed to inform the reader of those studies on the vertical axis that have particularly influenced the approaches and analyses in this multi-part work. Their intellectual

[118] See §§47-50 above on Koier's analysis of the Dutch particle *ergens*, published in the same monograph.

footprint is discernible in our efforts to be sensitive to the kind of discourse being studied (as in coherence approaches), to the communicative actions performed by speakers (as in CA), to the constraints on interpretation that particles may encode (as in RT), and to the specific co-textual features that influence our interpretation (as in CxG). In other words, the insights of these and similar approaches have led us to approach Greek particles the way we do: not as syntactically irrelevant parts of sentences, but as pragmatically crucial parts of verbal interactions.

I.4

General Conclusions

§1. In this chapter we outline the value of our work for the study of Greek particles on the one hand, and archaic and classical Greek literature on the other. By "conclusions" we do not mean that we will be summarizing the outcomes of our various analyses on particles, particle combinations, and discourse phenomena. For these discussions we direct your attention to the *ad hoc* conclusions found in each chapter. Instead, here we present the methodological advances that our study offers to literary and linguistic scholarship on ancient Greek.

4.1 Particles Invite Sensitivity to Discourse

§2. There is a striking incongruity between what scholars have said about particles and how they are commonly treated in current teaching and study of the Greek language. Almost a century before Denniston, Schraut called particles the "nerves that pervade the body of speech",[1] and comparable claims have been made by numerous scholars—Aristotle and Apollonius Dyscolus in antiquity, and Hoogeveen, Hartung, Stephens, Paley, and Hancock in the eighteenth to early twentieth centuries.[2] It cannot be a coincidence

1 Schraut 1849:9.

2 In *Rhetoric* 3.5, Aristotle discusses the importance of speaking good Greek, enumerating several ways in which this is done, of which the first he mentions is the correct use of connective particles (σύνδεσμοι). Apollonius Dyscolus claims in *Syntax* III.379.1 that every particle has a certain force: ἕκαστος αὐτῶν ἔχει τινὰ δύναμιν "every one of them [i.e. filling combiners] has some force" (see I.2 §63). See also the following statements by modern scholars: *Quod si particula salva orationis structura abjici possit, non statim ea dicenda otiosa, vel expletiva, cum, hac neglecta, pereat vel emphasis, vel perspicuitas, quam orationi suppeditat, vel simile quid, propter quod vel additur, vel repetitur; atque ita suo semper officio fungens, ob id ipsum non abundat.* "[What else is it but a mistake of the language or of a writer to add words that do not mean anything?] Because, if a particle could be left out without changing the structure of a discourse, it should not immediately be called empty, or expletive, because, when this particle is ignored, either emphasis would be lost, or clarity, with which [a particle] supplies the discourse, or something similar, for which reason [the particle] is added or repeated; and so, since it always carries out its own function, for that very reason it is not redundant" (Hoogeveen 1769:vi); "*Es ist dieß [i.e. the explanation of particles] keine Sache, die Jemand nur nebenbei mit abmachen kann; denn es handelt sich um nichts Geringeres, als einzudringen in die innersten und geheimsten Gesetze des Organismus der Sprache ....*" ("This [i.e. the explanation of

that anyone who turns their mind to these smallest parts of speech realizes their importance on every level of analysis.

§3. Particles are constitutive elements of ancient Greek. They deserve the same kind of attention that was paid to them in early modern scholarship (see the introductory note in Part V), when they were studied just as much as all the other recurrent components of the language. In this monograph we demonstrate new ways in which the importance of ancient Greek particles can be revealed. To this aim we provide a number of methodological and terminological tools, all based in the underlying idea that discourse is the point of reference for understanding how particles function.

§4. As Apollonius Dyscolus observed, particles typically co-signify (συσσημαίνειν) with other constituents. In our approach we have considered all possible factors that could be relevant to particle use in each of the different genres, even the non-linguistic contexts that Apollonius does not take into account. On the methodological level, this means to take a holistic approach to discourse, in which syntax, semantics, and pragmatics are all taken into consideration. Our analyses have shown that sensitivity to specific contextual and co-textual features is crucial to understanding particle use in ancient Greek discourse.

§5. One advantage of the discourse perspective is that it shows that all particles are multifunctional. Not only can they do different things in different contexts, but they can also do multiple things at the same time. In certain instances the pragmatic contribution of particles is best compared to that achieved by intonation in spoken English. Intonation is an important carrier of signification, and like particles it can do many things at the same time. Most important, the same sentence produced with different intonational contours will carry different implications, and this is consistent with our findings on particles. While not often adding propositional meaning, the use of a certain particle will lead to certain implications, which will strongly influence the communicative effect of the utterance.

§6. Particles may signal the sequence of acts and moves in the discourse (organizational functions), and qualify the attitude of the speaker towards the content (modal functions) at the same time. In other words, our analysis of so-called "modal" particles takes into account their potentially co-existing organizational functions. By analogy, instead of assigning *either* connective *or* adverbial functions to particles (which largely

particles] is no task that one could absolve merely in passing; for it concerns nothing smaller than invading into the innermost and most secret laws of the language's organism ..." (Hartung 1832:50); "[In certain compounds particles] are most liable to the imputation cast on them by grammarians of being idle particles (otiosae particulae) or expletives in the fullest sense of that term; namely, sounds without a meaning. But this (...) they never really are, except to those who are ignorant of their signification (...)" (Stephens 1837:29); "[Particles] so greatly affect the tone, connexion, or irony of a passage, that a correct knowledge of their uses is quite a necessary condition of accurate Greek scholarship" (Paley 1881:v); "The Greek particle is a gem with many facets (...)" (Hancock 1917:26).

coincide with organizational vs. modal functions), we find that it is better to think of functions as existing on a continuum. The continuum we envision allows for the consideration of multifunctionality beyond syntactic roles.

4.2 What to Look Out For in Connection with Particles

§7. While any aspect of the co-text or context is potentially important in understanding particle use, our research shows that a number of features tend to be particularly relevant in particle studies. Three factors are fundamental and must always be taken into consideration: first, particles frequently occur in combinations; second, particles affect the process of segmentation; and third, particles have bearing on the author-audience vector across genres.

§8. Attention to particle combinations goes back to early modern scholarship, but recent work has not appreciated the full range of their functions. Typically, combinations are regarded as derivations of their constituent parts, so that the function of the whole is usually viewed as based on the function of one or more of its constituents. Although this is often true, there are two further facets to their functionality. First, particle combinations can preserve functions of the constituent particles that are no longer present when the constituents are used alone.[3] Second, some particle combinations go through further development, so that they become clusters with functions that reach beyond the sum of their parts.[4] Particle clusters in particular are understudied, because of the aforementioned tendency to base a combination's function on those of its constituents. Moreover, particles can also combine into recurrent constructions with other parts of speech, such as anaphoric pronouns.[5]

§9. The second guiding factor is discourse segmentation. In a number of chapters, we demonstrate the link between particles and subdivisions of discourse into acts and moves. With this approach we challenge the (often implicit) assumption that particles modify either single phrases or whole sentences. Some particles can indeed have scope over only an adjacent word or phrase, but beyond that particles may mark transitions between acts *within* sentences, or transitions between units (moves) that comprise *multiple* sentences.

§10. What our research indicates is that particles—especially but not exclusively—mark discourse segmentation in the Greek language; they can guide us better than

3 See e.g. Denniston 1950:57: "Further, as with δή and μήν, so with γάρ, the original asseverative force remains in existence after the development of the connective, and side by side with it, *at any rate in combinations* (just as the asseverative force of μήν persists in ἀλλὰ μήν, καὶ μήν, and ἦ μήν)" (our emphasis).

4 E.g. μὲν δή in Herodotus (see IV.3.11), or μὲν οὖν in drama (see III.2.2).

5 E.g. ὅ γε in Homer (II.5.3) and οὗτος forms + δή in Herodotus (IV.3.11).

modern punctuation, indentation, and chapter divisions. Attuning ourselves to the segmentation of discourse puts us in a better position to see the existence throughout our corpus (and beyond) of small projecting phrases, priming acts, guiding the reader or listener through complex discourse. At the larger scale, we can see how particles compartmentalize units of multiple sentences, turns of speech, or even prose sections and chapters.

§11. The extra-linguistic context is the third factor that we have prioritized in our study of particle use. No discourse is conceived in a vacuum: the performer or author constantly has the audience in mind while producing his discourse. Accordingly, we demonstrate how particles help anchor the current discourse to knowledge shared between speaker/author and audience. In drama particles perform this function by interacting with conventions of conversation, marking speaking turns as certain social actions. In epic and lyric, performers work in constant interaction with a tradition, which restricts their narrative possibilities but at the same time greatly increases their potential frame of reference. The knowledge shared between performer and audience is in constant flux, and particles play an important part in the performer's strategies of audience involvement. Herodotean irony can be interpreted as a manifestation of this process in historiography: the ironic effect of some particles springs from the fact that they highlight a discrepancy in the knowledge shared between author and audience on the one hand, and characters on the other.

4.3 Particles, Text, and Literature

§12. Although particles are typically regarded as belonging to the minutiae of discourse, the range of literary and philological observations made in this monograph demonstrates their importance for issues of text and interpretation. For all genres discussed, the role of particles in marking the boundaries of discourse units and signaling the relations between them directly impacts the way we read these texts. The flow of discourse[6] is primary, not secondary, and it is largely guided by particles. Our work demonstrates why it is necessary to analyze a text at its micro-level, by examining the smallest lexical items: they form the basis for any further interpretation. Before entering into a discussion over what a text means, we have to take a step back and first establish as well as we can what it actually says.

§13. This approach to the language of Greek literature has yielded results that in many cases are in line with observations made by literary scholars. We found that differences in the way Herodotus and Thucydides use δή directly reflect differences in their historiographical methods. Whereas Herodotus aims to align author and audience as much as possible, Thucydides invites readers to align with characters, thus facilitating

[6] See IV.3 §9 and n11.

the audience's immersion in the narrative. Dramatic speeches that commentators characterize as calm and collected or rather as highly emotional or angry can be shown to make use of certain particles and other linguistic features rather than others. On the more general level of the linguistics of literature, our attention to discourse phenomena builds on the work of several Dutch scholars on particles in specific genres (e.g. by Sicking, Van Ophuijsen, Wakker). In addition, our exploration of discourse act boundaries harmonizes with studies (e.g. by Devine and Stephens, Bakker, Scheppers, and Goldstein) that make the notion of intonational phrase central to word order and the construction of meaning.[7]

§14. At the same time, we have challenged some ideas that are solidly established in literary scholarship. For example, we found that the distribution patterns of certain particles are strongly correlated to the type of discourse they appear in (e.g. direct speech versus narrator text). These patterns challenge the claim that small lexical items such as γε, ἄρα, and τε are distributed randomly and function solely as metrical fillers in poetic discourse. Other assumptions about τε, which are deeply engrained in the collective scholarship, must also be revised as a result of the data we have uncovered. The particle that is most typically connected to epic is in fact more frequent in Pindar and tragic lyric, and it occurs less in the "Homeric" language of Herodotus than in Thucydides. Moreover, we have shown across genres that the canonical view that τε has two mutually exclusive functions (copulative or non-copulative) is neither sufficient nor productive.

§15. Our close attention to discourse segmentation has also yielded some surprising results. Contrary to common belief, Thucydides builds his discourse out of units as small as those in Herodotus. Thucydides may be syntactically and lexically more sophisticated than his predecessor, but on the level of discourse he presents his story in equally small increments. The language of Pindar's lyric reveals a similar pattern: its syntax is often baroque, but the progress of its discourse is clearly suited to on-line reception by a listening audience. Along the same lines the language of drama is both literary and accessible. Dramatic dialogue is of course stylized, but close study of their linguistic patterns shows that they in fact follow the same conversational rules that are employed in everyday interaction.

§16. In general this project has revealed various phenomena in language use that tend to be overlooked in traditional grammars and literary criticism. In this respect our attention to the occurrence and distribution of particles across genres brings our knowledge of ancient Greek grammar more up-to-date, and advances current studies in ancient Greek literary discourse. In fact, our chapters show that sensitivity to discourse reaches beyond particles and linguistics. Narrative transitions, discourse memory, anaphoric choices, resonance, conversational rules, emotional states of mind, stancetaking,

7 See in particular II.2 §§16-17; IV.3 §§70-71.

segmentation, and coordination strategies affect our comprehension of meaning and appreciation of artfulness *tout court*.

4.4 Directions in Ancient Greek Particle Studies

§17. We have tested the soundness of theories and methodologies through practical analyses of select genres. Those analyses may be extended in a number of ways. Not only can each discourse topic be applied to examine any of the other genres we cover (so, for example, one may explore discourse patterns in historiography, stance in Homer, or discourse memory in tragedy), but, further afield, such analyses may also be conducted on genres we exclude (so, for example, one may consider resonance in Hellenistic poetry, segmentation in Plato, anaphoric reference in Imperial novels, etc.). In fact, the concepts we introduce are not solely applicable to questions of particle use, but can throw light on multiple aspects of a discourse and its language.

§18. We see particular further potential in statistical approaches to word use, the unframed/framed discourse distinction, and the stance triangle. In multiple contexts we have demonstrated that a statistical approach to word use (explored especially in III.2) reveals patterns that otherwise remain undiscussed. With sufficient and clear parameters, and with a primary focus on the bare text at our disposal, statistical differences between parts of a discourse can provide a starting point for innovative analyses in any genre. The distinction between framed and unframed discourse (introduced in II.4) will be a productive approach for all kinds of ancient Greek narrative. It can clarify issues of tense use, particle use, and anaphoric reference. Finally, the stance triangle (introduced in IV.4) can create new insights in multiple genres. In the recent developments of research more and more attention is given to how an audience experiences a discourse, and how the author guides this process. The stance triangle provides an efficient framework for unraveling and describing the intricate relationships between author, audience, and characters.

§19. In more general terms, the future of Greek particle studies must lie in a further rapprochement with recently developed models for discourse segmentation, with views of grammar inspired by discourse phenomena and social interaction, and in particular with the field of discourse marker studies in contemporary languages. While there has been contact between ancient Greek particle studies and discourse marker studies, it has been limited in two ways. First, the interaction has been largely unidirectional: contemporary methods have been applied in order to better describe ancient Greek particles, but thorough knowledge of Greek particles is rarely shared within the field of linguistics. For example, μέν appears to be a lexical marker of pragmatic projection that is hardly paralleled (if at all) in contemporary western languages. Second, classicists have been extremely selective in borrowing from contemporary linguistics, with the effect that the majority of relevant publications apply only a very small number of methods, especially

Functional (Discourse) Grammar and coherence approaches. For further advances in our understanding of particles in all languages, we need to bring together the two millennia of scholarship on Greek particles and the past century of studies on modern languages, and continue the work as one field that will be all the stronger for its unification.

PART II

PARTICLE USE IN HOMER AND PINDAR

BY

MARK DE KREIJ

II.1
Introduction

§1. Homer and Pindar[1] represent the earliest and most important poetic genres of Archaic and Classical Greece: epic and lyric. Similar to drama, epic and lyric performance was social, interactive, and often ritual. There was a rhythm to Homeric epic and a melody to Pindaric song that is lost to us, which can at best be approximated with the aid of meter. Although we cannot reconstruct the performance, we must constantly keep it in mind as we consider the text. Unlike drama, however, the epic and lyric performer form the single source of their discourse, which means that their role is closer to that of the author in historiography. Part II examines the role of particles in Homer and Pindar, highlighting relations between language and those aspects of the performance context that are not typically taken into account. The corpus used for analysis consists of the *Iliad*, the *Odyssey*, and Pindar's *Victory Odes*.[2]

§2. For Homer, this approach is exemplified by the work of Nagy, Bakker, Kahane, and Minchin.[3] Homeric discourse "was a matter of speech and voice, and of the consciousness of the performer and his audience."[4] An important implication of this approach is that it is not essential to know when the *Iliad* and the *Odyssey* were written down, nor to what time exactly different parts of the texts can be traced back. It is unlikely that the *Iliad*

1 Regardless of authorship, I use Homer and Pindar as metonyms for "Homeric epic" and "Pindar's song" throughout. Cited texts are from the Thesaurus Linguae Graecae Online unless noted otherwise: Allen 1931 for the Iliad, Von der Mühll 1946 for the Odyssey, and Snell/Maehler 1971 for Pindar's Victory Odes. Frequencies are based on the same editions. Translations are by the author, except for those cases where he adduces an existing translation to make a point.

2 In editions given in the *Thesaurus Linguae Graecae Online* unless noted otherwise: Allen 1931 for the *Iliad*, Von der Mühll 1946 for the *Odyssey*, and Snell/Maehler 1971 for the *Victory Odes*. Translations are my own, except for those cases where I adduce an existing translation to demonstrate a point.
Although in principle the entire corpus is considered in the analyses, the statistical analysis of particle use in narrator text and direct speech covers four books of the *Iliad* (4, 5, 6, and 17) and four books of the *Odyssey* (9, 10, 17, and 18), which amounts to 4917 lines, containing 6259 particles.

3 See Nagy 1979, 1990, and 1995, Martin 1989, Kahane 1994, Bakker 1997b and 2005, and Minchin 2001. Consider also Martin 1997:141, "...[epic] performers enact what audiences want, using all the poetic and musical resources at their disposal."

4 Bakker 1997b:1.

was ever performed in Archaic or Classical Greece in exactly its current form (e.g. the edition in West 1999), or even in the form given in any of our manuscripts. Nonetheless, the language with all its layers, complexities, and inconsistencies, as we find it in the manuscripts and editions, adequately reflects the language that may have been used in composition-in-performance. There are undoubtedly different diachronic layers in Homeric language, but the differences in particle use that emerge (at least within the *Iliad* and the *Odyssey* respectively) may equally well reflect synchronic multifunctionality. In short, the written texts represent the words of a potential unique performance, and the language can be analyzed accordingly.

§3. As for Pindar, the many facets of his lyric language have been illuminated especially by the work of Bundy, Mackie, Bonifazi, and Wells:[5]

(t1)

> "It is necessary to think away the boundaries of the material text and to see each victory song as an emergent communicative event in order to grasp that at the moment of performance the composer would have been in the process of demonstrating his artistic skill and vying for a positive evaluation of his work from the audience."
>
> Wells 2009:141

Unlike Homeric epic, the texts of Pindar's lyric do not reflect composition-in-performance, but they were still composed *for* performance: Pindar composed them with an occasion, a performer, and an audience in mind.[6]

§4. Both Pindar and the Homeric performer constantly operate on a set of assumptions about the knowledge shared between him and the audience, and always intend their communication to be successful.[7] However, the fact that the performances of Homeric epic and Pindar's lyric were communicative events does not entail any limitations on their potential literary artfulness.[8]

§5. The on-line interaction between performer and audience is foundational: issues of internal and external narrators and of implicit or ideal hearers or readers all derive from this situation.[9] Likewise, the question of the historical "ego" in Pindar's individual

5 See Bundy 1962, Mackie 2003, Bonifazi 2001, 2004a, 2004b, 2004c, and Wells 2009.

6 See also Wells 2009:30-36 on the interactive nature of Pindaric song: we happen to have the written libretto of a song composed with only performance in mind.

7 See Bundy 1962:35 quoted in chapter 3 §68.

8 See e.g. Kahane 1994:143.

9 For the movement of perspectives between narrators and characters in the *Iliad* and *Odyssey*, see especially the work of De Jong 2001 and 2004b.

odes, though important, is not central in this study.[10] In both the epic and lyric corpora, the performer (a singer or rhapsode for Homer, a singer or chorus for Pindar) will have been the natural referent for the first person singular or plural, barring explicit information to the contrary, such as in direct speech. Even in direct speech, moreover, the performer is the speaker, and at that moment embodies the "I". For these reasons, I will speak of "performer" and "audience" throughout.[11]

1.1 Starting Points

§6. Particle use in Homer and Pindar is an infinitely large topic, and no study can address it in all its aspects. Numerous articles, essays, and even monographs have been devoted to single particles like γάρ, δή, and τε,[12] and issues surrounding δέ, μέν, and ἄρα in Homer have vexed commentators from the scholiasts onward. In the following chapters, I explore four aspects of Homeric and Pindaric language that come to the fore when we regard the texts as elements of a performance. If we can come to a better understanding of these larger topics, it will illuminate a number of old and new questions surrounding particle use in Homer and Pindar.

§7. Consider this passage from the *Iliad*:

(t2)

(...) ἀτὰρ μεγάθυμοι Ἐπειοὶ
ἀμφέσταν <u>δὴ</u> ἄστυ διαρραῖσαι μεμαῶτες·

Iliad 11.732-733

But the great-hearted Epeians
were marshalled about the city, eager to raze it utterly.

[Translation Murray]

If we follow the translation given by Murray, it appears that δή is in fifth position in a sentence (ἀτάρ ... μεμαῶτες), and moreover the particle remains untranslated. This position does not fit well with what we know about postpositive particles like δή. In fact, the position and force of δή here cannot be explained sufficiently if one regards the sentence or clause as the main domain of analysis. As an alternative to established explanations, in

10 The discussion of the "I" in Pindaric lyric is complex and ongoing, and it is typically linked to the question of who performed the *Odes*, see e.g. Davies 1988, Heath 1988, Lefkowitz 1988, 1991 and 1995, and Carey 1991.

11 For the sake of convenience I speak of "narrator text" to distinguish it from "direct speech."

12 Consider e.g. Misener 1904 on γάρ, Thomas 1894 on δή and ἤδη in Homer, and Ruijgh 1971 on "τε épique."

chapter II.2 "Discourse Acts" we discuss ways to segment discourse at the subsentential level, and re-examine the function of particles in this new light.

§8. Now compare the following use of γάρ in Pindar (see II.3 §§74-75):

(t3)

> θεῶν δ' ἐφετμαῖς Ἰξίονα φαντὶ ταῦτα βροτοῖς
> λέγειν ἐν πτερόεντι τροχῷ
> παντᾷ κυλινδόμενον·
> τὸν εὐεργέταν ἀγαναῖς ἀμοιβαῖς ἐποιχομένους τίνεσθαι.
> ἔμαθε δὲ σαφές. εὐμενέσσι γὰρ παρὰ Κρονίδαις
>
> γλυκὺν ἑλὼν βίοτον, μακρὸν οὐχ ὑπέμεινεν ὄλβον.
>
> Pindar, *Pythian* 2.21-26
>
> By the orders of the gods, they tell that Ixion says the following to mortals,
> on his feathered wheel,
> spinning in all directions:
> to go to one's benefactor and pay him back with good deeds.
>
> And he learned it clearly. Indeed, among the kind children of Kronos,
> having obtained a sweet life, he did not endure his bliss for long.

The relation between the γάρ clause and the one that precedes it cannot be construed as causal. Ixion did not learn his lesson "because" he had a sweet life among the gods, nor "because" he could not endure his bliss. Rather, he was punished "because" he made advances on Hera, and this causal link is expressed by ὅτ(ι) in line 27. The link marked by γάρ is a different one, and it does not concern a relation between two adjacent clauses, but between one clause (ἔμαθε δὲ σαφές) and the following narrative (25-34). Commentaries do not address these subdivisions of the discourse above the clause or sentence level, and translations cannot easily render it. The problem of γάρ can be better understood if we examine more closely the segmentation of discourse above the sentence level: this is the topic of II.3 "Moves."

§9. The Homeric simile is of course very familiar to the reader of epic; here is a typical example (see II.4 §31):

(t4)

(...) ὥς τε λέοντα,
ὅς ῥά τε βεβρωκὼς βοὸς ἔρχεται ἀγραύλοιο·
πᾶν δ᾽ ἄρα οἱ στῆθός τε παρήϊά τ᾽ ἀμφοτέρωθεν
αἱματόεντα πέλει, δεινὸς δ᾽ εἰς ὦπα ἰδέσθαι·
ὣς Ὀδυσεὺς πεπάλακτο πόδας καὶ χεῖρας ὕπερθεν.

Odyssey 22.402-406

Just like a lion,
which, having fed, comes from an ox in the field,
completely then his breast and both his paws
are bloody, and terrible for the eyes to see.
Just so Odysseus was bespattered, his feet and his hands above.

Odysseus is compared to a lion covered in blood, and in the language we find two instances of so-called "epic" τε, in lines 402 (ὥς τε) and 403 (ὅς ῥά τε), along with two instances of "copulative" τε in line 404 (στῆθός τε παρήϊά τ᾽). "Epic" τε is most commonly described as denoting a habitual action, a permanent fact, or a temporary fact. On the one hand, this broad description deserves elaboration, and on the other one might ask what makes the τε in lines 402 and 403 different from the two in line 404. The Homeric and Pindaric material in fact suggests that these instances represent two aspects of the same τε, a particle that reflects an ongoing negotiation with tradition. Chapter II.4 "Discourse Memory" explores this constant interaction between current discourse and knowledge shared between performer and audience.

§10. Finally, this occurrence of δ᾽ ἄρα in Pindar deserves closer attention (see II.5 §52):

(t5)

θάνεν μὲν αὐτὸς ἥρως Ἀτρεΐδας
ἵκων χρόνῳ κλυταῖς ἐν Ἀμύκλαις,

μάντιν τ᾽ ὄλεσσε κόραν, ἐπεὶ ἀμφ᾽ Ἑλένᾳ πυρωθέντας
Τρώων ἔλυσε δόμους ἁβρότατος. ὁ δ᾽ ἄρα γέροντα ξένον
Στροφίον ἐξίκετο, νέα κεφαλά, Παρνασσοῦ πόδα ναίοντ᾽·

Pindar, *Pythian* 11.31-35

> He himself died, the hero son of Atreus [Agamemnon],
> arriving in time in renowned Amyklai,
>
> and he brought death on the seer girl, after over Helen he had despoiled
> the burnt down houses of the Trojans of their luxury. So HE [sc. Orestes], the young boy,
> went to his aged host, Strophius, living at the foot of Parnassus.

The particle ἄρα has confused classicists and linguists for centuries, in Homer more than in Pindar, but one thing that is clear here is that it cannot mark an inference or conclusion from the preceding. It does not mean: Agamemnon died, "and because of that" Orestes went to Strophius. In fact, when Agamemnon is murdered, Orestes is saved by Arsinoe, and later he goes to Strophius: there is no direct temporal or causal connection between the two events, so (δ') ἄρα must be doing something different. An understanding of the cognitive underpinnings of anaphoric reference combined with particles will provide better tools to deal with examples like this one, and this topic is elaborated in II.5 "Particles and Anaphoric Reference."

1.1.1 Sneak preview

§11. The first half of part II considers particles as clues to the articulation of discourse, both below and above the sentence level. In scholarship on Homer and Pindar, the existence of syntactically multiform units below the sentence level, which we call "discourse acts," and suprasentential units, "moves," has never been linked systematically to particle use. Chapter II.2 introduces the discourse act, ranging from phrases to full clauses or sentences, as the primary frame of reference for the function of particles. This approach illuminates the use of δέ in Homer (and beyond), and it allows us to better describe the projecting function of μέν. A discourse also consists of larger units of fluctuating size, which we call moves, made up of acts that cohere for different reasons. Chapter II.3 investigates the occurrence of particles at boundaries between such units, considering first the use of καὶ γάρ and ἤδη at the beginning of embedded stories. Within Pindaric narratives, the functions of δέ and ἄρα receive particular attention. Finally, a new analysis of δή in Homer demonstrates that part of the particle's function is the segmentation of narrative discourse.

§12. The second half of Part II is concerned with how performer and audience co-create and access a mental representation of the discourse. Having established that γάρ can introduce moves such as an embedded narrative, chapter II.4 further explores the kinds of discourse transitions at which γάρ occurs. It turns out that in Homer and Pindar γάρ is perhaps the most important marker of a new move that is different in nature from—but strongly associated with—the preceding move. Just like γάρ, τε and ἄρα are often involved in managing and accessing the knowledge shared between performer and audience. Chapter II.5 then focuses on shared discourse: what tools does the performer use to guide his audience? Particles such as γε and δή, and combinations such as (δ') ἄρα collaborate with anaphoric reference to help the hearer draw the right inferences, and understand where the discourse is going.

§13. The progression of Homeric and Pindaric discourse is linear, since it is bound to its realization in time. The tools of the Homeric performer differ from Pindar's, but both performers shape their discourse in order to accommodate this reality. A factor that permeates both epic and lyric discourse is that of projection, pointing forward to ease the audience's comprehension. Both in Homer and Pindar we find syntactically incomplete, short units ("priming acts") that presage the subject of the upcoming part of discourse. Despite the obvious differences between epic and lyric, particle use is also often comparable. For example, δέ and ἄρα play an important role in narrative discourse, in both genres, while τε can be much better understood if the different ranges of use in Homer and Pindar are taken into account.

§14. Particles in Homer and Pindar differ in frequency as well as usage. First of all, particles are much more frequent in Homer than in Pindar, both individually and as a group, except τε, which abounds in Pindar.[13] Second, Homer employs particles like ἄρα and δή in a wider range of co-texts than Pindar. Third, Homeric discourse shows a clear distinction in particle use between direct speech and narrator text; no such discourse-bound patterns occur in Pindar. There are many more small differences in particle use between Homer and Pindar, some of which will be discussed in the upcoming chapters, and they may be the result of generic differences, diachronic development, or even idiosyncracies. The following chapters show that it is productive to juxtapose epic and lyric language: the different performance contexts help illuminate the many aspects of particle use in Homer and Pindar.

§15. The following table gives an impression of the use of particles across the two Homeric epics and Pindar's *Victory Odes*. The numbers represent the occurrences of a certain particle per 100 lines, rounded off to a single decimal. These numbers will be referred to at different points in vol. II, and further explored where relevant.

13 Particles make up around 17.1% of words in the *Iliad*, 18% of words in the *Odyssey*, and 12.7% of words in Pindar.

	Iliad		*Odyssey*		Pindar
	Narrator text	Direct speech	Narrator text	Direct speech	
δέ	50,5	23	53	21	24,7
τε	15,4	13,4	13,3	13	13,4
καί	14,3	23	17,4	20,9	16,9
ἄρα	10,7	2,9	11,9	1,5	0,8
μέν	5,9	6,8	6,6	5	5,4
γάρ	3,2	7,6	2,7	7,9	4,9
ἀλλά	2,8	7,3	4,2	8	3,5
γε	2,7	6,4	2,9	6,5	0,8
αὐτάρ	1,9	1,1	5,9	2	0
δή[14]	1,7	5,1	3,8	4,7	0,5

Table 1: Particle frequencies in Homer and Pindar[15]

14 The analysis of δή is from a more comprehensive corpus, based on an analysis of twelve books of the *Iliad* (13-24) and twelve books of the *Odyssey* (1-12).

15 For Homer they are the result of a statistical analysis of δέ, γάρ, δή, μέν, τε, καί, ἄρα, ἦ, ἤ, ἀλλά, τοι, γε, αὖ, αὖτε, αὐτάρ, ἄταρ, νυ, ἄν/κε, περ, πω, που, πη, πως, ἠδέ, ἠμέν, οὖν, μάν, οὐδέ, οὔτε, μήδε, μήτε in four books of the *Iliad* (4, 5, 6, and 17) and four books of the *Odyssey* (9, 10 {the stretches where Odysseus is narrator have been analyzed as narrator text}, 17, and 18), which amounts to 4917 lines, containing 6259 particles. For Pindar, I have analyzed the *Victory Odes*; the table lists only the most frequent particles.

II.2

Discourse Acts

The Domain of Particle Analysis

§1. The present chapter builds on the discussion of discourse segmentation set out in IV.3, so to facilitate understanding I briefly summarize the ideas set out there, where the reader may find a fuller discussion and references. In ancient philosophy and rhetoric, language was described in terms of *períodoi*, *kôla*, and *kómmata*. All three terms are hard to define, and our understanding of them is often strongly determined by English translations. It appears that the term *períodos* initially described an intonation curve between two prosodically similar moments. The *kôlon* is a subdivision of the *períodos*: either a complete thought or a complete part of a thought, with distinct parts, and easy to repeat in a breath. *Kómma*, finally, is a term applied to particularly short *kôla*. What underlies all three terms is a focus on performance rather than on syntactical shape (e.g. sentence, clause, phrase), and in this chapter I trace modern and contemporary research that takes the same perspective on discourse.

§2. To ancient scholars, discourse consisted of different-sized units not based primarily on syntactical division, but rather on the sense of completion on the one hand and the speaker's physical limitations on the other. From the nineteenth century onwards, conversely, the approach to discourse segmentation in ancient Greek texts reveals a strong tendency to regard syntax as the primary structure. This exclusive focus on syntax obscures the important role of particles in the articulation of discourse. A greater sensitivity to the linear presentation of both epic and lyric is needed for an understanding of the function of particles and their host units. The present chapter gathers the relevant evidence, both cross-linguistic and specific to ancient Greek, for the contention that not the sentence or clause, but the discourse act is the basic unit of language use. It is with regard to this smallest subdivsion of discourse that the function of particles is to be understood.

2.1 Introduction

§3. In speech, language is more malleable than the grammatical handbooks would have us believe, as we may note from the loose adherence to grammar even academics reveal in their day-to-day conversations.[1] This is not to say that a grammatical analysis is not a valid approach to such performed texts; both the Homeric and Pindaric corpora show a distinct tendency to obey a set of rules that largely conforms to what the handbooks call Greek grammar. A thorough knowledge of the grammar is indispensable for understanding the texts and allows the reader to note deviations from the standard and to hypothesize explanations for them.[2] Anyone interested in gaining a better understanding of the text's impact in performance, however, cannot stop at contemplating grammar alone.[3] What we wish to challenge here is not the *relevance* of a prescriptive syntax for the study of Homer and Pindar, but its *primacy*.

§4. Consider the following example from the *Odyssey*, followed by Murray's translation:

(t1)

(...) ὁ δ' ὁρμηθεὶς θεοῦ ἤρχετο, φαῖνε δ' ἀοιδήν,
ἔνθεν ἑλών, ὡς οἱ μὲν ἐϋσσέλμων ἐπὶ νηῶν
βάντες ἀπέπλειον, πῦρ ἐν κλισίῃσι βαλόντες,
Ἀργεῖοι, (...)

Odyssey 8.499-502

(...) *and* the minstrel, moved by the god, began, and let his song be heard,
taking up the tale *where* the Argives had embarked on their benched ships
and were sailing away, after casting fire on their huts (...)

Translation Murray

Murray's pleasant translation tells the story adequately, but it obscures the original word order. In the translation the reader is given a neat sentence, which begins before this excerpt and continues after it. It is worth comparing the punctuation in the Greek (from Von der Mühll's edition) to that in the English translation. Although the placement of some commas corresponds in the two texts, there are discrepancies. First of all,

1 Tannen 1984 presents a study of talk-in-interaction between academics.

2 In fact, we believe that there is a strong link between discourse and grammar: with Du Bois and others we assume that it is language-in-use that shapes grammar, not the other way around.

3 See II.1 for more on this issue.

in the translation there is a comma after "the minstrel," which allows the reader to focus on the new source of the upcoming discourse, but this comma is left out in the Greek.[4] Conversely, Von der Mühll prints a comma before ὡς, but Murray leaves it out before the corresponding "where" in the translation.

§5. These differences may be partly (or even wholly) due to the fact that English has more or less established rules for comma placement in written texts, whereas such a system did not exist for ancient Greek.[5] However, the choices in the Greek edition are revealing: they show that Von der Mühll feels there should be a comma before the "first-position word" ὡς, while he regards the participial construction ὁρμηθείς θεοῦ as too closely connected to the pronoun ὁ to permit a comma to intervene. Commas in written English are largely syntactic markers, since they mark the segments they divide as parts of the same superstructure: the sentence, which is in turn bounded by full stops. In (t1) above this convention explains the placement of a comma rather than a period after βαλόντες: the following nominative Ἀργεῖοι is taken as the subject of a long subclause, itself part of the sentence of which ὁ is the subject. However, it is open to discussion whether or not the syntactical unit of the sentence has true analytical value in a study of Homer, Pindar, or any other discourse produced in, or meant for, performance.

§6. The reception of a performed text is at least partly linear: the hearer cannot hear the second word before the first word, and likewise the second verse only after the first verse.[6] In cognitive studies it has been established that the working memory used for processing aurally received text is not all that large.[7] Still, we find numerous instances in Greek epic and lyric where the grammatical subject of a clause is not given until two verses after the verb, as in the *Odyssey* passage above. A close translation looks as follows:[8]

(t2)

And he, having started from the god, began. He made the song appear,
starting from there, where they, on their well-benched ships,
sailed off on their way, having thrown fire on their tents,
the Argives,...

4 See below §§63-79 for this kind of construction.

5 See IV.3.4.

6 See Kahane 1994:143, "The *pace*, *direction*, and *sequence* of any particular performance is fixed" [italics original].

7 See Chafe 1994:53-55 and Rubin 1995:69, "...each intonation unit corresponds to the contents of working memory."

8 Bakker 1997b and Edwards 2002 also advocate closer translations. However, Edwards proposes a translation into "conversational English" (2002:11), and he says: "this is the way a bard would address his audience." I follow both Bakker and Edwards in staying very close to the original order of the Greek, especially as regards the act-by-act progression.

If the Greek audience truly needed the subject from line 502 to complete the construction begun in line 500, one would have to conclude that in performance this text would become rather unsuccessful. In fact, the nominative follows at a point where the audience would have been expected to already know who the story was about; it must therefore be regarded as serving another function. My translation focuses on the articulation of discourse in separate acts, each of which serves at least one purpose in furthering the discourse.

§7. This chapter traces the history of this approach to discourse articulation in Greek in general and Homeric epic in particular. I first outline the ideas presented by Wackernagel and refined by Fraenkel and later scholars (§§9-15), which several contemporary scholars have recently revisited (§16). Then I trace contemporary work on discourse articulation, especially in English, which has focused on spoken discourse (§§17-20). The earlier scholarship on ancient Greek, together with contemporary scholarship on modern languages, provides the foundation for the study of discourse acts (§§21-23).

§8. There are several ways in which we regard the study of discourse articulation as relevant to the analysis of the functions of particles. First of all, particles are important boundary markers in ancient Greek, revealing the production of discourse in manageable chunks in Homer (§§24-30) and Pindar (§§37-45).[9] Second, establishing act boundaries allows for a better appreciation of the host units of different particles (δέ §§31-36 and μέν §§46-62). Third, a close examination of discourse segmentation in Homer and Pindar reveals that particles, particle clusters, or a particle in concert with one word (group) function as separate acts. Closely examining the way particles work on the small scale allows for a more precise understanding of the role of some particles in navigating larger discontinuities in discourse, especially in Homeric narrative (§§64-71) and Pindaric performance (§§72-79).

2.1.1 *Kôlon*, intonation unit, discourse act

§9. In 1892 Wackernagel published a seminal article about a rule in the word order of Indo-European languages that he felt was followed so strictly that it deserved the predicate "law."[10] As Goldstein rightly observes, Wackernagel 1892 presented neither the beginning nor the final form of the argument, but it has become the reference point for the large body of literature that has built upon its ideas.[11] The gist of Wackernagel's argument is that a group of words, including particles, tend to occur in the second position

9 See IV.3.10 for the same phenomenon in Herodotus and Thucydides.

10 Wackernagel 1892: "Über ein Gesetz der indogermanischen Wortstellung."

11 Goldstein 2010:9. Wackernagel later attributed the discovery of the law to Delbrück (Wackernagel 1920:46); he had already mentioned the phenomenon himself in 1879. In 1892:342 he also refers to Bergaigne 1877 who had mentioned the second-position tendency of personal pronouns in Greek.

of a clause, be it a main or a subclause.[12] His argument initially excludes enclitic particles that join sentences,[13] as their role of conjoining the host sentence to the preceding one gives them a natural reason to be in second position. His analysis consequently focuses on κε, which does not function on the level of *Satzverbindung*.[14] For this enclitic particle, as well as for θην, νυ, and τοι, Wackernagel finds that they have a strong tendency to occur in second position of the sentence. Finally, he notes that a number of non-enclitic particles, called *postpositive Partikeln* by Krüger, follow the same pattern of eschewing initial position.[15]

§10. Some forty years later, Eduard Fraenkel refined and extended Wackernagel's ideas[16] in two publications, with the intention of better explaining the many apparent exceptions to the law in extant Latin and Greek literature.[17] Fraenkel's contention is that the postpositives, such as particles, come in the second position not necessarily only of sentences, but also of smaller syntactical units.[18] He calls these smaller units *Kola* (henceforth *kôlon, kôla*), a term inherited from ancient scholarship on the units that make up prose and poetry.[19] Fraenkel analyzes the use of ἄν in Greek classical prose,[20] and concludes that it can generally be considered to occupy the second position of a *kôlon*,

12 Initially he focuses on enclitic personal pronouns (μιν, νιν, οἱ, ἑ, σ*, μ*, σφ*) in second position.

13 Wackernagel 1892:370-371 mentions τε and ῥα. He mentions in passing that the position of ῥα in *Iliad* 2.310 βωμοῦ ὑπαΐξας πρὸς ῥα πλατάνιστον ὄρουσεν is not problematic since the participle acts like a subclause here: "[hier] ist das Partizip einem Nebensatz gleichwertig" 1892:370-371; this comment foreshadows Fraenkel's approach to *kôla*.

14 Wackernagel 1892:371.

15 Wackernagel 1892:377 lists ἄν, ἄρ, ἄρα, αὖ, γάρ, δέ, δῆτα, μέν, μήν, οὖν, τοίνυν, but his analysis focuses almost exclusively on ἄν (379-402).

16 Fraenkel 1933:336n2 refers to Müller who had shown that Plato's prose proceeds in short *kôla* in his 1927 dissertation. In this work, Müller compares the language of the *Nomoi* with the language of the *Epinomis*, in order to show that the latter was not written by Plato. In the process, he shows the intricate construction of the Platonic sentences, but apparently inadvertently also that Plato constructs his lines from relatively small building blocks, with enclitics in the second position of many of the *kôla*.

17 E. Fraenkel 1932 and 1933, both gathered in Fraenkel 1964, 73-130, with additional "Nachträge zu 'Kolon und Satz II' " on pages 131-139; he adds his final thoughts in 1965: "Noch einmal Kolon und Satz."

18 In "Kolon und Satz I" Fraenkel argues that in Latin elegy (Propertius, Horace, Martial) pentameter end almost always counts as a break of some sort, even if the sentence runs in into the next distich. A purely syntactic reading, which may conclude that a subject is divided from its verb by distich end, does not do justice to the *Bau*, the build-up of the sentence. The insertion of a parenthetical phrase at the end of a pentameter, for example, creates a syntactical *Fuge*, a joint: if we can speak of a syntactic break, there cannot be enjambment.

19 See IV.3.6 for more on *kôla* in prose, with an overview of ancient and recent literature as well as new analyses of Herodotus and Thucydides. For more on the metrical *kôlon*, see §§24-26 below and e.g. Gentili and Lomiento 2003.

20 His corpus is Herodotus, Thucydides, Lysias, Plato, Demosthenes, Aeschylus, Sophocles, Euripides, Aristophanes, and Menander (details in Fraenkel 1965:3).

when it occurs later in a clause.[21] Having established this principle, Fraenkel revisited the topic in 1965 in order to show that vocatives generally occur at *kôlon* boundaries.[22]

§11. We might describe Fraenkel's approach as a shift from a "map view" to a "route view" of language.[23] That is to say, he regards the text as first and foremost a syntactic construct, but rather than contemplating every sentence as an architectonic whole, he assumes that reception was realized in smaller units, which he calls "*syntaktische Kola.*"[24] These *kôla* the listener or reader receives in sequence, and they make sense in their linear order. Speakers group their words and thoughts in these smaller units, and it is the existence of these units that explains supposed enjambment in Roman elegy, "abnormal" placement of ἄν in Greek prose, and improves our understanding of how vocatives are used. Fraenkel's work would form the basis for a series of studies in Greek linguistics in the following decades; his intuitions have pointed the way for the approach I elaborate in this chapter.

§12. Now with regard to second, or peninitial, position, some explanation is warranted. In the majority of cases, especially in classical prose, a "postpositive" particle occurs in second position in a clause. However, second position does not necessarily mean the second lexical item in a clause. If the preceding word is part of a tight group, such as article and noun or preposition and noun, it is possible for the whole word group to precede the particle. In such cases this positioning of the particle is unproblematic, although it is worth considering why it occurs on some but not all occasions. A first-position particle, like ἀλλά and καί,[25] may similarly cause a particle that comes after it to appear as the third rather than second word. Diagnostically most relevant, then, are those cases where a postposed particle occurs later than in second position in a clause even when none of the two abovementioned situations apply. In these instances it is probably the case that what comes before the peninitial particle and its preceding word is not a full syntactical clause, but a separate *kôlon* nonetheless.

21 The only exception to this rule is when it comes directly before or after the verb that it accompanies: Fraenkel 1933:320.

22 Fraenkel 1965; in later oratory, at least already in the fifth century BCE, vocatives are used much more as a means of "*Gliederung und Hervorhebung*," ("subdivision and emphasis") helpful for the hearer, crucial for the reader.

23 This terminology is more typically applied to (oral) narrative, compare Zoran 1984, Landau and Jackendoff 1993, Herman 2002, and Ryan 2003; applied to classics by Bonifazi 2008 and 2012, Minchin 2001, Purves 2010, and Strauss Clay 2011. Consider also Collins 1991, who says in his *The Poetics of the Mind's Eye* (98): "the consecutiveness of speech accords with the consecutiveness of visual perception."

24 Fraenkel 1932:204.

25 καί especially can in some functions be completely mobile, whereas in other functions it is generally in initial position. See IV.2.4 and especially §§117-132 for more on the scope and position of καί.

§13. In his 1959 work on word order in Pindar, Lauer retrieves Fraenkel's work on *kôla* to apply it to Pindar's songs.[26] Like Fraenkel before him, he uses the idea of *kôla* to demonstrate that apparently divergent and problematic word order in fact obeys the rules of word order with regard to *kôla*, if not with regard to sentences. Lauer argues that the Pindaric corpus offers more insight into the performative reality than prose does, because of its metrical form. That is to say, whereas prose is only divided into syntactical units (which may or may not have a specific relation to the discourse units it was realized in), poetry is divided into both syntactical and metrical units, which provides slightly more handholds for establishing possible and even probable discourse division.[27]

§14. Throughout his study Lauer adheres closely to Fraenkel's method, establishing *kôlon* boundaries by using criteria such as the placement of postpositives, quasi-independent grammatical constructions (such as *participia coniuncta*), and stylistic practices (such as parallel constructions). Having established these boundaries, he goes on to describe the *kôla* that emerge. Most of them fall under the open-ended list of types offered by Fraenkel,[28] but Lauer makes a few additional observations. Most importantly, Lauer observes that quite regularly there is a very short *kôlon* at the beginning of sentences, which he calls *Kurzkola*, short *kôla*, but does not further define them.[29] He is similarly taciturn about the term *potentielle Kola*, potential *kôla*, which he uses to describe these same short opening *kôla*, but which might be much more broadly applicable, on which see below.[30] Sometimes these initial *kôla* are so short that they consist of nothing more than a conjunction, which leads Lauer to conclude that conjunctions can stand outside the *kôlon*.[31] Finally, Lauer notes that in case of *hyperbaton*, the two (or more) members, typically an adjective (or a participle in attributive position) and a noun, can be *Kolonbildend*, opening and closing them.[32]

§15. In his analysis of vocatives, Fraenkel hints at the phonetic realization of *kôla* and *kôlon* boundaries, namely that the insertion of a vocative would result in a pause, with different possible effects.[33] For Stinton 1977, phonetic realization is the crucial

26 The more recent study by Hajdú 1989 does not refer to Lauer, and as a result many of Hajdú's findings about *kôla* and word order in Pindar had been anticipated by Lauer.

27 Turner and Pöppel 1983 claims that the notion of breaks at line end is a general characteristic that will be noticed even when one does not know the language of the poetry. As noted above, Fraenkel actually used supposed rules governing the coincidence of syntactical breaks with metrical breaks in Latin elegy to establish his *kôlon* idea.

28 Fraenkel 1932:212-213, 1933:320-347.

29 In the 1964 edition of *Kolon und Satz* II Fraenkel uses the term *Kurzkolon* in his footnotes, and expands briefly on particles forming *Kurzkola* in "Nachträge zu 'Kolon und Satz, II'" 135-137.

30 Lauer 1959:46; I expand on such acts in §§63-79.

31 For καί forming a separate discourse act, see IV.2.4.4.

32 Lauer 1959:54-58. The idea is taken up by Race 2002 and by Markovic 2006. Markovic makes no reference to Lauer's work.

33 Fraenkel 1965:17.

question: can we establish where pauses might have been heard in Greek discourse?[34] His corpus, lyric passages of Greek tragedy, is quite different from Fraenkel's material, but "the categories he [sc. Fraenkel] establishes for Greek prose can be readily adapted to the more condensed language of lyric poetry."[35] Using Fraenkel's categories on the one hand, and metrical responsion on the other, he makes the argument that both *brevis in longo* and hiatus are generally allowed only where there is a syntactical pause. His research into the intricate language of lyric shows that meter and sense stand in a somewhat natural relationship.[36]

§16. Recently, the concept of the *kôlon* has resurfaced in Scheppers' *The Colon Hypothesis*.[37] His work is an important step forward because he includes literature from contemporary linguistics. Scheppers builds on the idea of *kôla* with help from research into modern languages, for which a spoken corpus is available. Like Bakker before him, whose work on Homer I discuss below, Scheppers incorporates the work done on "intonation units." As the term suggests, the units are parts of spoken discourse that cohere by virtue of forming a single intonational contour, generally bounded by pauses. Scheppers combines the concept of *kôlon* and that of intonation unit to analyze the prose discourse of Lysias and Plato "as literary representations of 'spoken' Greek."[38] Goldstein likewise turns to intonation in order to further our understanding of the position of enclitics and postpositives. In a thorough study of fifth-century Greek prose, he demonstrates that Wackernagel's law is best understood as not primarily a syntactic phenomenon, but rather bound to intonational phrases.[39] Scheppers, Goldstein, and Bakker urge us to attempt to hear the intonational division of Greek discourse, and acknowledge its importance to word order and construction of meaning. In our work on particles in poetry and prose we subscribe to this approach to Greek discourse and hope to contribute to its further development. Their work has a solid basis in research on contemporary spoken discourse.

34 Rather than Fraenkel's cola, Stinton consistently uses "(atomic) sense-groups," imported from contemporary studies on English phonetics.

35 Stinton 1977:29.

36 Stinton's argument is long and intricate, aimed mainly at proving the correlation between metrical period-end and pause. In the final pages he discusses the different gradations of pause that may be found: from the tightest connection of preposition and noun divided by verse end (no pause expected) to a verb divided from its direct object, where the pause is more probable.

37 Scheppers builds on the word order publications by Dik (1995, 2007). Dik 1995:36 builds on Fraenkel's work and regards the intonation unit or *kôlon* as "the basic units for the analysis of word order, taking precedence, in principle, over syntactically defined clauses." Goldstein 2010 proposes another approach to word order, but also regards *kôla* as basic units. See IV.3.6 for more on Scheppers' work.

38 Scheppers 2011:x. Markovic 2006:127-129 also builds on Bakker's ideas about intonation units and *kôla*.

39 Goldstein 2010 is concerned with this issue throughout, but especially chapters 3 and 4 are crucial.

§17. Research on intonation units starts with Halliday's concept of the "tone group," which can be distinguished as a separate unit by virtue of having only one "tonic element." In later scholarship the focus shifts to the "intonational contour," to fit better with actual practice.[40] Speakers portion their discourse by proceeding in units that are marked by an independent intonational contour, and are often bounded by pauses. This segmentation, it appears, is not (or not only) a function of the physical need to breathe at regular intervals, but rather of the cognitive effort involved in planning speech.[41] Brown and Yule 1983 follow this line of reasoning and choose to call the small segments "information units," since they reflect the piecemeal addition of information to the discourse. Chafe proposes to use the term "intonation units," and adds that they are generally a combination of given and new information.[42] The combination of given and new information in intonation units is only a trend: some intonation units in fact contain only new, or, more rarely, only given information. Similarly, he notes that in his corpus of spoken English the correspondence between intonation units and syntactical clauses is in fact quite low.[43]

§18. It is one thing to observe that a certain kind of unit exists in discourse, but quite another to explain *why* it occurs. There is a range of explanations available, each reflecting the particular approach used in establishing the smallest discourse unit. One group of scholars, represented by Roulet on the one hand (Geneva School) and Sinclair and Coulthard on the other (Birmingham School), approach discourse as a strategic construct with a certain aim, and smaller discourse units as having a certain function in reaching that goal. In their seminal 1975 article on classroom discourse, Sinclair and Coulthard establish the term "discourse act," analogous to Austin's speech act.[44] They define discourse acts as the smallest step toward reaching a (sub)goal of the discourse, hierarchically ordered on a scale of act - move - exchange - transaction - lesson.[45] Roulet

40 Halliday 1967; his method is adapted especially by Chafe 1979, (ed.) 1980, and by Brown and Yule 1983.

41 See Pawley and Hodgetts Syder 2000:172-173.

42 See II.5 §9 for a discussion of Chafe's work and what he calls "activation cost."

43 Even of the substantial intonation units (see note 49 below), only sixty percent coincides with syntactical clauses. The numbers are inevitably much lower for regulatory and fragmentary intonation units.

44 Sinclair and Coulthard 1975:23; Austin established the term speech act in his 1962 work *How to Do Things with Words.*

45 Sinclair and Coulthard use as their corpus recordings of school lessons, and attempt to describe the structure of the strongly dialogic discourse. They first divide the lesson into "transactions," encompassing the entire discussion of a certain topic. Within those transactions, they establish "exchanges," typically a dialogue between teacher and student. These exchanges can then be subdivided into "moves," actions with a specific goal, such as "getting an answer to a question." There are of course many ways of asking a question, and more often than not a teacher does not simply ask a question outright, but introduces or embeds it in some way, or never even actually asks anything.

1984 adopts part of this terminology (act - move - exchange),[46] and proceeds to apply the ideas to different kinds of material, including both spoken discourse and written texts. Over two decades of work, Roulet redefines his conceptualization of the discourse act several times, but in Roulet et al. 2001 he settles on the discourse act as every "update to the discourse memory," [47] basing his idea on the work done by Berrendonner.[48]

§19. More recently, cognitive linguists have engaged with the smallest steps in discourse. Chafe regards the intonation unit as a focus of consciousness, "typically expressed with four words of English." [49] Langacker talks about the same process in terms of "attentional frames," which function "as instructions to modify the current discourse space in particular ways."[50] As regards form, attentional frames may well coincide with grammatical constituents, but this is "only a tendency, not an inviolable principle."[51] The relation between the empirically observable intonation unit and the cognitive process of language production may be linked productively to the work of the Birmingham and Geneva schools. The new focus of consciousness forms an update to the discourse memory (on which see II.4), which is verbalized in a new intonation unit.[52]

46 In his 1984 article, Roulet says (31-32): "[attempting] to describe the speech acts which constitute authentic (French) conversations and texts—as we have been doing in Geneva since 1979—(...) has ultimately led us to postulate a hierarchical structure composed of at least three levels: exchange, move, and speech act." In a later publication, he clarifies that he borrows the terminology exchange-move-act from Sinclair and Coulthard (Roulet et al. 2001:53).

47 Roulet et al. 2001:64-65.

48 Berrendonner 1990, who speaks of the "memoire discursive" or "savoir partagé" [shared knowledge]. He calls the smallest unit of discourse a clause or utterance ("énonciation"). His analysis suggests that he does not take a primarily syntactic approach to establishing these units, but it is not entirely clear what factors he does regard as relevant. Only in his conclusion ("En guise de conclusion" 35) does he bring up prosody: "les segments qui sont prosodiquement '*détachés*'" [italics original].

49 See Bakker 1997b:44-53 for a discussion of the concept of intonation units. Chafe's intonation units fall into three functional categories: fragmentary, substantive, and regulatory intonation units. Fragmentary are those that remain unfinished, like false starts, and whose function as such is generally hard to establish. Most frequent are the substantial intonation units, containing substantive ideas, states, or referents. The third are the regulatory intonation units, with the function of regulating the flow of discourse, the interaction between speaker and hearer, the cognitive process, and the speaker's attitude toward what she is saying (Chafe 1994:62-64).

50 Langacker 2001:151, quoting from Harder 1996. Langacker and Roulet's discourse space or discourse memory are echoed in what Steen 2005 calls "mental representations of discourse." Unhappy with the *ad hoc* approach applied by his predecessors, Steen introduces the "basic discourse unit." This ideal unit is at the same time a proposition and a clause and an intonation (or punctuation) unit and an illocutionary act. The strength of Steen's approach is that he states explicitly what many other researchers do implicitly: that they operate with the idea of an ideal discourse act and categorize the others based on their relation to the ideal (note, for example, Halliday's positing of a marked and unmarked information unit, Chafe's "fragmentary intonation unit," and the like).

51 Langacker 2001:162.

52 Chafe 1994 throughout explicitly links these two ideas about the intonation unit: it represents a focus of consciousness, and it is an update to the mental representation of discourse.

§20. There is one more element that contributes to our understanding of the discourse act. In the field of functional discourse grammar, scholars like Kroon, Hannay, and Hengeveld have approached language in a way largely similar to that of the Geneva and Birmingham schools. They have, however, a slightly different perspective: they define acts specifically as the smallest steps toward the main goal of the discourse. Hannay and Kroon, looking back to Kroon's earlier work on Latin discourse particles, define discourse acts as "the smallest identifiable unit of communicative behaviour,"[53] but they expand it by stipulating that all acts are "strategic steps which the speaker wishes to make."[54] Hannay and Kroon conclude that focus should shift from a link between discourse units and grammatical units to a link between discourse units and prosodic/orthographic units.[55] To bring all the above elements together: an intonation unit verbalizes a focus of consciousness, which is both an update to the discourse memory and a new step toward the overarching discourse goal.

2.1.2 Distinguishing potential discourse acts

§21. Discussions of the non-grammatically defined smallest units of discourse have followed divergent paths, but their results converge. The conclusions that contemporary linguists have come to share are worth revisiting briefly. First, it is generally agreed that there is more than one kind of organization at work at the same time in any discourse. This position accords with the view that different kinds of subdivision are possible, whether based on syntax, content, discourse steps, performance, or other criteria.[56] Second, discourse units are not building blocks of a grammatical structure, but the verbalization of frames or foci of consciousness. Third, discourse acts function in terms of updates to discourse memory. Fourth, the smallest discourse unit tends to align with the strategic function of the smallest step toward a discourse goal. By and large, the smallest subdivisions of discourse are no larger than clauses (often smaller), do not consistently map onto syntactical units, represent some elemental progression within

53 Kroon 1995:65. Hannay and Kroon elaborate in 2005:93, "In the 1997 model of FG [Functional Grammar] (...) the speech act (the precursor to the discourse act) was described in terms of clausality. In FDG [Functional Discourse Grammar] this problem is resolved, since discourse acts can also be realized by a variety of non-clausal structures."

54 Hannay and Kroon 2005:104.

55 Hannay and Kroon 2005:88. Note that their conclusion was anticipated by, among others, Chafe 1994:63-69 (whom they cite), Brown and Yule 1983:159-164, and Langacker 2001:154-163 (not cited in their references).

56 Arguably, the lack of clarity about these different possible levels is part of the reason why "acts" are defined differently among different scholars; see Hannay and Kroon 2005:103-104. They separate "ideas" from "acts," and they argue that the units that the Geneva school has focused on are in fact "ideas" whereas they themselves focus on "acts." See IV.3.6 and 7 for a discussion of other discourse segmentation criteria in contemporary discourse analysis.

a discourse strategy, represent the current cognitive focus of the speaker, and generally manifest in prosodically independent units.[57]

§22. Building on these separate but connected bodies of research, we will henceforth call the smallest subdivisions of discourse "discourse acts." This choice is not only based on the belief that we should where possible avoid adding to the plethora of terminology used in linguistics, but also on the conviction that the term captures two important features of these units. First, it categorizes the unit as a subdivision of discourse, in whatever form, rather than a subdivision of a text or a sentence. Second, it characterizes the unit as an action, a word or word group used by the speaker to do something. This resonates with the concept of "action" in Conversation Analysis, which describes what speakers do with their utterances.[58]

§23. Establishing where divisions lie between discourse acts is inevitably tentative, as may be concluded from the outline of the literature on contemporary languages above. In particular Roulet and the Functional Discourse Grammar researchers have discussed the problem of establishing discourse act boundaries in sentences like:

(t3)

(1) Pierre est sorti malgré la pluie
Pierre went out despite the rain

(2) Pierre est sorti bien qu'il pleuve.
Pierre went out even though it's raining

The only apparent difference between these two examples is that in (1) the concessive is expressed through an adverbial phrase, whereas in (2) it takes the form of a subclause. The Geneva School regards both of these discourses as consisting of two acts, whereas Hannay and Kroon agree with them only if the prepositional phrase is realized as a separate intonation or punctuation unit.[59] The deciding factor, then, is performance: whatever the linguistic form of the text, the speaker decides what to present as separate intonation units, and thus as separate discourse acts.[60] In the following analysis of discourse

57 Prosodically independent units have their parallel in punctuation units in written text, on which see especially Hannay and Kroon 2005:108-116; compare IV.3.4.

58 See III.4 §§19-22 on "action" in Conversation Analysis.

59 In practice, however, Roulet and Hannay and Kroon are closer together than we are led to believe. The question is whether we see the sentence as a generic example or as a unique event. In the former case, the sentence is open to different kinds of performance, and thus can be rendered potentially in one or two (or more) acts. In the latter case, as an actual event, it is rendered in *either* one *or* two acts (or possibly more, for whatever reason), but this cannot be extrapolated from the written form.

60 This holds independently of whether the discourse is poetry or prose. See IV.3.5 for *kôla* and *kómmata*, ancient terms that are partly equivalent to intonation units or discourse acts.

acts in Homer and Pindar, any marking of discourse division necessarily represents a conjecture about the work's realization in performance: we cannot fully reconstruct how the text was intended to be realized, and we can never establish how it was actually realized. Any division we propose, then, can only be into potential discourse acts, parallel to Lauer's *potentielle Kola*.[61] To this we would add one *caveat*, posited by Bright: *factum valet* "an action otherwise prohibited by rule is to be treated as correct if it happens nevertheless."[62] Bright's general observation may be extended to the idea of a prescriptive definition: whatever definition of discourse act we establish, actual discourse will always prove it inadequate—there is simply no limit to linguistic creativity.

2.2 Discourse Acts in Homer

§24. Contemporary scholarship on non-syntactic units in Homeric discourse starts with Egbert Bakker. In his extensive work on Homer from the end of the eighties onward, Bakker has engaged with Chafe's ideas about intonation units.[63] Transcripts of descriptions of Chafe's film, *The Pear Film*, by individuals who just watched it show language use that is remarkably similar to that in Homer. Bakker urges us to consider this spoken narrative style as the blueprint for epic. Let us consider a passage discussed by Bakker, with his division into chunks, or intonation units:

(t4)

ἔνθ' ἄρα τοι, Πάτροκλε,
φάνη βιότοιο τελευτή· /
ἤντετο γάρ τοι Φοῖβος
ἐνὶ κρατερῇ ὑσμίνῃ /
δεινός·
ὃ μὲν τὸν ἰόντα κατὰ κλόνον
οὐκ ἐνόησεν, /
ἠέρι γὰρ πολλῇ
κεκαλυμμένος ἀντεβόλησε· / (790)

Iliad 16.787-790, as given in Bakker 1997b:113

(t5)

οἱ δ' ὅτε δὴ
κλισίῃσιν ἐν Ἀτρεΐδαο γένοντο, /

61 Lauer 1959:46, see also Scheppers 2011:40-42.
62 Bright (ed.) 1966:323.
63 Especially Bakker 1993b and 1997b.

τοῖσι δὲ βοῦν ἱέρευσεν
ἄναξ ἀνδρῶν Ἀγαμέμνων /
ἄρσενα πενταέτηρον
ὑπερμενέϊ Κρονίωνι /

Iliad 7.313-315, as given in Bakker 1997b:97

One of the contentions in Bakker's *Poetry of Speech* is that what Chafe and others call intonation units have their stylized counterpart in metrical *kôla* in Homer, generally about half a line long. Like intonation units, the metrical *kôla* that make up the hexameter are a few words long, probably reflecting "the amount of information that is active at one time in a speaker's consciousness."[64] Working from this view, Bakker divides each line in the examples above into two "chunks," which he assumes to have been "a prosodic, intonational reality."[65] Each line above represents one intonation unit, and the slash (/) marks verse end. In positing a boundary Bakker takes two factors into account: first the meter, second the content of phrases.

§25. The Homeric hexameter is a metrical form of remarkable consistency. Since it is a particularly long verse form, it generally consists of two or more metrical cola.[66] In ninety-nine percent of verses there is a caesura (called the B caesura) after the first heavy syllable of the third foot (masculine) or between its two light syllables (feminine).[67] Here is an example of each from (t4):

(t6)

Masculine B caesura:
ἠέρι γὰρ πολλῇ ¦ κεκαλυμμένος ἀντεβόλησε·

Feminine B caesura:
ἔνθ' ἄρα τοι, Πάτροκλε, ¦ φάνη βιότοιο τελευτή·

Beyond this mid-verse metrical break, there are two further frequently occurring breaks: A caesura (ninety percent of verses), in the first foot or after the first syllable of the second foot, and C caesura (eighty-six to eighty-seven percent), either between the fourth and fifth foot (called "bucolic diaeresis") or after the first syllable of the fourth foot. The common metrical breaks are also points where syntactical and sense breaks typically occur, which

64 Bakker 1997b:48.

65 Bakker 1997b:50.

66 Literature on Homeric colometry is extensive, but H. Fraenkel 1926 (revised in H. Fraenkel 1955) is the seminal publication; see for later studies, all building on Fraenkel, Barnes 1986, Edwards 1966, 2002, and 2011 (in Finkelberg), and Bakker 1997b.

67 Edwards in Finkelberg 2011:II.518-519.

brings us back to Bakker's intonation units, or chunks, and our discourse acts. Bakker's analyses demonstrate that the mid-verse caesura in particular often serves as a place for a sense boundary. On the other hand, this need not be the case, and even the strong metrical break of verse end does not always coincide with the end of a discourse act.[68] Edwards, who anticipated some of Bakker's points, bases his analysis of the Homeric verse into four units on Hermann Fraenkel's observations.[69] Edwards argues for a strict correlation between metrical boundaries and sense units, clear linguistic evidence to the contrary notwithstanding, leading to divisions such as | ὃ δὲ τὸν μέν | ἔασε |.[70]

§26. Homeric meter is an important guide in suggesting discourse act boundaries, along with syntax, sense, and boundary markers. Building on Bakker's approach I consider all these factors in establishing discourse act boundaries in Homer. There are often several possibilities of dividing the verse, depending on which criteria one gives priority to. [71] Consider once more the following line from (t5), first according to Bakker's division and then ours, with a vertical bar to mark a discourse act boundary:[72]

(t7)

οἱ δ' ὅτε δή
κλισίῃσιν ἐν Ἀτρεΐδαο γένοντο, /

Iliad 7.313, in Bakker 1997b:97

οἱ δ' | ὅτε δὴ κλισίῃσιν ¦ ἐν Ἀτρεΐδαο γένοντο

Bakker keeps οἱ δ' ὅτε δή together, despite the position of δή, yet divides after δή, even though it means dividing the temporal conjunction ὅτε from its clause.[73] Bakker's reason for dividing after δή in (t7) is that the particle occurs right before a common position

68 As Bakker demonstrates in 1997b:151-154; see especially the example of *Iliad* 22.451-455 on page 154.

69 Compare Edwards 1966:117 "[T]here is a close relationship between the sense-units of the sentence and the metrical *kôla*, or, putting it another way, between the pauses in sense and the caesurae of the verse." In his work, he considers every caesura a possible boundary, yielding more than just half-line *kôla*. Blankenborg (unpublished thesis, Radboud Universiteit Nijmegen) is currently working on a more dynamic model of establishing the likelihood of prosodic pauses at different points in the Homeric verse.

70 Edwards 2002:4. Edwards argues that this half line may resolve as one or two units, i.e. with or without the boundary, but his system does not allow for a boundary to occur after ὃ δέ, which is where I would put it. More on such small discourse acts in §§63-79.

71 However, see Kahane 1994:26-29 for a discussion of five separate readings of "sense-pauses" in the Homeric hexameter, which show remarkable convergence.

72 From this point onward, I will divide all examples into potential discourse acts. Vertical bars are used to identify units of discourse in prose by Blass 1887 and Scheppers 2011, in prose and poetry by Fraenkel 1932, 1933, 1964, and 1965, and in poetry by Bonifazi and Elmer 2012a.

73 See for the οἱ δ' | ὅτε δή construction §§64-66, §71, and De Kreij 2016.

of the A caesura, the trithemimeris.[74] However, οἱ δ' is an important separate cognitive act, and therefore I propose to divide directly after.[75] This boundary coincides with another variant of the A caesura, and similar breaks occurs elsewhere in Homer; see also (t8).[76] In (t7) the feminine B caesura (marked by ¦) does not coincide with a discourse act boundary: a metrical break is an attractive place for an act boundary, but it does not entail an act boundary. In the excerpts from Homer given here and in other chapters, discourse act boundaries will be seen to regularly coincide with one of the three common metrical breaks in the hexameter, or with verse end.

§27. A longer excerpt better illustrates the many possible positions of discourse act boundaries, and the many forms acts take. At the end of the *Catalogue of Ships* there is a description of Achilles and his men loitering near the ships while the other Greeks are advancing on Troy. Taking into account meter and all the other factors outlined above, I divide the fifteen lines into potential discourse acts marked by vertical bars; boundary markers are underlined.

(t8)

ἀλλ' ὅ μὲν | ἐν νήεσσι κορωνίσι ποντοπόροισι |
κεῖτ' | ἀπομηνίσας Ἀγαμέμνονι ποιμένι λαῶν |
Ἀτρεΐδῃ· | λαοὶ δὲ | παρὰ ῥηγμῖνι θαλάσσης |
δίσκοισιν τέρποντο | καὶ[77] αἰγανέῃσιν ἱέντες |
τόξοισίν θ'· | ἵπποι δὲ | παρ' ἅρμασιν οἷσιν ἕκαστος |
λωτὸν ἐρεπτόμενοι | ἐλεόθρεπτόν τε σέλινον |
ἕστασαν· | ἅρματα δ' εὖ πεπυκασμένα κεῖτο | ἀνάκτων
ἐν κλισίῃς· | οἳ δ' | ἀρχὸν ἀρηΐφιλον ποθέοντες |
φοίτων ἔνθα καὶ ἔνθα κατὰ στρατὸν | οὐδὲ μάχοντο. |
οἳ δ' ἄρ' ἴσαν | ὡς εἴ τε πυρὶ χθὼν πᾶσα νέμοιτο· |
γαῖα δ' ὑπεστενάχιζε | Διὶ ὣς τερπικεραύνῳ |
χωομένῳ | ὅτε τ' ἀμφὶ Τυφωέϊ γαῖαν ἱμάσσῃ |
εἰν Ἀρίμοις, | ὅθι φασὶ Τυφωέος ἔμμεναι εὐνάς· |
ὣς ἄρα | τῶν ὑπὸ ποσσὶ | μέγα στεναχίζετο γαῖα |
ἐρχομένων· | μάλα δ' ὦκα διέπρησσον πεδίοιο. |

Iliad 2.771-785

74 Bakker 1997b:150.

75 Compare Kahane 1994:18, who speaks of the "intricate interrelationships between metrical units and sense-units."

76 Compare *Iliad* 4.29 (=16.443 and 22.181): ἕρδ'· | ἀτὰρ οὔ τοι πάντες ἐπαινέομεν θεοὶ ἄλλοι; see also Goldstein 2010:41 who claims that "it is possible for an intonational phrase to be as small as a syllable," with reference to Cruttenden 1997:68.

77 καί frequently occurs directly after the caesura (see Von Hartel 1874 and Eberhard 1889), in which case it often starts a new *kôlon* (discussed in Bakker 1997b:71-74).

This is a very turbulent passage from the *Iliad*:[78] out of fifteen verses, only lines 774 and 781 can be divided roughly into two half lines.[79] Most of the discourse act boundaries are based on the words in bold that tend toward peninitial or initial position in the act. Furthermore, I take adverbial phrases as separate, as well as participial phrases.[80] In the first part of the passage (771-779, the description of Achilles' camp) these participial and adverbial phrases separate the subject from its verb (an adverbial phrase intervenes in 771 and 773, a participial phrase in 776 and 778-779) with only one exception (ἅρματα 777).[81] The verbs, moreover, are isolated to such an extent that they appear only in the following line. Fifteen out of thirty acts are introduced by a boundary marker, thirteen of which are particles. In line 779 οὐδέ begins an act, illustrating the strong tendency for negatives to be act-initial.[82] It becomes clear from this passage why Bakker would characterize δέ as a "boundary marker," as it accompanies many small and large steps in the narrative.[83]

§28. The description of Achilles' camp, placed just after the catalogue of ships and just before the return to the battlefield, reveals the full extent of its mastery only when read as a sequence of small steps. A discourse analysis of any stretch of text must take into account semantics, syntax, pragmatics, meter, and cognition—discourse analysis is a holistic approach to the text.[84] The narrative presents us with a "wide" shot of the camp with Achilles and the Myrmidons. It brings us first to the ships, where Achilles indulges in his wrath; then shows us his people, by the sea, keeping themselves busy; then the horses, which stand idle by their chariots, which in turn are parked in the tents of their owners. My reading reveals the clustering of subjects + δέ throughout the passage. The arrangement is not uncommon in Homer, but the symmetry here is striking. Moreover, the (pro)noun + δέ combinations are consistently postponed until the middle of the

78 This turbulence, among other things, leads Kirk 1985:242-243 to say about lines 761-779 that it might be "a singer's expansion, and not by Homer himself."

79 In many cases the emergent discourse articulation will match metrical division, in the sense that Edwards adopts from H. Fraenkel. Consider in the example above especially the verse-initial acts in 773, 775, 777, 778, 780, 782, 783, and 785, as well as the verse-final act in 779. This match is attractive and complements the argument that these acts had some prosodic independence.

80 The decision to regard adverbial phrases as separate is influenced by how English works. In none of the cases above does the adverbial or participial phrase limit the preceding (pro)noun, in which case prosodic continuity would be necessary: we do not find "the men by the sea" (which implies an opposition with "the men inland") but "the men, by the sea," etc; see Langacker 2001:161-162 with example 7.

81 In line 777, κεῖτο does occur directly after the bucolic diaeresis, which may have led to a discontinuity before *and* after κεῖτο.

82 Moorhouse 1959 argues that the negation was originally sentence-initial in Greek, but note the objections raised by Gonda 1963, especially that Moorhouse does not sufficiently take into consideration the role of style and genre. Fraenkel appears to agree with Moorhouse, and in his 1964 edition of *Kolon und Satz* II he marks in the footnotes the many instances of negations at *kôlon* beginning; Scheppers 2011:74-75 notes the same tendency in Lysias and Plato.

83 See Bakker 1993b and IV.2.2; more on δέ in §§31-36 below.

84 See IV.3 for a holistic approach to Herodotean and Thucydidean discourse segmentation.

verse, whereas typically δέ follows a (pro)noun immediately at the head of the verse.[85] Finally, in three places (lines 773, 775, and 778) we find the subject plus particle isolated as a separate discourse act. This is complemented by the isolation of the finite verbs, also consistently produced as separate acts in this passage. In lines 772, 777, and 779 the verb stands almost alone, and up to 779 even the ones that are less independent are separated from their subjects by at least a participle. The position of the verbs, either at line beginning (772 and 777) or at line end (779), suggests that they were prosodically set apart from their context by pauses or other discontinuities.[86] Their isolation will have lent emphasis to the words, putting the spotlight on their sense—which is one of inactivity: κεῖτο, ἕστασαν, οὐδὲ μάχοντο.[87]

§29. The narrative and visual path from one subject to the next, each highlighted in turn, and the overall sense of inactivity bring us to the reversal in 780, where the audience is presented with the act οἳ δ' ἄρ' ἴσαν. The beginning of line 780 is a heavy transition, which supports the choice by most editors to indent before this line—it is natural to print it as a new paragraph. The pronoun οἵ here is completely ambiguous, since it comes after a section containing a large selection of referents, but in fact it refers to none of the subjects in the description of Achilles' camp. Rather, it marks the return to the battlefield before Troy, and functions as the cap of the entire *Catalogue*. The surprise effected by the narrative turn would not have had as much impact if it were not for the careful build-up of the preceding ten lines. After dwelling on the picture of soldiers lounging and killing time, the performer brings our attention back to the advancing army with three constituents: the pronoun οἵ, the particle combination δ'ἄρα, and the verb ἴσαν. The use of a particle combination to follow the pronoun instead of just a simple δέ provides some warning that we are being presented with a different kind of transition from the preceding ones,[88] but undoubtedly the verb here is the crucial factor. For the audience to be abruptly confronted with "they went", after encountering a series of static verbs, requires quite a bit of cognitive processing on their part, as they search for the group of appropriate referents.

§30. To seal the return, Homer introduces a simile, comparing the army to an advancing, all-consuming forest fire (780). This image effectively redirects the audience's attention to the battlefield, for it recalls another simile at the beginning of the *Catalogue* (lines 2.455-458) in which the shine of the Greeks' armor is likened to the blaze of a forest

[85] For the combination of pronoun + particle see below in §§63-79 but especially II.5.

[86] For more on prosody see IV.3.2.

[87] *Gesamtkommentar* 2003:II.2.250, "Ausdrücke des Liegens, Stehens und zweckfreien Tuns (...) bzw. unfreiwilligen Nichtstuns (779) sind vorherrschend und stehen oft am [Versanfang]." The Basel commentary to the *Iliad* will be referred to throughout volume 2 by '*Gesamtkommentar*, year, volume number, fascicle number, page number.' The individual volumes are edited by different scholars, and can be found under their names in the Bibliography.

[88] As regards the combination's use here, let me anticipate that ἄρα often serves to accomplish "frame recall," a return to the main narrative thread, on which see II.4 §18 and §38, and II.5.3.3.

fire on a mountain.[89] The simile serves to accommodate the cognitive effort required to travel back to the army advancing, that was last referred to in 2.455-473. The similes before and after the *Catalogue* are further connected in the sense that the one just before it describes a glinting army seen far off while the simile at line 780 gives an image of a Greek horde about to engulf the Trojans. The echo of the imagery must have helped the audience negotiate a considerable narrative and spatial discontinuity.[90]

2.2.1 Homeric δέ

§31. The scene at Achilles' camp is a linguistically turbulent passage, produced in a stream of short acts that stand in no fixed relation to syntax or meter. The acts direct attention to different aspects of the scene, and allow the audience to take everything in step by step. δέ is instrumental in accomplishing this compartmentalizing effect, and in fact is essentially omnipresent in Homer. Yet the particle, despite its prevalence in the text, has not been the object of as much close analysis as might have been expected. The particle's fundamental function in Homer has most recently been described by Bakker:

(t9)

> δέ "marks no more than a new step, a moment in time at which a new piece of information is activated in his [the narrator's] consciousness. The particle *dé* is the most widely used linguistic *boundary marker* between foci of consciousness. And as an observable syntactic cue for such cognitive breaks in our text it is an important element for the study of how consciousness is turned into speech."
>
> Bakker 1997b:63 [italics original].

Before Bakker, δέ had been viewed as a primarily "connective" particle, sometimes with adversative force.[91] However, especially in Homer, δέ can occur at the boundary between two clauses, two phrases, between main clause and subclause, or vice versa, or between a vocative and what follows. In other words, δέ is not in the first place a syntactic marker.[92] Bakker, however, argues that it reflects the production of discourse in small steps. As

89 Scott 2005:38 remarks that the simile at *Iliad* 2.780 "is responding to the first simile in the earlier cluster at 455" but does not expand on the possible performative effectiveness of this "responsion"; see also Kirk 1985:243 and *Gesamtkommentar* 2003:II.2.253.

90 Consider Auer 2005:27, "Memory for form is much shorter than memory for content," and Langacker 2001:180: "While the essential content may be retained, memory of how it was presented linguistically will soon be lost". The new image, in other words, may well remind the audience of the earlier one.

91 See for the *communis opinio* in earlier scholarship Denniston 1950^2:162.

92 See IV.2 §§14-25 for the syntactic flexibility of δέ-acts, especially in Herodotus and Thucydides.

such, δέ has little to do with content, and everything with form: the term connective thus is useful only if it concerns discourse rather than content.

§32. One aspect of the previous scholarship on δέ that Bakker preserves is the idea of δέ as in some way weak or "bleached. " From the earliest studies onward δέ has been regarded as etymologically connected to δή; Bakker, like others before him, views δέ as a bleached version of δή.[93] This sense of δέ as a bleached form of δή, however, focuses overmuch on the semantic load of the particle.

§33. Indeed, Homeric δέ often goes (and should go) untranslated in English, but that is because its function does not have its equivalent in English in a lexical item, but in punctuation or prosody. Rather than anything bleached, as a boundary marker δέ is in fact the strongest of all second-position words: the only one that is practically never moved from its position in Homer and to a lesser extent in lyric.[94] The particle's strength on a purely functional level has seldom been discussed, yet it is crucial to a number of other questions involving δέ. For instance, the fact that δή (or at least one of its aspects) seems to have been a mobile in early Greek, of which some trace remains in Homer,[95] speaks against the close relation envisioned between the two words by Bakker and most earlier scholars. Indeed δή's mobility all but eliminates the possibility that in Homer δέ functioned as a bleached version of δή.[96]

§34. To better understand the differences between δέ and δή, consider first the instances where both particles occur, as in the following haunting scene from the *Odyssey*:

(t10)

οἱ δ' ἤδη γναθμοῖσι γελώων ἀλλοτρίοισιν, |
αἱμοφόρυκτα *δὲ δὴ* κρέα ἤσθιον· | ὄσσε δ' ἄρα σφέων
δακρυόφιν πίμπλαντο, | γόον δ' ὠΐετο θυμός. |

Odyssey 20.347-349

And they were now laughing with lips not their own,
actually they were eating meat defiled with blood, and then their eyes
were filled with tears; their heart presaged grief.

[93] Bakker captures the *communis opinio* when he says (1997b:75) that the etymological connection of δέ with δή, "as a phonetically shortened and weakened version of this latter particle" is "commonplace."

[94] Not strong in the sense of marking the strongest pause (as a period does in punctuation), but strong in the sense of its adherence to its position—it is clearly strongly connected to the start of new acts. See note 97 for the exceptions.

[95] See II.3.3.2 for the relevant evidence and literature.

[96] This is not to say that they may not be etymologically connected, but in Homer the two lexical items have clearly gone separate ways. Alternatively, the particle δή might be a strengthened version of δέ (parallel to ἆρα which seems to have developed from ἄρα, see Braswell 1988:173-174 and De Kreij 2015) in one of its functions; more on this in II.3 §§56-57.

Here and in all thirty-one other instances of the combination δέ precedes δή.[97] The same thing holds for the combination of δέ with ἄν/κε(ν); remember that Fraenkel actually chose ἄν as a case study for his research into *kôlon* boundaries. The reason must quite simply be that δέ, at least in Homer, cannot leave its peninitial position for another second-position word. This tenacity suggests that its function is tightly connected to its position, which supports Bakker's description of δέ as the quintessential boundary marker.

§35. The boundary that δέ marks can be that between a main and a subclause, between two parallel phrases, or after a vocative in direct speech, but the particle can also occur at stronger discontinuities in the discourse, as in the following example:

(t11)

εὖτ' ἀστὴρ ὑπερέσχε φαάντατος, | ὅς τε μάλιστα
ἔρχεται | ἀγγέλλων φάος Ἠοῦς ἠριγενείης, |
τῆμος δὴ νήσῳ προσεπίλνατο | ποντοπόρος νηῦς. |
Φόρκυνος[98] δέ τίς ἐστι λιμήν, | ἁλίοιο γέροντος, |
ἐν δήμῳ Ἰθάκης· | (...)

Odyssey 13.93-97

When that brightest star rose, the one that most of all
comes, heralding the light of early-born Dawn,

97 The parallels are *Iliad* 7.94, 7.399, 8.30, 9.31, 9.245, 9.432, 9.696, 10.252, 11.524, 13.52, 16.763, 17.466, 18.20, 18.290, 18.291, 19.345, 20.23, 20.307, 21.92, 22.300, 24.398; *Odyssey* 1.26, 2.176, 3.168, 4.706, 5.302, 5.322, 7.155, 13.178, 14.24, and 20.321. The postpositive that Fraenkel took as his case study, ἄν, occurs 30 times with δέ, always following it; the pattern persists in the 130 instances of δέ κ(εν). There are relatively few examples in Homer (out of 10.969 instances in total) of δέ leaving its peninitial position, only after prepositional constructions (the list is not exhaustive): ἀνὰ ῥῖνας δέ (1x: *Odyssey* 24.318), ἀπ' αὐτοῦ δέ (2x: *Iliad* 11.829 = 11.845), δι' ὤμου δέ (2x: *Iliad* 13.519 and 14.451), διὲκ προθύρου δέ (1x: *Odyssey* 21.299), ἐκ θαλάμου δέ (1x: *Iliad* 24.275), ἐκ κεφαλῆς δέ (1x: *Odyssey* 6.226), ἐκ πάντων δέ (2x: *Iliad* 4.96 and *Odyssey* 2.433), ἐκ πυκινῆς δέ (1x: *Odyssey* 6.128), ἐκ τοῦ δέ (3x: *Iliad* 13.779, 15.69, and *Odyssey* 1.212), ἐν μέσσῃ δέ (1x: *Odyssey* 5.326), ἐν θυμῷ δέ (1x: *Iliad* 15.566), ἐν βουλῇ δέ (1x: *Iliad* 2.194), ἐν τῇ δέ (1x: *Iliad* 7.248), ἐν δοιῇ δέ (1x: *Iliad* 9.230), ἐν καυλῷ δέ (1x: *Iliad* 17.607), ἐν λεχέεσσι δέ (1x: *Iliad* 18.352), ἐν γαίῃ δέ (1x: *Iliad* 22.276), ἐν κλισίῃσι δέ (1x: *Iliad* 23.254), ἐν νύσσῃ δέ (1x: *Iliad* 23.338), ἐν Λέσβῳ δέ (1x: *Odyssey* 3.169), ἐν νόστῳ δέ (1x: *Odyssey* 11.384), ἐν πρύμνῃ δέ (1x: Odyssey 15.285), ἐν προχοῇς δέ (1x: *Odyssey* 20.65), ἐν δαπέδῳ δέ (1x: *Odyssey* 22.188), ἐπὶ πολλὰ δέ (1x: *Odyssey* 14.120), ἐπὶ στήθεσσι δέ (1x: *Iliad* 21.254), ἐπὶ δηρὸν δέ (1x: *Iliad* 9.415), ἐπ' αὐτῷ δέ (2x: *Iliad* 4.470 and 14.419, once ἐπὶ δ' αὐτῷ *Odyssey* 22.75 [in ἐπὶ δέ, ἐπί is otherwise used adverbially, without a complement following the particle]), ἐπ' αὐτῶν δέ (4x: *Iliad* 1.461 and 2.424, *Odyssey* 3.458 and 12.361), ἐς νῆας δέ (1x: *Iliad* 11.513), ἐς ἀλλήλας δέ (1x: *Odyssey* 18.320), ἐς Φηρὰς δέ (2x: *Odyssey* 3.488 and 15.186), πρὸ Φθίων δέ (1x: *Iliad* 13.693), πρὸς Θύμβρης δέ (1x: *Iliad* 10.430), ὑπὸ γλωχῖνα δέ (*Iliad* 24.274).

98 Practically every edition indents before Φόρκυνος, and likewise before "There is" in the translation; see also De Jong 2001a:317-318 and Bowie 2013:114, "new episodes in Greek (and Latin) literature are often marked by an *ecphrasis*, a formal description of a place or scene, regularly in the form 'There is a certain...'."

just then it approached an island, the sea-faring ship.
There is a harbor of Phorcys, the old man of the sea,
in the land of Ithaca. (...)

After describing how the sun comes up and the ship carrying the sleeping Odysseus reaches Ithaca, the performer devotes some attention to the place where Odysseus will be left by the Phaeacians.[99] This new section is set apart by the present tense and starts with δέ but is not otherwise marked, yet it represents a significant redirection from action to image and from movement to stasis. The two parts of discourse are divided by nothing more than δέ.[100]

§36. This passage is one example of how the particle can occur in any kind of transition, because of its ability to occupy the second position of any discourse act. Δέ in Homer is the simplest metalanguage: its syntactic and semantic flexibility shows that its function does not primarily lie on those levels, but is concentrated on marking a discourse boundary.[101] In Homer, δέ is markedly more frequent in narration than in direct speech. The imbalance suggests that there is something in the steps of narrative discourse that allows or requires more neutral boundaries than in direct speech.[102] Over time δέ develops from being an omnipresent boundary marker to a particle used to start new *períodoi*, and eventually to a marker of adversativity. This development is accompanied by a steady decline in the particle's frequency in later texts, as well as a looser adherence to its peninitial position.[103]

2.3 Discourse Acts in Pindar

§37. Pindaric language is widely regarded as difficult. This view is implicitly reflected in the punctuation practices found in modern editions, which give the impression that

[99] See for this discursive device ("unframed discourse") and the role of particles in it II.4.2 (γάρ) and II.5.3.3-4 (ἄρα and δή).

[100] On this kind of discourse transition see also II.3 §49, where I discuss a similar construction without a particle; IV.2.2 examines the different kinds of divisions that may be marked by δέ.

[101] As the instance of δή in line 95 illustrates, there is a construction where δή is used with temporal markers to signal boundaries in discourse. It is in this function that δή and δέ may be connected; see II.3 §§56-57 for a discussion.

[102] In Homer's narrative passages, δέ makes up 6,8% of the words in the *Iliad* and 7,4% in the *Odyssey*, whereas in direct speech it makes up only 3,1% in the *Iliad* and 2,9% in the *Odyssey*.

[103] The details of this development are not easily mapped, since diachronically diverse texts are generally also generically diverse. For the frequency of δέ, it is around 5.4% in Homer, which is never matched in later literature, where only Herodotus approaches it at 4.2%. However, the strong variation within Homer between narrative and direct speech suggests that the differences with other authors too need not all be the result of diachronic development.

Pindar sometimes wrote monstrously long sentences.[104] This syntactical approach does not do justice to how the songs were received by a listening audience. Like Homeric epic, Pindaric song proceeds in small acts. The most important difference between the two corpora is the music that was an integral part of Pindar's songs.

§38. The melodies of Pindaric song are all lost to us, and we must keep in mind that the melody may have mitigated the apparent complexity of Pindaric discourse. The melodic dimension may have clarified constructions, created breaks and links, and overall made linguistic construction quite secondary. Moreover, music changes the way the lyric language is received and understood on a level above the discourse act. As opposed to the repetitive rhythm of Homer, the division of Pindaric song into strophe, antistrophe, and epode creates an intermittent recurrence of rhythmic (and melodic) units. Songs exploit the audience's "melodic memory" to create resonance beyond the linear production of verse after verse, in a phenomenon called "tautometric responsion."[105]In the example of *Pythian* 6 (t12 and t13 below), for instance, the phrases ἄγεις ἐφημοσύναν (20, about the victor's son) and νόημα τοῦτο φέρων (29, about Antilochus), occupy the same metrical position in strophe and antistrophe. In this case, the resonance reinforces the comparison that Pindar proposes between the victor's son and Antilochus.

§39. The one aspect of Pindaric song that is still accessible to us is its meter. Therefore, in dividing Pindar's songs into discourse acts, metrical considerations play an important role. Since the verses are decidedly shorter than the Homeric hexameter, they are not often broken up into separate metrical *kôla*.[106] Although verse end does not coincide with act boundary quite as regularly as in Homer, this is still a strong tendency. Moreover, the strong metrical boundary after strophe, antistrophe, and epode always coincides with act boundary.

§40. Consider the third strophe of *Pythian* 6. After two *strophai* introducing the event (the chariot race in the *Pythian* games), the winner (Xenocrates), and his clan, Pindar focuses on Xenocrates' son, who is addressed in line 15 with the vocative Θρασύβουλε, and again in line 19 with σύ τοι:[107]

(t12)

σύ τοι | σχεθών νιν ἐπὶ δεξιὰ χειρός, | ὀρθὰν ἄγεις ἐφημοσύναν, |
21 τά ποτ' ἐν οὔρεσι φαντὶ | μεγαλοσθενεῖ

[104] See II.3.4.2 for a discussion of a twelve-line "sentence" at the beginning of *Pythian* 2. The same prejudice exists about the length and complexity of Thucydides' *períodoi*, see IV.3.10.2 for a discussion.

[105] The idea of tautometric responsion is presented in Metzger 1880:33-41, and critiqued by Gildersleeve 1885:l-li.

[106] There is a lot of scholarship on Pindaric colometry, and different scholars have proposed different metrical articulations of his songs; see e.g. Irigoin 1953, Cole 1988, Gentili and Perusino 1999, and Itsumi 2009.

[107] I here follow the colometry given in Gentili et al. 1995.

Φιλύρας υἱὸν ὀρφανιζομένῳ
Πηλεΐδᾳ παραινεῖν· | μάλιστα μὲν Κρονίδαν, |
βαρύοπα στεροπᾶν κεραυνῶν τε πρύτανιν, |
θεῶν σέβεσθαι· |
ταύτας δὲ μή ποτε τιμᾶς
ἀμείρειν | γονέων βίον πεπρωμένον. |

Pindar, *Pythian* 6.19-27

Now you, keeping him at your right hand, you keep the command straight,
which they say that once in the mountains to the greatly powerful—
that Philyras' son advised to the orphaned
son of Peleus: to honour especially Kronos' son,
loud-voiced lord of lightning and thunder,
of all the gods.
And to never of those honours
deprive the given life of one's parents.

In the passage above, I mark discourse act boundaries on the basis of syntax and sense (e.g. the apposition βαρύοπα...πρύτανιν), but also considering postpositives (νιν, ποτε, μέν, and δέ) and hyperbaton constructions (ὀρθὰν...ἐφημοσύναν). After σύ τοι[108] follows a participial phrase with the enclitic νιν in second position.[109] The first two lines of this third strophe thus proceed in three acts, the first to direct attention to the focus of the upcoming two strophai ("You then"), the second to provide a link to the preceding ("keeping him [sc. Thrasyboulos' father] at your right hand"),[110] and the third to look ahead to the upcoming discourse ("straight you keep the command").

§41. The next act starts with a neuter pronoun (τά, "those things") that retrieves the referent of ἐφημοσύναν "command." At the same time, the pronoun functions as a transition into a little mythical reference (23-26).[111] The clause that provides an orientation for this narrative neatly demonstrates the difference between Pindar and Homer. Line 21 ends with the dative adjective μεγαλοσθενεῖ, which can in no natural way be construed with what preceded; it thus projects[112] an indirect object (dative) of an upcoming new

[108] See §§72-79 for a discussion of similar transitions (2nd person pronoun + particle) in Pindar.

[109] In Pindar, νιν is not limited to second position, but it does tend toward it. Here the participial phrase following the nominative gives sufficient reason to assume a discontinuity between τοι and σχεθών.

[110] Scholars are not undivided on this point (see Gentili et al. 1995:545-546 for an overview of the possibilities), but I see no reason to read νιν here as referring to the victory.

[111] See II.3 §50 on relatives (+ποτε) introducing embedded narratives in Pindar.

[112] See below §§49-51 on the concept of (pragmatic) projection.

action that will fit the epithet. The first words that follow are Φιλύρας υἱόν, a circuitous way of naming Cheiron, who after φαντί will naturally be taken as the agent in the emerging construction. At this point the audience may already have the information they need: Pindar is elaborating on a saying that Cheiron once taught someone in the mountains (ἐν οὔρεσι), someone as yet unnamed to whom the (rare) epithet μεγαλοσθενής can suitably apply. The combination of cues will have activated the figure of Achilles in the audience's minds. The suspicion gains strength in line 22 when the audience encounters a second epithet, ὀρφανιζομένῳ, and finally is confirmed with the patronymic in line 23 (Πηλεΐδᾳ). Because of the interweaving construction, it is hard to establish where this relatively long act (21-23) may have been subdivided. The adjective in the dative (μεγαλοσθενεῖ) creates the expectation of a noun, and the thought is not yet complete at the end of line 22. Despite its length, however, the audience would still have been able to semantically process the construction on-line.

§42. In Homer, this act would probably have been broken in two, presented with the different components clustered together. Note, however, that such syntactical and discursive flourishes in Pindar are designed precisely to be flourishes; they function as verbal (and perhaps musical) *tours-de-force* that stand out against the general piecemeal progression of the discourse in his songs.[113] The saying itself is introduced at μάλιστα μέν and illustrates how so-called μέν - δέ constructions are often not symmetrical in early Greek poetry (more on this in §56-§59). Finally, line 24 (βαρύοπα στεροπᾶν κεραυνῶν τε πρύτανιν) contains another idiosyncrasy of Pindar's. Lauer first observed that Pindar has a tendency to demarcate his *kôla* using hyperbata, which Lauer called *Kolonbildend*.[114] The suggestion is that a lone adjective (βαρύοπα) at the beginning of an act (or *Kolon* in Lauer's terms) creates the expectation of a noun, and the eventual occurrence of the noun (πρύτανιν) then marks the end of the discourse act.[115] Markovic remarks that throughout early Greek literature, hyperbaton is a tool frequently used especially for "signaling or reinforcing the *end* of syntactical and semantic units" [my emphasis], and regards it as a feature "of oral tradition."[116]

§43. The wisdom that Pindar offers in *Pythian* 6.23-25 is that one should honor Zeus most out of all the gods, and that one should honor one's parents. The second part of the

113 This observation resonates with the claims about tragic lyric in Stinton 1977:29.

114 Lauer 1959:54-58; see also Race 2002 and Markovic 2006:138-140. Race 2002:21 believes that Lauer pays "little attention" to hyperbata, and does not refer to Lauer's idea of *Kolonbildende* hyperbata. Markovic does not cite Lauer, but describes this kind of hyperbaton similarly, calling it a "framing hyperbaton."

115 Especially remarkable are instances where Pindar postpones a word that would otherwise have been in initial position in order to achieve hyperbaton, as ὅς in *Olympian* 1.12 θεμιστεῖον ὅς ἀμφέπει σκᾶπτον and τόν in *Isthmian* 1.13 παῖδα, | θρασεῖαι τόν ποτε Γηρυόνα φρῖξαν κύνες.

116 Markovic 2006:128-129.

gnṓmē ("honor your parents") introduces an important theme in the ode which provides the starting point for the following strophe:[117]

(t13)

ἔγεντο καὶ πρότερον | Ἀντίλοχος βιατὰς | νόημα τοῦτο φέρων, |
ὃς ὑπερέφθιτο πατρός, | ἐναρίμβροτον
ἀναμείναις στράταρχον Αἰθιόπων |
Μέμνονα. | Νεστόρειον γὰρ ἵππος ἅρμ' ἐπέδα |
Πάριος ἐκ βελέων δαϊχθείς· | ὁ δ' ἔφεπεν
κραταιὸν ἔγχος· |
Μεσσανίου δὲ γέροντος |
δονηθεῖσα φρὴν | βόασε παῖδα ὅν, |

χαμαιπετὲς δ' ἄρ' ἔπος οὐκ ἀπέριψεν· | αὐτοῦ μένων δ' ὁ θεῖος ἀνήρ |
πρίατο μὲν θανάτοιο κομιδὰν πατρός, |

Pindar, *Pythian* 6.28-39

This happened in earlier times too. Strong Antilochos, keeping this in mind,
he died for his father, standing up to the man-slaying general of the Ethiopians,
Memnon. For Nestor's horse entangled the chariot,
struck by Paris' arrows, and he [Memnon] brandished his powerful spear.
The old man from Messene's
mind in panic, he called to his son.

And not an earthbound word escaped from him: staying put, the godlike man
bought with his death his father's escape.

The theme established by the end of the third stanza is explored in the fourth, which here takes the form of a little narrative. The transition to the past (ἔγεντο καὶ πρότερον) and the introduction of the story are clear. The pronoun in νόημα τοῦτο secures the connection to the preceding discourse, and the next act, starting with the personal pronoun ὅς referring to Antilochus, begins a little abstract of the entire story.[118] Μέμνονα in apposition at the head of line 32 is semantically superfluous, but the name here serves to close

[117] See Gentili et al. 1995:547.
[118] For the typical components of a narrative see II.3.2.1.

the ring begun at the naming of Antilochus, a ring from victim to killer.[119] Furthermore, placing the name here enables Pindar to juxtapose Memnon with Nestor: a reflection in the language of the situation on the battlefield. The narrative proper follows, beginning with the particle γάρ,[120] and proceeds in six subsequent acts, no fewer than four of which start with δέ.[121] Use of δέ in Pindar is noticeably different from Homer's usage: the particle occurs much less frequently, and is more often used to mark more significant boundaries in the discourse.[122] It is in Pindar's narrative sections that we find a distribution of δέ closer to that found in Homer, but even in Pindaric narrative the particle is not used quite as frequently as in Homer. As for the particle's position, in line 37 δέ is postponed until after the word group αὐτοῦ μένων, a license that does not occur in Homer.[123]

§44. The function of μέν in line 39 is not immediately obvious. It occurs in the line that appears to function as the resolution of the narrative (see II.3 §14), the end of the story. The sense of resolution is confirmed when we consider how the strophe continues:

(t14)

ἐδόκησέν τε τῶν πάλαι γενεᾷ
ὁπλοτέροισιν | ἔργον πελώριον τελέσαις |
ὕπατος ἀμφὶ τοκεῦσιν ἔμμεν πρὸς ἀρετάν. |

Pindar, *Pythian* 6.40-42

And he was regarded among the race of the men of old,
by latter generations, having done that great deed,
to be foremost as regards virtue toward the parents.

Line 39, then, functions as the end of the narrative proper, while 40-42 are a reflection on the story's outcome. If we take the classical approach to μέν as a "preparatory" particle, we find no satisfactory explanation for its occurrence here, in the act πρίατο μὲν θανάτοιο κομιδὰν πατρός. On a semantic level there is no parallellism or contrast with the following ἐδόκησέν τε τῶν πάλαι γενεᾷ. Syntactically, the verbs πρίατο and ἐδόκησεν do resonate with each other, as both have Antilochus as their subject. Scholars

[119] See IV.3.5 on the sense of completion inherent in the idea of *períodos*.

[120] For this function of γάρ at the beginning of an embedded narrative see II.3.2.2.

[121] See Gentili et al. 1995:548, "sono descritti con evidenza quasi figurativa, accentuata dall' andamento rapido e paratattico delle frasi, i particolari dell' episodio."

[122] See II.3 §65 for more on δέ at significant discursive transitions in Pindar. δέ makes up 5.4% of the words in the *Iliad* and *Odyssey*, while it makes up 4% of the words in the *Victory Odes*. The contrast is starker when one considers the difference between narration and direct speech in Homer (see note 102).

[123] See note 97 above; Gentili et al. 1995:37 punctuates between αὐτοῦ and μένων; I follow the punctuation and colometry of Gildersleeve and Snell/Maehler.

have consequently argued that μέν in such occurrences is "answered" by τε instead of δέ in Pindar.[124] But the two acts that would here be connected through μέν - τε diverge in their discursive nature. The first (39) rounds off the narrative, while the second (40) functions as a postscript.

§45. How, then, should we understand this μέν? In the following section I argue that μέν must be taken in instances like this as a metalinguistic cue: its host act rounds off one move, while μέν projects that a new move is coming up. The particle μέν possesses this function regardless of what introduces the upcoming act, be it δέ, τε, καί or no particle at all.

2.4 μέν in Homer and Pindar

§46. In the passages from *Pythian* 6 above (t12-t14), there are two instances of the particle μέν, both of which may offer insight into the workings of the particle. In Attic Greek prose, μέν mostly has a narrow function, that is, it marks the first part in a μέν - δέ construction. In such contexts it may be translated "on the one hand," or remain untranslated. Schömann first argued that μέν developed from μήν, and that its original force was affirmative.[125] This view is compatible with the argument put forward by Spitzner, and soon promoted to *communis opinio*, that μέν in Homer is simply a dialectal variant (Ionic) of μήν (Attic) and μάν (Doric).[126] Spitzner's observation led to the argument that μέν *tout court* is descended from μήν and its variants, both on a formal and on a functional level. Leumann further hypothesizes that the μέν - δέ construction preserves the Ionic variant of μάν because the construction found its way into Greek discourse through the scientific works from Ionia. At the same time, all dialects kept their own variant of μάν for all other instances, that is, where it affirms its clause.[127] Among these scholars, some also regard the fact that μέν is a shorter form of μήν as a sign of a bleaching or weakening of the function performed by its ancestor.[128]

124 See Bury 1892a:156, Gildersleeve 1885:164, and Hummel 1993:388-389.

125 Schömann 1831:176; he revisits the topic in 1862:188.

126 Spitzner 1832:I.2 xx-xxxi, picked up by Hartung 1833:390, expanded by Nägelsbach 1834:I.153-175; see also Bäumlein 1861:160 μέν "[versichert] einfach die Aussage und speziell den voranstehenden Begriff," Ebeling 1885:1046-1061, Wackernagel 1916:117, Denniston 1950²:359-397, Ruijgh 1971:202.

127 Leumann 1949:87-88 is the first to attempt a coherent answer to the question: if μέν is indeed historically connected to μάν, why do we not find different dialectal forms of the μέν - δέ construction?

128 Matthiae 1845:3, Passow 1852:175, Bäumlein 1861:159, Bakker 1997b:80, Beekes 2010:930. In some cases, an analogy is proposed with the relation between δέ and δή, on which see more in §§26-29 above.

§47. Thus the particle's origin in μήν and its more common Attic use in a μέν - δέ construction have been linked.[129] One thing that has been lost in this development of scholarship is the forward-looking force of μέν. If μέν is from affirmative μήν, it implies contrast with the following by strongly affirming the present clause, phrase, or constituent.[130] I follow the majority of scholars in assuming a formal (i.e. diachronic) relation between μέν on the one hand and μήν and μάν on the other. However, unlike the majority I do not believe that μέν is always functionally connected to μήν and μάν by the time of Homer (i.e. synchronically), since to describe the use of μέν in Homer as "affirmative" is insufficient.

§48. Before the link between μήν and μέν became central to the analysis of μέν, scholars paid more attention to how μέν was actually used by Greek authors. This led Hoogeveen to say the following: "when a speaker uses μέν, he warns the reader or hearer that he should not agree to this first part, but should wait for the ἀπόδοσις, which resolves the utterance."[131] In other words, with μέν the speaker promises to add something after the current clause, phrase, or constituent.[132] Rather than a development from the particle's putative original affirmative force, this "anticipatory" sense is primary in μέν. The question now remains how to read μέν in Homer, since it can either be the Ionic form of Attic μήν, that is with the function of μήν, or the μέν shared by all dialects. In practice, this question would have to be answered per instance, but we may follow the generalization offered by Hartung that μήν is only shortened to μέν when it is used with other particles.[133] In my analysis of μέν in Homer and Pindar, I have found no instances of μέν on its own (i.e. except in particle combinations and after οὐ) where it cannot be explained as forward-pointing.

2.4.1 μέν projecting acts and moves

§49. The next step is to come to a better understanding of this "anticipatory" function of μέν. The words of Hoogeveen may be linked to the idea of metalanguage: μέν is first and foremost an instruction to the hearer. Discourse acts are not strung together at random, but rather stand in some kind of logical relationship to each other. As I discuss in more

[129] There is a useful overview of the early literature on the topic in Mutzbauer 1884:4-9; Ruijgh 1971:202 argues that already in Homer the majority of instances of μέν is of the coordinating μέν - δέ construction.

[130] See Hartung 1833:402-403.

[131] Hoogeveen 1769:639, "qui enim primo vocabulo apponit τὸ μέν, lectorem vel auditorem monet in hoc tanquam principio ne acquiescat, sed exspectare jubet, donec sequatur ἀπόδοσις, quae orationem absolvat."

[132] See also Stephens 1837:74, "μέν informs the reader that some statement is about to follow which ought to be considered in connection with that in which μέν itself occurs."

[133] Hartung 1833:393, see more specifically Ruijgh 1981:274, who lists ἦ μέν, οὐ μέν, οὐδὲ μέν, καὶ μέν, and μὲν δή.

detail in II.3, different kinds of multi-act discourse units ("moves") cohere for different reasons. The acts within a move may share a common topic, or in narrative they may share a place of action and set of characters (in what we call "contextual frames"). As a result of the coherence that acts possess in relation to each other, acts create expectations in the discourse, in a process called projection.[134] This phenomenon may help explain the workings of μέν, the particle that appears to have specialized in cueing projection.[135]

§50. In his work on projection, Auer describes the pragmatic process of how one word, utterance, or conversational action projects another. In conversation, speakers are remarkably capable of predicting what is coming next, often even beyond the interlocutor's upcoming turn. This predictability is a result of experience, but more basically it depends on relevance. Any conversational action restricts the range of possible consequent actions:

> (t15)
>
> "By projection I mean the fact that an individual action or part of it projects another. In order to understand what is projected, interactants need some kind of knowledge about how actions (or action components) are typically (i.e., qua types) sequenced, i.e. how they follow each other in time."
>
> Auer 2005:8[136]

An act can project several others, and in practice these possibilities form a limited set. Beyond conversation, projection can become inherent in syntactical constructions, such as "the thing is,..."[137] Therefore, Auer speaks of pragmatic projection: "one act or action projects another" and syntactic projection: "one syntactical constituent projects another." Projection can work on the microlevel (syntax: a preposition projects a noun to follow)[138] and on the macrolevel (genre: the first part of a priamel projects at least one more).[139]

[134] The term projection has its origins in Conversation Analysis, beginning with Sacks, Schegloff, and Jefferson 1974 (Schegloff offers a comprehensive definition in 1984:267), and it has been explored by Streeck 1995 and 2009, Goodwin 1996:372 ("prospective indexicals"), Auer, Couper-Kuhlen, and Müller 1999, Hopper 2004, 2008 (with Thompson) and 2011, Günthner 2008 and 2011, Auer 2005, 2009, and 2011 (ed. with S. Pfänder).

[135] Scholars working on projection (be it pragmatic or syntactic) do not explore (to our knowledge) the possibility that certain particles can be linked directly to the process, but Auer 1992:8 (introduction to Auer and Di Luzio (eds) 1992) does say about an occurrence of *allora* in a conversation that it is to be interpreted there as a "projective particle instead of an adverb," and this "prospective particle foreshadows the upcoming joke-telling."

[136] For the cognitive relevance of the second part of this definition, see II.4.4 on scripts and Homeric type-scenes.

[137] See Günthner 2008 for such constructions in German.

[138] See Auer 2005:16, "a preposition prestructures the following slot in a highly compelling way (a noun phrase is bound to follow)."

[139] The audience are familiar with the genre and know "how actions (or action components) are typically (i.e., qua types) sequenced" in a *Victory Ode*.

Moreover, projection can be more specific (preposition projects noun) or less specific ("and" after a syntactic closure "leave[s] all options open apart from *not* continuing").[140]

§51. The concept of projection can offer better understanding of μέν in its entire range of pragmatic functions in ancient Greek, including the Homeric corpus and Pindar's *Victory Odes*. In the present section I discuss the functions of μέν in terms of projection. First, the focus is on μέν creating pragmatic projection across discourse transitions. Second comes a discussion of the ultimate pragmatic projection: μέν at the beginning of discourse units, performative units, and even whole works. Finally, I consider the μέν - δέ construction, which works differently when μέν has large scope than when it has small scope.

§52. One aspect of μέν that has suffered in particular from the scholarly focus on μήν is its use in discourse transitions. In his list of functions of μέν - δέ constructions, the first function Hoogeveen lists is μεταβατικός ("transitional").[141] In recent scholarship this has been retrieved by Bakker: rather than signaling a juxtaposition in states of affairs, μέν - δέ signals a juxtaposition of two discourse units.[142] As Devarius noted (see fn. 141), μέν can have this function on its own as well, without a following δέ. Consider the beginning of book ten of the *Iliad*:

(t16)

καὶ τότε δὴ σπείσαντες | ἔβαν κλισίηνδε ἕκαστος, |
ἔνθα δὲ κοιμήσαντο | καὶ ὕπνου δῶρον ἕλοντο. |

Ἰλιάδος κ΄

Ἄλλοι <u>μὲν</u> παρὰ νηυσὶν | ἀριστῆες Παναχαιῶν |
εὗδον παννύχιοι | μαλακῷ δεδμημένοι ὕπνῳ· |
ἀλλ' οὐκ Ἀτρεΐδην Ἀγαμέμνονα ποιμένα λαῶν |
ὕπνος ἔχε γλυκερὸς | πολλὰ φρεσὶν ὁρμαίνοντα. |

Iliad 9.712-713 and 10.1-4

And at that point, after pouring libations, each went to his tent.
There they lay down and received the gift of sleep.

Iliad 10

140 Auer 2005:16 [italics original].

141 Hoogeveen 1769:655; see also Devarius 1588:122, who describes the first of μέν's functions as περιγραφικός, "summarizing." In later Greek this function is mostly taken over by the combinations μὲν δή (see also IV.3.11.4) and μὲν οὖν (μέν νυν in Herodotus, see IV.3.11.4 and 5): Hoogeveen 1769:672-685, Hartung 1832:263, 1833:16, 19, and 399-402, Bäumlein 1861:178-179, Denniston 1950²:258-259 and 472-473.

142 Bakker 1993b:302-305. In 1997b he phrases his point yet more eloquently: "μέν and δέ mark events in performance time, not in story time." See IV.3.8 for the use of μέν and δέ at endings and beginnings of chapters and even books in both Herodotus and Thucydides.

The others around the ships, the best of all the Achaeans
slept through the night, overcome by soft sleep.
But not Atreus' son Agamemnon, the shepherd of men,
did sweet sleep hold, as he pondered many things in his mind.

After ending the scene in book nine with all the leaders of the Greeks returning to their tents for the night, at the beginning of book ten the focus shifts to Agamemnon. In contexts like this, Apollonius Dyscolus describes μέν as marking a περιγραφή, a conclusion or summary.[143] Devarius took up this same term, calling μέν περιφραγικός, whereas Hoogeveen speaks of μεταβατικός ("transitional"); I believe Hoogeveen's description is more helpful. In discourse terms, μέν does not function so much to mark a conclusion, since that is contained within its host act, but to point ahead. In instances like (t16) μέν pragmatically projects a new move, even as its host act rounds off the preceding one. As (t16) shows, the continuation of the discourse does not have to start with δέ: in line 3 ἀλλά introduces the new focus of discourse.

§53. Compare one further example, from the *Catalogue of Ships*:

(t17)

τῶν μὲν ἄρ' Ἰδομενεὺς δουρὶ κλυτὸς ἡγεμόνευε |
Μηριόνης τ' ἀτάλαντος Ἐνυαλίῳ ἀνδρειφόντῃ· |
τοῖσι δ' ἅμ' ὀγδώκοντα μέλαιναι νῆες ἕποντο. |
Τληπόλεμος δ' Ἡρακλεΐδης | ἠΰς τε μέγας τε |
ἐκ Ῥόδου ἐννέα νῆας ἄγεν | Ῥοδίων ἀγερώχων, |

Iliad 2.650-654

Of them, then, Idomeneus famed for his spear was leader,
and Meriones, peer of Enyalios, slayer of men,
and with them eighty black ships followed.
And Tlepolemus the Heraclid, strong and tall
from Rhodos led nine ships of noble Rhodians.

The *Catalogue* consists of a list of entries that describe a people and their leaders, one by one.[144] The entries are linguistically quite consistent, giving first the people and the leader in the first line, then often a little narrative, then naming the leader again, and giving the number of ships that he brings. In the renaming of the leader, which starts the final element of the entry, we often find μέν, as in (t17). Just like in (t16) μέν in (t17)

[143] Apollonius Dyscolus, *Combiners* 251.19-26 (edition Dalimier 2001), discussed in I.2 §74.

[144] See *Gesamtkommentar* 2003:II.2.148-150 for the language of the *Catalogue* entries.

prepares the hearer for the transition to a new focus, in this case a new entry. Here μέν is followed by δέ (line 653), but there is no syntactical symmetry between the two constructions. Rather, the μέν act looks like a conclusion, with the anaphoric pronoun retrieving the people named in the preceding discourse, whereas the δέ act looks like a new beginning, since it introduces a new name in first position.

§54. The function of μέν, however, is not itself "summarizing," nor does it only juxtapose two list items or states of affairs.[145] The particle provides a metalinguistic cue for the upcoming entry even while its host act rounds off the present one: μέν projects an upcoming move.[146] In (t17) the information about the ships intervenes after the projection (652), but, as Auer shows, the "trajectory" of a projection may be quite long.[147] The audience will not have regarded the projection as resolved until the start of a new entry; they are able to mentally carry the projection over the intervening discourse.[148]

§55. In (t16) and (t17) μέν is not attached to one particular word in the act. That is to say, I do not take μέν as having small scope over the word preceding it. Its scope extends over the entire act, and its influence in fact reaches beyond. Compare this similar example from Pindar, where δέ marks the resolution of the pragmatic projection triggered by μέν:

(t18)

μάλα *μὲν* ἀνδρῶν δικαίων περικαδόμενοι. | *καὶ μὰν* θεῶν πιστὸν γένος. |
μεταμειβόμενοι δ' ἐναλλὰξ ἁμέραν | τὰν μὲν παρὰ πατρὶ φίλῳ Δὶ νέμονται, | (...)

Pindar, *Nemean* 10.54-56

taking good care of just men. Yes, the race of gods is truly trustworthy.

[145] Compare Bakker's description of *Iliad* 8.256-58 (1997b:84): "Instead of a referential or stylistic contrast, then, μέν in unit d marks a *moment at which a switch is withheld*, a moment consciously marked as something other than a new step with a new item coming into focus, and a characteristic way of guiding the listener's consciousness through the flow of speech" [emphasis original].

[146] Compare also the μέν in *Pythian* 6.39 (t13) which occurs in the line that rounds off the narrative, yet points ahead to the discussion of the story's relevance for the laudandus.

[147] Auer 2005:8, "An action (or action component) may project onto the timing slot immediately following it, and make some next activity (component) expectable in this slot. But it may also allow other things to happen 'in-between', before the projected unit legitimately can or should occur, and it may project more than one 'next' in a sequence."

[148] See also Stephens 1837:74 on μέν, "[the hearer] is kept in expectation, and takes care to retain the former statement distinctly in his view, till he has heard that which he ought to consider it in connection with."

> And alternately changing the day, the one with their beloved father Zeus they live (...)

In *Nemean* 10 Pindar tells the story of Castor and Pollux, who have here just been introduced as the stewards of the *agones* in Sparta. In line 54 this is expanded in an additional participial phrase, introduced by μέν. Now, this participial phrase rounds off the topic of Castor and Pollux as stewards of the Games. The final act of line 54 introduces a new grammatical subject and contains a gnomic thought. Then the epode ends, and at the beginning of the new strophe Castor and Pollux are retrieved as subject (μεταμειβόμενοι), but as part of a new topic: their mortal/immortal status. In this case, then, μέν serves to project a new move, yet it also projects the current discourse topic (Castor and Pollux) across a *gnṓmē* and the strong performative discontinuity between the epode and a new strophe.[149]

§56. In early Greek poetry, the relation between a μέν act and the following discourse is decidedly loose: μέν projects pragmatically, so it does not determine how discourse continues, only that it does. This touches upon another function of the particle often addressed in earlier scholarship: its so-called "inceptive" function which in turn is inherently connected to the "asseverative" function of the particle.[150] Bakker links the transitional function of μέν to its inceptive use as follows: "[μέν] is often used to mark a statement that clears the ground, establishing a framework for discourse to come, and as such it tends to be used at the beginning of a speech."[151] Consider the following statement by Denniston about the frequent occurrence of μέν at the beginning of speeches:

(t19)

> "It is difficult to resist the impression that the budding speaker, at the turn of the fifth and fourth centuries, was recommended, as a kind of stylistic convention, to start off with a μέν, and to trust more or less to luck that he would find an answer to it, and not to care greatly if he did not."
>
> Denniston 1950^{2}:383.

However difficult we may find it to resist this impression, Denniston here presents as a special use of μέν something that represents a central and original function of the particle. Although any initial act may be said to naturally project by virtue of being initial

[149] See II.3 §73n241 for more instances of μέν used in this way by Pindar. Compare III.4.2 for μέν used by speakers in tragic and comic dialogue to "hold the floor," that is, to extend their utterance over the upcoming line end.

[150] For descriptions of μέν as "inceptive" or "asseverative" see Matthiae 1845:5, Schömann 1862:188, and Denniston 1950^{2}:382-384.

[151] Bakker 1997b:82.

(projection on a macrolevel), this use of μέν should be regarded as pragmatic projection. In practice, instances of μέν at the beginning of a new discourse rarely represent a balanced combination of a μέν and δέ act. Consider the famous beginning of *Olympian* 1:

(t20)

Ἄριστον μὲν ὕδωρ, | ὁ δὲ χρυσὸς | αἰθόμενον πῦρ
ἅτε διαπρέπει νυκτὶ | μεγάνορος ἔξοχα πλούτου· |

Pindar, *Olympian* 1.1-2

Best is water, but that gold, a blazing fire
alike that stands out in the night, beyond lordly wealth.

The priamel to *Olympian* 1 starts with a juxtaposition of water and gold, or so it appears. The particles μέν and δέ in the second position of the first two clauses suggests that we are faced with a classic parallel construction, but the reality is more complex. Gildersleeve's translation nicely brings out the asymmetry in the construction: "...but there is another—gold—a blazing fire like it loometh—a night fire far above all proud wealth."[152] Rather than just an article, ὁ in Pindar is "still largely deictic";[153] because of that and for metrical reasons Gildersleeve translates ὁ δέ as a separate step ("but there is another"), a separate act in our terms. The first act with μέν grounds the song and performance, upon which the next act starting with δέ builds. Then follows another foil before the priamel's climax is reached in line 7. μέν thus marks a discursive beginning, not one half of a syntactically or propositionally symmetrical construction. The fact that μέν so often occurs at the beginning of strophes, antistrophes, epodes, and songs is an extension of this same function.[154]

2.4.2 Small-scope μέν

§57. Until this point, I have focussed on the function of μέν on its own, with large scope, projecting the progression of discourse. We must also consider the construction μέν—δέ, however, which occurs from the earliest Greek literature onward. Since the most basic cue for discursive progress in Homer is δέ,[155] it comes as no surprise that at some stage the frequent act projection of μέν and act introduction of δέ led to a grammaticalization

152 Gildersleeve 1885:129.

153 See II.5 §25 for more on the demonstrative pronoun and the article in Pindar.

154 μέν in peninitial position of a new strophe: *Olympian* 10.64, *Pythian* 3.47 (μὲν ὦν), 4.93, 4.116, 4.139, 5.94, *Nemean* 7.85; antistrophe: *Olympian* 2.48, *Pythian* 3.8, 3.77, *Nemean* 1.62, 11.6, *Isthmian* 4.7 (μὲν ὦν), 4.61; epode: *Olympian* 7.32, *Pythian* 2.65, 4.86, *Isthmian* 1.30; and song: (t20), *Olympian* 9, *Pythian* 4, and *Isthmian* 2. This makes up 22 out of a total of 182 instances of μέν in the *Odes*.

155 See above §§31-36, IV.2.2, and Bonifazi 2015:253.

of the μέν - δέ construction.[156] In this construction, μέν does not project "a continuation of discourse" but it grammatically projects "a δέ act."[157] The following two examples from Pindar illustrate the difference between μέν on its own marking pragmatic projection, and μέν in a μέν - δέ construction:

(t21)

πολλὰ <u>μὲν</u> ἀρτιεπής
γλῶσσά μοι τοξεύματ' ἔχει | περὶ κείνων
κελαδέσαι· | <u>καὶ νῦν</u> (...)

Pindar, *Isthmian* 5.46-48

Many arrows does my fluent
tongue have, about them
to celebrate; and now (...)

In a typical Pindaric transition, the *Isthmian* ode proceeds from the manifold possible topics to the one the composer wants to focus on.[158] μέν creates a ground, yet points ahead,[159] and is followed by καὶ νῦν, which pins down what Pindar will in fact focus on.[160] Some view the relation between the μέν act and what follows as that of general to particular, or of secondary to primary.[161] However, in practice this is often clearly not the case, and moreover when it does occur, it may quite simply reflect the presentation of

[156] Auer 2005:28, "the same linguistic element can either constitute an independent action to be dealt with and responded to, or be a grammatical element of a syntactic construction. There is reason to believe that the second is a grammaticalized version of the first. Vocatives (...) are a case in point." Auer expands on the different uses of the vocative on pages 31-32.

[157] See Ford, Fox, and Thompson 2002:20: "certain recurrent kinds of interactional activities precipitate certain recurrent kinds of grammar, and (...) important cues to an understanding of what grammar is can be found in considering how grammar works in everyday social interactions"; see also Hopper and Traugott 2003.

[158] See also Patten's note (2009:201) on πολλὰ μέν in *Isthmian* 5.46: "...it plays the same role [as πολλά μοι in *Olympian* 2] within the conventional rhetoric of the ode: it *prepares* the listener for the reduction of the theoretically possible diversity of topics (πολλὰ μέν) to the one topic that the singer intends to choose..." [my emphasis].

[159] Especially in this context consider how Cooper 2002:2655 aptly describes the function of μέν: "μέν stops the movement and develops a need for and expectation of reinstituted movement."

[160] See IV.2.4.2 for the generally climactic or pinning-down function of καί; on καί νυν/καὶ νῦν in Pindar, see Privitera 1982:198, Felson 1999:8: "καὶ νῦν, (...) and νῦν δέ (...) regularly function as 'shifters' from mythic time to the epinician here and now," see also Felson 2004:374n21 and 378 with n29.

[161] This is frequently noted as typical of μέν and δέ constructions, e.g. Devarius 1588:123: "Interdum enim universale aliquod proponentes sub μέν particula, postea sub δὲ, strictius aliquod subiicimus," Bäumlein 1861:168-169, and Kühlewein 1870:21.

discourse in order of increasing relevance or importance, more than any particular function of the μέν - δέ construction.

§58. With an apparently similar turn of phrase, Pindar rounds off one of his *Pythian* odes:

(t22)

(...) πολλὰ μὲν κεῖνοι δίκον
φύλλ' ἔπι | καὶ στεφάνους· |
πολλὰ δὲ πρόσθεν πτερὰ δέξατο νικᾶν. |

Pindar, *Pythian* 9.123-125 (end)

(...) Many did they shower
leaves on him and wreaths;
and many wings of victory did he receive before.

Here full symmetry is achieved through the verbal resonance of πολλὰ μέν - πολλὰ δέ, and this parallellism may have been marked prosodically, as happens with juxtapositions in spoken English.[162] Rather than read (t21) as an instance where the δέ component of the juxtaposition is "omitted," one might say conversely that Pindar creates a beautiful symmetry in (t22) by adding a parallel δέ act. In this construction, one can also see how both μέν and δέ have small scope, to emphasize the symmetry. The particle μέν lends itself to this kind of construction, but the occurrence of μέν does not—or at least not in archaic and early classical Greek—*entail* the construction in every instance.[163]

§59. In its use with small scope, which may have been rendered prosodically, μέν has another pragmatic function. As in the μέν - δέ construction, small scope μέν can project something very specific, dependent on the word preceding the particle; one can think for example of ἄλλοτε μέν (which projects ἄλλοτε δέ).[164] A special use of this small-scope μέν is with personal pronouns in the nominative, as in the following example from the *Iliad*. Personified Sleep reminds Hera of a time that Hera had commanded Sleep to distract Zeus:

162 Compare the instance in *Pythian* 6.23 (t12) where the μέν act is also part of a closed juxtaposition. About the so-called "list intonation," see, for example, Liberman and Pierrehumbert 1984, Selkirk 1984 (English), and Truckenbrodt 2004 (southern German); see also IV.2.3.7 for a link with τε.

163 This was the belief of Hoogeveen 1796:660-672, Thiersch 1826:571-576, and Bury 1892b; consider also the comment of the scholiast to μέν in *Iliad* 4.301: ποῦ ὁ δέ; ("Where is the δέ?"), see I.2 §44.

164 *Iliad* 18.472, 21.464, 23.368, 24.530; *Odyssey* 4.102, 5.331, 11.303, 16.209, 23.94.

(t23)

ἤτοι | ἐγὼ μὲν ἔλεξα Διὸς νόον αἰγιόχοιο |
νήδυμος ἀμφιχυθείς· | σὺ δέ οἱ κακὰ μήσαο θυμῷ |
ὄρσασ' ἀργαλέων ἀνέμων ἐπὶ πόντον ἀήτας, |

Iliad 14.252-254

Yes, *I* put the the aegis-bearing Zeus to sleep,
sweet me shed about him, and *you* contrived evil for him in your mind
stirring up blasts of cruel winds on the sea,

Examples like this are rare in Homer, but in this instance there appears to be a close relation between ἐγὼ μέν and σὺ δέ. That is to say, uttering ἐγὼ μέν, when the particle has small scope, limits the possibilities of the following to σὺ δέ, ὑμεῖς δέ, ὁ δέ, or similar.[165] This projection can even reach across utterances, see this example from Aeschylus (— marks a new speaker):

(t24)

Χ. τοὖργον εἰργάσθαι δοκεῖ μοι βασιλέως οἰμώγμασιν·
ἀλλὰ κοινωσώμεθ' ἤν πως ἀσφαλῆ βουλεύματ' ᾖι.
— ἐγὼ μὲν ὑμῖν τὴν ἐμὴν γνώμην λέγω,
πρὸς δῶμα δεῦρ' ἀστοῖσι κηρύσσειν βοήν.
— ἐμοὶ δ' ὅπως τάχιστά γ' ἐμπεσεῖν δοκεῖ
καὶ πρᾶγμ' ἐλέγχειν σὺν νεορρύτωι ξίφει.

Aeschylus, *Agamemnon* 1346-1351

Chorus: The deed is done, it seems to me by the king's cries.
Now let us deliberate if perchance there is a safe course of action.
— *I* tell you what I think:
to proclaim a call to the citizens to return to the palace.
— It seems to *me* that we should barge in as soon as possible,
and prove the fact with a newly-blooded sword.

The chorus hear Agamemnon's cries as he is attacked, and consider what to do. The deliberations proceed chorus member by chorus member, each sharing his thoughts. The first chorus member in the excerpt starts his utterance with ἐγὼ μέν, which implicitly

[165] The parallels of ἐγὼ μέν are *Iliad* 22.123; *Odyssey* 11.82, 15.515, 17.593, 22.367.

juxtaposes his opinion to the others to follow.[166] Two lines later, a second speaker starts with ἐμοὶ δέ, reacting to the first speaker and continuing the discussion of possible courses of action that runs on until line 1371. That is to say, μέν serves to project an act or in this case utterance that is in a significant way parallel to the present act: it has small scope, which limits the possibilities of what follows. The projection is fulfilled with δέ in the following utterance.[167]

§60. If μέν can thus project a δέ act across speakers, it follows that μέν can be used to exploit this function even when the projection is never fulfilled.[168] In (t25) μέν projects a specific act, which remains unspoken:

(t25)

Ath. οὔκουν γέλως ἥδιστος εἰς ἐχθροὺς γελᾶν;
Od. ἐμοὶ μὲν ἀρκεῖ τοῦτον ἐν δόμοις μένειν.
Ath. μεμηνότ' ἄνδρα περιφανῶς ὀκνεῖς ἰδεῖν;
Od. φρονοῦντα γάρ νιν οὐκ ἂν ἐξέστην ὄκνῳ.

Sophocles, *Ajax* 79-82

Ath. Is it not the sweetest laughter to laugh at enemies?
Od. *Well*, it suffices for me if he stays in the house.
Ath. Do you shrink from seeing a man who is clearly mad?
Od. If he had been sane I would not have avoided him in fear!

Athena tries to convince Odysseus to gloat over the downfall of Ajax, but Odysseus is hesitant, and uses ἐμοὶ μέν to disalign himself with Athena: "it suffices for *me* if he stays in the house. [But *you* do not seem to agree.]" Quite specifically, in instances like (t25) μέν locates the referent over which it has scope (ἐμοί) with respect to other available (textually explicit or implicit) referents.[169] This use of μέν is especially frequent in drama.[170]

§61. Small-scope μέν following a pronoun or name can thus create a contrast by projecting a viewpoint that differs at least in part from the one held by the first referent.

[166] See Chafe 1994:77 on the influence of the factor of contrastiveness on pronoun selection in English; see also II.5 §§41-43 for the use of ὅ γε to mark contrastiveness.

[167] See III.4 §§37-38 on the rarity of turn-initial δέ in responses of one speaker to another.

[168] See for the possible effects of unfulfilled projection Auer 2005:25-27.

[169] The pragmatic force of such answers beginning with μέν approaches that of "well" in question—answer sequences. Lakoff 1973:463 describes its use in answers when the speaker "senses some sort of insufficiency in his answer, whether *because he is leaving it to the questioner to fill in information on his own or because he is about to give additional information himself*" [my italics]. Schiffrin 1987:126-127 offers a slightly different analysis of this function of "well," she explains it as marking how the upcoming statement will not directly answer the *expectations* of the interlocutor; this latter approach is endorsed by Blakemore 2002:133.

[170] See Denniston 1950²:380-382 for parallels.

As we explore in a later chapter (II.5), γε after names or pronouns can have the same pragmatic effect of creating contrast, but for a different reason. Whereas μέν creates contrast through projection of another referent (who is often later expressed), γε creates it through emphasis on the current referent.[171]

§62. Projection can account for a range of pragmatic functions that μέν has in Homer, Pindar, and beyond. First, the particle serves as metalanguage to guide the hearer through the discourse, often foreshadowing transitions to new moves within the discourse. In this function, its scope extends over its entire host act, and there is no particular relation between μέν and the word that precedes it. Second, μέν can have scope over the preceding word, with a range of possible effects. In Homer and Pindar not every μέν entails a δέ: when μέν has large scope, the projection can be fulfilled with any particle that can continue the discourse, or no particle at all. If μέν has small scope, it most typically forms part of a μέν - δέ construction, which in later literature covers the majority of μέν instances.

2.5 Priming Acts

§63. Projection is omnipresent in ancient Greek discourse, reaching far beyond the specialized lexical item μέν. It manifests itself in syntactic constructions, semantic interlinking, and discourse articulation. In contemporary texts, an indentation creates certain expectations in the reader about the relation between the upcoming discourse and the preceding discourse (some kind of discontinuity) and about the nature of the upcoming discourse (in some way coherent). In spoken discourse other tools are available to obtain similar effects, first and foremost utterance- and sentence-initial discourse markers, which are generally intonationally independent from what follows (such as "First, I would like to welcome you all" or "Sadly, Sarah could not make it").[172] This section focuses on short acts in epic and lyric that share important characteristics with such discourse markers, especially their syntactic and presumably prosodic independence, which creates a projecting effect over the following discourse. The acts under examination are those consisting of nothing more than a (pro)noun and a particle, which reflect *ad hoc* cognitive processing while projecting the referent's relevance for the upcoming discourse. I propose to call such phenomena priming acts.[173] In the section on Homeric discourse the focus is on the narrative function of these priming acts, while the section

[171] See II.5.3.2 on ὅ γε in Homer and III.4 §§62-64 on γε in turn-initial position tragic and comic dialogue.

[172] For sentence adverbials in English see e.g. Swan 1988; Schiffrin 1987:228-266 discusses the discourse marking function of temporal adverbs like "now" and "then."

[173] See De Kreij 2016. The term builds on Emmott 1997:123, who uses "priming" to describe the activation of a contextual frame.

on Pindaric song considers the performative effect of priming acts involving a second-person pronoun.

2.5.1 Priming acts in Homeric narrative

§64. To illustrate the nature of priming acts, consider again Bakker's reading of *Iliad* 7.313-314 (see t5), repeated here. Each line represents, in Bakker's terms, one chunk or intonation unit, forward slash (/) marks hexameter end:

(t26)

οἱ δ' ὅτε δὴ
κλισίῃσιν ἐν Ἀτρεΐδαο γένοντο, /
τοῖσι δὲ βοῦν ἱέρευσεν
ἄναξ ἀνδρῶν Ἀγαμέμνων /

Iliad 7.313-314, as given in Bakker 1997b:97

The boundary marker δή is, without further explanation, put here in fourth position of an intonation unit.[174] In performance, it is not inconceivable that οἱ δ' ὅτε δὴ was performed as part of one intonation unit.[175] Cognitively, however, the first intonation unit in (t26) contains two acts, or rather one act and the beginning of a second, which concludes with the second chunk in Bakker's division. Consider again my alternative presentation of line 313:

(t27)

οἱ δ' | ὅτε δὴ κλισίῃσιν ἐν Ἀτρεΐδαο γένοντο, |
τοῖσι δὲ βοῦν ἱέρευσεν | ἄναξ ἀνδρῶν Ἀγαμέμνων

Iliad 7.313-314

And when they came to the huts of the son of Atreus,
then did the lord of men, Agamemnon, slay a bull

Translation Murray

174 δή in Homer as a rule has the second position in clause or subclause, and can only be moved by another first- or second-position word. The clear exceptions to this rule are the instances of δὴ τότε and δὴ γάρ, where δή is in first position. A possible counterexample is *Iliad* 7.359 εἰ δ' ἐτεὸν δή, but the scholia already regarded it as a problematic passage, probably because of the position of δή, and Aristarchus did not in fact read the δέ. More on the different aspects of Homeric δή in II.3.3.

175 See the discussion of the example in §26 above.

When we read these two lines as four acts—with the nominative ἄναξ ἀνδρῶν Ἀγαμέμνων taken as a separate act expanding the subject contained within ἱέρευσεν - οἱ δ' turns out to be a subject without a verb, a phenomenon generally called a pendant nominative.[176] Most translations, like Murray's above, solve this problem by taking the pronoun as the subject of the following act (a subclause). As a result, the independence of the pronoun is lost in the translation, obscuring the emergent discourse articulation.[177] Consider an alternative translation:

(t28)

> And they, when they came to the tents of Atreus' son,
> for them he sacrificed a bull, Agamemnon lord of men.

Syntactically, the isolation of οἱ δ' is troubling, which is probably why instances such as this one are generally read as Murray does, without further discussion.

§65. Fraenkel had already noted the existence of such short initial *kôla* containing particles like μέν, δέ, τε, and others in second position.[178] He notes that when a constituent is brought to the front of the sentence, it receives strong emphasis:

(t29)

> "Ein starkes Pointieren einzelner Satzglieder wird auch da hervorgerufen, wo (...) ein Glied in auffälliger Weise an die Spitze des Satzes gerückt und so bis zu einem gewissen Grade isoliert wird."[179]
>
> Fraenkel 1933:336

176 See for example Chantraine 1953a. Ruijgh 1990 and De Jong in her 2012 commentary on *Iliad* 22 use this term with little elaboration. When the noun or pronoun at the head of the sentence is not a nominative but in another case, the grammars speak of prolepsis. Bertrand 2010 applies a pragmatic model to word order in Homer, and regards these constructions as "undetermined" (page 322, "indeterminée").

177 Murray's reading, tacitly accepted by many, may be based on the assumption that for some reason ὅτε δή as a unit is transposed until after the pronoun, some sort of anastrophe, to avoid the metrically intractable *ὅθ' οἱ δή or equivalent. However, this reasoning is insufficient. After all, there are adequate metrical equivalents for this construction, especially ἀλλ' ὅτε δή and καὶ ῥ' ὅτε. Thus, if indeed this construction is some transposition of ὅτε, the reason is most likely not metrical. Rather, it appears that the desire to use the nominative pronoun, which is syntactically optional, demands this construction rather than another.

178 Though sometimes discourse unit-final; see Fraenkel 1933:337, where he gives a few examples of summarizing *kôla*.

179 "A strong emphasis on individual constituents is also accomplished there, where (...) a constituent is conspicuously put at the head of the sentence, and is thus isolated up to a point."

As Fraenkel saw, the act containing the pronoun + particle is a normal and productive rather than anacolouthic construction.[180] Classicists have more recently described the phenomenon in Greek as a sign of "oral syntax, "[181] a characterization that, like earlier views, marks this kind of construction as divergent from a supposed standard syntax.

§66. At certain points in narratives, but also in other kinds of discourse, we find such short discourse acts, comprising a (pro)noun and often a particle, set apart from their main verb by a participle, adverbial phrase, or temporal subclause, or even lacking a main verb, as in (t28). These acts make sense if we consider their possible function not at the level of the sentence, but of the larger discourse. From that perspective *Iliad* 7.313, for example, reveals itself as a narrative transition. In fact, Murray indents the line, which suggests that he interprets it as the start of a new scene or episode. At the beginning of this new scene, its main characters are activated and primed first of all, with the pronoun, before moving on to a new action: the priming act aids the redirection of the audience's attention.

§67. In contemporary linguistic studies scholars have observed a similar phenomenon in spoken language, generally called left dislocation.[182] More specifically relevant is Ochs Keenan and Schieffelin's discussion of a phenomenon that they call referent + proposition.[183] In these constructions, the subject of a proposition is presented as a separate intonation unit, followed by a proposition with the subject repeated (or changed). Consider the following typical example:

180 Compare ὁ δ' followed by a participle in *Iliad* 6.510-511 ὁ δ' ἀγλαΐηφι πεποιθώς / ῥίμφα ἑ γοῦνα φέρει; Slings 1992b:100 says about this example: "[f]rom a point of view of oral communication (...) the sentence is completely well-formed." Like Slings, Goldstein 121-171 applies an information structure approach to such constructions. On pages 136-143 he discusses what I call priming acts in fifth-century prose in terms of "new subjects" and "topic resumption," among other things.

181 De Jong 2012:122 ad *Iliad* 22.248-249: "... a pendant nominative (or frame) (...) This is a fairly common phenomenon in the Homeric epics, a clear manifestation of their oral syntax"; Hajnal 2004:243-244 calls the construction of verse-final αὐτάρ Ἀθήνη in *Odyssey* 6.2 a "Spur mündlicher Syntax," ("a trace of oral syntax"); see also Slings 1992b, referred to above.

182 Established by Van Riemsdijk and Zwarts 1974 (re-published in 1997), see also Ochs Keenan and Schieffelin 1976, Geluykens 1992, Pekarek Doehler 2011b. Ochs Keenan and Schieffelin 1976:240-241 already eschewed the term "left-dislocation," and more recently Pekarek Doehler 2011b:50 has added that she finds "such a view (..) both pragmatically and cognitively implausible."
The verse-final αὐτὰρ+(pro)noun construction (see t32) is another good illustration of the problem of the term left-dislocation. Because of its position at verse end, it is in the right periphery of the performative unit, i.e. the hexameter verse, and probably in some way independent from the rest of the line. Syntactically it may be in the left periphery of its sentence, but most importantly, it is both performatively and syntactically independent. A more promising approach is to regard the act not at the level of the sentence, but at the level of discourse. From that angle, the act is neither left nor right of anything, and least of all is it dislocated in any way. Rather, it is exactly where it should be to provide a cognitive reorientation.

183 See also Berrendonner 1990:29 on "syntagme nominal + proposition": the referent "nomme ou met en mémoire un objet de connaissance que Z [sc. the proposition] présuppose ensuite comme thème."

(t30)

"My sister, she and her boyfriend just broke up..."

Ochs Keenan and Schieffelin 1976:243 (adapted)

As οἱ δέ in (t27), the noun phrase "My sister" stands on it own: it does not form part of a clause finished at a later point. Chafe discusses the same kind of construction, but he calls the initial unit an "isolated referent." In his analysis of oral narratives he comes to the conclusion that "[i]t is not unusual for an intonation unit to verbalize little or nothing more than a referent."[184] Left-dislocated elements in contemporary discourse are typically associated with topic status: the terms found in the left periphery of the sentence often reflect what a significant part of the upcoming discourse is about.[185]

§68. Greek is a Pro-Drop language, which means that its verb forms do not require the addition of a grammatical subject in the nominative. Since a nominative is often not strictly speaking necessary, its addition can be regarded as marked. This brings us to examples like the following passage, where the referent in the priming act takes the form of a name, and the main clause has a coreferential verb:

(t31)

Τηλέμαχος δ', | ὅθι οἱ θάλαμος περικαλλέος αὐλῆς
ὑψηλὸς δέδμητο | περισκέπτῳ ἐνὶ χώρῳ |
ἔνθ' ἔβη εἰς εὐνὴν | πολλὰ φρεσὶ μερμηρίζων |

Odyssey 1.425-427

And Telemachus, where for him the bedroom of the magnificent house
was built up high, in a place with a view,
there he went to his bed, pondering many things in his mind.

In this example the name in the priming act (Τηλέμαχος) cannot be constructed with the verb in the immediately following act (δέδμητο), since it is not coreferential: it supports the validity of likewise regarding οἱ δέ as independent in (t27).[186] Here, Telemachus is

[184] Chafe 1994:67, and on page 68: "[t]ypically, such *isolated referents* (expressed as so-called free NPs) are subsequently included as participants in events and states. But intonation units like these show that it is quite possible for speakers to focus on a referent alone" [italics original].

[185] I use "topic" in the sense of discourse topic, as described by Brown and Yule 1983:71; see also Chafe 2001:673-674.

[186] Consider also *Odyssey* 13.81-88 ἡ δ' | ὥς τ' ἐν πεδίῳ τετράοροι ἄρσενες ἵπποι (...) ὣς ἡ ῥίμφα θέουσα θαλάσσης κύματ' ἔταμνεν. Here after the loading of the ship and two lines about Odysseus falling asleep, the attention is directed back to the ship, captured in nothing more than a feminine pronoun. After the pronoun a simile that introduces a new subject begins. This

singled out from a larger group and remains the main referent in the last lines of book one of the *Odyssey*. Despite the slight variations in form, in all incarnations the priming act reflects a cognitive process: the reorientation of the mind's eye. From a discourse perspective, these priming acts typically occur at narrative transitions, redirecting the joint attention of the performer and audience to a character that has been out of focus for a time. When a referent is retrieved in a priming act, it creates an expectation of (i.e. projects) an upcoming action done by (or to, if the (pro)noun is in an oblique case)[187] the character.

§69. In a long and complex narrative, neither the audience nor the performer can keep track of every detail or character in the imagined world. Rather, a traditional storyworld is a construction based on the discourse as well as the whole body of knowledge and assumptions about that world shared by audience and performer.[188] A great deal of cognitive processing is involved in keeping track of who is where doing what at any particular point in the narrative. For this complex task the mind is well equipped, and Emmott has studied this cognitive process for readers of English literature. She speaks of "contextual frames," a concept that regards people and places in a narrative as interconnected in networks.

§70. Emmott describes how characters are bound to certain places in the storyworld unless we are cued to change our knowledge of their location. The storyworld is only theoretically a whole world: in practice it is a string of discrete spaces containing certain characters and thus not others.[189] "Thus a narrative has *regions*, filled by *landmarks* (=reference objects) through which a *path* is established."[190] Just as one word or construction will activate a whole semantic frame, the mention of one referent will make the entire contextual frame accessible. Thus a priming act can accomplish more than just re-orient the performer's and audience's attention on a specific character. The reference

construction with a simile (there are 9 parallels in Homer: *Iliad* 4.433, 11.67, 12.167, 13.62, 15.271, 15.323, 15.381, 16.428; *Odyssey* 22.302) clearly demonstrates that the initial (pro)noun is syntactically independent. For the function of τε in similes see II.4.3.1.

187 Note that when the pronoun in the priming act is in the nominative a following complementary construction is optional (pragmatic projection) whereas if the pronoun is in an oblique case, it is always integrated into a construction (syntactic projection).

188 The concept of a storyworld, or the mental representation of the implied (and not always explicitly discussed) world where a narrative takes place, comes from Herman 2002. For the storyworld as a mental representation of the narrative, see II.4.1.

189 Some places are of a specific "nature," such as Olympus, which has an effect on its contextual frame (some characters are naturally assumed to be there unless we know otherwise, while other characters are by nature excluded from the space).

190 Landau and Jackendoff 1993:223; compare Chafe 1979:179: "Rather than think of an experience as being stored in memory in terms of distinct episodes, it seems preferable to think of a more complex storage in terms of coherent spaces, coherent temporal continuities, coherent configurations of characters, coherent event sequences, and coherent worlds."

to a character activates the entire contextual frame to which the character is bound.[191] That is to say, the priming act has a potential double relevance: it is quite likely that it had a performative relevance in allowing the audience to follow the complex narrative of long epics, but it is also quite possible that the language accommodates the cognitive processing of the Homeric performer as he produces his instantiation of, for example, the story of how Telemachus reaches the decision to stand up to the suitors, in the first book of the *Odyssey* (t31). They might be signs of the performer navigating his memory by navigating the storyworld, moving from place to place and focusing on different characters as they become relevant.[192]

§71. In the ongoing narrative, priming acts may also serve to prime a character that has been covertly present in the ongoing contextual frame.[193] This is what happens in example (t32): after a long speech by Telemachus, at which Odysseus and the suitors are present, Odysseus is set apart from the others (πάντες) and primed as the character whom we will be following in the upcoming stretch of narrative.[194]

(t32)

ὣς ἔφαθ', | οἱ δ' ἄρα πάντες ἐπῄνεον. | <u>αὐτὰρ Ὀδυσσεύς</u> |
ζώσατο μὲν ῥάκεσιν περὶ μήδεα, | φαῖνε δὲ μηροὺς

Odyssey 18.66-67

Thus he [sc. Telemachus] spoke, and they all approved. And Odysseus,
he girded rags around his loins, and he showed his thighs

Here the act αὐτὰρ Ὀδυσσεύς is divided from what follows by verse end, as well as the boundary marker μέν in the following line.[195] Denniston says the following about such constructions:

[191] This is what Emmott 1997:123 calls "priming." Sometimes this priming of an entire new scene is encoded in the rest of the verse, as for example in *Iliad* 6.237-238: Ἕκτωρ δ' | ὡς Σκαιάς τε πύλας καὶ φηγὸν ἵκανεν / ἀμφ' ἄρα μιν, and 6.323-324: Ἀργείη δ' Ἑλένη | μετ' ἄρα δμῳῇσι γυναιξὶν / ἧστο.

[192] See Schank and Abelson 1977:19: "If we ask a man 'Who was your girlfriend in 1968?' and ask him to report his strategy for the answer, his reply is roughly: 'First I thought about where I was and what I was doing in 1968. Then I remembered who I used to go out with then.' (...) Lists of 'past girlfriends' do not exist in memory. Such a list must be constructed. The process by which that list is constructed is a search through episodes *organized around times and locations in memory*" [my emphasis]. For Schank and Abelson's work on "scripts" see II.4 §§46-47.

[193] See Emmott 1997:122-126 for overt and covert characters in contextual frames.

[194] This reading is supported by Bonifazi's recent work on the particle αὐτάρ; see Bonifazi 2012:218-243. On page 222 she speaks of "the visual and presentational function of αὐτάρ."

[195] See Kahane 1994:114-119 on the name Odysseus in verse-final position; Clark 1997:107-158 (especially 140-142) calls such line endings that open new narrative units "bucolic anticipations."

(t33)

> "Normally μέν and δέ stand second in their respective clauses, and everything between the last stop and the word preceding μέν applies to the whole μέν... δέ complex. (Strictly speaking, one should say, not 'clause' but 'word-group', which does not necessarily coincide with punctuation.)"
>
> Denniston 1950²:371

This clearly holds for (t32), where αὐτὰρ Ὀδυσσεύς provides the "subject" of both the μέν and the following δέ clause. However, Denniston fails to address the question of why this construction occurs, nor does he allow for the fact that the act preceding the μέν - δέ construction may project beyond it (i.e. "apply" to more than "the whole μέν...δέ complex").[196] The priming act αὐτὰρ Ὀδυσσεύς redirects the performer's and audience's focus, and projects the character's relevance for the upcoming discourse.[197] It may not be a coincidence that this kind of short act, which occurs in a myriad of contexts, has been incorporated in the quasi-fixed constructions of the form X δ' | ὅτε δή, X δ' | ἐπεὶ οὖν (and 3x τ' ἐπεὶ οὖν), and X δ' | ὥς οὖν. The beginnings of new scenes, often marked by indentation in the editions, typically require extra attention to be placed on particular referents. In such contexts, priming acts have become part of the verse that concerns itself with framing the upcoming scene.[198]

2.5.2 Priming acts in Pindar

§72. Narrative priming acts are especially suited to the performance situation of the Homeric epics, but they can be found even in Pindar's songs. [199] Examples of the kind described above are few, however, and the units are syntactically fully integrated, as opposed to many instances in Homer. The following passage may function as an exemplar of the narrative priming act in Pindar:

196 Moreover, the act preceding a μέν - δέ construction can take many forms, and it can be only a particle. See IV.2.4.4 for the construction καὶ | X μέν.

197 Here again the terminology of projection is informative, as Streeck and Jordan 2009:95 define "pre's" as "the small behavioral units that precede larger behavioral units or adjustments."

198 See De Kreij 2016; the instances of these constructions are: (X δ' ὅτε δή) *Iliad* 1.432, 3.15, 4.446, 5.14, 5.630, 5.850, 6.121, 7.313, 8.60, 9.669, 10.180, 10.526, 11.232, 11.618, 13.240, 13.604, 16.462, 18.67, 18.520, 20.29, 20.176, 21.148, 22.248, 23.38; *Odyssey* 1.126, 1.332, 2.314, 6.85, 7.3, 16.324, 18.208, 18.217, 19.532, 21.42, 21.63, 24.362; (X δ' ὡς οὖν) *Iliad* 3.21, 3.30, 3.154, 5.95, 5.711, 7.17, 8.251, 11.248, 11.575, 11.581, 14.440, 16.419, 17.198, 18.222, 18.530, 21.49, 21.418; *Odyssey* 3.34, 8.272, 15.59, 17.492, 22.407, 24.232, 24.391; (X δ' επεὶ οὖν) *Iliad* 1.57, 2.661, 3.340, 4.382, 5.573, 10.272, 11.642, 13.1, 16.394, 18.333, 22.475, 23.813, 24.329, 24.587; *Odyssey* 4.49, 8.372, 8.454, 16.478, 17.88, 19.213, 19.251, 21.57, 21.273, 23.300, 24.384, 24.489.

199 The occurrence of the priming act outside epic may suggest that the construction was simply entrenched in language, quite independently of epic. In any case, the priming act serves an important function in accommodating the cognitive processing of performer and audience.

(t34)

(…) βασιλεὺς δ' | ἐπεί
πετραέσσας ἐλαύνων ἵκετ' ἐκ Πυθῶνος | ἅπαντας ἐν οἴκῳ
49 εἴρετο παῖδα | τὸν Εὐάδνα τέκοι |
(…)
52 ὣς ἄρα μάνυε. | τοὶ δ' | οὔτ' ὦν ἀκοῦσαι |
οὔτ' ἰδεῖν εὔχοντο (…)

Pindar, *Olympian* 6.47-49 and 52-53

(…) *And the king*, when
he came driving out of rocky Pytho, everyone in the house
49 he asked <about> the child, whom Euadne bore,
(…)
52 Thus he prophesied. *And they*, neither having heard,
nor having seen it they swore (…)

In this passage in *Olympian* 6, where king Aipytus returns from Pytho to search for Iamos, the offspring of Euadne and Apollo, the priming act | βασιλεὺς δέ | effects a transition back to the king, who is subject and protagonist for the next five lines. The isolated | τοὶ δ' | in line 52 effects another transition, this time to the king's listeners, who had been passive bystanders until then.[200] In both cases the nominatives fit neatly into the syntactic structure, but as in the Homeric examples their function is not to be sought on a syntactic level only. Here, too, the priming acts function as cognitive pivots, accommodating the redirection of attention.[201]

2.5.2.1 Pindaric priming acts with second-person pronouns

§73. The Pindaric corpus features a different category of priming act, which may serve to illustrate a generic difference between epic and lyric. As songs composed for an occasion and for a specific audience, Pindar's *Victory Odes* display a more direct interaction

[200] The other instances of priming acts in narratives are: *Olympian* 6.39: ἁ δὲ | φοινικόκροκον ζώναν καταθηκάμενα; *Olympian* 8.67: ὃς | τύχᾳ μέν; *Olympian* 10.43: ὁ δ'ἄρ' | ἐν Πίσᾳ ἔλσαις; *Pythian* 4.111: τοὶ μ' | ἐπεὶ; *Pythian* 9.18: ἁ μὲν | οὔθ' ἱστῶν; *Pythian* 9.111: πατὴρ δὲ | θυγατρὶ φυτεύων; *Nemean* 1.43: ὁ δ' | ὀρθὸν μὲν ἄντεινεν κάρα ; *Nemean* 5.25: αἱ δὲ | πρώτιστον μέν; *Isthmian* 6.41: ὁ δ' | ἀνατείναις οὐρανῷ. A slightly larger fronted unit is found in *Pythian* 3.100: τοῦ δὲ παῖς | ὅνπερ. Not narrative, but similar in function are *Olympian* 1.30: Χάρις δ' | ἅπερ ἅπαντα τεύχει τὰ μείλιχα θνατοῖς | ἐπιφέρουσα τιμὰν | καὶ ἄπιστον ἐμήσατο πιστόν ἔμμεναι τὸ πολλάκις and *Olympian* 6.80: κεῖνος | ὦ παῖ Σωστράτου.

[201] See also *Olympian* 7.49: κείνοις | ὁ μέν, for an instance where the pronoun is in the dative, and its referent is thus primed as the patient in a following event.

between performer and audience than the Homeric epics do. As a result, priming acts in Pindar typically do not shift perspective or focus solely *within* the storyworld, but shift from one world to the other, such as from the storyworld to the *hic et nunc*.[202] Second-person discourse is especially effective for moving out of the storyworld and into the here and now. Even in the interactive performance situation of Pindaric song, a singular or plural second-person reference has a strong effect. In the following paragraphs I show how the disruptive effect of a transition to second-person discourse can be linked to the occurrence of second-person pronouns in priming acts.[203] These priming acts can take different forms, and can be syntactically integrated to greater or lesser extent into the following discourse. Finally I discuss the frequent co-occurrence of second-person priming acts and names in the vocative.

§74. Pindaric discourse is a complex negotiation between speakers and addressees, who can be physically present (the performer(s), the audience, the victor, and his clan), vicariously present (as the composer through his song), or treated as present (ancestors, heroes, and gods). That is to say, not every "you" has to refer to someone physically present at the performance.[204] When a second-person pronoun or verb occurs at the beginning of a new act or move, moreover, the audience cannot know who is being addressed unless it is made clear through extra-linguistic means, or until the addressee's identity is specified in what follows.[205] Therefore, when a you-reference occurs (especially outside direct speech), the audience cannot but be highly involved.[206] More than third-person forms, and even more than first-person references, second-person forms create an immediacy in the performance that lends itself well to transitions in the discourse, and especially to marking an upcoming passage as significant.

§75. Taking into account this performative effect of you-references, it is not surprising that we often find a second-person pronoun occurring in a priming act, as at the end of *Nemean* 3:

[202] Apart from priming acts, which consist of (pro)nouns and particles, different but comparable constructions occur at discourse transitions in Pindar: *Olympian* 1.67 πρὸς εὐάνθεμον δ' | ὅτε φυάν, 6.4 εἰ δ' | εἴη μὲν, 10.45, περὶ δὲ πάξαις | Ἄλτιν μὲν ὅγ', 13.104 νῦν δ' | ἔλπομαι μέν; *Pythian* 1.17-18 νῦν γε μάν | ταί θ' ὑπὲρ Κύμας, 1.75-76 ἀρέομαι | πὰρ μὲν Σαλαμῖνος; *Nemean* 9.39 λέγεται μάν | Ἕκτορι μέν, 10.90 ἀνά δ' | ἔλυσεν μέν, 11.11 ἄνδρα δ' ἐγὼ | μακαρίζω μέν, 11.29 ἀλλὰ βροτῶν | τὸν μέν; *Isthmian* 2.41 ἀλλ' ἐπέρα | ποτί μὲν, 8.11 ἀλλ' ἐμοὶ | δεῖμα μέν.

[203] "Second-person priming acts" are all those instances where a second-person pronoun makes up a separate discourse act, typically accompanied by one or more particles.

[204] This aspect of Pindaric performance is discussed in Felson 1999 and 2004; Bonifazi 2004a:396-400 discusses the range of functions of "you"-reference in Pindar.

[205] See Bonifazi 2004a:400 on *Isthmian* 6.19 ὔμμε τ' | ὦ χρυσάρματοι Αἰακίδαι: ὔμμε can be "an *am Phantasma* reference to the Aeginetan ancestors, an ocular reference to some artistic representation of the Aeacids, or an ocular reference to the Aeginetan clan."

[206] See for example Felson 2004:382-383 on the second-person forms in *Pythian* 9.90-100.

(t35)

(…) ἔστι δ᾽ αἰετὸς ὠκὺς ἐν ποτανοῖς, |
ὃς ἔλαβεν αἶψα, | τηλόθε μεταμαιόμενος, | δαφοινὸν ἄγραν ποσίν· |
κραγέται δὲ κολοιοὶ ταπεινὰ νέμονται. |
τίν γε μέν, | εὐθρόνου Κλεοῦς ἐθελοίσας, | ἀεθλοφόρου λήματος ἕνεκεν |
Νεμέας Ἐπιδαυρόθεν τ᾽ ἄπο καὶ Μεγάρων δέδορκεν φάος. |

Pindar, *Nemean* 3.80-84 (end)

(…) The eagle is swift among birds:
he seizes quickly, chasing from afar, the bloodied prey with his claws.
And the chatterers, the jackdaws live down below.
And for *you*, by the will of fair-throned Kleo, because of a desire to win,
out of Nemea, from Epidauros, and out of Megara *light has gleamed*.

The last epode of the song starts with a metaphor that sets up a comparison between the eagle, best of birds, and the victor.[207] Then in line 83 we find a priming act that consists of the dative τίν and the particles γε and μέν. Unlike the nominatives in Homer, discussed above, the pronoun here is fully part of the syntactical construction, but the verb and subject that complete the construction are postponed to the very end of the song (δέδορκεν φάος). A priming act in this form, consisting of a second-person pronoun and a particle, is comparatively rare in Homer.[208]

§76. In (t35), I take μέν as the Ionic variant of μάν in a cluster with γε. The function of γε μέν is not to mark an adversative relation (Denniston 1950²:387, with Bowra's reading of the passage), but to mark a conceptual connection. As in the cluster νῦν γε μάν, the first word (τίν) introduces a concept ("the present" for νῦν and "the victor" for τίν) that is emphatically juxtaposed with the preceding. The juxtaposition is in itself neutral, but in the majority of instances of γε μέν/γε μάν the relation between the preceding and the

[207] With Bury 1890:60-61 and Pfeijffer 1999:418 (who reads μέν differently). Bowra, conversely, reads the eagle as referring only to Pindar, and regards the image as unconnected to the final praise of the victor.

[208] One possible exception with σὺ δέ is *Odyssey* 17.379 σὺ δὲ | καί ποθι τόνδ᾽ ἐκάλεσσας, and with ὑμεῖς *Iliad* 7.73 ὑμῖν δ᾽ | ἐν γὰρ, 13.116 ὑμεῖς δ᾽ | οὐκέτι; *Odyssey* 20.266 ὑμεῖς δέ | μνηστῆρες. In Homer ἀλλὰ σύ is more frequent, with the inherent reorienting function of ἀλλά: *Iliad* 1.393 ἀλλὰ σὺ | εἰ δύνασαί γε, 9.600 ἀλλὰ σὺ | μή μοι, 18.134 ἀλλὰ σὺ μὲν | μή πω; *Odyssey* 16.256 ἀλλὰ σύ γ᾽ | εἰ δύνασαί τιν᾽ and especially 21.234 ἀλλὰ σύ | δῖ᾽ Εὔμαιε; Drummen 2009 explores the reorienting function of ἀλλά in Greek drama.

following tends to be one of similarity rather than one of difference.[209] Here, eagle and victor are united by the conceit of distant sight; the eagle sees things from afar (τηλόθε), while the victor has light gleaming from afar on his behalf. Despite the syntactic integration of τίν here, the act τίν γε μέν has a force of its own. Irrespective of what follows, the second-person reference at once redirects attention to the "you," linking the victor to the image of the eagle. By emphatically directing attention to the victor at the end of the song, the most important person of the event is primed and will remain in the audience's mind even when the music dies down.

§77. The cognitive and performative usefulness of second-person priming acts like the one in (t35) readily suggests itself: just like priming acts that occur in narrative, these redirect joint attention to a new referent. This referent may be physically present at the performance, such as the victor or a member of his clan,[210] or not.[211] Since even deceased people, heroes, and gods can be made present through Pindar's use of "you," the potential absence of the referent does not significantly influence the performative impact of uttering the second-person pronoun.[212] The performative effect, in turn, leads to a higher level of audience involvement directly following the priming act. As a result, second-person pronouns have a natural place right before discursive peaks, such as the final line of the song in (t35). The position of the priming act has a particularly poignant peak effect in the second epode of *Isthmian* 7:

(t36)

ἴστω γὰρ σαφὲς | ὅστις ἐν ταύτᾳ νεφέλᾳ χάλαζαν αἵματος πρὸ φίλας
πάτρας ἀμύνεται, |

†λοιγὸν ἀμύνων† ἐναντίῳ στρατῷ, |
ἀστῶν γενεᾷ μέγιστον κλέος αὔξων |

209 νῦν γε μάν occurs in *Pythian* 1.17 and 1.50; νῦν γε μέν in *Pythian* 4.50, and the remaining instances of γε μέν/γε μάν are *Olympian* 12.5, *Olympian* 13.104, *Pythian* 3.88, *Pythian* 7.19, *Nemean* 8.50, *Nemean* 10.33, *Isthmian* 3.18b.

210 Second-person priming acts, of referent(s) potentially present: *Olympian* 5.21 σὲ τ' | Ὀλυμπιόνικε (see Kambylis 1964:132n5), *Olympian* 13.14 ὔμμιν δὲ | παῖδες Ἀλάτα, *Pythian* 2.18 σὲ δ' | ὦ Δεινομένειε παῖ, *Pythian* 2.57 τὺ δὲ | σάφα νιν ἔχεις (strophe beginning), *Pythian* 6.19 σύ τοι | σχέθων νιν (t11, strophe beginning), *Nemean* 3.83 τίν γε μέν | εὐθρόνου Κλεοῦς ἐθελοίσας. Formally different but functionally similar are *Olympian* 11.11-12 ἴσθι νῦν | Ἀρχεστράτου / παῖ, *Nemean* 5.48 ἴσθι | γλυκεῖάν τοι Μενάνδρου / σὺν τύχᾳ μόχθων, and *Isthmian* 6.44 νῦν σε | νῦν εὐχαῖς ὑπὸ θεσπεσίαις / λίσσομαι.

211 Second-person priming acts, of referent(s) not physically present: *Olympian* 9.17 σόν τε | Κασταλία | πάρα, *Pythian* 6.50 τὶν τ' | Ἐλέλιχθον, *Pythian* 8.8 τὺ δ' | ὁπόταν (strophe beginning), *Pythian* 8.61 τὺ δ' | Ἑκαταβόλε (strophe beginning), *Isthmian* 6.19 ὔμμε τ' | ὦ χρυσάρματοι Αἰακίδαι, *Isthmian* 7.31 τὺ δέ | Διοδότοιο παῖ; in *Nemean* 5.41 we find τὺ δ' Αἰγίναθε δίς | Εὐθύμενες.

212 Consider also the possibility that a hero or god may be present in the form of a tomb and/or a statue.

ζώων τ' ἀπὸ καὶ θανών. |
<u>τὺ δέ</u>, | Διοδότοιο παῖ, | μαχατάν
αἰνέων Μελέαγρον | αἰνέων δὲ καὶ Ἕκτορα |
Ἀμφιάραόν τε, |
εὐανθέ' <u>ἀπέπνευσας</u> ἁλικίαν |

Pindar, *Isthmian* 7.27-34

So may he know well, whoever in that cloud wards off the hailstorm
of blood for the beloved fatherland,

<...> to the opposing army,
that for his townsmen's race he magnifies the greatest glory
in life as well as after death.
You, son of Diodotos, glorifying the warrior
Meleager, and glorifying Hector even,
and Amphiaraon,
you breathed out your flowering youth.

In the ode for Strepsiades of Thebes, Pindar reserves most of his praise for Strepsiades' uncle and namesake who had died fighting for Thebes. In these lines, the song transitions from praising this ancestor's virtues to addressing him directly.[213] Consider especially the stark contrast between the third person imperative ἴστω in 27 and the second-person pronoun followed by the vocative in 31. Lines 27-30 are the expression of a wish (ἴστω, "may he know"), and line 31 appears to immediately fulfill that wish. In performing 31-36, the performer(s), especially if it was a chorus of citizens, enact the praise of the uncle Strepsiades.[214] The transition from the expression of the wish to its fulfillment is reflected in a change from the third person to the second person, and the pivotal act is τὺ δέ, with the pronoun in the vocative or the nominative.[215]

§78. Considering the effect of the second-person priming act, it does not come as a surprise that it often co-occurs with a name in the vocative. Just as a second-person

[213] Felson 1999 and 2004 discuss deictic shifts marked among other things by first, second, and third person pronouns. Pfeijffer 1999:479 and 550 discusses the instances of τὺ δέ in *Pythian* 8 (8.8 and 8.61) as markers of topic shift, but this does not sufficiently explain the performative impact of such acts.

[214] The date and context of *Isthmian* 7 are obscure, see Privitera 1982:103-107.

[215] The pronoun's case is important in that if it is a vocative there is no good reason to assume a discourse act boundary before the name in the vocative. If the pronoun is a nominative, however, it is likely that there was a discontinuity between pronoun and name; i.e. τὺ (nom.) δέ | Διοδότοιο παῖ, or τὺ (voc.) δέ Διοδότοιο παῖ; a similar case is *Pythian* 8.61 τὺ δ' | Ἑκαταβόλε | (...) ὤπασας. In *CEG* 326.2 τὺ δέ, Φοῖβε, δίδοι, the verb form is an imperative, so the pronoun probably should be read as a vocative.

reference does, a vocative turns attention to a new addressee,[216] and in combination the two are complementary. As noted above, at the moment of utterance the referent of a second-person pronoun is underdefined. The most natural way to resolve the ambiguity through verbal means is to provide a name, which after a second-person pronoun inevitably takes the form of a vocative.[217] Vocatives in Pindar have been decribed as adding "liveliness" to the songs,[218] or as reminiscences of epic and hymns,[219] but other scholars have noted their discursive importance.[220] Names in the vocative in Pindar may be compared to apostrophes of characters in Homer. Characters in the epic narrative tend to be addressed at or just before important moments.[221] In Pindar the vocatives likewise occur at discursive transitions, both within the mythical narrative and between myth and *hic et nunc*.

§79. The effect of second-person references in priming acts in a Pindaric performance must have been profound. By devoting a separate discourse step to redirecting attention, Pindar made sure that the audience would be able to follow the path of his song. Moreover, the second-person pronoun primes the audience to focus on the directly upcoming discourse as an important new action. The difference between second-person priming acts and priming acts in narrative is that they do not only effect a cognitive redirection of attention, but may also trigger a physical shift of gaze, especially when Pindar turns to the victor, as in (t35). The cognitive usefulness of the priming act always goes hand in hand with its discursive importance. The fact that a discourse act is entirely devoted to directing attention to a new referent naturally creates anticipation about the upcoming discourse.

2.6 Conclusions

§80. The first sections of this chapter have sketched the scholarship on the smallest subdivisions of discourse in ancient Greek and contemporary languages. The importance of the concept of the discourse act reaches beyond this chapter and beyond the study

216 The major study of vocatives in Pindar is Kambylis 1964. The peculiarities of their linguistic form are briefly discussed by Hummel 1993:71-73.

217 There is also a group of instances where the vocative and the pronoun are inverted. In these cases the second-person pronoun does not form a priming act: *Olympian* 6.12 Ἁγησία | τὶν δ' αἶνος ἑτοῖμος, 8.15 Τιμόσθενες | ὔμμε δὲ, 9.112 Αἶαν | τεόν τ'; *Pythian* 4.59 ὦ μάκαρ υἱὲ Πολυμνάστου | σὲ δ', 5.5-6 ὦ θεόμορ' Ἀρκεσίλα | σύ τοί νιν, 5.45 Ἀλεξιβιάδα | σὲ δ'; *Nemean* 1.29 Ἁγησιδάμου παῖ | σέο δ', 2.14 ὦ Τιμόδημε | σὲ δ', 6.60 Ἀλκίμιδα | σέ γ', 7.58 Θεαρίων | τὶν δ', 7.94-95 ὦ μάκαρ | τὶν δ'.

218 E.g. Gerber 2002:29, "Pindar elsewhere enlivens the style by addressing one of a pair directly," Meyer 1933:55, "Verlebendingung der (...) Erzählung," and Hummel 1993:67.

219 See Braswell 1988:141-142 *ad Pythian* 4.59.

220 Bundy 1962:6-7 (and *passim*) discusses apostrophe in Pindar in terms of "name caps" and "pronominal caps," and notes that they occur often directly after a priamel; see also Bonifazi 2001:117 for discussion of the vocative in *Olympian* 6.22.

221 See Block 1982, Richardson 1990:170-171, Kahane 1994:154-155, Mackay 2001, and De Jong 2009:94-95 for literature and discussion of apostrophe of characters in Homer.

of particles. In language, the act—consisting of a few words that verbalize the focus of consciousness—has more claim to the status of the basic linguistic unit than the clause or the sentence. Based on the argument that the discourse act is the most basic unit in the language-producing mind, the functions of particles are to be understood primarily with regard to discourse acts rather than to clauses or sentences. Discourse acts and particles exist independently from each other, but each is relevant to the other: discourse acts are the domain over which most particles exercise their force.

§81. δέ in Homer is inherently linked to the discourse act, by consistently marking boundaries between many different kinds of act. Its function is analogous to the use of "stop" to mark boundaries in telegrams written in English. The other particle discussed in terms of discourse acts is μέν. I describe this particle's pragmatic functions in terms of projection: μέν projects that another act is to be expected. This force of the particle is further exploited in the μέν - δέ construction, when μέν has small scope and specifically projects a contrasting or complementary δέ act. Finally, the priming act, a strongly "incomplete" chunk of discourse in syntactic and semantic terms, illustrates an important discourse function of discourse acts. Priming acts typically occur at the beginning of new scenes, a type of transition that demands significant cognitive processing. To accommodate the speaker and audience's cognitive needs, the "who" precedes the "what". This reading of syntactically "dislocated" or "pendant" units recognizes their cognitive efficiency rather than focusing on their grammatical deficiency.

§82. An analysis of Homeric and Pindaric discourse demonstrates that the language of the two performative genres is more similar than one might have expected. Despite the fact that the syntax of Pindar's songs is occasionally more intricate than that of Homeric epic, the discourse still generally progresses in small-ish acts. Both epic and lyric discourse proceed in small strategic steps, discourse acts, each with their own function in reaching the discourse goals.

II.3

Moves

Particles at Discourse Transitions

§1. The present chapter builds directly on chapter II.2 and presupposes knowledge of its main points; our understanding of discourse acts is summarized in II.2.1.2. Greek particles reflect the production of discourse in cognitively manageable units—discourse acts—which are the building blocks of epic and lyric compositions. The analysis in II.2 reveals how a performer or author produces his work in small increments to guide his audience through the discourse. In this chapter I am concerned with all kinds of larger discourse units, such as narrative episodes or scenes, and the function of particles with relation to them.[1] First, I introduce the term "move" to describe coherent discourse units consisting of at least one, but generally of multiple discourse acts (§§6-11). An understanding of this phenomenon in discourse then informs my reading of γάρ (§§22-29), καὶ γάρ (§§30-32), and ἦ (§§33-43) in Homer and Pindar, focusing on the introduction of Homeric embedded narratives as a case study. After examining a few other ways in which the poets embed narratives within the larger discourse (§§45-50), I examine how those narratives themselves are articulated. In this section I explore the different functions of δή, considering also the diachronic development of the particle that may emerge from the Homeric corpus (§§53-64). A narrative from Pindar provides the backdrop for a discussion of his consistent use of ἄρα to round off larger units in discourse (§§65-67). Finally, I consider the role of particles in one of Pindar's compositions (*Pythian* 2), especially in the many transitions between different kinds of discourse (§§68-76).

3.1 Moves

§2. Discourse acts, the smallest functional subdivisions of discourse, are the building blocks of larger sections called "moves."[2] The term originated in the analysis of dialogic

1 Compare IV.3 for a similar consideration of differently-sized units in discourse.

2 Sinclair and Coulthard 1975; Roulet 1984, Roulet et al. 1985, Roulet 1997, Roulet et al. 2001; Risselada 1993; Kroon 1995; Langacker 2001; Hannay and Kroon 2005. Move is not an unproblematic term, as it is used in different ways and has been applied in different fields: compare

discourse, where it makes sense to divide conversation into different moves conceived by the interlocutors.[3] An often-cited example is that of the invitation:[4]

(t1)

A: Are you free tonight? | 'Cause I have an extra ticket for the symphony orchestra. |

B: Well, | I really should work on this paper tonight. | Sorry, | maybe next time? |

In two turns, which could be expanded almost infinitely, speakers A and B go through an exchange that consists of an "invitation" and "rejection."[5] Each of the two turns consists of multiple acts that are united by the fact that they share a common communicative goal.[6]

§3. In the example above, the move starts with an unannounced question, but in practice the context will provide some kind of embedding. We may expect a prefatory remark like, "Oh, by the way, are you...", when the invitation comes after another move (such as a greeting), or, if the interlocutors have just met face-to-face, "Hey, I wanted to ask you something: are you..." On the whole, when speakers are initiating a new move, they feel a strong need to mark the transition. At the "end" of moves, conversely, there is typically less explicit marking in the language.[7] Of course, some moves have inherent

for example Ryan 1991:130, who uses "move" as follows: "I call a 'move' an action with a high-priority and a high risk of failure."

3 In this sense the concept of move has been applied to Homeric epic by Beck in Grethlein and Rengakos 2009, where she says (146) that "[a] 'move' is essentially a speech act in a conversational context" (she repeats the definition in Beck 2012:12, with reference to Kroon 1995, Risselada 1993, and Roulet 1984). This is a narrower definition of move than the one we (and most of her sources) employ.

4 This is a constucted example for the sake of illustration.

5 See III.4.1 for the Conversation Analysis approach to interactions. In Conversation Analysis these two "turns" form a "sequence," and the invitation and rejection are an "adjacency pair."

6 The establishment of this common goal is inevitably subjective, and it cannot always be ascertained. Consider the final acts by speaker B: | Sorry, | is still part of the rejection move, as an attempt to mitigate the interlocutor's loss of face. The final act, | maybe next time? | however, could either be regarded as a continuation of this attempt at mitigation, or as an actual question about "next time" in which case it might be regarded as the start of a new move. In practice, it is the reaction of the interlocutor that establishes the "right" interpretation of this act: if speaker A responds "Sure!" the exchange ends without any new moves, but if she responds "OK, | they are also playing next Thursday, | how's that?" she has clearly taken speaker B's question as a new move.

7 Roulet's analyses reveal the same tendency in French: the beginnings of moves are often marked by what he calls "pragmatic markers" (see I.3 for the terminology), while the linguistic form of the ends of moves is never discussed (see especially Roulet 1984:36-39, on a newspaper article). Compare Langacker 2001:178 who remarks that the intonation group "Now Bill," "serves to announce that structure building is going to start in a new place." Chafe 2001:674 says the following about "topic": "Topics generally have clear beginnings, although that is not always

endings, like the invitation above, but just as often the end of one move is recognizable only because another move begins.[8]

§4. The terminology of moves and acts forms part of a larger framework concerning the subdivision of discourse, and it is most often applied to analyze dialogic discourse.[9] In this framework, researchers are concerned with establishing the structure of an exchange, which they divide into main and subsidiary elements.[10] Since I approach epic and lyric from the perspective of performance, I do not believe such a hierarchical analysis to be the most productive. Rather, I choose to focus on the on-line delivery and processing of the discourse.[11] Whatever structure may emerge from the written text, in performance the cues to structure would have worked mostly on a local level, guiding the audience linearly through the discourse.[12] What one expects to be marked, then, are the transitions to new moves, since these are the places where both performer and audience need a cue for cognitive reorientation. Since epic and lyric performance make reception linear, the most important thing is that a move beginning is recognized as some sort of redirection.[13]

---

the case (...) and their endings are sometimes well defined, sometimes not"; compare Tannen 1984:41-43.

8 Consider Langacker's insightful comment (2001:177): "at any point in a discourse can we stop working on one structure and start building another." See IV.3 §§94-98 for the discursive discontinuities that can accompany move starts in historiography.

9 The terminology was established initially by Sinclair and Coulthard 1975 (who founded the so-called Birmingham school). Their work was picked up by Stenström 1994 and by members of the "Geneva school", represented especially by Roulet 1984, Roulet et al. 1985, Roulet 1997, Roulet et al. 2001; see II.2 §18. Kroon 1995 applies the Geneva model to written Latin discourse in her discussion of discourse particles.

10 Consider Kroon's definition (1995:66): a move is "the minimal free unit of discourse that is able to enter into an exchange structure. (...) A move usually consists of a central act (which is the most important act in view of the speaker's intentions and goals) and one or more subsidiary acts..."

11 Roulet insists upon the hierarchical approach, but he suggests that the hierarchy is not absolute when he argues that moves can contain other moves: in 1981:10-11 the examples suggest that an *intervention* (move) can itself be part of larger *interventions*, see Roulet 1984:45 "...moves [can] constitute a larger move and are tied together by interactive functions"; see also Roulet 1997:134 figure 2, and Roulet et al. 2001:53.

12 This matches the idea of "stucturing" instead of the static "structure"; see Sherzer 1982:389, "I use the term *structuring* rather than structure in order to stress the dynamic process which is involved" [emphasis original]. Kroon 1995 focuses on rhetorical prose and is more optimistic about establishing the structure of her corpus (66-67): "Many particles (both in Latin and in other languages) appear to be involved predominantly or partly in marking the linear or hierarchical structure of a discourse as outlined above. This means that they mark out the separate units of discourse by indicating how these are structurally tied up with other units of the same discourse, both linearly (i.e. involving relations between units of the same rank) and hierarchically (i.e. involving the relationships that units maintain with 'higher' or 'lower' units). As such these particles can be said to have a mainly organizational function."

13 Even the speech-capping formulae are generally more forward than backward looking. Many of them mark the end of the direct speech rather by focusing on the upcoming narrative move

§5. The most recognizable transitions in Homer are the beginnings and endings of direct speech. Metalinguistically, every start of direct speech is marked explicitly with a speech-introduction verse, probably because the transition from one speaking source (the narrator) to another (a character) is crucial to following the narrative. The same holds for the great majority of transitions after direct speech.[14] The performer of the *Iliad* or the *Odyssey* had only one voice, but comparative evidence from other epic material suggests that transitions from direct speech to narrator text may have been marked prosodically.[15] In the remainder of Homeric epic, most moves are less obviously recognizable as units than stretches of direct speech. Only by considering both the content and the linguistic form can we come to an informed analysis of transitions in discourse. Such moments are often marked by some kind of linguistic turbulence,[16] in the form of a change in tense, orientation, or source, or through the occurrence of metalanguage, often in the form of particles. Attention to the path of the discourse, with all its bends and sudden turns, may thus reveal certain functions of particles. At the same time, the occurrence of certain particles may serve as a cue that the discourse is taking a new direction.

3.1.1 Move transitions

§6. Because epic and lyric have been transmitted in written form, it is all too easy to consider the genres as ultimately monologic discourse, structured by an author according to a functional hierarchy. As argued in the II.4, however, it is important to keep in mind that both epic and lyric represent interactions between performer and audience. In fact, traces of this ultimately interactive nature are present throughout the discourse, not only in the use of particles that mark its production in acts, but also in more explicit metanarrative comments. Consider the introduction to the Homeric *Catalogue of Ships*:

(t2)

ἔσπετε νῦν μοι Μοῦσαι Ὀλύμπια δώματ' ἔχουσαι· |[17]
(...)
οἵ τινες ἡγεμόνες Δαναῶν καὶ κοίρανοι ἦσαν· |
πληθὺν δ' οὐκ ἂν ἐγὼ μυθήσομαι | οὐδ' ὀνομήνω, |

Iliad 2.484 and 487-488

(such as the announcement of a new speaker) than on rounding off the preceding move of direct speech.

14 See Louviot 2013 on speech-capping in Old-English poetry.

15 See Bonifazi and Elmer 2012:246.

16 I borrow the term from Longacre 1996², discussed in footnote 46 below.

17 The vertical bars mark discourse act boundaries, see II.2.1.2.

Tell me now, Muses who have Olympian houses,
(...)
who were the leaders of the Greeks and the captains.
Their multitude I would not be able to speak nor name,

In a gesture rare in Homeric epic, the (persona of the) narrator breaks the spell of the narrative and foregrounds his role as a performer. Most of the Homeric narrative effaces the presence of the performer and audience as much as possible; in order to maintain the illusion of their absence, the performer divides his discourse by more subtle means. In this instance, however, a special piece of discourse is set apart by a special introduction.[18] The performer professes his inability to complete his intended move without help from the Muses, which he apparently receives, [19] since he concludes:

(t3)

οὗτοι ἄρ' ἡγεμόνες Δαναῶν καὶ κοίρανοι ἦσαν·

Iliad 2.760

These then were the leaders of the Danaans and the captains.

The listing of the leaders of the Greek army is thus composed as a separate move, explicitly demarcated by metanarrative comments.[20]

§7. When I call the *Catalogue* a separate move, I mean this in a relative sense. Above the level of the act, different-sized units are hard to distinguish on any absolute basis.[21] In the *Catalogue*, for example, it would be fully justified to call each geographical subsection a "move" within the larger whole. Rather than assigning different names to moves of different sizes, we use a single term—move—with the understanding that the concept is a relational one: the *Catalogue* is a move within the *Iliad*, the subsection on the men from Pylos (2.591-602) is a move within the *Catalogue*, and the story of the singer Thamyris

[18] See II.4 §§11-14 for the comparable "framed" vs. "unframed" discourse, with further examples of this temporary breaking of the spell.

[19] The actual interpretation of the passage is contested, and this summary represents only one possible reading, but the discussion is not relevant to my contention that the *Catalogue* is presented as a separate move.

[20] For a discussion of metanarrative passages in the *Iliad*, with literature, see De Jong 2004b:45-53, and see De Jong 2001a:119-120 for a listing of narratorial interventions in the *Odyssey*. For this specific line and the cognitive importance of οὗτοι see Bakker 2005:80-81 and 143 (although I would propose a different reading of ἄρα, see for the similar function of ἄρα after the simile II.4.3.2).

[21] See IV.3 §100 for moves linked to genre expectations in historiography.

(2.594-600) is a move within that subsection.[22] With these *caveats* we may productively approach ancient Greek epic with the terminology employed by the Birmingham and Geneva schools.[23] The performer of epic is engaged in a constant interaction with his audience, the reflections of which must inform our understanding of the language.

§8. For Pindar's lyric compositions the term move is not only helpful, it is, as we shall see, indispensable.[24] While it is not intuitive to describe narrative scenes or episodes in terms of moves, lyric discourse invites it. The work of Schadewaldt and Bundy has taught us to see Pindar's *Victory Odes* as coherent wholes conceived with a single goal in mind: praise. This praise can be multi-faceted, but it is present in every component part of the ode. The priamels, the praise of the family, the reflections upon humanity and the gods, the narrative sections, and of course the praise of the victor are all moves in the larger interaction that is the song, which in turn is part of the festive occasion. The component parts of Pindar's songs, different yet fitting into a larger whole, represent Pindar's many moves toward his goal of praising the victor.[25] Just as a speaker might prepare his interlocutor for an actual invitation by starting with "Are you free tonight?" Pindar often primes his audience for the praise of the victor by starting with a priamel. Another clearly observable kind of move are the gnomic, evaluative statements that occur within narratives, or at transitions between myths and direct praise.[26] Just like scenes and

22 We want to avoid any attempt to define "move" in an absolute sense, as some scholars attempt to do. One can imagine that it is very possible to name the different layers of the hierarchy in the *Catalogue*, which is so clearly divided, but such a system would not easily translate to the rest of the Homeric corpus. If we call the *Catalogue* an "episode," the different entries "subsections," and then the smallest discourse units above the sentence level "moves," this distinction may be useful on a local level, but it becomes difficult, and perhaps unproductive, outside of the *Catalogue*. Using a different set of terms, Givón 2005:141 (with reference to Givón (ed.) 1997) does offer a full terminology for what he regards as the different levels of discourse.
Do note that the *Catalogue* is not representative for the rest of Homeric discourse. It is a very strict, ringed piece of discourse that—not despite but because of its intricacy—allows the performer to reperform a large body of specific knowledge, such as a list of places and their leaders; see for the cognitive aspect of catalogues in Homer Bakker 1997b:60, Minchin 2001:73-99, Tsagalis 2010, and Strauss Clay 2011:117, with note 59.

23 See II.2 §18 for more on the Birmingham and Geneva schools.

24 Bundy describes the Pindaric odes as unities built up out of different pieces all aimed at praising the victor, but defines the separate pieces, which we would call moves, only on a functional level (a gnomic passage, a priamel, a narrative, etc.). The closest he comes to a description in terms of moves is in the conclusion of his second paper: "[T]o follow the movement of the ode is not to follow the development of a thought that has a beginning, a middle, and an end, but to pursue the fulfillment of a single purpose through a complex orchestration of motives and themes that conduce to one end: the glorification, within the considerations of ethical, religious, social, and literary propriety." See also Felson 2004:387, about *Pythian* 9: "Despite these ruptures, a set of real-world "moves" can be retrieved by an audience informed about pan-Hellenic contests and the epinician genre." It is unclear how Felson uses "move" here, but it may be in a deictic sense (compare "shifters").

25 Wells 2009:61-128 speaks of the different "speech genres" that alternate in Pindaric discourse.

26 See II.4 §§22-23 for more on this view of *gnômai.*

episodes in epic narratives, Pindaric moves are distinguished by linguistic markers, and are characterized by a specific linguistic form.

§9. We call larger and smaller subdivisions of epic and lyric discourse "moves," and we assume that these linguistic units in discourse represent specific aspects of a composer or performer's discourse strategy. This assumption is implicit in our belief that the discourse units we identify represent a textual reality and are not just abstractions projected upon the text. Our interpretations always go hand in hand with an analysis of the linguistic form at what we believe are move transitions. For Homer, I focus on the transition into and out of self-contained stories, as well as the navigation of transitions within narrative.[27] For Pindar's lyric, my analysis involves transitions between one kind of discourse and another, as from narrative to *gnṓmē*, or from an address of a god to praise of the victor's clan.

§10. A performer has a number of tools at his disposal to mark new beginnings. One basic difference we can establish is between transitions with and those without metalanguage. Non-metalinguistic transitions include instances like the priming discourse acts discussed in the preceding chapter, which entail no metalanguage, or language that "discusses" the transition. Instead, the narrative is presented in such a way as to accommodate the cognitive processing needed to navigate the discontinuity.[28] Metalinguistic transitions, on the other hand, are those where the performer uses language that is relevant not to the propositional content, but to the ongoing interaction between him and the audience. Metanarrative questions or comments (such as the opening of the *Catalogue*) are the prime example of this kind of transition, but they occupy only one end of the scale. The rest of the spectrum is taken up mostly by particles or combinations of particles.[29]

§11. Awareness of different moves in discourse is indispensable for gaining a full understanding of certain particles. In narrative contexts, as in many others, particles are better understood as relevant to the interaction than to the content or syntax.[30] Herman

[27] The term "move" is not commonly applied to narrative, but consider Roulet et al. 2001, especially the example on page 328-329.

[28] Included in this category are the performative tools that the epic performer has at his disposal to make a transition within the narrative seamless, such as by using sightlines or sounds *et cetera*.

[29] See Maschler 2009, who explores the link between discourse markers and metalanguage in the talk of bilingual speakers of English and Hebrew. Grosz and Sidner 1986:177 talk about "discourse segments" and describe the relation between linguistic form and discourse in the following terms: "There is a two-way interaction between the discourse segment structure and the utterances constituting the discourse: linguistic expressions can be used to convey information about the discourse structure; conversely, the discourse structure constrains the interpretation of expressions." The first part of their two-way interaction is what I call metadiscursive language.

[30] See Grosz and Sidner 1986:177-178 on what they call "discourse segment boundaries": "The explicit use of certain words and phrases (...) and more subtle cues, such as intonation or changes in tense and aspect, are included in the repertoire of linguistic devices that function (...) to indicate these boundaries."

says the following when discussing cognitive narratology: "At issue is how stories reflexively model cognitive, interactional, and other dimensions of acts of narration along with other forms of communicative practice."[31] His corpus is written discourse, and in the case of performed narratives like the Homeric epics and Pindar's songs we may focus not only on "how stories model cognitive and interactional acts," but also on how the language of Homeric and Pindaric stories *reflects and encodes* such cognitive and interactional acts. Particles are crucial tools for locating and understanding such metalinguistic actions behind and beyond the texts.

3.2 Particles in Narrative

§12. Narrative has received special attention as an object of research ever since the work of the structuralists in the mid-twentieth century,[32] but especially since the advent of narratology.[33] The approach has gained considerable popularity in the field of literary studies and has engendered a significant number of studies in Classics.[34] On the whole, narratology's focus is on the relation between narrator (as removed from author or performer) and narrative, and it considers the latter more as a product than as an ongoing event. As a result, the linguistic form of a story is relevant mainly when it informs the researcher of the narrator's manipulation of time or space.[35] In the following, we examine the role of particles in articulating and guiding narrative, approaching the texts as encodings of an interactive process between performer(s) and audience. By treating Homeric and Pindaric stories as acts of narration and studying the ways in which language reflects

31 Herman 2010:140.

32 It started in the study of folktales and myth; the landmark works are Propp [1928] 1958, Lévi-Strauss 1960 (review of Propp), Bremond 1973, Todorov et al. 1979, Detienne 1981, and Vernant and Vidal-Naquet 1986; see also Hansen 2002:1-31 for an overview of the earlier folktale studies and the (limited) application of the methodology in classical studies.

33 See especially Barthes 1957 and Genette 1972; Prince 1997:39-42 gives a very compehensive history of narrative and narratology up to the late nineties, and includes a rich bibliography. A central question that has arisen in the last decades is: what makes a discourse narrative? The discussion is too complex to present here, but studies that address the question include Fludernik 1996, Ryan 2007, and Herman 2009a. A commonly held principle is to regard something as narrative when it contains at least two unique events in a temporal sequence (see e.g. Labov and Waletzky 1967, Couper-Kuhlen 1988:353).

34 De Jong 1987, 2001, 2007 (ed.), 2012 (ed.); Rood 1998; De Jong and Sullivan (eds.) 1994, De Jong, Nünlist, and Bowie (eds.) 2004; Stoddard 2004; Grethlein and Rengakos (eds.) 2009; Köhnken 2006; Grethlein, and Rengakos (eds.) 2009.

35 E.g. De Jong (ed.) 2007 and 2012. Prince 1997:40 says that it is "the narrating as opposed to the narrated, (...) the signs in a narrative representing the narrating activity, its origin, its destination, and its context (...) that narratologists have explored most thoroughly." However, none of his following examples discusses the language of narrative and its relation to the narrating activity, which is exactly what I focus on in the present chapter.

the narrative process we aim to provide a complement to the traditional narratological analyses.[36]

§13. If a narrative is perceived as an ongoing interaction between a performer and an audience, it will yield linguistic signs of the composer's cognitive processes as well as his assumptions about the hearer's cognitive processing. In the production of a discourse, whether fully composed beforehand or in situ,[37] multiple cognitive processes simultaneously affect the linguistic realization. At the most basic level, the composer's linguistic competence and his training in composing are important determinants. This largely unconscious dimension of language production includes considerations of linguistic limitations, social conventions, and his own cognitive limitations.[38] More conscious is the influence of his expectations about what the audience will be able to process, what relevant pre-existing knowledge they have, and of course what they will appreciate. Such cognitive processes are inherent to all communication,[39] but since epic and lyric are not day-to-day speech, but rather "special discourse" meant for performance before a listening audience, their literary language may more visibly reflect this active consideration of the audience.[40] With this in mind, let us consider how these processes manifest themselves in the performer's construction of his discourse in acts and moves.

3.2.1 Narrative moves

§14. In the emergent structure of discourse in corpora like Homeric epic and Pindar's lyric, the component parts of stories are most clearly delineated, especially in Homer. Things do not just happen in stories, but situations are set up, characters are introduced,

36 See Longacre's work on the linguistic form of narrative discourse (1985, 1990, and 1995). Pseudo-Longinus, in his work *On the Sublime* (chapters 23- 29) already discusses the linguistic changes at certain moments in the narrative. His work considers discourse transitions above the sentence level, and suggests that he considers the pragmatic perspective on language; see the summary of Terry 1995:119-120, "Among those changes which he discusses are the expansion of the singular into the plural to convey the idea of multitude (23.2-3), the contraction of the plural into the singular to give an effect of sublimity (chap. 24), the use of the present tense in narrating past time in order to increase vividness (chap. 25), the change of the person addressed from the whole audience to a single individual also to give a vivid effect (chap. 26), the use of the first person for one of the characters to show an outbreak of emotion (chap. 27), and the use of periphrasis or circumlocution to give the work a far richer note (chap. 28-29)."

37 In its original incarnation, I assume that Homeric epic was composed in performance (see e.g. Nagy 1996 and Bakker 1997b), while Pindar's victory odes were probably composed beforehand. If we assume that a number of odes were performed by a chorus, they must in fact have been finished well before the occasion; see II.1 §§1-5 for more on the topic.

38 There are also relevant non-cognitive processes, such as the limitations imposed by the need to breathe.

39 See Enfield 2006, especially 409-412. This touches upon the topic of common ground, which I explore in terms of discourse memory in II.4.1.

40 See e.g. Reynolds 1995, a comprehensive study about performances of the Sirat Bani Hilal oral epic.

a complication is presented, and after things come to a head a resolution is achieved. This basic structure of narrative first proposed by Labov and Waletzky has been shown to be inherent in stories across languages, cultures, and media.[41] Their narrative scheme looks as follows (after adaptation in later publications):[42]

> (t4)
>
> Abstract (a short preview/overview of the narrative)
>
> Orientation (introduction of time, place, and characters)
>
> Complicating Action (the body of the narrative)
>
> Resolution (the complication is resolved)
>
> Coda (a metanarrative comment to cap the narrative)
>
> Evaluation (the point of telling the story. In the earliest versions of the scheme "evaluation" was placed between "resolution" and "coda," but in later publications Labov, Waletzky, and others argued that evaluation is generally present throughout the narrative, in the choice of vocabulary, syntax, evaluative metacomments, gestures and facial expressions, et cetera.)[43]

The construction of narrative along these lines may be regarded as the result of social convention, but this convention in turn probably has a cognitive basis.[44] Whatever form the narrative takes, verbal or not, it is often possible to distinguish the different constituent parts. The omnipresence of this narrative structure suggests either that the storyteller is aware of the differences between sections and presents them differently, or that a certain linguistic form comes automatically with a certain part of the story—it is hard to establish the extent to which some of this linguistic marking is conscious. Regardless, in the Homeric and Pindaric corpora there appears to be a consistent marking of

41 See especially Bamberg (ed.) 1997, which contains a re-publication of Labov and Waletzky's 1967 article; and additions to the scheme offered by Fleischman 1990 (who introduces "peak" between complicating action and resolution), Fludernik 1996, and Klapproth 2004. Minchin 2001:186-196 applies the scheme to Homeric narratives.

42 These are the terms given by Labov and Waletzky, and the brief explanations between parentheses are paraphrases of their longer discussions of the parts.

43 The first explanation of "evaluation" is given in Labov and Waletzky 1967:28-35, with a substantial revision in Labov 1972. In the 1997 anniversary volume, several people expand on the topic: Daiute and Nelson 1997 (evaluation as an emergent point of view) and Fleischman 1997:165-166; see also Fleischman 1986 and Bower 1997 (syntax and word order as a possible marker of evaluation).

44 See for the cognitive basis of narratives: Schank 1995, Talmy 1995, Turner 1996, Herman 2011, and Sanford and Emmott 2012.

boundaries between Labovian sections of narrative, and they are realized in different linguistic forms. In the following, I first study embedded narratives as moves within the larger discourse, with a focus on Homer, and I then examine different narrative sections as moves within those stories.

§15. Of all the components in the Labovian model, the complicating action and the resolution are the minimal requirements for something to be perceived as a narrative. When either or both of those components are missing, the most we can say is that an expected narrative is lacking, but not that an actual narrative is presented. Most commonly, a narrative will have a complicating action and a resolution, often preceded by at least some kind of orientation. Multiple scholars have proposed to include an additional component between complicating action and resolution, alternatively called "climax" or "peak."[45] From a linguistic perspective this claim is sound, since the language of climactic scenes commonly differs from that of the surrounding discourse. Therefore I employ the terms climax and peak to denote the pivotal scene between complicating action and resolution. In Labovian terms, the climax may be regarded as the last part of the complicating action, or the start of the resolution.[46]

§16. Consider the following example of a two-sentence narrative in Pindar's first *Pythian Ode*. It tells how the Greek heroes on their way to Troy came to get Philoctetes, son of Poias, on Lemnos:

(t5)

(...) νῦν γε μὰν | τὰν Φιλοκτήταο δίκαν ἐφέπων |
ἐστρατεύθη | σὺν δ᾽ ἀνάγκᾳ νιν φίλον
καί τις ἐὼν μεγαλάνωρ ἔσανεν.| φαντὶ δὲ Λαμνόθεν | ἕλκει
τειρόμενον | μεταβάσοντας ἐλθεῖν |
ἥροας ἀντιθέους | Ποίαντος υἱὸν τοξόταν· |
ὃς Πριάμοιο πόλιν πέρσεν, | τελεύτασέν τε πόνους Δαναοῖς, |
ἀσθενεῖ μὲν χρωτὶ βαίνων, | ἀλλὰ μοιρίδιον ἦν. |

Pindar *Pythian* 1.50-55

(...) Yes, just now, following Philoktetes' way,
he campaigned, and in need even a proud one

[45] Chafe 2001:677 notes that the idea of "climax" is missing from the Labovian narrative schema. He himself proposes an alternative schema; for the use of the term peak see Longacre 1996^{2}.

[46] Longacre 1996^{2} designates peaks in narrative as "zones of turbulence" and shows how they can be marked (1996^{2}:39-48) by: (1) rhetorical underlining, (2) a "crowded stage" i.e. many characters in the frame, (3) heightened vividness, (4) a change of pace, (5) a change of vantage point, and/ or (6) the sudden occurrence or disappearace of certain particles as well as use of onomatopoeia.

> greeted him as a friend. They say that from Lemnos they came to
> take him, tired out by his wound,[47]
> the godlike heroes, Poias' archer son.
> He razed Priam's city, and ended the Danaans' troubles.
> Though walking with flesh infirm, still it was fated.

After a brief orientation (50-51), consisting in the naming of a main character (Philoctetes) as a parallel for the *laudandus* (Hieron), Pindar presents a famous narrative in an extremely condensed form. The actual start of the complication is marked by φαντὶ δέ, which shows once more that δέ in Pindar regularly marks major discourse boundaries.[48]

§17. The complicating action takes up no more than one sentence (52-53 Λαμνόθεν... τοξόταν) before coming to the climax (ὃς Πριάμοιο πόλιν πέρσεν) and then the resolution (τελεύτασέν τε πόνους Δαναοῖς). Note that the run-up to the most important event is presented in the form of an *accusativus cum infinitivo*, while the climax—Philoctetes' role in bringing down Troy—is in the form of a finite clause. This climactic clause, moreover, is formally a relative clause, which is perhaps not expected to drive the narrative forward.[49] It is likely that Pindar is influenced by the use of the relative pronoun in Homer, where its value is regularly closer to that of a demonstrative. Hence, my translation reflects the narrative force of the act (He razed Priam's city, and ended the Danaans' troubles) rather than the grammatical form of the clause (...Poias' archer son / who razed Priam's city...).

§18. The point of the story is the analogy between Philoctetes, who went to battle wounded, and the *laudandus* Hieron, who did so as well. Here the evaluation (ἀλλὰ μοιρίδιον ἦν), in Labov's term, follows the resolution. The punctuation chosen by Snell and Maehler reflects the interpretation that the participial clause ἀσθενεῖ μὲν χρωτὶ βαίνων following the resolution is still part of the narrative. On several linguistic grounds, however, it is more attractive to regard this act as the start of a new move.[50] First of all the act would be superfluous on the level of content if it were part of the preceding narrative (see ἕλκει τειρόμενον, 52). More important, however, is the use of the particle μέν. As I argue in II.2, μέν has a projecting function, carrying a constituent, thought, or action forward.[51] As a result it also often has an asseverative function, starting a new move, here with the pragmatic enrichment that gives it a concessive force. Rather than

47 In the translation of lines 51 and 52 I have had to change the word order to obtain understandable English.

48 Note, moreover, that φαντί consistently occurs at the start of (little) narratives in Pindar: *Olympian* 7.54; *Pythian* 2.21, 4.88, 4.287, 6.21, 7.19; *Isthmian* 8.46a.

49 Compare Couper-Kuhlen 1988, who discusses subordinated when-clauses in narrative, which provide foreground rather than background information. See II.5 for more on relative clauses in narrative.

50 Compare the discussion of section beginnings and endings in IV.3.11.

51 See II.2.4.

to the preceding finite verbs, μέν connects its host act to the ἀλλά clause that follows: "Though walking with flesh infirm, still it was fated [that he would win the battle]." If taken in this form, the statement is readily applicable to both Philoctetes and Hieron, the *laudandus*. This reading is supported by the imperfect ἦν, which follows the aorists in the complicating action (μεταβάσοντας ἐλθεῖν 52), climax (πέρσεν 54), and resolution (τελεύτασεν 54): a change of tense suggests a new move, and the imperfect often occurs in evaluative statements.[52]

§19. This brief example illustrates two things: on the one hand the fact that narrative transitions can be explicitly marked in the language, and on the other hand that different narrative sections may manifest themselves through different linguistic patterns.[53] By analyzing these two factors we can observe how certain particles or strings of particles are relevant to transitions between narrative moves.

3.2.2 Narrative beginnings: γάρ

§20. The Homeric *Iliad* and *Odyssey* are practically all narrative, in the narrow sense. So most relevant for the current chapter are the transitions to the many discrete narratives embedded within the larger plots of the two epics.[54]

§21. Literature on self-contained stories in Homeric epic abounds, and the scholarship has established an impressive set of terms to describe the phenomenon from different angles. One kind is what Slater called the lyric narrative, characterized especially by its ring-compositional form. This form is not unconnected from the idea of epic regression, although it has sometimes been treated separately.[55] Slater, following West, notes that the lyric narrative in Homer is often introduced by a relative pronoun + aorist + ποτε + aorist participle.[56] Contrary to what Slater suggests, however, this kind of construction does not hold the monopoly on introducing embedded narratives in epic. Each component of Slater's construction in combination with other elements can start a self-contained narrative, which is not by nature different from the "lyric narrative" described by Slater. In all such constructions, the pronoun often does not have a relative

52 See IV.2 §§ 112-113 for the use of ἐτελεύτα in Thucydides, and Allan 2007:113-115 for the use of the imperfect in evaluative statements in Thucydides.

53 See III.2.1 for the concept of discourse patterns.

54 Other scholars choose to distinguish between the narrative and descriptive mode in epic, but I agree with most current narratologists who argue that description in any form typically performs a narrative function (e.g. Tsagalis 2012: De Jong (ed.) 2012:1-3). By extension, it is unproductive to regard them as two different discourse modes (for the term, see Smith 2003). At the same time, however, the action of a character and the setting of that action may be presented in different linguistic forms, the transition between which we do regard as a narrative transition.

55 See Slater 1983. Lyric narrative is related to the idea of "epic regression", on which see Schadewaldt 1938:84 who speaks of "zeitlich rückschreitend" ("walking backward in time"); the term "epic regression" was coined by Krischer 1971:136-140.

56 Slater 1983:118, referring to West 1966:161, on Hesiod, *Theogony* 22; see also Calame 1985.

but rather a demonstrative force: not "..., who" but ".... *S/He*." As for ποτε, although it is by nature an ideal marker to use for displacing performer and audience to a moment before the narrative *hic et nunc*, parallels show that it is by no means the performer's only or even the most frequently used tool. The particular construction described by Slater is an asyndetic transition into an embedded narrative, which is only one of many ways to embed a narrative in the larger plot. I revisit the construction briefly toward the end of this section.[57]

§22. The transition is more often accompanied by one or more particles, instead of or in addition to the use of ποτε. Very common in Homer is the combination of a pronoun followed by a particle (for which see II.5), but here I focus on the beginnings of embedded narratives marked by (combinations of) particles, sometimes along with other words. One of the particles most at home in the beginning of embedded narratives is γάρ.[58] Consider this passage from Agamemnon's speech to Diomedes in book 4:

(t6)

(...) περὶ δ' ἄλλων φασὶ γενέσθαι. |
ἤτοι μὲν <u>γὰρ</u> ἄτερ πολέμου εἰσῆλθε Μυκήνας |
ξεῖνος | ἅμ' ἀντιθέῳ Πολυνείκεϊ | λαὸν ἀγείρων· |

Iliad 4.375-377

(...) And they say he was beyond others.
Oh yes, *for*[59] he came to Mycene in peace
as a guest, with godlike Polyneices, to collect an army.

Agamemnon is talking to Diomedes about the latter's father Tydeus, in an attempt to get him back into the fight. Although he has never met Tydeus himself, Agamemnon has heard good things about him (line 375), which leads him to narrate the story about Tydeus' visit to Mycene (lines 376-398). Traditionally, γάρ is explained in this and other instances as providing the justification for what precedes, which would fit into its generally understood main "causal" or "explanatory" function.[60] Consider this relatively recent description by Sicking of γάρ in Lysias: "The purpose of sentences introduced by

[57] See also II.5 for the different combinations of pronouns + particles and their functions.

[58] See Slings 1997a and De Jong 1997. The observation that γάρ often occurs at the beginning of embedded narratives has been noted before, e.g. by Sturz 1801:565 and Slater 1969:99.

[59] Although in some of the examples I have chosen to render this force of γάρ with "for", this practice should not lead the reader to infer that γάρ always has a causal value, but rather that "for" also has a wider range of functions than just the causal.

[60] See γάρ in ORPS (our online database).

γάρ is primarily explanatory: they provide answers to all sorts of questions raised by the speaker's utterances."[61]

§23. For ancient Greek in general, Slings argues that "the most typical PUSH particle is γάρ," which is to say that it is the particle most typically used to mark the displacement to a new "frame of reference."[62] The PUSH is answered by a POP, which marks the return to the main line of narrative or argumentation.[63] De Jong has approached the use of γάρ in Homeric embedded narratives from a different angle, that of epic regression.[64] It appears to be a typical tool of the epic performer to work his way back from the outcome to the beginning of a story, at which point he tells it from beginning to end in more detail: D-C-B-A-A'-B'-C'-D' in De Jong's notation.[65] Since γάρ is the particle used to provide the cause or justification of something just mentioned, it fits quite naturally at the beginning of the receding steps C-B-A: D happened because C happened, C happened because B happened, and so on. Over time, a variant on this pattern emerged, D-A-B-C-D', where the narrator tells the outcome and then skips immediately to the start of a story, which is thus as a whole introduced by γάρ.[66]

§24. Both Slings and De Jong's approach to γάρ at the beginning of embedded narratives start from the idea that the essence of γάρ, and its basic function, is to provide explanation or justification. However, scholarship on γάρ is divided on the issue of what the original force of the particle was and—by extension—how that original force led to its different uses in later literature.[67] The *communis opinio* emerging from the end of the nineteenth century, and set in stone by Denniston, is that the causal function of γάρ is a development from an earlier affirmative function, which reflects the particle's origins in the combination γε + ἄρ.[68] Denniston, among others, argued that this force had been lost by the time of the earliest extant Greek literature, except in combinations.[69]

61 Sicking 1993:23.

62 Slings 1997a:101: "Embedded sequences are characterised by the fact that they have a different 'frame of reference' from the embedding sequence."

63 See Slings 1997a:101, who takes the PUSH-POP model from Polanyi and Scha 1983.

64 De Jong 1997 "γάρ Introducing Embedded Narratives."

65 The typical example of this pattern is *Iliad* 1.8-16 (discussed in De Jong 1997:177), where we are brought from the outcome to the beginning of the story in successive steps, after which the full story is told from beginning to end.

66 De Jong 1997:176-179; this is in essence the same kind of construction that Slater discusses, though using different terminology.

67 Those scholars who regard γάρ as one of the easily understood particles (e.g. Hummel 1993:406) have focused on classical Attic literature in their analysis of the particle, where its use is quite narrow and specialized.

68 Denniston 1950:56, "The derivation of γάρ from γε and ἄρ, though occasionally challenged (...), has been pretty generally accepted by scholars." Bäumlein 1861:68 exemplifies the approach to the original value of γάρ: "Es wird mithin durch γάρ der ganze Satz als unmittelbar gewiss und unbestreitbar, als eine Thatsache, die nun einmal so ist, nachdrücklich hervorgehoben" ("Through γάρ, the entire sentence is emphatically stressed as immediately certain and incontestable, as a fact that is simply the case").

69 Denniston 1950:57, referring to Misener 1904:7-10.

§25. One view that recurs throughout scholarhip is that γάρ is relevant to starting new parts of discourse.[70] Hoogeveen initially called it "inchoative," while in later scholarship it is more generally called asseverative.[71] The focus has been on γάρ in embedded narratives, as in the studies by Slings and De Jong discussed above, and parentheticals.[72] Although asseverative and inchoative are neutral adjectives, since they denote nothing more than a discontinuity, an assumption underlies many of these studies that γάρ marks its host act or move as in some way subordinate to its co-text.[73]

§26. The recent scholarship on γάρ, then, is characterized by these two tendencies, first the tendency to attribute some causal or explanatory value to all instances of γάρ, and second to regard the discourse introduced by γάρ as new, but also somehow backgrounded or subsidiary to the text that precedes it.[74] Both of these ideas may profit from a re-examination of γάρ from the perspective of the division of discourse into acts and moves. Like most particles—and like "because" or "for" in English—γάρ can mark relations both between acts and between moves.[75] Moreover, it can mark relations on a propositional or on a metalinguistic level. When γάρ is used as metalanguage it will most often function on the level of the move, but this is only a tendency, not a rule.

§27. This distinction is relevant to the occurrence of γάρ at the beginning of embedded narratives, since γάρ in those instances should be regarded as metanarrative. The particle says something about the direction of the upcoming discourse, not so much about the content of the upcoming sentence. Slings implies as much in his discussion of γάρ as a PUSH particle, but Bakker's dicussion of γάρ in terms of the "flow of speech" or "movement in speech" is clearer.[76] Bakker argues that the particle in Homer marks necessary steps in the flow of discourse, to develop something mentioned earlier;[77] this

70 Bakker 1997b:116-118 notes that γάρ often occurs at the start of the "anecdote" in the structure of the ἀνδροκτασία proposed by Beye 1964.

71 Hoogeveen 1769:187-188; see also Sturz 1801:565-569 (on Xenophon) and Ebeling 1885:160-164 (on Homer). Denniston believes that the primary use of γάρ is asseverative (1950:57), but he argues that this force is retained only in combinations. Compare also Bakker 1997b:114 "...it is not surprising that *gár* is particularly at home in the vicinity of the starting point of all starting points, the very beginning of the epic tale."

72 For γάρ-parentheticals in Herodotus see IV.5 §68 and the insightful analysis in Kerschensteiner 1964. Kerschensteiner 1964:36 argues that parentheticals often add crucial, rather than secondary, information (page 36); see also Lang 1984a:6-12, although she does speak of "background digressions."

73 E.g. Sicking 1993:20 "subordinating the stretch (...) within the scope of the particle," Slings 1997a:102 "subsidiary," Wakker 2009b:69 "subsidiary explanation introduced by γάρ." A similar view of the particle is held in the the paper presented by Luraghi and Celano 2012. De Jong and Bakker have actively opposed this notion.

74 For more on γάρ introducing apparent background information, see II.4.2.

75 Consider again Sicking's note about "the purpose of *sentences* introduced by γάρ" [my emphasis]: he regards the force of γάρ as working on the level of the sentence only.

76 Bakker 1997b:112.

77 Bakker 1997b:112, see Hummel 1993:406 (on Pindar) for the same point.

development has nothing to do with foreground or background.[78] He thus redirects attention to another aspect of the use of γάρ in Homer that vindicates the idea of an "explicative" function, but with a more literal understanding of its root "explic-": "unfold".

§28. Bakker's terminology of "developing" captures well what happens in the ongoing epic discourse. Every embedded narrative in Homer represents a choice, since with every character or event he refers to, the epic performer has the freedom to move on or to expand.[79] γάρ at the beginning of embedded narratives marks sections that are associative unfoldings of the collective memory that is the realm of the Homeric performer.[80] It represents the link that the performer perceives between the preceding and subsequent discourse, even if on the surface the two may seem unconnected. γάρ marks the activation by the performer of a narrative that relates to the ongoing narrative in some way: by enriching the story, reflecting upon it, or putting it in a different light. Sometimes the information provided in the γάρ move proves to be nonessential to the narrative, but more often it is indispensable to the development of the ongoing action. In (t6) above, for example, the story invoked by the performer, in the voice of Agamemnon, is a crucial part of Agamemnon's rhetorical strategy in his effort to persuade Diomedes.[81]

§29. In these contexts, it is thus best not to regard γάρ as explanatory, ("[I say this] because…"),[82] but as a marker of the cognitive act of association.[83] This association, moreover, occurs not on a microlevel but on a macrolevel: it is often not the sentence containing γάρ itself that is particularly relevant to the preceding, but the whole move that follows. That is to say, γάρ at the beginning of embedded-narrative moves marks

[78] See Bakker 1997b:113n50, with reference to Hopper 1979:215-216. Bakker's description of γάρ is partly anticipated by Reynen 1958:89-90, who describes its use in *Iliad* 1.55 as making explicit something that has been implicit up to that point. See III.3.3.1.5 for a discussion of γάρ at the beginning of conversational turns, where the contention is likewise that γάρ does not introduce discourse that is in any sense secondary.

[79] See II.5 for more on expansions about characters and the crucial role of particles in guiding such passages.

[80] The use of γάρ to mark unframed discourse, as discussed in II.4, is not so much an unfolding as it is an associative insertion. In both cases there is a displacement, but here it is from one "frame of reference" to another, while in II.4 I discuss the movement between framed and unframed discourse. Regardless, it is never productive to talk about these displaced pieces of discourse as "background."

[81] Note, however, Kirk's comment (1985:I.368) that "such a *digression* was itself attractive from a narrative point of view" [my emphasis]. De Jong 2004^2:155-157 rightly notes the function of the story here, anticipated by Austin 1966:300.

[82] This would be the equivalent of "epistemic because" in constructions like "John's out, because the light is off," discussed by Dancygier and Sweetser 2000:120-122.

[83] A combination that I will not discuss extensively is αἴ γάρ/εἰ γάρ (on which see Misener 1908 and Tabachovitz 1951), which introduces wishes. This is the best construction to illustrate that γάρ can not always be "explanatory" (*pace* Misener 1904 and 1908, who would see a causal relation even in these instances). However, these wishes always arise directly from a preceding thought or utterance, and γάρ signals how the upcoming move arises from the preceding discourse through cognitive association.

the theme or idea represented by the move as relevant to the ongoing discourse.[84] The linguistic form of this move may be of any size, but it is more likely to be a multi-act unit than not.[85] A look through Homer and through Homeric scholarship shows that γάρ often occurs at the beginning of embedded narratives, so in the following discussion I focus more specifically on καὶ γάρ and ἤδη (γάρ) in Homer. In Pindaric song the range of functions of γάρ is the same as in Homer; in chapter II.4 I explore one aspect of the particle's use by Pindar further.[86]

3.2.2.1 καὶ γάρ

§30. About καὶ γάρ De Jong says the following, in a note on *Iliad* 22.46: "καὶ γάρ typically signals the introduction of an example which must back up a general claim."[87] More recently, Aftosmis has made the same claim for καὶ γάρ in Pindar.[88] De Jong's reading is appropriate for *Iliad* 22.46, and there are a number of parallels,[89] but the characterization of καὶ γάρ as introducing examples or paradeigmata oversimplifies the combination's workings. This should not be a surprise, since καὶ γάρ is a combination of two particles and thus also a collocation of two spectra of functions, which would make it unlikely for the combination to have only a limited function.[90] In the forty-five instances of καὶ γάρ in Homer, we find combinations of the whole range of functions of both particles. De Jong chooses to focus on καὶ γάρ used to introduce *exempla*, but her claim that this is "typical" is unfounded. I am more interested in the combination's use in introducing associative narratives, a group of twelve instances that overlap in part with De Jong's paradigmatic narratives.[91] The following example of καὶ γάρ from the last book of the *Iliad* represents

84 This function is by its nature of course not limited to embedded narratives, but may also introduce other moves.

85 Compare the discussion of καί in IV.2 §§133-137, concerning the boundaries of the second conjunct. The process described there for establishing the function of καί could similarly be applied to better understand this function of γάρ.

86 A selection of examples of γάρ starting embedded narratives in Pindar: *Olympian* 1.55 (ἀλλὰ γάρ), 2.48 (μὲν γάρ), 7.27 (καὶ γάρ), 7.48 (καὶ τοὶ γάρ); *Pythian* 2.25, 3.25, 5.83, 6.32, 9.114; *Nemean* 6.34 (καὶ γάρ), 8.26, 9.13, 10.60; *Isthmian* 1.17.

87 De Jong 2012:71, *ad* 22.46; the passage reads as follows:
καὶ γὰρ νῦν δύο παῖδε Λυκάονα καὶ Πολύδωρον /
οὐ δύναμαι ἰδέειν.
Gesamtkommentar 2009:VIII.2.216 makes the same observation about καὶ γάρ at *Iliad* 24.602.

88 Aftosmis 2010:244-270, where he also discusses οὐδὲ γάρ (on which see note 96 below). καὶ γάρ occurs eleven times in Pindar: *Olympian* 7.27, *Pythian* 1.10, 4.181, 9.42, 10.59, *Nemean* 1.50, 1.67, 6.34, *Isthmian* 2.30, 5.4, 5.26; οὐδὲ γάρ once: *Olympian* 14.8.

89 There are 10 instances out of 45 (22+23) total occurrences of καὶ γάρ in Homer that may be said to introduce particular "examples" in the sense perhaps meant by De Jong 2012 (she does not offer any parallels *ad loc.*): *Iliad* 2.292, 2.377 (example in the form of a little narrative), 5.478 (example in the form of a little narrative), 9.502, 16.810, 22.46, 24.602 (example in the form of a little narrative); *Odyssey* 4.199, 14.70, 17.566.

90 See I.1 on combinations in general, and §42 below on ἦ in combinations.

91 *Iliad* 2.377, 9.502, 9.533, 11.698, 19.52, 19.95, 24.602; *Odyssey* 2.17, 17.419, 18.138, 19.75, 19.186.

De Jong's idea of the introduction of an example, while it takes the form of an associative narrative:[92]

(t7)

(...) νῦν δὲ μνησώμεθα δόρπου. |
<u>καὶ γάρ τ'</u>[93] ἠΰκομος Νιόβη ἐμνήσατο σίτου, |
τῇ περ δώδεκα παῖδες ἐνὶ μεγάροισιν ὄλοντο |

Iliad 24.601-603

(...) Now let us remember the meal.
After all even pretty-haired Niobe thought of food,
though for her twelve children died in the halls

As in (t6), the narrative serves as a persuasive device, and again it is triggered by association in the performer's mind. The example of Niobe's story is triggered by the parallel with Priam: just as she ate despite her grief, so Priam should too. It is the association between the two episodes that explains why we find γάρ.[94] In this instance, there is no doubt that the story introduced by γάρ represents a paradigmatic narrative meant to persuade the interlocutors to have dinner. As such, it is a particular example that follows after a general claim. However, association is the key element in the relation between the preceding and upcoming move signalled by γάρ. As a result, the new move can also be a general statement following upon a particular one; the inverse of an example backing up a general claim.[95]

§31. The apparently specialized function of the combination καὶ γάρ in these instances to introduce associative narratives in fact follows naturally from the combination of καί and γάρ. The twelve instances where καὶ γάρ introduces an associative narrative involve three different funtions of καί, while the function of γάρ remains constant. The relevant functions of καί, discussed at length in IV.2, are the scalar function, the function of pinning down, and the more common function of marking similarity. In the

92 The Niobe narrative is a classical example of a ring-composition; see Richardson 1993:339-340 and *Gesamtkommentar* 2009:VIII.2.212-215.

93 A possible explanation for the occurrence of τε in instances like this is that it marks a tradition shared between performer and audience, here the famous story of Niobe; I translate "after all." For an extensive discussion of this aspect of τε see IV.2.3.1 and for the particle's use in Homer see II.4.3.1 and II.4.4.

94 De Jong 1997 quotes a few more instances of γάρ introducing embedded narratives: *Iliad* 4.467, 6.38, 6.130 (see below), 14.315; *Odyssey* 1.260, 3.262, 3.276, 4.677, 14.244, 14.317. These narratives are listed not only because of the use of γάρ, but also because of their regressive structure. As the examples cited here and in the rest of the chapter show, however, it does not look as though the function of γάρ in such contexts should be linked to the recessive nature of the narrative.

95 See for an example of this (t29) below.

little narratives, the inset story features either *better* men, women, or gods doing something that should enlighten the course of action in the current situation,[96] or something that happened to one person or group *in particular*,[97] or something that was *also* once the case for someone else.[98]

§32. The scalar force of καὶ X ("even X…") is especially suited to introducing a paradigmatic story, since if even in more dire situations better men did something, how could we not follow their example?[99] The second group involves the pinning-down function of καί, where one person or group is singled out from an earlier collective.[100] Finally the last four instances, all in the *Odyssey*, show perhaps the most familiar face of καί marking a perceived parallel, to be translated as "too" or "also."[101] The function of γάρ in all these instances does not fluctuate as that of καί does, but in all cases it marks an association between the new move and the ongoing narrative. Because of the differences among even these few cases, it is unproductive to think of καὶ γάρ as working in a cluster with one specific function in Homer. In Homer the two particles work separately, combining different functions of καί with γάρ to introduce different kinds of moves. The new move may be a paradigmatic narrative, as in the case of the Niobe story, but it may also be associated to the surrounding discourse in other ways, depending on the function of καί.

3.2.3 ἤδη and ἦ marking beginnings

§33. The function of γάρ to introduce associative narratives illustrates the particle's importance for the process of producing, unfolding the narrative. Not surprisingly, then, γάρ can introduce narratives in other combinations than only with καί, as in the following passage from *Iliad* book 3, where Antenor describes Odysseus to Priam. We are on the walls of Troy, and Helen is pointing out the best of the Achaeans at Priam's request. After her brief introduction of Odysseus, Antenor pitches in with an associative narrative to illustrate where Odysseus' real talents lie:

96 Zeus in *Iliad* 19.95 and Niobe in *Iliad* 24.602. Note also *Iliad* 6.130-131 οὐδὲ γὰρ οὐδὲ Δρύαντος υἱὸς | κρατερὸς Λυκόοργος / δὴν ἦν and 18.117 οὐδὲ γὰρ οὐδὲ βίη Ἡρακλῆος φύγε κῆρα, which show that the opposite of the scalar function of καί can be rendered with οὐδέ "not even." These are the only two cases where οὐδὲ γάρ introduces an associative narrative (out of 9 + 3 instances in Homer). On οὐδέ as the "negative scalar particle" see Cooper 2002:4.3069 (*sub* P), Denniston 1950:196, Ruijgh 1971:190, and Willmott 2011:13-15.

97 The *Curetes* had been the victim of Artemis' wrath in *Iliad* 9.533; *Neleus* was owed a debt from the Eleians in *Iliad* 11.698; *Aegyptius*' son was killed by the Cyclops in *Odyssey* 2.17.

98 Agamemnon *too* had been wounded by Coön in *Iliad* 19.52; Odysseus *too* had once lived in a house amongst his men in *Odyssey* 17.419, 18.138, and 19.75; Odysseus-in-disguise speaks of seeing himself coming to Crete *too* in *Odyssey* 19.186.

99 In the words of Richardson 1993:340 on the Niobe narrative (t7), these are arguments "*a fortiori*." See for καί as a scalar particle IV.2 §123 and Bakker 1988:75, 84, 113-119, and 205.

100 See IV.2.4.2 for καί used to pin down something specific.

101 See IV.2 §124 for καί rendered as "also"; Denniston 1950:293 calls this function "responsive," but without clarification of the term.

(t8)

Τὴν δ’ αὖτ’ Ἀντήνωρ πεπνυμένος ἀντίον ηὔδα·
“ὦ γύναι | *ἦ μάλα* τοῦτο ἔπος νημερτὲς ἔειπες· |
ἤδη γὰρ καὶ δεῦρό *ποτ’*[102] ἤλυθε | δῖος Ὀδυσσεύς” |

Iliad 3.203-205

Her in turn did Antenor the prudent respond:
“Milady, *really* you told that story truthfully.[103]
For already here *too once* came noble Odysseus.”[104]

In a valiant attempt to do justice to the string ἤδη γὰρ καὶ δεῦρό ποτ’, Murray translates line 204 as: “for (γάρ) once (ποτ’) before (ἤδη) also (καί) noble Odysseus came here (δεῦρο).”[105] This translation sounds forced because, among other reasons, it stretches the meaning of ἤδη. The presence of ποτε (“once”) means that the most common sense of the temporal adverb, “already”, would be superfluous. Murray here translates it to mean “at some point before the present,” when elsewhere in Homer it always bears a relation to the present, so “now” or “already” in the sense of “by now.”[106] Adverbs like ἤδη are called “mobile,” since they can occur in any position in an act. Thus we find it at the beginning (*Odyssey* 2.89 ἤδη γὰρ τρίτον ἐστὶν ἔτος, “it is already the third year”), in the middle (*Iliad* 7.293 νὺξ δ’ ἤδη τελέθει “and night is already here”), or at the end (*Odyssey* 1.303 αὐτὰρ ἐγὼν ἐπὶ νῆα θοὴν κατελεύσομαι ἤδη “and I will go to my swift ship now”).[107] In (t8) and a number of parallels, however, I believe that we are not looking at ἤδη at the beginning of an embedded narrative, but at ἦ δή. In the following section, I argue that a number of instances of ἤδη γάρ in the *Iliad* may in fact represent ἦ δὴ γάρ. To back up that argument, I discuss the relevant passages in relation to the instances where our manuscripts

102 Note that this construction brings to mind the introduction of the “lyric narrative” as discussed by Slater and West (see fn. 56), including ποτε and the aorist, but without the pronoun.

103 νημερτές is an adjective that goes with ἔπος, but I translate it as an adverb, in order to better render τοῦτο.

104 Here and in the following examples I give the text of the editions (ἤδη) and translate accordingly (“already”).

105 *Gesamtkommentar* 2009:III.2.84 takes γάρ as explanatory: “γάρ leitet eine Erzählung ein, die als ganze zur Erklärung der vorausgehenden Aussage dient” (“γάρ introduces a narrative, which as a whole serves to explain the preceding utterance”).

106 See Thiersch 1852:427.

107 Thomas 1894:81-83 notes rightly that in Homer in a large number of cases ἤδη is limited to the initial position. This may suggest that ἤδη evolved out of (initial) ἦ + δή, as Thomas believes (84: “In the first part of ἤδη we have plainly nothing but the common circumflexed asseverative particle [ἦ]”). Thiersch 1852:427, conversely, assumes that the manuscripts wrongly render ἤδη in initial position for a certain number of instances and proposes to read ἤδη with a purely temporal sense especially where ἤδη is found in non-initial position (*fit hoc imprimis, si ἤδη in media sententia aut post alias particulas infertur*).

do read ἦ δή. Finally, I offer a possible explanation of ἦ in these and similar contexts. Since the relevant instances of ἤδη γάρ are limited to the *Iliad*, in this section there are no examples from the *Odyssey*.

§34. Although the manuscripts—especially Venetus A and B—offer valuable readings, strings of letters like HΔH are often ambiguous, and the choices made by the medieval scribes and more recently by editors are to some extent arbitrary.[108] When found at act beginning, HΔH may equally resolve as either ἤδη or ἦ δή.[109] The combination ἦ δή is restricted to act-initial position, since ἦ is initial in Homer. The use of ἤδη throughout the Homeric epics shows beyond doubt that it can be a mobile adverb with the meaning of "already" or "(by) now." However, it is not to be taken for granted that whenever our manuscripts have ἤδη it is the adverb that we should read. The nature of the textual transmission of the Homeric corpus means that it is possible that HΔH (ΓAP) at verse beginning was simply rendered homogeneously as ἤδη γάρ despite the fact that in some cases it stood for ἦ δὴ γάρ.[110]

§35. Now to return to (t8) above, I propose the following reading: ἦ | δὴ γάρ καὶ δεῦρό ποτ' ἤλυθε | δῖος Ὀδυσσεὺς | ("Oh yes (ἦ), for actually (δὴ γάρ) he came right here[111] once, god-like Odysseus"). This reading of ἦ as a separate act with interjectional value and a distinct prosodic contour marks a strong discontinuity in the discourse, here the start of an embedded narrative. This use of ἦ at move beginning has many parallels in Homer. We find this asseverative force of ἦ in the string ἦ δή at the start of direct speech (see below), in ἤτοι (or ἦ τοι),[112] ἤδη, the swearing formula ἦ μήν, and possibly even the apparent verb form ἦ ("he spoke", from ἦμι) in Homeric discourse.[113] Moreover, the

[108] Consider, for example, the reading of *Iliad* 1.453 in Ven. A and B: ἤδη μέν (ἦ μὲν δή or ἠμὲν δή edd.)

[109] ἢ δή and ᾗ δή are also possible, but it is normally easier to establish if a feminine relative pronoun is warranted in a sentence.

[110] The instances of ἤδη γάρ at the beginning of narratives are: *Iliad* 1.260, 1.590, 3.205, 5.188, 14.249; in all of these cases ἤδη γάρ is verse-initial. The same use may be found in Hesiod *Theogony* 645-646: ὄφρ' εἴπω τά με θυμὸς ἐνὶ στήθεσσι κελεύει / ἤδη γὰρ μάλα δηρὸν ἐναντίοι ἀλλήλοισι, which is one of only two instances of verse-initial ἤδη γάρ in Hesiod. Since ἤδη is a mobile, there are also instances where ἤδη in first position does mean "already" or "(by) now," and as a result ἤδη γάρ does not begin new embedded narrative, namely: *Iliad* 5.206, 6.361, 14.206 (=14.305), 15.110, 15.139, 15.613, 19.334, 20.306, 23.623, 24.765; In the *Odyssey*, ἤδη γάρ is never used to introduce an embedded narrative; the instances are: 2.89, 2.211, 3.335, 5.161, 5.223, 6.34, 10.381, 12.451, 13.40, 15.16, 15.66, 17.606, 19.160, 19.222, 20.309. In the majority of instances the adverb is here followed by a present, an imperative, or νῦν.

[111] See IV.2.4.2 for this pinning-down function of καί.

[112] Thiersch 1852:428 argues that ἤτοι never serves to introduce the first part of an antithesis (against Apollonius Dyscolus and the recent *communis opinio*, see also Ruijgh 1981), but in fact always serves to start something new (*asseverat*) with a conclusive force from τοι. Ruijgh 1981 reads ἤτοι in narrative and ἦ τοι in direct speech, but Thiersch 1852:452-453 argues that we should read ἦ τοι everywhere in Homer.

[113] Compare the use of interjections after direct speech in the Serbo-Croatian epic song discussed in Bonifazi and Elmer 2012a, with examples from PN 662, line 32"..." *Hey, when the serdar's company*

string δὴ γάρ at act beginning is uniquely Homeric. In Homer we find a limited number of constructions that allow δή at act beginning: δὴ γάρ (never at verse beginning), δὴ τότε, δή ῥα τότε (both always at verse beginning). In four other separate instances the position of δή is debatable.[114] In later Greek δή becomes mostly restricted to peninitial position in the act.[115] The fact that δὴ γάρ is never found at verse beginning[116] may be another reason why we find the string ἦ δὴ γάρ.[117]

§36. Compare the following introduction of another associative narrative in *Iliad* 1:[118]

(t9)

(...) ἀργαλέος γὰρ Ὀλύμπιος ἀντιφέρεσθαι· |
ἤδη γάρ με καὶ ἄλλοτ' | ἀλεξέμεναι μεμαῶτα |
ῥῖψε ποδὸς τεταγὼν ἀπὸ βηλοῦ θεσπεσίοιο, |

Iliad 1.589-591

(...) Because the Olympian is dangerous to oppose.
For already also another time, as I was trying to save you,
he threw me, having seized my foot, from the divine threshold.

Line 589 may be read alternatively, with my emendation, as follows: ἦ | δὴ γάρ με ("Yes, for actually (καί) another time, as I was trying to save you, he threw me..."). If we want to read ἤδη with the manuscripts, the same temporal problem holds as in (t8) above. The event has direct relevance to the present, but if ἤδη indeed is a temporal marker here, its function is not to emphasize that it has "already happened," but that it "happened at some point before the present" which is in fact fully expressed by ἄλλοτε, as it is by ποτε in (t8).

§37. These two examples may suggest that we should always translate ἦ as "(Oh) yes..." but the exact translation is not the point.[119] The force of ἦ is connected to its

---

heard this on page 302 and line 476 "..." *Oh, when Halil understood these words* on page 304.

114 *Iliad* 15.437, 19.342, 23.785, and 24.243, see §§57-63 for a discussion of all four passages. Note that these cases are restricted to the *Iliad*, just like the instances of ἦ δὴ γάρ starting an embedded narrative. See IV.4 §§101-102 for a discussion of γὰρ δή in Herodotus and IV.4 §147 on ἤδη γάρ and γὰρ ἤδη in Herodotus and Thucydides.

115 Except in Hesiod (8 instances of δή in initial position) and later imitations of the Homeric style. See IV.3.11.3-4 for δή in μὲν δή and other combinations in Herodotus and Thucydides.

116 Metrically it would be quite at home at verse beginning, since the combination often forms a trochae within the verse.

117 For a discussion of further instances of δὴ γάρ, see §62.

118 *Gesamtkommentar* 2000:I.2.180 calls the narrative a paradigm, which serves to justify ("*begründen*") Hephaestus' warning.

119 The association of ἦ with affirmation is widespread in earlier scholarship, but Ruijgh 1971:192-194 first argues that it was actually the positive antithesis of οὐ ("Or, il nous paraît possible que dans la préhistorie du grec, ἦ ait eu la fonction et la valeur représentées plus tard par ναί

prosodic contour, and carries no fixed semantic load. Compare this example from *Iliad* book 14:

(t10)

Ζηνὸς δ' | οὐκ ἂν ἔγωγε Κρονίονος ἆσσον ἱκοίμην |
οὐδὲ κατευνήσαιμ', | ὅτε μὴ αὐτός γε κελεύοι. |
ἤδη γάρ με καὶ ἄλλο τεὴ[120] ἐπίνυσσεν ἐφετμὴ |

Iliad 14.247-249

To Zeus, I would not go any closer to Cronus' son,
nor would I lull him into sleep, if it were not he himself that ordered me.
For already also another time your command taught me,

If we read ἦ | δὴ γάρ με here, the thought expressed is perhaps best rendered in English as "no" ("No, for actually also another time your command taught me"). A little narrative of that earlier event then follows.

§38. All of the examples above occur in direct speech, where ἦ might at the same time be regarded as a sign of the character's involvement.[121] In fact, where the manuscripts consistently give ἦ δή rather than ἤδη, the particles always occur at the start of direct speech.[122] These passages provide another argument to read ἦ | δὴ γάρ rather

'oui!'" 192), and his argument is followed by Sicking 1993:55. The problem of paraphrasing ἦ is well illustrated by Stephens 1837:43, when he paraphrases ἦ πολλά (Sophocles, *Ajax* 1418) as "Much, *yes, much*" [italics original], but does not put forward "yes" as one of the possible ways to render ἦ. "Yes" + repetition happens to be a way to emphasize a word in English (which is what Stephens wants to render), but this does not mean he regards ἦ and "yes" as equivalent in that passage.

120 See Janko 1992:190-191 for the textual problems in this line, especially regarding ἄλλο τεή.

121 See especially Cuypers 2005 for Homer, who argues that ἦ almost exclusively occurs in direct speech. This is a problematic statistic, however, because ἦ is a typical lexical item that is subject to a lot of editorial interference. For example, there is no consensus about whether the string HTOI should be rendered always as ἤτοι, always as ἦ τοι, or one or the other depending on the context. Ruijgh 1981 reads ἤτοι in narrative and ἦ τοι in direct speech, but consider Thiersch 1852:452-453, who argues we should read ἦ τοι everywhere in Homer. Murray's Loeb text gives ἦ τοι everywhere, while Van Thiel 1996 and West 1999 give ἤτοι in narrator text in the *Iliad*; but compare Garvie 1994 and Steiner 2010 (with note on page 96) who consistently print ἦ τοι in their *Odyssey* texts.

122 The instances of ἦ δή in Homer are: *Iliad* 1.518, 1.573, 2.272, 2.337, 14.53, 15.467, 17.538 (ἦ δὴ μὰν), 21.583 (ἦ δή που), 24.518, compare moreover 17.629 ἤδη μέν (ἦ δὴ μέν N; West does not note the variant in his apparatus); *Odyssey* 1.253, 5.182. Compare also ἦ καί at the start of direct speech in *Iliad* 6.441 and *Odyssey* 1.158, 21.131; ἦ μάλα δή in *Iliad* 6.518, 8.102, 11.441, 15.14, 22.229, 22.297, 22.373 and *Odyssey* 1.384, 4.169, 4.333, 4.770, 5.286, 9.507, 11.436, 12.297, 13.172, 13.383, 15.486, 17.124, 17.264, 22.151, 23.149; ἦ μέγα θαῦμα in *Iliad* 21.54.

than ἤδη γάρ in the examples discussed above and their parallels. Three instances are especially relevant: *Iliad* 15.467, 17.538, and 21.583. For *Iliad* 15.467 the Venetus A manuscript offers an informative reading: "ὢ πόποι· ἦ, δὴ πάγχυ..."[123] The comma after ἦ suggests a pause after this single syllable, which matches my reading of the instances of ἤδη γάρ under discussion, listed in note 110.[124] The other two relevant instances of ἦ δή at the start of direct speech, *Iliad* 17.538 and 21.583, are similar to ἤδη γάρ in that another second-position word follows δή: it is followed by μάν in *Iliad* 17.538 and που in *Iliad* 21.583. Whereas που, being an enclitic, is often pushed back,[125] μάν is accented and is never pushed from its second position by another second-position word in Homer,[126] except in this passage, *Iliad* 17.538.[127] This exception suggest that here μάν is in fact in its normal second position, and that ἦ, as in the beginnings of embedded narratives in ἤδη γάρ (or ἦ δὴ γάρ), forms its own discourse act.[128] Seeing Hector and Aeneas flee before the Aiantes, Patroclus' charioteer Automedon rejoices for having killed Aretus:

(t11)

τεύχεά τ' ἐξενάριξε καὶ εὐχόμενος ἔπος ηὔδα· |
"ἦ | δὴ μὰν ὀλίγον γε | Μενοιτιάδαο θανόντος |
κῆρ ἄχεος μεθέηκα | χερείονά περ καταπέφνων." |

Iliad 17.537-539

He stripped him of his armor he spoke this word in prayer:
"*Yes! Surely* at least a little, now that Menoetius' son died,
I have eased my heart, having killed only a lesser one."

123 Compare the act-initial δὴ πάμπαν in *Iliad* 19.342, see §60-§61.

124 See IV.3.4 for the relation of prosody to punctuation in ancient and medieval scholarship.

125 Although even the position of που seems to have caused some confusion in 21.583: Herodian notes that some manuscripts wrongly (οὐκ εὖ) read ἤδη here.

126 Only by the first-position word ἀλλά followed by οὐ: *Iliad* 5.895, 17.41, 17.448, 23.441.

127 There are no instances of μάν δή, but this may be the result of the fact that μάν, μήν, and μέν before consonants were normalized to μέν. There are 59 (33+26) instances of μὲν δή in Homer, of which nine are ἦ μὲν (or ἠμὲν) δή: *Iliad* 1.453, 2.798, 3.430, 7.97, 9.348, 16.362; *Odyssey* 4.33, 14.216, 18.257. See Nägelsbach 1834: 153-176, Friedländer 1859a:820-823, Bäumlein 1861:153-154, and Wackernagel 1916:177-182 on μέν, μάν, and μήν in Homer, and specifically on the interchangeability of μέν and μήν/μάν in Homer see Nägelsbach 1834:159-167, Cobet 1875:365-367, and Leumann 1949:85-89. One of their conclusions is that μέν was probably written before consonants and μάν before vowels.

128 This would mean that there was one other construction which retained δή in act-initial position: δὴ μάν before vowel, as in *Iliad* 17.538 and ἤδη (ἦ δὴ?) μέν before consonant as in *Iliad* 17.629, with possible parallels in *Iliad* 20.187 ἤδη (ἦ δὴ?) μέν and *Odyssey* 24.506 ἤδη (ἦ δὴ?) μέν. In the other instances of ἤδη μέν in Homer, the adverb ἤδη looks like the best reading.

As a marker of discursive discontinuity, ἦ is not limited to introducing embedded narratives, which it does in the cluster ἤ | δὴ γάρ. In (t11) ἦ starts direct speech (with numerous parallels in note 123) and it regularly occurs at the start of oaths (in the cluster ἦ μήν). In both cases one can imagine the effectiveness of a prosodic interruption in the form of ἦ to mark the transition to a new kind of discourse, a new move.[129]

§39. This correlation between the occurrence of ἦ and the start of a new move supports several scholars' characterization of ἦ as asseverative.[130] More often, however, descriptions of ἦ focus on the function of affirming what the speaker is saying, as a marker of (emotional) involvement.[131] Whether it is actually used in dialogue, as in drama, or not, its force is generally understood as dialogic in nature. For the passages cited above, we have translated ἦ as a reaction to an implicit question, to better render the discontinuity in discourse.[132] It marks the speaker anticipating a likely question from his audience, and answering it with the narrative (or other kind of move) that is relevant to the imagined question. At the start of direct speech, ἦ rather marks a reaction to something that just happened, as Automedon reacts to what he has done in (t11).

§40. The majority of approaches to ἦ have focused on its possible force and function on the sentence level, with little attention to its place within the larger discourse. Despite etymologists' observations that the particle may derive from an interjection, few scholars have regarded ἦ from this angle.[133] Primary interjections are linguistic renderings of often non-lexical exclamations, and as a result their force lies less in their semantic content (if there is any)[134] and much more in their prosodic contour.[135] Consider the following definition of an interjection by Ameka: "Primary interjections are little words or non-words which (...) can constitute an utterance by themselves. (...) They could be uttered as co-utterances with other units."[136] And this same author adds

[129] See also Scodel 2012:329, "ἦ (...) most often appear[s] at this boundary where an individual, internal judgment meets the outside world—or the judgment of others."

[130] See Thiersch 1852:424-440, Thomas 1894:81-85, Smyth 1956:649, Slater 1969:223; compare also Kühner 1835:391 where he argues that ἦ μήν introduces an autonomous expression.

[131] See ἦ in ORPS (our online database); most recently, Sicking 1993, Van Erp Taalman Kip 1997, Wakker 1997b, Cuypers 2005, and Caspers 2010 have discussed the particle in terms of the interaction between speaker and hearer. See III.2.2.10 and III.4 §47 on the function of ἦ in tragic and comic dialogue, IV.4.3.1 for ἦ μήν and IV.4.8 for ἤδη linked to speaker involvement.

[132] See Humbert 1960:406, who imagines the speaker talking to himself: "comme qui se dirait: 'Oui, c'est bien ainsi'" ("as if someone said to himself: 'Yes, it is really like that'.").

[133] See Schwyzer and Debrunner 1950:II.564, Ruijgh 1971:192, Chantraine 2009^2:387, Beekes 2010:I.507.

[134] Although Nordgren 2012 attempts to establish the semantics of interjections in ancient Greek drama.

[135] See Biraud 2010 for a discussion of the possible prosodic realization of ancient Greek interjections, compare Norrick 2009a:868-869 for the prosodic quality of interjections in English.

[136] Ameka 1992, with the definition on page 105; see also Nordgren 2012:8-15 for the discussion of the term as applied to ancient Greek.

that interjections are "always separated by a pause from the other utterances with which they may co-occur."[137]

§41. The pronunciation of ἦ appears to have been a continuum ranging from a full interjection,[138] reflecting its possible origin, to the disjunctive particle ἤ, which has a rather narrow and clear function. This continuum might be regarded as the synchronic reflection of a diachronic evolution.[139] Likewise, the Homeric corpus shows traces of δή as a mobile adverb but also as a particle restricted to second position, while the combination ἦ + δή = ἤδη became a mobile adverb, possibly under the influence of δή.[140] If ἦ was indeed originally an interjection, it would have constituted a discourse act by itself, as a vocative does, for example.[141] ἦ's origin as an interjection would explain why it developed into a particle restricted to act-initial position. An independent interjection would always be used before (or after) another act, and if it were to be assimilated into one of the surrounding acts, the interjection would most naturally come at the end of the preceding act or the beginning of the following. Since interjections in Greek are often turn-initial,[142] it makes sense that ἦ would become restricted to act-initial position.[143]

§42. Because of its initial position, ἦ will have become collocated with peninitial words, often other particles. The resulting collocations then specialized into combinations with specific functions (such as ἦ μέν/μήν/μάν to introduce oaths, and ἦ γάρ as a tag question requesting confirmation). The existence of these specializations, however, should not blind us to the original force of the component parts, for two reasons. First, the specialized combination could only come to work as it does because of the function of the particles that originally formed it; a cluster does not form arbitrarily. Second, the fact that a certain cluster specializes into a specific function does not mean that every instance of the combination must have this specialized function.[144] For example, ἦ μέν does not always have to introduce an oath: it may also occur where ἦ is used to mark another kind of new move and μέν marks its host act as the beginning of a larger part of discourse. Likewise HΔH is not always ἤδη, HTOI can be both ἦ τοι and ἤτοι, and so on.[145]

137 Ameka 1992:108.

138 As apparently imagined by the scribe of Venetus A at *Iliad* 15.467, see §38.

139 Given the apparent different linguistic layers in the Homeric corpus, it may even be a direct representation of the diachronic development, with different uses of ἦ reflecting different stages in the creation of the text. However, we insist that it is not problematic to assume that a certain lexical item is used in different ways at one moment in time, with the native speakers often not even conscious of the differences between them, or, conversely, of their common ancestry; see Koier 2013:19-23 for more on this concept.

140 For a discussion of the different functions of δή in Homer see §§53-64.

141 See Fränkel 1965 for more on the vocative and act boundaries (*Kolon*-boundaries in his terms).

142 Nordgren 2012:52-55.

143 Of course, they share this characteristic with discourse markers or pragmatic markers (see Norrick 2009:870), under which many particles may be subsumed.

144 Compare the discussion of καὶ γάρ in the Homeric epics in §30-§31.

145 This includes the start of an associative narrative in *Iliad* 6.414 ἦ τοι γάρ, 19.100 ἤτοι ὁ γε, as well as instances where ἦ τοι introduces indirect speech or indirect thought, as in also *Iliad* 15.699

§43. It is important to remember that even the consensus readings of Homeric manuscripts, scholia, and editions are fallible. By exercising due skepticism, we may identify phenomena that orthography has obscured. As becomes clear only when one takes into account the larger discourse, the instances of ἦ (δή) above form a separate group that shows a specific (perhaps older) function of ἦ. On its own and in combination with other particles in Homer, ἦ may serve as a prosodic marker of the beginning of a new move, a paralinguistic means to signal discontinuities in the discourse.[146] However, this does not mean that it does not function at the same time as a marker of speaker involvement, as it has been described in most of the recent publications.[147] The particle can mark a discontinuity or salient moment in the interaction, and at the same time it may reflect the emotional engagement of the speaker.[148]

§44. For different reasons, then, both γάρ and ἦ occur at the beginning of embedded narratives or other moves. The force of γάρ is too often regarded as clearly causal or explanatory, but the causal function does not best describe its force when used in epic or lyric. As for ἦ, I have offered an analysis that considers its function in the flow of discourse, taking into account its possible origin. Whereas the use of γάρ must perhaps be seen as a result of the cognitive activities of composer or performer, the use of ἦ is a direct reflection of an interactional situation, either real or imagined.

3.2.4 Other narrative beginnings

§45. Embedded narratives in epic represent unfoldings on the path through the Homeric storyworld. Beside ἦ and γάρ there are multiple other linguistic means to start embedded narratives, such as adverbs of time and place. Certain locales in the storyworld bring with them longer or shorter stories. These can be told at any point when a place is mentioned in the narrative, and the stories can therefore be activated with locative adverbs. Consider the following excerpt from one of Odysseus' stories:

ὅδ' ἦν νόος | ἦ τοι Ἀχαιοὶ and *Odyssey* 5.383: αὐτὰρ Ἀθηναίη κούρη Διὸς ἄλλ' ἐνόησεν / ἦ τοι τῶν ἄλλων; compare IV.4.3.1 (ἦ μήν) and IV.4.8 (ἤδη).

146 The corpus of these instances is not complete. There are several other instances of ἤδη at move beginnings, and probably others of ἦ + X as well; consider for instance ἤδη νῦν at *Odyssey* 10.472, 15.65, 16.168, and perhaps ἤδη τοι in *Odyssey* 22.101. For now I have focused on ἤδη γάρ and ἦ δή in the manuscripts.

147 See note 130 above.

148 I maintain this point in spite of Norrick's remark (2009a:868) that in his sizeable English corpus "many primary interjections do not express emotions, as is often maintained of interjections generally, but rather information states."

(t12)

> Θρινακίην δ' ἐς νῆσον ἀφίξεαι· | ἔνθα δὲ πολλαὶ
> βόσκοντ' Ἠελίοιο βόες | καὶ ἴφια μῆλα.
>
> *Odyssey* 12.127-128

> And you will come to the island of Thrinacia. There in numbers
> graze the cattle of Helios and his strong flocks.

ἔνθα is here clearly used in a spatial sense, its core value. In that capacity it serves well to initiate a little narrative associated with a place. The word, however, is used more broadly in Homeric epic—in fact, the majority of instances in Homer marks the start of a new move within a narrative, generally translated with "then."[149] ἔνθα thus straddles a fuzzy semantic border where it can mean either (or both) "then" and "there". When ἔνθα means "there" it refers to a geographical place in the storyworld, but when it is most naturally translated as "then," it may well be a marker of a certain "place" on the unfolding path of the narrative.[150]

§46. Another marker often occurring in move-initial position is ὡς/ὥς. Like ἔνθα, this word is multi-faceted: it can mean "just like..." or the corresponding "that's how," typical of the Homeric simile, but it can also start a "when" clause, often preposed to the initial action of a new scene. The function of such constructions in providing a static setting before the dynamic action makes complete sense with regard to the build-up of narratives in general.[151] As such, it is important to consider their discursive or narrative function, and unproductive to focus on their syntactical subordinate status.[152]

§47. There are, then, several ways to mark narrative beginnings linguistically. My analysis of γάρ, ἦ, and other words demonstrates that it is important to be aware of such macro-discursive divisions when looking at particles. Only then can they be seen as what they are: reflections of an ongoing interactive exchange. Particles mark moments in the act of narration rather than syntactical relations in a text, and as such provide invaluable insight into the interaction between performer and audience.

§48. On occasion, however, there is no explicit linguistic marking of important transitions in the discourse. Since we must start from the assumption that the performer would not have wanted to confuse the audience, a lack of linguistic signs would necessitate some kind of non-linguistic or paralinguistic marking. In Pindar, every new strophe

149 Note, for example, how often ἔνθα occurs after an indentation in modern editions, and even at the very beginning of book 5 of the *Iliad*. Bonifazi 2012:283-284 hints at a similar interpretation of ἔνθα as a discourse marker.

150 See Bakker's separation between "performance time" and "story time" 1997b:68.

151 Compare the function of the priming acts described in II.2.5.

152 For more on such "when clauses" see Bakker 1991.

or antistrophe is a new beginning, and the performative discontinuity is even stronger with the start of a new epode. Since the Homeric epics were not generally performed in one go, or not by a single performer,[153] we may assume that they too offered possibilities to break off and start again and thus creating very clear boundaries of which very little trace remains in the text.

§49. Whether or not we may find traces of such heavy performative discontinuities in our texts, on a local level there are passages where a strong discontinuity on the level of content or orientation remains without syndetic marking. In the famous battlefield encounter between Glaucus and Diomedes in book six of the *Iliad*, Glaucus embarks on a long story about the fame of his forefathers at line 152:

(t13)

> ἔστι πόλις Ἐφύρη | μυχῷ Ἄργεος ἱπποβότοιο, |
> ἔνθα δὲ Σίσυφος ἔσκεν, | ὃ κέρδιστος γένετ᾽ ἀνδρῶν, |
>
> *Iliad* 6.152-153
>
> *There is a city*[154] *Ephyre*, in a corner of Argos grazed by horses.
> And there Sisyphus lived, who was the craftiest of men.

With the story Glaucus starts a new move, but contrary to expectation we do not find any syndetic marking at its beginning. This start of a new move in asyndeton is informative. The lack of metalinguistic marking suggests that the discontinuity must have been marked by the performer in some non-linguistic or paralinguistic manner.[155] This is not to say that the presence of a metalinguistic marker voids the possibility of extralinguistic or paralinguistic marking. The example shows that there are multiple strategies to negotiate discourse transitions, involving metalinguistic marking to a greater or lesser extent, and always possibly marked otherwise in performance.

153 See e.g. Ford 1997.

154 The construction ἦν or ἔστι followed by a geographic location recurs in Homer, both with and without particles, see *Gesamtkommentar* 2003:II.2.262 *ad* 2.811 for all parallels and literature. The other asyndetic constructions with ἦν or ἔστι are: *Odyssey* 7.244, 9.116, 15.403, 19.172. Givón 2005:131-133 discusses the following constructions in English: "There's this guy..." and finds that the "cataphoric persistence" of those referents in the following discourse is very strong. That is to say that referents introduced through this kind of "existential presentative construction" tend to persist as discourse topics in the following discourse. Recently, Auer and Maschler 2013 have described the narrative function of VS (verb subject) constructions in spoken stories in Hebrew and German, but they do not discuss the construction with existential verbs.

155 A parallel instance is *Iliad* 9.529 Κουρῆτές τ᾽ ἐμάχοντο καὶ Αἰτωλοὶ μενεχάρμαι, but there the story is announced more explicitly by the *verbum dicendi* ἐρέω (*I will tell*, 528). This verb is in turn a metanarrative comment by the secondary narrator, Phoenix, who is telling this story.

§50. Another kind of asyndetic start of narratives is represented by the example below. It consists in a relative or demonstrative pronoun in an oblique case, followed by a little narrative about its referent.

(t14)

> (...) γλαυκόχροα κόσμον ἐλαίας, | <u>τάν ποτε</u>
> Ἴστρου ἀπὸ σκιαρᾶν παγᾶν ἔνεικεν Ἀμφιτρυωνιάδας |
>
> Pindar *Olympian* 3.13-14
>
> (...) the graycolored adornment of olive, *which once*
> from the shady springs of the Ister Amphitryon's son brought,[156]

Here we see a narrative of the kind described by Slater and West as a "lyric narrative", introduced by a pronoun, ποτε, and an aorist.[157] The transition to the narrative falls on a metrical boundary in the song, which would allow for some prosodic marking on τάν ποτε to signal that it is the start of a new move.[158] For the present study it suffices to note that asyndeton, the start of a new sentence without the use of a conjunction, conjunctive adverb, or particle, often occurs at the beginning of new moves. For Homer asyndeta occur mostly at the start of embedded narratives or subsections of narratives, while in Pindar asyndeton can occur at the start of an embedded narrative, at narrative transitions, introducing a gnomic statement, or at the transition to the *hic et nunc*.[159] The lack of any metalinguistic marking of so strong a discursive transition suggests some kind of prosodic discontinuity such as an extended pause.[160]

3.3 Move Transitions in Homeric Narrative

§51. The preceding section concerned itself with the range of possible methods of marking embedded narratives linguistically. The next step is to discuss the transition between different components of a certain narrative, taking the Labovian division (§14) into consideration. Let us return to Antenor's story about Odysseus (t8). After making some initial remarks about Odysseus' earlier visit at Helen's summons, Antenor continues:

[156] Translation Race 1997, order adapted.

[157] See Gentili 2013:421. Slater 1983 discusses parallels for this in Homer, with a focus on those narratives introduced by a relative pronoun + ποτε; see above §§21-22. Compare also Pindar *Olympian* 3.29, 6.75, 7.30, 9.9, 10.104, 13.63; *Pythian* 1.16, 4.20, 4.107, 4.152, 9.15, 10.31, 12.6; *Nemean* 4.25.

[158] τάν ποτε makes up the final dactyl of the third verse of the epode, Snell/Maehler 1971:11 regard this as a separate metrical colon.

[159] See Xanthou 2007 on asyndeton in Pindar, and below §§65-76 for transitions in Pindar involving particles and other markers.

[160] Compare IV.3.4 for Nicanor's contention that asyndetic transitions were accompanied by the longest pause in his system, of four *khronoi*.

(t15)

τοὺς δ' ἐγὼ ἐξείνισσα | καὶ ἐν μεγάροισι φίλησα, |
ἀμφοτέρων δὲ φυὴν ἐδάην | καὶ μήδεα πυκνά. |
ἀλλ' ὅτε δὴ Τρώεσσιν ἐν ἀγρομένοισιν ἔμιχθεν |
στάντων μὲν Μενέλαος ὑπείρεχεν εὐρέας ὤμους, |
ἄμφω δ' ἑζομένω | γεραρώτερος ἦεν Ὀδυσσεύς· |
ἀλλ' ὅτε δὴ μύθους καὶ μήδεα πᾶσιν ὕφαινον |
ἤτοι μὲν Μενέλαος ἐπιτροχάδην ἀγόρευε, |
παῦρα μὲν ἀλλὰ μάλα λιγέως, | ἐπεὶ οὐ πολύμυθος |
οὐδ' ἀφαμαρτοεπής· | ἦ[161] | καὶ γένει ὕστερος ἦεν. |
ἀλλ' ὅτε δὴ πολύμητις ἀναΐξειεν Ὀδυσσεὺς |
στάσκεν, | ὑπαὶ δὲ ἴδεσκε | κατὰ χθονὸς ὄμματα πήξας, |
σκῆπτρον δ' | οὔτ' ὀπίσω οὔτε προπρηνὲς ἐνώμα, |
ἀλλ' ἀστεμφὲς ἔχεσκεν | ἀΐδρεϊ φωτὶ ἐοικώς· |
φαίης κε | ζάκοτόν τέ τιν' ἔμμεναι | ἄφρονά τ' αὔτως. |
ἀλλ' ὅτε δὴ ὄπα τε μεγάλην ἐκ στήθεος εἵη |
καὶ ἔπεα νιφάδεσσιν ἐοικότα χειμερίῃσιν, |
οὐκ ἂν ἔπειτ' Ὀδυσῆΐ γ' ἐρίσσειε βροτὸς ἄλλος· |
οὐ τότε γ' ὧδ'[162] Ὀδυσῆος ἀγασσάμεθ' εἶδος ἰδόντες." |

Iliad 3.207-224

The progress of Antenor's story exemplifies the way Homeric epic habitually signals each narrative step with a temporal marker combined with particles. At the same time, this excerpt is special in that it has the same combination four times within thirteen lines: ἀλλ' ὅτε δή (209, 212, 216, 221).[163] Despite the high frequency of the combination in the Homeric corpus, this four-fold clustering is limited to only three places.[164] The effect in

[161] This reading of ἦ is again quasi-interactional, in this case relevant to the stance of the narrator: compare III.2.2.10 and III.4 §47 (ἦ in tragic and comic dialogue), IV.4.3.1 (ἦ μήν), and IV.4.8 (ἤδη).

[162] Although generally translated "thus", ὧδε in fact represents a more complex meaning that often marks particular relevance of this statement for the zero-point of the utterance, the here-and-now (Bonifazi 2012:85). The tensions between τότε "then" and ὧδε "in this way here" represent how the story about Odysseus in the past has direct relevance for how he is now being perceived from the walls of Troy.

[163] The repeated ἀλλ' ὅτε δή serves to mark new points in a report or narrative (*Gesamtkommentar* 2009:III.2.85).

[164] Out of 106 instances of ἀλλ' ὅτε δή in the corpus, there are only three passages where four instances are found so closely together: here, in *Iliad* 6.172-200 (the embedded narrative by Glaucus to Diomedes) and *Iliad* 10.338-365 (the embedded narrative of Diomedes' and Odysseus' pursuit of Dolon); there is a cluster of three instances in *Odyssey* 14.287-301, but more frequently it occurs in twos: *Iliad* 5.773-780, 11.170-181, 17.728-732, 23.768-773, *Odyssey* 3.269-286 (with ἀλλ' ὅτε in line 278), 4.514-519, 10.144-156, 12.329-335, 12.399-403, 14.472-483, 15.457-477.

this passage, as in the two parallel passages, is one of crescendo. The audience is kept in suspense as Antenor works toward the climax of his narrative: Odysseus was older than Menelaus, and the latter spoke briefly but very well, and Odysseus did not look impressive; only when he started speaking could one see his true character.

§52. The quadruple ὅτε is answered by ἔπειτα, introducing the climax of the story: "when...and when...and when...and when...*then*..."[165] In the Labovian model, line 223 is the resolution, the final line of the story. The fact that ἔπειτα is followed by a second temporal marker in 224 (τότε) is marked, suggesting a special addition. This interpretation is supported by the switch to the first person plural (ἀγασσάμεθ'). The last line places the point of view firmly with Antenor (and perhaps the other Trojans), giving it a more explicitly evaluative character. Antenor's personal involvement in these lines evinces itself in another, more subtle manner. The final two lines contain the only two instances of γε in the entire speech, directing attention first to Odysseus himself, and then to τότε, "at that very moment." The sudden occurrence of γε here illustrates our belief that a higher frequency of γε may correlate with more personal involvement of the speaker, such as in emotional passages.[166] Not surprisingly, in the Homeric corpus γε occurs more than twice as much in direct speech as in narrator text.[167]

3.3.1 Homeric δή I: Marking narrative steps

§53. Using temporal markers is a very natural way of navigating the narrative, especially in the complicating action. In Homer, however, the temporal marker does not typically occur on its own; among other particles, δή tends to gravitate toward such markers in Homer.[168] This tendency is well-known to readers of Homer, and it has led scholars to posit that the original value of δή was temporal.[169] Given its formal likeness to ἤδη, this theory is intuitively attractive. As a result, however, these scholars have attributed a temporal value to all instances of δή in Homer, whether combined with temporal markers or not. In opposition to this approach, there is a theory that δή is in fact etymologically connected

165 In *Iliad* 10.366 τότε δή introduces the climax of the story, compare *Iliad* 5.775 ἔνθ', 11.182 τότε δή ῥα, 23.774 ἔνθ', *Odyssey* 3.288 τότε δή, 4.520 ἄψ δέ, 10.145 καὶ τότ', 10.157 καὶ τότε, 12.405 δὴ τότε, 14.303 δὴ τότε, 14.484 καὶ τότε, 15.478 μὲν ἔπειτα.

166 In III.3 §§76-83 and III.5 §§51-63 γε is connected to a speaker's emotional involvement.

167 The frequencies are based on an analysis of four books of the *Iliad* and four books of the *Odyssey* (4917 lines). In the *Iliad* it occurs 2,7 times per 100 lines of narrator text, and 6,4 times per 100 lines of direct speech. In the *Odyssey*, it occurs 2,9 times per 100 lines of narrator text, and 6,5 times per 100 lines of direct speech.

168 Edwards 2002:38-61 makes a number of important observations considering narrative transitions in Homer. His argument is that the transitional constructions in Homer have the effect of avoiding narrative breaks (see especially 58).

169 See Devarius 1588:63-64, Hoogeveen 1769:276, Hartung 1832:245-246, Nägelsbach 1834:48 and 62, Kühner 1835:386, Ellendt 1835:166-167, Döderlein 1858:362, Wetzell 1879:14, Ebeling 1885:291, Thomas 1894:85, Navarre 1904b:93-94 (but he argues against the idea in 1932:667-679).

to δῆλον (clear, visible),[170] which would better explain its generically emphatic function in *koinḗ* Greek.[171]

§54. However, attempting to establish a general value of δή in Homer passes over an important particularity in the distribution of δή in the corpus. If the value of δή were indeed evidential (or more generally emphatic), one would expect it to occur more frequently in direct speech than in narrative (which it does, by a factor of almost 3 to 1 in the *Iliad*, and less markedly by 1.2 to 1 in the *Odyssey*),[172] but one would not expect the use of the particle to be *qualitatively* different between direct speech and narrative. The same presupposition would hold if δή were to be read everywhere as having some temporal value. Neither of these explanations of the particle can account for the remarkable pattern emergent from the Homeric material, which begs closer analysis. In the entire text, around half of the instances of δή coincide with a temporal marker (-οτε, ἔπει-, νῦν, τῆμος, ἔνθα),[173] but in narrator text the average increases to 75-85%.[174] As a result, the relative frequency of δή with temporal markers in direct speech is quite a bit lower, and in direct speech the particle in fact occurs in a much larger spectrum of cotexts.[175]

§55. These numbers urge us to consider that δή in combination with temporal markers is inherently different from other collocations, which allows it to be used freely in narrator text. In what follows, I present a closer analysis of two groups of instances of δή, which provide a basis for more nuanced descriptions of the particle's function in epic and lyric: (1) δή in peninitial position with a temporal marker, (2) instances of δή in initial or otherwise marked position. The second category also provides material to understand δή in peninitial position without a temporal marker. Since δή is very rare in Pindar (twenty instances in the *Odes*), and use of the particle in Pindar matches that in Homer, the discussion below concerns itself only with Homer; I cite Pindaric parallels for each kind in footnotes.[176]

§56. In its most common use, in peninitial position in combination with a temporal marker, δή articulates the progression of discourse in larger steps. For example in the

170 See Schweighaeuser 1824:150, Heller 1853:277, Döderlein 1858:362, and Bäumlein 1861:98.

171 On the broad application of δή in Hellenistic and later Greek see δή in ORPS (our online database) and I.2 §35.

172 The frequencies for δή are based on an analysis of 12 books of the *Iliad* (13-24) and 12 books of the *Odyssey* (1-12), and the numbers are the following: in the *Iliad* 1,7 instances of δή per 100 lines of narrator text and 5,1 per 100 lines of direct speech, and in the *Odyssey* 3,8 per 100 lines of narrator text and 4,7 per 100 lines of direct speech.

173 Overall, in the *Iliad* 39.9% of δή instances are with a temporal marker, while this number is 58.3% in the *Odyssey*.

174 In narrator text, in the *Iliad* 75% of δή instances occur with a temporal marker, 25% without; in the *Odyssey* this is 84.3% with and 15.7% without temporal marking.

175 In direct speech, in the *Iliad* 23.1% of δή instances occur with a temporal marker, 76.9 % without; in the *Odyssey* this is 38.4% with and 61.6% without a temporal marker.

176 The exceptions are *Olympian* 9.9, *Pythian* 11.17, and *Isthmian* 2.27, discussed in II.5 §70n194, and *Olympian* 10.60, *Nemean* 5.15, *Nemean* 10.76, where δή occurs in (indirect) questions. In the latter three instances I take δή as intensifying the entire act.

combination ἀλλ' ὅτε δή, where δή is in its expected peninitial position,[177] the particle signals a narrative boundary on the level of the move. The act introduced by δή is often not an especially salient new step in the narrative, nor does the act require any kind of intensification. Likewise, the temporal adverb it follows in such contexts does not appear to need particular stress. Consider the following excerpt from (t16):

(t16)

τοὺς δ' ἐγὼ ἐξείνισσα | καὶ ἐν μεγάροισι φίλησα, |
ἀμφοτέρων δὲ φυὴν ἐδάην | καὶ μήδεα πυκνά. |
ἀλλ' ὅτε δὴ Τρώεσσιν ἐν ἀγρομένοισιν ἔμιχθεν |

Iliad 3.207-209

Them I welcomed and hosted in my halls.
Of both of them I learned the nature, and the cunning tricks.
Now when[178] among the assembled Trojans they mingled...

After the introductory two lines (207-208), ἀλλ' ὅτε δή marks the progression to the complicating action. The move introduced by the combination is not a narrative peak, nor does it in any other way seem to be emphasized. That is to say, it does not seem to be the case that the passage reads with small-scope δή as "very much at that moment" (i.e. "just when").[179] Its function, which is perhaps impossible to render into English, is to mark in concert with ἀλλά that there is some kind of narrative discontinuity, which coincides with the start of a new move.[180] The function of δή along with a temporal marker to mark new moves in the narrative correlates with the findings of Bestgen and Vonk.[181] In a study of the effect of the use of temporal markers versus "and" at narrative transitions, they found that temporal markers (segmentation markers in their terms) reduced the availability of words in the preceding discourse. This suggests that readers regard those temporal markers as some kind of new beginning. In Greek, the temporal adverb marks the progression, while δή marks the discontinuity.[182] It is no coincidence that in this func-

177 For a discussion of the peninitial position see II.2 §12.

178 Murray translates "Now when...," which has a similar function of moving the discourse along in English, semantically independent of the temporal value of "now."

179 This is how Denniston 1950:219 reads such instances: δή used with "[r]elative temporal adverbs, 'precisely when', 'just when'." His reading is followed by the comment on this passage in *Gesamtkommentar* 2009:III.2.85.

180 "Demetrius" says in his treatise on style (Pseudo-Demetrius of Phaleron *Style* 56) that in *Iliad* 21.1 δή is used to mark a new beginning, and that, if the combiner had not been used, the reader might have thought Homer was still talking about the same thing.

181 Bestgen and Vonk 1995, especially 20-21.

182 See also *Nemean* 8.19 ἵσταμαι δή, where the discursive discontinuity is implicit in the present tense following upon a narrative act in the aorist; in *Nemean* 10.75 θερμὰ δὴ τέγγων likewise the

tion δή often occurs in a subordinate clause, which syntactically projects an answering main clause, and thus a longer piece of discourse. There is a productive analogy for this effect of a subordinate clause in recent research on aspect in English. In an experiment, readers were asked to predict what was to follow after a clause with imperfective or perfective aspect: "The diver was snorkeling..." versus "The diver had snorkeled...". The latter of the two led to the inference that the details of the snorkeling event are less relevant for the ongoing interpretation than whatever follows in the discourse.[183] Likewise, a when-clause of the form ἀλλ' ὅτε δή suggests that the information in the subsequent act will be more salient than that of the when-clause itself.[184] This formulation makes it less likely that δή here functions to intensify its host act.

§57. For this function of δή it is productive to retrieve the possible etymological relation between δέ and δή.[185] Most scholars believe that δέ and δή are to be regarded as formally related, regarding δέ as a bleached development from δή. Alternatively, I propose the possibility that δή is a lengthened form of δέ, analogous to the development of ἆρα (with long alpha) from ἄρα. This morphological relation is then, for one function of δή, mirrored in a functional relation: δέ marks boundaries between discourse acts, while δή divides the discourse into larger steps, consistently occurring at the start of new moves.[186]

§58. There is also a group of instances where δή occurs with temporal markers, in narrator text, but in initial position: δὴ τότε and δὴ ῥα τότε. The act-initial position of δή as well as its position in the larger discourse suggests that the particle has a different function in this construction. A different interpretation of ὅτε δή on the one hand and δὴ τότε on the other is moreover suggested by the fact that the former introduces a subordinate clause, whereas the latter introduces a main clause. Consider the following passage from the *Odyssey*:

function of δή is less to intensify than to mark the narrative progression; *Isthmian* 8.65 ἐνίκασε δή ποτε may represent this function too, or it may represent δήποτε, a result of grammaticalization in which the added value of δή has all but disappeared "once upon a time" (LSJ). See IV.4.5.1 on δή marking narrative steps in Herodotus.

183 Ferretti, Kutas, and McRae 2007.

184 See Bakker 1991 for the narrative function of temporal clauses in Herodotus, Buijs 2005 for temporal and participial clauses in Xenophon, and Muchnová 2003 for the narrative function of ἐπεί clauses in Homer.

185 See II.2.2.1.

186 Compare the three instances of ὅτε δ(έ): *Iliad* 16.690, 17.178, 19.134. Especially the last of the three is a good comparandum for ὅτε δή clauses in narrative transitions. In the literature, the relation between the two particles is without exception regarded as a development from δή to a (weaker) δέ. However, the possibility of δή being a prosodically strengthened form of δέ cannot be excluded. This would be a situation comparable to the possible development of ἄρα to ἆρα in second position (different from ἆρα in initial position) as attested in Pindar and drama (see Braswell 1988:173-174 and De Kreij 2015).

(t17)

ἡμεῖς δ' | αἶψ' ἀναβάντες | ἐνήκαμεν εὐρέϊ πόντῳ, |
ἱστὸν στησάμενοι | ἀνά θ' ἱστία λεύκ' ἐρύσαντες. |
ἀλλ' ὅτε δὴ τὴν νῆσον ἐλείπομεν | οὐδέ τις ἄλλη
φαίνετο γαιάων, | ἀλλ' οὐρανὸς ἠδὲ θάλασσα, |
δὴ τότε κυανέην νεφέλην ἔστησε Κρονίων |
νηὸς ὕπερ γλαφυρῆς, | ἤχλυσε δὲ πόντος ὑπ' αὐτῆς. |

Odyssey 12.401-406

And we, getting on board quickly, set out on the wide sea,
setting up the mast and hoisting up the white sail.
But when we left the island behind, and no other part
appeared of the lands, but only sky and sea,
right at that moment Cronos' son raised a black cloud
over the hollow ship, and the sea grew dark under it.

In line 403, ἀλλ' ὅτε δή introduces a new step in the narrative, but the crucial event occurs with δὴ τότε. Whereas δή in peninitial position merely marks progression of the narrative, in initial position it marks a salient moment. Here and in a number of parallels, δὴ τότε introduces a peak in the narrative, the moment that has been worked up to until then.[187] The scope of δή in such instances is debatable: it either intensifies τότε or the entire act. The translation shows that I take it as intensifying τότε, but δὴ τότε together introduces the entire move: the intensified temporal adverb functions as what we call a "peak marker."[188] Compare the same narrative moment in this passage from the *Iliad*:

(t18)

ἐννῆμαρ ξείνισσε | καὶ ἐννέα βοῦς ἱέρευσεν. |
ἀλλ' ὅτε δὴ δεκάτη ἐφάνη ῥοδοδάκτυλος Ἠὼς |
καὶ τότε μιν ἐρέεινε | καὶ ᾔτεε σῆμα ἰδέσθαι |

Iliad 6.174-176

For nine days he hosted him, and nine cows he sacrificed.
But when the tenth rosy-fingered Dawn appeared,
right then he questioned him and asked to see the token,

187 See also Pindar, *Olympian* 3.25.

188 The combination τότε δή serves a similar function, and illustrates that in its intensifying function too δή can occur in peninitial position.

The function of καί to introduce a peak or climax is discussed elsewhere, and the combinations δὴ τότε and καὶ τότε have the same function in Homer: to introduce a narrative peak.[189] In the combination καὶ τότε δή, finally, it is hard to establish whether δή marks a move boundary or intensifies the act, along with καί. The construction may serve as a reminder that boundaries are fuzzy, and that the following conclusions are based on patterns we perceive. Since in the end δή is just one word, its multiple functions may have blended into one another, and more than one of the particle's aspects may be relevant in a single instance.

3.3.2 Homeric δή II: Intensifying constituents or acts

§59. Particle scholarship has disregarded the discourse-articulating function of δή outlined in the previous section, and instead focused on its emphatic function. More recently, Bakker has suggested that δή "is better characterized as a marker of evidentiality":[190] "[t]he use of this particle draws the hearer into the story by marking the narration as deriving from a shared basis, a common experience that binds the narrator and listeners together as if they were actually jointly witnessing a given scene."[191] Bakker's reading of δή in Homer is part of his argument that Homeric language suggests that the performance was a process of bringing the mountain to Mohammed, bringing the narrative into the here and now instead of displacing the audience into the past.[192] He sees a trace of this same function in the omnipresent Homeric δέ, which he regards as a bleached version of δή: "[i]f *dé* is a weak form of *dḗ*, then its meaning is similar but weaker."[193]

§60. As argued above, I do not think that emphasis or evidentiality is necessarily to be sought in those constructions where δή occurs in peninitial position with a temporal marker. Now, in the Homeric corpus δή is not always a peninitial particle, but is also allowed in act-initial position. The instances of δή in this position—limited to a few constructions: δὴ τότε, δή ῥα τότε, δὴ γάρ, and three isolated examples[194]—reveal a

189 Bakker 1997b:79 notes that καὶ τότε marks "significant events or breaks in the story"; for this passage, see Graziosi and Haubold 2010:127, "καὶ τότε μιν (...) emphasizes that we have reached a crucial point in the story" and *Gesamtkommentar* 2008:IV.2.70. See IV.2 §§100-101 on καὶ δή at narrative peaks in Herodotus.

190 Bakker 1997b:75.

191 Earlier scholars have linked δή to perception; see Döderlein 1850:III.362, Thiemann 1881: 530-531, Paley 1881:21, Sicking 1986:133. A similar link between δή and perception is drawn in III.2 §§73-79 for tragedy and comedy and in IV.4.5.2 for historiography. Scholars have also spoken of δή in terms of "evidentiality," see Bakker 1997b:78-79, Van Ophuijsen 1993:141 and 146 "self-evidential," Cuypers 2005:38 and 55-59, De Jong 2007:14-15, Van Erp Taalman Kip 2009:114. Wakker 1994, 1995, 1997b argues that it more generally emphasizes the importance of the utterance (1994:351 "δή draws special attention to the (...) proposition").

192 See further Bakker 1993b:15-25 and 2005:146.

193 Bakker 1997:79.

194 The third example follows below as (t23). There is one other puzzling position of δή, in *Iliad* 24.243 ῥηΐτεροι γὰρ μᾶλλον ?|? Ἀχαιοῖσιν δὴ ἔσεσθε; this instance is unique and as yet unclear.

different function, closer to the "emphatic" or "evidential" function posited by earlier scholarship. However, a close analysis of δή in apparently divergent position reveals a more detailed picture. Consider first the following two instances:

(t19)

τέκνον ἐμόν | <u>δὴ</u> πάμπαν ἀποίχεαι ἀνδρὸς ἑῆος

Iliad 19.342 (direct speech)

My child, utterly you forsake your own warrior

(t20)

Ἀντίλοχος δ' ἄρα <u>δὴ</u> λοισθήϊον ἔκφερ' ἄεθλον[195]

Iliad 23.785 (narrator text)

Antilochus, then, carried off the very last prize.

The instance from direct speech (t19) reveals the act-initial position of δή because it follows a vocative. The instance in *Iliad* 23 is less straightforward, but I argue that δή is a mobile here, with scope over the following word.[196]

§61. In (t19) δή is arguably act-initial modifying the following word: πάμπαν.[197] The combination of δή and comparatives or superlatives, including "first," "last," "all," and "many," is widespread enough for me to consider it as a special construction with the particle, where δή functions as an intensifier of an adjective at one end of a scale. If we then consider (t21), δή seems to modify λοισθήϊον ("the very last"), and therefore occurs just before the adjective, in act-medial position.[198] As far as position is concerned, (t19) and (t20) show that δή in its intensifying function is moderately mobile. The Homeric corpus suggests that δή in some functions can precede its host adjective or adverb,

The scribe of the Venetus A manuscript chose to place the particle between commas, apparently as a parenthetical discourse act: ῥηΐτεροι γὰρ μᾶλλον Ἀχαιοῖσιν, δὴ, ἔσεσθε.

195 This line seems to have been a textually problematic place: British Library add. mss. 17210 reads Ἀντίλοχος δ' ἄρα οἱ λοισθήϊον ἔκφερ' ἄεθλον, while a papyrus (P.Lond.Lit 27) has δή added above the line in a second hand.

196 There are seven other instances of the combination ἄρα δή, all in the *Iliad*, and in most cases I believe that δή has scope over the entire act (the one possible exception is *Iliad* 17.85 δὴ πρίν).

197 *Gesamtkommentar* 2009:VI.2.147 notes the remarkable position of δή, and takes the particle to have scope over the entire utterance: "[δή] verleiht der folgenden Aussage bes. Emphase."

198 Denniston 1950:204 calls this the "emphatic" use, and the intensifying function I posit matches in particular Denniston's decription of its use to denote "that a thing (...) is very much so." Moreover, passages in tragedy (Denniston 1950:212) show that small-scope, forward-looking δή could still occur: δὴ μάλιστα. See also Pindar *Nemean* 8.51 δὴ πάλαι in act-medial position "really long ago."

which allows it to occur anywhere from act-initial to act-medial position.[199] Already in Homer δή does not always precede the constituent it modifies, like in (t19) and (t20), but can also follow it.[200] Because of this mobility, the collocation of δή directly in front of polar adjectives (adjectives near either end of a scale, e.g. first and last) also occurs with δή in its typical peninitial position.[201] As far as the division between direct speech and narrator text is concerned, the use of δή as intensifier is largely limited to direct speech, most likely because the narrator does not tend to offer intensifications. In order to better understand this intensifying function of δή, a study of the combination δὴ γάρ is informative.

§62. The peculiar combination δὴ γάρ is largely limited to Homer, with an additional three instances in the *Homeric Hymns* and two in Hesiod.[202] In principle, there are two ways to explain such a combination of particles: either δή and γάρ occur together because they work together, or they occur together because their positions (initial and peninitial) happen to be contiguous. Now, δή in Homer occurs more frequently in peninitial than in initial position, but a pattern emerges from the analysis of the exceptions above. At first glance the δὴ γάρ group might be read like (t19) and (t20) above, as γάρ intervening in a unit of δή X, where δὴ has scope over the constituent that immediately follows γάρ.[203] Keeping in mind the possibility that one aspect of δή is its use to intensify a following adjective, consider this passage:

199 Denniston 1950:212 regards this positioning as secondary ("Originally, perhaps, δή was regarded as going with the preceding word."), whereas I believe that the material suggests that the construction where δή precedes its host disappears from Greek quite early on. The formation δὴ ποτέ (sometimes δήποτε) may invite several explanations, but the simplest one is that in the string at act beginning ποτε would naturally follow δή (ποτε δή only occurs twice, in the construction εἰ ποτε δή). When it is the accented interrogative πότε it does shift to initial position, and may be followed by δή. The following are the relevant instances of the combination ἦ δή where δή intensifies an adjective at one end of a scale: *Iliad* 1.518 (=1.573) ἦ | δὴ λοίγια, 2.272 ὢ πόποι | ἦ | δὴ μυρί' (compare Euripides *Heraclids* 331 πόνους δὴ μυρίους), 15.467 ὢ πόποι | ἦ | δὴ πάγχυ, 24.518 ἆ δείλ' | ἦ | δὴ πολλά, *Odyssey* 1.253 ὢ πόποι | ἦ | δὴ πολλόν, 5.182 ἦ | δὴ ἀλιτρός γ'; I believe that ἦ in these instances is at least partly interjectional (§33-§43). The group may be expanded with Pindar *Olympian* 6.79 πολλὰ δὴ πολλαῖσιν; see also Archilochus fragment 172.3 νῦν δὲ δὴ πολύς.

200 The construction that illustrates this best is εἰ δ' ἐτεὸν δή: *Iliad* 7.359, 12.233 and *Odyssey* 23.107. This is the standard order in later Greek; in Thucydides and Herodotus it occurs frequently just after superlatives, e.g. μεγίστη δή (with δή in act-medial position) in Thucydides, see IV.4.6.2.

201 This happens particularly with forms of πρῶτ-, πᾶς*, and πολ-; the *loci* are *Iliad* 1.235, 1.545, 2.117, 4.97, 7.207, 9.24, 9.348 (ἦ μὲν δὴ μάλα πολλά), 10.173, 11.219, 11.559, 11.825, 13.275, 14.187, 14.509, 15.291, 15.616, 16.23, 16.113, 16.198, 16.538, 17.427, 18.103, 19.9, 19.54, 19.342, 23.490, 23.607, 24.65, 24.167, 24.713; *Odyssey* 3.183, 4.414, 5.76, 5.300, 6.227, 7.134, 8.131, 8.282, 13.155, 14.149, 14.289, 15.401 (ὅς τις δὴ μάλα πολλά), 16.340, 16.469, 17.174, 17.217 (νῦν μὲν δὴ μάλα πάγχυ), 22.195 (=17.217), 22.440, 22.457, 23.49, 24.528.

202 *Hymn to Demeter* 76, 148, and 159; Hesiod, *Works and Days* 417 and *Fragment* 204.96 (in both instances δὴ γὰρ τότε).

203 As I argue for καὶ γάρ, §§30-32. Alternatively, one could read it as δή intensifying the force of γάρ, as Denniston 1950:243 does: "The reverse order, δὴ γάρ, which gives an even stronger emphasis

(t21)

αὐτὰρ ὁ βῆ κατὰ δῶμα | φίλον τετιημένος ἦτορ, |
νευστάζων κεφαλῇ· | δὴ γὰρ κακὸν ὄσσετο θυμῷ |

Odyssey 18.153-154

And he went down the hall | sorrowful in his own heart |
bowing his head. | *For* his spirit boded a *truly bad* thing. |

The translation above represents the reading of δή with small scope, intensifying κακόν; Murray appears to give a similar reading, with "for his spirit boded ill indeed," but the English is ambiguous. This reading, however, only works in this and two other instances of δὴ γάρ,[204] too low a number to sufficiently explain the combination's function. In the fourteen remaining cases δή cannot be read as intensifying the word immediately following γάρ, but rather appears to modify the entire act. This passage from the *Odyssey*, where δὴ γάρ is in act-initial position but not followed by an adjective, exemplifies these cases:

(t22)

ἀλλ' | ἦ τοι παύεσθαι ἀνωγέμεν ἀφροσυνάων, |
μειλιχίοισ' ἐπέεσσι παραυδῶν· | οἱ δέ τοι | οὔ τι
πείσονται· | δὴ γάρ[205] σφι παρίσταται αἴσιμον ἦμαρ. |

Odyssey 16.278-280

Now, I tell you, order them to cease from their follies,
coaxing them with gentle words. And they, not at all
will they obey you. *For really*, their fated day is at hand.

We have rendered δὴ γάρ as a separate punctuation unit in English, which is how sentence adverbs are generally rendered to signal that they have scope over the entire sentence.[206]

[sc. on γάρ], is also frequently found in [Homer]." However, what is intensified is not the relation between the current act and the preceding, but the current act in itself.

204 *Iliad* 13.122 and 15.400, both have the form δὴ γὰρ μέγα νεῖκος ὄρωρεν. A similar reading could be proposed for *Hymn to Demeter* 76, 148, and 159.

205 See II.4 §19 for the function of γάρ in δὴ γάρ.

206 Denniston, conversely, insists that δή always modifies one word, which tends to be, but does not have to be, adjacent to the particle. This would mean that in this example δή "modifies" παρίσταται, probably. Although this reading makes sense, it does not recognize the difference in the Greek: it would be very hard to mark that δή is supposed to be construed with a word that occurs much later in the act.

Whereas with scope over one adjective δή intensifies the meaning of that word, with a larger scope it rather marks an intensity behind the utterance of the act: not "very X" but "take note that X" or "I insist that X." This reading of δὴ γάρ is supported by a final example of δή in act-initial position:

(t23)

Τεῦκρε πέπον | *δή* νῶϊν ἀπέκτατο πιστὸς ἑταῖρος

Iliad 15.437 (in direct speech)

Good Teucer, *truly* a trusted friend of ours was slain.

The context and content strongly suggest that there is no reason to read δή as intensifying νῶϊν here; the focus of the act is on conveying that a close friend has passed away, not that he has passed away *particularly for them*. The most natural reading is that δή marks the intensity behind the utterance, and does not function to intensify one of the constituents in the act. Therefore, δή has scope over at least its entire act, and its force modifies the act of uttering rather than the content of the utterance.[207] This use of the particle is inextricably linked to the "voice" of a subjective speaker, and as such is more frequent in direct speech than in narrator text. At the same time, when it does occur in narrator text, the particle may reveal something of the "voice" of the narrator. This aspect of δή is explored further in IV.4.5.3-4.5.5 and 4.6.1, considering the particle in direct speech, indirect speech and thought, and authorial statements in Herodotus and Thucydides.

§63. In its intensifying function, then, δή can modify the content conveyed (with small scope) or it can mark the intensity of the speaker in conveying his discourse (with act scope), and the boundary between these two options is inevitably fuzzy. To clarify how δή works as a mobile in Homer, I suggest an analogy with καί, a particle that knows a similarly strong correlation between position in the act and scope. If καί has scope over (at least) its host act, it occurs in act-initial position, while if it has scope over one word (group) it immediately precedes that word.[208] Homer shows remnants of a similar distribution of δή, either directly preceding a constituent that it modifies (t19 and t20), or occurring in act-initial position if it modifies (at least) its host act (t22 and t23).

[207] Bakker 1997b:75-76 reads this instance of δή as creating involvement through a shared visible reality: "*Dḗ* conveys that the consciousness verbalized receives its input from the speaker's immediate environment, from what is perceptually clear and evident."

[208] See I.1 on the link between position and scope.

3.3.3 Homeric δή: Conclusions

§64. Recent scholarship on δή has focussed largely on its function of emphasizing, and the tendency has been to see the discourse-articulating function of the particle as a branch of this main function, if it is discussed at all. For δή in the Homeric epics it is important to be aware of the clear discursive differences between the two functions, and for the so-called "emphatic" function we can come to a more nuanced differentiation. When δή marks larger narrative steps, it freely occurs in any kind of discourse, both within and outside direct speech. In this function, δή does not serve to intensify either the content or the act, but along with a temporal marker it signals a progression in the articulation of moves in discourse. In its intensifying function δή modifies either single words or entire discourse acts, originally occurring in act-initial position when it has scope over the act, or directly preceding the word (group) it modifies when it has smaller scope. By Homer already, but especially in later literature, intensifying δή with scope over the entire act gravitates more and more to act-peninitial position.[209] However, δή has small scope in some constructions: preceding the constituent it modifies in fixed constructions like δὴ μάλα, δὴ μάλιστα and following it in constructions like superlative + δή.[210] In its peninitial position, the two functions still discernible in Homer start to flow together, but even in authors like Herodotus both of them may still be identified.[211] Only through a close examination of context and cotext is it possible to gain a deeper understanding of the many faces of δή in Greek literature.[212]

3.4 Move Transitions in Pindaric Discourse

3.4.1 Particles at move transitions in narrative

§65. The longest narrative in Pindar provides a good counterpoint to Homer's style. His narrative of Jason and Medea in *Pythian* 4 is complex and plays with several narrative voices, but it too guides its audience from scene to scene. In the following I pick out a number of transitional passages that illustrate the linguistic and extra-linguistic tools available to Pindar to mark discontinuities. In the first part of the lengthy song (lines 4 - 58), Pindar adduces Medea as the narrator of the first part of the story regarding the foundation of Cyrene. Medea's words are introduced by a speech formula in 11-12, and

209 In Homer, δή in peninitial position has an intensifying function with act scope in constructions like εἰ δή (also in Pindar *Olympian* 1.54) and ἦ μάλα δή (also in Pindar *Pythian* 4.64).

210 It is in the latter category that we should place Pindar, *Olympian* 13.99 ἑξηκοντάκι δή (Race translates "full sixty times"), *Pythian* 4.273 δυσπαλὲς δή "difficult indeed," *Pythian* 9.91 τρὶς δή "full three times" (Race), *Nemean* 1.17 θαμὰ δή "often indeed" (Race), and *Nemean* 8.48 δὶς δή "full twice."

211 See the observations in IV.3.11.3-4 and IV.4.5.

212 There is one specific aspect of δή as yet undiscussed, which is the use of the particle after pronouns; see II.5.3.4.

start with a story of one of the Argonauts receiving a clod of earth as a guest gift from Triton, which is presented first in regression (lines 20-25)[213] and then recounted from the beginning (line 25 and further):

(t24)

(...) δώδεκα δὲ πρότερον
ἁμέρας ἐξ Ὠκεανοῦ φέρομεν | νώτων ὕπερ γαίας ἐρήμων |
ἐννάλιον δόρυ, | μήδεσιν ἀνσπάσσαντες ἁμοῖς. |
τουτάκι δ' οἰοπόλος δαίμων ἐπῆλθεν, | φαιδίμαν
ἀνδρὸς αἰδοίου πρόσοψιν θηκάμενος· | φιλίων δ' ἐπέων
ἄρχετο, | ξείνοις ἅ τ' ἐλθόντεσσιν εὐεργέται |
δεῖπν' ἐπαγγέλλοντι πρῶτον. |

ἀλλὰ γὰρ νόστου πρόφασις γλυκεροῦ
κώλυεν μεῖναι. | φάτο δ' Εὐρύπυλος | Γαιαόχου παῖς ἀφθίτου
Ἐννοσίδα |
ἔμμεναι· | γίνωσκε δ' ἐπειγομένους· | ἂν δ' εὐθὺς ἁρπάξαις ἀρούρας |
δεξιτερᾷ προτυχὸν ξένιον μάστευσε δοῦναι |

Pindar, *Pythian* 4.25-35

(...) Before, twelve
days from the Ocean we carried it, across empty ridges of land,
the spear of the sea, drawing it according to my plans.
And then the solitary god came to us, with the radiant
features of a respectable man. With friendly words
he began, as when to arriving guests generous men
first announce dinner.

But of course the excuse of our sweet return
kept us from staying. He said that Eurypulos, son of the immortal
earthholder and -shaker,
he was; he noticed that we were pressed. At once having picked up soil,
with his right hand he strove to offer it as a makeshift guest-gift.

The narrative progresses at a steady pace, with δέ occurring at every significant narrative step (lines 25, 28, 32, 34, 34). In such narrative passages Pindaric use of δέ may appear to

213 Here too the narrative is introduced by τόν ποτε; see §48-§50 for more on such asyndetic narrative beginnings.

approach that of Homer, but in practice the particle is not as flexible in the *Victory Odes*. Note that, unlike in editions of Homer, δέ is always preceded by a high dot or a period. In Homer, δέ can introduce practically any kind of act, ranging from prepositional phrases to full main clauses. In Pindar the range is similarly large, but most commonly it serves to separate periods or sentences, as in all 5 examples above. Not only are the discourse segments separated by δέ all syntactic wholes, they also form discrete narrative events.[214] That is to say, δέ in Pindar serves as a boundary marker on a slightly higher level of discourse division than in Homer, closer in fact to the function of δή in the latter (see §61-§62).

§66. After a few lines of reflection, Medea's speech ends, and it is capped with the intriguing construction ἦ ῥα Μηδείας ἐπέων στίχες (line 57).[215] For the current purpose, the occurrence of the particle ἄρα is most relevant. Like δή, ἄρα occurs much less in Pindar than in Homer, with only 30 instances in the *Victory Odes*.[216] Of those, seven occur in *Pythian* 4, which is not so surprising if one keeps in mind that in Homer ἄρα is extremely frequent in narrative, but much less so in direct speech.[217] In Pindar this pattern continues, with the great majority of instances of ἄρα occurring in narrative sections.[218] In this construction in *Pythian* 4, ἄρα is not only part of a narrative, but also within that context a part of a speech-capping construction, which is an environment where we often find ἄρα.[219] The verse that follows direct speech represents a return to the action, after the special kind of move that direct speech is. In this kind of context, ἄρα marks the expected outcome of what precedes, consider this parallel from later in *Pythian* 4:

214 See also Braswell 1988:284-285 (*ad Pythian* 4.202-203), but he wants to differentiate between those instances where δέ marks temporally sequential steps, and those where these steps are not temporally sequential. Against the background of the discussion of δέ in II.2 §§31-36, I do not believe such a differentiation is productive.

215 The construction is reminiscent of the Homeric ἦ ῥα, καί after direct speech, but represents an interesting variation on this theme. In my reading (as in Race's) ἦ is not the *verbum dicendi*, but the particle ἦ: "Such were the verses of Medea's speech" (Race). Gentili et al. 1995:444 and Braswell 1988:138-139 take ἦ as the verb of speech, with στίχες as subject in a *schema pindaricum* (singular verb with plural subject); Segal 1986:154 proposes a similar reading.

216 The edition of Snell/Maehler only has twenty-five, but five instances should be added where Snell/Maehler give ἦρα (ἄρα mss.). I follow Braswell 1988:173-174, who reinstates Boeckh's reading of ᾱρα as a prosodically lengthened form of ἄρα; see also De Kreij 2015. This gives a total of thirty instances of the different forms of ἄρα.

217 In Homer, there are between 8 and 10 instances of ἄρα per 100 lines of narrative, versus between 2 and 3 instances per 100 lines of direct speech. In Pindar, throughout the *Odes* ἄρα occurs 0.9 times per 100 lines, while in *Pythian* 4 the seven instances represent 2.3 occurrences per 100 lines.

218 Out of the 30 instances in the *Odes*, in only three cases does ἄρα clearly occur outside of a narrative context: *Isthmian* 5.41, *Olympian* 10.52, *Nemean* 8.32.

219 For Pindar, 9 out of 30 instances of ἄρα are in speech-capping phrases (in one instance it caps indirect speech: *Olympian* 6.52); in *Pythian* 4 it is at line 57, 156, and 232. This makes up more than a third of a total of 22 speech-capping phrases in the *Odes*.

(t25)

ἀλλ' ἐν ἕκτᾳ | πάντα λόγον θέμενος σπουδαῖον ἐξ ἀρχᾶς | ἀνήρ
συγγενέσιν παρεκοινᾶθ'· | οἱ δ' ἐπέσποντ'. | αἶψα δ' ἀπὸ κλισιᾶν |
ὦρτο σὺν κείνοισι· | καί ῥ' ἦλθον Πελία μέγαρον· |

Pindar, *Pythian* 4.132-134

But on the sixth, laying out the entire serious story from the beginning, the man
shared it with his relatives. And they followed him. At once from the couches
he rose with them, and they came to Pelias' palace.

After telling the story of the homecoming of Jason, who spends five days catching up with his father and family (lines 124-131), Pindar moves on to the peak of the encounter between Jason and Pelias. The peak is introduced with ἀλλ' ἐν ἕκτᾳ (line 132), which follows a typical pattern: "for five days nothing happened, but on the sixth..."[220] As in the ἀλλ' ὅ γε construction, a negative statement is followed by a positive one, introduced by ἀλλά. The negative statement inherently projects that a change will come, often from inactivity to action.[221] Thus, ἀλλ' ἐν ἕκτᾳ in itself promises the peak, and the participial clause that follows (πάντα...ἀρχᾶς, line 132) serves to postpone the crucial events. As the action starts (from οἱ δέ, line 133) the acts become shorter, and we find three finite verbs in three lines. The final act (καί ῥ' ἦλθον Πελία μέγαρον, line 134) contains ἄρα. Although the act is clearly connected to the preceding two, it represents a shift of frame: they arrive at Pelias' palace. In fact, the act is the outcome of the preceding scene, and as such functions as a hinge between one scene and the next.[222] This discourse function matches directly the use of ἄρα after direct speech and in the second half of the Homeric simile,[223] and it recurs in its use after pronouns (as *Pythian* 4.78), especially after unframed discourse.[224]

§67. *Pythian* 4 is an exceptional ode, but quite representative regarding its narrative transitions. Pindar's narratives are less linear than Homer's, proceeding in a more complex manner, but discontinuities are still typically accompanied by particles or

220 See Braswell 1988:214 for the Homeric origin of this convention; the number of days is not fixed.

221 See II.5 §35 and §46-§47 on ἀλλ' ὅ γε.

222 Compare ἄρα at the end of the arrival scene in line 121 and rounding off the gathering of the Argonauts in 189. Gentili et al. 1995:465 and Braswell 1988:220 rather read ῥα as marking immediate succession, following Denniston 1950:42-43.

223 More on particles in the similes in II.4.3. In that same chapter the higher frequency of the particle in Homer is discussed. This function of ἄρα with regard to discourse articulation is surprisingly absent in the scholarship on the particle, most notably in Denniston.

224 See II.5.3.3.

particle combinations pointing the way for the audience. Different from epic, Pindar's odes contain many discursive discontinuities outside of the narrative, which are best illustrated by a close reading of a representative ode.

3.4.2 The discursive flow of lyric song: *Pythian* 2

§68. In narrative discourse in Pindar, δέ remains the most common marker of progression, though used more sparsely than in Homer. In the same contexts, ἄρα functions to round off scenes or to cap direct speech. Beyond narrative, however, Pindar has a whole array of linguistic and extra-linguistic means at his disposal to steer his song. When considering his navigation of the many (apparent) discontinuities in his discourse, we must remember Bundy's warning:

(t26)

> We forget that this is an oral, public, epideictic literature dedicated to the single purpose of eulogizing men and communities; that these eulogies are concentrated upon athletic achievement; *that the environment thus created is hostile to an allusiveness that would strain the powers of a listening audience,* hostile to personal, religious, political, philosophical and historical references that might interest the poet but do nothing to enhance the glory of a given patron, hostile to abruptness in transitions, to gross irrelevance, to lengthy sermonizing, to literary scandals and embarrassments...
>
> Bundy 1962:35 [my emphasis]

Pindar's discourse of praise consists of endless twists and turns, transitions from present to past perhaps reflected in the back-and-forth of a dancing chorus. Despite the decidedly lower frequency of particles in Pindar than in Homer (12.7% of words versus 17.1% in the *Iliad* and 18% in the *Odyssey*), they are just as important metalinguistic markers of transitions in the discourse. More so than in Homer, however, asyndeton is the polyfunctional transitional device *par excellence* and can initiate every imaginable new move.[225] At the same time, the many different kinds of transition have caused several markers to become specialized in certain discourse functions. In the present section I discuss several excerpts from Pindar's second *Pythian*, describing its linear progression in acts and moves, along with all the relevant markers occurring at important transitions.

§69. The second *Pythian* is a good example of the many turns one finds in a Pindaric ode. As often in the corpus, the first strophe and part of the antistrophe are taken up by a complex *tour-de-force* introducing the *laudandus* (Hieron), his home, and the gods to whom the ode is directed especially. On the basis of syntax, modern editors take this

225 See §48-§50 above.

construction of mounting intricacy and interconnectedness as one sentence, a beautiful piece of language architecture, which is reflected in the recent Loeb translation.[226] Pragmatically, however, the passage consists of a number of separate moves that are themselves articulated in manageable discourse acts. Consider the first strophe:

(t27)

Μεγαλοπόλιες ὦ Συράκοσαι, | βαθυπολέμου

τέμενος Ἄρεος, | ἀνδρῶν ἵππων τε σιδαροχαρμᾶν δαιμόνιαι τροφοί, |
ὔμμιν τόδε τᾶν λιπαρᾶν ἀπὸ Θηβᾶν φέρων
μέλος | ἔρχομαι | ἀγγελίαν τετραορίας ἐλελίχθονος, |
εὐάρματος Ἱέρων | ἐν ᾇ κρατέων |
τηλαυγέσιν ἀνέδησεν Ὀρτυγίαν στεφάνοις, |
ποταμίας ἕδος Ἀρτέμιδος, | ᾇς οὐκ ἄτερ |
κείνας ἀγαναῖσιν ἐν χερσὶ ποικιλανίους ἐδάμασσε πώλους. |

Pindar, *Pythian* 2.1-8

Great city—Syracuse! Of deep-in-war
Ares a sanctuary, of men and steel-clad horses[227] a divine nurse.
To you, bringing from Thebes-the-Shining this
song, I come, <with> news of the four-horse chariot that shakes the earth:[228]
Hieron of the good chariots, prevailing in that <contest>,
crowned Ortygia with far-shining garlands,
seat of the river-goddess Artemis. Not without her
did he master those pretty-reined mares with his gentle hands.

The intricacy of the syntactic construction of the first strophe belies its performative clarity; consider first the sequence of acts. The first two lines, in three discourse acts, form a tricolon building up to Syracuse's largest boon: her men and horses. The occasion of this song, victory in a chariot race, is thus suggested, and Pindar moves on: with a second-person plural pronoun he involves the audience, followed by a participial act whose final boundary is determined by the hyperbaton of τόδε and μέλος (ὔμμιν τόδε τᾶν λιπαρᾶν ἀπὸ Θηβᾶν φέρων / μέλος).[229] The "you" implies an "I," which is realized

[226] Race uses all of eleven commas in his translation until he comes to the full stop after "trident" (12).

[227] Lit. "horses that fight in iron-mail," see Gildersleeve 1885:256.

[228] I am aware that ἀγγελίαν is an apposition of μέλος, but the addition of <with> is the most economical way of translating this line into comprehensible English without interfering too much with the Greek word order.

[229] See Lauer 1959:54-58, Race 2002, and Markovic 2006:138-140.

in line 4 (ἔρχομαι). The apposition to μέλος that closes the line (ἀγγελίαν...) projects a report of the actual news, and the audience's expectation is fulfilled immediately in line 5, in two acts: the first mention of the *laudandus* is accompanied by the third reference to the event (εὐάρματος Ἱέρων), which gives Pindar the possibility to refer to the actual victory—already abundantly in focus—with the minimal participial phrase ἐν ᾇ κρατέων. The following act (τηλαυγέσιν ἀνέδησεν Ὀρτυγίαν στεφάνοις) contains the main verb of which Hieron is the subject, but cognitively the act brings the audience from the athletic event to Syracuse, describing how the victor "crowned Ortygia," which primes the goddess Artemis, named in the following act (ποταμίας ἕδος Ἀρτέμιδος).[230] This then allows the poet to set up the theme of divine aid in the victory, to be elaborated in the antistrophe.

§70. These acts together make up three coherent moves. The first move of the ode consists of three vocatives (Μεγαλοπόλιες ὦ Συράκυσαι, | βαθυπολέμου / τέμενος Ἄρεος, | ἀνδρῶν ἵππων τε σιδαροχαρμᾶν δαιμόνιαι τροφοί, lines 1-2), which establish a marked directionality of the discourse, from chorus or singer to audience. Line 3 marks the transition to the second move with ὔμμιν.[231] Since the pronoun is plural, its referent is potentially ambiguous: it may refer to the city of Syracuse or to its inhabitants. However, deictically ὔμμιν must have been a very strong moment in the song, and the audience cannot but have felt addressed. The second move lays down a foundation for the performance: it establishes the relation between "I" and "you," it summarizes the nature of the song, and it does all this in the form of a quasi speech-introduction: φέρων μέλος | ἔρχομαι. The third move (lines 5-8) contains the actual ἀγγελία announced at the end of the second move. It follows in asyndeton, and we would expect it to have been performatively marked as different from the preceding. The news is that of Hieron's victory, probably superfluous to the audience, and it leads the song back to Syracuse, and to Artemis. The hinge act is ποταμίας ἕδος Ἀρτέμιδος (line 7), which describes Ortygia and at the same time serves to introduce the goddess. Lines 7-8, from ἇς οὐκ ἄτερ onward, present Artemis as a divine helper to Hieron, while cohesion with the preceding acts is achieved with yet another reference to the athletic event (ποικιλανίους ἐδάμασσε πώλους, line 8).

§71. It will not have escaped the reader that I have yet to mention particles in this discussion. The simple reason is that apart from τε (line 2), the first strophe of *Pythian* 2 contains no particles, but its relevance derives precisely from this absence. First, the beginnings of Pindaric odes regularly have very few particles. Second, this strophe illustrates well that move transitions are inherent in any kind of discourse, whether it has particles or not. However, when particles do occur at move beginnings, their function should be understood with respect to those larger movements in the discourse. Consider the first antistrophe of *Pythian* 2:

230 Ortygia is the little island on which Syracuse was built, just off the coast of Sicily; see Gentili et al. 1995:366-367.

231 For the pragmatic effect of using the second person see II.2.5.2.1.

(t28)

ἐπὶ γὰρ ἰοχέαιρα παρθένος | χερὶ διδύμᾳ |
ὅ τ᾽ ἐναγώνιος Ἑρμᾶς | αἰγλάεντα τίθησι κόσμον, | ξεστὸν ὅταν δίφρον |
ἔν θ᾽ ἅρματα πεισιχάλινα καταζευγνύῃ |
σθένος ἵππιον, | ὀρσοτρίαιναν εὐρυβίαν καλέων θεόν. |
ἄλλοις δέ τις ἐτέλεσσεν ἄλλος ἀνήρ |
εὐαχέα βασιλεῦσιν ὕμνον ἄποιν᾽ ἀρετᾶς. |
κελαδέοντι μὲν ἀμφὶ Κινύραν πολλάκις |
φᾶμαι Κυπρίων, | τὸν ὁ χρυσοχαῖτα προφρόνως ἐφίλησ᾽ | Ἀπόλλων, |

Pindar, *Pythian* 2.9-16

No, on them the virgin archeress, with both hands,
and Hermes of the games, place the shining harness, whenever <to> the polished car
and under the bit-steering chariot he [sc. Hieron] yokes
the strength of horses, calling on the trident-wielding, wide-ruling God.
Now, to different people does each man pay tribute,
a resounding hymn for kings as recompense for their excellence.
They often sing about Kinyras,
the voices of the Cyprians, whom the golden-haired loved willingly, Apollo

γάρ, or more precisely ἐπὶ γάρ, introduces the antistrophe and functions as a join after the performative discontinuity. ἐπί is not followed by a dative (the word following γάρ is in the nominative) which suggests that it refers back to πώλους in line 8.[232] γάρ, meanwhile, points ahead, marking the current act as an elaboration, an unfolding of the claim made earlier (line 8). There is a shift in tense from aorist (ἀνέδησεν 6, εδάμασσε 8) to present (τίθησι), which accompanies a shift from the specific victory to the regular aid that Hieron receives from the gods (ὅταν 10), an extension of the general theme of divine aid.[233]

§72. Race's translation of γάρ with "because" renders the function of the word well enough here, but the simplicity of the translation hides the complexities of the

232 The argument can be made that we should read it as an anastrophe (or as an adverb), in which case the accent should be written on the first syllable: ἔπι. Regardless of this editorial decision, we may assume that a preposition that is not followed by a noun and a pre-verb in tmesis were pronounced with a different intonational contour to avoid ambiguity.

233 See Gentili et al. 1995:368.

construction. It is not the case that "Hieron mastered the horses with Artemis' help, *because* she puts the harness on." That is to say, there is no causal relation on the propositional level between the γάρ act and what preceeds. One could say that γάρ is used to mark what Sweetser would call an epistemic relation between the two clauses: "I can *say* that Hieron had divine help, *because* Artemis <always> puts the harness on..."[234] More practically, however, γάρ marks its host move (ἐπὶ γάρ...θεόν, 9-12) as one that is triggered by the preceding discourse: the association here is of a general statement with a particular event.[235] Hence my translation of γάρ as "No, ..." which marks the current move as an expansion on the preceding, while at the same time clearly signalling the start of something new; an effect that is lost if one translates "because" or "since."[236]

§73. I do not dwell here on the instances of τε in line 10 and 11, which represent a typical use of the particle after a pronoun to mark a piece of knowledge as shared or to-be-shared.[237] More noteworthy is the occurrence of δέ in line 13, since it illustrates a difference in the way that the particle functions in Homer and Pindar.[238] Pindar uses δέ more frequently in narrative than in other parts of his discourse, but in both contexts he uses the particle to mark significant discontinuities. Here it accompanies the transition from the specific case of Hieron (line 11) to the gnomic (or at least general) statement that different men honor different heroes (ἄλλοις δέ...ἀρετᾶς, 13-14). In discourse terms, both the content and orientation of lines 13 and 14 differ strongly from what precedes and what follows, suggesting that it is a separate move.[239] It is relevant that in this case δέ is not only in act-peninitial position, but also in verse-peninitial position. The fact that this metrical boundary matches the boundary marked by δέ suggests that the discontinuity perceived is stronger than when δέ is in verse-medial position.[240] The next move is marked by μέν (line 15), which projects the theme introduced in the act into the upcoming discourse. Pindar uses the particle more than once to carry a theme or narrative over the metrical boundary between strophe and antistrophe or, as here, between antistrophe and epode.[241]

234 Dancygier and Sweetser 2000:120-122; see also Slings 1997:104-106.

235 See §§22-29 above on γάρ in Homer: γάρ can also introduce an example following a general claim.

236 Compare again Sicking's claim that "sentences introduced by γάρ (...) provide answers to all sorts of questions raised by the speaker's utterances," in Sicking 1993:23; if we substitute "moves" for "sentences" in this statement, I would be inclined to agree.

237 This aspect of τε is explored in IV.2.3.1 and II.4.3.1, and particularly for Pindar in II.4.5.

238 See II.2.2.1 for more on δέ in Homer, and §65 above for δέ in Pindar.

239 Compare the discussion of independent thoughts inserted by means of δέ in Herodotus and Thucydides in IV.2 §§26-28.

240 Compare the use of δέ in a narrative section of *Pythian* 6 (three instances of δέ in a narrative, all mid-verse), discussed in II.2 §43, or the narrative section from *Pythian* 4 (t24), where in ten lines δέ occurs five times (25, 28, 32, 34, 34), of which four are in verse-medial position, before a stronger transition with a first-person verb followed by δέ in verse-peninitial place (38, πεύθομαι δέ).

241 Compare the discussion in II.2 §55, and further *Olympian* 6.41, 7.69, 7.88, 8.67; *Pythian* 2.15, 2.31, 4.53, 4.154, 11.31, 11.46; *Isthmian* 2.37. A metrical boundary may be compared to what is known as

§74. In the epode that follows, Pindar does not proceed with a narrative about Kinyras, as the audience may have expected, but rather makes a direct comparison between the Cyprian hero and Hieron (lines 17-20). Subsequently he launches into a narrative about Ixion, a paradigmatic narrative of divine punishment for overreaching.[242] Consider the end of the epode and the beginning of the second strophe:

(t29)

θεῶν δ' ἐφετμαῖς | Ἰξίονα φαντὶ ταῦτα βροτοῖς
λέγειν | ἐν πτερόεντι τροχῷ |
παντᾷ κυλινδόμενον· |
τὸν εὐεργέταν ἀγαναῖς ἀμοιβαῖς ἐποιχομένους τίνεσθαι. |

ἔμαθε δὲ σαφές. | εὐμενέσσι γὰρ παρὰ Κρονίδαις |
γλυκὺν ἑλὼν βίοτον | (...)

Pindar, *Pythian* 2.21-26

By the orders of the gods, they tell that Ixion says the following to mortals,
on his feathered wheel,
spinning in all directions:
to go to one's benefactor and pay him back with good deeds.

And he learned it clearly. Indeed, among the kind children of Kronos,
having had a sweet life, (...)

In the epode Pindar introduces the story of Ixion with φαντί (compare the example from *Pythian* 1, t4), followed by a gnomic thought attributed to Ixion. Since the *gnṓmē* occurs at the end of the epode, Pindar could have left it at that, but in the following line the third-person aorist form (ἔμαθε) followed by δέ suggests that the audience should assume continuity of grammatical subject at the start of the new strophe: Ixion is still in focus.[243] The actual narrative begins with γάρ (line 25), which introduces a clause that serves as an orientation for the narrative, in the form of a participial construction. The complication is introduced in the apodosis: μακρὸν οὐχ ὑπέμεινεν ὄλβον (line 26), and then the

a "Transition Relevance Place" in Conversation Analysis: a point where a switch of speaker may occur. In Pindar, it is a likely place for a change of discourse topic. The use of μέν to signal the continuity of discourse topic across the metrical boundary may be compared to the use of μέν to "hold the floor" across TRPs in tragic and comic dialogue; see III.4 §28-§30.

242 See Burton 1962:116-119 on the story of "one of the great sinners of Greek legend" (116).

243 See II.5 §19 on finite verb + δέ to mark continuity of grammatical subject.

narrative unfolds. Only in lines 34-35 is it interrupted briefly by a gnomic thought, introduced by χρὴ δέ, a cluster that almost invariably starts *gnômai* in Pindar.[244] After Ixion's misdeeds and his punishments have been discussed (26-41), the resolution of the story (starting with asyndeton, ἄνευ οἱ Χαρίτων τέκεν, 42) tells of the birth of a son from the union of Ixion and Hera-as-cloud, called Centaur, whose offspring with a mare in turn yields the familiar creatures that are half horse and half man. This rounds off the second epode (41-48).

§75. The third strophe starts with an expanded statement of the principle that gods can put down or raise up any mortal, already brought up in lines 7-11. Pindar then redirects attention to the here and now with a metadiscursive statement in 52 (ἐμὲ δὲ χρεών). This leads to a piece of advice to himself in the form of a *gnṓmē* at the end of the strophe, urging him to focus on praising positive things rather than blaming (lines 54-56). This advice he immediately applies in the antistrophe to his *laudandus*: τὺ δὲ σάφα νιν [sc. πλοῦτον] ἔχεις ("But you have it [sc. wealth] with wisdom," line 57) starts a new expansive move dedicated to praising Hieron's money and power. Note how once again the explicit mention of a first or second person followed by a particle accompanies move transitions in the songs. The remainder of the song alternates between commenting on Hieron's prowess and alluding to some people who seem to have slandered either Hieron or Pindar. At the end of the fourth antistrophe these topics are left behind for another *gnṓmē*, in this case acting as a bridge to the last epode, which stresses once more that gods decide the fate of men.

(t30)

(...) χρὴ δὲ πρὸς θεὸν οὐκ ἐρίζειν |

ὃς ἀνέχει | τοτὲ μὲν τὰ κείνων, | τότ' αὖθ' ἑτέροις ἔδωκεν μέγα
κῦδος. | ἀλλ' οὐδὲ ταῦτα νόον
ἰαίνει φθονερῶν· | στάθμας δέ τινες ἑλκόμενοι
περισσᾶς | ἐνέπαξαν ἕλκος ὀδυναρὸν ἑᾷ πρόσθε καρδίᾳ, |
πρὶν ὅσα φροντίδι μητίονται τυχεῖν. |
φέρειν δ' ἐλαφρῶς ἐπαυχένιον λαβόντα ζυγόν
ἀρήγει· | ποτὶ κέντρον δέ τοι
λακτιζέμεν | τελέθει
ὀλισθηρὸς οἶμος· | ἁδόντα δ' εἴη με τοῖς ἀγαθοῖς ὁμιλεῖν. |

Pindar, *Pythian* 2.88-96 (end)

(...) One should not contend with god.

[244] Of the eight instances in the *Odes*, only one (*Isthmian* 8.16) does not introduce a generic piece wisdom. This generalization may be extended to most instances of clause-initial χρή; see on this instance Gentili et al. 1995:378.

He raises up, sometimes the fate [lit. "things"] of those people,[245]
then again to others does he gives great honor. But not even that
warms the mind of jealous men. Pulling some line
too far, they fix a painful wound into their own heart,
before they succeed in those things that they plan in their minds.
To carry lightly the yoke one has taken on one's neck
is helpful. And I tell you, kicking against the goad
is a slippery course. Pleasing them, may it be granted to me to
consort with the good.

Once again χρὴ δέ (line 88) introduces the gnomic thought, but it is followed by a change in direction marked by ἀλλά (line 89). ἀλλά here expresses no semantic contrast but rather marks a redirection of the discourse, and this use of the particle is decidedly more frequent in Homer and Pindar than it is in Attic Greek. In Homer this use appears most commonly in constructions where ἀλλά marks transitions to a move containing an imperative or a wish at the end of direct speech. In Pindar, however, it occurs at all kinds of re-orientations, thus often coinciding with move beginning. Here, the penultimate move of the song (lines 89-96) is concerned with the theme of envious men, but the meaning of the passage is ambiguous.[246] It leads on to the final act and final move of the song, introduced by δέ and containing a first-person pronoun (line 96), in which Pindar expresses a hope for himself.[247] As all Pindaric discourse, even this apparent personal statement implicitly praises the laudandus and the present audience.

§76. The second *Pythian* ode provides a good case study to support the argument that considering Pindaric discourse as a sequence of moves by the poet offers insight into the use of language in general and of particles in particular. This ode is particularly illustrative since it contains so many different kinds of discursive transitions, but this kind of approach will illuminate the reading of any Pindaric ode. Therefore we apply the terminology of acts and moves throughout the other chapters.

245 See Gildersleeve 1885:267, "the fortunes of those whisperers."

246 Pindar argues that man should bear the fate he is given, without attempting to overreach. It might be read as advice for Hieron, or as an illustration of Pindar's own attitude toward life, and toward his host Hieron; see Gentili et al. 1995:405.

247 Gentili et al. 1995:405 calls it a "final prayer" ("preghiera finale").

3.5 Conclusions

§77. In this chapter I have shown that in order to understand why certain particles occur in certain places, we need to look at the larger movements of discourse at all levels beyond that of the sentence. Earlier studies on ἦ and δή have focused mainly on their role within the scope of the sentence, or in relation to adjacent words. Moreover, there is a tendency in the scholarship on almost all particles to find a general description that covers all the different aspects of the particle. Both tendencies have obscured certain patterns that can refine our understanding of what particles do.

§78. ἦ, δή, and γάρ all have a facet that is connected to the start of new moves. For ἦ it is its interjection-like value that makes it performatively effective at discourse transitions. δή's occurence at narrative transitions, often in concert with temporal markers, is not as easily explained. It is clear, however, that these occurrences should not be regarded as representatives of its intensifying function. In fact, the Homeric corpus reveals that δή possesses a whole spectrum of functions, each of which is bound to specific contexts and to δή's position in the act. Finally, as regards γάρ, apparently simple translations often belie the particle's more complex functions. Like "for" in English, the particle can signal relations among many different elements in discourse. In narrative, the use of γάρ often marks the start of a new move, which is associatively connected to the surrounding discourse. Understanding this use of γάρ opens up a range of alternative translations that do not foreground the close causal relation that is rendered by "for" or "since", but rather render the sense of discursive discontinuity between the preceding move and the one introduced by γάρ.

§79. The Attico-centric approach to particles has left its traces everywhere. The focus on the causal/explanatory function of γάρ, the attempt to find a single function for δή, the reading of ἦ as a basically affirmative or emphatic particle, the reading of δέ as adversative, and the assumption that every μέν implies a δέ, are all examples of the orthodoxy that is especially misleading when working with corpora like that of Homer and Pindar. Starting from Attico-centric assumptions prevents us from perceiving the richness of metalinguistic functions that these particles perform, and it leads to the mislabeling of Homeric and Pindaric usage as odd, anacolouthic, or simply metrically convenient. We should rather view their usage as signs of earlier stages in the grammaticalization of certain constructions, or as due to the particularities of performative genres.

§80. A significant part of the chapter considers particles not in isolation, but in clusters and in constructions with other word groups. Particle combinations are not monolithic: the same combination may combine different functions of the particles involved. Hence we should be wary of attributing fixed functions to a certain combination. Furthermore, there is a difference between a combination (where the sum is no more than its parts) and a cluster (where the sum is more than its parts, and the cluster has evolved to become somewhat detached from its origins). Especially for early Greek, but perhaps for ancient Greek in general, it is risky to make generalizing statements about the force of a particle combination. Only when it has completely grammaticalized so as to be regarded as essentially one word can we speak of a coherent function, and even in that case one can never exclude the possibility that in some instances the particles have ended up next to each other by happenstance. To understand particle combinations, one must appreciate the richness in function of all the constituent elements, and search for patterns in the different contexts in which the combination is found.

§81. A final thought to take from this chapter is that editions are not sacred. Especially for vulnerable little words like particles, and even more so for ambiguous lexemes like H, the normalizing practices of the Alexandrians, scribes, and modern editors may have obscured subtle but important differences. Detailed studies of all these different stages of textual transmission combined with an informed scepticism toward the sources at our disposal allow us to propose new readings of particles, where the content and the form of the discourse provide enough material to make an argument. In short, paying attention to the larger discursive context in which individual sentences are situated can enable more nuanced readings of even the smallest details in a text.

II.4

Discourse Memory

The Negotiation of Shared Knowledge

§1. In the present chapter I discuss language that refers to the level of interaction not overtly, but through indirect means. This language is not self-referential, but rather marks the relation of the performer to the content in a manner that reveals his expectations about the knowledge of the audience. We are concerned here with the dimension of shared experience, shared knowledge, shared beliefs, and shared discourse.

§2. Tradition is an important part of this dimension, for both Homeric and Pindaric discourse. Consider what Foley says about the function of tradition in the generation and reception of Homeric epic:

(t1)

> "The poetic tradition properly understood is not at all a limiting but rather a connotatively explosive medium, a touchstone or nexus of indication and reference wholly different from the medium at the disposal of the "non-traditional" artist, *for such a diction and narrative structure have obvious and necessary reference not only to the present poem, poet, and time but also to an enormous number of other poets, poems, and eras.*"
>
> Foley 1990:2 [my emphasis]

Any performance of Homeric epic represents a moment in the continuum of tradition. Whichever part of the tradition is in current focus, the whole remains constantly relevant and accessible as a body of knowledge shared between performer and audience.[1]

§3. Pindar's engagement with tradition is complex, and his songs must be regarded as both a product and a producer of traditional knowledge. That is to say, his songs stand

1 Havelock 1963:88-93 speaks of tradition in terms of a house full of furniture through which the Homeric performer threads a path.

in a continuum, at once forming and being formed by tradition.[2] The difference between lyric song and epic poetry lies in the fact that lyric has to take into account both local and Panhellenic tradition.[3] As Wells puts it:

(t2)

> "Pindar's compositions entail a dynamic process of fluid interchange with the past of tradition, the present of original performance, and the future of subsequent reperformance."
>
> Wells 2009:137

In the Panhellenic culture of the fifth century these three temporal dimensions are inextricably linked, and therefore always intertwined in Pindaric song.

§4. The present chapter studies the linguistic reflection in Homer and Pindar of engagement with tradition and other kinds of shared knowledge, a phenomenon that has been termed "discourse memory." I argue that apparently random use of certain particles—γάρ, ἄρα, and τε in particular—can be understood as metalanguage reflecting the performer's assumptions about a shared body of knowledge. First, I introduce the term "discourse memory" and locate it within the larger framework of this study (4.1). Then I discuss how the Homeric performer monitors the discourse memory, supplementing it with pieces of knowledge introduced by γάρ (4.2.1). In Pindar's *Victory Odes* we find a similar use of γάρ, but, beyond introducing information about the storyworld, Pindar uses γάρ to insert *gnômai* (4.2.2). A special kind of traditional discourse is that of the Homeric simile, of which a linguistic analysis is presented in the third section, with a focus on τε and ἄρα (4.3). The fourth section of the chapter studies recurrent or common event sequences ("typical scenes") in Homer, in which ἄρα is important again (4.4). In the final section , I present an analysis of τε in Pindar (4.5).

4.1 Discourse Memory

§5. Before going on to discuss how epic and lyric discourse reflect the process of negotiating shared knowledge, it is necessary to consider what form this body of information takes in our minds. In a 1981 article, Lord describes the role of memory in the performance of epic:

2 See Nagy 1990:128-129, where he argues that the Pelops narrative in *Olympian* 1 need not have been Pindar's invention.

3 See also Nagy 1990:114, "Though each of Pindar's victory odes was an occasional composition, centering on a single performance, each containing details grounded in the historical realities of the time and place of performance, still each of these victory odes aimed at translating its occasion into a Panhellenic event."

(t3)

> "...we could safely say for the whole song that Salih has not either memorized or even "remembered" a *text*, but he has remembered the essential elements in each section, and he has remembered the story. It is in *these* areas, i.e., essential elements in the themes or segments and the overall story, that memory plays its role."
>
> Lord 1981:456 [emphasis original]

Lord highlights two aspects of memory relevant to the epic performance: knowledge of the narrative sequence on the one hand (the "overall story"), and the crucial elements to every segment of the story on the other. Both of these elements are to a large extent prescribed by tradition, a fact that is not limited to epic. In both lyric and epic, the content and structure of stories is therefore to a certain extent shared by performer and audience. [4] Besides the narratives within epic and lyric, the genres themselves are traditional too: the performer is aware of the audience's expectations about both form and content. More generally, in a performance at a certain time and place, there exists a body of shared experiences and beliefs, resulting from a world and a culture shared by performer and audience. Finally, the performer can build upon what was said before within the same performance, the shared discourse: he can assume, rightly or not, that the audience remembers the most important events of the preceding discourse.

§6. This pool of information that constantly serves as a background to the unfolding discourse has been discussed in several forms, but I will follow Berrendonner and Roulet in calling it the discourse memory.[5] In II.2 I note that Roulet eventually defines the discourse act as every "update to the discourse memory," building on the work done by Berrendonner. [6] Cornish, conversely, speaks of "discourse model" rather than "discourse memory," but he equates his term to Berrendonner's "mémoire discursive." In this chapter I follow Berrendonner and Roulet in using the term "discourse memory," but will also refer to Cornish's "discourse model," using the two terms to denote two different things.

4 See Havelock 1963:88-93 and Nagy 1979:3, "To my mind there is no question, then, about the poet's ability to say accurately what he means. What he means, however, is strictly regulated by tradition. The poet has no intention of saying anything untraditional. In fact, the poet's inherited conceit is that he has it in his power to recover the exact words that tell what men did and said in the Heroic Age."

5 Roulet et al. 2001:64-65 and Berrendonner 1990, who speaks of the "memoire discursive" or "savoir partagé" [shared knowledge].

6 Roulet et al. 2001:64-65.

§7. The discourse model (Cornish) is "a coherent [mental] representation of the discourse,"[7] while the discourse memory (Berrendonner) contains "the information that, at every moment, is valid for the two interlocutors and shared among them."[8] Building on Berrendonner's brief description, I believe discourse memory can be defined more fully. The work by the cognitive linguist Langacker is especially helpful in this respect. He defines the "current discourse space (CDS)" as follows:

(t4)

"[b]esides the context of speech, the CDS includes a body of knowledge presumed to be shared and readily accessible. It also includes the speaker's and hearer's apprehension of the ongoing discourse itself: a series of previous usage events, as well as subsequent events that might be anticipated. Any facet of this can be drawn upon or alluded to in the current utterance."

Langacker 2001:144

I understand the difference between discourse memory and the discourse model as follows: the discourse memory is the whole body of shared knowledge that underlies the current discourse,[9] whereas the discourse model is that part of the discourse memory that has been activated to create a mental representation of the current discourse. In other words, the discourse model is part of the working memory, while the rest of the discourse memory is that part of the long term memory that is shared between performer and audience.[10]

§8. For Homeric and Pindaric discourse, the three components of the discourse memory that exert influence on the linguistic formation and subsequent interpretation of any discourse act in Homer and Pindar are (1) the tradition, (2) the shared knowledge of the world, and (3) the preceding discourse. Every discourse act may thus engage in an interaction with the current discourse model as well as with any other relevant information in the discourse memory.

§9. The world evoked in the narrative of epic or lyric is up to a point removed from the here and now, yet the composer constantly counts on his audience's basic knowledge

7 "Discourse model" was coined by Prince 1981, and is used by Cornish 1999:5, with the following definition: "This model is a coherent representation of the discourse being evoked via the co-text and its context in terms of the speaker's or writer's hypothesized intentions." I employ the term throughout II.5.

8 Berrendonner1990:25, "(mémoire discursive ou savoir partagé), contenant les informations qui, à chaque instant, sont valides pour les deux interlocuteurs et publique entre eux."

9 Compare also Venneman 1975:314 who speaks of a "presupposition pool," which contains information "constituted from general knowledge, from the situative context of the discourse, and from the completed part of the discourse itself."

10 For this relation between working memory and the discourse model, see Cornish 1999:159, 166.

of the world. The world created to serve as the theater for a narrative has been called a storyworld.[11] The form of a storyworld is subject to what Ryan calls the "principle of minimal departure," which states that the storyworld is the same as the "real" world (i.e. the world in which performer and audience live) except for those aspects explicitly mentioned.[12] So in the storyworld of the *Iliad*, the Greek heroes are taller and stronger than the men of Archaic Greece, but wood still burns, the sea has tides, the sun goes down and comes up again, and so on. Unless the audience receives an instruction to adapt the image, they will project the world they know onto the storyworld.

§10. The discourse memory covers the entire body of relevant knowledge that the performer assumes to be shared between him and the audience at any particular point in the discourse. This cognitive process is a matter of assumption and prediction, since the performer cannot know exactly to what extent the audience shares his knowledge. For that very reason, it is only of limited relevance to know what knowledge exactly is actually shared between performer and audience at a certain point in time. We may compare the use of "of course" in academic papers to indicate that some piece of information is expected to be shared, even if in practice only part of the audience may actually know it. Expressing such assumptions linguistically may thus be as much a rhetorical device as a reflection of reality. In the following sections I trace different linguistic elements that to my mind reflect these assumptions and predictions on the part of the performer.

4.2 Unframed Discourse

§11. As a story progresses, every discourse act is an implicit instruction to update the storyworld. However, narration of the action is not the only way for the performer to develop the discourse model; he can also choose to engage with the discourse memory more explicitly.[13] At any moment in the narrative the performer may feel the need to explain something, which he cannot always do while staying in the background.[14] To discuss this phenomenon of narrative discourse in particular, I introduce the concepts of framed and unframed discourse.

§12. In her 1997 monograph, Emmott explains narrative as being built around spaces, contexts that contain certain characters at certain times, and are placed relatively

[11] I borrow the term "storyworld" from Herman 2002; see also II.5.1.

[12] Ryan 1991:51.

[13] Beyond language, extralinguistic and paralinguistic information can also influence the discourse model. When a performer points (or even looks) at something in the direct performance context, this may from then on form part of the discourse model without ever having been expressed verbally (see also II.5 §37). Likewise, an emphasized personal pronoun may imply a contrast with another referent (e.g. "YOU are not like that"), who at that point becomes a part of the discourse model without ever being mentioned.

[14] See Richardson 1990:5 and 197-198 on the absence and presence of the narrator in Homeric discourse.

or absolutely within the storyworld. Such a space is a "contextual frame" in Emmott's terms,[15] and it plays a central role in how a narrative is managed.[16] One may imagine a contextual frame as a space in the mental representation of the discourse, which functions as a receptacle for specific characters, items, and events. A character is "bound" to a contextual frame until the performer provides explicit information to the contrary ("covert continuity").[17] Once characters are bound to a location, activating that character gives both performer and audience access to the entire contextual frame.[18] Emmott demonstrates that the largest part of conventional narratives occurs within contextual frames: this she calls "framed" discourse.[19]

§13. Framed discourse consists of those acts that are temporally and spatially positioned within a contextual frame in the storyworld. They tell of the events that occur in a certain time and place within the frame of the narrative. To these framed acts, Emmott contrasts "unframed" discourse: acts that do not present narrative events, but rather inform the audience about the storyworld and its inhabitants. Consider the following example:

(t5)

"How's the baby?"

"Little bleeder never sleeps, he's wearing us out, but he's fine."

The baby was six years old. Having the baby was a definite achievement: getting it safely conceived and born had taken a couple of years.

Doris Lessing 1965 'A Man and Two Women' in
A Man and Two Women, 91; given as an example
by Emmott 1997:246 [emphasis Emmott]

15 Emmott's contextual frames are an application of the idea of [semantic] frames—interconnected semantic networks, on which see Fillmore 1976—to characters in narrative discourse. Cornish 1999:44-45 speaks of "referential space" which appears to approach Emmott's idea of "contextual frame."

16 Emmott 1997:121-122. Emmott's point can be linked directly to the observation by the psychologists Winograd and Church (1988:6-7, referred to by Minchin 2008:10), who claim that spatial information can cue the recall of associated material; see also Rothkopf, Fisher, and Billington 1982:126.

17 See Emmott 1997:125-129.

18 The relevance of contextual frames to the linguistic realization of narrative is manifold: see II.2.5 on the link between transitions between contextual frames and the use of priming acts, and II.5 throughout for how the concept of the contextual frame can explain apparent problems of reference.

19 Emmott speaks of "framed text," but "text" is a problematic term with regard to the Homeric and Pindaric corpora.

The narrator shifts from reporting direct speech to describing a character. The italicized passage is unframed, since it is not concerned with what is happening at a certain point in time. In English unframed discourse is marked by its form as generalizations, often a description or backstory, as here.[20] The information given in unframed text is true beyond the current scene in the storyworld: it is not happening in a narrative "here and now." Since unframed discourse often takes this form, scholars have described it in terms of "descriptive mode" or "background discourse,"[21] but unframed is a more inclusive term: it covers not only descriptions, but also expressions of stance, and it avoids the hierarchical implications of foreground versus background. Most importantly, the status of the discourse as framed or unframed is not dependent on content (i.e. descriptions) but on the attitude of the performer towards the discourse. In many cases, the performer can choose between presenting discourse as framed or unframed: compare "they saw her stride in through the gate. She was a tall woman..." (framed) against "She strode in through the gate. *She had always been the tallest of three sisters...*" (unframed).[22]

§14. The unframed nature of a piece of discourse is reflected through language in multiple ways. First of all, there is often a tense shift after the transition to unframed discourse, and again when the framed text is resumed. Second, the occurrence of unframed discourse has an effect on the flow of discourse. Although unframed discourse typically has direct relevance to the surrounding framed discourse, the change in perspective means that other discourse processes are interrupted. Anaphoric reference in particular is affected: when a character is introduced into a frame, that character remains available in that frame until we are informed otherwise ("covert continuity"). Characters introduced in unframed discourse, however, do not remain available when framed discourse is resumed.[23] In the example above, the "sisters" are not normally available when the "striding through the gate" frame is resumed.[24] Third, metalinguistic markers occur at the transitions into and out of unframed discourse. Emmott observes

20 Emmott 1997:252-258.

21 Emmott discusses the different terms with extensive literature in 1997:141-145. For Homer, Bakker 2005:123-135 uses both the terms "background" and "off-sequence."

22 These are constructed examples for the sake of illustration.

23 See Emmott 1997:239 and 248-252.

24 See also Grosz and Sidner 1986:178 "...the discourse segmentation affects the interpretation of linguistic expressions in a discourse. (...) The segmentation of discourse constrains the use of referring expressions by delineating certain points at which there is a significant change in what entities (...) are being discussed. For example there are different constraints on the use of pronouns and reduced definite-noun phrases within a segment than across segment boundaries." On pages 193-194 they describe what happens in a shift between two discourses: "Because the second discourse shifts attention totally to a new purpose (...), the speakers cannot use any referential expressions during it that depend on the accessibility of entities from the first discourse."

that in English written narrative temporal markers often serve to mark such frame transitions,[25] and she concludes:

(t6)

> "Markers such as ["once"] suggest that the distinction between (framed) events in context and (unframed) decontextualized generalizations is important and has a textual realization which needs to be taken into account."
>
> Emmott 1997:248

In addition to the linguistic marking mentions above, ancient Greek likewise employs metalinguistic markers at the transitions between framed and unframed discourse. I now turn to the most important of these markers in Homer and Pindar.

4.2.1. γάρ and unframed discourse in Homeric epic

§15. The Homeric performer is omniscient, so he can report not only the observable actions of the protagonists, but also their backstories and their thoughts. Moreover, the performer can reflect upon the narrative situation himself, either as a narrating persona or as a performer in the here and now. These steps out of the storyworld into unframed discourse are often introduced by γάρ. They reveal the performance's nature as an interactive activity,[26] acting as a sign of the performer assessing the knowledge shared between him and audience, and providing crucial information when needed. In Homeric narrative γάρ has three functions: (1) to introduce information about characters or the storyworld, (2) to blend the perspectives of the performer with that of a character, and (3) to introduce evaluative comments about the ongoing narrative. My contention throughout is that it is unproductive to link γάρ to the idea of background, since from a narrative and discourse perspective the acts and moves introduced by γάρ are important.[27] They supply information indispensable for the narrative, heighten suspense, and invite audience involvement.

§16. As discussed in II.3, the performer can use γάρ to unfold certain story paths. The mention of a place, item, or character may trigger an association with another narrative, which is then introduced by γάρ. In the following passage Odysseus, a first-person

25 Such as "now" and "once," see Emmott 1997:246-250.

26 Compare Barthes 1977:110 about signs of the narrator and of the hearer/reader in the text. When a first-person narrator in a novel says: "Leo was the owner of the joint..." he is not "giving himself information," so he must be "turning to the reader." For more on transitions between the storyworld and the realm of the Homeric performance see Richardson 1990:66, Minchin 2001:43, Bakker 2005:114-135, Strauss Clay 2011:21, and Tsagalis 2012:19.

27 See II.3 §§25-26 for the recent tendency in scholarship to associate γάρ with the introduction of background information.

internal narrator, introduces his plan (βουλή) to defeat the Cyclops. Before he can outline his plan to his audience, however, he has to explain to them that there is a club in the Cyclops' cave, a crucial element in the plan:

(t7)

ἥδε δέ μοι κατὰ θυμὸν ἀρίστη φαίνετο βουλή· |
Κύκλωπος γὰρ ἔκειτο μέγα ῥόπαλον | παρὰ σηκῷ, |
χλωρὸν ἐλαΐνεον· | (...)
(...)
τοῦ μὲν | ὅσον τ' ὄργυιαν | ἐγὼν ἀπέκοψα | παραστὰς |
καὶ παρέθηχ' ἑτάροισιν, | ἀποξῦναι δ' ἐκέλευσα· |

Odyssey 9.318-320, 325-326

And this seemed in my mind to be the best plan:
You see, there *lay* a big club of the Cyclops near the pen,
of green olivewood;
(...)
Of that, then, *I cut off* about a fathom's length, standing near it,
and *put it near* my comrades; *I ordered* them to sand it down.

In lines 319-324 a passage is inserted to give information that the audience needs to understand the point of the narrative. The information that Odysseus offers is in the form of a piece of knowledge about the storyworld of his Cyclops narrative. This shift to the unframed move is marked by γάρ and a change to the imperfect tense (ἔκειτο etc), as typically occurs in such situations. The return to framed discourse is marked by μέν and three verbs in the aorist.[28]

§17. It is clear that in passages like (t7) there is no sense of causality inherent in the γάρ clause.[29] Not even if we take into account the possibility of "anticipatory γάρ"—i.e. the γάρ clause providing the cause before the result—can we explain this instance as causal.[30] Nor can we describe this as "background information," since in narrative terms the unframed discourse occurs exactly because it is indispensable to understanding the

[28] See II.5 for more on the use of pronouns and particles near transitions between framed and unframed discourse.

[29] See De Jong 2004b:91-93, who explains this use of γάρ as answering implied questions of the audience, and takes it as a sign that the Iliad is a "récit motivé" in Genette's terms.

[30] The discussion of the possibility that a γάρ clause can give a cause before the clause that contains the result goes back to Aristarchus (see I.2 §31); the existence of "anticipatory" or "proleptic" γάρ is accepted by Schraut 1849:16, Schraut 1857, Fritsch 1859, Hoffmann 1880, Monro 1882a, and Ebeling 1885, and opposed by Döderlein 1858.

ongoing narrative. The nature of the discourse changes for a limited time, but its importance does not. Consider one more example from the Cyclops narrative:

(t8)

τρεῖς δὲ ἕκαστον φῶτ' ὄϊες φέρον· | αὐτὰρ ἐγώ γε, |
ἀρνειὸς γὰρ ἔην μήλων | ὄχ' ἄριστος ἁπάντων, |
τοῦ κατὰ νῶτα λαβών, | λασίην ὑπὸ γαστέρ' ἐλυσθεὶς |
κείμην· | (...)

Odyssey 9.431-434

And three ewes carried each man; but then I—
there was a ram, far the best of all the sheep;
grabbing him down the back, curled under his haired belly
I lay;

Again, γάρ is used to introduce a piece of knowledge that the speaker thinks the hearer may not, or cannot, know. In both (t7) and (t8) the piece of unframed discourse interrupts the flow of the narrative, in (t8) actually interfering with a syntactical construction.[31]

§18. Compare the following excerpt from an informal conversation recorded by Chafe, about an old-fashioned Swiss professor:

(t9)

13. ... a—nd he— .. wou-ld immédiately open his ... nótes up,

14. ... in the front of the róom,
15. .. and he st
16. and évery ... évery lecture,
17. ... áfter the fírst,
18. .. stárted the same wáy.
19. *This was .. u—m at Wésleyan,*
20. *when Wesleyan was still ... a mén's school.*
21. ... *So* évery lecture after the first would begin,
22. ... Géntlemen,
23. ..ze lást time,

Chafe 1987:23 [my emphasis]

[31] A similar construction occurs in Herodotus I.126 ἐνθαῦτα ὁ Κῦρος | ἦν γάρ τις χῶρος τῆς Περσικῆς ἀκανθώδης (...) | τοῦτόν σφι τὸν χῶρον; see for this passage Kerschensteiner 1964:40 and IV.3 §108.

There is no clear marking of the beginning of the unframed discourse, but the return to the narrative frame is marked with "so"; Emmott calls this "frame recall."[32] The similarity with (t7) and (t8) is striking: as the speaker comes to the *pointe* of his story, he introduces a crucial piece of information: the presence of the club in (t7), the ram in (t8), and the fact that Wesleyan was still a men's school in (t9). The speaker then proceeds to tell the rest of the story so that Odysseus has a club to make a weapon, an animal to cling to, and so that the "[g]entlemen" in (t9) makes sense. There may be another motivation behind this strategy: by inserting the information at this point in the narrative, in this form, the climax of the story is briefly postponed. Thus introducing this kind of unframed discourse may serve to build up tension in the unfolding of the framed discourse.

§19. There are countless examples of γάρ introducing pieces of important knowledge in narrative. Beyond the instances discussed above, I simply note examples throughout the other chapters where they occur. For now, I turn to another kind of unframed discourse commonly introduced by γάρ. In II.3 I discuss δὴ γάρ with regard to the function of δή, but now I focus on the function of γάρ in the combination. I have noted before that δή in narrator text occurs in the great majority of cases with a temporal marker, signaling larger steps in the narrative. Much less often, it occurs in narrator text in its intensifying function, either with large or with small scope. One example of this latter category is δὴ γάρ in narrator text: in act-initial position, δή does not appear to have its discourse-segmenting function.[33]

§20. Consider the following example about Deïphobus:

(t10)

τοῦ δὲ βάδην ἀπιόντος <u>ἀκόντισε</u> | δουρὶ φαεινῷ |
Δηΐφοβος· | <u>δὴ γάρ</u> οἱ <u>ἔχεν</u> κότον ἐμμενὲς αἰεί. |
ἀλλ' ὅ γε[34] καὶ τόθ' <u>ἅμαρτεν</u>, | ὃ δ' Ἀσκάλαφον βάλε δουρὶ |

Iliad 13.516-518

And him, as he retreated step by step, *struck* with his shining spear
Deïphobus. *For* he *had had* a hate for him, ever unceasing.
But HE *missed* right then. He hit Ascalaphus with his spear,

In this prototypical example, it seems almost like we get a glimpse of Deiphobus' thoughts at the moment that he attacks Idomeneus "I have really always hated him!" However, the addition of ἐμμενὲς αἰεί, as well as the imperfect (ἔχεν) within the narrative in the aorist,

[32] I take the expression "frame recall" from Emmott 1997:150-157; see §§38-41 below and II.5.3.3 for more on the topic.

[33] δὴ γάρ in narrator text: 3 out of 8 instances in the *Iliad*, 3 out of 9 in the *Odyssey*.

[34] See II.5.3.2 for ὅ γε after unframed discourse.

strongly suggest the omniscient perspective of the narrator. In contrast to the unframed discourse discussed above, the kind of information introduced by δή γάρ here is not about the external world, but about the thoughts of a character.[35] The performer uses γάρ to introduce a little insight into a character's psyche, creating the impression of what we might call free indirect thought. In this form of representing thought, there is no cue like "he thought: ..." (direct thought) or "he thought that ..." (indirect thought), but a character's thoughts are represented more obliquely.[36] The use of intensification through δή within the narrator text may also be a sign of empathy of the narrator with that character: there is a blurring of perspectives.[37] In the parallel instances of δή γάρ there is always some similar insight into the feelings of a character.[38] Unframed discourse in narrative, in short, concerns not only information about the storyworld, but also about the thoughts and feelings of characters.[39]

§21. The expression of omnitemporality ἐμμενὲς αἰεί in (t10) brings us to the final kind of unframed discourse in Homer introduced by γάρ: *gnômai*, or generalizing statements about the world, which function as comments on the ongoing narrative. Lardinois has noted the possibility of connecting "a gnomic statement to the particular situation to which [the poet] wants the saying to apply, by inserting a particle or conjunction, such as γάρ or ἐπεί, at the beginning of the gnomic expression."[40] He discusses the phenomenon in Sophocles, but it also occurs in Homer, especially in the combination γάρ τε.[41] Consider the following example from the *Odyssey*, where Nestor is speaking of Agamemnon's decision to stay in Troy and attempt to appease Athena:

35 The parallels are *Iliad* 17.546, 17.625; *Odyssey* 10.160 (Odysseus as narrator), 13.30, 18.154. There is one exception of δή γάρ in narrator text: *Iliad* 24.351, where δή γάρ introduces a piece of knowledge about the storyworld. The role of δή in this passage is unclear, and it is one of the passages often adduced to argue that δή has a temporal value in Homer (= ἤδη: "by now"); see e.g. Thomas 1894:94 where it is listed under "the purely temporal use [of δή]."

36 See IV.4 §97 with n. 146 for a similar reading of δή in indirect thought in Herodotus, and IV.4 §113 and §121 on γὰρ δή in Thucydides.

37 Compare the instances of γάρ marking "double focalization" in discourse (i.e. focalized both through the narrator and through a character) discussed by De Jong 2004b:111-112. An especially attractive example of possible empathy of the narrator/performer is *Odyssey* 13.30, about Odysseus: δή γάρ μενέαινε νέεσθαι ("he very much wanted to return home").

38 This kind of blurring also occurs in one of the few instances of γὰρ δή in narrator text: *Iliad* 12.331-333 τοὺς δὲ ἰδὼν ῥίγησ' υἱὸς Πετεῶο Μενεσθεύς· / τοῦ γὰρ δὴ πρὸς πύργον ἴσαν κακότητα φέροντες. / πάπτηνεν δ' ἀνὰ πύργον Ἀχαιῶν εἴ τιν' ἴδοιτο. The performer explains Menestheus' shudder (ῥίγησε) by verbalizing the character's perception of the army approaching his part of the wall. I infer a shift in perspective from the use of δή and the fact that the combination γὰρ δή rarely occurs in narrator text without a temporal marker (only here and in *Odyssey* 5.276 τὴν γὰρ δή μιν ἄνωγε Καλυψώ, δῖα θεάων).

39 More on the link between δή and the blurring of perspective in narrative in IV.4.5.3-5.

40 Lardinois 2006:216.

41 See Ruijgh 1971:720-721, who speaks of permanent and temporary facts introduced by γάρ τε.

(t11)

> <u>νήπιος</u>, | οὐδὲ τὸ ᾔδη, | ὃ οὐ πείσεσθαι ἔμελλεν· |
> οὐ <u>γάρ τ'</u> αἶψα θεῶν <u>τρέπεται</u> νόος <u>αἰὲν</u> ἐόντων. |
>
> *Odyssey* 3.146-147
>
> *Fool*, he did not know that she [sc. Athena] would not be persuaded.
> *No*, not quickly *is* the mind *turned* of the gods who are *forever*.

Nestor is acting like an internal narrator, and his use of νήπιος clearly shows his non-neutral stance.[42] Here and in other examples of γάρ τε moves in Homer, the pattern is clear: after the two adjacent particles there is a shift to present tense (or an elided ἐστι),[43] and this is often accompanied by a form of αἰεί.[44] Finally, this kind of gnomic unframed discourse typically occurs in direct speech, and is practically limited to the *Odyssey*.

§22. It is telling that we find the combination γάρ τε in these gnomic statements by characters. The discourse function of γάρ can now be explained as introducing unframed discourse, while its logical function here is that of signalling the reason or cause for the preceding. What, then, is the function of τε here? I argue that the addition of τε in this construction serves to mark the statement as referring to a large body of shared knowledge, which we might term tradition. The particle's use in Homeric *gnômai* can be compared to that in similes, other instances of timeless discourse, and to its use in Pindaric song. Finally, it may be brought into connection with the occurrence of τε in proverbs in archaic epic.[45] I cannot, therefore, agree with Denniston's contention that in combinations τε's "association with particular particles" (i.e. γάρ in this case) is rather "loose and fortuitous."[46]

§23. There is a correlation in Homer between the occurrence of unframed discourse and the particle γάρ. Whether to introduce additional information that is crucial to the narrative, or to reflect upon the situation, the performer turns to γάρ to mark the transition and to signal the associative link. Any transition between framed and unframed discourse is neutral with regard to the importance of the unframed move. The correlation emerges clearly from the material, but the performer does not have to use the particle when he introduces unframed discourse.[47]

42 See also Bakker 2005:84, who calls such *nḗpios* passages "direct interaction between the poet and his audience."

43 *Odyssey* 1.152 (=21.430) τὰ γάρ τ' ἀναθήματα δαιτός.

44 *Iliad* 1.63; *Odyssey* 1.351, 4.397, 5.78, 7.294, 7.307, 12.105, 14.228, 15.54 (ἤματα πάντα), 20.75, and 20.85. One may also compare the unique ὣς γὰρ θέσφατόν ἐστι, spoken by Zeus in *Iliad* 8.477.

45 See IV.2 §§55-56 with further examples from Homer and Hesiod.

46 Denniston 1950:528.

47 Consider by way of example *Iliad* 16.688, right after a *nḗpios* statement (16.686): ἀλλ' αἰεί τε Διὸς κρείσσων νόος ἠέ περ ἀνδρῶν.

4.2.2 γάρ and unframed discourse in Pindar

§24. The examples of gnomic unframed discourse provide a natural bridge to Pindaric song: their tendency to occur in direct speech in Homer brings us closer to the communicative situation in Pindar. Pindar's movements between framed and unframed discourse are both more numerous and more explicit than Homer's, and he too avails himself of γάρ to add pieces of information about the storyworld where needed.[48] His songs differ from Homeric epic in that Pindar explicitly engages with the real world. Consider the following example:

(t12)

'χρήματα χρήματ' ἀνήρ' | ὃς φᾶ | κτεάνων θ' ἅμα λειφθεὶς καὶ φίλων. |
ἐσσὶ γὰρ ὦν[49] σοφός· |

Isthmian 2.11-12

'Means, means make the man' says he who has been left by both possessions and friends.
You see, you are well-versed in song.

After the gnomic statement of line 11, Pindar turns to Thrasyboulus, son of the laudandus and addressee for most of this song.[50] The act ἐσσὶ γὰρ ὦν σοφός· marks a discursive discontinuity: it directs attention away from a general statement to Thrasyboulus in particular. The implication is that the preceding expression is not applicable to Pindar's addressee. Pindar, addressing Thrasyboulus directly and calling upon his authority as poet, seems to say: "You are wise, do not try to deny it, I just proclaimed it."[51] Here, and in several other instances where γάρ introduces unframed information about the victor

48 γάρ introduces unframed discourse about the storyworld in *Pythian* 2.38, 4.209, *Nemean* 10.46, 10.62, 11.34, *Isthmian* 1.26.

49 ὦν in Pindar occurs only in combination with other particles, which makes it hard to establish its function. Here I have taken it to mark an inference from the extralinguistic context. About γάρ in Pindar, Hummel says that it is without doubt one of the particles with the clearest semantic value (1993:406, "C'est sans doute une des particules les plus claires du point de vue de la valeur sémantique..."). However, instances like (t12) stretch her classification of γάρ as causal or explicative.

50 See II.5.4 for a complete analysis of *Isthmian* 2, with additional comments on this passage.

51 See Bäumlein's characterization (1861:68) of γάρ as marking something as a fact that "nun einmal so ist."

or his family, some kind of extralinguistic reference to them would also be appropriate; perhaps in the form of a gesture or a gaze, just before or along with the γάρ act.[52]

§25. Just as the Homeric performer does, but much more often, Pindar provides reflections on the story or the praise event with interjected pieces of wisdom. These *gnômai* are a common way in Pindaric song to put the rest of the discourse in perspective, and like the γάρ moves in Homer serve to create or recall a shared ground between performer and audience.[53] τε fits gnomic contexts in Homer very well, and it is to some extent surprising that τε does not frequently occur in Pindaric *gnômai*.[54] Consider the following *gnṓmē* from the seventh *Isthmian* ode:

(t13)

ὅ τι τερπνὸν ἐφάμερον διώκων |
ἕκαλος ἔπειμι γῆρας | ἔς τε τὸν μόρσιμον
αἰῶνα. | θνᾴσκομεν γὰρ ὁμῶς ἅπαντες· |
δαίμων δ' ἄϊσος· |

Pindar, *Isthmian* 7.40-43

Pursuing what is pleasant every day
calmly I go to old age, and to the fated
life's end. *For* we all die the same;
but our fortune is distinct.

Here the *gnṓmē* occurs in first-person discourse, it puts Pindar's statement about his old age in relief. The transition between different moves of the performer becomes even clearer in the following example, called "parenthetical" by Hummel:[55]

(t14)

ἀλλ' ὅμως, | κρέσσον γὰρ οἰκτιρμοῦ φθόνος, |
μὴ παρίει καλά.

Pindar, *Pythian* 1.85-86

[52] γάρ further introduces unframed discourse about the real world in *Olympian* 4.10, 6.25, 7.23, 10.13, 10.50, 11.19, *Pythian* 5.34, *Isthmian* 2.30, 4.40, 4.45, 4.49, 6.60, 8.70.

[53] I align with Wells 2009:150, "...gnomic style renders statements couched in that style as relevant to all participants in the speech event of performance."

[54] The reason is probably that τε is almost always copulative in Pindar (see §§54-68 below), whereas *gnômai* are expressly separated from the preceding discourse. In this kind of context, a copulative particle would be infelicitous.

[55] Hummel 1993:407.

But still—*after all*, envy is better than compassion—
do not pass over good things.

Pindar advises Hieron not to be too humble, it seems, and supports his advice with reference to a common piece of wisdom.[56] As in (t8), the γάρ act (and move) interrupts a syntactical whole, and for this reason Hummel calls it a parenthetical construction. She adds: "In this type of structure, the particle *serves to signal the change of syntactical and logical level of the utterance*" [my italics].[57] Despite the difference in terminology, Hummel's assessment resonates with my analysis of γάρ as marking that the speaker is (however briefly) performing a different kind of move. *Gnômai* introduce knowledge necessary to understand the workings of the world of the discourse.[58] In Homer this world is generally the storyworld, sometimes extended to include the world at large, while in Pindar the emphasis is more on the latter.

4.2.3 γάρ in Homer and Pindar: An overview

§26. The particle γάρ has been called the "most typical PUSH particle," marking displacement to a new frame of reference.[59] This characterization is important, since in most of its functions γάρ aids in negotiating different strands of discourse, but both in II.3 and here I have described in detail its function in different contexts: II.3 focused on γάρ's role at the beginning of new moves, especially embedded narratives; here I have described its use in transitions between framed and unframed discourse. From a certain perspective, γάρ's function of introducing embedded narratives may be described in terms of starting unframed discourse.[60] An embedded narrative takes the form of framed discourse, but is "unframed" with regard to the ongoing narrative.[61]

56 Commentators point to the same proverb in Herodotus' *Histories* 3.52.2 (φθονέεσθαι κρέσσον ἐστὶ ἢ οἰκτίρεσθαι) and as a saying attributed to Thales by Stobaeus (*Seven Sages* 10.3.δ17, Diels/Kranz 1951-1952:I.64, φθονοῦ μᾶλλον ἢ οἰκτίρου. The text is an emendation by Diels; Stobaeus has φθόνου χάριν μὴ οἰκτίρου); see Gentili et al. 1995:359.

57 Hummel 1993:407 "Dans ce type de structure, la particule *a pour fonction de signaler le changement de niveau syntaxique et logique de l'énoncé*" [my italics].

58 γάρ introduces *gnômai* in *Olympian* 8.23, 9.28, 9.104, 14.5, 14.8, *Pythian* 1.41, 1.82, 3.85, 4.263, 4.272, 4.286, 8.73, 10.53, 10.59, 11.29, *Nemean* 1.32, 1.53, 6.29, 7.12, 7.30, 7.52, 8.17, 9.27, 9.33, 11.45, *Isthmian* 1.47, 4.30, 4.33, 7.16, 7.42, 8.14.

59 Slings 1997a:101; see II.3 §23 for more on the PUSH-POP distinction.

60 It is worth noting that in Pindar ἐπεί can serve this same function, to introduce embedded narratives or *gnômai*, see e.g. the beginning of an embedded narrative in *Olympian* 9.29 and a *gnṓmē* in *Olympian* 10.88. For the narrative function of ἐπεί-clauses in Homer, see Muchnová 2003, and ancient Greek narrative in general, see Muchnová 2006 and 2009.

61 Emmott 1997:244 discusses flashbacks in similar terms: they are formally most often "located in a specific context" and thus framed, but they have in common with unframed text that they often provide a "comment on the main narrative."

§27. Through an unframed move introduced by γάρ, the performer introduces a piece of information (in the form of a motivation, narrative, *gnṓmē*, or description) into the discourse model, and thus it becomes part of the discourse memory. Another important factor is that a performer can use γάρ to introduce this different kind of discourse exactly when he means to. By choosing the right moment, the performer manages the knowledge shared between him and the audience, but can also manipulate the flow of the narrative and the performance. Below and in II.5.3.3 I discuss ἄρα in unframed narrative, where the performer assumes that the following information is already part of the discourse memory, but activates it again in the current discourse model. Both ἄρα and γάρ can thus serve to manage the discourse memory.

§28. In order to identify the type of move that γάρ introduces, the tense that follows γάρ offers a cue: (1) when γάρ introduces embedded narratives it is commonly followed by an aorist, (2) when γάρ introduces unframed information about the (story)world it is commonly followed by an imperfect, and (3) when γάρ (τε) introduces an unframed *gnṓmē* it is followed by a verb in the present tense.[62] Of course, patterns involving γάρ are tendencies rather than rules, and since the different uses represent aspects of the same particle we must keep in mind that boundaries will be fuzzy. Notwithstanding this fact, an analysis of γάρ in terms of introducing different kinds of unframed discourse reveals that the particle is involved in at least three different constructions.[63] This discourse-sensitive approach may serve as a step toward explaining γάρ's multifunctionality across register, genre, and time.

4.3 Particles in the Homeric Simile

§29. The simile is one of the most recognizable kinds of Homeric discourse,[64] and it touches upon discourse memory in at least two ways. On the one hand it presupposes shared knowledge about the world, while on the other hand it presents itself as a body of tradition within epic discourse recognized by the audience. The simile aids in visualizing a complex scene by imposing a somehow different (if not always simpler) image upon it.[65] In a simile such as "Achilles faught like a lioness who, when she sees her cubs attacked, comes snarling at her prey. Just so Achilles attacked..." "Achilles" is the tenor,

[62] In a corpus study of γάρ, Luraghi and Celano 2012 found that the particle is frequently followed by tense shift with respect to the immediately preceding clause.

[63] This use of γάρ is not limited to early literature; consider a clear example of unframed discourse in the *New Testament, Mark* 5:42 καὶ εὐθὺς ἀνέστη τὸ κοράσιον καὶ περιεπάτει, ἦν γὰρ ἐτῶν δώδεκα. καὶ ἐξέστησαν [εὐθὺς] ἐκστάσει μεγάλῃ ("And immediately the girl stood up and walked. She was twelve years old. And [at once] they were amazed with great joy.").

[64] Influential studies on the Homeric simile include H. Fränkel 1921, Shipp 1972²:3-222, Scott 1974, Moulton 1977, Nimis 1987:23-95, Muellner 1990, Martin 1997 (with a discussion of Fränkel, Scott, and Moulton on 142-143), Minchin 2001:132-160, and Ready 2011.

[65] Minchin 2001:137-139 presents a cognitive approach to the Homeric simile, and on 137 says: "[similes] provide listeners (...) with a schema, a conceptual outline, which enables them to focus

"lioness" is the vehicle, and the whole desciption of the vehicle ("like a lioness...prey") is the "vehicle portion."[66] By its very nature the simile presupposes that the image in the vehicle portion is recognizable, even if in reality the audience may never have seen a lion.[67] The recognizability derives from the fact that the image is part of the tradition familiar to both performer and audience. In this section I argue that the simile's dependence on tradition is one of the determinants of the Homeric performer's use of particles.[68]

§30. My results are based on a study of the language of the similes listed in the appendix of Scott's study: 341 in the *Iliad* and 134 in the *Odyssey*.[69] A number of these similes take the form of only a marker of comparison (ὡς, ἠύτε, (ε)ἴκελος, etc.) and a noun phrase, and are therefore too short for the study of particle use in the simile. The corpus that remains is made up of all those instances where the vehicle portion of the simile is expressed with a clause containing at least one finite verb. This kind of construction occurs 215 times in the *Iliad* (making up 708 lines) and 47 times in the *Odyssey* (148 lines). Of this group, the tenor is repeated in the majority of cases, 182 times in the *Iliad* and 38 times in the *Odyssey*.

§31. Typically, the simile takes the form of the following two examples, one drawn from the *Iliad* and the other from the *Odyssey*:[70]

their attention and to organize their ideas appropriately, in order to build a mental model for understanding what is being presented to them in words."

66 I take the term "vehicle portion" from Ready 2011:4-5, with note 10.

67 Martin 1997:152-153 comments on the observation by Shipp 1972 that the similes contain late language: "[asides, digressions, and similes] must change from year to year or even from one performance to the next (...) since they refer to the 'real' world of the audience, are more likely to be in less standardized, 'later' language."

68 The language of the simile has been regarded by some scholars as significantly different from the rest of the epics (e.g. Tsagalis 2012:18 on dual coding), but the study of Ingalls 1979 shows at least that similes are no less formulaic than the rest of the narrative. Bakker 2005:114-135 thoroughly studies tense and augment in the simile, while De Jong 2004b:93-94 notes the recurrence of τε and present tense.

69 Scott 1974:191-205; De Jong 2001a:105 offers slightly different numbers: 346 similes in the *Iliad* and 136 in the *Odyssey*. Since she does not offer a list, I have not been able to compare the numbers.

70 As the numbers suggest, the simile has a different place and a different form in the *Odyssey* than in the *Iliad*. Not only does the simile occur significantly less in the *Odyssey*, around two thirds of the total take the simple form ("like X"), while this kind makes up only about one third of the instances in the *Iliad*. Of the similes of the complex form that do occur, however, the size in the two epics is similar: the vehicle part of the simile has an average of 3.3 lines in the *Iliad*, next to 3.1 lines in the *Odyssey*. See Moulton 1977:117-119 and De Jong 2001a:105 for other differences and similarities between similes in the *Iliad* and the *Odyssey*.

(t15)

ὡς δ' ὅθ' ὑπὸ λιγέων ἀνέμων σπέρχωσιν ἄελλαι |
ἤματι τῷ ὅτε τε πλείστη κόνις ἀμφὶ κελεύθους, |
οἵ τ' ἄμυδις κονίης μεγάλην ἱστᾶσιν ὀμίχλην, |
ὣς ἄρα τῶν ὁμόσ' ἦλθε μάχη, | (...)

Iliad 13.334-337

Just as when by the whistling winds gusts are driven,
on a day when there is a lot of dust on the roads,
which, full of dust, raise a large mist,
just so their battle joined.

(t16)

(...) ὥς τε λέοντα, |
ὅς ῥά τε βεβρωκὼς βοὸς ἔρχεται ἀγραύλοιο· |
πᾶν δ' ἄρα οἱ στῆθός τε παρήϊά τ' ἀμφοτέρωθεν |
αἱματόεντα πέλει, | δεινὸς δ' εἰς ὦπα ἰδέσθαι· |
ὣς Ὀδυσεὺς πεπάλακτο πόδας καὶ χεῖρας ὕπερθεν. |

Odyssey 22.402-406

Just as a lion,
which, having fed, comes from an ox in the field,
completely *then* his breast *and* both his paws
are bloody, and terrible for the eyes to see.
So Odysseus was bespattered, his feet and his hands above.

Both these similes follow the basic pattern of the Homeric simile: (1) the vehicle is introduced by a marker, here ὡς, as in the large majority; (2) a combination of a relative pronoun and a particle introduces the information in the vehicle relevant to the comparison; (3) cohesion in the first part of the simile is attained by the recurrence of τε;[71] (4) the simile is rounded off with another marker—here ὥς, which is the rule—in (t15) followed by ἄρα. The particles τε and ἄρα are particularly frequent in similes: τε most typically occurs in the first part of the simile, the vehicle portion, while ἄρα generally occurs at the start of the simile's resolution, with the re-introduction of the tenor.

71 As observed by Ruijgh 1971:352-353, 382-383 and De Jong 2004b:93-94.

The first element in the simile, the introductory marker of comparison, varies in form but is always present.[72] The latter three elements deserve more discussion.

4.3.1 τε in the Homeric simile

§32. τε is inherently bound to the vehicle portion of the simile, where it occurs on average once every two lines in the *Iliad*, and once every three lines in the *Odyssey*.[73] The high frequency of τε is remarkable, and suggests that it is connected to the simile's strong dependence on discourse memory. Scholarship has sought to link the value and function of τε, especially when it is not copulative, to the permanent truth of the content of the clause in which it appears.[74] Rather, the particle should be linked to the interaction between performer and audience: τε marks not a *state* of the propositional content of its host act, but an *assumption* by the performer that this piece of knowledge is shared between him and the audience.[75] In other words, the performer uses τε to mark its host act as accessible in the discourse memory. To be more precise, τε refers either to the "tradition" part of the discourse memory (consider especially its use with names and places) or to the "shared experience" part. In similes, the performer accesses on the one hand shared daily experience (as in shepherd or weather similes), and on the other hand the shared experience of epic: it is unlikely that the audience learned the image of the bloody lion from anywhere other than epic. In the end, this use of τε is a discourse strategy: regardless of whether a piece of information is "permanently true," the performer presents it as something shared between him and the audience.

§33. Aside from this general high frequency of τε in the vehicle portion, there is a further interesting element to the use of τε in similes. The vehicles introduced in similes, gusts of wind in (t15) and a lion in (t16), do not carry the comparison *per se*—the armies and Odysseus are not compared to winds or a lion, but rather to these things in a specific state.[76] This closer approximation is introduced by a relative pronoun accompanied by τε—οἵ τε in (t15), and by ὅς ῥά τε in (t16). In this way the expanded vehicle portion makes the scene more vivid for the audience while at the same time enabling the poet to convey

72 In the *Iliad*, the variants are ὡς, ὥς τε, ὡς ὅτε, ὡς δ'ὅτε, ὡς ὁπότε, ὡς εἰ, ὡς εἴ τε, ὥς τε γάρ, ἠύτε, εὖτε, φή, ὅσσος, ὅσσος τε, οἷος, οἷος τε, ἐοικώς, εἴκελος, ἐοικέω, εἴσκω, ἐναλίγκιον, ἶσος, ἅ τε. In the *Odyssey*, they are: ὡς, ὥς τε, ὡς ὅτε, ὡς δ'ὅτε, ὡς εἴ τε, ὥς τε γάρ, ὡς δ'ὁπότε, ὥς τίς τε, ὅσσος, ὅσσος τίς τε, ἐοικέω, οἷος περ.

73 This should be compared to the normal frequency of once every 7 or 7,5 lines in both the *Iliad* and the *Odyssey* (in both epics it occurs between 13 and 15,5 times per 100 lines, both in direct speech and in narrator text). The numbers in the *Iliad* are 369 occurrences in 708 lines of simile, and in the *Odyssey* 53 in 148 lines. For the frequencies, I make no distinction between copulative and non-copulative ("epic") τε; compare the discussion in IV.2.

74 See IV.2.3, with an overview of literature, and below §§55-57.

75 See IV.2.3.1 for a more elaborate presentation of this argument in Herodotus and Thucydides.

76 See Scott 1974:7-8, with literature, for the discussion about the exact point of comparison in Homeric similes.

what he views as the crux of the comparison.[77] In (t15) it is the combination of dust and wind that creates the necessary image, and likewise in (t16) it is the lion after feeding that provides the image of Odysseus that the poet wants to invoke.[78]

§34. The following example from the beginning of *Iliad* 3 illustrates this use of τε:

(t17)

εὖτ' ὄρεος κορυφῇσι Νότος κατέχευεν ὀμίχλην |
ποιμέσιν οὔ τι φίλην, | κλέπτῃ δέ τε νυκτὸς ἀμείνω, |
τόσσόν τίς τ' ἐπιλεύσσει | ὅσον τ' ἐπὶ λᾶαν ἵησιν· |
ὣς ἄρα τῶν ὑπὸ ποσσὶ κονίσαλος ὄρνυτ' ἀελλὴς |
ἐρχομένων· | (...)

Iliad 3.10-14

As on the peaks of a mountain the South Wind pours a mist,
not at all loved by shepherds, *yet* to the thief better than night,
and one can see only so far as he could throw a stone,
just so under their feet a dust-filled cloud rose up
as they came on.

The entry of the Greek and Trojan armies on the battlefield is accompanied by a series of similes. The second, given in (t17), is used to describe the advance of the Greeks. The advance of the Trojans has just been compared to that of a flock of twittering birds, noisy and without order, and now the performer turns to the Greeks. They come on in silence, and the dust their feet throw up provides a cover for them as if they were thieves. Since we are in a situation of war rather than peace, the fact that the mist is a nuisance to shepherds suggests the perspective of the Trojans: the Greeks are hidden from their view, just as a mist may hide a flock from shepherds. The image of the thief, in turn, matches the Greeks who benefit from the dust that hides them. The crucial link proposed by the simile is that between the advancing Greeks and the thief taking advantage of the mist, and this is the element introduced by τε.

§35. Despite the frequency of τε in similes, it does sometimes occur that the particle is absent from the vehicle portion of a simile. In the following example from *Iliad* 9, Achilles compares himself to a mother bird: [79]

77 Cf. Bakker 2005:149 on ὅν τε in line 2 of the *Homeric Hymn to Apollo*: "The relative clause gives the *specific respect* under which the god is evoked" [my italics]. Relative clauses in similes work much the same way.

78 I would like to thank Philippe Rousseau for helping me refine my thoughts regarding τε clauses in the first part of the simile.

79 For some discussion of this interesting simile see Lohmann 1970:240; Ready 2011:140-145 solves the apparent mismatch between the tenor and the vehicle by demonstrating that invoking the

(t18)

ὡς δ' ὄρνις ἀπτῆσι νεοσσοῖσι προφέρῃσι |
μάστακ' ἐπεί κε λάβῃσι, | κακῶς δ' ἄρα οἱ πέλει αὐτῇ, |
ὣς καὶ ἐγὼ |[80] πολλὰς μὲν ἀΰπνους νύκτας ἴαυον, |

Iliad 9.323-325

As a bird to her fledgling youngs brings
mouthfuls whenever she has found some, bad though it is for herself,
so I too, many sleepless nights did I spend

Here we find a whole simile without τε, the absence of which is especially remarkable in the second half of 324, since this act provides the simile's key as in the examples above. A closer look at the editions reveals that most manuscripts as well as a third-century papyrus read κακῶς δέ τέ οἱ.[81] It appears to be mainly the testimony of Aristarchus, transmitted in the scholia, that has led to most editions giving δ'ἄρα.[82] Considering the frequency of τε in the vehicle portion of the simile, the frequent link between τε and the key of the simile, and finally the manuscript evidence, I would propose that δέ τέ οἱ is the more attractive reading.

§36. The following two similes feature similar textual variants:

(t19)

ὡς δ' ὅτε καπνὸς ἰὼν εἰς οὐρανὸν εὐρὺν ἵκηται |
ἄστεος αἰθομένοιο, | θεῶν δέ ἑ μῆνις ἀνῆκε, |
πᾶσι δ' ἔθηκε πόνον, | πολλοῖσι δὲ κήδε' ἐφῆκεν, |
ὣς Ἀχιλεὺς Τρώεσσι πόνον καὶ κήδε' ἔθηκεν. |

Iliad 21.522-525[83]

As when smoke goes and reaches the wide sky
from a burning city, the wrath of the gods sends *it* up,

selfless efforts of the mother bird directs attention toward the similar plight of the warrior who has to give up all the spoils of battle.

[80] Quite frequently, as here, the simile's tenor is resumed with a priming act.

[81] See West 1999:I.266 for the few manuscripts that read δ' ἄρα; the papyrus is *P. Oxy.* 4.765.

[82] See II.5.3.3 for a discussion of δ'ἄρα: δ'ἄρα typically introduces framed acts that are either fully accessible in the discourse memory or expected; this passage does not easily match either option. This is not in itself enough to dismiss the reading δ'ἄρα, however.

[83] Discussed, with literature, in Ready 2011:47.

makes an ordeal for all, and brings grief upon many,
thus Achilles brought toil and grief to the Trojans.

(t20)

ὡς δ' ὁπότ' | ἐν ξυλόχῳ ἔλαφος κρατεροῖο λέοντος |
νεβροὺς κοιμήσασα | νεηγενέας γαλαθηνοὺς |
κνημοὺς ἐξερέῃσι | καὶ ἄγκεα ποιήεντα |
βοσκομένη, | ὁ δ' ἔπειτα ἑὴν εἰσήλυθεν εὐνήν, |
ἀμφοτέροισι δὲ τοῖσιν ἀεικέα πότμον ἐφῆκεν, |
ὣς Ὀδυσεὺς κείνοισιν ἀεικέα πότμον ἐφήσει. |

Odyssey 4.335-340

As when a hind, in the thicket of a strong lion
having put her fawns to sleep, new-born and still suckling,
seeks pastures and grassy hollows,
roaming, and HE then comes to his lair,

and brings to both of them an unseemly fate,
thus Odysseus will bring an unseemly fate to them.

In line 523 of (t19), several manuscripts and papyri give τε as a variant reading for ἑ. Editors appear to prefer ἑ as the *lectio difficilior*, but the statistics for τε in similes support reading τε. The same goes for *Odyssey* 4.338 in (t20), where a group of manuscripts reads ὁ δέ τ' ὦκα rather than ὁ δ' ἔπειτα.[84] I cannot establish here what has led editors to prefer the latter reading, but nothing textual or metrical speaks against reading the former. The more common ὁ δ' ἔπειτα might be argued to be the *lectio facilior*, while at the same time this construction never occurs in a simile.[85] A further argument for reading ὁ δέ τ' ὦκα is that in *Iliad* 21.261 we find τὸ δέ τ' ὦκα, in the same metrical position, in a simile describing how the river Scamander overtakes Achilles. From the discourse perspective, in both (t19) and (t20) the acts that have τε in a variant reading introduce the simile's salient element: the gods who drive on the smoke is compared to Achilles driving on the Trojans, and the lion who enters his lair is compared to Odysseus returning to his palace.

§37. To sum up, the function of τε in the vehicle portion of the Homeric simile is roughly twofold. On the one hand the particle creates cohesion on the level of language

84 The simile is repeated in *Odyssey* 17, and for line 17.129 the same two variant readings are found in the manuscripts.

85 *Iliad* 6.240, 15.430, 20.342, 23.569, 23.613; *Odyssey* 2.406, 3.30, 3.437, 5.193, 7.38, 8.262, 9.480, 9.526, 14.490.

and on the level of knowledge shared between performer and audience.[86] With τε, the performer marks a certain piece of knowledge as available in the discourse memory.[87] On the other hand, when it occurs in the crucial act like in (t14) and (t15)—especially when it occurs only there in the vehicle portion—τε appears to mark its host act as the *pointe*, the salient element of the simile.[88]

4.3.2 ἄρα in the Homeric simile and beyond

§38. Now let us consider the end of the simile. As mentioned above, the comparison is always capped by a marker, generally ὥς, sometimes followed by ἄρα. The occurrence of ἄρα in the final part of the simile accompanies the return to the narrative frame. Scholars have noted that across languages conclusive particles (e.g. "so" in English (t9), *also* in German, and *igitur* in Latin) often serve to pick up or recall the main thread.[89] ἄρα in the return to the tenor of the simile does precisely that.[90] This function of ἄρα can also be seen in its occurrence directly after direct speech, as well as after different kinds of unframed discourse.

§39. Earlier scholarship on ἄρα vacillates between two extremes: some scholars view it as marking the upcoming sentence as expected from the preceding,[91] while others assert that the particle marks the new sentence as something unexpected and noteworthy.[92] Denniston's analysis, following Hartung's position that ἄρα indicates surprise, is still most commonly held to be right. He explains ἄρα as expressing a "lively feeling of

86 Moreover, it may be relevant to the link that Martin 1997:153-166 draws between the language of the Homeric simile and the language of lyric. As noted in III.2 §§39-49, τε is especially frequent in tragic lyric, and only in Pindar is the particle more frequent than in Homer. If Martin is right in suggesting that similes were lyric in origin, the high frequency of τε in both corpora may be another relevant correlation.

87 Compare the similar recurrence of non-copulative τε in passages about constellations: *Iliad* 22.29-31 ὅν τε κύν' Ὠρίωνος ἐπίκλησιν καλέουσι. / λαμπρότατος μὲν ὅ γ' ἐστί, κακὸν δέ τε σῆμα τέτυκται, / καί τε φέρει πολλὸν πυρετὸν δειλοῖσι βροτοῖσιν· and *Odyssey* 5.272-275, Πληϊάδας τ' ἐσορῶντι καὶ ὀψὲ δύοντα Βοώτην, / Ἄρκτον θ', ἣν καὶ ἄμαξαν ἐπίκλησιν καλέουσιν, / ἥ τ' αὐτοῦ στρέφεται καί τ' Ὠρίωνα δοκεύει, / οἴη δ' ἄμμορός ἐστι λοετρῶν Ὠκεανοῖο·. De Jong 2004b:95 has observed the same pattern, and discusses it in terms of "presupposed knowledge."

88 This may be further explored in combination with the possible demonstrative origin of τε, on which see the discussion in IV.2 §52 and Bakker 2005:148-149.

89 See Schraut 1857:29-30 for ἄρα, οὖν, νύ, and ὦν in Greek, *also* in German, and *igitur* in Latin; Polanyi and Scha 1983:265 for "so" in English; Sicking 1993:25-27, Slings 1997a:101, and Wakker 2009b:69-70 for οὖν in Greek. In Homer, one of the particles used to mark frame recall is ἄρα, see II.5.3.3.

90 Before Schraut 1857:29-30, Nägelsbach 1834:193-196 notes and discusses the use of ἄρα in recaps; Haacke 1857:3-12 in fact lists it as the first of three functions of ἄρα.

91 Ellendt 1835:85-87, Rost (ed.) 1836:1011, Stephens 1837:11-12 and 101-112, Klotz 1842:160-195, Matthiae 1845:1-3, Schraut 1849:12-17, Classen 1854:21, Heller 1858, Bäumlein 1861: 19-39, Rhode 1867:iii-xxxiv, Brugmann 1883:36-70, Humbert 1960³:380-383, and Grimm 1962.

92 Hartung 1832:419-427, Denniston 1950:32-43, Ruijgh 1971:432-443, and Wakker 1994:213 and 343.

interest," since "[f]or Homer, as for a child, the most ordinary things in daily life are profoundly interesting." The main reason for Denniston's choice is that the particle occurs so often in Homer that it is unlikely to confer an idea of connection (as held by other scholars), "except in so far as some kind of connexion must be present in all speech or action."[93] Ironically, in his attempt to refute connection as the central value of ἄρα, Denniston may have pointed exactly to how the particle works.

§40. Whereas τε is used to refer to knowledge shared beyond the current discourse, ἄρα introduces information that is assumed to be available or inferrable from the preceding discourse. It is thus used in rephrasings, quasi-repetitions, and recaps, after similes, direct speech, and excursus. Moreover, ἄρα is used when the action or event in its host act follows naturally from the preceding.[94] That is to say, it occurs with expected actions in typical sequences (see below §§45-52), and with other logical consequences of preceding discourse. The use of ἄρα in similes matches perfectly the fact that it marks something readily accessible in the mental representation of the discourse. Consider the following examples:

(t21)

τῶν δ' ὁμὸν ἵστατο νεῖκος | ἐπὶ πρυμνῇσι νέεσσιν. |
(...)
ὣς ἄρα τῶν ὁμόσ' ἦλθε μάχη, | (...)

Iliad 13.333 and 337

And among them joint strife rose up at the sterns of the ships.
(...)
just so their battle joined.

In (t21) ἄρα accompanies the return to the narrative frame in a verse that recapitulates the line just preceding the simile. There is clear resonance on the level of content as well as on the lexical level, as the bold words show. In (t22), conversely, the link established is more tenuous, but the image of the Achaeans advancing is retrieved with the expression "under their feet":

93 All the quotes are from Denniston 1950:33; this is one of the few non-explanations in Denniston's seminal work. However, relatively recent works still refer to the description "expressing a feeling of lively interest," e.g. De Jong 2004b when discussing ἄρα used in negative statements by the Homeric narrator.

94 See also Bäumlein 1861:31 "wir begegnen (...) vielen Stellen, in welchen ἄρα ausdrückt (...), dass etwas natürlich und *nach dem Vorhergehenden zu erwarten* ist" [my italics].

(t22)

> οἱ δ' ἄρ' <u>ἴσαν</u> σιγῇ | μένεα πνείοντες Ἀχαιοὶ |
> ἐν θυμῷ μεμαῶτες ἀλεξέμεν ἀλλήλοισιν. |
> (...)
> ὣς <u>ἄρα</u> <u>τῶν ὑπὸ ποσσὶ</u> κονίσαλος ὄρνυτ' ἀελλὴς |
>
> *Iliad* 3.8-9 and 13
>
> But they of course advanced in silence, the Achaeans,
> desiring in their heart to defend one another.
> (...)
> Thus under their feet rose an eddying dust cloud

In both instances, ἄρα marks the return to the narrative frame, and the projection of the simile's image on the situation in the storyworld.

§41. ἄρα's presence is not required after a simile, however: it occurs 30 times in the second half of the simile out of a total 182 in the *Iliad*, versus 9 times out of 38 in the *Odyssey*.[95] When ἄρα is absent, no other particle follows, except for μέν on five occasions.[96] Since the second half of the simile signals the return to the narrative and thus the beginning of a new move, the occurrence of μέν is not surprising,[97] nor is the high frequency of asyndeton.

4.3.3 The linguistic form of the simile

§42. Out of 262 full similes in Homeric epic, there is really only one example that diverges significantly in its particle use, from *Iliad* 23. After Diomedes has won the chariot race at Patroclus' funeral games, Menelaus and Antilochus battle for second place, which is finally taken by Antilochus—though apparently not entirely fairly. The minuscule distance between the two chariots is described by the following simile:

(t23)

> <u>ὅσσον δὲ</u> τροχοῦ ἵππος ἀφίσταται, | ὅς ῥα ἄνακτα
> ἕλκῃσιν | πεδίοιο τιταινόμενος σὺν ὄχεσφι· |
> τοῦ μέν τε ψαύουσιν ἐπισσώτρου τρίχες ἄκραι |

[95] This gives 16.5 instances per 100 lines in the *Iliad* and 23.7 in the *Odyssey*, versus a normal frequency of 10,7 per 100 lines of narrator text in the *Iliad* and 11.9 per 100 lines of narrator text in the *Odyssey*. Given the small size of the data, however, these differences may be the result of chance.

[96] *Iliad* 12.436, 15.413, 17.740; *Odyssey* 10.487, 23.162.

[97] See the discussion of μέν in terms of projection in II.2.4.

οὐραῖαι· | ὃ δέ τ' ἄγχι μάλα τρέχει, | οὐδέ τι πολλὴ
χώρη μεσσηγὺς | πολέος πεδίοιο θέοντος· |
τόσσον δὴ Μενέλαος ἀμύμονος Ἀντιλόχοιο
λείπετ'· |

Iliad 23.517-523

As much as a horse is removed from the wheel, one who draws
his master across the plain, straining with the chariot.
He touches the wheel with the hindmost hairs
of his tail, it rolls close behind, and not much
space is there in between, as he runs over the long plain;
That much did Menelaus trail noble
Antilochus.

This little-discussed simile seems, at first glance, to have all the characteristics of a Homeric simile, but it is remarkable in several ways. Rather than illustrating the scene by means of unrelated imagery, the simile retains the image of a horse and chariot in order to establish quite precisely the distance between Antilochus and Menelaus.[98] The mention of the horse drawing its lord (ἄναξ) through the plain does not remove the image from the current scene, for Menelaus qualifies as an ἄναξ, and the venue for the games is the Trojan plain. Beyond making an analogy, then, the passage is an attempt to more precisely establish the physical position of the characters in the storyworld. From a narrative perspective, moreover, the tension evoked by the image seems to miss its mark since the outcome of the scene has already been reached: Antilochus has beaten Menelaus.

§43. The language adds to these peculiarities, in the form of τόσσον δή just after the vehicle portion. This is the only occurrence of δή in the resolution of a simile, and the particle does not fit the context as readily as τε and ἄρα. The function of δή in this situation is more likely to be one of intensification rather than of marking a narrative boundary.[99] The only comparable instance is in *Odyssey* 21.253, ἀλλ' εἰ δὴ τοσσόνδε βίης ἐπιδευέες εἰμὲν / ἀντιθέου Ὀδυσῆος..., where δή appears to have a small-scope intensifying force over τοσσόνδε: "but if we are *really that much* weaker in might than god-like Odysseus...." As noted in II.3, δή in peninitial position of the act may have scope over the following word, as possibly in the *Odyssey* example,[100] or over the entire act, as appears to be the case here in *Iliad* 23.522. It cannot be excluded that δή has a small scope over

98 See Richardson 1993:226, "The comparison in 517-521 is unusual in being taken from the activity described, like expressions such as 'leading by a head'."

99 See II.3.3.2 for a discussion of the intensifying function of δή.

100 A small scope for δή is easier to exclude than to confirm, when the following word (group) clearly cannot be intensified. The *Odyssey* example allows both a reading of small and act scope.

the preceding τόσσον, which gives the most natural reading, but this use of δή is rare in Homer, and only becomes more frequent in later Greek.[101]

§44. Now, the nature of δή does not exclude its use after the vehicle portion of the simile, but the question remains why it is employed only here. The answer may lie in the key of the simile, which is the distance between two competing chariots. In all other instances of ὅσσος—τόσσος similes,[102] the comparison is one of approximation, whereas in this case the image is very specific: as closely as a chariot follows the horse—so close that its tail can touch the wheel—exactly as closely behind Antilochus was Menelaus. With scope over the entire act, δή places emphasis on the exactness of the entire act—they were *that* close. This emphasis serves moreover a narrative purpose, since it vindicates Menelaus' claim that if Antilochus had not cheated, the former would certainly have beaten Nestor's son.

§45. The linguistic make-up of the Homeric simile is thus rather uniform, and a good illustration for the relation of τε and ἄρα with discourse memory. The difference between τε and ἄρα may be illustrated by the fact that ἄρα can occur within the first half of the simile, while τε never occurs after the final ὥς in the simile. In Homeric discourse, ἄρα is used especially to mark the assumption that the preceding discourse provides the background for understanding what follows. More restricted than ἄρα, τε is used to introduce pieces of knowledge that the performer treats as shared between him and the audience, on the basis of shared experience and tradition. In his similes, the Homeric performer adduces evocative images to both clarify and intensify particular moments in the narrative. The simile illustrates these functions of τε and ἄρα particularly well, but they are relevant to the interaction between performer and audience in all Homeric discourse.

4.4 Scripts, Scenarios, and Traditional Knowledge

§46. The discourse memory contains any kind of information: not just facts, descriptions, names, and events, but also experience-based knowledge of event sequences. This latter

In *Iliad* 23.522 it is clear that δή cannot intensify Μενέλαος ("*very Menelaus"). In this kind of construction, καί would have been used: καὶ Μενέλαος, "Menelaus in particular".

101 See IV.4.5-6 for δή in Herodotus and Thucydides.

102 They are the following, listed by the line number containing the form of τόσσος: *Iliad* 2.472 (a swarm of flies - the Greek army), 5.772 (a man's range of sight - the jump of a divine horse), 8.560 (stars - campfires), 14.150 (the cry of 10,000 warriors - Poseidon's cry), 14.400 (wind - the cry of the Trojans), 16.592 (the throw of a javelin - the retreat of the Trojans), 17.23 (the pride of a lion - the pride of Euphorbus), 17.266 (the roar of the sea against a river - the cry of the onrushing Trojans), 23.433 (the throw of a discus - the run of Antilochus' chariot), 23.847 (the throw of a shepherd's crook - the throw of the iron ingot), 24.319 (the width of a rich man's door - the wingspan of an eagle); *Odyssey* 4.793 (the fear of a lion among men - Penelope's fear), 5.251 (the width of a freight ship - the width of Odysseus' raft), 8.125 (the range of a mule - Clytoneüs' lead), 9.324 (a ship's mast - the Cyclops' club).

kind of knowledge is called a scenario or a script.[103] Scenarios or scripts are packages of associated knowledge about certain activities, such as a sacrifice or an assembly, that are activated as soon as the relevant activity or event is evoked. "[T]he basic *structural* tenet of scenario theory is that much of the information that we store about the world is stored as situation-specific representations."[104] When a scenario becomes relevant, the knowledge shared between performer and audience creates expectations that can either be met or frustrated in the following discourse. As with the storyworld, the natural reaction to the activation of a scenario is to assume that it follows the known path, unless it is stated explicitly that it does not.[105] In epic, scenarios or scripts are most clearly visible in passages known as type scenes or themes.

§47. The heroes of the *Iliad* and *Odyssey* typically engage in activities that the audience may not be familiar with, such as debating with kings or laying siege to a city; in addition, they engage with gods and monsters. Besides these special activities, however, Homeric heroes must still perform the mundane acts of eating, washing, and travelling from place to place. These activities may seem ordinary, but they are not in traditional epic, and accordingly have received a considerable amount of attention.[106]

§48. The first to study this corpus of recurrent scenes was Arend, who coined the term typical scenes ("*typische Szenen*"). His intent was to show what connects them and how Homer uses variation for rhetorical and stylistic purposes.[107] In his review of Arend's work, Parry makes one important addition.[108] Parry argues that the origin of the type scene must be sought in the nature of oral poetry. Born of tradition, the type scene is a resource in composition, a pattern that the singer learns in his training and can access at will. Lord expands on Parry's claims, but he speaks of "themes" rather than of type scenes. In a comparative study of Homeric and Yugoslav epic, Lord defines theme more broadly than Arend's *typische Szene*, and speaks of "a process of composition by theme among oral poets."[109] In Lord's analysis, themes are not a special kind of discourse, but the main building blocks of epic composition, important aids to the composer's memory. Nagler pushes this final idea a bit further when he speaks of a theme as a "preverbal Gestalt for the spontaneous generation of a "family" of meaningful details."[110]

[103] Sanford and Garrod 1998 speak of scenarios, Schank and Abelson 1977 speak of scripts.

[104] Sanford and Emmott 2012:24, emphasis original.

[105] This section builds especially on the work done by Minchin 1992, 2001, and 2007.

[106] Arend 1933:27 notes that this may seem strange to the modern reader, and his explanation is that the pleasure for the Greeks lay in presenting the perfect version of a certain activity: "...der Anblick dieses Volkommenen (...) ist für den Griechen zugleich schön und des Erzählens wert."

[107] Arend 1933, especially 22-27.

[108] Parry 1936, reprinted in 1971:404-407.

[109] Lord 1951:80, he defines theme on page 73: "a recurrent element of narration or description"; more on theme in Lord 1960:68-98.

[110] Nagler 1974:82; note also the strong resonance between Nagler's idea and that of the (semantic) frame. See also Havelock 1963:82 "...the real and essential 'formula' in orally preserved speech consists of a total 'situation' in the poet's mind."

§49. Minchin draws a direct link between Nagler's idea and the cognitive concept of scripts.[111] Her adaptation of Arend's type scene and Lord's theme is that she does not (only) regard the epic theme as a product of epic tradition, but (also) of human experience.[112] The poet does not narrate the epic theme of saddling a horse, he merely activates his own (and depends on the audience's) memory of preparing a horse for riding. In my terms, then, Minchin proposes that the performer taps into a different part of memory: that of experiential knowledge in addition to that of epic tradition.[113] Minchin describes the relation between formula and theme as follows:

(t24)

> "...a singer will acquire scripted material in the normal course of life; the metrical language which will give it expression is, by contrast, actively learned by the young singer during his apprenticeship, at the same time as he commits to memory the storypaths of the songs he proposes to sing."
>
> Minchin 2001:15

That is to say, whereas the formulaic language is part of what the epic singer learns in his craft, the use of themes in composition follows naturally from human experience. I concur with Minchin that a natural connection is to be drawn between the epic phenomenon of typical scene or theme and the cognitive concept of the script. However, the origin of the script need not always lie in common human experience, but may well be the specific epic experience of the performer.

4.4.1 Particles in two recurrent themes

§50. In the following analysis of two recurrent scenes (bathing and arming) I address the question whether typical scenes are instantiations of elements inherent to epic (traditional) or whether they may also be regarded as verbalizations of common scripts (universal). I study the linguistic make-up of the scenes with special attention to particles. The typical scenes of "bathing" and "arming/clothing" demonstrate how the scripts in the performer's mind project a sequence known to the audience, the fulfillment of which is marked by ἄρα.

111 Minchin 2001:40.

112 See also Havelock 1963:77 "After this fashion, the verse composes itself so that the specific situations which are necessary to make a story are put together out of behaviour patterns which are typical. They are all bits and pieces of the life and thought of the day as it is lived in this kind of society."

113 Minchin 2001:39.

§51. The typical scene of bathing occurs only in the *Odyssey*, but it serves as a good starting point because of its brevity and relative uniformity throughout its different instantiations. Consider the fullest example from 17.87-90:

(t25)

ἐς δ' ἀσαμίνθους βάντες ἐϋξέστας | λούσαντο. |
τοὺς δ' | ἐπεὶ οὖν δμῳαὶ λοῦσαν | καὶ χρῖσαν ἐλαίῳ, |
ἀμφὶ δ' ἄρα χλαίνας οὔλας βάλον | ἠδὲ χιτῶνας, |
ἔκ ῥ' ἀσαμίνθων βάντες | ἐπὶ κλισμοῖσι καθῖζον. |

Odyssey 17.87-90

Going toward the baths, well-polished, they washed.
And them, when the maids had washed them, *and* anointed them with oil,
around them woolly cloaks they threw, and tunics.
Going out of the baths, they sat down on the couches.

The parallels are largely the same, though in some instances the scene is shorter.[114] As here, the particles that appear most frequently in these scenes are δέ and ἄρα. The frequency of δέ roughly matches its average in narrator text, but the same is not true of ἄρα. Especially in the second part of the scene, the particle recurs consistently. Its presence thus marks the bathing scene as a little narrative (the progression of which is marked by δέ) that happens to be predictable. Washing, clothing, and returning to the public space are details that can always be expected. The underlying script explains why the performer marks the later narrative steps with ἄρα. To put it in different terms, the activation of the "bathing" script projects a sequence of actions, and the fulfilment of this projection is marked with ἄρα.

§52. Another recurrent scene is that of clothing the hero. Consider this clothing scene from *Iliad* 2, when Agamemnon has just woken from his prophetic dream:

(t26)

ἕζετο δ' ὀρθωθείς, | μαλακὸν δ' ἔνδυνε χιτῶνα |
καλὸν νηγάτεον, | περὶ δὲ μέγα βάλλετο φᾶρος· |
ποσσὶ δ' ὑπὸ λιπαροῖσιν | ἐδήσατο καλὰ πέδιλα, |
ἀμφὶ δ' ἄρ' ὤμοισιν | βάλετο ξίφος ἀργυρόηλον· |
εἵλετο δὲ σκῆπτρον πατρώϊον | ἄφθιτον αἰεὶ |

Iliad 2.42-46

[114] *Odyssey* 3.464-469, 4.48-51, 8.454-456, 10.361-365, 23.153-155, 24.365-370.

He sat up, *and* put on a soft tunic,
fine, newly made, *and* around it he threw his great cloak,
under his smooth feet he tied fair sandals,
then around his shouldes he put his silver-studded sword.
He took the sceptre of his forefathers, ever imperishable.

The clothing[115] or arming[116] scene has numerous parallels, mostly in the *Iliad*, that all follow the same pattern. As in the bathing scene in (t25), the sequential actions are separated by δέ. Even more than the bathing scene, the linguistic make-up of the clothing scene is indistinguishable from the surrounding narrative.

§53. An important implication of this conclusion is that the use of ἄρα throughout Homeric narrative may be connected to the existence of knowledge stored in the form of scripts.[117] This supports Lord's idea that themes are not a special kind of discourse, but the main building blocks of epic. This knowledge available in the discourse memory includes those scripts learned through the experience of epic. That is to say, the origin of the scripts that underlie the building blocks of oral epic is not just daily experience, but also the daily experience *of the epic poet as epic poet*. Likewise, the knowledge that the performer assumes that his audience possesses derives from their experience as an audience at epic performances. Let me give one example, often adduced as proof that ἄρα marks "surprising" information:

(t27)

καί νύ κέ οἱ πόρεν ἵππον, | ἐπῄνησαν γὰρ Ἀχαιοί, |
εἰ μὴ ἄρ' Ἀντίλοχος μεγαθύμου Νέστορος υἱὸς |
Πηλεΐδην Ἀχιλῆα δίκῃ ἠμείψατ' ἀναστάς· |

Iliad 23.540-542

And now he would have given him [sc. Admetus] the mare, for the Achaeans agreed,
if Antilochus, son of great-hearted Nestor, had not
gotten up and rightly answered Peleus' son Achilles:

[115] The Homeric clothing scenes are *Iliad* 2.42-46, 10.21-24, 10.131-134; *Odyssey* 2.2-4, 4.303-305, 20.124-127.

[116] In the arming scenes of *Iliad* 3.328-338, 16.130-139, 11.16-43, and 19.364-391 use of δέ is even more consistent.

[117] The description of ἄρα by Schraut 1849:14 resonates particularly strongly with this idea: "Through ἄρα the sentence (...) is connected to the memories, the images, and the feelings that fill the soul of both the listener and the speaker" ("durch ἄρα [wird] der Satz (...) mit den Erinnerungen, den Bildern, den Gefühlen, die des Zuhörers wie des Sprechenden Seele füllen, verknüpft").

If we imagine being one of the characters, we may agree with Ruijgh's claim that "the fact marked by ἄρα is surprising."[118] However, the audience of an epic performance knows that the linguistic construction καί νύ κε always projects its opposite.[119] In other words, the narratively surprising event is rendered in a projected and thus expected discourse act. ἄρα, as often, functions as metalanguage to mark its host act as expected, irrespective of the discourse act's content.

4.5 τε in Pindar

§54. Out of all archaic and classical Greek authors of whom a significant corpus is extant, Pindar's songs have the highest frequency of τε, higher even than Homeric epic.[120] In the great majority of cases, τε in Pindar is copulative. Keeping in mind the strong influence of Homer on Pindaric language and its overall archaic nature, it is surprising that so-called "epic" τε is rare in Pindar. In this section I first discuss these few instances of "epic" τε in terms of activating shared, traditional knowledge in the discourse memory. Second, I examine copulative τε's range of uses, on the one hand to conjoin constituents and on the other hand to connect phrases or clauses. Then I argue that there is a clear common element in the function of τε across copulative and non-copulative uses. Even in its copulative function, τε signals that a fact or a relationship between facts or constituents is available in the discourse memory. Finally, I take the instances of τε in *Olympian* 1 as a case study to demonstrate that the choice for τε over καί is not arbitrary.

4.5.1 "Epic" τε in Pindar

§55. Ruijgh defines "epic" τε as those instances of the particle where τε is not copulative, that is, where it cannot be substituted by καί.[121] There are around sixteen instances (out of 526[122] total instances in the *Victory Odes*) where τε is not copulative; in each case after a relative or demonstrative pronoun.[123] Ruijgh divides the cases into two categories: τε introducing digressions containing "permanent facts" and τε introducing relative clauses containing "temporary facts." Based on my argument in the present chapter

118 Ruijgh 1971:436 on εἰ μὴ ἄρα in *Iliad* 3.374, "Il est évident que le fait marquée par ἄρα est surprenant."

119 See Ruijgh 1971:185-186 on καί νύ κε and De Jong 2004b:68-81 on what she calls "if not-situations"; the parallels of καί νύ κε followed by εἰ μή are *Iliad* 3.373, 5.311, 5.388, 7.273, 8.90, 8.131, 11.311, 11.750, 17.530, 18.165, 18.454, 23.382, 23.490, 23.733, 24.713; *Odyssey* 4.363, 4.502, 24.528.

120 There are 526 instances of τε in the *Victory Odes* (2.37% of words), and 4090 in the *Iliad* and the *Odyssey* (2.01%).

121 Ruijgh 1971:1, "on pourrait définir 'τε épique' comme l'emploi de τε dans les constructions où il serait impossible de substituer καί à τε."

122 Give or take a few instances, depending on how one chooses to read the different instances of ἅτε: as ἅτε or ἅ τε; see also Ruijgh 1971:983-984.

123 Ruijgh 1971:984-987 finds eighteen in the odes, but I do not include *Pythian* 11.59 and *Isthmian* 2.23.

about τε accompanying knowledge in the discourse memory, and particularly knowledge shared beyond the present discourse, the distinction between "permanent" and "temporary" facts is perhaps not productive. Consider an example from Ruijgh's category of permanent facts:

(t28)

τὸ μὲν ἐμόν, | Πηλέϊ γέρας θεόμορον
ὀπάσσαι γάμου Αἰακίδᾳ, |
<u>ὅν τ’</u> εὐσεβέστατον φάτις[124] Ἰαολκοῦ τράφειν πεδίον· |

Pindar, *Isthmian* 8.38-40

It is my <opinion>, to give this divine gift of marriage
to Peleus, son of Aiakos,
who is said to be the most pious man that the plain of Iolkos has produced.

Themis speaks to Zeus and Poseidon, who have been quarreling over Thetis. Themis prophesies that if Thetis will indeed lie with Zeus or his brother, the offspring of that union will be more powerful than his father. Instead, she proposes, Thetis should be married to the mortal Peleus. The relative clause introduced by ὅν τε adds that he is "said to be" the most pious man in Iolkos. Most of Ruijgh's permanent facts concern gods, but he explains the use of τε here because it concerns the fame ("*renommée*") of a hero.[125]

§56. This complication can be avoided altogether if we consider the two relevant contexts of this utterance. On the one hand Themis makes a claim about Peleus' piety among the gods, and on the other hand Pindar declares Peleus the most pious man from Iolkos. In the first context, it is the gods who judge who is most pious, which explains why Themis seeks to create intersubjective agreement through the use of τε. In the second context, Pindar appeals to the audience's knowledge of the story of Peleus, who came to Aegina from Iolkos. The fact of Peleus' piety may be traditionally accepted or not, but what is important is that the particle marks the fact as shared in nature, and by extension possessing intersubjective truth.

§57. Compare the following example of a "temporary" fact quoted by Ruijgh:

[124] φάτις is Bothe's emendation, the manuscripts read φασιν (unmetrical); Bergk proposes φράσι and changes τράφειν to τράφει.

[125] Ruijgh 1971:985, "Il est vrai que la relative mentionne un mortel, mais d'autre part, elle signale la renommée permanente du héros" ("It is true that the relative mentions a mortal, but on the other hand it signals the fame of the hero").

(t29)

(…) ἐπεὶ νεφέλᾳ παρελέξατο |
ψεῦδος γλυκὺ μεθέπων | ἄϊδρις ἀνήρ· |
εἶδος γὰρ ὑπεροχωτάτᾳ πρέπεν Οὐρανιᾶν |
θυγατέρι Κρόνου· | ἄν τε δόλον αὐτῷ θέσαν
Ζηνὸς παλάμαι | καλὸν πῆμα. |

Pindar, *Pythian* 2.36-40

since he [sc. Ixion] lay with a cloud,
pursuing a sweet lie, the ignorant man.
For in form it resembled the most eminent of the goddesses,
the daughter of Kronos. *Her* [sc. the cloud] Zeus' plans had put there
for him as a beautiful bane.

The only explanation Ruijgh offers for this passage is "fait mythique," "<it is a> mythical fact."[126] The effectiveness of Ruijgh's dichotomy between permanent and temporary facts appears to break down here. After all, if a mythical fact is not permanent, then what is? The passage introduced by ἄν τε appears to be the salient element in the mythical narrative about Ixion's attempt on Hera (announced in lines 26-33).[127] The reason he was caught is that Zeus tricked him. This is a fact that Pindar takes from tradition, which he conveys with the addition of τε—whether the entire audience actually knows this exact detail or not. To come back to Ruijgh's definition, it is neither important whether τε marks a fact or not, nor whether this fact is permanent or temporary. All that matters is the social contract of the lyric performance: performer and audience partake in the same world, culture, tradition, and event: τε appeals to *and* creates exactly this shared knowledge.

4.5.2 Copulative τε in Pindar

§58. So far the use of τε in Pindar is largely consistent with its use in Homer. However, there is a basic quantitive difference between use of τε in Homer and in Pindar: whereas in Homer non-copulative τε makes up a fifth of the total, in Pindar τε is copulative in the absolute majority of instances.[128] These numbers reflect the tendency of "epic" τε's decline after Homer, except in hexameter and elegiac poetry.[129] This quantitive

[126] Ruijgh 1971:986.

[127] For further instances of τε introducing the salient element of a shared image or narrative, see §§32-37 above on τε in similes and §§66-68 below on *Olympian* 1.

[128] Ruijgh 1971:351 gives 831 instances of "epic" τε, out of a total of 4090 instances of τε in Homer (20.3%): for Pindar Ruijgh gives 18 out of 528 (3.4%).

[129] See Ruijgh 1971:5.

development notwithstanding, the copulative and non-copulative uses of τε may be more closely connected synchronically than Ruijgh and most other grammarians concede. In fact, I believe that τε's pragmatic function of marking knowledge as shared is common to both the copulative and non-copulative uses. The difference between the two uses of τε lies only in their syntactic function.[130]

§59. To support this claim, let me now turn to copulative τε in Pindar. Hummel distinguishes the following kinds of conjuncts connected by τε (with my numbering):[131] (1) τε can connect clauses ("sentential τε"); (2) τε can connect phrases; (3) τε can connect "paires idiomatiques": two items that exist as a pair not only in Pindar, but independently in language;[132] (4) τε conjoins pairs unique to Pindar; (5) τε conjoins complementary pairs, sometimes in the form of a hendiadys.

§60. The last three entries in the list all concern τε connecting constituents. Except for the examples of hendiadys, all these instances may be understood better when we consider the cross-linguistic notion of "natural coordination," as proposed by Viti.[133] Viti's point of departure is Wälchli's definition of "natural coordination" as opposed to "accidental coordination":

(t30)

> Natural coordination is the "coordination of items which are expected to co-occur, which are closely related in meaning, and which form conceptual units, such as 'father and mother,' (...) rather than 'the man and the snake', 'toe and belly', (...) which are instances of accidental coordination, coordination of items which are not expected to co-occur, and which do not have a close semantic relationship."
>
> Wälchli 2005:5

In two recent studies, Viti has argued that in Homer copulative τε is used more for natural coordination, and καί more for accidental coordination. For both Homer and Pindar, I believe we may apply the idea of natural coordination even more productively to the use of τε if we bring it in connection with the concept of discourse memory.

§61. Wälchli speaks of pairs that are "closely related in meaning, and (...) form conceptual units." However, I submit that the natural association of any pair depends

130 See IV.2.3 for the argument that the so-called "connective" and "adverbial" functions of τε should be regarded as two ends of a continuum, rather than mutually exclusive. The material discussed there is mainly from Herodotus and Thucydides.

131 Hummel 1993:390-393.

132 Hummel 1993:392, "une paire qui n'est pas propre à Pindare, mais existe pour ainsi dire en langue."

133 Viti 2006 and Viti 2008, with reference to Gonda 1954.

on the cultural, performative, and discursive context. In the right situation, almost any two items may be regarded as naturally connected. The factor that makes any coordination natural is shared knowledge: the whole of the discourse memory. Consider the pairs "earth and sky," and "blood, sweat, and tears." The perceived natural association between these terms has its origin in different parts of the discourse memory: "earth and sky" is shared human experience, "blood, sweat, and tears" depends on a shared culture, and will only be a natural tricolon for a limited group of people. I will apply natural coordination as a relative term, depending on the context, language, and the participants in the discourse.[134]

§62. In the context of Pindaric performance, many items can be presented as naturally associated. Consider an example from each of Hummel's last three categories:

(t31)

νέκταρ ἀμβροσίαν <u>τε</u>

Pindar, *Olympian* 1.62

nectar *and* ambrosia

Nectar and ambrosia are related as the drink and food of the gods, but this link is limited to a context of people who share this tradition. Hummel lists it among the examples of "paires idiomatiques." Slightly more specific is the relation between the following two items:

(t32)

(...) ἐν ἀέθλοις |
ἐν μάχαις <u>τε</u> πολέμου | (...)

Pindar, *Olympian* 2.43-44

in athletics
and in battles of war

Hummel lists this passage as an example of a pair that is unique to Pindar. However, the relation between athletic games and battle is inherent in the ritual dimension of the games. It is generally assumed that in essence athletic contests are mock battles that allow participants to win honour outside of actual war.[135] In the epinician genre, we may

[134] See IV.2.3.1 for the idea that "natural" is better regarded as "culturally shared," with a study of relevant instances of τε in Herodotus and Thucydides.

[135] See Nagy 1990:121-122 on athletic games as mock combat.

say that it is a natural pair from the perspective of the generic conventions. Finally, there are pairs that are related on a more *ad hoc* basis:

(t33)

(...) πατρῴας ἀπὸ γᾶς | ἀπό τε κτεάνων |

Pindar, *Pythian* 4.290

from his fatherland *and* from his possessions

In the final lines of *Pythian* 4, Pindar asks Arkesilas to allow the exiled Damophilos to return to Cyrene, since he has been away "from his fatherland and his possessions." The two are no natural pair (Hummel lists the passage under complementary pairs) but they presuppose some specific knowledge about the exile, presumably shared between performer and at least a part of the audience.

§63. The combination τε καί serves even more consistently than τε alone to mark "natural" coordination.[136] In the great majority of instances, the construction X τε καί Y in Pindar conjoins two constituents that are closely connected, for several possible reasons. Closest to Wälchli's idea of "natural coordination" come examples like the following:[137]

(t34)

(...) γᾶν τε καὶ πόντον κατ' ἀμαιμάκετον |

Pindar, *Pythian* 1.14

over land *and* over unfathomable sea

Combinations like land and sea appear to be expressions of shared human experience, but even they are context-based: this one will not be natural to people from a land that knows no coastline. Other pairs conjoined by τε καί are even more clearly bound together by a relation that is natural within a specific context.[138] Finally, τε καί occurs

[136] Hummel 1993:397 believes that τε καί serves to connect two conjuncts that are typically complementary elements of a whole: "La coordination est le plus souvent à deux termes qui peuvent constituer une totalité dont les deux éléments sont complémentaires."

[137] I do not see why in this case Hummel does not speak of a "paire idiomatique." Compare especially *Olympian* 2.10 πλοῦτον τε καὶ χάριν, *Olympian* 9.65-66 μορφᾷ τε καὶ ἔργοισι, *Pythian* 8.3 βουλᾶν τε καί πολέμων, *Pythian* 8.3 ἔρξαι τε καὶ παθεῖν, *Pythian* 10.24 τόλμᾳ τε καὶ σθένει, *Pythian* 11.45 εὐφροσύνα τε καὶ δόξα, *Nemean* 1.57 λῆμα τε καὶ δύναμιν, *Nemean* 5.9 εὔανδρον τε καὶ ναυσικλυτάν, *Isthmian* 1.42 δαπάναις τε καὶ πόνοις.

[138] *Olympian* 10.62 ποσίν τε καὶ ἅρματι, *Pythian* 4.195 νύκτας τε καί πόντου κελεύθους, *Pythian* 8.31 λύρᾳ τε καὶ φθέγματι μαλθακῷ, *Isthmian* 6.62 ἄγλαοὶ παῖδές τε καὶ μάτρως.

particularly often with geographical locations and names.[139] In the remaining cases, τε καί either does not conjoin two syntactically symmetrical constituents, or τε and καί work separately.[140]

§64. Beyond τε καί, in the two semantic fields of geography and proper names, Pindar prefers τε coordination over καί coordination. Overall, τε is directly adjacent to a place or name in almost a third of instances.[141] Often, the relation between the conjuncts is expressed as natural for contextual reasons. Consider the following passage from Pythian 11:

(t35)

Ὀλυμπίᾳ τ' ἀγώνων πολυφάτων |
ἔσχον θοὰν ἀκτῖνα | σὺν ἵπποις, |
Πυθοῖ τε | γυμνὸν ἐπὶ στάδιον καταβάντες | ἤλεγξαν
Ἑλλανίδα στρατιὰν ὠκύτατι. | (...)

Pindar, *Pythian* 11.47-50

In the famous contest at Olympia
they gained swift glory with horses,
and in Pytho, entering in the naked footrace, they put
the Greek host to shame with their speed.

The venues for the two most important Panhellenic games are listed with the use of τε only.[142] The relation between Olympia and Pytho is obvious in the context of an epinician ode. The same natural connection exists between the siblings Castor, Pollux, and Helen:

139 See IV.2 §70 for τε καί linking such pairs in Herodotus and Thucydides, as well in combinations of geographical locations and names of people. *Olympian* 1.18 Πίσας τε καὶ Φερενίκου, *Olympian* 2.78 Πηλεύς τε καὶ Κάδμος, *Pythian* 10.4 Πυθώ τε καὶ τὸ Πελινναῖον, *Nemean* 3.50 Ἄρτεμίς τε καὶ θρασεῖ' Ἀθάνα, *Nemean* 4.46 Οἰώνᾳ τε καὶ Κύπρῳ, *Nemean* 4.75 Οὐλυμπίᾳ τε καὶ Ἰσθμοῖ, *Isthmian* 9.2 Ὕλλου τε καὶ Αἰγιμιοῦ.

140 E.g. *Isthmian* 2.23, see II.5 §78.

141 143 out of 526 instances.

142 For the natural pair of Olympia and Pytho, compare *Olympian* 7.10 Ὀλυμπίᾳ Πυθοῖ τε νικώντεσσιν, *Pythian* 9.101-103 ἐν Ὀλυμπίοισί τε καὶ βαθυκόλπου Γᾶς ἀέθλοις ἔν τε καὶ πᾶσιν ἐπιχωρίοις, and *Isthmian* 1.65 ἔτι καὶ Πυθῶθεν Ὀλυμπιάδων τ'; compare also τε used with other venues for games: *Olympian* 2.49-50 Πυθῶνι δ' ὁμόκλαρον ἐς ἀδελφεόν / Ἰσθμοῖ τε κοιναὶ Χάριτες, *Olympian* 7.81-82 κλεινᾷ τ' ἐν Ἰσθμῷ τετράκις εὐτυχέων, Νεμέᾳ τ' ἄλλαν ἐπ' ἄλλᾳ, *Olympian* 12.17-18 νῦν δ' Ὀλυμπίᾳ στεφανωσάμενος / καὶ δὶς ἐκ Πυθῶνος Ἰσθμοῖ τ', *Olympian* 13.34-37 Νέμεά τ' οὐκ ἀντιξοεῖ· / πατρὸς δὲ Θεσσαλοῖ' ἐπ' Ἀλφεοῦ / ῥεέθροισιν αἴγλα ποδῶν ἀνάκειται, / Πυθοῖ τ', *Olympian* 13.98 Ἰσθμοῖ τά τ' ἐν Νεμέᾳ, *Pythian* 8.36-37 Οὐλυμπίᾳ τε Θεόγνητον οὐ κατελέγχεις, / οὐδὲ Κλειτομάχοιο νίκαν Ἰσθμοῖ θρασύγυιον· *Pythian* 11.9-12 Πυθῶνά τε (...) ἀγῶνί τε Κίρρας, *Nemean* 2.9 θαμὰ μὲν Ἰσθμιάδων δρέπεσθαι κάλλιστον ἄωτον ἐν Πυθίοισί τε νικᾶν, *Nemean* 4.75 Οὐλυμπίᾳ τε καὶ Ἰσθμοῖ Νεμέᾳ τε συνθέμενος, *Isthmian* 8.4-5 Ἰσθμιάδος τε νίκας ἄποινα, καὶ Νεμέᾳ / ἀέθλων.

(t36)

> Τυνδαρίδαις τε φιλοξείνοις ἁδεῖν | καλλιπλοκάμῳ θ' Ἑλένᾳ |
>
> Pindar, *Olympian* 3.1
>
> To please the hospitable Tyndarids *and* Helen of the pretty hair

This kind of connection between people or gods that are naturally associated in a specific context recurs throughout the *Odes*.[143]

§65. In all these cases, it is the knowledge shared between performer and audience that makes two conjuncts a natural pair. From this perspective, the copulative use of τε and so-called "epic" τε are no longer so far apart. Whether τε introduces a relative clause or conjoins two naturally connected items, τε consistently denotes a known relation: either between a referent and something about him or between a number of items, referents, or places.

§66. In addition to marking constituents as a natural pair, τε signals this kind of coordination on a macro-discursive level. In the final paragraphs of this section, I discuss the use of τε in the narrative of Pindar's first *Olympian*. This most well-known of Pindar's songs in part owes its fame to the intriguing aetiology it presents of the Olympic Games. In his telling of the myth of Pelops, Pindar ostensibly rejects one version of the tradition and substitutes a more politically correct one. However, Pindar does not actually substitute a new story for an old one, but places two available stories in a hierarchy.[144] The first aetiology mentioned in *Olympian* 1 is the story of Pelops being cooked and eaten. This particular narrative correlates with the footrace, the earliest event in the Games. This footrace ended at the ash heap where the thigh pieces of a slaughtered ram would then be burnt by the victor.[145] By the fifth century, however, the chariot race had become the

[143] *Olympian* 2.82-83 Κύκνον τε θανάτῳ πόρεν, / Ἀοῦς τε παῖδ' Αἰθίοπα, *Olympian* 7.74 εἷς μὲν Κάμιρον / πρεσβύτατόν τε Ἰάλυσον ἔτεκεν Λίνδον τ', *Olympian* 9.43 Πύρρα Δευκαλίων τε, *Olympian* 9.69-70 υἱὸν δ' Ἄκτορος ἐξόχως τίμασεν ἐποίκων / Αἰγίνας τε, *Olympian* 13.42 Τερψίᾳ θ' ἕψοντ' Ἐριτίμῳ τ', *Olympian* 14.13-15 <ὦ> πότνι' Ἀγλαΐα / φιλησίμολπέ τ' Εὐφροσύνα, θεῶν κρατίστου / παῖδες, ἐπακοοῖτε νῦν, Θαλία τε, *Pythian* 4.182 Ζήταν Κάλαΐν τε, *Pythian* 5.71-72 Ἡρακλέος / ἐκγόνους Αἰγιμιοῦ τε, *Nemean* 5.25-26 Θέτιν / Πηλέα θ', *Nemean* 8.6 οἷοι καὶ Διὸς Αἰγίνας τε λέκτρον ποιμένες ἀμφεπόλησαν, *Nemean* 10.11 Ζεὺς ἐπ' Ἀλκμήναν Δανάαν τε μολὼν, *Nemean* 10.39-40 ἐὼν Θρασύκλου / Ἀντία τε σύγγονος, *Nemean* 10.84 σύν τ' Ἀθαναίᾳ κελαινεγχεῖ τ' Ἄρει, *Isthmian* 5.33 Κάστορος δ' αἰχμὰ Πολυδεύκεός τ', *Isthmian* 6.57-58 ταμίας / Πυθέᾳ τε κώμων Εὐθυμένει τε·, *Isthmian* 8.54-55 Μέμνονός τε βίαν / ὑπέρθυμον Ἕκτορά τ'.

[144] See Nagy 1990:126-128.

[145] See Burkert 1972:108-119 and Nagy 1990:123-125, both referring to Philostratus, *On Gymnastics* 5-6.

most important event in the Olympic Games. It is this shift in popularity that explains why Pindar gives priority to another version of the story.[146]

§67. The foregrounded story in *Olympian* 1 is the episode where Pelops has to race Oinomaos in a chariot to win his daughter Hippodamia. Pindar does not treat this as a new version of the myth, but the "Pelops is eaten" episode precedes the "chariot race" in time. In Nagy's analysis, *Olympian* 1 presupposes the following elements of the story:

(t37)

(a) Tantalos perverts feast by serving up inappropriate food (the flesh of Pelops) to immortals.
(b) Tantalos is punished by the gods.
(c) Pelops survives cauldron. (c2) Pelops abducted by Poseidon. (c3) Tantalos gets nectar and ambrosia (as compensation?)
(a') Tantalos perverts feast by serving up inappropriate food (nectar and ambrosia) to mortals.
(b') Tantalos is punished by the gods. (b'2) Pelops is exiled from Olympus to Peloponnesus. (b'3) Pelops calls on Poseidon for help.
(c') Pelops survives chariot race against Oinomaos. (c'2) Pelops settles Peloponnesus.

Nagy 1990:133, numbering and layout adapted

Now let us consider the linguistic realization of these elements (/ marks line end):

(t38)

(a) ὁπότ' ἐκάλεσε πατὴρ τὸν εὐνομώτατον / ἐς ἔρανον φίλαν τε Σίπυλον, (37-38)
ὕδατος ὅτι τε[147] πυρὶ ζέοισαν εἰς ἀκμάν / μαχαίρᾳ τάμον κατὰ μέλη, / τραπέζαισί τ' ἀμφὶ δεύτατα κρεῶν / σέθεν διεδάσαντο καὶ φάγον. (48-51)
(b) Ø
(c) ἐπεί νιν καθαροῦ λέβητος ἔξελε Κλωθώ (26)
(c2) χρυσέαισί τ' ἀν' ἵπποις / ὕπατον εὐρυτίμου ποτὶ δῶμα Διὸς μεταβᾶσαι· (41-42)
(c3) [νέκταρ ἀμβροσίαν τε] / δῶκεν οἷσιν ἄφθιτον / θέν νιν (62-64)

146 See Wells 2009:139 "...it is not that selection itself is new in the process of Panhellenism, but that the criteria for selection change."

147 Bergk proposes to read this τε as Doric for σε, but since this form is not attested in Pindar or Bacchylides, I follow Gerber 1982:84 and Hummel 1993:399 in reading the particle.

(a') ἀθανάτους ὅτι κλέψαις / ἁλίκεσσι συμπόταις / νέκταρ ἀμβροσίαν <u>τε</u> / δῶκεν (60-63)
(b') κόρῳ δ' ἕλεν / ἄταν ὑπέροπλον, ἅν τοι πατὴρ ὕπερ / κρέμασε καρτερὸν αὐτῷ λίθον (56-57b)
(b'2) τοὕνεκα προῆκαν υἱὸν ἀθάνατοί <οἱ> πάλιν / μετὰ τὸ ταχύποτμον αὖτις ἀνέρων ἔθνος (65-66)
(b'3) τὸν μὲν ἀγάλλων θεός / ἔδωκεν δίφρον <u>τε</u> χρύσεον πτεροῖσίν <u>τ'</u> ἀκάμαντας ἵππους. (86b-87)
(c') ἕλεν δ' Οἰνομάου βίαν παρθένον <u>τε</u> σύνευνον· (88)
(c'2) ∅

Out of Nagy's nine elements of the story that are expressed in the text, six contain τε (one shared between (c3) and (a')). These passages account for eight out of thirteen instances of τε in *Olympian* 1; the other five instances are outside the narrative.

§68. In these narrative acts, τε almost completely supplants καί (one instance in the acts above, out of nine total instances in the ode). Moreover, τε highlights specifically the essential elements of the tradition, a phenomenon that we might compare to the high frequency of τε in the salient parts of a simile. Whether in specific pairs of people, places, items, and ideas or in crucial elements of a traditional narrative, the distribution of τε follows a consistent pattern. It may not always be clear to us what determines the choice of τε over καί, but it cannot be a coincidence that in contexts of shared tradition and shared knowledge τε is preferred.

4.6 Conclusions

§69. The language of any discourse is to a large extent determined by what came before, and what comes before a current discourse act reaches far beyond what has been said before: "The meaning of a text is more than the sum of the meanings of the individual sentences that comprise it."[148] The reason behind this claim by Schank and Abelson is that every discourse act interacts with the discourse memory to create a fuller meaning, and a fuller representation in the discourse model than the words alone add up to. In this chapter I have described some of the many possible interactions between current discourse and the larger discourse memory, and its marking through metalanguage.

§70. The particle γάρ serves to introduce acts that ensure a shared ground, a shared mental representation of the discourse (discourse model) between the performer and the audience. Engagement with the discourse memory is a question of attitude rather than of fact, so in the case of γάρ it is the performer's *belief* that a piece of knowledge is missing from the discourse memory that determines its use. Both in Homer and Pindar γάρ is

[148] Schank and Abelson 1977:22.

thus used to introduce information about the storyworld, but also to insert comments on the ongoing discourse. One subset of the latter, *gnômai*, generally occur in direct speech in Homer, and are introduced by γάρ τε. In Pindar, gnomic acts account for a much larger proportion of the instances of γάρ than in Homer.

§71. In the Homeric simile, interaction between discourse and discourse memory is constant and particularly visible. Whereas γάρ serves to introduce additional information into the discourse memory, ἄρα and τε accompany knowledge already shared. Both particles do this in their own way, and again they are relevant to the performer's expectations. ἄρα occurs in practically every context in Homeric discourse, and I align with the scholarship that links ἄρα to "expectedness." Rather than focus on the audience's perspective, however, I propose that ἄρα reflects the performer's stance toward his discourse. By uttering ἄρα, the performer metalinguistically marks the current discourse act as either known or naturally expected from what comes before. Since ἄρα works as metalanguage, this value of ἄρα does not necessarily mean that the propositional content of an act is expected, but typically it is.

§72. As emerges from its use in the Homeric simile, τε occurs in more specific contexts. In terms of discourse memory, the difference between ἄρα and τε concerns the part of the discourse memory that is accessed. ἄρα typically—but not exclusively—refers to the current or past discourse, whereas τε refers to the discourse memory beyond the preceding discourse. An analysis of τε in the Homeric simile and Pindar has revealed that τε marks both facts and relations between facts, concepts, places, and people as shared between performer and audience beyond the present discourse. Thus it typically co-occurs with names, places, or actions that are part of the shared experience or tradition. In Homeric epic, this pattern holds for those instances where τε is copulative as well as for those where it is not. In Pindar τε has specialized in its copulative function, but its use still shows clear traces of interaction with the discourse memory.

II.5

Particles and Anaphoric Reference

A Discourse Perspective on Particles with Third-Person Pronouns

§1. In ancient Greek, pronouns and particles have a special relationship: the two are often found together and intrinsically connected. They are not only frequently adjacent, but they work together to guide the discourse, and may even form a single unit. II.2 demonstrates how the Homeric and Pindaric performers produce their discourse piecemeal, each piece adding a bit of information to the preceding. As a speaker focuses on the ideas in her mind she verbalizes her words according to the flow of her thoughts, and in the form of discourse acts. Chafe argues that only one new idea can be in focus in the mind at one time.[1] This is reflected in the form and content that discourse acts take: established knowledge tends to appear towards the beginning of the act and new information tends to follow.[2] Because anaphoric pronouns recall referents that are already in the hearer's mind, they must appear within the body of established, given knowledge (more on "given" below) in order to be effective.

§2. Anaphoric reference directs attention to a referent about which something new will be added, and pronouns are the prototypical markers of anaphoric reference. Combinations or clusters of pronouns and particles are not used randomly; a deeper understanding of the pronoun illuminates the workings of the particle and vice versa. Only by comparing a larger number of instances of different collocations can it become clear that there are significant and consistent differences between them. The ideas established in the preceding chapters are relevant to the role that particles play in guiding reference. In particular the distinction between framed and unframed discourse (II.4.2) provides an important analytical tool for the study of anaphoric pronouns in Homer and Pindar.

1 See Chafe 1994:108-119 for the discussion of his "one new idea constraint." He applies it to intonation units, but we use the term "discourse act," see II.2.

2 For early literature on the idea of topic, see Chafe 1976 and Givón (ed.) 1983. H. Dik 1995 and 2007 applies a pragmatic approach to word order in ancient Greek. Scheppers 2011 employs similar methodology to his idea of the "colon" in prose, a close cognate of what we call a discourse act.

§3. In this chapter I examine how the use of different particles interacts with different nuances of anaphoric reference. In order to understand these nuances it is first necessary to arrive at a good understanding of how anaphora works, both inside and outside the text. In the first section (5.1) I outline recent approaches that interpret the process of anaphoric reference as an interaction between a speaker and hearer rather than as a set of immanent relations between textual constituents. In the next section (5.2) I address the peculiar place of the nominative pronoun in a pro-drop language like Greek. Moreover, I discuss the ambiguous function of ὁ and ὅς as both demonstrative and relative pronouns. After addressing these issues, I present a representative case study (5.3) of combinations of the most frequent third-person pronoun in the nominative (ὅς and ὁ) and different particles in Homeric narrative: ὁ δέ, ὅ γε, ὁ δ'ἄρα, ὅ/ὅς ῥα, and ὁ/ὅς δή.[3] The analysis aims to show that the combinations have consistently and significantly different functions, depending on the particle used.[4] I do not engage in particular with pronouns (and particles) at the beginning of embedded narratives, but this theme has been studied extensively for both Homer and Pindar.[5] The final section (5.4) traces anaphoric reference through an entire Pindaric ode: *Isthmian* 2. In this close reading, I consider not only pronouns and particles, but also nouns and verb forms, to sketch a picture of the audience's on-line processing of anaphoric reference.

5.1 A Discourse Approach to Anaphoric Reference

§4. Classically, anaphora has been regarded as a relation that functions within a text.[6] An anaphoric relation is typically expressed as one between an anaphoric pronoun and a textual antecedent. However, recent research that focuses on naturally occurring discourse demonstrates that the textual approach often does not explain what actually happens. Consider the following example:

3 So-called "epic" τε after pronouns has already been discussed for Homer in II.4.3.1 and for Pindar in II.4.5. See also IV.2.3 for a more complete discussion of τε's functions; for ὁ καί I refer the reader to the extensive discussion of the particle's functions in IV.2.4. Finally, the function of γάρ after pronouns falls under the discussion of "γάρ introducing unframed discourse" in II.4.2.1.

4 The topic of referents in narrative is to a significant extent more relevant for Homer than for Pindar. First of all, the Homeric epics offer a reasonable number of instances of the phenomena, whereas Pindar's *Victory Odes* have only a very limited number of the kinds of constructions under examination. This is the result of the fact that the Pindaric corpus is smaller, and less of it is narrative. Second, even in narratives, Pindar is much less concerned with scenes involving multiple characters. As a result, Pindar is less prominent in section 3, the comparative analysis, but the close reading of *Isthmian* 2 in 5.4 balances out the asymmetry.

5 See e.g. Des Places 1947 and Bonifazi 2004c for Pindar, and Slater 1983 and Calame 1985 for Homer.

6 Cornish 1999:116-117.

(t1)

Wash and core six apples. Put them into a fireproof dish.[7]

This simple example demonstrates the problem of a purely textual approach. If a reader regards "them" as referring to the textual antecedent "six apples," the utterance would be infelicitous. After all, the referent of "them" must be described as "the six washed and cored apples." In practice, of course, the reader or hearer has no trouble making the inferences necessary to understand the two sentences in the cookbook. This is a relatively simple example of anaphoric reference, but even here an analysis in purely textual terms does not explain the cognitive process sufficiently.[8] It is not enough to say that "six apples" is the textual antecedent of "them."

§5. To solve problems such as this one, Cornish redefines the term "antecedent" as follows: "I take [antecedent] to be a description of the referent (...) in terms of its salient attributes."[9] The generally understood meaning of antecedent, namely the textual antecedent, Cornish calls the "antecedent-trigger":

(t2)

The antecedent trigger "introduces an entity into the discourse via its predicational and utterance context, and an anaphor of a particular type and form accesses that mentally represented discourse entity at a later point in the discourse, adding to this representation further properties resulting from the processing of the anaphoric clause as a whole."

Cornish 1999:4

Cornish's description points to the importance of the cognitive processes involved in the production and processing of discourse. The textual antecedent problem is one of the factors that have led to a cognitive approach to reference.

§6. Another relevant factor is the relationship between different anaphoric expressions and the kinds of referents that they can retrieve. In early pragmatic accounts, unaccented anaphoric pronouns were regarded as expressing "given" information, while the

7 This is an example from a cookbook, quoted by Halliday and Hasan 1976:2. One may compare the more famous, but constructed, example from Brown and Yule 1983:202, "Kill an active, plump chicken. Put it in the oven." Consider another example, from Dinsmore 1987:15, "If J. Edgar Hoover had been born a Russian, he would have been a Communist." Here the named character refers to a historical person, but the personal pronoun "he" refers to a hypothetical referent. Emmott 1997: 179-180 discusses this gap in coreferentiality.

8 See Berrendonner and Reichler-Béguelin 1995 for their arguments against what they call the "*antecedentiste*" (26-27) approach to reference.

9 See Cornish 1999:7 and 41-51; this description of the antecedent is influenced by Ariel 1996:17.

following predication contains the "new" information of the sentence. If a full noun phrase or name is used instead of a pronoun, however, this generally introduces new information into the discourse. The form of the referential expression was thus linked to its status of given versus new.[10] In English, the possible forms of referring expressions range from full noun phrases, via prosodically emphasized pronouns (SHE), to unaccented pronouns (she), and null anaphor (the absence of a verbally expressed subject or object). Along a scale between "given" and "new," established information should receive light linguistic and prosodic marking, whereas new information is made explicit and receives prosodic emphasis.[11] Consider the following examples:[12]

(t3)

"John called Mary a Republican, and then SAM [new] walked in."

(t4)

"Mary paid John and he [given] bought himself a new coat."

It is important to be aware that the labels of "given" and "new" in this framework do not relate to the status of the referent in the speaker or hearer's knowledge. In fact, (t3) reads most naturally when we assume that both speaker and hearer know who "Sam" refers to. The newness or givenness is rather a status relative to the ongoing discourse, which has led people to prefer the terms discourse-old and discourse-new. However, even this terminology is insufficient for explaining the forms of referential expressions used in naturally occurring discourse. Most obviously problematic are referents that are introduced into the discourse, then not mentioned for a certain span of text, and then retrieved. Although they are discourse-old (i.e. "given"), they cannot generally be retrieved by an unaccented pronoun.

§7. As an alternative to the discourse-old and discourse-new distinction, scholars have come to describe anaphora in terms of the "accessibility"[13] of referents or, alternatively, in terms of a givenness hierarchy.[14] The aim of these approaches is to account for the form of the referential expression in every conceivable reference relation in discourse.[15] What the approaches have in common is that they assume a match (more or

10 See especially Halliday 1967 and Halliday and Hasan 1976.

11 See e.g. Prince 1981 and Brown and Yule 1983:190-222.

12 Slightly adapted from Prince 1981:226-227.

13 Ariel 1988, 1990, and 1991.

14 Gundel, Hedberg, and Zacharsky 1993, expanded in multiple later publications.

15 The main difference between the two approaches is that whereas Ariel (accessibility) maps referential expressions directly on a status on the accessibility scale, Gundel's approach (givenness hierarchy) allows for upward implication (see most recently Gundel, Hedberg, and Zacharsky 2012:252-254). That is to say that a referential expression that is marked low for givenness may

less strict) between the accessibility/ givenness of a referent, and the different available referring expressions.[16] Since it is not my goal to be able to predict the referential expression for each instance of anaphora or deixis in Homer and Pindar,[17] I focus on the thing that these approaches have in common: the supposition that there is a relation between the accessibility of a referent and the referring expression a speaker may use. The next question, then, is what this accessibility consists of.[18]

§8. In the production of a discourse, the aim of the speaker is to guide the hearer's creation of a mental representation of the discourse that is as close as possible to the speaker's. This mental representation, the "discourse model," is the framework within which reference functions.[19] With each new discourse act the discourse model is updated, while at the same time the production of each discourse act presupposes a certain state of the discourse model. There needs to be a minimal correspondence between the speaker's and the hearer's discourse model for us to be able to speak of successful communication. This minimal value is hard to establish, but one crucial factor is the mutual tracking of referents. That is, for us to speak of a successfully communicated narrative, the speaker and the hearer need to agree about who did what to whom. It is the speaker's task, therefore, to assess the salience, accessibility, or givenness of a certain referent in the hearer's current discourse model, if she wishes to successfully refer to the relevant character:

(t5)

> "[I]t is incumbent upon the speaker to use the discourse procedure which is in accordance with both his/her referential intention and with his/her *assessment* of the current state of the interlocutor's discourse model."
>
> Cornish 1999:20 [my emphasis]

This description of the process of reference has been widely taken up, as witnessed by the following relatively recent quotes:

---

be used for entities that are in fact higher on the givenness hierarchy in the minds of speaker and hearer. In simpler terms, it is "allowed" to overdetermine referents, but not to underdetermine them (since in the latter case the communication would probably be unsuccessful).

16 Consider the scheme proposed for English by Gundel *et al.* 2012:251:
in focus > activated > familiar > uniquely identifiable > referential > type identifiable
(*it*) > *that/this/this N* > *that N* > *the N* > indef. *this N* > *a N*
In the Accessibility Marking scale by Ariel 1991:449, the list is even more extensive; see Cornish 1999:6-8 for a discussion of both approaches.

17 Bakker 1997b:111 attempts to create such a scheme for Homer.

18 For the reader's convenience, I henceforth use the term accessibility to cover both the ideas of givenness and accessibility.

19 Cornish 1999:5-6, but the term goes back to Prince 1981:235. On page 5 Cornish defines discourse model: "This model is a coherent representation of the discourse being evoked via the co-text and its context in terms of the speaker's or writer's hypothesized intentions."

(t6)

> "[T]he grammar of reference and topicality in human language is keyed delicately to *anticipate* the epistemic mental states of the interlocutor."
>
> Givón 2005:133 [my emphasis]

Gundel, Hedberg, and Zacharsky focus on the presuppositions inherent in referential expressions:

(t7)

> "The major premise of the Givenness Hierarchy theory (Gundel et al., 1993) is that different determiners and pronouns encode, as part of their conventional meaning, information *assumed* by the speaker about the cognitive status of the intended referent in the mind of the addressee."
>
> Gundel, Hedberg, and Zacharsky 2012:251 [my emphasis]

What all authors agree on[20] is that anaphora is not to be understood as a relation between a referential expression and its antecedent in the co-text, but as an instruction to the hearer to focus on a certain referent in his discourse model. It is not primarily a process of verbal memory, but of cognitive focus within the mental representation of discourse.[21] As a result, the accessibility of a referent is its status in the current representation of the discourse: regardless of whether it has been mentioned before and how long ago, the referent's current status as more or less in focus determines the anaphoric expression used.

§9. Over recent decades, Chafe has applied this cognitive perspective to narrative. Chafe follows the basic idea that accessing referents that are already in focus requires less cognitive effort than accessing referents that are out of focus at the moment of utterance. This difference in effort is what explains the use of different referring expressions, with generally less linguistic marking for referents that are in focus, and more for referents that are out of focus.[22] A good illustration of the cognitive approach to anaphoric reference in narrative is the case of (apparent) underdetermination:

[20] See also Ariel 1991:444 "[T]he claim is that addressees are guided in antecedent retrievals by considering the degree of Accessibility signalled by the marker, rather than by noting the contextual source marked (general knowledge, physical salience, linguistic material), as had commonly been assumed by pragmaticists (Clark and Marshall 1981, Prince 1981, *inter alia*)."

[21] Bonifazi 2012:19-38 proposes a similar approach to anaphoric markers in Homer, with a main focus on (ἐ)κεῖνος and αὐτός.

[22] Chafe 1994:75 "For the most part, both new and accessible information are expressed with accented full noun phrases, whereas given information is expressed in a more attenuated way."

(t8)

"Jane hit Abby. She fell."

Since we have two female referents in this narrative the "she" in the second sentence is underdetermined at first sight. However, we have no problem interpreting the line since we visualize the scene and imagine the victim falling, rather than the aggressor. From Homer, we might compare the moment of Patroclus' death by the hands of Hector:

(t9)

ἀγχίμολόν ῥα οἱ ἦλθε κατὰ στίχας, | οὖτα δὲ δουρὶ |
νείατον ἐς κενεῶνα, | διαπρὸ δὲ χαλκὸν ἔλασσε· |
δούπησεν δὲ πεσών, | (...)

Iliad 16.820-822

close to him *he [sc. Hector] came* through the ranks, and thrust with his spear
at the lower belly, and right through he drove the bronze.
He [sc. Patroclus] clattered when he had fallen, (...)

In English we find the unaccented personal pronoun "he," where in Greek we find the equivalent least marked reference, null anaphor, within the third-person singular verb (δούπησεν). Despite the change of grammatical subject (from Hector to Patroclus), the lack of an expressed new subject does not lead to confusion, for three reasons. First, the semantics of πεσών makes Patroclus the logical subject, since he has just been wounded. Second, δούπησεν δὲ πεσών is a formula that always refers to the stricken hero, so the audience's knowledge of epic will prevent any potential ambiguity of reference.[23] Third, the form of the formula in itself suggests that not just "the referent Patroclus" is in focus, but the entire image of his fall. The finite verb does not strictly refer to the noise Patroclus makes, but to that of his armor and weapons.[24] The Homeric performer can present this complete, synaesthetic image, since from the moment that he is stabbed and wounded (line 821), Patroclus is in focus in the mind's eye. It is the idea of "focus" that explains the two examples above: in both cases the mind's eye inevitably moves to the

[23] It occurs 21 times: *Iliad* 4.504, 5.42, 5.540, 5.617, 11.449, 13.187, 13.373, 13.442, 15.421, 15.524, 15.578, 16.325, 16.401, 16.599, 16.822, 17.50, 17.311, 17.580, 20.388; *Odyssey* 22.94, 24.525; see Kirk 1985:392.

[24] Although the LSJ s.v. δουπέω takes the main meaning of the verb to be "sound heavy or dead," I follow Chantraine 2009:282 in reading it as "the clatter or noise (of battle)" ("fracas des lances" "bruit de la bataille"), since outside of this formula the verb is used chiefly to describe the sound of battle or of the sea.

recipient of the attack, putting them in mental focus, and thus making them accessible.[25] In earlier work, Chafe speaks of the "subject of consciousness" in terms of attention, "the mechanism by which the spotlight of consciousness is directed at one or another area of the material accessible to the mind."[26] A higher accessibility leads to a lower "activation cost," in Chafe's terms, which in turn translates to a less specific referring expression.[27] The focus of the mind's eye is an important factor in the process of anaphoric reference. It is especially relevant in passive constructions, where there is a clear distinction between subject/object and patient/agent. In Homer and Pindar, moreover, the grammatical subject can be a part of the body or a hero's weapon or armor, as it might be here, while the subject of consciousness always remains the character (see also t13 below).

§10. In the field of ancient Greek literature, Bakker and Bonifazi have applied the cognitive approach to examine anaphoric reference in several works. Bakker has applied Chafe's ideas on activation cost to expressions of anaphoric reference in Homeric epic.[28] Expanding on Bakker's work, Bonifazi further has addressed the need for a cognitive perspective on anaphoric reference in ancient Greek literature more generally. She has argued that accessibility or activation cost does not sufficiently account for all forms of anaphoric reference, especially in literature.[29] Her study focuses on αὐτός and (ἐ)κεῖνος, but her brief analysis of anaphoric reference in the first ten lines of the *Odyssey* points the way for further research.[30] The present chapter builds on the work of Bakker and Bonifazi, applying the cognitive perspective particularly to third-person demonstrative pronouns in the nominative (ὁ and ὅς) followed by particles.

5.2 ὁ and ὅς

§11. In order to establish similarities and differences between the possible clusters of pronoun and particle I will take retrieval of a singular masculine referent in the nominative as my core material. In the ongoing narrative, the Homeric performer constantly manages the relevant referents in multiple ways. Frequently, as in (t9) above, a verb form suffices to successfully select the correct referent in the discourse model. In this chapter I have chosen to focus on lexical items that serve specifically to retrieve referents: pronouns.

[25] See also Chafe 1994:175: "Whether or not a referent is assumed to be newly activated in the listener's consciousness is a different question from whether or not it is assumed to be already part of the listener's knowledge." Chafe describes these two separate domains in terms of "active/inactive" versus "shared/unshared."

[26] Chafe 1994:122.

[27] Chafe 1994:71-81.

[28] Bakker 1997b:108-111 and *passim*.

[29] Bonifazi 2012:19-26.

[30] Bonifazi 2012:28-38.

§12. Such lexical items still cover a wide range of words, including αὐτός, ἐγώ, σύ, μίν, ἑ, τοι, οὗτος, κεῖνος,[31] ὅδε, ὅς, and ὁ. The lexical item most frequently used to retrieve referents in a narrative is the anaphoric third-person pronoun referring to a character. Within this category, ὅς[32] and ὁ[33] give the lightest marking short of a verb form only (null anaphor). Because these forms are by far the most frequent, and are commonly accompanied by particles, they form the core material for my comparative study. Finally, I focus on the nominative rather than the oblique cases because the nominative form is often syntactically superfluous. After all, in a pro-drop language like ancient Greek the grammatical subject is encoded in the verb form. That is to say, ὁ is not equivalent to τόν in referential terms, since the former may in the right context be elided, while the latter is more often indispensable.[34] Although I do not focus on the oblique forms of the anaphoric pronoun, I discuss a small number of instances, mostly in the footnotes.

§13. Among the masculine singular nominative forms, the relationship between ὅς and ὁ is complex in archaic Greek.[35] In classical Attic prose, ὅς is the masculine singular of the relative pronoun, while ὁ is the masculine singular definite article or a weak demonstrative pronoun.[36] In Homeric epic, and through its strong influence in Pindar and other lyric as well, the distinction is not so clear. In this early Greek, the two words can have the respective values they have in classical Greek, but beyond that both can function as demonstrative or relative pronouns. This dual functioning presents significant problems, since it is not always clear from the Greek if a clause should be taken as a relative clause introduced by the pronoun or as a new main clause with a demonstrative pronoun as the grammatical subject. Consider the following example:

(t10)

(...) τοῖσι δ' ἀνέστη |
Κάλχας Θεστορίδης | οἰωνοπόλων ὄχ' ἄριστος, |
ὃς ᾔδη τά τ' ἐόντα τά τ' ἐσσόμενα πρό τ' ἐόντα |

Iliad 1.68-70

(...) And amongst them stood up

[31] For κεῖνος and αὐτός forms referring to Odysseus in the *Odyssey* see Bonifazi 2010 and 2012:38-183.

[32] ὅς: 375x in the *Iliad* and 229x in the *Odyssey*.

[33] ὁ/ὅ: 751x in the *Iliad* and 164x in the *Odyssey*.

[34] This distinction is not addressed in Des Places 1947:35-50, Hummel 1993:174-177, or Bonifazi 2004c.

[35] For a concise exploration of the issue, see Bonifazi 2004c (with a focus on Pindar); see also Bakker 1999 and 2005:77-80 on ὁ and οὗτος in Homer.

[36] ὁ represents the pronoun from the PIE root *to, i.e. ὁ, ἡ, τό, while the relative pronoun from the PIE root *yo gives the paradigm ὅς, ἥ, ὅ. The TLG edition of the *Odyssey* does not accentuate the demonstrative pronoun, while the edition of the *Iliad* does. For reasons of consistency, and in accordance with common practice, I have chosen to give ὁ throughout.

Kalchas son of Thestor, among augurs by far the best,
who knew what was, what would be, and what had been.

An alternative reading of the final line is: "...by far the best. He knew..," if we interpret the pronoun as demonstrative rather than relative.[37] In (t10) it is perhaps unnecessary to choose a demonstrative reading, but consider this parallel:

(t11)

ἡ δ' αἶψ' ἐξ ἀγορῆς ἐκάλει κλυτὸν Ἀντιφατῆα, |
ὃν πόσιν, | ὃς δὴ τοῖσιν ἐμήσατο λυγρὸν ὄλεθρον. |
αὐτίχ' ἕνα μάρψας ἑτάρων | ὁπλίσσατο δεῖπνον |

Odyssey 10.114-116

At once she called from the place of assembly the glorious Antiphates,
her husband, and he devised for them woeful destruction.
Instantly he seized one of my comrades and made ready his meal,[38]

Here, Murray prefers to read the pronoun as demonstrative (rather than relative), and translates accordingly. In the language there is no formal distinction between the two possible readings of the pronoun, which suggests that Murray was guided by the context.

§14. In (t11) one reason for translating ὅς as "he" rather than "who" is the fact that it constitutes a narrative transition. The act following the mention of the husband (ὃν πόσιν) is not so much a description of this new referent—as might be expected in a relative clause—but rather an act introducing a new event, with the freshly introduced husband as the grammatical subject.[39] The fact that in (t11) an aorist (ἐμήσατο) follows the pronoun, whereas in (t10) it is a pluperfect (ᾔδη), standing in for the imperfect of οἶδα, contributes to this reading.[40] On a macrolevel the δή act in (t11) marks the beginning of

[37] Probert 2015:17-18 quotes this passage as an early example of a relative clause in ancient Greek, and says: "it is not difficult to think of the structure found in (2.1) [sc. "Calchas, who..."] as having come from a structure of type (2.2) [sc. "Calchas. He..."]."

[38] Translation Murray. This is in fact a unique instance of ὃς δή in Homer; only here does it introduce framed discourse. See below §59-§65 for the more common pattern of use of this pronoun and particle combination.

[39] Behind Murray's translation there might also be a presupposition about the status of main clauses and subordinate clauses. The former are generally regarded as carrying the narrative forward, while the latter offer "background" information. This view is challenged by Cristofaro 2003, and specifically for ancient Greek by De La Villa 2000 and Bonifazi 2004c; see also Probert 2015. For further discussion of background and foreground see II.3 §§25-27, II.4.2, and IV.5 §68.

[40] See below, especially §§59-62, for the possible relevance of the use of the imperfect (sometimes present or pluperfect) in a context of narrative told in aorists.

a new scene within the narrative, which leads to Odysseus' departure from the island of the Laestrygones. In discourse terms, ὅς in (t10) introduces an act that is unframed (the performer informs us about the character Kalchas), while ὃς δή in (t11) introduces a framed act, a continuation of the narrative.[41] This distinction may (unconsciously) play an important part in decisions of editors, regarding punctuation, and of translators.

§15. In Homer and Pindar both ὅς and ὁ are used to retrieve a masculine character.[42] To understand the use of ὁ/ὃς + particle, we must understand the nature of referent tracking in ancient Greek. To an English reader, ὁ may look like "he," but the two pronouns are not equivalent. Because ancient Greek is a pro-drop language, neutral continuity of grammatical subject is signaled by null-anaphor constructions, with a predicate consisting of a finite verb only.[43] In a similar construction, English supplies the unaccented pronoun. ὁ in Homer, then, is not equivalent to unaccented "he" but to accented "HE."[44]

(t12)

πρόσθε δ' Ἀλέξανδρος προΐει δολιχόσκιον ἔγχος, |
καὶ βάλεν Ἀτρεΐδαο κατ' ἀσπίδα πάντοσε ἴσην, |
οὐδ' ἔρρηξεν χαλκός, | ἀνεγνάμφθη δέ οἱ αἰχμὴ |
ἀσπίδ' ἐνὶ κρατερῇ. | ὁ δὲ δεύτερον ὄρνυτο χαλκῷ |
Ἀτρεΐδης Μενέλαος | (...)

Iliad 3.346-350

First *Alexander* sent off his far-shadowing spear,
and *he hit* on Atreides' shield, perfectly balanced,
but the bronze did not break through, and its point was turned
on the mighty shield. *And HE* in turn rushed with his bronze,
Atreus' son Menelaus (...)

In this passage the narrator describes the fight between Paris (Alexander) and Menelaus. For this narrative stretch, those two characters are the only relevant referents, and the

[41] See II.4 §§11-14 for the terms "framed" and "unframed" discourse.

[42] I exclude the feminine singular pronoun in the nominative for practical reasons. First, the feminine pronoun (ἡ and ἥ) occurs much less frequently; second, the constructions in which it partakes do not differ from that of the masculine pronoun that I discuss below.

[43] For a discussion of pronoun use in pro-drop languages, see Frascarelli 2007:694-696, with extensive references.

[44] See Cornish 1999:63 on pronouns in English and French: they "signal referential and attentional continuity." He adds, "this is the case where they are unaccented in English, and clitic in French. Where they are accented, their indexical properties change: in particular, they are capable of referring to entities which, though assumed to be recoverable by the addressee, are not the ones enjoying the highest degree of focus at the point of use."

focus of the mind's eye shifts steadily from one to the other. In lines 346 and 347, agency remains with Paris and as a result the new act in 347 is introduced without a pronoun (Ø βάλεν).[45] A few lines later we have followed the thrown spear to its mark, Menelaus, who has now become focused in the mind's eye. As Tomlin explains, the nominative case is a grammatical reflex of attention management: in English the nominative typically refers to the referent that has become the focus of attention in the directly preceding discourse.[46] However, in instances like (t12) the new grammatical subject (Menelaus) is in focus in the mind's eye, but has not yet been primed in the language when he is activated with ὁ δέ in 349. This is the reason that we find the pronoun ὁ, and not just the verb.[47] Contrary to our intuition, then, ὁ is a marked rather than an unmarked anaphoric expression and should be taken as such.[48]

§16. In other words, it seems that Menelaus was not completely accessible in the middle of line 349, and therefore was activated with a pronoun. However, activation cost is only one of many factors affecting the use of ὁ or ὅς in Homer and Pindar.[49] The corpus of Homeric epic and Pindaric song differs to a significant extent from the discourse that contemporary linguists generally engage with. Although Homeric and Pindaric discourse must still, by and large, follow the unwritten rules of communication, they possess an additional layer of artfulness and traditionality that will have an effect on the linguistic form beyond cognitive requirements. Chafe's account of referent retrieval, which proposes that accessibility is only one of many factors determining the form of a referring expression, offers additional avenues of analysis.[50]

45 If there is no ambiguity of anaphoric reference, there is a tendency in English to keep reference to the subject "light," called the "light subject constraint" by Chafe 1994:82-92; Greek appears to function similarly.

46 Tomlin 1997:181-186 discusses the nominative in terms of attention: the nominative marks the referent being attended to, and this "being attended to" is generally initiated in the preceding act. Consider especially the note on 182: "That is, the grammar of English does not look at the semantic role of an argument when determining subject selection; it only looks for the current output of attention system [sic]—the attentionally detected event parameter."

47 Compare the following constructed example from Prince 1981:227 "John called Sam a Republican and then HE insulted HIM." The accented pronouns (as opposed to "John called Sam a Republican and then he insulted him") suggests that there is a shift of subject, leading to the assumption that "HE" refers to Sam, whereas "he" would most naturally have referred to John. See also the example in Prince 19n34. Fox 1987:172 shows that in written English narrative the accented pronoun would most probably take the form of a full noun phrase. Givón 2005:136 shows that zero anaphora and unstressed pronouns in English signal maximal referential continuity whereas constructions containing a stressed pronoun or even stronger marking signal referential discontinuity.

48 I use marked/unmarked in the sense proposed by Givón 2005:139: "maximal-continuity anaphoric devices—zero-anaphor and unstressed/clitic pronoun—are the *least marked* devices, carrying the smallest phonological weight and lacking independent lexical status" [emphasis original].

49 See Bonifazi 2012:26.

50 First in Chafe 1976.

§17. To handle a complex narrative, the speaker's mind attempts to maximize clarity while minimizing explicit reference;[51] and the hearer's mind works on the assumption that this is indeed what the speaker does.[52] Therefore, when a referential expression appears to give more information than required (i.e. when it exceeds the referent's required activation cost) an explanation is called for.[53] In the vast majority of cases, such instances of apparent overdetermination can be explained by considering other factors. Beyond activation cost I consider the relevance of discourse transitions, frame switches, contrastiveness, and "zooming" of the mind's eye.[54]

5.3 ὁ/ὅς + Particle in Homer

§18. The following discussion of ὁ/ὅς + particle combinations focuses on the pragmatic functions of the acts they introduce. It is from the pragmatic perspective that the particles' force can be understood, and a comparative study shows that the speaker's choice for one particle over another is rarely arbitrary. I first explore the combination ὁ δέ (and ὅς δέ) since it is one of the most common combinations, and has come to be associated with the very specific grammatical function of marking subject change. Our analysis aims to separate the different contributions of the two elements (pronoun and particle) in order to come to a better understanding of the whole in its many contexts. Subsequently I turn to the other extremely frequent collocation ὅ γε, which has also received some attention in the literature, in this case as a marker of subject continuity. As with ὁ δέ, the reality in Homer is more complex, but unlike ὁ δέ the combination ὅ γε appears to be working as a cluster.[55] After these frequent and known combinations, I turn to those pronoun and particle combinations that generally go undiscussed, but are in fact crucial in guiding the narrative: ὁ δ'ἄρα, ὅ(ς) ῥα, and ὁ(ς) δή.

51 See Levinson 1987:68 "The less you say, the more you mean."

52 See Cornish 1999:6 "[T]he speaker's task in referring must be to choose a referring expression marking the level of cognitive accessibility of the intended referent which matches that which s/he assumes the entity in question currently enjoys in his or her addressee's mental model of the discourse under construction," and 20, "the type of signalling device (...), which is most likely to get the addressee to grasp the referent intended in the most economical manner possible."

53 Gundel *et al.* 2012:251: "A speaker, in producing a particular determiner or pronoun, thus provides a processing signal to the addressee that helps restrict the set of possible referents." On pages 252-253 they explain how the hierarchy works on the basis of how informative the linguistic referring expression is.

54 Chafe 1994:77-78 discusses the factor of contrastiveness (creating contrast between one referent and another, which may or may not be expressed) as a reason for using accented forms in spoken English when unaccented forms might have been expected; Emmott 1997:86 (with reference to Longacre 1974 and 1996[2]) notes that there may be literary reasons for "lexical reiteration" instead of pronominalization.

55 I use "combination" as a neutral term for two or more particles or other words that co-occur, and "cluster" for recurrent combinations whose resulting function either extends beyond, or is significantly different from, the sum of its parts; see I.1.

5.3.1 ὁ δέ

§19. The cluster ὁ δέ is probably the most well-known combination of pronoun and particle, but despite its frequency the collocation is not well understood. In order to gain a better understanding of the combination, it is paramount to separate the functions of its two constituent parts, contrary to common practice. The pronoun ὁ works like an accented pronoun in English, roughly equivalent to emphatic "HE," and as such it is used regularly in instances featuring discontinuity of grammatical subject or another kind of referent switch. In II.2 I outlined the main function of δέ as the "quintessential boundary marker," following Bakker's work.[56] This function suggests that the particle has nothing specifically to do with continuity or discontinuity in the tracking of referents in Homeric discourse. In fact, a combination of a finite verb + δέ is a common way of maintaining subject continuity.[57] If one wishes to link ὁ δέ to changes of subject one should be aware that the reason for this correlation is ὁ, not δέ.[58]

§20. There is more to be said about the combination and its relation to referential continuity or discontinuity. Janko writes that ὁ δέ "normally marks a change of grammatical subject."[59] His claim is often true, especially after Homer, but it does not address the question of why ὁ δέ serves this purpose so well. In the combination ὁ δέ in Homer, the lightly emphatic pronoun invites the audience to find a reason for the emphasis—often a change of grammatical subject—whereas δέ simply marks the progress of the discourse.

§21. Since δέ marks the progress of discourse, and because most of Homeric discourse is framed narrative, δέ in Homer typically marks a continuation of framed discourse. In combination with the pronoun ὁ/ὅς, then, it is no surprise that ὁ δέ in Homer often introduces an act with a new grammatical subject. However, we must remember that ὁ as an anaphoric pronoun is only lightly emphatic; it is not as strong an anaphoric expression as a strong demonstrative, for example. Therefore, even when ὁ δέ marks change of grammatical subject, the referent of ὁ must be highly accessible. Consider the following instance at the end of book twenty of the *Iliad*. After a long list of Achilles' exploits on the battlefield the narrator caps the episode with two similes:

56 See II.2 §§31-36.

57 See for example ἷξε δέ in (t15) below.

58 Chantraine 1953a:159 remains vague when he says "[l]a particule et l'article servent souvent à indiquer un changement de sujet." Since he discusses ὁ much more as a pronoun than as an article, it is striking that he calls it an "article."

59 Janko 1992 *ad Iliad* 16.467, where ὁ δέ occurs despite continuity of grammatical subject. It is probably comments like this that lead to claims like that in Raible 2001:593 "Languages using this [zero anaphor] technique tend to develop a special morpheme signaling a different subject (...) in the subsequent clause. In classical Greek this is the function of the particle *de*." While Janko's generalization holds, Raible's claim for δέ alone oversimplifies. He might rather have said that in combination with a pronoun in the nominative, δέ often signals a change of subject.

(t13)

ὡς δ᾽ ἀναμαιμάει βαθέ᾽ ἄγκεα θεσπιδαὲς πῦρ |
οὔρεος ἀζαλέοιο, | βαθεῖα δὲ καίεται ὕλη, |
πάντῃ τε κλονέων | ἄνεμος φλόγα εἰλυφάζει, |
ὣς ὅ γε[60] πάντῃ θῦνε | σὺν ἔγχεϊ | δαίμονι ἶσος |
κτεινομένους ἐφέπων· | ῥέε δ᾽ αἵματι γαῖα μέλαινα. |
ὡς δ᾽ ὅτε τις ζεύξῃ βόας ἄρσενας εὐρυμετώπους |
τριβέμεναι κρῖ λευκὸν | ἐϋκτιμένῃ ἐν ἀλωῇ, |
ῥίμφά τε λέπτ᾽ ἐγένοντο | βοῶν ὑπὸ πόσσ᾽ ἐριμύκων, |
ὣς ὑπ᾽ Ἀχιλλῆος μεγαθύμου | μώνυχες ἵπποι |
στεῖβον ὁμοῦ νέκυάς τε καὶ ἀσπίδας· | αἵματι δ᾽ ἄξων |
νέρθεν ἅπας πεπάλακτο | καὶ ἄντυγες αἳ περὶ δίφρον, |
ἃς ἄρ᾽ ἀφ᾽ ἱππείων ὁπλέων ῥαθάμιγγες ἔβαλλον |
αἵ τ᾽ ἀπ᾽ ἐπισσώτρων· | ὁ δὲ ἵετο κῦδος ἀρέσθαι |
Πηλεΐδης, | λύθρῳ δὲ παλάσσετο χεῖρας ἀάπτους. |

Iliad 20.490-503

As a portentous fire rages up deep glens
of a dry mountain, and the deep forest burns,
and driving it everywhere, the wind whirls the flame about.
Thus *HE* rushed everywhere with his spear, like to a god,
driving on his victims. And the black earth ran with blood.
As when someone yokes broad-fronted bulls,
to crush white barley on the well-built threshing floor,
and soon they are threshed out under the loud-bellowing bulls' feet.
Thus under brave-hearted *Achilles* the *single-hoofed horses*
trampled corpses and shields alike; and with blood the *axle*
was all spattered below and the rims, those around the chariot,
for them the *drops* from the horses' hooves struck,
and those from the wheels. *And HE* went to win glory,
Peleus' son, and with gore were spattered his invincible hands.

The audience cannot but picture the scene of Achilles tearing through the enemy ranks like a forest fire spurred on by the wind, trampling their bodies like grain on a threshing floor. In the final lines the narrator sketches an image of Achilles triumphant on a chariot spattered with blood, riding over the bodies of his adversaries. Although he has not been

[60] For this use of ὅ γε—to help retrieve the referent after an intervening discourse discontinuity of some sort (here a simile)—see §§27-50 below.

the grammatical subject over the last eight lines, and has not been named in four lines, ὁ δέ suffices to restore Achilles as grammatical subject in 502. The images evoked are strong, but unlike some other similes they apply readily to the current situation on the battlefield. In 498 the horses are the subject (ἵπποι) and the axle (ἄξων) in 499, but Achilles is constantly at the forefront of our mind, literally in the center of the image, in focus. As in the case of Jason below (t32), ὁ in 502 does not just retrieve "Achilles" but it retrieves the raging and bloody Achilles that has just been created in the mental representation of the discourse.

§22. However, because ὁ/ὅς can retrieve all accessible masculine singular referents in the frame, ὁ δέ in framed discourse cannot be mapped directly onto the function "grammatical subject change." There are several instances where a pronoun is used despite clear continuity of grammatical subject. Such cases of apparent overdetermination deserve closer inspection, as they may occur for several cognitive or stylistic reasons. In book nine of the *Odyssey*, Odysseus relates how he acquired the wine with which he would later intoxicate the Cyclops, saying:

(t14)

(…) ὅν μοι δῶκε Μάρων, | Εὐάνθεος υἱός, |
ἱρεὺς Ἀπόλλωνος, | ὃς Ἴσμαρον ἀμφιβεβήκει, |
οὕνεκά μιν σὺν παιδὶ περισχόμεθ' ἠδὲ γυναικὶ |
ἁζόμενοι· | ᾤκει γὰρ ἐν ἄλσεϊ δενδρήεντι |
Φοίβου Ἀπόλλωνος. | ὁ δέ μοι πόρεν ἀγλαὰ δῶρα· |

Odyssey 9.197-201

(…) [the wine], which Maro gave me, son of Euanthes,
the priest of Apollo, who had encompassed the Ismarus,
because we had protected him with his son and his wife
out of reverence. *For he* [sc. Maro] *lived* in a wooded grove of
Phoebus Apollo. *And HE* [sc. Maro] *gave* me splendid gifts:

After the first plural form περισχόμεθα, the singular verb form ᾤκει suffices to avoid ambiguity. It might seem all the more surprising, then, that the pronoun is used in the following act, even though there is total continuity of grammatical subject.

§23. An explanation for this overdetermination is readily available after the discussion of framed and unframed discourse in II.4. Both the imperfect tense of ᾤκει[61] and the particle γάρ suggest that the move in lines 200-201 is different from its surroundings.

61 ᾤκει is a single imperfect among aorists (δῶκε, 197, περισχόμεθα, 199, πόρεν, 201): this is typical for unframed discourse in Homer; see II.4.2, and §§51-62 below on ἄρα.

It is in fact a little piece of unframed discourse, where the performer turns to the audience and offers some information needed in order to understand the ongoing action in the narrative. In cognitive terms, the act starting with ᾤκει γάρ does not create the image of Maro in any kind of activity, but rather of his house in a sacred grove. The retrieval of Maro after that is therefore more fraught.[62] As we return to the contextual frame of the action, the pronoun (ὁ) turns attention from Maro "living in a grove" to Maro as he is in the embedded narrative, having just been saved by Odysseus and his men.

§24. Similarly, in the following narrative about Poseidon intervening in the battle between Aeneas and Achilles, the anaphoric pronoun is used at one point despite continuity of grammatical subject:

(t15)

αὐτὰρ ἐπεὶ τό γ' ἄκουσε | Ποσειδάων ἐνοσίχθων, |
βῆ ῥ' ἴμεν | ἄν τε μάχην καὶ ἀνὰ κλόνον ἐγχειάων, |
ἷξε δ' ὅθ' Αἰνείας ἠδ' ὁ κλυτὸς ἦεν Ἀχιλλεύς. |
αὐτίκα | τῷ μὲν ἔπειτα κατ' ὀφθαλμῶν χέεν ἀχλὺν |
Πηλεΐδη Ἀχιλῆϊ· | ὁ δὲ | μελίην εὔχαλκον
ἀσπίδος ἐξέρυσεν | μεγαλήτορος Αἰνείαο· |

Iliad 20.318-323

Now, when Poseidon the earth-shaker heard this,
he set to go up through the battle and the hurtling of spears,
and he reached where Aeneas and glorious Achilles were.
At once, he then shed a mist over the eyes of the one,
Peleus' son Achilles. And HE, the ashen spear well-shod in bronze
he drew from the shield of great-hearted Aeneas,

In this passage ὁ δέ is problematic, since it would most naturally establish Achilles as the grammatical subject of the new act, instead of continuing to refer to Poseidon as it actually does. This apparent mismatch may have been Aristarchus' reason for athetizing lines 322-324, since taking out these lines creates an attractive symmetry between τῷ μέν (sc. Achilles, 321) and Αἰνείαν δέ (325).[63] As we follow the reading of the manuscripts and editions, however, this requires an explanation. In II.2.5 we devote some attention

[62] See II.4 §14 and Emmott 1997:239 and 248-252.

[63] The reason given in the scholia is that Poseidon could not have drawn the spear from the shield since in lines 276-279 the spear is described as landing on the ground. Edwards 1991:327 plausibly defends the lines by taking it to mean that the shield had been pinned to the ground by the spear, "which is realistic enough."

to small fronted acts that serve to guide the mind's eye of the audience. These priming acts take the form of a referential expression + a particle (often δέ), and are followed by some performative discontinuity. Even though nothing linguistically suggests that there is a boundary after δέ (the accusative that follows seems in no way to be independent), the manuscripts suggest that some kind of discontinuity was assumed after ὁ δέ.[64] Here, the reason for such a discourse act is not obvious, but the motivation may be visual. After his arrival Poseidon sheds mist over Achilles' eyes, which leads the mind's eye to focus on Achilles. The expectation of the audience might have been that focus and agency stayed with Achilles, but in fact the scene moves back to Poseidon with ὁ δέ (322). The god then first enacts a ritual return of the spear to the hero, after which he performs a truly awesome deed: he throws Aeneas over the entire army to the other side of the battlefield. The scene is climactic and highly vivid,[65] and the use of the pronoun rather than a null anaphor may serve to prepare for the upcoming image that has Poseidon as its center.

§25. A study of ὁ δέ in Pindar reveals the same range of possibilities as in Homer, the difference being that ὁ δέ almost always marks change of grammatical subject.[66] Since in Pindaric song δέ marks boundaries between larger units of discourse (see II.3 §65), this need not come as a surprise. Besides this difference, ὁ δέ in Pindar has two additional functions. First, Pindaric ὁ sometimes comes close to its classical function as an article[67]—a use rare in the Homeric epics[68]—while retaining its Homeric function as a relative or demonstrative pronoun.[69] In two instances, ὁ δέ precedes a proper name, and there the boundary between demonstrative pronoun and article is more fuzzy than elsewhere in

64 The codex Marciana 458 has a comma after ὁ δέ, while both Escorial Ω and Venetus B have a sign of a double grave over δέ: "δὲ̏ ", which I interpret to be some kind of instruction for prosodic discontinuity. This is why I use a comma in the English translation. It resembles *Iliad* 20.455-456, where there is a clear boundary after ὁ δέ: ὣς εἰπὼν Δρύοπ' οὖτα κατ' αὐχένα μέσσον ἄκοντι· / ἤριπε δὲ προπάροιθε ποδῶν· ὁ δὲ | τὸν μὲν ἔασε. In this passage ὁ δέ does mark a change of subject (ἤριπε has Druops as its subject), but as in 20.322 there is a transition to a new episode of the narrative. See IV.3.4-5 on more about ancient and medieval punctuation and its links to our act boundaries.

65 The use of αὐτίκα may also have contributed to the vividness of the scene, see Bonifazi 2012:273-281, with reference to the present passage in 280n40.

66 ὁ δέ accompanies continuity of grammatical subject only in *Pythian* 4.78, see (t32).

67 See Gildersleeve 1885:ci and Bonifazi 2004c:49-54. In the present and following notes I give a list of the uses of ὁ δέ in Pindar. I read the article ὁ in *Olympian* 1.1, 8.28; *Pythian* 1.35, 9.78, 11.30; *Nemean* 7.67; *Isthmian* 7.39.

68 See Chantraine 1953a:160-162, 165-166; Chantraine notes that in the Homeric books generally regarded as more recent, the use of the "article" is closer to that in classical Greek (165), and adds "on a pu supposer qu'à l'époque d'Homère, la langue courante connaissait déjà l'article, mais que l'épopée conservait traditionellement l'emploi démonstratif de l'article." Bakker 2005:76n12 adds that "in many cases the "article" is more marked [in Homer] than in Attic Greek."

69 I read ὁ as a relative pronoun in *Olympian* 1.73, 10.43 (δ' ἄρα); *Pythian* 1.8, 4.78 (δ' ἆρα), 3.92, 6.33, 9.17, 11.34 (δ'ἄρα); *Nemean* 1.43, 1.61, 7.36, 10.13; *Isthmian* 6.41.

Pindar.[70] As in Homer, "there is an uncertainty about the relative vs. the demonstrative use of the pronouns, and (...) a complex interlacing of (...) functions among relative pronouns, definite articles, and articles used as pronouns."[71] Second, the pronoun can be used as a forward-looking demonstrative in constructions like this gnomic expression:

(t16)

(...) ὁ δ' ὄλβιος, | ὃν φᾶμαι κατέχωντ' ἀγαθαί |

Olympian 7.10

(...) He is fortunate, who is held in good repute[72]

Here and in the parallels, the sense of the act introduced by ὁ δέ is gnomic.[73] In all cases I read the first part of the thought as a copulative construction with ἐστί left out, which means that ὁ must be read as a demonstrative pronoun rather than as an article. Because in this context ὁ δέ introduces a *gnṓmē*—unframed, generalizing discourse—there is always a change of grammatical subject. However, in *gnômai* the referent of ὁ can be ambiguous; either it can be the indefinite "he", or it can be the main referent of the preceding discourse, often the victor.

§26. Examples (t14) and (t15) demonstrate that ὁ δέ may accompany continuity of grammatical subject, provided that there is some other reason for emphasizing the referent. The combination ὁ δέ in Homer and Pindar reflects the whole range of its constituent elements: ὁ/ὅς as a marked anaphoric expression, sometimes only lightly marked, sometimes almost deictic, and δέ as the marker of discourse progression, marking stronger boundaries in Pindar than in Homer.

5.3.2 ὅ γε

§27. ὅ γε enjoys a special status among combinations of pronoun and particle: the LSJ, for example, specifically lists ὅ γε as a special construction under its discussion of ὁ.

70 *Pythian* 2.73 ὁ δὲ Ῥαδάμανθυς ("(that) Rhadamanthys") and 5.60 ("(that) Apollo"). Bonifazi 2004a links this to the idea of "recognitional deixis," from Diessel 1999, to mark a referent that is new in the discourse, but already known to speaker and listener. Using an article with a name is the exception rather than the rule in Pindar, which suggests that at least some demonstrative force may be attributed to ὁ in these cases.

71 Bonifazi 2004b:50.

72 Literally: "whom good rumours hold."

73 The parallels are: *Olympian* 10.66 ("He, who"); *Pythian* 8.48 ("He, who"; in this instance as for *Pythian* 4.78-79, (t33) below, Giannini in Gentili et al. 1995:575 reads ὁ as an article), 8.88 ("He, who"); *Nemean* 5.34 ("He, (...) Zeus"), 9.24 ("He, (...) Zeus").
The construction does occur in the *Hymns*: *Homeric Hymn to the Muses and Apollo* 4 ὁ δ' ὄλβιος and *Homeric Hymn to the Earth Mother* 7 ὁ δ' ὄλβιος; and there is a rare instance in Homer *Iliad* 1.139 ὁ δέ κεν κεχολώσεται ὅν κεν ἵκωμαι "he will be angry, to whom I will come."

They describe the combination as follows: “Pron. ὁ, ἡ, τό made slightly (if at all) more emphatic by the addition of γε.”[74] This description of the function of γε exemplifies most scholarship on the particle, and it covers well the sense that is common to most instances of the particle. Denniston discusses γε in terms of “concentration,” which leads to the two further functions of marking limitation and intensification.[75] About γε after pronouns, Denniston says the following: “Naturally, in many cases γε is limitative: but in many others it is determinative: often it seems to be otiose, the pronoun apparently requiring no stress, or at most a secondary stress.”[76] By limitative, Denniston means that γε marks its host word (group) as the thing that the current claim holds true for *at least*; “determinative” fits his idea of “concentration,” and what other scholars (and the LSJ) describe as “emphatic”; “otiose” appears to mean redundant.

§28. As we shall see, the limitative function of γε (as described by Denniston) does not emerge from the cluster ὅ γε, and yet the particle is clearly not redundant. Rather, γε in ὅ γε mainly lends emphasis, but this idea needs refinement. What does it mean for a particle to make a pronoun (and specifically ὁ) more emphatic? In the following section I demonstrate three things: (1) distributionally, ὁ and ὅ γε are complementary: they occur in mutually exclusive positions in the act and the verse; (2) functionally, ὅ γε serves to retrieve a referent of which some aspect has to be supplied through inference; (3) when ὅ γε appears in contexts where there is continuity of grammatical subject, several factors contribute to the choice of ὅ γε over a null anaphor, including frame switches and transitions between narrator text and direct speech.

§29. First consider the position of ὅ γε, which provides the clearest indication that we are dealing with a cluster rather than a combination. In the discussion above, I have taken ὁ as the equivalent of the accented pronoun in English. In its relative and anaphoric functions, the pronoun tends to occur in act-initial position in Homer. It is thus a statistical anomaly that ὅ γε *never* occurs in act-initial position. Of course, γε is more mobile than δέ, which means that it can occur later in the act as well as in peninitial position. However, the positional tendency of the pronoun would suggest that at least in some cases we would find ὅ γε at the start of a new act. For metrical reasons ὅ γε cannot occur at verse beginning, but this does not hold for οἵ γε, which still shares the same positional limitation: it never occurs at act or at verse beginning. That is to say, the nominative pronoun occurs in act-initial position, and γε occurs in peninitial position in the act, but ὅ γε as a combination is never act initial. This makes the combination different from the sum of its parts in a significant way, and therefore we shall treat ὅ γε as a cluster. If the

[74] Liddell, Scott, Jones, and McKenzie 1940⁹:1195b (s.v. ὅ γε).

[75] Denniston 1950:114-115.

[76] Denniston 1950:122. He provides an analogy from English: “The same tendency occasionally shows itself in English, as when we say ‘Not I’, meaning ‘I certainly did not.’” De Jong 2012:68 *ad Iliad* 22.33 (ὅ γε) comments that “the anaphoric pronoun is often redundant and γε unnecessary (...). The combination is found very often, however, and may have been of metrical use to the singer.”

positional limitations of the cluster differ from that of its components, the same may be possible for the cluster's function. Unlike ὁ δέ, the function of ὅ γε may be more limited than the range of functions ὁ and γε have on their own.

§30. In commentaries, ὅ γε is regularly described as resuming the subject of the current sentence; that is, it is regarded as marking grammatical subject continuity.[77] Considering once more the masculine nominative pronoun's range of functions, however, we may predict that this generalization will not hold, and the numbers show that it does not: almost half of all instances in the *Iliad* and *Odyssey* mark change of grammatical subject.[78] Consider the following passage from *Iliad* book one, where Achilles considers whether he should attack Agamemnon or not:

(t17)

ὣς φάτο· | Πηλεΐωνι δ' ἄχος γένετ', | ἐν δέ οἱ ἦτορ |
στήθεσσιν λασίοισι | διάνδιχα μερμήριξεν, |
ἢ ὅ γε | φάσγανον ὀξὺ ἐρυσσάμενος παρὰ μηροῦ |
τοὺς μὲν ἀναστήσειεν, | ὃ δ' Ἀτρεΐδην ἐναρίζοι, |

Iliad 1.188-191

Thus he spoke. Peleus' son was distressed, and his heart
in his shaggy breast debated two ways:
whether *HE*, having taken his sharp sword from his thigh,
should make the others leave, *and HE* should kill Atreus' son...

The text illustrates neatly how problematic generalizations about ὁ δέ and ὅ γε in Homer are: ὅ γε in 190 marks change of grammatical subject from ἦτορ, "heart," to Achilles, whereas ὁ δέ in 191 accompanies subject continuity.[79] The choice of the pronoun over null anaphor is expected in 190, since null anaphor would have led to the jarring image of the heart drawing a sword. In 191 the anaphoric pronoun serves to juxtapose the image of the assembly dispersing with the image of Achilles and Agamemnon staying and fighting. This explains the use of the pronoun in both instances, but the question remains what the function of γε is in ὅ γε.

§31. The reason for the addition of γε, although hard to determine, may have been prosodic: ὁ alone is more easily lost than ὁ followed by a clitic and at times a whole

77 See Leaf 1900:149 on *Iliad* 3.409, about ὅ γε in general: "ὅ γε (...) merely resumes the original subject" and Neitzel 1975:47 "ὅ γε steht bei Homer immer demonstrativ als masc. nom. Es nimmt das Subjekt des Satzes betont wieder auf."

78 Out of a total of 128 instances in the *Iliad*, ὅ γε marks grammatical subject change in 58 instances. This number is 27 out of 62 for the *Odyssey*, so slightly less than half in both epics.

79 Leaf 1900:18 rightly notes that "ὁ δέ as often repeats the subject of the first clause."

syllable.[80] However, this does not explain why we find γε instead of another enclitic, such as ῥα. Whatever the range of functions of ὅ γε when it is grammaticalized as a cluster, a particular function of γε must have led to the development of the cluster in the first place. Before moving on to more instances of ὅ γε in Homer, let us examine this question more closely.

§32. One way to analyze the function of γε is to describe it in terms of focus. The term focus has multiple uses, both technical and intuitive, and use of the term in classical scholarship is diffuse. Denniston spoke of γε as a "limitative" particle, reducing an expression's applicability to "at least" the word (group) marked by γε. Building on Denniston's ideas with the addition of the terminology of functional grammar, Bakker speaks of γε in wishes as marking "exclusive focus," to contrast its function with the inclusive focus marked by περ.[81] Both Sicking and Wakker build on Bakker's work but describe γε more generally as a "focus particle."[82]

§33. A number of scholars have attempted to adapt or refine the idea of γε as a focus particle. About γε in Aristophanes, Tsakmakis says: "γε is not a focalizer which can be indiscriminately attached to any element of the utterance (even if that is focalized), but it can only be attached to a word which coheres with the preceding utterance."[83] About ὅ γε specifically, Bonifazi says: "γε gives prosodic and semantic prominence to ὁ." This interpretation conflates two elements that are consecutive, I believe: γε does indeed give prosodic prominence to ὁ, and it is this prosodic prominence that leads to an interpretation of ὅ γε as in some way emphatic ("semantic prominence"). Then she argues that in ὅ γε, γε "emphasizes something relationally new about somebody referentially old."[84] This claim requires some unpacking. If the "somebody referentially old" is the referent of the pronoun ὁ, then the "something relationally new" must be contained in the rest of the discourse act in which ὅ γε occurs. However, I believe that γε in ὅ γε has scope only over the pronoun, not over the entire act.

§34. In my reading, γε emphasizes the pronoun, which would then have to be both "relationally new" and "referentially old." I agree with Tsakmakis and Bonifazi that in ὅ γε the pronoun refers to someone who is referentially old and thus "coheres with the preceding utterance." In line with Bonifazi's argument, moreover, we may consider that

80 Consider also that Homer has the elided form ὅ γ' 104 times and the full form ὅ γε 86 times.

81 When used in scalar wishes, περ marks something that is still attainable ("inclusive") while γε marks something that is impossible to attain ("exclusive"), see Bakker 1988:97-98.

82 See Sicking 1986:125 and Wakker 1994:308.

83 Tsakmakis 2010:350; see also Slings 1997a:126, who believes that the idea of γε as a focus marker "cannot do justice to its use in adding constituents to already complete sentences (quite apart from the fact that γε hardly ever accompanies the true Focus of a sentence)."

84 See Bonifazi 2012:31.

the pronoun can refer to something at once old and new. More specifically, I argue that ὅ γε retrieves an accessible referent in a form that is to be inferred.[85]

§35. Consider the following passage from the *Odyssey*. While Odysseus is sailing past the Sirens, they call to him in an attempt to make him stop:

(t18)

οὐ γάρ πώ τις τῇδε παρήλασε | νηῒ μελαίνῃ, |
πρίν γ' ἡμέων μελίγηρυν ἀπὸ στομάτων ὄπ' ἀκοῦσαι, |
ἀλλ' <u>ὅ γε</u> τερψάμενος νεῖται | καὶ πλείονα εἰδώς. |

Odyssey 12.186-188

For never yet has a man rowed by here in a black ship,
before hearing the honey-sweet voice from our lips;
no, *HE* enjoys it and travels on, knowing more in fact.

The passage seems straightforward, but on closer inspection it involves an interesting shift. Whereas in the majority of instances of ἀλλ' ὅ γε there is a single referent who functions as the agent in both parts of the construction, here the tracking of referents is more complicated.[86] The initial assertion is that "no-one sails by before hearing the Sirens," so what does ὅ γε refer to? To no-one? The participle τερψάμενος makes it clear that who is meant by ὅ γε is the sailor who did indeed stay and listen, and was pleased as a result. The automatic inference triggered by "no-one sails by" creates a pool of available referents who *did not* sail by, one of whom can then be referred to with ὅ γε.[87] A similar example occurs in the following gnomic thought that Odysseus imparts to the suitors:

(t19)

τῷ μή τίς ποτε πάμπαν ἀνὴρ ἀθεμίστιος εἴη,
ἀλλ' <u>ὅ γε</u> σιγῇ δῶρα θεῶν ἔχοι, ὅττι διδοῖεν.

Odyssey 18.141-142

[85] See III.3.3.1.1-2 for an exploration of this aspect of γε marking dialogic resonance across utterances in tragic and comic dialogue, and see III.4.5.2 for γε in answers to express a speaker's stance.

[86] See §§48-49 below for more on ἀλλ' ὅ γε.

[87] Compare Berrendonner 1990:28 "Au pronom ne s'attache donc pas nécessairement une assomption d'existence: il ne comporte en lui-même aucune présupposition concernant des objets de connaissance qui devraient déjà figurer dans M [=mémoire discursive]."

> Therefore let no one ever be an altogether lawless man,
> No may *HE* keep in silence the gifts of the gods, whatever they may have given.

Again, an unproblematic reading belies the underlying referential complexity. As in (t18) ὅ γε directs attention to the indefinite referent that we infer from the preceding act.[88] Alternatively, one might say that ὅ γε triggers the creation of a generic referent, about which the only inferrable information at the point of utterance is that he has not "been a lawless man." It is this cognitive action, I propose, that justifies the use of ὅ γε over null anaphor or the pronoun only.[89]

§36. The process of inference also applies in the occurrences of ὅ γε in the following passage from the *Iliad*. The episode reveals more about anaphoric reference than just the use of ὅ γε, however, so allow me a brief excursus. Pandarus is distraught by Diomedes' relentless attack on the Trojans, and says to Aeneas:

(t20)

> "Αἰνεία | Τρώων βουληφόρε χαλκοχιτώνων |
> Τυδεΐδῃ μιν ἔγωγε δαΐφρονι πάντα ἐΐσκω, |
> ἀσπίδι γιγνώσκων | αὐλώπιδί τε τρυφαλείῃ, |
> ἵππους τ' εἰσορόων· | σάφα δ' οὐκ οἶδ' εἰ θεός ἐστιν. |
> εἰ δ' ὅ γ' ἀνὴρ ὅν φημι | δαΐφρων Τυδέος υἱὸς |
> οὐχ ὅ γ' ἄνευθε θεοῦ τάδε μαίνεται, |

Iliad 5.180-185

> "Aeneas, counsellor of the bronze-clad Trojans,
> to Tydeus' battle-minded son *I* liken *him* completely,
> recognizing his shield and his crested helmet,
> and looking at his horses. With certainty I do not know if he is a god.
> And if *HE* is the man I mean, the battle-minded son of Tydeus,
> then *HE* does not rage like that without a god.

88 If one wishes to find a textual antecedent for ὅ γε, one can choose to read "Let it not be that someone is a wholly godless man, but let him own his gifts from the gods in silence." In this reading ὅ γε could be taken as referring to τις, and a similar reading could be wrangled out of (t19). However, ὅ γε here is better understood as triggering the creation of a generic referent than retrieving an earlier one.

89 See *Iliad* 21.113 for another instance of ὅ γε retrieving τις, and similarly ὅ γε retrieving ᾧ κεν in 24.530; compare Cornish 1999:54-56 with examples 2.20a and 2.20b for similar constructions in English and French.

Before we look at the two instances of ὅ γε, consider the use of μιν in line 181. μιν is an unstressed (enclitic) third-person pronoun in the accusative that serves to retrieve accessible referents. Pandarus' speech starts in line 180, and he has not mentioned the referent of μιν ("that man") up to this point. However, in the preceding turn Aeneas has already pointed the man out (τῷδ'...ἀνδρί 174). The referent of the strong demonstrative ὅδε is the man they both see, and Pandarus retrieves him with the much less emphatic μιν, since by now he is well established in both their mental discourse models (as well as in that of performer and audience, of course).

§37. To better explain this passage, we must turn to the difference between anaphora and deixis. I follow Cornish' definition of the terms, which can be explained simply: a speaker uses deixis when she wants to bring a referent into focus in the current discourse model, and anaphora when she retrieves one that is already accessible.[90] Just before (t20), Aeneas introduces "the man" into the conversation with the expression τῷδ'...ἀνδρί, "that man," a combination of demonstrative pronoun and noun—this is deixis.[91] This same referent, who is still in the discourse context (i.e. visible) for the two interlocutors, is from that moment onward in focus in their discourse model, and can be referred to with the enclitic anaphoric pronoun μιν. Deixis is thus not inherently linked to a reference to something outside of the discourse: the crucial question is whether a referent is part of the current discourse model or not. In fact, both anaphora and deixis function outside the text, since they do not primarily interact with the preceding text but with the mental representation of the discourse.

§38. This brings us to ὅ γε in lines 184 and 185. The first ὅ γε refers again to "that man there," who Pandarus is not quite sure is even human.[92] Pandarus speculates that it may be Diomedes, since the man seems to bear Diomedes' shield. The following conditional clause shows that the referent is interactionally clear, but undetermined in textual terms: "If THAT ONE is the man I mean, the battle-minded son of Tydeus...". Both interlocutors know who they are talking about, but his identity is unknown. Thus, ὅ γε refers to the entirety of Aeneas and Pandarus' suppositions about the man, including the possibility that he is a god or that he is Diomedes. Finally comes the apodosis, with the second instance of ὅ γε. If ὅ γε in 184 refers to the man in the middle of the spectacle, ὅ γε in 185 no longer has the same referent, since an assumption underlies the utterance of line 185 that the man is indeed human and in fact Diomedes: "if THAT (ὅ γε) is Diomedes, then HE [sc. Diomedes] (ὅ γε) cannot be raging without divine help." The second ὅ γε

90 See Cornish 1999:112-148 for a discussion, with extensive literature.

91 See Cornish 1999:30, who discusses a speaker using an "accented demonstrative pronoun (*THAT*) fulfilling a deictic function, in order to render accessible and salient an item of information which (...) was in the background, not the foreground, of attention." There are several similar cases: *Iliad* 13.53 (Poseidon speaking of Hector who is in sight), 13.70 (about Poseidon/Kalchas), and 19.344 (κεῖνος ὅ γε, Zeus to Athena about Achilles).

92 Especially in instances like this I cannot agree with Bakker 1999:6 that "ὁ is used (...) to refer to any person or thing that the speaker cannot actually point at."

marks this discontinuity of reference in the mental representation of the discourse: it refers no longer to "that man" but to "that man, Diomedes." The audience can follow this interaction only by taking into account the development of the referent in the mental representation of the discourse, and this inferential process is foregrounded through the use of ὅ γε.

§39. The implied elements pertaining to the referent of ὅ γε can have local relevance, as in (t20) above, but they can also reach beyond the current narrative scene. Telemachus describes the fight between the stranger (Odysseus) and the beggar Irus to his mother Penelope:

(t21)

> οὐ μέν τοι ξείνου γε καὶ Ἴρου μῶλος ἐτύχθη |
> μνηστήρων ἰότητι, | βίῃ δ' ὅ γε φέρτερος ἦεν.
>
> *Odyssey* 18.233-234
>
> Although, the fight of this stranger and Irus did not end according to the will of the suitors: in might, *HE* was stronger.

The situation here is different from most preceding examples, since the two available referents have both been mentioned only in an oblique case. Neither a null anaphor nor a pronoun suffices to retrieve Irus or the stranger. In the earlier narrative, however, it was told that the "stranger" was indeed the stronger, and in fact the whole co-text suggests that the suitors backed Irus. As a result, the referential ambiguity is resolved by the time that φέρτερος was uttered.[93] There is yet another layer to this reference. In the mind of Telemachus, who is speaking, and in the minds of performer and audience, ὅ γε refers not to a stranger but to Odysseus. The reference means something different to the internal audience (Penelope and the suitors) than to the performer and his audience, and this layering has its effect on the content. Bonifazi has demonstrated convincingly that references to the disguised Odysseus are particularly sophisticated in this part of the *Odyssey*, and there is no doubt in my mind that this instance is another example of this complexity.[94] The performer uses ὅ γε because the referent—and the sense of Telemachus' utterance—can only be grasped fully if the listener makes the necessary inferences. It may be surprising to Penelope and the suitors that the stranger beat Irus, but this is decidedly not the case for Telemachus or the audience: obviously Odysseus is stronger in might than the resident beggar of his own palace.

93 Compare (t8) and (t9) above.

94 Bonifazi 2012, especially 159-172. Compare also ὅ γε in *Odyssey* 19.575 (reference to Odysseus by Penelope, spoken to Odysseus-in-disguise).

§40. The consideration of the larger discourse is likewise indispensable in the following case of apparently superfluous reference to Telemachus. After he has been washed by Nestor's youngest daughter, he is retrieved with ὅ γε:

(t22)

αὐτὰρ ἐπεὶ λοῦσέν [sc. Πολυκάστη] τε καὶ ἔχρισεν λίπ' ἐλαίῳ, |
ἀμφὶ δέ μιν φᾶρος καλὸν βάλεν | ἠδὲ χιτῶνα, |
ἔκ ῥ' ἀσαμίνθου βῆ | δέμας ἀθανάτοισιν ὁμοῖος· |
πὰρ δ' ὅ γε Νέστορ' ἰὼν | κατ' ἄρ' ἕζετο, | ποιμένα λαῶν. |

Odyssey 3.466-469

Now, when she had washed him and anointed him richly with oil,
around him she threw a beautiful cloak, and a tunic.
Out of the bath he came, in physique the immortals alike,
and *HE* went next to Nestor, and sat down by the shepherd of men.

The addition of γε in this instance may not appear to be needed, since Telemachus is surely constantly in focus as he is being washed and clothed. His continued prominence in the mental representation of discourse is confirmed by the fact that he is retrieved in line 468 as the unexpressed subject of βῆ. Since Telemachus remains the subject, ὅ γε looks marked in 469. I propose that we read the overdetermination here as an instruction to visualize not just Telemachus, but Telemachus as he is after the ablutions described in the preceding lines. The instruction is perhaps anticipated by the description δέμας ἀθανάτοισιν ὁμοῖος (469). It is not just Telemachus who joins Nestor, but it is Telemachus looking like a god. The same expression is used of Odysseus when he arrives at the palace of the Phaeacians and after he has been washed by Eurynome in book twenty-three.[95] Even more salient, Telemachus himself utters similar words when he mistakes his father for a god during the recognition scene in book sixteen.[96] The scene in book three thus reveals its importance on a macro-discursive level. The first books of the *Odyssey* are about how Telemachus finds himself in the role of man of the house. Perhaps the moment when he joins Nestor is the moment when he finally becomes a worthy heir to his father, and thus like his father looks "like a god." If so, it really is a new Telemachus that sits down next to Nestor.[97]

95 *Odyssey* 8.14 and 23.163.

96 *Odyssey* 16.182-183: ἄλλα δὲ εἵματ' ἔχεις καί τοι χρὼς οὐκέθ' ὁμοῖος. / ἦ μάλα τις θεός ἐσσι.

97 Another possible reason for the strong referring expression is the fact that there is a scene boundary after line 468. Compare *Odyssey* 1.443 for ὅ γε marking a similarly strong visual focus on Telemachus, as he sits on his bed and ponders his future.

§41. Now, since ὁ is itself a lightly emphatic pronoun, ὅ γε can also function to create an explicit or implicit contrast.[98] In this case, ὁ and γε work together: the emphatic pronoun suggests a contrast, while the particle triggers the implied opposite of the stressed referent. Contrastiveness can be marked with regard to referents already mentioned, to upcoming referents, or to implied referents.[99] Consider the following example of the construction ἦ τοι ὅ γε, from Theoclymenus' words to Penelope:

(t23)

"ὦ γύναι αἰδοίη Λαερτιάδεω 'Οδυσῆος, |
ἦ τοι ὅ γ' οὐ σάφα οἶδεν, | ἐμεῖο δὲ σύνθεο μῦθον· |

Odyssey 17.152-153

"Revered wife of Laertes' son Odysseus,
Let me tell you, *HE* does not know it clearly, do listen to my word.

ὅ γε creates the contrast: "Don't listen to *him*, listen to *me*." The referent of ὁ is highly accessible, since it refers to the last speaker (Telemachus), to whom both current interlocutors have presumably been listening.[100] Thus he is part of the speech situation, visually accessible, and in focus in the discourse model.[101]

§42. Consider one final example of subject continuity where ὅ γε serves to set up a contrast with an upcoming referent:[102]

(t24)

αἶψα δὲ νῆας ἔπηξε, | πολὺν δ' ὅ γε λαὸν ἀγείρας |
βῆ φεύγων ἐπὶ πόντον· | ἀπείλησαν γάρ οἱ ἄλλοι |
υἱέες υἱωνοί τε βίης 'Ηρακληείης. |

Iliad 2.664-666

Quickly he built ships, and *HE*, after gathering many men,

98 See also Monro 1882a:258, who argues that γε after pronouns serves "to bring out the contrast which (...) Pronouns [sic] more or less distinctly imply." More generally, Hartung 1832:371, Kühner 1835:398, and Stephens 1837:92 remark that γε can mark a contrast with something left implicit; see III.3.3.1.1 for a closer analysis of γε marking a contrast with something implicit in tragic stichomythia.

99 Chafe 1994:76-78, examples on 77: "ín" in example 7b (backward), and "dóctor" in example 8c (forward). Compare Grégoire 1930:163, who notes that when γε in Homer has the ictus, it usually follows a form of ὅ. In these cases, he believes that the pronoun-particle combination is in some kind of opposition with a preceding element.

100 The other instances of ἦ τοι ὅ γε where there is no subject continuity are *Iliad* 11.94 and 19.100.

101 Compare the discussion of ὅ γε in direct speech to refer to "that man there" in (t20).

102 It is not "semantisch redundant" as *Gesamtkommentar*:II.2.215 claims.

> went fleeing over the sea. For the others threatened him,
> the sons and grandsons of mighty Heracles.

In the little narrative about Tlepolemus we hear how he kills his uncle, and then starts building ships: *he* has to flee, because the *other* children of Heracles are on his tail. The contrast is made explicit by the adjective ἄλλοι, which justifies the use of ὅ γε in 664. As (t24) demonstrates, contrastiveness is a factor that functions separately from activation cost: at that point Tlepolemus is clearly accessible.[103]

§43. In the following complex instance ὁ is placed relative to a contrasted, hypothetical version of its referent. This hypothetical version of the referent is triggered by the very utterance of ὅ γε. In her conversation with Aphrodite about Paris, Helen accuses the goddess of weakness:

(t25)

> μηδ' ἔτι σοῖσι πόδεσσιν ὑποστρέψειας Ὄλυμπον, |
> ἀλλ' αἰεὶ περὶ κεῖνον ὀΐζυε | καί ἑ φύλασσε, |
> εἰς ὅ κέ σ' ἢ ἄλοχον ποιήσεται| ἢ ὅ γε δούλην. |

Iliad 3.407-409

> May you not turn your feet toward Olympus yet,
> but always suffer for him and guard him,
> until he makes you his concubine or *HE* makes you a slave.

The passage is far from straightforward, but in line 409 ποιήσεται retrieves Paris, who is clearly very accessible at that point (κεῖνον, ἑ 408). Since the construction changes from imperative to indicative in 409, the third person verb form suffices to disambiguate among the three available referents: I (Helen), you (Aphrodite), and he (Paris). Then follows ὅ γε in the second part of the disjunction. The occurrence of ὅ γε in either part of a disjunctive construction is well documented, but little discussed.[104] Contrary to expectation, ὅ γε in disjunctions is not used to juxtapose two referents, but rather two possible events involving the same referent.[105] Here the two items in disjunction, ἄλοχον and δούλην, are syntactically symmetrical and semantic opposites. However, the addition of ὅ γε to the second suggests that the expression ἢ ὅ γε δούλην must be read with emphasis placed on ὁ ("or *he* makes you a slave"). The opposite of this statement is not "until he

[103] Chafe 1994:77, "Contrastiveness is independent of activation cost."

[104] See Monro 1882a:258-259, Denniston 1950:119, Chantraine 1953a:II.159.

[105] See *Gesamtkommentar* III.2.143, "ὅ γε betont im zweiten Satzglied die Identität der (...) unterschiedlich handelnden Person," with parallels.

makes you a *concubine*"[106] (this is the opposite of "until he makes you a *slave*") but rather of "*you* make him a slave." It is exactly this presupposition that is triggered through the use of ὅ γε.[107] The expected situation in Greek culture is that the goddess of love makes a human her slave, not the other way around.[108] The markedness of the (hypothetical) situation is brought out by the combination of the pronoun and the particle.[109]

§44. The previous examples all illustrate that some of the force of γε remains in the cluster ὅ γε. However, because ὅ γε functions as a cluster, the force of γε sometimes appears to be extremely weak or even lost. In those instances, ὅ γε looks like a formal and metrical variant of ὁ, a weak demonstrative with no further pragmatic enrichment. In the second book of the *Iliad* we are told the story of Agamemnon's scepter, a piece of unframed discourse introduced just before the king starts to speak in the council.

(t26)

> ἔστη σκῆπτρον ἔχων | τὸ μὲν Ἥφαιστος κάμε τεύχων. |
> (...)
> αὐτὰρ ὃ αὖτε Θυέστ' Ἀγαμέμνονι λεῖπε φορῆναι, |
> πολλῇσιν νήσοισι καὶ Ἄργεϊ παντὶ ἀνάσσειν. |
> τῷ ὅ γ' ἐρεισάμενος | ἔπε' Ἀργείοισι μετηύδα· |

Iliad 2.101, 107-109

> He stood up holding the scepter, over which Hephaestus toiled to make it.
> (...)
> Now this Thyestes in turn left it to Agamemnon to carry,
> to rule over many islands and all of Argos.
> *HE*, leaning on this, spoke words to the Argives:

After the story of the scepter, the current frame is recalled with τῷ ὅ γε, the first pronoun retrieving the scepter, and the second guiding attention toward Agamemnon.[110] The

[106] ἄλοχος does not mean "wife" here, but "concubine of equal <social> class" (*Gesamtkommentar* III.2.143, "'Konkubine, Geliebte' von ebenbürtigem Stand.").

[107] It does not "merely resume the original subject," as Leaf 1900:I.149 believes.

[108] Shipp 1972:240 rather believes that δούλη here means "slave-concubine," but this is rejected by Krieter-Spiro in the *Gesamtkommentar*, with references. Regardless of the exact meaning of ἄλοχος and δούλη here, the scalar sense is clear: "until he makes you a concubine" (unexpected), and "until HE makes you a slave" (even more unexpected).

[109] See Bonifazi 2012:37 "The particle γε might contribute (...) by stressing the paradoxical novelty introduced by the ongoing discourse act."

[110] See II.4.3.2 and below §§51-62 for frame recall after unframed discourse. The same construction occurs after an intervening relative clause, as in *Odyssey* 15.252-255, or after a simile, see ὅ γε in (t13) above. Sometimes the gap between the final mention of the referent and the retrieval

latter had been out of focus for several verses, and even though his name is mentioned in the oblique in line 107, this is not actually the referent of ὅ γε. Rather, the act containing ὅ γε re-establishes the frame of Agamemnon in the council, and that is why the pronoun is used rather than a simple verb form. There is, however, no need for further emphasis: γε is there only to accompany the pronoun in its non-initial position. Compare the following example from the *Odyssey*:

(t27)

οἶσιν δ' Εὐπείθης ἀνά θ' ἵστατο καὶ μετέειπε· |
παιδὸς γάρ οἱ ἄλαστον ἐνὶ φρεσὶ πένθος ἔκειτο, |
Ἀντινόου, | τὸν πρῶτον ἐνήρατο δῖος Ὀδυσσεύς· |
τοῦ ὅ γε δάκρυ χέων ἀγορήσατο καὶ μετέειπεν· |

Odyssey 24.422-425

Among them Eupeithes stood up and spoke—
for over his child comfortless grief lay on his heart,
over Antinous, whom godlike Odysseus first killed—
HE, weeping over him, addressed the assembly and said:

The co-text is essentially the same as in (t27): a speaker is introduced, then follows a brief piece of unframed discourse (γάρ),[111] and finally a pronoun referring to the unframed discourse (τοῦ) and a second pronoun with γε, in the act that re-establishes the narrative frame.

§45. In the above two examples ὅ γε is uttered just before the start of direct speech. This may not be a coincidence. In about a quarter of the instances where ὅ γε accompanies subject continuity, it is in the line right before or after direct speech.[112] The explicit marking of the referent in these instances serves to avoid confusion about the source of the upcoming thoughts or words, or to re-establish the speaker as an agent after his

through ὅ γε is rather long, as in *Iliad* 17.108 and *Odyssey* 17.514. A change of subject while the referent is in focus occurs in *Odyssey* 18.398.

[111] De Jong 2001a:584 reads lines 423-424 as focalized through Eupeithes, upon which the narrator intrudes with his knowledge of whom Odysseus killed first: "The narrator intrudes upon his embedded focalization (...) by adding the detail 'first' (something which the father cannot know)." Unlike the instances of δὴ γάρ (see II.4 §19), however, there is nothing in the language here to suggest a blurring of perspectives. I read the lines as unframed discourse, directly from performer to audience, where he shares knowledge only he can have. The Homeric performer knows Eupeithes' mind and he can tell the audience that his son Antinous was in fact the first to be killed.

[112] ὅ γε right before direct speech: *Iliad* 1.93, 2.55, 2.109, 4.357, 8.138, 13.94, 13.480, 17.219, 19.100, 21.367, 23.5, 23.42; *Odyssey* 1.31, 2.24, 4.189, 13.254, 17.466, 18.110, 24.425, ; ὅ γε right after direct speech: *Iliad* 1.68, 1.101, 2.76, 2.207, 4.250, 7.354, 7.365, 9.620; *Odyssey* 2.224.

speech has finished. The construction ἦ τοι ὅ γ' generally occurs in the following formulaic speech-capping verse:[113]

(t28)

ἦ τοι ὅ γ' ὣς εἰπὼν κατ' ἄρ' ἕζετο, τοῖσι δ' ἀνέστη

Hey[114] *HE*, having spoken thus, sat down. And among them stood up

Since this verse follows direct speech, subject continuity is implicit. It is not hard to see that in this construction ὅ γε serves to set up a light contrast between this speaker and the next.

§46. Immediately after direct speech is one context where ὅ γε consistently differs from ὁ δέ. While ὅ γε marks continuity of grammatical subject after direct speech, ὁ δέ marks subject change.[115] This difference can be explained from the constituent order of the two constructions. With ὅ γε, we find "X ὅ γε | participle | finite verb," whereas with ὁ δέ we find "finite verb | ὁ δέ." In the latter construction, null anaphor would have been the natural marker of subject continuity.

§47. An extension of the use of ὅ γε to put particular cognitive focus on a referent can be found in the following example. Like the priming acts discussed in II.2.5, an emphatic pronoun may serve to direct extra attention to a certain referent. A priming act serves to mentally (or visually) turn to or zoom in on a referent,[116] which may in turn create the expectation that this referent will project over a significant piece of upcoming discourse. We can find a cognate of this construction in a small number of instances of ὅ γε,[117] especially just before direct speech or indirect thought.[118] In other contexts, it can also project the prominence of a character, as in the introduction of Alcinous, in Nausicaä's description of the palace of the Phaeacians to Odysseus:[119]

113 *Iliad* 1.68, 1.101, 2.76, 7.354, 7.365; *Odyssey* 2.224.

114 For this interjection-like reading of ἦ at strong discursive discontinuities, see II.3.2.3.

115 In both *Iliad* (8x) and *Odyssey* (8x) there is the speech-capping construction ὣς φάθ', ὁ δέ, always marking subject change. A similar construction occurs in the *Odyssey* only, but accounts for 14 out 41 instances of ὁ δέ: ὣς ἐφάμην, ὁ δέ.

116 ὅ γε is especially visually relevant in *Iliad* 5.585 (the image of the warrior standing upright with his head in the sand) and *Odyssey* 17.302 (Odysseus' dog Argos).

117 There are even a few instances where the two constructions intersect, as in *Iliad* 21.550, 21.581, and *Odyssey* 11.190, 20.140, 22.116.

118 The cognitive priming is primarily local and visual/experiential in the construction φῆ δ' ὅ γε: *Iliad* 2.37; *Odyssey* 17.142, 24.470. For the loci of ὅ γε near the beginning of direct speech, see note 112 above.

119 I read a similar projecting function of ὅ γε in: *Iliad* 15.455, 24.189; *Odyssey* 22.480.

(t29)

ἔνθα δὲ πατρὸς ἐμοῖο θρόνος ποτικέκλιται αὐτῇ, |
τῷ ὅ γε οἰνοποτάζει ἐφήμενος | ἀθάνατος ὥς. |

Odyssey 6.308-309

And there is my father's throne, leant against that <pillar>.
On that *HE* sits and drinks his wine, like unto an immortal.

The reference to Alcinous here serves at once as the climax of the imagined entrance into the palace, and as the beginning of the long episode in which Alcinous and Odysseus are the main characters. At this crucial moment Alcinous is granted agency with some emphasis, which prepares the audience for his importance in the upcoming narrative.

§48. As a final consideration, we turn to the construction ἀλλ᾽ ὅ γε, which almost exclusively accompanies continuity of grammatical subject.[120] In the vast majority of cases, the construction takes the following form: "he did not do X, ἀλλ᾽ ὅ γε did Y." [121] That is to say, these are occurrences of ὅ γε within the classical "οὐ X ἀλλά Y" construction, where ἀλλά equals German *sondern*.[122] This juxtaposing construction can be used with scope over single noun phrases or over (generally longer) verb phrases. The combination ἀλλ᾽ ὅ γε in Homer always juxtaposes an entire verb phrase with a preceding negated one: after positing what the referent will not do, the action resumes with the statement of what he will do. Consider the following typical instance, where Sarpedon has just heard of the wounding of Glaucus:

(t30)

Σαρπήδοντι δ᾽ ἄχος γένετο Γλαύκου ἀπιόντος |
αὐτίκ᾽ ἔπειτ᾽ ἐνόησεν· | ὅμως δ᾽ οὐ λήθετο χάρμης, |
ἀλλ᾽ ὅ γε | Θεστορίδην Ἀλκμάονα δουρὶ τυχήσας |
νύξ᾽, |

Iliad 12.392-395

To Sarpedon sorrow came at Glaucus' leaving,
right when he had noticed; still he did not forget the fight.

[120] There are also 6 instances of the construction where there is no subject continuity: *Iliad* 2.3, 15.676, 17.705, 24.14, *Odyssey* 5.82, 14.526.

[121] 20 times in the *Iliad* and 9 times in the *Odyssey*; the 4 exceptions are *Iliad* 1.281, 5.434 (but this instance is textually uncertain), and 8.311 (=13.518), where we find a different construction. I am not sure what Denniston 1950:12 means by: "Often the emphatic word or phrase in the ἀλλά-clause (which word or phrase follows immediately, or almost immediately, after the particle) is limitatively qualified by γε (...). Homer never has ἀλλά ... γε," especially since he quotes *Iliad* 1.281 ἀλλ᾽ ὅ γε on page 11.

[122] See ἀλλά in ORPS (our online database).

> *No, HE*, coming upon Thestor's son Alcmaon with his spear,
> struck him,

There is clear subject continuity from line 393 onward, yet after two verbs with null subjects (ἐνόησεν, λήθετο) we find ἀλλ' ὅ γε. There is a significant difference between the sense of the verbs before and after the pronoun and particle combination, marking the contrast between inaction and action.

§49. ἀλλ' ὅ γε consistently introduces a new action, often marking the beginning of a new scene. The verb in the negated act of the construction is generally a reflection of some inner state of the referent (he was not afraid),[123] a static verb (he did not stay),[124] or a forward-oriented statement (he did not fulfill).[125] What these verbs have in common is that they interrupt the action by explicitly considering and dismissing a counterfactual situation.[126] Pragmatic projection is inherent in the construction, since the assertion that someone did not do one thing suggests that he *did* do another. The *onus* of the construction, then, is on the second part, for which the first part serves as a foil. From this perspective, ἀλλ' ὅ γε works to resume the action, and this new beginning justifies the use of the pronoun even if the referent is already in focus. The occurrence of ἀλλ' ὅ γε even when there is apparent subject continuity can thus be explained because some kind of cognitive redirection is needed—suggested by ἀλλά—just before the occurrence of the cluster ὅ γε. The apparent overdetermination can be read as an attempt to bridge this gap and direct attention toward the right referent.

§50. I have devoted a great deal of attention to ὅ γε for the simple reason that it is a very hard combination to pin down. With due attention to the direct co-text, context, and the larger narrative, however, its functions can be better understood. The function of γε that manifests in ὅ γε is the particle's ability to activate an implication about its host word (group). This means that in a number of instances ὅ γε serves to retrieve an inferrable referent, or an accessible referent in an inferrable new form. Since ὅ γε is a grammaticalized cluster, this pragmatic enrichment of γε is not evident in every instance. In a number of cases ὅ γε appears to be nothing more than a formal variant of the

123 The parallels are (line numbers refer to the instances of ἀλλ' ὅ γε): *Iliad* 1.320 (λῆγ' ἔριδος), 4.389 (τάρβει), 5.321 (ἐλήθετο), 12.305 (μέμονε), 12.394 (λήθετο), 13.523 (πέπυστο, but the text is uncertain for ἀλλ' ὅ γε), 15.676 (Αἴαντι .. ἥνδανε θυμῷ), 17.705 (ἤθελε), 21.581 (ἔθελεν), 24.14 (μιν λήθεσκεν); *Odyssey* 5.82 (ἠγνοίησεν), 9.554 (ἐμπάζετο), 14.422 (λήθετο), 14.526 (συβώτῃ ἥνδανεν).

124 *Iliad* 2.3 (Δία δ' οὐκ ἔχε .. ὕπνος), 6.504 (δήθυνεν), 15.586 (μεῖνε), 23.5 (εἴα ἀποσκίδνασθαι); *Odyssey* (5.33 the negation takes the form of an adverbial phrase "without interference by gods or men"), 11.190 (οἱ <ἐστι>), 12.188? (παρήλασε, see t18), 18.142 (εἴη).

125 *Iliad* 2.420 (ἐπεκραίαινε), 22.92 (ἔπειθον); *Odyssey* 9.288 (ἀμείβετο).

126 For the more well-known variant of a counterfactual construction ("καί νύ κεν...εἰ μή) see Louden 1993. His argument is that these constructions occur at pivotal moments in the narrative.

demonstrative pronoun in limited positional contexts. The use of ὅ γε in these instances can be explained from the function of the lightly emphatic pronoun, and serves to put the referent firmly into cognitive focus. In this function, ὅ γε occurs particularly often right after frame switches and before and after direct speech. The function of the cluster must be regarded as a continuum with at one end ὅ γε as a variant of ὁ, and at the other end ὅ γε carrying a complex of inferences to be added to the referent. This continuum can be explained from the cluster's origin in ὁ and γε. Every instance of ὅ γε in Homer represents a point on the sliding scale. In any case, it does not do justice to the discourse function of the cluster to remark that ὅ γε is "semantically redundant."[127]

5.3.3 ὁ δ' ἄρα and ὅ(ς) ῥα

§51. In contrast to the flexible cluster ὅ γε, ἄρα only follows anaphoric pronouns in very limited contexts. In the present section, I first discuss the cluster ὁ δ' ἄρ(α) in Pindar and Homer, which typically works as a marker of frame recall. Then follows an analysis of ὅ(ς) ῥ(α), a combination that can introduce two distinct constructions: either an unframed act with a verb in the imperfect tense, or a framed act with an aorist verb.

§52. In II.4, I argue that the use of ἄρα in Homer and Pindar is a sign of the speaker's management of discourse memory.[128] The particle introduces acts containing information that the speaker expects to be accessible in the hearer's mind. When ἄρα comes after anaphoric and relative pronouns, it likewise accompanies accessible information in the discourse memory that is not currently being attended to. Consider first this instance of ὁ δ'ἄρα in Pindar:

(t31)

(...) ξένου Λάκωνος Ὀρέστα.

τὸν δή[129] φονευομένου πατρὸς
...(18-30)
θάνεν μὲν αὐτὸς ἥρως Ἀτρεΐδας
ἵκων χρόνῳ κλυταῖς ἐν Ἀμύκλαις,

μάντιν τ' ὄλεσσε κόραν, ἐπεὶ ἀμφ' Ἑλένᾳ πυρωθέντας
Τρώων ἔλυσε δόμους ἁβρότατος. ὁ δ' ἄρα γέροντα ξένον
Στροφίον ἐξίκετο, νέα κεφαλά, Παρνασσοῦ πόδα ναίοντ'·

Pythian 11.16-17 and 31-35

[127] See *Gesamtkommentar* II.2.215, "semantisch redundant."
[128] See II.4 §§34-37 and §§46-49.
[129] See below note 159 as well as (t48) with note 198 for δή after pronouns in Pindar.

(...) of Orestes the Laconian guest.

Him actually, at the slaughter of his father [sc. Agamemnon],
18–21 how Orestes escaped from Klytaemnestra
22–25 Klytaemnestra's motives
25–30 *gnômai*
He himself died, the hero son of Atreus [sc. Agamemnon],
arriving in time in renowned Amyklai,

and he brought death on the seer girl, after over Helen he had despoiled
the burnt down houses of the Trojans of their luxury. *So HE* [sc. Orestes], the young boy,[130]
went to his aged host, Strophius, living at the foot of Parnassus.

After a gnomic passage, a demonstrative pronoun and a full noun phrase serve to retrieve Agamemnon (αὐτὸς ἥρως Ἀτρεΐδας 31).[131] Although he had been mentioned in the oblique before (φονευομένου πατρός 17, σὺν Ἀγαμεμνονία 20), he had not yet been fully attended to, only mentioned as part of an event relevant to Orestes. Then Pindar narrates a selection of Agamemnon's adventures in reverse: he elliptically retrieves the story of Agamemnon's taking of Priam's daughter Cassandra, and then bringing her to Mycenae where she too is killed by Clytaemnestra (in Pindar's version, lines 19-21) with the four words μάντιν τ' ὄλεσσε κόραν. The particle τε here, I submit, serves to mark the sharedness of this episode, and allows Pindar to waste no more words in telling it.[132] The mention of Agamemnon's death activates the event of line 16 again in the hearer's mind. This makes Orestes, who has not been named or even mentioned for seventeen lines, accessible enough to be referred to with ὁ. In the preceding lines Agamemnon has been the grammatical subject, so the pronoun suggests a change of subject; the only other available masculine singular referent is Orestes.[133] The possible ambiguity in the anaphoric expression is perhaps the reason for the apposition νέα κεφαλά in line 35,[134]

[130] The parenthetical apposition comes much later in the Greek, but sticking to this position would yield an ambiguous English translation.

[131] See Bonifazi 2012:137-184 for more on the layered meaning of αὐτός, noting especially the strong link with death (141-143 for the body of Patroclus); I merely point out the proximity of θάνεν here.

[132] See II.4 §§57-71 for more on the link between τε and tradition in Pindar.

[133] I take issue with Des Places' reading, 1947:45 "11, 34 : ὁ δ' (= Oreste) après (θάνεν) μὲν αὐτὸς ἥρως (31), qui tient lieu d'ὁ μέν." From the point of view of discourse and performance there is no reason to see a link between μέν and δέ in this passage.

[134] Snell/Maehler give the nominative νέα κεφαλά, following Heyne's reading, rather than the dative νέᾳ κεφαλᾷ of the manuscripts (followed by Gentili et al. 1995); either reading suits my

since this can only refer to Orestes. This passage demonstrates that ἄρα functions on the level of the larger discourse or interaction rather than as a link between two contiguous clauses. In narrative terms, ἄρα recalls the frame of the main storyline: lines 32-34 function as a little flashback, told regressively, and δ' ἄρα serves to re-activate the main narrative frame of Orestes' story. At the same time ἄρα marks its host act, as well as the upcoming narrative, as a part of the tradition shared between Pindar and his audience.

§53. This reading of (t31) is supported by both other instances of ὁ δ' ἄρα in Pindar (*Olympian* 10.43 and *Pythian* 4.78),[135] one of which deserves fuller discussion. Pindar's fourth *Pythian* ode is famous for its intricate narrative, an impression reinforced by the passage containing ὁ δ' ἄρα. In a song that is at least partly about his quest, Jason is mentioned once in the beginning of the song (in an oblique case: εἶπε [sc. Medea] δ' οὕτως ἡμιθέοισιν Ἰάσονος αἰχματᾶο ναύταις, "Medea spoke thus to the demi-god sailors of Jason the spearman," lines 11-12), but is never named again. First Pindar gives Medea's long prophecy and then he turns, in line 70, to the start of the journey of the Argonauts. This leads him to the episode of Pelias and Jason. Pelias receives a prophecy that a stranger with one sandal will come and be a threat to him and his throne. Later, this man actually arrives:

(t32)

ἦλθε δέ οἱ κρυόεν πυκινῷ μάντευμα θυμῷ, |
πὰρ μέσον ὀμφαλὸν εὐδένδροιο ῥηθὲν ματέρος |
τὸν μονοκρήπιδα πάντως ἐν φυλακᾷ σχεθέμεν μεγάλᾳ, |
εὖτ' ἂν | αἰπεινῶν ἀπὸ σταθμῶν | ἐς εὐδείελον
χθόνα μόλῃ κλειτᾶς Ἰαολκοῦ, |

ξεῖνος αἴτ' ὦν ἀστός. | ὁ δ' ἆρα [sc. Iason] χρόνῳ
ἵκετ' αἰχμαῖσιν διδύμαισιν | ἀνὴρ ἔκπαγλος· |

Pythian 4.73-79

And there came to him [sc. Pelias] a prophecy chilling to his shrewd heart,
spoken at the central navel of the well-wooded mother:
to always be fully on guard against *the man with one sandal*,

interpretation, although in the manuscript reading it is not an appositive.

[135] *Olympian* 10.43-45 is a good parallel (ὁ δ' ἄρ' ἐν Πίσᾳ ἔλσαις ὅλον τε στρατόν / λᾴαν τε πᾶσαν Διὸς ἄλκιμος / υἱὸς) with the difference being that the referent in that song, Heracles, is not retrieved by association as Orestes is here. However, Heracles is available at the occurrence of ὁ δ'ἄρα by virtue of the death of the main referent in focus (θάνατον αἰπὺν οὐκ ἐξέφυγεν, 42). Just as in *Pythian* 11, the pronoun is followed by a clarifying appositive later in the sentence (Διὸς ἄλκιμος / υἱὸς).

> when, from the high dwellings, he came to the sunny
> land of famous Iolkos;
>
> be he a stranger or a townsman. *And HE of course* in time
> did come, with two spears, a terrible man.

I read ἆρα rather than the ἦρα proposed by Schroeder and printed in most editions.[136] Braswell regards ἆρα as a prosodically enriched form of ἄρα, and I would add that it may be regarded as pragmatically enriched as well. Again, ὁ δ' ἆρα marks the recall of the main narrative frame, after the explanation of the prophecy. The "one-sandaled man" of the prophecy is Jason, as Pindar's audience would have known. What makes this instance different from (t31) is that here there is apparent continuity of grammatical subject, so the use of the nominative pronoun must be explained otherwise.

§54. The reason for this overdetermination is that the pronoun ὁ has an ambiguous referent. Since *Pythian* 4 activates the narrative of the Argonauts right from the song's beginning, we can say that Jason has been covertly present throughout the narrative. When Pindar turns to the specific episode of Pelias' prophecy, the knowing audience will activate the figure of Jason, making ὁ in line 78 a referential nexus. ὁ refers to the one-sandaled man (τὸν μονοκρήπιδα, 75) who comes to Iolkos, but at the same time it refers to Jason. The pronoun conflates the stranger of the prophecy and the Jason of myth. The function of ἆρα is similarly layered: the particle accesses both the local expectations ("of course the prophecy comes true")[137] and the global discourse memory that consists in the tradition shared by composer and audience ("as we both know, Jason did indeed come to dethrone Pelias").[138] As in (t31) and the one other parallel (*Olympian* 10.43-45, see note 135), an appositional cap follows, ἀνὴρ ἔκπαγλος, to dispel any possible ambiguity: ἔκπαγλος strongly suggests that the referent is now supposed to be a hero rather than an unknown man with one sandal.[139]

§55. In the three instances in Pindar, the combination δ' ἄρα (or δ' ἆρα) after pronouns serves to recall the main narrative frame. I read ἄρα as having scope over the entire act rather than just over the pronoun (I imagine prosodic emphasis as falling on the most important part of the clause, perhaps the verb phrase: "And so he DID come...").

136 The manuscripts have ἄρα, which in most current editions is emended to ἦρα since a heavy syllable is desired; see Braswell 1988:173-174 and De Kreij 2014 for discussion; Gentili et al. 1995:128 and Liberman 2004:100 also read ἆρα.

137 Even if some members of the audience may not have known the episode well enough, the fact that something is fated (θέσφατον ἦν, 71) implies that it will happen.

138 See Bonifazi's comment at 2004b:63 about pronouns in Pindar: "[t]hrough them both the performer and the audience enter in the dimension of epic memory."

139 ἔκπαγλος is most likely (through dissimilation *ἔκπλαγλος > ἔκπαγλος) from ἐκπλήσσω "expel," "hunt." If this is correct, the original sense of "outcast" might interact here with the more generic "terrible." Pindar refers at once to the "terrible" hero and the "exiled" hero.

Thus, ἄρα modifies the act by marking its contents as shared between performer and audience. In narrative terms, the acts introduced by ὁ δ' ἄρα are always framed: they continue the action of the narrative.

§56. The use of ὁ δ' ἄρα in Homer is slightly more varied, but it falls within the same range as that in Pindar. The following example is representative for the majority of instances. During the battle at the wall of the Greek camp, Ajax gets angry and decides to take drastic measures:

(t33)

Αἴας δὲ πρῶτος Τελαμώνιος ἄνδρα κατέκτα |
Σαρπήδοντος ἑταῖρον | Ἐπικλῆα μεγάθυμον |
μαρμάρῳ ὀκριόεντι βαλών, | ὅ ῥα τείχεος ἐντὸς |
κεῖτο μέγας παρ' ἔπαλξιν ὑπέρτατος· | οὐδέ κέ μιν ῥέα |
χείρεσσ' ἀμφοτέρῃς | ἔχοι ἀνὴρ | οὐδὲ μάλ' ἡβῶν, |
οἷοι νῦν βροτοί εἰσ'· | ὁ δ' ἄρ'[140] ὑψόθεν ἔμβαλ' ἀείρας, |
θλάσσε δὲ τετράφαλον κυνέην, | σὺν δ' ὀστέ' ἄραξε |
πάντ' ἄμυδις κεφαλῆς· | ὁ δ' ἄρ' | ἀρνευτῆρι ἐοικὼς |
κάππεσ' ἀφ' ὑψηλοῦ πύργου, | λίπε δ' ὀστέα θυμός. |

Iliad 12.378-386

Ajax Telamon's son first killed a man,
brave-hearted Epicles, a comrade of Sarpedon,
throwing a jagged rock. This of course lay inside the wall
large and topmost near the battlements. And not easily
with both hands could a man hold it, even in his prime,
as mortals are now. *So HE* threw it, lifting it high,
he crushed the four-ridged helmet, and crushed together
all at once the bones of his head. *HE*, *then*, an acrobat alike,
fell down off the high wall, and life left his bones.

I discuss the use of ὅ ῥα to introduce unframed discourse, as in line 380, in §§58-59 below. For the present, I focus on the instances of ὁ δ' ἄρα in lines 383 and 385. In 383 ὁ δ' ἄρα retrieves Ajax, last named in 378, who picks up a stone no normal man could have lifted. The referential expression comes after the description of the rock, and ὁ δ' ἄρα serves to

[140] Most editions print ὃ δ' ἄρ' both here and in 383, but since I regard ὁ as referring to Ajax, I give ὁ δ' ἄρ', in this instance supported by the best manuscript (Venetus A gives ὁ δ'ἄρ' in both 383 and 385).

retrieve the narrative frame.[141] After the image of Ajax throwing the rock at someone, his victim is made an agent by ὁ in 385, while what happens to him (he tumbles off the wall head first) is marked by ἄρα as the expected outcome. In addition, the next words (ἀρνευτῆρι ἐοικώς) suggest that the hearer is invited to imagine the scene by superimposing upon it the (shared) image of a diver. The vivid nature of the acts introduced by ὁ δ' ἄρα is paralleled elsewhere in Homer, and it may be linked to Bakker's reading of ἄρα as an "evidential" particle.[142]

§57. It cannot be established for every instance why we find ὁ δ' ἄρα rather than ὁ δέ in Homer, but some pragmatic difference must underlie their linguistic divergence. The much higher frequency of ἄρα in Homer suggests that the range of functions of δ' ἄρα is larger than in Pindar. Whereas in Pindaric song ὁ δ' ἄρα consistently serves to recall the main narrative frame, in Homer the common element is that ἄρα expresses the performer's assumption that the content of the act resonates strongly with the current state of the discourse memory.[143] What happens after ὁ δ' ἄρα is expected, either based on common sense or social convention (obviously the messenger obeys Agamemnon),[144] or based on traditional knowledge (of course a plan by Odysseus works).[145] The combination in Homer always retrieves an accessible referent, but in many cases it accompanies not only a change of grammatical subject, but also a visual transition.[146]

§58. The combination δ' ἄρα thus introduces new framed events that feature a referent who is thought to be retrievable but not necessarily in focus at the moment of reference. When one removes δέ from the combination, what is lost is the sense of a discourse boundary. That is to say, whereas pronoun + δ' ἄρα moves the narrative ahead, no such thing need be expected of pronoun + ἄρα. In ὅ(ς) ῥα the particle still marks its

141 Similar instances of ὁ δ' ἄρα clearly marking frame recall in *Iliad* 2.268, 10.354, 19.367, 21.174, 21.246; *Odyssey* 5.392, 5.453, 19.447, 19.464, 20.275, 23.90.

142 See Bakker 1993d:15-25 and 1997b:17-20. As for the combination ὁ δ' ἄρα, compare *Iliad* 19.367, where the terrifying image of Achilles as he prepares to re-enter the battle is followed by ὁ δ' ἄρα; similarly *Iliad* 12.462 (Hector leaps through the broken gates, followed by a vivid description), *Odyssey* 5.456 (note Murray's translation "So he lay breathless..."). Finally, in 23.90, it appears the hearer is invited to share a character's perception, when Penelope has just entered the hall and sits across from Odysseus, after which: ὁ δ' ἄρα πρὸς κίονα μακρὴν / ἧστο κάτω ὁρόων, which I am tempted to read as "And there he sat..."

143 See the discussion of discourse memory in II.4.1

144 *Iliad* 3.120, compare *Iliad* 5.836, 7.188, 7.416, 8.319, 10.374, 12.385, 13.192, 15.543, 16.413, 16.579, 16.742, 21.118; *Odyssey* 5.456, 8.450, 12.411, 12.413, 14.485, 15.98, 15.121 (this instance is special in the sense that it retrieves specific information that was added to the discourse memory in lines 102-104), 18.396.

145 *Iliad* 10.350; the boundary between common sense and traditional knowledge was probably fuzzy in the Greek world, but I would offer the following *loci* as parallels: *Iliad* 6.154 (genealogy), 17.196 (Achilles' armor), 20.239 (genealogy), 21.189 (genealogy), 23.642 (the sons of Actor); *Odyssey* 11.257 (genealogy).

146 The one exception where ὁ δ' ἄρα accompanies grammatical subject continuity is *Iliad* 11.426.

host act as shared between performer and audience, but the act itself need not necessarily be framed, nor need it move the narrative forward.

§59. The combination ὅ ῥα is very rare in Homer and not attested in Pindar. Of the six instances, two do not in fact contain the demonstrative or relative pronoun, but rather the equivalent of ὅ τι, which is suggested by the preceding verb of perception or knowing.[147] Of the remaining four instances, two are followed by an imperfect and two by an aorist.[148] The meaning of these numbers becomes clearer when we consider that ὅς ῥα occurs in two constructions: (1) ὅς ῥα with an imperfect introduces unframed discourse,[149] and (2) ὅς ῥα with an aorist introduces framed discourse.[150] The following passage illustrates both constructions with ὅ(ς) ῥα:

(t34)

ἔνθά οἱ υἱὸς ἐπᾶλτο Πυλαιμένεος βασιλῆος |
Ἁρπαλίων, | ὅ ῥα πατρὶ φίλῳ ἕπετο πτολεμίξων |
ἐς Τροίην, | οὐδ' αὖτις ἀφίκετο πατρίδα γαῖαν· |
ὅς ῥα τότ' Ἀτρεΐδαο μέσον σάκος οὔτασε δουρὶ

Iliad 13.643-646

There jumped on him the son of king Pylaemenes,
Harpalion, *who of course followed* his beloved father, so that he could fight,
to Troy, and not again did he reach his fatherland.
So HE then in the middle of Atreides' shield *thrust* with his spear

ὅ(ς) ῥα introducing unframed discourse serves to recall little bits of information about the referent which the speaker expects to already be part of (or inferrable from) the discourse memory.[151] In line 643 the next assailant of Menelaus enters the scene,

147 Namely *Iliad* 16.120 and *Odyssey* 24.182.

148 *Iliad* 12.380 (imperfect, see t34 above), 13.644 (imperfect), 22.470 (aorist); *Odyssey* 22.327 (aorist).

149 The parallel instances of ὅ(ς) ῥα + imperfect introducing unframed discourse are: *Iliad* 2.77, 2.752, 5.70, 5.612, 5.708, 6.18, 6.131, 11.123, 13.665, 15.431, 15.461, 16.178, 16.464, 16.572, 17.611; *Odyssey* 1.154, 2.225, 9.187, 16.396, 22.331. Sometimes with the pluperfect: *Iliad* 5.77, 12.445, 13.364, 17.350; *Odyssey* 24.445 or present: *Iliad* 15.411, 22.23, 22.27, 23.517; *Odyssey* 15.319, 22.403. The present tense is generally used with ἄρα when it occurs in the first part of a simile, see e.g. II.4 (t16).

150 The parallel instances of ὅ(ς) ῥα + aorist to effect frame recall are: *Iliad* 1.405, 10.318, 11.231, 15.584 (after an apostrophe of a character), 15.644, 17.72 (after ἔνθα κε...εἰ μή flash-forward), 23.384 (after καί νύ κε...εἰ μή flash-forward); *Odyssey* 10.158 (beginning of little narrative), 14.380, 20.291, 21.184.

151 See for another interpretation of ὅς ῥα (τε) Ruijgh 1971:432-443; he follows Hartung and Denniston and believes that ἄρα in this construction serves to mark a certain measure of surprise or interest on the part of the speaker.

Harpalion son of Pylaemenes. After the name is stated in line 644 we find ὅ ῥα and a verb in the imperfect: the pronoun and particle introduce a piece of unframed discourse that consists of a flashback and a flash-forward. In this instance, one can just as well translate "Harpalion. He followed"; either way the act introduced by ὅ ῥα is unframed. Both the flashback and the flash-forward (οὐδ'...γαῖαν 645) are unframed discourse in the sense that the performer reveals his omniscience and informs the audience outside the frame. The use of ἄρα in unframed discourse marks a piece of knowledge from the discourse memory that is retrieved to become part of the current discourse model: it may be regarded as activating a piece of information in the long-term memory to become part of the working memory.

§60. After the unframed discourse in (t34) ὅς ῥα τότε follows at verse beginning, followed by an aorist. Functionally, there is a clear overlap with δ' ἄρα: ὅς ῥα τότε here recalls the frame and introduces a new action, expressed by an aorist.[152] It is possible that the ὁ δ'ἄρα and ὅς ῥα (τότε) functioned as metrical alternatives to effect the same transition in a different place in the verse. In line with this use, ὅ(ς) ῥα followed by an aorist starts an embedded narrative in two instances in the *Odyssey* and once in a fragment of Pindar, where we might have expected to find γάρ.[153]

§61. In a small number instances ὅ(ς) ῥα is followed by an aorist when the act appears unframed:

(t35)

αὐτὰρ ὑπέρθυμον Πολυφείδεα | μάντιν Ἀπόλλων
θῆκε | βροτῶν ὄχ' ἄριστον, | ἐπεὶ θάνεν Ἀμφιάρηος· |
ὅς ῥ' Ὑπερησίηνδ' *ἀπενάσσατο* | πατρὶ χολωθείς, |
ἔνθ' ὅ γε ναιετάων | μαντεύετο πᾶσι βροτοῖσι. |

Odyssey 15.252-255

And proud Polypheides, a seer Apollo
made him, by far best of mortals, since Amphiaraos died.
He had moved to Hyperesia, angry with his father.
Living there, he prophesied for all men.

My translation and punctuation reflect a reading of line 254 as unframed, despite the presence of the aorist. Two things support this reading: (1) ἀποναίω is not attested in the

[152] *Odyssey* 12.281 is different: a present in direct speech which actually refers to the present.

[153] *Odyssey* 10.158, 14.380. The only extant instance of ἄρα after a pronoun in Pindar is found in fr. 125.1 τόν ῥα, where it also appears to introduce an embedded narrative about how Terpander invented the *bárbiton* (note the aorist εὗρεν). See II.3.2.2 on γάρ beginning embedded narratives.

imperfect, and (2) there is a parallel passage in the *Iliad*. Compare this passage from the *Catalogue of Ships*, from the entry about the people from Doulichion:

(t36)

τῶν αὖθ' ἡγεμόνευε Μέγης ἀτάλαντος Ἄρηϊ |
Φυλεΐδης, | ὃν τίκτε Διῒ φίλος ἱππότα Φυλεύς, |
ὅς ποτε Δουλίχιονδ' *ἀπενάσσατο* πατρὶ χολωθείς· |

Iliad 2.627-629

Them in turn led Meges, equal to Ares,
Phyleides, him bore the horseman Phyleus, beloved to Zeus,
who one day *had moved* to Doulichion, angry with his father.

It is clear that the resemblance between these two passages reaches beyond the repetition of the verb.[154] For the current purpose, it suffices to note that the information about Phyleus moving from Elis to Doulichion is necessary, yet clearly out of the current frame, as the use of ποτε confirms. I believe this justifies a similar reading of the passage from the *Odyssey* (t35): ὅς ῥα in line 254 introduces a piece of unframed discourse containing shared knowledge.[155] The passage preceding (t35) is a genealogy leading up to Polypheides and eventually his son, Theoclymenus. At this point in the genealogy, the family is in Argos, but it appears that the performer knows that Polypheides is connected to Hyperesia rather than to Argos. That would explain why he adds the line, with ὅς ῥα, to avoid a discrepancy between his performance and shared tradition.

§62. The combination ὅ(ς) ῥα thus serves two main purposes: (1) to introduce unframed discourse containing shared knowledge about a certain referent (accessing global discourse memory), and (2) to return to the frame after intervening unframed discourse of some sort (accessing local discourse memory). Moreover, there is a strong tendency for the performer to use the imperfect tense in unframed acts, and the aorist in framed acts.

5.3.4 ὁ δή and ὅς δή

§63. The combination ὁ δή/ὅς δή is not quite as flexible as ὅ(ς) ῥα. In II.3.3 and II.3.4 I set out an analysis of the pragmatic functions of δή in Homer and Pindar. The particle is only used with a limited range of co-texts outside of direct speech: with temporal expressions,

154 These are the only two instances of πατρὶ χολωθείς in Homer. Moreover, there is a strong phonetic resonance between Φυλεΐδης and Πολυφείδης; see Minchin 2001:88-90 for this kind of "auditory memory" in Homer.

155 Other instances of ὅ(ς) ῥα apparently introducing unframed discourse with the aorist: *Iliad* 5.612 (in direct speech), 5.650 (in direct speech), 6.158, 16.328; *Odyssey* 3.161 (in a σχέτλιος comment).

in certain combinations, and after pronouns. When used after pronouns, δή typically occurs in a relative clause.[156] The main functions of δή in early epic and lyric may be summarized as follows: (1) as a mobile (rare), it occurs in any position and has an intensifying force over the following word group, or else in act-initial position has scope over the entire act; (2) in peninitial position in the act, it generally has an intensifying force over the act it is in, or over the preceding word group, but it can sometimes have scope only over the following word group; (3) in narrator text, in peninitial position with a temporal marker of some sort, it marks larger narrative moves.

§64. One might expect that δή in relative clauses would not mark larger narrative steps. This intuition is corroborated by the fact that of the twenty-seven instances of ὁ δή and ὃς δή in Homer only four are accompanied by a temporal adverb, and none of these occurrences appears to mark larger discourse steps.[157] Rather, the particle consistently intensifies either the entire act or the following word (group).[158] Before moving on to a discussion of the range of functions of δή in these clauses, let me establish some common characteristics of the clauses introduced by pronoun + δή. In contrast to δέ and δ' ἄρα, δή after pronouns rarely serves to introduce a new *event*. Rather, it provides information about the internal or external *state* of the referent in focus: like the majority of ὅ(ς) ῥα instances, ὁ δή and ὃς δή introduce unframed discourse. Unlike ὅ(ς) ῥα, ὁ δή and ὃς δή introduce information about a referent that the speaker regards as inaccessible to the audience.[159]

§65. Since both anaphoric and relative pronouns most commonly occur in initial position, there are no instances of act-initial δή with scope over the act (function (1) in the list above) in this construction.[160] There is a link between the position of δή in the act and the scope of the particle: when δή occurs in peninitial position, it typically has scope at the minimum over the entire act, whereas in any other position its scope is more restricted, over only the following word. I first consider the instances where δή appears to have act scope. Since ὁ and ὅς δή are always at act beginning, however, the fact that δή occurs in second position does not exclude the possibility of mobile δή. After a discussion of the instances of δή with act scope, I explore the possibility of small-scope δή in some borderline instances. Finally, I show that sometimes the intensifying function of δή

156 However, whether to read a pronoun as relative or demonstrative is always a subjective decision to some extent.

157 ὁ δή occurs four times in the *Iliad* and five times in the *Odyssey*, ὃς δή eight and ten times, respectively. See my discussion of those four instances in §69 below; also compare the plural 3.134 οἳ δὴ νῦν.

158 About the latter combination, note Denniston 1950:123 "The particle which normally stresses a relative relation is δή."

159 In Pindar this pattern does not hold, as τὸν δή in *Pythian* 11.17 starts a little embedded narrative.

160 In fact, even καί sometimes abandons its strict initial position (with scope over the act) for the sake of a pronoun, see IV.2 §103.

reaches beyond the reported interaction between two characters (in direct speech), and touches instead upon the interaction between performer and audience.

§66. δή occurs with intensifying force over the act in instances when the speaker urgently wishes to underscore an assertion. In English, this is often best rendered by adding an intensifier to the verb phrase (as in t37).[161] This construction only occurs in direct speech in Homer. Consider the following exhortation by Ajax to the other Greeks:

(t37)

ἦ οὐκ ὀτρύνοντος ἀκούετε λαὸν ἅπαντα |
Ἕκτορος, | <u>ὃς δὴ</u> νῆας ἐνιπρῆσαι μενεαίνει;

Iliad 15.506-507

Do you not hear Hector encouraging all his people?
He is *fairly* raging to raze the ships!

The Trojans are at the wall, and Ajax does all he can to get the Greeks to fight back and keep them from the ships. His rhetorical question has a note of incredulity, and in the next utterance he vehemently adds some information that his audience apparently does not yet know. Although I do not see δή as directly connected to what is evident and visible, I do believe that some of the utterance's tone of insistence comes from the implication that the speaker directly perceives what he is claiming.[162]

§67. In ten or eleven instances of ὅς δή / ὁ δή[163] the particle modifies first and foremost the following adverb or adjective, and it is thus most likely to be unrelated to the preceding pronoun. This happens with forms of πολύς, for example in this passage from the *Odyssey*:[164]

[161] ὁ δή/ὅς δή (and because of its frequency I include neuter ὃ δή) with act scope is paralleled in *Iliad* 1.388 ὃ δὴ τετελεσμένος ἐστί (Achilleus about Agamemnon's threat), 2.436 ἔργον ὃ δὴ θεὸς ἐγγυαλίζει, 17.202 ἃ δείλ' οὐδέ τί τοι θάνατος καταθύμιός ἐστιν / ὃς δή τοι σχεδὸν εἶσι· (Zeus, as if to Hector); *Odyssey* 4.777 ἀλλ' ἄγε σιγῇ τοῖον ἀναστάντες τελέωμεν / μῦθον, ὃ δὴ καὶ πᾶσιν ἐνὶ φρεσὶν ἤραρεν ἡμῖν (Antinous about the suitors' plan), 10.514 Κώκυτός θ', ὃς δὴ Στυγὸς ὕδατός ἐστιν ἀπορρώξ (Circe to Odysseus), and 15.490 ἠπίου, ὃς δή τοι παρέχει βρῶσίν τε πόσιν τε. Compare Pindar *Isthmian* 2.27 τὰν δὴ καλέοισιν.

[162] See II.3.3.2n192 for scholars linking δή to perception or evidentiality. A similar link between δή and perception is drawn in III.2 §§73-79 for tragedy and comedy and in IV.4.5.2 for historiography.

[163] Ten or eleven depending on the reading of *Odyssey* 2.16.

[164] The parallels are *Iliad* 15.291 (ὃς δὴ πολλῶν), 2.117 (ὃς δὴ πολλάων), 9.24 (ὃς δὴ πολλάων). See II.3 §61n201 for more parallels of δὴ + πολύς and similar adjectives.

(t38)

δὴ τότε Φοῖνιξ ἦλθεν | ἀνὴρ ἀπατήλια εἰδώς, |
τρώκτης, | ὃς δὴ πολλὰ κάκ' ἀνθρώποισιν ἐώργει·

Odyssey 14.288-289

And at that moment a Phoenician arrived, a man skilled in wiles,
a greedy man, *who* had done *very many* evils to men.

This instance, like the majority of ὅς/ὁ δή instances, occurs in direct speech. Here Odysseus introduces a new character, a Phoenician (288), about whom he introduces several descriptions that his audience cannot yet know. One aspect of the "newness" inherent in relative clauses introduced by pronoun + δή is that it generally contains an expression of stance, a personal judgment or feeling of the speaker.[165]

§68. Similar is the use with superlatives (more frequent in historiography, see IV.4.6.2), which occurs twice in the *Iliad*, both in Aeneas' boast to Achilles:

(t39)

Δάρδανος αὖ τέκεθ' υἱὸν Ἐριχθόνιον βασιλῆα, |
ὃς δὴ ἀφνειότατος γένετο θνητῶν ἀνθρώπων· |
(...)
Ἶλός τ' Ἀσσάρακός τε | καὶ ἀντίθεος Γανυμήδης, |
ὃς δὴ κάλλιστος γένετο θνητῶν ἀνθρώπων·

Iliad 20.219-220, 233-234

Dardanus then begot a son, king Erichtonius,
who was *by far the richest* of mortal men.
(...)
Ilus, Assaracus, and god-like Ganymedes,
who was *by far the fairest* of mortal men.

Aeneas' intensified superlatives serve to strengthen his boast about his forefathers. The second of the two examples shows that the link between relative clauses introduced by δή and "new information" is relative. There can be no doubt that both the internal audience (Achilles) and the audience at the performance was expected to know that Ganymedes was the most beautiful man of all. However, the presence of δή here, rather than ἄρα or

[165] δὴ γάρ also often introduces personal viewpoints of some kind, see II.3 §62 and II.4 §19. For the concept of stance and for its relevance to the use of δή in Herodotus and Thucydides, see IV.4.4-6.

τε, presents the statement not so much as a foregone conclusion, but as an expression of a personal opinion, with a clear rhetorical goal.

§69. Finally, we find small-scope forward-oriented δή in four (or five) final instances in temporal expressions, where again δή serves to intensify the sense of the following word. Here Eumaeus speaks to Telemachus of his trip to the palace:

(t40)

ὡμήρησε δέ μοι παρ' ἑταίρων ἄγγελος ὠκύς, |
κῆρυξ, | ὃς δὴ πρῶτος ἔπος σῇ μητρὶ ἔειπεν.

Odyssey 16.468-469

There joined me a quick messenger from among your friends,
a herald, *who as the very first* gave word to your mother.

Here, as in all the parallels,[166] the intensified expression occurs in direct speech. In all instances, the scope of δή is ambiguous, but here at least there seems to be a reference to a specific earlier scene (335-341). Eumaeus and the herald sent by Telemachus arrive at the palace at the same time, and the herald gives his news first (337). It is for this reason, I believe, that δή intensifies πρῶτος here: to render precisely what happened.[167]

§70. Finally, there is an instance of ὅς δή that appears to strongly appeal to the visual imagination of the audience. In narrator text, the performer introduces Dolon, a character central to the upcoming narrative, and gives a vivid description:

(t41)

ἦν δέ τις ἐν Τρώεσσι | Δόλων Εὐμήδεος υἱὸς |
κήρυκος θείοιο πολύχρυσος πολύχαλκος, |
ὃς δή τοι | εἶδος μὲν ἔην κακός, | ἀλλὰ ποδώκης· |

Iliad 10.314-316

There was someone among the Trojans, Dolon son of Eumedes,
the godlike herald, rich in gold and rich in bronze.
And this guy—let me tell you—he was ugly of face, but quick of feet.

This is one of only two instances of δή τοι in narrator text, and one of the relatively few instances in Homer where τοι is clearly the particle rather than the dative second person

166 Parallels: *Iliad* 21.315 δὴ νῦν; *Odyssey* 1.49 δὴ δηθά and 2.48 δὴ τάχα; perhaps also Odyssey 2.16 δὴ γήραϊ κυφός "bowed through great age."

167 Compare the use of δή after τόσσον in *Iliad* 17.522, discussed in II.4 §§42-44.

pronoun. Just as in (t39), this piece of discourse introduces a character.[168] The difference is that the introduction here first mentions the father of the character in focus. The performer brings the attention back to Dolon with the priming act ὅς δή τοι.[169] The priming act also projects Dolon's importance in the upcoming long episode (316-457).[170] The presence of the particle τοι especially suggests that there may be one more factor at work in this passage. It is as if the performer turns to the audience and speaks to them directly, inviting them to imagine this Dolon, and to share the performer's opinion of him. Since it occurs in the priming act, I believe that δή may be regarded as having scope over the entire line, the entire description of this antagonist.

§71. Whether δή following an anaphoric pronoun has small scope or act scope, it generally introduces a subjective view of a character, either by another character or by the narrator. The difference between unframed discourse introduced by ὅς ῥα on the one hand and by ὁ δή and ὃς δή on the other can be put in the following terms: unframed discourse introduced by ὁ δή or ὃς δή contains information that the performer assumes to be as yet unavailable to the audience. As a result, the function of pronoun plus δή overlaps partly with that of γάρ introducing unframed discourse. In general, however, unframed discourse introduced by γάρ is more directly associated with the preceding discourse than that introduced by δή. The following passage from Pindar will serve as illustration:

(t42)

ἀπὸ Ταϋγέτου πεδαυγάζων | ἴδεν Λυγκεὺς | δρυὸς ἐν στελέχει |
ἡμένους. | <u>κείνου γὰρ</u> ἐπιχθονίων πάντων γένετ' ὀξύτατον
ὄμμα. | (...)

Pindar *Nemean* 10.61-63

Peering down from the Taugetus, Lynkeus saw them in the trunk of
an oak,
hidden. *For* of all the men on earth *his* was the sharpest
sight. (...)

[168] Compare also ὅς δή in *Odyssey* 7.156; the line recurs in *Odyssey* 11.343 (about the same character), but is there omitted by many manuscripts.

[169] The other instance is *Odyssey* 20.289, where ὅς δή τοι similarly forms a priming act, but where the visual component is not clearly present; Hainsworth 1993:186 notes the structural similarity of *Iliad* 10.314-318 and *Odyssey* 20.287-291.

[170] Book ten of the *Iliad* is often called the *Doloneia* after this episode; see e.g. Danek 1988, Dué and Ebbott 2010, and Alden in Finkelberg (ed.) 2011:I.216-217.

The use of γάρ after pronouns in both Homer and Pindar often introduces unframed discourse, as here.[171] γάρ introduces a fact about Lynkeus' sight, which is triggered by association with the preceding narrative. The difference between unframed discourse introduced by δή and γάρ is that δή typically introduces a personal judgment. This does not mean that γάρ cannot introduce a personal judgment, as δὴ γάρ in Homer illustrates (see II.4 §20). Unframed discourse introduced by ἄρα, conversely, is expressly presented as shared between performer and audience or between speaker and internal audience. The difference between ὅς ῥα on the one hand and ὁ/ὅς δή and ὁ/ὅς γάρ on the other may be represented quite well with the paraphrase "who of course" for ὅς ῥα and "who actually" for ὁ/ὅς δή and ὁ/ὅς γάρ.

5.4 Participant Tracking in a Pindaric Ode: *Isthmian* 2

§72. Whereas until now I have limited my analysis to ὅς and ὁ, the masculine singular demonstrative or relative pronoun in the nominative, for my study of *Isthmian* 2 I take a more inclusive approach. Pronouns, nouns, and verbs all serve the performer's efforts to guide the audience's attention. Within this overall process of participant tracking—that is, the cognitive process of monitoring which character is in focus and which others should be attended to—the specific role of particles bears close study. In mainstream commentaries, most entries concern nouns, adjectives, adverbs, and verbs. Moreover, the entries show a distinct focus on semantics over discourse progression or participant tracking.[172] This illustrates the point I make at the beginning of this chapter: participant tracking does not generally cause problems for comprehension. Nonetheless, the complex process of referring to people both inside and outside the direct performance context deserves close attention. In what follows I present a line-by-line commentary to Pindar's *Isthmian* 2 with a focus on referent tracking.

§73. The second *Isthmian* is a special victory ode. Unlike most other odes written for an athletic victory, *Isthmian* 2 is addressed for the most part to the victor Xenocrates' son Thrasyboulus. The reason for this appears to be the fact that by the time the song was composed, Xenocrates had already died. The exact context of the song has been debated, especially the questions of whether Pindar makes reference to the occasion of *Pythian* 6, an earlier victory ode for Xenocrates (probably at least twenty years before), and

[171] Compare in Homer for example *Odyssey* 17.256-257: αὐτίκα δ' εἴσω ἴεν, μετὰ δὲ μνηστῆρσι καθῖζεν,/ ἀντίον Εὐρυμάχου· τὸν γὰρ φιλέεσκε μάλιστα; "At once he went inside, and sat among the suitors, / across from Eurymachus; for him he liked most"; note especially the iterative φιλέεσκε which demonstrates the unframed nature of the act. The parallels in Pindar are *Olympian* 3.36, 6.25, 7.23, 9.28, 13.6; *Pythian* 4.281; *Nemean* 6.17; *Isthmian* 1.17.

[172] By way of example, in Verdenius' 1982 commentary on *Isthmian* 2 there are 138 lemmata, of which only 18 do not concern verbs, nouns, adjectives, or adverbs; 10 of these 18 lemmata concern particles. Out of the total 138, only 11 lemmata discuss problems concerning the referent of a (pro)noun or verb.

whether at that time Pindar and Thrasyboulus may have been romantically involved.[173] Finally, opinions differ on the question of date, with proposals ranging from 474 BCE to 471 BCE. If the song was composed and performed after 472, this means that Xenocrates' brother Theron would also have passed away, and the reign of the Emmenids at Akragas would have ended.[174]

§74. Before moving on to the running commentary, let me broadly sketch the developments of referents within the ode, and the juxtaposition of individual and collective. From the start of the performance, the first person refers most naturally to the performer—be it a singer or a chorus.[175] Behind that performer lies always the voice of Pindar, so first-person references will often have been ambiguous, possibly on purpose. In this song, Thrasyboulus is established as the main second-person referent immediately with a vocative in line 1. He is picked up again in the first epode, in a verb form, and the part of the discourse addressed directly to Thrasyboulus is rounded off in the second epode, with another vocative. Next, Pindar starts the third triad with a *gnṓmē*, which introduces an extensive eulogy of Xenocrates, addressed perhaps to the wider audience. If Thrasyboulus is here still to be understood as the second person, it no longer emerges in the language. The final epode reveals this implicit change, with a third-person imperative that has to refer to Thrasyboulus. This opens up the second-person slot for another referent, Nicasippus, whose identity remains unclear. It is typically reserved for the laudandus to be juxtaposed with Pindar in the final lines of the song, so whoever Nicasippus was, the very fact that he is referred to in the second person in the last epode strongly suggests that he was a person of some importance to Pindar, the laudandus, and/or the audience.

§75. With Thrasyboulus established as second person, Xenocrates—the actual victor—is automatically relegated to the third person. Since all referents besides the performer, Thrasyboulus, and Nicasippus occur in the third person, Pindar has to disambiguate every time he talks of Xenocrates. To that end the victor is introduced by name at the end of the first epode, which runs over thematically into the second strophe. Pindar describes his athletic victories, and Xenocrates remains in focus until the shift to his charioteer just before the end of the strophe. After rounding off the second triad, Pindar has to activate Xenocrates again by naming him, before launching into a praise of his virtuous life. The eulogy reaches a climax in the third antistrophe, where Xenocrates is really the only referent. Then at the beginning of the final epode the marker νυν brings the audience back to the here-and-now, and makes Xenocrates an unlikely referent for

173 Bury 1892a:26-37 offers an excellent introduction on the song's context. Bury believes that there may have been an amorous connection between Pindar and the young Thrasyboulus (33), but he is not followed by Privitera 1982:29 or Verdenius.

174 Bury 1892a:31 prefers the later date, Privitera 1982:27-28 the earlier; Verdenius 1982:1 proposes 472 BCE, but does not discuss the implications.

175 See II.1 §5 for the issue of the "I" persona in Pindar, and its relevance to questions of performance.

the third-person imperative. He moves to the background, referred to only as "the father of", and Thrasyboulus takes his place as the main third-person referent.

§76. Throughout the song we find juxtapositions of individuals and groups, both mortal and immortal, but in the end the central figures are individuals. Thus in the first strophe and antistrophe the Muses are first activated as a group, but later represented by the Muse Terpsichora. Even more clearly, in the second strophe two groups are adduced, but only to better demonstrate the κλέος of Xenocrates: he was a light for the Akragantines, and he pleased the Erechtheids.[176] After the praise of Nicomachus the charioteer, there is an interesting exception: Pindar links Ainesidamus' descendants, that is Xenocrates and his brothers, as a group to an Olympic victory. It seems likely that he is being purposefully vague since neither Xenocrates nor Thrasyboulus had been involved in this victory, but another of their clan. Finally, we find the townsmen and the gods mentioned as groups who were treated well by Xenocrates; again the collective serves as a foil for the praise of the individual.

§77. To sum up, the special nature of *Isthmian* 2 is reflected in the linguistic forms of anaphoric reference. Whereas the laudandus is typically in the second person, in this case it is an absent father in the third person who receives the most resounding words of praise. The son Thrasyboulus is the addressee in the first and second triads, but has to make way for the mysterious Nicasippus in the final epode. The first-person referent is embedded in the the here-and-now of the performance, and his linguistic presence is linked in particular to places where the song references the event. Thus besides in direct addresses to the second person we find the "I" in transitions and metanarrative statements.

§78. The text below visually highlights the elements of the discourse that guide the audience's referent tracking. Linguistic markers of frame switches are instrumental in this process, since a change of frame determines which referents are accessible. For this reason, I have marked not only act boundaries (|) but also frame shifts, marked with a double vertical bar (||).[177] All particles are in bold (also when combined with a negative). In green I have indicated all relative and demonstrative pronouns, including articles, as well as all pronouns, and nouns (including names) referring to characters outside or inside the discourse. The verb forms (finite verbs and participles) are also in green, when they are instrumental to participant tracking. These form the majority of the items discussed in the entries, but here and there I go slightly off topic in order to address an issue in the text or in current scholarship. After each metrical unit of strophe, antistrophe, or epode follows the translation, the list of referents, and then the commentary.

176 Athanassaki 2012:199 takes this presentation as emphasizing the audience's reaction to Xenocrates' and Nicomachus' athletic feats in the games.

177 Frame shift always coincides with move transitions, but there may be (and often are) multiple moves between frame shifts. In IV.3 §110, we use || to mark the boundaries between moves. Since the commentary concerns anaphoric reference, frame transitions are most important to mark.

(t43)

οἱ μὲν πάλαι, | ὦ Θρασύβουλε, | φῶτες, | οἳ χρυσαμπύκων
ἐς δίφρον Μοισᾶν ἔβαινον | κλυτᾷ φόρμιγγι συναντόμενοι, |
ῥίμφα παιδείους ἐτόξευον μελιγάρυας ὕμνους, |
ὅστις | ἐὼν καλὸς | εἶχεν Ἀφροδίτας
εὐθρόνου μνάστειραν ἁδίσταν ὀπώραν. ||

First strophe, 1-5

The ancients, Thrasyboulus, men who mounted
the chariot of the Muses with gold headbands, using the renowned lyre,
lightly shot honey-sounding hymns for boys.
Whoever, being beautiful, had
the sweetest bloom reminiscent of fair-throned Aphrodite.

Participants: the ancients, Thrasyboulus, the Muses, ὅστις, Aphrodite | 1-2 οἱ... ἔβαινον: The first line has οἱ and οἵ, the first demonstrative and the second relative. The placement of the vocative (Thrasyboulus, see §§74-75) between οἱ and φῶτες argues against reading οἱ as a definite article with φῶτες. This is supported by the fact that οἱ πάλαι on its own can mean "the ancients."[178] φῶτες οἵ...ἔβαινον should then be read in apposition to οἱ πάλαι. | 2-3 συναντόμενοι...ἐτόξευον: Subject continuity, frame continuity: null anaphor. | 4-5 ὅστις...ὀπώραν: New grammatical subject introduced at line beginning with the relative ὅστις. Change of subject is accommodated by a possible pause before and/or after the independent participial phrase ἐὼν καλός. The relation between lines 3 and 4 is close at the semantic level, but syntactically loose. The asyndetic beginning of line 4 suggests that 4-5 stand somewhat apart,[179] which complements the lack of a clear syntactic link. The semantic coherence of 1-3 and 4-5, however, is promoted by strophic contiguity, and there is no need to create a more integrated syntactical construction in the translation.[180]

(t44)

ἁ Μοῖσα γὰρ | οὐ φιλοκερδής πω τότ' ἦν | οὐδ' ἐργάτις· |
οὐδ' ἐπέρναντο γλυκεῖαι | μελιφθόγγου ποτὶ Τερψιχόρας |

[178] LSJ s.v. πάλαι I.2.

[179] See II.3 §§ 49-50 for asyndeton at move beginning.

[180] Bury, *ad* ὅστις: "The antecedent is παῖδες implied in παιδείους"; Race: "shot...at any boy who was beautiful"; Privitera 1982:35, "per chi era bello."

ἀργυρωθεῖσαι πρόσωπα μαλθακόφωνοι ἀοιδαί. |
νῦν δ’ ἐφίητι <τὸ> τὠργείου φυλάξαι |
ῥῆμ’ ἀλαθείας < ‿_ > ἄγχιστα βαῖνον, |

First antistrophe, 6-10

For the Muse, she was then not yet profit-loving, nor for hire.
Not yet were they sold by honey-voiced Terpsichora,
sweet songs with silvered faces and lovely voices.
And now she [sc. the Muse] commands us to heed that of the Argive
[sc. Aristodemus]
an adage that comes closest to <...> reality.[181]

Participants: the Muse, Terpsichora, the Argive (Aristodemus) | 6 ἁ Μοῖσα γάρ: New grammatical subject introduced through article and noun, separated from the following in a priming act. γάρ accompanies the switch of grammatical subject, and serves to expand on the Muses mentioned before (line 2). The topic of the "mercenary Muse" persists throughout the first antistrophe.[182] Although lines 6-8 appear to continue the frame of πάλαι based on the continuation of past tense, the string of negations foregrounds the current situation over the old. The discontinuity of orientation, of reference (the men of old are no longer in the frame), and the occurrence of γάρ all suggest that a frame switch co-occurs with the performative discontinuity of strophe end after line 5. | 7-8 γλυκεῖαι...ἀοιδαί: The grammatical subject of this passage is ἀοιδαί, but the logical subject is Terpsichora. | 9 νῦν δ’ ἐφίητι: Combined with the present tense, νῦν δέ marks a clear transition to the present. Commentators wish to see νῦν δέ as anwering the οἱ μέν πάλαι in line 1, but for the reasons given *ad* 6 I believe that the switch in orientation occurs between lines 5 and 6. On a more local level, νῦν interacts with τότε (6): the antistrophe concerns the Muse (announced in a priming act in 6), both in the past (τότε) and in the present (νῦν). Therefore I take the Muse as the subject of ἐφίητι. The anaphoric and cognitive continuity across line 8 and 9 suggests that there is no frame switch here. | 9 <τὸ> τὠργείου... βαῖνον: τό (conjectured) may be a demonstrative pronoun or an article. As in line 1, I read it as a demonstrative, with the following noun phrase ῥῆμα ... βαῖνον, as an appositive.[183]

[181] I follow the reading of line 10 suggested by Verdenius 1982:9.

[182] For a productive analysis of this passage, see Cairns 2011.

[183] For parallels of demonstrative τό followed by a genitive, yielding the meaning "that of..." or "that pertaining to...," see e.g. Euripides *Ion* 742 and *Trojan Women* 43.

(t45)

“χρήματα χρήματ’ ἀνήρ” | ὃς φᾶ κτεάνων θ’ ἅμα λειφθεὶς καὶ φίλων. ||
ἐσσὶ γὰρ ὦν σοφός· | οὐκ ἄγνωτ’ ἀείδω |
Ἰσθμίαν ἵπποισι νίκαν, ||
τὰν Ξενοκράτει Ποσειδάων ὀπάσαις, |
Δωρίων αὐτῷ στεφάνωμα κόμᾳ
πέμπεν ἀναδεῖσθαι σελίνων, |

First epode, 11-16

‘Means, means make the man’ says he who has been left by both possessions and friends.
You see, you are well-versed in song. Nothing unknown to you do I sing,
<I sing> the Isthmian chariot victory.
Having granted that <victory> to Xenokrates, Poseidon
sent a wreath of Dorian wild celery to him
to put over his hair,

Participants: a man, friends, Thrasyboulus, the “I” persona, Xenocrates, Poseidon | 11 ὃς φᾶ...φίλων: ὅς can be a relative or demonstrative pronoun. Although the relative pronoun can be postponed in Pindar (see II.2 §42n113), I do not follow Verdenius in reading it as postponed until after the quasi-direct speech here.[184] The performative discontinuity between antistrophe and epode is too strong for such a complex relative construction to be felicitous. ὅς is better read as demonstrative. Moreover, I do not think we should take ὅς as referring to Aristodemus here (the Argive, τὠργείου), but as indefinite. Of course there is room for ambiguity, so depending on the audience ὅς may be interpreted as either general or specific. | 12 ἐσσὶ...σοφός: The transition from generic discourse to the *hic et nunc* is immediately accomplished with ἐσσί. The interaction between performer and the specific addressee Thrasyboulus initiated with the vocative in line 1 is picked up again here. The role of γάρ and ὦν in the transition has vexed commentators. I do not have the answer, but there are several things we can establish with a reasonable degree of certainty: (1) γὰρ ὦν in Pindar is not like the cluster γὰρ ὦν in Herodotus, where it tends to follow resumptive pronouns;[185] (2) γάρ introduces some salient information

[184] Verdenius 1982:10.
[185] *Contra* Bury 1892a:42.

to the discourse model—even if the distinction framed/unframed may not be the most helpful in this non-narrative context; (3) ὦν in Pindar only occurs in combinations with other particles, which complicates the understanding of its function.[186] I have read γὰρ ὦν as establishing common ground: any relation with the preceding must be inferred in English, as it is in the Greek. | 12 οὐκ...ἀείδω: ἐσσί, a few words before, establishes the *hic et nunc* as the relevant frame, and by expressing the "you" it makes the "I" readily accessible: an act-final first-person verb with null anaphor thus creates no difficulty. If ἄγνωτ' is indeed to be read as ἄγνωτα, then it must be indefinite. Thus, it is an expansion of the thought expressed in the first part of line 12. | 14-17 τὰν...φάος: τάν is anaphoric, directly retrieving the νίκα of line 13. The change in grammatical subject and the ring construction in lines 14 to 17 (participial clause—main clause—participial clause) suggest that 14 should be taken with the following rather than the preceding verse; thus I have marked a frame switch just before 14. | 15 αὐτῷ: The anaphoric pronoun looks superfluous, since Xenocrates has already been established as the indirect object of the construction. Verdenius proposes that it is added "for the sake of clarity: it prevents us from connecting κόμᾳ with πέμπεν," but this explanation is insufficient. Rather, use of the pronoun may be connected to the fact that αὐτός here refers to the *recently deceased* Xenocrates. Whereas the participle concerning the victory is in the aorist (ὀπάσαις), πέμπεν is in the imperfect, suggesting a change in perspective. This change may be from the victory at the Isthmian games to the more current event of his death. The σέλινον was associated with death and sickness: "persons dangerously ill were said δεῖσθαι τοῦ σελίνου."[187] Pindar appears to combine this expression with that of crowning victors with σέλινον, to create a complex reference to the victory and to Xenocrates' death. It is in this context that we may reconsider αὐτός, which has a special relationship with the body of a hero as a deictic center.[188]

(t46)

εὐάρματον ἄνδρα γεραίρων, Ἀκραγαντίνων φάος. ||
ἐν Κρίσᾳ δ' εὐρυσθενὴς εἶδ' Ἀπόλλων νιν | πόρε τ' ἀγλαΐαν ||
καὶ τόθι | κλειναῖς Ἐρεχθειδᾶν χαρίτεσσιν ἀραρώς |
ταῖς λιπαραῖς ἐν Ἀθάναις, | οὐκ ἐμέμφθη

[186] Unlike for other particles, Hummel 1993:410 does not offer any explanation for ὦν in Pindar.

[187] LSJ s.v. σέλινον I.1.

[188] See Bonifazi 2012:141-143; Bury 1892a:43 also explains αὐτῷ with reference to Xenocrates' recent death, but rather because the wreath was intended for Xenocrates *himself*, but once it arrived he was no longer alive to receive it.

ῥυσίδιφρον χεῖρα πλαξίπποιο φωτός, |

Second strophe, 17-21

honoring the man who knows the chariot well, a light for the
Akragantines.
In Krisa mighty Apollo saw him, and gave him splendor.
And there, pleasing to the renowned favors of the Erechtheids,
in shining Athens,[189] he did not complain about
the chariot-saving hand of the horse-striking man,

Participants: Xenocrates, the Akragantines, Apollo, the Erechtheids, the charioteer | 18 ἐν Κρίσᾳ...νιν: There is a change of grammatical subject, introduced by a name (Ἀπόλλων); the tense returns to aorist (εἶδε, as ὀπάσαις), and the object (Xenocrates) remains the same and can be picked up with the enclitic νιν. | 18 πόρε τε: Subject continuity, frame continuity: null anaphor. τε adds an entire clause, generally called "sentential τε" or "consecutive τε." | 19 καὶ τόθι: There is discussion about whether this should be connected to the preceding (in which case τε is inserted after κλειναῖς): "And he [sc. Apollo] granted him glory, there too. And to the renowned..." or to the following: "And he [sc. Apollo] granted him glory. And there <he [sc. Xenocrates] was> pleasing to the renowned favors of the Erechtheids..."[190] Prior to answering the question of how καὶ τόθι should be constructed, we need to consider the referential transition. In the middle of a symmetrical construction about gods granting Xenocrates victories, Xenocrates is here made an agent and grammatical subject himself. This kind of transition is unlikely after τόθι, since τε with a participial clause and no other marker would strongly suggest subject continuity (there is subject continuity in lines 18, 25, and 38; in 23 the relative in the oblique projects subject change: ὅν τε). Therefore I propose keeping the reading of the manuscripts (without τε), as do Fennell, Dornseiff, and Thummer, and I take καὶ τόθι as a transitional priming act,[191] projecting "there" forward. Thus there are three contextual frames: one in the Isthmus (introduced by ['Ισθμίαν

[189] Pindar appears to denote Athens alternately with and without the article. The extant instances do not show a clear pattern; I have here not translated the article to avoid awkward English.

[190] Bury 1892a:44 reads καὶ τόθι as forward looking, but retains τε and says that "τ' connects τόθι and ταῖς λιπαραῖς ἐν 'Αθάναις ἀραρώς." He translates: "And, both there and in rich Athens..." He offers no parallels of this use of καί...τε in Pindar, and he appears to translate καί twice: both as a sentence connective ("And...") and as anticipating τε ("both..."); Hummel 1993:399 remarks that καί...τε only ever connects 3 items: X καί Y, Z τε.

[191] Privitera 1982:36 adopts καὶ τότε, but reads it like me as effecting a transition. His reading is attested only in a scholion, and I see no need for the emendation (*pace* Privitera 1982:161 who calls καὶ τόθι "grottesco").

νίκαν] τάν 14), one in Krisa (near Delphi, introduced by ἐν Κρίσᾳ δέ 17), and one in Athens (introduced by καὶ τόθι). That is to say, καί works *de dicto*, not *de re*. The reason for the variation in form may be that καὶ τόθι introduces a longer section of discourse, from line 19 to line 27. The length in turn may be because the Athenian victory was the most recent.[192] | 20 οὐκ ἐμέμφθη: The change in contextual frame effected by καὶ τόθι means by definition that there is a new pool of potential referents (there is no covert continuity across frame boundaries). In the preceding discourse, across the different frames, the only common element is Xenocrates. Therefore, he is the most accessible, and the only referent that can be retrieved with null anaphor (Ø ἐμέμφθη) at this point. | 21 φωτός: A new referent is introduced into the frame with a full noun and adjective. The full line devoted to introducing him—without naming him—at the end of the strophe projects his relevance into the antistrophe. φωτός thus works cataphorically: a name is expected and anticipated.

(t47)

τὰν Νικόμαχος κατὰ καιρὸν νεῖμ' ἁπάσαις ἁνίαις· |
ὄν τε καὶ κάρυκες ὡρᾶν ἀνέγνον, | σπονδοφόροι Κρονίδα
Ζηνὸς Ἀλεῖοι, | παθόντες πού τι φιλόξενον ἔργον· |
ἁδυπνόῳ τέ νιν ἀσπάζοντο φωνᾷ |
χρυσέας ἐν γούνασιν πίτνοντα Νίκας |

Second antistrophe, 22-26

that <hand> Nicomachus plied rightly to all the reins.
And him the heralds of the season also recognized, the truce-bearers of Cronus' son
Zeus from Elis; they had probably experienced some deed of hospitality.
And they welcomed him with sweetly breathing voice,
as he fell in the lap of golden Victory,

Participants: Nicomachus, the heralds from Elis, Zeus, Victory | 22 τάν Νικόμαχος: The relative only has one locally available referent: χεῖρ, and the name is automatically connected to the charioteer introduced in 21. His name at the very beginning of the antistrophe suggests that he will be its main topic (cf. ἁ Μοῖσα in line 6). | 23 ὅν τε: The pronoun retrieves the most accessible masculine referent: Nicomachus. Although τε occurs right after a relative

[192] Bury 1892a:30-31. Both Xenocrates' *Pythian* and *Isthmian* victories are mentioned in the 476
Olympian odes for Theron (*Olympian* 2 and 3), while his Athenian victory is not.

pronoun, it appears to be at least partly copulative, in a bisyndetic construction with the τε in line 25.[193] | 23 καὶ κάρυκες: καί should not be connected with τε, but has small scope over κάρυκες.[194] This can mean either: "the heralds, too" (as Privitera 1982:37), or καί can have a pinning-down function,[195] perhaps to be rendered through prosodic emphasis: "the HERalds." Since the introduction of the κάρυκες ὡρᾶν marks the transition to the Olympic games, "also" is not unfelicitous. | 24 παθόντες πού: The plural participle picks up κάρυκες, and I agree with Bury 1892a:45 that the aorist participle places παθόντες before ἀνέγνον in time.[196] που might serve to interact with the audience at the performance, if we follow Koier's argument that που with verbs of knowing marks something as shared between speaker and hearer.[197] Thus it serves to reinforce a sharedness in the praise of Nicomachus' hospitality. | 25 νιν: The enclitic pronoun marks continuity of object. | 26 πίτνοντα: Co-referential with νιν. Despite the semantic difficulties in this line (see Verdenius 1982:22), it is clear that the referent concerned is Nicomachus. | 26 Νίκα: This ode is only marginally concerned with an athletic victory, but Pindar still introduces personified Victory here. It is remarkable that the word Νίκα is so far separated from the names of Xenocrates and Thrasyboulus, and instead directly associated with the charioteer Nicomachus.

(t48)

γαῖαν ἀνὰ σφετέραν, || τὰν δὴ καλέοισιν Ὀλυμπίου Διός
ἄλσος· | ἵν' ἀθανάτοις Αἰνησιδάμου
παῖδες ἐν τιμαῖς ἔμιχθεν. ||
καὶ γὰρ οὐκ ἀγνῶτες ὑμῖν ἐντὶ δόμοι |
οὔτε κώμων, | ὦ Θρασύβουλ', | ἐρατῶν, |
οὔτε μελικόμπων ἀοιδᾶν. ||

Second epode, 27-32

in their land, which men actually call a sanctuary of Olympian
Zeus. There the descendants of Ainesidamus
joined in immortal honors.
And thus, your house is no stranger

[193] See II.4 §§58-61 about the rarity of so-called epic τε in Pindar.

[194] See II.4 §63 about τε καί in Pindar: it is never used as a combination with sentence scope (*pace* Thummer 1969:II.44 and Verdenius 1982:20).

[195] See IV.2.4.2 for this function of καί.

[196] Bury 1892a:45.

[197] See Koier 2013:258-259.

to either beloved revels, Thrasyboulus,
or to sweet-sounding songs.

Participants: the heralds, <men>, Zeus, Ainesidamus' descendants, Thrasyboulus | 27 γαὶαν... σφετέραν: Nicomachus won "in their land," σφετέραν still refers to the κάρυκες. | 27 τὰν δή: The pronoun followed by δή consistently marks a new beginning of some sort in Pindar.[198] Here it introduces unframed discourse, which allows for a new, generic referent "men."[199] The act introduced by τὰν δή resolves any possible ambiguity in the preceding passage, where Olympia has only been referred to obliquely. | 28-29 Αἰνησιδάμου παῖδες: The new grammatical subject is introduced by a full noun phrase. The re-introduction of the descendants of Ainesidamus (his sons Xenocrates and Theron, but including grandson Thrasyboulus too, I believe; see note *ad* ὑμῖν 30) also accommodates the upcoming return to the *hic et nunc*. Only Theron won at the Olympic games, so I would take it as a generic statement that the family gained honor at the games.[200] | 30 καὶ γάρ...δόμοι: γάρ introduces the return to the present, and is best left untranslated. I disagree with Verdenius and Thummer that καὶ γάρ should be taken as affirmative and that the transition should be read as an asyndeton.[201] γάρ serves precisely to mark the associative link between the preceding move about the past and the current move about the present, and as such has scope over the entire move; καί, conversely, has scope over the act only. | 30 ὑμῖν: The combination of ὑμῖν with the vocative Θρασύβουλε in the next line suggests that Pindar here takes all descendants of Ainesidamus together: Thrasyboulus, his father Xenocrates (deceased), and his uncle Theron (perhaps still alive). δόμοι "house," the grammatical subject in this move, reflects this inclusiveness.

(t49)

οὐ γὰρ πάγος | οὐδὲ προσάντης ἁ κέλευθος γίνεται, |
εἴ τις εὐδόξων ἐς ἀνδρῶν ἄγοι τιμὰς Ἑλικωνιάδων. ||

[198] In Pindar, δή occurs twice after a pronoun (here and in *Pythian* 11.17, I do not count *Olympian* 9.9 τὸ δή ποτε, since I believe that δή should there be taken with ποτε). In both cases it marks the introduction of a frame switch (into an embedded narrative at *Pythian* 11.17 and into unframed discourse at *Isthmian* 2.27). In *Pythian* 11.17 Pindar introduces the element that Arsinoe saved Orestes, which may have been an innovation by him. This could explain the intensification conveyed by δή.

[199] As Bury 1892a:45, against Verdenius 1982:22.

[200] Thummer 1969:II.45-46, Privitera 1982:162, and Verdenius 1982:23 believe it only refers to Xenocrates and Theron, and is purposely vague in order to imply that Xenocrates won at Olympia too.

[201] Thummer 1969:II.46 and Verdenius 1982:24.

μακρὰ δισκήσαις ἀκοντίσσαιμι τοσοῦθ’, | ὅσον ὀργάν
Ξεινοκράτης ὑπὲρ ἀνθρώπων γλυκεῖαν
ἔσχεν. || αἰδοῖος μὲν ἦν ἀστοῖς ὁμιλεῖν, |

Third strophe, 33-37

For there is no obstacle, nor is the road steep,
if one brings honors of the Heliconians to <the house> of famous men
Having thrown the discus far may I cast the javelin just as far, as
Xenocrates has a temperament sweeter than that of all other
men. He was respectful in dealing with his townsmen,

Participants: one (= the “I” persona), famous men, the Heliconian Muses, Xenocrates, men, townsmen | 33 οὐ γὰρ πάγος: γάρ is directly followed by a new grammatical subject, which cannot naturally be connected to the preceding move. In combination with the strong performative discontinuity between epode and strophe, this would probably have created the expectation of a frame switch. Only in the course of the following line does it become clear that γάρ introduces a gnomic reflection on the preceding. | 34 τις: The indefinite pronoun is only nominally indefinite: it refers generically to poets who sing the praises of good men, but at the same time specifically to Pindar himself singing the praises of Thrasyboulus’ clan.[202] | 34 τιμὰς Ἑλικωνιάδων: The “honors of the Heliconian muses” here stand for Pindar’s song. | 35 μακρά... ἀκοντίσσαιμι: The tightly knit combination of participle and finite verb directly projects an athletic image onto the poetic activity. The first-person verb places the act firmly in the *hic et nunc*, however metapoetic the comment may be. | 35-37 ὅσον...ἔσχεν: The athletic image leads into further praise of Xenocrates, who is introduced by a full name, and in an integrated construction. | 37 αἰδοῖος μέν ἦν: After the introduction in lines 35-36, a frame switch occurs in 37 with μέν and a switch from aorist to imperfect. μέν is used here, as often in Pindar, to project a topic (and a grammatical subject) across the performative boundary between strophe and antistrophe.[203]

(t50)

ἱπποτροφίας τε νομίζων ἐν Πανελλάνων νόμῳ· |
καὶ θεῶν δαῖτας προσέπτυκτο πάσας· | οὐδέ ποτε ξενίαν
οὖρος ἐμπνεύσαις ὑπέστειλ’ ἱστίον ἀμφὶ τράπεζαν· |

202 Bury 1892a:46 construes τις with Ἑλικωνιάδων.
203 See II.2 §55 and II.3 §73 with note 241 for more on this function of μέν.

ἀλλ' ἐπέρα | ποτὶ μὲν Φᾶσιν θερείαις, |
ἐν δὲ χειμῶνι πλέων Νείλου πρὸς ἀκτάν. ||

Third antistrophe, 38-42

practicing horsebreeding according to the Panhellenic ways,
and he welcomed all the feasts of the gods. And never did an
adverse wind furl his sail at his hospitable table;
no, he travelled on, toward Phasis in summer,
and in winter sailing to the shore of the Nile.

Participants: Xenocrates, the gods | 38 τε νομίζων: Without explicit marking to the contrary, τε suggests continuity of grammatical subject. | 39 καί: As in 19 (Ø, δέ, καί), καί introduces a third consecutive item: μέν, τε, καί.[204] | 39 οὐδέ ποτε: The linguistically more extensive transition introduces the fourth topic of hospitality, which will remain in focus until line 42. | 41-42 ἀλλά, μέν, δέ: The discourse progresses in clear steps. Because of constant subject continuity there are no (pro)nouns referring to the grammatical subject.

(t51)

μή νυν, || ὅτι φθονεραὶ θνατῶν φρένας ἀμφικρέμανται ἐλπίδες, ||
μήτ' ἀρετάν ποτε σιγάτω πατρῴαν, |
μηδὲ τούσδ' ὕμνους· || ἐπεί τοι
οὐκ ἐλινύσοντας αὐτοὺς ἐργασάμαν. ||
ταῦτα, | Νικάσιππ', | ἀπόνειμον, | ὅταν
ξεῖνον ἐμὸν ἠθαῖον ἔλθῃς.

Third epode, 43-48

Now may he not, since envious hopes surround the minds of men,
may he never be silent about his paternal virtue,
nor about these hymns. Since, you know,
I did not craft these to remain idle.
Give him this, Nicasippus, as his due, when
you come to my trusted guest-friend.

Participants: men, Thrasyboulus, Xenocrates, Nicasippus, the "I" persona | 43 μή νυν: Right after the discontinuity between antistrophe and epode we find νυν: even in its enclitic form it will have activated the *hic et nunc* after μή at the

204 Thummer 1969:II.49 adduces *Olympian* 4.14-16 for the exact same sequence of particles.

beginning of act, verse, and epode. | 43 ὅτι...ἐλπίδες: The unframed nature of this insertion gives it the sense of a parenthetical right after the beginning of the epode. The gnomic thought serves as a backdrop for the wish started by μή νυν. | 44 μήτε: The negative resumes the interrupted construction in 43, and τε is probably to be understood as anticipatory in some sense to the negatives at the start of the following two lines. | 44 σιγάτω: One of the hardest forms in the song as regards referent tracking. Xenocrates has been the grammatical subject throughout the last passage, but that is no longer the case after the strong discontinuity marked by μή νυν. As soon as the frame of the here and now is activated, the most accessible referents are the performer (first person) and the audience or Thrasyboulus (second person). There is no logical referent for the third person imperative σιγάτω, however, since the wish is unlikely to refer to the dead Xenocrates. On the basis of sense, all commentators read σιγάτω as referring to Thrasyboulus, albeit in the third person. Bury rightly notes that πατρῴαν immediately helps to disambiguate.[205] Verdenius suggests that the performer addresses Nicasippus from μή νυν onward (see the vocative in line 47).[206] This would certainly explain the shift to third person, and it may be supported by one more argument. Verdenius believes that ταῦτα refers to the present song,[207] but I believe Privitera rightly reads it as referring specifically to the two pieces of advice introduced by ταῦτα: "riferisci a Trasibulo questa mia raccomandazione di celebrare suo padre."[208] If ταῦτα indeed refers to these specific elements, then it is likely that the performer already turned (mentally or physically) to Nicasippus with μή νυν in line 43, and σιγάτω refers to Thrasyboulus. | 45 μηδέ: Perhaps the second limb of μήτε...μηδέ is indeed more poignant than the first.[209] This asymmetry appears to be corroborated by the following line, which expands on the hymns. | 45 ἐπεί τοι: As in line 43 (ὅτι), a causal conjunction introduces a motivation, in this case for the preceding wish. τοι must be the particle, since if it were the second person, it would only make sense if it referred to Thrasyboulus, which it cannot do here. | 46 αὐτούς: Since there is clear object continuity, Bury is probably right in regarding αὐτούς as implying a contrast with "other hymns."[210] | 47 Νικάσιππε: Whoever

[205] Bury 1892a:48.

[206] Verdenius 1982:34.

[207] Verdenius 1982:35.

[208] Privitera 1982:166.

[209] Compare Thummer 1969:II.53, "das μή wird aufgegliedert in μήτε...μηδέ"; Verdenius 1982:34 further adduces Denniston 1950:193 on οὔτε...οὐδέ "giving the effect of climax in the second limb."

[210] Bury 1892a:49; other commentaries do not discuss the pronoun.

this man was,[211] I believe his presence at the performance must be presupposed. If he was indeed a *khorēgós*, the last epode is apparently some kind of personal message. However, in performance the addressee of the chorus might then have been unclear to the audience. In any case, he must have been present at the occasion, and Nicasippus must have been an accessible referent for (the majority of) the audience. For σιγάτω to be easily understandable, a physical shift of gaze by the performer would have been helpful. I find it doubtful that Nicasippus was a mere professional of any kind: the position so close to the end of the song is extremely marked. | 48 ξεῖνον ἐμόν: The guest-friend must be Thrasyboulus, but the first-person reference is inherently ambiguous, referring at once to the composer Pindar and the current performer. The ambiguity may not have been felt by the audience at all, but a full understanding of the final expression depends again on the question of who Nicasippus was.

§79. Many of the passages discussed in the running commentary above may appear at first sight not to be problematic at all. However, it is my point to reveal how complex the process of referent tracking is, which normally works automatically in our minds as we read or listen. The focus in this section has not been to solve problems, but to attempt to explain why we have relatively few problems in following Pindar's discourse. Along the way, I have discussed more general problems with the second *Isthmian* from the perspective of anaphoric reference. The analysis only proposes an alternative road to solutions, arriving sometimes at conclusions similar to, sometimes different from, the commentaries. Finally, considering an entire discourse illustrates best how referent tracking and particle use mutually influence each other. Understanding better what particles do helps us to gain a fuller understanding of the process of reference tracking, and vice versa.

5.5 Conclusions

§80. In the discussion of particles that come after ὅς or ὁ in Homer, we must consider at least the following factors in order to perceive the relevant patterns. First, what is the exact referent of the anaphoric pronoun? That is, not its textual antecedent, but the mental representation of the referent at the moment that the pronoun is uttered. Second, does the anaphoric pronoun continue framed or unframed discourse, mark a transition from framed to unframed discourse, or a transition from unframed to framed? Third, who is the referent for the speaker or audience: is the referent present in the physical discourse context? Is there a particular emotional connection between speaker and referent? Does the referent have a particular relevance to the larger narrative or tradition? Do speaker and audience have the same referent in mind?

211 Bury 1892a:49 believes that Nicomachus was a *chorēgós*, and is followed by Thummer 1969:II.53, and Verdenius 1982:35; Privitera 1982:165 says that he was perhaps "just a messenger."

§81. As regards the difference between ὁ and ὅς, it is clear that they are used interchangeably in Homer. For both third-person pronouns the following pattern occurs: when ὁ/ὅς introduces framed discourse, all masculine singular referents within the frame are in principle accessible. When ὁ/ὅς introduces unframed discourse, conversely, the performer picks out one character who *must* be highly accessible: that is, the referent must be overt in the directly preceding discourse, typically as subject or as object. Therefore ὁ/ὅς introducing framed discourse more often marks change of grammatical (and logical) subject than ὁ/ὅς introducing unframed discourse.

§82. The different particles that follow the pronoun introduce very particular kinds of acts. ὁ δέ marks a continuation of framed discourse or a resumption of framed discourse after unframed discourse. The cluster ὅ γε can carry the force of γε to a greater or lesser extent, thus offering a functional continuum. At one end of the continuum ὅ γε serves to activate a referent who is completely or largely to be inferred, that is, who has not been expressed linguistically in the preceding discourse. At the other end, ὅ γε is indistinguishable from the anaphoric pronoun ὁ itself, serving particularly to retrieve or pin down the character currently in focus near discursive transitions. As for Homer, neither the numbers nor current understanding of the anaphoric pronoun justify the widespread belief that ὁ δέ marks change of grammatical subject, whereas ὅ γε serves to mark grammatical subject continuity.

§83. Both ἄρα and δή after anaphoric pronouns have commonly been described as lending emphasis to the pronoun.[212] In translations, in fact, their presence is often not reflected at all, particularly in Homer. Thus, these particles go undiscussed, and patterns of use have remained unstudied. In the sections above I have provided one possible way of describing the differences between the use of ὅ/ὅς ῥα and ὁ/ὃς δή. When it introduces unframed discourse, ὅ/ὅς ῥα accompanies a verb in the imperfect tense that imparts a piece of shared or expected knowledge about the referent. In framed discourse, conversely, a verb in the aorist typically follows ὅ/ὅς ῥα, describing an action that is either already known or logically expected. ὁ/ὃς δή in Homer always introduces unframed discourse, barring one instance, mostly in direct speech, and offers new information about a referent. Often the newness of the act lies in the fact that it is a personal reflection of some sort. It is this last aspect that sets ὁ/ὃς δή slightly apart from ὁ γάρ. This last combination also typically serves to introduce new information, but γάρ, unlike δή, betrays no particular personal involvement, and can therefore be used freely by the narrator as well as by internal speakers.

§84. Both the corpus study of particle use after anaphoric pronouns in Homer and the "anaphora commentary" to Pindar's *Second Isthmian* are meant as sorties into a huge field that has yet to be explored further. Building on the work of Bakker and

212 See also Ruijgh 1971:435, "Après tout, ἄρα a donc a peu près la même valeur que δή, particule qui est moins fréquente chez Homère."

Bonifazi I have attempted to demonstrate the importance of taking a discourse approach to anaphoric reference. Not only does this offer a deeper understanding of the process of anaphoric reference itself, but it provides a solid basis for better explaining certain aspects of difficult Homeric particles such as ἄρα and δή. The complexities of anaphoric pronouns are yet another element of discourse to take into account when searching for patterns of particle use in Homer and Pindar.

PART III

PARTICLE USE IN AESCHYLUS, SOPHOCLES, EURIPIDES, AND ARISTOPHANES

BY
ANNEMIEKE DRUMMEN

III.1
Introduction

§1. A number of similarities and differences between Attic drama and other parts of our corpus has naturally given rise to research questions and approaches that both converge and diverge. Tragedy and comedy share with Homeric epic and Pindaric song their poetic form and an original performative and ritual context. Dating from the fifth century BCE, these texts are close in time to the work of Pindar as well as Herodotus and Thucydides. With Thucydides the four playwrights share their Athenian background and thus features of culture and dialect.

§2. The corpus for this volume's research consists of a selection of three plays per author: Aeschylus' *Agamemnon*, *Libation Bearers*, and *Persians*; Sophocles' *Ajax*, *Antigone*, and *Oedipus King*; Euripides' *Bacchae*, *Hippolytus*, and *Medea*; and Aristophanes' *Birds*, *Frogs*, and *Lysistrata*.[1] These twelve plays are widely viewed as canonical: they are frequently read, studied, translated, and performed around the world. However, the upcoming chapters will occasionally adduce examples and parallels from other plays by the same authors as well. Since tragedy takes up the lion's share of my corpus, it will receive more attention than comedy in my discussion, but most observations based on tragic material have also been checked in the comic material. Every chapter includes examples from each of the four playwrights.

1.1 The Performative Context

§3. The dramas in the corpus were written for embodied performances, consisting of several actors and chorus members who moved, gestured, danced, spoke, and/or sang. Most important for my current examination, in their capacity as characters they

[1] Unless otherwise noted, the editions from the *Thesaurus Linguae Graecae Online* are used: Page 1972 for Aeschylus, Lloyd-Jones and Wilson 1990 for Sophocles, Diggle 1984 and 1994 for Euripides, Wilson 2007 for Aristophanes. The translations from the most recent Loeb editions are cited, unless indicated otherwise: for Aeschylus Sommerstein 2008a, 2008b; for Sophocles Lloyd-Jones 1997, 1998; for Euripides Kovacs 1998, 2001, 2002, 2005; for Aristophanes Henderson 1998a, 1998b, 2000, 2002.

interacted, verbally as well as nonverbally.[2] And of course, an audience was present at the performances to hear and see all of this.

§4. The performative context has many implications, three of which are especially relevant to the research in this part. First, the language used in the plays can be assumed to be closer to real spoken dialogue than texts that were written to be either read or performed entirely by a single performer or single group of performers. At the least, the process of turn-taking (several speakers taking turns-at-talk after one another) found in normal spoken conversation is still present in dramatic dialogue, even if it is obviously stylized.[3] Second, there are particularly salient and crucial differences among the parts of the plays. Dialogues, monologues, and lyric songs—the three main components of the plays—do not only differ in their metrical structures and linguistic features, but they were performed in fundamentally divergent ways, because of variation in the number of the speakers (one or more) and their type (character or chorus). This is considerably different for non-dramatic texts: although these may include passages of direct speech or variations in meter, they were continuously performed, or read, by one person or one group. This observation is related to a third point: while polyphony and multiple stances are regularly signaled implicitly in non-dramatic texts, in drama they are often explicitly present. That is to say, the utterances attributable to different (fictional) sources, i.e. the characters, were actually spoken by different actors embodying these characters.

§5. These preliminary observations make it clear that the tragedies and comedies of this part's corpus are approached as discourse[4] meant for performance, rather than as (later) texts that we happen to have available to read.[5] Even though the texts are all that remains from the performances of the fifth century BCE, this written language represents part of an originally multimodal event.[6]

§6. Recent literary and historical research has thrown light on various performative aspects of Classical drama. For example, costumes, masks, props, and gestures played a crucial role in the plot and meaning of tragedies.[7] Numerous studies, in addition, focus on

2 See I.1 §§12-17 on the connectedness of verbal and nonverbal communication.

3 See e.g. Schuren 2015 for a recent study on Euripides that takes turn-taking into account.

4 See I.1 §§12-21 for an introduction to the concept of discourse, and to our use of it in this monograph.

5 This general view on Greek drama has been common at least since Taplin's influential publications on tragedy (especially 1978 and 1989). See also e.g. Bain 1977 and Revermann 2006b (on drama generally), Foley 2003 (on tragedy), Budelmann 2000 (on Sophocles), Hesk 2007 (on Aristophanes). Meineck 2011 (on tragedy) combines this performative view with insights from neuroscience.

6 See also part II on particle use in Homer and Pindar, where the originally multimodal performance event of these poems is likewise emphasized. This basic approach is outlined in II.1.

7 On costumes in Euripides, see e.g. Worman 1999. On tragic masks, see e.g. Wiles 2007 and Meineck 2011. On props in tragedy, see e.g. Sommerstein 2010 (on Aeschylus) and Mueller 2015. On gestures in tragedy, see e.g. Csapo 2002, and Mueller 2011. On gestures in tragedy and comedy, see e.g. Boegehold 1999. On various methodologies for analyzing all these performative aspects

the fifth-century audience, in particular their theatrical competence,[8] and their response to the performances.[9] Tragedy and comedy also carry political significance in their original context.[10] Analyses of the plays' later reception often focus on performance as well.[11] The work presented in the current part is complementary to the research on all of these topics, in that the focus here is on the linguistic part of the dramatic performance.

1.2 Themes and Findings

§7. The specific contexts of the plays make certain pragmatic phenomena particularly relevant for linguistic analysis. The following chapters deal with four general phenomena that are related to analyze particle use. Let me illustrate these here with an example for each.

§8. First, the considerable situational differences among the various parts of the plays are connected to recurrent patterns of language use. III.2 accordingly discusses several linguistic tendencies in dialogues, monologues, and choral songs. Based on insights from Construction Grammar (see especially Östman 2005), the term "discourse patterns" is applied to describe and analyze these tendencies.

§9. For example, the particle τε turns out to be much more frequent in choral songs than in other parts of the plays. The following lyric excerpt from Euripides (see III.2 §41, (t8)) illustrates this phenomenon: the song contains more τε instances than is usual in tragedy.

(t1)

(Χο.) †οὐδὲ γὰρ ἐν† πόλεσι δίπτυχοι τυραννίδες
μιᾶς ἀμείνονες φέρειν,
ἄχθος τ' ἐπ' ἄχθει καὶ στάσιν πολίταις·
τεκόντοιν θ' ὕμνον ἐργάταιν δυοῖν
ἔριν Μοῦσαι φιλοῦσι κραίνειν.

Euripides' *Andromache* 471-477

---

in tragedy, see e.g. Powers 2014. On comic masks, see e.g. Wiles 2008. On several performative aspects in Aristophanes, see e.g. Slater 2002 and Revermann 2006a.

8 See Revermann 2006b.

9 See e.g. Gruber 1986 on the audience response to Aristophanic and other comedies; Ruffell 2008 on audience response to Greek drama in general.

10 See e.g. Goldhill 2000 on tragedy and comedy; Slater 2002 on Aristophanes; Carter 2007 on tragedy; Sommerstein 2010 on Aeschylus.

11 On modern performances of tragedy, see e.g. McDonald 1992; Foley 1999; Meineck 2013 (specifically on the chorus). On modern performances of Aristophanic comedy, see e.g. Van Steen 2000, and papers in Hall and Wrigley 2007 (eds.).

> (Ch.) For cities, likewise, double kingship is worse than single to endure, grief piled on grief for the citizens and the cause of faction. When two poets produce a hymn, the Muses are wont to work strife between them.

On the one hand, τε does have one clear syntactic function which operates in virtually all cases in the drama corpus, and that is the connective one. On the other, this single, widespread function does not adequately explain why τε's distribution over different kinds of discourse in the plays is variable. That is to say, the variation in the distribution is significant enough to require an explanation. Apart from signaling a connection, τε must provide another pragmatic contribution to the discourse. III.2 discusses this contribution, which is connected to shared encyclopedic and cultural knowledge. The chapter presents analyses of eleven particles with this approach, using distribution as input for interpretation.

§10. The prominence of dialogue in the plays provides an excellent opportunity to consider how speakers build on the words of previous speakers. The ways in which speakers explicitly and implicitly refer to other speakers' utterances fall within the domain of dialogic syntax, a recently developed linguistic framework (see Du Bois 2014). If speakers deliberately stress certain similarities between their utterance and previous ones, we can speak of "resonance"—the pragmatic phenomenon that III.3 delves into. The highlighted similarities may be lexical, semantic, syntactic, morphological, phonological, metrical, and/or pragmatic. Playwrights may use such resonance for goals that lie beyond the specific interaction of the characters, such as stressing a main theme of a play.

§11. Particles may indicate how a speaker uses such resonance. Consider the following Sophoclean passage (see III.3 §81, (t16)):

(t2)

> Με. ἤδη ποτ' εἶδον ἄνδρ' ἐγὼ γλώσσῃ θρασὺν
> ναύτας ἐφορμήσαντα χειμῶνος τὸ πλεῖν,
> ᾧ φθέγμ' ἂν οὐκ ἐνηῦρες, ἡνίκ' ἐν κακῷ
> χειμῶνος εἴχετ',
> (...)
> Τευ. ἐγὼ δέ γ' ἄνδρ' ὄπωπα μωρίας πλέων,
> ὃς ἐν κακοῖς ὕβριζε τοῖσι τῶν πέλας.

Part of Sophocles' *Ajax* 1142-1151

> Me. In the past I have seen a man of reckless speech urging sailors to sail during a storm. But one heard no word from him when he was in the grip of the storm's attack; (...)

Te. And I have seen a man full of stupidity, who harried others in their time of troubles.

In his reply to Menelaus, Teucer echoes the other man's linguistic construction ("I have seen a man…").[12] The particle combination δέ γε clarifies how the speaker intends this echo to be understood: as a hostile new step in the discourse, in reaction to the previous insult. The two particles occur together several times in pragmatically similar contexts.

§12. III.4 applies the framework of Conversation Analysis. Recent scholarship has identified many regularities in modern talk-in-interaction. A close look at the stylized dialogues in tragedy and comedy reveals that such general patterns play a role there as well. The use of certain particles is clearly related to turn-taking strategies, conversational structure, and the communicative actions performed by turns of speaking.

§13. An example is the use of δέ—a particle that marks discourse boundaries of various kinds—at the beginning of a turn. When δέ is in turn-initial position, the directly preceding change of speaker already establishes that a new unit has just started, namely a new turn of speaking. The particle therefore marks a specific discourse boundary in this initial position. The following Aeschylean dialogue (see III.4 §§34-36, (t8)) contains a case in point:

(t3)

Δα. τίνι τρόπωι; λοιμοῦ τις ἦλθε σκηπτὸς ἢ στάσις πόλει;
Βα. οὐδαμῶς, ἀλλ' ἀμφ' Ἀθήνας πᾶς κατέφθαρται στρατός.
Δα. τίς δ' ἐμῶν ἐκεῖσε παίδων ἐστρατηλάτει, φράσον.
Βα. θούριος Ξέρξης, κενώσας πᾶσαν ἠπείρου πλάκα.

Aeschylus' *Persians* 715-718

Da. How has it happened? Has our state been stricken by a virulent plague, or by civil strife?
Qu. Not at all; what has happened is that our entire army has been destroyed in the region of Athens.
Da. And tell me, which of my sons led the army there?
Qu. The bold Xerxes; he emptied the whole expanse of the continent.

δέ in this environment marks its host turn as the first part of a new question-answer pair within a series of such pairs. That is, the particle combines with the signal conveyed by

[12] Throughout the chapters, formulations such as "Teucer says to Menelaus" are used as convenient shorthands for those such as "Sophocles writes as Teucer's utterance" or "the audience will have heard the actor performing Teucer say to the actor performing Menelaus."

the conversational structure, in order to indicate how the turn is intended to fit into its surrounding co-text. III.4 analyzes this and similar relations between particle use and conversational phenomena.

§14. Another phenomenon especially relevant in multi-party discourse is the linguistic reflection of emotional states of mind. This process usually involves several verbal and nonverbal signals at the same time. Clues about the play's plot and semantic or syntactic patterns are used in III.5 to detect how particle use relates to calmness, agitation, and the specific agitated state of anger.

§15. In the dialogue from Aristophanes cited in (t4) (see III.5 §§57-58, (t12)), for example, several cues make it clear that the two speakers are angry:

(t4)

556bis Πα. οὐ μὲν οὖν με προσεδόκας,
557 ὁτιὴ κοθόρνους εἶχες, ἀναγνῶναί σ' ἔτι;
τί δαί; τὸ πολὺ τάριχος οὐκ εἴρηκά πω.
Πλ. μὰ Δί' οὐδὲ τὸν τυρόν γε τὸν χλωρόν, τάλαν,
560 ὃν οὗτος αὐτοῖς τοῖς ταλάροις κατήσθιεν.

Aristophanes' *Frogs* 556bis-560

Innkeeper. Hah! You didn't think I'd recognize you again with those buskins on. Well? I haven't even mentioned all that fish yet.

Plathane. Right, dearie, or the fresh cheese that he ate up, baskets and all.

γε is particularly frequent in contexts like this one. III.5 explains the connection of this particle to certain affective environments. In general, the chapter illuminates how particles can contribute to expressions of calmness or agitation without ever being the only signs of a particular feeling.

§16. The analysis of how particle use relates to several pragmatic phenomena in dramatic texts provides new tools for understanding particles.[13] The approach taken

[13] Several of these phenomena are also linguistically analyzed, albeit usually without an explicitly pragmatic framework, by e.g. Hancock 1917 on stichomythia in tragedy and other genres; Werres 1936 on swearing expressions in Aristophanes; Earp 1944 on the style of Sophocles, and 1948 on the style of Aeschylus; Ireland 1974 on stichomythia in Aeschylus; Stevens 1976 on colloquial expressions in Euripides; Mastronarde 1979 on contact among tragic characters; Stanford 1983 on emotions in tragedy; Pfeiffer-Petersen 1996 on repetition in Sophocles; Kloss 2001 on pragmatic humor in the language of Aristophanes; J. Barrett 2002 on tragic messenger speeches; Van Wolferen 2003 on Euripidean prologues; R.J. Allan 2009 on narrative modes in Euripides; Van Emde Boas 2010 and 2017b on conversational phenomena in Euripides; Willi 2010a on register variation in drama and other genres; Goldhill 2012 on the language of Sophocles; Rutherford

here makes it possible to explain not only the pragmatic functions of certain particles, but also why they occur in the particular co-texts and contexts they do.

§17. A better understanding of particles, in turn, leads to a stronger basis for interpreting dramatic texts. Taking into account the distribution of particles across different kinds of discourse enables a reader to notice when a certain particle is in fact peculiar to its context, a realization that affects interpretation. For example, the presence of τε in stichomythia, where it is atypical, may carry a sense of solemnity (see III.2). Similarly, sensitivity to a speaker or writer's uses of resonance and the role of particles within this strategy illuminates content. By considering the presence of certain particles or particle combinations together with resonating elements in an utterance, we may better appreciate how, for example, an utterance works as an insult or sarcastic joke (see III.3). Further, examining particle use in relation to conversational features helps explain the communicative actions of characters. Particles may for instance signal that a speaker wants to keep the floor. Even the fictional language of Greek drama shows that dialogues are constructed jointly by several speakers (see III.4). Finally, characters' emotional states of mind are connected to the ways in which they structure their discourse. This includes patterns of particle use, even though particles do not directly indicate specific emotions (see III.5).

§18. In sum, particles were crucial to the communicative strategies that the fictional characters represented on stage used to interact with each other, as well as to the strategies used by the authors themselves to communicate with their original fifth-century audiences. If viewed through the analytic tools offered here, particles can once again be of aid to the modern readers of these fascinating literary works.

2012 on tragic language; and Schuren 2015 on Euripidean stichomythia. These works contain remarks on particle use, but this is not their main focus.

III.2

Varying One's Speech

Discourse Patterns

2.1 Introduction

§1. Every speaker is familiar with the use of different varieties of her language for different communicative situations. The language we encounter and use varies, for example, when we are talking to friends, reading a newspaper, or writing an article. In other words, many linguistic choices depend on the communicative situation.[1] Linguistic variation based on situational context has been the subject of the fields of register studies and Construction Grammar, which have developed the concepts of "register" and "discourse pattern." In this chapter I will build on this research to explore particle use in Greek drama.

§2. I will argue that dialogues, monologues, and choral songs in Greek drama may be considered discourse patterns—that is, conventional pairings of certain functional and formal characteristics. Because of the differences in these characteristics, a particle's distribution across the three discourse patterns illuminates its functions and uses. If a particle is usually more frequent in one discourse pattern rather than another, this means that it is connected to specific pragmatic goals associated with that discourse pattern. Consequently, the non-random distributions of particles contribute to the interpretation of their functions: macro-pragmatics illuminates the micro-pragmatics of particles' local functions. My analysis in this way refines specific readings of particles, and at the same time highlights pragmatic characteristics of each discourse pattern, which inform, and are informed by, the use of linguistic features other than particles as well. We shall see that the distributions differ widely across the particles, and that each particle has different associations that explain why it is more or less frequent in a certain situation.

1 On the fundamental dependency of linguistic choices on communicative situations, see, among many others, Schegloff, Ochs, and Thompson 1996 (they speak of "the thoroughgoing situatedness of language's observable engagement with the world," 26); Linell 2009 (e.g. 16: "sense-making processes and situated discourse are *always* interdependent with contexts." [emphasis original]).

Accordingly a variety of topics, such as shared knowledge, the speaker's prominence, and allusions to other genres, will play a role in my explanations.

§3. I begin by introducing the concepts of "discourse pattern" and "register" (§§4-9), and then discuss previous research on linguistic variation in Greek drama (§§10-15), and situate my analytical method within the scholarship (§§16-21). The main part of the chapter (§§22-89) discusses the distributions of eleven particles (ἀλλά, γάρ, γε, δέ, δή, δῆτα, ἦ, καί, μέν, οὖν, and τε) in order of their frequencies, and uses these distributions as input for interpretation. In other words, I will argue that analyzing dialogues, monologues, and choral songs as discourse patterns sheds light on the use of linguistic features such as particles. §§90-95 present the chapter's conclusions. Finally, an appendix (§96) gives the particle distributions that were found to be statistically non-significant.

2.1.1 Theoretical background: Discourse patterns and registers

§4. Scholars who study discourse patterns or registers aim to learn about the interrelation between situational and linguistic variation. The situational variation includes, in the case of different formats within tragedy or comedy, sub-situations within one larger situation. The term "discourse pattern" was developed in Construction Grammar (CxG), a cognitive approach to language use. This approach assumes that all the linguistic knowledge of speakers and writers is stored in symbolic pairings of form and meaning, called "constructions."[2] The form can be anything, from a morpheme to a word, a phrase, a sentence, or an intonation pattern. Like the form, the meaning may also be as specific or abstract as the construction in question requires. Examples of constructions that have been studied from this perspective are the classical Greek potential optative, and pragmatic particles in several languages.[3]

§5. Östman 2005 argues that even whole texts, such as recipes, novels, or conversations, should be considered constructions, because their general make-up is part of the linguistic knowledge of speakers and writers.[4] That is, speakers and writers know which

2 See e.g. Croft and Cruse 2004; Hoffmann and Trousdale (eds.) 2013 for general overviews of CxG; see also I.3 §§41-51.

3 On the classical Greek potential optative, see Drummen 2013a; on pragmatic particles, see e.g. Fischer 2010 (on English); Fried 2009 (on Czech); Fried and Östman 2005 (on Czech and Solv, a Swedish dialect spoken in Finland).

4 In his 2005 article, Östman builds on his 1999 article, in which he introduces the cognitive concept of discourse pattern but does not elaborate on its possible link to Construction Grammar. Leino and Östman 2005 use the notion of discourse pattern to describe several forms of linguistic variation from a CxG perspective. Östman and Trousdale 2013 discuss the use of discourse patterns within a broader attempt to describe several kinds of linguistic variety in a CxG framework. Antonopoulou and Nikiforidou 2011 apply Östman's concept of discourse pattern to an analysis of discoursal incongruity, which may have humorous effects. For example, when formal features that are part of the discourse patterns "classroom discourse" or "philological text edition," such as footnotes, are taken over in a different context, the borrowing may signal a parody of the genre of origin. In a related way but more generally, Hollmann 2013

specific forms are allowed and appropriate in which kinds of text. An entire text, Östman argues, can thus be one construction, with a "form" pole and a "meaning" pole. He calls these large constructions "discourse patterns": they are "conventionalized associations between text type and genre" (132), just as constructions are conventionalized form-meaning pairings. What is acceptable as a whole text, he argues (127), is subject to similar conventionalizations as what is grammatical as a sentence.

§6. The form pole, called "text type" by Östman, is highly general, and much less filled in with specific words and forms than a small construction such as a word or a phrase. It includes information about the relative frequency of linguistic features, in comparison to other discourse patterns. The meaning pole, which Östman calls "genre,"[5] is also general: it can be a designation such as "an academic article," "a recipe," or, we may infer, "an Aristophanic lyric song." The broad, overarching meaning is not derivable from the parts of the construction, such as a high frequency of nouns, imperatives, or a certain particle.

§7. The concept of discourse pattern is very close to the concept of "register," a language variation depending on the communicative situation.[6] Halliday 1978 argues that registers mainly differ semantically; their lexicogrammatical differences derive from these semantic differences.[7] Similarly, Agha 2001:212 defines a register as "a linguistic repertoire that is associated, culture internally, with particular social practices and with persons who engage in such practices." A main method developed in register studies, which are part of sociolinguistics, is to study the co-occurrence patterns of linguistic features in different texts.[8] Co-occurrence tendencies tell us something about the functions of the counted linguistic features, for "co-occurrence reflects shared function."[9]

---

argues that cognitive linguistics, such as CxG, should include social factors in its analysis. He cites examples of constructions in several languages whose use is constrained or determined by social factors.

Note that the main goal of Östman 2005 in identifying discourse patterns is not to find genre-based constraints on the use of specific, local constructions; for that kind of analysis see e.g., concerning different languages, Matsumoto 2010 and Nikiforidou 2010 (who both cite Östman 2005; Nikiforidou explicitly describes her own research as different), and Ruppenhofer and Michaelis 2010 (who do not refer to Östman). Those articles, then, do not intend to describe entire genres or text types as constructions.

5 Note that the term "genre" is used in a different way in this monograph, that is, to refer to established literary genres, such as epic, tragedy, and historiography. See I.1 §2. On the dynamic nature of this concept, see e.g. Nagy 1999, who argues that genre is not an absolute concept, but different genres are interdependent; likewise Mastronarde 2000, who argues that a genre such as tragedy is a moving, not a frozen form.

6 On registers and register variation, see e.g. Agha 2001; Biber 1994, 1995, 2006, 2010; Biber, Conrad, and Reppen 1998; Conrad and Biber (eds.) 2001; Dittmar 2010; Halliday 1978; Quaglio 2009.

7 Halliday 1978:185.

8 See e.g. Biber, Conrad, and Reppen 1998.

9 See e.g. Biber 1994:36; 2006:178; Biber, Conrad, and Reppen 1998:147; Conrad and Biber (eds.) 2001:6.

§8. Furthermore, register studies provide evidence for different dimensions of variation in order to interpret the co-occurrence patterns. These dimensions have both linguistic and functional content: they are sets of co-occurring linguistic features that can be tied to a certain communicative aspect, such as the degree of formality or narrativity.[10] For example, a high frequency of first- and second-person pronouns, imperatives, questions, and a low frequency of nouns typically co-occur in certain English registers, such as informal conversation. These linguistic characteristics belong to the same dimension of variation; together they indicate high involvement of the speaker, and little time for speech production. Other dimensions concern, for example, narrative versus non-narrative discourse, or the presence of an impersonal style.

§9. The terminology used in register studies is not always clearly defined. In particular, researchers use the term "register" to refer to extralinguistic, situational characteristics, or to linguistic co-occurrence patterns, or to the combination of both. In other words, it is ambiguous whether form, meaning, or both are included in "register." As Lee 2001 and Sampson 1997 point out, there is much terminological confusion in the scholarly literature about terms such as "genre," "register," and "text type": different authors use these terms in a different way, without clearly distinguishing between them.[11] Lee 2001 attempts a clarification: he notes that "genre" is sometimes set in opposition to "text type," with "genre" referring to criteria external to the text (such as the audience and nonverbal activity), and "text type" referring to internal criteria (such as lexical and grammatical co-occurring features). Additionally, he observes, "genre" tends to be associated with social purposes of language, while "register" tends to be associated with the situation or immediate context. Despite Lee's efforts to clarify, however, "genre," "register," and "text type" are often used interchangeably. Östman's term "discourse pattern" is problematic as well, since he uses the poorly defined terms "text type" and "genre" to define it. However, it is clear that "discourse pattern" includes both form and meaning. Because of this clarity, I employ the term "discourse pattern" rather than "register" in this chapter.[12]

10 See e.g. Biber 1988:*passim*; 1994:35-36; Biber, Conrad, and Reppen 1998:148. Willi 2010a:309, on ancient Greek registers, also discusses multidimensional analysis.

11 Lee 2001 and Sampson 1997 do not include Construction Grammar in their discussion; even though Östman 2005 uses the terms "genre" and "text type," they are not frequent within Construction Grammar.

12 What I am not exploring here are related concepts such as key words (for which see e.g. Scott and Tribble 2006), formulaic language, as investigated in modern languages (for which see e.g. Corrigan, Moravcsik, Ouali, and Wheatley (eds.) 2009, Wray and Perkins 2000), and discourse modes (for which see e.g. Smith 2003 on English; Adema 2007 on Virgil; R.J. Allan 2007 on Thucydides; 2009 on Euripides). The investigation of key words tends to focus on (clusters of) words only, not on grammatical features or the co-occurrence of several features. Studies of key words therefore do not aim to give an overview of the linguistic differences between language varieties. The study of formulaic language (not to be confused with Homeric formulae) concerns expressions that are restricted in form and in distribution (Corrigan *et al.* 2009: xv). The aim of

2.1.2 Research on linguistic variation in ancient Greek drama

§10. Linguistic variation in Greek drama has been studied from different perspectives using different terminology. For example, Earp discusses several aspects of style in two monographs, one written in 1944 on Sophocles, and the other in 1948 on Aeschylus.[13] The major stylistic difference he identifies is between "elevated" and "colloquial" style.[14] Earp describes several factors that influence differences in frequency and use of associated linguistic features. One factor is time: because Aeschylus and Sophocles developed their styles over the course of their careers, fewer ornamental epithets appear in the later Aeschylean plays than in the earlier ones, and similarly the use of amplification declines in Sophocles. Two other factors influencing stylistic difference are a play's subject matter and the purpose of each individual scene. Earp finds that "intense emotion leaves little room for conventional ornament" in Aeschylus (1948:57), and that Sophocles uses antithesis mainly in argumentative contexts (1944:95).[15] Perhaps the most important factor is the difference between lyric parts and what Earp calls "dialogue," i.e. all non-sung parts. "Ornament" and other "elevated" features are more frequent in lyric, "for the same mood which impels us to sing impels us also to use heightened language" (1948:78). Even though Earp does not pay attention to particle use, here and in many other places he shows great sensitivity to the influence of external factors, such as communicative situation and a speaker's goals, upon language variation.[16]

§11. Other scholars note similar linguistic tendencies, though without analyzing as many details as Earp does. Examples are Ruijgh 1971:988-989, H.J. Dik 2007:6, and Rutherford 2010:441, 443-444, who draw attention to the linguistic differences between lyric and iambic parts of tragedies. According to Ruijgh, the non-sung parts are mainly based on contemporary Attic, whereas the sung parts are strongly modeled on choral lyric, usually from different dialects. Baechle 2007 provides metrical and prosodic evidence for the similar claim that "the tragedians had a very highly developed sense of

this research on formulae is to analyze their frequency, distribution, change, acquisition, use, explanations, and functions. That is, it focuses on several aspects of specific formulae, rather than on entire language varieties in different situations. Discourse modes or narrative modes are very similar concepts to discourse patterns. However, discourse modes are linguistic units, close to the concept of "text type" as used by Östman. They are mainly identified by the patterns of linguistic features found; discourse patterns and registers, in contrast, are identified first by the communicative situation, after which their linguistic shape is investigated.

13 Earp does not define "style" precisely, but his use of this term roughly equals the use of "register" in later research.

14 On colloquialisms in tragedy, see also Stevens 1976 on Euripides, West 1990 on Aeschylus, and Halla-aho and Kruschwitz 2010 on early Roman tragedy.

15 Concerning antithesis in tragedy, Finley 1939:57-59 argues that Sophocles and Euripides were both influenced by the antithetical style of the sophists. Sophocles *Antigone*, Finley claims (58), is "in style the most antithetical (...) of all extant Greek tragedies." This play therefore shows the influence of prose style on Sophocles. See also Navarre 1900:106 on antithesis in tragedy.

16 For recent discussion of different styles in tragedy, see e.g. Rutherford 2010 and 2012.

what style was appropriate to dialogue, as opposed to tragic lyric" (4). Rutherford 2010 juxtaposes a lyric passage, an excerpt from a long *rhesis*, and a stichomythic passage, in order to illustrate the main "modes" (448) of tragic language. Barlow 1971, a study on imagery in Euripides, emphasizes different distinctions: this author includes separate discussions of (1) choral odes, (2) monody and lyric dialogue, (3) messenger speeches, and (4) *rheseis* and iambic dialogues. She notes for example that the two lyric "modes" employ an "elevated tone" (43).

§12. With a different perspective, Sideras 1971 demonstrates that Aeschylus employs many Homerisms, in lexicon, syntax, morphology, word order, and rhetorical figures.[17] Sideras does not mention particle use, but we will see in this chapter that also in that domain Aeschylus resembles Homer more than the other tragedians. Stevens 1976, furthermore, discusses "colloquialisms" in Euripides, using other genres, mainly Aristophanes, as evidence that certain expressions, including specific particle constructions, were felt as "colloquial."[18] With this term he means less suited for "poetic," "prosaic," or "neutral" language (2). However, as he admits (64), most of these expressions are not frequent enough to provide statistically significant information about their distributions, and the effect of different expressions varies. On top of that, any classification of certain features as colloquial involves a certain degree of subjectivity, as e.g. Collard 2005:358 points out.

§13. Concerning Aristophanes, likewise, Dover 1972 notes the linguistic differences between lyric and iambic parts. Lyric passages share vocabulary with "the serious lyrics of tragedy," but are still more similar to comic dialogue, even though "the expression is more concentrated" (71).[19] In other words, we may infer, lyric parts are generally more concerned with *what* is said, and *how*, than iambic parts, and less with *who* is saying it to *whom*. Comedy as a whole, Dover argues, "combines all the registers of Greek utterance which are known to us: at one extreme a solemnity evocative of heroic warfare and gorgeous processionals, at the other a vulgarity inadmissible in polite intercourse" (72).

§14. Willi's exploration of "registers" in classical Greek (2010a) is an important precedent to the current study.[20] The author builds upon register studies in order to analyze linguistic differences across Greek (parts of) texts in a detailed manner. He undertakes a

17 On linguistic and other similarities between Aeschylus and Homer, see also e.g. Schnyder 1995:24-25.

18 Collard 2005 supplements Stevens' work, adding many examples from Euripides as well as Aeschylus and Sophocles. See also López Eire 1996 on colloquialisms in Aristophanes.

19 Compare Rutherford's remarks on tragic lyric: "imagery is denser and more complex than in the iambic parts (2010:444).

20 Also Willi's 2010b publication on the language of comedy is relevant: there the author notes that comic dialogue is characterized by colloquialisms, such as a high frequency of parataxis, "certain particles or function words" (483), and oaths (488). See now also Willi 2017 on register variation in tense, aspect, and mood (especially the use of the perfect, as opposed to the aorist) in various ancient Greek authors. In this article he pays attention to synchronic and diachronic aspects of register variation, as well as to dialectal factors.

sample study of three registers: that of forensic oratory, that of historiography, and that of (the approximation of) casual conversation. He gives the number of occurrences of 23 linguistic features in six roughly contemporaneous text samples of 1,000 words each.[21] Several of these features indeed seem to be influenced by the register that is appropriate to the text in question. For example, nouns are more common in historiography than in the other genres, whereas the inverse distribution is found for first-person verbs.[22]

§15. The underlying assumption of all the preceding scholarship is that situational differences within plays are reflected in linguistic differences. Singing a song, for example, constitutes a different communicative situation in drama than having a dialogue: the meter, music, speakers, length of the turns, and communicative goals are different. The assumption that these differences influence language also informs the current work.

2.1.3 Methodology in this chapter

§16. This chapter builds on Willi's study and the other research described above, focusing on the main discourse patterns of Greek drama, and specifically using the results as input for the interpretation of particles. Because of the specific focus on particle use, information about the distributions of 14 individual particles is taken into account. In scope and detail, my study fills a gap in previous work, as Earp does not discuss particle use at all, and Willi mentions particles only as a group, without considering the distribution of individual items.[23] I also refine earlier work by distinguishing three different discourse patterns, rather than only a iambic and lyric part.[24]

§17. The frequencies of 25 linguistic features have been collected in three different communicative formats within tragedy and comedy: (1) iambic dialogues with short turns of speaking, (2) iambic monologues, and (3) lyric choral songs. These settings constitute the bulk of tragedy and comedy, and have a clearly distinct linguistic shape. Delving into the three discourse patterns associated with these communicative formats therefore

21 The features that Willi takes into account and that are also considered here are nouns, first- and second-person references (in his study only verbs), future indicatives, finite passives, participles, oaths; features appearing in his study but not counted by me are adjectives, pronouns, past-tense indicatives, perfect indicatives, subjunctives, potential optatives, imperatives (I included imperatives in the category of second-person references), relative clauses, conditional clauses, direct questions, average sentence length, vocative phrases (I included these in the category of second-person references). Note that Willi has counted "particles" as one feature comprising a group of 21 lexical items (ἀλλά, ἄν, ἄρα, ἀτάρ, αὖ, γάρ, γε, γοῦν, δέ, δή, δήπου, δῆτα, ἤ, καίτοι, μέν, μέντοι, μήν, οὖν/ὦν, περ, τοι, τοίνυν), but excluding e.g. καί and τε.

22 I will refer to specific results of Willi's study at several points below.

23 Concerning a different language, Horie and Iwasaki 1996 describe some aspects of register influence on the use of pragmatic particles in Thai conversation. They show, for example, that differences in formality of the register may lead to a different particle use.

24 See Rutherford 2010:448-453, mentioned in §11 above. Another addition is the use of a statistical chi-squared test to verify the significance of my findings; see §21 below.

forms a natural starting point for this type of investigation in drama. Indirectly, my study may shed light on the linguistic tendencies of rarer formats as well, such as anapaests and lyric parts sung by individual characters, which I leave out of consideration here. For my data collection, turns in the dialogue patterns are no more than 4 lines long; monologues are at least 15 lines long in Aristophanes, and at least 25 lines long in tragedy. The corpus used for this collection is made up of a collection of passages, rather than entire plays.[25] The passages have the following total size:

	Aeschylus	Sophocles	Euripides	Aristophanes	*total*
dialogues	2,235	6,424	5,152	3,636	*17,447*
monologues	3,729	7,732	9,554	1,997	*23,012*
choral songs	3,881	3,076	3,199	1,715	*11,871*
total	*9,845*	*17,232*	*17,905*	*7,348*	*52,330*

Table 1: Number of words in the selected passages[26]

§18. The account includes a selection of 14 different particles: ἀλλά, ἄρα/ἆρα,[27] γάρ, γε,[28] δέ, δή, δῆτα, ἦ, καί,[29] μέν, μέντοι, μήν, οὖν,[30] and τε. Other linguistic features

25 It includes passages from my twelve core texts as well as from other plays, namely dialogues, monologues, and choral songs from Aeschylus *Eumenides*, Euripides *Andromache*, and Aristophanes *Assemblywomen*; monologues and choral songs from Aristophanes *Clouds*; and choral songs from Sophocles *Women of Trachis*. For the twelve core plays of my general corpus, see I.1 §2 and III.1.

26 For the linguistic features nouns and participles I used a smaller tragic corpus. Because of the high average frequency of these features, a smaller tragic corpus was sufficient to get statistically significant results: 5,075 words from dialogues (1,455 Aeschylus, 1,975 Sophocles, 1,645 Euripides); 7,599 words from monologues (1,280 Aeschylus, 3,573 Sophocles, 2,746 Euripides); and 5,103 words from choral songs (2,311 Aeschylus, 1,455 Sophocles, 1,337 Euripides).

27 I did not distinguish between ἄρα and ἆρα for this count, because the difference in function depends primarily on its position in an act, rather than on whether the alpha is long. That is, in act- or clause-initial position ἆρα is the question particle, while in peninitial position both ἄρα and ἆρα can be found. The distribution of ἄρα/ἆρα turned out not to be statistically significant, as the particle is relatively infrequent in drama; see note 39 below. On the use of ἄρα in Homer, see II.4 §§34-37; II.5 §§49-58; in Pindar, see II.3 §66 and De Kreij 2014.

28 The instances of γε counted include those of γοῦν. This latter particle is still clearly recognizable as a combination of γε and οὖν; see e.g. Hoogeveen 1769:232-233, Kühner 1835:399, and Bäumlein 1861:188. Denniston 1950 [1934]:448 notes that it is even disputed when to write γ' οὖν as two words. In any case, γοῦν is infrequent compared to γε (on average 0.02% in Aeschylus, 0.02% in Sophocles, 0.01% in Euripides, and 0.05% of all words in Aristophanes).

29 The instances of καί counted include all crasis forms.

30 The instances of οὖν counted include those of οὔκουν, οὐκοῦν, and γοῦν. See note 29 above; in these forms οὖν is usually considered to be recognizable. See e.g. Rost 1859 and Bäumlein

selected are nouns, participles, finite verbs, imperfects, present indicatives, future finite verbs, finite passives, first-person references, second-person references,[31] negations, and swearing expressions.[32] These can be compared to features of modern languages that are analyzed in register studies.[33]

§19. Note that it is not my goal to describe all characteristics of the three discourse patterns. Differences in lexical semantics, for example, are not taken into account here, despite their relevance for situationally-motivated linguistic variation; these differences involve subjective judgments, and are therefore harder to quantify.[34] The current study uses the frequencies of a limited number of linguistic features;[35] my objective is to use these distributions in order to understand particle use better. The features chosen have a relatively clear general function, and can be compared to modern-language features that have been analyzed in register studies. For example, Biber 1995:94-104 mentions nouns, past tense (markers), present tense (markers), passives, first- and second-person pronouns, and negations as among the features that distinguish registers in English, Tuvaluan, Korean, and Somali. I use these comparisons from modern languages on the assumption that situational variation functions similarly across languages. That is, I assume that the use of, for example, first-person references or negations in ancient Greek drama is so similar to their use in different modern languages that a high or low frequency of these features reflect similar fundamental aspects of verbal communication, such as a high level of interactiveness, as in modern-language registers that have been investigated.

§20. Biber 1995 also includes English discourse particles and Tuvaluan discourse linkers (in his terminology) in his register analysis, but only as a group. In his comparison of registers in ancient Greek, Willi 2010a similarly reports the combined frequency of 21 particles (see note 22 above). In my analysis, on the contrary, the distributions of each

---

1861:173-198 for discussion of οὖν and several of its combinations.

31 First- and second-person references include personal and possessive pronouns as well as verb forms and vocatives.

32 Only swearing expressions in the form of νή or μά plus the name of a god or gods were included, not those with other than deities' names. I do not call these constructions "oaths," as e.g. Willi 2010b:488 does, because in most cases in comedy they are not used in this manner (see (t10) on τε below for an example of a real oath).

33 See §§19-20, §45, and §59 below for discussions of such features from modern languages.

34 Clarke 2010 also points out other problems concerning the lexical semantics of ancient Greek.

35 I did not count the frequencies of, for instance, demonstratives, infinitives, imperatives, perfects, subjunctives, (potential or other) optatives, relative or conditional clauses, and questions. These features do appear in the sample study of Willi 2010a (see p. 307). Neither do I take into account the feature of sentence length, which he does mention. Where a "sentence" starts and ends in ancient Greek is partly a subjective decision by the editors; see IV.3 §§16-18 for more on this issue. Since a "sentence" tends to contain at least one finite verb, short sentences in a certain passage are usually connected to a high frequency of finite verbs. I have chosen to focus on the frequencies of verbs and particles directly, rather than on their indirect reflection in punctuation choices by editors.

particle have been collected separately, which has allowed me to perceive distributional differences across particles.[36]

§21. To test the statistical significance of the attested distributions, I used the software of Preacher 2001 to calculate a chi-squared (χ^2) test of independence.[37] A chi-squared test calculates the probability that a certain attested distribution of a feature is found in samples from groups with the same average frequency of that feature, in which case that distribution would not be meaningful ("significant"). In our case, the "groups" are texts, that is, groups of words. The features are particles and other linguistic items with a certain number of occurrences in the different samples. An attested distribution yields a chi-squared value; from this value Preacher's software calculates the probability, called p-value, that the given distribution would be attested in two random samples from the same text. If the p-value is very low (it may range between 0 and 1), then this attestation is very unlikely, and we may assume that the text A and B in fact do differ in their overall frequency of the feature in question. Normally a distribution with a p-value below 0.05 is considered statistically significant; this means that there is a less than 5% chance that the distribution is due to chance. For example, if a sample of 1,000 words from text A contains 22 δέ instances, and a sample of the same size from text B contains 45 δέ instances, the chi-squared value is 8.169; the p-value is 0.00426 (or 0.426%). This is smaller than 0.05 (or 5%), so the distribution is significant. Once significance has been established, we may then turn to explaining the difference in frequency of δέ between text A and B.

2.2 Distribution as Input for Interpretation

§22. In this main part of the chapter I discuss particle distributions across the three discourse patterns, and use this information as input for interpreting the particles' functions. If several playwrights consistently choose a certain particle more often in one of the discourse patterns, this suggests that that particle is associated with some communicative purposes or circumstances of the situation related to that discourse pattern. For example, a consistently higher frequency in dialogues may reflect the particle's association with more interactive speech. If no such consistent frequency differences can be detected for a certain particle, then this particle has several functions, each of which is associated with different communicative aspects, or its functions are equally relevant to all situations. In either case, tendencies on a macro-level can be illuminating.

[36] It would be interesting to investigate whether functionally similar words in English or other languages also differ in their distribution across registers, since particles and discourse markers tend to show a wide functional variety in any language. See I.3 for more on this general functional variety.

[37] I wish to thank Maxim Hendriks and Alessandro Vatri for their help in the use and explanation of the chi-squared test.

§23. The analyses focus on different particles in order of their average frequency, starting from the most frequent ones. I will only discuss the eleven particles that have a statistically significant distribution in at least two out of four authors.[38]

2.2.1 δέ

§24. The most frequent particles overall are δέ and καί.[39] The distribution of δέ is as follows:

Author	Dialogues	Monologues	Choral songs	Significant?[40]
Aeschylus	2.46	4.13	5.20[41]	yes
Sophocles	2.13	2.55	2.47	no
Euripides	2.41	3.68	3.38	yes
Aristophanes	2.56	2.90	1.98	no

Table 2: Frequencies of δέ in percentages of all words

Aeschylus uses δέ especially often in choral songs, such as the one in *Agamemnon* 367-474:

(t1)

(Χο.) (...) | φθονερὸν δ' ὑπ' ἄλγος ἕρ-
πει προδίκοις Ἀτρείδαις.
| οἱ δ' | αὐτοῦ περὶ τεῖχος
| θήκας Ἰλιάδος γᾶς
εὔμορφοι κατέχουσιν, | ἐχ-
θρὰ δ' ἔχοντας ἔκρυψεν.
(ἀντ. γ) | βαρεῖα δ' ἀστῶν φάτις σὺν κότωι,
| δημοκράντου δ' ἀρᾶς τίνει χρέος·
| μένει δ' ἀκοῦσαί τί μου

[38] The distributions of ἄρα/ἆρα, μέντοι, and μήν are not statistically significant in most authors, because they are too infrequent overall; see the appendix in §96 below.

[39] These particles are also the most frequent ones in the other genres discussed in this monograph; see our frequency graphs (available online as I.5) for an overview of particle frequencies.

[40] This column reports whether the chance that the situations had no influence on the attested distribution is less than 5% or not, based on a chi-squared test for independence. See §21 above.

[41] In all tables of frequencies, the lowest frequency for each author is marked with a white cell; the middle and highest frequencies with light and dark grey, respectively.

μέριμνα νυκτηρεφές [42]

Aeschylus *Agamemnon* 450-460

(Ch.) And grief steals over them, mixed with resentment against the chief prosecutors, the Atreidae. And over there, around the city wall, the men in their beauty occupy sepulchres in the land of Ilium: the enemy's soil covers its conquerors.

The talk of the citizens, mixed with anger, is a dangerous thing: it is the equivalent of a publicly ordained curse: I have an anxiety that waits to hear of something happening under the cover of night.

The several instances of δέ in this song mark boundaries between discourse acts, short communicative steps that may or may not coincide with a clause.[43] The particle has a relatively neutral function, signaling that a new step in the discourse has begun. The step can correspond to anything: a new event in a narrative, an argumentative point, a vocative, a contrastive noun phrase, an apposition, and so on. In this passage, for example, the act φθονερὸν δ' ὑπ' ἄλγος ἕρπει προδίκοις Ἀτρείδαις (450-451) describes one aspect of the scene "Greeks grieving over men lost in Troy" that the singing elders are depicting. οἱ δ' in 452 constitutes a new step, signaling a switch from the grieving family at home to the deceased warriors themselves.[44] The next δέ, in 455, introduces a new act again, adding another facet to the "deceased warriors at Troy" picture. In 456 δέ starts a gnomic act,[45] and simultaneously accompanies the start of a new antistrophe, a larger boundary than just a new discourse act. In fact, throughout this whole first stasimon (367–474) every strophe and antistrophe except for the very first strophe starts with a δέ. The parallels show that this is a typically Aeschylean phenomenon.[46] Admittedly, apart from this

42 The vertical bars added to this passage indicate potential boundaries of discourse acts; see II.2 §§26-27; IV.2 §24; IV.3 §45.

43 On the concept of discourse act, see esp. II.2 and IV.3 §§71-72. On the general function of δέ marking a new or different step, see e.g. Bäumlein 1861:89; Bakker 1993b; 1997:62-68. See also II.2 §§31-36 on δέ in Homer; II.3 §65 on δέ in Pindar; IV.2 §§14-46 on δέ in Herodotus and Thucydides.

44 On the construction ὁ δέ or οἱ δέ as a separate discourse act, see II.2 §64 on Homer, §72 on Pindar; IV.2 §24 on Thucydides; IV.3 §115 on Herodotus.

45 On δέ introducing *gnômai* in Pindar, see II.3 §§74-75.

46 Other δέ instances at the start of choral (anti)strophes include Aeschylus *Persians* 74, 81, 86, 93, 106, 133, 576, 584; *Seven Against Thebes* 304, 333, 345, 357, 727, 734, 758, 778, 785, 900, 922; *Suppliant Women* 40, 57, 91, 96, 104, 122, 144, 154, 538, 547, 556, 565, 595, 688, 704, 743, 750, 757, 784, 792, 800, 1026, 1034, 1043, 1057; *Agamemnon* 122, 192, 205, 218, 228, 248, 385, 403, 420, 437, 699, 717, 727, 737, 750, 763, 772, 988; *Libation Bearers* 55, 603, 613, 623, 631, 639, 646, 794, 812, 831, 946, 965; *Eumenides* 155, 169, 366, 377, 550, 558, 938, 956, 976, 1040, 1044; Sophocles *Antigone* 117, 134, 955, 966, 1126; *Oedipus King* 883; *Oedipus at Colonus* 681, 694, 707; *Philoctetes* 719; *Women of Trachis* 962; Euripides *Alcestis* 121, 578, 973; *Andromache* 479, 1019, 1028, 1037; *Electra* 442, 452, 713; *Hecuba* 923,

pragmatic boundary-marking function, the δέ instances in this passage work to prevent hiatus. However, other words could have been used for that as well, so its metrical function cannot have been the only justification for the use of δέ. In other words, the particle's non-random distribution proves that it cannot have been mainly a metrical tool.

§25. The relatively high frequency of δέ in all three communicative settings in all four authors can be connected to the particle's relatively neutral, "minimal" function, which makes it compatible with many different contexts and co-texts. The especially frequent use in Aeschylean choral songs makes their discourse appear less explicitly subjective, since the nature of the connections between most discourse acts is not spelled out. That is, the singers do not make it explicit how exactly they consider the acts to be related.[47] The "neutral" presentation fits the specific context at this moment of the *Agamemnon*: as Raeburn and Thomas 2011 point out in their commentary on this stasimon, the song contains many "shifts of thought," but the idea of retribution unites the different topics. From the other instances of punishment in the song, Raeburn and Thomas note, the chorus can draw the obvious conclusion about Agamemnon's upcoming fate, "but dare not voice it." The audience, of course well aware of what will happen to the king, will understand what the song is hinting at.[48] In this context with emphasis on implicit meaning, the minimal boundary signals conveyed by the δέ instances are appropriate.

§26. The high frequency of δέ in Aeschylean songs may at the same time lend these passages an epic air, since δέ is very frequent especially in Homeric narrator text.[49] The songs share with epic a concern with famous, traditional stories and a general tendency to avoid explicitly encoding subjectivity. The same holds true for non-dramatic lyric, where δέ is similarly frequent.[50] The allusion to epic and lyric helps establish Aeschylean songs *qua* songs, that is, underscore their genre affiliations, as well as endow them with an authoritative voice, typically associated with these genres.

§27. Aeschylus uses δέ especially often in songs, but in monologues too he employs it more frequently than the other dramatists. As for Euripides, he uses δέ most in his

---

933; *Helen* 1122, 1337; *Heracles* 655; *Hippolytus* 742; *Ion* 1061; *Iphigeneia in Aulis* 185, 231, 242, 253, 265, 557, 762; *Medea* 421, 431, 439, 636, 990, 996; *Phoenician Women* 239, 250; *Trojan Women* 531, 551.

47 This less explicit organization of the discourse is also reflected in an extremely low frequency of the particles γε and ἀλλά in Aeschylean choral songs: see below, Table 11 on γε and Table 16 on ἀλλά, with discussions.

48 See also Fraenkel 1950 *ad* 429, earlier in this same song: "*by smooth and almost imperceptible transitions*, we are led from the picture of the departing Helen and the sorrows of her husband back to the wretched victims of her rashness" (my emphasis). Also 429 contains a δέ.

49 The average frequency of δέ in Homer is 5.4% (7.0% in narrator text and 2.9% in direct speech). See II.2 §36. There are also several Homeric words in this song: see e.g. E. Fraenkel 1950 *ad* ῥίμφα 407, τλησικάρδιος 430, and οὐκ ἄσκοποι 462.

50 The average frequency of δέ in Pindar is 4.1% of all words. See II.2 §44.

monologues.[51] Consider the following passage from a messenger speech, which describes how Dionysus bent down a fir tree:

(t2)

(Αγ.) κυκλοῦτο δ' ὥστε τόξον ἢ κυρτὸς τροχὸς
τόρνωι γραφόμενος περιφορὰν ἑλικοδρόμον·
ὣς κλῶν' ὄρειον ὁ ξένος χεροῖν ἄγων
ἔκαμπτεν ἐς γῆν, ἔργματ' οὐχὶ θνητὰ δρῶν.
Πενθέα δ' ἱδρύσας ἐλατίνων ὄζων ἔπι
ὀρθὸν μεθίει διὰ χερῶν βλάστημ' ἄνω
ἀτρέμα, φυλάσσων μὴ ἀναχαιτίσειέ νιν,
ὀρθὴ δ' ἐς ὀρθὸν αἰθέρ' ἐστηρίζετο
ἔχουσα νώτοις δεσπότην ἐφήμενον.
ὤφθη δὲ μᾶλλον ἢ κατεῖδε μαινάδας·

Euripides *Bacchae* 1066-1075

(Me.) It [i.e. the tree] began to curve like a bow or a rounded wheel when its shape is being traced by the peg-and-line with its spiraling rotation. So the stranger, drawing down with his hands the mountain tree, bent it to the ground, a deed no mortal could do. Then, having set Pentheus atop the fir branches, he set the tree straight again by letting the branches slip upwards through his hands—gently, taking care not to unseat Pentheus—and sheer to sheer heaven it towered, with my master on its back. He now was seen by the maenads more than he saw them.

Again, δέ marks the boundaries of discourse acts, which in this context are part of narrative steps.[52] Each narrative step in this excerpt is in fact constituted by several discourse acts; because of its neutral function, δέ may also appear at the boundaries of such moves (multi-act units).[53] First the messenger describes the bending of the fir tree (1066-1069).

51 Unlike Aeschylus and Euripides, Sophocles and Aristophanes employ this particle roughly equally often throughout the three communicative situations. Aristophanes is especially fond of turn-initial δέ in quickly alternating dialogue; this construction occurs in Aeschylus as well, but in Aristophanes these instances make up a larger part of the total number of δέ. See III.4 on turn-initial δέ in drama: §§34-38 for discussion and parallels, §73 for its frequencies in the four authors.

52 Other Euripidean messenger speeches with a high number of δέ instances are *Hippolytus* 1173-1254 and *Medea* 1136-1230. However, Hippolytus' argumentative and angry speech in *Hippolytus* 616-668 has an even higher frequency of δέ (19 instances in 333 words) than the narrative speech by the messenger; yet four of these δέ instances are in dubious, probably interpolated lines; see e.g. W.S. Barrett 1964 *ad loc.*

53 On the concept of move, see II.3 (with §65 and §73 specifically on δέ in Homer and Pindar); IV.3.11 (specifically on Herodotus and Thucydides).

Next (δέ 1070) Dionysus places Pentheus on top of the tree and sets it straight again. Subsequently, the acts starting with δέ in 1073 describe what happened to the tree as a consequence. In 1075, finally, the particle introduces the next narrative event: the bacchants see Pentheus on the tree. This next step is in fact the climax of the story, as reflected in the change from imperfects to aorist (ὤφθη, 1075). δέ thus helps to move the story forward from one event to the next, marking discrete steps in continuous discourse, in a manner similar to its use in Homeric or Pindaric narrative.

§28. Although commentators do not remark on the high frequency of δέ in Euripidean speeches, they often note that messenger speeches in general resemble epic language. For example, Page 1938 *ad* Euripides *Medea* 1141 explains that messenger speeches are modeled upon epic.[54] Similarly, Palmer 1980 notes that in tragedy, "Homerisms are particularly frequent in messenger speeches" (133). J. Barrett, in his 2002 study of messenger speeches, argues that "the messengers' narrative voice typically resembles that of epic" (xvi). In such epic environments, then, a higher frequency of δέ is also appropriate.[55]

§29. In the next paragraphs I will discuss the distribution of other linguistic features than particles, in order to establish an interpretive link between these other features and the distribution of δέ. I will focus on imperfect forms, present indicatives, and participles. Imperfects are relatively frequent in monologues in all four authors. In (t2), for example, we find κυκλοῦτο (1066), ἔκαμπτεν (1069), μεθίει (1071; this form could also be present tense), and ἐστηρίζετο (1073). This high frequency of imperfects can be connected to a frequent occurrence of narratives in monologues. The distribution of imperfects across the discourse patterns is as follows:

Author	Dialogues	Monologues	Choral songs	Significant?
Aeschylus	4	18	7	yes
Sophocles	8	13	6	yes
Euripides	3	11	4	yes
Aristophanes	3	17	8	yes

Table 3: Frequencies of imperfects in percentages of all finite verbs

54 He writes that messenger speeches "are the least dramatic parts of the drama: they are full of description, and while they are being spoken the action of the play is at a standstill. Their literary model is therefore the narrative of epic poetry, which they resemble in being descriptions of action rather than action itself. In this least dramatic, most epic, part of his play the poet turns to the language of the epic poets for one or two tricks of style." See also e.g. Mastronarde 2002 *ad* Euripides *Medea* 1116-1250, who speaks of "reminiscences of epic" in messenger speeches, and Rutherford 2010:444: tragic messenger speeches "often include reminiscences of epic narration."

55 See note 49 above on the high frequency of δέ in Homer.

On imperfects, Rijksbaron writes that it is "crucially connected with historical narrative" (1988:254): the imperfect "unequivocally locates a state of affairs in the past." Likewise, Bakker 1997e:20-21 considers the imperfect, but not the aorist, to be a true past tense. Rijksbaron observes (248) that in Herodotus, the imperfect is much more frequent in narrative than in direct speech.[56] In all four Greek dramatists, the imperfect's distribution is in line with these observations: it is most common in monologues, the best setting for telling a story.[57] This distribution indirectly confirms the affinity of δέ for narrative contexts.

§30. The distribution of present indicatives is useful in so far as we can interpret it in light of general, cross-linguistic functions of these forms and of other tense-mood combinations, that is, bound to characteristics of ancient Greek as well as other languages. Sophocles uses present indicatives most in choral songs, Euripides most in dialogues:

Author	Dialogues	Monologues	Choral songs	Significant?
Aeschylus	37	35	40	no
Sophocles	40	35	43	yes
Euripides	42	36	36	yes
Aristophanes	39	35	35	no

Table 4: Frequencies of present indicatives in percentages of all finite verbs

[56] Similarly, in English the past tense is more common in fiction texts than in other registers (Biber, Conrad, and Reppen 1998:143).

[57] While the imperfect is generally less frequent in choral songs, there are exceptions. E.g. the third stasimon in Aeschylus *Persians* (852-907) contains a remarkably high frequency of imperfects: 4 to 8 forms out of all 12 finite verbs. The exact number of imperfects is unclear because of ambiguous forms (that can be both imperfect or aorist) and textual problems (that lead to ambiguity as to whether a form is imperfect or present). The Persian chorus members here relate how pleasant life was during the reign of king Darius. This song takes the audience out of the events of the play itself—the recent disaster and current lamentation—not into timeless considerations, as in many other choral songs, but into the chorus' and the characters' past. As Broadhead 1960 *ad loc.* points out, this praise of Darius' deeds is fitting, because it follows naturally upon the previous ghost-scene; it also throws into relief the humiliation and misery of Darius' son Xerxes. Italie 1953 and De Romilly 1974 also note the contrast between Darius and Xerxes.

Another choral song with many imperfects, relating past events from the play's characters' lives, is Sophocles *Women of Trachis* 497-530.

In dialogues, the present tense tends to be communicatively appropriate because of the implied attention to the current speech situation.[58] In choral songs, conversely, the present tense fits references to general or timeless states. I relate the lower frequency of present indicatives in monologues to analogously general tendencies: this communicative setting is especially used in Classical drama for narratives about the past, and for argumentative purposes. Both scenarios typically require other verb forms besides present indicatives. The distribution of present indicatives, then, on a general level confirms my claim that the communicative situation determines linguistic choices, and more specifically strengthens the connection that I have drawn between monologues and narrative purposes. This indirectly supports my interpretation of δέ's distribution as reflecting, among other things, an affinity for narrative contexts.

§31. The distribution of participles provides input for our interpretation of δέ as well. This distribution is similar to that of δέ: participles are most frequent in Aeschylean choral songs and Euripidean monologues:

Author	Dialogues	Monologues	Choral songs	Significant?
Aeschylus	3.5	6.1	6.3	yes
Sophocles	4.5	5.1	4.1	no
Euripides	3.2	5.5	3.7	yes
Aristophanes	3.2	5.5	5.2	yes

Table 5: Frequencies of participles in percentages of all words

In the register study by Willi 2010a, participles are found to be more frequent in oratory and historiography, and less frequent in texts that represent conversation. More participles, he observes, seem to be related to a greater average sentence length. Indeed, participles help to segment the discourse into small chunks, just as δέ, but they achieve this syntactically;[59] we can imagine that such syntactic chunking would be especially helpful in a long, complex turn of speaking.[60]

58 See Biber 1995:143 on the English present tense. He explains that the concern with immediate circumstances that present tense verbs reflect can be connected to interactiveness and involvement.

59 See IV.3 §78, and IV.5 §§19-20, §§23-24, §53 for analysis of certain participial phrases in Herodotus and Thucydides as separate discourse acts.

60 Besides this general function, participles' similarity to nouns may play a role in their distribution. They seem to be closer to nouns than finite verbs in this respect; see Tables 8 and 9 below for the distributions of nouns and verbs. Fox 1983 explores the hybrid nature (between noun and verb) of the participle in Herodotus and argues that participles are backgrounding devices.

§32. To sum up the findings of this subsection, δέ is very frequent (compared to other particles) throughout the discourse patterns in all authors, and especially so in Aeschylean choral songs. In this communicative environment, I have argued, the high frequency of δέ reflects a seemingly neutral presentation of the discourse in which the speaking "I" does not come to the fore, and evokes a Homeric style. Euripides' preference for the particle in monologues may be explained by δέ's affinity with narratives, and from the well-known link between messenger speeches and epic story telling. Other linguistic characteristics of the discourse patterns, such as the imperfect and present tenses and participles, also reflect such pragmatic associations in their distributions.

2.2.2 καί

§33. The other frequently occurring particle, καί, shows a striking distribution across the three discourse patterns. Aeschylus uses καί more often in dialogues, but Sophocles and Euripides prefer to use it in monologues. Aristophanes, however, uses it more often in songs:

Author	Dialogues	Monologues	Choral songs	Significant?
Aeschylus	3.09	2.90	1.67	yes
Sophocles	2.52	3.50	2.15	yes
Euripides	2.45	2.89	1.19	yes
Aristophanes	2.86	3.61	4.14	yes

Table 6: Frequencies of καί in percentages of all words

The distribution of καί, then, reflects differences in particle use across the playwrights. In fact καί has multiple functions in all authors, but each author tends to exploit this variety in different contexts.

Hopper and Thompson 1984:741 argue that participles cross-linguistically tend to share more with nouns than with verbs. I remind the reader here that I did not count the frequencies of adjectives, to which participles are closest in function. Observations on English registers (Biber 2006:14; Biber, Conrad, and Reppen 1998:7) suggest that adjectives, like nouns, are connected to formality. Infinitives are also missing from my counts; according to Fox 1983:28, infinitives in Herodotus are functionally closer to finite verbs than participles, which are closer to nouns.

§34. Aeschylean dialogues are a case in point: they contain various καί constructions. Consider the following excerpt, from a scene in which the messenger is telling the Persian queen about the army's defeat:

(t3)

Βα. αἰαῖ, κακῶν δὴ πέλαγος ἔρρωγεν μέγα
Πέρσαις τε καὶ πρόπαντι βαρβάρων γένει.
Αγγ. εὖ νυν τόδ' ἴσθι, μηδέπω μεσοῦν κακόν·
τοιάδ' ἐπ' αὐτοῖς ἦλθε συμφορὰ πάθους,
ὡς τοῖσδε καὶ δὶς ἀντισηκῶσαι ῥοπῇι.
Βα. καὶ τίς γένοιτ' ἂν τῆσδ' ἔτ' ἐχθίων τύχη;

Aeschylus *Persians* 433-438

Qu. Aiai, what a great sea of troubles has burst upon the Persians and the whole Eastern race!

Me. Well, be sure of this, the tale of disaster is not yet even half told: such a calamitous event has occurred, on top of what I have told you, that it outweighs that in the scale fully twice over.

Qu. What possible misfortune could be even more hateful than the one we have heard of?

Each of the three instances of καί in this passage is part of a different construction. The first has a small scope and marks a close connection, together with τε,[61] between Πέρσαις, "the Persians," and πρόπαντι βαρβάρων γένει, "the whole race of the barbarians." The two items are semantically and morphologically similar, so there can be no doubt about the function of the particle combination. The second instance of καί, in 437, is not surrounded by two items that could be connected. It must be interpreted as pinning down and highlighting the adverb δίς: "even twice" or "really twice."[62] The third instance is found in turn-initial position at the start of a question, and has a large scope over that entire question. In this construction the use of καί may imply the speaker's

61 On τε, see §§39-49 below; II.4 §§31-37 (in Homer), §§54-68 (in Pindar); IV.2 §§47-92, and IV.5 §11, §14, §17, §27, §36, §44, §62, §77, §108 (in historiography). On the cluster τε καί in Herodotus and Thucydides, especially in connection with names of people and places, see IV.2 §66, §80, §92.

62 See Roussel 1960 *ad loc.* for this interpretation here; see IV.2 §§102-105 for discussion of this function of καί in general. Other examples of καί with this pinning-down function include Aeschylus *Persians* 1045; *Seven against Thebes* 657, 760; Sophocles *Antigone* 772 (see IV.2 §104), 1253; *Oedipus King* 557; Euripides *Medea* 526; Aristophanes *Knights* 342.

surprise.[63] All of these specific functions interact with the dialogic situation at hand. The close connection marked by τε καί in 434 indicates that the two interlocutors share certain knowledge (see the subsection on τε below), drawing them closely into the interaction. The "even twice" highlight in 437 fits the messenger's current dialogic task: to announce a further shocking narrative in addition to his earlier speeches. Finally, the implied surprise in 438 relates to the high interactiveness of this situation in which the speakers immediately react to each other after short utterances.[64] In other words, the larger context of the discourse pattern throws light on the interpretation of καί's local functions that depend on the direct co-text.

§35. In Sophocles we find the highest frequency of this particle in monologues.[65] The following passage from a speech by Tecmessa, relating Ajax' actions in his madness, illustrates this tendency:

(t4)

(Τε.) ὁ δ' εἶπε πρός με βαί', ἀεὶ δ' ὑμνούμενα·
"γύναι, γυναιξὶ κόσμον ἡ σιγὴ φέρει."
κἀγὼ μαθοῦσ' ἔληξ', ὁ δ' ἐσσύθη μόνος.
  καὶ τὰς ἐκεῖ μὲν οὐκ ἔχω λέγειν πάθας·
εἴσω δ' ἐσῆλθε συνδέτους ἄγων ὁμοῦ
ταύρους, κύνας βοτῆρας, εὔερόν τ' ἄγραν.
καὶ τοὺς μὲν ηὐχένιζε, τοὺς δ' ἄνω τρέπων
ἔσφαζε κἀρράχιζε, (...)

Sophocles *Ajax* 292-299

(Te.) But the words he spoke to me were few and hackneyed: "Woman, silence makes a woman beautiful." Hearing this, I ceased, and he sped off alone. What happened there I cannot tell you; but he came in bringing with him bound bulls, herdsmen's dogs, and woolly prizes. Some he

63 See Broadhead 1960, Pontani 1951, Italie 1953, and Hall 1996 *ad loc.* Other examples of turn-initial καί with this "zooming-in" function, implying surprise or indignation, include Aeschylus *Agamemnon* 280; *Libation Bearers* 179, 776; *Eumenides* 204, 206, 898; *Suppliant Women* 509; Sophocles *Oedipus King* 976, 1019, 1023; *Oedipus at Colonus* 73, 414; Euripides *Alcestis* 43; *Andromache* 917; Aristophanes *Birds* 829, 963bis, 1437bis. On turn-initial καί in drama, see also III.3 §§89-94 and III.4 §36. I observe in III.4 §73 that the three Aeschylean plays in my corpus have a higher relative frequency of turn-initial καί than those of the other dramatists: 7.2% of the turns start with καί, whereas this percentage is 5.4 in Sophocles, 3.4 in Euripides, and 6.0 in Aristophanes.

64 For my use of the term "utterance," i.e. as everything that is said by one speaker until she stops talking and a new speaker starts, see III.4 §9.

65 My corpus does not even contain any Sophoclean monologue without καί.

> decapitated, others he turned upside down and cut their throats or clove their spines, (...)

Again, we see the multifunctionality of the particle. The different καί instances have different scopes: the first three introduce whole clauses, the fourth one only one verb form. According to Stanford 1963 *ad* line 294, this καί indicates a consequence, and at the same time emphasizes the pronoun ἐγώ. The "consequence" Stanford refers to is a pragmatic enrichment of the connection marked by καί: "and therefore"; we can infer this enrichment from the co-text.[66] Jebb 2004 [1896] translates this καί with "and." The instances in 295 and 298 (both untranslated by Jebb) each form a fronted discourse act on their own—we can infer an act boundary from the μέν instances in the following acts. These two καί instances each project an upcoming multi-act move, encompassing a μέν act, a δέ act, and more.[67] Each καί connects the upcoming move as a whole to the preceding discourse.[68] Finally, καί in 299 connects two items that are morphologically and semantically similar, just as we had seen for τε καί in the *Persians* example.[69] Jebb's choice of "or" to translate this καί reflects that the particle here may work differently from the other three instances.[70] In the καί constructions in this monologue, then, the particle has slightly different pragmatic functions. These functions relate less to interactiveness, as we found in the dialogic example, and more to a speaker taking her time to formulate her utterance.

§36. In some cases, mainly found in monologues, the two conjuncts connected by καί are so close in meaning that the second one can be interpreted as a specification or reformulation of the first one. καί then receives the enrichment "that is," "better to say," "in other words," or "to be more precise." Here is an example of this construction from a monologue by Pentheus:

(t5)

> (Πε.) ταῦτ' οὐχὶ δεινὰ <u>κἀ</u>γχόνης ἔστ' ἄξια,
> ὕβρεις ὑβρίζειν, ὅστις ἔστιν ὁ ξένος;

Euripides *Bacchae* 246-247

[66] On enrichments of καί, see IV.2 §§93-137.

[67] See III.5 §§30-31 on such so-called priming acts typically used in calm contexts in drama.

[68] On such καί priming acts, see IV.2 §108.

[69] Other Sophoclean monologues with a high frequency of καί (more than 4% of all words) are *Ajax* 646-692; *Antigone* 162-210, 249-277, 280-314, 407-440, 998-1032; *Oedipus King* 771-833. In all of these speeches we find the particle in several different constructions, such as combined with τε (e.g. *Antigone* 176, 177, 181), with καί itself repeated (e.g. *Ajax* 669; *Antigone* 264-265), with small scope (e.g. *Antigone* 436; *Oedipus King* 787), with large scope (e.g. *Antigone* 260, 422), "pinning down" one constituent rather than connecting two items (e.g. *Ajax* 680, 692; *Antigone* 296), and as a fronted discourse act (e.g. *Antigone* 434).

[70] For καί meaning or implying "or," see IV.2 §§117-121.

(Pe.) Is it not dreadful and enough to make a man hang himself, <if we are to allow this> stranger, whoever he is, to commit such an outrage (...)?[71]

ἀγχόνης ἄξια ("worthy of death by hanging") can be considered a specification of the first conjunct ("terrible"). This use of καί is described by Hartung 1832, who speaks of "eine nähere Bestimmung des Vorangehenden" (145), and by Humbert 1960: καί marks a "meilleure approximation" (412).[72] All four playwrights employ this construction: other examples are κατεῖχε κἀπράυνεν ("he tried to restrain and, that is to say, to calm them," Aeschylus *Persians* 190, in a monologue), ὑπερμαχοῦμαι κἀπὶ πάντ' ἀφίξομαι ("I will fight and, that is, go to all lengths," Sophocles *Oedipus King* 265, in a monologue), and ἐχθρῶν κοὐ φίλων ("from enemies, I mean, not from friends," Aristophanes *Birds* 378, in an utterance of six lines).[73] This use of καί shows again how a specific co-text leads to a certain enrichment of the particle's force. Just as καί may mark a large-scope "zooming in" at the start of questions, likewise it may specify, with smaller scope, a noun phrase or verb phrase when it connects two semantically similar items. The tendency for this function to occur mainly in monologues can be connected to a general pragmatic need of monologues, which is to hold the floor: only when a speaker has ample time to put her message into words, she can "afford" to describe a certain action or concept in two slightly different ways. In addition, using such specifications may support an argumentative goal, which speakers often pursue in uttering a long speech.[74]

§37. Unlike the tragedians, Aristophanes exploits the multifunctionality of καί most in choral songs. The following example from *Lysistrata* contains many instances; the singers are the united choruses of both men and women, who have finally decided to make peace.

(t6)

(Χο.) ἀλλὰ πολὺ τοὔμπαλιν πάντ' ἀγαθὰ καὶ λέγειν
καὶ δρᾶν· ἱκανὰ γὰρ τὰ κακὰ καὶ τὰ παρακείμενα.

71 Kovacs takes ἀγχόνης ἄξια to refer to suicide; Dodds 1960 [1944] and Seaford 1996 *ad loc.* argue against such a reading, and think that Pentheus is threatening to hang the stranger. For my interpretation of καί here this issue is irrelevant: in both cases the particle can be read as marking a specification.

72 On this use of καί in several other authors, see IV.2 §§96-101 (on καί in combinations), §§102-105 (on καί alone).

73 Other examples of καί marking the second conjunct as a specification of the first one include Aeschylus *Libation Bearers* 1028 (in a monologue); Sophocles *Ajax* 496 (in a monologue), 808 (in a 10-line utterance); *Antigone* 718 (in a monologue), 1193 (in a monologue); *Oedipus King* 593 (in a monologue); *Philoctetes* 71 (in a monologue); Euripides *Bacchae* 198 (in a one-line utterance), 308 (in a monologue); *Hippolytus* 457 (in a monologue); *Medea* 560 (in a monologue), 1152 (in a monologue); Aristophanes *Birds* 499 (in a one-line utterance that is in fact part of a longer speech with interruptions), 1683 (in a two-line utterance; see III.5 §33 for discussion); *Lysistrata* 227 (in a one-line utterance that is in fact part of a longer speech), 529 (in a one-line utterance).

74 On monologues often having an argumentative goal, see §30 above and §67 below.

ἀλλ' ἐπαγγελλέτω πᾶς ἀνὴρ καὶ γυνή,
εἴ τις ἀργυρίδιον
δεῖται λαβεῖν, μνᾶς ἢ δύ' ἢ
τρεῖς· ὡς ἔσω 'στὶν κἄχομεν βαλλάντια.
κἄν ποτ' εἰρήνη φανῇ,
ὅστις ἂν νυνὶ δανείσηται παρ' ἡμῶν,
ἂν λάβῃ μηκέτ' ἀποδῷ.
ἑστιᾶν δὲ μέλλομεν ξένους τινὰς Καρυστίους, ἄνδρας καλούς τε κἀγαθούς.
κἄστι <μὲν> ἔτνος τι· καὶ δελφάκιον ἦν τί μοι,
καὶ τοῦτο τέθυχ', ὥστε γίγνεσθ' ἁπαλὰ καὶ καλά.

Aristophanes *Lysistrata* 1046-1064

(Ch.) but quite the opposite: to say and do only what's nice, because you've already got more than enough troubles. So let every man and woman tell us if they need to have a little cash, say two or three minas; we've got it at home, and we've even got purses to put it in. And if peace should ever break out, anyone that borrows from us now need no longer repay it—if he's had it! We're getting set to entertain some visitors from Carystus today; they're fine and handsome gentlemen. There's some soup, and I had a nice piglet and sacrificed it, so it's turning into tasty tenders.

In καὶ λέγειν καὶ δρᾶν (1046-1047), the repetition of the particle emphasizes the addition of the two items: "*both* to say *and* to do." The καί in τὰ κακὰ καὶ τὰ παρακείμενα (1047) has a small scope, like the first two instances, but in this case the element before it and the one after it refer to the same entity: the current troubles. That is why the translation "and" is less appropriate here; Henderson 1987 *ad loc.* calls this καί "emphatic." In fact, its function is not really distinct from a καί that we do translate as "and": it binds the two aspects of the troubles closely together, creating a hendiadys.[75] At the same time, it contributes to the κ-alliteration here. The instance in 1049 (ἀνὴρ καὶ γυνή) has a small-scope connecting force; those in 1052, 1053, 1061, 1062, and 1063 have a larger scope, since they connect entire verb phrases or clauses. The καί in 1052 may trigger an enrichment as "even," as Henderson's translation shows. The instance in 1060, finally, is found in the fixed phrase καλούς τε κἀγαθούς, another hendiadys as in 1047; also καί in ἁπαλὰ καὶ καλά (1064) works in a similar way. All in all, the particle binds together discourse segments of different size and nature. In this specific song, the staggering number of καί instances may iconically underline that the two semi-choruses are now united. As

[75] See IV.2 §140 on the view that the different functions of καί exist on a continuum.

Wilamowitz 1927 *ad loc.* remarks, the male and female chorus members possibly form pairs while singing this song. This would be especially apt, we can imagine, for the phrase ἀνὴρ καὶ γυνή in 1049. Thus, the local functions of these καί instances are either appropriate to any communicative situation (1049, 1052, 1053, 1061, 1062, 1063) or reflect the general poetic attention—high in choral language—to how things are said (1046, 1047 (twice), 1060, 1064).[76] The particle's repetition is especially related to the song's overarching pragmatic goals, namely to underline and celebrate the union of the two semi-choruses.

§38. The above passages show that καί participates in several different but related constructions, and that these constructions tend to occur mostly in one of the discourse patterns.[77] Aeschylus' preference for using καί especially in dialogues may additionally reveal influence of Homeric particle use: in Homer καί is more frequent in direct speech than in narrator text.[78] Sophocles and Euripides employ a broad range of καί constructions especially in monologues, where some of its functions are related to holding the floor for an extended period of time. Aristophanes uses καί mostly in choral songs. The multifunctionality of this particle seems to make it especially suitable for exaggerated repetition, a strategy that fits the mocking tone of many comic songs.

2.2.3 τε

§39. Like καί, τε marks connections, but it differs in its implications, possible enrichments, and specific constructions.[79] τε also has a distribution unlike that of any other particle. The use called "epic," discussed in IV.2 §§47-69, does not occur in tragedy and comedy, except for the idiomatic construction οἷός τε "able to": all other instances of τε here have a connective function.[80] However, that does not mean that these instances in drama are in no way related to the "epic" ones. The distributions of τε prove that it does more than merely connect; after all, the action of connecting items is not tied to a particular communicative situation, and τε in fact displays relatively large frequency differences across the three discourse patterns. Most authors prefer to use it in choral songs:

76 See §13 above on this general characteristic of the language of choral songs in Aristophanes.

77 However, since I did not count the relative frequencies of the different constructions—an enterprise which would moreover be subjective—the exact distributions of each construction cannot be established.

78 See II.1 §14. See §26 above on δέ in Aeschylus for another potential link to Homeric particle use in this author.

79 See IV.2 §§47-92 for elaborate discussion of the uses of τε in several authors.

80 See Ruijgh 1971:990 on οἷός τε in tragedy, 1004 on οἷός τε in comedy. On 991-1004 he discusses the other fixed constructions in drama containing an original "epic" τε. These are usually written as one word: ἅτε, ὅστε, and ὥστε.

Author	Dialogues	Monologues	Choral songs	Significant?
Aeschylus	0.58	2.15	1.67	yes
Sophocles	0.44	1.22	1.43	yes
Euripides	0.74	1.63	2.47	yes
Aristophanes	0.22	0.80	2.57	yes

Table 7: Frequencies of τε in percentages of all words

This distribution can be explained from several related associations of the particle. First and most fundamentally, τε marks certain knowledge as shared between speaker and addressee. In arguing this I follow the descriptions of τε in Wentzel 1847:2, Bloch 1955:147, and Gonda 1954:207, and build on this monograph's analyses of τε in epic, lyric, and historiography.[81] Second, what is shared is often traditional or even part of a traditional performance or ritual: τε may imply a link to tradition and rituality as well. Third, a high frequency of the particle may trigger an allusion to epic or lyric, genres where τε is naturally frequent because of the importance of traditional knowledge. Fourth, because of these associations, τε can convey a generally solemn and formal tone. I will discuss each of these implications in turn.

§40. First consider the many τε instances in this excerpt from a speech by the messenger in Aeschylus *Persians*, shortly after he brought the news of the Persian defeat:

(t7)

(Αγ.) Ἄμιστρις Ἀμφιστρεύς τε πολύπονον δόρυ
νωμῶν, ὅ τ' ἐσθλὸς Ἀριόμαρδος, Σάρδεσιν
πένθος παρασχών, Σεισάμης θ' ὁ Μύσιος,
Θάρυβίς τε πεντήκοντα πεντάκις νεῶν
ταγός, γένος Λυρναῖος, εὐειδὴς ἀνήρ,
κεῖται θανὼν δείλαιος οὐ μάλ' εὐτυχῶς·

Aeschylus *Persians* 320-325

[81] See II.4 §§32-37 on τε in Homeric similes; II.4 §§57-71 on connective τε in Pindar; IV.2 §§47-92 on τε in Herodotus and Thucydides.

> (Me.) and Amistris, and Amphistreus who wielded a spear that caused much trouble, and brave Ariomardus who dispensed grief with his arrows, and Seisames the Mysian, and Tharybis, admiral of five times fifty ships, a Lyrnaean by birth and a handsome man, lies wretchedly dead, having enjoyed no very good fortune.

The messenger here sums up the names of commanders who died in the recent battle, connecting them with τε. These names are well-known to the speaker and his addressee, the queen (as well as possibly the audience). That is, they represent shared knowledge.[82] At the same time, the high frequency of τε in this speech (as many as 10 instances out of 147 words total) lends a Homeric note to the messenger's voice.[83] As J. Barrett 2002 shows, tragic messengers in general, and this one in *Persians* in particular (23-54), are consistently portrayed as resembling an epic storyteller.[84]

§41. The prototypical kind of shared knowledge is the knowledge associated with traditions and rituals. Since the singing of choral songs is a traditional, ritual activity, the use of τε is especially suitable for this environment, regardless of the specific elements that the particle connects.[85] This is a further connection, then, between a particle's local function, depending on the immediate co-text, and a co-existing global function, depending on the discourse pattern. An example of a lyric passage with many instances is the following part of a Euripidean song:

(t8)

(Χο.) †οὐδὲ γὰρ ἐν† πόλεσι δίπτυχοι τυραννίδες
μιᾶς ἀμείνονες φέρειν,
ἄχθος τ' ἐπ' ἄχθει καὶ στάσιν πολίταις·
τεκόντοιν θ' ὕμνον ἐργάταιν δυοῖν
ἔριν Μοῦσαι φιλοῦσι κραίνειν.
πνοαὶ δ' ὅταν φέρωσι ναυτίλους θοαί,
κατὰ πηδαλίων διδύμα πραπίδων γνώμα

[82] Other examples of τε connected to shared knowledge (not necessarily traditional; see note 88 below) include Aeschylus *Suppliant Women* 256, 257, 258; Sophocles *Oedipus at Colonus* 551, 553, 555, 765; *Philoctetes* 314; Euripides *Heracles* 1290.

[83] τε's frequency in Homer is 2.0%, much higher than the average in drama: see our frequency graphs (available online as I.5). τε is roughly equally distributed across narrator text and direct speech in Homer, though in the *Iliad* slightly more common in narrator text; see II.1 §15.

[84] See §28 with note 55 above on the similarity between messenger speeches and epic language in general.

[85] See e.g. Nagy 1995:45 on the ritual dimension of choral lyric performance in the Athenian theater, and Calame 2013 and Grethlein 2013a:96-98 on several ritual functions of tragic songs. See also Burton 1980 on the Sophoclean chorus ("Many of the odes take the form of conventional types of ritual utterance," 3). On rituality and comic songs, see e.g. Bierl 2001 and Auffarth 2007.

> σοφῶν τε πλῆθος ἀθρόον ἀσθενέστερον
> φαυλοτέρας φρενὸς αὐτοκρατοῦς.
>
> Euripides *Andromache* 471-482

> (Ch.) For cities, likewise, double kingship is worse than single to endure, grief piled on grief for the citizens and the cause of faction. When two poets produce a hymn, the Muses are wont to work strife between them. When swift breezes are hurtling sailors along, a double intelligence at the helm and a throng of wise men conjoined is not as effective as a lesser mind with full authority.

At this point in the play it is becoming clear how disastrous it is that Neoptolemus has "a double marriage," as the chorus calls it: his jealous wife Hermione is threatening to kill his concubine Andromache and her child. In the song the chorus expands on the topic of disastrous rivalry, generalizing it to other spheres of private and public life. As Stevens 1971 and Lloyd 1994 *ad loc.* point out, this song fits into "a common pattern in Greek lyric" (Lloyd) through generalization, development, and then applying the general themes to the current situation. Indeed, the τε instances in 476 and 481 are found in *gnômai*.[86] In general the traditional context is a fitting environment for the particle. In 475 it is combined with καί, closely connecting two noun phrases; in 476 τε has a larger scope, introducing a whole clause;[87] in 581 it has a small scope again. All these instances of τε, then, have a connecting function, but the particle's distribution over the discourse patterns shows that there is more to the use of τε than this local function. More globally, the many τε occurrences here strengthen the ode's link to tradition.[88]

§42. There are only five tragic songs without τε in my corpus (which contains 55 tragic choral songs in total).[89] These songs happen to be exceptional in other ways as well: they contain, for example, more first- or second-person references than the average choral ode, and fewer nouns. Their style is in certain respects closer to that of the average dialogue than to that of the average song. In terms of content, they are all directly tied to the immediate context of the play, and do not take the audience out of the ongoing

[86] On γάρ τε in *gnômai* in Homer, see II.4 §§21-22 and IV.2 note 90.

[87] See IV.2 §§76-77 on "sentential" τε in Herodotus and Thucydides.

[88] On τε and tradition, see II.1 §13; II.4 §§31-37 (on Homer); II.4 §§55-72 (on Pindar); IV.2 §§54-69 (mainly on historiography). Other τε instances in drama connected to traditional knowledge include Aeschylus *Seven against Thebes* 128, 130, 135, 147; Sophocles *Oedipus at Colonus* 793; *Philoctetes* 726; Euripides *Hecuba* 18, 19, 21 (two τε instances), 22; *Heracles* 1274, 1275.

[89] The five tragic songs without τε are Aeschylus *Eumenides* 254-275; Sophocles *Ajax* 172-200, 1185-1222; *Oedipus King* 1086-1109; Euripides *Andromache* 117-146.

story as many other songs do.[90] One of them is the parodos by the Salaminian sailors in Sophocles *Ajax*:

(t9)

> (Χο.) οὔποτε γὰρ φρενόθεν γ' ἐπ' ἀριστερά,
> παῖ Τελαμῶνος, ἔβας
> τόσσον ἐν ποίμναις πίτνων
> ἥκοι γὰρ ἂν θεία νόσος ἀλλ' ἀπερύκοι
> καὶ Ζεὺς κακὰν καὶ Φοῖβος Ἀργείων φάτιν

Sophocles *Ajax* 182-186

> (Ch.) Never were you in your right mind when you went so far astray as to fall upon the flocks! No, a godsent sickness must have come upon you; but may Zeus and Phoebus avert the evil rumour of the Argives!

The song as a whole (lines 172-200) contains 12 references to a "you" (about 10% of all 126 words), a much higher frequency than the average of about 5% for Sophoclean songs.[91] Indeed, three out of four songs in *Ajax* have a higher frequency of references to either first or second person.[92] These chorus members, in other words, advance themselves as communicators more than is usual for a tragic chorus. This is also reflected in the occurrence of γε in two of the songs, such as here in line 182—this particle is normally absent from tragic choral songs.[93] Moreover, these linguistic features accompany atypical content: the songs concern Ajax himself, or the influence of his troubles on the lives of the chorus members, rather than general or timeless considerations.[94] In different

[90] For example, the songs in Aeschylus *Libation Bearers* 585-652; Sophocles *Antigone* 332-375; *Oedipus King* 863-910; Euripides *Andromache* 274-308; *Hippolytus* 525-564, 732-775.

[91] See Table 14 below for the frequencies of second-person references across the discourse patterns. Burton remarks on this ode that the chorus members "address Ajax in the second person, even though he is not present on stage, because he dominates their thoughts and because they urgently need his presence." (1980:11)

[92] In 693-718 there are 6 first-person references (frequency of 6%) and 11 second-person references (frequency of 10%); in 1185-1222, there are 7 first-person references (frequency of 6%). See Tables 13 and 14 below for the average frequencies of first- and second-person references across the discourse patterns. These other stylistically exceptional songs contain two τε instances (one of which is not found in all manuscripts) and no τε instances, respectively.

[93] See §§58-61 below on the distribution of γε, and the association of this particle with the explicit expression of the speaker's stance. The other γε is in line 716. No commentator comments on the particle's unusual environment.

[94] The one song which does not have a strikingly high frequency of references to the "I" or "you" (596-645) zooms out slightly more from the immediate context of the play: it still concerns the troubles of Ajax, but now from the perspective of his mother's expected reaction. This song has 4% references to the first person (more than the average of 2.8% in Sophoclean choral songs, but

ways, then, the singing sailors show their personal involvement in what they are singing about,[95] that is, the fate of their leader Ajax, and their emotional nearness to him. This fits well with their identity as his followers and friends.[96] Such a chorus of Greek men of military age was unusual in tragedy.[97] In this case, Sophocles has matched the unusual choral identity with unusual language use. The chorus' characterization is therefore strengthened by the linguistic choices in the odes.

§43. τε tends to appear also in ritual contexts other than choral lyric, such as prayers, prophecies, or the swearing of an oath. This includes instances in dialogues, even though the particle is less frequent there than in monologues and choral songs. In tragic dialogues the τε frequency is significantly higher than in comic dialogues. Consider the following instances:

(t10)

Μη. ὄμνυ πέδον Γῆς πατέρα θ' Ἥλιον πατρὸς
τοὐμοῦ θεῶν τε συντιθεὶς ἅπαν γένος.
Αι. τί χρῆμα δράσειν ἢ τί μὴ δράσειν; λέγε.

Euripides *Medea* 746-748

Me. Swear by the plain of Earth, by Helios, my grand-father, and by the whole race of gods all together.

Ae. To do what or refrain from what? You must say.

Mastronarde 2002 *ad loc.* notes that the "generalizing formula" in Medea's list of gods is typical of "ritual contexts." Similarly, Page 1938 comments that Euripides "is using conventional language" in 747, and Mossman 2011 observes "the solemnity of the ritual." A solemn tone fits the situation, because Medea's life might later depend on the oath that she is now proposing. The double τε is repeated by Aegeus when he indeed swears the oath in lines 752-753. In addition to emphasizing the ritual activity of swearing an oath,

less than in the other songs in *Ajax* (see note 92 above), and 5% to the second person (which is the average for Sophoclean choral songs).

95 See §8 above and §59 below on the degree of explicit personal involvement as one of the factors that influence linguistic differences between registers in modern languages.

96 Finglass 2011 *ad* 134-200; Garvie 1998 *ad* 134-200; Hesk 2003:30, 48; Jebb 1896:xlvi; Kamerbeek 1953 *ad* 134-200; and Stanford 1963:li-lii, *ad* 134-200 all note the chorus' exceptional loyalty to and dependence on Ajax. See also Burton 1980:39: "The lyrics are (...) a mirror in which we see reflected the characters of Ajax and of his sailors, and their mutual relationship of devotion and interdependence."

97 See Foley 2003:26-27: there were more female choruses, and most male ones consisted of old or foreign men.

τε here marks the entities it connects (the Earth, the Sun, and all gods) as belonging to shared encyclopedic knowledge.[98]

§44. Besides these associations with shared knowledge, tradition, and rituality, a high τε frequency may remind the audience of epic, of non-dramatic lyric, and, in Aristophanes, of tragic lyric.[99] The allusion to other genres is especially apparent in Aristophanic choral songs, where the average frequency of τε is more than eleven times as high as in dialogues. Consider the following example:

(t11)

(Χο.) οὗ σέβας ἀρρήτων ἱερῶν, ἵνα μυστοδόκος δόμος
ἐν τελεταῖς ἁγίαις ἀναδείκνυται,
οὐρανίοις τε θεοῖς δωρήματα,
ναοί θ' ὑψερεφεῖς καὶ ἀγάλματα,
καὶ πρόσοδοι μακάρων ἱερώταται,
εὐστέφανοί τε θεῶν θυσίαι θαλίαι τε
παντοδαπαῖσιν ὥραις,

Aristophanes *Clouds* 302-310

(Ch.) where ineffable rites are celebrated, where the temple that received initiates is thrown open during the pure mystic festival; and where there are offerings of the heavenly host, temples with lofty roofs and statues, most holy processions for the Blessed Ones, well-garlanded victims for the gods, and feasts in all seasons; (...)

Aristophanes' overuse of the particle in this choral song (six instances in 56 words in total) mockingly mirrors τε's traditional implications, and at the same time parodies epic and tragic lyric. Echoes from epic are also apparent in the lexical choices: words like ὑψερεφεῖς ("high-roofed," 306) and εὐστέφανοι ("well- garlanded," 308) are taken

98 On oath swearing in Euripidean stichomythia and the length this takes up, see Schuren 2015:38. On various aspects of performing oaths in tragedy and comedy, see Fletcher 2012.

Other τε instances in contexts of oath swearing are found in Aeschylus *Agamemnon* 1433 and *Seven against Thebes* 45 (both in monologues), similarly connecting names of deities. Note also the τε instances in addresses to deities in Aeschylus *Agamemnon* 509, 513-514, 516, 519, and Sophocles *Philoctetes* 134; in official advice by the seer Teiresias in Sophocles *Antigone* 1016-1017; in references to prayers in Sophocles *Antigone* 1200 and *Philoctetes* 738 (cited in (t20) below); in a supplication in Sophocles *Philoctetes* 468, 469, 472; in reporting a prophesy in Sophocles *Oedipus King* 995; and in reporting an official message from Zeus in Aristophanes *Birds* 1232-1233.

99 See Swift 2010 about the influence of lyric poetry on tragedy, esp. tragic songs. The lyric poets Pindar and Bacchylides use τε in frequencies of 2.11% and 1.67%, respectively, whereas in the tragedians its overall frequencies are 0.85%, 0.89%, and 1.36%, respectively. Aristophanes has 0.58%. See II.4 §§32-37 on uses of τε in Homer; II.4 §§54-68 on τε in Pindar.

from epic vocabulary. The clouds, who form the chorus here, are thus presented as exaggeratedly solemn and divine creatures.[100] τε contributes to this image, beyond its local connecting function in the specific instances.[101]

§45. This example of parody also illustrates the last, related association of τε in my corpus: the particle's connection to a generally formal or solemn tone. Not only τε's frequent occurrence in contexts of shared knowledge, tradition, and rituality suggests this formal or solemn implication, but also the distribution of other linguistic features over the discourse patterns, such as nouns and finite verbs. The distributions of these features are illuminating, because they are connected to levels of formality in modern-language registers. For example, in the four languages analyzed in Biber 1995 (English, Nukulaelae Tuvaluan, Korean, and Somali), a higher frequency of nouns is associated with discourse that is less involved, less interactive, and has a less overt expression of personal stance than other texts.[102] This means, for example, that English academic prose, a relatively formal register, has a noun-verb ratio twice as high as spoken conversation, which is relatively informal.[103] Biber, Conrad, and Reppen 1998:69 explain that nouns typically convey something more abstract and more information-focused than verbs. Verbs, in contrast, refer to actions, and also often to thoughts and feelings of the speaker.[104] This makes verbs more suitable for highly interactive situations.[105]

100 Similarly, the 18 τε instances (2.4% of 752 words) in the parabasis of Aristophanes *Birds* (676-800) contribute to an exaggeratedly solemn presentation of the bird chorus. τε is found, in Wilson's 2007 edition, in lines 691 (4 instances!), 693, 701, 702, 704 (here τε is a conjecture), 718, 719, 720, 734, 740 (here τε καί is a conjecture), 746, 778, 782, 790, 793. In 777 τε in the manuscripts has been changed into τά by Bentley, which is accepted by Wilson; Dunbar 1995 however retains τε, albeit in a different position of the verse.

101 In lines 308-309, τε also contributes to the alliteration between the τ- and θ-sounds. In 306, as often in Aristophanic choral songs, τε is combined with καί; we saw in Table 6 that the frequency of καί is also relatively high in this environment. Together the two particles indicate an especially tight link between two items, as well as an association with shared or ritual knowledge. Other examples of the combination τε καί/τε... καί in Aristophanic songs are found in e.g. *Birds* 1069, 1332, 1697, 1701; *Clouds* 567; *Frogs* 388, 407, 1107, 1489; *Lysistrata* 323, 1060 (cited in (t6) above), 1067; *Peace* 348, 779, 809, 1129; *Women at the Thesmophoria* 669, 975. See IV.2 §70, where it is argued that τε καί in historiography often carries an implied meaning related to encyclopedic and cultural knowledge.

102 Biber 1995:142, 173, 194, 206, 242, 249.

103 Biber 2006:14; Biber, Conrad, and Reppen 1998:67-69.

104 See Biber, Conrad, and Reppen 1998:69: there is an "emphasis in academic prose on objects, states, and processes—all referred to with nouns—rather than human agents and their actions (described with verbs)."

105 This observation might also be connected to the findings discussed by Pennebaker 2011:42-43 that in English, men use on average more nouns than women, and women more verbs than men. Also in other characteristics of their language use, men tend to focus more on abstract objects, and women more on (social) actions. These differences suggest that women, more than men, tend to use linguistic features that reflect interactiveness. Such evidence demonstrates

§46. The distributions of nouns and finite verbs over the discourse patterns in my corpus are as follows:

Author	Dialogues	Monologues	Choral songs	Significant?
Aeschylus	23.2	30.9	30.1	yes
Sophocles	16.4	19.7	31.1	yes
Euripides	21.6	24.9	34.1	yes
Aristophanes	16.2	21.0	25.3	yes

Table 8: Frequencies of nouns in percentages of all words

Author	Dialogues	Monologues	Choral songs	Significant?
Aeschylus	15.4	11.3	10.0	yes
Sophocles	15.9	12.5	9.8	yes
Euripides	16.5	12.6	10.7	yes
Aristophanes	15.7	14.7	11.4	yes

Table 9: Frequencies of finite verbs in percentages of all words

Dialogues tend to have a higher frequency of finite verbs and a lower frequency of nouns than monologues and choral songs. Stichomythic conventions may play a role in the high frequency of verbs in dialogues: the tight schema of turns ensures that a speaker has only a short time to utter her turn. Since a finite verb is often needed for that, this increases the frequency of verbs in such an environment.[106] This conventional "pressure" may mirror a similar situation for speakers in face-to-face conversation, to which dramatic dialogues are closer than monologues or songs.[107] More generally, a lower verb frequency and a higher noun frequency are found in formal, less interactive, and less

once again the influence of situational characteristics on linguistic choices, in particular on the frequency of nouns and verbs (see also §§1-2 and §§4-8 above).

106 I thank the audience of my paper "Discourse Patterns in Aristophanes" at the *2013 Classical Association Annual Conference* in Reading, UK, for this suggestion.

107 See e.g. Biber 2006:213-218 on the influence of production circumstances on patterns of linguistic variation across registers.

explicitly involved discourse in the modern languages analyzed in register studies.[108] The language used in tragic and comic monologues, as compared to that used in dialogues, thus reflects these situational characteristics, and choral lyric language even more so. Not only nouns and verbs indicate these correlations, but also the distributions of first- and second-person references, negations, and swearing expressions.[109]

§47. In formal or solemn communicative environments, we find a corresponding high frequency of τε. Consider the following passage from an Aeschylean monologue, the environment in which this author uses τε most:

(t12)

124a[110] Ηλ. κῆρυξ μέγιστε τῶν ἄνω τε καὶ κάτω
124b < > Ἑρμῆ χθόνιε, κηρύξας ἐμοὶ
τοὺς γῆς ἔνερθε δαίμονας κλύειν ἐμὰς
εὐχάς, πατρῴων δωμάτων ἐπισκόπους,
καὶ γαῖαν αὐτήν, ἣ τὰ πάντα τίκτεται
θρέψασά τ' αὖθις τῶνδε κῦμα λαμβάνει.
κἀγὼ χέουσα τάσδε χέρνιβας νεκροῖς
λέγω καλοῦσα πατέρ' "ἐποίκτιρόν τ' ἐμὲ
φίλον τ' Ὀρέστην φῶς τ' ἄναψον ἐν δόμοις.

Aeschylus *Libation Bearers* 124-131

El. Great Herald who communicates between those above and those below, Hermes of the Underworld, <aid me> by making proclamations on my

108 With "less interactive" I do not mean that there is less interaction going on in choral songs, because the songs are crucial for the audience, but that the singers do not expect to receive an immediate explicit reply, as a speaker of a dialogue or monologue would expect.

109 These features are discussed in §59 (first- and second-person references, and swearing expressions) and §66 (negations) below.

Passive finite verbs seem to point in the same direction: they are the most frequent in choral songs in all authors, but their distribution is significant in Sophocles only (4% of all finite verbs in dialogues, 6% in monologues, 7% in choral songs). Van Hell, Verhoeven, Tak, and Van Oosterhout 2005:245 claim that passive constructions in several modern languages are typically associated with "a more detached, distanced, generalized, and objective stance" than the active voice, and a higher degree of formality. In the same vein, Biber 1995:70-71 observes that impersonal constructions in Somali and passive constructions in English can be used "to suppress the source of information and the role of the author in the assertion of information." The passive, then, may help to make the speaker "invisible" concerning her influence on what she is saying. Concerning the ancient Greek passive, George 2005:13 observes its high frequency in administrative Mycenaean documents, and proposes to "compare the widespread use of the passive in contemporary bureaucracy." Similarly, Schironi 2010:349 notes that the ancient Greek passive is relatively frequent in mathematical texts.

110 Line 124a was originally line 165, transposed here by Hermann 1852. See III.4 (t5).

> behalf both to the powers under the earth, who watch over my father's house, that they should hear my prayers, and to Earth itself, who gives birth to all things, nurtures them, and then receives that fruit of her womb back into herself. And I, as I pour these lustral libations, call on my father and say: Have pity on me, and kindle a light in your house in the shape of my beloved Orestes.[111]

Electra is here performing a prayer to Hermes and the dead Agamemnon: a solemn tone can be expected in such a context. Praying is also a ritual activity; the solemn-tone association of τε in this case overlaps with this other implication. The entire speech (124-151) contains 46 nouns (26.6% of its 173 words), 17 finite verbs (a low frequency of 9.8%), and as many as seven τε instances (4.0%).[112] Together these features reflect a formal style, appropriate to the praying activity. The two τε in 124a (=165) and 128 signify a tight connection of their conjuncts as well as an allusion to traditional knowledge. In 130-131, the first two instances establish a close link between the elements "me" and "Orestes"; the τε after φῶς[113] has a larger scope, adding a new verb phrase.[114]

§48. Choral songs exceed the spoken parts in their formal and ritual nature. In addition to all the features mentioned, other characteristics of lyric language, such as more semantically obscure words and Doric coloring, contribute to the defamiliarizing style of choral songs, since they remove the language even more from daily spoken Attic than the general stylization throughout tragedy already does.[115] The characteristics of the songs' melodic patterns and accompanying dances will have played a role in the overall defamiliarization of this communicative situation as well.[116]

§49. The distributions of τε as well as of other linguistic features over the three discourse patterns make it apparent that this particle contributes more to the discourse than only its local connecting force. I associate τε with several implications deriving

[111] φῶς τ' ἄναψον in 131 is an anonymous conjecture of the manuscript reading πῶς ἀνάξομεν. Sommerstein translates Wilamowitz' alternative conjecture without τε after φῶς. See Garvie 1986 *ad loc.*

[112] Blass 1906, Groeneboom 1949, and Garvie 1986 do not remark on these τε occurrences.

[113] These words are a conjecture: see note 110 above.

[114] There is also a metrical function in the first four cases, but the particle's distribution proves that metrical considerations cannot have been decisive for its use. Other examples of τε contributing a formal or solemn tone include Sophocles *Oedipus King* 253 (three τε instances), 1184-1185 (three τε instances); Euripides *Heracles* 1325 (two τε instances); Aristophanes *Birds* 379 (two τε instances); *Lysistrata* 502 (one τε instance).

[115] See Battezzato 2005:149; Silk 2010.

[116] An effect of this style, in combination with a certain content, may be "to draw us away for the moment from the happenings on the stage," as argued by W.S. Barrett 1964 for the song in Euripides *Hippolytus* 732-775. See also Burton 1980 about Sophocles in particular: a choral song may create a pause, "diverting the audience with mythical parallels" (132) just before quick plot movements need their attention again. Similarly, he writes on the ode in Sophocles *Oedipus King*

from their performative context: shared knowledge, tradition, rituality, an allusion to epic, a parody of tragic lyric, and a generally solemn or official tone.

2.2.4 γάρ

§50. The distribution of γάρ in my corpus is as follows:

Author	Dialogues	Monologues	Choral songs	Significant?
Aeschylus	15.7	1.10	1.11	no
Sophocles	1.85	1.33	1.14	yes
Euripides	1.11	1.21	0.84	no
Aristophanes	1.84	0.95	1.11	yes

Table 10: Frequencies of γάρ in percentages of all words

In Aeschylus and Euripides γάρ is roughly equally distributed across the three discourse patterns, whereas in Sophocles and Aristophanes it is used more frequently in dialogues.[117] Compared to τε, γάρ has a more complex distribution pattern, a probable result of its use in several constructions, in which it has varying functions.

§51. γάρ in drama often marks its host act as the cause, explanation, or clarification of a preceding (or sometimes following) act.[118] This cause or explanation may relate to the other act in two ways, either alone or simultaneously: *de re* (concerning content) or *de dicto* (concerning the discourse acts).[119] An example of a content relation is "I did this *because* my master ordered me to": the "because" clause introduces a state of affairs that plays a role in the realization of the main clause. Here is an instance of this kind of γάρ in Aeschylus:

863-910: "the song provides a pause for reflection within the gathering menace of the tragedy" (157). In general, tragic choral songs are usually seen as "more weakly contextualized" than other parts of the plays (Silk 1998:15). See also Battezzato's remark that the tragic chorus is often seen as "an impersonal entity" (2005:155).

117 See II.1 §15 for γάρ's distribution in Homer: there it is on average more than twice as frequent in direct speech as in narrator text.

118 See e.g. Hartung 1832:457-459; Bäumlein 1861:82; Denniston 1950 [1934]:58-62. This use is much less frequent in epic and lyric discourse: see II.3 §§22-32, §§78-79; II.4 §§15-28, §70 on γάρ in Homer and Pindar. On γάρ in Herodotus and Thucydides, see IV.2 §59, §98; IV.3 §§108-110.

119 On *de re* vs. *de dicto* as used in linguistic research, see Torck 1996:48; Slings 1997a:104-106; Ferrari, Cignetti, De Cesare, Lala, Mandelli, Ricci, and Roggia 2008:37; Béguelin 2010:18-19.

(t13)

Χο. γύναι, κατ' ἄνδρα σώφρον' εὐφρόνως λέγεις·
ἐγὼ δ' ἀκούσας πιστά σου τεκμήρια
θεοὺς προσειπεῖν εὖ παρασκευάζομαι·
χάρις γὰρ οὐκ ἄτιμος εἴργασται πόνων.

Aeschylus *Agamemnon* 351-354

> Ch. Lady, you have spoken wisely, like a sensible man; and having heard trustworthy evidence from you, I am preparing to address the gods in an appropriate manner, for a reward, which ought not to go unhonoured, has been given in return for our sufferings.

Now that Troy has been captured, the chorus has decided to address the gods appropriately. The γάρ act explains why the speakers are getting ready (παρασκευάζομαι) to sing the upcoming song.[120]

§52. As represented in the above example, γάρ typically expresses a *de re* relation (signaling a cause on the level of content) when a speaker has just referred to her own actions or feelings, a natural consequence of the fact that one normally knows the reason(s) for one's own actions or feelings.[121] When the discourse concerns agents other than the speaker herself, it is more likely that γάρ signals a *de dicto* relation. For example: "what time is it?—*because* you have a watch." Here the "because" clause explains why the speaker felt she could direct her question to this specific addressee. The following excerpt contains an instance of γάρ in this use:[122]

120 See Aristophanes *Wealth* 828 for a γάρ instance in a similar context: the speaker is coming to thank the god "because (γάρ) he is responsible for my great blessings."

121 Other examples of γάρ marking a *de re* reason in a first-person context are found in e.g. Aeschylus *Agamemnon* 10 (see E. Fraenkel 1950 *ad loc.*: "[t]he sentence gives the reason why the Watchman has fulfilled night after night for a whole long year a task which is to him a waeriness of the flesh."), 32, 105, 259, 461, 584, 601; Sophocles *Ajax* 21, 106 ("he is inside" refers indirectly to the speaker's own action), 125, 205; Euripides *Medea* 38, 44, 215, 228, 267, 278, 303, 309; Aristophanes *Birds* 255; *Wealth* 822, 828. Some of these instances mark a *de dicto* relation at the same time.

122 "Bis" and "ter" are designations from the *TLG*, where *bis* indicates the second turn of speaking within the same line, and *ter* the third. Other examples of γάρ marking a *de dicto* relation include Aeschylus *Agamemnon* 134, 154, 214, 326, 343, 350, 381, 522, 524, 534, 555; Sophocles *Ajax* 23, 182, 257, 279, 328, 393, 397; *Antigone* 20, 96; *Oedipus King* 147, 231, 291, 724, 981; *Philoctetes* 1450; Euripides *Medea* 6, 66, 80, 83, 89, 92, 125, 183, 263, 314; Aristophanes *Birds* 21, 32, 97, 132, 199, 253, 349, 376, 432, 452, 458; *Peace* 321, 337.

(t14)

(Ευ.) οὗτος δὲ δὴ τίς ἐσθ’ ὁ μετ’ ὀρνίθων βίος;
σὺ γὰρ οἶσθ’ ἀκριβῶς.
Επ. οὐκ ἄχαρις εἰς τὴν τριβήν·

Aristophanes *Birds* 155-156

Pe.[123] But what about this life with the birds? Tell me about it; you know every detail.
Te. It wears quite nicely.

In this case the particle does not refer to a causal relation in the reported world, but marks its host act as clarifying why the preceding interrogative act was uttered. The speaker can ask this question, he assumes, because the Hoopoe knows the answer.

§53. A γάρ act may also signal a *de re* and a *de dicto* relation at the same time. This dual signification regularly occurs when a speaker explains why she has just used a certain evaluative expression. On the *de re* level, the γάρ act explains why the evaluated object of thought really fits the given characterization; simultaneously, the γάρ act clarifies, *de dicto*, the speaker's use of that evaluative expression in the preceding act. Here is an example from Euripides:[124]

(t15)

(Μη.) κἀν τῷδ’ ἀγὼν μέγιστος, ἢ κακὸν λαβεῖν

ἢ χρηστόν· οὐ γὰρ εὐκλεεῖς ἀπαλλαγαὶ
γυναιξὶν οὐδ’ οἷόν τ’ ἀνήνασθαι πόσιν.

Euripides *Medea* 235-237

(Me.) The outcome of our life's striving hangs on this, whether we take a bad or a good husband. For divorce is discreditable for women and it is not possible to refuse wedlock.

The γάρ act in 236 explains, *de re*, why it is the ἀγὼν μέγιστος ("the greatest issue") for women whether their husband is good or bad: that is, women have no choice but to get

123 In the Greek text, edited by Wilson 2007, Euelpides speaks this line; in Henderson's 2000 Loeb edition, from which the translation is taken, it is given to Peisetaerus.

124 Other examples of γάρ marking simultaneously a *de re* and a *de dicto* relation after an evaluation are found in e.g. Aeschylus *Agamemnon* 14, 267, 423, 433, 469, 506, 532, 559; Sophocles *Ajax* 9, 20, 150, 185, 215, 216, 264, 327, 432; *Antigone* 389; *Oedipus King* 137, 288, 1268; Euripides *Medea* 17, 140, 325; Aristophanes *Birds* 202, 273, 317, 342.

married and stay with their husbands. At the same time, Medea explains why she has just uttered that qualification ("I said that because...").[125] This reason may well contain another evaluative expression,[126] such as here οὐ εὐκλεεῖς ("not reputable"), which may subsequently trigger more γάρ acts clarifying the use of that assessment.

§54. Just as in Homer, Pindar, and historiography, γάρ in drama is also regularly found in gnomic contexts.[127] Since *gnômai* concern general matters, they represent a stepping out of the surrounding discourse: they are "unframed."[128] γάρ does not necessarily imply any causality when it introduces unframed discourse (see II.4). A *gnôme* in drama may however imply a *de dicto* causal relation that can be paraphrased as "(I know that this is the case) because that is how things always go." An example of γάρ introducing a *gnôme* occurs in this song by the frightened Danaids:

(t16)

(Χο.) κυσὶν δ' ἔπειθ' ἕλωρα κἀπιχωρίοις
ὄρνισι δεῖπνον οὐκ ἀναίνομαι πέλειν·
τὸ γὰρ θανεῖν ἐλευθεροῦ-
ται φιλαιάκτων κακῶν.

Aeschylus *Suppliant Women* 800-803

(Ch.) Thereafter, I do not refuse to become prey for the dogs, a dinner for the native birds: for he who dies[129] is freed from evils that cry to be bewailed.

As Wecklein 1902 and Friis Johansen and Whittle 1980 *ad loc.* point out, the idea that the dead are free from misery is proverbial in tragedy. γάρ marks this *gnôme* as backing up

125 See Denniston 1950 [1934]:60-61 on this use: γάρ "gives the motive for saying that which has just been said: 'I say this because...'."

126 See IV.4 §59 and §101 on γάρ with stancetaking expressions in authorial statements in Herodotus and Thucydides.

127 See II.4 §§20-23 (on Homer and Pindar); IV.3 §108 (on historiography).

128 Especially in narrative discourse, where the ongoing story provides a consistent frame, unframed discourse is conspicuous. Unframed discourse includes not only *gnômai*, but also e.g. embedded narratives; γάρ may mark the start of different kinds of such narrative expansions. For the concepts of unframed versus framed discourse, and the role of γάρ to mark a switch to unframed discourse, see II.4 §§15-28 (on Homer and Pindar). See IV.2 §§98-99 and IV.3 §110 on γάρ marking an expansion in historiography. See De Jong 1997 on γάρ introducing embedded narratives in several authors. My corpus presents only few examples of γάρ marking a switch to unframed discourse in narrative (e.g. Sophocles *Ajax* 319), since drama contains little narrative overall.

129 Sommerstein reads Hartung's conjecture ὁ γὰρ θανὼν instead of τὸ γὰρ θανεῖν. See Friis Johansen and Whittle 1980 *ad loc.* for discussion of the probable corruption.

the maidens' death wish.[130] Most other gnomic statements with γάρ are preceded by a discourse act with a third person. The speaker in those cases has to infer why a certain situation is or was as she perceives it, as she cannot know it from her own experience.

§55. At the beginning of utterances in dialogues γάρ usually does not signal any cause or explanation, whether *de re* or *de dicto*. Rather, it signals explicitly that the speaker is expanding on the preceding utterance, and that she infers something from it. For example, after Euelpides in Aristophanes *Birds* 109bis-110 has clarified that he and his friend are no jurors, but jurophobes from Athens, the Hoopoe asks σπείρεται γὰρ τοῦτ' ἐκεῖ /τὸ σπέρμ'; (110bis-111), "(are you saying that) that seed sprouts there?" The Hoopoe, accepting the two men's claim to be jurophobes, infers that jurophobes exist in Athens; the question with γάρ indicates his inference, and implies his surprise at the realization.

§56. The expansion or inference signaled by turn-initial γάρ often implies indignation or anger.[131] Examples are mainly found in Sophocles and Aristophanes, who use γάρ especially often in dialogues, such as in this altercation between Menelaus and Teucer:

(t17)

Με. ἡ γλῶσσά σου τὸν θυμὸν ὡς δεινὸν τρέφει.
Τευ. ξὺν τῷ δικαίῳ γὰρ μέγ' ἔξεστιν φρονεῖν.
Με. δίκαια γὰρ τόνδ' εὐτυχεῖν κτείναντά με;
Τευ. κτείναντα; δεινόν γ' εἶπας, εἰ καὶ ζῇς θανών.
Με. θεὸς γὰρ ἐκσῴζει με, τῷδε δ' οἴχομαι.
Τευ. μή νυν ἀτίμα θεούς, θεοῖς σεσωμένος.
Με. ἐγὼ γὰρ ἂν ψέξαιμι δαιμόνων νόμους;

Sophocles *Ajax* 1124-1130

Me. What fierce anger your tongue supplies with sustenance!
Te. Yes, one can feel pride when one has justice on one's side.
Me. Is it just that this man should be honoured when he was my murderer?
Te. Your murderer? You have said a strange thing, if you have died but are alive.
Me. Yes, a god has kept me safe, but for Ajax I am dead.

[130] Other examples of γάρ marking a *de dicto* relation in a gnomic context include Aeschylus *Agamemnon* 76, 222, 254; *Seven against Thebes* 77, 338; Sophocles *Ajax* 154, 157, 160, 260, 330, 378; *Antigone* 127; *Oedipus King* 198; Euripides *Hippolytus* 530, 563, 1108; *Medea* 48.

[131] On this use of γάρ, see Viger 1752 [1627]:492; Bäumlein 1861:74 (γάρ gives questions more "Ton und Lebhaftigkeit"); Denniston 1950 [1934]:77 (these γάρ questions are "surprised and incredulous, often ironical"); Van Erp Taalman Kip 1997. See also III.3 §§95-98 for the repeated use of turn-initial γάρ in tragic stichomythia with angry speakers.

Te. Then do not refuse honour to the gods, seeing that the gods preserved you.
Me. Why, would I find fault with the laws of the gods?

In 1125 Teucer expands on what Menelaus has just said, angrily implying that this reproach about his own "terrible temper" (θυμὸν ὡς δεινὸν, 1124) can in fact be turned into an argument for Teucer's side: "yes, (it is right for me to have a terrible temper) for with justice it is allowed to be high-minded."[132] The γάρ instances in questions, in 1126 and 1130, suggest that Menelaus has made an inference from the preceding utterance: "are you really saying that...?"[133] The γάρ in the answer in 1128 signals an expansion on the preceding question ("did you die and yet stay alive?"), as well as a *de dicto* explanation: "yes, I said that, because..."[134] The inferences that are communicated in all cases signal the speakers' strong indignation.[135] γάρ thus indirectly contributes to the expression of this emotion.

§57. The above examples show that γάρ's distribution may help to distinguish among several different uses of the particle. Sophocles and Aristophanes are fond of a use of γάρ in questions or answers, where the particle indicates that an inference has been drawn, which may arouse indignation in the speaker. This use is highly interactional and fits dialogues best. In contrast, the constructions in which γάρ marks a *de re* and/or *de dicto* cause or explanation occur in all three discourse patterns. Finally, the use of γάρ to introduce *gnômai*, which occurs less frequently than the causal uses, seems to occur especially in choral songs, where one of the general communicative goals is to recall and reinforce communal values. For the understanding of γάρ's function in a certain tragic or comic passage, then, it is crucial to take into account the global pragmatic functions of the specific discourse pattern.

132 At the same time, Teucer frames his response as a gnomic thought; see §54 above. Note that the position of γάρ in this utterance (1125) implies that the words ξὺν τῷ δικαίῳ were considered, and probably pronounced as, one unit.

133 Other examples of turn-initial γάρ in questions, marking an inference from the preceding utterance, are found in e.g. Sophocles *Ajax* 282; *Oedipus King* 1000, 1029; Euripides *Medea* 59; Aristophanes *Birds* 74, 110bis (see §55 above), 289, 300, 355bis, 369; *Frogs* 25bis, 29 (both *Frogs* examples are cited in (t18) on γε and δῆτα below); *Lysistrata* 497bis.

134 Other examples of turn-initial γάρ in answers and other statements, marking an expansion on the preceding utterance, are found in e.g. Aeschylus *Agamemnon* 271, 551; Sophocles *Ajax* 82; *Antigone* 511, 555, 569; *Oedipus King* 731, 1024; Euripides *Medea* 327; Aristophanes *Birds* 285; *Lysistrata* 55.

135 See Jebb 1896, Kamerbeek 1953, and Stanford 1963. Viger 1752 [1627]:492 already notes the connection between γάρ in questions and indignation. See also Goldhill 2012:58-62 about the use of turn-initial γάρ in Sophocles.

2.2.5 γε and δῆτα

§58. γε and δῆτα have consistent and significant distributions across the three discourse patterns. I discuss these two particles together, because their distributions are very similar.

Author	Dialogues	Monologues	Choral songs	Significant?
Aeschylus	0.58	0.35	0.08	yes
Sophocles	1.53	0.50	0.26	yes
Euripides	1.51	0.40	0.13	yes
Aristophanes	2.48	0.60	0.17	yes

Table 11: Frequencies of γε in percentages of all words

Author	Dialogues	Monologues	Choral songs	Significant?
Aeschylus	0.09	0	0	yes
Sophocles	0.39	0.09	0	yes
Euripides	0.33	0.05	0.06	yes
Aristophanes	0.41	0.25	0	yes

Table 12: Frequencies of δῆτα in percentages of all words

The consistent distribution of these two particles suggests that their pragmatic functions are most suitable for the dialogue setting. Indeed, we will see below that they are connected to interactiveness. First I will discuss the distribution of several other features in order to strengthen my claim that linguistic choices reflect the degree of interactiveness of the different discourse patterns. Then I will focus on the particles themselves.

§59. We already saw in §§45-46 above that the distributions of nouns and finite verbs reflect that dialogues are less formal, but more interactive and explicitly involved, than the settings of monologues and choral songs. The distributions of first- and second-person references and of swearing expressions strengthen this impression as well. They all have their highest frequency in dialogues.[136]

Author	Dialogues	Monologues	Choral songs	Significant?
Aeschylus	5.8	4.5	1.8	yes
Sophocles	7.3	6.5	2.8	yes
Euripides	8.4	6.7	2.5	yes
Aristophanes	6.7	6.7	5.4	no

Table 13: Frequencies of first-person references in percentages of all words

Author	Dialogues	Monologues	Choral songs	Significant?
Aeschylus	9.9	2.1	2.1	yes
Sophocles	11.4	6.0	4.9	yes
Euripides	13.8	5.9	6.9	yes
Aristophanes	7.7	6.6	6.0	no

Table 14: Frequencies of second-person references in percentages of all words

Author	Dialogues	Monologues	Choral songs	Significant?
Aristophanes	1.1	0.1	0.06	yes

Table 15: Frequencies of swearing expressions in percentages of all words

[136] Also future finite verbs have their highest frequency in dialogues in all authors, but their distribution is only significant in tragedy as a whole, not in any of the individual authors. The future is inherently subjective: it is the speaker's expectation that something will happen later, not an observable fact. See e.g. Bakker 2005:99-101, 144-145 for a performative reading of the future in Homeric Greek; and Rijksbaron 2002 [1984]:33 on the future in classical Greek: "Since 'fact' and 'future' are, strictly speaking, incompatible, the future indicative naturally does not have the same factual value as the past and present tenses."

Scholars connect functionally similar features in modern languages to the speaker's explicit involvement. First- and second-person references, in this count including personal and possessive pronouns as well as verb forms, make the speaker more present as a communicator. That is, explicitly mentioning an "I" or "you" emphasizes that an interaction involves not only a message, but also a speaker communicating it to an addressee. Biber, Conrad, and Reppen 1998:147 and Quaglio 2009:126 similarly find that English first- and second-person pronouns are related to interactiveness and involvement. Aristophanic swearing expressions, in the form of νή or μά followed by the name of one or more gods, display a similar distribution. Werres 1936:20-22 notes that swearing expressions often co-occur with first-person pronouns and the particle γε. They can to a certain extent be functionally compared to English expletives and taboo words, which are associated with informality and emotionally-loaded language.[137] Werres (11) describes Greek swearing expressions as colloquial expressions serving to emphasize utterances, or parts of them. The term "colloquial" in scholarly literature tends to refer to interactional discourse situations, mostly in drama (see §12 above). Regardless of whether the Aristophanic swearing expressions were actually common in fifth-century spoken Attic, then, they do seem to reflect the high interactiveness of a communicative situation.

§60. In short, several linguistic characteristics of tragic and comic dialogues suggest speakers who come to the foreground, and a strong focus on the ongoing interaction. Since γε and δῆτα are highly preferred in dialogues, we may conclude that they are functionally related to this explicit presence of the speaker and this interactiveness. In general, the particle γε can be compared to prosodic emphasis: it highlights a specific part of an utterance, and it often contrasts this part implicitly to something else.[138] This highlighting reflects the speaker's view or attitudes, and implies that the γε utterance is reacting to certain previous discourse.[139] If speakers using γε react to the view or the utterance of others, the subjectivity and the sense of contrast implied by γε acquire an interactional character. This connection to interactiveness is what makes γε especially

[137] Quaglio 2009:101, 109-111.

[138] On the highlighting function of γε, see Hartung 1832:348-349 and Bäumlein 1861:54. On the implicit contrast conveyed by γε, see Hartung 1832:371, Kühner 1835:398, and Stephens 1837:92. On γε in drama, see also III.3 §§76-79; III.4 §§62-64; III.5 §§45-47 and §§51-63; on ὅ γε in Homer, see II.5 §§27-50; on γε in historiography, see IV.4 §§40-44 (the particle is here interpreted as a sign of the historians' voice in authorial statements).

[139] On the connection, in Aristophanes, between γε and discourse-old information, see Tsakmakis 2010. On the similar connection between discourse-old information and German modal particles, see Diewald 1999 (she argues that an utterance with a modal particle appears as a reaction to a preceding turn in a real or supposed dialogue). See also III.3 §§76-79 on γε in contexts of resonance. In Van Leeuwen's edition of Aristophanes *Lysistrata* we find some exclamation marks after γε acts, such as in 252.

compatible with a dialogic environment.[140] Consider the following passage from an Aristophanic dialogue containing both γε and δῆτα:[141]

(t18)

25 Ξα. οὐ γὰρ φέρω 'γώ;
25bis Δι. πῶς φέρεις γάρ, ὅς γ' ὀχεῖ;
Ξα. φέρων γε ταυτί.
26bis Δι. τίνα τρόπον;
26ter Ξα. βαρέως πάνυ.
Δι.οὔκουν τὸ βάρος τοῦθ', ὃ σὺ φέρεις, οὖνος φέρει;
Ξα. οὐ δῆθ' ὅ γ' ἔχω 'γὼ καὶ φέρω, μὰ τὸν Δί' οὔ.
Δι. πῶς γὰρ φέρεις, ὅς γ' αὐτὸς ὑφ' ἑτέρου φέρει;

Aristophanes *Frogs* 25-29

Xa. Well, aren't I bearing one [a load]?
Di. How can you be bearing anything when you're riding?
Xa. Well, I'm bearing this.
Di. How?
Xa. Quite unbearably!
Di. But doesn't the donkey bear what you're bearing?
Xa. Not what I've got here and bear myself, it certainly doesn't.
Di. But how can you bear anything, when something else bears you?

The speakers, Xanthias and Dionysus, use several γε instances to single out certain elements of their short utterances. In 25bis γε qualifies the whole discourse act ὅς ὀχεῖ ("[you] who are riding"). By highlighting this piece of information, Dionysus implies that Xanthias' claim to be bearing a load cannot hold because he is himself being carried. Xanthias in turn underlines his answer in 26 with γε—the luggage he *is* carrying (ταυτί) is obviously the most relevant part of the discussion to him. With the γε element in 28 he refers to his luggage again,[142] whereas Dionysus' γε act in 29 repeats his point about the donkey. The highlighting in each case implies a contrast between the speaker's view and that of his interlocutor.

[140] Out of the thirteen Aristophanic dialogues I analyzed, there is none without γε. See also II.1 §15 and II.3 §52 on γε's distribution in Homer: it is much more frequent in direct speech than in narrator text.

[141] Other examples of dialogues with both these particles are Sophocles *Ajax* 1346-75; *Oedipus King* 1141-1185; Euripides *Andromache* 435-444; *Bacchae* 922-972; Aristophanes *Assemblywomen* 755-816; *Frogs* 1423-1481; *Lysistrata* 46-123. See also Sophocles *Philoctetes* 732-741 in (t20) below.

[142] Stanford 1958 *ad* 28 notes the great emphasis conveyed by this line through the particles used, the swearing expression, and the accented οὔ.

§61. For an example of γε from a completely different context, consider this passage from Aeschylus *Libation Bearers*:

(t19)

(Ηλ.) ἀλλ' εἰδότας μὲν τοὺς θεοὺς καλούμεθα
οἵοισιν ἐν χειμῶσι ναυτίλων δίκην
στροβούμεθ'. εἰ δὲ χρὴ τυχεῖν σωτηρίας,
σμικροῦ γένοιτ' ἂν σπέρματος μέγας πυθμήν.
καὶ μὴν στίβοι γε, δεύτερον τεκμήριον,
ποδῶν, ὅμοιοι, τοῖς τ' ἐμοῖσιν ἐμφερεῖς·

Aeschylus *Libation Bearers* 201-206

(El.) We appeal to the gods, who know what kind of storm are whirling our ship around—though if we are destined to find safety, a great tree-trunk can spring from a tiny seed. And look, a second piece of evidence—footprints, resembling and similar to my own!

γε is infrequent in monologues, and generally in Aeschylus: he uses γε less than the other authors in all three discourse patterns. These distributional facts warn us that the particle's occurrence here is especially striking. γε appears in an emotionally highly involved, even agitated observation by Electra, a context that makes the speaker's own experience come to the foreground. Electra had inferred that Orestes had *sent*, not personally brought, his lock of hair, which is the first sign she had found on her father's tomb (lines 168-180). The sudden discovery of the footprints—καὶ μήν marks this observation as an unexpected appearance[143]—is a highly emotional moment for her.[144] She stresses the word στίβοι with γε, marking the discovered footprints as bearing special importance.[145] Again, we may compare γε to prosodic emphasis.[146] In this case, Electra does not react to someone else's utterance, but rather to her own earlier remarks on the first sign of Orestes.

§62. As for the less frequent particle δῆτα, it is almost completely restricted to dialogues.[147] In the quoted passage from Aristophanes *Frogs* (line 28) δῆτα indicates

143 On καὶ μήν in drama, see Van Erp Taalman Kip 2009.

144 On the connection between γε and agitation in drama, see III.5 §§45-47.

145 See II.5 §40 for discussion of an instance of ὅ γε in Homer where the visual appearance of the referent plays a role in the choice of the referring expression.

146 Indeed, in this play's performance in the original Greek that I attended (November 2011 in Oxford), this line was pronounced in a marked way: louder and with a higher pitch than the surrounding lines. Also note the exclamation mark in Sommerstein's translation.

147 Denniston 1950[2]:269 notes: "δῆτα is a lively particle, far more at home in question and answer than elsewhere."

Xanthias' strong personal involvement with the item to which it is attached, in this case the negation. He emphasizes that the donkey is "absolutely not" carrying his luggage; later in the line he does so again with the swearing expression μὰ τὸν Δία. This denial is of emotional importance to Xanthias, as he is (apparently) suffering from his heavy load.[148] δῆτα always conveys such an emphatic signal of personal involvement when it occurs in answers or other reactions.[149] This function is linked to the alternation of speakers, as is δῆτα's use in questions.[150]

§63. To recap: the distributions of γε and δῆτα have led me to establish a connection between these particles and the communicative activities that characterize dialogue in general. My interpretations are strengthened by the distributions of nouns, finite verbs, first- and second-person references, and swearing expressions. These features do not only imply that the speaker explicitly comes to the foreground in dialogues, but also enhance, in different ways, the interactiveness of the discourse. The particles γε and δῆτα achieve this by juxtaposing the views of different speakers (γε), and by marking the emotional charge of answers and questions (δῆτα).

2.2.6 ἀλλά

§64. The particle ἀλλά shows the following distributions in the passages analyzed:

Author	Dialogues	Monologues	Choral songs	Significant?
Aeschylus	0.98	0.40	0.08	yes
Sophocles	1.11	0.94	0.59	yes
Euripides	0.43	0.72	0.09	yes
Aristophanes	1.13	1.30	0.99	no

Table 16: Frequencies of ἀλλά in percentages of all words

148 On the connection between δῆτα and emotional agitation in drama, see III.5 §§49-50.

149 On the function of δῆτα in assertions to emphasize a certain element with agreement, see especially Bäumlein 1861:108; Hartung 1832:305; Kühner 1835:389-390; Paley 1881:25.

150 In questions δῆτα indicates that the speaker has made an inference from the preceding discourse. Regarding δῆτα in assertions as well as in questions in drama, see III.3 §§84-88; both constructions can be linked to the picking up of elements from preceding utterances. When δῆτα does occur outside of dialogues, it helps create the impression that an imaginary dialogue is embedded within the longer utterance. See III.3 §88 and III.5 §49 and §§70-71 for discussion of δῆτα examples in monologues.

Sophocles shows a significant preference for ἀλλά compared to the other two tragic poets throughout the three patterns.[151] He and Aeschylus use the particle most often in dialogues; Euripides most often in monologues.

§65. The general function of ἀλλά can be described as the substitution of one alternative with another, which can include the correction of an explicit element, an implicit element, and the switch to a different topic.[152] That is, the substitution can be *de re* or *de dicto*. Consider the following examples from Sophocles:

(t20)

Φι. ἆ ἆ ἆ ἆ.
Νε. τί ἔστιν;
Φι. οὐδὲν δεινόν. ἀλλ' ἴθ', ὦ τέκνον.
Νε. μῶν ἄλγος ἴσχεις σῆς παρεστώσης νόσου;
Φι. οὐ δῆτ' ἔγωγ', ἀλλ' ἄρτι κουφίζειν δοκῶ.
ὦ θεοί.
[153] Νε. τί τοὺς θεοὺς ὧδ' ἀναστένων καλεῖς;
Φι. σωτῆρας αὐτοὺς ἠπίους θ' ἡμῖν μολεῖν.
ἆ ἆ ἆ ἆ.
Νε. τί ποτε πέπονθας; οὐκ ἐρεῖς, ἀλλ' ὧδ' ἔσῃ
σιγηλός; ἐν κακῷ δέ τῳ φαίνῃ κυρῶν.

Sophocles *Philoctetes* 732-741

Ph. Ah, ah, ah, ah!
Ne. What's the matter?
Ph. Nothing grave. Come, my son!
Ne. Are you in pain because your sickness is with you?
Ph. No, I think I am just getting better. O gods!
Ne. Why do you thus groan and call upon the gods?
Ph. I am calling on them to come as preservers and be kind to us.
Ah, ah, ah, ah!
Ne. What is the matter with you? Will you not tell me, but remain
silent as you are? You seem to be in some trouble.

[151] ἀλλά in turn-initial position is also more common in Sophocles than in the other tragedians; see Drummen 2009:143-144.

[152] On the functions of ἀλλά in general, see e.g. Hoogeveen 1769:1-53; Kühner 1835:436-440; Krüger 1842:340-342; Dindorf 1873:19 (on Aeschylus); Bodin and Mazon 1902:337-339 (on Aristophanes); Denniston 1950 [1934]:1-17; Ruijgh 1971:135-136; Sicking 1986:129. On this specific description, see Basset 1997 (on Aristophanes); Drummen 2009 (on drama).

[153] Lloyd-Jones and Wilson 1990 read *antilabe* here; other editors, such as Schein 2013, read ἰὼ (or ὦ) θεοί as 736, *extra metrum*.

Philoctetes is suffering a painful attack from his sickness. He does not want Neoptolemus to notice, however, so tries to deny that anything serious is happening. In 733bis, after a short answer to Neoptolemus' question, Philoctetes quickly shifts to a directive discourse act: ἀλλ' ἴθ'.[154] In this case, ἀλλά and the preceding negation οὐδέν are not part of the same construction; rather, the particle marks a switch to a different kind of act. That is, ἀλλά here marks a *de dicto* rather than a *de re* substitution. In 735 and 740, conversely, one element is first negated, and then its substitution is explicitly mentioned. Sophoclean characters frequently bring up such substitutions, especially in dialogues.[155] The speaker first utters an act (often including a negation) that is to be substituted, either *de re* or *de dicto*; the following act effects the substitution, and the speaker marks this by means of ἀλλά. She thereby emphasizse the ἀλλά act. That is, a formulation such as "will you not tell, but remain silent?" is more emphatic than just "will you remain silent?" In other words, I consider ἀλλά to contribute to emphasizing the subjective character of a speaker's substitutions in front of the interlocutor. In Greek drama such emphasis is most often needed in dialogues, and also more at home in monologues where there is an individual speaker, than in choral songs.[156]

§66. ἀλλά in drama is often combined with a negation, another sign of this subjective emphasis. The distributions of negations (both οὐ and μή forms) across the discourse patterns are as follows:

Author	Dialogues	Monologues	Choral songs	Significant?
Aeschylus	3.2	2.4	2.2	yes
Sophocles	4.9	4.0	2.7	yes
Euripides	4.2	3.4	2.0	yes
Aristophanes	3.7	2.5	1.5	yes

Table 17: Frequencies of negations in percentages of all words[157]

[154] The construction of ἀλλά followed by an imperative is especially frequent in Homer: see II.3 §75.

[155] Other examples of ἀλλά marking a switch to a different discourse act include Sophocles *Women of Trachis* 616,627; Euripides *Medea* 688; Aristophanes *Frogs* 507, 512, 517. Other examples of ἀλλά marking a substitution of an explicitly mentioned element include Sophocles *Antigone* 446, 564, 577; *Philoctetes* 861; Aristophanes *Frogs* 488bis, 527bis, 1066.

[156] On the chorus as a group, see e.g. Budelmann 2000, who argues that the Sophoclean chorus is particularly engaging because it communicates "to the spectators the group experience that is enacted on stage." (268). The chorus is connected to "uncountable multitudes" which "resemble civic communities.(269)"

[157] R.J. Allan 2009 on narrative modes in Euripidean messenger speeches also finds both ἀλλά and negations to be frequent in the same contexts (175-176).

Sophocles, who is fond of ἀλλά, has the highest frequency of negations in all discourse patterns. In all authors negation is the most frequent in dialogues.[158] This can be explained because negation is both functionally and formally marked across languages.[159] One of the reasons is that negation is cognitively more demanding than affirmation: it requires more cognitive effort to process negated information than to process positive information.[160] An utterance such as "I am not in pain at all" (see (t20) above) inevitably refers to a situation in which the speaker *is* in pain. As Miestamo 2009 puts it, negation "is a mental process added by language users" (211). A hearer needs to imagine both the situation with pain, in this case, and its negation. This markedness, in turn, helps the speaker to emphasize part of her utterance: she is not just describing a situation, for example, but also defining it in terms of what it is not.

§67. ἀλλά, then, verbally encodes and emphasizes the substitutions (*de re* or *de dicto*) that speakers perceive or construct in their discourse. This function makes the particle suitable for argumentative situations as well: speakers in such contexts want to substitute certain views with certain others. I interpret the high frequency of ἀλλά in Euripidean monologues along this line. Whereas Aeschylus and Sophocles tend to use monologues for narrative or descriptive purposes, Euripidean speeches tend to serve an argumentative function, as they are often integrated within disputes between characters.[161] Euripidean monologues may thus be considered to be more interactive, more strongly oriented toward a specific interlocutor, and hence closer to both dialogue within drama and rhetoric speeches beyond drama, for example in oratory, philosophy, and historiography.[162] An example of this kind of argumentative speech is Jason's monologue in Euripides *Medea* 522-575, which contains as many as six instances of ἀλλά (in 339 words). Two of these instances are shown here:

[158] Similarly, Biber 1988:245 observes that in English negation occurs more often in speech than in writing. R.J. Allan 2009:176; 2011:41 also mentions frequencies of negations as characterizing different ancient Greek passages.

[159] See for example Miestamo 2009:210-211. See also e.g. Horn 1989:154-203 on the markedness of negation.

[160] Miestamo 2009:210-211.

[161] See e.g. Scodel 2000 on the importance of rhetorical performance in Euripides; see e.g. Conacher 1998 and W. Allan 2000 on connections between Euripides and the sophists. Also in historiography speeches tend to be the moments where people's arguments and rhetoric come to the fore.

[162] In messenger's stories, for example, the speaker tries to be more invisible, and let the story tell itself (see J. Barrett 2002 for an elaborate and insightful analysis of tragic messenger speeches); see §28 above. Note that the messenger speech in Euripides *Hippolytus* 1173-1254, mentioned in note 53 above for its remarkably high frequency of δέ (4.7%), does not contain any ἀλλά instance, despite its great length of 471 words. The other δέ-rich Euripidean messenger speech, in *Medea* 1136-1230, contains two ἀλλά's in 558 words; a low frequency of 0.4%.

(t21)

(Ια.) σοὶ δ' ἔστι μὲν νοῦς λεπτός· ἀλλ' ἐπίφθονος
λόγος διελθεῖν ὡς Ἔρως σ' ἠνάγκασεν
τόξοις ἀφύκτοις τοὐμὸν ἐκσῶσαι δέμας.
ἀλλ' οὐκ ἀκριβῶς αὐτὸ θήσομαι λίαν·
ὅπηι γὰρ οὖν ὤνησας οὐ κακῶς ἔχει.

Euripides *Medea* 529-533

(Ja.) As for you, I grant you have a clever mind—but to tell how Eros forces you with his ineluctable arrows to save me would expose me to ill will. No, I will not make too strict a reckoning on this point. So far as you *did* help me, you did well.

In this monologue, Jason is arguing with Medea, carefully answering her reproaches against him. Jason's style is reminiscent of the sophists.[163] The first ἀλλά in the passage (529) marks a correction of an implied element from the preceding act. Medea may have a delicate or clever mind (νοῦς λεπτός),[164] but she is telling an invidious story about saving Jason; it was in fact Eros who had forced her to save him. The second instance (532) marks a larger shift or "switch" in the discourse. Although the remark about Eros in 530-531 may have given rise to an expectation that Jason would go on about this point, with ἀλλ' οὐκ he signals a different direction in the discourse: other arguments against Medea's position are more important to him. The particle thus helps in shifting to different points, and so in marking out the steps in one's argument more precisely.[165] As Mossman 2011 *ad loc.* remarks, there is a "play of assertion and partial withdrawal" in these lines.

§68. As we have seen, in all of its constructions ἀλλά marks some kind of substitution or correction. The tendency of ἀλλά to appear most often in Aeschylean and Sophoclean dialogues, as well as its frequent co-occurrence with negations, support a connection to the speaker's subjectivity and to interactiveness. Euripides' preference for ἀλλά in monologues can be explained with reference to the rhetorical purposes of many of these speeches.

[163] See Mossman 2011 in her commentary on the speech. The sophists' influence on speeches in *Medea* is also discussed by Finley 1939:51-52. He notes, for example, that "antithesis strongly marks the debate of the *Medea*" (57).

[164] μέν projects more to come, here creating the expectation that a hostile counterargument will follow this positive statement ("yes, but..."). See §§69-72 below on μέν, and II.2 §§49-62 on μέν and projection in Homer and Pindar.

[165] See Thyresson 1977:103 on ἀλλά in Epicurus: its eliminative use is "the most important weapon in the polemic arsenal. The construction of the clauses allows one first to attack that which is wrong, incorrect, untrue, etc. and then to introduce with ἀλλά one's own personal standpoint of what is correct and right as far as opinions and arguments are concerned."

2.2.7 μέν

§69. μέν is generally described as setting up an expectation for some part to follow.[166] That is, in pragmatic terms, it projects another discourse act, in fifth-century Attic often a δέ act.[167] In drama μέν occurs most frequently in monologues:

Author	Dialogues	Monologues	Choral songs	Significant?
Aeschylus	0.45	0.99	0.59	yes
Sophocles	0.45	0.97	0.59	yes
Euripides	0.41	0.95	0.34	yes
Aristophanes	0.63	1.05	0.64	no

Table 18: Frequencies of μέν in percentages of all words

Besides indicating that more narrative steps will follow in story-telling monologues,[168] speakers can also use μέν, for example, to mark a juxtaposition of (parts of) conditions, arguments, or points of view.[169] μέν therefore does not seem to be especially associated with narratives, unlike δέ (see §§27-30 above).

§70. An example of a monologue with many μέν instances is the priest's speech in Sophocles *Oedipus King* 14-57. It contains six occurrences of the particle in 267 words in total (a frequency of more than two percent). Here is the beginning of this monologue:

(t22)

ΙΕΡΕΥΣ ἀλλ', ὦ κρατύνων Οἰδίπους χώρας ἐμῆς,
ὁρᾷς μὲν ἡμᾶς ἡλίκοι προσήμεθα
βωμοῖσι τοῖς σοῖς, οἱ μὲν οὐδέπω μακρὰν
πτέσθαι σθένοντες, οἱ δὲ σὺν γήρᾳ βαρεῖς·
ἱερεὺς ἐγὼ μὲν Ζηνός, οἵδε τ' ᾐθέων

[166] See Hartung 1832:403; Stephens 1837:74; Bäumlein 1861:164; Denniston 1950 [1934]:359. On μέν in Homer and Pindar, see II.2 §§46-62; on μέν at the beginning and at the end of moves in Herodotus and Thucydides, see IV.3.11, and IV.5 §32, §56, §58, §95.

[167] See II.2 §§49-62 on μέν and projection. In Homer and Pindar, the expectation created by μέν is usually that of a new discourse act in general; in later Greek it tends to be more specifically that of a δέ act (see II.2 §§56-57).

[168] Examples of this use include Sophocles *Oedipus King* 781; Euripides *Andromache* 1086; *Children of Heracles* 818, 834; *Hippolytus* 1173, 1190, 1219.

[169] As e.g. several times in Menelaus' monologue in Euripides *Andromache*: 648, 663, 666, 675, and 689.

λεκτοί· τὸ δ' ἄλλο φῦλον ἐξεστεμμένον
ἀγοραῖσι θακεῖ, (...)

Sophocles *Oedipus King* 14-20

Pr. Why, Oedipus, ruler of my land, you see the ages of us who are seated at your altars, some not yet able to fly far, others weighed down with age. I am the priest of Zeus, and these are chosen from the unmarried young; the other crowd that carries chaplets is seated in the market-place (...)

These μέν occurrences have different scopes. The first one, in line 15, helps to establish that the priest is starting a long, elaborate answer to Oedipus' questions.[170] The second one (16) falls within the scope of this first instance. As part of a οἱ μέν... οἱ δέ construction, μέν simultaneously marks one discourse act as preliminary, and projects another act.[171] The μέν in 18 signals an implicit contrast between the priest himself and other persons.[172] Though this last use of the particle could work in short utterances just as well, the former two are especially appropriate to utterances with a certain length of speaking.

§71. When an Aristophanic character manages to utter a substantial monologue, μέν also appears regularly. In the following passage from *Birds* a herald has arrived in the bird city to inform Peisetaerus of the bird mania in Athens:

(t23)

(Κη.) πρῶτον μὲν εὐθὺς πάντες ἐξ εὐνῆς ἅμα
ἐπέτονθ' ἕωθεν ὥσπερ ἡμεῖς ἐπὶ νομόν·
κἀκεῖθεν ἂν κατῆραν εἰς τὰ βιβλία·
εἶτ' ἂν ἐνέμοντ' ἐνταῦθα τὰ ψηφίσματα.
ὠρνιθομάνουν δ' οὕτω περιφανῶς ὥστε καὶ
πολλοῖσιν ὀρνίθων ὀνόματ' ἦν κείμενα.
Πέρδιξ μὲν εἷς κάπηλος ὠνομάζετο
χωλός, Μενίππῳ δ' ἦν Χελιδὼν τοὔνομα,

Aristophanes *Birds* 1286-1293

(He.) For starters, at the crack of dawn they all fly the coop together, just like us, to root for writs; then they flock to the archives and there sharpen their bills. They're so blatantly bird-crazy that many even had bird names

170 See III.4 §55 on this use of μέν in drama.

171 See II.2 §§58-59 on μέν followed by δέ in Pindar and Homer.

172 See Jebb 1893 and Kamerbeek 1967 *ad loc.* for this interpretation of μέν in 18; Kamerbeek cites Denniston 1950:380-381, who calls this a "μέν solitarium."

added to their own. There's one lame barkeep called Partridge; Menippus took the name swallow; (...).

The herald's entire speech runs from 1277 to 1307 (180 words in total), an impressive length for a comic utterance. As Dunbar 1995 *ad* 1298 remarks, such "lengthy narrative speeches" are rare in Aristophanes. The speaker therefore needs linguistic signals in order to clarify that he still has more to say. In the quoted passage the two μέν instances are among these signals.[173] The one in 1286 creates the expectation, together with πρῶτον, that the first action described will not be the only one. μέν in 1292 projects more entries in a list of bird nicknames, after the announcement of this topic in 1291. The communicative setting also helps the herald to hold the floor: his addressee, Peisetaerus, actually wants to hear the message, which makes interruptions less likely. The herald's speech, as Dunbar points out, is a parody of a tragic messenger speech, a dramatic subgenre that by definition requires some length.

§72. In general, then, μέν's projective function is more appropriate when the speaker goes on talking than in short utterances. Though the projected next act or entity may be left implicit, in my corpus usually the projection is indeed fulfilled in the discourse acts following a μέν act. In this way I connect μέν's relatively high frequency in dramatic monologues to its basic pragmatic function, which is to project one or more discourse acts.

2.2.8 δή

§73. Aeschylus uses δή most in dialogues, Euripides most in monologues. Interestingly, in Homer δή is more frequent in direct speech than in narrator text: the Aeschylean distribution of this particle may thus form another link to Homeric particle use.[174] δή's relatively low frequency in songs mirrors its rarity in lyric in general.[175]

Author	Dialogues	Monologues	Choral songs	Significant?
Aeschylus	0.54	0.19	0.15	yes
Sophocles	0.27	0.22	0.13	no
Euripides	0.23	0.27	0.03	yes
Aristophanes	0.39	0.15	0.35	no

Table 19: Frequencies of δή in percentages of all words

173 See also III.4 §§28-30 for discussion of μέν as a floor-holding device.

174 See II.1 §15 for δή's distribution in Homer. See §26 above on δέ and §38 above on καί for other links between Homeric and Aeschylean particle use.

175 Its overall frequency in Pindar, for example, is only 0.07 per 100 words. See our frequency graphs (available online as I.5).

Various uses of δή, found mainly in dialogues or in somehow dialogic contexts (see e.g. (t25) below), tend to be connected to the speaker's expression of stance, and the interaction between speaker and hearer. Sometimes it intensifies part of an utterance; in other contexts it marks the event referred to as perceivable, obvious, or expected, or it marks the discourse act as such. The use of δή to mark narrative steps, which is common in Homeric narrator text and in Herodotus, occurs as well, but is rare in drama; this use requires relatively long stretches of narrative.[176]

§74. Just as in Homer and historiography, δή in drama may occur in stancetaking expressions, where it is used in order to intensify these expressions. The co-text in such cases contains an adjective or an adverb that expresses an extreme of some kind, such as superlatives or words like "all" or "alone."[177] Here is an example from a 6-line utterance from Aeschylus *Persians*:

(t24)

Βα. αἰαῖ, κακῶν ὕψιστα <u>δὴ</u> κλύω τάδε,

Aeschylus *Persians* 331

Qu. Aiai, this is truly the most towering disaster I have ever heard of,

δή here emphasizes the subjective judgement κακῶν ὕψιστα.[178] The particle's late position in the act (the discourse act arguably starts directly after the interjection αἰαῖ) suggests that δή here has small scope, over only the superlative preceding it. This subjectivizing function can be connected to descriptions of δή as expressing affirmation or the

[176] See II.3 §§56-57 for discussion of this use of δή in Homer; see IV.3.11.3 and IV.5 §80 for discussion of this use of δή (especially in combinations) in Herodotus and Thucydides. Examples from drama are Aeschylus *Seven against Thebes* 214 (Tucker 1908 and Hutchinson 1985 *ad loc.* note that the construction is epic); *Suppliant Women* 571 (Friis Johansen and Whittle 1980 *ad loc.* note that the construction is epic); Sophocles *Women of Trachis* 772 (Jebb 2004 [1892] and Davies 1991 indent the text at this point); Euripides *Andromache* 1147 (Stevens 1971 *ad loc.* notes that "the particle marks the decisive point"); *Hippolytus* 38, 1181; Aristophanes *Frogs* 816, 826; *Lysistrata* 523.

[177] This is how e.g. Stephens 1837:63, Krüger 1842:347-348, and Denniston 1950 [1934]:204-207 describe the use of δή with superlatives and other words that express an extreme. In a slightly different way, e.g. Hoogeveen 1769:290-294 and Monro 1882a:256 argue that δή in this use indicates that the highest stage of something has been reached. See II.3 §61 for discussion of this use of δή in Homer, mainly in direct speech; see IV.4 §113, §116, and IV.5 §38 for discussion of this use of δή in Herodotus and Thucydides.

[178] Other examples of δή intensifying an extreme expression include Aeschylus *Persians* 236, 382, 490, 548, 583, 1013; *Libation Bearers* 897; Sophocles *Antigone* 173, 615, 821, 823, 895; *Electra* 202; Euripides *Hippolytus* 462, 834, 982, 1246; *Medea* 1067; Aristophanes *Frogs* 1254.

speaker's certainty.[179] The particle's higher frequency in Aeschylean dialogues supports a connection to the speaker's own view or attitude. However, the use of this particle does not in itself imply a contrast with different views, as γε does.[180]

§75. When it has scope over an entire act, δή may have a number of functions that are related to each other. One is to mark the content of its act as visible or otherwise perceptible to speaker and addressee. Many scholars in fact argue for "clearly," "obviously," or referring to something known or visible as the basic meaning of δή.[181] While I do not claim that this nuance is present in every instance of the particle in drama, I do consider it part of its functions. The following Euripidean example stems from a 12-line utterance in which Hippolytus says goodbye to several addressees, among whom the goddess Artemis:

(t25)

> (Ιπ.) ὦ φιλτάτη μοι δαιμόνων Λητοῦς κόρη,
> σύνθακε, συγκύναγε, φευξούμεσθα δὴ
> κλεινὰς Ἀθήνας. (...)

Euripides *Hippolytus* 1093-1094

> (Hi.) Dearest of gods to me, daughter of Leto, you I have sat with, you I have hunted with, I shall leave glorious Athens as an exile.

δή is in peninitial position in its act here, since an act boundary after a vocative is likely.[182] Hippolytus addresses Artemis at the moment of his exile. He assumes that the goddess sees or hears what is happening to him (if she can hear this very utterance, she will also have heard Theseus' preceding order to Hippolytus to leave the country). Thus the particle δή accompanies the description of an action that is perceptible to speaker and

[179] An affirmative meaning is considered δή's primary meaning by Thiersch 1826:193, 549 (on Homer); Stephens 1837:9; Navarre 1932; Denniston 1950 [1934]:203-204; Leumann 1949; Humbert 1960:403; Ruijgh 1971:646-647; Wakker 1994:351, 1997a:216 (on tragedy), 1997b:239 (on Herodotus and Thucydides).

[180] See §§58-63 above on γε, with references. Van Emde Boas, Rijksbaron, Huitink, and De Bakker 2019:686-687 (on Classical Greek).

[181] An evidential meaning of δή is considered the primary one by Hartung 1828:4 (though in 1832 he changed his mind); Döderlein 1858:362-363 (on Homer); Rost 1859:2n3; Bäumlein 1861:98-99; Wähdel 1869:2 (on Aristophanes); Hoffmann 1884:9 (on Herodotus); Smyth 1956 [1920]:646-647; Sicking 1986:133; 1993:51-53 (on Lysias); Van Ophuijsen 1993:141-148 (on Plato); Bakker 1997b:78-79 (on Homer); Cuypers 2005:38, 55-59 (on Homer and Apollonius); Van Emde Boas, Rijksbaron, Huitink, and De Bakker 2019:686-687 (on Classical Greek).

[182] See II.2 §10, §15, §31.

addressee alike, and marks the act as such.[183] Though there is no quick dialogic exchange here, the δή act does convey the speaker's attention to his addressee.

§76. A similar situation, where δή also has scope over an entire act, is when a speaker refers back to what the addressee has just said. An example is found in the magistrate's reaction (1.5 lines long, see 571-572) to Lysistrata's utterance in the following passage:

(t26)

Λυ. ὥσπερ κλωστῆρ', ὅταν ἡμῖν ᾖ τεταραγμένος, ὧδε λαβοῦσαι,
ὑπενεγκοῦσαι τοῖσιν ἀτράκτοις, τὸ μὲν ἐνταυθοῖ, τὸ δ' ἐκεῖσε,
οὕτως καὶ τὸν πόλεμον τοῦτον διαλύσομεν, ἤν τις ἐάσῃ,
διενεγκοῦσαι διὰ πρεσβειῶν, τὸ μὲν ἐνταυθοῖ, τὸ δ' ἐκεῖσε.
Πρ. ἐξ ἐρίων δὴ καὶ κλωστήρων καὶ ἀτράκτων πράγματα δεινὰ
παύσειν οἴεσθ'; ὡς ἀνόητοι.

Aristophanes *Lysistrata* 567-572

Ly. It's rather like a ball of yarn when it gets tangled up. We hold it this way, and carefully wind out the strands on our spindles, now this way, now that way. That's how we'll wind up this war, if we're allowed: on snarling it by sending embassies, now this way, now that way.

Ma. You really think your way with wool and yarnballs and spindles can stop a terrible crisis? How brainless!

δή in 571 co-occurs with a lexical echo from the preceding utterance (κλωστήρων καὶ ἀτράκτων, echoing κλωστῆρ' (...) τοῖσιν ἀτράκτοις from 567-568). A heavy paraphrase of the particle in this context would be "as you say." The information referred to in such quoting contexts may not be directly perceptible, but will nevertheless be

[183] See IV.4 §§92-93 on δή in Herodotus in contexts of direct speech that are linked to perceptions of evidence.

Other examples of δή (sometimes combined with καί; see §77 below) marking its act as referring to a perceptible event or feature include Aeschylus *Libation Bearers* 565, 874, 1057; Sophocles *Antigone* 155, 441, 939; Euripides *Hippolytus* 778, 1007, 1342, 1447; Aristophanes *Frogs* 270bis, 1476; *Lysistrata* 65, 77, 83, 312, 327, 557, 601, 683, 909, 925.

I do not agree with the interpretation of W.S. Barrett 1964 and Halleran 1995 *ad loc.*, who claim that δή adds a pathetic emphasis. The pathos resides rather in the content of the passage; it is not contributed by the particle.

obvious to both of the interlocutors. This use of is δή close to the one found in historiography to resume a narrative thread after an interruption or another topic ("as I was saying").[184] The difference, however, is that in those cases δή refers back to the narrator's own previous discourse, whereas in drama speakers refer to utterances by their addressees.[185]

§77. If certain information or a certain event is perceptible, or has just been mentioned, this means, more generally, that it is *evident* for speaker and addressee, or at least it can be presented as such. The content of δή acts can also be evident, obvious, or expected for reasons other than being directly perceptible or quoted.[186] In this use the particle is sometimes combined with καί; together the two particles have become a cluster to mark the noticing of a new character on stage,[187] as well as the speaker's obedience to a directive.[188] These uses, again, directly concern the interaction among the characters on stage.

§78. Related to this use is δή's ability to mark not the content of its act, but the very utterance of an act as expected or obvious.[189] This is the most natural interpretation of many δή instances in questions, such as in the *Lysistrata* dialogue directly after the lines cited in (t26):[190]

(t27)

Πρ. ἐξ ἐρίων δὴ καὶ κλωστήρων καὶ ἀτράκτων πράγματα δεινὰ
παύσειν οἴεσθ'; ὡς ἀνόητοι.

[184] On this use of δή, see IV.4: §89 on Herodotus and §110 on Thucydides. See also Van Ophuijsen 1993:143 on this use ("what may be called anaphoric δή") in Plato, and Wakker 1997b:241-242 on this use ("so-called anaphoric" δή, 241) in Herodotus and Thucydides.

[185] Other examples of δή with references to the addressee's utterance are found in e.g. Sophocles *Antigone* 91, 726; Euripides *Bacchae* 652, 822; *Hippolytus* 233, 948, 962, 1071; Aristophanes *Lysistrata* 146, 1102bis.

[186] Examples of δή marking the content of its act as obvious, evident, or expected are found in e.g. Aeschylus *Seven against Thebes* 655; *Libation Bearers* 532, 891; Sophocles *Antigone* 80, 923, 1202; Euripides *Alcestis* 5; *Bacchae* 291, 934; *Hippolytus* 7, 688, 1093; Aristophanes *Lysistrata* 1301.

[187] This use of καὶ δή is found in e.g. Euripides *Medea* 1118; Aristophanes *Lysistrata* 65, 77; *Wasps* 1324. See Van Erp Taalman Kip 2009 for discussion.

[188] καὶ δή marking an evident or perceptible obedience to a directive is found in e.g. Sophocles *Electra* 317, 892, 1436; *Philoctetes* 818; Euripides *Alcestis* 1118; Aristophanes *Birds* 175bis, 550; *Wealth* 227, 414; *Women at the Thesmophoria* 214bis. See III.4 §§51-52 for discussion. On the use of καὶ δή in Herodotus, see IV.2 §§100-101.

[189] Bäumlein 1861:104 interprets δή with imperatives in a similar way: he argues that the particle marks the order as natural and justified under the current circumstances.

[190] Other examples of δή marking its discourse act as an obvious or expected one are e.g. Aeschylus *Libation Bearers* 569, 732; *Eumenides* 431; Sophocles *Electra* 376, 1400; *Oedipus King* 655ter; Euripides *Hippolytus* 722; Aristophanes *Lysistrata* 503bis, 503ter, 769bis, 941, 1100, 1108, 1295.

572bis Λυ. κἂν ὑμῖν γ' εἴ τις ἐνῆν νοῦς,
ἐκ τῶν ἐρίων τῶν ἡμετέρων ἐπολιτεύεσθ' ἂν ἅπαντα.
Πρ. πῶς δή; φέρ' ἴδω. (...)

Aristophanes *Lysistrata* 571-574

Ma. You really think your way with wool and yarnballs and spindles can stop a terrible crisis? How brainless!
Ly. I do think so, and if you had any brains you'd handle all the polis' business the way we handle our wool!
Ma. How then? I'm all ears.

I interpret the δή in 574 as marking its host question as an expected action in its context. After Lysistrata's vague statement about applying wool strategies to politics, the magistrate considers it a logical communicative action to ask what she means exactly. That is, the particle does not concern logical relations between the content of different utterances (as δῆτα signals in questions), but indicates in this case that the action of asking is an obvious one. This signal is most appropriate in dialogues, the setting in which the focus on the ongoing interaction is the highest.

§79. To sum up: δή in drama, is most frequent in situations with high interactiveness: that is, in relatively short turns of speaking, or those that otherwise betray attention to the interaction, for example by using vocatives (see (t25)). In choral songs, a setting where a face-to-face interaction on the stage is hardly present, δή has a relatively low frequency. Based on this distributional input as well as co-textual patterns and the behavior of δή in other genres, I interpret its functions as follows. When δή has small scope, over an adjective or adverb that describes a quality in the extreme, it intensifies an expression of the speaker's stance, a function that is also common in Homer and historiography. With act scope δή either marks the *content* of its act or the *uttering* of the act as perceptible, evident, or expected to the speaker. These functions reflect the speaker's attention to her addressee: she presents the content or the action as evident to both herself and a "you." They do not, however, require an immediate verbal reaction from this addressee, as is likely in the case of γε and δῆτα (see §§58-63 above), particles that favor dialogues in an even stronger way. Finally, monologues display some uses of to δή to mark narrative progression (frequent in Homer and Herodotus), but because of the relatively small proportion of narrative in drama, this concerns a minority of instances.

2.2.9 οὖν

§80. This particle is the most frequent in dialogues, in Sophocles and Euripides significantly so:

Author	Dialogues	Monologues	Choral songs	Significant?
Aeschylus	0.36	0.13	0.15	no
Sophocles	0.47	0.12	0.07	yes
Euripides	0.39	0.25	0.03	yes
Aristophanes	0.55	0.50	0.12	no

Table 20: Frequencies of οὖν in percentages of all words

As for οὖν's low frequency in choral songs, at least in Sophocles and Euripides, it is relevant that the particle is rare in epic and Pindar.[191] As I have argued in my discussion of δέ and τε above, we can see once more that choral songs tend to be linguistically closer to epic and lyric than monologues and dialogues.[192] In general, the playwrights' preference to use οὖν in dialogues can be explained from the greater explicit presence of the speaker in this situation, and the high level of interactiveness among the characters.[193]

§81. With οὖν a speaker may present an utterance as an inference or conclusion, as in this excerpt from a monologue by Hippolytus:

(t28)

(Ιπ.) ὡς καὶ σύ γ' ἡμῖν πατρός, ὦ κακὸν κάρα,
λέκτρων ἀθίκτων ἦλθες ἐς συναλλαγάς·
ἁγὼ ῥυτοῖς νασμοῖσιν ἐξομόρξομαι
ἐς ὦτα κλύζων. πῶς ἂν <u>οὖν</u> εἴην κακός,
ὃς οὐδ' ἀκούσας τοιάδ' ἁγνεύειν δοκῶ;

Euripides *Hippolytus* 651-655

(Hi.) It is in this fashion, despicable creature, that you have come to traffic with me in the sacred bed of my father. I shall pour running water into my

[191] The overall frequency of οὖν in Homer is only 0.04% of all words; In Hesiod, there are only 2 instances, which means a frequency of less than 0.01%. Pindar has one of 0.05%. The later epic authors Apollonius Rhodius, Oppian of Anazarbus, and Oppian of Apamea, all use οὖν in a frequency of 0.04%, just like Homer.

[192] See §25 above on δέ and §43 above on τε.

[193] For an οὖν construction that is not discussed here, i.e. the one in pre-expansions, see III.4 §§43-45.

> ears to wash away your proposals! How could I be such a traitor? The very sound of such things makes me feel unclean!

Hippolytus here expresses his shock and disgust at the proposal of Phaedra's nurse that he start an affair with Phaedra. οὖν occurs in a rhetorical question that implies "I could never be (so) base." The rejected idea is based on the following premises: (1) someone who would violate his own father's bed would have a strong desire to do so, and (2) Hippolytus himself is too pure to ever have such a desire. Premise (1) is left implicit; (2) is mentioned in the following relative clause. οὖν, by marking its host act as an inference or conclusion, shows the speaker's choice to present his discourse as such, in pursuing his goal to communicate his view to the nurse. That is, instead of leaving it to the addressee to detect a specific relation between parts of the utterance, the particle explicitly marks the kind of connection that the speaker wants to be understood.[194]

§82. οὖν may also be combined with μέν. In some instances, as in (t29), each particle retains its own separate function; in others it is used as a cluster (see (t30) below). Both uses are slightly different from those of μὲν οὖν in Thucydides, discussed in IV.3 §§144-146. While the historian uses μὲν οὖν to introduce new discourse threads within extended narratives, in drama the combination contributes to the interpersonal level of communication, in several ways. What remains the same across these genres, however, is the contribution to the structuring of the discourse: μὲν οὖν connects different acts to each other in a specific way. Consider this example from a 20-line utterance by Ismene to Antigone:

(t29)

> (Ισ.) ἔπειτα δ' οὕνεκ' ἀρχόμεσθ' ἐκ κρεισσόνων
> καὶ ταῦτ' ἀκούειν κἄτι τῶνδ' ἀλγίονα.
> ἐγὼ μὲν οὖν αἰτοῦσα τοὺς ὑπὸ χθονὸς
> ξύγγνοιαν ἴσχειν, ὡς βιάζομαι τάδε,
> τοῖς ἐν τέλει βεβῶσι πείσομαι. (...)

Sophocles *Antigone* 63-67

[194] Other οὖν instances marking its utterance or act as an inference or a conclusion include Aeschylus *Libation Bearers* 114 (in a question), 177 (in a question); *Eumenides* 219 (in an assertion); *Seven against Thebes* 704 (in a rhetorical question); *Suppliant Women* 340 (in a question); Sophocles *Ajax* 1215 (in a rhetorical question); *Women of Trachis* 550 (in an assertion), 1162 (in an assertion); Euripides *Andromache* 82 (in a rhetorical question), 1165 (in a rhetorical question, very similar to the example quoted here); *Medea* 289 (in an assertion); Aristophanes *Frogs* 274 (in a question), 1056bis (in a question), 1064bis (in a question), 1420 (in an assertion), 1458 (in a rhetorical question); *Wealth* 83 (in a question), 518bis (in a question).

> (Is.) and then [we must remember] that we are ruled by those whose power is greater, so that we must consent to this and to other things even more painful! So I shall beg those beneath the earth to be understanding, since I act under constraint, but I shall obey those in authority;

In this case, as commentators point out, the two particles work separately.[195] μέν, on the one hand, has a projecting function. It therefore places emphasis on ἐγώ in a way that sets it in contrast against something implied. Here the speaker Ismene, in outlining her intention to obey Creon's injunction against burying her brother, suggests that her plan of action may diverge from Antigone's, her addressee.[196] οὖν, on the other hand, marks the upcoming acts as a conclusion from the preceding discourse. Ismene should bury her brother, but has to consent to the king; *therefore* she will ask the deceased for understanding, and obey. That is, μέν helps to indicate potential disagreement; οὖν underlines how the speaker interprets a certain situation—in Ismene's view one has to conclude that obedience is inevitable. Both particles thus relate to both the discourse organization (connections among different acts) and the interaction between the speaker and addressee (disagreement, and Ismene's responsibility for her conclusion).

§83. When the two particles work together as a cluster, μὲν οὖν may mark a correction of a preceding element. The corrected element is often from an utterance spoken by the addressee, which clearly connects this function to the ongoing interaction. An example is found in the following Aristophanic scene. Hermes and Trygaeus are talking about the Spartans:

(t30)

> (Ερ.) κᾆτα τἀκείνων γε κέρδη τοῖς γεωργοῖς ἦν κακά·
> αἱ γὰρ ἐνθένδ' αὖ τριήρεις ἀντιτιμωρούμεναι
> οὐδὲν αἰτίων ἂν ἀνδρῶν τὰς κράδας κατήσθιον.
> Τρ. ἐν δίκῃ μὲν οὖν, ἐπεί τοι τὴν κορώνεών γέ μου
> ἐξέκοψαν, ἣν ἐγὼ 'φύτευσα κἀξεθρεψάμην.
>
> Aristophanes *Peace* 625-629

[195] See Jebb 1888, Kamerbeek 1978, and Griffith 1999 *ad loc*. Other examples of μὲν οὖν not working as a cluster include Aeschylus *Suppliant Women* 133; Sophocles *Antigone* 925; *Electra* 459, 549; *Women of Trachis* 1270; Euripides *Andromache* 554; *Children of Heracles* 818; *Hecuba* 16, 51; *Hippolytus* 393, 451, 1249, 1318.

[196] On μέν creating contrasting emphasis when a projected new act is left implicit, see II.2 §60.

(He.) And their [i.e. the Spartans'] gain became the farmers' loss, for the warships despatched from here to retaliate would consume the figs on trees belonging to wholly blameless men.

Tr. No, they deserved it! You see, they cut down that black fig tree of mine, which I'd planted and nurtured.

As Platnauer 1964 and Olson 1998 *ad loc.* note, μὲν οὖν indicates that Trygaeus does not agree with the previous utterance, but corrects part of it: in his view the Spartan farmers were not innocent in the war. Since the Spartans were responsible for Trygaeus' loss of his fig tree, in his view they deserved to lose some figs themselves. Olson interprets the combination as "no, to the contrary."[197] Since this corrective use cannot be inferred from the normal pragmatic contributions of each of the two particles, I speak of a cluster in this case.[198] It occurs especially in turn-initial position, which makes it more frequent in the discourse pattern connected to dialogues.[199] The cluster's predominance in this communicative setting is understandable in view of its interactional value.

§84. Just as several other particles that tend to be most frequent in dialogues, then, οὖν fits situations with high interactiveness. More specifically, with οὖν a speaker may mark a discourse act as her own conclusion or inference from the preceding. Such a relation is not inherent in the semantic content of an utterance, but, crucially, betrays the speaker's interpretation of that content, and the way she wants to present it to the addressee. The cluster μὲν οὖν is even more strongly subjective: the speaker presents her discourse act as a correction, usually of an act uttered by the addressee.

2.2.10 ἦ

§85. ἦ is used the most in tragic dialogues, less often in songs, and hardly ever in monologues:

[197] The cluster καὶ μήν has a similar use at the beginning of turns, indicating a correction or objection, especially in Aristophanes: see Devarius 1588:114-115; Bodin and Mazon 1902:354-355; Smyth 1956 [1920]:658-659; Wakker 1997a:217-218; Van Erp Taalman Kip 2009:125. Examples include Aristophanes *Clouds* 1185, 1441; *Frogs* 612bis, 1036; *Lysistrata* 588bis; *Wealth* 1073, 1139.
In Thucydides τοίνυν may have a similar function, signaling disalignment: see IV.4 §61.

[198] On the difference between combination and cluster, see I.1 §19.

[199] Rost 1859:7 and Bäumlein 1861:174 note that combinations such as μὲν οὖν are frequent in answers. Other examples of the cluster μὲν οὖν marking a correction include Aeschylus *Persians* 1032; *Agamemnon* 1396; *Libation Bearers* 999; *Eumenides* 38; Sophocles *Ajax* 1363; *Electra* 1503bis; *Oedipus at Colonus* 31; Euripides *Alcestis* 821, 1113; *Hippolytus* 821, 1012; Aristophanes *Frogs* 612, 626; *Wasps* 898; *Wealth* 270, 287, 347, 390, 914, 1009.

Author	Dialogues	Monologues	Choral songs	Significant?
Aeschylus	0.45	0.08	0.13	yes
Sophocles	0.50	0.09	0.16	yes
Euripides	0.29	0.05	0.09	yes
Aristophanes	0.11	0	0.06	no

Table 21: Frequencies of ἦ in percentages of all words

In general, ἦ is considered to have two functions, an interrogative and an affirmative one.[200] In fact, the particle's two different functions are divided across the two dramatic communicative settings in which it is mainly used: we tend to find ἦ in questions in dialogues, and in assertions in choral songs.[201] However, we shall see that its uses in these two contexts are related.

§86. For a few examples in questions, consider the following passage from Sophocles *Oedipus King*. It is part of the dialogue with the highest number of ἦ instances in my corpus (six instances in 517 words in total). The speakers are Oedipus and a Corinthian messenger.

(t31)

Οι. ὦ πρὸς θεῶν, πρὸς μητρός, ἢ πατρός; φράσον.
Αγ. οὐκ οἶδ'· ὁ δοὺς δὲ ταῦτ' ἐμοῦ λῷον φρονεῖ.
Οι. ἦ γὰρ παρ' ἄλλου μ' ἔλαβες οὐδ' αὐτὸς τυχών;

200 On the particle ἦ and these two uses, see e.g. Estienne (Stephanus) 1572a:1415-1422; Devarius 1588:92-102; Viger (Vigerus) 1752 [1627]:409-413; Ellendt 1835:299-300 (on Sophocles); Stephens 1837:42-49; Ebeling 1885:528-531 (on Homer); Denniston 1950 [1934]:279; Humbert 1960[3]:406-409; Berrettoni 1969:53-56 (on Homer); Scodel 2012 (on Homer).

201 ἦ is found in questions in dialogues in e.g. Aeschylus *Agamemnon* 269, 276, 942; *Libation Bearers* 220, 526, 774; *Eumenides* 424, 434, 717; Sophocles *Ajax* 38, 44, 48, 97, 103 (see III.4 §47 for discussion), 1133; *Antigone* 44, 574, 752; *Electra* 385, 663, 1177, 1503; *Oedipus King* 368, 429, 622, 757, 943, 1000, 1012, 1039, 1041, 1043, 1045 (see (t31) with discussion below for the instances in 1039, 1041, 1043, and 1045), 1120, 1130, 1173; *Philoctetes* 121, 322, 565, 654; Euripides *Andromache* 249, 437, 441, 581, 1062; *Bacchae* 828, 834, 1032; *Hecuba* 1047, 1124; *Hippolytus* 97, 1448.

It is found in assertions in choral songs in e.g. Aeschylus *Persians* 648 (see (t32) with discussion below), 852; *Eumenides* 144; Sophocles *Ajax* 621; *Women of Trachis* 846, 847; Euripides *Andromache* 274; *Hippolytus* 758, 1102.

Some ἦ instances in questions in choral songs are found in Sophocles *Ajax* 172, 176. This song is exceptional—that is, dialogue-like—in several other respects as well: see the discussion in §42 above.

Αγ. οὔκ, ἀλλὰ ποιμὴν ἄλλος ἐκδίδωσί μοι.
Οι. τίς οὗτος; ἦ κάτοισθα δηλῶσαι λόγῳ;
Αγ. τῶν Λαΐου δήπου τις ὠνομάζετο.
Οι. ἦ τοῦ τυράννου τῆσδε γῆς πάλαι ποτέ;
Αγ. μάλιστα· τούτου τἀνδρὸς οὗτος ἦν βοτήρ.
Οι. ἦ κἄστ' ἔτι ζῶν οὗτος, ὥστ' ἰδεῖν ἐμέ;
Αγ. ὑμεῖς γ' ἄριστ' εἰδεῖτ' ἂν οὑπιχώριοι.

Sophocles *Oedipus King* 1038-1046

Oe. By heaven, did my father or my mother name me? Tell me that!
Me. I do not know; the man who gave you to me knows it all better than I did.
Oe. Then did you not find me, but received me from another man?
Me. Yes, another shepherd gave you to me.
Oe. Who was he? Do you know how to tell this truly?
Me. I think he was said to be one of Laius' men.
Oe. The man who long ago was ruler of this land?
Me. Yes; that was the man whose shepherd he was.
Oe. Is he still alive, so that I could see him?
Me. You who are the people of the country would know that best.

In each case ἦ starts a question. Since none of these questions contains a question word, I interpret ἦ as one of the signals that the upcoming utterance is a question. Several indications lead to this interpretation. First and most important, there are no elements that would point to ἦ's other use, which is connected to stancetaking (see on (t32) below). Second, the replies to the turns in 1039, 1043, and 1045 start with οὐκ (1040), μάλιστα (1044) and a turn-initial γε (1046): since these words are typical for answers to questions, they retrospectively suggest that the earlier turns were questions. Third, the ἦ in 1041 occurs after τίς οὗτος, a clear question; therefore it is logical to take the ἦ act as an appendix to that question.

§87. The question in 1039 is marked with turn-initial γάρ as an inference from the preceding utterance,[202] and asks for confirmation of this inference. ἦ γάρ together can be translated as, "are you really (ἦ) saying that...?" Oedipus' other three questions in this passage likewise ask for confirmation of their suggested statements. However, unlike ἦ questions or ἦ statements in Homer, which always seem to concern an evaluation of a character, these suggestions here concern facts.[203] In general, asking for confirmation is

202 See §§55-56 above.
203 See Scodel 2012 on the use of ἦ in Homer, e.g. 321: "The particle only rarely affirms the truth of what could actually be known, but insists on the rightness of inferences, predictions, and

close to the affirmative force that the particle has in assertions.[204] At the same time, the ἦ instances imply that Oedipus is highly emotionally involved in this interrogation.[205] The facts he is asking about are not just plain facts; they have emotional significance to him. This involvement is indeed apparent from his insistence, throughout this scene, to find out everything about his own origin.[206]

§88. The emotional charge of ἦ questions is present in ἦ assertions as well, which are mainly found in choral songs. Such utterances generally do not concern facts, but the speaker's stance. Consider the following excerpt from a song by the Persian elders, who ask Earth and the underworld gods to send up their dead king Darius:

(t32)

(Χο.) πέμπετε δ' ἄνω
οἷον οὔπω
Περσὶς αἶ' ἐκάλυψεν.
ἦ φίλος ἀνήρ, ἦ φίλος ὄχθος·
φίλα γὰρ κέκευθεν ἤθη.

Aeschylus *Persians* 644-649

(Ch.) and send him up here, one like no other whom Persian soil has ever covered. Truly we love the man, we love the mound; for it conceals a man of lovable character.

The elders underscore the attitude they are expressing toward Darius with ἦ: it is φίλος, the word of emotion, that receives the emphasis.[207] It is disputed whether there should be one or two instances in this line;[208] in any case their function here is clearly connected to the emotional evaluation. The contribution of ἦ to emotional evaluation blurs the borderline between a particle and an interjection, a connection strengthened by ἦ's capacity to form a discourse act on its own (as e.g. in 1045 in (t31) above).[209] Several

evaluations." 331: "(...) interrogative ἦ is very close to the affirmative, since the speaker seeks agreement not about what has taken place, but about his interpretation of it (...)."

204 See e.g. Schwyzer and Debrunner 1950:564-565, who claim that ἦ in questions keeps its affirmative value.

205 On ἦ and emotional involvement, see also II.3 §§38-39 (on Homer) and III.4 §47 (on tragedy).

206 See e.g. ὦ πρὸς θεῶν in 1037, and his strong refusals to listen to Iocaste in e.g. 1058-1059 and 1065.

207 On the emotional charge of φίλος and φιλία in tragedy, see e.g. Stanford 1983:39-40, 45.

208 Groeneboom 1930, Broadhead 1960, Roussel 1960, and De Romilly 1974 all read only the first ἦ. Denniston 1950 [1934]:281 also thinks that the second ἦ is unmetrical.

209 See II.3 §§33-42 on the closeness of Homeric ἦ to an interjection, and on interpreting it, accordingly, as a potentially independent prosodic unit, and as a sign of a character's emotional involvement.

interjections are typically at home in choral songs. Their pragmatic function, like that of ἦ, primarily concerns the expressive level of communication; it is less focused on eliciting a certain reaction from the addressee. I interpret the distribution of ἦ's use in assertions in light of this connection: choral songs imply less individuality than the other settings, but emotional involvement may still be high.

§89. In short, in both of its uses in drama the particle ἦ conveys the speaker's involvement. ἦ questions ask for confirmation of the suggested assertion. Unlike in Homer, such questions may concern facts as well as opinions. Since questions are inherently dialogic, this use is most frequent in dialogues. In assertions the particle affirms an assessment, an usually emotionally-laden one. In this use, found mainly in choral songs, ἦ's function is similar to that of an interjection, by expressing the speaker's involvement without necessarily asking for a reaction.

2.3 Conclusions

§90. In this chapter I have argued that paying attention to the distribution of particles over different communicative situations and their co-occurrence patterns with other features improves our understanding of these particles' functions. That is to say, exploring dialogues, monologues, and choral songs as discourse patterns with specific formal as well as functional features has proven useful for linguistic analysis, and promises to be a fruitful avenue for further research. One could, within drama, delve into hybrid communicative situations such as lyric dialogues,[210] or into the distributions of linguistic features other than the ones analyzed here, such as adjectives or certain subordinating conjunctions. In other genres, it would be interesting to compare similar distributional patterns across, for example, narrative and direct speech,[211] as well as across authors of the same genres.

§91. The general pictures of the three discourse patterns are the following. Dialogues usually have a relatively high frequency of γε and δῆτα in all authors; ἦ in tragedy; γάρ in Sophocles and Aristophanes; οὖν in Sophocles and Euripides; and καί and δή in Aeschylus. Other features that tend to be relatively frequent in this environment are finite verbs, first- and second-person references, negations, and (in Aristophanes) swearing expressions. Nouns tend to be relatively infrequent. These features reflect a high degree of on-stage interactiveness and individual involvement, and a low degree of formality. In monologues relatively common particles are μέν in tragedy; καί in Sophocles

[210] These other discourse patterns, however, would need to form a large enough corpus to yield statistically significant data concerning frequencies of linguistic features.

[211] For several such comparisons of particle frequencies in Homer, see II.2 §36 on δέ; II.3 §§38-39 on ἦ, with the nuancing note 122; §52 on γε; §§54-55 and §§60-61 on δή; §66 on ἄρα. For several particles being related to the reflection of a character's or the author's voice in Herodotus and Thucydides, see IV.4.3.

and Euripides; δέ, δή, and ἀλλά in Euripides; and τε in Aeschylus. In this discourse pattern we find the highest relative number of imperfects: a sign of this setting's affinity to narratives. Aeschylus also uses the most nouns in his monologues. The linguistic shape of monologues reflects a lower degree of involvement and interactiveness than in dialogues, but a higher degree than in choral songs. It can also be connected to floor-holding: the features reflect that speakers take more time to formulate their utterance than in the short turns of dialogues. Choral songs, finally, have the greatest density of the particle τε (except in Aeschylus) and of nouns. Aeschylus tends to use many δέ in these lyric parts, and Aristophanes many καί. The distributions of the selected features reflect that choral songs have a low degree of interactiveness among characters, a low degree of individual involvement, a high degree of formality, and a particular connection to tradition and rituality. Certain features, such as a high frequency of δέ, also help to regularly allude to the style of epic.

§92. In general, this information about relative frequencies of particles and other features may be used as a blueprint, so to speak, for the three discourse patterns. It will for example help us to tell, when reading tragedy and comedy, if a certain particle is marked in its current context (see e.g. (t19)), or if in fact the absence of a particle is striking (see e.g. (t9)). The distributional tendencies also clarify which particles are expected to co-occur more or less often: at least for drama, we do not need to share Denniston's surprise at the rarity of τε and γε occurring together.[212] On the contrary: the functions of these two particles fit different communicative settings.

§93. The observations also throw light upon differences in particle use across the four authors and two genres. Aeschylus is the king of δέ among these playwrights: especially in his choral songs, the particle is extremely frequent. Sophoclean and Aristophanic dialogues often resemble each other in their particle use: they share a high frequency of γάρ, ἀλλά, οὖν, and δῆτα. Aristophanic dialogues, however, surpass all other contexts in their frequency of γε.[213] Aristophanes further shows an extreme fondness for καί and τε in choral songs, although the latter particle is about as common in Euripidean songs.

§94. By using the distributions of the particles and co-occurring features as input for interpretation, I have connected the particles' local functions to several global

[212] Denniston wonders why τε and γε are rarely found together, "since the combination is a perfectly natural one" (1950 [1934]:161).

[213] And even all other Greek literature: a *TLG* survey of γε's frequency in 51 authors from Homer to the third century CE demonstrates that the author with the second highest average γε frequency, i.e. Plato, still uses it only 0.92 times per 100 words. In Aristophanes the frequency is 1.07%, if all speaker names and indications of line numbers are taken into account as well—the real frequency of γε is therefore even higher (see our frequency graphs [available online as I.5]). For more correct frequencies in drama, but concerning only parts of the plays, see Table 11 above for the average γε frequencies in the three discourse patterns. See III.5 §52 on probable reasons for the high γε frequency in Aristophanes.

associations invited by each discourse pattern. That is, the local co-text is not enough to interpret a particle's pragmatic contribution: knowledge about its distribution enhances our understanding of why a certain particle fits a certain context. For example, the distribution of δέ can be connected to its relatively neutral local function, and, more globally, to allusions to epic in specific contexts such as messenger speeches. καί is particularly multifunctional: some of its uses fit the high interactiveness of dialogues, others the longer floor-holding of monologues. τε does not only mark coordination between two items: its higher frequency in certain contexts demonstrates its overarching connection to shared encyclopedic or cultural knowledge and several related associations. This interpretation of τε's large-scale pragmatics echoes its associations in other genres. Along the same lines, I interpret the contrastive function of γε as related to the interaction between characters, more specifically to their engagement with each other's varying opinions. For δή, the local co-text is required to distinguish between its several functions; most of these signpost personal and/or interpersonal attitudes that have a bearing on the global communicative situation. All in all, my results serve as a warning not to treat all these particles together as one linguistic feature. Their distributions, local functions, and global associations vary greatly, even within the dramatic corpus.

§95. In other words, then, the small-scale pragmatics of particles can be connected to their large-scale pragmatics. This illustrates the necessity of a discourse perspective on particle use: since particles are used differently in different discourse patterns, and since they carry additional implications beyond their local function, the sentence in which they occur is not sufficient for their interpretation. Large-scale patterns of distribution are crucial for understanding the particles' functions, uses, and implications.

Appendix: Non-Significant Distributions

§96. For the sake of completeness, I give here the distributions of ἄρα/ἆρα, μέντοι, and μήν. They are not discussed in the chapter, because they are not statistically significant in most authors. This has to to do with their generally low frequency, compared to that of other particles.

Author	Dialogues	Monologues	Choral songs	Significant?
Aeschylus	0.22	0.03	0.08	yes
Sophocles	0.17	0.15	0.20	no
Euripides	0.16	0.12	0.28	no
Aristophanes	0.41	0.10	0.06	no

Table 22: Frequencies of ἄρα/ἆρα in percentages of all words

Author	Dialogues	Monologues	Choral songs	Significant?
Aeschylus	0.05	0.03	0	no
Sophocles	0.09	0.06	0	no
Euripides	0.08	0.07	0	no
Aristophanes	0.08	0.05	0	no

Table 23: Frequencies of μέντοι in percentages of all words

Author	Dialogues	Monologues	Choral songs	Significant?
Aeschylus	0.22	0.11	0.03	no
Sophocles	0.25	0.03	0	yes
Euripides	0.10	0.03	0	no
Aristophanes	0.14	0.10	0	no

Table 24: Frequencies of μήν in percentages of all words

III.3

Reusing Others' Words

Resonance

3.1 Introduction

§1. Whenever we speak or write, we inevitably use words and constructions that others have already used, or that we ourselves have used on previous occasions. Recurrence of elements from previous discourse is therefore common in language use, both spoken and written. Types of recurrence include reusing certain words, echoing sounds, reproducing syntactic constructions, and recycling pragmatic functions such as questioning or evaluating. Sometimes we use such repetition across utterances[1] consciously to achieve specific communicative goals. We might, for example, echo an interlocutor as a way to join her in her action. In a different context, we might use an opponent's own words, concepts, or constructions to defeat him rhetorically. In yet another situation, we might mimic someone else's intonation pattern to amuse our listeners.

§2. The process of exploiting linguistic echoes for pragmatic reasons is called resonance in the theory of dialogic syntax, developed by John Du Bois. This chapter will discuss the use of resonance in Greek tragedy and comedy, and the roles that particles play in this process. The aim of applying this modern linguistic approach to an ancient corpus is not to advance our knowledge about (dialogic) communication in general; spoken conversations form better material for investigating those aspects. Rather, as holds for the theory applications in III.2 (discourse patterns) and III.4 (Conversation Analysis), the goal is a better understanding of language use in the corpus of Greek drama, and of particle use in particular.

1 I use the term "utterance" in a neutral way, for pieces of discourse continuously "uttered" in any medium. If a change of speaker occurs, I consider this the end of an utterance: see III.4 §9.

3.1.1 What is dialogic resonance?

§3. The concept of resonance has been developed by Du Bois, in the framework of dialogic syntax.[2] This theory stresses the dialogic nature of communication: that is, every piece of discourse is shaped by a context, and in its turn shapes the new context. The approaches to language use upon which Du Bois' theory builds consider discourse a dynamic and joint construction by all participants, rather than a static product by one speaker or writer, as some other linguistic theories assume. Among the dialogic approaches we can find the joint-action theory of language use (Clark 1996), Conversation Analysis (see III.4 for discussion and references), and dialogism (Voloshinov 1973 [1929]; Bakhtin 1981 [1934]; Linell 1998, 2009). They all share the view that every communicative act is context-shaped and context-renewing; that is, communicative acts respond to some prior context and at the same time serve as context for subsequent contributions.[3]

§4. Although these frameworks are based on spoken language use, they are also useful for understanding written discourse. These theories as well as others have demonstrated that spoken language should be considered the primary and most basic form of language use, from which all others are derived. Hopper and Thompson 2008 convincingly argue that the simpler forms of certain constructions used in spoken language should not be viewed as degenerate versions of the written norm. Rather, written constructions are better considered "normativized and extended versions" (119) of the spoken ones.

§5. Starting from general ideas on dialogism, Du Bois has developed the framework of dialogic syntax, which focuses on dialogic engagement across pieces of discourse, both spoken and written, and (in conversation) both across turns of speaking and within single turns. The approach is not restricted to dialogues; as Du Bois puts it, "[w]hat is essential to dialogicality is not dialogue in the narrow sense, but engagement with prior words and structures" (2014:372). As case studies he analyzes the relations among separate turns in American English conversations, since spoken exchanges between two speakers are the canonical realizations of dialogic syntax. He observes that speakers often pick up certain elements from previous utterances in order to achieve some pragmatic goal(s). A speaker, for example, might reuse her interlocutor's words, constructions, intonation patterns, etc. to express disagreement:

2 Du Bois' seminal work on dialogic syntax has been in circulation for several years before publication in 2014. The scholar has presented these ideas on various conferences since 1998, and the paper has been distributed since 2001.

3 See also II.4 on discourse memory, especially §§5-10.

(t1)

Joanne: It's kind of like *you* Ken.
Ken: That's not at *all* like me Joanne.

Fragment of spoken dialogue, from
Du Bois 2014:362

In this exchange, Du Bois points out, the second speaker Ken picks up lexical items, syntactic structures, and the intonation pattern of the first speaker Joanne's utterance. He thereby highlights his disagreement. Similarly, picking up a specific part of another's utterance may serve to signal doubt or objection:

(t2)

Wendy: Eight-ounce measuring cup. Is virtually unbreakable.
Kevin: Virtually.

Fragment of spoken dialogue, from
Sakita 2006:472

Here Kevin, by repeating Wendy's "virtually," draws attention to this part of her utterance to characterize it as the crucial part of her overall claim: the cup is not completely unbreakable.

§6. Du Bois calls this process of "activating affinities across utterances" dialogic resonance. Note that resonance is not merely repetition. Only when the repetition in question draws attention to itself, and when it accomplishes specific ends, resonance is triggered. It is therefore a more dynamic process than repetition: the speaker or writer actively does something by picking up some previous element. On top of that, resonance is broader than lexical repetition: building upon a syntactic construction or mirroring an intonation pattern can also trigger resonance. The difference between these two processes, however, is not clear-cut. Du Bois, for example, is dubious as to whether the repetition in the following excerpt should be considered a trigger of resonance. Ken has just asked Lenore what kind of vitamin tablets she brought:

(t3)

Lenore: This is liver.
Ken: How many different liver things do you have?

Fragment of spoken dialogue, from
Du Bois 2010:32

As the word repeated here, "liver," is not a very common one, the repetition seems at first sight to be significant. It is ambiguous, however, whether Ken has a specific intention in repeating Lenore. Du Bois points out that in all likelihood Ken simply does not have an appropriate synonym available to him.

§7. The current corpus of tragedy and comedy displays similar borderline cases. This chapter assumes that if we can plausibly infer conscious pragmatic goals for certain repetitions that occur across utterances, we may interpret these repetitions as resonance triggers.[4] For a fictional drama corpus, we should keep in mind the added dimension of the author: on top of the characters' pragmatic goals, those of the playwright may be involved in resonance.[5]

3.1.2 Studies on resonance in modern languages

§8. To date we have several applications of dialogic syntax using corpora from different modern languages. This new body of work shows that resonance takes place in a variety of linguistic forms and with several functions, and has yielded a number of theoretical refinements. This section gives an overview of these applications, in order to illustrate that resonance is a productive concept.[6] It is relevant to many languages and types of discourse, and it has points of contact to several other concepts.

§9. Giora and Balaban's 2001 article is the first application of resonance theory. The authors mention resonance as an explanation for the use of metaphors in Hebrew newspapers. The metaphors' literal meaning is processed alongside their figurative, metaphoric one, which often leads to recurrence of the literal meaning in following discourse. Haddington 2004 looks at stancetaking in American English news interviews through the lens of dialogic syntax, following Du Bois 2007[7] in describing stancetaking as "a dynamic, dialogic, intersubjective, and collaborative social activity" (111).[8] In the process of stancetaking in news interviews, interviewees frequently pick up linguistic features from their interviewers' utterances to express their own stance. Laury 2005 focuses on topicality in Finnish interactions, and shows that "speakers use the recycling of linguistic elements as a resource in maintaining topical continuity in conversational interaction" (165).

§10. Sakita 2006 extends the theory of dialogic syntax by uniting it with ideas drawn from cognitive linguistics. Analyzing some of the same American English examples as

4 Pickering 1999:34, discussing lexical repetitions in tragedy, adds a similar warning. He points out that not all repetitions can or should be considered intentional and meaningful; yet at the same time, he argues strongly against the view that all are unconscious and "careless."

5 See §§29-32 below on resonance used by playwrights (rather than by characters).

6 See also Du Bois 2014:365 for an overview of resonance studies.

7 Du Bois has presented his ideas on stancetaking at several conferences before publishing them in 2007, which is why Haddington can already refer to them in 2004.

8 On stancetaking, see IV.4.4.

Du Bois, Sakita points out that many instances of resonance depend on the speakers' capacity for schematization. That is, speakers need to "instantly abstract a schema from a priming utterance" (494) before they can use this schema to build their own utterance upon. Giora 2007, using examples from newspapers and webpages in English and Hebrew, proposes further theoretical refinements. This author distinguishes between "backward" and "forward" resonance, that is, resonance "between a given utterance and a previous one" and resonance "between a given utterance and a future one" (142). Giora makes this distinction because, in her view, "the speaker's choice of a given constituent may be determined by the next constituent she is planning to use" (144). Forward resonance, then, is a concept that is relevant only in restricted cases, when we are dealing with separate utterances spoken by the same speaker. Furthermore, while a speaker's intentions may indeed play a role in her use of conscious repetitions, resonance can only be triggered once the second utterance has been heard. It is therefore better to keep to one clear definition of resonance, and to treat only echoes of *earlier* elements as resonance triggers.

§11. Zima, Brône, Feyaerts, and Sambre 2008 show that speakers frequently employ resonance in contexts of disagreement during French and Austrian political debates. In their words, "[f]ormal mapping relations are intentionally used to convey interpersonal pragmatic differential" (144). Speakers especially tend to pick up the syntax from an earlier speaker. Here is an example:

(t4)

Speaker 1: Es war einmal ein Professor,
Speaker 2: Der wollte Vizekanzler werden!
Speaker 1: Der wollte etwas Gutes tun—nicht für sich, sondern für nachwachsende Generationen
(...)

Fragment of a debate in the Austrian parliament, March 2006,
from Zima *et al.* 2008:144 (their translation)

S1. Once upon a time, there was a professor
S2. Who wanted to become vice-chancellor!
S1. Who wanted to do good—not for himself but for the succeeding generations
(...)

In this exchange, the two speakers take turns stealing their opponents' syntax and semantics. Speaker 1, intending to characterize himself as a do-gooder, begins with a typical fairytale beginning. Speaker 2 then interjects, commandeering the first speaker's syntax and semantics to throw doubt on his good intentions. In the third utterance, however, Speaker 1 mirrors the second speaker's utterance to reassert his own attitude on the matter. Resonance is thus useful for conveying differences, Zima *et al.* conclude, such as to express disagreement or sarcasm, to ridicule, or to claim intellectual superiority. Nuolijärvi and Tiittula 2011 extend the work of Zima *et al.* in their discussion of Finnish political debates. This article also describes how speakers employ resonance to convey pragmatic differences. Resonance can "be used for marking a stance toward the previous speaker's utterance" (578). The authors focus on the use of irony, which always seems to involve some kind of intentional "echoing" of another speaker.[9]

§12. Oropeza-Escobar 2011, in a book-length study on resonance in contemporary Mexican Spanish interactions, demonstrates that resonance can be used in joking contexts. Speakers also often use resonance to signal agreement or disagreement, or, more generally, to indicate their stance.[10] In the following passage, two speakers mock the first by exploiting the phonological similarity between (the Spanish equivalents of) "election" and "erection":

(t5)

Speaker 1: Sabe qué tipo de *erección* tendremos en el dos mil tres?
Speaker 2: Perdón?
Speaker 3: Qué tipo de qué?
Speaker 2: *Erección*?
Speaker 1: Qué tipo de *elección*.
Speaker 3: Sí yo también oí...
Speaker 2: Sí, ándale.
Speaker 3: Porque dijo *erección*, verdad?

Fragment of informal Mexican Spanish conversation, from Oropeza-Escobar 2011:32-33 (her translation)

S1. Do you know what type of *erection* we will have in 2003?
S2. Pardon?
S3. What type of what?
S2. *Erection*?
S1. What type of *election*.
S3. Yes I also heard...

9 Nuolijärvi and Tiittula build on Wilson and Sperber's 1992 view on irony. On stance and irony in Herodotus and Thucydides, see IV.4.4.6; on δή connected to this, see IV.4 §§104-108 on Herodotus, and §§123-126 on Thucydides.

10 Despite the length of her book, Oropeza-Escobar does not seem to add much theoretical insight to the ideas expressed by, especially, Du Bois 2010 [2001] and Linell 1998, both of whom she frequently cites.

S2. Yeah, that's right.
S3. Because he said *erection*, right?

As Oropeza-Escobar (33, 44) points out, the second and third speakers mock and embarrass the first speaker by repeating his "slip of the tongue" with a marked intonation.

§13. Finally, the 2011 article by Takanashi provides a detailed discussion of resonance in playful informal Japanese conversations. She shows that speakers may perform a switch in speech style in response to a similar shift by a previous speaker. For example, one participant she studies playfully enacts the speech style of a stereotypical professor; his friend replies by acting out the response of a stereotypical student. In another example, speakers enact the personae of stereotypical wife and husband, and stereotypical American versus Japanese. Takanashi calls this phenomenon "pragmatic resonance," and more specifically "stylistic resonance."[11]

§14. To sum up: the recent work on resonance in modern languages shows that this process is ubiquitous, and that its analysis can throw light on different aspects of communication. So far we have evidence from English, Finnish, French, German, Hebrew, Japanese, and Mexican Spanish; and from both spoken and written language taking place in both informal settings (such as daily conversation) and formal ones (such as political debates and newspapers). These analyses bring to light the many forms and functions that resonance can take. We will see in this chapter that Greek drama, likewise, displays a variety of resonance uses.

3.1.3 Studies on resonance in ancient Greek

§15. Let us now turn to ancient Greek. Indeed, scholars have long observed that speakers in Greek tragedy and comedy exploit linguistic similarities across turns of speaking to achieve different effects. Thus, the existing work is compatible with this framework, even though none of the authors so far explicitly applies Du Bois' concept of resonance.

§16. Hancock's 1917 dissertation on tragic stichomythia is a particularly good example of this convergence of thought. He observes that it is characteristic in stichomythia for one speaker to pick up and emphasize another speaker's words or constructions (6, 35-36), often in an angry or mocking way (33). Hancock analyzes this process in detail and outlines its forms and functions. He also notes the different ways in which each of the major tragedians employs this type of recurrence. Most relevant for us, his study includes observations on the use of particles in such processes.[12]

11 Takanashi seems to gloss over the fact that several other types of resonance, such as prosodic and syntactic ones, are occurring at the same time. Beside that, Du Bois already mentions the possibility of pragmatic resonance as well.

12 Hancock incidentally notes (53-57) that the same repetition across utterances is also present in the Platonic dialogues, where it takes its own set of forms and functions.

§17. Ireland 1974 on Aeschylus similarly focuses on the way speakers during stichomythia pick up elements from each other's utterances. In this author's view, stichomythia does not just present an "arbitrary juxtaposition of independent statements," but an "interaction of intellectual and emotional responses" connected to the dramatic situation (513). He gives many examples of "the syntactic completion of one line by the other" (511), and discusses the role of particles in them.

§18. Pfeiffer-Petersen 1996 on Sophocles looks specifically at repetition in conflict stichomythia. This scholar analyzes several linguistic strategies employed in agonistic dialogues, which range from the repetition of words and morphemes across utterances ("Wortaufnahmen") to syntactic, phonological, and semantic similarities. Her conclusions closely align with the work on dialogic syntax previously surveyed, as she finds that repetitions frequently occur to emphasize a speaker's main ideas or emotions, or to "fight back" an opponent with his own words. Such repetitions are especially prominent in scenes of vehement disagreement.

§19. Pickering is a particularly prolific scholar of repetition in tragedy, with several rich publications and presentations to his name from 1999 to 2003.[13] His main focus is verbal or literal repetition: that is, lexical echoes across different lines.[14] Pickering 1999 stresses that since repetition is "natural in human communication" it lends an air of realism to tragic dialogues (152-154, 231). He writes (154): "there is nothing in the least odd about the repetition of words in the tragedians. Not only are the authors behaving in the common human way, but they are also accurately representing their characters as behaving in the common human way."[15] Developing this work, Pickering and Pickering 2002 analyze lexical repetition from one line to the next in twenty-one Greek tragedies (seven by each poet). They find that such repetition appears in stichomythia about twice as often as it does in spoken parts of tragedy overall. Characters in tragedy, Pickering and Pickering conclude, repeat each other's words much more often when their speaking turns are short.

§20. Collins 2004 investigates the use of competitive "capping" in tragic and comic stichomythia. Capping is a conversational practice of verbal one-upmanship, central to

[13] Pickering 1999 is Peter E. Pickering's dissertation on repetition in tragedy. In an article labeled 2000a, he discusses repetitions and their removal by the copyists of tragedy. The publication called 2000b focuses on repetition in *Prometheus*. Pickering and Pickering 2002 is a conference paper of Peter Pickering and his son Martin Pickering, who is a cognitive linguist. Furthermore, in an article published in 2003, Peter Pickering discusses so-called "careless" repetition in Greek. Pickering's work is referred to by Schuren 2015:15, 132 on Euripidean stichomythia; this author adds in her interpretations of specific passages that lexical repetition may reflect impatience (32) or sarcasm (173), and that a story may be repeated in different forms across a tragedy, with several effects (216-217).

[14] Pickering confines his analyses to "lexical words." That is, particles, conjunctions, prepositions, the definite article, forms of "to be" etc. have been excluded. Repetitions of "non-lexical words" are considered by Pickering to be usually irrelevant.

[15] This naturalness of repetition is again stressed in Pickering 2000a:135.

symposia, whereby one speaker sets a theme and another responds by modifying that theme in some way. Parodies and riddles result, or in case of a lament, the emotional effect is heightened. Extending Collins' work, Hesk 2007 describes some specific cases of competitive capping in Aristophanes, which involve (141-142) "lexical repetition, structural mirroring and quasi-improvised responsion." Hesk argues that capping in comedies is a parody of the real poetic competitions that occurred for example in sympotic games.

§21. Willi 2003 and 2010b also look at comedy. The author observes linguistic features which create a parody of tragic language. He finds that one of the ways in which Aristophanes parodies tragedy is by mirroring, and thus mocking, tragedy's "stylistic grandeur" (138). A notable example is the liberal use of abstract nouns ending in -μα, a signal feature of tragic language.[16]

§22. An unpublished paper on Sophocles by Lucci 2012 points out that Sophocles sometimes uses lexical repetition in stichomythia in order to create humorous wordplay. This wordplay can function as a comic foil to subsequent horrifying tragic events, Lucci argues.

§23. Similarly, Rutherford, in his book on tragic language and style, notes that repetition of one speaker's words by another is a frequent feature of tragic stichomythia (2012:173). Rutherford mentions several functions of lexical repetition, both in stichomythia and other parts of a play. First, it may underline not only disagreement between speakers, but also their unity, as between Orestes and Electra in Sophocles *Electra* (173). Second, terms used in a prologue may reappear throughout a play, which highlights their thematic importance (Sophocles is especially fond of this technique (181)). Third, a speaker might sarcastically reuse a previous speaker's words, as Antigone does when echoing Ismene's οἴμοι in Sophocles *Antigone* 86 (185). Finally, a playwright may put certain words or constructions repeatedly in a speaker's mouth to characterize him or her in a certain way (185).

§24. Altogether the above studies provide an abundance of data on the use of similarities across utterances in Greek drama. All the analyses fit well with the concept of resonance observed in the modern-language corpora discussed in the previous section. However, the studies tend to focus on lexical repetition and syntactic continuation only; resonance is broader, as it can also be triggered by semantic, pragmatic, metrical, and other similarities across utterances. On top of that, analyzing resonance entails taking into account the speaker's pragmatic goals in echoing a previous utterance.

3.1.4 This chapter

§25. This chapter analyzes similarities, mainly across different utterances, in tragedy and comedy using the modern linguistic concept of resonance. As will be demonstrated, resonance is an important communicative strategy of characters and playwrights. We

[16] On the use of -μα nouns in tragedy, see Barrett 2007.

can detect various forms, beyond lexical repetition and syntactic parallelism, as well as a wide range of functions. The study of resonance throws light on many aspects of communication in the corpus, including particle use.

§26. The next section distinguishes two groups of functions of resonance in Greek drama. First, resonance may serve the speaking character's goals; second, it may serve the playwright's goals. Examples and analyses will show for which functions the linguistic echoes are employed, as well as which forms are involved. Subsequently, I discuss the roles that particles play in the process of resonance. There are two ways in which they do so. Most important, particles indicate how a speaker uses resonance between her utterance and a previous utterance. Second, they may trigger resonance themselves when repeated across utterances.

3.2 Resonance in Tragedy and Comedy

3.2.1 Functions of resonance

§27. Recall from our survey of resonance studies in modern languages that conscious linguistic repetition (lexical or otherwise) may have several pragmatic functions. Repetition may, for example, stress the unity of two speakers: in using similar words and constructions, the speakers stress that they belong together and that they have similar communicative goals. In tragedy, such resonance may be due to the ritual context. If two speakers are performing a ritual together, such as invoking a dead relative (see (t6)), they tend to use highly similar language.

§28. A second, antithetical, function of resonance is to express semantic or pragmatic difference from a previous utterance, such as to disagree with one's interlocutor. We have seen some examples of this function from modern languages: politicians tend to pick up their opponents' language in order to defeat their arguments. In tragedy and comedy we see this function especially in quick stichomythic exchanges; scholars often note the high degree of lexical repetition there. As the practice in Greek drama and modern languages attests, it is a rhetorically effective strategy to contradict an opponent with his own words.

§29. In addition to the pragmatic purposes of the speakers, we must also consider those of the playwright. Similarities and recurrences across utterances may serve ends that transcend the immediate concerns of the communicating characters. The reappearance of a certain semantic concept may, for instance, underline its importance as a theme in the play. Phonological or metrical resonance may also have the same effect.[17]

§30. Similarly, when a speaker habitually uses certain words or constructions over the course of a play, this recurrence becomes a way of characterizing her. For example, if a character repeatedly uses directive or interrogative utterances and does so much more

[17] See II.2 §38 on metrical resonance and its possible effects in Pindar.

often than her interlocutors, this repetition may trigger a resonance of illocutionary force.[18] The habitual use of directives may characterize the speaker as, for instance, more powerful than her addressees, while the habit of asking questions is particularly fitting for characters who are ignorant of everything they should have known.

§31. In comedy, resonance that functions at the metadramatic level includes the following forms. First, there is the type of resonance that is triggered through repetition of unusual words or of whole situations within the scope of a play. Such resonance may work to create a humorous effect. Second, there is the type that is triggered by recurrence of forms across plays, especially between comedy and tragedy. The comedian's purpose here is to create paratragedy or to parody a different genre. So, for example, the extensive lexical quotation that Aristophanes makes use of in *Frogs* highlights the play's reference to tragedy. Less conspicuous similarities may achieve this effect as well.

§32. We should also consider resonance in comedy that serves dual functions, both the character's purposes and the playwright's. When one speaker is sarcastic with another, the character's pragmatic goal is to disagree with her interlocutor. At the same time, sarcasm works at the metadramatic level, to amuse the audience.

3.2.2 Resonance used by speaking characters

3.2.2.1 Resonance stressing unity of speakers and actions

§33. It must be noted that the typically agonistic nature of Greek drama does not leave much room for the type of resonance that stresses the unity of speakers and their actions. Nonetheless, there are two contexts that are highly compatible with this type of resonance, ritual (see (t6) with discussion) and, more specifically, lament (see (t7) with discussion). Consider this first example, from Aeschylus *Libation Bearers*. Orestes and Electra are together invoking the ghost of their dead father Agamemnon, as well as the chthonic powers, to summon their help in the vengeance they plan to take against Clytemnestra. The two siblings' utterances display much lexical and syntactic repetition:

(t6)

Ορ. ὦ γαῖ', ἄνες μοι πατέρ' ἐποπτεῦσαι μάχην.
Ηλ. ὦ Περσέφασσα, δὸς δέ γ' εὔμορφον κράτος.
Ορ. μέμνησο λουτρῶν οἷς ἐνοσφίσθης, πάτερ.
Ηλ. μέμνησο δ' ἀμφίβληστρον ὡς ἐκαίνισας.
Ορ. πέδαις γ' ἀχαλκεύτοισι θηρευθείς, πάτερ.
Ηλ. αἰσχρῶς τε βουλευτοῖσιν ἐν καλύμμασιν.

18 "Illocutionary force" refers to the intended function of an utterance in communication, such as assertive, interrogative, or directive. It is a term from speech-act theory, originally developed by Austin 1962 and Searle 1969.

Ορ. ἆρ' ἐξεγείρῃ τοῖσδ' ὀνείδεσιν, πάτερ;
Ηλ. ἆρ' ὀρθὸν αἴρεις φίλτατον τὸ σὸν κάρα;

Aeschylus *Libation Bearers* 489-496

Or. Earth, send me up my father to watch over my fight.
El. Persephassa, give him to us in his beauty and power.
Or. Remember the bath in which you were done to death, father!
El. Remember how they devised a new kind of net!
Or. And you were caught in fetters that were not made of metal, father.
El. Yes,[19] in the shroud that was part of their shaming plot.
Or. Are you awakened by the thought of that disgrace, father?
El. Are you raising your beloved head erect?

There are repetitions of words at the beginning of lines 489-490, 491-492, and 495-496. Groeneboom 1949 *ad loc.* explains these similarities as references to cult formulas. Both he and Garvie 1986 observe that this prayer continues or repeats the theme of the directly preceding lyric section, the *kommos* (lines 306-478), sung by the chorus, Electra, and Orestes in alternation. According to Garvie, the lexical repetitions and other similarities across turns by the different speakers in 489-496 recall the strophic correspondences of the *kommos*.

§34. We can make these similarities more visible in so-called diagraph visualizations. The diagraph is "a higher-order, supra-sentential syntactic structure that emerges from the structural coupling of two or more utterances (or utterance portions), through the mapping of a structured array of resonance relations between them" (Du Bois 2014:376). Illustrating this structure in a schematic form clarifies the resonance relations in a certain stretch of discourse. Elements which are seen as resonating with elements from another utterance are boldfaced and placed in the same column. The method helps make clear how exactly the elements resemble and differ from each other. In Figure 1, for example (Diagraphs of Aeschylus *Libation Bearers* 489-496[20]), resonance takes place simultaneously on several levels. First, there are several lexical echoes: some words are taken over literally (μέμνησο, πάτερ/πατέρ', ἆρ'). Second, the utterances show similar syntactic structures: 489-490 both start with a vocative and contain an imperative singular; 491-492 contain an imperative singular and a subordinate clause dependent on an argument of the main verb; 493-494 contain a dative plural argument of θηρευθείς; and 495-496 feature interrogative main clauses with a second person singular verb. Third, there are

[19] Sommerstein 2008a reads and translates the conjecture γε instead of τε in this line.

[20] The symbols { } mark that the position of an element has been changed, in order to make the resonance clearer. See Du Bois 2014:374n5.

489 OR.	**ὦ γαῖ'**	**ἄνες**	μοι	**ἐποπτεῦσαι μάχην**	**{πατέρ'}**
	oh Earth	send up	for me	to watch over the fight	[my] father
490 EL.	**ὦ Περσέφασσα**	**δὸς**	δέ γ'	**εὔμορφον κράτος**	
	oh Persephassa	give	and	[his] beautiful strength	
491 OR.	**μέμνησο**	**λουτρῶν**		**οἷς ἐνοσφίσθης**	**πάτερ**
	remember	[the] bath		in which you were killed	father
492 EL.	**μέμνησο δ'**	**ἀμφίβληστρον**		**ὡς ἐκαίνισας**	
	and remember	[the] net		how you put it to a new use	
493 OR.	**πέδαις γ' ἀχαλκεύτοισι**			θηρευθείς	**πάτερ**
	with *non-metal fetters*			you were caught	father
494 EL.	**αἰσχρῶς τε βουλευτοῖσιν ἐν καλύμμασιν**				
	and with a shamefully plotted net				
495 OR.	**ἆρ'**	**ἐξεγείρῃ**		τοῖσδ' ὀνείδεσιν	**πάτερ**
	[question]	you are awakened		by this disgrace	father
496 EL.	**ἆρ'**	**ὀρθὸν αἴρεις**		φίλτατον τὸ σὸν κάρα	
	[question]	you raise erect		your beloved head	

Figure 1: Diagraphs of Aeschylus *Libation Bearers* 489-496

semantic links: between the meanings of "Earth" and "Persephassa"; between "send up"and "give"; "watching over a fight"and "being strong and beautiful" (helpful characteristics of Agamemnon); "bath" and "net" (deadly tools used by Agamemnon's killers); "fetters" and "net"; "awaking"and "raising your head." Fourth, there are pragmatic similarities, where the second of each pair of utterances takes over the first utterance's pragmatic goal. These goals are, respectively, (1) to entreat the Underworld powers to send up a strong Agamemnon, (2) to entreat Agamemnon to remember the murder, (3) to detail the murder weapons, and (4) to ask Agamemnon whether the prayer has successfully roused him.

§35. The diagraphs also highlight that the essential word "father" (once as the object of a verb, three times as vocative) is uttered only by Orestes in this excerpt. This stresses his dominance over his sister. In addition, the fact that Electra is always the one taking over elements from Orestes' utterances, rather than the other way around, further stresses her dependent position.[21]

§36. All these resonances work together to convey the unity of the speakers and their action. Electra does not change the pragmatic goals of Orestes' utterances when she takes over elements from them, but simply mirrors those goals. In the words of Hancock 1917:9, the passage displays "balance but no opposition." Du Bois 2007 calls this kind of unity "alignment."[22] Speakers often assess objects in relation to previous assessments by others, and then "align" or "disalign" with them. That Electra so closely mimics Orestes' speech patterns suggests her strong accordance with Orestes' sense of loyalty to Agamemnon. Moreover, it fits the ritual nature of the scene: the two speakers are together invoking their dead father.

§37. The exodus at the end of Aeschylus *Persians* (908-1077, containing first anapaests, then lyrics) uses resonance to emphasize the unity of the speakers and their actions as well. The chorus and the Persian king Xerxes are together lamenting the Persian defeat. Again, resonance is triggered on several linguistic levels at the same time. There is, for instance, a syntactic similarity in the many doublings of words, by both the chorus and the king: e.g. αἰνῶς αἰνῶς (930) and ἔλιπες ἔλιπες (985) by the chorus, and βοᾷ βοᾷ (991) and νέαι νέαι δύαι δύαι (1010) by Xerxes. Repeating words fits the ritual purpose of their song, to perform a lament. That both speakers are doing this at the same time highlights their unity in performing this ritual.[23] Besides words that are uttered twice directly after each other, there are some "refrains" in the song that are verbally repeated across different utterances by the same speaker. For example, Xerxes sings βόα νυν ἀντίδουπά μοι three times (1040, 1048, 1066). Other words are literally repeated across utterances by different speakers: the chorus picks up πεπλήγμεθ' in 1009 from Xerxes' turn in 1008. These lexical repetitions may trigger resonance, and highlight the joint action of ritual lament.

§38. In some parts of this passage, we can also see—or, rather, hear—repetition of the sound αι. The frequency of this sound throughout the exodus as a whole is not striking: it occurs 93 times in the 170 lines, which means about 55 times per 100 lines on average. This frequency does not differ much from that found in the first 100 lines of *Persians* and *Agamemnon*, which respectively yield 41 and 50 occurrences. Nevertheless, if the sound

21 Rutherford 2012:170 notes that Electra's role is in fact subordinate to that of Orestes throughout the play.

22 See IV.4 §§45-84 (section 4.4) on the application of Du Bois' notion of stance to historiography, with §§47-49 and §§61-63 on alignment and disalignment in particular. On alignment, see also Pickering and Garrod 2006.

23 See the *kommos* at Sophocles *Ajax* 330-427, where we also find several doublings of words.

αι appears at a higher rate than usual in the close affinity of the interjection αἰαῖ, then the sound αι and its wailing function receive greater emphasis.[24] In other words, if the phonological repetition is striking enough, it may trigger resonance, and achieve certain pragmatic goals.[25] Here the resonance of αι underlines the chorus and the king's purpose to lament as well as the fact that they are making a common effort to do so.

(t7)

Χο. παπαῖ παπαῖ.
Ξε. καὶ πλέον ἢ παπαῖ μὲν οὖν.
Χο. δίδυμα γάρ ἐστι καὶ τριπλᾶ.
Ξε. λυπρά χάρματα δ' ἐχθροῖς.
Χο. καὶ σθένος γ' ἐκολούθη.
Ξε. γυμνός εἰμι προπομπῶν.
Χο. φίλων ἄταισι ποντίαισιν.
Ξε. δίαινε δίαινε πῆμα, πρὸς δόμους δ' ἴθι.
Χο. αἰαῖ αἰαῖ δύα δύα.

Aeschylus *Persians* 1031-1039

Ch. Papai, papai!
Xe. No, "papai" is too mild!
Ch. Yes, the disaster was twice and thrice as great.
Xe. Painful, and a delight to our enemies!
Ch. Cut short, too, was the strength—
Xe. I am denuded of escorts!
Ch. —of our friends, by calamaties at sea.
Xe. Wet, wet your cheeks in grief, and go with me to the palace.
Ch. Aiai, aiai! Sorrow, sorrow![26]

In this passage, we find 14 instances of αι in 9 lines. This high frequency was probably striking for the audience. Note that the particle καί, with its similar sound, also forms parts of the resonating elements.

[24] On the meaning and function of αἰαῖ, see Nordgren 2015:130-133, 212-215.

[25] See II.5 §61 with note 154 for an example of phonological as well as lexical and thematic resonance between two passages in Homer; these resemblances invite a similar interpretation of both passages.

[26] This translation by Sommerstein 2008b is slightly adapted to fit the order of lines as given in the TLG text by Page 1972.

1363	JA.	**ὦ** oh	**τέκνα** children	**μητρὸς** mother	**ὡς** how	**κακῆς** bad	**ἐκύρσατε** you have
1364	ME.	**ὦ** oh	**παῖδες** sons	**{πατρῴαι}** fatherly	**ὡς** how	**{νόσωι}** by sickness	**ὤλεσθε** you perished
1370	ME.	**οἵδ'** these	**οὐκέτ' εἰσί** are no more	τοῦτο γάρ for that	**σε δήξεται** will hurt you		
1371	JA.	**οἵδ'** these	**εἰσίν** are		**οἴμοι** ah me!	σῶι κάραι μιάστορες avengers for your head	

Figure 2: Diagraphs of Euripides *Medea* 1363-1364 and 1370-1371

3.2.2.2 Resonance stressing differences

§39. Sometimes linguistic similarities work to effect something quite the opposite from what I have just discussed. In these cases a speaker picks up a word or construction from a previous utterance, usually by a different speaker, and uses this element in a new semantic context, and/or for a different pragmatic goal. The result is that the very similarity in form highlights the divergence between the two utterances. Such resonance stressing semantic or pragmatic differences may involve disagreement. Two speakers who are fighting over something may pick up parts of each other's utterances in order to defeat their opponent with his very own words. We have seen in the introduction that such use of resonance is frequent in modern languages as well.

§40. Collins 2004:30 points out that speakers in tragedy and comedy may express disagreement by picking up each other's words during stichomythia. As an example, Collins cites Aristophanes *Lysistrata* 371-374, a dialogue with many similarities across utterances, in which the female chorus leader picks up words from the men's leader. These verbal echoes, he argues, produce "subtle but powerful shifts of meaning (30)." Resonance can also stress semantic or pragmatic differences without outright disagreement between speakers. For example, as mentioned by Hancock 1917:36, two characters may construe a certain word differently, and thus use the same word to mean different things. In such cases, the poet usually wants to convey something more in addition to what the character herself is saying, for example the character's ignorance about a certain topic.

§41. The following passage from Euripides *Medea* is described by Hancock 1917:18 as "very effective in form and spirit." Mastronarde 2002 *ad loc.* notes that these lines "present a good example of violently argumentative stichomythia (...) with a characteristic echoing and contrasting of specific words in successive lines."

(t8)

Ια. ὦ τέκνα, μητρὸς ὡς κακῆς ἐκύρσατε.
Μη. ὦ παῖδες, ὡς ὤλεσθε πατρῴωι νόσωι.
Ια. οὔτοι νιν ἡμὴ δεξιά γ' ἀπώλεσεν.
Μη. ἀλλ' ὕβρις οἵ τε σοὶ νεοδμῆτες γάμοι.
Ια. λέχους σφε κἠξίωσας οὕνεκα κτανεῖν;
Μη. σμικρὸν γυναικὶ πῆμα τοῦτ' εἶναι δοκεῖς;
Ια. ἥτις γε σώφρων· σοὶ δὲ πάντ' ἐστὶν κακά.
Μη. οἵδ' οὐκέτ' εἰσί· τοῦτο γάρ σε δήξεται.
Ια. οἵδ' εἰσίν, οἴμοι, σῶι κάραι μιάστορες.
Μη. ἴσασιν ὅστις ἦρξε πημονῆς θεοί.
Ια. ἴσασι δῆτα σήν γ' ἀπόπτυστον φρένα.

Euripides *Medea* 1363-1373

Ja. Children, what an evil mother you got!
Me. Children, how you have perished by your father's fault!
Ja. It was not my hand, you know, that killed them.
Me. No: it was the outrage of your new marriage.
Ja. Did you really think it right to kill them because of a marriage?
Me. Do you imagine that loss of this is a trivial grief for a woman?
Ja. For a woman of sense, yes. But you find everything a disaster.
Me. But the children are dead: this will wound you to the quick.
Ja. They live, alas, as spirits to take vengeance on your crimes!
Me. The gods know who struck the first blow.
Ja. Yes, they know indeed your loathesome heart.

Two pairs of utterances, at 1363-1364 and 1370-1371, are especially notable here.[27] Observe that in the repeated elements, not only the meaning, but also the form of each of the second utterances (lines 1364 and 1371), is dependent on the first ones (1363 and 1370). Again, we may use diagraph representations to visualize the affinities (See Figure 2:

[27] On the use of γε in lines 1369 and 1373, and the use of δῆτα in 1373, see below, §79 and §84; on ἀλλά in line 1366, see Drummen 2009:148.

Diagraphs of Euripides *Medea* 1363-1364 and 1370-1371). In both pairs of utterances, resonance again occurs on several levels. There are lexical similarities, the straight repetition of words (ὦ, ὡς, οἴδ', εἰσί(ν)).[28] Syntactic repetitions are the following: 1363 and 1364 both have the form "vocative + ὡς-exclamative with second person plural verb"; 1370 and 1371 are short declarative sentences with the same verb and the same subject. On a semantic level, the following words have related meanings: τέκνα and παῖδες, μητρός and πατρώιαι, κακῆς and νόσωι (both referring to something bad), and σε δήξεται and οἴμοι (both referring to Jason's pain).

§42. The speakers in this passage change the pragmatic goals of the words and constructions they choose to echo. In 1363, Jason addresses the children in order to blame Medea. She picks up this construction in her utterance, also addressing the children, but in order to blame Jason. In 1370, Medea rubs it in that Jason has lost his children; in his reaction he turns part of the same linguistic material into a threat against her. The passage demonstrates, then, the way resonance occurs in ancient Greek drama to express disagreement and hostility.[29] The phenomenon seen here bears resemblances to the samples observed by Nuolijärvi and Tiittula 2011, and Zima *et al.* 2008 (see section 3.1.2 above) in the modern political debates they study. Zima *et al.* 2008 point out that resonance may involve irony, sarcasm, ridiculing, or expressing intellectual superiority; in short, it may "convey dissociative pragmatic purposes" (144).

§43. Aristophanes *Frogs* provides an example of resonance stressing differences in comedy. In the following passages we find lexical, phonological, semantic, syntactic, and morphological similarities, all working to sarcastic effect. For the audience, this resonance will have been humorous. The context is as follows. The god Dionysus is wearing a Heracles costume, but discovers that it has made him unpopular with some people. As a result he orders his slave Xanthias to wear the costume. But it turns out that "being Heracles" also comes with advantages, and Dionysus wants the costume back (lines 528-531). As soon as Dionysus is wearing the costume again, however, some enemies of Heracles enter. So the frightened god wants to return the dangerous outfit to Xanthias.

28 As Page 1938 *ad loc.* puts it, εἰσίν in 1371 "replies to" οὐκ εἰσί in 1370.

29 Similarly, Van Emde Boas 2017b:216-217 discusses examples of resonance with *matr-/patr-* showing the difference between Electra's and Orestes' views in Euripides' *Electra*. Further examples of resonance stressing differences include Sophocles *Oedipus King* 547-552 (Oedipus accuses his brother-in-law Creon of a conspiracy, picking up words and constructions from the latter's utterances); 1018-1019 (ἴσος has different implications in the two utterances); Euripides *Hippolytus* 1456-1457 (Theseus uses the same word to ask Hippolytus to stay alive as Hippolytus uses to describe his death). See also Sophocles *Ajax* 485-524 for a more general instance of resonance stressing differences, with the discussion by Hesk 2003:66. He draws attention to the allusions to Ajax' preceding speech in Tecmessa's monologue. She underlines, Hesk writes, "the appropriate nature of her rebuttal by imitating the *form* of Ajax's discourse (maxims, *polyptota*) at the same time as she alters the content" (italics in original). He argues that Sophocles often uses such repetitions "to emphasise meaning and/or lend emotional force to their words."

(t9)

(Δι.) κατάθου τὸ δέρμα.
Ξα. ταῦτ' ἐγὼ μαρτύρομαι
καὶ τοῖς θεοῖσιν ἐπιτρέπω.
Δι. ποίοις θεοῖς;
τὸ δὲ προσδοκῆσαί σ' οὐκ ἀνόητον καὶ κενὸν
ὡς δοῦλος ὢν καὶ θνητὸς Ἀλκμήνης ἔσει;
(...)
Ξα. οἶδ' οἶδα τὸν νοῦν· παῦε παῦε τοῦ λόγου.
οὐκ ἂν γενοίμην Ἡρακλῆς ἄν.
Δι. μηδαμῶς,
ὦ Ξανθίδιον.
Ξα. καὶ πῶς ἂν Ἀλκμήνης ἐγὼ
υἱὸς γενοίμην, δοῦλος ἅμα καὶ θνητὸς ὤν;
Δι. οἶδ' οἶδ' ὅτι θυμοῖ, καὶ δικαίως αὐτὸ δρᾷς·
κἂν εἴ με τύπτοις, οὐκ ἂν ἀντείποιμί σοι.

Aristophanes *Frogs* 528-531 and 580-585

(Dionysus wants the Heracles costume back)
Di. Off with that lionskin.
Xa. Witnesses take note! I'm putting this in the gods' hands.
Di. Gods indeed! And how brainless and vain of you, a mortal slave, to think that you could be Alcmene's son!
(...)
(Dionysus wants Xanthias to wear the costume again)
Xa. I know what you're thinking, I know. Stop talking, stop it. I'm not going to be Heracles again.[30]
Di. Don't be that way, Xanthikins.
Xa. And how could I, a mere mortal slave, become Alcmene's son?
Di. I know you're angry, I know, and you've every right to be. You could even take a punch at me and I wouldn't complain.

Xanthias picks up several words from Dionysus' utterances and thereby draws attention to Dionysus' pragmatic goals. Van Leeuwen 1896 clarifies the similarity with *Dionysi verba imitatus* as a stage direction in his text.[31] The following diagraph visualization illustrates the instances of resonance triggered (See Figure 3: Diagraph of Aristophanes *Frogs* 531

[30] Henderson reads Hermann's conjecture αὖ instead of the second ἄν.

[31] Tucker 1906 and Stanford 1958 also note the similarity between Dionysus' and Xanthias' utterances. Stanford comments on the sarcastic nature of Xanthias' references.

531 DI.	ὡς that	**Ἀλκμήνης** Alcmene's [son]	**ἔσει** you'll be	**{δοῦλος ὢν καὶ θνητὸς}** being a slave and mortal
582-3 XA.	καὶ πῶς ἂν and how [would]	**Ἀλκμήνης {υἱὸς}** Alcmene's son	**{ἐγὼ} γενοίμην** I become	**δοῦλος ἅμα καὶ θνητὸς ὢν** being both a slave and mortal

Figure 3: Diagraph of Aristophanes *Frogs* 531 and 582-583

and 582-583). Dionysus finds his own words thrown back at him now that he has changed his mind (again). The sarcastic resonance has a humorous effect: not only is Dionysus in this scene extremely inconsistent and opportunistic, Xanthias even manages to point his behavior out to him by reusing the god's own words.

§44. The word order in the diagraph has been altered to show the similarities between the two utterances more clearly (see note 20), but in the original passages the repetition is done chiastically: δοῦλος ὢν καὶ θνητὸς Ἀλκμήνης ἔσει (531) vs. Ἀλκμήνης ἐγὼ /υἱὸς γενοίμην, δοῦλος ἅμα καὶ θνητὸς ὢν (582-583).[32] In fact the chiastic ordering strengthens the sarcastic effect. Dionysus had first mentioned Xanthias' characteristics as a mortal slave, and then the idea of him becoming Alcmene's son. Xanthias in his retort first mentions the idea of him becoming Alcmene's son—in itself not yet enough to trigger the resonance, because the current scene is about the costume as well—and only then utters the most important words: isn't he just a slave and a mortal, as Dionysus has said himself?

§45. A question starting with καὶ πῶς often indicates the speaker's indignation about the addressee's words, as the construction implies that what the addressee said is impossible.[33] This implication is even stronger with a potential optative. All the linguistic ingredients of this construction work together to convey the sense of indignation, in the following way. First, the particle καί links the new utterance closely to the previous one.[34] The speaker picks up an element from the preceding utterance, such as its main point or topic, and goes on to say something new which involves this element. Second, with the interrogative πῶς the speaker asks "how" a certain event could take place or be carried out. The combination καὶ πῶς therefore often implies that the speaker has

32 The word Ἀλκμήνης is however in the same metrical position twice.

33 See Hancock 1917:29, who notes that καὶ πῶς often introduces an incredulous question in tragic dialogues, and Garvie 1986 *ad* the καὶ πῶς-question in Aeschylus *Libation Bearers* 179: "It is equivalent to a statement of impossibility."

34 See the discussion of καί and resonance below, §§89-94.

his doubts about how something from the previous utterance could be realized. Third, a potential optative concerns the possibility of an event in some circumstances.[35] When the potential optative is employed in combination with καὶ πῶς, the suggestion of impossibility becomes even stronger. Asking about how (πῶς) something would be possible in some circumstances (potential optative), rather than just how it could take place in a concrete situation, usually implies that the event in question is impossible in all circumstances. Since this event tends to be something the other speaker has just spoken of (καί), the current speaker conveys that he is surprised, incredulous, indignant, or even angry, about his addressee's ridiculous suggestion.[36]

§46. In this case, Xanthias is echoing Dionysus' earlier indignation in order to express sarcasm. Dionysus was the one who suggested earlier (in 531) that it would be impossible for a mortal slave to "become" Heracles. Now he hears his own suggestion thrown back at him, after he has begged Xanthias to put the costume on again.

§47. Besides these striking similarities, lines 580-585 trigger another instance of resonance. The words οἶδ' οἶδ(α) ("I know I know") from Xanthias' utterance in 580 are repeated by Dionysus in 584. As Dover 1993 *ad* 584 remarks, the second instance has "an entirely different tone" from the first. The first "I know I know" conveys Xanthias' intransigent attitude toward Dionysus: "I know what you want, and I won't grant it, so don't even ask."[37] The second conveys understanding on Dionysus' part, his effort to placate Xanthias by assuming an attitude of mildness and humility: "I know you're angry, I understand how you feel, you are right." Dionysus tries to propitiate Xanthias by reusing Xanthias' words, in the hope that the slave will grant his request.

§48. Finally, the passage twice features a double ἄν with an optative,[38] in 581 and 585, resulting in the following resonance (see Figure 4: Diagraph of Aristophanes *Frogs* 581 and 585). Dionysus echoes Xanthias' entire construction: he repeats the

35 See Drummen 2013, with further literature.

36 Such questions occur seven times in Aristophanes, excluding fragments: *Birds* 829, 1437; *Clouds* 1333; *Frogs* 582; *Knights* 773; *Lysistrata* 912; *Peace* 1076a. Of these, *Knights* 773 is exceptional, because it is *not* addressed to the previous speaker, but to a third person present. Therefore, this question still implies impossibility of the event suggested, but there is no sense of indignation. The other cases do convey an indignant or rejecting tone. See Van Leeuwen 1898 *ad Clouds* 1333 and Dunbar 1995 *ad Birds* 829.

Note, furthermore, that a πῶς question with a potential optative functioning as an indirect wish (see Drummen 2013a:85-89, 104-105) is never preceded by καί. A wish typically stands on its own and is addressed to a deity or the world in general, rather than to an interlocutor in the dialogue at hand.

37 The repetition of οἶδα itself in 580 is explained by Stanford 1958 *ad loc.* as emphatic. In this case, this explanation works well, as Xanthias can be understood as angry or indignant. In Dionysus' utterance at 584, however, the repetition seems rather to serve the triggering of resonance with 580; extra emphasis would be less appropriate to Dionysus' flattering pragmatic goal.

On first-person verbs in expressions of the speaker's stance in historiography, see IV.4 §55 and §66.

38 In both cases the two ἄν instances syntactically belong to the main-clause verb.

581 XA.	**οὐκ ἂν**	**γενοίμην**	Ἡρακλῆς	**ἄν**	
	not would	I become	Heracles	[would]	
585 DI.	**οὐκ ἂν**	**ἀντείποιμί**	σοι	**{κἂν**	εἴ με τύπτοις}
	not would	I contradict	you	and [would]	if you would hit me

Figure 4: Diagraph of Aristophanes *Frogs* 581 and 585

οὐκ ἄν... ἄν,[39] and uses a formally similar verb (first person aorist optative). In both utterances the potential optative is used to express a strong refusal.[40] Such negative contexts are suitable for the repetition of ἄν.[41] Tucker 1906 *ad loc.* writes that the repeated ἄν in 581 helps amplify the negative tone. His translation "I wouldn't—no!—I wouldn't" also reflects the speaker's intent to refuse, rather than just negate.

§49. The pragmatic function of the potential optative must therefore be counted as one of the sources of resonance here. In this case Dionysus is using the same verbal construction to ingratiate himself with Xanthias. We can imagine that it would have been amusing for the audience to recognize the similarities across these utterances, and the very different uses to which the same words or constructions are put.

3.2.3 Resonance used by playwrights

3.2.3.1 Resonance stressing a theme

§50. So far I have discussed the pragmatic goals of speaking characters in using resonance. Two uses of resonance have been examined, one where a character repeats elements in order to emphasize unity with the other speaker and his actions, and the other where a character tries to emphasize semantic or pragmatic differences. Yet the characters are not the only ones communicating in a tragedy or comedy. On a metadramatic level, the playwright communicates something to the audience through his characters' voices.[42]

39 The second ἄν in 581 has been emended to αὖ by Hermann. I follow Wilson's text, and as is clear from the discussion in the main text, I think a repeated ἄν works very well in this context.

40 A potential optative can express a strong refusal when combined with a first person aorist verb denoting a controllable action. In this case, γίγνομαι refers to a controllable action, because it implies "putting on a costume," rather than simply "become" (which is usually uncontrollable). See Drummen 2013a for the different uses of the potential optative, including discussion of the instance in 581 (p. 101).

41 See Drummen 2013a:99-102. On the pragmatic meaning of ἄν repetitions, see Goldstein 2012.

42 On character's voice in other genres, see II.3 §28 on Homer, §65 on Pindar; IV.4.2-3 on Herodotus and Thucydides (also on the authors' voices).

One of the objectives that a poet may achieve on this level, by conspicuously repeating certain linguistic forms, is to stress the play's central themes.[43]

§51. Let us return to our first Greek example, from Aeschylus *Libation Bearers*. We have seen in (t6) how Orestes and Electra together invoked their dead father Agamemnon in a prayer. One of the words triggering resonance in (t6) was Orestes' repetition of the word πάτερ. This word was already prominently used in the *kommos* (306-478) preceding the prayer (479-510).[44] This resonance strengthens the prominence of the "father" theme. In addition, both the lyric *kommos* and the iambic prayer that follows contain many other words and forms that bring the vocative πάτερ to mind. The following table gives an overview of all the forms which resonate with πάτερ in these two parts. The vocative πάτερ itself is found twelve times in this passage, a remarkably high number. In all of extant Aeschylus (including fragments), this form is found twenty-nine times; it is by far the most frequent in *Libation Bearers*, which contains fifteen instances. (See Table 1: Resonance with πάτερ in Aeschylus *Libation Bearers* 306-510.) As the table shows, the most obvious type of resonance is lexical, triggered by all words with the root πατρ-. Such words produce semantic and phonological resonance as well; vocative forms also share morphology and the pragmatic function of direct address. Furthermore, the words τεκόντων (329), τοκεῦσι (385), τεκομένων (419), ματρός (422), and μᾶτερ (430) trigger semantic resonance, as they all belong to the same semantic sphere as "father."

§52. The other forms listed in the table, ἄτερ (338), ἅπερ τε (381), ἐπ' ἄτῃ (404),[45] τάπερ πάθομεν (418-419), and ἅπερ (440), do not resemble πάτερ in meaning or function, but they do reflect its sound. The form τάπερ in 418 especially stands out: this is its only occurrence in all of extant tragedy. Similarly, the combination ἐπ' ἄτῃ occurs only in one other place in tragedy.[46] The other words occur more often, but in the context of *Libation Bearers* it is striking that they all happen to be concentrated in this song: ἄτερ (338) and the two instances of ἅπερ (381 and 440) occur nowhere else in *Libation Bearers*. These forms may therefore be read as triggering phonological resonance with πάτερ: they ensure that the sound of the πάτερ-address rings in the audience's ears throughout the

43 See II.4 §40 on lexical and semantic resonance in Homer as a structuring device used by the narrator, and the role of ἄρα in such resonating contexts.

44 In lines 306-510, eight of the occurrences of πάτερ are uttered by Orestes, and four by Electra. The chorus can of course not address Agamemnon as "father." Sier 1988:84 observes that they even do not address him at all: they refer to him only in the third person. That Orestes uses this vocative more often than his sister might contribute to his authoritative status during the prayer, alongside Electra picking up his words and constructions (see §35 above). This effect of characterizing the relationship between speakers is actually another function of resonance, which is discussed below, §§57-62.

45 Lines 403-404 display even more phonological similarities: <u>πα</u>ρὰ τῶν <u>πρ</u>ότερον φθιμένων <u>ἄτ</u>ην / ἑ<u>τέ</u>ραν ἐ<u>πά</u>γουσαν <u>ἐπ' ἄτ</u>ῃι.

46 Sophocles *Electra* 1298: ἀλλ' ὡς ἐπ' ἄτῃ τῇ μάτην λελεγμένῃ.

line	form	speaker	types of similarity triggering resonance with πάτερ
315	πάτερ αἰνόπατερ	Orestes	lexical, phonological, morphological, semantic, pragmatic
329	πάτερων	chorus	lexical, phonological, semantic
329	τεκόντων	chorus	semantic
332	πάτερ	Electra	lexical, phonological, morphological, semantic, pragmatic
338	(δ') ἄτερ	Electra	phonological
346	πάτερ	Orestes	lexical, phonological, morphological, semantic, pragmatic
364	πάτερ	Electra	lexical, phonological, morphological, semantic, pragmatic
381	ἅπερ τε	Orestes	phonological
385	τοκεῦσι	Orestes	semantic
404	ἐπ' ἄτῃ	chorus	phonological
418-419	τάπερ πάθομεν	Electra	phonological
419	τεκομένων	Electra	semantic
422	ματρός	Electra	semantic
430	μᾶτερ	Electra	semantic
435	πατρός	Orestes	lexical, phonological, semantic
440	(δ') ἅπερ	chorus	phonological
443	πατρῴους	chorus	lexical, phonological, semantic
444	πατρῷον	Electra	lexical, phonological, semantic
456	πάτερ	Orestes	lexical, phonological, morphological, semantic, pragmatic
479	πάτερ	Orestes	lexical, phonological, morphological, semantic, pragmatic
481	πάτερ	Electra	lexical, phonological, morphological, semantic, pragmatic

line	form	speaker	types of similarity triggering resonance with πάτερ
487	πατρῴων	Electra	lexical, phonological, semantic
489	πατέρ'(α)	Orestes	lexical, phonological, semantic
491	πάτερ	Orestes	lexical, phonological, morphological, semantic, pragmatic
493	πάτερ	Orestes	lexical, phonological, morphological, semantic, pragmatic
495	πάτερ	Orestes	lexical, phonological, morphological, semantic, pragmatic
500	πάτερ	Electra	lexical, phonological, morphological, semantic, pragmatic

Table 1: Resonance with πάτερ in Aeschylus *Libation Bearers* 306-510

scene. Phonological resonance works to emphasize the prominence of the target word, here πάτερ, and thus of its function (appealing to Agamemnon).[47]

[47] Similar phonological similarities functioning as a trigger for resonance may be that of the name Ξέρξης in Aeschylus *Persians*. The recurrence of a similar sound subtly underlines Xerxes' decisive role in the terrible events, or help to evoke the disastrous situation connected to this character in the audience's minds.

Besides seventeen occurrences (with different endings) of the name itself, there are in the edition by Page 1972 at least eight other words that clearly resemble Ξέρξης in sound. They are, however, distributed over the whole play more widely than the resonating elements in the *kommos* prayer scene in *Libation Bearers*.

Words starting with ἠρξ- or ἐρξ- are infrequent in Aeschylus: there are seventeen instances in total, when fragments and *Prometheus bound* are included. Of these, six occur in *Persians*, the highest number for a single play: 236 ἔρξας by the chorus, 353 ἦρξεν by the messenger, 409 ἦρξε by the messenger, 774 ἦρξεν by the ghost of Darius, 786 ἔρξαντες by the ghost of Darius, and 1058 ἔρξω by the chorus. A similar form is 351 κατῆρξαν by queen Atossa. Furthermore, the participle ῥήξας in 468 by the messenger, with Xerxes as subject, is one out of two words starting with ῥηξ- in all of Aeschylus (the other is ῥῆξιν in the very short fragment 313a). This ῥήξας in 468 at the same time activates a lexical and semantic resonance with ῥήγνυσιν in line 199 by the queen, where it is accompanied by an explicit mentioning of the name Ξέρξης. (Words with ξε- do not seem relevant for this resonance, because they are much more frequent: these mainly involve forms or derivations of ξένος.) Note that none of these possibly resonating words is uttered by Xerxes himself.

The similarity between 199 and 468 is noted by Broadhead 1960, Hall 1996, and Roussel 1960 *ad loc.* The latter commentator also refers to the parallel occurrences of ἔρξας, ἦρξεν, and ῥήξας within the play, but does not discuss a possible sound similarity among these forms, or

line	speaker	Greek	translation	(implied) subject
350	Teiresias	ἐννέπω (σε)	"I tell (you)"	Teiresias
351	Teiresias	προεῖπας	"you have proclaimed"	Oedipus
352	Teiresias	προσαυδᾶν (μήτε)	"(not) to address"	Oedipus
354-5	Oedipus	(ἐξεκίνησας) τόδε /τὸ ῥῆμα	"(you have started) this story"	Teiresias
358	Teiresias	(προὐτρέψω) λέγειν	"(you urged me) to speak"	Teiresias
359	Oedipus	(ποῖον) λόγον	"(which) word"	Teiresias
359	Oedipus	λέγ' (αὖθις)	"say it (again)"	Teiresias
360	Teiresias	λέγειν	"to say"	Teiresias
361	Oedipus	(οὐχ ὥστε γ') εἰπεῖν	"(not in order) to say"	Oedipus
361	Oedipus	(αὖθις) φράσον	"tell it (again)"	Teiresias
362	Teiresias	(σέ) φημι	"I say (that you)"	Teiresias
363	Oedipus	ἐρεῖς	"you will say"	Teiresias
364	Teiresias	εἴπω (τι)	"shall I say (something)"	Teiresias
365	Oedipus	(μάτην) εἰρήσεται	"(in vain) it will be said"	Teiresias
366	Teiresias	(σέ) φημι	"I say (that you)"	Teiresias
368	Oedipus	λέξειν (δοκεῖς)	"(you think) that you will say"	Teiresias

Table 2: Constructions referring to "saying" in Sophocles *Oedipus King* 350-368

§53. At this global level, then, resonance is an important communicative strategy

between them and Ξέρξης. Groeneboom 1930 remarks, *ad* 1058 ἔρξω, that this is a future form because the chorus has not yet started the action; no acoustic explanation is suggested.

Another resonance in *Persians* might be triggered by πᾶς κατέφθαρται στρατός ("the entire army has been destroyed") and lexically or semantically similar expressions. These occur several times throughout the play (e.g. 244, 251, 278-279, 345, 716, 728, 729). Note that none of them is uttered by Xerxes.

at the poets' disposal to stress the themes of a play. Let us consider some more cases of this function. For example, in the dialogue between Oedipus and Teiresias in Sophocles *Oedipus King* 350-368, the concept of "saying" is repeated many times. Pfeiffer-Petersen 1996:79 notes this repetition and interprets it as emphasizing a main theme (96).

§54. The relevant passage is presented in (t10) below. Table 2 gives an overview of the resonance in question and includes the (implied) subject of each "saying" word. (See Table 2: Constructions referring to "saying" in Sophocles *Oedipus King* 350-368)

(t10)

Τε. ἄληθες; ἐννέπω σὲ τῷ κηρύγματι
ᾧπερ προεῖπας ἐμμένειν, κἀφ' ἡμέρας
τῆς νῦν προσαυδᾶν μήτε τούσδε μήτ' ἐμέ,
ὡς ὄντι γῆς τῆσδ' ἀνοσίῳ μιάστορι.
Οι. οὕτως ἀναιδῶς ἐξεκίνησας τόδε
τὸ ῥῆμα; καὶ ποῦ τοῦτο φεύξεσθαι δοκεῖς;
Τε. πέφευγα· τἀληθὲς γὰρ ἰσχῦον τρέφω.
Οι. πρὸς τοῦ διδαχθείς; οὐ γὰρ ἔκ γε τῆς τέχνης.
Τε. πρὸς σοῦ· σὺ γάρ μ' ἄκοντα προὐτρέψω λέγειν.
Οι. ποῖον λόγον; λέγ' αὖθις, ὡς μᾶλλον μάθω.
Τε. οὐχὶ ξυνῆκας πρόσθεν; ἦ 'κπειρᾷ λέγειν;
Οι. οὐχ ὥστε γ' εἰπεῖν γνωστόν· ἀλλ' αὖθις φράσον.
Τε. φονέα σέ φημι τἀνδρὸς οὗ ζητεῖς δίκας.
Οι. ἀλλ' οὔ τι χαίρων δίς γε πημονὰς ἐρεῖς.
Τε. εἴπω τι δῆτα κἄλλ', ἵν' ὀργίζῃ πλέον;
Οι. ὅσον γε χρῄζεις· ὡς μάτην εἰρήσεται.
Τε. λεληθέναι σέ φημι σὺν τοῖς φιλτάτοις
αἴσχισθ' ὁμιλοῦντ', οὐδ' ὁρᾶν ἵν' εἶ κακοῦ.
Οι. ἦ καὶ γεγηθὼς ταῦτ' ἀεὶ λέξειν δοκεῖς;

Sophocles *Oedipus King* 350-368

Te. So? I call on you to abide by the proclamation you made earlier, and from this day on address neithe these men nor me, since you are the unholy polluter of this land!
Oe. Have you so shamelessly started up this story? How do you think you will escape its consequences?
Te. I have escaped; the truth I nurture has strength.
Oe. From whom have you learned it? Not, I think, from your prophetic art.
Te. From you; it was you who forced me to speak against my will.

Oe. To say what? Tell me again, so that I can understand it better!
Te. Did you not understand before? Are you trying to test me?
Oe. Not so that I can say I know it; come, say it again!
Te. I say that you are the murderer of the man whose murderer you are searching for!
Oe. You shall not get away with speaking disaster twice!
Te. Shall I tell you another thing, to make you even angrier?
Oe. Tell me as much as you please, since your words will be wasted!
Te. I say that you are living unawares in a shameful relationship with those closest to you, and cannot see the plight in which you are.
Oe. Do you believe that you will continue to repeat such things and go scot-free?

These sixteen resonating elements in nineteen lines emphasize the importance of the "saying" theme at this point in the play. Thirteen of these constructions have or imply Teiresias as subject, a fact that highlights the special nature and power of his utterances. As Bollack 1990 *ad* lines 356-358 points out, Oedipus himself is the "author" of Teiresias' words.[48] That is, though Oedipus does not know it, he is actually responsible for Teiresias' "story."[49]

§55. In *Oedipus King* we also find a resonance of the theme "parents," for instance in the following passage. Oedipus has just revealed the prophecy concerning his parents in the course of explaining why he never returned to Corinth. The Corinthian messenger now tells Oedipus that he was wrong to stay away for this reason.

(t11)

Αγ. ἦ μὴ μίασμα τῶν φυτευσάντων λάβῃς;
Οι. τοῦτ' αὐτό, πρέσβυ, τοῦτό μ' εἰσαεὶ φοβεῖ.
Αγ. ἆρ' οἶσθα δῆτα πρὸς δίκης οὐδὲν τρέμων;
Οι. πῶς δ' οὐχί, παῖς γ' εἰ τῶνδε γεννητῶν ἔφυν;
Αγ. ὁθούνεκ' ἦν σοι Πόλυβος οὐδὲν ἐν γένει.
Οι. πῶς εἶπας; οὐ γὰρ Πόλυβος ἐξέφυσέ με;
Αγ. οὐ μᾶλλον οὐδὲν τοῦδε τἀνδρός, ἀλλ' ἴσον.

[48] "Oedipe est lui-même, sans le savoir, l'auteur du discours que Tirésias lui tient, sans le vouloir." Bollack does not comment, though, on this possible resonance throughout the passage; neither do Dawe 2006 [1982], Van Herwerden 1866, Jebb 2004 [1893], Kamerbeek 1967, Markantonatos 1986, and Ritter 1870.

[49] Pfeiffer-Petersen 1996:68 draws attention to a similar repetition of the theme of "saying" in another Sophoclean tragedy: *Antigone* 1048-1063. Teiresias is involved (speaking to Creon, the king of Thebes) in that dialogue as well. The seer's involvement in dialogues emphasizing the theme of "saying" in two different plays highlights the sense that his words have special value.

Οι. καὶ πῶς ὁ φύσας ἐξ ἴσου τῷ μηδενί;
Αγ. ἀλλ᾽ οὔ σ᾽ ἐγείνατ᾽ οὔτ᾽ ἐκεῖνος οὔτ᾽ ἐγώ.
Οι. ἀλλ᾽ ἀντὶ τοῦ δὴ παῖδά μ᾽ ὠνομάζετο;

Sophocles *Oedipus King* 1012-1021

Me. Is it so that you shall not acquire pollution through your parents?
Oe. Exactly that, old man, that is what always frightens me.
Me. Do you not know that you have no reason to be afraid?
Oe. But I must, if indeed these are my parents!
Me. Because Polybus was no relation to you!
Oe. What are you saying? Was not Polybus my father?
Me. No more than I was, but just as much!
Oe. And how can my father be as much my father as one who is nothing to me?
Me. Well, neither he nor I begot you.
Oe. But why did he call me his son?

The concept of "parent" recurs in seven out of the ten speaking turns in this passage. A diagraph visualization clarifies the similarities and differences among the resonating elements. (See Figure 5: Diagraph of Sophocles *Oedipus King* 1012-1021: parental terms.) The passage displays a high frequency as well as a great variety of parental terms. This underlines the paramount importance of (the identity of) Oedipus' parents. The word πατήρ itself is conspicuously absent here, but it was used shortly before in the same dialogue (line 1001).[50] The idea of "father" or "parents" ominously hovers over the words of the two speakers, and, as the audience knows, over Oedipus' head.

§56. Note also the repetition of Πόλυβος in lines 1016-1017. Mentioning this name is a semantically heavy choice, as it is not needed for retrieving the right referent.[51] Especially in 1017, a demonstrative pronoun would certainly have been sufficient for that. The repetition of the name thus places an ominous emphasis on Polybus and the crucial issue of his true relationship to Oedipus.[52] Comparison with the other instances of the word confirms the reading of Πόλυβος in 1016 and 1017 as a strikingly heavy refer-

50 Similarly, as Kamerbeek 1967 *ad* 1012 points out, φυτευσάντων refers back to φυτεύσασιν in line 1007.

51 See II.5 on different ways to retrieve referents in Homer and Pindar.

52 Metrical resonance may in this case strengthen the lexical and referential resonance: Πόλυβος is in the same metrical position in both lines, with five syllables preceding and five following. This may however be irrelevant, as seven instances of the name (in any inflected form) are in this position, out of its nine occurrences (or ten, depending on the edition) in the iambic trimeters of the play. This is not surprising, since the second metron is the most usual place for the resolution which Πόλυβος requires.

1012 ME.	ἦ μὴ μίασμα really? so that not a pollution	**τῶν φυτευσάντων** of the begetters	λάβῃς you would get
(...)			
1015 OE.	πῶς δ' οὐχί {εἰ} but how not if	**{παῖς γ'} τῶνδε γεννητῶν** a *child* of these parents	ἔφυν I am (born)
1016 ME.	ὁθούνεκ' ἦν σοι Πόλυβος οὐδὲν since Polybus was nothing to you	**ἐν γένει** in kinship	
1017 OE.	πῶς εἶπας οὐ γὰρ Πόλυβος how did you say, for not Polybus	**ἐξέφυσέ με** begot me	
(...)			
1019 OE.	καὶ πῶς and how	**ὁ φύσας** the father	ἐξ ἴσου τῷ μηδενί equally to the nothing
1020 ME.	ἀλλ' οὔ but not	**σ' ἐγείνατ'** he begot you	οὔτ' ἐκεῖνος οὔτ' ἐγώ nor that man nor I
1021 OE.	ἀλλ' ἀντὶ τοῦ δὴ but why then	**παῖδά μ' ὠνομάζετο** he called me his son	

Figure 5: Diagraph of Sophocles *Oedipus King* 1012-1021: parental terms

ence, because not all other cases are semantically optional. For example, in 774 we find ἐμοὶ πατὴρ μὲν Πόλυβος ἦν Κορίνθιος, "my father was Polybus the Corinthian...".

3.2.3.2 Resonance characterizing a speaker and an interaction

§57. A playwright can also use resonance to characterize a speaker, or an interaction and the interlocutors' relationship to each other, in a certain way.[53] For example, a speaker's repeated use of a certain word may signal her special preoccupations and concerns. If she uses certain grammatical constructions or literary figures of speech very often, this may mark her habits of interaction.

[53] On linguistic and stylistic characterization in tragedy, see e.g. Katsures 1975.

§58. Griffith 1999:36 observes that the differences between Antigone and Creon in Sophocles *Antigone* are reflected in "their respective diction and speech patterns." For instance, the king often uses generalizations and *gnômai*.[54] Similarities across Creon's utterances, then, trigger resonance in ways that reveal aspects of his character.

§59. Aeschylus *Libation Bearers* provides an example of resonance characterizing an interaction, namely the one between Electra and Orestes (see (t6) and Figure 1 above). Since Electra is always echoing Orestes, her communicative style reflects her assumption of the subordinate position. As noted by Groeneboom and Garvie, Orestes is taking the lead in this prayer. Garvie points out that it is natural for Orestes to be leading: he has just made the decision to perform the murder, so he is now taking the initiative.[55]

§60. In Sophocles *Oedipus King* 1015-1019, cited in (t11), we find Oedipus beginning three questions with πῶς: the lexical repetition highlights the illocutionary function (asking for information) shared by the utterances. Kamerbeek 1967 *ad loc.* notes the repetition and adduces a comparable sequence of questions in lines 99-131, where Oedipus is addressing Creon. That earlier dialogue presents a sequence of eight interrogatives by the king (one with πῶς).

§61. The recurrence of an interrogative illocutionary force can trigger resonance, just as lexical, semantic, or syntactic similarities do. In this case this "illocutionary resonance" is strengthened by phonological similarities. Seven out of the eight questions in 99-131 start with the sound π(ο)-: ποίῳ (99), ποίου (102), ποῦ (108), πότερα (112), ποῖον (120), πῶς (124), and ποῖον (128).[56] Such resonance across utterances by the same speaker helps characterize him.[57] Oedipus is presented as a fanatic investigator who asks many questions—which stresses that he nevertheless does not know anything about his own identity.

§62. We can also see resonance characterizing an interaction in Sophocles *Ajax* 527-545, an exchange between Ajax and Tecmessa:

54 In Drummen 2013a:94, I draw attention to Creon's frequent use of "mitigating" potential optatives, which can be seen as part of this rhetorical strategy.

55 However, Garvie 1986 also notes that in line 493, Orestes does develop what Electra has just said.

56 The other one, Oedipus' question in 116-117, is a yes/no-interrogative.

57 The repetition of πῶς alone already triggers this kind of resonance, because Oedipus utters eleven of the twenty instances of this word in *Oedipus King*. In Sophocles' plays *Ajax*, *Antigone*, and *Women of Trachis*, πῶς is less frequent (ten, five, and thirteen occurrences, respectively), and less typical of one specific character. However, also in *Electra* (22 cases), *Oedipus at Colonus* (21 cases), and *Philoctetes* (30 cases), we find a higher frequency of πῶς, and one character uttering most of the instances (Electra, Oedipus, and Philoctetes). Analysis of the other questions or question words uttered by these characters may clarify how such resonance contributes to the depiction of their personalities.

(t12)

Αι. κόμιζέ νύν μοι παῖδα τὸν ἐμόν, ὡς ἴδω.
(...)
Τε. τί δῆτ' ἂν ὡς ἐκ τῶνδ' ἂν ὠφελοῖμί σε;
Αι. δός μοι προσειπεῖν αὐτὸν ἐμφανῆ τ' ἰδεῖν.
Τε. καὶ μὴν πέλας γε προσπόλοις φυλάσσεται.
Αι. τί δῆτα μέλλει μὴ οὐ παρουσίαν ἔχειν
Τε. ὦ παῖ, πατὴρ καλεῖ σε. δεῦρο προσπόλων
ἄγ' αὐτὸν ὅσπερ χερσὶν εὐθύνων κυρεῖς.
(...)
Αι. αἶρ' αὐτόν, αἶρε δεῦρο· (...)

Part of Sophocles *Ajax* 530-545

Aj. Then bring me my son, so that I can see him!
(...)
Te. What can I do to help you as things stand now?
Aj. Let me speak to him and see him face to face!
Te. Indeed, the servants are guarding him near by.
Aj. Why am I kept waiting for his presence?
Te. My son, your father is calling you! Come, whichever of you
attendants is guiding him, bring him here!
(...)
Aj. Lift him up, lift him up here!

The dialogue from lines 527 to 545 contains seventeen utterances: nine by Ajax, eight by Tecmessa. Of these, Ajax utters four directive utterances (530, 538, 540,[58] 545), three addressed to Tecmessa, one to a different servant. Tecmessa utters only one directive (542), addressed to another slave. That Ajax's speech has directive illocutionary force so much more often than Tecmessa's underlines the power differential between the two interlocutors.[59]

[58] The utterance in 540 does not contain an imperative form, but I think we can reasonably interpret it as having directive illocutionary force. By uttering τί δῆτα μέλλει μὴ οὐ παρουσίαν ἔχειν;, Ajax mainly wants to get Tecmessa to fix this problem, not to answer his question.

[59] Note further that Ajax uses more verbs in the second person in this dialogue, and Tecmessa more first-person verbs. Out of Ajax's thirteen finite verbs, two are first person, seven are second person, and three are third person. Of Tecmessa's ten finite verbs, she utters four first-person forms, two second-person ones, and four third-person ones. This perhaps strengthens the characterization of Ajax as the dominant figure, and Tecmessa as the social inferior, in this dialogue. Pennebaker 2011 points out for the English language that insecure people tend to use more first-person singular pronouns than self-confident speakers and writers. As Greek is a pro-drop

3.2.3.3 Resonance used for humor

§63. A use of resonance typical in comedy is making jokes. Lucci 2012 discusses wordplay in tragedy (which includes repetition and antithesis) in a similar vein: he considers wordplay to be "inherently comic" because it yields "situations of surprise, coincidence, and incongruity." In contrast to wordplay, the broader process of resonance is not humorous in principle. The examples I discussed in the previous subsections show that highlighting affinities across utterances may have very different functions from joking, such as stressing disagreement or a play's themes. However, I do see humor as one of the possible functions of resonance, at least in Aristophanes.

§64. In addition to repetition of words or constructions, repetition of particular actions can increase a scene's humorous effect, as in the following passage, from a dialogue involving the Athenian magistrate and several women (Lysistrata and three others) on the Acropolis. Several moves (that is, multi-act units) performed in this passage are echoes of earlier moves:[60]

(t13)

Πρ. ἄληθες, ὦ μιαρὰ σύ; ποῦ 'στι τοξότης;
ξυλλάμβαν' αὐτὴν κὠπίσω τὼ χεῖρε δεῖ.
Λυ. εἰ τἄρα νὴ τὴν Ἄρτεμιν τὴν χεῖρά μοι
ἄκραν προσοίσει, δημόσιος ὢν κλαύσεται.
Πρ. ἔδεισας, οὗτος; οὐ ξυναρπάσει μέσην
καὶ σὺ μετὰ τούτου χἀνύσαντε δήσετον;
ΓΡΑΥΣ Α΄. εἰ τἄρα νὴ τὴν Πάνδροσον ταύτῃ μόνον
τὴν χεῖρ' ἐπιβαλεῖς, ἐπιχεσεῖ πατούμενος.
Πρ. ἰδού γ' ἐπιχεσεῖ. ποῦ 'στιν ἕτερος τοξότης;
ταύτην προτέραν ξύνδησον, ὁτιὴ καὶ λαλεῖ.
ΓΡ. Β΄ εἰ τἄρα νὴ τὴν Φωσφόρον τὴν χεῖρ' ἄκραν
ταύτῃ προσοίσεις, κύαθον αἰτήσεις τάχα.
Πρ. τουτὶ τί ἦν; ποῦ τοξότης; ταύτης ἔχου.
παύσω τιν' ὑμῶν τῆσδ' ἐγὼ τῆς ἐξόδου.
ΓΡΑΥΣ Γ΄ εἰ τἄρα νὴ τὴν Ταυροπόλον ταύτῃ πρόσει,
ἐγὼ 'κποκιῶ σου τὰς στενοκωκύτους τρίχας.
Πρ. οἴμοι κακοδαίμων· ἐπιλέλοιφ' ὁ τοξότης.

Aristophanes *Lysistrata* 433-449

language (i.e. finite verbs do not require an explicit subject), personal pronouns are much less frequent than in English. It would nevertheless be interesting to see if we could find similar patterns in other Greek dialogues.

60 On the concept of move, see II.3, especially §§2-11, and IV.3.11.

> Ma. Really, you witch! Where's a policeman? Grab her and tie both hands behind her back.
> Ly. If he so much as touches me with his fingertip, mere public servant that he is, so help me Artemis he'll go home crying!
> Ma. What, are you scared? You there, help him out; grab her around the waist and tie her up, on the double!
> Woman 1. If you so much as lay a hand on her, so help me Pandrosos, I'll beat the shit out of you!
> Ma. Beat the shit out of me? Where's another policeman? Tie her up first, the one with the dirty mouth!
> Wo.2. If you raise your fingertip to her, so help me our Lady of Light, you'll be begging for an eye cup!
> Ma. What's going on? Where is a policeman? Arrest her. I'll foil at least one of these sallies of yours!
> Wo.3. If you come near her, so help me Tauropolus, I'll rip out your hair till you scream!
> Ma. Damn my luck, I'm out of policemen.

In this scene, four actions are repeated: the magistrate calls out for a policeman, the magistrate orders this policeman to grab and/or tie up one of the women, a woman threatens to do him some violence, and the policeman runs away. The last repeated action is not expressed in words, and can therefore not be shown in a diagraph, but it can be inferred from the fact that the magistrate has to call out for a new policeman. We can imagine the humorous effect of the policemen running away one by one. The repetition of all these actions naturally leads to many similarities in the language of the successive utterances, as shown in diagraph representations. (See Figure 6: Diagraphs of Aristophanes *Lysistrata* 433-449.) The first diagraph shows how the beginnings of the magistrate's utterances resemble each other: he utters first a reaction to the unfortunate situation he finds himself him, and then a call for a policeman. The second of these calling moves (καὶ σὺ μετὰ τούτου) is very different in form from the others, but it still has the same pragmatic function as those, to signal a switch to a new policeman. The last instance of τοξότης "policeman" in 449 is part of the scene's climax, which the audience expects: the magistrate has no more policemen left.[61]

§65. In the second diagraph, we can see the magistrate's orders. Though each order is different in form (different verbal roots, both singular and dual forms, interrogative as well as imperative sentence types, aorist next to present imperatives), they all share the

[61] After this defeat, the magistrate tries again: he sends against the women a group of Scythians, who are similarly defeated. This is however a new attack, not part of the policemen sequence anymore. For other kinds of pragmatic jokes in Aristophanes, see Kloss 2001. These forms of humor, Kloss points out (32), are on the borderline between the verbal and situational.

same function, to order someone to grab one of the women and tie her up. Regardless of how the magistrate formulates his command, he is equally unsuccessful.

§66. The third diagraph concerns the women's threats. These moves have a similar function as well as strongly resemble each other in form. They all have the structure "oath + protasis (condition) + apodosis (consequence)." All the oaths invoke some female goddess (appropriate in a fight between women and men). All the protases involve a policeman starting or trying to do some harm.[62] All the apodoses predict violence or someone's reaction to violence. The utterances also trigger a lexical resonance of εἰ τἄρα νὴ τὴν. As Henderson 1987 *ad loc.* points out, the ἄρα marks the threat's connection to the previous utterance by the magistrate: "if that's the way you want it... ."[63] The τοι, paraphrased by Henderson as "be sure," underlines what the women say and addresses the threatened man even more directly.[64]

§67. All in all, the women's threats, though spoken by four different speakers, are more similar to each other than the magistrate's orders, spoken by one person. The women thus prove themselves loyal and cooperating, whereas the men are presented as chaotic and disobedient, with the magistrate standing alone. However, Henderson 1987 *ad loc.* also notes a difference among the women's threats: unlike the other women, Lysistrata does not address the policeman directly (Henderson explains this as "beneath her dignity").

§68. What makes the scene amusing is the very recurrence of this sequence of four actions. It would have been hardly remarkable if Lysistrata had frightened away just one policeman: the scene would have told us something about this character's power, but it would not have made the audience laugh, to see cowardly men being repeatedly defeated. The second, third, and fourth occurrences of the actions draw attention to the first ones through their form and/or function: they resonate. This resonance becomes a source of humor in itself: it is not only humorous that the magistrate and his armed policemen are defeated easily by verbally aggressive women, it is also humorous that the defeat happens again and again.

§69. A similar joke involving repetition occurs in *Frogs* 1198-1247, where the character Aeschylus verbally "attacks" the character Euripides with a little oil flask: Aeschylus repeatedly attaches the oil flask as a tag to the prologues recited by Euripides. In a detailed discussion of this passage, Collins 2004:32-43 points out that the action revolves around a game of capping.[65] Participial enjambment, Collins argues, makes it possible for

62 Van Leeuwen 1903 *ad* 435-448 calls attention to a similar threat by one of the women in line 365 (with the condition and the consequence expressed in separate utterances). However, there the man is not frightened at all by the woman's threat.

63 On ἄρα in drama, see e.g. Hermann 1825: xv-xxviii; Ellendt 1835:85-87; Klotz 1842:160-195; Heller 1858; Fritsch 1859; Bäumlein 1861:21-39. On ἄρα in Homer and Pindar, see II.3 §§65-67; II.4 §§38-41, §§50-53; II.5 §§51-62; in Herodotus and Thucydides, see IV.4 §§165-172.

64 On τοι in drama, see III.4 §§58-61, with references. On τοι in Herodotus, see IV.4 §§34-39; IV.5 §§75-76, §84, §86, §93.

65 See above, §20, on Collins' work.

433 MA.	**ἄληθες ὦ μιαρὰ σύ**	**ποῦ 'στι τοξότης**	
	really you ugly one	where is a policeman	
437-8 MA.	**ἔδεισας οὗτος (…) /**	**καὶ σὺ μετὰ τούτου**	(...)
	are you afraid, you	you too, with this one	
441 MA.	**ἰδού γ' ἐπιχεσεῖ**	**ποῦ 'στιν ἕτερος τοξότης**	
	well well, he shit	where is another policeman	
445 MA.	**τουτὶ τί ἦν**	**ποῦ τοξότης**	ταύτης ἔχου
	what was this	where [is] a policeman	get her
449 MA.	**οἴμοι κακοδαίμων**	**ἐπιλέλοιφ' ὁ τοξότης**	
	ah me, my bad luck	the policeman has left	

---

434 MA.	**ξυλλάμβαν' αὐτὴν κὠπίσω τὼ χεῖρε δεῖ**	
	grab her and bind her hands behind her back	
437-8 MA.	(...) **οὐ ξυναρπάσει μέσην/χἀνύσαντε δήσετον**	{καὶ σὺ μετὰ τούτου}
	won't you seize her waist/and both of you quickly tie [her] up	you too, with him
442 MA.	**ταύτην προτέραν ξύνδησον**	(...)
	tie this one up first	
445 MA.	(...) **ταύτης ἔχου**	
	get her	

435-6 LY.	**εἰ τἄρα νὴ τὴν Ἄρτεμιν**	**τὴν χεῖρά μοι /ἄκραν προσοίσει (...)**	**κλαύσεται**
	if hey by Artemis	he'll stretch the tip of his hand to me	he'll cry
439-40 WO1;	**εἰ τἄρα νὴ τὴν Πάνδροσον**	**ταύτῃ μόνον/τὴν χεῖρ' ἐπιβαλεῖς**	**ἐπιχεσεῖ πατούμενος**
	if hey by Pandrosos	you'll just touch her with your hand	you'll be beaten and shit
443-4 WO2;	**εἰ τἄρα νὴ τὴν Φωσφόρον**	**τὴν χεῖρ' ἄκραν / ταύτῃ προσοίσεις**	**κύαθον αἰτήσεις τάχα**
	if hey by Phosphoros	you'll stretch the tip of his hand to her	you'll soon ask an eye cup
447-8 WO3;	**εἰ τἄρα νὴ τὴν Ταυροπόλον**	**ταύτῃ πρόσει**	**/ἐγὼ 'κποκιῶ σου τὰς στενοκωκύτους τρίχας**
	if hey by Tauropolos	you'll go near her	I'll pull out your hair till you scream

Figure 6: Diagraphs of Aristophanes *Lysistrata* 433-449

Aeschylus to repeatedly substitute the end of the lines with ληκύθιον ἀπώλεσεν "lost his little oil flask."[66] Hence in this scene it is not only the literal repetition of Aeschylus' utterances that triggers resonance to comic effect, but also the repetitive grammatical construction of Euripides' recited prologues, which all contain participles. Collins adduces a number of other examples for comparison, the most notable being a scene in *Birds* 974-990 in which Peisetaerus is harassed by a deceitful oracle monger. Here the move λαβὲ τὸ βιβλίον "take the book" is uttered three times by the same speaker, the oracle monger. Peisetaerus subsequently echoes these words in a hostile fashion. The addressee is thus "defeated" by having his own words hurled back at him.

3.2.3.4 Resonance creating parody

§70. Another Aristophanic use of resonance involves referring to tragedy or other genres through direct quotation or allusion to themes or linguistic characteristics. Aristophanes *Frogs* 1119-1410, with its literal citations of tragedy, constitutes an obvious example. This comedy is also full of subtler references to the style of the tragedians. For example, it parodies tragic metre.[67]

66 On such connections across stichomythic utterances with participles, see also Ritter 1870 *ad* Sophocles *Oedipus King* 1015, where he notes "die durch Participien aus einem Verse in den nächsten übergeleitete Structur."

67 See Collins 2004:36, 42; Stanford 1958:173-187; Tucker 1906:232-233, 238.

§71. An utterance by the Athenian magistrate in Aristophanes *Lysistrata* 450, ἀτὰρ[68] οὐ γυναικῶν οὐδέποτ' ἔσθ' ἡττητέα ("but we must never be defeated by women"), provides us with a more specific instance of such cross-genre resonance. As Van Leeuwen 1903 and Griffith 1999 note, this line refers to Sophocles *Antigone* 678, in which Creon says, κοὔτοι γυναικὸς οὐδαμῶς ἡσσητέα ("and not, you know, should we in any way be defeated by a woman"). The linguistic similarities are striking: both utterances contain a double negation, the word γυνή in the genitive, and ἡττητέα/ἡσσητέα in their only occurrences in extant Greek literature. Since the first performances of *Antigone* and *Lysistrata* were about thirty years apart, it is unclear whether the audience of *Lysistrata* would have noticed the allusion to Sophocles.[69] The spectators may have been familiar with *Antigone* through reperformance or quotations. Perhaps they only noted a general similarity in tone between the two utterances. In the tragedy, Creon's attitude has fatal consequences, first for Antigone, and later for Creon and his family as well. The echo in Aristophanes, on the other hand, signals that the magistrate would like to emulate Creon's authoritarianism, but he ends up being defeated by women after all. The audience of *Lysistrata* could have been amused by this mentality resonance between the magistrate and Sophocles' Creon.

§72. Another feature of Aristophanic parody involves his use of abstract nouns ending in -μα, discussed by Willi 2003:136-139 and 2012 (see further Barrett 2007). Willi points out that this morphological echo occurs in combination with other typically tragic features, signaling paratragedy. The "tragic" character Euripides in Aristophanes *Acharnians* 393-434 uses many of such features, whereas his "comic" interlocutor Dicaeopolis does not.

3.2.4 Conclusions about resonance in tragedy and comedy

§73. To sum up, the communicative strategy of resonance is relevant to Greek drama in general. We have so far seen several functions and forms: speakers achieve their communicative goals within an interaction by exploiting similarities between one utterance and another, and playwrights employ this strategy for their own goals on a different level. Characters use resonance to stress solidarity with another speaker and to express dissent. Poets make use of resonance to underline a play's themes, to depict character, to make jokes, and to parody. As for different forms, we have seen examples of lexical, phonological, morphological, syntactic, semantic, pragmatic, and illocutionary similarities, all of which may trigger resonance. Very often these kinds of similarities are found working in combination with each other in a single passage. The variety in functions

[68] On the function and use of ἀτάρ in tragedy and comedy, see III.4 §§39-40.

[69] Sophocles *Antigone* was probably first performed around 441, Aristophanes *Lysistrata* in 411. See Griffith 1999:1-2 and Henderson 1987:xv.

and forms of resonance reflects its communicative importance, for characters as well as playwrights.

3.3 The Role of Particles in the Process of Resonance

3.3.1 Particles indicating how resonance is used

§74. When a speaker is deliberately echoing a certain element from a previous utterance and wishes to call attention to this resonance, she may stress and clarify it with a particle. That is, some particles are suitable for indicating what a speaker does in picking up a certain element from a previous utterance.

§75. Such resonance-clarifying particles tend to be found at the beginnings of utterances: a natural position to echo an element from the previous utterance. Exceptions do occur, for example when a speaker in a long monologue appears to conduct a "dialogue with herself," as we shall see. The focus will be on five particles or particle combinations that can be linked, in some of their functions, to the process of resonance: γε, δέ γε/δέ... γε, δῆτα, καί, and γάρ.

3.3.1.1 γε

§76. The particle γε is ideally suited to signaling that a speaker picks up and singles out one specific element from the last utterance; it has a "zooming-in" effect. In addition, γε indicates that the speaker is giving a new twist to the element that was singled out. In such contexts γε not only indicates how resonance is used but also emphasizes the resonance itself, by drawing particular attention to the repeated element's use in the original utterance.[70]

§77. The general function of γε in drama can be described as as singling out one element of the discourse, in implicit contrast to something else.[71] This function is subjective, that is, it refers to attitudes of the speaker towards the discourse, as well as intersubjective, which means that this function is connected to the speaker's interaction with her addressee.[72] This description of γε mainly follows those of Hartung 1832, Kühner 1835, Stephens 1837, and Bäumlein 1861.[73] Hancock 1917 in his study on tragic stichomythia also remarks on γε. He notes that the particle is frequently used at the beginning

[70] See II.5 §§33-34 for a similar analysis of γε, combined with the pronoun ὁ, in Homer: the cluster ὅ γε is interpreted as referring to an accessible referent, thus establishing a link to previous discourse, but in a somehow new form, thus adding a new twist.

[71] On γε in drama, see also III.2 §§58-61; III.4 §§62-64; and III.5 §§45-47 and §§51-63.

[72] On subjectivity and intersubjectivity, see e.g. Traugott and Dasher 2002:19-23. On the connection between intersubjectivity and stance, see IV.4 §§51-52. On γε as a marker of voice and subjectivity in authorial statements in Herodotus and Thucydides, see IV.4 §§40-44.

[73] According to Hartung 1832:348-349, γε implies that one element is more important or relevant than the rest. By singling out this one element, γε puts emphasis on it (Bäumlein 1861:54).

of utterances (27) "to pick up a whole phrase or sentence in assent which is at once qualified by a further clause."[74] That is, in Du Boisian terms, γε can be used at the start of utterances that trigger resonance with a preceding utterance; the particle then signals that the speaker puts a new spin on the echoed material.

§78. With these considerations in mind, let us look at the uses of γε in resonating contexts. The element highlighted by γε does not have to be uttered explicitly in the original turn of speaking: it is usually an implicit element that can be inferred from this earlier utterance. The speaker of the γε turn presents this element as highly relevant. Here is an example:

(t14)

Λυ. συνεπόμνυθ' ὑμεῖς ταῦτα πᾶσαι;
ΠΑΣΑΙ νὴ Δία.
238bis Λυ. φέρ' ἐγὼ καθαγίσω τήνδε—
Κα. τὸ μέρος γ', ὦ φίλη.
239bis Λυ. ὅπως ἂν ὦμεν εὐθὺς ἀλλήλων φίλαι.

Aristophanes *Lysistrata* 237-239

Ly. So swear you one and all?
All. So swear we all!
Ly.[75] All right, then, I'll consecrate the cup.
Ca. Only your share, my friend; let's make sure we're all on friendly terms from the very start.

Calonice builds upon the meaning and structure of the preceding utterance, yet adds a crucial qualification: Lysistrata should drink only part of the wine. As Henderson 1987 *ad loc.* remarks, Calonice "fears that Lysistrata might drink all the wine herself." It is this—for Calonice frightening—alternative that is implicitly invoked by τὸ μέρος γ'. The scope of γε does not extend beyond this discourse act,[76] but because τὸ μέρος builds upon the

Additionally, Hartung 1832:371, Kühner 1835:398, and Stephens 1837:92 point out that the element set in contrast to the one accompanied by γε is often left implicit.

74 Werres 1936:36 on γε in combination with swearing expressions such as νὴ Δία also notes that γε often occurs in utterances that grammatically depend on a previous utterance.

75 The Greek text edited by Wilson 2007 attributes the lines differently from Henderson's 2000 translation. This is irrelevant for the interpretation of γε.

76 A discourse act is a short communicative step, expressed in language, with a certain pragmatic goal; it may but does not need to coincide with a syntactic clause. The concept of discourse act is employed throughout this monograph; for elaborate discussion, see II.2, especially §§3-23, and IV.3 §§70-91.

preceding utterance, the particle's contribution—highlighting this element and hinting at implicit alternatives—clarifies how the speaker intends to use the resonance here.[77]

§79. A speaker using γε in a resonating utterance, then, singles out a specific element to steer the discourse in a new direction. Therefore this use of γε is quite compatible with contexts of disagreement. Consider the example below, part of the dialogue between Jason and Medea already cited in (t8).[78]

(t15)

Ια. λέχους σφε κἠξίωσας οὕνεκα κτανεῖν;
Μη. σμικρὸν γυναικὶ πῆμα τοῦτ' εἶναι δοκεῖς;
Ια. ἥτις γε σώφρων· σοὶ δὲ πάντ' ἐστὶν κακά.

Euripides *Medea* 1367-1369

Ja. Did you really think it right to kill them because of a marriage?
Me. Do you imagine that loss of this is a trivial grief for a woman?
Ja. For a woman of sense, yes. But you find everything a disaster.

In line 1369, Jason's construction ἥτις γε, which stands elliptically for [ταύτῃ] γ' ἥτις (Flacelière 1970 *ad loc.*), refers to Medea's γυναικί from 1368. γε signals and highlights that he is putting a new spin on this word: the particle emphasizes the discourse act "woman with sense" (ἥτις σώφρων), implying a contrast to a woman without sense, the kind of woman Jason suggests Medea is.[79] In the rest of his utterance he makes explicit this contrast between Medea and a sensible woman, through the pronoun σοί and the boundary-marking particle δέ.

77 See also Van Leeuwen 1903 ("'pro rata certe parte!' exclamat") and Wilamowitz-Moellendorff 1927 ("Kleonike protestiert") *ad loc.*

78 Other examples of γε marking this kind of resonance include Sophocles *Ajax* 78, 1132; *Oedipus King* 365 (cited in (t10) and Table 2), 570; Euripides *Bacchae* 499, 970; *Helen* 1633; *Medea* 1397bis, 1398bis; Aristophanes *Birds* 1680; *Frogs* 1045bis; *Knights* 1100, 1151bis; *Lysistrata* 238bis, 441 (cited in (t13) and Figure 6), 530; *Wealth* 155. See Lucci 2011 for discussion of γε in Sophocles *Ajax* 78 (ἐχθρός γε τῷδε τἀνδρι καὶ τανῦν ἔτι). Odysseus here picks up the word ἀνήρ from the preceding utterance by Athena. As Lucci points out, Odysseus alters the meaning of the word: "ἀνὴρ now refers to Odysseus himself, not Ajax, and so Athena's emphasis on mortality is lost. Instead Odysseus introduces a new word, ἐχθρός, which is both stressed and placed in implicit opposition to Athena's statement by the particle γε. Odysseus is unconcerned with Ajax's status as a human being per se; the problem is that Ajax is a human being who has been and still is hostile to Odysseus." Incidentally, Pickering 1999:180 notes that ἀνήρ is the word most frequently repeated in Sophocles *Ajax* (47 times).

79 See IV.5 §73 for an example of γε in a very similar context in Herodotus.

3.3.1.2 δέ γε/δέ... γε

§80. More often than turn-initial γε on its own, we find the turn-initial combination δέ γε/δέ... γε in resonating utterances. For the particular interpretation that described here, the two particles do not need to be contiguous,[80] nor to both have scope over their entire discourse act; they only need to occur within the same discourse act.[81] The construction is the most frequent in the aggressive dialogues of Aristophanes, especially in *Knights*, where combative capping plays an important role.[82] Hartung 1832:382 describes δέ in this combination as introducing an adversative element, while γε indicates "Entgegensetzung" ("opposition," "contrast," "confrontation"). In milder terms, Paley 1881:17 writes that δέ γε expresses "assent" with "some demur or reservation." Neil 1901:191 and Denniston 1950:153 observe that the combination is often used in drama and Plato in "retorts."[83] In such contexts, Neil writes, the second speaker "wishes to cap [the statement of the first] or to bring in a consideration on the other side."

§81. The following passage from Sophocles *Ajax* presents an example of turn-initial δέ γε in a resonating context. In this scene Menelaus wants to forbid Teucer to bury his half-brother Ajax.

(t16)

Με. ἤδη ποτ' εἶδον ἄνδρ' ἐγὼ γλώσσῃ θρασὺν
ναύτας ἐφορμήσαντα χειμῶνος τὸ πλεῖν,
ᾧ φθέγμ' ἂν οὐκ ἐνηῦρες, ἡνίκ' ἐν κακῷ
χειμῶνος εἴχετ',
(...)
Τευ. ἐγὼ <u>δέ γ'</u> ἄνδρ' ὄπωπα μωρίας πλέων,
ὃς ἐν κακοῖς ὕβριζε τοῖσι τῶν πέλας.

Part of Sophocles *Ajax* 1142-1151

[80] That is, I agree with Denniston 1950:152 that the meaning of the combination does not depend on δέ and γε being directly next to each other.

[81] In e.g. Euripides *Iphigeneia at Aulis* 1134 (σὺ δ', ἤν γ' ἐρωτᾷς εἰκότ', εἰκότ' ἂν κλύοις), we find δέ and γε close to each other at the start of an utterance, but the presence of ἤν before γε makes it clear that there is an act boundary directly after δέ. The two particles are therefore not in the same discourse act in this case. See IV.3 §57, §110 on subordinating conjunctions as one of the signs for act boundaries.

[82] See Hesk 2007.

[83] Denniston notes that δέ γε/δέ... γε may also be used to pick up the thread of the speaker's own previous words (1950 [1934]:154). This latter interpretation is appropriate, I find, when the host utterance does not resonate with *the directly preceding utterance*, but the speaker instead adds a new step to *her own previous utterance*. Examples include Aristophanes' *Assemblywomen* 279ter; *Birds* 514; *Clouds* 169, 175, 681; *Frogs* 914bis; *Wasps* 605, 776bis.

> Me. In the past I have seen a man of reckless speech urging sailors to sail during a storm. But one heard no word from him when he was in the grip of the storm's attack; (...)
> Te. And I have seen a man full of stupidity, who harried others in their time of troubles.

Teucer takes over Menelaus' construction "I have seen a man" as well as his move's pragmatic goal: to compare the interlocutor to a negative image.[84] Both speakers mention "a man" in general, and then make it clear that they are in fact insulting their addressee. With the particle δέ, Teucer marks his new turn as a separate, new step in the discourse.[85] At the same time, γε indicates that he builds upon the previous utterance, putting a new spin on the echoed material and highlighting his own subjective view. The construction consisting of (1) δέ, (2) γε (both in the turn's first discourse act), and (3) resonance with the preceding utterance has a very specific function: it marks the juxtaposition of a particular new step—a step that conveys hostility—to the preceding utterance. The particle combination clarifies how the speaker intends to use his echo; paying attention to the use of resonance therefore helps to understand why we find δέ γε/δέ... γε here and in other resonating and hostile contexts.

§82. The hostile new step in this and several other cases contains a reference to the first person. In this way the speaker juxtaposes her own (current or future) action, view, or experience to that of her addressee, for instance to threaten him. Another example is Pentheus' order to tie up Dionysus (ἐγὼ δὲ δεῖν γε, "and I [say]: 'do bind him!'" Euripides *Bacchae* 505) in reaction to Dionysus' "I say: 'do not bind me'" αὐδῶ με μὴ δεῖν, 504).[86] In other resonating utterances with δέ γε/δέ... γε we find a second-person reference:

(t17)

> (Πε.) οἶσθ' ᾧ μάλιστ' ἔοικας ἐπτερωμένος;
> εἰς εὐτέλειαν χηνὶ συγγεγραμμένῳ.
> Ευ. σὺ <u>δὲ</u> κοψίχῳ <u>γε</u> σκάφιον ἀποτετιλμένῳ.

Aristophanes *Birds* 804-806

[84] The tense change (εἶδον, 1142 vs. ὄπωπα, 1150) further highlights Teucer's new spin on the echo. On tense and tense change in connection with particles, see II.4 §§15-28 on γάρ in Homer and Pindar, and IV.4 on Herodotus and Thucydides: §107 and §114 on δή; §149, §151, §153 and §160 on ἤδη; §169 on ἄρα.

[85] See III.4 §§34-38 for discussion of turn-initial δέ in drama.

[86] Other δέ γε/δέ... γε utterances with this function are e.g. Aeschylus *Seven against Thebes* 1026; Sophocles *Ajax* 1150; *Philoctetes* 1293; Euripides *Cyclops* 708; *Iphigeneia in Tauris* 749; Aristophanes *Acharnians* 623, 1216; *Assemblywomen* 261, 1010; *Birds* 1042, 1053; *Frogs* 236, 253, 570, 575a, 1395; *Knights* 356, 363, 364, 365, 432, 744, 906, 967, 1105, 1154, 1156, 1171, 1178, 1191; *Lysistrata* 104, 105, 115, 374, 1158; *Wasps* 1230bis; *Wealth* 296, 770, 1090, 1091.

(Pe.) Know what you look just like in those wings? A painted goose, done cheaply!
Eu. And you look like a blackbird with a bowl cut!

Peisetaerus describes his friend's new bird costume in 804-805 in a rather unfriendly way. In response, Euelpides utters a hostile, scornful description of Peisetaerus' own appearance.[87] Together with σύ and the resonance triggered by utterance's similarity to the previous utterance, the turn-initial particle combination δέ γε/δέ... γε marks the juxtaposition of an insult or reproach in reaction to a previous insult or reproach.[88]

§83. Other resonating utterances with δέ γε/δέ... γε put a counter-argument next to a previously uttered argument. An example occurs in Aeschylus *Libation Bearers* 921: Clytemnestra has just argued that it is painful for women to be kept apart from their husband (ἀνδρός), but Orestes counters τρέφει δέ γ' ἀνδρὸς μόχθος ἡμένας ἔσω, "it's the man's labour that feeds the women sitting at home."[89] Also in this case the particle combination clarifies the use of conscious engagement between utterances. For the analysis of these particles it is therefore essential to take into account more co-text than just their host utterance.

3.3.1.3 δῆτα

§84. The *Medea* dialogue cited in (t8) also contains an occurrence of the particle δῆτα, here repeated:

(t18)

Μη. ἴσασιν ὅστις ἦρξε πημονῆς θεοί.
Ια. ἴσασι δῆτα σήν γ' ἀπόπτυστον φρένα.

Euripides *Medea* 1372-1373

Me. The gods know who struck the first blow.
Ja. Yes, they know indeed your loathesome heart.

[87] See Kock 1864 ("gegenseitige Sticheleien"); Zanetto in Zanetto and Del Corno 1987 (as at symposia, the victim of a joke responds with his own fantastic and ridiculous comparison); Dunbar 1995 ("sequence of fantastic comparison and counter-comparison") *ad loc.*

[88] Other δέ γε/δέ... γε utterances with this function include Aeschylus *Suppliant Women* 1056; Sophocles *Oedipus King* 372; *Fragment* 187.2; Aristophanes *Birds* 845bis, 1044, 1053; *Clouds* 915bis, 920bis, 1277; *Knights* 444.

[89] Other δέ γε/δέ... γε utterances with this function include Aeschylus *Agamemnon* 939, 941; Euripides *Andromache* 584; *Bacchae* 490; *Children of Heracles* 109; *Ion* 368, 1256, 1330; *Iphigeneia in Aulis* 21, 334; Aristophanes *Clouds* 914; *Frogs* 1395. The three sub-functions of the construction can overlap, as in the *Ajax* passage cited in (t16), where the resonating utterance refers to both the first and, indirectly, the second person.

The role of this particle, which is confined almost entirely to dialogues,[90] depends on the illocutionary force of the utterance, that is whether the utterance is an assertion or a question (or, more rarely, a directive). Let us first consider δῆτα in assertions, such as in the *Medea* dialogue. According to Hartung 1832:305 and Kühner 1835:389-390, δῆτα in answers emphatically expresses total agreement. Similarly, Bäumlein 1861:108 and Paley 1881:25 note that δῆτα may affirm a word repeated from another speaker. This affirming function is what we have in our example: Jason echoes ἴσασι from the previous utterance, apparently to concur with the claim that "the gods know." However, the rest of his utterance shows that the initial "agreement" was ironic, and turns it into a hostile sentiment. Again γε is used to zoom in on a specific element that was not explicitly mentioned by the previous speaker. This element, σὴν ἀπόπτυστον φρένα, "your detested mind," changes the utterance's pragmatic goal.[91] Thus in this case a speaker employs resonance to highlight his disagreement with another speaker.

§85. This use of δῆτα, marking complete and often vehement agreement with a word taken over from a previous utterance, is relatively frequent in tragedy and comedy.[92] The echoed element is often a negation, which consequently receives strong emphasis.[93] Paley 1881:25 speaks of "strong and indignant denial" expressed by οὐ δῆτα, translating it as "no indeed!" with an exclamation mark. In several cases, δῆτα with a negation (whether repeated or not) is followed by γε: thus δῆτα emphasizes the negation, and γε then marks which specific element involved in this negation is singled out as the most relevant by the speaker.[94] δῆτα is also found, especially in comedy, after lexical echoes in directive utterances, such as orders or requests, where it has a similar emotional strengthening effect. For example, Pfeiffer-Petersen 1996:84 draws attention to δῆτα in Sophocles *Oedipus King* 445. Here the angry Oedipus picks up κόμιζε from

90 See III.2 §58 and §§62-63 for the distribution of δῆτα over the different parts of the plays, with discussion.

91 Page 1938 *ad loc.* remarks that γε and δῆτα are often used when a speaker echoes a word from another speaker, but does not discuss their functions.

92 Examples of δῆτα in resonating assertions include Aeschylus *Persians* 1072; *Prometheus Bound* 770; *Seven against Thebes* 879, 888, 932, 982; *Suppliant Women* 207, 216, 359; Sophocles *Electra* 845, 1198, 1455; *Philoctetes* 419; *Women of Trachis* 1127; *Oedipus at Colonus* 536; Aristophanes *Birds* 269, 275, 1548; *Frogs* 28, 914, 1089; *Lysistrata* 524, 836, 848, 882, 930, 972.

93 See e.g. Hartung 1832:306, who translates οὐ δῆτα as "ganz und gar nicht."

94 An example from tragedy is found in Sophocles *Antigone* 762: Κρ. (...) /ἄγετε τὸ μῖσος ὡς κατ' ὄμματ' αὐτίκα /παρόντι θνήσκῃ πλησία τῷ νυμφίῳ /Αι. οὐ δῆτ' ἔμοιγε τοῦτο μὴ δόξῃς ποτέ. "Cr. Bring the hateful creature, so that she may die at once close at hand, in the sight of her bridegroom. Ha. She shall not die close to me, never imagine it (...)!" An example from Aristophanes is found in *Birds* 1670: Πε. (...) ἤδη σ' ὁ πατὴρ εἰσήγαγ' εἰς τοὺς φράτερας /Ηρ. οὐ δῆτ' ἐμέ γε καὶ τοῦτ' ἐθαύμαζον πάλαι. "Pe. Tell me, has your father inducted you into his phratry yet? He. Not me he hasn't, and that's always made me wonder."

Teiresias' utterance in 444 with the stronger κομιζέτω δῆθ'. In such cases impatience is often implied.[95]

§86. δῆτα appears most frequently in questions. The function of such questions—the function, that is, of δῆτα in combination with the interrogative illocutionary force of the utterance—is to pass over to something new, which is nonetheless linked to the preceding utterance. More specifically, the particle indicates that the question springs from what was just said.[96] Even when there are no explicit repetitions from a previous utterance, δῆτα points in this way to the dialogic relation between the speaker's and her interlocutor's speech. Thus, a δῆτα question highlights a conscious topical similarity with a previous utterance. At the same time, by asking about something which would otherwise not be discussed, it opens a new move, and a new direction in the discourse.[97] Since the speaker usually expects an immediate answer, δῆτα questions tend to carry an air of impatience or urgency.[98]

§87. The new topic raised by the speaker through δῆτα questions sometimes seem completely unrelated to the preceding conversation, but in these cases the relevance of the new topic becomes clear a few speaking turns later.[99] A striking instance of this use

95 So Hartung 1832:308, Kühner 1835:390, and Stanford 1958 *ad* Aristophanes *Frogs* 11. Other examples of δῆτα in resonating directives include Euripides *Electra* 673, 676; *Hercules* 900; *Trojan Women* 1231; Aristophanes *Lysistrata* 96, 1245. On δῆτα being linked to emotional agitation, see III.5 §§49-50.

96 See Denniston 1950 [1934]:269-70: δῆτα in questions has "a logical connective force." The particle indicates "that the question springs out of something which another person (or, more rarely, the speaker himself) has just said." Wiesner 1999:356 similarly notes that δῆτα carries a logical function, as δῆτα questions arise from the preceding context. Also Goldhill 2012 on Sophocles notes that δῆτα "normally has a consequential force with questions" (43).

97 Examples of such δῆτα questions include Aeschylus *Agamemnon* 1211, 1286 (see (t20) below); *Libation Bearers* 218, 916; *Eumenides* 206; *Suppliant Women* 302; Sophocles *Ajax* 42, 109, 518, 537, 1360; *Antigone* 449, 1099; *Electra* 1037; *Oedipus King* 364, 558, 577, 622, 651, 765, 1014; *Oedipus at Colonus* 52, 258, 643, 1018, 1308 (see note 103 below); *Philoctetes* 54, 757, 1352, 1393; *Women of Trachis* 73, 76, 342, 400, 410, 1219, 1245; Euripides *Alcestis* 39, 380, 530, 689, 822, 960; *Bacchae* 1277 (see (t19) below), 1351; *Medea* 1056; Aristophanes *Birds* 201, 817, 911, 969, 1025, 1147, 1152, 1217, 1585, 1671, 1689; *Frogs* 12, 194, 200, 296, 635, 654, 768, 784; *Lysistrata* 54, 181, 399, 753, 912, 914, 1103, 1159.

This description of δῆτα in questions resembles that of German modal particles by Diewald 1999: she points out that particles such as "denn" produce a backward connection to the pragmatic context (194), whereas questions are always initiating conversational steps (192). It would be interesting to compare the use of δῆτα to that of other particles in questions. See III.2 (passim) for observations on the distribution of several such particles in drama, and III.4 §§43-45 for discussion of a particular οὖν construction in questions in drama.

98 See Hartung 1832:306-307 (δῆτα in questions either indicates a strong increase, or the impatience of the speaker, who immediately wants an answer); Bäumlein 1861:108 (δῆτα may give emphasis to a question word); Hancock 1917:30 (δῆτα questions are "questions of surprise, logical doubt, impatience, or anger"). See note 95 above.

99 Examples of this use of δῆτα questions, referring to something new, the relevance of which becomes clear only later, are: Sophocles *Oedipus at Colonus* 52; *Oedipus King* 364, 1002, 1014; *Philoctetes* 895; *Women of Trachis* 76, 400, 410, 1219.

of δῆτα comes from Euripides *Bacchae*, where the δῆτα question produces an ironic effect for the audience.[100] The dialogue excerpted below takes places between Cadmus and his daughter Agaue, after she has unknowingly killed her son Pentheus. Cadmus already knows about this disaster—and so does the audience.

(t19)

Κα. ἐς ποῖον ἦλθες οἶκον ὑμεναίων μέτα;
Αγ. Σπαρτῶι μ' ἔδωκας, ὡς λέγουσ', Ἐχίονι.
Κα. τίς οὖν ἐν οἴκοις παῖς ἐγένετο σῶι πόσει;
Αγ. Πενθεύς, ἐμῆι τε καὶ πατρὸς κοινωνίαι.
Κα. τίνος πρόσωπον δῆτ' ἐν ἀγκάλαις ἔχεις;
Αγ. λέοντος, ὥ γ' ἔφασκον αἱ θηρώμεναι.

Euripides *Bacchae* 1273-1278

Ca. To what household did you come at your marriage?
Ag. You married me to Echion, one of the Sown Men, they say.
Ca. Well, what son was born in that house to your husband?
Ag. Pentheus, his father's son and mine.
Ca. Whose head do you have in your hands then?
Ag. The hunters told me it is a lion's.

With his first two questions about Agaue's husband and son, Cadmus tries to bring her to her senses after her Bacchic frenzy. If she does remember these persons, she might realize that she is holding the head of this very son. As in other interrogative instances, δῆτα in 1277 marks the question's inferential link to a preceding utterance and draws attention to semantic or pragmatic similarities across these utterances.[101] Here Cadmus' question builds on Agaue's reference to Pentheus (a semantic similarity) as well as on his own previous questions (an illocutionary similarity). Agaue cannot realize that τίνος in 1277 in fact refers to the same referent as τίς in 1275, but for the audience the repetition of the question word may highlight this irony. Since Agaue cannot understand that Cadmus' question is related to her own preceding utterance, as the audience can, δῆτα emphasizes the dramatic irony of the passage.

§88. Though it is rare, δῆτα questions may also be used in monologues. Because δῆτα in dialogues signals a reaction to a previous utterance, in monologues the presence of the

[100] See IV.4 on irony in the use of δή: §§104-108 on Herodotus, and §§123-126 on Thucydides.

[101] I do not agree with Dodds 1960 [1944] *ad loc.*, who claims that δῆτα indicates that "Cadmus has reached what he was leading up to." In my view this is not what the particle indicates, although it is true in this case that Cadmus has reached his most important question. I do agree with Dodds' paraphrase "well, then" of δῆτα, since it reflects the inferential link that the particle indicates. See also Fraenkel 1950 *ad* Aeschylus *Agamemnon* 1286-1290, quoted below in (t20).

particle gives the impression that the speaker is conducting a "dialogue with herself." The following example from *Agamemnon* is taken from a long speech by Cassandra. She knows that there is no escape, and that she will die very soon.[102]

(t20)

(Κα.) φυγὰς δ' ἀλήτης τῆσδε γῆς ἀπόξενος
κάτεισιν ἄτας τάσδε θριγκώσων φίλοις.
ὀμώμοται γὰρ ὅρκος ἐκ θεῶν μέγας,
ἄξειν νιν ὑπτίασμα κειμένου πατρός.
τί δῆτ' ἐγὼ κάτοικτος ὧδ' ἀναστένω;
ἐπεὶ τὸ πρῶτον εἶδον Ἰλίου πόλιν
πράξασαν ὡς ἔπραξεν, οἳ δ' εἷλον πόλιν
οὕτως ἀπαλλάσσουσιν ἐν θεῶν κρίσει,
ἰοῦσ' ἀπάρξω, τλήσομαι τὸ κατθανεῖν.

Aeschylus *Agamemnon* 1282-1290

(Ca.) (an avenger will come) An exile, a wanderer, banished from this land, he will return to put the coping-stone on these disasters for his family; that the gods have sworn a great oath that his father's corpse lying helpless will draw him back. So why do I lament and groan aloud like this? Now that I have seen the city of Ilium suffer as it suffered, now that those who captured the city are getting this kind of verdict before the tribunal of the gods, I too shall go and have the courage to face death.

E. Fraenkel 1950 *ad loc.* remarks: "a sentence beginning with τί δῆτα draws the conclusion from a preceding statement (this need not be by a different person (...))." The reason for the δῆτα question, he adds, is always to be found in the preceding discourse, never in what follows. In this case, the rhetorical δῆτα question in line 1286 presents a new association prompted by the speaker's own words. Fraenkel paraphrases Cassandra's argumentation as, "it is quite certain that my death will be avenged; why then do I lament?" Thus, also in this monologue a δῆτα question looks backward (marking an inference from preceding discourse) and forward (opening up a new topic) at the same time; this construction is however more at home in dialogues.[103]

[102] There is a similar instance of a δῆτα question shortly before in the same monologue: line 1264.

[103] Another clear example of such a δῆτα question in a monologue is Sophocles *Oedipus at Colonus* 1308, where the speaker Polyneices also uses the question to switch to something new, while at the same time marking an inferential link to the preceding. His question is prefaced by the interjection εἶέν, which seems to signal a "jump" to something new (albeit connected) in the speaker's thoughts. In the Loeb edition by Lloyd-Jones 1994b, the switch is visually emphasized

3.3.1.4 καί

§89. When a character's utterance starts with καί, the particle usually marks a close connection to a preceding utterance. The new utterance may, for example, continue or mirror the previous speaker's communicative action, such as a directive following a directive (see (t21) below). καί helps to trigger resonance in such cases: the particle makes it explicit that the speaker is picking up something from the preceding utterance in order to do something with it herself. This interpretation fits with the descriptions of καί in the scholarly literature. Hartung 1832:153 describes the particle as marking a union ("Vereinigung") between two elements. Similarly, Bäumlein 1861:145 holds that καί introduces a new thought or concept that belongs in the same line of thinking ("unter den gleichen Gesichtspunkt") as what came before. He adds (146) that καί may mark the second element in a combination as a more specific qualification of the first element ("nähere Bestimmung"). The Homerist Bakker follows these scholars in calling καί a particle of "inclusion" (1997b:71) and "integration" (72). When linking two different clauses, Homeric καί marks that the focus on a given idea continues, but that a different aspect of it is highlighted (72).

§90. Consider the following example from Euripides *Hippolytus*. Phaedra has decided to commit suicide and informs the chorus of this decision.

(t21)

Χο. μέλλεις δὲ δὴ τί δρᾶν ἀνήκεστον κακόν;
Φα. θανεῖν· ὅπως δέ, τοῦτ' ἐγὼ βουλεύσομαι.
Χο. εὔφημος ἴσθι.
724bis Φα. <u>καὶ</u> σύ <u>γ'</u> εὖ με νουθέτει.

Euripides *Hippolytus* 722-724

Ch. What harm past cure do you mean to do?
Ph. To die. But the manner of it—that shall be *my* devising.
Ch. Say no more shocking words!
Ph. And you, give advice that is good!

The chorus' request εὔφημος ἴσθι, "say good-omened words," in fact means "please change your mind and don't commit suicide." Phaedra in her response mirrors the utterance's directive illocutionary force, her νουθέτει picks up on the imperative singular

by a paragraph break from this point in both the Greek text and the translation. See IV.3 §§53-64 on such paralinguistic discourse segmentation in ancient Greek texts, and its relation to particle use.

morphology of ἴσθι, and her εὖ echoes the chorus' εὔφημος.[104] καί at the beginning of Phaedra's turn highlights the resonance, by explicitly linking the two utterances.[105] However, Phaedra also employs the particle γε, which highlights σύ and thereby points to the new spin she is putting on the echoed material: she implies that the chorus' utterance was in fact not good advice at all.

§91. Turn-initial καί may also link utterances by signaling a speaker's intention to deal in more detail with an existing point.[106] In these cases, it is not a communicative goal that is being echoed, but a topic or claim from the preceding utterance. A speaker may for example zoom in on something to ask a detailed question about it, as in (t22), where the chorus asks Clytemnestra how she knows about the recent fall of Troy. Perhaps she had received signs in a dream?

(t22)

Κλ. οὐ δόξαν ἂν λάβοιμι βριζούσης φρενός.
Χο. ἀλλ' ἦ σ' ἐπίανέν τις ἄπτερος φάτις;
Κλ. παιδὸς νέας ὣς κάρτ' ἐμωμήσω φρένας.
Χο. ποίου χρόνου δὲ καὶ πεπόρθηται πόλις;
Κλ. τῆς νῦν τεκούσης φῶς τόδ' εὐφρόνης λέγω.
Χο. καὶ τίς τόδ' ἐξίκοιτ' ἂν ἀγγέλων τάχος;
Κλ. Ἥφαιστος, Ἴδης λαμπρὸν ἐκπέμπων σέλας·

Aeschylus *Agamemnon* 275-281

Cl. I wouldn't accept the mere fancy of a slumbering mind.
Ch. Then has some unflegded rumour swelled your head?
Cl. You really disparage my intelligence, as if I were a young child!
Ch. Within what time has the city actually been sacked?
Cl. Within the night, I say, that has just given birth to the present day's light.
Ch. And what messenger could come here with such speed?
Cl. Hephaestus, sending a bright blaze on its way from Mount Ida.

[104] Barrett 1964 and Halleran 1995 *ad loc.* note the echo of the chorus' εὔφημος in Phaedra's εὖ.

[105] Other examples of turn-initial καί highlighting resonance between utterances by different speakers are found in e.g. Aeschylus *Persians* 236, 723 (see III.4 §36 for discussion); *Libation Bearers* 183, 223, 500, 503; Sophocles *Ajax* 45, 527; *Antigone* 322, 577, 749; *Oedipus King* 630, 963, 1019, 1023, 1170; Euripides *Bacchae* 1372bis; *Hippolytus* 326; *Medea* 608, 906; Aristophanes *Birds* 325bis, 976, 1349, 1437bis; *Frogs* 67bis, 582bis (see §§43-49 above), 1393ter; *Lysistrata* 6bis, 88bis, 603, 604, 752bis, 1221. *Ad* Euripides' *Electra* 976, Van Emde Boas 2017b:217 similarly notes that Electra indicates with καί "that this line adds directly to the preceding one."

[106] On this function of καί in several genres of ancient Greek literature, especially in narrative contexts, see IV.2.4.4.

The turn-initial καί in 280 indicates that the chorus is taking up the substance of Clytemnestra's utterance (i.e. resonance is triggered) and is delving into it in further detail: if the capture of Troy only took place the night before, the chorus would like to know, then how can the queen already know about it?[107]

§92. In the next passage from Aristophanes *Frogs*, we see an utterance starting with καί that triggers resonance not with the immediately preceding utterance, but with an earlier turn by the same speaker. The similarities between these utterances would have been striking even without the particle, but καί draws attention to the resemblance more explicitly, by marking the new utterance as linked. Two furious innkeepers are complaining about Heracles' gluttony. The slave Xanthias throws some oil on the fire, because he would like to see the innkeepers punish his master Dionysus, who is wearing the Heracles costume.[108]

(t23)

Πα. κἄπειτ' ἐπειδὴ τἀργύριον ἐπραττόμην,
ἔβλεψεν εἴς με δριμὺ κἀμυκᾶτό γε—
Ξα. τούτου πάνυ τοὔργον· οὗτος ὁ τρόπος πανταχοῦ.
Πα. καὶ τὸ ξίφος γ' ἐσπᾶτο, μαίνεσθαι δοκῶν.
Πλ. νὴ Δία, τάλαινα.
Πα. νὼ δὲ δεισάσα γέ πως
ἐπὶ τὴν κατήλιφ' εὐθὺς ἀνεπηδήσαμεν·
ὁ δ' ᾤχετ' ἐξᾴξας γε τὰς ψιάθους λαβών.
Ξα. <u>καὶ</u> τοῦτο τούτου τοὔργον.
(...)

Aristophanes *Frogs* 561-568

In. And when I presented the bill, he gave me a nasty look and started bellowing.
Xa. That's his style exactly; he acts that way everywhere.
In. And he drew his sword like a lunatic.
Pl. Amen, my poor dear.
In. And we were so scared I guess we jumped right up to the loft, while he dashed out and got away, taking our mattresses with him.
Xa. That's his style, too.

[107] See also the discussion of turn-initial καὶ πῶς in the example from Aristophanes *Frogs* above, §§43-46.

[108] See III.5 §§57-58 for discussion of different aspects of this same scene.

Xanthias' remark in 568 repeats the one in 563, as noted by Van Leeuwen 1896 *ad loc.* By marking the second utterance with turn-initial καί, Xanthias makes it explicit that his comment is an addition to or a continuation of the comment he is echoing. That Xanthias can make this comment *again* humorously increases the women's anger, which makes the situation all the more dangerous for his terrified master.[109]

§93. Because of its general linking function,[110] καί is well-suited to starting off resonating utterances. The particle does not itself trigger resonance, but helps to draw attention to meaningful similarities across utterances. Lexical, phonological, syntactic, and other types of resonance stand out more clearly when the second utterance is marked with καί. Because resonance can be triggered by similarities on different levels, this highlighting may occur both when καί has small scope ("that too," "even that") and when it has large scope, linking entire discourse acts ("and who could come?"). That is, the use of resonance does not depend on the particle's scope.

§94. The linking nature of καί and its affinity with resonance-triggering contexts make it clear that καί functions very differently from δέ, even though both of them are often translated "and." Turn-initial δέ marks its utterance as a new, separate step in the discourse, rather than as a pursuing of or "zooming in" on the preceding utterance.

3.3.1.5 γάρ

§95. When a speaker uses γάρ at the beginning of a resonating utterance, she indicates that her use of resonance involves an inference on her part. Hancock 1917:27 translates this use of γάρ as "yes, for...," or "no, for...". He notes (31) that γάρ marking an ellipsis of a whole phrase is very common in tragic stichomythia. When it comes to the use of γάρ in questions, Denniston 1950:77 notes that it is frequent at the beginning of "surprised and incredulous questions, where the speaker throws doubt on the grounds of the previous speaker's words. (...) Frequently the second speaker echoes, with contempt, indignation, or surprise, a word or words used by the first." Viger (Vigerus) 1834 [1627]:492 also notes that γάρ in questions may signal indignation.

§96. γάρ's role in resonance contexts, then, is to indicate that a speaker refers to a preceding utterance because she infers a certain (in her view) outrageous implication from that utterance. That is, the logical link between the two utterances signaled by the particle conveys that the speaker is indignant about what was said. The causal use of γάρ

[109] The passage also contains instances of turn-initial καί in 561 and 564, where the women use them to underline the connectedness and the extent of their complaints. Stanford 1958 *ad loc.* paraphrases καί in 564 as "Yes, and what's more...". The particles δέ and γε in 565bis are not connected to resonance, as the construction discussed in §§80-83 above, because they do not occur within the same discourse act; the position of πως suggest an act boundary before δεισάσα. Turn-initial δέ here marks the utterance as a new step in the discourse (see III.4 §§34-38).

[110] This general function of καί leads to many different uses in different contexts. See III.2 §§33-38 for several uses in drama. See IV.2.4 on the multifunctionality of καί in Herodotus and Thucydides.

also plays a role in its resonance-marking function: it introduces, at the beginning of an utterance, why a speaker does or does not agree with a previous suggestion.

§97. In the following passage from Sophocles *Antigone*, we can see as many as eight instances of the particle marking a relation across different speakers' turns.[111] It is an angry dialogue between Creon and his son Haemon, who is trying to convince his father not to kill Antigone.[112]

(t24)

Αι. μηδέν γ' ὃ μὴ δίκαιον· εἰ δ' ἐγὼ νέος,
οὐ τὸν χρόνον χρὴ μᾶλλον ἢ τἄργα σκοπεῖν.
Κρ. ἔργον γάρ ἐστι τοὺς ἀκοσμοῦντας σέβειν;
Αι. οὐδ' ἂν κελεύσαιμ' εὐσεβεῖν ἐς τοὺς κακούς.
Κρ. οὐχ ἥδε γὰρ τοιᾷδ' ἐπείληπται νόσῳ;
Αι. οὔ φησι Θήβης τῆσδ' ὁμόπτολις λεώς.
Κρ. πόλις γὰρ ἡμῖν ἁμὲ χρὴ τάσσειν ἐρεῖ;
Αι. ὁρᾷς τόδ' ὡς εἴρηκας ὡς ἄγαν νέος;
Κρ. ἄλλῳ γὰρ ἢ 'μοὶ χρή με τῆσδ' ἄρχειν χθονός;
Αι. πόλις γὰρ οὐκ ἔσθ' ἥτις ἀνδρός ἐσθ' ἑνός.
(...)
Κρ. ὦ παγκάκιστε, διὰ δίκης ἰὼν πατρί;
Αι. οὐ γὰρ δίκαιά σ' ἐξαμαρτάνονθ' ὁρῶ.
Κρ. ἁμαρτάνω γὰρ τὰς ἐμὰς ἀρχὰς σέβων;
Αι. οὐ γὰρ σέβεις, τιμάς γε τὰς θεῶν πατῶν.

Sophocles *Antigone* 728-737 and 742-745

(Cr. Should young men teach sense to the old?)
Ha. Nothing but what is right! If I am young, one must not consider my age rather than my merits.
Cr. Is it a merit to show regard for those who cause disorder?
Ha. It is not that I would ask you to show regard for evildoers.
Cr. Is not she afflicted with this malady?
Ha. This people of Thebes that shares our city does not say so.
Cr. Is the city to tell me what orders I shall give?
Ha. Do you notice that what you have said is spoken like a very young man?

[111] In the lines left out, there is another γάρ (741), but this one marks an utterance-internal relation.

[112] A similar angry dialogue full of γάρ instances and repetitions of words and concepts is the one by Menelaus and Teucer in Sophocles *Ajax* 1120-1141, about (not) burying Ajax. Another example of turn-initial γάρ clarifying resonance is found in Sophocles *Philoctetes* 250.

Cr. Must I rule this land for another and not for myself?
Ha. Yes, there is no city that belongs to a single man!
(...)
Cr. You villain, by disputing against your father?
Ha. Because I see that you are offending against justice!
Cr. Am I offending when I show regard for my own office?
Ha. You show no regard when you trample on the honours due to the gods!

We see γάρ co-occurring with a chain of semantic (and sometimes lexical) echoes, all of which produce resonance. The following overview shows that each resonating element that contains γάρ refers back to a previous utterance by the other speaker.

resonating element	resonating with
730 Creon: ἔργον γάρ	729 Haemon: ἔργα
732 Creon: (...) γὰρ τοιᾷδ' (...) νόσῳ	730 Haemon: τοὺς κακούς
734 Creon: πόλις γὰρ	733 Haemon: Θήβης τῆσδ' ὁμόπτολις λεώς
736 Creon: (...) γὰρ (...) τῆσδ' ἄρχειν χθονός	733 Haemon: Θήβης τῆσδ'
737 Haemon: πόλις γὰρ	736 Creon: τῆσδ' (...) χθονός
743 Haemon: οὐ γὰρ δίκαιά	742 Creon: διὰ δίκης ἰὼν
744 Creon: ἁμαρτάνω γὰρ	743 Haemon: σ' ἐξαμαρτάνονθ' ὁρῶ
745 Haemon: οὐ γὰρ σέβεις	744 Creon: σέβων

Table 3: Resonating elements marked with γάρ in lines 728-745[113]

γάρ in this series of resonance signals that the speaker is making an inference in regards to the element he picks up from the earlier utterance. The use of γάρ, in other words, suggests that the speaker has a specific reason to echo his addressee. The preceding utterance is thus marked as a logical starting point for the current utterance.[114] In English we

[113] Creon's utterance in 736 also refers back to Haemon's line of argumentation as a whole, besides the specific element of the city.

[114] On γάρ marking an expansion or unfolding of the previous discourse in Homer and Pindar, see II.3 §28, §§71-72; II.4 §§15-28; in Herodotus and Thucydides, see IV.3 §§109-110; IV.5 §19, §39, §68, §95.

can render this specific resonance signal with phrases such as "so are you saying that...?" (in questions) and as "yes, for..." or "no, for..." (in answers).

§98. Kamerbeek 1978 and Griffith 1999 *ad loc.* note that γάρ in this context implies indignation.[115] Indeed the lexical echoes in this passage create an emotional impression of the speakers. This expression of emotions is not, however, a function of the particle by itself.[116] Rather, indignation follows pragmatically from what a speaker is doing with a γάρ echo. One speaker may say something with an implication that infuriates the other one. This second speaker can express her indignation by repeating the relevant element and indicating her inference based on that. In questions, such use of resonance leads to an indignant implication along the lines of, for example: "... merits."—"What?! Merits?! Are you saying that it's a merit to...". In responses, an angry speaker may suggest her superiority by implying that this inference is the only right response to the question just asked.[117]

3.3.2 Particles triggering resonance themselves

§99. In (t24), there are so many instances of resonance-marking γάρ that we can say that the particle in itself triggers resonance. The audience will have noticed the exceptional frequency of γάρ in this dialogue (as does e.g. Hancock 1917:28). That is, attention is drawn to the particle's own recurrence across utterances. Pickering does not take echoes

[115] See also Goldhill's discussion of this stichomythia, including ample attention to the many γάρ instances (2012:58-63), as well as the elaborate discussion of this dialogue and the lexical repetitions in it by Pfeiffer-Petersen 1996. The latter author writes (62) that at 730, Creon tries to make his opponent insecure with a rhetorical question echoing Haemon's ἔργα. Creon's echo in 734 has a similar function: he repeats πόλις with "apparent amazement" ("mit offensichtlichem, rhetorischem Erstaunen," 62). Pfeiffer-Petersen then notes (63) that the formal resemblance between 742 (διὰ δίκης ἰὼν by Creon) and 743 (οὐ γὰρ δίκαιά by Haemon) emphasizes the contrast in the content of the two utterances. Finally, she points out (63-64) that line 744 also receives emphasis by repeating the concept of ἁμαρτάνω from 743. Pfeiffer-Petersen concludes (65) that the numerous lexical repetitions across utterances in this dialogue show the intensity ("Heftigkeit") of the conflict. She also notes that most of these echoes are Haemon's (seven out of eleven repetitions in lines in 726-765), which indicates his interest in influencing Creon's views as well as his willingness to respond to Creon's arguments. Budelmann 1998:6 adds, in his review of Pfeiffer-Petersen's book, that "many of the words Haemon repeats are prominent elsewhere in the play." The resonance triggered by these words may thus not only serve communicative purposes of the speaking characters, but also those of the playwright, on a different level.

[116] See also III.5 §19 and §88 on this general point concerning particles and emotion expression.

[117] The angry dialogue between Oedipus and Teiresias in Sophocles *Oedipus King* 316-462 also contains many instances of γάρ, nine times uttered by Teiresias, and four times by Oedipus. During the workshop *Word Play: Ancient Greek Drama and the Role of Particles* in November 2012 in Heidelberg, it was suggested by Andreas Willi and Evert van Emde Boas that Teiresias perhaps uses these γάρ-instances in an "arrogant" way, claiming to have more knowledge than his interlocutor. However, only four of Teiresias' γάρ's in this passage are turn-initial (one by Oedipus), marking a relation across turns; the others mark a turn-internal relation.

of particles into account in his studies on repetition in tragedy (see §19 above). As these words are frequent throughout the texts, he generally does not consider their repetition meaningful. However, it is reasonable to take so many occurrences of the same particle within so few lines as a trigger of resonance. This occurs especially in Aristophanes.

§100. The resonance of γάρ in the *Antigone* passage may underline the speakers' angry mood, since this construction usually implies indignation. A similarly high density of an individual particle is found in the following passage from Euripides *Andromache*:[118]

(t25)

Ορ. μῶν ἐς γυναῖκ' ἔρραψας οἷα δὴ γυνή;
Ερ. φόνον γ' ἐκείνηι καὶ τέκνωι νοθαγενεῖ.
Ορ. κἄκτεινας, ἤ τις συμφορά σ' ἀφείλετο;
Ερ. γέρων γε Πηλεύς, τοὺς κακίονας σέβων.
Ορ. σοὶ δ' ἦν τις ὅστις τοῦδ' ἐκοινώνει φόνου;
Ερ. πατήρ γ' ἐπ' αὐτὸ τοῦτ' ἀπὸ Σπάρτης μολών.
Ορ. κἄπειτα τοῦ γέροντος ἡσσήθη χερί;
Ερ. αἰδοῖ γε· καί μ' ἔρημον οἴχεται λιπών.

Euripides *Andromache* 911-918

Or. Did you perchance plot against her like a woman?
He. Yes, death for her and for her bastard son.
Or. Did you kill them, or did some mischance prevent you?
He. Old Peleus stopped me, favoring the lowly.
Or. But was there one who shared this murder with you?
He. My father, come from Sparta for this purpose.
Or. Yet he was bested by an old man's hand?
He. Yes, by his sense of shame—and then he left me!

Hermione underlines all of her four answers in this dialogue with γε at the start. In this way she presents all the highlighted elements as extremely relevant to her in her current state of anxiety and despair. The resonance triggered by the γε repetition across her

118 Other examples include Sophocles *Ajax* 1121-1135 (seven instances of turn-initial γάρ); *Oedipus King* 549-551 (two instances of turn-initial τοι in resonating utterances); Aristophanes *Acharnians* 407-409 (five instances of turn-initial ἀλλά); *Assemblywomen* 773bis-776bis (four instances of turn-initial γάρ in resonating utterances, all by the same speaker), 799bis-804bis (six instances of turn-initial δέ, all by the same speaker); *Clouds* 914-920bis (three instances of turn-initial δέ γε/δέ... γε); *Knights* 363-365 (three instances of turn-initial δέ γε/δέ... γε), 1154-1156 (two instances of turn-initial δέ γε/δέ... γε); *Wealth* 164-168 (seven instances of δέ γε/δέ... γε, here not marking resonance themselves, but adding new steps); 1090-1091 (two instances of turn-initial δέ γε/δέ... γε), 1155-1159 (five instances of turn-initial ἀλλά).

turns helps to characterize her as being agitated.[119] The individual instances of γε in this excerpt are not related to resonance-marking, however, but rather demonstrate the particle's affinity for answers.[120]

§101. In the following example from Aristophanes *Lysistrata*, the relevant particle (τοιγάρ) appears only twice, but because it is used very infrequently in comedy, this single repetition is unusual enough to trigger resonance. In the scene in question, the Athenian Cinesias tries to convince his wife Myrrhine, who is participating in Lysistrata's sex strike, to come home.

(t26)

(Κι.) οὐ βαδιεῖ πάλιν;
900 Μυ. μὰ Δί' οὐκ ἔγωγ', ἢν μὴ διαλλαχθῆτέ γε
καὶ τοῦ πολέμου παύσησθε.
901bis Κι. τοιγάρ, ἢν δοκῇ,
ποιήσομεν καὶ ταῦτα.
902bis Μυ. τοιγάρ, ἢν δοκῇ,
κἄγωγ' ἄπειμ' ἐκεῖσε· νῦν δ' ἀπομώμοκα.

Aristophanes *Lysistrata* 899-903

(Ci.) Won't you come home?
My. I certainly will not, not until you men agree to a settlement and stop the war.
Ci. All right, if that's what's decided, then that's what we'll do.
My. All right, if that's what's decided, then I'll be coming home. But meanwhile I've sworn to stay here.

τοιγάρ,[121] uttered in 901 by Cinesias and in 902 by Myrrhine, occurs only three times in Aristophanes, all in this play. Therefore, as Denniston 1950:565 notes, we may consider its use by Cinesias "pompous," which is then "mockingly" picked up by Myrrhine in her reply. Of course, in this case the whole clause τοιγάρ ἢν δοκῇ is repeated, not just the particle τοιγάρ; yet it is clear that the particle is not excluded from such mocking echoes.

§102. Besides being part of a larger repeated expression, particles may also participate in resonance by sounding like other words. We have seen an example of that in (t7) from Aeschylus *Persians*, where καί resonates with the αι-sound in the lament by

[119] See III.5 §§45-47 on γε in contexts of agitation in drama.
[120] See III.4 §62 on γε in answers in drama.
[121] As for the function of τοιγάρ, Hartung 1833:354 and Bäumlein 1861:253-254 describe it as marking a decisive or natural conclusion from the preceding.

Xerxes and the chorus. Similarly, τε in *Libation Bearers* 381 can be seen as part of the large number of words resonating with πάτερ, listed in Table 1 above.

3.4 Conclusions

§103. This chapter has argued that resonance is an important communicative strategy in Greek drama, and that the study of resonance is useful for our understanding of particles. Past observations on the use of repetition in tragedy and comedy have laid the groundwork for examining how resonance works in these texts. By examining relevant passages through the lens of this concept, the different functions of resonance were identified more clearly, as well as the different forms it takes. Employing the concept of resonance as a research tool for investigating other genres will likewise be useful. It is in the first place illuminating for texts that represent utterances by several speakers; in less dialogic texts, criteria will be needed to determine when a new segment is sufficiently different from the preceding discourse to be compared to what would be a new turn in a dialogue.

§104. With regard to the functions of resonance, one can distinguish between goals of the speaking character, and goals of the playwright. The fact that both of these levels are continually present is an important difference between the communication found in literary drama and daily conversation. Speaking characters may pick up elements from previous utterances in order to emphasize their solidarity with the other speaker and his actions. Or, in other contexts, they highlight similarities across turns precisely to stress differences between what they want to say and what was said before. Playwrights may highlight linguistic echoes in order to stress a play's theme, to depict characters' personalities or characterize their interactions, or to make jokes or parody.

§105. Resonance is triggered by similarities on several linguistic levels. Examples have been given of lexical, phonological, syntactic, morphological, semantic, pragmatic, and illocutionary resonance triggers. Usually similarities work on several levels at the same time, regardless of the function of the resonance.

§106. Focusing on the use of resonance has thrown light on the use of particles and particle combinations. They play a role in this process in two different ways. First, they indicate the way in which a speaker is using resonance. The focus here has been on γε, δέ γε/δέ... γε, δῆτα, καί, and γάρ; other particles have similar uses as well. It is, however, important to keep in mind that marking a certain use of resonance is in no way the only function of a particle, not even in its turn-initial position. Not every utterance triggers resonance, and resonance is certainly not a prerequisite for the use of particles. Second, particles sometimes trigger resonance themselves, when they are repeated often enough to draw attention to their own recurrence. Whether or not a particle (combination) may trigger resonance or not depends on its usual frequency: for a highly infrequent particle two occurrences in quick succession may already be striking (see (t26) with discussion).

§107. There is no need to postulate new general functions for particles in order to describe what they do in resonance contexts; rather, resonance deepens what we already know about the functions that different particles serve. For example, the particle handbooks describe γε as indicating that a specific element from a previous statement is being singled out, or γάρ as signaling a causal relation. If we combine this general knowledge about a particle's function with the observation that a speaker consciously picks something up from a previous turn of speaking, we see the two strategies interacting: we then understand *why* the speaker singles a certain element out, or *why* she indicates a causal relation in a certain context. That is, she wants to engage with a previous piece of discourse in a specific way, in order to achieve a certain pragmatic goal. These specific resonance-marking functions of γε, γάρ, and καί can only work in a dialogic context of speakers interacting with each other. Similarly, the interpretation of the particle combination δέ γε/δέ... γε is different in resonating turns of speaking (juxtaposing a hostile new step) than in ones that do not resonate with the directly preceding utterance (adding a new step to the speaker's own previous words). As for δῆτα, the particle handbooks claim that in assertions it signals agreement; the very word "agreement" implies dialogicality, since a speaker can only agree *with* someone or something else.

§108. Thus, the Du Boisian concept of resonance enables us to understand better why a certain function for a given particle works well in a certain context, and how this function interacts with the highlighting of similarities across utterances. The dialogic interaction becomes clearer. In this way we can better understand that particle use should be considered a communicative strategy, one that interacts with the communicative strategy known as resonance.

III.4

Speaking in Turns

Conversation Analysis

4.1 Introduction

4.1.1 Tragic and comic conversation

§1. Characters in tragedy and comedy talk in turns. Aeschylus' Persian queen and the ghost of Darius converse about the army's defeat through a series of questions and answers. Sophocles' Oedipus gets angrier at Teiresias with every line he utters. Medea and Jason in Euripides' play express their feelings both in long argumentative speeches and in more rapid dialogues. In Aristophanes, characters regularly interrupt each other with short comments. Characters advance the plot in their spoken interactions by asking questions, giving orders, expressing opinions, and so on.[1]

§2. This turn-taking is one of tragedies' and comedies' formal aspects that distinguishes the genres from most other Greek texts: dramatic texts directly reflect the voices of different speakers who were physically co-present in a theatre, communicating with each other in real time. The dialogic nature of plays influences the use of particles, as argued in this chapter. It is fruitful, therefore, to approach particle use in these texts through a framework that deals with the functioning of dialogic interaction: Conversation Analysis (CA).

§3. Naturally the dialogues of Greek drama are stylized and formalized versions of real spoken conversation, but since they are ultimately based on spoken language, we may reasonably assume that these texts contain remnants of the rules of real conversation. CA can teach us something about these rules. The difference between our material and that of most CA research—written texts rather than recorded spontaneous conversation—means that our goals are accordingly different: we do not aim to understand conversation in general by looking at ancient drama texts. Rather, insights from CA, based on real conversation, can clarify the language used in these plays.

1 The importance of dialogue is not the same in every play, however. The plot of Aeschylus *Persians*, notably, is carried less by dialogue, and more by song, narration, and lamentation.

§4. Recent scholarship has begun to apply CA methods to the study of ancient Greek literature: Minchin 2007 on Homer, and Van Emde Boas 2010 and 2017b and Schuren 2015, all on Euripides, make use of the framework.[2] Minchin mainly focuses on how linguistic forms are linked to certain social actions, such as rebuking, declining an invitation, and asking a (specific kind of) question. She also discusses aspects of turn-taking in Homer. Van Emde Boas uses CA alongside several other modern linguistic approaches in his analysis of Euripides *Electra*. He argues that the characters' linguistic patterns play an important role in their characterization. Furthermore, he discusses how approaches such as CA can help in the case of textual problems, particularly concerning speaker-line attribution. Schuren applies a broad pragmatic framework, including insights from CA as well as speech-act theory, as well as narratology, in her monograph on Euripidean stichomythia. She focuses in particular on turn-taking, social deixis, and storytelling. These three scholars observe, by adopting a CA perspective, phenomena that would otherwise go unnoticed or remain unexplained. At the same time, they strengthen our awareness of the general similarities between our own everyday conversation and the language use in ancient literature: the same communicative principles are often at work. As Van Emde Boas (2010:8) rightly points out, "for dramatic dialogue to be comprehensible to an audience, it still must use the same linguistic resources that are familiar to them from their own daily conversations."[3]

§5. Earlier remarks on the structure of conversations in ancient Greek drama can be found in Hancock 1917 on stichomythia in different genres, Gelzer 1960 on the Aristophanic agon, Ireland 1974 on Aeschylean stichomythia, Bain 1977 on asides, Mastronarde 1979 on tragic dialogue, and Dover 1987a on language and character in Aristophanes, among others. However, CA raises, and provides answers for, a number of important questions which these scholars have not addressed, and which still require systematic analysis. Indeed Mastronarde 1979 assumes that real conversation is simply a "chaos" without any regularity.[4] Yet CA has shown that conversation in fact exhibits a

2 Schuren builds on a limited number of CA references, apparently ignoring any works published after 1996. Beck 2005 in *Homeric Conversation* also mentions the approach of CA (but only briefly; esp. 20-21). She is mainly concerned with aesthetic and poetic effects of Homeric conversation types: these are different issues from those normally discussed in CA.

3 See also Schuren 2015:5 on the necessary similarity between Euripidean stichomythia and real conversation: "stichomythia is a dramatic representation of conversation just as tragedy in general represents lived experience, and similarity between the two spheres is a necessary prerequisite for dramatic effect on the audience." On the usefulness of analyzing fictional discourse in general from a CA perspective, see e.g. McHoul 1987 and, more generally linguistic, Dynel 2011. Dynel argues (p. 56) that "[f]ictional discourse is not strange and should not be treated as if it were." For a CA study comparing spontaneous speech and dramatic dialogue (in performance), see Hafez 1991 on Egyptian Arabic.

4 Mastronarde 1979:1 writes of "the naturalistic disorder of spontaneous conversation, with its repetitions, dead-ends, misunderstandings, and unheralded transitions"; at page 5: "the disordered brokenness of real conversation." 52: "It is characteristic of real, informal conversation that more than one person may speak at once, that a speaker may fall silent in

great deal of systematic organization, a view supported in the Greek by the recurrence of certain forms in certain turn positions and sequential positions. The framework thus has the potential to offer important explanations about these recurrences.

§6. This chapter uses the CA approach to show that conversational structures and practices influence language production in tragic and comic dialogues, and thus also the selection and use of particles. I begin by introducing CA, its terminology and its various aspects. Textual analysis follows, mainly focused on the dialogic parts of the plays,[5] the communicative environment that CA has the most to say about.

4.1.2 Conversation Analysis (CA)

§7. CA focuses on talk-in-interaction, that is, on language used for performing social actions.[6] The approach originated in sociology, with Sacks' lectures on conversation (1964-1968),[7] Schegloff's work on conversational openings (1967; 1968), and, most well-known, the seminal article by Sacks, Schegloff, and Jefferson 1974 on the systematics of turn-taking in conversation. Further explorations along these lines followed.[8] Conversation analysts aim to describe and understand the system, rules, and practices of talk-in-interaction. They emphasize that we can better understand utterances if we pay attention to what they are *doing* rather than to what they are about.[9] Here CA builds on Austin's 1962 claim that words do things: utterances do not merely describe the world, but perform actions.[10]

§8. The basic unit of conversation is the "turn," also called "turn of speaking," or "turn-at-talk." Conversation, like other forms of coordinated, joint activities, requires some kind of turn-taking to manage the contributions of the different participants.[11] Examples of such joint activities, noted by Sidnell 2010:36, are ballroom dancing, road work, and open heart surgery. Clark 1996:59 also gives analogous examples of other

mid-sentence, and that speaker B may begin to speak in the middle of A's utterance. Theater-dialogue, in most traditions, dispenses with much of the chaos of real conversation in the interests of clarity." 73: "the chaotic informality of real conversation."

5 Long monologues and especially choral songs form a very different discourse situation from rapid dialogues: see III.2 on discourse patterns for linguistic differences across these three situations in tragedy and comedy.

6 See also I.3 on approaches to particles and discourse markers.

7 Posthumously published as Sacks 1995.

8 CA has grown into a widely practiced research field; helpful recent introductions can be found in Schegloff 2007 and Sidnell 2010, and in shorter form in Gardner 2005 and Heritage 2010.

9 See e.g. Schegloff 2007:1; Sidnell 2010:60-61.

10 The joint-action approach to language described by Clark 1996 is similar to CA, although the scholar does not directly work within a CA framework. On 341-342 he underlines the importance of action over topic. Interactional Linguistics also resembles CA (see e.g. Selting and Couper-Kuhlen [eds.] 2001); this is a research field combining linguistics, Conversation Analysis, and anthropology.

11 See e.g. Schegloff 2007:1.

non-verbal joint actions, such as playing music or paddling a canoe; as well as of different activities involving talk as part of them, such as a business transaction. In the case of conversation, participants take turns-at-talk. These turns are themselves composed of one or more turn-constructional units (TCUs), the smallest units that may constitute a turn.[12]

§9. The word "turn," as I use it here, refers to the linguistic realization of actions, that is, to a string of words uttered by one speaker, rather than to the action(s) performed by these words.[13] In my use "turn" is equivalent to "utterance"; these two terms only differ in the perspective they offer.[14] "Utterance" neutrally refers to everything that is said by one speaker until she stops talking; "turn" refers to the positioning of a stretch of talk by one speaker with respect to other stretches of talk by other speakers.[15] Consider the following example:

(t1)

Θεράπων. Δικαιόπολι.
959bis[16] Δι. τίς[17] ἐστι; τί με βωστρεῖς;
959ter Θε. ὅ τι;
ἐκέλευε Λάμαχός σε ταυτησὶ δραχμῆς
εἰς τοὺς Χοᾶς αὐτῷ μεταδοῦναι τῶν κιχλῶν,
τριῶν δραχμῶν δ' ἐκέλευε Κωπᾷδ' ἔγχελυν.

Aristophanes *Acharnians* 959-962

[12] On TCUs, see e.g. Sacks, Schegloff, and Jefferson 1974:702; Schegloff 1987:77; 2006:79; 2007:3-7; Sidnell 2010:41-42, 113.

[13] The possible confusion concerning "turn" as referring to actions, or as referring to the linguistic realizations of actions, arises mainly from the different use of "turn" and "turn beginning." A "turn beginning" is not just the beginning of any "turn," but a specific action. See e.g. Schegloff 1987:74 and 1996:74-75 for formulations indicating that "turn beginning" refers to an action. See e.g. Levinson 2013:126; Sacks, Schegloff, and Jefferson 1974:702-703; Schegloff 1987:77; 2007:4 for uses of the term "turn" as referring to the linguistic realization of an action. In order to avoid confusion, I will not use the term "turn beginning" at all, but speak instead of "turn-initial position," or "utterance starts," both referring to the *linguistic realization of* actions. I thank Geoffrey Raymond for clarifying this point with me (personal communication).

[14] See e.g. the terminology of Kent 2012:719: she writes that a certain "utterance performs a number of actions." Like a "turn," an "utterance" *is* not an action, it *performs* actions.

[15] A choral song, then, is technically one utterance and one turn, unless it is interrupted by speech of another character; however, the conversational regularities of turn-taking, sequence organization, and preference organization are less relevant in this communicative environment than in the iambic parts of the plays. Therefore I do not discuss choral songs in this chapter. See III.2 for several discussions of particle use in choral songs, e.g. in §§24-25, §37, §§41-42, §44, §§88-89.

[16] "Bis" and "ter" are designations drawn from the *TLG*, where *bis* indicates the second turn of speaking within the same line, *ter* the third, and so on.

[17] Van Leeuwen 1901 and Olson 2002 read τί, a conjecture by Elmsley; they claim that a hiatus is allowed after τί. Although this choice changes the meaning of the question, it is not relevant for my illustration here.

> Slave. Dicaeopolis!
> Di. Who's that? Why are you yelling for me?
> Sl. Why? Lamachus orders you, for this drachma here, to give him some of your thrushes for the Pitcher feast, and he orders a Copaic eel for three drachmas.

The first turn (or, more neutrally, utterance) by the slave is only one word long: its function is to address Dicaeopolis and catch his attention.[18] Dicaeopolis reacts immediately, starting a turn in the middle of the verse.[19] This turn performs two related requests for information: who the speaker is (or what is going on; see note 17), and why he addressed Dicaeopolis. To respond to these requests, the slave needs a longer turn (slightly more than three lines), built out of several parts or TCUs. With the first TCU, ὅ τι; "(you ask me) why?", he projects a relatively long answer.[20] Subsequently, he reports Lamachus' two orders, in this way indirectly ordering Dicaeopolis to provide the requested items. We can interpret the projection and the two reports as three separate actions. Regardless of the number of actions performed by a turn, however, I speak of one turn when it is continuously uttered by one speaker.[21]

§10. An important part of a turn is its start: the start frequently gives indications as to how a turn fits into a sequence or a series of sequences.[22] Turn-initial items also often project what kind of turn the speaker has just started: they foreshadow a certain syntax and/or a certain action.[23] As Sidnell 2010:143 puts it, "the initial components of a turn can strongly project the type of turn underway." The role of Greek particles in a conversational structure is therefore most visible when they occur in turn-initial position. For this reason my discussion in this chapter focuses mainly on turn-initial particles.

§11. I define turn-initial particles as the first particle occurring in its earliest possible position in the first discourse act of a turn.[24] For second-position particles (in the classical sense), I will still speak of turn-initial position when they are found directly

18 Similar one-word vocative turns with similar reactions in Aristophanes may be found in *Acharnians* 410, 1048, 1085; *Frogs* 40, 464, 1220; *Women at the Thesmophoria* 193. See also below, §41, on οὗτος as a vocative construction.

19 This short sequence of two turns may be described as a summons-answer pair. See below, §15, on adjacency pairs, and §41 for another example from Aristophanes.

20 See my discussion of (t6) in §30 below on such echo questions at the beginning of answers. See note 23 below for the notion of (pragmatic) projection.

21 See Aristophanes *Acharnians* 607bis-617: the addressees of Dicaeopolis (members of the Acharnian chorus) reportedly shake their heads during the course of uttering these lines; yet since the Acharnians do not give a verbal reaction, the lines still count together as one turn.

22 On (the importance of) the start of turns, see e.g. Schegloff 1987; 1996; Sidnell 2010:140-152.

23 On projection, see Auer 2002:*passim*; Schegloff 2007:e.g. 30, 44-47, 127-128; Sidnell 2007:235 (projectability "allows participants to anticipate the probable course, extent, and nature of the talk in progress"); 2010:e.g. 143; 232-233; Pekarek Doehler 2011a; and II.2 §§49-50.

24 On discourse acts, see below, §20, and especially II.2.

after the first constituent of a turn. Thus, for instance, the "postponed" δέ in Aeschylus *Persians* 719 (see (t8) with note 68) is considered turn-initial, but for example particles occurring in the discourse act after the one constituted by a vocative are not.[25] If a turn starts with a swearing expression in Aristophanes, a particle following that is not considered turn-initial, because swearing expressions can constitute separate discourse acts, just as vocatives and interjections do; for example, καὶ μήν after νὴ τὸν Δία in Aristophanes *Frogs* 285 is therefore not considered turn-initial. However, since establishing the start and end of discourse acts involves interpretation, the determination of a particle's turn-initial position can be subjective. The chapter focuses on the clearest instances of turn-initial particles.[26]

§12. Most turns without turn-initial particles are explicitly connected to their co-text and context by other turn-initial expressions. I call these expressions "contextualization cues," a term coined by Cook-Gumperz and Gumperz,[27] and I include the following forms apart from particles. First, a turn is immediately situated if it starts with a reference to the speaker or addressee(s), which can be realized by first- or second-person verb forms, vocatives, and pronouns. Second, subordinating conjunctions and demonstrative pronouns and adverbs also make it clear at the outset how a new turn is responding to the preceding one. Third, lexical repetitions of an element from the preceding turn clarify the response's focus. Fourth, primary interjections and (only in comedy) swearing expressions indicate a reaction to a previous turn or nonverbal action.[28] Fifth, turn-initial question words and negations usually project part of the nature of the new turn. We will see below that turns without turn-initial particles or any of these other turn-initial contextualization cues tend to be found in particular contexts, and that the conversational structure is crucial for situating these turns.[29]

§13. One area of research in CA is how turn-taking is organized, that is, when exactly speakers start and end their turns. Sacks, Schegloff, and Jefferson 1974 show that usually one party talks at a time; pauses and overlaps in talk tend to be brief. Participants in

25 An exception is Aristophanes *Frogs* 300, where the vocative is used in a "quotative" way: the speaker comments on his own use of this vocative with the following particle τοίνυν; it is therefore part of the first discourse act of this turn, it could not have occurred earlier in the turn, and it is considered turn-initial.

26 E.g. γε in μὴ σοί γέ in Sophocles *Ajax* 533 is not counted as turn-initial, because its theoretical first possible position would be directly after μή.

27 See Cook-Gumperz and Gumperz 1976, and the discussion by Auer 1992. Auer defines (p. 24) contextualization cues as "all the form-related means by which participants contextualize language." His discussion includes non-verbal and paralinguistic cues. I use the term here only for linguistic expressions. See this chapter's appendix for the numerical frequencies of the different turn-initial contextualization cues in the twelve plays of my corpus.

28 On the difference between primary and secondary interjections, see e.g. Norrick 2009a. Aristophanic swearing expressions can be considered secondary interjections. On the use of primary interjections in Greek drama, see Nordgren 2015.

29 See §42, §48, and §§62-66.

an interaction monitor when there is a "transition relevance place" (TRP) in a turn of speaking, and pay attention to these TRPs in their conversational behavior.[30] Speakers make sure, for example, to leave no pause at a TRP if they want to hold the floor. Listeners tend to start a new turn exactly at the moment of a TRP, such as when a syntactic unit is complete. In English this means, for example, that tag questions are relatively frequently overlapped by the first part of a new turn. In the formalized speech of Greek drama, the end of a verse line is typically a TRP.

§14. CA has also developed the study of what it calls "sequence organization." Sequences are "courses of action implemented through talk."[31] For example, a sequence may consist of one speaker asking a question or requesting a certain action, and another speaker's response. The organization of sequences involves "the ways in which turns-at-talk are ordered and combined to make actions take place in conversation."[32] Research on sequence organization looks at how speakers make their turns coherent with prior turns.[33] This research thus focuses on the specific actions performed by turns, and the structuring of those actions, rather than the moments at which turns may start or end.

§15. Crucially, sequences are built around "adjacency pairs." An adjacency pair is a unit of two turns by different speakers that are placed next to each other, are relatively ordered, and are of the same pair type.[34] That is, the order of the two turns matters, and the actions they perform belong together. The first turn, called the "first pair part," makes only certain responses relevant; this second turn is termed "second pair part." Some examples of adjacency pairs are greeting-greeting, question-answer, assessment-(dis)agreement, offer-acceptance/rejection. If the expected second pair part is absent, this is an "official absence" for the participants. Speakers often indicate in their response that they notice this absence, as in this example from Aristophanes:

(t2)

120 (Δη.) ὢ λόγια. δός μοι, δὸς τὸ ποτήριον ταχύ.
Νι. ἰδού. τί φησ' ὁ χρησμός;
121bis Δη. ἑτέραν ἔγχεον.
Νι. ἐν τοῖς λογίοις ἔνεστιν "ἑτέραν ἔγχεον;"

Aristophanes *Knights* 120-122

(first slave reads oracles, second slave pours wine)
Fi. What prophecies! Give me the cup, give it here quickly!

30 On TRPs, see also Clayman 2013.

31 Schegloff 2007:3.

32 Schegloff 2007:i.

33 See e.g. Schegloff 2007:xiv.

34 On adjacency pairs, see e.g. Schegloff 2007:13-14; Sidnell 2010:63-66. The concept is also explained by Van Emde Boas 2010:13-14.

Se. Here. What's the oracle say?
Fi. Pour me a refill!
Se. The prophecies say "pour me a refill"?

The second slave's question in 121 is the first part of an adjacency pair; an answer to it is the expected second pair part. The first slave does not answer the question, however, but instead orders his friend to pour him another glass of wine. But since, in general, answers are normatively expected[35] after questions, the second slave takes the order as an answer—the oracle says, "pour me a refill"—or pretends to do so for the sake of the joke.

§16. Although a sequence in principle consists of a single adjacency pair, the pair can also be expanded by other pairs placed before, after, or in between it. These other pairs are called pre-, insert, and post-expansions:

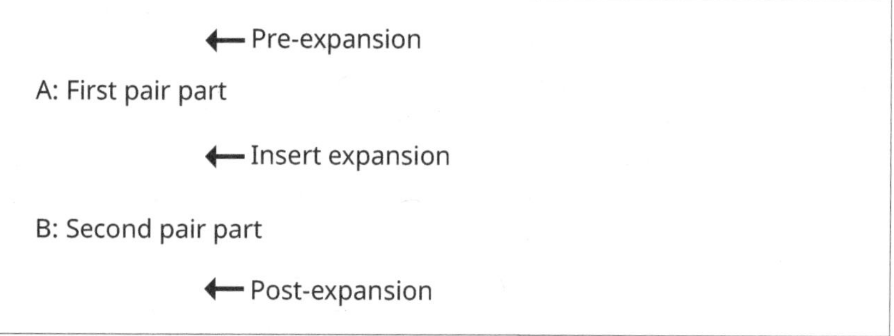

Figure 1: An adjacency pair with possible expansions, from Schegloff 2007:26

Which turns are considered the base pair and whether other turns are seen as expansions on it depends on one's interpretation of the whole sequence. In the case of our ancient plays, we can of course rely only on indications in the texts, as we do not have access to nonverbal cues such as pauses, intonation, or gestures. In addition, the expansions themselves may be subject to further expansions, which can lead to highly complex sequences.

§17. Pre-expansions, as Sidnell 2010:103 puts it, "are recognizably preliminary to some other action whose production they project." For example, a question about availability typically precedes an invitation sequence. An insertion sequence delays the second pair part to deal with issues that need to be resolved before the second pair part can be produced. Such insert expansion may occur, for example, because a participant has misunderstood the first pair part.[36] Finally, a post-sequence expands on the base sequence after the second pair part. Post-expansions can be "sequence-closing thirds,"

[35] On normative constraints in CA, at least for English, see e.g. Schegloff 2007:67n5, 203; Hayashi 2013:*passim*.

[36] On insert expansions, see e.g. Schegloff 2007:97-114.

with which the speaker intends to close a sequence.[37] Common forms of sequence-closing thirds in English are *oh*, *okay*, and assessments, as in the following excerpt. It starts with person A asking his friends B and C, who are a couple, a question.

(t3)

A: So how are you people?	⟵ FPP: question
B: We're fine.	⟵ SPP: answer
C: No complaints.	⟵ SPP: answer
A: Good.	⟵ post-expansion: assessment
So listen, are you, uh, this thing is still off?	⟵ new FPP: question

Example of a post-expansion from Schegloff 2007:125
(simplified, and explanations added)

Schegloff 2007:124-125 points out that the assessment "good" by speaker A function as a sequence-closing third. After uttering this post-expansion, speaker A launches a new sequence with "so listen...".

§18. Adjacency pairs are also structured according to what is known as a "preference organization." Usually a certain type of second pair part is interactionally preferred over some other type, namely the kind of response that "promotes the accomplishment of the activity underway."[38] For example, an acceptance is a "preferred response" to an invitation, a rejection a "dispreferred" one. Note that this is a structural, interactional preference that speakers orient to and that deals with normative expectations; it is independent from the speaker's actual, psychological preference. (A speaker may, after all, be relieved if her invitation is rejected.) As part of preference organization, dispreferred responses are marked, both in form and in delivery. They often contain explanations about why they are produced, for example why an offer is declined or a request refused. As Levinson 2006:48 writes, "[r]esponses that are in the expected direction are immediate and brief, responses that are in the opposite direction are typically delayed, marked with hesitations and particles like *well*,[39] and accompanied by explanations."

37 On sequence-closing thirds, see e.g. Schegloff 2007:118-142.

38 On preference organization, see e.g. Pomerantz 1984; Schegloff 2007:58-81; Sidnell 2010:77 (from which the quote is taken).

39 This is not meant to imply that marking a dispreferred response is the only function of English *well*. See I.3 §§21-23 for a discussion of a number of *well* instances. See below, §55, as well as II.2 §§59-60 for a use of turn-initial μέν comparable to that of turn-initial *well*.

§19. Finally, CA scholars stress that turns perform actions. The term "action," used in CA, is different from the term "(discourse) act" used in Discourse Analysis. The two concepts are not mutually exclusive; rather, the terms reflect different perspectives on the same idea, that language is used for doing things.

§20. A discourse "act," on the one hand, is viewed in relation to the surrounding whole: an act is a small step within a larger discourse.[40] Each act has a certain function contributing to the main goal of the discourse. Acts are often described as prosodic or orthographic units.[41] Much research on such acts looks at which segments of discourse can be said to form a small step, and where these segments start and end.[42] Thus, in (t3) above, the second turn by speaker A, "Good. So listen, are you, uh, this thing is still off?", could be described as consisting of five acts, based on its prosodic realization as reflected in the punctuation of the transcription. In written language, act boundaries manifest themselves through certain linguistic indications; particles constitute one set of important signs in Greek.[43] The concept in CA which is closest to the discourse act is the turn-constructional unit (TCU).[44]

§21. "Action" in CA, on the other hand, focuses on what the speaker wants to accomplish in a social situation: actions are "things that people do in their talking in interaction."[45] Sidnell and Enfield 2012:328 list "requesting, inviting, offering, complaining, excusing, agreeing, and disagreeing" as examples of what they consider actions. As Levinson 2013:104 points out, the assignment of a certain action to a turn tends to be revealed by the response of a next speaker. Accordingly, Levinson considers the primary action performed by a turn to be "what the response must deal with in order to count as an adequate next turn" (107). To put it in more general terms, an action needs to be something recognizable to the participants, an identifiable communicative doing, for which they hold the speaker accountable.[46] Note that "action" does not refer to the words and nonverbal signs used to accomplish communicative goals, but rather to the thing accomplished itself—the invitation, the summoning, the questioning, and so on. Thus CA scholars are more interested in understanding what a turn or part of a turn is doing in a social situation than they are in identifying the boundaries of an action's realization in words.

40 On acts, see II.2, especially §§9-20, with further literature.

41 E.g. by Hannay and Kroon 2005; see II.2 (especially §20) and IV.3 (especially §§71-72) for discussion.

42 See e.g. the discourse segmentation in acts of passages from Herodotus and Thucydides, as proposed in IV.5.

43 See II.2 *passim* and IV.3 §§57-64.

44 See above, §8.

45 Schegloff 2006:73. On actions in CA, see also e.g. Schegloff 2007:xiv; Sidnell 2010:61.

46 Accountability of actions means that they are observable and reportable by other people, who can put responsibility on the speaker for her actions. See Garfinkel 1967:1, 33-34; and more recently Auer 2002:4; Firth 2009:68.

§22. We can combine the two concepts to say that (discourse) acts perform (social) actions—short segments of talk, alone or in groups, perform questions, invitations, summonings, and so on. Actions can be realized in single acts—such as a vocative, which performs the action of addressing someone—as well as in multi-act moves—such as a series of acts performing an invitation.[47] In what follows I will use both terms in the way described above: "act" will refer to short stretches of discourse, which have an arguable start and end, and "action" to the social doings performed by talk.

§23. To sum up: this section has sketched the main concepts that CA scholars use to describe how people interact by means of turns-at-talk. We can now move on to the application of those concepts to the study of particle use in Greek drama.

4.1.3 Applying CA to particles in tragedy and comedy

§24. Greek particles often signal something on a conversational-structural level, in the process of performing other functions, such as signaling contrast between entities or marking discourse boundaries. CA therefore enriches our understanding of particles. Examining the role that particles play in the organization of turns, sequences, preference, and action helps us understand why and how particles are used in the contexts in which they are used.

§25. This chapter applies four concepts of CA: turn-taking organization (§§26-31), sequence organization (§§32-48), preference organization (§§49-56), and the actions performed by turns (§§57-70). The main focus is on question-answer pairs, because they appear frequently in the corpus and are clearly recognizable as pairs. That is to say, a question as a first pair part sets up strong expectations about the relevant second pair part: the norm is that this second part is an answer (see (t2)). These sections are followed by concluding remarks on what we can learn from CA about ancient Greek particle use (§§71-72), and an appendix with quantitative observations on turn-taking and on turn-initial expressions in the corpus (§§73-75).

4.2 Turn-Taking

§26. This section looks at the interaction between turn-taking organization and particle use. Particles play a role in the turn-taking process by indicating the speaker's lack of acknowledgement of a previous turn (τε), or by helping her hold the floor for a turn of multiple lines (μέν).

§27. The following passage from Euripides *Hippolytus* illustrates the use of turn-initial τε. In this scene Phaedra is suffering heavily from being in love with her stepson; her nurse, unaware that Phaedra is lovesick, tries to find out the cause of Phaedra's

[47] On moves, see II.3 *passim*; IV.3 §§92-146; IV.5 *passim*.

illness. Finally Phaedra consents to the questioning, and starts to give hints about her trouble.

(t4)

Τρ. σιγῷμ’ ἂν ἤδη· σὸς γὰρ οὑντεῦθεν λόγος.
Φα. ὦ τλῆμον, οἷον, μῆτερ, ἠράσθης ἔρον.
Τρ. ὃν ἔσχε ταύρου, τέκνον; ἢ τί φῂς τόδε;
Φα. σύ τ’, ὦ τάλαιν’ ὅμαιμε, Διονύσου δάμαρ.
Τρ. τέκνον, τί πάσχεις; συγγόνους κακορροθεῖς;
Φα. τρίτη δ’[48] ἐγὼ δύστηνος ὡς ἀπόλλυμαι.
Τρ. ἔκ τοι πέπληγμαι· ποῖ προβήσεται λόγος;

Euripides *Hippolytus* 336-342

Nu. I’m silent now. The word henceforth is yours.
Ph. Unhappy mother, what a love you felt!
Nu. For the Cretan bull? Or what is this you mean?
Ph. And you, poor sister, Dionysus’ bride.
Nu. What’s wrong with you, daughter? Why defame your kin?
Ph. And I the third, how wretchedly I perish!
Nu. I am astonished. Where will these words lead?

In 339, we find τε in the first act of Phaedra’s turn. The particle marks that she continues her own previous turn, in this case by adding another vocative. She thus does not answer the nurse’s question of 338. Indeed, Phaedra’s σύ does not refer to the nurse, her interlocutor present on stage. When τε occurs in turn-initial position, the speaker is ignoring (or pretending to ignore) the turn just uttered by the interlocutor—in other words, the speaker is continuing her own previous turn.[49] The particle is however infrequent in this position.[50]

[48] For discussion of turn-initial δέ, see §§34-38 below.

[49] The other instances of turn-initial τε in this function are found in Aeschylus *Libation Bearers* 494; *Persians* 1020; Euripides *Bacchae* 497; Aristophanes *Birds* 599, 1591; *Frogs* 809, 956; *Lysistrata* 35. Similar instances outside my core corpus are found in Sophocles *Oedipus at Colonus* 221; Euripides *Hecuba* 428. This reading is further supported by the fact that in historiography τε may convey continuation as well, by expressing a tight link with the previous conjunct, or by marking the similarity of parallel entries in lists. See IV.2 §§78-84.

[50] There are only thirteen instances out of 4,402 turns in the corpus (see this chapter’s appendix for quantitative observations on turn-initial expressions). The low frequency of τε in turn-initial position is also noted by Hancock 1917:26. Apart from the turn-initial τε quoted in (t4) and the eight parallels mentioned in the previous note, three cases involve a construction with several particles starting with τε; these constructions have a turn-internal function, and thus are irrelevant for turn-taking organization: τε δὴ καί in Aeschylus *Persians* 735, τε... καί in Euripides

§28. In multi-line turns, we can often identify certain expressions that help these speakers hold the floor beyond the TRPs[51] constituted by line-ends. The particle μέν is one of these floor-holding devices. Because this particle's function is to project upcoming discourse acts,[52] it can effectively signal that the speaker wants to hold the floor for some time.[53] At the same time, μέν carries out its general projecting function, marking for example an upcoming change in addressee[54] or a juxtaposition of several items (with δέ following).[55]

§29. The following passage from Aeschylus *Libation Bearers* features this floor-holding use of μέν: the particle suggests that Electra's turn will not be over after one line.[56]

(t5)

160 (Χο.) ἴτω τις δορυσθενὴς ἀνὴρ
ἀναλυτὴρ δόμων †Σκυθιτά τ' ἐν χεροῖν
παλίντον' ἐν ἔργωι† βέλη 'πιπάλλων Ἄρης
σχέδιά τ' αὐτόκωπα νωμῶν ξίφη.
164[57] Ηλ. ἔχει <u>μὲν</u> ἤδη γαπότους χοὰς πατήρ·
166 νέου δὲ μύθου τοῦδε κοινωνήσατε.
Χο. λέγοις ἄν· ὀρχεῖται δὲ καρδία φόβωι.
Ηλ. ὁρῶ τομαῖον τόνδε βόστρυχον τάφωι.

Aeschylus *Libation Bearers* 160-168

Bacchae 935, and τε… τε in Aristophanes *Lysistrata* 1036ter. Similar examples from outside my core corpus are τε… καί in Sophocles *Philoctetes* 119; τε… τε in Sophocles *Oedipus at Colonus* 1514. For the projecting function of τε in such constructions, see IV.2 §§80-84. The last instance, in Aristophanes *Frogs* 1402, is in a quotation from tragedy. It is unknown whether this line was at the start of a turn in the original play (Euripides *Meleager*), since we only have fragments of it. The presence of τε as well as the narrative content of the line suggest that it is unlikely to have been turn-initial.

51 See §13 above for the term TRP.

52 For discussion of this function of μέν, see II.2 §§46-62.

53 Compare the use of "projector constructions" in spoken French, e.g. "je veux dire" (roughly "I mean"), as floor-holding devices, discussed by Pekarek Doehler 2011a.
When the expectation of floor-holding raised by μέν is not fulfilled, the presence of μέν suggests that there is something more that remains unsaid. Examples include Aeschylus *Eumenides* 418, *Suppliant Women* 338; Sophocles *Ajax* 80; Euripides *Medea* 703. See II.2 §60 for discussion of this function of μέν.

54 E.g. Sophocles *Antigone* 444 (σὺ μέν; σὺ δ' follows).

55 E.g. Sophocles *Antigone* 561 (τὴν μέν; τὴν δ' follows), 1100 (μέν with imperative; δέ with imperative follows); *Philoctetes* 123 (σὺ μέν; ἐγὼ δέ follows).

56 Other examples of μέν (not necessarily turn-initial) as a floor-holding device include Aeschylus *Agamemnon* 264; Sophocles *Ajax* 121, *Antigone* 223, 444, 561, 1100; *Oedipus King* 927; *Philoctetes* 123, 453, 981bis; Euripides *Bacchae* 775, 787; *Hippolytus* 695, 1257; Aristophanes *Acharnians* 608; *Birds* 76; *Wasps* 650.

57 Blass 1906, Garvie 1986, Groeneboom 1949, Murray 1955 [1937], Page 1972, and West 1990 all follow Hermann in moving line 165 (an invocation of Hermes) to after 123.

> (Ch.) Oh, if only there would come a man, mighty with the spear, to set the house free again, brandishing in his hands Scythian weapons in the work of war and wielding a sword, of one piece with its hilt, for close fighting!
> El. Now my father has the drink-offerings—the earth has swallowed them; but here is something new about which I want to share a word with you.
> Ch. Speak on; my heart is leaping with fear.
> El. I see this cut lock of hair on the tomb.

During the preceding choral song (152-163), Electra has poured libations on Agamemnon's grave. She makes it explicit (164) that this ritual has been performed, and that her father has received the libations. However, μέν implies that this was not all she wanted to say. Within the same turn, she switches to a new action (with the act νέου δὲ μύθου τοῦδε in 166): announcing an upcoming piece of news to the chorus.[58] Subsequently, a stichomythic exchange ensues until line 180.

§30. μέν is often found together with other floor-holding markers. In this example from Aristophanes, Peisetaerus manages to speak for more than six lines in a row (164bis-170)—remarkably long in this rapid conversation, and in comedy in general.[59] μέν alone is therefore not enough as a floor-holding device in this case, but is used together with syntactic and semantic incompleteness at the ends of lines:

(t6)

(Πε.) ἦ μέγ' ἐνορῶ βούλευμ' ἐν ὀρνίθων γένει,
καὶ δύναμιν ἣ γένοιτ' ἄν, εἰ πίθοισθέ μοι.
Επ. τί σοι πιθώμεσθ';
Πε. ὅ τι πίθησθε; πρῶτα μὲν
μὴ περιπέτεσθε πανταχῇ κεχηνότες·
ὡς τοῦτ' ἄτιμον τοὔργον ἐστίν. αὐτίκα
ἐκεῖ παρ' ἡμῖν τοὺς πετομένους ἢν ἔρῃ,
"τίς ἐστιν οὗτος;" ὁ Τελέας ἐρεῖ ταδί·
"ἄνθρωπος ὄρνις ἀστάθμητος πετόμενος,
ἀτέκμαρτος, οὐδὲν οὐδέποτ' ἐν ταὐτῷ μένων."

[58] The two particles in this case do not signal a propositional juxtaposition, but a succession of two different discourse acts. Garvie 1986 ad loc. calls μὲν... δέ a "transitional formula." This implies that μέν announces the transition. On μέν at discourse transitions in Homer and Pindar, see II.2 §§52-55. On μέν at transitional points in historiography, see IV.3 §§125-146; IV.5 §32, §56, §58, and §96.

[59] See §74 in the appendix to this chapter below.

Επ. νὴ τὸν Διόνυσον εὖ γε μωμᾷ ταυταγί.

Aristophanes *Birds* 162-171

(Pe.) Oh what a grand scheme I see in the race of birds, and power that could be yours, if you take my advice!
Ho. What advice would you have us take?
Pe. What advice should you take? For a start, don't fly around with in all directions with your beaks agape; that's discreditable behavior. For example, back where we come from, if among the flighty crowd you ask, "Who's that guy?" Teleas will reply, "The man's a bird, unstable, flighty, unverifiable, never ever staying in the same spot."
Ho. By Dionysus, that's a fair criticism.

How does Peisetaerus make sure in 164bis-170 that his interlocutor, the Hoopoe, does not interrupt whenever he reaches line-ends, typical TRPs in drama? First, he repeats the Hoopoe's question in indirect form (ὅ τι;), producing the expectation that he intends to answer it elaborately.[60] At the start of this answer, and notably at the very end of the line, we find πρῶτα μέν: a strong sign that (much) more will definitely follow.[61] Then, in 166, Peisetaerus again starts a new sentence just before line-end.[62] The next line similarly ends with an incomplete subordinate clause: ἔρῃ lacks its object, and the ἥν-clause as a whole lacks a main clause.[63] At the end of 168, it is semantics rather than syntax that is incomplete: the verse-final demonstrative ταδί cannot refer to anything preceding it, so it must refer to something that follows.

§31. This section has argued that paying attention to turn-taking organization improves our understanding of linguistic forms found in tragic and comic dialogues. In particular, the use of turn-initial τε and μέν has been illuminated. In the next section, we will look at the structuring of several turns in a row.

60 Other turn-initial indirect repeats of a preceding question are found in e.g. Aristophanes *Acharnians* 595, 959ter (cited in (t1) above); *Wealth* 462ter, 465bis; *Women at the Thesmophoria* 203ter. All of these except *Acharnians* 595 occur at the end of a line, an especially strategic position for a floor-holding device, since this tends to be a TRP.

61 See Dunbar 1995 *ad loc.*: this part of Peisetaerus' proposal "is marked as preliminary." Note πρῶτον μέν in *Lysistrata* 574bis for a similar start to a long answer.

62 All editors read the full stop before αὐτίκα in line 166.

63 See Auer 2000:184-188, 2002, and 2009b on how syntax projects more to come in modern spoken languages. Other instances of incomplete syntax at line-end that help the speaker hold the floor include Sophocles *Antigone* 45 (noun lacking after adjectives); *Oedipus at Colonus* 396 (complement of verb lacking); *Women of Trachis* 739 (noun lacking after adjective); Euripides *Andromache* 885 (complement of genitive lacking); *Bacchae* 788 (main verb lacking); *Hippolytus* 1257 (main verb lacking; μέν also helps here), 1258 (main verb lacking), 1259 (main verb lacking); Aristophanes *Lysistrata* 894 (main verb lacking); *Women at the Thesmophoria* 64 (main verb lacking).

4.3 Sequence Organization

§32. Sequence organization explains how each turn responds to the previous one and points forward to further talk. Particles help indicate how a speaker intends her current turn to fit in the ongoing sequence and series of sequences. This section discusses how the concepts of (series of) adjacency pairs and pair expansions help to understand particle use. The first subsection will discuss the role of particles in series of adjacency pairs, in first pair parts, and in second pair parts. The second subsection will present observations on particle use in pre-, insert, and post-expansions.

4.3.1 Adjacency pairs and adjacency-pair series

§33. Several adjacency pairs may follow each other in a series.[64] In such series, the particle μέν may signal that the speaker intends to perform several actions that are similar to the one marked by μέν. The particle may, in other words, not only project more within a single turn (§§28-30), but also on a larger scale. A question containing a turn-initial μέν, for example, can set up the expectation of more questions:[65]

(t7)

Τρ. ὁρᾷς; φρονεῖς μὲν εὖ, φρονοῦσα δ' οὐ θέλεις
παῖδάς τ' ὀνῆσαι καὶ σὸν ἐκσῶσαι βίον.
Φα. φιλῶ τέκν'· ἄλληι δ' ἐν τύχηι χειμάζομαι.
Τρ. ἁγνὰς μέν, ὦ παῖ, χεῖρας αἵματος φορεῖς;
Φα. χεῖρες μὲν ἁγναί, φρὴν δ' ἔχει μίασμά τι.
Τρ. μῶν ἐξ ἐπακτοῦ πημονῆς ἐχθρῶν τινος;

Euripides *Hippolytus* 313-318

Nu. You see? You are in your right mind, but though you are sane,
you are not willing to benefit your sons and to save your own life.
Ph. I love my children. It is another fate that buffets me.
Nu. Your hands, may I presume, are clean of blood?
Ph. My hands are clean. It is my heart that's stained.
Nu. Not spells, I hope, launched by some enemy?

μέν in 316 does not function as a floor-holding device, because the nurse first needs an answer to her question. It is more likely signaling that the nurse is just asking the first

64 See e.g. Schegloff 2007:207-213 on sequence series in general, and Heritage and Sorjonen 1994 for an application of the concept.

65 See also Page 1938, citing Verrall 1881, on μέν (not turn-initial) in Euripides *Medea* 1129 marking the messenger's question as preliminary.

of a series of questions, as indeed she proceeds to do.[66] The particle also hints at other possible troubles, left implicit for now, from which Phaedra might be suffering.[67] This suggestion of implicit alternatives in fact helps to create the sequential expectation: that the nurse may go on with asking about those other possibilities. In contrast, the expectations raised by the two other instances of μέν in this passage (313 and 317) are fulfilled within the same turn, through the addition of a complementary δέ-act.

§34. In a series of questions and answers, turn-initial δέ is often employed to signal a new question, that is, a new first pair part within the series. Several examples are found in (t8) from a dialogue between the ghost of the Persian king Darius and queen Atossa. The queen has just told her dead husband, in a turn of six lines, that the Persian kingdom has been ruined. The dialogue then goes on as follows:

(t8)

Δα. τίνι τρόπωι; λοιμοῦ τις ἦλθε σκηπτὸς ἢ στάσις πόλει;
Βα. οὐδαμῶς, ἀλλ' ἀμφ' Ἀθήνας πᾶς κατέφθαρται στρατός.
Δα. τίς δ' ἐμῶν ἐκεῖσε παίδων ἐστρατηλάτει, φράσον.
Βα. θούριος Ξέρξης, κενώσας πᾶσαν ἠπείρου πλάκα.
Δα. πεζὸς ἢ ναύτης δὲ πεῖραν τήνδ' ἐμώρανεν τάλας;
Βα. ἀμφότερα· διπλοῦν μέτωπον ἦν δυοῖν στρατευμάτοιν.
Δα. πῶς δὲ καὶ στρατὸς τοσόσδε πεζὸς ἤνυσεν περᾶν;
Βα. μηχαναῖς ἔζευξεν Ἕλλης πορθμὸν ὥστ' ἔχειν πόρον.
Δα. καὶ τόδ' ἐξέπραξεν ὥστε Βόσπορον κλῇσαι μέγαν;
Βα. ὧδ' ἔχει, γνώμης δέ πού τις δαιμόνων ξυνήψατο.

Aeschylus *Persians* 715-724

Da. How has it happened? Has our state been stricken by a virulent plague, or by civil strife?
Qu. Not at all; what has happened is that our entire army has been destroyed in the region of Athens.
Da. And tell me, which of my sons led the army there?
Qu. The bold Xerxes; he emptied the whole expanse of the continent.
Da. And did the wretched boy make this foolish attempt by land or by sea?
Qu. Both; it was a double front composed of two forces.

66 Other μέν-instances in tragedy indicating that the turn is preliminary to another pragmatically similar turn include Aeschylus *Agamemnon* 1203; *Eumenides* 589, *Libation Bearers* 111; *Suppliant Women* 917; Sophocles *Oedipus King* 1234; Euripides *Bacchae* 493, 831, 1264.

67 See II.2 §§59-60 for discussion of μέν in drama projecting an upcoming δέ act even when this projection is not fulfilled.

> Da. And how did a land army of that size manage to get across the water?
> Qu. He contrived means to yoke the strait of Helle, so as to create a pathway.
> Da. He actually carried that out, so as to close up the mighty Bosporus?
> Qu. It is true. Some divinity must have touched his wits.

Prompted by the general news of a disaster, Darius asks in 715 in which way Persia has been ruined. The queen's answer in 716 starts without a turn-initial particle: we will see below that this is no coincidence. Since an answer forms the expected second pair part of a question-answer pair, it does not need an explicit signal clarifying how the turn is linked to the previous one. The queen's other answers in this passage (718, 720, 722, 724) similarly lack any turn-initial particle.

§35. Darius' second, third, and fourth questions (717, 719, 721) contain a turn-initial δέ.[68] In each case the particle marks the turn as the next first pair part, here a new question, in the same series of sequences.[69] Within this series of questions, each δέ question is somehow "new," that is, there is a change of topic. Turn-initial δέ thus helps to locate a turn within the series of pairs—a frequent use of the particle in my corpus.[70]

§36. Notice that the question in 723 starts with καί: an indication that this question fits differently in the series from those marked with δέ. Here Darius does not simply accept the answer from the previous turn and go on to the next question, but lingers

68 Broadhead 1960 and Italie 1953 *ad loc.* refer to Denniston 1950:187-188 on the "postponement" of δέ in 719. Since it is sensible here to take the words preceding δέ as one unit (all commentators read them this way) we can still consider δέ turn-initial, that is, as occurring in the first discourse act of the turn. See §11 above.

69 On δέ's general function of marking new steps in a discourse, see II.2 §§31-36 on Homer, and IV.2 §46 on Herodotus and Thucydides. Note that Sommerstein translates the three questions with turn-initial δέ in this passage as beginning with *and*. See Heritage and Sorjonen 1994 on English questions starting with *and* in medical institutional settings. They show that *and*-prefaced questions are typically new questions within a list: they are part of a larger agenda-based activity. Those without turn-initial *and*, by contrast, tend to be prompted by new information just provided.

70 Other examples of turn-initial δέ in following questions include Aeschylus *Agamemnon* 274, 278, 935; *Eumenides* 593; Sophocles *Electra* 392; *Oedipus King* 89, 108, 112, 128, 528, 579, 938, 954, 991, 1025, 1027, 1031; *Oedipus at Colonus* 68, 302, 391, 401, 412, 471; *Philoctetes* 102, 112; Euripides *Andromache* 439, 915; *Bacchae* 465, 467, 469, 471, 473, 481, 485, 832, 1290 (see below, (t9)), 1292, 1294, 1298; *Hecuba* 767, 773, 777, 1015, 1017; *Hippolytus* 95, 280, 282; *Medea* 668; Aristophanes *Assemblywomen* 254; *Birds* 67, 1203; *Knights* 204, 206; *Lysistrata* 835, 997; *Peace* 186, 187. In the "interrogation" scene in Euripides *Bacchae* 460-491, Pentheus also uses δέ-turns to return to his list of questions after some other action, such as an assessment of a previous reply. In Euripides' *Electra* 977-978, as described by Van Emde Boas 2017b:217, both Orestes and Electra here try to start new sequences with questions containing turn-initial δέ.

on the current topic, the news he has just received. That is, whereas δέ marks discourse discontinuity (such as a change of topic), καί indicates continuity. The fact that the καί turn is a question suggests that the speaker is surprised or indignant about the previous statement, or has doubts about it.[71] Darius here asks for confirmation of the answer given in 722: did Xerxes *really* yoke the Hellespont?[72] Because the queen has just provided this information, Darius' request for repetition indicates his surprise. Hancock 1917:29 describes καί questions similarly: they "[leap] spontaneously from the lips as the significance of the other speaker's words reaches the mind. Sometimes they merely serve to repeat the amazing fact just stated, sometimes they raise a fresh point arising from the other." With a καί question, in other words, a speaker "zooms in" on a previous utterance, implying surprise, doubt, or even indignation about that utterance.[73] The particle δέ, by contrast, cannot give the signal that the speaker is further pursuing some element of the previous turn.[74]

§37. Sometimes the playwrights exploit the sequential signal conveyed by turn-initial δέ to indicate something more than just a next question in a series. For example, a δέ-turn after receiving dreadful news implies the speaker's absence of (emotional) reaction to the news. An example from Euripides *Bacchae* is Agaue's response upon hearing that she and her sisters have killed her son Pentheus:

(t9)

Αγ. τίς ἔκτανέν νιν; πῶς ἐμὰς ἦλθ' ἐς χέρας;
Κα. δύστην' ἀλήθει', ὡς ἐν οὐ καιρῶι πάρει.
Αγ. λέγ', ὡς τὸ μέλλον καρδία πήδημ' ἔχει.
Κα. σύ νιν κατέκτας καὶ κασίγνηται σέθεν.
Αγ. ποῦ δ' ὤλετ'; ἦ κατ' οἶκον, ἢ ποίοις τόποις;

Euripides *Bacchae* 1286-1290

[71] Note *actually* in Sommerstein's translation. See Broadhead 1960, Groeneboom 1930, Italie 1953, and Roussel 1960 *ad loc.*, and the translation of Hall 1996. They all explicitly or implicitly interpret the question in this way.

[72] Because of its act-initial position, καί in 723 can have either small scope over τόδ' only, or act scope over τόδ' ἐξέπραξεν. The "zooming-in" effect of the question fits both scope interpretations, as τόδ' by itself refers to the action described in the previous utterance. In 721, by contrast, the position of καί later in the act suggests a small scope over στρατὸς τοσόσδε only, while turn-initial δέ presents the entire question as a next step in a series. See I.1 §20 on the relevance of position and scope to particle interpretation.

[73] Other examples of surprised, doubtful, or indignant questions with turn-initial καί include Aeschylus *Agamemnon* 280; *Libation Bearers* 179, 776; *Eumenides* 898; *Persians* 438; *Suppliant Women* 509; Sophocles *Oedipus King* 976, 1019, 1023; *Oedipus at Colonus* 73, 414; Euripides *Andromache* 917; Aristophanes *Birds* 829, 963bis, 1437bis. On connections between particles and emotional states of mind in drama, see III.5.

[74] See IV.2 §§14-46 and §§93-146 for elaborate discussion of different functions of both δέ and καί, and their differences.

Ag. Who killed him? How did he come into my hands?
Ca. Unhappy truth, how untimely you have come!
Ag. Speak: my heart leaps at what is to come!
Ca. You killed him, you and your sisters.
Ag. Where did he perish? At home, or where?

The particle δέ in 1290 marks the turn as a new step in Agaue's series of questions, rather than a reaction to the terrible news. Asking "where did he die" after "you killed your own son" is an unexpected and striking response. It shows that the speaker has not (yet) fully understood the disastrous message, or somehow wants to refrain from giving a reaction to it, such as an emotional assessment.[75] This use of δέ is a specific exploitation of its more general function to mark new or different discourse acts.[76]

§38. Similarly, turn-initial δέ may signal that a turn following a question is not an answer to that question; the speaker starts a new action in her δέ-turn instead.[77] Consider Chremylus' turn after Blepsidemus' question in the following dialogue from Aristophanes *Wealth*:[78]

(t10)

Βλ. ἀλλ' οὐδὲ τὸ βλέμμ' αὐτὸ κατὰ χώραν ἔχει,
ἀλλ' ἐστὶν ἐπιδηλοῦν τι πεπανουργηκότος.
Χρ. σὺ μὲν οἶδ' ὃ κρώζεις· ὡς ἐμοῦ τι κεκλοφότος

75 Darius' δέ question in Aeschylus *Persians* 717, cited in (t8) above, is also a response that does not emotionally react to news brought in the preceding turn. Another example is Creon's δέ question in Sophocles *Antigone* 401, after the guard has told him that Antigone is the criminal he is looking for. Contrast these turns to the ones starting with an interjection, conveying the speaker's emotional reaction: see §65 below for discussion.

76 On this general function of δέ, see e.g. Bäumlein 1861:89; Bakker 1993b; 1997b:62-68. See also II.2 §§31-36 on Homeric δέ, III.2 §§24-32 on the distribution of δέ in drama, and IV.2 §§14-46 on δέ in historiography.

77 This description does not contrast with Denniston's remark that Sophocles "not infrequently uses δέ in answers, to introduce a protest or objection" (1950 [1934]:166): as his examples show, he does not mean "answers" in a strict sense (i.e. after questions), and his point is exactly that the δέ-turn always introduces some new point.

78 Similar turns starting with δέ after a question that do not function as an answer include Aeschylus *Libation Bearers* 123; Sophocles *Oedipus King* 379 (Brunck proposes a conjecture γε instead of δέ here; see Bollack 1990 *ad loc.* for discussion), 1030, 1056, 1144; *Oedipus at Colonus* 1488; *Women of Trachis* 403; Euripides *Bacchae* 830; *Heracles* 1253; *Hippolytus* 341 (see (t4) above); Aristophanes *Assemblywomen* 520bis, 636bis; *Birds* 1205; *Frogs* 275, 936; *Knights* 1198bis. The turn-initial discourse acts πῶς δ' οὐ in Aeschylus *Libation Bearers* 123 and σὺ δ' οὐ in *Frogs* 275 do function as an answer, but only indirectly, i.e. by requiring inference; in form they are new questions. Sophocles *Oedipus King* 1030 is translated with "Yes, and..." by Lloyd-Jones 1997 [1994], but the turn-initial δέ rather suggests that the preceding question is ignored or treated as irrelevant (see the turn in *Oedipus King* 379).

ζητεῖς μεταλαβεῖν.
Βλ. μεταλαβεῖν ζητῶ; τίνος;
Χρ. τὸ δ' ἐστὶν οὐ τοιοῦτον, ἀλλ' ἑτέρως ἔχον.

Aristophanes *Wealth* 367-371

Bl. Why, even the look in his eye is shifty; yes, he's obviously done something bad.
Ch. I know what *you're* clucking about; you think I've stolen something and want a cut.
Bl. Me want a cut? Of what?
Ch. It's not like that; it's something else entirely.

Instead of answering the question, Chremylus adds more acts to his own previous turn, which was marked with μέν as projecting something more. The two turns roughly amount to: "you (σὺ μέν), I know what you think. But (δέ) the situation is not like that." Because Chremylus treats Blepsidemus' question as an irrelevant interruption, the position of δέ was not intended to be turn-initial. Therefore δέ does not mark the start of a new adjacency pair within a series here, but only the start of a new act, in this case an act that semantically contrasts with Chremylus' previous acts.[79] In discourse-analytic terms, we can say that δέ always marks an act boundary, while intentionally turn-initial δέ even marks the boundary of a move, a larger unit that probably corresponds to at least an adjacency pair in dialogue.[80]

§39. Another particle that may signal the start of a new adjacency pair is ἀτάρ. It differs, however, from δέ in that it is almost never found in turn-initial position. Out of the total number of 86 instances of ἀτάρ, 83 occur later in a turn.[81] In this mid-turn position, the particle signals that the speaker moves on to a new sequence after she herself ended the previous one. ἀτάρ may for instance occur after an answer to a question,[82] or

[79] In Euripides *Hippolytus* 341, cited in (t4) above, we find a similar turn-initial δέ after an interrupting question. Also here, the speaker (Phaedra) does not reply to the question, but adds a new act to her own previous turn. This turn-initial δέ differs from the turn-initial τε in line 339, however, in that τε marks the new vocative as closely linked to the vocative in 337, whereas δέ marks a new step: Phaedra now turns to her own fate. See Wecklein 1885 *ad* line 341, who remarks that δέ is more appropriate than τε here because of the switch to a new thought, whereas 339 continued the thought of 337.

[80] See II.3 §§2-5 and IV.3 §§92-106 for elaborate discussion of the term move.

[81] There are 39 cases of this particle in extant tragedy (excluding fragments) and 47 cases in Aristophanes. The three instances occurring immediately after a speaker change are Euripides *Medea* 80; Aristophanes *Birds* 69, 648. There are however variant readings: see below, §40, for discussion. For an analysis of ἀτάρ in Homer, Euripides, and Aristophanes, including consideration of interactional contexts, see Inglese 2018.

[82] Examples of ἀτάρ preceded by answers to questions include Sophocles *Oedipus King* 1052; Euripides *Andromache* 883; *Trojan Women* 63; Aristophanes *Assemblywomen* 376, 551; *Clouds* 187,

after an assessment of the previous turn.[83] An example from Euripides *Hecuba* is shown in (t11). In this scene a servant comes to Hecuba, bringing her the corpse of her son Polydorus. Hecuba does not know that he is dead, however, and thinks she sees the body of her daughter Polyxena.

(t11)

Θε. ὦ παντάλαινα κἄτι μᾶλλον ἢ λέγω,
δέσποιν', ὄλωλας κοὐκέτ' εἶ, βλέπουσα φῶς,
ἄπαις ἄνανδρος ἄπολις ἐξεφθαρμένη.
Εκ. οὐ καινὸν εἶπας, εἰδόσιν δ' ὠνείδισας.
ἀτὰρ τί νεκρὸν τόνδε μοι Πολυξένης
ἥκεις κομίζουσ', ἧς ἀπηγγέλθη τάφος
πάντων Ἀχαιῶν διὰ χερὸς σπουδὴν ἔχειν;

Euripides *Hecuba* 667-673

Se. Mistress, woman utterly undone beyond my power to describe, you are lost; though you see the light of day you are dead, without child, without husband, without city, utterly destroyed!

He. This is no news you bring: you say these hard words to one who knows them well. But why have you come bringing the body of Polyxena when it has been reported that her burial was being eagerly carried out by all the Achaeans?

Hecuba gives an assessment of the servant's words, and then goes on to ask her a question—a first pair part that opens a new sequence. ἀτάρ signals that the upcoming words will not be part of the assessment anymore, but the start of a new action. With this ἀτάρ question Hecuba turns her attention towards the tableau she sees in front of her. This quick switch from her brief and dismissive assessment to her naive question underlines her ignorance about Polydorus' fate.

§40. My analysis of ἀτάρ as marking a switch to a new sequence *within* a turn suggests that a widely accepted reading in Aristophanes *Birds* should be revised:

801; *Wealth* 1111.

83 Examples of ἀτάρ preceded by assessments include Aeschylus *Persians* 333; *Bacchae* 516; Euripides *Hecuba* 671 (see (t11) below); *Hippolytus* 1398; Aristophanes *Acharnians* 448; *Assemblywomen* 248, 358, 394; *Birds* 144, 916; *Clouds* 382, 677, 693; *Wasps* 28, 652, 815; *Wealth* 749; *Women at the Thesmophoria* 87.

(t12)

Θε. ὁδὶ δὲ δὴ τίς ἐστιν ὄρνις; οὐκ ἐρεῖς;
Ευ. Ἐπικεχοδὼς ἔγωγε Φασιανικός.
Πε. ἀτὰρ σὺ τί θηρίον ποτ᾽ εἶ, πρὸς τῶν θεῶν;
Θε. ὄρνις ἔγωγε δοῦλος.

Aristophanes *Birds* 67-70

Sl. And this other one, what kind of bird is he? Speak up.
Eu. I'm a brownbottom, from the Phaesance.
Pe. Say, what kind of creature might you be, in heaven's name?
Sl. Me, I'm a slavebird.

Almost all editions read ἀτάρ in 69 in turn-initial position,[84] but as we have seen this is an unlikely choice in view of the fact that ἀτάρ hardly ever occurs in this position. Moreover, manuscript R, the only one which transmits the form ἀτάρ instead of ἀλλά[85]—all editors rightly adopt the former as *lectio difficilior*—is also the only one which has no speaker change here.[86] It is therefore better to keep the speaker in 69 who also uttered 68 (whether this is Peisetaerus or Euelpides).[87] ἀτάρ would then mark, as it normally does, a turn-internal switch from a second pair part (in this case an answer) to a new first pair part (in this case a question).

§41. Going on to a different adjacency pair, that of the summons and answer, we find a construction in its first pair part that is never accompanied by a particle. This is οὗτος in its use as a summoning expression:[88]

[84] Bothe 1829 and Schröder 1927 give 68 to Peisetaerus, and 69 (with ἀτάρ) to Euelpides; Dunbar 1995, Kakridis 1974, Kock 1864, Mastromarco and Totaro 2006, Sommerstein 1987, Wilson 2007, and Zanetto (in Zanetto and Del Corno 1987) give 68 to Euelpides and 69 (with ἀτάρ) to Peisetaerus. Only Van Leeuwen 1902 has no speaker change at this point, yet he changes the text in other aspects: he gives 68 to Peisetaerus, moves 66, spoken by the slave-bird, to after 68, with 66bis spoken by Euelpides, and lets Euelpides continue his turn in 69 with ἀτάρ.

[85] ἀλλά does regularly mark a switch to a new adjacency pair in turn-initial position, e.g, Aristophanes *Birds* 54; *Frogs* 123, 646; *Wasps* 173bis, 428.

[86] This is noted only by Dunbar 1995 and Zanetto in Zanetto and Del Corno 1987 in the apparatus.

[87] Also for the seemingly turn-initial ἀτάρ in *Birds* 648, Dunbar 1995 and Zanetto in Zanetto and Del Corno 1987 reports that the same manuscript R has no speaker change here. But if we follow that reading, who else would then speak this line as well as the previous word? Schröder 1927 seems to hint at a compromise interpretation: his paraphrase "Doch, was ich sagen wollte" implies that Peisetaerus wants to give the impression of continuing with his own turn, even though there has actually been a short interrupting turn.
The ἀτάρ in Euripides *Medea* 80 has a variant reading αὐτάρ in some manuscripts; however, that particle does not occur elsewhere in tragedy. Perhaps the ἀτάρ-instance in line 80 has been influenced by the one in 83, which is (as usual) not the start of a new turn.
Bonifazi 2012:212n84 writes that ἀτάρ in Homer is found in contexts where "the flow of discourse is interrupted by the introduction of a comment, or an exclamation, or a self-correction."

[88] See Dickey 1996: esp. 154-155 on οὗτος in Aristophanes as "an attention-getting vocative"; she notes that it is rare in tragedy and prose.

(t13)

225 Πε. οὗτος.
225bis Ευ. τί ἐστιν;
225ter Πε. οὐ σιωπήσει;

Aristophanes *Birds* 225

Pe. Hey there.
Eu. Yes?
Pe. Be quiet!

With οὗτος Peisetaerus demands the attention of Euelpides, who gives a reaction to indicate that he is listening. While οὗτος in its summoning function does not always constitute a turn all by itself, and is sometimes followed by σύ in the same discourse act,[89] vocative οὗτος is never accompanied by a second-position particle.[90] It thus differs from the vocative pronoun σύ, which regularly precedes a δέ.[91] If a particle such as γε or δέ does follow οὗτος, then οὗτος is always used in its more common function as a nominative third-person demonstrative pronoun, rather than as a vocative expression.[92]

§42. Let us move on to a particular *second* pair part: the answer to a question. Numerous answers in the corpus share a distinctive trait: they lack any turn-initial particles or other turn-initial contextualization cues.[93] One of the numerous instances is the messenger's answer in this scene from Sophocles *Antigone*:

[89] E.g. in Sophocles *Oedipus King* 532, 1121; Euripides *Hecuba* 1280; Aristophanes *Acharnians* 564.

[90] Other cases of οὗτος as a summoning expression (without particles) include Sophocles *Ajax* 1047; *Women of Trachis* 402; Aristophanes *Birds* 49; *Clouds* 732; *Frogs* 198; *Lysistrata* 878; *Peace* 268; *Wasps* 1, 854. An explicit second pair part does not always follow.

[91] E.g. in Aeschylus *Agamemnon* 617, 1061; *Eumenides* 89; *Persians* 478; Sophocles *Ajax* 684, 845; *Antigone* 446, 1087; *Electra* 891, 1472; *Oedipus King* 980; *Women of Trachis* 1157; Euripides *Alcestis* 1112; *Children of Heracles* 565; *Hippolytus* 1431; Aristophanes *Acharnians* 191, 262, 1033, 1119; *Birds* 457, 926; *Knights* 118, 891, 1065; *Wasps* 6, 1154bis.

[92] E.g. οὗτος δέ in Sophocles *Oedipus King* 954, and οὗτος γ' in Aristophanes *Birds* 75. See II.2 §§73-79 on σὺ δέ and similar constructions in Pindar.

[93] See Ireland 1974:517n10, on stichomythia in Aeschylus: "in many cases the natural answer to a question does not require the introduction of a connecting particle (...)."See now also Battezzato and Rodda 2018 on the use of particles versus asyndeton in dialogic contexts, especially in questions—frequently with particles—and answers—strikingly often starting without a particle. As these authors emphasize, "[p]article usage is determined by the structure of linguistic interaction" (3). On contextualization cues, see §12 above. The particle γε is, however, regularly used in turn-initial position in answers; see §62 below for discussion.

(t14)

ΕΞΑΓΓΕΛΟΣ ὦ δέσποθ', ὡς ἔχων τε καὶ κεκτημένος,
τὰ μὲν πρὸ χειρῶν τάδε φέρεις, τὰ δ' ἐν δόμοις
ἔοικας ἥκειν καὶ τάχ' ὄψεσθαι κακά.
Κρ. τί δ' ἔστιν αὖ κάκιον ἐκ κακῶν ἔτι;
Εξ. γυνὴ τέθνηκε, τοῦδε παμμήτωρ νεκροῦ
δύστηνος, ἄρτι νεοτόμοισι πλήγμασιν.

Sophocles *Antigone* 1278-1282

Me. My lord, you carry this sorrow in your arms with full rights of ownership, and it seems that soon you will enter and see other sorrows in the house.
Cr. What is there that is yet more evil, coming after evils?
Me. Your wife is dead, own mother of this dead man, unhappy one, through wounds newly inflicted!

After the messenger's announcement of bad news, Creon asks for clarification of the disaster, to which the messenger gives a straightforward answer (1282).[94] Even without a turn-initial contextualization cue such as a particle, the connection between the two turns of the adjacency pair is clear because of the function of the second one as answer to the first. In other words, the build-up of a dialogue in adjacency pairs has an influence on the linguistic form of this second pair part, i.e. without turn-initial contextualization cues.[95]

94 This second pair part is a preferred response: see §18 above for the term and §§50-52 below for discussion of particle use in preferred responses.

95 Other answers without turn-initial particles or other turn-initial contextualizing cues include Aeschylus *Persians* 794; *Agamemnon* 269, 279, 544, 936, 1208; *Libation Bearers* 119, 121, 180, 215, 769, 886; *Eumenides* 210, 432, 602, 892; Sophocles *Ajax* 801, 874, 1134; *Antigone* 513, 575, 1100; *Electra* 927, 929, 943; *Oedipus King* 87, 100, 103, 114, 122, 130, 292, 362, 561, 578, 623, 656, 703, 729, 742, 752, 756, 766, 934, 936, 939, 955, 961, 990, 992, 1022, 1032, 1044, 1125, 1173bis, 1176bis; *Oedipus at Colonus* 39, 42, 67, 69, 1508; *Philoctetes* 54bis, 113, 162; Euripides *Alcestis* 513, 519, 521, 531, 533, 535, 712; *Andromache* 884; *Bacchae* 466, 470, 472, 478, 482, 486, 833, 1267, 1274, 1276, 1278; *Children of Heracles* 664, 669, 695, 713; *Hecuba* 768, 770, 772, 776, 778, 780, 1016; *Heracles* 1129, 1139; *Hippolytus* 93, 348, 723, 800, 802; *Medea* 667, 669, 671, 675, 677, 702, 706, 1125; *Suppliant Women* 132, 138, 759; Aristophanes *Assemblywomen* 376bis, 383bis, 468, 1135bis; *Birds* 90ter, 99, 104, 226, 409, 411bis, 416, 965bis, 1030bis, 1537bis, 1583bis; *Clouds* 483bis (see (t17) below); *Frogs* 131, 133ter, 139, 142bis, 169bis, 207, 286bis, 618bis, 919, 1021, 1129bis, 1220ter, 1405, 1415bis; *Lysistrata* 162bis, 496ter, 744bis, 748bis; *Wealth* 392ter, 393bis, 402.

4.3.2 Pair expansions

§43. As described in §§16-17 above, adjacency pairs may be expanded with pre-, insert, and/or post-expansions to form a complex sequence. Pre-expansions, which project specific adjacency pairs, regularly feature the particle οὖν:

(t15)

Οδ. τί γάρ σ' ἔδρασεν, ὥστε καὶ βλάβην ἔχειν;
Αγ. οὔ φησ' ἐάσειν τόνδε τὸν νεκρὸν ταφῆς
ἄμοιρον, ἀλλὰ πρὸς βίαν θάψειν ἐμοῦ.
Οδ. ἔξεστιν οὖν εἰπόντι τἀληθῆ φίλῳ
σοὶ μηδὲν ἧσσον ἢ πάρος ξυνηρετεῖν;
Αγ. εἴπ'· ἦ γὰρ εἴην οὐκ ἂν εὖ φρονῶν, ἐπεὶ
φίλον σ' ἐγὼ μέγιστον Ἀργείων νέμω.
Οδ. ἄκουέ νυν. τὸν ἄνδρα τόνδε πρὸς θεῶν
μὴ τλῇς ἄθαπτον ὧδ' ἀναλγήτως βαλεῖν·

Sophocles *Ajax* 1325-1333

Od. What did he do to you so as to injure you?
Ag. He says he will not leave this corpse unburied, but will bury it against my will.
Od. Then may a friend tell the truth to a friend and assist you no less than I have done till now?
Ag. Speak! Indeed I should be foolish not to let you, since I regard you as my greatest friend among the Argives.
Od. Listen, then! I beg you not to venture to cast this man out ruthlessly, unburied.

Agamemnon has been arguing with Teucer about the possible burial of Ajax, and Odysseus has just arrived to help settle the argument. After the sequence consisting of Odysseus' question and Agamemnon's answer in 1325-1327, Odysseus intends to give his friend advice. He does not give his suggestion directly, however, but first inquires about his right to speak (1328-1329). Since the conversation's further development depends on Agamemnon's answer to this inquiry, this question and its answer can be called a pre-expansion.[96] The particle οὖν in general marks an inferential link to the preceding

96 See the following remarks *ad loc.* by several commentators. Stanford 1963: "Odysseus, before he tries to persuade Agamemnon to permit the burial of Ajax, makes sure that Agamemnon is in a friendly mood towards him." Garvie 1998: "Odysseus cleverly begins by establishing that Agamemnon is prepared to treat him as a friend and to observe the traditional code of

discourse,[97] as well as the start of a new move, a discourse unit larger than one act.[98] In this case, the interrogative nature of the turn is already enough to signal the start of a new adjacency pair, as questions are always first pair parts. The presence of οὖν therefore projects an even bigger move than just a new sequence, that is, a new *expanded* sequence. οὖν implies that the speaker's current action requires more words than the current turn, which can consequently be interpreted as a pre-expansion (or sometimes an insert expansion).[99]

§44. The first pair part of Odysseus' base adjacency pair—i.e. his advice—contains enclitic νυν in turn-initial position (1332). This particle does not mark the start of a new move, as οὖν, but has a backward-oriented force only. νυν marks a logical connection between its host act and the preceding discourse: the previous utterances, in this case the pre-expansion, form the necessary background for uttering the current turn.[100] As Finglass 2011 *ad loc.* remarks, with νυν "Odysseus emphasises that he will hold Agamemnon to his word." This "word" is what Agamemnon has just given in his response to Odysseus' preliminary question. Pre-expansions and insert expansions by definition deal with matters on which the decision to utter or continue the base sequence depends; νυν is therefore particularly at home at the start of such subsequent base sequences.[101]

---

friendship. By agreeing to do so Agamemnon dooms himself to lose the ensuing argument." Finglass 2011: "(...) Odysseus, rather than immediately attacking Agamemnon's case, politely requests permission to speak (...)."

97 On οὖν marking an inferential link, see Stephens 1837:11-12, 101-102; Dindorf 1873:260 on οὖν in Aeschylus; Navarre 1908:299 and Denniston 1950 [1934]:416 on οὖν in questions in fifth-century Greek. See Bäumlein 1861:182; Wähdel 1869:6 on οὖν in questions in Aristophanes; Hoffmann 1884:6 on ὦν in Herodotus; these three authors all argue that the particle indicates a general "Zusammenhang" (coherence) with the preceding.

98 On οὖν marking the start of a new substantial unit, see Schütz 1806 [1782]:510-511 (an edition of Hoogeveen); Des Places 1929:56-65 on οὖν in Plato; Sicking 1986:134 on οὖν in classical Greek; Van Ophuijsen 1993:84 on οὖν in Plato; Slings 1997a:101; Wiesner 1999:316; Revuelta Puigdollers 2009b:95-96; Wakker 2009b:67, 80 on οὖν in Lysias. For the concept of move, see §22 above, II.3 §§2-5, and IV.3 §§92-106.

99 Other examples of οὖν in pre-expansions include Aeschylus *Libation Bearers* 766; Sophocles *Oedipus King* 562, 564, 568, 655, 1517; *Women of Trachis* 1191; Euripides *Bacchae* 819, 1271, 1275; *Cyclops* 131; *Hecuba* 998, 1008 (in this case the addressee Polymestor immediately infers what Hecuba's base first pair part was intended to be; compare the English example of "sequence truncation" in Levinson 2013:111); *Helen* 315, 1233; *Hippolytus* 91; *Ion* 1029; *Iphigeneia at Aulis* 725; Aristophanes *Birds* 80; *Frogs* 1010bis; *Knights* 1158 (see (t16) with discussion in §45 below). Of these pre-expansions, those in Euripides *Helen* 315, 1233, *Ion* 1029, and Aristophanes *Birds* 80 lack a verbal response to the pre-expansion's first pair part: the speaker immediately goes on with the base first pair part. Examples of οὖν in insert expansions include Sophocles *Women of Trachis* 1247; Aristophanes *Frogs* 642, 1141; *Lysistrata* 122ter, 861bis. In Aristophanes *Frogs* 1139 we find οὔκουν in an insert expansion.

100 On the function of the enclitic particle νυν, see e.g. Hoogeveen 1769:II.804-806. See Swift 2010:362 on νυν in Euripides *Alcestis* 1097: the particle indicates, she writes, that the speaker "does not regard what he is saying to be in conflict with Admetus' statement [i.e. the preceding turn]."

101 Other examples of turn-initial νυν after a pre-expansion include Aeschylus *Libation Bearers* 770 (with οὖν in the pre-expansion); Euripides *Bacchae* 821 (with οὖν in the pre-expansion); *Cyclops*

§45. A common way to start a pre-expansion is to ask the addressee about certain knowledge (compare the English "you know what just happened?" and similar pre-expansions). If he turns out already to know, the speaker will not start the base adjacency pair in the way she had planned it.[102] The associations of both "do you know" questions and the particle οὖν with pre-expansions lead to the regular occurrence of οἶσθ' οὖν in such environments.[103] In the following passage from Aristophanes *Knights*, the playwright makes fun of the conventional sequential structure:

(t16)

Αλ. οἶσθ' οὖν ὃ δρᾶσον;
1158bis Δημ. εἰ δὲ μή, φράσεις γε σύ.
Αλ. ἄφες ἀπὸ βαλβίδων ἐμέ τε καὶ τουτονί,
1160 ἵνα σ' εὖ ποιῶμεν ἐξ ἴσου.
1160bis Δημ. δρᾶν ταῦτα χρή.

Aristophanes *Knights* 1158-1160

(Demos is annoyed by the competition between the sausage seller and Paphlagon)
Sa. Do you know what you should do?
De. If I don't, you'll tell me.
Sa. Start me and this guy from the same gate, so we have an equal shot at serving you.
De. That's what we should do.

The character Demos immediately understands that the sausage seller's "question" in 1158 is actually an announcement of a directive.[104] "Do you know what you should do?" is a rather petrified form of pre-expansion, since the speaker does not really expect the

440; *Iphigeneia at Aulis* 872; *Phoenician Women* 907, 911; Aristophanes *Frogs* 129; *Knights* 1011. Several of these instances are cited by Lobeck 1866 *ad* Sophocles *Ajax* 1332. An example of turn-initial νυν after an insert expansion is found in Aristophanes *Lysistrata* 864 (with οὖν in the insert expansion). Aristophanes *Frogs* 1013 (with οὖν in the pre-expansion) and *Lysistrata* 124 (with οὖν in the insert expansion) contain the similar particle τοίνυν in turn-initial position.

[102] See Mastronarde 1979:43: many stichomythic question-answer scenes in tragedy unfold gradually, often with "a formulaic οἶσθα-question or equivalent expression." See Schuren 2015:187-188, 200 on οἶσθα questions in Euripides combined with different deictic pronouns.

[103] Pre-expansions with οἶσθ' (...) οὖν include Sophocles *Oedipus King* 655, 1517; *Women of Trachis* 1191; Euripides *Cyclops* 131; *Hecuba* 998, 1008 (see note 99 above); *Helen* 315, 1233; *Hippolytus* 91; *Ion* 1029; *Iphigeneia at Aulis* 725; Aristophanes *Birds* 80. Several of these instances are cited by Van Leeuwen 1900 *ad* Aristophanes *Knights* 1158.

[104] Van Leeuwen 1900 *ad loc.* notes that similar sequences are found in Sophocles *Oedipus King* 1517 (with οὖν); Aristophanes *Peace* 1061 (with ἀλλά instead of οὖν; also noted by Ribbeck 1867 *ad* the *Knights* passage).

addressee to already know the upcoming advice.[105] Demos' reaction humorously makes this discrepancy between the pre-expansion's form and function explicit: he does not answer the question (note the turn-initial δέ), but dryly remarks that the sausage seller will tell him the advice anyway.

§46. Insert expansions are most easily discerned when a question or order (a first pair part) is followed by another question instead of the expected response (a second pair part).[106] The insert question does not necessarily contain a turn-initial particle, since its nature as a question[107] already makes it clear that it forms a new first pair part.[108] However, turn-initial δέ helps clarify the signal that an insert expansion has started, especially in the construction τί δέ. We have already seen (§38) that a turn-initial δέ after a question makes it clear that the turn is not a straightforward answer to that question. With τί δέ in such a context, a speaker indicates that she cannot yet answer because some preliminary issue first needs to be clarified.[109] Here is an example.[110]

(t17)

Σω. ἄγε δή, κάτειπέ μοι σὺ τὸν σαυτοῦ τρόπον,
ἵν' αὐτὸν εἰδὼς ὅστις ἐστὶ μηχανὰς
ἤδη 'πὶ τούτοις πρός σε καινὰς προσφέρω.
Στ. τί δέ; τειχομαχεῖν μοι διανοεῖ, πρὸς τῶν θεῶν;
Σω. οὔκ, ἀλλὰ βραχέα σου πυθέσθαι βούλομαι,
εἰ μνημονικὸς εἶ.

105 In terms of Searle 1975, we would call this an "indirect speech act": though the turn has the form of a question, pragmatically the turn functions as an announcement of the upcoming main action. Describing the same phenomenon, Schegloff 2007:73-78, 151 and Levinson 2013:112 speak of certain actions, such as questions, being a "vehicle" for many other actions.

106 Concerning tragedy, Mastronarde 1979:37 in such cases speaks of a "counter-question" that causes an answer to be delayed, for example by seeking clarification.

107 We can infer this nature from the presence of question words, from general semantic cues, or sometimes from the question's response; originally it must have been signaled prosodically as well.

108 Examples of questions without a turn-initial particle starting an insert expansion may be found in Aeschylus *Agamemnon* 268; *Libation Bearers* 120, 767; Sophocles *Ajax* 532, 1322; *Antigone* 316, 317; *Oedipus King* 360, 1129; Euripides *Hippolytus* 100; *Medea* 1368; Aristophanes *Birds* 180, 1212bis, 1213bis; *Frogs* 40quat.

109 Rijksbaron 2007:244-257 discusses τί δέ in Plato. He focuses on its function as a marker of topic shift and on issues of punctuation, rather than on the organization of the conversational sequences. Nevertheless, he does remark that τί δέ "signals that during a conversation the speaker is making a new move" (256).

110 Other insert expansions with turn-initial τί δέ include Sophocles *Antigone* 318; *Oedipus King* 1056, 1144; Euripides *Ion* 284; *Iphigeneia among the Taurians* 496; Aristophanes *Assemblywomen* 525; *Birds* 358 (after a request instead of a question), 1205; *Lysistrata* 514 (not really turn-initial, but at the start of a quoted turn by another speaker).

Στ. δύο τρόπω, νὴ τὸν Δία.

Aristophanes *Clouds* 478-483

So. Now then, describe for me your own characteristics; when I know what they are, on that basis I can apply to you the latest plans of attack.
St. How's that? Are you thinking of besieging me? Good heavens!
So. No, I just want to ask you a few questions. For instance, do you have a good memory?
St. Yes and no, by Zeus (...)

At 478-480, Socrates produces a request for information: a first pair part making relevant the provision of that information by Strepsiades. Instead of giving the expected answer, Strepsiades responds by asking a question of his own, thereby beginning an insert sequence. The particle δέ in 481 marks the turn as a new step and not the expected response. The construction τί δέ as a whole suggests that it is a request for certain additional information, the lack of which motivates the refusal to answer the question.

§47. Since an insert expansion often starts with a question, also a question particle such as ἦ may begin insert expansions, as in (t18).

(t18)

Αθ. εἶέν· τί γὰρ δὴ παῖς ὁ τοῦ Λαερτίου;
ποῦ σοι τύχης ἕστηκεν; ἦ πέφευγέ σε;
Αι. ἦ τοὐπίτριπτον κίναδος ἐξήρου μ' ὅπου;
Αθ. ἔγωγ'· Ὀδυσσέα τὸν σὸν ἐνστάτην λέγω.
Αι. ἥδιστος, ὦ δέσποινα, δεσμώτης ἔσω
θακεῖ· θανεῖν γὰρ αὐτὸν οὔ τί πω θέλω.

Sophocles *Ajax* 101-106

At. So! But what of the son of Laertes, what is his situation? Did he escape you?
Aj. Did you ask me where the cunning fox was?
At. I did; I mean your rival, Odysseus.
Aj. Mistress, he sits inside, the most welcome of prisoners! I do not want him to die yet.

Ajax does not answer Athena's question in 103, but instead asks for clarification. According to Garvie 1998 *ad loc.*, this is a "predictable" reaction the hero would have "to the name of his enemy." Finglass 2011 *ad loc.* similarly remarks that "Ajax's counter-question indicates his contempt for Odysseus." Ajax has clearly understood to whom Athena is referring, but does not agree on her manner of referring to him: because of his hatred for Odysseus, Ajax avoids direct mentioning of Odysseus' name or father.[111] The particle ἦ marks the turn as a request for clarification, and simultaneously reflects Ajax' emotional involvement.[112] If such a question is found after another question, where an *answer* is expected, the ἦ turn can be interpreted as starting an insert expansion.[113]

§48. Post-expansions, finally, seem generally to lack a turn-initial particle. Such turns are often sequence-closing thirds, in the form of assessments of the second pair part just received, such as an answer to a question.[114] As argued in section 4.5 below, there is a connection between such evaluating turns and their starts without a particle or other linguistic contextualization cue. Post-sequences can also be opened with a question that is prompted by a preceding answer.[115]

4.4 Preference Organization

§49. Earlier I noted that most first pair parts have a preferred and a dispreferred response. The latter is usually marked in some way, whereas preferred responses tend to be more straightforward in form.[116] In tragic and comic dialogue, certain turn-initial particles and

[111] Later in the play (line 380), however, Ajax does utter τέκνον Λαρτίου once (the commentators do not remark on his use of this referring expression). See Stivers, Enfield, and Levinson 2007 on the social importance of different forms of person reference. They note e.g. that "reference is not just, indeed not primarily, about giving and receiving information but about navigating social relationships." (19) See Haviland 2007:250-251 in the same volume for discussion of an actual example of hostile person reference.

[112] On ἦ in questions marking a request for clarification, see e.g. Bäumlein 1861:122; Humbert 1960:407; Van Emde Boas, Rijksbaron, Huitink, and De Bakker 2019:689. On ἦ and emotional involvement, see II.3 §§38-39, and III.2 §§87-89. ἦ's capacity to start a question-answer pair can be related to its function of marking a new narrative move in Homer; see II.3 §§33-43.

[113] In fact, however, asking for clarification with ἦ is more common after answers or otherwise news-bringing turns than after questions. The only other ἦ questions in my corpus that can be interpreted as starting an insert expansion are found in Aeschylus *Agamemnon* 942 (ἦ καί: also zooming in on the preceding turn) and Sophocles *Antigone* 44 (ἦ γάρ).

[114] Examples of post-expansions without a turn-initial particle that function as assessments after a question-answer pair include Aeschylus *Agamemnon* 270; *Eumenides* 900; Euripides *Hippolytus* 278; Aristophanes *Birds* 79bis.

[115] Examples of post-expansions without a turn-initial particle that function as new questions after a complete adjacency pair are e.g. Sophocles *Ajax* 532; *Oedipus King* 1047, 1124, 1126; *Oedipus at Colonus* 388; Euripides *Hippolytus* 803; Aristophanes *Birds* 70bis. Of these, the instance in *Ajax* is after a request-refusal pair, all others after a question-answer pair.

[116] For an exception see Medea's rejection of Jason's offer of money in Euripides *Medea* 616-617. As Buffing 2011 notes, her response is very strong and straightforward. The response's unusual character strengthens the characterization of Medea as angry, and behaving impolitely as a result. On this passage see also Goldstein 2012:10-11, who points out that Medea's answer is strengthened, "in response to the strength of Jason's directive" (sc. to accept the money).

particle combinations fit the context of preferred responses, others that of dispreferred ones.

4.4.1 Preferred responses

§50. A common case of preferred response is an information-providing answer to an information-seeking question. It has been argued in §42 above that such answers often lack turn-initial particles or other linguistic contextualization cues. Since an answer is the normatively expected response to a question, no specific signal is needed to mark the upcoming turn as such. Similarly, preferred responses to requests and offers, i.e. turns expressing compliance and acceptance, may also start without a particle. Such responses often signal their connection to the speech situation by starting with a verb in the first person, which indicates that the speaker is obeying the request or accepting the offer.[117]

§51. In some cases preferred responses do contain turn-initial particles. Descriptions of compliance after a command can be preceded by the particle combination καὶ δή, as in (t19), in which the chorus of suppliants expresses their obedience to Pelasgus, the king of Argos, who has asked them to leave their boughs on the altar:[118]

(t19)

Βα. κλάδους μὲν αὐτοῦ λεῖπε, σημεῖον πόνου.
Χο. <u>καὶ δή</u> σφε λείπω χειρία λόγοις σέθεν.

Aeschylus *Suppliant Women* 506-507

Ki. Leave the branches here as a symbol of your distress.
Ch. Look, I am leaving them, obedient to your words.

καὶ δή in the chorus' turn can be connected to their (immediate) obedience, which they explicitly describe with the first-person present form λείπω.[119] The particle καί indicates

[117] Examples of preferred responses to directives and offers with a turn-initial first-person verb, but without turn-initial particles, include Sophocles *Ajax* 116 (response to an encouragement/statement of permission); *Oedipus King* 700 (response to a request), 861 (response to a request/order); Euripides *Alcestis* 376 (response to an offer); *Hippolytus* 250 (response to a request); *Medea* 184 (response to a request), 267 (response to a request), 752 (response to a request, after an insert expansion), 1019 (response to a piece of advice); Aristophanes *Birds* 176 (response to a request), 1276 (response to an offer); *Women at the Thesmophoria* 27ter (response to a request), 28bis (response to a request). As in answers to questions, in such preferred responses "the relation between two turns is predetermined," as Battezzato and Rodda 2018:3 put it; as I do, they find that turn-initial particles are often absent in such environments.

[118] Other instances of turn-initial καὶ δή with a first-person verb expressing compliance to a directive include Sophocles *Electra* 317, 1436; *Philoctetes* 818; Aristophanes *Birds* 175bis, 550; *Wealth* 227, 414; *Women at the Thesmophoria* 214bis.

[119] See Wecklein 1902 and Friis Johansen and Whittle 1980 *ad loc.*

a link to the preceding co-text or context, and a zooming in on something specific, whereas δή in drama is regularly associated with referring to perceivable elements.[120] Together the particles work as a cluster, marking a specific event or place as clearly and immediately perceivable.[121] If a speaker starts to carry out a requested action, καὶ δή is thus a fitting signal to draw attention to this obedience. Wecklein 1902 *ad loc.* adds that καὶ δή is like ἰδού. This latter expression, sometimes similar to English *okay*, is another explicit indication of a preferred response to a directive, besides explicitly describing that the request is being carried out.[122]

§52. The position of καὶ δή in the turn and sequence makes a difference in its function. In modern languages, too, certain words work differently depending on their placement in a conversation—English *oh*, for example, does one thing when uttered at the start of an answer (a second pair part), another in an expansion after an answer (a first pair part).[123] Likewise, the function of the polyfunctional discourse marker *okay* depends partly on its position in a turn.[124] The particular function of καὶ δή connected to expressing compliance thus applies only when the combination appears in turn-initial position in a second pair part.[125]

4.4.2 Dispreferred responses

§53. If a speaker cannot or does not want to provide an answer to a question, grant a request, or otherwise utter a preferred response to a certain first pair part, the response tends to be formally marked. Dispreferred responses are less straightforward in form in English conversation, as pointed out in §18 above. Speakers of dispreferred responses tend to start speaking after a pause, use turn-initial discourse markers, be indirect in their formulation, and give accounts for why they do not answer, grant, accept, or obey.

[120] On these functions of καί, see III.2 §§34-37, and IV.2 §§102-105. On δή referring to something perceivable, see III.2 §§75-78, and e.g. Döderlein 1858:362-363; Bäumlein 1861:98-99; Humbert 1960:404; Sicking 1986:133; Van Ophuijsen 1993:141; Bakker 1997b:75. Possibly Stephens 1837:65, Paley 1881:21, and Thiemann 1881:530-532 hint at this force as well. See also II.3 §§53-64 on δή in Homer, and III.2 §§73-79 on δή in drama.

[121] On this function of καὶ δή, see Bäumlein 1861:98-102; Cooper 2002:2940; Denniston 1950 [1934]:250. These scholars also note the occurrence of (turn-initial) καὶ δή in responses to commands: Bäumlein at 102; Cooper at 2940; Denniston at 251. See also Van Erp Taalman Kip 2009 on καὶ δή in drama in utterances referring to expected character entrances, and IV.2 §§100-101 for a cluster reading of καὶ δή in Herodotus and Aristophanes. On the notion of cluster, see I.1 §19.

[122] Turn-initial ἰδού in obedient turns after directives is found in Sophocles *Ajax* 346; *Philoctetes* 776; Aristophanes *Acharnians* 583; *Assemblywomen* 132; *Clouds* 82; *Frogs* 200bis, 201bis; *Lysistrata* 924; *Women at the Thesmophoria* 25, 255.

[123] See Heritage 1984, 1998, 2002; see I.3 §§29-32 for discussion.

[124] For several uses of *okay* as a discourse marker, see Gaines 2011, with further literature.

[125] The use of καὶ μάλα to indicate an affirmative response to a yes-no question in Xenophon is similar; see Jiménez Delgado 2013.

§54. In the stylized discourse of tragic and comic dialogues, we cannot identify pauses between turns, but we do find dispreferred responses with justifying accounts. An example is the servant's reply to Peisetaerus' request in (t20).

(t20)

(Πε.) οἶσθ' οὖν ὃ δρᾶσον, ὦ τροχίλε; τὸν δεσπότην
ἡμῖν κάλεσον.
81bis Θε. ἀλλ' ἀρτίως νὴ τὸν Δία
εὕδει καταφαγὼν μύρτα καὶ σέρφους τινάς.

Aristophanes *Birds* 80-82

(Pe.) So, roadrunner, you know what you should do? Call your master for us.
Se. Oh no: he's just started his nap, after a lunch of myrtle berries and gnats.

The hoopoe's servant feels compelled to explain why he does not want to comply with Peisetaerus' request: he does not want to wake up his master. The turn-initial ἀλλά signals a correction or switch concerning the explicit or implicit content of the previous turn.[126] In this case, the imperative κάλεσον implies that the servant would carry out the calling, or that there would be no obstacles to do so. The turn starting with ἀλλά corrects such implications, thereby conveying that the servant does not obey.[127]

§55. μέν can signal a dispreferred response in answers to questions, by suggesting that the answer is not straightforward. Consider the start of Ismene's answer to Antigone's question:

(t21)

Αν. ἔχεις τι κεἰσήκουσας; ἤ σε λανθάνει
πρὸς τοὺς φίλους στείχοντα τῶν ἐχθρῶν κακά;
Ισ. ἐμοὶ μὲν οὐδεὶς μῦθος, Ἀντιγόνη, φίλων
οὔθ' ἡδὺς οὔτ' ἀλγεινὸς ἵκετ' ἐξ ὅτου
δυοῖν ἀδελφοῖν ἐστερήθημεν δύο,
μιᾷ θανόντοιν ἡμέρᾳ διπλῇ χερί·

126 See Drummen 2009 on turn-initial ἀλλά in tragedy and comedy.

127 Other instances of turn-initial ἀλλά in dispreferred responses are found in Aeschylus *Agamemnon* 1248 (after a request); Sophocles *Ajax* 1141 (after an order); *Oedipus King* 1020 (after a question); *Oedipus at Colonus* 1418 (after a request); Aristophanes *Birds* 153bis (after a piece of advice), 1450bis (after a suggestion); *Frogs* 134 (after a suggestion and an insert expansion), 481bis (after a request); *Lysistrata* 504bis (after a request), 713 (after a request for information), 758 (after a request), 947bis (after a request).

ἐπεὶ δὲ φροῦδός ἐστιν Ἀργείων στρατὸς
ἐν νυκτὶ τῇ νῦν, οὐδὲν οἶδ' ὑπέρτερον,

Sophocles *Antigone* 9-18

An. Have you any knowledge? Have you heard anything? Or have you failed to notice the evils from our enemies as they come against our friends?

Is. To me, Antigone, no word about our friends has come, either agreeable or painful, since we two were robbed of two brothers, who perished on one day each at the other's hand. Since the Argive army left during this night, I know nothing further (...)

Ismene could simply have answered "no, I don't know," but instead she elaborates on what she does know. As Jebb 1888 and Griffith 1999 *ad loc.* point out, the emphatic position of ἐμοί and the presence of μέν imply a contrast between Ismene herself and unspecified others. While this implication may be present, μέν at the same time conveys that its own discourse act is not all that the speaker wants to say.[128] In this way the particle indicates that the answer, or at least its first act, is insufficient, incomplete, or different from expected. We may compare this use of μέν to English turn-initial *well* in answers.[129]

§56. Different linguistic forms, then, tend to introduce preferred and dispreferred responses. Preferred responses to questions, directives, and offers often start without any contextualization cue. A directive may elicit a turn-initial καὶ δή or ἰδού from its addressee, who thereby draws attention to his visible compliance. Dispreferred responses to various first pair parts may start with ἀλλά; those reacting to a question sometimes contain turn-initial μέν.

4.5 The Actions Performed by Turns

§57. According to CA, it is possible to identify linguistic constructions that regularly perform particular actions.[130] We can also correlate certain actions with the presence or absence of certain particles.

[128] See my discussion of μέν as a floor-holding device in §§28-30 above.

[129] See also II.2 §60 for discussion of μέν at the start of answers. On English *well*, see e.g. Jucker 1993; Aijmer 2013, with further literature. Other examples of turn-initial μέν in non-straightforward answers are found in Aeschylus *Agamemnon* 1203; *Persians* 337, 353; Sophocles *Ajax* 80 (see (t25) in II.2 with discussion), 121; *Oedipus King* 527, 1051, 1234; Euripides *Bacchae* 493, 831, 1264; Aristophanes *Birds* 124, 358bis; *Frogs* 866, 1063; *Lysistrata* 142bis, 574bis.

[130] See e.g. Heritage 2010:*passim*; Sidnell 2010:61-62, 75; Enfield 2013:94-100.

4.5.1 τοι

§58. The particle τοι, for example, works to further a speaker's persuasive ends.[131] The particle's function is to signal an appeal to the addressee, who is strongly encouraged to take note of, and believe, the statement being uttered.[132] For this function the particle's position in a turn does not make a difference. Bäumlein 1861:239 and Denniston 1950:539 note that τοι is mainly used in assertions, and give as paraphrases German "sag' ich dir," "darfst du glauben," and English "you know," "I tell you."[133] τοι has a frequency of about 0.1% of all words in the four dramatists: less than, for example, δή or οὖν (roughly 0.2% on average), but more than for example δῆτα (roughly 0.05% on average).[134] The quite specific pragmatic meaning of τοι makes it a relatively marked, and therefore infrequent form of expression.[135]

§59. Appealing an addressee is particularly appropriate to turns that are meant to persuade. In (t22) the slave Andromache tries to persuade Hermione, the wife of her master Neoptolemus, that Andromache herself is not the cause of Hermione's childlessness, as Hermione had angrily claimed. Rather, Andromache argues, Neoptolemus does not like Hermione because of her arrogance and temper.

(t22)

(Αν.) σὺ δ' ἤν τι κνισθῇς, ἡ Λάκαινα μὲν πόλις
μέγ' ἐστί, τὴν δὲ Σκῦρον οὐδαμοῦ τίθης,
πλουτεῖς δ' ἐν οὐ πλουτοῦσι, Μενέλεως δέ σοι
μείζων Ἀχιλλέως. ταῦτά <u>τοί</u> σ' ἔχθει πόσις.

Euripides *Andromache* 209-212

(An.) But if *you* get angry, you argue that Sparta is a great city and Scyros is of no account, that you are a rich woman living in the midst of the poor,

[131] τοι does not contribute to the positive or negative tonality of an utterance: it implies neither hostility nor friendliness, and may be used in both kinds of contexts. The instance in (t22) is an example of a hostile context, just as Sophocles *Electra* 582. Examples of τοι used in a friendly context include Sophocles *Electra* 871; Aristophanes *Lysistrata* 16.

[132] See IV.4 §§34-39 for similar observations on τοι in Herodotus.

[133] On the interpretation of τοι as an affirmative particle, i.e. as working to underscore the strength of an assertion to the addressee, see Stephens 1837:49-50; Bäumlein 1861:236-239; Denniston 1950 [1934]:537-542. On alternative views, see Hoogeveen 1769:566, who interprets τοι as conclusive, and Hartung 1833:338-370, who interprets τοι as restrictive. As Denniston 1950 [1934]:542 notes, τοι may be used in gnomic contexts as well as in specific statements (as in (t22)).

[134] See our frequency graphs (available online as I.5).

[135] See IV.4 §177 on the lower frequency of particles that contribute a more specific meaning than those that add something more general; the particles discussed there are δῆθεν (highly specific function, very infrequent) versus δή (more general functions, more frequent) in Herodotus.

and that Menelaus is a greater man than Achilles. It is for this that your husband hates you.

Although Andromache knows that she does not have much chance to persuade this angry woman, she nevertheless urges Hermione, with τοι, to believe her statement in 212.[136] "It is because of this that your husband hates you" is one of the most important points in Andromache's argument: if it is really Hermione's own fault that Neoptolemus dislikes her, then she has no reason to hate his concubine. The use of the particle, then, can be connected to the action that the turn is intended to perform.

§60. Aristophanes also uses τοι in this addressee-appealing way in assertions with persuasive purposes:

(t23)

Λυ. ἆρ' οὐ παρεῖναι τὰς γυναῖκας δῆτ' ἐχρῆν;
Κα. οὐ γὰρ μὰ Δί', ἀλλὰ πετομένας ἥκειν πάλαι.
Λυ. ἀλλ', ὦ μέλ', ὄψει τοι σφόδρ' αὐτὰς Ἀττικάς,
ἅπαντα δρώσας τοῦ δέοντος ὕστερον.
ἀλλ' οὐδὲ Παράλων οὐδεμία γυνὴ πάρα,
οὐδ' ἐκ Σαλαμῖνος. (...)

Aristophanes *Lysistrata* 54-59

Ly. So shouldn't the women have arrived by now?
Ca. By now? My god, they should have taken wing and flown here ages ago!
Ly. Well, my friend, you'll find they're typically Athenian: everything they do, they do too late. There isn't even a single woman here from the Paralia, nor from Salamis.

The use of τοι in Lysistrata's utterance of 3,5 lines (56-59) is similar to the tragic examples: the speaker encourages the addressee, her neighbor Calonice, to accept her statement.[137]

[136] Other examples of τοι in tragic monologues that can be connected to the speaker's persuasive intentions include Aeschylus *Agamemnon* 877, 903; Sophocles *Ajax* 520; *Electra* 582, 916, 984; *Philoctetes* 480; *Oedipus at Colonus* 1187; Euripides *Children of Heracles* 533; *Hippolytus* 467. Examples in shorter speeches include Aeschylus *Prometheus Bound* 39 (1-line utterance); Sophocles *Electra* 871 (4-line utterance); *Oedipus at Colonus* 1407 (15-line utterance). The instance in Euripides *Bacchae* 1118 occurs in a messenger speech, which as a whole does not have a primarily persuasive goal, but it is part of a quotation from Pentheus, who is cited as trying to persuade his mother Agaue not to kill him.

[137] See also IV.5 §§75-76, §84, §86, and §93 on τοι in discourse acts with persuasive purposes in historiography. Other examples of τοι in Aristophanes where the hearer is invited to accept the τοι statement include *Assemblywomen* 604; *Birds* 308, 600, 1225, 1437, 1438bis, 1642; *Clouds* 365, 878;

In this case the speaker's persuasive purposes do not reach beyond the single statement, as they may do in a long tragic monologue.

§61. In a few cases in tragedy and comedy τοι is used as as a general intensifier and attention-getting device, unrelated to making a statement credible. An example from Aristophanes *Wealth* may clarify the difference.[138] In this other, less frequent use τοι is also connected to the action performed by the host turn: the interpretation is appropriate when τοι is used outside of assertions, or when the speaker describes her own action of calling someone. In (t24) the god Hermes has just secretly knocked on the door; Cario opens it and does not immediately see him. Then Hermes makes himself visible:

(t24)

Κα. τίς ἔσθ' ὁ κόπτων τὴν θύραν; τουτὶ τί ἦν;

οὐδείς, ἔοικεν· ἀλλὰ δῆτα τὸ θύριον
φθεγγόμενον ἄλλως κλαυσιᾷ;
1099bis Ερ. σέ <u>τοι</u> λέγω,
1100 ὦ Καρίων, ἀνάμεινον.
1100bis Κα. οὗτος, εἰπέ μοι,
σὺ τὴν θύραν ἔκοπτες οὑτωσὶ σφόδρα;

Aristophanes *Wealth* 1097-1101

Ca. Who's that banging on the door? What's going on? No one around, apparently. This door will have plenty to cry about if it's making noise for nothing.
He. You there, Cario, hold on!
Ca. Hey, was that you banging on the door so loud?

Hermes' utterance at 1099bis-1100 is a multi-act move that aims to attract Cario's attention. That is, the move, including the discourse act σέ τοι λέγω, does not state anything that the addressee is encouraged to "believe." σέ τοι λέγω approximates the attention-getting use of οὗτος, found in 1100bis.[139] In a move such as the one by Hermes the force

Frogs 73bis, 509, 1039, 1046, 1047bis (Henderson aptly translates νὴ τὸν Δία τοῦτό γέ τοι δή as "That's the truth, all right!"); *Lysistrata* 16, 46, 626; *Peace* 628 (see III.2 §83); *Wasps* 934.

138 Other examples of τοι in this use are Aeschylus *Libation Bearers* 456 (σέ τοι λέγω); Sophocles *Ajax* 1228 (σέ τοι); *Electra* 1445 (σέ τοι); *Oedipus at Colonus* 1578 (σέ τοι κικλήσκω); Euripides *Iphigeneia at Aulis* 855 (σέ τοι λέγω); Aristophanes *Birds* 274 (σέ τοι), 356ter (ἐγώ τοί σοι λέγω), 406 (σέ τοι καλῶ); *Peace* 934 (εὖ τοι λέγεις); *Wealth* 1099 (σέ τοι λέγω). As the immediate co-text makes clear, τοι cannot be interpreted as a second-person pronoun in these cases either, as it often is in Homer and in Herodotus, because the second person is either already referred to by another pronoun, or is the subject of the verb. I have not found any instances of this use of τοι in drama.

139 On the use of this expression in drama, see §41 above.

of τοι needs to be interpreted as weaker than in assertions. It does still appeal to the addressee: not to believe anything, but simply to pay attention.

4.5.2 Turn-initial γε

§62. Another particle that is connected to the actions performed by its host turn is γε. It is often found at the beginning of answers to questions. The questioner has implied, by the very action of asking, that he is not yet fully aware of the answer; therefore the answerer may feel the need to highlight the most important part of her answer with γε. Consider the following example from Euripides *Medea*:

(t25)

Μη. γυναῖκ’ ἐφ’ ἡμῖν δεσπότιν δόμων ἔχει.
Αι. οὔ που τετόλμηκ’ ἔργον αἴσχιστον τόδε;
Μη. σάφ’ ἴσθ’· ἄτιμοι δ’ ἐσμὲν οἱ πρὸ τοῦ φίλοι.
Αι. πότερον ἐρασθεὶς ἢ σὸν ἐχθαίρων λέχος;
Μη. μέγαν <u>γ’</u> ἔρωτα· πιστὸς οὐκ ἔφυ φίλοις.

Euripides *Medea* 694-698

Me. He has put another woman over me as mistress of the house.
Ae. Surely he has not dared to do such a shameful deed?
Me. He has indeed. Once he loved me, but now I am cast off.
Ae. Was it some passion, or did he grow tired of your bed?
Me. A great passion. He has been unfaithful to his family.

The first discourse act of Medea’s answer in 698, μέγαν γ’ ἔρωτα, picks up the construction with ἐρασθείς from the previous turn.[140] As Mastronarde 2002 *ad loc.* notes, γε is common in such resonating answers.[141] With the particle, Medea emphasizes μέγαν ἔρωτα, thereby inviting the addressee (Aegeus) to infer a contrast between this element and others she does not explicitly state (such as a better reason her husband might have had to leave her).[142] In this case, the emphasis thus created leads to a sarcastic

[140] Elliott 1969, Flacelière 1970, and Mastronarde 2002 *ad loc.* all make note of this echo.

[141] See III.3 §§76-79 on γε and resonance.

[142] On this function of γε, see e.g. Hartung 1832:371, Kühner 1835:398, Stephens 1837:92, and Bäumlein 1861:54. Other examples of turn-initial γε in answers are found in Aeschylus *Persians* 800; Sophocles *Ajax* 104, 876, 1347, 1365; *Antigone* 404, 728, 1103; *Electra* 319; *Oedipus King* 365, 563, 628bis, 994, 1001, 1011, 1046, 1171, 1175bis; *Oedipus at Colonus* 387; *Women of Trachis* 1214; Euripides *Andromache* 254, 912, 914, 916, 918; *Bacchae* 835, 966bis; *Hecuba* 766; *Hippolytus* 96, 98, 1053; *Medea* 698, 1369, 1398bis; Aristophanes *Birds* 56bis, 75, 178bis, 1360; *Frogs* 5bis, 26, 125, 313bis; *Lysistrata* 29, 148bis, 862, 882, 897bis, 1162, 1167. Sometimes resonance is involved in the answer (see III.3 §§76-79), or an agitated emotion (see III.5 §§45-47 and §56).

nuance: later in the dialogue Medea shows her conviction that Jason's great "passion" did not concern the other woman, but the royal power he would receive through his new marriage.[143] The function of γε to emphasize one element by invoking implied others makes it suitable for the start of answering turns.

§63. Turn-initial γε is also regularly found in turns performing a stancetaking. This common action in talk-in-interaction involves a speaker evaluating something, and thereby positioning herself and (dis)aligning with others.[144] Stancetaking is pragmatically close to answering: after all, when asked a question, a speaker gets the opportunity to express her own view on something.[145] In the following Aristophanic passage, Dionysus assesses Heracles' suggestion of a route to the Underworld:

(t26)

Ηρ. ἀλλ' ἔστιν ἀτραπὸς ξύντομος τετριμμένη,
ἡ διὰ θυείας.
124bis Δι. ἆρα κώνειον λέγεις;
125 Ηρ. μάλιστά γε.
125bis Δι. ψυχράν γε καὶ δυσχείμερον·
εὐθὺς γὰρ ἀποπήγνυσι τἀντικνήμια.

Aristophanes *Frogs* 123-126

He. Well, there's a shortcut that's well-beaten—in a mortar.
Di. You mean hemlock?
He. Exactly.
Di. That's a chill and wintry way! It quickly freezes your shins solid.

143 Elliott 1969 and Mossman 2011 *ad loc.* argue for such an interpretation. The sarcastic reading is strengthened by our knowledge that Medea is very angry with Jason about this; see III.5 §§56-58 for γε in contexts of anger.

144 See also III.5 §§59-63 on γε in contexts of stancetaking in Aristophanes. We adopt the model on stancetaking by Du Bois 2007; see also Du Bois and Kärkkäinen 2012. On stance and particle use, see IV.4.4-9. Often only one of the three dimensions evaluating, positioning, and alignment is made explicit; however, as Du Bois 2007:164 argues, the other two are always implied. Strictly speaking, every utterance is a subjective judgment by the speaker: she considers the current utterance the most relevant thing to say at the current moment, whether it is a question, an answer, an assessment, or something else. In the words of Du Bois and Kärkkäinen 2012:438, "every utterance in interaction contributes to the enactment of stance, even if this stance is only evoked and not explicitly spelled out (...)." However, I here speak of "stancetaking" only when an evaluation, positioning, or alignment is made explicit. On assessments (generally the evaluation part of stancetaking) in a CA perspective, see e.g. Pomerantz 1984; Schegloff 2007:59-60, 71, 73-74, 123-126.

145 In fact, most turns containing a turn-initial γε can arguably be classified as either answers to questions (or less frequently to requests) or stancetakings. It seems somewhat suspicious to me that some of the turn-initial γε instances that cannot clearly be so categorized are actually conjectures. Examples are Aeschylus *Libation Bearers* 493; Euripides *Bacchae* 1297; *Hippolytus* 1404.

By using γε, Dionysus commits himself emphatically to the assessment ψυχράν, "cold" (note the exclamation mark in Henderson's translation). This stancetaking turn functions as a second pair part, indirectly rejecting Heracles' suggestion in 123-124 after the insert expansion in 124bis-125. γε at the same time implies a contrast between its host act and an implicit alternative, such as, in this case, a positive adjective that would convey acceptance of the suggested route.[146] The function of γε, then, is not only appropriate to answers, but also to assessments.

§64. It is not surprising that we often find γε in the context of stancetaking: this communicative action makes explicit a subjective—and sometimes particularly emotional—view of the speaker.[147] γε is comparable to the prosodic prominence rendered by an exclamation mark: a verbal equivalent, we can say, of banging one's fist on the table, or of stamping one's feet.[148] It is noteworthy in this respect that turn-initial γε is very rare in questions.[149] Such "stamping" of one's words is appropriate when expressing an opinion or giving an answer that is deemed highly relevant, but less so when asking a question, where the speaker tends to primarily ask the addressee for a certain response.

[146] On γε implying a contrast to an implicit alternative, see e.g. Bäumlein 1861:54; Hartung 1832:371; Kühner 1835:398; Stephens 1837:92; and III.3 §§77-79 and III.5 §47.

[147] On the connection between stancetaking and emotion, see Du Bois and Kärkkäinen 2012. On the connection between γε and anger, and between γε and stancetaking—sometimes combined—see III.5 §§51-63. Other examples of turn-initial γε in turns performing stancetaking are found in Aeschylus *Agamemnon* 938, 1213; *Persians* 286, 1023; Sophocles *Ajax* 78, 534, 589, 983; *Antigone* 241, 573; *Oedipus King* 1035, 1159; *Philoctetes* 755; Euripides *Andromache* 909; *Bacchae* 800, 824; *Hippolytus* 1080; *Medea* 588; Aristophanes *Assemblywomen* 213; *Birds* 158, 1208, 1268, 1692; *Frogs* 125bis, 228, 491, 1149, 1261, 1430, 1451; *Knights* 470; *Lysistrata* 81bis, 148bis, 205, 498quat, 499bis, 521, 777, 988bis, 992, 1228.

[148] Of course the addition of γε may also have a metrical advantage, as in Sophocles *Oedipus King* 1035 (a stancetaking) and Euripides *Medea* 698 (an answer), where γ' provides the necessary lengthening of the previous syllable. Nevertheless, its pragmatic function must be contextually appropriate at the same time; otherwise the poet could have used another way of lengthening. In the two instances cited, for example, δ' or τ' in the same position would have produced the same metrical advantage, but would have been pragmatically impossible, or at least extremely odd. (See §27 above on turn-initial τε and §35, §§37-38 on turn-initial δέ.)

[149] Possible examples of turn-initial γε in questions are found in Aristophanes *Birds* 1446 (γ' ἆρα), 1542 (γ' ἆρ'); *Frogs* 138bis (in a later position, εἶτα πῶς γε περαιωθήσομαι;); 515 (πῶς γε λέγεις). All of these have textual variants, however, and are disputed by editors. I therefore do not agree with Lowe 1973:50 that γε at the beginning of a question is generally unproblematic. Dover 1993 *ad Frogs* 138bis and 515 argues that these γε instances were probably added to the manuscripts in later transmission. Denniston 1950 [1934] mentions that the examples he cites (124-125) are "for the most part textually doubtful" as well.

4.5.3 Utterance starts without particles

§65. Turn-initial interjections are also related to stancetaking: they indicate an emotional reaction to the previous turn.[150] Interjections usually form a separate discourse act on their own, without any accompanying particles.[151] An example is οἴμοι τάλας by Oedipus:

(t27)

(Οι.) τὸν δὲ Λάιον φύσιν
τίν' εἶρπε φράζε, τίνα δ' ἀκμὴν ἥβης ἔχων.
Ιο. μέλας, χνοάζων ἄρτι λευκανθὲς κάρα.
μορφῆς δὲ τῆς σῆς οὐκ ἀπεστάτει πολύ.
Οι. <u>οἴμοι τάλας</u>· ἔοικ' ἐμαυτὸν εἰς ἀρὰς
δεινὰς προβάλλων ἀρτίως οὐκ εἰδέναι.

Sophocles *Oedipus King* 740-745

(Oe.) but tell me about Laius, what he looked like and what stage in manhood he had reached.
Io. He was dark, but just beginning to have grizzled hair, and his appearance was not far from yours.
Oe. Ah me! It seems that all unknowing I have exposed myself to a dread curse.

The turn starting in 744 is a post-expansion after a question-answer pair: a natural position for expressing a stance about the received answer. With the interjection, Oedipus directly expresses his emotional reaction to Iocaste's answer. As opposed to a stancetaking response containing an adjective or adverb assessing the evaluated object (possibly followed by γε), an interjection indicates more focus on its speaker.[152]

§66. Stancetaking turns can also start without any particles or other linguistic contextualization cues. In these cases the speaker expresses an opinion without

[150] Though the category of interjections is ill-defined, just as that of particles, and the functions of these two categories occasionally overlap, an important difference is that interjections can form an utterance on their own, whereas particles generally do not. See Nordgren 2015:11–12, 16–17. On interjections in drama, see also III.5 §15.

[151] As with vocatives (see note 25), there are exceptions, in which the interjection is used as a quote, rather than directly expressing an emotion: Aeschylus *Persians* 1032, 1071, 1072.

[152] See Nordgren 2015:17 on Greek interjections being speaker-oriented. Other examples of turn-initial interjections are found in e.g. Aeschylus *Persians* 725 (see (t8) above), 731; *Agamemnon* 1214; *Libation Bearers* 691, 875, 928, 1007; Sophocles *Ajax* 332, 336, 737, 791, 800, 1266; *Antigone* 82, 1105, 1294, 1306, 1317; *Oedipus King* 316, 754, 1308; Euripides *Bacchae* 805, 1259, 1350; *Hippolytus* 353, 806, 1064; *Medea* 277, 330, 1310, 1393, 1399; Aristophanes *Birds* 62, 86, 272bis, 1501; *Frogs* 307, 653, 657, 1214; *Lysistrata* 198, 449, 462, 845, 1078.

highlighting one specific part of it (as with γε) and without making her emotions explicit (as with an interjection). An example is the last turn by Medea in the following passage:[153]

(t28)

Μη. ὄμνυ πέδον Γῆς πατέρα θ'[154] Ἥλιον πατρὸς
τοὐμοῦ θεῶν τε συντιθεὶς ἅπαν γένος.
Αι. τί χρῆμα δράσειν ἢ τί μὴ δράσειν; λέγε.
... (lines 749-751 left out)
Αι. ὄμνυμι Γαῖαν φῶς τε λαμπρὸν Ἡλίου
θεούς τε πάντας ἐμμενεῖν ἅ σου κλύω.
Μη. ἀρκεῖ· τί δ' ὅρκωι τῶιδε μὴ 'μμένων πάθοις;

Euripides *Medea* 746-754

Me.
Swear by the plain of Earth, by Helios, my grandfather, and by the whole race of gods all together.
Ae.
To do what or to refrain from what? You must say.
(Medea answers)
Ae.
I swear by Earth, by the holy light of Helios, and by all the gods that I will do as I have heard from your lips.
Me.
That is good. But what punishment do you call down on yourself if you do not abide by your oath?

Medea's request for the oath and Aegeus' compliance (after an insert expansion in which he asks for more details) are followed by Medea's assessment of Aegeus' oath in a sequence-closing third:[155] ἀρκεῖ, "it is good." Because the assessment is sequentially dependent on what preceded it, its linguistic form does not need to tie the turn explicitly to its co-text and context right at the beginning.

§67. We also find several borderline cases of stancetaking turns that contain a contextualization cue as their second or third word, but still within the first discourse act. Since these cues often form a syntactic construction with the turn's very first word,

153 Other examples of stancetaking without turn-initial contextualization cues include Sophocles *Ajax* 1120, 1137; *Antigone* 88, 576; *Oedipus King* 616; Euripides *Alcestis* 706; *Bacchae* 193, 197, 838; *Medea* 364, 520, 684; Aristophanes *Acharnians* 479; *Birds* 95bis; *Frogs* 606bis, 652, 1411.

154 For the use of τε in this passage, see III.2 §43.

155 See (t3) with discussion in §17 above.

their turns appear very similar to ones that are immediately contextualized. That is to say, whereas I employ a narrow definition of "turn-initial position" in this chapter,[156] I am aware that the linguistic reality is more flexible. Consider the following example:

(t29)

480 Χρ. τί δῆτά σοι τίμημ' ἐπιγράψω τῇ δίκῃ,
ἐὰν ἁλῷς;
481bis Πε. ὅ τι σοι δοκεῖ.
481ter Χρ. καλῶς λέγεις.

Aristophanes *Wealth* 480-481

Chr. And what penalty shall I impose if you lose your case?
Poverty. Whatever you like.
Chr. Excellent.

Chremylus' assessment καλῶς λέγεις of Poverty's answer (a sequence-closing third) is contextualized by referring explicitly to the addressee. The verb phrase as a whole can probably be felt as a turn-initial contextualization cue, even though the second-person verb form is not the turn's very first word.[157]

§68. Turns without turn-initial contextualization cues may take on a particularly important or formal character. A turn's gnomic nature, content of special significance for the speaker, or uncommon words or constructions may help create this impression.[158] The five quotes from tragedy in Aristophanes *Frogs* without turn-initial contextualization cues probably have a formal ring to them as well.[159] Consider the following example from Aeschylus *Agamemnon*:[160]

156 See §§11-12 above.

157 Other examples of stancetaking turns with a contextualization cue as their second or third word, but within the first discourse act, include Sophocles *Ajax* 94; *Antigone* 561, 571, 1059; *Oedipus King* 545, 859, 1160; *Women of Trachis* 1238; Euripides *Bacchae* 193; *Hippolytus* 278; *Medea* 522, 741, 1127; Aristophanes *Birds* 79; *Frogs* 169ter.

158 Perhaps the "independent" form of these utterances was sometimes chosen by the poets to make them more amenable to being taken out of their context for purposes of quotation. Wright 2013 argues that some lines in tragedy may well have been designed by the playwright to be easily quoted outside their original context. The absence of a particle or other contextualization cue at the start, I suggest, may be one feature contributing to such a movable character.

159 Aristophanes *Frogs* 1152, 1182, 1211, 1225, 1471.

160 Other examples of turns without turn-initial contextualization cues that sound gnomic, extra important, or formal include Sophocles *Ajax* 383, 1163 (starting with ἔσται), 1352; *Antigone* 561, 576; *Oedipus King* 1069; Euripides *Bacchae* 193, 1348; *Hecuba* 1000 (starting with ἔστ'); *Heracles* 93; *Medea* 520, 700, 1231, 1367; Aristophanes *Birds* 903, 1213, 1581 (see Dunbar 1995 *ad loc.*), 1626; *Lysistrata* 501. Several such turns without a turn-initial contextualization cue are also found in

(t30)

(Αγ.) ἐπεὶ δ' ἀκούειν σοῦ κατέστραμμαι τάδε,
εἶμ' ἐς δόμων μέλαθρα πορφύρας πατῶν.
Κλ. ἔστιν θάλασσα, τίς δέ νιν κατασβέσει;
τρέφουσα πολλῆς πορφύρας ἰσάργυρον
κηκῖδα παγκαίνιστον, εἱμάτων βαφάς·
οἶκος δ' ὑπάρχει τῶνδε σὺν θεοῖς, ἄναξ,
ἔχειν, πένεσθαι δ' οὐκ ἐπίσταται δόμος.

Aeschylus *Agamemnon* 956-962

(Ag.) Now, since I have been subjugated into obeying you in this, I will go, treading on purple, to the halls of my house.

Cl. There is a sea—who will ever dry it up?—which breeds an ever-renewed ooze of abundant purple, worth its weight in silver, to dye clothing with. So with the gods' help, my lord, we can remedy this loss; our house does not know what poverty is.

Clytaemnestra reacts to Agamemnon's worries about spoiling the purple fabrics (expressed in lines 948-949): the sea will never cease to abundantly supply purple, and the royal family is rich enough. It is not immediately clear, however, that this turn responds to Agamemnon's earlier words, since other remarks by him came in between, and the relation between the turns is not made explicit. Instead, Clytaemnestra "begins in a tone of magnificent emphasis," as Fraenkel 1950 *ad loc.* notes. He does not specify which features of her utterance convey this tone; I argue that the start without contextualization cues plays a role. Besides conveying a sense of formality, ἔστιν here also alludes to the use of this word at move beginnings in Homer.[161]

§69. The pragmatic analysis of linguistically uncontextualized utterance starts can throw light on textual problems involving the addition or removal of a turn-initial particle. In the following passage from Aristophanes *Lysistrata*, several editors add a turn-initial δέ, while others retain the reading of the manuscripts, which show that the turn starts without a contextualization cue.[162] The desperate Athenian Cinesias tries to convince his wife Myrrhine in this scene to end her sex strike, which was contrived by

lyric parts. These are not discussed here, because lyric songs generally have a different style than iambic dialogues.

161 See II.3 §49 with note 155 on move beginnings with ἔστι or ἦν, with further literature.

162 Van Leeuwen 1903, Sommerstein 1990 and Wilson 2007 add δέ to 898; Von Wilamowitz-Moellendorff 1927, Coulon (ed.) 1958, and Henderson 1987 defend the reading without a particle.

the women in order to force the men to make peace. Cinesias introduces his most important point in lines 898-899.

(t31)

Κι. ὀλίγον μέλει σοι τῆς κρόκης φορουμένης
ὑπὸ τῶν ἀλεκτρυόνων;
897bis Μυ. ἔμοιγε νὴ Δία.
Κι. τὰ τῆς Ἀφροδίτης <δ’> ἱέρ’ ἀνοργίαστά σοι
χρόνον τοσοῦτόν ἐστιν. οὐ βαδιεῖ πάλιν;
Μυ. μὰ Δί’ οὐκ ἔγωγ’, ἢν μὴ διαλλαχθῆτέ γε
καὶ τοῦ πολέμου παύσησθε.

Aristophanes *Lysistrata* 896-901

Ci. It doesn’t bother you that the hens are pulling your woolens apart?
My. Not a bit.
Ci. And what a long time it’s been since you’ve celebrated
Aphrodite’s holy mysteries. Won’t you come home?
My. I certainly will not, not until you men agree to a settlement and
stop the war.

While a turn-initial δέ would be appropriate here—it often introduces new questions in a series (see §§34-35 above), and it is very frequent in turn-initial position in Aristophanes (see Table 1 in the appendix below)—certain linguistic features better support the reading of the manuscripts. The turn contains the unusual word ἀνοργίαστα, “uncelebrated,” in its first occurrence in extant Greek literature.[163] The utterance would have a more humorous effect if a husband’s complaint about “Aphrodite’s holy rites” is presented as something formal, as the remark would exploit the incongruity of speaking in a “high” style in a “low” context. To add δέ to this line would spoil an opportunity for a joke.[164]

§70. In general, this section on connections between particle use and the actions performed by turns has shown that turns starting with γε are pragmatically similar to those without any turn-initial contextualization cue: both are mainly used for answering and stancetaking. Indeed, γε does not directly mark a relation between its turn and the

[163] One form of the verb ὀργιάζω is found in Euripides *Bacchae* 416, but this play was performed in 405 BCE, several years after Aristophanes *Lysistrata* (411 BCE).

[164] On other instances of humor in Aristophanes deriving from the pragmatic level of communication, see Kloss 2001. Other examples of textual problems involving turn-initial particles include Aeschylus *Persians* 480 (δέ or γε), *Libation Bearers* 494 (γε or τε); Sophocles *Ajax* 82 (γε or γάρ), 879 (δῆτα or δή); Euripides *Bacchae* 1297 (γε or no particle); Aristophanes *Birds* 273 (γε or no particle), 1693 (no particle or ἀλλά); *Frogs* 515 (no particle or γε; see note 149 above); *Lysistrata* 945 (γε or no particle). I intend to discuss these cases elsewhere.

previous discourse—its scope does not exceed its host act[165]—but highlights a specific element by implicitly contrasting it to a different element. The actions of answering and stancetaking both tend to be uttered in non-initial positions in a conversational sequence: the preceding discourse sets up the relevance of an answer or (usually) a stancetaking; therefore their relationship to the previous turns does not need to be made explicit.

4.6 Conclusions

§71. This chapter has argued that CA illuminates particle use in tragedy and comedy. Despite their stylized language, the plays still reflect many practices of everyday spoken conversation. Just as in conversation, in Greek drama speakers often use special signals to hold the floor (§§28-30). Furthermore, turns relate to each other either by initiating (first pair parts) or by reacting (second pair parts); the pairs of turns thus formed can be structured in a series, and expanded with preliminary, intervening, or appending material (§§32-48). Again, just as in conversation, responses that fit the goal of the preceding turn best (preferred responses) tend to start with different constructions than responses that were not called for (dispreferred responses; §§49-56). Finally, speakers habitually perform certain actions such as answering and stancetaking by using certain linguistic constructions (§§57-70). Most important, it has been shown that the use of particles is sensitive to the interactional aspects that are clarified by CA. That is to say, particles reveal how turns relate to each other and to the structure of an ongoing interaction.

§72. By taking into account the interactional context surrounding every turn, a CA approach helps us understand why different particles are appropriate in different communicative contexts. For example, one of the known functions of τε is to mark two elements as closely connected; paying attention to the structure of a conversation makes us understand why this particle is highly infrequent in turn-initial position, and why it does occur there in rare cases (§27). The particle μέν may project an upcoming move of multiple discourse acts; speakers exploit this projecting function within turns (§§28-30) as well as within series of similar turns (§33). δέ generally indicates a new step in the discourse; CA makes it clear why this kind of signal is relevant in a series of questions, in response to news, or when a speaker ignores a previous turn (§§34-38). Similarly, we understand better how καί's zooming-in force can interact with its turn-initial position (§36). ἀτάρ has a specialized function in drama, confined to non-initial position in turns (§§39-40). ἦ, οὖν, and καὶ δή all have their own pragmatic functions; CA allows us to clarify how these functions interact with certain positions within a sequence or within a turn (§43, §47, and §§51-52). τοι and turn-initial γε have been shown to be connected to the communicative actions that their turns perform (§§58-70).

165 Denniston 1952:111 on Greek prose style speaks of γε as a particle that may "soften" asyndeton: "though not strictly connective, [γε and some other particles] seem to have been regarded by the Greeks as to some extent mitigating the lack of connexion."

Turn-initial forms	Aeschylus	Sophocles	Euripides	Aristophanes
ἀλλά and combinations	28 (4.9%)	52 (5.1%)	13 (1.6%)	98 (4.9%)
γε and combinations	7 (1.2%)	34 (3.4%)	21 (2.5%)	52 (2.6%)
γάρ and combinations	24 (4.2%)	49 (4.8%)	21 (2.5%)	52 (2.6%)
δέ and combinations	32 (5.6%)	59 (5.8%)	53 (6.4%)	148 (7.4%)
δῆτα and combinations	3 (0.5%)	26 (2.6%)	14 (1.7%)	47 (2.4%)
καί and combinations	41 (7.2%)	55 (5.4%)	28 (3.4%)	120 (6.0%)
μέν and combinations	30 (5.3%)	29 (2.9%)	20 (2.4%)	40 (2.0%)
other particles and particle combinations	67 (11.8%)	108 (10.7%)	51 (6.2%)	224 (11.2%)
Number of starts with particles	232 (40.7%)	412 (40.7%)	221 (26.8%)	781 (39.2%)
finite verb in 1st/2nd person, imperative	67 (11.8%)	102 (10.1%)	138 (16.7%)	261 (13.1%)
question word	53 (9.3%)	106 (10.5%)	83 (10.1%)	216 (10.8%)
negation	38 (6.7%)	94 (9.3%)	68 (8.2%)	153 (7.7%)
vocative	36 (6.3%)	66 (6.5%)	81 (9.8%)	82 (4.1%)
pronoun (demonstrative/ personal/relative)	30 (5.3%)	93 (9.2%)	50 (6.1%)	169 (8.5%)
interjection(s)	64 (11.2%)	74 (7.3%)	68 (8.2%)	91 (4.6%)
lexical repetition from preceding turn	10 (1.8%)	19 (1.9%)	20 (2.4%)	68 (3.4%)
swearing expression, e.g. νὴ/ μὰ Δία	—	—	—	116 (5.8%)
other connection, e.g. conjunction adverb	17 (3.0%)	55 (5.4%)	31 (3.8%)	121 (6.1%)

Table 1: Overview of turn-initial forms in three plays per author

Appendix: Quantitative Observations on Turn-Initial Expressions

§73. The following is an overview of all turn-initial expressions in the twelve plays of my corpus.[166] The table (see Table 1: Overview of turn-initial forms in three plays per author)[167] documents the frequency of several particles at the start of turns, and the differences in distribution among the authors. It also indicates what other linguistic forms tend to be found in turn-initial position, along with their frequencies.[168] In all four authors turns tend to be explicitly contextualized at their start in some way. Most often speakers do this by referring to the speaker or addressee with a verb form, vocative, or pronoun, by projecting the nature of the upcoming turn with a question word or negation, or by indicating an emotional reaction with an interjection. As for turn-initial particles, δέ and καί are the most frequent ones, not surprising in view of their overall high frequency.[169] For ἀλλά, γε, γάρ, δῆτα, and μέν, the frequencies vary quite widely across the authors. As also observed in III.2 on discourse patterns, Aeschylus tends to avoid γε and δῆτα. He is, however, relatively fond of turn-initial μέν.[170] Euripides is the exception in his avoidance of turn-initial ἀλλά.[171] Furthermore, in his plays overall fewer turns start with a particle, and we find a higher frequency of non-contextualized starts. A more detailed comparison of these turn starts in Euripides versus the other authors might reveal whether he uses them in different ways.[172] As for turn-initial interjections: they are typical of tragedy, while comic characters more often start speaking with a swearing expression.[173] The uses of and differences across these turn-initial expressions other than particles can, I expect, be fruitfully explored in a CA approach as well.

166 Aeschylus *Persians, Agamemnon, Libation Bearers*; Sophocles *Ajax, Antigone, Oedipus King*; Euripides *Bacchae, Hippolytus, Medea*; Aristophanes *Birds, Frogs, Lysistrata.*

167 For the term “combination,” see I.1 §19. It includes both “clusters,” in which more than one particle pragmatically work together, and combinations in which several particles simply happen to be adjacent, but have their own separate functions.

168 These numbers are lower than the sum of all starts with particles and those with other contextualization cues, because turns may start with both a particle and another contextualization cue. If so, they are only counted once for this subtotal. Question words, especially, are frequently combined with a turn-initial particle in second position: e.g. Aeschylus *Persians* 1016 (τί δ’); Sophocles *Oedipus King* 1177 (πῶς δῆτ’); Euripides *Medea* 689 (τί γάρ); Aristophanes *Frogs* 1162 (πῶς δή).

169 See our frequency graphs (available online as I.5). See also Hancock 1917 on the frequency of different turn-initial particles in tragic stichomythia: he notes (26) that τε is infrequent, καί frequent, and δέ even more so. Asyndeton is even more frequent (28): “Particles are largely used because they save phrases, asyndeton because it saves both phrases and particles.”

170 See III.5 §§34-37 for some specific uses of μέν in Aeschylus *Agamemnon.*

171 See also Drummen 2009 on turn-initial ἀλλά in these four authors, with similar numbers.

172 The difference may of course also be due to chance.

173 On swearing expressions in Aristophanes, see e.g. Dillon 1995. These “oaths,” he argues (137), “usually indicate only the speaker’s emotional state.”

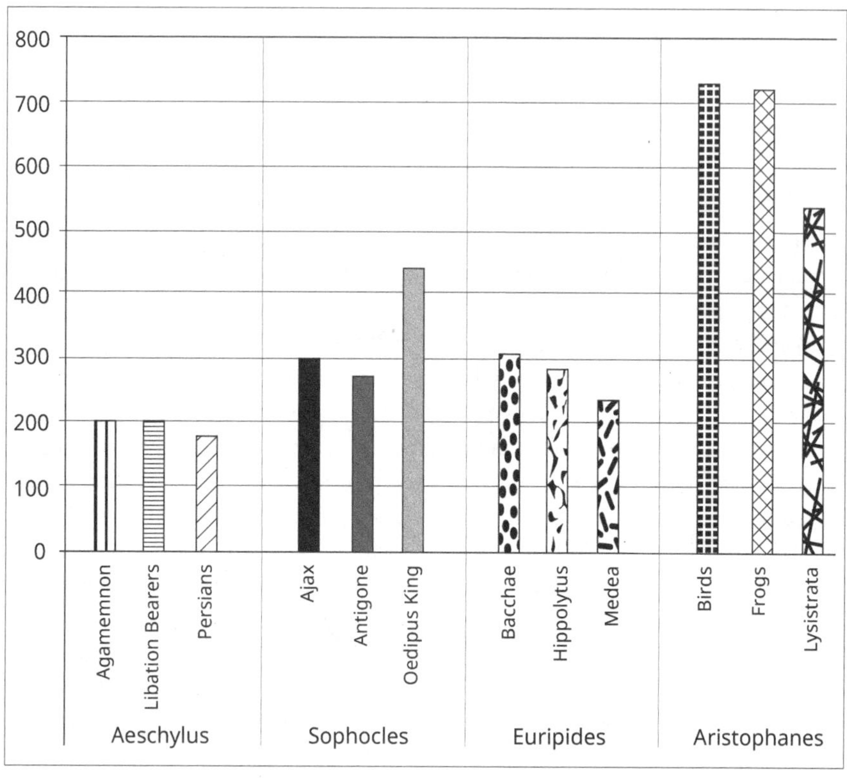

Figure 2: Number of turns in the three plays per author

§74. Concerning the total number of turns per play, comedies feature more turns than tragedies, and the plays of Aeschylus contain the fewest turns. The following diagram shows that this holds true for all individual plays. In my corpus, there are many more turns in each play of Aristophanes than in any individual tragedy. These quantitative differences reflect different conversational styles. (See Figure 2: Number of turns in the three plays per author.) The three comedies are on average longer than the tragedies,[174] but comic turns also tend to be shorter than tragic turns. The average turn lengths are 6.7 lines per turn in Aeschylus; 4.3 lines per turn in Sophocles; 5.2 lines per

[174] The plays consist of the following number of lines: Aeschylus *Persians*: 1077; *Agamemnon*: 1673; *Libation Bearers*: 1076; Sophocles *Ajax*: 1420; *Antigone*: 1353; *Oedipus King*: 1530; Euripides *Bacchae*: 1392; *Hippolytus*: 1466; *Medea*: 1419; Aristophanes *Birds*: 1765; *Frogs*: 1533, *Lysistrata*: 1321. On average, Aeschylus writes 1275, Sophocles 1434, Euripides 1426, and Aristophanes 1540 lines per play.

turn in Euripides; and only 2.3 lines per turn in Aristophanes.[175] Comic speakers more often "interrupt" each other: a conversational style leading to Slings' remark (2002:101) that most Aristophanic speakers are characterized by "aggressiveness."

§75. In tragedy, the plays of Aeschylus have the fewest speaking turns: only 190 on average. This is primarily because the long lyric sections make up a large part of Aeschylean plays. These three tragedies also contain fewer and shorter stichomythic passages than those by Sophocles and Euripides. The higher relative frequency of turn-initial interjections in Aeschylus is due to the extremely high number in *Persians*, where lamenting—with which many interjections tend to be associated—is one of the main communicative actions of the play. Furthermore, in this sample Sophocles *Oedipus King*, with 441 turns, appears as the tragedy of dialogue and of stichomythia *par excellence*: it has many more turns of speaking than any of the other eight tragedies. We can connect the high number of turns to the play's plot: Oedipus' quest for information is enacted in his many stichomythic exchanges with other characters.[176] Not surprisingly, this play also has a higher frequency of turn-initial question words than the other tragedies (51, whereas the other tragedies have no more than 34 per play).[177]

175 In this respect, comedy can be said to be closer to spoken conversation, where turns tend to be short. See e.g. Schegloff 2007:3-4, who explains that turns may consist of only one turn-constructional unit, that is, one grammatical unit with a certain intonational packaging, and Sidnell 2010:41-43, 139 on turn-constructional units and transition-relevance places.

176 See also Hancock 1917:17 on Euripides *Medea*: "we should expect from the nature of the plot and the character of the heroine a great deal of vigorous stichomythia. In fact, however, most of the bitterness is vented in longer speeches and there is comparatively little line-dialogue."

177 The absolute numbers of turn-initial question words are: Aeschylus *Persians*: 12; *Agamemnon*: 24; *Libation Bearers*: 17; Sophocles *Ajax*: 32; *Antigone*: 24; *Oedipus King*: 51; Euripides *Bacchae*: 34; *Hippolytus*: 25; *Medea*: 24; Aristophanes *Birds*: 84; *Frogs*: 77, *Lysistrata*: 55.

III.5

Reflecting Emotional States of Mind

Calmness Versus Agitation

5.1 Introduction

§1. Drama texts incorporate a multitude of characters' voices, embodied by different actors.[1] These multivocal performative aspects furnish ideal opportunities to explore various pragmatic phenomena in the plays' language, three of which are discussed in III.2, III.3, and III.4. The characters' verbal expressions of their emotional states of mind are an essential component of dramatic interactions, and thus deserve pragmatic analysis as well. Particles are among the linguistic features that may reflect emotional states of mind; it is the goal of the present chapter to illuminate how they do so.[2]

§2. The concept of emotions is notoriously difficult to define and describe consistently.[3] As Sanford and Emmott 2012:191-192 outline, theories of emotion tend to either "emphasize the role of an experiencer's judgment (appraisal)," or "highlight the role of an experiencer's body (...) in producing an emotion." The authors note that there are many variants of both theories.[4] Often the cognitive and somatic sides are combined: a person's

1 Voice in other genres is discussed in II.3 §28 (on the voice of a character in Homer) and especially IV.4 §§15-44 (on direct and indirect voices of characters in Herodotus and Thucydides).

2 It is not my goal here to examine how the audience's emotions are aroused by a performance. Though these emotions are part of the communicative process of drama, they are less directly relevant to particle use. For emotional responses of the ancient audience, see e.g. Budelmann and Easterling 2010 (on tragedy); Grethlein 2010:88 (on Aeschylus *Persians*); Munteanu 2011 (on comedy) and 2012 (on tragedy). At Oxford University, the project "Adults at play(s)" (started in 2014) has investigated the psychology of dramatic audiences, using both Greek and Shakespearean tragedy as research corpus. For modern readers' emotional responses to narrative, and their mental representations of characters' emotions, see Sanford and Emmott 2012:191-232.

3 In general, emotions are seen as "relatively brief and intense reactions" to changes in a person's environment (Altenmüller, Schmidt, and Zimmermann 2013:344). The transitory nature of emotions is also mentioned in the definitions by e.g. Caffi and Janney 1994:327; Mortillaro, Mehu, and Scherer 2013:4; Owren, Philipp, Vanman, Trivedi, Schulman, and Bachorowski 2013:175; Schwarz-Friesel 2013:70.

4 On (problems in) defining and classifying emotions, see also e.g. Reisenzein 1994; Wierzbicka 1999; Altenmüller, Schmidt, and Zimmermann 2013; Juslin 2013; Schwarz-Friesel 2013:43-87.

appraisal of an event influences her bodily reaction, that is, her tendency to be drawn toward or away from an object.[5] On top of the definition problem, the term "emotion" and its conceptualization are highly culture-dependent, as many scholars point out.[6] The ancient Athenians will therefore have conceptualized emotions differently from modern English-speaking scholars. However, the terms "emotion" and "emotional state of mind" will be used here nevertheless, as this chapter does not aim to investigate historical or philosophical elements that inform the cultural side of emotions.

§3. A caveat specific to the study of emotionality in drama is that the speakers are fictional characters. The emotions themselves and the ways of revealing them may very well be based on idealizations and stereotypes, rather than on actual human experience. However, any interaction of the characters on stage has to be at least recognizable and comprehensible to the audience—an assumption that underlies also III.2, III.3, and III.4.[7] Even if these interactions are stylized, they are grounded in reality. The actors' masks expressed only part of the characters' emotions; any nuance and alteration had to come from language, prosody, and gesture.

§4. This chapter complements previous research on emotions in Greek literature by analyzing linguistic signs of calmness and agitation, in particular by means of particle use. The way in which characters (in fact the playwrights) organize the flow of discourse is explored, in particular the use of particles, under these states of mind. In addition, examples of particle use are discussed that are influenced by the more global temperament of certain tragic characters (see §§78-87 below).

§5. The chapter mainly discusses broad states of mind, rather than specific emotions such as sadness or fear. The reason is that calmness and agitation[8] are often clearly indicated by the context, and reflected in discourse organization and particle use, whereas specific emotions tend to require specific clues, such as the explicit mentioning of the feeling. The focus here is not on such semantic expressions, but on the pragmatic and

5 See Sanford and Emmott 2012:192-193, with reference to Arnold 1961:177.

6 See e.g. Stanford 1983:21-46; Wierzbicka 1999:esp. 3-4; Konstan 2006:*passim*; Cairns 2008; Theodoropoulou 2012:433; Schwarz-Friesel 2013:59; Sanders 2014:*passim*. Along the same lines, Sidnell and Enfield 2012:321 argue more generally: "the language you speak makes a difference in the social actions you can perform."

7 See e.g. III.4 §§3-4 for discussion of the unrealistic nature of tragic and comic dialogues and why we can nevertheless use Conversation Analysis to analyze them. More generally, Hogan has convincingly shown in numerous publications (e.g. 2010; 2011) that literature is a crucial source for learning about emotions and how they are expressed. He illustrates (2010:188-194) the usefulness of literature for emotion research by analyzing the levels of (1) literature's existence, (2) universal genres such as romantic and heroic narratives, and (3) individual literary works.

8 I use "agitation" as a shorthand for "a relatively high degree of arousal"; see §§22-23 below. That is, "agitation" does not refer to one particular emotion, but is used as the contrary of the equally broad term "calmness"; whether the agitation is linked to a positive or a negative emotion needs to be understood or inferred from the context. In practice, I will be concerned almost entirely with negative emotions; see §22 below.

performative side of communication. However, anger *is* discussed separately: the broad co-text and context usually indicate the presence of anger better than other specific emotions, if no explicit label is given.

§6. The expression of calmness and agitation is closely linked to the interaction on stage; while some emotions are more interactive than others (see §53 below on anger), it is always crucial to take into account the interactional context for the interpretation of linguistic patterns. A speaker's specific communicative goal in a certain situation may require the display of a higher or lower degree of arousal (see §25 below).

§7. Another important general point to keep in mind is that linguistic features associated with a certain emotional state, whether a particle, a syntactic construction, or a strategy like repetition, do not encode this emotion all by themselves, but only in combination with certain co-texts and contexts. That is, the same linguistic feature may carry a different function in another co-text and context. The chapter illustrates this multifunctionality for several linguistic features: see §28 on the order of subordinate and main clauses, §67 on appositions, §77 on repetition, §§34-42 on μέν, §§51-63 on γε, and §§85-86 on δέ. In other words, some functions unrelated to emotionality will also be discussed, in order to clarify the role of the different co-texts and contexts.

§8. The chapter starts with an overview of the scholarship, both on emotions in ancient Greek texts (§§9-21) and on calmness versus agitation in general (§§22-25), and a discussion of my use of its insights and methods. 5.2 analyzes linguistic reflections of a calm state of mind (§§27-43), and of an agitated state of mind (§§44-50). 5.3 devotes attention to γε in different comic contexts (§§51-63). This is followed by two tragic case studies that contrast calm discourse to agitated discourse (§§64-87), and by the conclusions (§§88-95).

5.2 Approaches to emotions

5.2.1 Emotions in ancient Greek texts

§9. The elaborate scholarship on emotions in ancient Greek literature in general, and in Classical drama in particular, can be divided into two groups. Most studies adopt a historical, literary, or philosophical approach, and focus on the macro-levels of cultural differences between Greek and English emotional terms, or the literary meaning of emotions. A smaller number of works delves into the micro-level of the linguistic expressions of emotions. This section gives examples of both kind of research.

§10. Recent publications on the ancient Greeks' conceptualization of emotions include Konstan 2006, Cairns 2008, Fulkerson 2013, and Sanders 2013 and 2014.[9] Konstan explores

[9] See §2 above. Stanford 1983 (see §18 below) also notes the difficulty in studying ancient Greek emotions, because terms and concepts cannot be translated one-to-one from the Greek language and culture to ours. See especially pp. 23-27 for problems surrounding "pity." However, it is not Stanford's main goal to examine the differences in emotion conceptualizations between us and

the differences between those conceptualizations and our modern ones.[10] Emotion terms such as ὀργή (~ "anger"), φιλία (~ "friendship"), and φθόνος (~ "envy") can in fact not be translated directly into English emotional labels. Greek terms may be more widely applicable, and specific English terms may be absent from the Greek vocabulary. However, Cairns argues that in the cases of pity, jealousy, and pride, Konstan sees larger differences between the Greek and the English conceptualizations than are in fact justified, because Konstan focuses too much on English labels for specific emotions. For example, the fact that classical Greek has no term for "pride" does not mean that the phenomenon was absent from classical Greek society or literature, in Cairns' view. Similarly, Sanders 2013 argues that sexual jealousy did exist in classical Greece, in contrast to Konstan's claim.

§11. Fulkerson 2013 is a monograph on regret in antiquity, describing, like Konstan's work, differences between the ancient and modern conceptions of this emotion. The author analyzes sources from Greek epic, tragedy, historiography, New Comedy, and several Latin genres. She argues, for example, that status was more important in the ancient conceptualization of remorse than in the modern one.

§12. Sanders 2014 argues for complementing the lexical approach to ancient emotions with a socio-psychological approach. This author offers an analysis of envy and jealousy in Classical Athens, describing the Athenians' experience, the expression, and the literary representation of these emotions. Tragedy and comedy are among the sources in which he analyzes φθόνος. Sanders outlines "scripts," that is, stylized cognitive scenarios, which correspond to certain emotion terms.[11] He concludes that φθόνος for example corresponds to twelve different scenarios, which are similar to those covered by English *envy*, *jealousy*, and *rivalry*.

§13. Visvardi 2015 adopts a literary approach to ancient Greek emotions, with a specific focus on the tragic chorus. The author analyzes choruses that enact fear and pity, and compares them to the depiction of emotions in Thucydides' *Histories*. Both the tragedians and Thucydides, she argues, display sensitivity to the motivational power of collective emotion in the Athenian institutions.

§14. Numerous scholars focus on the literary function of specific emotions in tragedy, analyzing individual plays, sometimes even in relation to individual characters.[12] For example, Thumiger 2013 analyzes the connections between *eros* and madness in several

the ancient Greeks; he focuses instead on the expressions and literary functions of emotions in tragedy.

10 See also Konstan 2001 on the differences between the modern concept of pity and those of the Greeks and Romans. On the emotions of the Romans, see also Kaster 2005.

11 See II.4 §46 on the notion of scripts, with references.

12 On the literary functions of emotions in Roman tragedy, see e.g. the book-length study of Seneca's revenge tragedies by Winter 2014. Instead of a literary perspective, Munteanu 2012 adopts a philosophical and historical one on pity and fear in several Greek tragedies. That is, her analyses aim to illuminate the ethical and social implications of these emotions. The papers in Chaniotis 2012 (ed.) and Chaniotis and Ducrey 2013 (eds.) similarly analyze emotions in various ancient sources as a historical phenomenon.

tragedies. She concludes that erotic emotion never brings comfort but only has negative consequences. This has to do with genre conventions, as well as with the strict individuality connected to *eros*. In the same volume, Sanders discusses several emotions of the Euripidean Medea, and argues that sexual jealousy is part of her motivation. Other examples are Gerolemou 2011 on female madness in tragedy, and Provenza 2013 on the portrayal and the function of madness in Euripides *Heracles*. All of these studies offer rich analyses of the specific emotion(s) in the play(s) they discuss; however, they do not examine the syntax, pragmatics, or discourse organization connected to emotional expressions.

§15. As for the linguistic expression of emotion, scholars focus on different possibilities.[13] First, emotions can be expressed with interjections, which is the topic of Nordgren's work on Greek drama (2012 and 2015). The category called expressive interjections, such as αἰαῖ, οἴμοι, and φεῦ,[14] express surprise, pain and vexation, lamentation, or joy, each of them with several specific nuances.[15] These interjections can be considered an unmediated way of emotion expression.

§16. Second, one can spotlight semantics, that is, when characters explicitly name their feelings. This is, for instance, the main focus of Schnyder 1995 on fear in Aeschylus. The author describes the vocabulary of fear used in several plays, including metaphors, thereby identifying differences in the fear vocabulary between Aeschylus, on the one hand, and epic and lyric, on the other.[16]

§17. More important to the current investigation are the levels of syntactic constructions and of discourse organization. The 2015 article by Luraghi and Sausa focuses on the linguistic constructions associated with different emotion verbs in Homer. The authors argue that verbs denoting anger, hate, and envy, which typically take a nominative-dative construction, "are construed as complex and potentially interactive, with experiencers that have agent properties" (16). The people or other agents that caused these feelings "are conceptualized as likely to react" (16). Verbs of longing, loving, and desiring, in contrast, often take a nominative-genitive construction: the subject is construed as having no control over the event, and no cause is mentioned. This group of emotion verbs, then, "does not imply any interaction." (18) Regarding other

13 On the importance of analyzing language when analyzing emotion in general, see e.g. Argaman 2010; Schwarz-Friesel 2013. On different linguistic and paralinguistic cues working together to convey emotions in any language, see e.g. Bazzanella 2004:62-63; Caffi and Janney 1994:348; Selting 1994; Van Lancker Sidtis 2008; Foolen 2012. A study of imitative constructions (onomatopoeic interjections) and their use to express emotions in Finnish is Jääskeläinen 2013. See also Theodoropoulou 2012 on the various linguistic means to express emotions, especially metaphors, and how these are employed in ancient texts.

14 On "expressive interjections" as a subcategory of Greek interjections, and on their function of expressing the speaker's mental state, see Nordgren 2015:17-19. On the connection between interjections and emotions in a modern language, see e.g. Schwarz-Friesel 2013:154-162 on German.

15 See Nordgren 2015:93-164.

16 Stanford 1983 on tragedy also pays attention to the semantic level of emotion expression.

verbs, "the NomDat construction is associated with verbs of social interaction, while the NomGen construction is associated with verbs of hitting, touching, reaching or trying to reach." (21) Luraghi and Sausa's results show that Homeric Greek displays syntactic differences between the representation of anger and similar emotions, on the one hand, and less interactive emotions, on the other hand.[17] Their case study thus illustrates that the expression of emotions influences grammatical choices in ancient Greek literature.

§18. The influence of emotions on discourse organization in tragedy is discussed by Mastronarde 1979 and Stanford 1983. Mastronarde's remarks are part of his argument about contact among tragic characters; for Stanford, conversely, emotions are his main focus. Both authors observe, for example, that *antilabe* may express agitation.[18] Mastronarde further discusses "suspension of syntax" beyond an utterance in stichomythia, that is, turns of speaking that are syntactically incomplete, and are potentially completed in a later turn; in Euripides this technique may emphasize a character's strong feelings, as it emphasizes the "self-absorbed continuation of her own thoughts" after an utterance by another speaker (62). In other words, Mastronarde shows that discourse organization, such as the build-up of syntactic structures, may be connected to characters' emotional states of mind. Stanford identifies several linguistic and stylistic markers of specific emotions, such as hyperbole, used to express anger, or single-word repetition, used to express excitement.[19] This scholar analyzes both the emotions experienced by characters or choruses and those aroused in audiences.

§19. As far as particles and emotion expression in ancient Greek are concerned, little has been written so far. Some remarks can be found in the ancient grammarians' writings. The treatise Περὶ Ἑρμενείας (*On style*)[20] states that δή contributes πάθος to a certain passage in Homer.[21] Similarly, Apollonius Dyscolus (second century CE) claims that γε may intensify the emotion expressed by καλῶς γε.[22] In modern times commentators offer notes on particles' emotional quality. They observe, for example, that καί in questions may indicate the speaker's surprise, doubt, or indignation when used at the start of questions.[23] However, commentators usually do not clarify which co-textual and contextual features

[17] See Foolen 2012:353 for reference to cross-linguistic research on the use of prepositions in relation to emotion words; the different prepositions attest to different construals of the emotions, just as the different syntactic constructions in Homeric Greek do.

[18] See Mastronarde 1979:59 and Stanford 1983:99.

[19] On hyperbole especially expressing anger in tragedy, see Stanford 1983:101; on single-word repetition indicating emotional agitation (especially connected to grief), see pp. 93-95.

[20] As discussed in I.2 §58, this work has been attributed to Demetrius of Phaleron, fourth to third century BCE, but was possibly written later.

[21] See I.2 §58 and De Jonge 2015:994 on this observation.

[22] See I.2 §75. Apollonius does not clarify which emotion is expressed; he simply speaks of ἔκπληξις ("consternation," "amazement," "agitation").

[23] See §83 with note 138 below. See also Hancock 1917:29 on this use of καί. This use is discussed in III.3 §45, with note 33; III.4 §36 with notes 72 and 73.

are relevant to their interpretation of a certain particle instance. In fact these features are crucial: particles never express an emotion or emotional state of mind by themselves.

§20. All in all, several approaches are available to emotions and emotional states of mind in ancient Greek. The present chapter fills a gap in previous investigations, in that it analyzes how certain emotional states of mind relate to particle use. That is, such states do not only influence linguistic choices in the direct description of emotions with verbs, discussed by Luraghi and Sausa, but also linguistic choices concerning discourse organization, which can be considered indirect manifestations of emotional states. Since particles only carry out their functions in combination with co- and contextual features, it is important to look at the connection between characters' emotional states and discourse organization more generally, including the contribution of particles. As it will turn out, stretches of discourse larger than sentences need to be taken into account, as well as the interaction among characters.

§21. In this analysis one should keep in mind that most utterances tend to perform multiple communicative actions simultaneously. The expression of emotions may be an utterance's main pragmatic goal, or may be a secondary goal accompanying a different main goal. The former is generally the case when a speaker utters no more than an interjection.[24] We encounter the latter situation when, for example, a threat or even the description of an outrageous past event conveys the speaker's anger.[25] Similarly, a carefully composed argumentative speech may show signs of the speaker's calmness while her main goal is to try to persuade the addressee.[26] Any utterance may be influenced by the speaker's emotional mindset to a higher or lower degree; there is no black-or-white distinction between utterances that express emotions and utterances that do not do so. I will therefore examine utterances that carry the reflection of some emotional state of mind while achieving various paragmatic goals.

5.2.2 Calmness versus agitation beyond ancient Greek

§22. Scholars of emotions often use a dimension of arousal for distinguishing among different emotions.[27] This dimension represents a continuum between calmness (or "deactivation"; see Reisenzein 1994) and agitation (or "activation" in Reisenzein's terms). The other dimension is that of valence (positive-negative). Juslin 2013 uses the following image, based on the work of Russell 1980, to show the possible distribution of emotions in

[24] Examples are Aeschylus *Persians* 1043; Sophocles *Ajax* 891; Euripides *Hippolytus* 310bis; Aristophanes *Frogs* 653. On interjections in Greek drama, see §15 above.

[25] As for example in (t12) below from Aristophanes *Frogs*.

[26] For examples of long speeches intended to persuade that reflect the speaker's calmness, see note 52 below.

[27] Beside the dimensional approach to emotion classification, the other main approach is the categorical approach, in which one has to decide the number and naming of emotional categories—a debated issue. See e.g. Altenmüller, Schmidt, and Zimmermann 2013:341-343; Schwarz-Friesel 2013:62-69 on both the categorial and the dimensional approaches.

a two-dimensional view.[28] The degree of arousal (calm-agitated) forms the vertical axis, the degree of pleasure or displeasure the horizontal axis:[29]

Alarmed • Aroused •
Afraid •
Tense •
Angry •
Distressed •
Annoyed •
Frustrated •
•Excited
•Astonished
•Delighted
•Glad
•Happy
•Pleased
Miserable •
Depressed •
Sad•
Gloomy •
Bored •
Droopy •
•Tired
•Sleepy
•Satisfied
•Content
•Serene
•Calm
•At Ease
•Relaxed

Figure 1: Two-dimensional emotions model, from Juslin 2013:256

In order to fully distinguish between emotions that occupy a similar location in this two-dimensional space, Reisenzein 1994 proposes to embed this theory within a cognitive theory that takes into account the appraisals themselves. He mentions the examples of disappointment, envy, and shame, which involve roughly the same proportions of displeasure and activation, but are caused by different (interpretations of) situations.[30]

§23. Though it is not my aim to classify the emotions found in tragedy and in comedy, the dimension of arousal and the notion of appraisal causes are relevant to the upcoming analyses. The valence dimension (see §22) will not concern us here, because positive emotions are less frequently expressed in the dramatic corpus, and are usually less clearly indicated on the linguistic level than negative emotions are.[31] The presence of positive emotionality is therefore harder to detect for us as readers. In contrast, the degree of calmness or of agitation brought about by a negative emotion tends to be identifiable, even if it is less clear which particular emotion is expressed that corresponds to a lower or higher degree of arousal. A linguistic expression might not make it clear exactly, for instance, whether the speaker is desperate, frustrated, or annoyed, but it usually communicates whether or not she is agitated. The contexts also tend to make clear the appraisals on which emotional states of mind are based. These appraisals, such

28 For an overview of several two-dimensional emotion models, see Barrett and Russell 2009.

29 Sometimes a third dimension is added, such as tension, intensity, or control. See e.g. Caffi and Janney 1994:338 on a three-dimensional model of "affective experience"; see also Schwarz-Friesel 2013:69 on the three "parameters" to describe the "wesentlichen Eigenschaften von Emotionen."

30 See also e.g. Sanford and Emmott 2012:191-193 on the relevance of appraisal in theories of emotion.

31 An exception is Aeschylus *Libation Bearers* 235-245, where Electra realizes that Orestes has returned alive and is standing in front of her. Blass 1906 *ad loc.* speaks of "leidenschaftliche Freude" ("passionate joy"), Garvie 1986 *ad loc.* describes Electra as "beside herself with joy." An Aristophanic example is the joyful greeting in *Lysistrata* 78-81.

as the interpretation of a past action as an insult causing anger, are among the nonverbal indications of a certain state of mind.

§24. Whether or not a speaker seems calm, in other words, can be inferred from the broad co-text and context. Relatively long speaking turns give more indications of a speaker's calmness or agitation than short utterances.[32] Nevertheless, also in short turns contextual cues such as an utterance's main goal or a speaker's social status provide hints about calmness. For example, a high-status speaker who gives an order or piece of advice to an inferior usually does not show agitation, because she has no reason to do so. Another context that is connected to calmness is an official speech by a leader figure (see e.g. (t2) below). Different contexts, then, can provide cues about a character's degree of arousal.

§25. Note that the literary functions of calmness in tragedy and comedy are different. Tragic calmness may betray characters' ignorance about advancing disaster (such as Oedipus in (t15) below),[33] demonstrate the secure power of gods,[34] or be needed for narrating a story, such as a messenger speech.[35] Comedy, conversely, does not contain "ironic" calmness before misfortune; the high social status that some comic characters adopt is not as absolute as that of tragic gods; and long narratives are rare. In both genres, nevertheless, calmness is associated with relatively long speeches that have a persuasive goal.[36] However, whereas in tragedy it is often a matter of life or death if someone is persuaded,[37] in comedy such speeches may concern absurd or mocking topics, such

32 This is why most parallel examples given in the footnotes are from relatively long turns of speaking, both calm and agitated ones. This is not meant to imply any influence of the degree of the speaker's agitation on her utterance length. Short and long utterances can both express calmness as well as agitation. In the case of long utterances, there simply tend to be more linguistic indications available from which to infer the speaker's state of mind.

33 Examples of tragic characters, who are unaware of upcoming doom and speak in a calm way, are Agamemnon in Aeschylus *Agamemnon* 810-854; the Pythia in *Eumenides* 1-33; Oedipus in Sophocles *Oedipus King* 1-13, cited in (t15); Andromache in Euripides *Andromache* 183-231 and 269-273.

34 Examples of gods speaking calmly in tragedy are Athena in Sophocles *Ajax* 1-13; Dionysus in Euripides *Bacchae* (throughout: see §§78-84 below), Aphrodite in *Hippolytus* 1-57.

35 Tragic messenger speeches reflecting calmness include Sophocles *Antigone* 1192-1243; Euripides *Medea* 1136-1230.

36 Apart from Aristophanes *Assemblywomen* 171-240 by Praxagora (see (t2) and notes 48 and 50 below), speeches meant to persuade that reflect calmness include Sophocles *Antigone* 683-723 by Haemon; *Oedipus at Colonus* 1181-1203 by Antigone; *Philoctetes* 1314-1347 by Neoptolemus; Euripides *Alcestis* 280-325 by Alcestis; *Bacchae* 266-327 by Teiresias; *Hecuba* 299-331 by Odysseus; *Hippolytus* 433-481 by the nurse, 983-1035 by Hippolytus; *Medea* 522-575 by Jason; Aristophanes *Acharnians* 496-556 by Dicaeopolis, *Wasps* 548-559 by Lovecleon.

37 For example, both Phaedra's nurse in Euripides *Hippolytus* 433-481 and Tecmessa in Sophocles *Ajax* 485-524 want to convince their masters not to commit suicide. Haemon in Sophocles *Antigone* 683-723 tries to persuade his father Creon not to kill Antigone. Andromache in *Andromache* 183-231 and Hippolytus in Euripides *Hippolytus* 983-1035 need to save their own life by arguing their cases. Hecuba in Euripides *Hecuba* 803-805 does not want to save anyone but tries to get help in taking violent revenge on her enemy Polymestor. See also McDonald 2007:475: "In Greek tragedy, many speeches justify murder."

as comparing the *pólis* to a woollen fleece,[38] or presenting birds as gods.[39] Despite these differences in underlying reasons, in my tragic and comic corpus the speakers of such long speeches must generally suppress their excitement, if present, in order to be persuasive.

5.3 Reflections of Calmness and Agitation

§26. Calm discourse has different linguistics characteristics from agitated discourse, and particle use is among the evidence for this difference. The reflections of calmness and agitation can be perceived on several linguistic levels.

5.3.1 Calmness

§27. One of the linguistic features that may be connected to calmness is the syntactic build-up in which a subordinate clause, or more, precedes its main clause. This type of composite sentence, in other words, begins with a clause that cannot syntactically stand on its own, but creates the expectation that something will follow. A few examples are found in Socrates' calm utterances in the following passage. He explains the clouds' appearance to Strepsiades, after the latter has expressed his surprise about that:

(t1)

Σω. ἀπόκριναί νυν ἅττ' ἂν ἔρωμαι.
Στ. λέγε νυν ταχέως ὅτι βούλει.
Σω. ἤδη ποτ' ἀναβλέψας εἶδες νεφέλην κενταύρῳ ὁμοίαν
ἢ παρδάλει ἢ λύκῳ ἢ ταύρῳ;
Στ. νὴ Δί' ἔγωγ'. εἶτα τί τοῦτο;
Σω. γίγνονται πάνθ' ὅτι βούλονται· κᾆτ' ἢν μὲν ἴδωσι κομήτην
ἄγριόν τινα τῶν λασίων τούτων, οἷόνπερ τὸν Ξενοφάντου,
σκώπτουσαι τὴν μανίαν αὐτοῦ κενταύροις ᾔκασαν αὑτάς.
Στ. τί γὰρ ἢν ἅρπαγα τῶν δημοσίων κατίδωσι Σίμωνα, τί δρῶσιν;
Σω. ἀποφαίνουσαι τὴν φύσιν αὐτοῦ λύκοι ἐξαίφνης ἐγένοντο.

Aristophanes *Clouds* 345-352

So. Now answer some questions for me.
St. Ask away, whatever you like.
So. Have you ever looked up and seen a cloud resembling a centaur,
or a leopard, or a wolf, or a bull?
St. Certainly I have. So what?

[38] *Lysistrata* 574bis-586 in Lysistrata's speech.
[39] *Birds* 481-538 in Peisetaerus' speech, with some interruptions.

> So. Clouds turn into anything they want. Thus, if they see a savage with long hair, one of these furry types, like the son of Xenophantus, they mock his obsession by making themselves look like centaurs.
> St. And what if they look down and see a predator of public funds like Simon, what do they do?
> So. To expose his nature they immediately turn into wolves.

The exchange of questions and answers is a parody of Socratic style, a way of speaking that generally does not require agitation. Especially Socrates is calm, since he possesses more knowledge than Strepsiades.[40] On multiple occasions in this scene Socrates utters subordinate clauses before their main clauses: an order that projects more to come through the syntactic incompleteness of the subordinate clauses.[41] In Socrates' utterance in 348-350 two such clauses (ἢν μὲν ἴδωσι κομήτην /ἄγριόν τινα τῶν λασίων τούτων and οἷόνπερ τὸν Ξενοφάντου) and a participial clause (σκώπτουσαι τὴν μανίαν αὐτοῦ) interrupt their main clause (κᾆτ'… κενταύροις ᾔκασαν αὑτάς). In 352 the participial clause ἀποφαίνουσαι τὴν φύσιν αὐτοῦ comes earlier than its main clause λύκοι ἐξαίφνης ἐγένοντο. In addition, the imperative ἀπόκριναι ("answer") in 345 semantically projects the utterance of an object such as "my question."

§28. Parallels from Aristophanes as well as tragedy suggest that this order of clauses is often found in calm situations.[42] The phenomenon may relate to a calm state of mind,

40 Starkie 1911 and Dover 1968 perhaps imply this in their comments *ad* 345, by noting Socrates' pedagogic style.

41 See IV.3 §24 on the difference between "ascending" (subordinate clause first) and "descending" periods (main clause first) in historiography.

42 Examples of elaborate subordinate clauses preceding their main clauses, or intervening within it, and certain similar structures from calm tragic monologues (see §24 with note 32 above) include Aeschylus *Agamemnon* 841-842, 846-847, 848-850, and 854 by Agamemnon; *Eumenides* 9-11 by the Pythia (two participial phrases preceding the main clause); Sophocles *Antigone* 170-174, 178-181, 182-183, 198-206, and 209-210 by Creon, 701-702 by Haemon (a genitive participial phrase preceding the comparative on which it depends); *Philoctetes* 70-71 by Odysseus; Euripides *Andromache* 29-30 by Andromache, 209-210 by Andromache; *Bacchae* 13-20 by Dionysus (a highly elaborate participial clause preceding its main clause); 288-290 by Teiresias (two subordinate clauses preceding their main clause); Euripides *Children of Heracles* 158-160 by the herald; *Hecuba* 802-805 by Hecuba; *Heracles* 1326-1328 by Theseus; *Hippolytus* 3-6, 21, 24-28 (an elaborate participial phrase preceding the main clause), and 34-40 by Aphrodite, 451-456 by the nurse; *Medea* 526-528 by Jason.

Sophocles *Women of Trachis* 1114-1115 by Hyllus also contains a subordinate clause preceding its main clause that may reflect calmness; it is however not part of a long speech, but of a 6-line utterance.

Other Aristophanic examples in calm contexts include *Acharnians* 520-522, 526 (a participial clause intervening between subject and finite verb), 541-543; *Assemblywomen* 517-518 (a second subordinate clause intervening within a first), 518-519 (several adverbial phrases preceding their main verb); *Birds* 1001-1004 (two participial clauses preceding their main clause, in this

because the speaker lingers on one hypotactic construction for a relatively long time.[43] This is not to say that it is the *function* of this clause order to "express" calmness; rather, it may be one of the *effects* of calmness that a speaker opts for this order in certain cases.[44] Moreover, to be more precise, subordinate clauses preceding their main clauses are not confined to calm contexts; but when this order occurs in agitated contexts, other features tend to be present to show the different state of mind (see e.g. Aristophanes *Frogs* 561, cited in (t12) below). As with the analysis of particles or other linguistic features, there is no one-to-one mapping of a certain emotional mindset and the language uttered; it is necessary to take into account the co-text and context beyond one sentence (see §7 above).

§29. Note that the mentioning of the projection that this clause order produces, or, conversely, of incremental style (see 5.3.2 below on agitation), is meant to refer to hearers' online reception of utterances. This kind of reception is different from the map view of readers, who easily connect a main clause to a subordinate clause that occurred several lines earlier, for example. For hearers the meaning of an utterance is incrementally updated, with every discourse act adding new information. It is for hearers, of course, that the ancient playwrights composed their poetry.

§30. Another feature connected to calmness is pragmatic projection, mainly through vocatives and priming acts.[45] Vocatives near the beginning of a speaking turn are pragmatically not complete on their own, but produce the expectation that several more acts, addressed to the particular addressee, will follow; therefore they have the potential to work as a floor-holding device, in order for the speaker to utter an elaborate turn.

---

case even interrupted by a different speaker), 1007-1009 (a participial phrase preceding the subject and main verb), 1355-1357, 1360-1361, 1368-1369; *Clouds* 404-405; *Frogs* 31; *Wasps* 552-553 (an object preceding its finite verb and subject).

43 Perhaps the association that I propose between subordinate clauses preceding their main clauses and calmness also has to do with speech planning. On speech planning in general, see e.g. Ferreira and Swets 2002; Konopka and Brown-Schmidt 2014. Ferreira and Swets 2002 point out, on the basis of psycholinguistic experiments, that it is partly under the speaker's control whether to plan an entire utterance in advance, or to speak incrementally. These authors write that "the extent to which planning occurs (...) depends on the intentions that motivate the speech" (80). Similarly, Konopka and Brown-Schmidt 2014 suggest (16) that complex messages probably require a more holistic planning before speaking than simple messages. The research on message planning so far, these authors note, "suggests considerable flexibility in the process of message planning and considerable sensitivity and perspective-taking on the part of the speaker when designing messages in different conditions and for different listeners" (17). It may be inferred, I suggest, that calmness and agitation may also play a role in the extent to which speakers engage in speech planning, and this may have an effect on their use of syntactic projection produced by the order of clauses.

44 A function of uttering a subordinate clause before its main clause may be to hold the floor; see III.4 §30 for discussion and an example. Compare also Auer 2000 on certain pre-posed subordinate clauses in spoken German.

45 On the term and concept of pragmatic projection, see Auer 2002, and II.2 §§50-57.

Vocatives are often combined with a calm attitude.[46] Priming acts are short discourse acts that start a multi-act move; "priming" refers to the cognitive priming of the concept or referent that the act mentions.[47]

§31. The following excerpt from *Assemblywomen* contains an example of a priming act. Here Praxagora begins a lengthy monologue after sending away an incompetent speaker from the assembly platform:[48]

(t2)

(Πρ.) αὐτὴ γὰρ |[49] ὑμῶν γ' ἕνεκά μοι λέξειν δοκῶ |
τονδὶ λαβοῦσα. | τοῖς θεοῖς μὲν εὔχομαι |
τυχεῖν κατορθώσασα τὰ βεβουλευμένα. |
ἐμοὶ δ' | ἴσον μὲν τῆσδε τῆς χώρας μέτα |
ὅσονπερ ὑμῖν· (...)

Aristophanes *Assemblywomen* 170-174

(Pr.) To judge from what I've seen of your abilities it seems best that I put on this garland and make a speech myself. I beseech the gods to grant success to today's deliberations. My own stake in this country is equal to your own, (...)

[46] Examples of vocatives in calm contexts projecting more than one act are Aeschylus *Agamemnon* 914 by Agamemnon; Sophocles *Ajax* 1 by Athena; *Antigone* 162 by Creon; *Electra* 1-2 by the old servant; *Oedipus King* 1 by Oedipus (see (t15) with discussion in §§67-68 below); *Oedipus at Colonus* 1 by Oedipus, 14 by Antigone; *Philoctetes* 3-4 by Odysseus; *Women of Trachis* 49 by the nurse; Euripides *Alcestis* 1 by Apollo; *Medea* 49 by the tutor, 869 by Medea, 908 by Jason; Aristophanes *Assemblywomen* 834 by the herald.

Cataphoric demonstratives announce their referent, and thereby contribute to the creation of elaborate coherent units as well: see e.g. Aristophanes *Clouds* 429, which contains both a turn-initial vocative (ὦ δέσποιναι) and a cataphoric demonstrative (τουτί). This utterance implies a certain degree of calmness because of its content's importance to the speaker. Shortly before, in 412, the elaborate turn-initial vocative uttered by the chorus of clouds also projects more discourse acts; the speakers are here arguably calm because of their exaggeratedly divine status and appearance. See III.4 §30 for more examples of syntactic and pragmatic projection, including a cataphoric demonstrative. On pragmatic projection realized by vocatives and other means in tragedy, see §§67-68 below.

[47] On the use and functions of priming acts in Homer, see De Kreij 2016, and II.2 §§63-79 on Homer and Pindar. On priming acts in Herodotus and Thucydides, see IV.2 §§38-41 and IV.3 §§107-116.

[48] Praxagora's monologue in 171-188 is 20 lines long; after interruptions it is followed by another 11.5 lines (192bis-203), then 8.5 more lines (204bis-212), and 97 more lines (214-240). All these parts together contain 415 words.

[49] A vertical bar indicates a (relevant) discourse-act boundary. See II.2 §26.

Praxagora's calm state of mind can be inferred from the official, serious content of this utterance and the parts of her speech that follow.[50] In 173 she uses a priming act ἐμοὶ δ', in order to project a series of acts related to "me." The position of μέν tells us, retrospectively, that ἐμοὶ δ' forms a separate discourse act. Note that at the same time this act involves a syntactic projection beyond an act: the dative in the act ἐμοὶ δ' is syntactically incomplete on its own. Additionally, even though γε may also occur in a later than act-peninitial position, it is probable that αὐτὴ γάρ in 170 is a priming act as well, which emphasizes Lysistrata's decision to take the floor.[51] Priming acts in drama are strikingly frequent in calm contexts, such as official speeches in Aristophanes, and certain monologues in tragedy.[52]

[50] On 171-172 Murphy 1938:87 writes, in connection to the rest of the speech, that Praxagora's "solemn prayer to the gods to prosper her plans indicates to her audience the gravity of the situation and the importance of her subject." See pp. 109-110 for Murphy's analysis of the argumentative build-up of 171-240.

[51] On priming acts with γάρ starting a move in Thucydides and Herodotus, see IV.3 §108.

[52] Other priming acts in calm, official speeches in Aristophanes include *Acharnians* 509 (ἐγὼ δὲ | μισῶ μὲν...), 513 (ἀτάρ, | φίλοι γὰρ...); *Assemblywomen* 84 (ἠκκλησία δ', | εἰς ἣν...); *Wasps* 678 (σοὶ δ' | ὧν ἄρχεις...). Priming acts in other calm contexts, namely orders or advice by high-status Aristophanic characters, include *Assemblywomen* 509 (καὶ μέντοι | σὺ μὲν...); *Birds* 837 (ἄγε νυν | σὺ μὲν...), 1363 (σὺ γὰρ | /τὸν μὲν...); *Frogs* 31 (σὺ δ' οὖν | ἐπειδὴ...). See note 55 below for priming acts in short utterances in Aristophanes.

Examples of priming acts in calm tragic monologues (at least 25 lines; see III.2 §17) include Aeschylus *Agamemnon* 854 (νίκη δ', | ἐπείπερ...); *Libation Bearers* 279 (νῦν οὖν | σὺ μὲν...); *Seven against Thebes* 24 (νῦν δ' | ὡς); Sophocles *Ajax* 487 (ἐγὼ δ' | ἐλευθέρου μὲν...); *Antigone* 722 (εἰ δ' οὖν, | φιλεῖ γὰρ...), 1226 (ὁ δ' | ὡς ὁρᾷ σφε; NB this is in a messenger speech; the form and function of the priming act resemble those in Homer; see II.2 §§64-71; and see III.2 §28 on messenger speeches' similarity to epic); *Electra* 577 (εἰ δ' οὖν, | ἐρῶ γὰρ...), 951 (ἐγὼ δ' | ἕως μὲν...); *Oedipus at Colonus* 377 (ὁ δ', | ὡς); *Oedipus King* 222 (νῦν δ', | ὕστερος γὰρ...), 258 (νῦν δ' | ἐπεὶ...); *Philoctetes* 1343 (ταῦτ' οὖν | ἐπεὶ...); Euripides *Alcestis* 313 (σὺ δ', | ὦ τέκνον μοι), 323 and 325 (καὶ σοὶ μέν, | πόσι,/ γυναῖκ' ἀρίστην ἔστι κομπάσαι λαβεῖν,/ ὑμῖν δέ, | παῖδες...); *Andromache* 6 (νῦν δ', | εἴ τις...), 209 (σὺ δ' | ἤν τι...); *Bacchae* 268 (σὺ δ' | εὔτροχον μὲν...), 274 (δύο γάρ, | ὦ νεανία), 1323 (νῦν δ' | ἄθλιος μέν...; this speaker, Cadmus, is in grief, but not agitated); *Children of Heracles* 23 (οἱ δ' | ἀσθενῆ μὲν...), 819 (μάντεις δ', | ἐπειδὴ...; NB this is in a messenger speech); *Hecuba* 51 (τοὐμὸν μὲν οὖν | ὅσονπερ...), 326 (ἡμεῖς δ', | εἰ...), 546 (ἡ δ', | ὡς...); *Heracles* 1331 (θανόντα δ', | εὖτ' ἂν...); *Hippolytus* 47 (ἡ δ' | εὐκλεὴς μὲν), 1025 (νῦν δ' | ὅρκιόν σοι...); *Medea* 244 (ἀνὴρ δ', | ὅταν...), 526 (ἐγὼ δ', | ἐπειδὴ...), 529 (σοὶ δ' | ἔστι μὲν...), 1141 (κυνεῖ δ' | ὁ μέν...; this is in a messenger speech), 1156 (ἡ δ', | ὡς ἐσεῖδε...; this is in a messenger speech; see the remark above on Sophocles *Antigone* 1226), 1177 (εὐθὺς δ' | ἡ μὲν...; this is in a messenger speech).

Other tragic examples of priming acts, in calm contexts but outside of long monologues, include Sophocles *Ajax* 1 (ἀεὶ μέν, | ὦ παῖ...) in a 13-line utterance by Athena; *Electra* 15 (νῦν οὖν, | 'Ορέστα...) in a 22-line utterance by the old slave; *Philoctetes* 1140 (ἀνδρός τοι | τὸ μέν...) in a 6-line utterance by the chorus; *Women of Trachis* 52 (νῦν δ', | εἰ...) in a 12-line utterance by the nurse; Euripides *Andromache* 269 (δεινὸν δ' | ἑρπετῶν μὲν) in a 5-line utterance by Andromache (see §25 with note 31 above on tragic characters' ignorance of upcoming disaster); *Hecuba* 900 (νῦν δ', | οὐ γὰρ...) in a 7-line utterance and 1243 (ἐμοὶ δ', | ἵν'...) in a 12-line utterance, both by Agamemnon.

See IV.3 §§107-116 for the observation that priming acts are frequent in Herodotus' and Thucydides' narrator text. This may be analogous, as the historians are usually not noticeably agitated about writing their chronicles.

These acts can be a sign of calmness in that the speaker promises, so to say, to stick with a certain concept or referent for at least one more discourse act.[53]

§32. As my discussion of (t2) shows, particles in and after priming acts are relevant to our interpretation in two ways. The priming act itself, on the one hand, tends to contain a particle, in this case δέ, that carries out its normal function by signaling how the act relates to the preceding discourse. The examples collected suggest that δέ is indeed the most frequent particle in priming acts. The next act, on the other hand, often includes a particle, in this case μέν, that retrospectively enables us as readers to see the boundary of the priming act—which the original audience was probably able to perceive via an intonational break.[54]

§33. The following passage from Aristophanes *Birds* illustrates the connection between priming acts and calmness in a rather different context: not an official speech, but a 2-line utterance. Three gods (Poseidon, Heracles, and the so-called Triballian) have come to Peisetaerus in order to discuss a settlement between him and the gods; Peisetaerus demands Zeus' girl Princess for himself in this negotiation. The three representative gods now discuss this proposal:

(t3)

Ηρ. παραδοῦναι λέγει.
Πο. μὰ τὸν Δί' οὐχ οὗτός γε παραδοῦναι λέγει,
εἰ μὴ βαβάζει γ' ὥσπερ αἱ χελιδόνες.
Πε. οὐκοῦν παραδοῦναι ταῖς χελιδόσιν λέγει.
Πο. σφώ νυν διαλλάττεσθε καὶ ξυμβαίνετε· |
ἐγὼ δ', | ἐπειδὴ σφῷν δοκεῖ, | σιγήσομαι.

Aristophanes *Birds* 1679bis-1684

He. He [i.e. the Triballian] says, hand her over.
Po. No, by Zeus, he's not saying hand her over; he's just twittering like the swallows.

53 Concerning structurally similar constructions in other languages, see e.g. Ochs Keenan and Schieffelin 1976; Salmon 2010. Admittedly, Ochs Keenan and Schieffelin consider the "Referent + Proposition construction" in spoken American English to be "a form of "unplanned" speech" (1976:248), which seems not to fit calm, well-thought-through utterances; however, the construction they discuss involves material that is not syntactically integrated in what follows. In my corpus of Greek drama priming acts do usually form a syntactic whole with subsequent acts. Salmon analyzes double-subject sentences in spoken Brazilian Portuguese, of the form "This president, taxes are getting higher." This construction does not involve syntactic integration either. Interestingly, Salmon considers this construction to be "a tool of style, of rhetoric" (2010:3441) and a reflection of the speaker's "attention to the informational needs of the audience" (3437).

54 This boundary may however also be indicated by another signal, such as a subordinating conjunction.

He.[55] All right, he's saying hand her over to the swallows.
Po. Very well, you two negotiate the terms of a settlement; if that's your decision, I'll keep quiet.

Poseidon's turn in 1680-1681 contains the swearing expression μὰ τὸν Δί' as well as two instances of γε, revealing a certain agitation (see §§45-47 below). However, after the squabbles, in 1683-1684 he gives in and leaves the final negotiation to the other two gods, declaring that he will "keep quiet" (σιγήσομαι). That is, he indirectly states that he will refrain from further agitation: he has decided to be calm from now on.[56] In 1683 he uses καί to combine διαλλάττεσθε "be reconciled" and ξυμβαίνετε "come to an agreement," two semantically similar words, the second of which may be considered a specification of the first. This use of καί is in fact most frequent in long monologues, where the speaker feels at leisure to formulate a concept in several slightly distinct ways;[57] the construction may therefore reflect calmness. Moreover, Poseidon's utterance features a subordinate clause (ἐπειδὴ σφῷν δοκεῖ) before its main verb σιγήσομαι in 1684. It also contains the priming act ἐγὼ δ'.[58] I interpret these features as discourse-organizational effects of Poseidon's calmness.

§34. Let us now consider more specific manifestations of calmness than subordinate clauses preceding their main clauses and forms of pragmatic projection. The case study of Aeschylean Agamemnon's particular use of μέν shows the influence of specific co-textual and contextual elements on how a particle may reflect calmness.[59] This example is followed by a discussion of several uses of μέν that do *not* reflect calmness, in order to clarify how co-text and context determine the emotional quality of particles.

55 It is unclear whether it is Peisetaerus or Heracles speaking this line; see Dunbar 1995 *ad loc.* and the apparatus of Wilson 2007. Both options would fit the context. Wilson opts for Peisetaerus; Henderson 2000 in his translation for Heracles.

56 See Schröder 1927 *ad loc.*, who interprets Poseidon's attitude as feeling too noble to deal further with that terribly rhetorical speaker Peisetaerus; the god gives in and keeps quiet ("Pos. hat kaum hingehört: zu vornehm, mit dem entsetzlich redegewandten weiter sich einzulassen gibt er nach und schweigt.").

57 See III.2 §36.

58 Other examples of priming acts in calm short utterances in Aristophanes are *Assemblywomen* 57 (official question of 3 lines; κάθησθε τοίνυν, | ὡς...), 601 (interested question of 1.5 lines; πῶς οὖν | ὅστις...), 610 (rhetorical argument of 2 lines; νῦν δ', | ἔσται γὰρ...), 728 (thoughtful decision of 2 lines; ἐγὼ δ' ἵν'...); *Lysistrata* 111 (official question of 2 lines, also containing syntactic projection across line-end; ἐθέλοιτ' ἂν οὖν, | εἰ...), 120 (official proclamation of 3.5 lines; ἡμῖν γάρ, | ὦ γυναῖκες, εἴπερ...); *Wasps* 764 (compromise of 3 lines; σὺ δ' οὖν, | ἐπειδὴ...). Calm short utterances can also form part of longer speeches: see note 52 above for priming acts in such contexts.

59 Tragic characters are more suitable for such a spotlight than comic ones, because tragic characters generally have a more consistent personality, with more complex life histories, which may lead to specific communicative goals. References to Agamemnon in this section only involve the character in Aeschylus *Agamemnon*, not in other plays.

§35. Agamemnon in his eponymous play utters μέν 7 times, or with a frequency of 1.5% (out of a total of 473 words), higher than any of the other 20 main characters in the 9 tragedies of my corpus.[60] This statistic alone cannot account for specific pragmatic goals; after all, particles are multifunctional. What is remarkable about Agamemnon's use of μέν is that he, despite his fondness for the particle, only employs certain uses of it.[61]

§36. Let us consider the following instance from the king's answer to Clytaemnestra's long welcome speech:

(t4)

Αγ. Λήδας γένεθλον, δωμάτων ἐμῶν φύλαξ,
ἀπουσίαι μὲν εἶπας εἰκότως ἐμῆι·
μακρὰν γὰρ ἐξέτεινας. ἀλλ' ἐναισίμως
αἰνεῖν, παρ' ἄλλων χρὴ τόδ' ἔρχεσθαι γέρας.
καὶ τἄλλα μὴ γυναικὸς ἐν τρόποις ἐμὲ
ἄβρυνε, (...)

Aeschylus *Agamemnon* 914-919

Ag. Daughter of Leda, guardian of my house, you have made a speech that was like my absence—you stretched it out to a great length; but to be

[60] For the comparisons of particle use across characters, the utterances of the following 21 tragic characters have been taken into account (in parentheses the total numbers of words spoken per character): Aeschylus: Agamemon (473) and Clytaemnestra (1927) in *Agamemon*, Electra (929) and Orestes (1864) in *Libation Bearers*, Xerxes (266) and the queen (1097) in *Persians*; Sophocles: Ajax (1629) and Tecmessa (1269) in *Ajax*, Antigone (1220), Creon (2117), and Teiresias (447) in *Antigone*, Creon (882), Oedipus (4258), and Teiresias (518) in *Oedipus King*; Euripides: Dionysus (1549), Pentheus (1119), and Teiresias (615) in *Bacchae*, Hippolytus (1644) and Phaedra (1088) in *Hippolytus*, and Medea (3447) and Jason (1225) in *Medea*. For characters that have relatively few lines to speak, their particle frequencies are influenced more by the specific scenes they appear in than by their personality or life-history features. This is especially striking in the case of Teiresias in *Oedipus King*: his utterances have a much higher frequency of γάρ (2.9%, 15 instances) and γε (1.2%, 6 instances) than usual. Emotionality, however, does play a role in these high frequencies: Teiresias in this play is relatively often engaged in angry stichomythia, where γάρ and γε are particularly at home (see III.3 §§76-79 on γε and §§95-98 on γάρ). For other analyses of particle distributions in tragedy and comedy, concerning different communicative situations rather than different characters, see III.2. See III.2 §69 for the average frequencies of μέν in different parts of tragedies and comedies, regardless of the specific speakers.

[61] Apart from the uses mentioned here, he utters μέν in 924 to imply that others may think differently (ἐμοὶ μέν, with a potential counterpart left implicit; see II.2 §60 on this use); and in 932 in a 1-line utterance to acknowledge that the conversation goes on, projecting further utterances within the dialogue rather than further acts within the utterance (see III.4 §33 on this use). Both of these uses differ from the ones discussed here, as they do not concern the discourse organization within one turn of speaking.

fittingly praised is an honour that ought to come to me from others. For the rest, do not pamper me as if I were a woman; (...)

With μέν in 915, Agamemnon projects the continuation of his discourse.[62] He warns Clytaemnestra immediately at the start of his speech that he will not only assess the length of her preceding monologue, but also, as it turns out, the content: her praise and her suggestion to walk on the purple fabric were in his view excessive. There is no δέ that answers this μέν in the discourse acts that follow it (916-919), which suggests that μέν's projecting signal here works more globally than to mark semantic or syntactic juxtaposition. In particular, the signal here pertains to the level of acts rather than content. As a signal of discourse organization, this μέν implies that Agamemnon feels he can go on speaking for some time without any problems. Thus the use of this particle displays calmness, and perhaps also an authoritative tone. Along these lines E. Fraenkel 1950 remarks: "[t]he king is, at least up till now, completely composed, he speaks with the gracious dignity of a great gentleman."[63] With this calmness Aeschylus in turn invites the audience to infer that Agamemnon does not suspect his upcoming murder.[64]

§37. Later in the play the king uses μέν together with a δέ in the next act, again to structure the presentation of his discourse, without indicating semantic contrast. Clytaemnestra has now persuaded her husband to walk on the fabric:

(t5)

(Αγ.) καὶ τοῖσδέ μ' ἐμβαίνονθ' ἁλουργέσιν θεῶν
μή τις πρόσωθεν ὄμματος βάλοι φθόνος.
πολλὴ γὰρ αἰδὼς δωματοφθορεῖν ποσὶν
φθείροντα πλοῦτον ἀργυρωνήτους θ' ὑφάς.
τούτων μὲν οὕτω, τὴν ξένην δὲ πρευμενῶς
τήνδ' ἐσκόμιζε· (...)

Aeschylus *Agamemnon* 946-951

(Ag.) and as I walk on these purple-dyed <robes>, may no jealous eye strike me from afar! For I feel a great sense of impropriety about despoiling this house under my feet, ruining its wealth and the woven work bought with

62 On the general function of μέν in tragedy and comedy, see III.2 §§69-72; on μέν as a marker of projection, see II.2 §§46-62; on μέν in Herodotus and Thucydides, see IV.3 §§125-146. A similar μέν instance by Agamemnon, also at the start of a speech, is found in 810.

63 Groeneboom 1966 [1944] *ad loc.* speaks of a cold stateliness.

64 See §25 with note 33 above on demonstrating ignorance about one's upcoming doom as one of the literary functions of ostensible calmness in tragedy.

its silver. Well, so much for that. This foreign woman—please welcome her kindly.

In this case μέν occurs in the last act of a move in which Agamemnon comments on the act of treading on the robes; the first act of the next move, about Cassandra, contains δέ. This construction, with μέν and δέ belonging to different moves, differs from the construction in which the two particles together imply semantic contrast.[65] Fraenkel 1950 *ad* 950 considers τούτων μὲν οὕτω "a dry, businesslike formula of transition."[66] Again, the careful articulation of discourse organization befits a calm state of mind. For the audience, well aware of what is about to happen to the king, the irony of his calmness may have heightened the tension.

§38. One μέν construction that Agamemnon does not use is that involving a strong semantic contrast between a μέν act and an immediately following δέ act. Sophoclean Antigone favors this particle construction, however.[67] Even though this use of μέν… δέ does not signal calmness or agitation, it will be discussed here in order to clarify the role of co-textual and contextual features in our interpretation of particle constructions. In Antigone's utterances, the μέν… δέ construction conveys the speaker's stance, more specifically her disalignment with her addressee Ismene, and even hostility towards her.[68] That is, this use is more connected to the emotional dimension of pleasure-displeasure, by conveying a negative stance, than to the dimension of arousal.

(t6)

Ισ. οἴμοι τάλαινα, κἀμπλάκω τοῦ σοῦ μόρου;
Αν. σὺ μὲν γὰρ εἵλου ζῆν, ἐγὼ δὲ κατθανεῖν.
Ισ. ἀλλ' οὐκ ἐπ' ἀρρήτοις γε τοῖς ἐμοῖς λόγοις.
Αν. καλῶς σὺ μὲν τοῖς, τοῖς δ' ἐγὼ 'δόκουν φρονεῖν.
Ισ. καὶ μὴν ἴση νῷν ἐστιν ἡ 'ξαμαρτία.
Αν. θάρσει. σὺ μὲν ζῇς, ἡ δ' ἐμὴ ψυχὴ πάλαι

65 On μέν at the end of moves, often followed by δέ at the start of the next move, see II.2 §§49-56 on Homer; IV.3 §§65-66 and IV.5 §32 and §§35-36 on historiography. Agamemnon utters similar μέν acts in 829 and 846, also here followed by δέ acts.

66 See IV.3 §§125-129 and IV.5 §32 on οὗτος forms + μέν, sometimes followed by δέ acts, in discourse transitions in historiography.

67 References to Antigone in this discussion only involve this character in Sophocles *Antigone*, not in other plays. Like Aeschylus' Agamemnon, Antigone is relatively fond of μέν: her utterances have a frequency of 0.9% (11 instances in 1220 words). Only those of Agamemnon (see §35 above), the queen in Aeschylus *Persians* (1.2%), and Jason in Euripides *Medea* (1.0%) have a higher frequency of μέν; the other 17 main characters in the 9 tragedies (see note 60 above) utter the particle less often.

68 See IV.4 on stance in general, with §§61-63 on (dis)alignment and its linguistic expression.

τέθνηκεν, ὥστε τοῖς θανοῦσιν ὠφελεῖν.

Sophocles *Antigone* 554-560

Is. Ah me, am I to miss sharing in your death?
An. Yes, you chose life, and I chose death!
Is. But I did not fail to speak out!
An. Some thought you were right, and some thought I was.
Is. Why, our offence is equal!
An. Be comforted! You are alive, but my life has long been dead, so as to help the dead.

Three times in this passage (555, 557, and 559) Antigone directly follows an act containing σὺ μέν with an act containing δέ and a first-person pronoun.[69] In this way she highlights her disalignment from her sister, that is, the contrast between their respective views—a rhetorical strategy that conveys emotional distance and hostility.[70]

§39. Ismene uses μέν... δέ constructions within one line as well, but never to stress an opposition to her sister. In 99 she even uses it to emphasize that Antigone is dear to her: ἄνους μὲν ἔρχῃ, τοῖς φίλοις δ' ὀρθῶς φίλη "in your going you are foolish, but truly dear to those who are your own."[71] The contrast expressed by the "local" μέν... δέ construction, then, may also be used to express emotional nearness.

§40. When μέν... δέ constructions contrast actions or situations, instead of decisions or opinions, they do not imply hostility, even if they do contrast the second and first person. For example, the angry Philoctetes in Sophocles *Philoctetes* 1021 and 1025-1026 uses the μέν... δέ construction twice in order to contrast his addressee (Odysseus) with himself, within a long monologue. However, he contrasts their respective situations, rather than their decisions; in this way he conveys more bitterness than hostility with these parts of the discourse. The differing nature of the co-texts, then, leads to a interpretation that is pragmatically different from the particles in Antigone's hostile utterances.

§41. Another example that clarifies the difference between μέν... δέ used to convey disalignment and μέν... δέ expressing another kind of contrast is the following passage

69 Griffith 1999 *ad loc.* notes that 555-560 refer back to the sisters' earlier argument at 71-81. Also in this earlier dialogue Antigone explicitly contrasts her own decisions to those of her sister, using μέν and δέ to signal the oppositions.

70 The use of antithesis and chiasmus (regardless of which particles are used) may also betray the influence of rhetoric on Sophocles' style. See Slings 1997b on such figures of speech (which he argues are not always literary language) in Sophocles and other authors. See e.g. McDonald 2007 and Pelling 2005 on the relation between rhetoric and tragedy in general; McDonald points out that rhetoric is more present in Sophocles than in Aeschylus, and even more in Euripides.

71 See Griffith 2001:127-129 on differences between Antigone's and Ismene's speech styles. See also Finley 1939, who argues that Sophocles *Antigone* is "in style the most antithetical (...) of all extant Greek tragedies" (58).

from Aristophanes *Women at the Thesmophoria*.[72] The character Euripides has just managed to distract the archer who was guarding Euripides' kinsman, and so has found an opportunity to rescue him.

(t7)

Ευ. Ἑρμῆ δόλιε, ταυτὶ μὲν ἔτι καλῶς ποιεῖς.
σὺ μὲν οὖν ἀπότρεχε, παιδάριον, ταυτὶ λαβών·
ἐγὼ δὲ λύσω τόνδε. σὺ δ' ὅπως ἀνδρικῶς,
ὅταν λυθῇς τάχιστα, φεύξει καὶ τενεῖς
ὡς τὴν γυναῖκα καὶ τὰ παιδί' οἴκαδε.

Aristophanes *Women at the Thesmophoria* 1202-1206

Eu. Trickster Hermes, just keep on giving me this good luck! You can run along now, kid; and take this stuff with you. And I'll release this one. As soon as you get loose you'd better run like a man away from here and head back home to your wife and kids.

After acknowledging that the god Hermes provided good luck (1202), Euripides first orders one of his slaves to leave, marking this order with μέν (1203) as only part of what he wants to say.[73] He then describes his own intended action in a δέ act (ἐγὼ δὲ λύσω τόνδε, 1204): he will free his kinsman. Another δέ act follows (σὺ δ' ὅπως ἀνδρικῶς, 1204), addressed to the kinsman, in which Euripides tells him, too, what he should do.[74] The acts thus juxtapose actions by different people; they do not refer to different decisions or opinions, as Antigone's hostile μέν and δέ acts did.

§42. The following passage from *Frogs* contains a further exploitation of μέν and δέ in successive acts, in this case with a metapoetic goal. No particular emotional state of mind is detectable from the context; again, the specific co-textual and contextual features determine the interpretation of the particle construction. The juxtaposition marked by μέν... δέ here combines with a figure of speech for parodic effect, as well as with a priming act. The god Dionysus has just told his half-brother Heracles that he wants to bring back Euripides from Hades.

72 Apart from the one in (t8), Aristophanic examples of such μέν-δέ constructions contrasting actions of first and second person without hostility include *Assemblywomen* 351-352, 509-510; *Frogs* 495-497; *Peace* 1122.

73 μέν and οὖν do not form a cluster in this case, but each carry out their own separate function. οὖν here marks a conclusion from the preceding discourse or situation: now that the archer is gone, the next planned actions can go on. See III.2 §§82-83 on μὲν οὖν as a cluster or as a combination of separate functions in drama; see IV.3 §§144-146 on μὲν οὖν in Thucydides.

74 Another example of σὺ μέν... ἐγὼ δέ in Aristophanes, contrasting actions rather than decisions, is found in *Assemblywomen* 509-510.

(t8)

Ηρ. εἶτ' οὐ Σοφοκλέα πρότερον ὄντ' Εὐριπίδου
μέλλεις ἀναγαγεῖν, εἴπερ ἐκεῖθεν δεῖ σ' ἄγειν;
Δι. οὐ πρίν γ' ἂν Ἰοφῶντ', ἀπολαβὼν αὐτὸν μόνον,
ἄνευ Σοφοκλέους ὅ τι ποιεῖ κωδωνίσω.
κἄλλως ὁ μέν γ' Εὐριπίδης πανοῦργος ὢν
κἂν ξυναποδρᾶναι δεῦρ' ἐπιχειρήσειέ μοι· |
ὁ δ' | εὔκολος μὲν ἐνθάδ', | εὔκολος δ' ἐκεῖ. |

Aristophanes *Frogs* 76-82

He. If you must resurrect someone, then why not Sophocles, who's better than Euripides?

Di. No, first I want to get Iophon alone by himself and evaluate what he produces without Sophocles. Besides, Euripides is a slippery character and would probably even help me pull off an escape, whereas Sophocles was peaceable here and will be peaceable there.

Slings 2002:101 argues that the repetition of εὔκολος in 82 make this verse "not only a tribute to Sophocles' character, but also to his style," because Sophocles regularly makes use of anaphora, that is, repetition of words at the beginnings of successive clauses.[75] Perhaps, I would add, Aristophanes also means the juxtaposition of a μέν act and a δέ act to allude to antithetic Sophoclean style.[76] The conspicuous act boundary after ὁ δ', possibly accompanied by a prosodic break, further helps the line stand out. Together with the anaphora this priming act—typical of calm, carefully structured discourse—makes the sentence appear like an official, important message. This form may have contributed to turning *Frogs* 82 into "probably the most famous anaphora from Aristophanes" (Slings 2002:101).

§43. To sum up my observations in this section: a speaker's calmness tends to be linguistically reflected in subordinate clauses preceding their main clauses, pragmatic projection through vocatives and priming acts, and certain uses of μέν. The particle δέ often figures in priming acts. However, μέν and δέ also occur in constructions that are unrelated to a certain emotional state of mind. The difference depends on several co-textual and contextual elements.

[75] See Slings 1997b:176-192 on anaphora in Sophocles *Electra* and several other authors.

[76] On antithesis in tragedy, see e.g. Navarre 1900:106; Finley 1939. See also note 70 above.

5.3.2 Agitation

§44. Let us now have a look at the way tragic and comic speakers linguistically express agitation (combined with negative feelings), the general state of mind at the other end of the arousal dimension. Commentators describe the following passage from Aeschylus *Seven against Thebes*, for example, as conveying "alarm" (Tucker 1908 *ad loc.*) or "intense emotion" (Hutchinson 1985 *ad loc.*).[77] Here a messenger informs the chorus (Theban women) of Eteocles and Polyneices' death:

(t9)

Αγγ. ἄνδρες τεθνᾶσιν ἐκ χερῶν αὐτοκτόνων.
Χο. τίνες; | τί δ' εἶπας; | παραφρονῶ φόβωι λόγου.

Aeschylus *Seven against Thebes* 805-806

Me. The men have died at each other's hands.
Ch. Who? What are you saying? Your words are frightening me out of my mind.

In his discussion of this example Stanford 1983 adds precision to the commentators' descriptions: he remarks that "jerky syntax often indicates emotion" (99).[78] Differently formulated, the three discourse acts in 806 are not syntactically integrated, but form syntactic units on their own. This incremental style is reminiscent of the so-called "adding style" that is often mentioned in connection to Homeric syntax. As Bakker 1997c:147 discusses, this style is defined by "the absence of syntactic anticipation."[79] It is my impression that several successive acts without syntactic integration are typical of agitated tragic utterances.[80]

77 Even though "intense emotion" does not necessarily refer to an intense emotion with a high degree of arousal (see §22 with Figure 1 above), in this case it is likely that this is what Hutchinson means.

78 A similar point is made by Mastronarde 1979:62 about suspension of syntax beyond a turn of speaking in Euripides; see §18 above. Also Schuren 2015:37 on Euripidean stichomythia notes that a "rapid succession of short questions [i.e. within one line] creates the impression of urgency, curiosity, and shock." This scholar provides several parallels of three or four "sentences in a single stichomythic line" in Euripides (2015:36n151).

79 On the connection that has been made between "adding style" and parataxis, see IV.3 §82.

80 Hutchinson 1985 *ad loc.* refers to two lines that are very similar in their syntactically incremental structure: Aeschylus *Agamemnon* 268, and Sophocles *Philoctetes* 1231. As in (t9), in both these cases the speakers themselves refer to their emotional state of mind as a clarification for why they are asking for more information. A similar utterance in Aristophanes is found at *Lysistrata* 830bis with three discourse acts in less than one line: τί δ' ἐστίν; | εἰπέ μοι, | τίς ἡ βοή; ("But what is it? Tell me, what is the shouting?"). The speaker's apparent agitation, as expressed by the

§45. As for particles, γε and δῆτα occur more frequently in agitated than in calm contexts. In general, these particles typically appear in dialogues with short turns, that is, in communicative situations in which speakers come to the foreground in their identity as communicators.[81] In such situations there is a clear focus on who is saying something, apart from the attention to what is said. The expression of agitated emotion, by its nature, tends to highlight the presence of the speaker, and therefore forms a suitable contexts for the two particles, just as dialogues in general do.

§46. Examples of γε in an agitated context are found at the end of a monologue by the dying Heracles in the *Women of Trachis*.[82] The hero in his rhesis speaks to the gods as well as to the people gathered at his deathbed: his son Hyllus, the chorus of Trachinian women, and an old man serving as a doctor.

(t10)

(Ηρ.) ἀλλ' εὖ γέ τοι τόδ' ἴστε, κἂν τὸ μηδὲν ὦ,
κἂν μηδὲν ἕρπω, τήν γε δράσασαν τάδε
χειρώσομαι κἀκ τῶνδε. προσμόλοι μόνον,
ἵν' ἐκδιδαχθῇ πᾶσιν ἀγγέλλειν ὅτι
καὶ ζῶν κακούς γε καὶ θανὼν ἐτεισάμην.

Sophocles *Women of Trachis* 1107-1111

(He.) But know this for certain, even if I amount to nothing and I cannot move, I shall chastise her who has done this, even in this condition! Let her only come near, so that she may be taught to proclaim to all that both in life and in death I have punished evildoers!

Heracles on his deathbed thinks (wrongly) that his wife Deianeira had intended to kill him, and he desperately wants to punish her for that. Here, γε works to highlight a specific part of the utterance: "but know this for certain" (ἀλλ' εὖ τοι τόδ' ἴστε) or only εὖ in 1107, "her who has done this" (τὴν δράσασαν) in 1108, and "evildoers" (κακούς) in

structure of her utterance, fits the parody of a (tragic) war situation, in which one suddenly sees an enemy approaching.

Examples of syntactic increments in agitated tragic monologues include the structures in Aeschylus *Agamemnon* 1266-1268 by Cassandra; Sophocles *Ajax* 1003-1007 by Teucer; *Philoctetes* 932-933 and 949-951 by Philoctetes; *Women of Trachis* 1086-1090 by Heracles; Euripides *Alcestis* 689-691 by Pheres, 781 by Heracles; *Andromache* 388-392 by Andromache; *Medea* 1327-1332 by Jason. A similar example from Aristophanes is *Birds* 1199-1201 (a 3-line utterance).

81 See III.2 §58.

82 Other examples of γε in agitated tragic monologues include Aeschylus *Agamemnon* 1267 (a generally accepted conjecture) and 1279 by Cassandra; Euripides *Andromache* 385 and 408 by Andromache.

1111. As Jebb 2004 [1892] *ad* 1111 remarks, "[t]he γε is very expressive"; he uses italics to render this in his paraphrase. The particle, in other words, works similarly to prosodic emphasis.[83] Heracles indicates that he considers his angry message and his wife's (presumed) responsibility highly important. Through this highlighting the particle indirectly betrays Heracles' emotional agitation. More specifically, these γε instances mark agitation in form of anger (see §§53-58 below). After 61 lines of mainly expressing pain, sadness, and desperation, but not anger (1046-1106)—without any γε—Heracles now turns his attention to the person he considers responsible for his situation, even though she is absent from the scene. That is, he turns to his feelings of anger.

§47. Recall from other chapters that γε's pragmatic function is to highlight a specific part of the utterance as highly relevant, according to the speaker, and as implicitly contrasted to something else; indeed the highlighted part often relates to the speaker's stance.[84] In this highlighting function, γε is comparable to the paralinguistic signs of prosodic emphasis or an exclamation mark.[85] That is to say, γε in itself does not express any emotion per se, but its use is very suitable for agitated contexts, just as prosodic emphasis and exclamation marks are.

§48. As a display of Heracles' agitation other than γε, the passage also contains a double repetition of καί, in both 1107-1109 (three instances) and 1111 (two instances), which emphasize the speaker's statements ("even if... even if... even" and "*both* in life *and* in death").[86] Moreover, in the online reception of these lines by hearers, it is not immediately clear whether the κἄν clauses syntactically belong to τόδ' ἴστε, and therefore follow their main clause, or to χειρώσομαι (1109), and therefore precede it. That is, even if they are retrospectively constructed with the latter, in their moment of utterance this structure is not yet apparent. The appearance of γε in both main clauses that frame the two

83 Note also the two exclamation marks in Lloyd-Jones' translation. On the comparison of γε to exclamation marks, see §47 and §§90-91 below; III.4 §64; IV.4 §44. Kamerbeek 1959 *ad loc.* merely calls γε in 1107 and 1111 "emphatic," and the instance in 1108 "between emphatic and limitative." Davies 1991 *ad* 1107 refers to E. Fraenkel 1977:37, who cites several semantically similar *loci*, including Sophocles *Antigone* 1064, which includes γε; however, neither commentator pays attention to the particle.

84 For discussions of γε in drama, see III.2 §§58-63 (distribution and general function), III.3 §§76-79 (in contexts of resonance), and III.4 §§62-64 (in answers and stancetaking utterances). Its uses in other genres is related but slightly different: see II.5 §§27-50 on γε in Homer, and IV.4 §§40-44 and IV.5 §20 and §34 on γε in Thucydides and §62,§§67-68, and §73 on γε in Herodotus. On γε in contexts of stancetaking, regardless of the speaker's emotional state of mind, see also §§59-63 below.

85 On the possibly emotional meaning of exclamation marks, it is interesting to note that Argaman 2010:92-94 includes "outstanding graphical means" such as certain forms of punctuation in her list of potential markers of emotional intensity in written Hebrew. Indeed, Argaman finds in her experiment that these features are more frequent in subjects' written expressions of more intense happiness than in those of less intense happiness. She does not, however, discuss the use, relevance, or statistical significance of these graphical means.

86 See also III.2 §37 on this highlighting effect of repeated καί in certain contexts.

κἄν clauses suggests that the prosodic emphasis is anyway on the pieces of information in the two main clauses. Regardless of the hypotactic structure, as received while hearing the lines or in retrospect, the first act κἂν τὸ μηδὲν ὦ (1107) does not project a second one of similar structure. This repetition therefore creates the impression that these remarks have great relevance to Heracles—which fits the emotionally agitated context.

§49. δῆτα, which in monologues is even more rare than γε, usually occurs in contexts of agitation. Consider the following speech by Euripidean Heracles, after he has unwillingly killed his own wife and children. He has elaborately described the miseries throughout his life, and now cries out:

(t11)

> (Ηρ.) τί <u>δῆτά</u> με ζῆν δεῖ; τί κέρδος ἕξομεν
> βίον γ' ἀχρεῖον ἀνόσιον κεκτημένοι;
>
> Euripides *Heracles* 1301-1302
>
> (He.) Why then should I live? What advantage shall I have if I
> possess an accursed and useless life?

Barlow 1996 *ad loc.* calls this rhesis (1255-1310) "a speech of despair"; she considers 1301-1302 its "emotional climax."[87] Indeed one can hardly imagine a more desperate question than "why then should I live?" δῆτα indicates a logical connection to the preceding discourse; at the same time, since it normally occurs in dialogues, where questions are immediately answered, δῆτα provides a tone of urgency, and draws attention to the speaker.[88] It thereby reflects and emphasizes the speaker's agitation and desperation.[89]

87 Also Bond 1981 *ad* 1255-1310 observes the strong emotionality of the speech, especially after line 1279. On Sophocles, Goldhill 2012:43 similarly suggests that δῆτα, especially when repeated, may indicate "emotional expressivity."

88 See III.3 §86 on δῆτα in questions marking a logical connection; see III.3 §88 on δῆτα questions in monologues creating the impression of a quasi-dialogue.

89 Other examples of δῆτα questions in emotional tragic monologues than in Oedipus' speech include Aeschylus *Agamemnon* 1264 and 1286 by Cassandra; Sophocles *Ajax* 518 by Tecmessa; *Philoctetes* 1348, 1352, and 1367 by Philoctetes; Euripides *Andromache* 404 by Andromache. The instance in Euripides *Children of Heracles* 162 occurs in a rational, non-emotional speech, but at this point of his speech the speaker, the herald, imagines hypothetical arguments against his own opinion (see W. Allan 2001 and Wilkins 1993 *ad loc.*); obviously he wants to present those counter-arguments as less rational.

Other examples of δῆτα questions in strongly emotional contexts (outside of long monologues) include Aeschylus *Prometheus Bound* 747 by Io (a 5-line utterance); Sophocles *Antigone* 230 by the guard (a 14-line utterance), 449 by Creon (a 1-line utterance; καὶ δῆτα is called "indignant" by Griffith 1999 *ad loc.*); Euripides *Electra* 967 by Orestes (a 1-line utterance); *Hippolytus* 806 (a 5-line utterance); Aristophanes *Frogs* 1399 by Euripides (a 1-line utterance).

Menge 1999 [1914]:246 implies this emotional implication of δῆτα questions in his general translation of τί δῆτα into German: "was denn nur?"[90]

§50. Agitated speakers, then, frequently employ an "incremental" style, where subsequent acts are not projected beforehand. Additionally, the particles γε and δῆτα are connected to agitation. γε highlights a specific part of an utterance and thereby emphasizes what the speaker is agitated about. δῆτα questions in monologues convey a sense of urgency, and appeal to hearers, since they are expected to be immediately answered. The particle γε may also reflect agitation in a more specific way, which is what we will turn to next.

5.4 The Different Emotional and Interactional Associations of γε in Aristophanes

§51. The connection of γε to agitated contexts merits closer attention, because more specific relations between the particle and certain emotional and interactional contexts can be identified. In fact the particle does not just fit agitation in general, but, as already suggested concerning (t10), at least in drama it is associated with angry contexts. In addition, γε tends to occur in contexts of stancetaking, which cross-cut those of anger: stancetaking contexts may or may not involve anger or agitation in general. This section analyzes examples from both of these—sometimes overlapping—contexts; together these two uses account for most of the γε instances of in tragedy and comedy.[91] Here the focus is on Aristophanes, since γε is much more frequent there than in tragedy; the functions mentioned here do however also occur in tragedy.[92]

§52. I connect the particle's unparalleled high frequency in Aristophanes to the playwright's tendency to let speakers refer explicitly to their own subjective opinions, judgments, attitudes, and feelings—often in potential contrast to those of others—rather than to speaker-external topics, such as those in arguments, narratives, or gnomic expressions. Although both tragedy and comedy contain all these communicative actions, comedy tends to draw more attention to the speaker of a message, but tragedy

90 Wiesner 1999:356 also suggests "denn (nur)" as a German translation for δῆτα in questions. A Google search of "was denn nur?" (23 December, 2014) shows entries with several question marks and/or exclamation marks, as well as contributions provided with explicit descriptions of the author's desperate feeling (e.g. "[ich] werd langsam wahnsinn[i]g" at www.urbia.de/archiv/forum/th-3517711/aaah-werd-langsam-wahnsinng-was-denn-nur-los.html). An expression such as "what the hell?" seems to work as an English paraphrase of "was denn nur?"

91 Two other uses of γε in drama, that can also overlap with contexts of anger and/or of stancetaking, are the one in resonance contexts, discussed in III.3 §§76-79, and the one at the beginning of answers, discussed in III.4 §62.

92 The frequency of γε in Aristophanes, more than 1.07% of all words, is higher than in any other author; see our frequency graphs (available online as I.5) and III.2 note 212 for discussion and clarification. See III.2 Table 11 for more accurate frequencies in drama, although concerning only parts of the plays.

more to the message itself.[93] This generalization may be connected to Taplin's claim that comedy tends to pay more attention to particulars, and tragedy more to general aspects: comedy, as he puts it, "cannot universalise for long without falling over a heap of dung" (1986:173).[94] The comic emphasis on particular things fits well with a linguistic emphasis on individual speakers. In addition to this, another reason for γε's much higher frequency in comedy seems to be the fact that comic language requires a higher degree of inferential activity from the audience than tragic language, because humor tends to be inferentially complex. γε *par excellence* invites inferences about elements that are implied, but not explicitly spelled out.

5.4.1 γε in angry contexts

§53. Anger is a specific kind of agitated emotion.[95] It is also an interactional emotion: it involves not only someone experiencing the emotion, but also an external agent to whom the angry person attributes responsibility for causing the anger. As Konstan 2006:45 puts it, anger "involves a judgment of intentions. That is why we do not normally get angry at stones: they can hurt us, but cannot insult us (...). Nor can we take revenge on them." Anger is inherently a reaction to a (real or supposed) action by someone else, unlike other feelings such as joy, happiness, sadness, grief, despair, or even fear, which can all be felt without the influence of other people.[96]

§54. Konstan warns that the ancient Greek conception of anger differs from the modern English one. That is, Aristotle describes one of the ancient Greek terms for anger, ὀργή, as "a realizable desire for revenge" (2006:64) in reaction to a slight that involves

93 As one illustration, consider the example of εὖ γε (or εὖ γ'), an expression with little semantic content but a strong connection to the speaker's personal view: it occurs once in Aeschylus, 5 times in Sophocles, 6 times in Euripides, and 17 times in Aristophanes. Stevens 1976:8 considers the expression "clearly colloquial." The subjectivity of speakers can be connected to their voice: see IV.4 §§40-44 on γε in connection to that in historiography.

94 Taplin discusses several differences between tragedy and Old Comedy, mainly concerning the relation of the play's worlds to the audience's world, and the related use of theatrical self-reference. He concludes that the two genres "are in essence fundamentally different" (1986:173).

95 See e.g. Kuppens 2009:32 (on anger in modern humans in general) and Figure 1 above for anger as an emotion with a relatively high degree of arousal.

96 On anger in general, see e.g. Kuppens 2009. On taking into account the appraisal causes of emotions in distinguishing between them (see also §22 above on such classification), see e.g. Reisenzein 1994:537. In this vein, anger typically presupposes that an action of some external agent has taken place in order to trigger the emotion. Kuppens 2009 notes that the agent who is blamed for a "goal-incongruent" situation does not necessarily have to be external, but typically is so. See Konstan 2006:38-40 on emphasis placed by Aristotle on emotions in social interactions, such as anger, rather than emotions arising without others' intentions, such as sadness. See also §17 above on the study by Luraghi and Sausa 2015 on emotion verbs in Homer: they find that verbs involving active reactions to other agents are construed with different grammatical constructions than verbs that only involve the experiencing subject. On fear in general, and the various stimuli that may cause it, see Öhman 2009.

contempt. Aristotle sharply distinguishes between anger on the one hand—a personal, temporary reaction to an intentional insult, with the possibility of revenge—and hatred or enmity on the other hand—a lasting, general attitude towards someone.[97] In English, by contrast, these two concepts overlap to a great extent, according to Konstan. Here we focus only on linguistic reflections of the personal, temporary feeling of anger, but the particular causes of this feeling are not analyzed; thus the appraisal causes may include not only contemptuous insults, but also general intentional harm.

§55. In tragedy and comedy anger plays a crucial role: it is often a driving force in the unfolding plot.[98] As Allen 2003 points out, anger was a central concept in fifth-century Athens, especially "in the ethical discourses that produced Athenian definitions of the good citizen, justice, and just behavior." (78) The author detects a positive view on male anger in Aristophanic comedies: there anger is treated as the source of Athens' independence, greatness, and egalitarianism (84). Tragedy, on the other hand, often revolves around "the angry woman" according to Allen (84), which is connected to the Athenian fear that anger would enter into the household, where it would be destructive.[99]

§56. The expression of anger in tragedy and comedy, then, tends to have different functions in terms of plot and character, just like the expression of calmness (see §25 above); nevertheless, in both genres the use of γε can be connected to this emotion. In fact γε appears in contexts of strong emotion since Homer;[100] for Aristophanes this usage has also been observed.[101] γε's function naturally fits angry contexts, for what is at stake when someone is angry is that she has a different opinion from someone else, at the very least.[102] Indeed, in both tragedy and comedy γε is particularly frequent in angry or otherwise agitated contexts.[103] In general, as discussed in III.2 §§58-63, γε is significantly

97 See Aristotle's definition of ὀργή at *Rhetoric* 2.1.1378a, cited by Allen 2003:79 and Konstan 2006:41. See Konstan 2006:46-76 for discussion of the differences, according to Aristotle. On another Greek term for anger, that is, μῆνις, which plays a central role in the *Iliad* and *Odyssey*, see e.g. Clay 1983:esp. 65-68 (specifically on the *Odyssey*); Frisk 1946; Muellner 1996 (specifically on the *Iliad* and Hesiod's *Theogony*); Watkins 1977. On μῆνις as well as other Greek terms for anger, such as χόλος, see Cairns 2003; Considine 1966; Irmscher 1950. Specifically on κότος and χόλος in Homer, see Walsh 2005.

98 This is the case also for the *Iliad* (see e.g. Irmscher 1950; Muellner 1996; Walsh 2005) and, as Clay 1983 argues, the *Odyssey*.

99 See also Konstan's discussion (2006:57-64) of the anger of Medea and Hecuba in Euripides' plays, and Gerolemou 2011 on "mad women" in tragedy.

100 See e.g. Monro 1882a:258 on γε in Homer: the particle "sometimes emphasises a word as a strong or appropriate one, or as chosen under the influence of a feeling (anger, contempt, etc.)."

101 On γε in Aristophanes connected to emotionality in general, see Neil 1901:188: "After the first word in a sentence, γε emphasizes the word and gives an emotional or 'pathetic' colour to the whole phrase."

102 On the pragmatic function of γε in drama, see §§46-47 above, with references to other chapters.

103 Examples of γε in angry contexts other than the ones discussed in this section include Aeschylus *Libation Bearers* 190 (though γε here, printed by Page 1972 and Sommerstein 2008a, is Porson's conjecture of δέ, and not accepted by Blass 1906, Garvie 1986, Groeneboom 1949, and Murray 1955 [1937]); Sophocles *Antigone* 70, 538, 739, 745, 747, 762; *Electra* 298, 341, 518, 520, 536; *Oedipus*

more frequent in dialogues than elsewhere.[104] This distribution makes it likely that γε's functions are connected to the speaker's personal involvement.

§57. In this scene from Aristophanes *Frogs*, two innkeepers (called "innkeeper" and Plathane in Henderson's translation)[105] in the Underworld are furious with Heracles for eating an enormous amount of food without paying. They obviously do not realize that the person looking like Heracles standing in front of them is actually Dionysus in a costume.

(t12)

Πα. οὐ μὲν οὖν με προσεδόκας,
ὁτιὴ κοθόρνους εἶχες, ἀναγνῶναί σ' ἔτι;
τί δαί; τὸ πολὺ τάριχος οὐκ εἴρηκά πω.
Πλ. μὰ Δί' οὐδὲ τὸν τυρόν γε τὸν χλωρόν, τάλαν,
ὃν οὗτος αὐτοῖς τοῖς ταλάροις κατήσθιεν.
Πα. κἄπειτ' ἐπειδὴ τἀργύριον ἐπραττόμην,
ἔβλεψεν εἴς με δριμὺ κἀμυκᾶτό γε—
Ξα. τούτου πάνυ τοὔργον· οὗτος ὁ τρόπος πανταχοῦ.
Πα. καὶ τὸ ξίφος γ' ἐσπᾶτο, μαίνεσθαι δοκῶν.

Aristophanes *Frogs* 556bis-564

In. Hah! You didn't think I'd recognize you again with those buskins on. Well? I haven't even mentioned all that fish yet.
Pl. Right, dearie, or the fresh cheese that he ate up, baskets and all.
In. And when I presented the bill, he gave me a nasty look and started bellowing.
Xa. That's his style exactly; he acts that way everywhere.
In. And he drew his sword like a lunatic.

In this case the speakers' angry mood is not demonstrated in an incremental syntactic style (in 557 and 561 a subordinate clause intervenes within the main clause) but the dialogue does contain a striking number of γε instances. The speaker's anger can be inferred from the content of the dialogue; linguistically it is here reflected especially in their particle use.

King 361, 363, 365, 369, 372 (δέ... γε; see III.3 §§80-83), 376, 383, 393; *Oedipus at Colonus* 1352, 1354; *Women of Trachis* 1107, 1106, 1111 (on these three cases see (t7) above with discussion), 1127; Euripides *Hippolytus* 1080; *Medea* 495, 514, 608; Aristophanes *Birds* 892, 894, 1208, 1210, 1216, 1220, 1575; *Frogs* 845; *Lysistrata* 529 (twice), 530; *Wasps* 416, 422 (see ὀργῆς in 424), 486.

104 See III.2 §58 on the distribution of γε over the different parts of tragedy and comedy.

105 Tucker 1906 argues that there is only one innkeeper with her maid in this scene, and attributes some of the utterances that others give to the second innkeeper to Dionysus instead.

§58. Tsakmakis 2010 interprets the use of γε in this scene as a marker of coherence. In this way, γε "highlights the common ground of the communication" (351). The use of γε in 562, for example, is in his view "a rhetorical strategy intended to make the new information appear consistent with existing contextual information. Consequently, the new information will appear less unbelievable" (351). However, in this angry context the innkeeper and Plathane are probably not primarily interested in emphasizing that the narrated events (eating cheese in 559, bellowing in 562, and drawing a sword in 564) form a coherent story.[106] After all, both interlocutors have witnessed the events. They rather want to stress the outrageous nature of Heracles' behavior. γε's local function is to single out τὸν τυρόν (559), κἀμυκᾶτο (562), and τὸ ξίφος (564)—implying, for example, that these events were extremely unexpected or outrageous. The women also emphasize stealing cheese, bellowing, and drawing one's sword as successive stages of escalation.[107] In 564 it is rather καί, in my view, that marks the link with the preceding utterance (here the speaker's own previous turn in 561-562), as well as a climax in the upcoming utterance.[108] More globally γε attests to the speakers' agitated state of mind, in this case anger. Moreover, the particle's distribution across tragedy and comedy makes Tsakmakis' interpretation improbable (see §56 above). If its function would be the marking of coherence, we would expect to find γε equally often in calm as in agitated contexts.[109]

5.4.2 γε in stancetaking contexts, with or without agitation

§59. Communicative situations involving anger, then, form highly suitable contexts for the pragmatic functions of γε. However, the particle also appears in contexts without anger or another kind of agitation. In these situations γε's function simply is to imply

[106] Tsakmakis notes (2010:347n11) that Bakker 1988:97-98 "rightly observes that γε is always related to a fact," which may lead one to think that truth is important in γε-utterances. However, Bakker's description exclusively concerns γε in Homer, whereas Tsakmakis discusses its use in Aristophanes; this does not need to be exactly the same as in Homer. See II.5 §§27-50 for the construction ὅ γε in Homer. Moreover, even when there is emphasis on facts, emotional or otherwise subjective implications can be attached to that emphasis. Note that in Aristophanes, γε is often found in stancetaking (see III.4 §63), which cannot be called pure "facts."

[107] The mentioning of these events are preceded by that of eating bread (551), meat (553, with γε), garlic (555), fish (558), and followed by a description of the women's fear (565bis, with γε), and of Heracles' departure with their mattresses (567, with γε).

[108] See IV.2 §§106-107 and §§122-132 on καί marking a narrative peak or a climax in Herodotus and Thucydides.

[109] Tsakmakis notes (2010:345n2) that his discussion of γε is influenced by Kroon's 2009 description of the Latin particle *quidem*, which she argues to be a signal (both backward- and forward-looking) of conceptual unity across several discourse acts. This description seems to work well for *quidem*, which according to Kroon (155) is relatively rare in dialogic contexts; this does not mean, however, that it would translate well to Greek γε, which favors dialogues and agitated contexts. Tsakmakis does note that "[t]he communicative situation is extremely important" (352n20), which includes the "degree of involvement," but in my view this observation does not influence his analysis enough.

a contrast with others' views.[110] The unifying factor in these cases is an explicit expression of stance.[111] Angry utterances generally tend to involve some stancetaking by the speaker as well, but this does not have to be made explicit.

§60. In the following passage from *Birds*, Tereus the Hoopoe has asked Peisetaerus and Euelpides, two Athenian visitors, what kind of city they are looking for. Peisetaerus has just answered that he would love to live in a city where his friends would insist on inviting him to parties. Tereus reacts:

(t13)

135 Επ. νὴ Δία ταλαιπώρων γε πραγμάτων ἐρᾷς.
τί δαὶ σύ;
136bis Ευ. τοιούτων ἐρῶ κἀγώ.
136ter Επ. τίνων;

Aristophanes *Birds* 135-136

Te. My word, it's miserable troubles you [i.e. Peisetaerus] long for!
And what about you [i.e. Euelpides]?
Eu. I long for much the same.
Te. Namely?

Tereus reacts to Peisetaerus' tastes by taking a clear stance: he finds them "miserable." This qualification is meant ironically, as the "troubles" that Peisetaerus longs for are in fact pleasant. That is, the utterance implies a contrast between its literal meaning and the conveyed ironic meaning. With γε Tereus highlights this implicit contrast, thereby emphasizing the irony.[112]

§61. Commentators observe emotions other than anger in this passage, which do not necessarily imply any agitation. Van Leeuwen 1902 *ad loc.* interprets Tereus as laughing (*ridens*) while saying this; Dunbar 1995 *ad loc.* considers Tereus' tone here "surprised." These feelings *may* involve a high degree of arousal, i.e. agitation, with a positive attitude, rather than a negative one as in the case of anger. However, the context here does not give clear indications about Tereus' level of agitation. In any case γε in Aristophanes does not in itself express anger; it can be employed in more friendly and calm contexts, in order to emphasize part of a stancetaking expression or answer. Probably these utterances do not have to involve some form of agitation.

110 On γε implying contrast in Homer, see II.5 §§27-50; in historiography, see IV.4 §§40-44 and IV.5 §20, §§67-68, and §73.

111 On stancetaking, see especially IV.4. On linguistic features of utterances that express stancetaking in drama, see III.4 §§63-67.

112 Note the exclamation mark in Henderson's translation. Dunbar 1995 *ad loc.* paraphrases γε's contribution with italics in her paraphrase of the utterance.

§62. γε also occurs in contexts that clearly relate to both explicit stancetaking and anger. An example is found in the utterance directly following (t13): Euelpides' answer to Tereus' question.

(t14)

Επ. τί δαὶ σύ;
136bis Ευ. τοιούτων ἐρῶ κἀγώ.
136ter Επ. τίνων;
Ευ. ὅπου ξυναντῶν μοι ταδί τις μέμψεται
ὥσπερ ἀδικηθεὶς παιδὸς ὡραίου πατήρ·
"καλῶς γέ μου τὸν υἱόν, ὦ Στιλβωνίδη,
εὑρὼν ἀπιόντ' ἀπὸ γυμνασίου λελουμένον
οὐκ ἔκυσας, οὐ προσεῖπας, οὐ προσηγάγου,
οὐκ ὠρχιπέδισας, ὢν ἐμοὶ πατρικὸς φίλος."

Aristophanes *Birds* 136-142

(Te.) And what about you [i.e. Euelpides]?
Eu. I long for much the same.
Te. Namely?
Eu. A city where a blooming boy's father would bump into me and complain in this fashion, as if wronged: "A fine way you treat my son, Mr. Smoothy! You met him leaving the gymnasium after his bath, and you didn't kiss him, didn't chat him up, didn't hug him, didn't fondle his balls—and you are my old friend!"

Euelpides explains what would present an "ideal problem" for him: namely, the possibility that the father of an attractive boy might complain if Euelpides did *not* kiss his son. The quoted man feels wronged and insulted by Euelpides' hypothetical behavior: one can infer that the imagined father is angry.[113] The quotation also involves irony or sarcasm, since the cited speaker could never mean καλῶς—an explicit expression of stance—in a serious way (cf. 137 μέμψεται, "complain," "blame").[114] γε after καλῶς in 139 highlights the contrast between the literal meaning of this evaluative adverb, and the implied negative meaning. The particle also helps to signal that the announced quotation is starting:

[113] Dunbar 1995 *ad loc.* explicitly describes this hypothetical father as angry. In line with the emotional tone, Henderson uses an exclamation mark in his translation of the γε utterance, as well as Dunbar 1995 and Van Leeuwen 1902 *ad loc.* in their paraphrases. Hartung 1832:372 also cites this instance, using boldface to convey the highlighting function of γε.

[114] On the irony or sarcasm in this utterance, see Bothe 1829, Dunbar 1995, Kock 1864, and Van Leeuwen 1902 *ad loc.*

in Aristophanes the particle frequently occurs in turn-initial position in utterances expressing stance.[115]

§63. γε's functions are associated, then, with several emotional and interactional contexts. Highlighting the speaker's own view, often in implicit contrast to others, is particularly suitable for utterances that express anger. The connection to the speaker's opinion also fits contexts of explicit stancetaking that are not accompanied by anger; in these cases other high-arousal emotions, perhaps on the pleasure side of the emotional field (see Figure 1 in §22 above) may be expressed. The implicit contrast that γε hints at can be part of an ironic expression, where the literal meaning of a word contrasts with its conveyed meaning. Irony always involves stancetaking; it may or may not be combined with anger.

5.5 Two Tragic Case Studies of Calm Versus Agitated Discourse

§64. This section spotlights calm and agitated discourse that simultaneously illustrate several of the findings discussed so far. The first case study compares utterances by the same character in different states of mind, the second involves the emotional inclinations of a play's two main characters.

5.5.1 Sophocles' calm versus agitated Oedipus

§65. Two speeches by Oedipus in *Oedipus King* well exemplify the two ends of the arousal spectrum. At the play's beginning, when Oedipus is unaware of his troubles, he appears calm, but at the end he becomes extremely desperate, that is, agitated in a certain (negative) way. The difference in these emotional states is reflected in several linguistic differences.

§66. At the very start of the play, Oedipus utters the following lines.

(t15)

Οι. Ὦ τέκνα, Κάδμου τοῦ πάλαι νέα τροφή,
τίνας ποθ' ἕδρας τάσδε μοι θοάζετε
ἱκτηρίοις κλάδοισιν ἐξεστεμμένοι;
πόλις δ' ὁμοῦ μὲν θυμιαμάτων γέμει,
ὁμοῦ δὲ παιάνων τε καὶ στεναγμάτων·
ἁγὼ δικαιῶν μὴ παρ' ἀγγέλων, τέκνα,
ἄλλων ἀκούειν αὐτὸς ὧδ' ἐλήλυθα,

115 See III.4 §63. In Birds 1327, Dunbar 1995 *ad loc.* and Neil 1901:190 consider the presence of γε an argument for reading a change in speaker. See also Neil 1901:190 on the general association of γε with speaker changes in Aristophanes.

A very similar expression of stance with γε in a hypothetical quotation is found in 1442 of the same comedy, where all commentators refer back to 139. The expression in 1442 is not ironic.

ὁ πᾶσι κλεινὸς Οἰδίπους καλούμενος.
ἀλλ', ὦ γεραιέ, φράζ', ἐπεὶ πρέπων ἔφυς
πρὸ τῶνδε φωνεῖν, τίνι τρόπῳ καθέστατε,
δείσαντες ἢ στέρξαντες; ὡς θέλοντος ἂν
ἐμοῦ προσαρκεῖν πᾶν· δυσάλγητος γὰρ ἂν
εἴην τοιάνδε μὴ οὐ κατοικτίρων ἕδραν.

Sophocles *Oedipus King* 1-13

Oe. Children, latest to be reared from the stock of Cadmus, why do you sit like this before me, with boughs of supplication wreathed with chaplets? and why is the city filled at the same time with incense, and with the sound of paeans and lamentations? Thinking it wrong to hear this from the report of others, my children, I have come myself, I who am called Oedipus, renowned to all. Come, aged man, tell me, since it is fitting you should speak for these, what is your state, one of fear or one of longing? Know that I am willing to render every kind of aid; I would be hard of heart if I felt no pity at such a supplication.

These words situate the audience in the play's opening state of affairs and enables them to infer Oedipus' specific state of mind at that point. He is here presented as a thoughtful and compassionate king, ready to help his people in times of need. He wants to inform himself well before taking action. As is usual for speakers at the beginning of tragedies,[116] the king appears calm, despite references to his own sense of worry and pity (κατοικτίρων, 13).[117]

§67. The speech contains an elaborate participial clause preceding its main clause, as well as examples of pragmatic projection through vocatives, ἀλλά, and a priming act.[118] In 6-7 a long participial clause, with the intervening vocative τέκνα in 6, precedes

[116] Other calm speakers are found at the beginning of Aeschylus *Eumenides* (Pythia), *Seven against Thebes* (Eteocles); Sophocles *Ajax* (Athena), *Electra* (old slave), *Philoctetes* (Odysseus), *Women of Trachis* (Deineira; she describes her fear, but in a calm way); Euripides *Andromache* (Andromache; she speaks of her misery, but without agitation), *Bacchae* (Dionysus), *Children of Heracles* (Iolaus), *Hecuba* (Polydorus), *Hippolytus* (Aphrodite).

[117] Bollack 1990, Dawe 2006 [1982], Van Herwerden 1866, and Jebb 2004 [1893] do not remark on the speaker's emotions in this passage. Ritter 1870 speaks of Oedipus' "Wahre Liebe und innige Theilnahme für die Bittenden" ("true love and heartfelt sympathy for the suppliants"; *ad* 6-8), and Kamerbeek 1967 mentions his "readiness to be helpful" (*ad* 6-7), remarks that can perhaps be connected to a relatively calm state of mind.

[118] Although the speech is only 75 words long and it is therefore hard to say anything about frequencies of linguistic items, perhaps another reflection of calmness is that the frequencies of first-person references (5 instances, that is 6.7%) and of negations (3 instances, that is 4.0%) are closer to the average frequencies in Sophoclean monologues of 25 lines or longer (6.5 and 4.0%, respectively) than to those in Sophoclean dialogues (7.3 and 4.9%, respectively). See §72 and note 126 below for the strikingly high frequencies of these items in Oedipus' agitated speech.

the finite verb ἐλήλυθα. In 1 the vocative ὦ τέκνα produces pragmatic projection: it is not complete on its own, but pragmatically requires the attachment of an utterance addressed to this addressee.[119] ὦ τέκνα projects more than one act: τίνας ποθ' ἕδρας τάσδε μοι θοάζετε, and ἱκτηρίοις κλάδοισιν ἐξεστεμμένοι. The extension of the already incomplete vocative with the apposition Κάδμου τοῦ πάλαι νέα τροφή in line 1 delays the fulfillment of the projection in this case. That is, even though appositions may be part of a purely incremental style, here the construction contributes to prolonging the vocative's pragmatic projection.

§68. Another vocative, ὦ γεραιέ "old man," occurs in 9, again triggering the expectation of subsequent acts—now addressed to the old priest rather than the group of young suppliants. In this case the main clause φράζ' "tell me" follows immediately afterwards. This verb in itself semantically projects a complement clause clarifying what the addressee should tell, even though the utterance would have been syntactically complete if it had ended here.[120] Moreover, the particle ἀλλά before the vocative enhances the pragmatic projection: whether we read it as an act on its own or as one act together with ὦ γεραιέ, ἀλλά always marks some shift in the discourse.[121] The shift to a different addressee in this case creates the pragmatic expectation that several upcoming discourse acts will be addressed to this person, not just one imperative.[122]

§69. Oedipus' speech also contains a priming act: πόλις δ' | ὁμοῦ μὲν θυμιαμάτων γέμει (4). As in the Aristophanic example of a priming act discussed in §31 above, the particle μέν retrospectively demonstrates the discourse-act boundary directly after δέ. The ὁμοῦ μέν and ὁμοῦ δέ acts following it both pertain semantically to "the city": together they form a multi-act move.[123] With δέ Oedipus presents πόλις δ' as a new step in the discourse, without making a more specific connection explicit.[124]

119 See §30 above. In Pindar vocatives serve to redirect the audience's attention (note its co-occurrence with ἀλλά here), and as such typically start new moves (see II.3 §70).

120 In this case the pragmatic projection is less strong than in the case of the vocative, because Oedipus has already asked the questions to which he would like his addressee to respond (lines 2-5).

121 On the functions and uses of ἀλλά in drama in general, see III.2 §§64-68.

122 On ἀλλά similarly introducing a multi-act move in Herodotus, see IV.5 §63.

123 See II.2 §71 for a similar example from Homer, where likewise a μέν act and a δέ act follow a priming act. As discussed there, Denniston 1950 [1934]:371 notes that such μέν and δέ acts often form one bigger unit together, but not that the preceding act may project this entire structure. See IV.2 §108 for καί as a priming act followed by a μέν act, a construction that is frequent in Herodotus and especially Thucydides.

In this case, the projection is simultaneously syntactic as well, because πόλις is the subject of the following finite verb γέμει, but since no full syntactic clause intervenes between them, the syntactic projection is less striking. That is, syntactically the structure πόλις δ' ὁμοῦ μὲν θυμιαμάτων γέμει is simply one independent clause distributed over two discourse acts, rather than preceded or interrupted by another, dependent clause, as in the stronger cases of syntactic projection.

124 On the possible exploitation of the "neutral" connection signaled by δέ in tragedy, see III.2 §§24-25.

§70. Now let us turn to Oedipus' later agitation. The following passage is part of the speech (1369-1415, 46 lines in total, 295 words) that he utters shortly after he has learned of his troubles and blinded himself.

(t16)

(Οι.) ἐγὼ γὰρ οὐκ οἶδ' ὄμμασιν ποίοις βλέπων
πατέρα ποτ' ἂν προσεῖδον εἰς Ἅιδου μολών,
οὐδ' αὖ τάλαιναν μητέρ', οἶν ἐμοὶ δυοῖν
ἔργ' ἐστὶ κρείσσον' ἀγχόνης εἰργασμένα.
ἀλλ' ἡ τέκνων δῆτ' ὄψις ἦν ἐφίμερος,
βλαστοῦσ' ὅπως ἔβλαστε, προσλεύσσειν ἐμοί;
οὐ δῆτα τοῖς γ' ἐμοῖσιν ὀφθαλμοῖς ποτε·
οὐδ' ἄστυ γ', οὐδὲ πύργος, οὐδὲ δαιμόνων
ἀγάλμαθ' ἱερά, τῶν ὁ παντλήμων ἐγὼ
κάλλιστ' ἀνὴρ εἷς ἔν γε ταῖς Θήβαις τραφεὶς
ἀπεστέρησ' ἐμαυτόν, αὐτὸς ἐννέπων
ὠθεῖν ἅπαντας τὸν ἀσεβῆ, τὸν ἐκ θεῶν
φανέντ' ἄναγνον καὶ γένους τοῦ Λαΐου.

Sophocles *Oedipus King* 1371-1383

(Oe.) For I do not know with what eyes I could have looked upon my father when I went to Hades, or upon my unhappy mother, since upon them both I have done deeds that hanging could not atone for. Then, could I desire to look upon my children, since their origins were what they were? Never could these eyes have harboured such desire! Nor to look upon the city, or the wall, or the statues of the gods or the temples, from which I, who had enjoyed the greatest luxury in Thebes, had in misery cut myself off, commanding with my own lips that all should drive from their houses the impious one, the one whom the gods had shown to be impure and of the race of Laius.

This rhesis is highly emotional. Commentators speak of Oedipus' dread in remembering his incest,[125] his "incommunicable anguish,"[126] and his "desperate state of mind."[127] Kamerbeek 1967 *ad* 1398-99 describes the whole speech as "Oedipus' most pathetic rhesis." Emotions such as desperation and anguish can be said to belong to the agitated pole of the arousal dimension.

125 Van Herwerden 1866 *ad* 1376.
126 Jebb 2004 [1893] *ad* 1415.
127 Kamerbeek 1967 *ad* 1389-1390.

§71. The use of particles is connected to Oedipus' emotionality. The entire speech contains, notably, four γε (1377, 1378, 1380, 1386) and two δῆτα (1375, 1377). The γε instances locally highlight specific parts of the discourse that are particularly connected to Oedipus' curse (the city of Thebes) or his current misfortune (his eyes), and globally reveal his state of mind. δῆτα in 1375 makes its host question resemble a dialogic turn of speaking, thus engaging potential hearers. Oedipus goes on to answer his rhetorical question himself with οὐ δῆτα in 1377: here the particle provides a strong emphasis on the negation.

§72. Numerous other linguistic features likewise relate to the agitation. Besides the semantic markers παντλήμων (1379), τοὐμὸν ἄθλιον δέμας (1388), and ἀνδρὸς ἀθλίου (1413), the abundance of first-person references (29 in total, 10% of all words) and negations (19 in total, 6% of all words) is remarkable.[128] The two devices work together to push the speaker into the foreground, the first-person references by directly pointing to the speaker, negations by displaying his subjective influence on his way of expression.[129] Oedipus now knows that all eyes are on him, because he himself has been the center of the story which he had been unraveling.

§73. Regarding syntax and discourse structure, this passage does not contain moves with a priming act followed by several acts fulfilling its projection, as the calm speech at the play's beginning did. Rather, the discourse structure mainly consists of a "spontaneous" adding of acts onto each other, as in ἐγὼ γὰρ οὐκ οἶδ' | ὄμμασιν ποίοις βλέπων | / πατέρα ποτ' ἂν προσεῖδον | εἰς Ἅιδου μολών, | /οὐδ' αὖ τάλαιναν μητέρ' ("For I do not know | [looking] with what eyes | I could have looked upon my father | when I went to Hades, | or upon my unhappy mother," 1372-1373). Here the syntax is complete after προσεῖδον, and does not project another act. Oedipus could have formulated the remarks about Hades and his mother in a separate construction; instead he adds them as increments to the already syntactically complete remark about his father.[130]

§74. Other examples of such syntactic increments in (t17), which do not project the structure beforehand, include οὐδ' ἄστυ γ', | οὐδὲ πύργος, | οὐδὲ δαιμόνων / ἀγάλμαθ' ἱερά ("nor to look upon the city, or the wall, or the statues of the gods or the temples," 1378-1379) and αὐτὸς ἐννέπων / ὠθεῖν ἅπαντας τὸν ἀσεβῆ, | τὸν ἐκ θεῶν /φανέντ' ἄναγνον | καὶ γένους τοῦ Λαΐου ("commanding with my own lips that all should drive from their houses the impious one, the one whom the gods had shown to be impure and of the race of Laius," 1381-1383). The syntax would not have required these acts to be

[128] The average frequency of first-person references in Sophoclean monologues is 6.5%; of negations 4.0%. See III.2 Tables 13 and 17. See note 118 above.

[129] On the relation of negations to the speaker's explicit presence, see III.2 §66.

[130] Only the first act of this structure does project, semantically, an object for οἶδ' "I [don't] know," which is fulfilled in the second and third acts ("[looking] with what eyes | I could have looked upon my father").

placed where they are. Therefore they give the impression that Oedipus only thinks of them at the very moment of utterance.

§75. The multi-act structure | τῶν ὁ παντλήμων ἐγὼ | / κάλλιστ' ἀνὴρ εἷς ἔν γε ταῖς Θήβαις τραφεὶς | / ἀπεστέρησ' ἐμαυτόν | (1379-1381) seems an exception to the incremental style in this speech, as the second act intervenes between the subject ἐγὼ in the first act and its syntactically projected verb ἀπεστέρησα in the third act. However, the intervening act is not a subordinate clause preceding and therefore projecting an entire main clause, but an apposition, not syntactically projected or required, within a subordinate clause. The multi-act structure is incremental in a different way: each of these acts adds information about Oedipus himself in a piecemeal fashion, which enhances the dramatic focus on his fate. Additionally, παντλήμων "utterly miserable" (1379) semantically does not project a word like κάλλιστ' "in a most beautiful way" (1380) so closely afterwards.

§76. One may object, justifiably, that an accumulation of increments may still form an elaborate structure of acts that syntactically, semantically, and/or pragmatically belong together. However, my point is that the earlier parts of such moves do not project or require the addition of the later parts. That is, we may identify multi-act moves such as ἀλλ' ἡ τέκνων δῆτ' ὄψις ἦν ἐφίμερος, | / βλαστοῦσ' ὅπως ἔβλαστε, | προσλεύσσειν ἐμοί; | (1375-1376) as coherent units. But in the moment of their utterance their combined structure is in fact incremental, literally: "but was my children's sight desirable, then? | [the sight that had] originated in such way as it had, | [was it desirable] for me to look at?" Line 1375 could have stood on its own; the two acts in 1376 only later turn out to belong, syntactically, semantically, and pragmatically, to the preceding line as well. The entire move appears more fragmented than a move in which earlier parts project the later ones.

§77. Note that in both Oedipus' calm and his agitated speeches he uses repetition in successive acts—ὁμοῦ-ὁμοῦ in the calm speech (lines 4-5), τόν-τόν in the agitated one (line 1382). These instances, however, serve different purposes. The ὁμοῦ acts are part of a carefully composed move, and pragmatically projected beforehand by a priming act, whereas the unannounced repetition of the definite article τόν contributes to an incremental style, and thus to the image of an agitated speaker.[131] Lexical repetition by itself, then, is not a sign of either calmness or agitation, but can be employed for different pragmatic goals. It is multifunctional and dependent on its specific context, just as other linguistic features, including particles, are (see §7 above).

[131] Other examples of lexical repetition reflecting emotional distress are the several word doublings spoken by Philoctetes in Sophocles *Philoctetes* 1169-1217, such as πάλιν πάλιν in line 1169 and φονᾷ φονᾷ in line 1209. In this lyric dialogue between Philoctetes and the chorus, some lines are distributed among several speakers (antilabe), which Stanford 1983:99 identifies as another sign of "emotional excitement."

5.5.2 Euripides' agitated Pentheus versus calm Dionysus

§78. So far I have discussed how a certain emotional state of mind at particular moments affects linguistic output. The second tragic comparison of calmness and agitation concerns how a character's speech style reflects a more permanent emotional state, that is, when emotionality is a feature of someone's temperament. As Revelle and Scherer put it, "personality is to emotion what climate is to weather" (2009:304). Because of the relation of γε to anger the particle also reflects, in specific cases, the more global feature of a tragic character's irascibility. The case of Pentheus in Euripides *Bacchae* illustrates γε's connection to anger as well as to temperament. His opponent, the god Dionysus, generally stays calm: this is reflected in his particular uses of δέ, among other features.

§79. Pentheus is presented as particularly short-tempered: Dodds 1960 [1944] for example mentions that "Pentheus is flurried, irascible, full of an unhealthy excitement" (xliv).[132] The character is fond of γε: he utters 11 instances, which means 1.0% of his 1119 words in the whole play. Most other tragic characters use the particle less often: for example, Clytaemnestra in Aeschylus *Agamemnon* 0.3% (6 instances in 1927 words in total); Antigone in the eponymous play by Sophocles 0.7% (8 instances in 1220 words); Hippolytus in his eponymous play by Euripides 0.8% (13 instances in 1644 words); Medea in hers 0.4% (14 instances in 3447 words).[133] These frequencies are of course only part of the information at our disposal, and do not tell us *how* a character uses a certain particle. Differences in frequencies across characters can, however, form a starting point for an analysis.

§80. In Pentheus' case, the high frequency of γε can be connected to his fiery temper. However, being angry by itself does not always entail that a character expresses this feeling in words, which is the aspect relevant to particle use. That is, if a character expresses her anger mainly through nonverbal means, then this feeling may not have clear reflections in her language use. It may seem surprising, for instance, that Euripidean Medea does not utter many instances of γε, but in fact she does not very often express her anger *verbally*. She spends most of her words for other communicative actions, such as lamenting her fate (e.g. lines 111-114, 144-147, 160-167), arguing her case (214-266), or explaining her plans (364-409, 764-810). Even when speaking directly to Jason she hides her anger in one of her speeches (869-905). In short, Medea expresses her anger especially in her nonverbal actions, but uses language to do other things, for which γε is less

[132] For example Pentheus' speech at 215-262 reflects anger (even though no γε is present here); Dodds 1960 [1944], Oranje 1984, and Seaford 1996 *ad loc.* remark on this anger, and all call the passage a "tirade" (so does Mastronarde 1979:23 on syntactic reflections of contact in tragedy).

[133] See note 60 above for the 21 tragic characters taken into account in my comparisons of particle frequencies. Oedipus in Sophocles *Oedipus King* is the only other character with a higher γε frequency than Euripides' Pentheus: 1.1% (48 instances in 4258 words). Oedipus speaks much of his text within angry dialogues.

fitting. Pentheus, in contrast, destined as he is to lose the battle with Dionysus, can only rage with words.

§81. The other main character of *Bacchae*, Dionysus, tends to remain calm. Dodds 1960 [1944]:xliv notes this general calmness, and writes *ad* 621-622: "amid the physical turmoil of the earthquake and the moral turmoil of the baffled Pentheus, the Stranger's calm marks him as something supernatural; it is like the sinister calm at the heart of a typhoon." Dionysus utters γε with a relatively low frequency of 0.6% (9 times in 1549 words). It is δέ that he uses more often than any other tragic character: its frequency in Dionysus' utterances is 4.1% (63 instances in 1549 words).[134]

§82. The following dialogue shows how emotional differences manifest in divergent particle use. Over the course of the exchange, Pentheus becomes increasingly agitated, while the Stranger (in fact Dionysus) remains calm throughout.

(t17)

Πε. πρῶτον μὲν ἁβρὸν βόστρυχον τεμῶ σέθεν.
Δι. ἱερὸς ὁ πλόκαμος· τῶι θεῶι δ' αὐτὸν τρέφω.
Πε. ἔπειτα θύρσον τόνδε παράδος ἐκ χεροῖν.
Δι. αὐτός μ' ἀφαιροῦ· τόνδε Διονύσωι φορῶ.
Πε. εἱρκταῖσί τ'[135] ἔνδον σῶμα σὸν φυλάξομεν.
Δι. λύσει μ' ὁ δαίμων αὐτός, ὅταν ἐγὼ θέλω.
Πε. ὅταν γε καλέσηις αὐτὸν ἐν βάκχαις σταθείς.
Δι. καὶ νῦν ἃ πάσχω πλησίον παρὼν ὁρᾶι.
Πε. καὶ ποῦ 'στιν; οὐ γὰρ φανερὸς ὄμμασίν γ' ἐμοῖς.
Δι. παρ' ἐμοί· σὺ δ' ἀσεβὴς αὐτὸς ὢν οὐκ εἰσορᾶις.
Πε. λάζυσθε· καταφρονεῖ με καὶ Θήβας ὅδε.
Δι. αὐδῶ με μὴ δεῖν, σωφρονῶν οὐ σώφροσιν.
Πε. ἐγὼ δὲ δεῖν γε, κυριώτερος σέθεν.

Euripides *Bacchae* 498-505

Pe. First I shall cut off your delicate locks.
Di. My locks are sacred: I grow them long in the god's honor.
Pe. Next, hand over that wand.

[134] Of the 21 tragic characters analyzed (see note 60 above), the next highest δέ frequencies are those of Clytaemnestra in Aeschylus *Agamemnon*, the queen in Aeschylus *Persians*, and Teiresias in Euripides *Bacchae* (all three 3.7%); those of Electra in Aeschylus *Libation Bearers* (3.6%); and those of Hippolytus in his eponymous play (3.4%). Although the frequencies by themselves do not yet tell us which communicative strategies these characters favor, since they may prefer different uses of the same particle, the quantitative comparison does make it clear that Dionysus utters δέ strikingly often. The next step is then to analyze in which way exactly he tends to use the particle; see the discussion of (t17) below for examples of such analyses.

[135] On turn-initial τε (a rare position for this particle), see III.4 §27, with note 50.

> Di. Take it from me yourself: I carry it, but it belongs to Dionysus.
> Pe. We will keep you penned up inside and under guard.
> Di. Dionysus himself will free me when I so desire.
> Pe. Sure, when you stand surrounded by bacchants and call on him.
> Di. Yes, even now he is near and sees what I am undergoing.
> Pe. Where is he? To my eyes he is not in evidence.
> Di. He's with me: since you are a godless man you do not see him.
> Pe. Seize him! He's treating me and Thebes with contempt!
> Di. And I forbid it: I am sane and you are not.
> Pe. I say bind him, and I have more authority than you.

Pentheus' use of γε keeps pace with his mounting frustration. In 499, γε marks a hostile use of resonance: Pentheus echoes his interlocutor's ὅταν, thereby extending its syntactic dependence on the main clause "the god himself will free me" (λύσει μ' ὁ δαίμων αὐτός, 498); he also picks up the reference to his interlocutor from the previous utterance. The addition of γε in resonating utterances emphasizes the speaker's hostile goal in echoing his opponent's words, and thereby implies anger or hate.[136] Line 505 contains another γε, in this case preceded by turn-initial δέ. As discussed in III.3, in contexts of resonance the combination of these two particles mark the echo from the preceding utterance as a hostile one.[137] In other words, Pentheus here employs γε as well as δέ... γε in such a way as to convey anger and hostility.

§83. Pentheus' utterance in 501 is a question starting with a καί act, which may imply indignation.[138] This implication fits the king's growing anger. His use of γε to highlight ὄμμασιν ἐμοῖς, "*my* eyes"—implying a contrast to what his addressee is claiming—accordingly receives a hostile function: the utterance implies that Pentheus' addressee is lying about the god's presence.

§84. In contrast to Pentheus, Dionysus stays calm in this scene. He adopts a solemn speaking style, which is reflected in his frequent use of αὐτός when it is semantically

[136] On this function of γε in contexts of resonance in tragedy and comedy, see III.3 §§76-79. On this instance of γε, Oranje 1984 notes that Pentheus speaks "mockingly" (60); he calls γε "emphatic" (61n154). Rijksbaron 1991 *ad loc.* cites Oranje and reads γε as implying assent through emphasis, while limiting that assent. Seaford 1996 *ad loc.* interprets the utterance as sarcastic (Pentheus "means, sarcastically, that the invocation will occur in prison"). On another note, Elmsley 1821 considers γε an argument against taking this utterance as a question (see III.4 §64 on the rarity of γε at the start of questions).

[137] See III.3 §§80-83, including discussion of this particular example. Again, Oranje 1984:62 notes the anger conveyed by Pentheus' words. Similarly, Wecklein 1903 *ad loc.* and Oranje 1984:77 note the sarcasm in Pentheus' utterance in 796, which contains another γε. On another particle implying emotion, see III.2 §87 on ἦ in tragedy.

[138] On this instance of καί marking a contemptuous or indignant question, see Dodds 1944 *ad loc.* and Oranje 1984:61n155. On this use of turn-initial καί in drama in general, see note 23 above.

redundant (494, 496, 498, 502),[139] and in starting several turns without turn-initial contextualization cues, even though these are not answers to questions (see 494, 496, 498).[140] In 500 the subordinate clause at the start (ἃ πάσχω) and the intervening participial phrase (πλησίον παρών) project that their main clause (ὁρᾶι) will follow.

§85. Both Pentheus and Dionysus use δέ, but in notably different constructions. These uses illustrate that in combination with several co-textual and contextual features, δέ may also contribute to the linguistic reflection of calmness or agitation. Dionysus twice uses δέ not in the first act of his turn, but later; this is in fact his usual habit.[141] When he utters δέ in turns longer than one line, which he often does, the particle also rarely appears in turn-initial position.[142] Pentheus, in contrast, usually uses δέ in turn-initial position.[143]

§86. I associate these different δέ constructions with different pragmatic goals. On the one hand, δέ marking an act boundary later in an utterance simply signals a new step in the discourse, without explicitly relating the host act to the preceding one; this use is for example frequent in long narratives.[144] On the other hand, δέ in the first discourse act of an utterance marks the start not just of a new act, but of an entire new adjacency pair, usually a new question-answer pair.[145] This turn-initial construction is therefore

139 In 498 αὐτός also hints at his double identity, since he is in fact "himself." αὐτός typically refers to gods or heroes. On the pragmatics of αὐτός, particularly in Homer, see Bonifazi 2012:137-183.

140 On turn-initial contextualization cues in tragedy and comedy, see III.4 §12.

141 The other one-line utterances by Dionysus with δέ in non-turn-initial position are *Bacchae* 464, 474, 484, 647, 833, 841, and 1345.

142 Dionysus utters δέ in non-turn-initial position in turns longer than one line in *Bacchae* 4, 6, 10, 11, 13, 23, 28, 33, 37, 48, 50, 62, 461, 617, 618, 621, 622, 624, 626, 627, 630, 632, 633, 634, 636, 638, 657, 659, 788, 847 (in the manuscripts this instance *is* turn-initial, but all editors accept Musgrave's transposition of 848 to before 847; indeed the text makes more sense like this, and as Seaford remarks *ad loc.*, in this way "δέ acquires its proper place"), 850, 853, 854, 859, 861, 917, 924, 944, 947, 948, 960, 965, 966, 975, 976, 1333, 1335, 1336, 1338, and 1341. He utters it in turn-initial position (that is, in the first discourse act of a turn) only four times: in 490, 654, 813, and 815.

143 Pentheus utters turn-initial δέ in *Bacchae* 465, 467, 469, 471, 473, 481, 485, 505 (see (t17); δέ... γε), 663, 830, 832, and 941.

144 On the "neutral" signal of δέ within turns, see III.2 §§24-25; on its relatively high frequency in messenger speeches, see III.2 §§27-28. A high frequency of δέ may also trigger an association to epic; see III.2 §26 on that. In angry or generally agitated contexts δέ seems to be less frequent. Speakers there tend to connect their discourse acts in a less neutral way, or use an incremental style without marking the start of new acts at all (see §§44 above). For example, in Oedipus' emotional speech at Sophocles *Oedipus King* 1369-1415 (on which see §§70-77 above), δέ is even completely absent. Heracles' emotional speech at Sophocles *Women of Trachis* 1046-1111 (on which see §46 above) has a low δέ frequency of 1.3% (5 instances in 387 words; the average δέ frequency in Sophoclean monologues is 2.6%; see III.2 Table 2); Hermione's angry 8-line utterance at Euripides *Andromache* 261-268 has 1.9% (1 instance in 52 words; the average δέ frequency in Euripidean dialogues [maximum of 4 lines per turn] is 2.4%, in monologues [minimum of 25 lines] 3.7%); Jason's angry speech at *Medea* 1323-1350 has 2.3% (4 instances in 171 words; the average δέ frequency in Euripidean monologues is 3.7% see III.2 Table 2).

145 See III.4 §§34-35 on this function of turn-initial δέ, and III.4 §15 for discussion of the concept of adjacency pair.

especially frequent in a list of questions, such as Pentheus' interrogation of the Stranger at *Bacchae* 460-486, where he utters 7 instances of turn-initial δέ. The one-line questions in that interrogation scene usually give little information about the speaker's emotional state; nevertheless, in the case of Pentheus' list of questions the god, who possesses the desired information, is calmer than the king, who tries to get it out.[146] Dionysus' preference for non-turn-initial δέ, then, implies that he tends to mark discourse connections of various kinds with the neutral signal of δέ, without making particular relations explicit; this reflects less communicative pressure, and therefore calmness. Pentheus usually employs the particle in its turn-initial construction, which is connected to interrogating, in his case in an agitated way. That is, δέ in itself indicates neither calmness nor agitation, but specific constructions of the particle in combination with other features do reflect these states of mind.

§87. The tragedians, then, represent some characters as more prone to certain emotions than other characters, and this leads to differences in particle use. In the case of *Bacchae*, Pentheus' frequent use of the particle γε and δέ in its turn-initial construction reflects his irascible personality. Dionysus' less frequent use of γε and his inclination for δέ in later than turn-initial position relates to his general calmness.

5.6 Conclusions

§88. In this chapter we have seen that particles do not directly express emotional states by themselves, but often play an important role in facilitating our interpretation of an utterance's emotional qualities. Calmness and agitation are two opposing states of mind that reveal themselves in divergent patterns of discourse organization and particle use. These linguistic tendencies are found in both tragedy and comedy, although the literary functions of the two emotional states tend to differ in the different genres.

§89. Calmness may be reflected in subordinate clauses that precede and thereby project their main clauses, as well as in pragmatic projection, especially through vocatives and priming acts. Several particles may play a role in priming acts, with δέ being the most frequent. Certain constructions with μέν tend to be found in calm contexts: they demonstrate that speakers who trust that they can keep the floor are at leisure to pay ample attention to structuring their discourse. In other words, I connect a discourse organization that involves several kinds of "stretching"—a strategy that all of these

[146] A similar stichomythic interrogation scene is Sophocles *Oedipus King* 1015-1046, where the questioner Oedipus utters 4 turn-initial δέ in his questions; he is clearly much more emotionally shaken by the answers than the shepherd who calmly gives his information. Compare in Aristophanes the question-answer scene of Socrates and Strepsiades cited in (t1) above. As in the Oedipus scene, here as well the one who possesses more knowledge (Socrates) is the calm, high-status character; however, in this case he is the questioner, as befits the philosopher's style (see §27 above).

features instantiate—to calmness. Certain uses of δέ also relate to calmness, by indicating emotionally neutral discourse boundaries within longer turns of speaking.

§90. In agitated contexts speakers tend to utter discourse acts that appear to be spontaneously added to one another. The particles γε and δῆτα especially fit such contexts as well. γε highlights a part of an utterance that expresses the speaker's subjective views, attitude, or feelings, potentially in contrast to those of other people. That is, the particle fits utterances that express the speaker's stance. Moreover, the contribution of γε is comparable to that of the emphatic prosody represented by an exclamation mark in English—an emphasis especially appropriate in contexts of high emotional arousal. δῆτα, which appears less frequently than γε, generally works to signal that a question arises from the preceding discourse; additionally it appears to directly reflect a speaker's sense of disquiet. The emotional prosody it conveys would be akin to a loud and desperate pronunciation of the entire utterance.

§91. γε can be more specifically connected to the agitated state of anger. The particle's pragmatic function, to highlight one element and stress the speaker's own views in contrast to others', makes it particularly useful for angry contexts. This interpretation again invites an analogy with the exclamation mark: like γε, this paralinguistic device does not signal anger by itself, but is expected to occur more frequently in angry contexts.

§92. As discussed in IV.4, taking stance usually involves some degree of emotional involvement. At the same time, expressing an emotion tends to involve an evaluation, positioning, or alignment by the speaker.[147] That is, even though expressing anger and expressing stance do not entail each other, they are communicative actions that can be combined. Both are more frequent in comedy, with its greater emphasis on particular speakers, than in tragedy, which focuses more on communicated content (see §52 above); the frequency of these actions in Aristophanes partly explains why this playwright uses γε so often.

§93. The results of this chapter show that Greek drama does not only provide information about the cultural and literary significance of emotional states of mind, which previous investigations have focused on. The texts are also an important source for the manner in which emotionality influences language use. By focusing on this influence, with special attention to calmness and agitation, the current analyses complement the approaches to ancient emotions that have been prevalent in recent research.

§94. All of these observations mean, once more, that it is necessary to look beyond the clause or the sentence, in order to fully understand the use of particles, and their

[147] See Du Bois 2007 and IV.4 §§46-51 for evaluation, positioning, or alignment as the three components of stancetaking. See §22 above on emotions involving a judgment. See IV.4.4.3 on the possible coexistence of epistemic and emotional stance in historiography.

pragmatic contributions to the discourse.[148] Particles do not just modify the single discourse act in which they occur; they also, at the same time, reflect the degree of emotional arousal of a passage, or aspects of a character's general emotional tendencies. In general, this chapter shows that the organization of discourse in drama (such as syntactic structure, pragmatic projection, and the marking of transitions) is connected to characters' calmness or agitation. That is to say, emotionality and discourse organization in drama are not only compatible, but also to some extent interdependent. More specifically, emotional arousal reveals itself through alterations in linguistic patterns, such as patterns of particle use.

§95. Since a speaker's emotional state of mind is relevant to this kind of linguistic choices, as this chapter has demonstrated, the study of discourse organization should not ignore the interactional level of discourse, including characters' attitudes towards their utterances and towards their addressees. Calmness and agitation are not an optional addition to the "dry" meaning of dramatic utterances; they are an inherent part of the embodied performance.[149] Both of these levels of emotional arousal have their own functions in the interaction among the characters, as well as in the literary communication between playwright and audience. The direction of investigation started in the current chapter therefore promises to illuminate the ancient dramas in many more ways.

[148] This holds also for the observations about connections between particle use and other general pragmatic phenomena, which can be found in the other research chapters of this monograph.

[149] See e.g. Foolen 2012:360-364 on the connection between emotion and embodied cognition in general. An indication for this connection is, for example, the finding that emotion-laden words are processed differently from non-emotional words.

PART IV

PARTICLE USE IN HERODOTUS AND THUCYDIDES

BY

ANNA BONIFAZI

IV.1

Introduction

§1. As a non-poetic genre, Classical historiography is not characterized by formal features such as meter or characters' appearances on stage.[1] Still, at the level of discourse articulation, historiography shares with epic, lyric, and drama some fundamental aspects. For example, it has in common with epic the use of different strategies to ensure a comprehensible narrative progression. It has in common with lyric the use of self-presentation devices to establish the authorial *persona*. Finally, it has in common with Classical drama the agonistic juxtaposition of different views on a common "stage," in line with contemporary oratory and philosophy. All these genres incorporate different voices and stances in various forms.

§2. Reflections on intertextuality, content patterns, and allusions to other genres in the language have always been part of scholarship on Classical historiography. The same holds for attention to keywords and motives underscoring crucial concepts, either in relation to the historians' methodology or their *Weltanschauung*. A more recent addition is the study of historiographical language with a focus on how content is presented. That is, scholars are beginning to pay more attention to the linguistic and narrative strategies enacted by Herodotus and Thucydides.[2]

1 Meter should not be completely ruled out from Greek Classical prose. Besides ancient and modern evidence about prose colometry (on which see IV.3.6), some scholarly attention has been devoted to *clausulae* that follow certain metrical schemes, partially inspired by *a posteriori* evidence from Cicero and Quintilian. Lamb (1914:241-272), for example, offers remarkable insights on *clausulae* and metrical features in Thucydides' narrative style. In this part, frequencies and quotations are based on the TLG online editions—Jones and Powell 1942 for Thucydides (which coincides with the OCT edition), and Legrand 1932-1954 for Herodotus. Section numbers in Herodotus follow Hude's edition (OCT)—they are not included in the TLG online. Differences between the editorial choices of Legrand and of Hude in Herodotus' text are occasionally noted. Translations include a mix of generally known (older as well as more recent) translations, and translations by the author. Several times commonly used translations become part of the discussion about interpretation.

2 Works that particularly influenced the writing of part IV include: Müller 1980 on clause combination in Herodotus; Bakker 1991 on temporal subclauses in Herodotus; Walker 1993 on *enargeia* in Greek historiography; Dik 1995 on word order and particles in Herodotus; Yaginuma 1995 on links between Thucydides' language and the process of reading; Lang 1995 on the use of participles in Thucydides; Wakker 1997b on modal particles in Herodotus and Thucydides; Bakker

§3. Part IV complements and adds to the existing literature on language in Herodotus' and Thucydides' *Histories*. The general theoretical framework used in the arguments and the analyses is the same as in Parts II and III. Particles and particle combinations are privileged linguistic items for the purposes of our investigations; however, they are consistently seen as a manifestation of more comprehensive features, all of them reflecting the holistic notion of discourse.[3] The following section illustrates what these comprehensive features are, and how they are thematized in the different chapters.

1.1 Themes and Examples

§4. The first two chapters discuss two fundamental mechanisms in the articulation of discourse—which in fact transcend the genre of historiography. One is the sequential addition of pieces of content through *and*-coordination. The other is segmentation, which encompasses larger and smaller units as well as stronger and weaker boundaries of discourse. IV.2 and IV.3 explore the contribution of particles to these mechanisms, with a view toward deepening our knowledge of particles' capabilities as discourse articulation devices.

§5. What motivates the study of the first mechanism, *and*-coordination, is that its apparent simplicity belies its real complexity. The complexity is due to the fact that coordinating conjunctions/particles give rise to a wide range of inferences. Canonical descriptions of their functions acknowledge only some of them. This is particularly true for δέ, τε, and καί. To exemplify the problem, let us consider καί in this passage (discussed in IV.2 (t65)):

(t1)

ὡς δὲ ἐχθροὶ *καὶ* ἔχθιστοι, πάντες ἴστε, οἵ γε ἐπὶ τὴν ἡμετέραν ἦλθον δουλωσόμενοι, ...

Thucydides 7.68.2

It will be clear to all of you that the Athenians are not only enemies but the worst of enemies. They came against our country to enslave it. (tr. Hammond)

1997c and 2007 on aspect and tense in Thucydides; Slings 2002, on several Herodotean "oral strategies"; Allan 2007 on complex sentences in Thucydides; De Bakker 2007 on direct speech in Herodotus; Scardino 2007 and 2012 on direct and indirect speech in both authors; Lallot, Rijksbaron, Jacquinod, and Buijs 2011 on the historical present in Thucydides. As for narratological aspects of Herodotus' work, I particularly profited from De Jong 2004a, 2013, and 2014:167-195. As for focalization in Thucydides, see n5.

3 See I.1 §7, and IV.3.9.

This is an excerpt from a speech by the Spartan commander Gylippus to the Spartans. In ἐχθροὶ καὶ ἔχθιστοι, is καί a conjunction or a focus particle? How do we explain the interpretation "or" in a reformulating function ("or, better to say")? Neither question is easy to answer if we assume that καί either means "and" or "also"/"even." Secondary literature is largely silent about *and*-coordination in Herodotus and Thucydides.[4] IV.2 shows that we can better understand δέ, τε, and καί if we take new factors into consideration, such as which portions of discourse are linked, what the linking signifies, and, in the case of δέ, what kind of discontinuity is expressed by its co-text.

§6. The second important mechanism of discourse articulation is segmentation. Segmentation ranges from boundaries between phrases to book divisions. IV.3 tackles the problem of how our modern segmentation strategies may obscure implications carried by particles and particle combinations. Modern segmentation strategies include syntactic interpretation of boundaries (a linguistic feature), and punctuation plus chapter/section divisions (paralinguistic features). To exemplify the problem, let us consider one of the passages commented on in the chapter (IV.3 (t30)):

(t2)

> Ὁ μὲν δὴ δίαιταν εἶχε ἐν Κροίσου, ἐν δὲ τῷ αὐτῷ χρόνῳ τούτῳ ἐν τῷ Μυσίῳ Ὀλύμπῳ ὑὸς χρῆμα γίνεται μέγα· ...
>
> Herodotus 1.36.1
>
> So Adrastus lived in Croesus' house. About this same time a great monster of a boar appeared on the Mysian Olympus, ... (tr. Godley)

The comma in print editions of the Greek text does not do justice to the scene change. While "So Adrastus lived in Croesus' house" temporarily closes a scene, "About this same time a great monster" opens a totally different one—in his translation Godley signals this change by turning the comma into a full stop. The use of μὲν δή and δέ reflects this major semantic and cognitive boundary more precisely than the comma does. IV.3 puts this disjunction in larger context by challenging secondary literature that attributes different periodic styles directly to the two historians rather than to the textual transmission and various "posthumous" segmentation strategies.

§7. The inclusion of voices and stances other than those of the author is another central topic in discourse articulation. This part of the analysis (IV.4) engages with recent literature that delves into the issues of point of view and focalization in Herodotus and Thucydides.[5] One important question to ask when tracking different voices and stances is

4 An exception is the discussion in Dover 1997a:71-77; see IV.2 n215.

5 E.g. Dewald 1999; Hornblower 1994; Allan 2013; Grethlein 2013b; Lamari 2013 (about focalization); Greenwood 2006:19-41 (about point of view and vantage point).

how and when particles reflect the speaker's attitude(s) in speeches, and how and when they reflect the author's in explicit and implicit authorial statements. We should also ask if particles contribute to signaling someone's voice and/or stance in third-person narration when that narration can be recognized as indirect speech, indirect thought, or free indirect thought. Once again, complexity is to be taken into account, as boundaries between the contributions of individuals are often blurred.

§8. The use of δή is paradigmatic in this respect; let us look briefly at one instance. Once the Athenians realize that the Syracusans have proved to be victorious at sea as well as on land, Thucydides describes their emotions as follows:

(t3)

... οἱ μὲν Ἀθηναῖοι ἐν παντὶ δὴ ἀθυμίας ἦσαν ...

Thucydides 7.55.1

The Athenians were in absolutely complete despair (tr. Hammond, slightly adapted)

It is difficult to judge how much δή, which in conveying conviction marks the expression of stance, is attributable to the Athenians, and how much to the historian. IV.4 discusses the communicative roles of γε, τοι, ἦ μήν, δή, δῆθεν, ἤδη, and ἄρα. The chapter not only shows that language can privilege stance (taken as a combination of positioning, evaluating, and aligning), but it also claims that irony and polyphony are deliberately generated to create alliances between author and audience, or between audience and characters.

§9. The observations contained in IV.2, IV.3, and IV.4 converge in a sample of close readings in IV.5. Four excerpts—a narrative section and a speech for each author—are closely examined to demonstrate how our comprehension of the flow of discourse changes if we consider segmentation clues alongside the syntactic ones, and clues about voice and stance. Chunking the discourse is a matter of inferring stronger and weaker boundaries from certain linguistic and paralinguistic features. I compare the segmentation indicated by canonical layouts of print editions with inferences that we can draw from the position of particles, from pragmatic interpretations of discourse acts, and from medieval punctuation. In addition, I consider the effects of lexical repetition, and the location of expressions attributable to someone's voice and/or someone's act of evaluating, positioning, and aligning. The difference resulting from the comparison is remarkable: reading and interpreting content depends very much on the kind of segmentation that is privileged, as well as on assumptions about whose voice and stance is conveyed at any moment.[6]

6 More specific topics and concepts are illustrated in the individual introductions (IV.2.1, IV.3.1, IV.4.1, and IV.5.1).

1.2 A Different Perspective on Historiographical Texts

§10. Paying attention to particles changes the way we read Herodotus and Thucydides, and shows the advantages of using a certain methodology. To be specific:[7] viewing δέ, τε, and καί as existing on a functional continuum, instead of making sharp dichotomous distinctions ("either this function or that"), allows us to explain phenomena that otherwise tend to end up in unspecified categories (such as "difficult cases,"[8] "emphatic" or "superfluous," functions[9]). Continuums range from connective to adverbial usages, and from propositional to nonpropositional contributions to meaning. To note a couple of cases in point: a discourse-based analysis of Herodotus' and Thucydides' texts better appreciates the uses shared by δή and ἤδη; it also allows us to differentiate between ὡς δ' ἄρα and εἰ ἄρα, even if both represent instances of ἄρα in subclauses. On a practical level, instead of applying standard translations of δέ, τε, and καί, the reader of the *Histories* is given a range of suggestions about implications or enrichments that she can consider: what is linked to what, what the underlying communicative actions are, and what counts as a new unit.

§11. An active reading that does not apply pre-fabricated translations but co-constructs meaning along with the author opens possibilities that for too long have been underestimated and understudied. Several of these possibilities have to do with the segmentation of the text. The primacy of syntactic divisions and hierarchies obscures the importance of further divisions, such as discourse units above and below the sentence level. The occurrence of ταῦτα μέν metalinguistically indicates the temporary closure of an episode or account; μέν in this case does not just anticipate a δέ clause (if it does at all). Likewise, phrases isolated by subsequent "second position" particles (e.g. Σικελίας γὰρ | περίπλους μέν..., Thucydides 6.1.2; see IV.3 (t15)) are fragmentary and semantically incomplete, but act as guiding elements of discourse that ensure the successful processing of several upcoming segments.

§12. If we conceive of the text as a sequence of moves achieving communicative goals, further articulated into acts, more attention is given to the words transmitted than to modern punctuation marks and chapter/section divisions. The reading procedure is inverted as a result: instead of almost exclusively relying on the modern paralinguistic segmentation of the text in order to frame and shape contents, we can observe word order and the location of particles and particle combinations, and derive segmentation of content from that.

7 For more specific findings, see IV.2.5; IV.3.12, IV.4.10, and IV.5.6.

8 See, for example, the fourth section of καί in Denniston (1950:325), which is devoted to "special difficulties."

9 See, for example, the view according to which τε in τε καί is superfluous (IV.2 n110).

§13. Particles offer a further kind of clue: some of them (δῆθεν and δή invariably, ἤδη in most co-texts, and ἄρα only to a limited extent) help track voice and stance. Their occurrence signals that an individual's sense of certainty or determination, her firsthand observation or perception, or simply her voice is accessed, for various purposes, and in various textual settings. On the practical level, this means that we count on some particles, among other co-occurring features, to detect the non-uniformity of third person narration, which includes indirect speech, indirect thought, and free indirect thought.

§14. Moreover, we may see the particles mentioned above as economical tools that compress in one word a pragmatically complex network of relations among subjects. Once again, thinking beyond "either or" solutions enhances our appreciation of literary subtleties, such as polyphony and irony. The pragmatic enrichment of a particle may pertain to the merging of voices and stances, or, conversely, it may signal a distance, a gap between the author's voice and a character's. In this case too readers must read actively: as subjects involved in the pragmatic network like characters and authors, readers are indirectly invited by the particles to react, to take position, and to evaluate events or further positions and evaluations.

§15. Let me conclude with remarks on similarities and differences in particle use between the two masterpieces. First, particles contribute to the segmentation of discourse in relatively small chunks in speeches as well as in narrator text in both works. This conclusion challenges the common view that Thucydides' sentences and periods are longer. Further, Herodotus is more generous than Thucydides in using particle combinations to round off or recap accounts. Herodotus also uses more particles than Thucydides to signal the author's voice, through explicit authorial statements and the marking of narrative progression. Perhaps this tendency reflects the aural character of Herodotus' reception. In any case, in both historians particles pertain to performance in a broad sense: in both authors they indicate how language is used; they are hinges between content and presentation.

IV.2

Multifunctionality of δέ, τε, and καί

2.1 *And*-Coordination

§1. This chapter explores a wide range of functions of δέ, τε, καί, and combinations involving them in historiographical discourse.[1] These particles appear the most often out of those used by the authors in our corpus.[2] They can all be translated in numerous contexts with "and." However, they express different aspects of *and*-coordination,[3] ranging from quasi-asyndeton to adversative implications.[4]

§2. The scope, or range of a particle's effect, varies for all of them: it can relate to full or parts of discourse acts, and to discourse moves, which may correspond to constituents of considerably different size.[5] Accordingly I will treat the three particles as affecting

1 This chapter will not delve into these particles' negative counterparts. One of the reasons is that a careful analysis of οὐδέ, for example, would probably occupy a separate chapter, as it would have to consider the distinction between οὐδέ as the negation of δέ, and οὐδέ as the negation of καί. Another reason is statistical: the frequency of negative coordination overall is much lower than the frequency of positive coordination (see, for example, Basset 1989); so, in view of the inevitably selective character of our monograph, we prefer to focus on numerically higher linguistic evidence. Finally, it makes sense to suppose that discourse-oriented suggestions about the pragmatic complexity of δέ, τε, and καί can shed light on the usages concerning both the "declarative" οὐ and the "modal" μή counterparts. For example, the difficulty of determining when negation covers whole sentences rather than single constituents is parallel to the difficulty of determining when καί and τε link or focus on clauses rather than on single constituents. On different markers of negation in Homeric Greek, see now Willmott 2011.

2 See the corresponding graphs in our frequency graphs (available online as I.5).

3 For an overview of coordination strategies in different languages, see Mithun 1988 and Raible 2001. About syndetic coordination in archaic IE languages, which is anything but uniform, see in particular Viti 2008. For a comprehensive analysis of conjunctions in archaic IE languages from a theoretical perspective, see Goldstein 2019.

4 Not only δέ but also τε and καί can be used to convey contrast. See below §72 and §115. By "implication" I mean what Grice (1975) called "implicature," that is, meaning inferred from words, but unspoken.

5 In logic, "scope" is the part of an expression that is governed by a given operator, such as a quantifier, a coordinator, or a negation. Scope ambiguities in syntax and in semantics are a long-standing subject matter; for an overview of earliest thoughts about it, see Partee and Hendriks 1997:37-61.

different segments of discourse, from single words and phrases, to clauses, to multi-clause units.

§3. By dealing with *and* particles we assume that they exist on a continuum with respect to two important distinctions. The first continuum ranges from propositional to non-propositional meanings.[6] That is to say, τε and καί may or may not affect truth conditions. *And* in English is open to the same variability. For example, in "they ate and drank," "and" modifies content in that the same proposition without reference to drinking would mean something different. But in "and(,) here is what happened:," "and" does not modify the content of whatever proposition follows "here is what happened"; rather, together with "here is what happened" it introduces a discourse unit whose clauses or sentences relate what happened (at a certain point, in a certain context). Finally, in "and it is a possession forever,"[7] "and" plays an intermediate role between linking the host clause with the preceding one (propositionally), and marking the host clause as a comment or a conclusion (non-propositionally). This continuum does not hold for δέ, which never modifies content. Whenever we associate δέ clauses with a strong sense of contrast, the contrast comes from the semantics of the co-text rather than from the particle δέ.[8]

§4. The second continuum is between the connective and the adverbial functions of δέ, τε and καί. Mithun (1988:345) states: "The lack of a clear distinction between adverbials and clause conjunctions is not unusual among languages." With regard to *and* cognates, consider "as well" or "in addition": grammatically these phrases function as adverbs, but at the same time they are used to add content not differently from the way *and* conjunctions do. A few years ago a sizable group of Hellenists working in Spain decided to label the subject of a joint research project "conjunctive adverbs." The basic idea is that ancient Greek grammars tend to neglect the fact that a number of adverbs—which prototypically do not connect clauses—in fact indicate the relation between the preceding and the following parts of discourse, thereby fulfilling the role of connectives.[9] Particles have the same problem: we can divide particles according to a syntactic generalization, that is, adverbial versus connective particles. However, borders sometimes are fuzzy, and possibly arbitrary. For example, we usually label δέ "particle" and καί "conjunction," and yet the connective functions of the former and the adverbial ones of the latter are amply exploited in our source texts. The idea that conjunctions and adverbs have fluid boundaries is hard to accept for classicists, because of a long-standing terminological tradition according to which syntactic distinctions suffice

6 See I.1 §§8; 10-11 on propositional and non-propositional meanings.

7 The clause deliberately evokes κτῆμά τε ἐς αἰεί (...), Thucydides 1.22.4, which will be analyzed in §78.

8 This view is already presented in Hoogeveen 1769:245; Schraut 1847:18; Ruijgh 1971:134; Brouwer 1975:46; Hummel 1993:381. See below §27, and IV.5 §35. In III.5 §§38-41 the whole texts of δέ acts following μέν acts are said to express semantic contrast—not the particle δέ per se. See also Klein 1992:36.

9 Crespo 2009 illustrates the general claim.

for determining the function of words. This chapter contends that the term "particle," however problematic, allows an interpreter of texts to maintain a neutral stance towards the discourse functions of words that may be syntactically quite diverse.[10]

§5. The view that functions exist on a continuum and do not fall into clear-cut categories underlies our method of analysis and our presentation of the results. The reader will not find quantitative overviews of functions, because functions are multidimensional most of the time, and especially because functions are based on inferences. Rather, the reader will find discussion of types of constructions, use of representative examples based on examining large amounts of text, or quotation of certain instances that illustrate a point better than others.

§6. Contemporary linguistics has considered, discussed, criticized, and revised the term "discourse markers" to avoid syntactically rigid divisions, and conversely to enhance the non-propositional relevance of several lexical items mono- and cross-linguistically.[11] Dealing with δέ, τε, and καί in ancient Greek literature means that one has to constantly cope with the propositional as well as the non-propositional levels of meaning, along with various clause positions that are not always easy to explain. However, the ancient grammarians attest to the use of a general term that modern analyses of ancient Greek would do well to adopt, since this term encourages us to be less oriented to syntactic classifications. This term is σύνδεσμος, "combiner,"[12] which refers to instances when clause combining is mediated through the use of lexical items. In Greek and in many other languages clause combining is possible through asyndeton[13] as well as through dedicated syndetic devices. "Combiner" simply is the equivalent of "syndetic device." It has the advantage of being more neutral than "conjunction," which derives from the literal translation of σύνδεσμος in Latin (*coniunctio*). In our modern mindset "conjunction" is syntactically strongly connoted, whereas "combiner" allows for a smoother inclusion of adverbs and sentence adverbials.

§7. A major challenge in understanding *and*-coordination strategies not only in historiography but also in epic, lyric, and drama is represented by the fact that translations regularly misrepresent the high frequency of δέ, τε, and καί, by replacing parataxis with hypotaxis. For example, a clause coordinated by δέ easily becomes a relative clause (see e.g. (t16)), whenever correspondence is established between a δέ clause conveying background information and a clause embedding information syntactically.[14] This is a

10 See I.1.3 on why we keep the term "particle." Laury and Seppänen 2008 and Fielder 2008 propose the notion of a continuum between conjunction and particle as far as Finnish and Bulgarian are concerned.

11 See I.3. The same attempt underlies the preference for "discourse markers" over "particles" in Bonifazi 2008, 2009, and 2012.

12 See I.1 §§1 and 9; I.2 §§14-16.

13 See, for example, Mann and Thompson 1987.

14 Cooper (2002:2705) notes: "Modern grammarians traditionally offer 'normalizations' of Greek paratactic expressions to hypotactic forms. ... the results are no fun to read."

predictable operation if we take into account the rules of our writing style.[15] But the rules of writing and of using texts in the archaic and classical Greek period are less clear; therefore, we should avoid making this substitution whenever possible, so as to preserve the original words, even if the resulting translation features a seemingly simple (or repetitive) "and." The problem is not merely formal, I suspect. Over the past centuries and even in the past decades, an aesthetically-based preference for hypotaxis over parataxis has led scholars to judge hypotaxis as an "improvement" over "primitive" parataxis. IV.3 will discuss how modern full stops in ancient Greek texts reveal hypotactic constructions of periodic discourse even when particles and independent clauses suggest otherwise. Here I will just mention a paradoxical fact: Thucydides, who is considered a master of hypotaxis, actually features an extraordinary amount of καί: 10,231 instances.[16]

§8. As for the seemingly plain role of *and*, many recent studies on *and* in English reveal a high degree of sophistication in its use, a fact that requires deep investigation. *And* is a profitable word to study precisely because it is multifunctional, and leaves most of its implied meanings to the receiver's understanding. I am going to list here four aspects of *and* in English that are crucially relevant to this chapter, and especially to καί.

§9. First, like many other conjunctions, *and* can connect facts but also acts. Consider these utterances:

(t1)

> Y. Yesterday we went to the movies and afterwards we went to the pub for a beer.
> X. Why didn't Peter show up? And, where were you that night?
>
> Van Dijk 1979:450

While in Y "and afterwards" connects the content segments "we went to the movies" and "we went to the pub for a beer," in X *and* connects the act of asking "why didn't Peter show up?" and the act of asking further "where were you that night?" Such a distinction is important as it clarifies that the connection does not need to be exclusively between states of affairs.

§10. The second aspect relates to the act of connecting in itself. Given that speakers may combine clauses without using any syndetic item, the use of *and* must be relevant in some way. Lang and Sköries[17] claim that *and* (in English as well as in German, at least)

[15] On the substantial differences between speaking and writing, see Chafe 1985; see also Biber 1988, 1995, and 2006.

[16] According to the *TLG* online Thucydides' *Histories* include 10,231 καί, against 7,623 in Herodotus' *Histories* (6.7% against 4% of total words).

[17] See Sköries 1999:52-60 and 142, recalling Lang 1977, and Sköries 1998:55. The preference for linking-and rather than adding-and also comes from Sköries 1999, who consistently mentions

combines items not only quantitatively but also qualitatively; it does not simply "add," it "links." The qualitative value of *and* consists in implying that the linked items are similar and diverse at the same time. Consider, for example, the title of the song "*Der Tod und das Mädchen*" ("Death and the Maiden"). "Death" and "maiden" share diversity and similarity through the link established by "*und*" ("and"). To use Pander Maat's terms, *and* creates a "joint relevance" of the two conjuncts.[18] The title announces such joint relevance; the words of Matthias Claudius and the music of Franz Schubert substantiate it. *And* in titles of scientific articles works in the same way.

§11. The third aspect is the capacity of *and* to be, as linguists have pointed out, "asymmetrical." The notion of asymmetry comes from logic. If *p and q* cannot equal *q and p*, then *and* is asymmetrical.[19] We might say, "Bring me my shoes and my jacket," which equals "Bring me my jacket and my shoes," but "the world will smile with you, and smile" does not equal "smile, and the world will smile with you." The following utterances show asymmetrical *and* in that in each of them *and* implies something more than *and*—for example, "and afterwards," "and so," etc. This makes the position of the two conjuncts unchangeable, or, in other words, if the order changes, the meaning changes as well. Let us think, for instance, of the quite different cause-effect relations of "He left her, and she took to the bottle" *versus* "she took to the bottle, and he left her."

(t2)

a. John took off his shoes and jumped in the pool

Sweetser 1990:8

b. It's my life and I do what I want.

Sköries 1999:19

c. They should have told you, and they didn't.

Sköries 1999:21

d. You give me your ice cream and I'll give you mine

Sköries 1999:22

e. He left her and she took to the bottle

Carston 2002:224

"'and'-links" ("*Undverbindungen*").

18 *And* conjuncts represent a "a joint-relevant unit " (Pander Maat 2001:202).

19 Early contributions on this include Lakoff 1971, then Grice 1975, Schmerling 1975, Posner 1980. In an article on the origins of *and* and *but* in English, Traugott (1986:147) confirms what previous scholars had claimed, that is, that "the basic meaning of 'and' is rich and asymmetric."

f. There are paperbacks and there is Penguin.

A Penguin slogan, Haaretz, August 2, 1995;
quoted in Ariel 2010:64[20]

The overarching point is that it is up to the receiver to infer what *and* specifically implies, as (s)he makes sense of the link being established. Carston (2002:222-264) discusses the notion of "enrichment" to explain the ability of *and* to convey more than simple addition.[21]

§12. The fourth and final aspect concerns discourse transitions. Sköries (1999:238) focuses on the imbalance characterizing the two conjuncts linked by *and* in the formulaic closure of folktales, "And they lived happily ever after." The second conjunct is the conclusion expressed by the *and* clause, while the first conjunct is the entire story preceding the conclusion. The author submits that *and* in fact compensates for this imbalance by stressing the narrative relevance of the closure: a series of discrete events that took place over a certain stretch of time is linked to one happy "ever after" state that seals the story.

§13. All these aspects of *and*-coordination (connecting facts and acts; establishing a qualitative link; asymmetry between the conjuncts; variable size of the two conjuncts) will be retrieved in the next sections, which explore the discourse functions of δέ, τε, and καί. The order of presentation is designed to progress from discussing a minimal to a "heavy" sense of addition. The main claims of this analysis, as far as the two *Histories* are concerned, are: the only consistent function of δέ is pragmatic; enriched (adverbial)

[20] While making sense of a. we read "and" as "and then" marking a temporal relation ("John took off his shoes and then jumped in the pool"); in b. we infer "and therefore" marking a causal relation ("It's my life and therefore I do what I want"); in c. "and by contrast," "but" marking a contrastive relation ("They should have told you, but they didn't"); in d. we infer a conditional relation ("If you give me your ice cream I'll give you mine"); in e. we infer "and in consequence" marking a consecutive relation ("He left her and in consequence she took to the bottle"); finally, f. leads us to infer an imbalance between the quality of anonymous paperbacks and Penguin paperbacks; the slogan plays with similarity and diversity by assuming the former and actually conveying the latter.

[21] A major debate among linguists concerns whether enrichment is part of the conceptual content of *and per se*, or if it is a matter of inference on the receiver's part; in the former case it is a semantic, in the latter a pragmatic, component of the meaning. For a recent semantic account of asymmetrical *and* see Bjorkman 2010. Pragmatic accounts of enrichments of *and* are offered in Txurruka 2003; Blakemore and Carston 2005; Zeevat and Jasinskaja 2007, and Ariel 2012. Ariel divides the pragmatic interpretations further. In a "relational" strategy, people combine the conjuncts; in an "independent" strategy the conjuncts contribute to a discourse point separately. An example of *and* that requires the conjuncts to be considered separately is "A woman told her friend, 'For eighteen years my husband and I were the happiest people in the world. Then we met'" (Ariel 2012:1693). From "then we met" we infer that in the previous clause the speaker does not consider the joint unit "my husband and I" (as a couple) but two independent people, "my husband" + "I." καί in my view always fits a "relational" strategy, except when the meaning is "or"; in those cases the conjuncts are presented as separate alternatives (see §§117-118).

understandings of τε are compatible with the syndetic role of τε; the dichotomous reading of καί either as 'and' or as 'also, even' obscures a number of further functions, such as pinning down, expanding the narration, and expressing 'or'. I shall make use of examples that are representative or particularly apt. I shall also include examples from other genres (prose and poetry). The non-historiographical examples will work either as initial input challenging canonical descriptions, or as evidence supporting the pragmatic readings of Herodotus and Thucydides that I am going to offer.

2.2 δέ Marking the Beginning of a New Discourse Act

§14. δέ is one of the most versatile particles. Unlike other particles, which can work on the propositional level in some usages (for example, ἀλλά replacing a chunk of content with a different content), δέ makes sense exclusively on a pragmatic level. Its versatility resides in its lack of semantic stability, and its complete dependence on context and co-text. δέ is used to introduce contrast and to mark topic continuation, and has a range of intermediate functions.

§15. When δέ is in a clause that has no adversative meaning, it is seen as "continuative" δέ. However, this label reveals problems with the way the particle's functions have been conceptualized. Denniston's classification system—and his own abandonment of it—exemplifies some of the problems. First he marks a category of connective roles, which he subdivides into "adversative" and "continuative."[22] However, soon after presenting them in a very few pages, he devotes attention to "particular uses of connective δέ" about which he immediately specifies in a parenthesis, "It will be convenient to drop the distinction between continuative and adversative, henceforward."[23] Such uses include "δέ for γάρ," δέ for οὖν or δή," "δέ marking the transition from the introduction to a speech to the opening of the proper speech," inceptive δέ, "apparently superfluous δέ," δέ in exclamations, and δέ in questions (sometimes preceded by apostrophes or imperatives).[24] So, one infers, these uses are neither adversative nor continuative. Then Denniston marks out a category of non-connective δέ, which he subsequently divides into "apodotic δέ," δέ occurring after various types of protases, δέ in participial phrases, "resumptive" δέ (that is, when it accompanies words that are picked up by repetition), and duplicated δέ (when it occurs in apodoses as well as in the preceding protases).[25]

22 Denniston 1950:162. In this introduction to δέ I am focusing particularly on Denniston not because he is the main source of insights on δέ—many other works preceding Denniston are equally helpful (if not more)—but because his classification of the roles of δέ is representative of a certain approach. This approach defines the particle's functions syntactically, and exhibits the heuristic habit of applying adjectives to describe these functions.

23 Denniston 1950:169.

24 Denniston 1950:169-177.

25 Denniston 1950:177-185.

§16. Denniston's need to abandon the dichotomous distinction "adversative" versus "continuative" so soon after he establishes it, and the fact that he groups several types of δέ under the rubric "non-connective," convey something significant. The uses of δέ encompass very different semantic contexts and very different syntactic constructions; therefore its functions must exceed matters of contrast and continuation, as well as matters of coordination and subordination. The conclusion I anticipate here builds on Bakker's reading of δέ's basic function, which is to mark discourse boundaries.[26] δέ in Herodotus and Thucydides marks boundaries between discourse acts, by indicating where a new act or move begins.[27]

§17. What makes a δέ utterance an act or move, and what makes it new or separate? Let me begin with a sample of occurrences in Herodotus and Thucydides. Over the first thousand words of the two *Histories*, δέ occurs 41 times in Herodotus and 29 times in Thucydides.[28] Even within such relatively small stretches of discourse, it is possible to detect interesting phenomena. Instead of using semantic or syntactic criteria to classify δέ (asking whether words surrounding δέ express contrast, in the case of the former, or in the latter case, asking whether δέ occurs in main or subclauses), my intent is to show the discourse relevance of using δέ *because* of its remarkable versatility, which encompasses both the semantic and syntactic domains. The only consistent meaning of δέ is pragmatic, and it consists in marking separate or new discourse acts.[29]

§18. In the selected Herodotean and Thucydidean excerpts δέ appears in different constructions. It occurs with (1) appositions (in Herodotus); (2) in main clauses that work as separate statements (both in Herodotus and in Thucydides); (3) with subordinating conjunctions (in both); (4) with participles and within infinitive constructions (mainly in Herodotus); and finally, (5) in short constructions projecting a multi-act discourse unit (mainly in Thucydides).

§19. In the first group, δέ in appositional phrases in Herodotus, we find the following instance:

26 On Bakker's account of δέ, and on δέ in Homer, see II.2.2.1 and II.5.3.1.

27 Acts and moves in this monograph are particularly discussed in II.2, II.3, IV.3, and IV.5.

28 In the count I included instances of οὐδέ as well. The percentage is very similar to the overall frequency of the particle in the two authors without negative counterparts (4.24% in Herodotus and 2.94% in Thucydides). One thousand words cover the proem to 1.8.2 in Herodotus, and 1.1 to 1.7 (almost entirely) in Thucydides.

29 Bäumlein (1861:89) captures this idea by saying that the earliest role of δέ is to represent the concept of "further," "new" as "different from the preceding" ("*das Weitere und Neue eben als ein vom Vorhergehenden Verschiedenes (...) sich darstellt.*"). For the pragmatic roles of δέ in drama, see especially III 2.2.1, and III.4 §§34-35, §§37-38, §46, §65.

(t3)

Κροῖσος ἦν Λυδὸς μὲν γένος, παῖς δὲ Ἀλυάττεω, τύραννος δὲ ἐθνέων τῶν ἐντὸς Ἅλυος ποταμοῦ, ...

Herodotus 1.6.1

Croesus was a Lydian by birth, son of Alyattes, and sovereign of all the nations west of the river Halys, ... (tr. Godley)

Usually δέ has clausal scope, but in these examples it frames information that lacks any predicate.[30] Nevertheless, the information, as I see it, is presented as a separate information unit. δέ marks this information unit as a separate discourse act.

§20. A second group of instances regards clauses that represent separate statements:

(t4)

φασὶ ... ἁρπάσαι τοῦ βασιλέος τὴν θυγατέρα Εὐρώπην· εἴησαν δ' ἂν οὗτοι Κρῆτες. Ταῦτα μὲν δὴ ...

Herodotus 1.2.1

[A]ccording to their story ... they carried off the king's daughter Europa. These Greeks must, I suppose, have been Cretans. So far then, ... (tr. Godley)

(t5)

ἔτι δὲ καὶ ἐν τοῖς βαρβάροις ἔστιν οἷς νῦν, καὶ μάλιστα τοῖς Ἀσιανοῖς, πυγμῆς καὶ πάλης ἆθλα τίθεται, καὶ διεζωμένοι τοῦτο δρῶσιν. πολλὰ δ' ἂν καὶ ἄλλα τις ἀποδείξειε τὸ παλαιὸν Ἑλληνικὸν ὁμοιότροπα τῷ νῦν βαρβαρικῷ διαιτώμενον..

Thucydides 1.6.5-1.6.6

Some barbarians even now, especially in Asia, hold boxing and wrestling bouts in which loincloths are worn. There are many other resemblances one could

30 This type of δέ is mentioned for example, by Denniston (1950:163), and Cooper (2002:2923). A further instance in the Herodotean thousand-word sample is 1.7.2 Ἦν Κανδαύλης, τὸν οἱ Ἕλληνες Μυρσίλον ὀνομάζουσι, τύραννος Σαρδίων, ἀπόγονος δὲ Ἀλκαίου τοῦ Ἡρακλέος "Candaules, whom the Greeks call Myrsilus, was the ruler of Sardis; he was descended from Alcaeus, son of Heracles" (tr. Godley). See also Sophocles *Oedipus at Colonus* 1275: ὦ σπέρματ' ἀνδρὸς τοῦδ', ἐμαὶ δ'ὁμαίμονες [Polynices to Antigone and Ismene] "Children of this man, and sisters of mine... [do you try to move my father's lips?]" (Lloyd-Jones 1998 [1994]).

point to between the old Greek and the present barbarian ways of life. (tr. Hammond)

"These Greeks must, I suppose, have been Cretans" (t4) and "There are many other resemblances one could point to..." (t5), from the cognitive point of view are unframed discourse: for a moment the historians step out of the account they are giving, to insert a narratorial comment.[31] δέ marks these statements as separate and different. As §30 will clarify, δέ is one of the linguistic devices that mark discourse discontinuity.

§21. The third group concerns δέ following subordinating conjunctions:

(t6)

Οὗτος δὴ ὦν ὁ Κανδαύλης ἠράσθη τῆς ἑωυτοῦ γυναικός, ἐρασθεὶς δὲ ἐνόμιζέ οἱ εἶναι γυναῖκα πολλὸν πασέων καλλίστην. Ὥστε <u>δὲ</u> ταῦτα νομίζων, ἦν γάρ οἱ τῶν αἰχμοφόρων Γύγης ..., τούτῳ τῷ Γύγῃ καὶ τὰ σπουδαιέστερα τῶν πρηγμάτων ὑπερετίθετο ὁ Κανδαύλης ...

Herodotus 1.8.1

This Candaules, then, fell in love with his own wife, so much so that he believed her to be by far the most beautiful woman in the world; and believing this, he praised her beauty beyond measure to Gyges ...; for it was to Gyges that he entrusted all his most important secrets. (tr. Godley)

(t7)

κίνησις γὰρ αὕτη μεγίστη δὴ τοῖς Ἕλλησιν ἐγένετο καὶ μέρει τινὶ τῶν βαρβάρων, ὡς <u>δὲ</u> εἰπεῖν καὶ ἐπὶ πλεῖστον ἀνθρώπων.

Thucydides 1.1.2

This was in fact the greatest disturbance to affect the Greek and a good part of the non-Greek world, one might even say the majority of mankind. (tr. Hammond)

In (t6) neither ὥστε nor ὡς introduces a proper subclause: in the former case we are dealing with "paratactic" ὥστε,[32] which serves to introduce the next piece of narration

31 Unframed discourse is defined in II.4.2.

32 Exploited by both historians. In modern editions the paratactic status is signaled by a full stop before ὥστε—even though punctuation marks are problematic (on which see IV.3). The *TLG* online records six instances of that in Herodotus (e.g. 1.8.1; 5.42.2; 9.122.4), and 38 in Thucydides

as a consequence or result of the preceding piece; in the latter, we are dealing with a parenthetical construction ὡς εἰπεῖν (equivalent to "so to say"). I submit that δέ, independently of the syntactic status of the host clause, qualifies it as discrete, as a unit that has its own separate illocutionary force. In the Herodotus passage, δέ signals that a new discourse act and move are beginning. The new act includes "resumptive" ταῦτα and the repetition of the verb νομίζω (see the preceding ἐνόμιζε), linguistic clues that go to support the hypothesis that a distinct discourse act is being enacted (ὥστε δὲ ταῦτα νομίζων, "he was believing so, and as a consequence of that..."). In addition, the subsequent γάρ signals that a different discourse act is going to follow. In the new move, which is larger than the first act, the historian links the king with Gyges.[33] In (t7) the presence of δέ in ὡς εἰπεῖν suggests that the stretch ὡς δὲ εἰπεῖν καὶ ἐπὶ πλεῖστον ἀνθρώπων is a separate act. Within this act, ὡς εἰπεῖν works as a discourse marker that attenuates—metalinguistically—the universalizing expression ἐπὶ πλεῖστον ἀνθρώπων.[34]

§22. The fourth group is represented by δέ after participles and in infinitive constructions. δέ in infinitive constructions appears several times in the thousand-word Herodotean sample, for the obvious reason that reported accounts and indirect speeches constitute the main narrative technique underlying those chapters. Here is an instance:

(t8)

Πέμψαντα δὲ τὸν Κόλχων βασιλέα ἐς τὴν Ἑλλάδα κήρυκα αἰτέειν τε δίκας τῆς ἁρπαγῆς καὶ ἀπαιτέειν τὴν θυγατέρα· τοὺς δὲ ὑποκρίνασθαι ὡς ...

Herodotus 1.2.3

When the Colchian king sent a herald to demand reparation for the robbery and restitution of his daughter, the Greeks replied that ... (tr. Godley)

(e.g. 1.18.3; 3.13.4; 8.68.4). In this passage several co-textual elements indicate that ὥστε δέ start a new thought: δέ, which is a minimal sign of discourse discontinuity; the resuming role of ταῦτα, which is a typical Herodotean feature at the beginning of new narrative steps; and the participle νομίζων, which usually precedes information about motivated action.

33 On γάρ moves in Herodotus, see IV.3 §108. In Herodotus 1.8.1 (t6) the previous δέ (ἐρασθεὶς δέ) signposts a separate act as well: ἐρασθεὶς δὲ ἐνόμιζέ οἱ εἶναι γυναῖκα πολλὸν πασέων καλλίστην in fact starts the piecemeal development of the macro-theme announced by the first utterance of the chapter, Οὗτος δὴ ὢν ὁ Κανδαύλης ἠράσθη τῆς ἑωυτοῦ γυναικός. The initial utterance shows several Herodotean characteristics of episode-starts: οὗτος, which projects a long discourse unit (on which see IV.3 §§120-123); the combination δὴ ὦν, which marks major narrative boundaries (see IV.4 §§86 and 89); the temporally unbound aorist ἠράσθη.

34 On the metalinguistic value of discourse markers, see Maschler 2009:1-2. See also I.1 §15.

Once again, regardless of the syntactic surface, which indicates dependent clauses, the two δέ signpost new steps in narrative: first, πέμψαντα ... αἰτέειν τε ... καὶ ἀπαιτέειν, with the Colchian king as the agent; second, ὑποκρίνασθαι, with the Greeks as agents.[35]

§23. The thousand-word Thucydidean sample offers the following instance of δέ with participles within an infinitive construction:

(t9)

δοκεῖ δέ μοι, ... κατὰ ἔθνη δὲ ... τὴν ἐπωνυμίαν παρέχεσθαι, Ἕλληνος δὲ καὶ τῶν παίδων αὐτοῦ ἐν τῇ Φθιώτιδι ἰσχυσάντων, καὶ ἐπαγομένων αὐτοὺς ...

Thucydides 1.3.2

I believe ... the various tribes took their own names, ... When Hellen and his sons grew to power in Phthiotis, and were called in ... (tr. Hammond)

The information about Hellenus and his sons arriving in Phthiotis represents a narrative step on its own; the subject is different from the previous δέ discourse act (κατὰ ἔθνη δὲ ...), but the verb forms of the entire passage (1.3.2) grant continuity to the discourse, as all participles and infinitives derive from δοκεῖ δέ μοι with which the subsection starts.

§24. Finally, Thucydides makes especial use of δέ in short constructions projecting a multi-act discourse unit. Projection takes place when short and syntactically incomplete phrases (whether noun or verbal phrases) are fronted to encompass multiple elements that are logically dependent on them. In the monograph we call them "priming acts."[36] The thousand-word sample includes the following instances:

(t10)

a. Τῶν δὲ πόλεων |[37] ὅσαι μὲν ...

Thucydides 1.7.1

[35] Within our sample, another clear instance is Χρόνου δὲ οὐ πολλοῦ διελθόντος, χρῆν γὰρ... (Herodotus 1.8.2) where δέ marks a genitive absolute as a discourse act.

[36] For the definition, and on priming acts that reorient the attention of performer and audience in Homer and Pindar, see II.2.5. On priming acts in drama, see III.5 §§30-33. On priming acts in Herodotus and Thucydides, see below 2.2.5; IV.3.11.1, and IV.5 §§11; 32; 42; 59; 63; 78; 103. On projection, see II.2 §§51-54 and III.4 §§9-10; on τε as a projection marker, see below §§80-84, and §§89-90.

[37] Vertical bars flag act boundaries; see II.2 §26, and IV.3 §46. Throughout the continuous texts of Herodotus and Thucydides analyzed in IV.5.2-5.5, act boundaries correspond to indentation (one act, one line).

b. δηλοῦσι <u>δὲ</u> | τῶν τε ἠπειρωτῶν τινὲς ...

Thucydides 1.5.2

c. οἱ <u>δ'</u> οὖν | ὡς ἕκαστοι Ἕλληνες ...

Thucydides 1.3.4

δέ marks the subjects in these three excerpts (the Greek cities; what shows piracy to be a good thing; the peoples who came to be called Hellenes), while the subsequent constructions (peninitial μέν; peninitial τε; subordinating conjunction ὡς) isolate them and make them separate *Kurzkola*, "short *kôla*."[38] The fronted phrases announce a macrotopic to be developed by additional clauses: they are what conjoin those clauses into a discourse unit or narrative move.[39] The fact that all three priming acts in (t10) coincide with the start of new sections in Stuart and Jones' edition converges on the idea that they encode discourse transitions.

§25. The element that underlies all the constructions and discourse functions under discussion is the "discretizing" force of δέ (to use Bakker's term[40]). δέ is a boundary marker that marks separate steps in the discourse, each of them with its own force. δέ maintains its discretizing force regardless of the syntactic status of the act it is in, and regardless of the specific communicative "point" associated with each δέ act.

2.2.1 δέ in phrases

§26. Let us now expand on the range of constructions I have just outlined. δέ sometimes marks acts that do not coincide with full clauses. One such type of act is represented by appositional phrases such as the following:[41]

38 On *Kurzkola* see II.2 §14.

39 Further examples of short constructions opening moves are discussed in IV.3.11.1. Besides δέ these constructions feature γάρ and καί.

40 Bakker 1997b:71.

41 The syntactic interpretation of appositions is controversial in linguistics; they are considered verbless adverbial clauses (e.g. Quirk *et al.*, 1985:996; 1314); nominal predications (e.g. Doron 1994); reduced relative clauses (e.g. Del Gobbo 2003). The pragmatic notion of discourse act overcomes the different syntactic interpretations by simply associating these phrases with strategic steps.

The possible mismatch between discourse acts and clauses in English is discussed especially in Hannay and Kroon 2005:100; a case in point is "I was robbed. By a six-year old." The full stop encodes an intonation break, which in turn signifies the split in two separate discourse acts, although the clause is one). For more discussion on this, see II.2.1.1. On such mismatches in Serbocroatian epics, see Bonifazi and Elmer 2012a.

(t11)

Πρῶτα μὲν ἐς Σάρδις ἐλθόντες ἅμα Ἀρισταγόρῃ τῷ Μιλησίῳ, δούλῳ <u>δὲ</u> ἡμετέρῳ, ἀπικόμενοι ἐνέπρησαν τά τε ἄλσεα καὶ τὰ ἱρά...

Herodotus 7.8.β.3

First they [the Athenians] came to Sardis with our slave Aristagoras the Milesian and burnt the groves and the temples; ... (tr. Godley)

Aristagoras, the orchestrator of the Ionian rebellion, had been enslaved by the Persians (his death is told at the very end of book 5). Herodotus organizes Xerxes' speech in such a way that the apposition (δούλῳ ... ἡμετέρῳ), thanks to δέ, becomes a parenthetical comment that stands out as a little separate act. The specific force of the comment resides in conveying scornful pride, which can be inferred by the whole co-text and context.[42] Godley's translation, however, evens out the message by putting "our slave" simply in attributive apposition, and giving priority to the macro-syntactic structure.

§27. In light of this passage, Legrand's editorial decision to put a comma after ἀνόλβιος in the following passage—where Hude (*OCT*), who keeps the more common form of the adjective ἄνολβος, does not punctuate—makes eminent sense:

(t12)

Ὁ μὲν δὴ μέγα πλούσιος, ἀνόλβιος <u>δέ</u>, δυοῖσι προέχει τοῦ εὐτυχέος μοῦνον ...

Herodotus 1.32.6

The man who is very rich but unfortunate surpasses the lucky man in only two ways, ...[43] (tr. Godley)

Solon is explaining to Croesus that wealth does not entail happiness. In ἀνόλβιος δέ the discourse function of δέ is not to mark a semantic contrast—ἀνόλβιος encodes that already; the function is to mark a separate act, which specifies that an unhappy state may well accompany a very rich state. A similar phenomenon occurs with δέ following a comparative:

42 Ophuijsen and Stork (1999:32) offer a similar reading of this Herodotean passage. It is tempting to recall here Clytemnestra's words in Aeschylus *Agamemnon* 1404-1405, similarly charged with scornful pride: ... οὗτός ἐστιν Ἀγαμέμνων, ἐμὸς / πόσις, νεκρὸς δέ, ... "This is Agamemnon, my husband. Dead. (...)" (tr. AB).

43 See also Herodotus 2.5.1 Δῆλα γὰρ δὴ καὶ μὴ προακούσαντι, ἰδόντι δέ, ὅστις γε σύνεσιν ἔχει, ὅτι ..., "For even if a man has not heard it before, he can readily see, if he has sense, that ...."

(t13)

Φροντίζων δὲ εὑρίσκω ἅμα μὲν κῦδος ἡμῖν προσγινόμενον χώρην τε τῆς νῦν ἐκτήμεθα οὐκ ἐλάσσω οὐδὲ φλαυροτέρην παμφορωτέρην δέ, ἅμα δὲ τιμωρίην τε καὶ τίσιν γινομένην.

Herodotus 7.8.α.2

... and my considerations persuade me that we may win not only renown, but a land neither less nor worse, and more fertile, than that which we now possess; and we would also gain vengeance and requital. (tr. Godley)

Xerxes, the speaker, marks his own considerations by using the explicit performative construction εὑρίσκω + φροντίζων (literally "while thinking I find that ..."), accompanied by δέ. Thus, δέ tells us that this is an act in itself, which in fact starts a move (see the multi-act unit ἅμα μέν, ... later answered by ἅμα δέ).[44] The δέ following παμφορωτέρην suggests that we should take παμφορωτέρην δέ as a separate discourse act. In Xerxes' words the semantic and pragmatic structure of what characterizes χώρην (the Greek land he wants to conquer) is clear: two negations and two pejorative comparative adjectives are followed by a comparative adjective that is positively oriented and accompanied by δέ. We process the three assessments through three distinct discourse acts and possibly three intonation units[45]: οὐκ ἐλάσσω | οὐδὲ φλαυροτέρην | παμφορωτέρην δέ: "we may win a land that is not less, that is not worse, that is more fertile."[46]

44 More on ἅμα μέν and ἅμα δέ sub-moves, see IV.5 §39.

45 On negatives as a criterion for establishing *kôlon* starts, see Scheppers 2011:76; 78; 243; see also II.2 §27 and IV.3 §46. ἀλλά would be an alternative to δέ (on ἀλλά expressing propositional contrast/replacement especially after negatives, see Drummen 2009). However, δέ suits the present piecemeal sequence of acts better than ἀλλά, as it presents the second and the third assessments as co-existing, rather than as contrasting alternatives to the first one. On the link between discourse and intonation boundaries, see below 2.2.3 on "inceptive δέ."

46 Even though more research should be done on δέ in Xenophon, here I record an instance that, in spite of its "final" position, is in line with the examples I have commented on. Xenophon *Anabasis* 5.3.9-5.3.10 παρεῖχε δὲ ἡ θεὸς τοῖς σκηνοῦσιν ἄλφιτα, ἄρτους, οἶνον, τραγήματα, καὶ τῶν θυομένων ἀπὸ τῆς ἱερᾶς νομῆς λάχος, καὶ τῶν θηρευομένων δέ. καὶ γάρ θήραν ..., "And the goddess would provide for the banqueters barley meal and loaves of bread, wine and sweetmeats, and a portion of the sacrificial victims from the sacred herd as well as of the victims taken in the chase" (tr. Brownson 1980). δέ serves to mark the information unit "and of the chased victims" as a separate discourse act (possibly corresponding to a separate intonation contour), albeit within the parallelism καὶ τῶν θυομένων - καὶ τῶν θηρευομένων. It also delimits the unit with respect to the following nexus καὶ γάρ. A further tripartite division of information and intonation units in Herodotus occurs at least at 8.67.2: ἵζοντο (...) πρῶτος μὲν ὁ Σιδώνιος βασιλεύς, μετὰ δὲ ὁ Τύριος, ἐπὶ δὲ ὦλλοι. "They [Persian tyrants and leaders] sat (...), first the king of Sidon, then the king of Tyre, then the rest" (tr. Godley).

§28. Notice that (t11)-(t13) have all been taken from speeches. Perhaps discourse acts that are marked by δέ and are not full clauses, are found more in direct speech than in narrative sections. Whether or not this is the case, these instances resonate with the short clauses, the parenthetical clauses, and the other syntactic constructions that δέ can accompany. Such phrases containing δέ are all meant to convey separate discourse acts.[47] What the instances in direct speech suggest overall is a great deal of vividness. In the following passage the Syracusan leader Hermocrates gives a speech against the Athenians in Camarina (6.76-80). The words below conclude its first part (chapter 76):

(t14)

περὶ δὲ οἱ μὲν σφίσιν ἀλλὰ μὴ ἐκείνῳ καταδουλώσεως, οἱ δ' ἐπὶ δεσπότου μεταβολῇ οὐκ ἀξυνετωτέρου, κακοξυνετωτέρου δέ. Ἀλλ' οὐ γὰρ δή ...

Thucydides 6.76.4

The Athenians were looking to replace Persian enslavement with theirs, and the Greeks to make a change of slave-master—to one just as clever, but clever for the worse. But enough of this ... (tr. Hammond)

I interpret κακοξυνετωτέρου δέ not just as a contrastive appendix, but as a full discourse step (however elliptical). It forcefully and vividly states something on its own: the new masters that the Greeks are going to have are wiser, but for evil.[48]

2.2.2 δέ in syntactically independent clauses

§29. When δέ appears in clauses with finite verbs, the particle marks with equal clarity the clause's status as a separate communicative act:

47 The fact that δέ may signal a separate discourse act is also shown by the occurrence of τί δέ in questions, particularly in classical Greek. Whether it stands alone or starts a more elaborate question, it signals the beginning of a new act. The role of τί δέ in Plato's dialogues (along with the different punctuation accompanying it in Byzantine manuscripts) is extensively discussed in Rijksbaron 2007:244-257. Denniston (1950:175-176) discusses several subtypes of it, including τί δέ as a "formula of transition." On the conversational role of τί δέ in drama, see III.4 §46.

48 The uniqueness of the adjective κακοξυνετωτέρου supports the idea that a separate and specific point is made by the utterance. Another instance of δέ marking exceptionally short discourse acts is Thucydides, at 7.3.1 ... ἐθορυβήθησαν μὲν τὸ πρῶτον, παρετάξαντο δέ. ὁ δὲ θέμενος... "They [the Athenians] were consternated at first, then formed in battle order. He [Gylippus] ..." (tr. adapted from Hammond).

(t15)

ὁ δὲ ... ξύλλογον ποιήσας (ἔτι δ' ἐστρατήγει) ἐβούλετο θαρσῦναί ...

Thucydides 2.59.3

He [Pericles] (...) called a meeting (he was still general) with the intention of stiffening ... (tr. Hammond)

Here ἔτι δ' ἐστρατήγει is not syntactically integrated with the rest of the sentence. The sign of parenthesis (which alternatively may be rendered by two dashes) is necessary in the English translation, but the Greek does not need it.[49] δέ suffices to mark discontinuity in discourse, and the syntactic impossibility of two contiguous finite verbs (ἐστρατήγει ἐβούλετο) enables readers to infer a boundary between them. This δέ in fact starts an unframed act: the narration of events (framed discourse) stops and gives way to a general (or omniscient) statement. A similar case in Herodotus occurs:

(t16)

... ἀπαγινέοντας δὲ φορτία Αἰγύπτιά τε καὶ Ἀσσύρια τῇ τε ἄλλῃ [χώρῃ] ἐσαπικνέεσθαι καὶ δὴ καὶ ἐς Ἄργος· τὸ δὲ Ἄργος τοῦτον τὸν χρόνον προεῖχε ἅπασι τῶν ἐν τῇ νῦν Ἑλλάδι καλεομένῃ χώρῃ. Ἀπικομένους δὲ τοὺς Φοίνικας ἐς δὴ τὸ Ἄργος τοῦτο διατίθεσθαι τὸν φόρτον.

Herodotus 1.1.1-2

Among other places to which they carried Egyptian and Assyrian merchandise, they came to Argos, which was at that time preeminent in every way among the people of what is now called Hellas. The Phoenicians came to Argos, and set out their cargo. (tr. Godley)

Note that Godley uses a relative clause, "which was at that time ...," to render the discontinuous piece of information. The Greek of Herodotus, however, conveys the break by using a syntactically independent δέ clause (τὸ δὲ Ἄργος τοῦτον τὸν χρόνον προεῖχε

[49] On parenthetical utterances and the problematic aspects of modern punctuation, see IV.3 §§ 59; 78; 80; 107; IV.5 §§16; 25; 68. Kerschensteiner (1964:38) acknowledges that sometimes the features we find in parentheses in Herodotus' text occur elsewhere without parentheses. Readers tend to associate discontinuous parenthetical utterances with prose rather than poetry; however, poets do use parenthetical δέ acts as well. E.g. Pindar, *Pythian* 10.44-46 ... θρασείᾳ δὲ πνέων καρδίᾳ / μόλεν Δανάας ποτὲ παῖς, ἁγεῖτο δ' Ἀθάνα, / ἐς ἀνδρῶν μακάρων ὅμιλον ... "Breathing boldness of spirit once the son of Danae [Perseus] went to that gathering of blessed men, and Athena led him there"—ἁγεῖτο δ' Ἀθάνα (tr. Race).

ἅπασι τῶν ἐν τῇ νῦν Ἑλλάδι καλεομένῃ χώρῃ). The grammatical subject coincides with the last word of the preceding clause,[50] but tense is discontinuous (imperfect προεῖχε, against the previous and the following aorists, ἐσαπικνέεσθαι and ἀπικομένους).[51] The subsequent δέ clause (ἀπικομένους δὲ...) assures us that we have resumed the narration of events; note the participle and the infinitive, which have the Phoenicians as their grammatical subject (see 1.1.1 τούτους γάρ).

§30. Before continuing the analysis, it is important to clarify the relationship between δέ acts and discourse discontinuity, which I briefly mentioned in §20. δέ is a particle that contributes to signal discourse discontinuity rather than continuity.[52] What does it mean? However similar in force and in grammar two contiguous δέ acts may be,[53] δέ keeps them distinct, because it marks their boundary. This is a minimal discontinuity, but it represents all what δέ does.[54] δέ acts may effect greater discontinuity in discourse, but in that case other linguistic features contribute to its greater extent, such as a change in tense, a change in mood, a change of grammatical subject, a marked form of pronoun, and further particles.[55] The more such features co-occur, the stronger the discontinuity is.[56] δέ in itself just keeps acts separate. As such, it never clarifies how acts differ, or which is the different force they convey.[57] It is the whole constituted by δέ and the co-occurring features that tells us the point of the act. Only then we can see the difference with respect to the previous act, whatever feature introduces it.

§31. Let us exemplify how δέ keeps acts separate by means of a Herodotean passage.

(t17)

Ὦ ξεῖνε Ἀθηναῖε, ἡ <u>δ᾽</u> ἡμετέρη εὐδαιμονίη οὕτω τοι ἀπέρριπται ἐς τὸ μηδέν, ὥστε οὐδὲ ἰδιωτέων ἀνδρῶν ἀξίους ἡμέας ἐποίησας;

Herodotus 1.32.1

50 On the Herodotean technique of repeating and resuming before moving on with narration, see in particular Müller 1980:51-63.

51 For tense change in unframed acts, see II.4 §14; for tense shift at move transitions, see IV.3 §95; §133; §134; IV.5 §16.

52 As for drama, see III.4 §§34-35 for δέ at the start of questions unrelated to the immediately previous turn of speaking, and III.4 §38 for turn-initial δέ signaling lack of answer to question.

53 As in Homeric epic, for example, where δέ mostly starts individual narrative steps. On the possible connection between δέ and narrative sections within tragedy, see III.2 §27. The idea of marking narrative progression is probably the main reason why scholars talk about the connective side of δέ. See, for instance, Cooper 2002:2922: "δέ is the most frequent conjunction"; "the connective force is commonplace from Homer."

54 See II.2 §36 "δέ in Homer is the simplest metalanguage."

55 In (t4) and (t5), for instance, ἄν happens to occur as well, which is the linguistic marker of a modal nuance. Modality is fully compatible with the expression of stance and subjectivity.

56 See IV.3 §95 for the connection between a high degree of discontinuity and the beginning of moves in historiography.

57 2.2.6 will discuss the different forces that contiguous δέ acts sometimes communicate.

> My Athenian friend, is our prosperity so worthless that you make us not even a match for private citizens? (tr. AB)

Solon has just argued, upon Croesus' inquiry, that Tellus, first, and Cleobis and Biton, second, are the happiest men he has ever heard of. At that point Croesus asks in disappointment the question here reported. The question proper starts after a vocative expression (ὦ ξεῖνε Ἀθηναῖε). In a discourse act perspective, δέ starts an act that spells out an inference from Solon's replies (that is, Solon despises Croesus' happiness), and in fact it introduces the question, while ὦ ξεῖνε Ἀθηναῖε constitutes a different act.[58] In virtue of that, there is no need to think of this δέ as "postponed."[59] The postponement relates to the beginning of the sentence, but in pragmatic terms the δέ is where it should be, that is, at the beginning of a new act.

2.2.3 "Inceptive" δέ

§32. δέ at the beginning of speeches, whether preceded by a vocative or not, is called "inceptive δέ" by Denniston (1950: 172) and by Cooper (2002:2935). Denniston, applying the concept only to speeches in Herodotus and Xenophon, explains inceptive δέ as follows: "Sometimes δέ marks a contrast with the preceding speech. (...) But in other

[58] This vocative act must correspond to some communicative strategic purpose beyond getting the attention of the interlocutor. The dialogic situation does not require any getting-attention device at that point, as Croesus and Solon are the only interlocutors, and the conversation started long before. Perhaps we can speculate about the ironic tone underlying the act.

[59] See Denniston 1950:189 for the description of δέ after vocative expressions as "postponed." In a note (1950:189n1) the author adds: "Pearson (on E.*Hel.* 1392) [Pearson ed. 1903] is hardly right in saying that δέ here is 'in its regular position with vocative outside the clause'." In fact I believe Pearson to be right, in light of what δέ effects on the discourse level. Already Thiersch 1826:477 notes the "autonomy" ("Selbständigkeit") of vocatives when δέ opens a sentence immediately afterwards. Cooper (2002:2923) offers the following interesting observation about the position of δέ in general: "The position of δέ is regularly postpositive and it comes after the first word in its sentence or clause. But if the first thought of the sentence is a unified idea represented by several words, there is a tendency for all these words contributing to the unified idea to precede δέ." A further instance of a δέ act after a vocative in Herodotus is 8.68α (Δέσποτα, τὴν δὲ ἐοῦσαν γνώμην με δίκαιόν ἐστι ἀποδείκνυσθαι ..., in Hude's edition—Legrand writes τήν γε). At Lysias 7.4 the manuscripts have ἦν μὲν γὰρ τοῦτο Πεισάνδρου τὸ χωρίον, δημευθέντων τῶν ὄντων δὲ ἐκείνου Ἀπολλόδωρος ὁ Μεγαρεὺς ... "This plot of ground belonged to Peisander; but when his property was confiscated, Apollodorus of Megara ..." (tr. Lamb). Bekker emended the "postposition" of δέ by moving it after δημευθέντων, and therefore normalizing its position. Denniston (1950:188-189) comments: "Bekker's δὲ τῶν is surely right." Yet, if we consider the genitive absolute as a "unified idea" (to use Cooper's terms), there is no need to emend the position of δέ. Grégoire 1930 shows that over time δέ's position in phrases and clauses becomes free more and more often.

places there is no obvious sense of contrast. (...) The object is, no doubt, to give a conversational turn to the opening ('Well,'), and to avoid formality."[60]

§33. Verdenius, in three articles and short notes (Verdenius 1947; 1955; 1974), gives a more comprehensive account of inceptive δέ. He broadens the category to include δέ after exclamations and apostrophes. He also takes account of δέ occurring at the *incipit* of works. Here is an example taken from the numerous beginnings he quotes:[61]

(t18)

Κατὰ τάδε ξύμμαχοι ἔσονται Λακεδαιμόνιοι <καὶ Ἀθηναῖοι> πεντήκοντα ἔτη. ἢν [δέ] τινες ἴωσιν ἐς τὴν γῆν πολέμιοι τὴν Λακεδαιμονίων καὶ κακῶς ποιῶσι Λακεδαιμονίους, ...

Thucydides 5.23.1

These are the terms on which the Spartans and the Athenians shall be allies for fifty years. [*indentation*] If any people enter Spartan territory with hostile intent and do harm to the Spartans ... (tr. Hammond)

Thucydides mentions the oaths and the terms of the alliance between Spartans and the Athenians after the peace of Nicias (καὶ ἐγένοντο ὅρκοι καὶ ξυμμαχία ἥδε, 5.22.3). Κατὰ τάδε starts a separate discourse, which is the record of the agreements. By means of τάδε the utterance projects that the details of these terms are about to come. ἢν [δέ] τινες starts the actual list of the agreements. This is why Verdenius regards this δέ as an example of "inceptive" δέ. The metalanguage of δέ in this case consists in marking the beginning of a series of entries; this is where the actual content of the oaths start.[62] The English translation of Hammond and Rhodes (2009:269) renders these discontinuities by presenting the

60 Denniston 1950:172. This type of δέ falls under the category "apparently superfluous δέ" (171), together with δέ in second answers to second questions, and in passionate exclamations.

61 In Verdenius 1947:274-275 they are: τοῦ δὲ λόγου τοῦδ' ἐόντος..., Heraclitus fr. 1 (δέ reported only by Hippolytus and not by Aristotle and Sextus; perhaps, Verdenius adds, there was a title Περὶ φύσεως preceding it); ἀρχὴ δέ μοι τοῦ λόγου ..., Ion of Chios fr. 1; ἁ φύσις δ' ἐν τῷ κόσμῳ ἁρμόχθη, Philolaus fr. 1; Σωκράτους δὲ ἀξιόν μοι δοκεῖ εἶναι μεμνῆσθαι, Xenophon *Apologia* 1; ἤκουσα δὲ ποτε αὐτοῦ ... Xenophon *Economics* 1; περὶ δὲ τῆς Ἀθηναίων πολιτείαι ..., Xenophon *Constitution of the Athenians* 1. In Verdenius 1955 he quotes ὧδε ἔχει περὶ αὐτέων· τὰ δὲ ἔθνεα ταῦτα ..., Hippocrates *Airs, Waters, Places* 13 (Wilamowitz and Heiberg delete δέ); σοὶ δ'ἐγὼ ἐσθλὰ νοέων ἐρέω ..., Hesiod *Works and Days* 286; τίς δὲ βίος ..., Mimnermus fr. 1.1; ἡμεῖς δ'οἷά τε φύλλα ..., Mimnermus fr. 2.1; ἡμετέρα δὲ πόλις ..., Solon fr. 3.1; σοὶ δ' ἐγὼ εὖ φρονέων ὑποθήσομαι, Theognides 27; χρημάτων δ' ἄελπτον οὐδέν ἐστιν, Archilochus fr. 74.1; Thucydides 5.23.1 (see main text); δοκεῖ δὲ μεγαλόψυχος εἶναι ..., Aristotle *Nicomachean Ethics* 1123b2.

62 A similar instance in Herodotus concerns the re-start of an actual account after the historian explicitly announces his intention to retrieve it (Herodotus 1.140.3-141.1 ἄνειμι δὲ ἐπὶ τὸν πρότερον λόγον. [141] Ἴωνες δὲ καὶ Αἰολέες, ὡς οἱ Λυδοὶ τάχιστα κατεστράφατο ὑπὸ Περσέων, ἔπεμπον ἀγγέλους ἐς Σάρδις παρὰ Κῦρον ... "I return now to my former story. [141] As soon as the

entire oaths' list in smaller font and as a spaced paragraph, and by indenting on "If any people...," which corresponds to the Greek ἤν [δέ] τινες. Verdenius notes that Hude and Krüger delete the particle, while Stuart and Jones put it between square brackets. I infer *ex silentio* that all the manuscripts report δέ, and, given the discourse function I tried to explain, I see no reason to remove the particle.[63]

§34. Verdenius' conclusion about inceptive δέ is that δέ originally was a weakened form of δή.[64] Beyond this thought, the interesting side of Verdenius' inquiry (and of Denniston's and Cooper's notes) is the association between δέ and the idea of a new start, in content and in performance. From a pragmatic perspective, discourse acts signaled by δέ are not only separated from whatever precedes them, but, in some cases at least, appear to signal a new start. The newness may involve a topical spin (whether at the absolute *incipit* or at an internal beginning of works), or it may mark a new intonational contour. This way of marking discourse discontinuity has to be taken into account as part of the communicative potential of δέ acts in historiography as well as in other genres.

§35. δέ is a syndetic device, but some scholars compare the occurrence of δέ with asyndeton.[65] What makes δέ comparable to asyndeton? The answer rests on what has been analyzed so far: δέ separates, it marks a boundary, and it may occur at beginnings. The particle's affinity with asyndeton probably also explains scholars' reluctance to classify δέ as a conjunction.

2.2.4 "Apodotic" δέ

§36. Earlier (§21) I noted that when δέ appears after subordinating conjunctions, the particle qualifies the host clause as a discrete unit with its own separate force, regardless of the host clause's syntactic status.

§37. My point about the irrelevance of the host clause's syntactic status may be further illustrated by considering the functionality of δέ when it appears in main clauses following causal or temporal subclauses. Denniston calls this "apodotic δέ" and lists it under the rubric "non-connective" δέ (along with duplicated δέ, which occurs in apodoses as well as in the preceding protases). The fact that δέ is used both in subclauses and "apodotic" main clauses (with no exception for Herodotus and Thucydides) means that δέ works on a level that is independent of syntactic hierarchies. That level is that

---

Lydians had been subjugated by the Persians, the Ionians and Aeolians sent messengers to Cyrus ..." (tr. Godley).

63 Another philological problem dealing with δέ in a passage from *Lysistrata* is examined from a pragmatic perspective in III.4 §69.

64 Many other scholars hypothesize the same thing, independently from "inceptive" δέ; see, for example, Thiersch 1826:549; Leumann 1949:87; Bakker 1997d:79. II.2 §§32-33 and II.3 §57 explore the possible link between the two particles.

65 Hummel 1993:382 about Pindar; Klein 1992:49 and Viti 2008:42 about Homer.

of the individual strategic steps forming any complex thought. Here is an instance of apodotic δέ in Thucydides:

(t19)

... καὶ ἐγένετο ἐπ' ἐκείνου μεγίστη, ἐπειδή τε ὁ πόλεμος κατέστη, ὁ <u>δὲ</u> φαίνεται καὶ ἐν τούτῳ προγνοὺς τὴν δύναμιν. ἐπεβίω δὲ δύο ἔτη καὶ ἓξ μῆνας· καὶ ἐπειδὴ ἀπέθανεν, ἐπὶ πλέον ἔτι ἐγνώσθη ἡ πρόνοια αὐτοῦ ἡ ἐς τὸν πόλεμον.

Thucydides 2.65.5

... and under his [Pericles'] guidance the city [Athens] reached its greatest height: and when the war came, it is clear that he provided for the strength of Athens in war too. He survived the outbreak of war by two years and six months. After his death the foresight he had shown in regard to the war could be recognized yet more clearly. (tr. Hammond)

In spite of the comma before ἐπειδή, which signposts a light pause, we may imagine a major pause before ἐπειδή τε, as τε, especially in Thucydides, is frequently used to introduce clauses that are independent from the preceding ones.[66] ὁ δέ appears as "apodotic δέ" after a temporal subclause. The reason why δέ is there is not so much to mark the change of grammatical subject,[67] as to qualify the clause as a new strategic step in the discourse ("he provided strength in war too"). This is what the next clause, which is still about Pericles and is still introduced by δέ (ἐπεβίω δὲ δύο ἔτη καὶ ἓξ μῆνας, "he survived the outbreak of war by two years and six months"), achieves as well.

2.2.5 δέ in priming acts

§38. In (t10) I gathered examples from the thousand-word sample of Thucydides, where δέ phrases project a multi-act unit (τῶν δὲ πόλεων | ὅσαι μὲν ... (1.7.1), δηλοῦσι δὲ | τῶν τε ἠπειρωτῶν τινὲς ... (1.5.2), and οἱ δ' οὖν | ὡς ἕκαστοι Ἕλληνες ... (1.3.4)). These phrases are pragmatically (and presumably also intonationally) isolated by the fact that the following particle or subordinating conjunction marks an act boundary (μέν, τε, and ὡς respectively). They invite us to cognitively keep the referents in focus for a while, even though the phrases appear syntactically incomplete and isolated ("anacoluthic").

§39. In IV.3.11.1 I analyze further parallels from the two *Histories*, and I claim that by projecting multi-act units short δέ constructions start a move. In this chapter I signpost a grammatical variation involving such constructions, which supports one of the points

66 See below 2.3.3; 2.3.4; 2.3.6. On the ambiguity of commas in modern punctuation, see IV.3 §58.

67 The pronouns preceding δέ already effect the change; see II.5.3.1.

already made about δέ, that is, syntactic diversity does not influence the pragmatic function of δέ. Consider the following adverbial phrase accompanied by δέ:

(t20)

τέλος <u>δὲ</u> | νεκρῶν τε πολλῶν ἐπ' ἀλλήλοις ἤδη κειμένων ἐν τῷ ποταμῷ καὶ διεφθαρμένου τοῦ στρατεύματος τοῦ μὲν κατὰ τὸν ποταμόν, τοῦ δὲ καί, εἴ τι διαφύγοι, ὑπὸ τῶν ἱππέων, Νικίας Γυλίππῳ ἑαυτὸν παραδίδωσι ...

Thucydides 7.85.1

In the end, when the bodies were lying heaped on one another in the river, and the army had been utterly destroyed, most of them there along the river and any who had escaped being accounted for by the cavalry, Nicias surrendered himself to Gylippus. (tr. Hammond)

This is one of the final poignant moments of the Sicilian expedition. τέλος δέ condenses the idea that a process has reached its completion; as such it semantically encompasses the content of the discrete steps that follow. On a pragmatic level it establishes projection by means of a short δέ phrase, grammatically isolated by the subsequent genitive absolutes νεκρῶν ... κειμένων and διεφθαρμένου τοῦ στρατεύματος, which are chiastically arranged and conjoined by τε ... καί.

§40. Even without subsequent act boundaries, clusters of words including δέ and occurring in first sentence position project arguments or sections that require more than one clause. Thucydidean examples include clusters that add evidence, proof, or authoritative evaluation about a certain fact, such as δηλοῖ δέ μοι (1.3.1) δηλοῖ δὲ μάλιστα (3.104.4); δηλοῖ δέ; δοκεῖ δέ μοι (1.3.2; 2.42.2; 6.34.2); σημεῖον δ' ἐστί (1.6.2); τεκμήριον δέ (1.73.5; 2.15.4; 2.39.2; 2.50.2; 3.66.1); and τεκμηριοῖ δέ (1.3.3).

§41. These constructions overall range from adverbial and verbal to noun phrases. Furthermore, in linguistics a univocal syntactic interpretation of noun phrases is not straightforward.[68] Still, in spite of this syntactic diversity, the pragmatic role of these constructions is consistent: they are all discourse acts that have a projecting force.

2.2.6 When the force of two contiguous δέ acts changes

§42. This final subsection focuses on the different force that contiguous δέ acts may convey. We have to retrieve, first, the idea that δέ *per se* does not tell anything about the specific force of the host act; it just marks its beginning (§§17; 21; 31). What characterizes

68 See above n41.

the force or *vis*[69] of the act is the co-occurrence of other semantic, syntactic, and pragmatic features.

§43. In light of that, the force of contiguous δέ acts sharing the same grammatical subject or the same topic (which are tokens of discourse continuity) may be assumed to be similar, if not the same. Towards the beginning of the section on δέ, I made an observation about δέ with infinitives (see §§22-23), where the grammatical subject usually carries over from the previous clause(s). The non-finite verb forms invite the reader or listener to keep in mind the action framework within which single narrative or argumentative steps are presented. δέ discretizes such steps, but the steps continue in the same direction. The more tokens of discourse continuity appear across δέ acts, the less the individual force changes. This also holds for δέ with finite verbs, and is what leads us to read contiguous δέ acts as marking "narrative steps" without further specification.

§44. However, contiguous δέ acts can also differ in force, if the co-text and context suggests it. Before quoting an Herodotean example of that (Thucydides hardly makes use of contiguous δέ acts[70]), let me point out an instance from Sappho:

(t21)

... ὄσσα δέ μοι τέλεσσαι
θῦμος ἰμέρρει, τέλεσον, σὺ <u>δ'</u> αὔτα
σύμμαχος ἔσσο.

Sappho *fr.* 1.26-28

... And what my heart desires to accomplish please accomplish it, and you yourself be my ally. (tr. AB)

The closure of Sappho 1 presents two contiguous δέ acts that have a different force in spite of a remarkably similar grammar. The first is an entreaty that Aphrodite make the wishes of the singing "I" come true (realized by the imperative form τέλεσον and by the attached relative clause (ὄσσα ... ἰμέρρει)). The second, σὺ δ'αὔτα / σύμμαχος ἔσσο, includes a further imperative with no change of the 'you'-referent. However, a mix of elements makes this second δέ act different from the first in force. These elements are the remarkable prominence of the personal pronoun in the vocative form, which cannot serve to disambiguate the referent;[71] the further emphasis given by αὔτα, which makes Aphrodite the absolute center of attention;[72] finally, the lexical choice σύμμαχος, which

[69] About the *vis* of particles, see I.1 §16.

[70] Thucydides prefers καί in contiguous acts that express narrative progress. See below n215.

[71] See II.2.5.2.1 for a cognitive reading of second-person nominative pronouns in Pindar.

[72] On αὐτός establishing a center and a periphery, see Bonifazi 2012:137-149 and Bonifazi 2019.

resonates with the lyric *tópos* of love-as-a-battle.[73] All of this signals the pragmatic force not just of a humble request for an action, but of an intense desire about the being of the goddess herself.

§45. Even though in historiography the genre and its communicative goals are quite different from lyric, each δέ act in the following Herodotean excerpt has a different force from the other. Denniston lists this passage under instances of "duplicated δέ":

(t22)

ὅθεν δὲ αὐτὰ ἔλαβε ἢ αὐτὸς ἐκτήσατο, τοῦτο δὲ οὐκ ἔχω εἰπεῖν· τούτοισι δ' ὦν πίσυνος ἐὼν κατήγαγε, ...

Herodotus 7.153.3

From where he [Telines] got these [men], and whether or not they were his own invention, I cannot say; however that may be, it was in reliance upon them that he restored the exiles, ... (tr. Godley)

Herodotus is telling how Telines, relative of Gelo (ruler of Gela and Syracuse) was able to reconcile his people after civil strife. He did so without the force of men, but by using the "holy instruments of these goddesses" (ἔχων οὐδεμίαν ἀνδρῶν δύναμιν ἀλλὰ ἱρὰ τούτων τῶν θεῶν, where τούτων refers to the previous mention τῶν χθονίων θεῶν, 7.153.2). The passage quoted above includes δέ in an indirect interrogative subclause (ὅθεν δέ ..., where the predicate is disjoined in αὐτὰ ἔλαβε and αὐτὸς ἐκτήσατο); δέ in the following main clause (τοῦτο δὲ οὐκ ἔχω εἰπεῖν); and a further δέ in the next main clause (τούτοισι δ' ... κατήγαγε). Regardless of the syntactic relation between sub- and main clause, three separate discourse acts with three different forces are performed: "how did this happen?," "I can't say that," and "he restored them."[74]

2.2.7 Interim conclusion

§46. δέ in both *Histories* shows semantic and especially syntactic versatility. I have given instances of δέ encompassing various syntactic configurations ((t3)-(t17)). The only consistent meaning of δέ derivable from its host constructions is pragmatic. This meaning consists in indicating that a new communicative act (or even move) is being performed. The new act may have a different subject (to speak in terms of content), or a

73 In her monograph on love as war in Sappho, Rissman (1983:10-11) comments about σύμμαχος: "[it] must be taken as a serious appeal for help, for an ally in the war of love. The poet does not consider her situation hopeless."

74 Over the first two books of each work, the instances of δέ (including δ') amount to 2,389 in Herodotus, versus 1,291 in Thucydides (1.26% vs. 0.84% respectively), which increases the probability of having more contiguous δέ acts in the former than in the latter.

different force (to speak in terms of intention), or both. Often δέ is attached to elements that in fact introduce new communication. Included in this use of δέ are points in the discourse when new content matches new performance (see "inceptive δέ" in 2.2.3), and when a short unit re-orients the audience's attention by establishing a relationship with an upcoming longer stretch of discourse ((t10) and (t20)). In both cases the use of δέ indicates a hierarchy different from the syntactic one: it is a discourse hierarchy, connected to the cognitive relevance of the re-orientation of attention.

2.3 The Continuum of τε

§47. τε is commonly understood as a particle that has a coordinating function in various grammatical contexts: when it connects two phrases by occurring twice (bisyndetic τε); when it appears before καί without intervening words (τε καί); when it appears before καί with intervening words (τε ... καί); finally, when it connects two (or more) phrases or clauses by occurring once, and without καί (τε "*solitarium*"). Conversely, τε is considered to have a non-coordinating (or non-connective) function when it occurs after relative pronouns, after a subordinating conjunction, or, as Ruijgh puts it (1971:1), whenever it cannot be substituted by καί. The standard label for the non-coordinating function is "epic τε."

§48. This section questions the validity of the dichotomous distinction between coordinating and non-coordinating functions of τε from a pragmatic perspective.[75] Our entire corpus, not just Herodotus and Thucydides, makes us view τε as existing on a continuum, a view that allows "connective" and "adverbial" functions to coexist in various degrees.[76] We combine syntax, semantics, and pragmatics to support our interpretations. We also take into account genre expectations and the discourse strategies suggested by the co-text of τε.[77]

§49. The label "epic" for non-connective τε appears first in Wentzel 1847 (1), a work that will be quoted later. Denniston (1950:496) provides a very concise description of "epic" τε: "epic τε of habitual action (...), which bears the same force when it follows relatives as when it follows other particles." Denniston derives "universalizing" τε (as in

[75] As for idiomatic constructions involving τε, the number of occurrences is not significant: Herodotus employs ἄλλ- τε καί forms four times; οἷο- τε forms 51 times, and ὅσον τε 22 times; Thucydides ἄλλ- τε καί forms (mainly ἄλλως τε καί) 47 times; οἷο- τε forms 29 times, and ὅσον τε two times.

[76] This continuum of functions is considered on the level of discourse functions, which is a synchronic level of analysis. It is not our purpose to chart the functions of τε diachronically, a task that would require a richer spectrum of texts and discussion of Indo-European comparanda. The only diachronic aspect that is taken into account is the adoption, by classical Greek genres, of features from earlier genres.

[77] Very similar conclusions are drawn about the pragmatics of τε in II.4 §§32-37 concerning τε in Homeric similes; in II.4 §58-68 concerning connective τε in Pindar; in III.2.2.3 concerning τε in tragedy and comedy.

ὅς τε meaning *quicumque*) from habitual τε. Ruijgh's definition of "epic" τε (which gives the title to his 1971 monograph) is slightly different: τε is "epic" when it is found after a relative or after a subordinating conjunction at the beginning of a clause that most of the time represents a digression and/or introduces a permanent reality ("*fait permanent*," 1971:2).[78]

§50. The following example, which comes from a genre that is neither epic nor historiography, challenges not only the distinction between connective and non-connective or "epic" τε, but also the traditional definition of "epic" instances.

(t23)

Πολλὰ μὲν οὖν ὑπῆρχε τοῖς ἡμετέροις προγόνοις μιᾷ γνώμῃ χρωμένοις περὶ τοῦ δικαίου διαμάχεσθαι. ἥ <u>τε</u> γὰρ ἀρχὴ τοῦ βίου δικαία· οὐ γάρ, ὥσπερ οἱ πολλοί, ...

Lysias 2.17

Now in many ways it was natural to our ancestors, moved by a single resolve, to fight the battles of justice: for the very beginning of their life was just. They had not been collected, like most nations, ... (tr. Lamb)

Lysias' point in this passage is to show that the Athenians occupied their own land by virtue of autochthony rather than by invasion. However, it is not clear which function τε fulfills.[79] If γάρ is the connector, τε cannot have a connective function. Is Lysias alluding to "epic" τε by means of a reference to something "habitual" (Denniston 1950:496) or "*digressif-permanent*" (Ruijgh 1971:1), even though τε does not follow any relative pronoun or subordinating conjunction?

§51. When a use of τε does not fit the standard definition of non-connective τε, or when it seems reductive to posit a connective function, I propose to apply a pragmatic reading in which the key point to keep in mind is that a shift is occurring. The shift is from a content-oriented view to an attitude-oriented view. Instead of associating τε with habitual, universal, or permanent content, several functions of τε may be seen in connection with the speaker's perspective on the content. The following examples will illustrate how this shift works. For now I anticipate that the speaker's perspective on the content is that of "presenting knowledge as shared."

78 The antiquity of "epic" τε is corroborated by Mycenaean Greek, which also had non-connective *qe*. Hajnal 2004 (242-243) sees in that use a sign of oral discourse—*qe* marks someone's name as left-dislocated with respect to the predicate about it. I thank Brent Vine for drawing my attention to the problem of how to interpret non-connective *qe* in Mycenaean.

79 Lysias does not employ τε very often. The *TLG* online records only 243 instances of τε (fragments included), of which 28 are οἷός τε forms.

§52. This reading rests on accounts offered by nineteenth century scholars. Particularly illuminating are the notes of Wentzel, in an essay on τε in Homer published in 1847.[80] According to his account, the originally demonstrative meaning of τε, "da" ("here/there," compare οἶος—τοῖος), gives rise to both the so-called "copulative" as well as the "purely epic" uses of τε.[81] In the epic use τε indicates something general or known to the readers or addressees ("*bekannt*"),[82] or something proven true through perception. It may also indicate well-known phenomena ("*allbekannte Erscheinungen*") regarding nature, human beings, gods, animals, or qualities and properties of objects and individuals; and it can be used in describing lands and items ("*Länder und Sache*").[83] The copulative function (which Wentzel prefers to characterize as partitive or distributive) derives from the demonstrative one, where a series of items is presented almost asyndetically: "there is this, there is that."[84] Setting aside the historical part of Wentzel's arguments about τε,[85] his views on the relatedness of τε's demonstrative and copulative functions is compatible with the model of a continuum: some demonstrative force underlies both the indication of something known and the presentation of different items in lists.

§53. Rather than setting a hard and fast rule where we divide all possible functions of τε in Archaic and Classical Greek between coordinating and non-coordinating roles,

80 Denniston and Ruijgh do mention this study, but do not acknowledge that it contributes anything more than a reference to the generalizing function of τε.

81 In Wentzel's terms, "*copulative*" and "*rein epischer*" respectively.

82 See Bloch 1955:147, which proposes "*bekanntlich*" as the translation of "epic" τε (and mentions Wentzel 1847).

83 Wentzel 1847:1-2, 31.

84 Different characteristics of items may be mentioned in a series, and still maintain a sense of separateness. Wentzel (1847:3) calls it "Getrenntheit": "Wir sagen ... : die Winkel sind theils rechte, theils stumpfe, theils spitze, d.h. die einen sind rechte, die andern sind stumpfe u.s.w. Der Grieche setzt hier τε-τε-τε und hat ursprünglich so gedacht: die Winkel sind rechte da, stumpfe da, spitze da, und bezeichnet dadurch eben ihr Getrenntsein in ihrer äußeren Erscheinung," "We say ... : the corners are partly fitting, partly dull-edge, partly acute; that is to say, some of them are fitting, others are dull-edge, etc. The Greek puts here τε ...τε ... τε, and originally thought the following: the corners are fitting here, dull-edge here, acute here, and through this he shows their separatedness in their exterior appearance."

85 Here is a compressed recapitulation of the main ideas on the development of the two syntactically diverse τε: Kühner and Gerth (1955: §81 take "epic" τε as deriving from coordinating τε (thus as a weak form of "also"); analogously, Gonda takes the complementarity expressed by τε as the primary function (from IE *-*kwe*, connected to Vedic *ca*, Latin -*que*), which is fully shown in its connective uses, while ὅς τε clauses convey a similar idea; they are "added mainly for the sake of completeness, for giving an addition, for expressing the idea of association" (1954:206-207); Ruijgh (1971:12; 15) also thinks a coordinating particle is where the adverbial "*digressif-permanent*" τε comes from. Conversely, Wackernagel (1920:118-119) and Chantraine (1953b:340) derive τε from **kwi*-, a IE marker of indefiniteness (see Latin *quis-que* and Greek οἱός τε), where the coordinating role comes from. Finally, Bloch (1955:152-153) holds that the two τε have different origins and different etymologies. In particular, "epic" τε may either come from a form of personal pronoun "you" (connected to Old Indic *tú*) or from a demonstrative form τῇ ("*sieh da*"). Beekes (2010:1457) only mentions IE *-*kwe*, the appearance of τε in adverbs as well (ὅτε, πότε, etc.), and the general meaning "and."

we should observe more closely what authors associate with τε, and how communication is improved by the use of τε. The following examples have either been left undiscussed, or labelled as "peculiar" or "superfluous," in secondary literature. However, we can better understand them by assuming that τε exists on a continuum ranging from the copulative to the adverbial pole.

2.3.1 τε and shared knowledge

§54. When we consider what is implied by inserting τε in an utterance, the heaviest enrichment that readers and listeners can supply regards the adverbial "epic" functions. By enrichment we mean the interpretation that individual words suggest but leave unsaid.[86] We can say that Ruijgh's adjectives "*digressif*" and "*permanent*" signpost enrichments attached to "epic" τε, namely the intention to digress in narrative ("*digressif*") and the marking of content as permanent ("*permanent*"). We invite the reader to view the matter in a different light: the enrichment of τε concerns the perspective or attitude of the speaker (and possibly of the receiver as well) towards the content. What makes states of affairs permanent, habitual, or general is the shared and consolidated knowledge about them. Wentzel's suggestion that "epic" τε connotes something "known" ("*bekannt*," 1847:2), Gonda's translation "you know" for some Homeric τε (1954:207), and, finally, Bloch's translation of τε "*bekanntlich*" (1955:147) hint at this. The idea of shared knowledge in fact can explain Homeric instances of non-copulative τε attached to non-permanent states of affairs, and instances of τε in clauses whose digressive character is questionable.[87] Here is an example:

(t24)

αἲ γὰρ ἐμοὶ τοσσήνδε θεοὶ δύναμιν περιθεῖεν,
τείσασθαι μνηστῆρας ὑπερβασίης ἀλεγεινῆς,
οἵ <u>τέ</u> μοι ὑβρίζοντες ἀτάσθαλα μηχανόωνται.

Homer *Odyssey* 3.205-207

O that the gods would clothe me with such strength, that I might take vengeance on the wooers for their grievous sin, who in wantonness devise mischief against me. (tr. Murray)

86 See above §11, as well as below §58; 2.3.2; §78 about τε; §§103-104; 2.4.6 about καί. We borrow "enrichment" from Carston's analysis of *and* (2002:227).

87 See Ruijgh's wording "*digressif-permanent*" (1971:1) for the use of how "epic" τε couples permanence of content with digression in narration. Digressing in narrative is commonly associated with providing backgrounding or with statements that are temporally unbound. "A digression, by its very name, is not bound by the constraints which limit the set of Relevant and Informative messages" (Giora 1990:300; capitals in the text).

Telemachus is speaking to Nestor. The propositional content of the relative clause is not a permanent fact, and it is unlikely to preface Telemachus' intention to digress. What τε could signal in this clause, conversely, is the articulation of shared knowledge about the suitors' mischief.[88]

§55. Further adverbial functions of τε in Homer, besides the construction "relative pronoun + τε," are connected either with the encyclopedic world of myths, or with sayings and proverbs, all of which represent shared knowledge. The following two examples feature the combinations καί τε and δέ τε.[89]

§56. The first passage regards sayings and proverbs:

(t25)

> ... οὔ μιν ἔγωγε
> φεύξομαι ἐκ πολέμοιο δυσηχέος, ἀλλὰ μάλ' ἄντην
> στήσομαι, ἤ κε φέρῃσι μέγα κράτος, ἦ κε φεροίμην.
> ξυνὸς Ἐνυάλιος, <u>καί τε</u> κτανέοντα κατέκτα.
> Ὣς Ἕκτωρ ἀγόρευ', ...

Homer *Iliad* 18.306-310

88 Speaker, interlocutor, and narrator are certainly part of the community sharing this knowledge. A further level on which shared knowledge can be incorporated in the text concerns the audience; recipients of epic stories represent the larger community of individuals sharing an entire tradition of known facts and actions. Ruijgh's comparison between epic τε-clauses and epithets (1971:27) indirectly confirms that. II.4 discusses the cognitive function of particles that, in the epic genre, signpost the accessing of tradition as discourse memory.

To further support the reading of (t24), I add a parallel that regards another resentful relative clause. Three times in the *Iliad* Agamemnon is defined by either Achilles or Patroclus as the one who "did no honor to the best of the Achaeans" (ὅ τ' ἄριστον Ἀχαιῶν οὐδὲν ἔτισεν, Homer *Iliad* 1.412 and 16.274; at 1.244 Achilles directly addresses Agamemnon: ὅ τ' ἄριστον Ἀχαιῶν οὐδὲν ἔτισας). Agamemnon's refusal to recompense Achilles happens at a certain point in the story and in a certain context. Also, all three occurrences of this relative clause appear after the mention of the sorrow or madness Agamemnon is driven to *as* he did not honor Achilles: γνῷ δὲ καὶ Ἀτρεΐδης εὐρὺ κρείων Ἀγαμέμνων / ἣν ἄτην ὅ τ' ἄριστον Ἀχαιῶν οὐδὲν ἔτισεν (Homer *Iliad* 1.411-412; 16.273-274); σὺ δ' ἔνδοθι θυμὸν ἀμύξεις / χωόμενος ὅ τ' ἄριστον Ἀχαιῶν οὐδὲν ἔτισας (Homer *Iliad* 1.243-244). The piece of information provided by the relative clause is a crucial part of the point the speaker wants to make. Ruijgh (1971:814-815) takes these passages as evidence supporting the view that holds that ὅ τε should always be read ὅτε (temporal conjunction)—see 1971:810-823 section "*La conjonction chimérique* ὅ τε." This would explain the temporal or clausal nuance of the purportedly relative clause, which would not fit the indication of permanent facts. *LSJ* offers a similar reading (s.v. ὅτε, II "introducing the reason for making a statement or asking a question"). Our suggestion about τε marking shared knowledge encompasses relative clauses with temporal or causal nuances beyond the form ὅ.

89 A table summarizing the occurrences of combinations involving δέ, τε and καί in the works of our corpus is available at the end of this chapter.

[Hector speaking] "I verily will not flee from him out of dolorous war, but face to face will I stand against him, whether he shall win great victory, or haply I. Alike to all is the god of war, and lo, he slayeth him that would slay." So Hector addressed their gathering, ... (tr. Murray)

In the final part of his speech to his fellow Poulydamas, Hector considers a direct attack on Achilles, and the possibility that either he or Achilles wins. He backs up his thought by affirming the impartiality of Ares, who can compensate a slaying by cutting down the one who slew. The enrichment of καί in this case consists in "in fact"; the pragmatic function of the particle is to introduce an illustration of the gnomic statement ξυνὸς Ἐνυάλιος (see below the section on καί). τε stresses the shared-knowledge, common-knowledge aspect of such sayings.[90]

§57. The second passage regards the encycopledic/cultural knowledge of myths:

(t26)

τῆς ἦ τοι πόδες εἰσὶ δυώδεκα πάντες ἄωροι,
ἓξ <u>δέ τέ</u> οἱ δειραὶ περιμήκεες, ἐν δὲ ἑκάστῃ
σμερδαλέη κεφαλή, ἐν δὲ τρίστοιχοι ὀδόντες,
πυκνοὶ καὶ θαμέες, πλεῖοι μέλανος θανάτοιο.

Homer *Odyssey* 12.89-92

[Circe speaking] Verily she [Scylla] has twelve feet, all misshapen, and six necks, exceeding long, and on each one an awful head, and therein three rows of teeth, thick and close, and full of black death. (tr. Murray)

The description of the monster's necks, head, and teeth fits traditional knowledge, with τε signposting its overall recall, and multiple δέ marking each detail. In the *Iliad* the

90 Edwards (1991:182) notes the wordplay around the sounds 'kt' and quotes *Iliad* 11.410 and 22.253 as parallels. I believe that the artful assonance of καί τε κτανέοντα κατέκτα fits the idea of a saying. At *Iliad* 23.590 double τε occur after two different coordinating conjunctions, possibly marking shared knowledge in a gnomic statement: κραιπνότερος μὲν γάρ τε νόος, λεπτὴ δέ τε μῆτις ("for [in a young man] thought is quicker, but guile is thin"). Further gnomic sentences in Homer contain γάρ τε, for example *Odyssey* 7.294 αἰεὶ γάρ τε νεώτεροι ἀφραδέουσιν ("for younger men always behave thoughtlessly"). In those cases the marking of common knowledge possibly deriving from τε nicely matches the insertion of story-world information or *gnômai* signaled by γάρ (on which see II.4 §21-22). Hesiodic poetry employs δέ τε in proverbial lines—the knowledge of which is quintessentially shared—in *Works and Days* 609, 818 and 824; the latter (ἄλλος δ' ἀλλοίην αἰνεῖ, παῦροι δὲ τε ἴσασιν) does not include τ' in Solmsen's edition (Solmsen and Merkelbach ed. 1970). III.2 §43 discusses an instance of τε in Euripides concerning swearing an oath.

combination δέ τε almost always occurs in similes.[91] Similes quintessentially contain encyclopedic or cultural knowledge that are shared through traditional poetry. The role of particles in similes is extensively discussed in II.4.3. The epic instances singled out in the current paragraphs complement the analyses included in II.4, but most of all they are instrumental to the upcoming argument about τε in Herodotus and Thucydides.

§58. The discourse functions of τε in the two *Histories* overall can be assessed as follows: (1) they presuppose familiarity with the epic genre and τε as one of its features.[92] (2) A significant portion of instances reveals a connection with encyclopedic knowledge essential to historical and geographical accounts. Especially in Herodotus this knowledge comprises myths as well. (3) The shared-knowledge attitude is conveyed almost exclusively by τε in its connective role. In other words, the pragmatic meaning related to shared knowledge is largely an enrichment of copulative τε. These aspects define the historiographical uses of τε in Herodotus and Thucydides. The next paragraphs detail them.

§59. The analysis starts with instances of τε that challenge standard grammatical interpretations. Consider this passage from Herodotus:

(t27)

... καὶ ὡς ἐγὼ συμβάλλομαι ... τῷ Ἴστρῳ ἐκ τῶν ἴσων μέτρων ὁρμᾶται. Ἴστρος <u>τε</u> γὰρ ποταμὸς ἀρξάμενος ἐκ Κελτῶν ... ῥέει ...

Herodotus 2.33.2-3

... and as I guess, ... it [the Nile] rises proportionally as far away as does the Ister. For the Ister flows from the land of the Celts ... (tr. Godley)

Lloyd (1989:258) notes that τε does not correspond with a καί here, but is answered by δέ later on, in the clause περὶ δὲ τῶν τοῦ Νείλου πηγέων (chapter 34). However, between Ἴστρος τε γὰρ (...) and περὶ δὲ τῶν (...) no fewer than 64 words occur, including three δέ, two γάρ, one μὲν δή, and one καί. Interpreting τε as a marker of shared knowledge about the river is a more economical solution, especially because it is placed adjacent to the river's name (I shall say more about τε and names).[93] In this passage γάρ may serve as a

[91] In fact, the combination δέ τε must be particularly old. The metrical analyses of the *Iliad* proposed by Eva Tichy (see the link https://www.freidok.uni-freiburg.de/pers/15752) reveals that δέ τε occurs in older rather than newer lines, where older means that they show traces of pre-hexametrical choriambs. I thank Eva Tichy for sharing her thoughts about Homeric δέ τε and καί τε.

[92] Tragic and comic choral songs show evidence of this presupposition as well. The relatively high frequency of τε contributes to their formal and ritual code. See III.2 §§44 and 47-48.

[93] In line with this argument, I do not think that an *and*-coordination is needed in interpreting Herodotus 9.57.2 περὶ ποταμὸν Μολόεντα ἱδρυμένον Ἀργιόπιόν τε χῶρον καλεόμενον, τῇ καὶ

further signal of the fact that some encyclopedic knowledge is incorporated at this point, to make the argument more compelling.[94]

§60. The next passage is from Thucydides:

(t28)

Κερκυραῖοι δὲ ἐπειδὴ ᾔσθοντο τούς τε οἰκήτορας καὶ φρουροὺς ἥκοντας ἐς τὴν Ἐπίδαμνον τήν τε ἀποικίαν Κορινθίοις δεδομένην, ἐχαλέπαινον·

Thucydides 1.26.3

When the Corcyraeans learnt of the arrival of settlers and troops at Epidamnus, and the handover of the colony to Corinth, their reaction was angry. (tr. Hammond)

The Corcyraeans are annoyed by the arrival of Corinthian settlers and troops in Epidamnus. They are also annoyed by the handover of Epidamnus to Corinth. The first τε signals a τε ... καί phrasal coordination between τούς οἰκήτορας and φρουρούς. From Hammond's translation it can be inferred that he interprets the second τε as a means to coordinate the two participles (ἥκοντας and δεδομένην) governed by ᾔσθοντο ("they realized"). A different grammatical reading is possible: τήν τε ἀποικίαν Κορινθίοις δεδομένην is an apposition of Ἐπίδαμνον,[95] and the discourse function of τε is to expand on Epidamnus by introducing a piece of shared knowledge about the handover.[96]

Δήμητρος Ἐλευσινίης ἱρὸν ἧστα, which Godley translates, "by the stream Molois *and* the place called Argiopium, where there is a shrine of Eleusinian Demeter" (my emphasis). τε may just mark encyclopedic knowledge about the area where the river is located—"by the stream Molois in the Argiopium area."

94 Both historians use τε γάρ (43 occurrences in Herodotus; 75 in Thucydides) mostly in a coordinating construction where γάρ has scope over the entire sentence, and the τε constituent is usually answered by a καί constituent. However, the coordinating function does not preclude an additional force related to encyclopedic knowledge, as in Herodotus 4.47.1 ἥ τε γὰρ γῆ ἐοῦσα πεδιὰς αὕτη ποιώδης τε καὶ εὔυδρός ἐστι, ποταμοί τε δι' αὐτῆς ῥέουσι ... "for their country is flat and grassy and well-watered, and rivers run through it (...). See above n90 for instances of τε γάρ in gnomic/proverbial contexts. On "anacoluthic" τε γάρ see Klotz 1842:749-750.

95 For appositions with τε (even if followed by καί), see Herodotus 3.70.1 Ὁ δὲ Ὀτάνης παραλαβὼν Ἀσπαθίνην καὶ Γωβρύην, Περσέων τε πρώτους ἐόντας καὶ ἑωυτῷ ἐπιτηδεοτάτους ἐς πίστιν ... "Otanes then took aside two Persians of the highest rank whom he thought worthiest of trust, Aspathines and Gobryas (...)."

96 It is not infrequent to find in both *Histories* an article/weak demonstrative followed by τε resembling "epic" τε after relative pronouns. See for instance Herodotus 1.74.6 Ὅρκια δὲ ποιέεται ταῦτα τὰ ἔθνεα τά πέρ τε Ἕλληνες ... "These nations make sworn compacts as do the Greeks." As for Thucydides, such τε regularly are either answered by καί or they link the previous sentence through coordination, but the contents suggest an overlapping function where geographical or historiographical knowledge is shared: e.g. 2.15.4 τό τε τοῦ Διὸς τοῦ Ὀλυμπίου καὶ τὸ Πύθιον καὶ τὸ τῆς Γῆς ...; 2.17.2 τό τε Πελαργικὸν καλούμενον τὸ ὑπὸ τὴν ἀκρόπολιν, ...; 1.104.2 καὶ

Accordingly, I translate: "The Corcyreans, when they realized that settlers as well as troops had arrived in Epidamnus—the colony passed to the Corinthians—had an angry reaction." This reading explains more satisfactorily the position of ἐς τὴν Ἐπίδαμνον, which would work better before ἥκοντας (τούς τε ... ἥκοντας, τήν τε ... δεδομένην) if τε had a coordinating function. Most of all, this reading better explains the reaction of the Corcyraeans. The text suggests that the Corcyraeans, rather than simply learning about the handover, as in Hammond's translation, already knew about it, and their anger is aroused by their discovery that material support had arrived from Corinth. τήν τε ἀποικίαν Κορινθίοις δεδομένην inserts a piece of information that seems to be shared not only among the Corcyraeans, but also by writer and readers.

§61. Even when τε is performing a copulative function (either in a τε ... καί construction or by connecting two clauses by itself), it can simultaneously imply the idea of shared knowledge. That is, an enriched (adverbial) understanding of τε is compatible with its syndetic role.[97] I can see this dual function occurring, for example, in this passage from Thucydides:

(t29)

ἔτη δ' ἐστὶ μάλιστα τριακόσια ἐς τὴν τελευτὴν τοῦδε τοῦ πολέμου ὅτε Ἀμεινοκλῆς Σαμίοις ἦλθεν. ναυμαχία <u>τε</u> παλαιτάτη ὧν ἴσμεν γίγνεται Κορινθίων πρὸς Κερκυραίους· ἔτη δὲ μάλιστα καὶ ταύτῃ ἑξήκοντα καὶ διακόσιά ἐστι μέχρι τοῦ αὐτοῦ χρόνου.

Thucydides 1.13.3-4

It is three hundred years up to the end of this war, since Ameinocles visited the Samians. The oldest sea-battle of which we know is that between the

ἀναπλεύσαντες ἀπὸ θαλάσσης ἐς τὸν Νεῖλον τοῦ τε ποταμοῦ κρατοῦντες καὶ τῆς Μέμφιδος ...; 1.2.2 ἥ τε νῦν Θεσσαλία καλουμένη καὶ Βοιωτία ...; 1.12.2 ἥ τε γὰρ ἀναχώρησις τῶν Ἑλλήνων ἐξ Ἰλίου χρονία γενομένη πολλὰ ἐνεόχμωσε, καὶ στάσεις ἐν ταῖς πόλεσιν ὡς ἐπὶ πολὺ ἐγίγνοντο. In his monograph, Hammer records examples of 'epic' τε in Herodotus (1904:36-38), and—in fact—analogous cases in Xenophon (1904:84).

97 See Mithun's quote in §4. A significant analogy—albeit dealing with a different grammatical item, and with no explicit mention of pragmatic values—can be found in Hoffmann's arguments about injunctive in Veda (Hoffmann 1967). The author opts for an enriched understanding of that mood by associating a general attitude of the speaker with its use. Besides the semantic and syntactic functions, in Veda the injunctive mood implies the intention to "mention/reference" ("*erwähnen*") as opposed to that of "report/give an account" ("*berichten*"; see Hoffmann 1967:163; 266-267). What makes this idea even closer to our proposal about τε is that Hoffmann, at the very end of the monograph (1967: 279) pins down the main function of the injunctive mood ("to mention") by calling it "commemorative": "*Die Hauptfunktion des Injunktivs ist also die Erwähnung: seine sachgemäße Benennung wäre demnach Memorativ.*" I thank David Goldstein for drawing my attention to this parallel.

> Corinthians and the Corcyraeans. As for the latter, it is two hundred and sixty years up to the same time. (tr. AB)

τε works as an *and* connecting the preceding clauses (ἔτη δ᾽ ἐστὶ ... ἦλθεν) to the following (ναυμαχία τε ... Κερκυραίους). At the same time τε signals that the information given is generally known.[98] Along the continuum between copulative *and* without any enrichment, and τε marking shared knowledge after relative pronouns, this τε is situated in the middle.

§62. The association of Homeric copulative τε with "natural" rather than "accidental" coordination by Viti (2006 and 2008) indirectly adds to the point of τε's continuum. "Natural" and "accidental" coordination are terms that Viti borrows from Wälchli (Wälchli 2005:5).[99] While "natural" coordination applies to conjuncts that are expected to co-occur, "accidental" coordination combines items that are accidentally related on a contextual base. Consider, for example, "land and sea" versus "the soil and the cherry tree." Viti argues that the copulative functions of τε in Homer largely deal with "natural" rather than "accidental" coordination. By comparing τε and καί in book 1 of the *Iliad* and book 1 of the *Odyssey*, she demonstrates that in Homer τε relates more to phrases, and καί more to clauses; τε relates more to nouns, and καί more to verbs, τε relates more to symmetrical, and καί more to asymmetrical expressions; finally, τε relates to static or contemporary situations, and καί more to progression. The same holds for *ca* in Vedic, and *-que* in Latin.[100] A good example of τε marking natural coordination is ἀνδρῶν τε θεῶν τε.[101] In that case τε appears in a bisyndetic construction involving noun phrases. Overall, the idea of natural coordination associated with several instances of τε in Homeric epic implies the following: a coordinating function can be combined with a joint semantic function of the two conjuncts. This thought fits the idea of a continuum: a connecting *and* is enriched by the implication "these two items are expected to occur together."

§63. In II.4 (about Homer and Pindar) and here (about Herodotus and Thucydides), a further step is proposed: what is "natural" to associate in a coordinating construction is

98 Later in chapter 13 of book 1 a further τε potentially serves two functions: the Corinthians are said to always have been involved with commerce, and to be capable of wealth. The information about wealth is marked by τε, and it is followed by a note about the poets who know that, as they call the area "rich": οἱ Κορίνθιοι ἐπὶ τοῦ Ἰσθμοῦ αἰεὶ δή ποτε ἐμπόριον εἶχον, ... χρήμασί τε δυνατοὶ ἦσαν, ὡς καὶ τοῖς παλαιοῖς ποιηταῖς δεδήλωται· ἀφνειὸν γὰρ ἐπωνόμασαν τὸ χωρίον "Corinth, being seated on an isthmus, was naturally from the first a centre of commerce .... Her wealth too was a source of power, as the ancient poets testify, who speak of 'Corinth the rich'" (Thucydides 1.13.5; tr. Jowett).

99 These notions are also discussed in II.4 §§60-61 along with Wälchli's definition.

100 Numbers and percentages appear in Tables 1 to 6 in Viti 2006.

101 Homer *Iliad* 1.544; 4.68; 5.426; 8.49 and 132; 11.182; 15.12 and 47; 16.458; 20.56; 22.167; 24.103; *Odyssey* 1.28 and 338; 12.445; 18.137. As for the use of τε for things that are naturally coupled ("naturellement couplés"), see also Humbert 1960:435-436.

a piece of encyclopedic or experiential or cultural knowledge that is shared by a collectivity. Let us consider the following Herodotean passage including bisyndetic τε:

(t30)

Ὁ μὲν δὴ Κλεομένης, ὡς λέγεται, ἦν τε οὐ φρενήρης ἀκρομανής τε, ὁ δὲ Δωριεὺς ἦν ...

Herodotus 5.42.1

Now Cleomenes, as the story goes, was not in his right mind and really quite mad, while Dorieus was ...

This is how Herodotus in book 5 sums up the personality of Cleomenes, unscrupulous but also brilliant king of Sparta, before moving on to Cleomenes' half-brother Dorieus. The passage features a peculiar example of bisyndetic τε in Herodotus. The peculiarity springs from the connection between two adjectival phrases (bisyndetic τε in Herodotus usually involves verbal phrases or clauses), and from the chiasmus τε—adjective—adjective—τε. The two τε can be interpreted as connective and "epic" at the same time: they associate quasi-synonyms, and they qualify the characterization of Cleomenes' personality as something known, a piece of knowledge presumably shared by the community—the phrase might even evoke a saying about him. ὡς λέγεται, which alludes to the circulation of information, reinforces this shared-knowledge function of τε.[102]

§64. The clearest cases of τε where the coordinating and the shared-knowledge adverbial roles fully coexist are lists of names, either of people or places. Let us first cite an example of that from the oldest surviving drama by Aeschylus:

(t31)

Μαγνητικὴν δὲ γαῖαν ἔς τε Μακεδόνων
χώραν ἀφικόμεσθ', ἐπ' Ἀξιοῦ πόρον,
Βόλβης θ' ἕλειον δόνακα Πάγγαιόν τ' ὄρος,
Ἠδωνίδ' αἶαν· ...

Aeschylus *Persians* 492-495

[Messenger] Then we reached the land of Magnesia and entered the country of the Macedonians, coming to the river Axius, the reed-swamps of Lake Bolbe, and Mount Pangaeum, in the land of Edonia... (tr. Sommerstein)

102 Separately, τε and noun phrases have their highest frequency in tragic and comic songs (see III.2 §46), which increases the chance that they occur together.

The messenger is recalling different landmarks on the route from Athens to Susa. These places and their names were important to Aeschylus' audience.[103] Through τε the language combines coordination with a shared-knowledge attitude, and perhaps also with a reminiscence of the epic genre.[104]

§65. Let us now switch to historiography. Some of the uses of τε in Herodotus and Thucydides involve encyclopedic knowledge, as befits a genre that has to incorporate a large number of personal and place names.[105] The very use of τε can imbue the conjuncts with an air of being widely known. Consider this example from Herodotus, one of many in the *Histories* that recall Aeschylus' method of listing places:

(t32)

Οὗτος δὲ Κυαξάρῃ τε τῷ Δηιόκεω ἀπογόνῳ ἐπολέμησε <u>καὶ</u> Μήδοισι, Κιμμερίους <u>τε</u> ἐκ τῆς Ἀσίης ἐξήλασε, Σμύρνην <u>τε</u> τὴν ἀπὸ Κολοφῶνος κτισθεῖσαν εἷλε, ἐς Κλαζομενάς <u>τε</u> ἐσέβαλε.

Herodotus 1.16.2

... [Alyattes] who waged war against Deioces' descendant Cyaxares and the Medes, drove the Cimmerians out of Asia, took Smyrna (which was a colony from Colophon), and invaded the lands of Clazomenae.[106]

During the account of the Lydian kingdom from Gyges to Croesus (1.6-29) the historian introduces Alyattes (Croesus' father), who succeeded king Sadyattes (1.16.1). The first τε in the excerpt signposts the coordination between king Cyaxares and his people, the Medes (Κυαξάρῃ τε ... καὶ Μήδοισι). The remaining τε coordinate clauses that summarizes further major endeavors of Alyattes. Notably, together with their syntactic function of coordinating conjunctions, all these τε occur near names (the Cimmerians, Smyrna, and

103 See Hall 1996:144. Broadhead 1960: 137-138 notes that there is a curious *hýsteron próteron* in space and time: geographically, from Greece comes the Edonian territory first and then mount Pangaeus, but here the order is inverted. On the messenger's voice resembling that of an epic narrator, see Barrett 2002:xvi-xvii.

104 III.2 §44 comments on an Aristophanic passage where the repeated use of τε in association with names alludes to the epic genre, and has a parodic effect.

105 See Cooper 2002:3116, who sees an idiomatic use of adverbial τε when it is used "in anatomical or geographical descriptions"; in that case τε, according to Cooper, expresses "clear perception" rather than generalization. I remind here the reader of Wentzel's remark that τε may indicate well-known phenomena ("*allbekannte Erscheinungen*") regarding nature, human beings, gods, animals, or qualities and properties of objects and individuals; also, it can be used in describing lands and items ("*Länder und Sache*"). See above §52. A connection between τε and names appears in Kühner and Gerth (1955:236).

106 I could not find notes in the commentaries about τε in this and in other passages, understandably because its use is not grammatically problematic, and because attention in such cases falls on the names.

Clazomenae, respectively). The degree of sharedness of this historical and geographical information cannot be established with precision; however, it is unlikely that Herodotus invents the information or presents it as something unheard of.[107]

§66. Thucydides, who uses τε more frequently than Herodotus,[108] associates the particle with names of people and places as well, both in τε ... καί constructions and in constructions termed "sentential" τε (about which more later).[109] In order to check how frequently τε is used with names, I chose the combination τε καί as a sample. Unlike τε ... καί, τε καί largely connects noun phrases, and it occurs 866 times in Herodotus, against 343 times in Thucydides. The higher count in Herodotus may suggest that he prefers to add τε to καί in connection with nouns or noun phrases.[110] A more important result, however, concerns the frequency with names: in 285 cases one or both conjuncts are names in Herodotus (32.9%), against fifty (14.5%) in Thucydides.

§67. A parallel count, to see whether the presence of τε makes a difference in that frequency, regards how many times καί alone in book 1 of the two works relates to names. Out of 1,175 instances in Herodotus 1, this use of καί happens 77 times (6.5%), while out of 1,453 καί in Thucydides 1 it happens 136 times (9.35%). Therefore, Herodotus uses τε with names more often than Thucydides, and Thucydides uses καί alone with names more often than Herodotus.

§68. A further analysis concerns whether τε καί appears in what Viti would call "natural coordination" (what I have presented as "encyclopedic/cultural shared knowledge") more in Herodotus than in Thucydides. Indeed, cases where, according to our interpretation, two items are coupled on the basis of a semantic association that depends more on general rather than on context-specific knowledge, are proportionally higher in Herodotus[111] than

[107] On Herodotus' sources for the account of the Lydian kings, see Pedley ed. 1972:22-25 and Asheri 1988:266-274.

[108] τε in Thucydides represents 1.70% of total words (one τε every 58 words on average), against 1.47% in Herodotus (one τε every 68 words). In our corpus the highest frequency of τε occurs in Pindar (2.11% of total words).

[109] See, for example, 1.9.1 (Ἀγαμέμνων τε μοι δοκεῖ ...); 1.9.2 (Πελοπά τε πρῶτον ...); 1.13.6 (Φωκαῆς τε Μασσαλίαν οἰκίζοντες Καρχηδονίους ἐνίκων ναυμαχοῦντες).

[110] Except for Hoogeveen 1769 and Gonda 1954, it is commonly assumed that τε in the combination τε καί (without intervening words) is superfluous.

[111] This and the next exceptionally long notes are meant to let the reader directly infer the kind of general knowledge emerging from the actual instances (104 in Herodotus vs. 44 in Thucydides). See Herodotus 1.17.1 ὑπὸ συρίγγων τε καὶ πηκτίδων and αὐλοῦ γυναικηίου τε καὶ ἀνδρηίου; 1.31.1 Κλέοβίν τε καὶ Βίτωνα (and 1.31.4 Κλεόβι τε καὶ Βίτωνι); 1.31.5 ὡς ἔθυσάν τε καὶ εὐωχήθησαν; 1.35.2 ἐπυνθάνετο ὁκόθεν τε καὶ τίς εἴη; 1.51.1 χρύσεόν τε καὶ ἀργύρεον; 1.59.6 καλῶς τε καὶ εὖ; 1.80.2 σιτοφόροι τε καὶ σκευοφόροι κάμηλοι; 1.88.3 φέρουσί τε καὶ ἄγουσι; 1.100.2 οἱ κατάσκοποί τε καὶ κατήκοοι; 1.121 πατέρα τε καὶ μητέρα; 1.128.2 νέους τε καὶ πρεσβύτας ἄνδρας; 1.129.1 κατέχαιρέ τε καὶ κατεκερτόμεε; 1.134.3 ἄρχον τε καὶ ἐπιτροπεῦον; 1.137.1 πλέω τε καὶ μέζω; 1.142.2 τὰ μὲν ὑπὸ τοῦ ψυχροῦ τε καὶ ὑγροῦ πιεζόμενα, τὰ δὲ ὑπὸ τοῦ θερμοῦ τε καὶ αὐχμώδεος; 1.165.3 πόθος τε καὶ οἶκτος; 1.186.2 σιδήρῳ τε καὶ μολύβδῳ; 1.201 πρὸς ἠῶ τε καὶ ἡλίου ἀνατολάς; 1.204.1 πρὸς ἠῶ τε καὶ ἥλιον ἀνατέλλοντα; 1.215.1 τοξόται τε καὶ αἰχμοφόροι; 2.4.2 βωμούς τε καὶ ἀγάλματα καὶ νηοὺς; 2.26.2 ὁ βορέης τε καὶ ὁ χειμὼν; 2.32.5 ὕδατί τε καὶ σιτίοισι εὖ ἐξηρτυμένους;

in Thucydides.[112] A final investigation regards how many instances of bisyndetic τε are found in the two works. In Herodotus the construction involves noun phrases as well as verbal phrases; interestingly enough, in ἤν τε ... ἤν τε ... the conjuncts tend to be short and symmetrical (syntactically and semantically).[113] Thucydides, conversely, who in general

---

2.35.2 ἤθεά τε καὶ νόμους; 2.35.5 πάντων τε καὶ πασέων; 2.42.2 Ἶσιός τε καὶ Ὀσίριος; 2.53.1 πρώην τε καὶ χθὲς; 2.53.3 τὰ ἐς Ἡσίοδόν τε καὶ Ὅμηρον ἔχοντα; 2.78 πῖνέ τε καὶ τέρπεο; 2.82.1 μείς τε καὶ ἡμέρη ἑκάστη; 2.113.3 περὶ τὴν Ἑλένην τε καὶ τὴν ἐς Μενέλεων ἀδικίην; 2.149.1 πρὸς βορέην τε καὶ νότον; 3.1.1 ἀποσπάσας ἀπὸ γυναικός τε καὶ τέκνων; 3.14.3 βοῇ τε καὶ κλαυθμῷ; 3.48.3 χοροὺς παρθένων τε καὶ ἠιθέων and τρωκτὰ σησάμου τε καὶ μέλιτος; 3.100 ἕψουσί τε καὶ σιτέονται; 3.119 τὸν ἄνδρα τε καὶ τὰ τέκνα; 4.132 γῆν τε καὶ ὕδωρ, (=5.18 twice; 5.17; 5.73; 6.48; 6.49; 6.94; 7.32; 7.163); 4.139 ἔργα τε καὶ ἔπεα; 4.142 κακίστους τε καὶ ἀνανδροτάτους; 4.180 λίθοισί τε καὶ ξύλοισι; 4.186 κρεοφάγοι τε καὶ γαλακτοπόται; 4.191 θηριωδεστέρη τε καὶ δασυτέρη; 4.199 ἀμᾶσθαί τε καὶ τρυγᾶσθαι; 4.205 τοιαύτη τε καὶ τοσαύτη; 5.14 τὰ τέκνα τε καὶ τὰς γυναῖκας; 5.24 συνετός τε καὶ εὔνοος; 5.31 καλή τε καὶ ἀγαθή; 5.45 τέμενός τε καὶ νηὸν; 5.58 αἰγέῃσί τε καὶ οἰέῃσι; 5.61 ἱρόν τε καὶ ὄργια; 5.67 θυσίας τε καὶ ὁρτὰς; 5.75 μετεβάλλοντό τε καὶ ἀπαλλάσσοντο; 6.11 μαλακίῃ τε καὶ ἀταξίῃ; 6.19 ὁ νηός τε καὶ τὸ χρηστήριον; 6.38 ἀγῶνα ἱππικόν τε καὶ γυμνικὸν; 6.42 φέροιέν τε καὶ ἄγοιεν; 6.56 τὰ δέρματά τε καὶ τὰ νῶτα; 6.58 ἄνδρα τε καὶ γυναῖκα; 6.83 ἄρχοντές τε καὶ διέποντες; 6.109 Ἁρμόδιός τε καὶ Ἀριστογείτων (=6.23); 6.137 ὑπὸ ὕβριός τε καὶ ὀλιγωρίης; 7.8 τιμωρίην τε καὶ τίσιν; 7.49 γῆ τε καὶ θάλασσα; 7.104 ἄπολίν τε καὶ φυγάδα; 7.201 ἀναιδείῃ τε καὶ ἀβουλίῃ 8.60 τέκνα τε καὶ γυναῖκες; 8.71 οὔτε νυκτὸ οὔτε ἡμέρης; 8.70.2 δέος τε καὶ ἀρρωδίη; 8.98.1 ἵππος τε καὶ ἀνὴρ τεταγμένος and ἵπποι τε καὶ ἄνδρες; 8.99 βοῇ τε καὶ οἰμωγῇ; 8.99 ἐν θαλίῃσί τε καὶ εὐπαθείῃσι; 8.100.2 ἀνδρῶν τε καὶ ἵππων; 8.100.3 νῦν τε καὶ πρότερον; 8.101 ἐχάρη τε καὶ ἥσθη; 8.109.3 θεοί τε καὶ ἥρωες; 8.108.3 κατὰ πόλις τε καὶ κατὰ ἔθνεα; 8.109 ἀνόσιόν τε καὶ ἀτάσθαλον; 8.110.1 σοφός τε καὶ εὔβουλος; 8.111.3 Πενίην τε καὶ Ἀμηχανίην; 8.113.3 στρεπτοφόρους τε καὶ ψελιοφόρους; 8.140 ἄνευ τε δόλου καὶ ἀπάτης; 8.144 ὅμαιμόν τε καὶ ὁμόγλωσσον; 9.21 λιπαρίῃ τε καὶ ἀρετῇ; 9.27 παλαιά τε καὶ καινὰ; 9.59 βοῇ τε καὶ ὁμίλῳ; 9.70.2 ἀρετῇ τε καὶ λιπαρίῃ; 9.80.1 κρητῆράς τε χρυσέους καὶ φιάλας τε καὶ ἄλλα ἐκπώματα; 9.80.2 χρύσεοί τε καὶ ἀργύρεοι; 9.80.2 ψέλιά τε καὶ στρεπτοὺς καὶ τοὺς ἀκινάκας; 9.82.1 χρυσῷ τε καὶ ἀργύρῳ; 9.92 πίστιν τε καὶ ὅρκια ἐποιεῦντο; 9.102.1 αἰγιαλόν τε καὶ ἄπεδον; 9.116.2 τάφος τε καὶ τέμενος.

112 See Thucydides 1.30.4 ναυσί τε καὶ πεζῷ (=3.13.4); 1.49.1 τοξότας τε καὶ ἀκοντιστάς; 1.90.3 ἀναχώρησίν τε καὶ ἀφορμὴν; 1.126.10 σίτου τε καὶ ὕδατος ἀπορίᾳ; 1.139.4 λέγειν τε καὶ πράσσειν; 2.4.2 κραυγῇ τε καὶ ὀλολυγῇ χρωμένων λίθοις τε καὶ κεράμῳ; 2.6.3 νενικημένων τε καὶ ξυνειλημμένων; 2.27.1 αὐτούς τε καὶ παῖδας καὶ γυναῖκας; 2.29.6 ἱππέων τε καὶ πελταστῶν; 2.35.3 βουλήσεώς τε καὶ δόξης; 2.75.3 ὕπνον τε καὶ σῖτον; 2.84.3 ἀντιφυλακῇ τε καὶ λοιδορίᾳ; 2.95.3 ναυσί τε καὶ στρατιᾷ; 2.97.3 χρυσοῦ τε καὶ ἀργύρου, and ὑφαντά τε καὶ λεῖα; 3.23.2 ἐτόξευόν τε καὶ ἠκόντιζον; 3.23.4 ἐτόξευόν τε καὶ ἐσηκόντιζον; 3.42.1 τάχος τε καὶ ὀργήν; 3.70.6 φίλους τε καὶ ἐχθροὺς; 3.97.3 διώξεις τε καὶ ὑπαγωγαί; 3.104.3 πυγμαχίῃ τε καὶ ὀρχηστυῖ καὶ ἀοιδῇ; 4.3.2 ξύλων τε καὶ λίθων; 4.8.6 ὑλώδης τε καὶ ἀτριβὴς; 4.12.3 τοῖς δὲ θαλασσίοις τε καὶ ταῖς ναυσὶ; 4.24.4 πεζῇ τε καὶ ναυσὶν; 4.34.1 λίθοις τε καὶ τοξεύμασι καὶ ἀκοντίοις; 4.69.2 τάφρον τε καὶ τείχη; 4.102.3 ἐς θάλασσάν τε καὶ τὴν ἤπειρον; 5.16.1 εὐτυχεῖν τε καὶ τιμᾶσθαι; 5.64.3 τὸ πρεσβύτερόν τε καὶ τὸ νεώτερον; 5.103.2 μαντικήν τε καὶ χρησμοὺς; 6.32.1 χρυσοῖς τε καὶ ἀργυροῖς; 6.46.3 φιάλας τε καὶ οἰνοχόας; 6.66.1 τειχία τε καὶ οἰκίαι; 7.30.3 ἱππέας τε καὶ ὁπλίτας; 7.31.5 σφενδονήτας τε καὶ ἀκοντιστὰς; 7.64.2 καθ' ἑκάστους τε καὶ ξύμπαντες; 7.71.6 οἰμωγῇ τε καὶ στόνῳ; 7.75.7 ἀντὶ δ' εὐχῆς τε καὶ παιάνων; 7.83.4 σίτου τε καὶ τῶν ἐπιτηδείων ἀπορίᾳ; 7.84.2 βάλλοντές τε καὶ κατακοντίζοντες; 8.1.1 τοῖς χρησμολόγοις τε καὶ μάντεσι; 8.1.2 φόβος τε καὶ κατάπληξις; 8.71.1 ἔνδοθέν τε καὶ ἔξωθεν.

113 See, for example, with noun phrases: Herodotus 7.190 ἄνδρας τε ἀναριθμήτους χρημάτων τε πλῆθος ἄφθονον; 9.122 ἀνθρώπων τε πολλῶν ἄρχομεν πάσης τε τῆς Ἀσίης. With verbal phrases: 1.15 Πριηνέας τε εἷλε ἐς Μίλητόν τε ἐσέβαλε; 3.35 Πρήξασπες, ὡς μὲν ἐγώ τε οὐ μαίνομαι Πέρσαι τε παραφρονέουσι; 3.50 διαλεγομένῳ τε οὔ τι προσδιελέγετο ἱστορέοντί τε λόγον οὐδένα ἐδίδου;

likes asymmetry, employs this construction less frequently;[114] he privileges the use of τε alone with scope over an entire sentence (see below). The construction οὔτε ... οὔτε, in which the related constituents show a great deal of symmetry (but hardly any "natural" coordination), abounds in both authors.

§69. From this discussion a diachronic, and perhaps stylistic, difference across the two authors can be inferred, as far as the use of τε is concerned. Herodotus uses τε in a way that recalls epic diction; that is, bisyndetic τε with relatively short conjuncts, τε in τε καί connecting noun phrases, and τε with names to present shared knowledge. Thucydides—who, I repeat, overall employs more τε than Herodotus[115]—also recalls epic diction, especially in lists involving names of people or places, but not as frequently. This practice is in line with his other uses of *and*: he uses more often "sentential" τε, which is rare in early epic, and, in absolute terms, he uses καί much more often than Herodotus (6.7% of the total words, against 4%).

2.3.2 Further enrichments

§70. τε in Herodotus and in Thucydides typically performs a connective role. Previous analyses have shown that a pragmatic enrichment may be attached to several instances, including τε in the τε καί combinations (without intervening words). The implied meaning relates to encyclopedic and cultural knowledge, whether geographical or historical. If we were to put this enrichment into words, we would use an adverbial phrase such as "as we know" (see Bloch's "*bekanntlich*"), or even a clause ("X is known with this name"). Those constituents would work non-propositionally, that is, they would indicate how to process the names or the encyclopedic information, rather than adding content to them.

§71. τε can convey further pragmatic meanings besides those related to shared knowledge. Some of them are indicated by Gonda (1954:195). They relate to the phrasal

8.108 ἐδόκεόν τε ναυμαχήσειν σφέας παραρτέοντό τε; 7.207 αὐτοῦ τε μένειν ἐψηφίζετο πέμπειν τε ἀγγέλους ἐς τὰς πόλις. Across sentences: Herodotus 8.141 κάρτα τε ἔδεισαν μὴ ὁμολογήσωσι τῷ Πέρσῃ Ἀθηναῖοι· αὐτίκα τέ σφι ἔδοξε πέμπειν ἀγγέλους. The construction ἤν τε ... ἤν τε ... stands out for its shortness and symmetry: Herodotus 2.65 ἤν τε ἑκὼν ἤν τε ἀέκων; 3.99 ἤν τε γυνὴ ἤν τε ἀνήρ; 4.28 ἤν τε θέρεος ἤν τε χειμῶνος; 7.35 ἤν τε σύ γε βούλῃ ἤν τε μή; 7.85 ἤν τε ἵππου ἤν τε ἀνθρώπου; 7.102 ἤν τε ἐλάσσονες τούτων, ἤν τε καὶ πλέονες (cf. 7.83 οὔτε πλέονες μυρίων οὔτε ἐλάσσονες).

114 Clausal level: see, for example, Thucydides 1.8.3 οἵ τε ἥσσους ὑπέμενον τὴν τῶν κρεισσόνων δουλείαν, οἵ τε δυνατώτεροι περιουσίας ἔχοντες προσεποιοῦντο ὑπηκόους τὰς ἐλάσσους πόλεις; 1.23.1 τούτου δὲ τοῦ πολέμου μῆκός τε μέγα προύβη, παθήματά τε ξυνηνέχθη γενέσθαι ...; 1.34.3 ὥστε ἀπάτῃ τε μὴ παράγεσθαι ὑπ' αὐτῶν δεομένοις τε ἐκ τοῦ εὐθέος μὴ ὑπουργεῖν; 1.57.2 οἵ τε γὰρ Κορίνθιοι φανερῶς ἤδη διάφοροι ἦσαν, Περδίκκας τε ὁ Ἀλεξάνδρου Μακεδόνων βασιλεὺς ἐπεπολέμωτο. A complex symmetry occurs at 1.41.3 φίλον τε γὰρ ἡγοῦνται τὸν ὑπουργοῦντα, ἢν καὶ πρότερον ἐχθρὸς ᾖ, πολέμιόν τε τὸν ἀντιστάντα, ἢν καὶ τύχῃ φίλος ὤν ....

115 See above n108. Blomqvist 1974:178 asserts that τε καί survives up to the Imperial Age in set phrases.

scope of τε in different genres. In our terms they represent possible further enrichments. At least two of them resonate with enrichments of καί that will be explored in the final section of this chapter: τε meaning "but" (e.g. Homer *Iliad* 1.167 ὀλίγον τε φίλον τε, "little but dear"), and τε meaning "or" (e.g. Homer *Iliad* 1.128 τριπλῇ τε τετραπλῇ τε, "three or four times"). In these cases τε fulfills its connective role, and at the same time it implies contrast (Gonda's "adversative" meaning), or no commitment to one of the two conjuncts (Gonda's "or" meaning).[116]

§72. Here I report a Herodotean passage where τε, according to Gonda, has an adversative value:

(t33)

ὁ δὲ Κώης, οἷά τε οὐ τύραννος δημότης <u>τε</u> ἐών, αἰτέει Μυτιλήνης τυραννεῦσαι ...

Herodotus 5.11.2

But Coes, inasmuch as he was no tyrant but a plain citizen, asked that he might be made tyrant of Mytilene (tr. Godley)

After the Scythian expedition Darius retreats to Sardis, where he meets Histiaeus, tyrant of Myletus, and Coes, a military commander of the same city. Both had helped Darius by preserving a bridge over the Ister, which had allowed the Persian retreat. To thank them Darius asks what they want as compensation. Histiaeus asks to rule over the area of Myrcinus, whereas Coes asks to rule Mytilene (topic of (t33)).[117] οὐ τύραννος δημότης τε ἐών clearly sets a contrast, which rests on the semantic opposition between τύραννος and δημότης. But the contribution of τε in this co-text does not need to be that of an adversative conjunction. τε may just serve to single out δημότης as a specific addition or gloss to οὐ τύραννος, a piece of knowledge perhaps shared. δημότης τε may also correspond to an intonationally marked unit of information.[118]

§73. The two last paragraphs indicate two aspects of the use of τε with respect to καί. On the one hand the interpretations of enrichments produced by τε and by καί may coincide. This indicates a partial overlap in function that is comprehensible. On the other hand, on closer inspection each particle means more than *and* in a different way. By taking the "adversative meaning" as an example, τε contributes to a contrastive utterance by

116 The idea of no commitment to one of the two conjuncts alludes to the recent scholarly discussion of English "or" as a means to express no commitment to one or even no commitment to either of two disjuncts by the speaker (see Ariel 2014).

117 Later (5.38) Herodotus informs us that during the Ionian revolt Coes was stoned to death by the Mytilenaeans.

118 §§89-90 provide input for different prosodic values of τε depending on whether the connection is forward- or backward-oriented.

underscoring a piece of knowledge relevant to the contrast, whereas καί's contribution—as we will see—is to underscore the link that still exists between two contrasting items.

2.3.3 τε "*solitarium*" and "sentential" τε

§74. I have not yet exhausted the multifunctionality of τε. οὐ τύραννος δημότης τε (t33) is an instance of τε followed by no καί and no τε. Scholars use the label τε "*solitarium*" for this τε construction.[119] In (t33) τε conjoins two noun phrases, τύραννος and δημότης. In the following passage τε comes with a verbal phrase:

(t34)

... μεταγιγνώσκω μετίημί <u>τέ</u> σε ἰέναι

Herodotus 1.40

... I change my thinking, and permit you to go to the chase (tr. AB)

The speaker here is Croesus, who, despite his anxiety, bows to his son's pressure and lets him go hunt.

§75. When τε introduces an entire clause, as in the passage below, that clause may be thematically attached to a previous unit (either one or more clauses) to complement it in some way:

(t35)

Σύ νυν ἐμὲ ἐκκομίσας αὐτὸν καὶ χρήματα, τὰ μὲν αὐτῶν αὐτὸς ἔχε, τὰ δὲ ἐμὲ ἔα ἔχειν· εἵνεκέν <u>τε</u> χρημάτων ἄρξεις ἁπάσης τῆς Ἑλλάδος. Εἰ δέ μοι ἀπιστέεις ...

Herodotus 3.122.4

Now if you will transport me and my money, you may take some yourself and let me keep the rest; thus you shall have wealth enough to rule all Hellas. If you mistrust ... (tr. Godley)

Here we have the central point of Oroetes (Persian governor of Sardis) in his message to the tyrant of Samos, Polycrates; it is part of the strategy that will bring the tyrant to death. After two coordinating main clauses (τὰ μὲν αὐτῶν αὐτὸς ἔχε and τὰ δὲ ἐμὲ ἔα ἔχειν) a further main clause occurs, introduced by τε. εἵνεκέν τε χρημάτων starts

[119] See, e.g., Levinsohn 1987:174; Cooper 1998:1428.

a thought that complements the previous thought (σύ νυν...): it resumes the topic "money," and it makes money the fundamental point of Polycrates' political ambitions.

§76. In spite of the modern semicolon before εἵνεκεν in (t35), the τε clause in fact is also a τε sentence. "Sentential" τε, as the adjective suggests, captures the fact that the scope of τε may be an entire sentence. Viger, originally writing in 1627, was the first to observe the phenomenon in Thucydides (Viger 1834⁴:518).[120] In our modern editions "sentential" τε occurs in second position after a full stop, which paralinguistically signals a major discourse boundary.[121] This kind of τε regularly occurs in both *Histories*, with no distinctions in use between speeches and narrative sections.

§77. Basically, a "sentential" τε is a τε "*solitarium*" that has sentential scope. Since in this monograph we prefer to look at multi-act units rather than at sentences,[122] the next paragraphs introduce discourse functions of τε that shed light on moves. Two pragmatic types of τε connections in moves are identified in the two *Histories*, one is backward-oriented, the other forward-oriented.

2.3.4 τε connections backward-oriented: The coda effect

§78. τε can signal the speaker's intention to attach some piece of information by suggesting, at the same time, an implied meaning dealing with the shape of the argument. Consider this famous Thucydidean passage:

(t36)

ὅσοι δὲ βουλήσονται τῶν τε γενομένων τὸ σαφὲς σκοπεῖν καὶ τῶν μελλόντων ποτὲ αὖθις κατὰ τὸ ἀνθρώπινον τοιούτων καὶ παραπλησίων ἔσεσθαι, ὠφέλιμα κρίνειν αὐτὰ ἀρκούντως ἕξει. κτῆμά <u>τε</u> ἐς αἰεὶ μᾶλλον ἢ ἀγώνισμα ἐς τὸ παραχρῆμα ἀκούειν ξύγκειται.

Thucydides 1.22.4

[120] See also Krüger 1842:327. Bodin-Mazon 1919:359 notes that in Aristophanes **τε** connects sentences frequently. See Hammer 1904:21-26 on the use of "sentential" τε in Herodotus; 43-47 on the same use in Thucydides.The author points out that Thucydides shows more than 400 instances: "*Atque primum quidem particula τε, cui altera non respondet, apud Thucydidem multo plus quadringenties exstat, sed paucis locis exceptis hac simplici particula semper sententiae adseruntur*" (Hammer 1904:38-39). As for Herodotus, see also Brouwer 1975:89. As for Thucydides, see also Cooper 1998:1341. "Sentential" τε is already used in Homeric epic, albeit sporadically (see, for example, Homer *Iliad* 1.256, as discussed in Klein 1992:17). (t29) above represents one of the many instances of "sentential" τε in Thucydides ("The oldest sea-battle τε of which we know was that between the Corinthians and the Corcyraeans"). On τε with sentential scope, see also Gonda 1954:197.

[121] See IV.3 §§3; 6; 9; 10 about punctuation as paralinguistic communication.

[122] See IV.3.7.

> I shall be content if it [my history] is judged useful by those who will want to have a clear understanding of what happened—and, such is the human condition, will happen again at some time in the same or a similar pattern. It was composed as a permanent legacy, not a showpiece for a single hearing. (tr. Hammond)

As in (t35) above, this passage also features a τε that helps establish a logical link, in the form of a consequence, with the preceding sentence. This famous clause (usually quoted without τε) shows not only a generic connection with the previous thoughts, but also constitutes the end of an argument, the conclusion of a point. Gonda (1954:197), recalling the observations of Classen and Steup (1892-1922, vol. I:8), views this τε as having a "conclusive force".[123] In Gonda's terms, τε marks a complementarity that extends over one or more clauses, and stresses thematic or argumentative coherence.[124] Such τε clauses produce a coda effect, in content and form; indeed, they tend to be short.[125] The pragmatic enrichment consists, in these cases, in providing a metalinguistic "warning" that regards a move, a multi-act discourse unit. When τε introduces a short independent clause, it notifies us to connect the host clause with the co-text and context of previous clauses, and it warns us that the host discourse act ends some narrative or argumentative move.

§79. We have seen that τε can link one or more preceding clauses. In the case of coda effects, the backward orientation of the connection is over a chain of thematically bound clauses. Now, when τε with clausal scope occurs in the middle of an account or an

123 As for such τε in Herodotus, see Hammer 1904:46, Lamberts 1970:118, and Brouwer 1975:86. According to Brouwer the function of τε in recapitulating statements is fulfilled also by the combination τε δή, which for Hammer (1904:36) is the most frequent τε combination used by Herodotus. IV.3 §128 takes up Brouwer's observation in connection with the discourse functions of δή.

124 The same principle applies to τε introducing the last item in a list, as Classen and Steup, and Gonda note. Denniston 1950:500, however, includes τε with conclusive force ("clinching or summing up of what precedes," especially in Thucydides) in a section on "peculiarities in the use of single τε." For Gonda's idea of "complementarity," see below §80.

125 See Cooper 1998:1428 for a similar observation. See, for example, Thucydides 1.73, end of section 1 ἥ τε πόλις ἡμῶν ἀξία λόγου ἐστίν. Up to chapter 23 of book 1, this kind of τε in Thucydides occurs six times (1, end of chapter 4; 1.5, end of section 3; 1.12, end of section 3; 1, end of chapter 16; 1, end of chapter 22; 1.23, end of section 1). An interesting variation on the construction τε ... καί occurs at 3.25.2 ὅ τε χειμὼν ἐτελεύτα οὗτος, καὶ τέταρτον ἔτος τῷ πολέμῳ ἐτελεύτα τῷδε ὃν Θουκυδίδης ξυνέγραψεν. Two different acts are performed: first, the τε clause closes the smaller narrative section on the winter; second, καί links all the sections on the fourth year to this conclusion (which is emphasized by the authorial seal). Herodotean instances of τε in "coda" effects include book 1, end of chapter 111; 2.82.2; 3.88.3; book 7, chapter 58, end of section 2; end of chapter 175; 8.57.3; book 8.60, end of section α; 8.76, end of section 1; 8.108, end of section 3; 8.136.3. Significantly, in both works the locus often coincides with section (and even chapter) boundaries in modern editions.

episode, it is not always clear whether the host act works as an intermediate conclusion, or as a springboard for further development. The next passage is a case in point:

(t37)

Οἱ δ' ἐκ τῆς αὐτῆς κώμης Μῆδοι ὁρῶντες αὐτοῦ τοὺς τρόπους δικαστήν μιν ἑωυτῶν αἱρέοντο· ὁ δὲ δή, οἷα μνώμενος ἀρχήν, ἰθύς τε καὶ δίκαιος ἦν. Ποιέων τε ταῦτα ἔπαινον εἶχε οὐκ ὀλίγον πρὸς τῶν πολιητέων, οὕτω ὥστε...ἄσμενοι ἐφοίτων παρὰ τὸν Δηιόκην καὶ αὐτοὶ δικασόμενοι, ...

Herodotus 1.96.2-3

Then the Medes of the same town, seeing his behavior, chose him to be their judge, and he (for he coveted sovereign power) was honest and just. By acting so, he won no small praise from his fellow townsmen, to such an extent that ... they came often and gladly to plead before Deioces ... (tr. Godley)

Herodotus is relating how the Median Deioces took control of his people. ποιέων τε ταῦτα effects two things at once: it introduces the consequence, the result of Deioces' behavior, and it starts a discourse unit that constitutes the climax of the story: Deioces wins the confidence of his people to such an extent that they end up believing he is the only reliable judge. Any connective word in a way is a hinge between previous and following material. My point here is that τε regards moves rather than single acts in both directions. As IV.3.11.2 will point out, a crucial feature that, especially in Herodotus, occurs in those moments is a οὗτος form. In (t37) we find ποιέων τε ταῦτα.

2.3.5 τε connections forward-oriented: τε as a projecting marker, and τε at the beginning of lists

§80. In this subsection I establish a correlation between a well-known function of τε and a move-scope function of τε that I define as "forward-oriented." The well-known function is easily explained if we think of an important feature of bisyndetic τε. In such a construction the first τε signals—in its postpositive position—where the first of two or more conjuncts starts. Any τε at the beginning of multi-item lists shares this feature. In the past the phenomenon has driven scholars to abstract an essential function for τε: Hartung associates τε with the idea of "equality" ("*Gleichmäßigkeit*"); Gonda with the idea of "complementarity."[126] This signalling function may seem obvious, but in fact it reveals

[126] Hartung 1832:88-89, 99; and Gonda 1954:199: τε indicates "virtually a complementary pair" (both in the connective and in the "epic" use). Denniston in 1934 could not foresee Gonda's study. Ruijgh 1971 does mention it, but also dismisses it; the conciseness of his summary does not reflect the length and richness of the analysis that Gonda presents over two sizable articles.

an aspect of τε that is fundamental to the approach of this chapter, an aspect I define in terms of a metalinguistic meaning associated with a connective role. In the τε ... καί constructions τε promises, so to speak, a correlation and metalinguistically guides us to find it. Whenever we come across a τε (say in Herodotus and in Thucydides), we look for a correlation. We fix in our mind the τε signal (which includes both τε and the constituent to which τε is attached), and, most probably, later in the text we find either another τε or, more typically, a καί that fulfills the promise together with a parallel constituent—not differently from what already Hammer notes (1904:47). In these cases τε acts as a projection marker. The connective function of τε in τε ... καί, far from being superfluous, resides in its metalinguistic meaning, which is to warn us that a correlation is going to be established, and to signal where it begins.[127]

§81. Such metalinguistic projection proves to be particularly useful when more words or even clauses intervene between τε and καί; when the two conjuncts differ syntactically from each other; and when τε constituents are parallel in sense and syntax but separated by other coordinating markers. The following three passages feature each construction listed above. First, a sentence exemplifying the separation of τε and καί by many words and clauses:

(t38)[128]

δηλοῦσι δὲ | τῶν <u>τε</u> ἠπειρωτῶν τινὲς ἔτι καὶ νῦν, οἷς κόσμος καλῶς τοῦτο δρᾶν, <u>καὶ</u> οἱ παλαιοὶ ...

Thucydides 1.5.2

Further illustration is given by some of the mainlanders even now, who take successful piracy as a compliment, and by the ancient poets ... (tr. Hammond)

τε projects complementarity as it invites a connection between τῶν ἠπειρωτῶν τινὲς and οἱ παλαιοί. At the same time, by virtue of signaling a specific upcoming correlation, the occurrence of τε assures us that δηλοῦσι δέ is a separate verbal phrase (which, in fact, is going to introduce a multi-act explanation).

§82. Now an example of τε conjoining syntactically different constituents:

A more recent echo of the idea of complementarity expressed by τε in Herodotus is found in Brouwer 1975:85-94.

[127] This projective role reminds us of μέν, which also works as a projection marker (II.2.4; III.5 §§35-36; IV.5 §33). In the case of μέν, the metalinguistic "warning" is different.

[128] The passage was already quoted and commented on; see above (t10, b).

(t39)

ἤν τε γνῶτε, Λακεδαιμονίοις ἔξεστιν ὑμῖν φίλους γενέσθαι βεβαίως, αὐτῶν τε προκαλεσαμένων χαρισαμένοις τε μᾶλλον ἢ βιασαμένοις.

Thucydides 4.20.3

And by decreeing the peace, you may make the Lacedaemonians your sure friends, inasmuch as they call you to it and are therein not forced but gratified. (tr. Hobbes)

Towards the end of a speech in which the Spartans, after being defeated in Pylos, propose a peace treaty with Athens, the chance of a firm friendship is put forward. Two circumstances (in fact alternative to each other) help ensure the anticipated bond: first, the Spartans themselves are the ones inviting peace; second, they are grateful for, not forced into, the peace. The two τε give balance to syntactic variation (the genitive absolute αὐτῶν τε προκαλεσαμένων, and the participles χαρισαμένοις ... βιασαμένοις agreeing with Λακεδαιμονίοις).

§83. Finally, an instance where parallel constituents are separated by other coordinating markers:

(t40)

τά τε πρότερον ἀκοῇ μὲν λεγόμενα, ἔργῳ δὲ σπανιώτερον βεβαιούμενα οὐκ ἄπιστα κατέστη, σεισμῶν τε πέρι, οἳ ἐπὶ πλεῖστον ἅμα μέρος γῆς καὶ ἰσχυρότατοι οἱ αὐτοὶ ἐπέσχον, ἡλίου τε ἐκλείψεις, αἳ πυκνότεραι παρὰ τὰ ἐκ τοῦ πρὶν χρόνου μνημονευόμενα ξυνέβησαν, αὐχμοί τε ἔστι παρ' οἷς μεγάλοι καὶ ἀπ' αὐτῶν καὶ λιμοὶ καὶ ἡ οὐχ ἥκιστα βλάψασα καὶ μέρος τι φθείρασα ἡ λοιμώδης νόσος

Thucydides 1.23.3

The phenomena in the old stories, more often told than attested, now became credible fact: earthquakes, which affected large areas with particular intensity; eclipses of the sun, occurring more frequently than in previous memory; major draughts in some parts, followed by famine; and, one of the most destructive causes of widespread death, the infectious plague. (tr. Hammond)

Here τε accompanies the mention of the cataclysmic events that characterized the Peloponnesian war, as a sign of its greater extent with respect to the Persian war. These elements of shared knowledge are earthquakes, eclipses, and draughts (σεισμῶν τε πέρι, ἡλίου τε ἐκλείψεις, and αὐχμοί τε).[129] Two καί conclude the list: καὶ λιμοί, and καί ἡ λοιμώδης νόσος. The discourse functions of καί are explored in the next section; here I anticipate that the way in which καί usually marks the last "spot" in lists is an enrichment that I render with "in particular."

§84. In the projecting function I described, τε can be said to signal a partition at the same time as it isolates a component of that partition. Viewed this way, τε works similarly to the one theorized by Wentzel; in its partitive/distributive role ("there is this, there is that") τε enables a series of items to maintain a sense of separateness.

2.3.6 τε starting moves

§85. Actually, a further τε occurs in (t40), that is, at its very beginning. τά τε invites considering the nouns that are attached to τά as a whole (τά πρότερον ἀκοῇ μὲν λεγόμενα, ἔργῳ δὲ σπανιώτερον βεβαιούμενα). In turn, this whole is completed by the predicate οὐκ ἄπιστα κατέστη. At the level of discourse units, this τε has scope over the entire list of phenomena. In light of that we may say that τε signals a move start.

§86. We may speculate about the lexical choice of the particle in connection with the mention of old and grand oral accounts (τά τε πρότερον ἀκοῇ μὲν λεγόμενα): if one of the potentials of τε is to recall shared knowledge, its use here seems almost *ad hoc*. In relation to that, I mention the fact that in Aristophanes τε occurs in choral songs ten times more than in dialogic parts.[130] The distribution of τε in comedy may reveal a genre-association with epic and lyric recalls of traditional material (whether to mock them or not), insofar as the content is about properties of entities, mythological accounts, similes, and names of people and places.[131] As for Thucydides, the allusions to the epic genre (ranging from lexicon to tone) are less explicit, albeit not absent.[132]

§87. The reading that the first τε in (t40) signals a move start is supported by the particles' positions in the first sentence. By using the segmentation criteria proposed in IV.3, the boundaries are the following: τά τε πρότερον | ἀκοῇ μὲν λεγόμενα | ἔργῳ δὲ σπανιώτερον βεβαιούμενα | οὐκ ἄπιστα κατέστη. In other words, τά τε πρότερον works as a priming act projecting a multi-act unit (see ἀκοῇ μὲν and ἔργῳ δὲ). Therefore, it starts a move. This is the same pattern I have previously discussed about δέ (§24). Here is another instance:

129 Herodotus 4.53.2 offers an example linguistically parallel to Thucydides 1.23.3: eight τε in seven *OCT* lines mark the list of benefits coming from the river Borysthenes, while the few καί in between mark sub-additions. Hammer analyzes variation in enumerations with τε and καί in Herodotus, Thucydides, and Xenophon (1904:22-26; 55-59; 76-77 respectively).

130 In tragedy τε occurs about three times as often in songs. See III.2 §39.

131 See, e.g., III.2 §40 and 44.

132 See, among others, Smith 1900; Jung 1991; Nicolai 2001; Rutherford 2012.

(t41)

Αἰγινῆταί τε | φανερῶς μὲν οὐ πρεσβευόμενοι, δεδιότες τοὺς Ἀθηναίους, κρύφα δὲ οὐχ ἥκιστα μετ' αὐτῶν ἐνῆγον τὸν πόλεμον, λέγοντες οὐκ εἶναι αὐτόνομοι κατὰ τὰς σπονδάς.

Thucydides 1.67.2

The Aeginetans did not send envoys openly, for fear of the Athenians, but in secret collaboration with the Corinthians they played a major part in instigating the war, claiming that they had lost the autonomy guaranteed under the treaty. (tr. Hammond)

Αἰγινῆταί τε opens and even dominates a multi-act unit about the initiatives of the Aeginetans before the Corinthians meet their allies in Sparta (in 432 BCE). The main subcomponents of this unit are signaled by φανερῶς μὲν and κρύφα δέ.

2.3.7 Backward and forward τε connections: Intonational parallels?

§88. As for prosodic equivalents of what ancient Greek particles seem to perform, in this monograph we limit ourselves to intuitive suggestions rather than claims.[133] The question in the title of this subsection reflects that. Nonetheless, we believe that making parallels with modulations in intonation, which are familiar to us, helps to understand that particles are integral to the meaning of messages.

§89. Earlier (§78; §80; nn85 and 126) I mentioned Gonda's idea that complementarity underlies most of the usages of τε. The domain within which the scholar sees complementarity is semantic and syntactic. We may translate the same idea into a different domain, that is, intonation. The metalinguistic projection that τε signposts whenever it accompanies the first conjunct of a τε ... καί construction can be compared to what in different modern Indoeuropean languages is a dedicated intonational contour. As for (t40), for example, τε may correspond to a paralinguistic sign; that is, τε may signal the start of an intonational pattern that is repeated over all the constituents of a list, which makes it a "list intonation."[134] Thus, metalinguistic projection would be combined with prosodic projection.[135]

133 Parallels between ancient Greek acts introduced by particles and intonational profiles are suggested also in II.2.5 concerning priming acts, and in IV.3 §65 about μέν.

134 See, for example, Liberman and Pierrehumbert 1984; Selkirk 1984 (about English); Truckenbrodt 2004 (about southern German).

135 Let us think of how we would utter a passage such as πλούτῳ τε ἰδίῳ καὶ δημοσίῳ καὶ ναυσὶ καὶ ἵπποις καὶ ὅπλοις καὶ ὄχλῳ (Thucydides 1.80.3); probably we would mark πλούτῳ ἰδίῳ prosodically (note the τε in between) by starting a list intonation profile.

§90 Just as τε projecting a complement in τε … καί may reflect a list intonation, τε in the coda effect may reflect an intonational contour that conveys the end of an argument. The contour would obviously differ from the list contour.[136] I wonder whether "epic" τε in relative clauses might have suggested some specific intonational pattern as well. What matters here is neither to demonstrate that this was the case, nor to show how general or specific τε patterns could have sounded (both being impossible tasks). Rather, the point is that we should entertain the possibility that ancient Greek τε in its various constructions marked various types of prosodic discontinuity.

2.3.8 Interim conclusion

§91. In this section I have shown that considering τε in dichotomous terms, *either* copulative *or* "epic," obscures the rich range of its discourse functions. The examples have illustrated how τε impacts phrases, clauses, and larger units; or in discourse terms, they affect both acts and moves. The forces of τε concern the presentation of conjuncts but also the perspective of speakers. Finally, the connective role may coexist with different types of enrichment pragmatically derived from the co-text. The example from Lysias I quoted at the beginning, (t23), condenses all these aspects: τε has scope over the main clause ("sentential" τε), which unquestionably is thematically connected to the preceding clauses. At the same time the statement about the rightness of Athenians' life from its origins most likely represented an opinion shared—and even endorsed—by the receivers. And last, τε carries an enrichment wherein the host clause is imbued with an epic tone, as befits the status of the speech as epitaph.[137]

§92. The main results of the investigation into the uses of τε in Herodotus and Thucydides are the following. Several times τε in both authors occurs together with names of people or names of places. This is how τε marks knowledge as shared in the historiographical genre. In the context of telling historical events and providing related accounts, shared knowledge amounts to encyclopedic and cultural knowledge. Except for a few cases where the correlation with a following καί is questionable, the shared-knowledge pragmatic enrichment coexists with the syndetic role. Another important enrichment is constituted by the metalinguistic signal provided by τε in the τε … καί constructions. In those cases τε projects a correlation (see Gonda's idea of complementarity). τε helps the receiver to track which constituents are conjoined, and where the

[136] The fact that different intonational contours are associated with the same lexical item in different positions or different constructions has been convincingly demonstrated by Ferrara 1997: the different sentence positions and the different pragmatic functions of "anyway" in English correspond to different intonational contours. A recent account of the prosodic spectrum of *and* in English conversation can be found in Barth-Weingarten 2012: variation in the phonetic design corresponds to variation in scope and in cognitive function.

[137] Lysias 2 is an epitaph dedicated to the Athenians who had died while assisting the Corinthians in the Corinth war.

correlation starts. The occurrences of τε "*solitarium*" (i.e. not accompanied by any τε or καί), once analyzed from a discourse perspective that considers multi-act units, reveal that they can serve to close as well as open discourse moves, and thus can possess a force beyond their actual scope, (that is, the single clause in which they are hosted). I have also made an open-ended observation on the correspondence between the occurrence of τε in lists, and the occurrence of a list intonation in modern languages. Finally, I have delineated some ways in which the two authors differ in their use of τε. From partial counts it seems that Herodotus uses more τε with noun phrases, and more τε καί with names. Thucydides uses fewer τε καί with names, and more τε with clausal scope.

2.4 καί Between Link and Climax

§93. Not differently from δέ and τε, καί in Classical historiography is employed in a variety of syntactic and semantic environments, where it reveals its potential beyond the connective and adverbial roles assigned by the *theoria recepta*. The scholarship does acknowledge peculiar functions of καί (for example, καί *adversativum*), but it usually presents them as peripheral uses, reserving center stage for καί in the senses of either "and" or "also/even." Moreover, we find few discussions of καί as such in Herodotus and Thucydides, largely due to commentators' understandable interest in the content of historical accounts. Yet, however simple the function of καί may be, its occurrence is indispensable. As we process words and clauses, καί enables us to link information, actions, thoughts, procedures, comments, and conclusions in an orderly fashion.

§94. In this section I argue that καί encompasses a range of meanings broader than what received scholarship has allowed it, such as "just" and "for example." Its very frequent employment (especially in Thucydides[138]) also calls for some explanation. My goals, then, will be to uncover the main discourse functions of καί in the two *Histories*, and to spotlight instances where καί is not discussed as it ought to be.[139] In line with our general methodology, I consider καί's roles beyond the clause and sentence level. I also continue to use the term enrichment to illustrate the particle's different implied meanings (what we as readers infer); these implied meanings correspond to adverbial meanings attached to connective roles. Finally, I retrieve and extend an idea that

[138] On average a καί occurs every 14.9 words (and every 24.8 words in Herodotus). Thucydides is not the only author using καί generously. The ratio for Xenophon is 1:18; Isocrates 1:20; Demosthenes 1:19. Trenkner (1960:1-5) calls this tendency in Attic and in later Greek (until the Greek of the New Testament) "καί-style."

[139] In several monographs and essays of the past centuries analyses of καί and καί combination include a richer spectrum of uses than in more recent works. See, for example, Devarius 1588:106-119 and Hoogeveen 1769:531-625. The latter divides the main functions of καί alone as follows: *potestate* συμμπλεκτικῆ ("combining," 531); χρονικῆ ("temporal," 535); προτρεπτικῆ ("hortatory/encouraging," 538); ἐπιδοτικῆ ("offering more," 541); ἐναντιωματικῆ ("opposing/adversative," 545); *usu* ἐλλειπτικῷ ("elliptical," 547). The discourse functions of καί in drama are mainly discussed in III.2.2.2 and III.3.3.1.4.

German philologists in the nineteenth century proposed about καί, namely the idea of "*Steigerung*" ("climax"). This idea constitutes what fundamentally distinguishes καί from τε and δέ.

2.4.1 καί in combinations

§95. Some forces of καί are underdiscussed in the literature. They can be observed when καί appears alone as well as when καί appears in combinations. Combinations are particularly revealing, for two reasons. First, combinations, more frequently than individual particles, contribute metalinguistic or metanarrative meaning above the clausal level (thus marking multi-clause units). Second, they illuminate the range of contributions of individual καί, in combinations where each particle has its own force, and in clusters where one overall force is conveyed.[140] My analysis starts from the combinations καὶ δὴ καί, καί τι καί, καὶ γάρ, and καὶ δή.

§96. καὶ δὴ καί occurs especially in Herodotus and Plato.[141] The literature agrees that its function in Herodotus is to introduce a topic that will be dealt with over subsequent clauses. Dik (1995:45-47) refers to Denniston (1950:254-255), who defines this function as a "secondary meaning of καὶ δὴ καί, marking a transition from general to particular";[142] she explains: "the 'and especially' part (καὶ δὴ καί) singles out *one* element, which then forms a convenient connection to the next stage in the narrative" (1994:46; italics in the text). Let us recall a representative example:

(t42)

τούτῳ τῷ Γύγῃ καὶ τὰ σπουδαιέστερα τῶν πρηγμάτων ὑπερετίθετο ὁ Κανδαύλης καὶ δὴ καὶ τὸ εἶδος τῆς γυναικὸς ὑπερεπαινέων.

Herodotus 1.8.1

"...Candaules not only discussed his most important business with him, but even used to make him listen to eulogies of his wife's beauty" (tr. De Sélincourt and Marincola).

[140] On combinations versus clusters of particles, see I.1 §3. Hartung 1832-1833, vol. II:390-402 sees the affirmative force of μέν operate through μέν combinations such as ἦ μέν, καὶ μέν, γε μέν, and μέντοι. Analogously, Denniston 1950:57 sees the original asseverative force of γάρ remain in γάρ combinations.

[141] 200 instances in Plato; 81 occurrences in Herodotus; 12 in the *Corpus Hippocraticum*; 4 in Xenophon; very few in other authors; none in Thucydides.

[142] The primary meaning of the cluster, for Denniston, is to join sentences, clauses, and single words not differently from καὶ ... δή (1950:254).

The beauty of Candaules' wife is singled out by καὶ δὴ καί, which warns us that the subject is going to be expanded and thematized over the next few acts. Building upon Denniston's and Dik's remarks, I suggest that the combination works as a cluster. Its overall force is both cognitive and metanarrative: on the cognitive side it triggers our interest in a particular element of the discourse and it invites us to narrow our attention to that element; on the metanarrative side it signals that that element is going to be developed further. Wennerstrom points out that in spoken narratives we may exploit emphatic prosody to mark a specific word or phrase that is going to play a significant role in what follows.[143] καὶ δὴ καί works similarly.[144]

§97. In Plato καὶ δὴ καί can perform a similar focusing discourse function.[145] In Thucydides this cluster does not occur at all, but the rare combination καί τι καί[146] is employed to convey a similar force in the following passage:

(t43)

τό τε Πελαργικὸν καλούμενον τὸ ὑπὸ τὴν ἀκρόπολιν, ὃ καὶ ἐπάρατόν τε ἦν μὴ οἰκεῖν καί τι καὶ Πυθικοῦ μαντείου ἀκροτελεύτιον τοιόνδε διεκώλυε, λέγον ὡς 'τὸ Πελαργικὸν ἀργὸν ἄμεινον,' ὅμως ὑπὸ τῆς παραχρῆμα ἀνάγκης ἐξῳκήθη.

Thucydides 2.17.1

The area below the Acropolis known as the "Pelargic" was under a curse prohibiting occupation, and there was also the tag-end of a Delphic oracle to

143 The example provided by Wennerstrom (2001:212) concerns a particularly high pitch, as well as lengthening of the vowels, put on the preposition "out" at the end of the following excerpt: [the teller conveys her excitement at going to a friend's house as a child] "So I went over and uhh she was at the door and I said 'Ask your mom' and she did and she could come *out*" (Wennerstrom's original prosodic transcription and pauses are dropped here; I just emphasize "out" by using italics). The clause "she could come out," the author comments, "sets up motivation for the primary complicating action of the story: because of her extreme excitement, the teller runs and jumps, falls, and breaks her ankle." The teller's excitement is combined with the plot-related relevance of the information being added. The performative sign becomes an organizational signpost related to the complicating action being triggered by "and she could come out."

144 Unlike γε, which also can be used to stress information for reasons that are left implicit, καὶ δὴ καί conveys an idea of narrowing down while adding, and it anticipates its effect over a multi-act unit.

145 See for example *Laws* 812d-e: " ... but as to divergence of sound and variety in the notes of the harp, when the strings sound the one tune and the composer of the melody another, or when (καὶ δὴ καί) there results a combination of low and high notes, of slow and quick time, of sharp and grave, [812e] and all sorts of rhythmical variations are adapted to the notes of the lyre—no such complications should be employed in dealing with pupils who have to absorb quickly, within three years, the useful elements of music." (tr. Bury).

146 Besides (t43), see Thucydides 1.107.7; 4.5.1 and 109.4; 5.90.1. The cluster occurs (sparsely) also in Sophocles, Aristophanes, Empedocles, Demosthenes, Aeschines, Antiphanes, the *Corpus Hippocraticum*, Plato, and Aristotle.

the same effect, saying "Best to let the Pelargic rest": but even so it was occupied in the immediate emergency. (tr. Hammond)

The communicative intention underlying the use of καί τι καί is to go into detail. In this passage καί τι καί introduces a specification on an oracle about the *Pelargikón*, which Thucydides then presents and comments on.[147] The discourse discontinuity marked by καί τι καί generates a narrative expansion-effect built upon a thematic link, which lasts until the end of the excerpt.[148]

§98. Another combination that conveys both the idea of expansion and the intention to specify things is καὶ γάρ.[149]

(t44)

Ἅτε δὲ ἐουσέων μυριάδων πολλέων καὶ παντὸς ἀνδρὸς ἐργαζομένου ἤνετο τὸ ἔργον· <u>καὶ γὰρ</u> λίθοι καὶ πλίνθοι καὶ ξύλα καὶ φορμοὶ ψάμμου πλήρεες ἐσεφορέοντο, καὶ ἐλίνυον οὐδένα χρόνον οἱ βοηθήσαντες ἐργαζόμενοι, οὔτε νυκτὸς οὔτε ἡμέρης.

Herodotus 8.71.2

Since there were many tens of thousands and everyone worked, the task was completed, as they brought in stones and bricks and logs and baskets full of sand. At no moment of the day or night did those who had marched out there rest from their work. (tr. Godley)

In order to avoid an inland attack by the Persians, the Peloponnesians rush to the Isthmus to build a defensive wall. In this passage Herodotus describes their intense work. After a general statement about the completion of the task, he specifies what the work consisted of, and how quickly it went. καὶ γάρ introduces that specification. While the pragmatic

147 The continuation of this text will be analyzed at a later point (see §103).

148 Denniston 1950:294 limits his explanation of καί τι καί to the definition of the syntactic roles of the two καί ("the first καί is copulative, the second adverbial"); he also records the variants καὶ δή τι καί and καὶ πού τι καί. In Thucydides 2.87.2 καὶ πού τι καί hedges (through που) an addition that specifies but also slightly contradicts the preceding conjunct; ξυνέβη δὲ καὶ τὰ ἀπὸ τῆς τύχης οὐκ ὀλίγα ἐναντιωθῆναι, καί πού τι καὶ ἡ ἀπειρία πρῶτον ναυμαχοῦντας ἔσφηλεν, "It so happened too that bad luck was largely against us, and it may be that (καί πού τι καὶ) in our first sea-battle inexperience brought some mistakes" (tr. Hammond)

149 65 occurences in Herodotus; 44 in Thucydides; see II.3.2.2.1 for a discussion of the combination in Homer.

role of καί is to signal the shift to the details of a certain circumstance,[150] the role of γάρ is to illustrate and to expand on the previous point by supplying further information.[151] Therefore, I regard καὶ γάρ as a combination rather than a cluster: each particle in the combination fulfills one of its discourse roles. What makes this combination work well is the fact that these two roles complement each other.

§99. In the next example, καί in the same combination καὶ γάρ shows a force that corresponds to "namely" in English:

(t45)

Οἱ δὲ ἀμφὶ τὸν Πείσανδρον ... ὁπλίτας ἔχοντες σφίσιν αὐτοῖς ξυμμάχους ἦλθον ἐς τὰς Ἀθήνας. καὶ καταλαμβάνουσι τὰ πλεῖστα τοῖς ἑταίροις προειργασμένα. <u>καὶ γὰρ</u> Ἀνδροκλέα τέ τινα τοῦ δήμου μάλιστα προεστῶτα ξυστάντες τινὲς τῶν νεωτέρων κρύφα ἀποκτείνουσιν, ὅσπερ καὶ τὸν Ἀλκιβιάδην οὐχ ἥκιστα ἐξήλασε, ...

Thucydides 8.65.1-2

Peisander and his colleagues, ... took on board hoplites who would support them. When they reached Athens they found most of the work already done by the members of the cabals. A group of younger men had conspired to have one Androcles quietly murdered: he ... had been instrumental in the banishment of Alcibiades ... (tr. Hammond)

The original text is much more discontinuous and vivid than the English translation, which by necessity conforms to its own stylistic and grammatical standards. Hammond groups the arrival in Athens and what Peisander and his fellows find; Thucydides devotes an independent clause to the finding, which starts with καί and the present tense καταλαμβάνουσι. Then, the general statement "they found most of the work already done by the members" is followed by καὶ γάρ, which introduces the name of Androcles, whose murder is subsequently related.[152] While the English translation focuses on clarity

150 In this passage the reading of γάρ with scope over the sentence, and καί parallel to the subsequent καί (γὰρ + καὶ λίθοι, καὶ πλίνθοι, καὶ ξύλα, etc.) is to disfavor, as in Herodotus the duplication of καί (καί X, καί Y) is restricted to binary additions (e.g. 1.68 καὶ συντυχίῃ χρησάμενος καὶ σοφίῃ).

151 In this monograph the discourse functions of γάρ in Homer and in Pindar are described in II.3.2.2, and II.4.2; those related to drama are described in III.2.2.4 and III.3.3.1.5. γάρ is particularly suitable to open moves in Herodotus and Thucydides; see IV.3 §107-109, and IV.5 §§16; 39; 61; 68.

152 According to Lardinois 2006, γάρ in itself can connect a gnomic statement to a particular circumstance; in his interpretation of Sophocles *Ajax* 669-670 (καὶ γὰρ τὰ δεινὰ καὶ τὰ καρτερώτατα / τιμαῖς ὑπείκει ...) γάρ is strengthened by καί.

in content and in agency, the Greek shows something more: the relation between the general statement and the plan to murder Androcles, by means of καὶ γάρ, which expands (γάρ) and specifies (καί); and the cognitive salience of Androcles, who is the target of the fellows' conspiration, by means of Ἀνδροκλέα immediately after καὶ γάρ. Incidentally, I let the reader note that τε accompanies Ἀνδροκλέα and is not followed by any καί; it signposts τινα τοῦ δήμου as an apposition, similarly to the apposition analysed in (t33), and it presents the information in terms of shared knowledge.

§100. The last combination that signals a change from general to particular is καὶ δή, which occurs 51 times in Herodotus, and not at all in Thucydides. The main discourse function of καὶ δή in Herodotus is related to the previous combinations in that it conveys the intention to detail and pin down. Here is an instance:

(t46)

Περὶ Σάρδις μὲν δὴ ἐγίνετο ταραχή, Ἱστιαῖον δὲ ταύτης ἀποσφαλέντα τῆς ἐλπίδος Χῖοι κατῆγον ἐς Μίλητον, αὐτοῦ Ἱστιαίου δεηθέντος. Οἱ δὲ Μιλήσιοι ἄσμενοι ἀπαλλαχθέντες καὶ Ἀρισταγόρεω οὐδαμῶς πρόθυμοι ἦσαν ἄλλον τύραννον δέκεσθαι ἐς τὴν χώρην, οἷα ἐλευθερίης γευσάμενοι. Καὶ δή, νυκτὸς γὰρ ἐούσης βίῃ ἐπειρᾶτο κατιὼν ὁ Ἱστιαῖος ἐς τὴν Μίλητον, τιτρώσκεται τὸν μηρὸν ὑπό τεο τῶν Μιλησίων.

Herodotus 6.5.1-2

So troubles arose in Sardis. Since he failed in this hope, the Chians brought Histiaeus back to Miletus at his own request. But the Milesians were glad enough to be rid of Aristagoras himself, and they had no wish to receive another tyrant into their country now that they had tasted freedom. When Histiaeus tried to force his way into Miletus by night, he was wounded in the thigh by a Milesian.

After setting out the general situation—Histiaeus trying to reach Miletus, and the Milesians unwilling to host him—Herodotus homes in on a specific fact and a specific moment, introducing this discourse act with καὶ δή. As a syntactically isolated cluster—note the subsequent νυκτὸς γάρ, which suggests an act boundary[153]—καὶ δή announces to listeners and readers that some exciting news is to follow. The present tense τιτρώσκεται adds to the vividness of the Greek. A translation closer to the Greek would be "Look what

[153] Act boundaries following καὶ δή can be frequently inferred from Herodotus (see, e.g., Herodotus 1.214.1 καὶ δή | οὗτος μέν ...; 3.64 καὶ δή | ὡς τότε ...). In a fragment of Eupolis (Austin *fr.* 92.1), the position of δέ attests to the perception of καὶ δή as a cluster: καὶ δὴ δὲ Πείσανδρ [...

happened. At night Histiaeus tried to enter Miletus. He is wounded in the thigh by some Milesian." The excitement relates to the instantaneity of an event.[154]

§101. Such a use of καὶ δή is not only Herodotean:

(t47)

> ... Φέρε, τίν' οὖν <ἂν> ἄγγελον
> πέμψαιμ' ἐπ' αὐτόν; Οἶδ' ἐγὼ καὶ δὴ πόρον
> ἐκ τοῦ Παλαμήδους. ...
>
> Aristophanes *Thesmophoriazusae* 769-770

... Let me see, whom could I best send to him? Ha! I know a means taken from Palamedes ... (tr. O'Neill).

The speaker, a relative of Euripides, realizes on the spot how he might send a message to Euripides, and καὶ δή signals the immediacy of the realization. Once again καὶ δή is syntactically isolated from the rest of the sentence (see the translation "Ha!"), and its position is in the middle of the clause.[155] Not differently from καὶ δὴ καί, καὶ δή works as a cluster. The individual forces of the two particles blend together and converge upon one pragmatic effect, which is to place focus on an instantaneous and perceptual fact.[156]

2.4.2 Using καί to pin down

§102. The καί combinations I have commented on so far carry an enrichment that we term, for convenience, "pinning down." I now turn to the same enrichment possessed by καί when it appears all by itself. καί sometimes pins down a preceding concept or information by expanding on it through concrete instances ("for example"), or through a

154 The sense of instantaneity conveyed by καὶ δή is perceived also by Budé, Devarius and by Hoogeveen, who translate καὶ δή as "continuo," "protinus" (Budé 1556:1292; Devarius 1588:118), and "protinus," "statim" (Hoogeveen 1769:573). IV.5 §83 and 86 discuss further occurrences of this cluster in Herodotus.

155 δή occurring in non-initial act position tends to have limited scope in our corpus; see II.3.3.2; III.2.2.8; IV.4 §100 and 4.6.2.

156 In Homer the same force can be detected in connection with the appearance of something exciting: ἐννῆμαρ μὲν ὁμῶς πλέομεν νύκτας τε καὶ ἦμαρ, / τῇ δεκάτῃ δ' ἤδη ἀνεφαίνετο πατρὶς ἄρουρα, / καὶ δὴ πυρπολέοντας ἐλεύσσομεν ἐγγὺς ἐόντας, "Nevertheless we sail on, night and day, for nine days, / and on the tenth at last appeared the land of our fathers, and—look!—we see people tending fires, very close," (Homer *Odyssey* 10.28-30; tr. adapted from Lattimore). On καὶ δή and καὶ μήν referring, in tragedy and comedy, to new entrances on stage, see Van Erp Taalman Kip 2009:112-123; Bari (2010:330) adds καὶ γάρ with reference to Aristophanes; Hartung 1833:389 (about καὶ μήν). καὶ δή in drama can be used also when a speaker signals obedience to a request (see III.4 §§51-52). What is in common to the examples in this section is the simultaneity between a certain action and its verbalization.

more detailed account ("namely"; German "*und zwar*").[157] The particle can also illustrate that concept in more specific terms ("that is to say," "that is").[158] Let us consider the following passage:

(t48)

ἐπεγένετο δὲ ἄλλοις τε ἄλλοθι κωλύματα μὴ αὐξηθῆναι, <u>καὶ</u> Ἴωσι προχωρησάντων ἐπὶ μέγα τῶν πραγμάτων Κῦρος καὶ ἡ Περσικὴ βασιλεία Κροῖσον καθελοῦσα ...

Thucydides 1.16.1

There ensued a range of obstacles to the progress of the various Greek states. The Ionians, for example, had been developing strongly, but then Cyrus and the Persian kingdom destroyed Croesus ... (tr. Hammond)

Hammond translates καί with "for example." The translation gives priority to the adverbial function entailed by the enrichment, "to pin down." In the Greek the use of καί simply means that the adverbial and the connective functions coexist.

§103. In the previous section I argued that τε shows the same functional overlap, in general terms: its connective function may have an adverbial enrichment. Similarly, when καί occurs after relative pronouns, it recalls aspects of τε's behavior. In these cases καί must be processed together with the preceding word instead of the following, unless the word after καί invites a scalar, or an "also," interpretation. Let me revisit the beginning of Thucydides 2.17.1 (earlier quoted because of καί τι καί):

(t49)

τό τε Πελαργικὸν καλούμενον τὸ ὑπὸ τὴν ἀκρόπολιν, ὃ <u>καὶ</u> ἐπάρατόν τε ἦν μὴ οἰκεῖν καί τι καὶ ...

Thucydides 2.17.1

157 A pragmatic analysis of "*und zwar*" is provided by Günthner 2012. "*Und zwar*" is the translation of several καί already proposed by Hartung 1832-1833, vol. I:145-147; Passow 1841-1857:1540; Bäumlein 1861:147-148; Schwyzer and Debrunner 1950:568; Trenkner 1960:35 ("*dans le sens de l'allemand 'und zwar, nämlich'*"). Verdenius 1956:249 adds "*en wel*" as a corresponding expression in Dutch. For καί at the start of questions that zoom in further on the content of the preceding utterance, see III.4 §36.

158 Pindar offers a clear example of this: ... τὸν Ἀργείων τρόπον / εἰρήσεταί που κἀν βραχίστοις. "The story will be told, I think, in the Argive manner—that is, very briefly" Pindar *Isthmian* 6.58-59 (tr. AB). I see an equivalent enrichment of καί in the Homeric formulaic line ἀλλ' ἄγε μοι τόδε εἰπὲ καὶ ἀτρεκέως κατάλεξον, "But tell me this, and give me an exact account" (e.g. Homer *Iliad* 24.380, tr. AB), where "give me an exact account" reformulates in more specific terms the content of "tell me."

The area below the Acropolis, called 'the Pelargic, which—let me add—was under a curse prohibiting occupation, and ... (tr. adapted from Hammond)

If we read the second τε in this passage (the one following ἐπάρατόν) as a marker of complementarity "answered" by καὶ τι καί, the two connected elements are ἐπάρατόν ... ἦν μὴ οἰκεῖν and everything that follows καὶ τι καί.[159] Therefore, the solo καί is attached to the relative pronoun.[160] Scholars who comment on relative pronouns followed by καί stress the effect of logical tightness between the contents of main and sub-clauses.[161] Denniston (1950:250) adds, "καί following a relative (...) often gives an effect of limitation by imposing an additional qualification." In this passage, ὅ initiates a little excursus on the Pelargic area,[162] and καί contributes the sense of an additional qualification with regard to that area.[163] The pragmatic function, then, of καί in syntactic contexts like this is to signal a narrative expansion (see the translation "let me add"), wherein a specific aspect of the relative pronoun's referent will be focused on.[164]

[159] I do not exclude that τε in ἐπάρατόν τε ἦν μὴ οἰκεῖν, besides marking complementarity, also implies shared knowledge, as presumably more people knew the curse. The same holds for τε in τό τε Πελαργικὸν καλούμενον, besides the value of "sentential" τε.

[160] The position of τε suggests a *kôlon* (and act) boundary before ἐπάρατόν; this element further supports that ὃ καί forms a unit (ὃ καὶ | ἐπάρατόν τε ...).

[161] καί in relative, causal, and final clauses "has the effect of putting such subordinate clauses on a plane with the main clause" (Smyth 1956:653); καί in subclauses (including relative clauses) strengthens the logical links of subordination (Humbert 1960:413); καί after relative pronouns expresses the accordance with a preceding concept (Bäumlein 1861:152). In subclauses or after conjunctions Verdenius and Waszink 1946:2-8 take καί to mean "really," "indeed", "in fact."

[162] Bonifazi 2004c argues that relative pronouns in early lyric and epic are devices often used to open narrative expansions about the referents.

[163] This use of καί is already exploited in Homeric poetry. See, for example, the relative pronoun that accompanies the first mention of Nestor in the *Iliad*: τοῖσι δὲ Νέστωρ / ἡδυεπὴς ἀνόρουσε λιγὺς Πυλίων ἀγορητής / τοῦ καὶ ἀπὸ γλώσσης μέλιτος γλυκίων ῥέεν αὐδή, "Then among them rose up Nestor, sweet of speech, the clear-voiced orator of the men of Pylos, he from whose tongue speech flowed sweeter than honey" (Homer *Iliad* 1.247-249; tr. Murray-Wyatt). καί pins down ἡδυεπὴς ... ἀγορητής, as it introduces a little expansion on a specific quality of the hero, namely his gifted voice. If καί would modify the comparative γλυκίων ("even sweeter"), it probably would occur immediately before it, as focus particles typically do; conversely, the peninitial clause position fits a clausal scope (see I.1 §20). In Modern Greek *και* in association with relative pronouns seems to have a similar "expanding" function; Canakis (1995:41) translates these *και* "besides," "among other things."

[164] Such a view allows readers to understand more precisely instances of καί (after relative pronouns) that are unrelated to "also" and "even," e.g. Thucydides 2.13.7 ἔστι δὲ αὐτοῦ ὃ καὶ ἀφύλακτον ἦν, "there was ... an unguarded section ..."; Thucydides 1.101.2 δὲ τῶν Εἱλώτων ἐγένοντο οἱ τῶν παλαιῶν Μεσσηνίων τότε δουλωθέντων ἀπόγονοι· ᾗ καὶ Μεσσήνιοι ἐκλήθησαν οἱ πάντες, "The Helots were mostly the descendants of the Messenians who had been enslaved long ago: hence the name 'Messenians' given to all the Helots" (tr. Hammond). Some occurrences of καί after subordinating conjunctions appear to have the same discourse function. For example, in Herodotus 9.116.3 Artauctes, a Persian ruler, deceives Xerxes into plundering Protesilaus' tomb by saying Τούτου μοι δός, τὸν οἶκον, ἵνα καί τις μάθῃ ἐπὶ γῆν τὴν σὴν μὴ στρατεύεσθαι, "give me this man's house, so that all may be taught not to invade your territory" (tr. Godley). καί

§104. I see a similar pragmatic function in καί after the interrogative marker ποῖος in Sophocles. The following French translation is drawn from an illuminating argument by Humbert about καί.

(t50)

Μόρῳ δὲ ποίῳ καί σφε βουλεύῃ κτανεῖν;

Sophocles *Antigone* 772

Quelle mort, au juste, as-tu le design de lui infliger? "Which death, exactly, do you plan to inflict on her?" (tr. Humbert 1960:412)

The chorus asks Creon how he intends to put Antigone to death.[165] Humbert quotes this line to exemplify καί's ability to express "better approximation" ("*meilleure approximation*," 1960:412). He posits that by means of καί the speaker either makes the conditions of reality more precise or asks the interlocutor to do so.[166] Griffith, in his commentary suggests (1999:253), "By what kind of death exactly?". Humbert's attention to this force of καί is unprecedented, although previous literature gestures toward the general idea;[167] it is his interpretation that correlates best with our own views about καί's capacity for specifying, detailing, pinning down, and gaining in precision.

§105. καί can be used to pin down in many ways; one of them is to focus in on a character, or on a moment in an ongoing account. The following passage, in which καί impacts a number of clauses, illustrates how καί marks the intention to elaborate:

(t51)

ἐνθαῦτα κατέβη αὐτὸς Ξέρξης ἐπὶ τὰς νέας, ... Ἐπεὶ δὲ ἀπικόμενος προΐζετο, παρῆσαν μετάπεμπτοι οἱ τῶν ἐθνέων τῶν σφετέρων τύραννοι καὶ ταξίαρχοι ἀπὸ τῶν νεῶν, καὶ ἵζοντο ὥς σφι βασιλεὺς ἑκάστῳ τιμὴν ἐδεδώκεε, πρῶτος μὲν

following ἵνα signals a focus on a specific aspect of the speaker's purpose. A separate argument should be developed about εἰ καί and καὶ εἰ, the difference between the former and the latter being an object of much discussion in earlier literature (see for example Hartung 1832-1833, vol. I:139-140; Denniston 1950:299-303).

165 For δέ at the start of new questions in drama, see III.4 §34-§35.

166 See also Aeschylus *Agamemnon* 278 and Euripides *Hecuba* 515.

167 E.g. Bäumlein 1861:146-147 ("nähere Bestimmung," "closer definition"), and Ebeling 1885:617 (καί can convey more accuracy). Smyth 1956:650 simply notes that καί often means "namely, for example." In his *Lexicon to Herodotus*, Powell (1938:176-180) calls "epexegetic" 88 instances of καί introducing illustrations or specifications. Denniston does not mention this aspect for καί alone in general, except in a gloss to line 17 of the *Homeric Hymn 3 to Apollo* (κεκλιμένη πρὸς μακρὸν ὄρος καὶ Κύνθιον ὄχθον) where he notes: "καί means 'and in particular'" 1950:291). Cooper 1998:1337 remarks that καί in drama and in invectives introduces the second element as a "characterization of the first."

ὁ Σιδώνιος βασιλεύς, μετὰ δὲ ὁ Τύριος, ἐπὶ δὲ ὧλλοι. Ὡς δὲ κόσμῳ ἐπεξῆς ἵζοντο ...

Herodotus 8.67.1-2

Xerxes himself went down to the ships. ... He came and sat on his throne, and present at his summons were the tyrants of all the peoples and the company leaders from the fleet. They sat according to the honor which the king had granted each of them, first the king of Sidon, then the king of Tyre, then the rest. When they sat in order one after another, ... (tr. Godley)

Here καί introduces a number of visual details. After priming us with references to the relevant characters (king Xerxes and the other prominent leaders), Herodotus, by means of καὶ ἵζοντο, proceeds to specify who was where, in what order they sat, and why.[168] καί's force—its connective function combined with the meaning of its enrichment—amounts to "and, let me zoom in and detail the scene." It takes many words to spell this out in English; in the Greek, καί alone is sufficient and economical.

2.4.3 Using καί to mark narrative peaks

§106. Let us turn to a function of καί where it marks narrative peaks. Pinning down in this case entails defining the highest moment of a course of action. These solo instances of καί, like καὶ δὴ καί and καὶ γάρ, have scope over multi-act units, and like καὶ δή, focus on a specific fact. Allan observes that Thucydides makes use of καί in combination with short paratactic clauses (often including an historical present-tense verb) at the peak of an episode (2007:93-94; 115).[169] A passage that I quoted earlier, (t45), contains an instance of this kind of καί:

(t52)

Οἱ δὲ ἀμφὶ τὸν Πείσανδρον ... ὁπλίτας ἔχοντες σφίσιν αὐτοῖς ξυμμάχους ἦλθον ἐς τὰς Ἀθήνας. <u>καὶ</u> καταλαμβάνουσι τὰ πλεῖστα τοῖς ἑταίροις προειργασμένα.

Thucydides 8.65.1-2

[168] The visual character of this description might echo some image. From Herodotus 4.88.1 we assume that the historian knew (or knew about) the illustration committed by Mandrocles of Samos, which depicted Darius on the throne facing his army. I thank Pietro Liuzzo for pointing out to me this and other connections between historiography and paintings (see Liuzzo 2012).

[169] Longacre 1985 argues that narrative peaks are usually accompanied by some turbulence on the linguistic level, which means, in our terms, that major discourse discontinuities occur. Short paratactic clauses and tense change in the peaks identified by Allan support Longacre's finding. Peaks and turbulence are discussed in II.3 §§15-17; for δὴ τότε and καὶ τότε as peak markers, see II.3 §58.

> Peisander and his colleagues, ... took on board hoplites who would support them. When they reached Athens they found most of the work already done by the members of the cabals. (tr. Hammond)

Hammond's translation opts for temporal continuity in the narration ("they took ...," "they reached ...," "they found ..."). The Greek, however, shows a change in tense from imperfect to present (ἦλθον—καταλαμβάνουσι), which enhances the foregrounding effect and sense of immediacy: Peisander and his colleagues' discovery, as a result, emerges as pivotal and particularly exciting.[170]

§107. This type of καί is related to what Basile (1998:714) calls "καί *di rottura*" ("breaking-off καί"); like *cum inversum* in Latin, καί may introduce a surprising, unexpected, new or simply exciting event. A fitting translation in Italian would be "*quand'ecco (che)/ed ecco*". In English, postponed when-clauses do the same thing (for instance, "I was sleeping, when the bell rang").[171] The following passage contains a τε ... καί construction, where the καί works in the manner just described. Fulfilling this function does not interfere with the correlating function it performs as part of a τε ... καί[172] unit:

(t53)

Ἠώς τε δὴ διέφαινε <u>καὶ</u> οἳ ἐγένοντο ἐπ' ἀκρωτηρίῳ τοῦ ὄρεος

Herodotus 7.217.2

170 A peak-marking καί that does not include the switch to a historical present is the following: ἤδη δὲ ἦν ὀψὲ καὶ ἐπεπαιάνιστο αὐτοῖς ὡς ἐς ἐπίπλουν, καὶ οἱ Κορίνθιοι ἐξαπίνης πρύμναν ἐκρούοντο κατιδόντες εἴκοσι ναῦς Ἀθηναίων προσπλεούσας, "It was now late in the day, and the paean for attack had already been sung when suddenly the Corinthians began to back water. They had caught sight of the approach of a further twenty Athenian ships..." (Thucydides 1.50.5; tr. Hammond). After the battle of Sybota in Thesprotia, the Corinthians sail to Corcyra to attack the Corcyraeans again. But off the coast they realize that twenty more ships of the Athenians reinforce the enemies, and decide to withdraw. The excerpt narrates the sudden moment when the Corinthians start to back water, which seems to be an unexpected move from the point of view of both Corcyreans and Athenians. The adverb ἐξαπίνης reinforces the climax.

Herodotus makes use of the same discourse strategy. For an instance see the long episode of Cyrus and Croesus: καὶ τὸν Κῦρον ἀκούσαντα ..., μεταγνόντα τε καί ἐννώσαντα ..., πρός τε τούτοισι δείσαντα ..., κελεύειν σβεννύναι τὴν ταχίστην τὸ καιόμενον πῦρ ..., "When Cyrus heard ... he relented and considered that .... In addition, he feared .... He ordered that the blazing fire be extinguished as quickly as possible" (Herodotus 1.86.6; tr. Godley). Cyrus had ordered Croesus to be burned alive. The fire was already burning when Apollo came to Croesus' rescue, and it started to rain. Cyrus understood that his opponent was enjoying divine protection. Within the general frame of reported speech, καί initiates a prolonged peak: the real climax (κελεύειν σβεννύναι) is delayed, and therefore made even more effective, by a long series of participles intervening in between, which motivates Cyrus' change of mind.

171 See Couper-Kuhlen 1988 about "postponed" when-clauses in English, where the comparison with Latin *cum inversum* is explicitly made.

172 Brouwer (1975:40) remarks that καί in τε ... καί in Herodotus may indicate further particularization.

Then dawn was appearing, when they [the Persians] reached the summit of the top of the mountain...[173] (tr. Godley)

The Persians have reached the top of mountain Oeta, through the track that takes them to the Thermopylae. All in all, καί seems to be capable of marking an increased degree of either precision (better approximation) or narrative interest. In a word, it leads to a climax.

2.4.4 Using καί to start narrative expansions

§108. The sole καί can perform a further discourse function in common with καὶ δὴ καί, καὶ γάρ, and καί after relative pronouns. This function relates to narrative expansion, and is recognizable in a particle pattern I already discussed in the sections on δέ and on τε. The pattern is "καί | x μέν"; it indicates that at least a second clause introduced by a particle will follow the x μέν clause, and that καί regulates both.

(t54)

καὶ μάχης γενομένης ἰσορρόπου πρὸς Κορινθίους διεκρίθησαν ἀπ' ἀλλήλων, καὶ ἐνόμισαν αὐτοὶ ἑκάτεροι οὐκ ἔλασσον ἔχειν ἐν τῷ ἔργῳ. <u>καὶ</u> | οἱ μὲν Ἀθηναῖοι ... τροπαῖον ἔστησαν· οἱ δὲ Κορίνθιοι ... ἡμέραις ὕστερον δώδεκα ... ἀνθίστασαν τροπαῖον καὶ αὐτοὶ ὡς νικήσαντες.

Thucydides 1.105.6

And when there was an well-balanced battle with the Corinthians, the two sides separated from each other. And each considered they had not the smaller part in the action. AND, the Athenians ... set up a trophy; the Corinthians ... after twelve days ... set a trophy in opposition, as if they too won. (tr. Hammond capital letters by AB)

After two καί that have a one-clause scope (καί ... διεκρίθησαν; καί ... ἐνόμισαν), the third appears more isolated, as it is followed by a οἱ μέν clause answered later by a οἱ δέ clause. This καί functions as a super-linker embracing the content of both the μέν and

173 In this passage I read τε δή as a cluster having scope over the entire sentence. More on τε δή in IV.3 §129. Further instances of "breaking-off καί" occur, e.g., in Plato *Euthydemus* 273a καὶ οὔπω τούτω δύ' ἢ τρεῖς δρόμους περιεληλυθότε ἤστην, καὶ εἰσέρχεται Κλεινίας ("And they took two or three turns, when Cleinias stepped in," tr. Lamb); Xenophon *Anabasis* 1.2.6 ἐνταῦθα ἔμεινεν ἡμέρας ἑπτά· καὶ ἧκε Μένων ὁ Θετταλὸς ("he [Cyrus] remained there seven days; at that point Menon the Thessalian arrived," tr. AB).

the δέ clause.[174] Earlier in the chapter (§46) I mentioned that these phenomena indicate a "discourse hierarchy," as opposed to a syntactic hierarchy, because it is a configuration of coordinating particles that signals it.[175] Prosodically emphatic *and* in English (see the capital letters in the translation) is applied when *and* has a scope larger than a clausal one.[176] In those cases it constitutes a separate intonation unit (rendered in writing by a comma after it). Pragmatically, this amounts to assigning an enriched metanarrative meaning to that "and," which I paraphrase as "and this is what happened."

§109. Other narrative expansions are introduced by καί together with wordings that explicitly tell, or enable us to predict, the communicative goal of the upcoming acts. After quoting an oracle about the Pelargic area (see above (t43) and (t49)), Thucydides gives us his own interpretation of it:

(t55)

<u>καί</u> μοι δοκεῖ τὸ μαντεῖον τοὐναντίον ξυμβῆναι ἢ προσεδέχοντο· οὐ γὰρ διὰ τὴν παράνομον ἐνοίκησιν αἱ ξυμφοραὶ γενέσθαι τῇ πόλει, ἀλλὰ διὰ τὸν πόλεμον ἡ ἀνάγκη τῆς οἰκήσεως, ὃν οὐκ ὀνομάζον τὸ μαντεῖον προῄδει μὴ ἐπ' ἀγαθῷ ποτὲ αὐτὸ κατοικισθησόμενον.

Thucydides 2.17.2

My view is that the oracle was fulfilled, but in the reverse of the general expectation. It was not the unlawful occupation which caused the disasters of the city, but the war which forced the occupation: without specific reference to the war the oracle was predicting that the area would never be occupied to a good end. (tr. Hammond)

[174] See II.2 §71 (t33) for a remark by Denniston about words preceding a μέν ... δέ complex. The pattern "| καί | x μέν" followed by a δέ clause, or by another particle, or by a subclause, occurs already in the *Iliad* (35 tokens) and in the *Odyssey* (25 tokens). In Herodotus it occurs 153 times; in Thucydides 348 times. In IV.3 §§111-112 the same pattern is analyzed in terms of a minimal act (just καί) projecting a multi-act discourse unit.

[175] In this respect, Rijksbaron's discussion of καί ... δέ in classical Greek (Rijksbaron 1997a), which centers on what is the connector and what is the adverb, should perhaps be examined more closely. Some of the instances may reveal a "καί | x δέ" pattern, which would change the segmentation of clauses and the discourse hierarchy. More in IV.3 §§110-111 on moves that start with this kind of καί. Contiguous καὶ δέ, conversely, occurs only in Homer, and infrequently (see the table at the end of the chapter). In those instances καί has scope over an entire act or entire move, while δέ further marks the beginning of that act or move.

[176] For a prosodic analysis of *and* across different scopes, see, recently, Barth-Weingarten 2012. The greater the syntactic-semantic scope, the less reduced the phonetic design is.

καί μοι δοκεῖ enacts a shift from reportage to commentary and evaluation. The word cluster warns us, metanarratively, that the historian is about to provide an assessment of the oracle, which in this case extends over several clauses.[177]

§110. We may say that καί μοι δοκεῖ starts a move, that is, the pursuit of a communicative goal by means of multiple acts. In this case μοι δοκεῖ works as a semantic clue substantiating the overarching evaluative goal of the move. This example further supports the idea that a καί move can only be understood through the syntax, semantics, and pragmatics of what surrounds καί.

§111. A similar use of καί marking a move transition is possible in forensic oratory:

(t56)

Καί μοι κάλει Καλλίαν καὶ Στέφανον. <Μάρτυρες> Κάλει δὲ καὶ Φίλιππον καὶ Ἀλέξιππον·

Andocides *On Mysteries* 17

Kindly call Callias and Stephanus—yes, and call Philippus and Alexippus. (tr. Maidment)

Andocides himself is talking to the court. The first καί ("And now ...") starts not only the sentence but also a new section of the defense. The men called by name are indirectly connected to Lydus, the last of the four witnesses Andocides recalls before defending himself. The text goes on with a brief presentation of the four individuals (chapter 18), after which the jury examines them.

2.4.5 Using καί to wrap accounts up

§112. Besides marking move starts, καί acts can mark move ends, especially in Thucydides.[178] At move ends the καί act wraps up major narrative sections. In these cases the first conjunct is a sizable multi-act unit that occurs before καί, while the second conjunct is just one act:

[177] IV.4 §§62-63 considers similar constructions, such as evaluative clauses starting with καί and including the verb δοκέω—for instance, Thucydides 1.143.3 Καὶ τὰ μὲν Πελοποννησίων ἔμοιγε τοιαῦτα καὶ παραπλήσια δοκεῖ εἶναι, τὰ δὲ ἡμέτερα ... , "Such is broadly my view of the Peloponnesian position. Our own position ..." (tr. Hammond).

[178] The use of καί (*usus* μεταβατικός) with reference to Thucydides is already noted by Hoogeveen (1769:533-534).

(t57)

καὶ τὸ θέρος ἐτελεύτα.

Thucydides, *passim*[179]

And so, summer ended. (tr. AB)

This simple Thucydidean discourse act regularly rounds off several chapters reporting the events of a particular summer. The narrative relevance is evident: the historian steps back from his piecemeal account, and establishes a link between the preceding utterances as a whole, and the present one.[180] Functionally this statement is similar to the "and they lived happily ever after" formula we find at the end of folktales, which I mentioned in the introduction.[181]

§113. So far I have mainly considered καί linking portions of discourse that exceed one clause or one act. The following passage shows more καί occurring near each other but having different scope and conveying different forces.[182] This use of καί does not represent an exception but rather a common feature we continually encounter in our reading, especially of Thucydides' text.[183]

(t58)

πάντα τε πρὸς τὸ παραχρῆμα περιδεές, ὅπερ φιλεῖ δῆμος ποιεῖν, ἑτοῖμοι ἦσαν εὐτακτεῖν. καὶ ὡς ἔδοξεν αὐτοῖς, καὶ ἐποίουν ταῦτα, καὶ τὸ.θέρος ἐτελεύτα.

Thucydides 8.1.4

179 See Thucydides 2.92.7; 3.86.5; 102.7; 4.49.1; 5.12.2; 50.5; 75.6; 82.6; 115.4; 6.62.5; 7.9.1; 8.1.4, and 28.5 (with θέρος), and 3.88.4; 4.51.1; 135.2; 5.51.2; 56.5; 83.4; 6.7.4; 93.4; 7.18.4; 8.6.5; 60.3 (with χειμών, winter).

180 Bakker (1997c:31), on 5.83.4 (mentioning the end of a winter which coincided with the end of the fifteenth year of war) points out: "in the recurrent year-end formula, the double use of *kaí* in combination with imperfects signals that the end of winter is not an assertion in its own right, but the end of a larger statement: the recording of a winter's events." The imperfect ἐτελεύτα can be seen as part of the rounding-off strategy as well. Again, Bakker remarks (1997c:30) "The imperfect verb *eteleúta* "ended" marking this transition does not denote an event as such in the narrative; rather, it is meant...to accommodate narrated events." The general quality of imperfect tense in Rijksbaron (1984:12) is that "it creates a framework within which other actions may occur." See also Allan 2007:106-107.

181 See §12. A similar use of καί in Herodotus occurs, for example, at 1.191.6 Καὶ Βαβυλὼν μὲν οὕτω τότε πρῶτον ἀραίρητο, "And Babylon, then, for the first time, was taken in this way"; 2.120.5 Καὶ ταῦτα μὲν τῇ ἐμοὶ δοκέει εἴρηται, "This is what I think, and I state it"; 9.121.1 Καὶ κατὰ τὸ ἔτος τοῦτο οὐδὲν ἐπὶ πλέον τούτων ἐγένετο, "This, then, is all that was done in this year."

182 For discussion of a passage in Aristophanes with a similar sequence of καί in close succession with different scopes, see III.2 §35.

183 See above, n16 and n138 about the extensive employment of καί in Thucydides.

> As tends to happen in a democracy, the people were ready to embrace any form of discipline in the panic of the moment, so they proceeded to implement the decisions they had taken. So the summer ended. {*Indentation*} (tr. Hammond)

The Greek narrative and syntactic pace of this passage can hardly be rendered in English. The three καί intensify the connection between different kinds of events, and almost iconically speed them up. At the same time, each καί introduces its own communicative act. The first καί links the description of the Athenians' attitude to its instantiation: Thucydides illustrates εὐτακτεῖν, perhaps with some nuance of distrust, as a smooth combination of planning and acting ("Which means: as things seemed good to them, ..."). This interpretation suits the Greek word order καί | ὡς ..., which suggests that καί's scope covers both the ὡς clause and the main clause ἐποίουν ταῦτα. The main clause, in turn, is introduced by the second καί, an "apodotic" καί.[184] The communicative act in this case involves signposting a climax as the narrative transitions from relating the Athenians' judgment to relating its exact implementation (ταῦτα being as salient as ἐποίουν).[185] Finally, the third καί introduces an act that rounds off the narration of summer events.[186]

2.4.6 Enrichments of καί when καί is untranslated

§114. In the introduction to this chapter (§11) I flagged that *and* in English sometimes possesses enrichments such as "and then," or "and on the other hand." The analyses of Greek texts so far suggested paraphrases of enriched καί such as "and in particular," "and here it what happened," "and—let me add— ..." In general, English translations of Herodotus and Thucydides do not omit καί, except when too many καί follow each other in Thucydides (which is not infrequent).[187] When they go untranslated and the co-text does not offer too many other καί, it is possbible that an enrichment occurs, which is difficult to render in words. Let us focus on three excerpts attesting to that:

184 For the notion of "apodotic," and instances of apodotic δέ, see above IV.2.2.4.

185 See Ὡς δέ οἱ ταῦτα ἔδοξε, καὶ ἐποίεε κατὰ τάχος, "This he [Cyrus] decided, and this he did immediately" (Herodotus 1.79.1; tr. AB). At 1.73 Herodotus narrates the details of the Scythians' resolute decision taken to avenge the bad treatment received by Cyaxares, king of Media. The details regard the plan of a macabre banquet, and Ταῦτα καὶ ἐγένετο (1.73.6) confirms the exact correspondence between thoughts and action. Ταῦτα καὶ ἐγένετο occurs also in Herodotus 6.78.2. See also τὰ δὴ καὶ ἐγένετο (Herodotus 1.22.2; 5.92.δ.1; 9.56.1) and τά περ ὦν/ἂν καὶ ἐγένετο (Herodotus 2.2.3; 7.168.3; 8.109.5; 9.113.2). καὶ ἐγένετο in Thucydides occurs 12 times. Hoogeveen (1769:536) interprets connective καί to convey, sometimes, promptness ("*celeritatis indicem*"), so that actions are connected without any delay ("*tempori nulla dilatio*"). Trenkner 1960:66 notes the use of καί near actions after *verba sentiendi* or *dicendi* to mark explicitly the accomplishment of an order, and takes it as a sign of λέξις εἰρομένη.

186 The entire first chapter of Thucydides 8 is analyzed act by act, and move by move, in IV.5.3.

187 Translators avoiding too many *and* in a row conform to the unwritten rules of texts meant to be read; the less parataxis, the better. On these non-neutral choices regarding discourse segmentation, see above §7, and IV.3.

(t59)

Ἐν δὲ τούτῳ, ὅσοι Ἑρμαῖ ἦσαν λίθινοι ἐν τῇ πόλει τῇ Ἀθηναίων ... μιᾷ νυκτὶ οἱ πλεῖστοι περιεκόπησαν τὰ πρόσωπα. καὶ τοὺς δράσαντας ᾔδει οὐδείς, ἀλλὰ μεγάλοις μηνύτροις δημοσίᾳ οὗτοί τε ἐζητοῦντο καὶ προσέτι ἐψηφίσαντο, καὶ εἴ τις ἄλλο τι οἶδεν ἀσέβημα γεγενημένον, μηνύειν ἀδεῶς τὸν βουλόμενον καὶ ἀστῶν καὶ ξένων καὶ δούλων. καὶ τὸ πρᾶγμα μειζόνως ἐλάμβανον· τοῦ τε γὰρ ...

Thucydides 6.27.1-2

While these preparations were still in train, most of the stone Herms in the city of Athens had their faces mutilated in one night ... . Nobody knew the perpetrators, but large rewards were publicly offered for information leading to their detection, and a decree was also passed giving immunity to any citizens, foreigner, or slave, who volunteered knowledge of any other desecration. The Athenians took the matter more seriously still, ... (tr. Hammond)

(t60)

Ἐθάμβεον δὲ ὁρέων χρυσῷ τε καὶ εἵμασι κεκοσμημένον, πρὸς δὲ καὶ κλαυθμὸν κατεστεῶτα ἐμφανέα ἐν Ἁρπάγου. Καὶ πρόκατε δὴ κατ᾽ ὁδὸν πυνθάνομαι τὸν πάντα λόγονθεράποντος ὃς ἐμὲ προπέμπων ἔξω πόλιος ἐνεχείρισε τὸ βρέφος, ὡς ἄρα Μανδάνης τε εἴη παῖς τῆς Ἀστυάγεος θυγατρὸς καὶ Καμβύσεω τοῦ Κύρου, καί μιν Ἀστυάγης ἐντέλλεται ἀποκτεῖναι. Νῦν τε ὅδε ἐστί.

Herodotus 1.111.4-5

But I was amazed at seeing him adorned with gold and clothing, and at hearing, too, the evident sound of weeping in the house of Harpagus. Very soon on the way I learned the whole story from the servant who brought me out of the city and gave the child into my custody: namely, that it was the son of Mandane the king's daughter and Cambyses the son of Cyrus, and that Astyages gave the command to kill him. And[188] now, here he is. (tr. Godley)

(t61)

[The Paeonians had given it [=..] to the Thracians, and when Xerxes demanded it back, they said that the horses had been carried off from pasture by the Thracians of the hills who dwelt about the headwaters of the Strymon.]

188 Incidentally, the speech ends with a "sentential" τε achieving a coda effect.

> Ἔνθα <u>καὶ</u> ὁ τῶν Βισαλτέων βασιλεὺς γῆς τε τῆς Κρηστωνικῆς Θρῆιξ ἔργον ὑπερφυὲς ἐργάσατο·
>
> Herodotus 8.116.1
>
> It was then that a monstrous deed was done by the Thracian king of the Bisaltae and the Crestonian country. (tr. Godley)

Perhaps the translators, perceiving that these καί logically link their respective conjuncts together in several possible ways, wished to leave the ultimate interpretation up to the reader. Let us see which implications of καί in these co-texts and contexts can be inferred. In the first passage, (t59), the first καί follows the news about the mutilation of the Herms: "καί nobody knew who had done this." Readers are invited to enrich the basic additive function. Possibly this καί clause implies some pinning-down with regard to the agents (after the passive περιεκόπησαν): "and the problem was that nobody knew who had done it."[189]

§115. The second excerpt, (t60), deals more directly with what scholars in the past have called καί *adversativum*.[190] The speaker is the herdsman who had been ordered to abandon on the hills the baby that Harpagus had given to him. By means of καὶ πρόκατε δὴ κατ' ὁδὸν πυνθάνομαι a significant shift is expressed, from the past in which he wondered at the baby's rich dress (ἐθάμβεον) to the *hic et nunc* (πρόκατε δή) in which he learns the whole story (πυνθάνομαι).[191] Verdenius (1975:190) sees in this use of καί an adversative nuance: the herdsman had only been able to surmise the origins of the baby before, *but* now he has confirmation, and knows the baby's identity.[192] The adversative nuance simply comes from the potential of καί. Like *and* in English, καί can convey several enrichments, *but* being one of them. If speakers choose *and* to imply *but*, it means that they prefer to stress the connection between two contrasting facts rather than their difference.[193] In the case of this Herodotean excerpt, the herdsman, by means of καί, not only juxtaposes his suspects and the truth, but he also marks the peak of his narration.

189 All the subsequent καί of the passage are translated, the last included. καὶ τὸ πρᾶγμα μειζόνως ἐλάμβανον is rendered with "the Athenians took the matter more seriously still;" καί is interpreted as reinforcing the comparative μειζόνως with a scalar meaning. On scalarity, see below §123.

190 See in particular Blomqvist 1979 and Slings 1980. An earlier discussion of καὶ ἐναντιωματική occurs in Hoogeveen 1769:545-547.

191 Given that πυνθάνομαι in fact governs several clauses, we may take this καί *adversativum* as a καί introducing a multi-act unit. In addition, the temporal expression πρόκατε δή reminds us of postpostive δή after temporal adverbs in Homer (on which see II.3 §56), which suggests an act boundary (καὶ | πρόκατε δή).

192 For a discussion of this καί, see Blomqvist 1979:34.

193 For example, in "They should have told you, and they didn't" (Sköries 1999:21; quoted in the Introduction), the speaker encodes with *and* her preference for expressing the link between the

§116. As for the third excerpt, (t61), I interpret καί as "exactly," "just," in combination with ἔνθα ("there," although Godley's translation opts for the temporal sense "then"). The sense is not so much to add further information about a previous topic, as to isolate with precision, and climactically, the site of the prodigious occurrence about to be described. I advance that ἔνθα may at the same time identify the "slot" in the narrator's mind devoted to the recall of that prodigious occurrence. In other words, ἔνθα may blend physical and mental geography.[194]

2.4.7 καί as "or"

§117. Let us now turn to the narrowest scope that καί can have, that is, over noun and adjectival phrases. In Herodotus I find instances of καί in co-texts that yield an enrichment apparently different from all those analyzed so far, that is, the implication "or." Let us consider one of them:

(t62)

καὶ λέγουσι οὗτοι ... ὡς τὰς βασιληίας ἱστίας ἐπιώρκηκε ὃς <u>καὶ</u> ὅς, λέγοντες τῶν ἀστῶν τὸν ἂν δὴ λέγωσι·

Herodotus 4.68.1

... and they generally tell him that such and such a man (naming whoever it may be of the people) has sworn falsely by the king's hearth; (tr. Godley)

The historian is describing the Scythian practice of divination when the king is sick. By means of ὃς καὶ ὅς the anonymous perjurers are taken into account separately ("such and such" equals "this or that").[195] The pragmatic implication of this use of καί is that the two items are treated as equivalent alternatives one of the other.[196]

§118. The enrichment of καί as "or" consists in adding an alternative. The force of this addition may reside in correcting, by means of the second conjunct, an aspect of the

two contrasting situations rather than conveying the (obvious) opposition between them.

194 See II.3 §45 for propositional and non-propositional readings of ἔνθα in Homer.

195 Powell 1938:180 records these further Herodotean instances of καί meaning "or": 2.121.α1 καὶ ὑπὸ δύο ἀνδρῶν καὶ ὑπὸ ἑνός; 3.101.1 ὅμοιον ... καὶ παραπλήσιον; 2.121β1 and 3.148.2 καὶ δὶς καὶ τρίς. In the scholion to Homer *Iliad* 15.634 the scholiast says that καί is used for disjunctive ἤ. For καί meaning "or," Sturz 1801-1804:614; see Schwyzer and Debrunner 1950:567n5; Denniston 1950: 292; Cooper 1998:1338.

196 In a footnote towards the beginning of the chapter (n21) I mentioned Ariel's argument about a "relational" versus "independent" interpretation of *and*-conjunctions (Ariel 2012). In my view the instances of καί as "or" are the only cases where an "independent" reading can be applied. The conjuncts have to be processed as separate alternatives, rather than as parts of a relational construct.

first. Let me flag this specific usage in other genres than historiography. Ramsay (1898) argues that some καί mean "or," and draws particular attention to this passage from Aristophanes' *Wasps* 433. He hypothesizes that Loathecleon summons two slaves instead of three.

(t63)

ὦ Μιδα καὶ Φρὺξ βοήθει δεῦρο καὶ Μασυντία

Aristophanes *Wasps* 433

Midas, Phryx, come here and help! Masyntias too! (tr. Sommerstein).

Ramsay believes that the first καί links two alternative names and means "alias," "or" (cf. Latin *sive*); thus, the imperative verb in second person singular refers to "Midas *or* the Phrygian," to which a second slave, Masyntias, is added (the second καί meaning "and"). This reading harmonizes with the general idea of enrichments of καί I have discussed so far. Sometimes the link established by καί implies (as a pragmatic enrichment) a reformulation/amelioration of the first conjunct through the second. A corresponding paraphrase would be "and, to say it differently/better."

§119. In the following passage from Plato, καί is directly translated "or":

(t64)

... τοῦτο λέγειν, ὅτι ἡ ἀνθρωπίνη σοφία ὀλίγου τινὸς ἀξία ἐστὶν καὶ οὐδενός.

Plato *Apology* 23a

... [the god] means this: "Human wisdom is of little or no value." (tr. Fowler)

In ὀλίγου τινὸς ... καὶ οὐδενός, καί introduces an alternative expression: Socrates adjusts his statement so that he corrects the preceding formulation. In this passage Socrates' communicative intention to adjust his formulation may lead to a scalar reading: "or" may be read as "or even"/"even," with ὀλίγου and οὐδενός marking the progression on the scale.[197] The point is that the scalar component provided by "even" does not cancel or contradict the intention to reformulate or ameliorate a thought.

§120. The following example from Thucydides illustrates the possible co-existence of "or" and "even" particularly well.

[197] The notion of scalarity will be resumed in §123.

(t65)

ὡς δὲ ἐχθροὶ καὶ ἔχθιστοι, πάντες ἴστε, οἵ γε ἐπὶ τὴν ἡμετέραν ἦλθον δουλωσόμενοι, ...

Thucydides 7.68.2

It will be clear to all of you that the Athenians are not only enemies but the worst of the enemies. They came against our country to enslave it. (tr. Hammond)

Gylippus is talking to the Syracusan troops. In spite of the syntactic and even morphological symmetry between ἐχθροὶ and ἔχθιστοι (phrasal scope), καί invites us to enrich the link being established. The possible translation "and even," indicating a scalar meaning, can be associated with an adjustment analogous to the one in Plato's passage, that is, "or, better to say." Hammond's "not only ... but" evokes scalarity in combination with an idea of correction. If we take καί to mean "better to say," we recognize both the scalar component in the argument, and the function of καί aiming at more precision: "That they are enemies, or, better to say, the worst of the enemies, you all know that."

§121. The last examples of this subsection show the connection between the implication "or" and the ideas of better approximation and closer determination. In fact, they introduce us to the next (and final) subsection, which is about καί suggesting a sense of climax.

2.4.8 καί and the idea of climax

§122. Denniston (1950:293) writes about καί: "... when the addition is surprising, or difficult of acceptance, and when a sense of climax is present, 'also' becomes 'even'." The present subsection expands on the idea of climax, by combining the roles of καί as "also" and "even," and two notions applied to καί in earlier particle literature, that is, *superaddendi vis* and "*Steigerung*."

§123. According to the canonical account of καί, whenever καί does not link two conjuncts but is attached to just one conjunct, it means "also" or "even." καί can unquestionably function as a focus particle,[198] and as a scalar particle.[199] In the past philologists used the term "*Steigerung*" ("intensification," "climax") to unify the meanings of "also" and "even," possibly embracing an upward as well as a downward progression ("even

198 On the different focusing effects of focusing adverbs see in particular De Cesare 2010.

199 Starting from Karttunen and Peters (1979:23-33), who introduce the notion of focus, scope, and scalar implicature in association with 'even'; 'even' not only evokes alternatives, but it also implies that the focus of 'even' is the extreme case of some state. A comparative account of additive focus particles in various IE languages is offered by König 1991. On modern Greek *kai* as "also," "too" ("emphatic or intensifying" *kai*) see Canakis 1995:32-40. On ancient Greek καί as a scalar particle, see Bakker 1988:75; 84; 113-119; 205.

more" as well as "merely").[200] A Herodotean passage illustrates quite clearly how the sense of "*Steigerung*" pertains to καί stressing an addition:

(t66)

Ἔστι δὲ ἄλλη πόλις ἀπέχουσα ὀκτὼ ἡμερέων ὁδὸν ἀπὸ Βαβυλῶνος·Ἶς οὔνομα αὐτῇ. Ἔνθα ἐστὶ ποταμὸς οὐ μέγας· Ἶς καὶ τῷ ποταμῷ τὸ οὔνομα·

Herodotus 1.179.4

There is another city, called Is, eight days' journey from Babylon, where there is a little river, also named Is ... (tr. Godley)

καί effects a micro-climax by doing more than establishing a link between the city and the river; it "superadds" that the river has the same name. The progress in the Greek takes four steps: "there is a city;" "its name is Is;" "nearby there is a river;" "the river's name is also Is" (Ἶς καὶ τῷ ποταμῷ).[201]

§124. At an earlier point (2.4.3-2.4.4) I explored the role of καί at narrative peaks, and at the beginning of moves that expand portions of accounts. Both contexts represent climaxes on a larger scale, that is, on the multi-act level of discourse.[202] Here I focus on the idea of intensification/climax by considering a smaller range of the effect of καί, which is the phrasal scope. I propose to extend the notion of climax from the adverbial level to the conjunctive level of καί. Such an extension allows us to recognize that καί can detail, specify, and pin down on a phrasal level.

§125. I first recall that the construction ἄλλως τε καί, which literally means "both otherwise and," is understood as "and especially."[203] The function of this καί combination is to gain in precision, and in this respect is in line with some of the discourse functions I discussed earlier in relation to καί and καί combinations with multi-act scope.

200 See in particular Hartung 1832-1833, vol. I:121; 133-136; 139-140. Devarius 1588:107; 109, and Hoogeveen 1769:541 call this force of καί *superaddendi vis*. In Homer the combination καί τε frequently introduces a specification; it can be translated as "and in particular". Gonda (1954:265) observes that the member introduced by καί in καί τε is "stronger, more special or important (...); it contains a climax" and translates: "and also, and particularly." See also Denniston 1950:291 "καί with a sense of climax," Kühner and Gerth 1955:246 and 257, and Cooper 2002:3016: "καί changing from simple conjunctional meaning into its adverbial acceptance (...) can introduce and effect either an ascending climax or a descending climax."

201 I see the *superaddendi vis* of καί also when it follows δέ (see the consistent occurrences of δὲ καί across the authors of our corpus in the table at the end of the chapter). In those cases καί intensifies the following phrase, while δέ performs, independently, its ususal boundary marker function.

202 König (1991:16) has already taken into account the extension of the value of focus particles such as "also" and "only" to sentences, thus becoming "conjunctional adverbs."

203 Thiersch 1826:571: καί after ἄλλος or ἄλλως provides a "closer link" ("*engere Verbindung*").

We may find slight variations in word order and in form (for example, different forms of ἄλλος may appear; τε, if present at all, may have a different position), but the function is the same. Perhaps the most famous ἄλλος form followed by καί in Herodotus is the one that occurs at the end of the proem:

(t67)

τά <u>τε ἄλλα καὶ</u> δι' ἣν αἰτίην ἐπολέμησαν ἀλλήλοισι.

Herodotus, proem

and especially (...) why the two peoples fought with each other. (tr. Sélincourt and Marincola)

The historian announces the intention not to leave the great and marvelous deeds of the Greeks and of the Persians without κλέος, and especially (τά τε ἄλλα καί) for which reason (αἰτίην) they warred. The "zooming in" effect of καί suits well not only the central subject of the work, but also the start of the historiographical narrative proper: the immediately following clause is about the Persians considering the Phoenicians responsible (αἰτίους).

§126. Here is a variant of the construction:

(t68)

Οἰκέουσι δὲ <u>καὶ ἄλλοι καὶ</u> Λακεδαιμονίων ἄποικοι Κνίδιοι, ...

Herodotus 1.174.2

Among those who inhabit it [Caria] are certain Cnidians, colonists from Lacedaemon. (tr. Godley)

The detailing effect is clear: various people inhabit Caria, but Herodotus wants to focus *in particular* on the Cnidians.[204]

§127. One more construction is regarded in literature as showing an imbalance in the conjuncts: the pattern includes any form of πολύς + καί + a qualifying adjective. Once again, an example from Herodotus:

[204] See also Herodotus 1.80.1 διὰ δὲ αὐτοῦ ποταμοὶ ῥέοντες καὶ ἄλλοι καὶ Ὕλλος συρρηγνύουσι ἐς τὸν μέγιστον ("the Hyllus and other rivers flow across it and run violently together into the greatest of them" tr. Godley).

(t69)

Ὡς δὲ τὰ κατὰ τὸν Τέλλον προετρέψατο ὁ Σόλων τὸν Κροῖσον εἴπας πολλά τε καὶ ὄλβια, ...

Herodotus 1.31.1

When Solon had provoked him [Croesus] by saying that the affairs of Tellus were so fortunate, ... (tr. Godley)

What irritates Croesus the most, according to Herodotus' lexical choice and word order, is the detail about the blessings Tellus could enjoy. Interestingly enough, in his monograph on particles, Bäumlein (1861:146) quotes this wording to explain that in such constructions, the addition expresses "nähere Bestimmung" ("closer determination") rather than a coordinating relationship.[205]

§128. Let us now turn to less discussed instances of καί triggering intensification or climax at the phrasal level.

(t70)

τὰ ἔτι καὶ ἀμφότερα ἐς ἐμὲ ἦν κείμενα ἐν Θήβῃσι, καὶ Θηβέων ἐν τῷ νηῷ τοῦ Ἰσμηνίου Ἀπόλλωνος.

Herodotus 1.52.1

Both of these [the shield and the spear that Croesus dedicated to Amphiaraus] were until my time at Thebes, in the Theban temple of Ismenian Apollo.[206] (tr. Godley)

The second καί introduces a discourse act conveying specification: the Theban *temple*, to be precise.[207] The occurrence of names is significant. Names represent ideal second conjuncts after καί, not because they pertain to shared knowledge (as with τε), but

205 See also Herodotus 3. 14 ἐκ πολλῶν τε καὶ εὐδαιμόνων; 9.107 πολλά τε καὶ κακά (=8.61=9.107); 9.37 πολλά τε καὶ λυγρά; 9.37 πολλά τε καὶ ἀνάρσια; 6.114 πολλοί τε καὶ ὀνομαστοί; 8.73 πολλαί τε καὶ δόκιμοι; 8.89 πολλοί τε καὶ ὀνομαστοὶ; 9.27 πολλά τε καὶ εὖ ἔχοντα. An earlier parallel is the Homeric hendiadys ... πολλὰ καὶ ἐσθλά, occurring eight times; the second adjective qualifies more specifically the items referred to. A different case is the hendiadys καλός κἀγαθός. Especially in Xenophon the wording becomes a unified concept that lets us think of καί replacing τε used in what some scholars call "natural" coordination (on which see §62).

206 Further examples are: ἐς ὃ στρατευσάμενος ἐπὶ τοὺς Ἀσσυρίους καὶ Ἀσσυρίων τούτους οἳ Νίνον εἶχον ..., "until he [Deioces] marched against the Assyrians; that is, against those of the Assyrians who held Ninus" (Herodotus 1.102.2; tr. Godley); τούτων Πασαργάδαι εἰσὶ ἄριστοι, ἐν τοῖσι καὶ Ἀχαιμενίδαι εἰσὶ φρήτρη ..., "The chief tribe is that of the Pasargadae; to them belongs the clan of the Achaemenidae, (...)" (Herodotus 1.125.3, tr. Godley).

207 I take the first καί as a particle intensifying ἀμφότερα (see below, καὶ ἅπαντα τοῦτο in (t72)).

because names often need specifying and pinning down. Aristophanes seems to play with this type of asymmetrical καί in association with names, in order to exploit the humorous implications:

(t71)

> [Μα.] ... ἡ δέ γ' Εὔβοι', ὡς ὁρᾷς,
> ἡδὶ παρατέταται μακρὰ πόρρω πάνυ.
> [Στ.] οἶδ'· ὑπὸ γὰρ ἡμῶν παρετάθη <u>καὶ</u> Περικλέους.
>
> Aristophanes *Clouds* 211-213
>
> [Dis.] ... And Euboea here, as you see, is stretched out a long way by the side of it to a great distance.
> [Strep.]
> I know that; for it was stretched by us and Pericles. (tr. Hickie)

Sommerstein (1991:171) translates παρετάθη as "render helpless, knock out," and recalls that the Euboean revolt of 446 had been suppressed by Pericles. While "us" is still ambiguous, καὶ Περικλέους makes the joke by clarifying retrospectively the pun in παρετάθη. καί is the hinge for the discourse act of joking.

§129. The idea of "*Steigerung*" or climax enables us to better understand instances of καί with narrow scope that fit neither of the canonical connective or adverbial meanings. Here is a case in point:

(t72)

τὰ στρατόπεδα ποιεῖ μὲν <u>καὶ</u> ἅπαντα τοῦτο·

Thucydides 5.71.1

All armies do thus. (tr. Hobbes)

This statement opens the rationale for Agis' tactically crucial decision in the battle of Mantinea, and τοῦτο has a proleptic function. Apart from the unusual clause position of μέν—which suggests that τὰ στρατόπεδα could have represented a separate intonation unit[208]—the role of καί is not classifiable within the canonical dichotomy. I propose to read καί as possessing an intensifying function as it spotlights ἅπαντα by way of

[208] Gomme *et al.* 1945-1981, vol. IV:119 considers the word order of this clause unexpected. In light of the analyses of isolated referents in this monograph (II.2.5; III.5 §§30-33; IV.3.11.1), I propose to read an act boundary after τὰ στρατόπεδα: τὰ στρατόπεδα | ποιεῖ μὲν καὶ ἅπαντα τοῦτο.

specification as well as by way of indicating its remarkableness ("absolutely all of them"); in a word, it triggers a little climax.

§130. The affirmative meaning attached to καί in answers, especially in combination with adverbs such as μάλα, κάρτα or ὀρθῶς[209] can be interpreted, along the same lines, as springing from καί's ability to intensify an expression, and to give it a climactic sense.

(t73)

Ἀστυάγης εἴρετό μιν εἰ ἡσθείη τι τῇ θοίνῃ. Φαμένου δὲ Ἁρπάγου <u>καὶ</u> κάρτα ἡσθῆναι παρέφερον τοῖσι προσέκειτο τὴν κεφαλὴν τοῦ παιδὸς ...

Herodotus 1.119.5

Astyages asked him, "Did you like your meal, Harpagus?" "Exceedingly," Harpagus answered. Then those whose job it was brought him the head of his son ... (tr. Godley)

One of the most horrifying moments in the episode of Harpagus and Astyages coincides with the tragic irony of Harpagus' answer—reported by Herodotus in the form of an indirect answer: "yes, absolutely" (καὶ κάρτα).[210]

§131. Finally, it is common for translators to take καί with phrasal scope as "also" when no further addition is indicated, as here:

(t74)

Λέγουσι δὲ <u>καὶ</u> τόδε Ἀράβιοι, ὡς ...

Herodotus 3.108.1

The Arabians also say that ... (tr. Godley)

"The Arabians also say" implies that the Arabians have just been reported as saying something. But this is not the case. In the preceding chapter (107), where the topic "Arabia" is introduced, the Arabians neither speak in direct or indirect speech. An alternative meaning for καί is therefore wanted. If we read this καί as a marker of "*Steigerung*" in

209 See, for example, Hoogeveen 1769:578 (about καὶ μάλα); Sturz 1801-4, vol. II:616 on Xenophon; Schwyzer and Debrunner 1950:567. Denniston 1950:325 lists the marking of affirmation in the paragraph devoted to "special difficulties" about καί.

210 Jiménez Delgado 2013 explores the development of the combination καὶ μάλα into an affirmative answer, starting from the use of the combination in Xenophon.

the sense of better approximation, we obtain an improved translation: "The Arabians say exactly/just this:," and their reported opinion follows.[211]

§132. The idea of "*Steigerung*," finally, can also be conveyed by intensifying the frequency of καί. This is a construction that Thucydides in particular favors. In these cases, the increase in καί produces what I call an "accumulation effect."[212]

2.4.9 Interim conclusion

§133. Let me now sum up by speaking in practical terms. Any continuous reading of the two *Histories* would prompt us to ask, what should we do when we come across καί (which in Thucydides appears on average once every fifteen words)? The first cognitive operation we instinctively activate is to find out whether there are two conjuncts or one, in other words, to find out what καί is linking. If there is only one conjunct, which is confined to the phrasal scope, besides "also" and "even" we may include in the range of meanings "in particular" or "exactly/just." If there are two conjuncts, we must establish the boundaries (the scope, in fact) of the second conjunct, and then of the first.[213] We are aided in establishing the boundaries of conjunct 1 if a τε is present to mark it.[214]

§134. The next step may consist in a deeper processing of the semantic and pragmatic information provided especially by conjunct 2, to identify the possible implications of καί. An implication that readers hardly realize, for example, regards καί as "and then" in narrative progression. We may say that this type of enrichment is typical of

211 I see a parallel in Pindar: ... τάχα δ' εὐθὺς ἰὼν σφετέρας / ἐστάθη γνώμας ἀταρβάκτοιο πειρώμενος / ἐν ἀγορᾷ πλήθοντος ὄχλου. / τὸν μὲν οὐ γίνωσκον· ὀπιζομένων δ' ἔμπας τις εἶπεν καὶ τόδε· / 'Οὔ τί ποὺ οὗτος Ἀπόλλων ... "Putting this intrepid resolve to the test, he quickly went straight ahead, and stood in the agora as a crowd was thronging. They did not recognize him, but awestruck as they were, one of them nevertheless said, among other things: 'Surely this is not Apollo, (...)' (Pindar *Pythian* 4.83-87, tr. Race). I claim that there is no need to translate καὶ τόδε, "also this" or "among other things," as if the anonymous onlooker actually delivered a longer speech than the reported one, as Giannini supposes in Gentili *et al.* (1995:453): "καὶ τόδε: 'anche questo' oltre 'al resto'"; or as if he were about to say extreme things, in accordance with scalar "even". Pindar simply makes him delineate a short mythological excursus establishing who the mysterious hero they are admiring (Jason in fact) is not (which triggers suspense). The onlooker says *just* or *exactly* this, with καί contributing a pinning down-effect further carried on by the proleptic τόδε, and, most of all, by the exact words uttered at that moment and re-performed in the song.

212 This typically happens in Thucydides. For example, the chapter on the plague symptoms (2.49) contains 35 καί over 351 words (1 καί every 12.2 words on average, against the overall average of once per 14.9 words). Beyond quantity, the series of καί additions concerning body parts being affected, and the devastating effects, contributes to the poignancy of the description.

213 Sköries (1998:53) notes that only after reaching the end of the second item linked by *and* it is possible to detect where the first item begins.

214 See above §§80-81 in the section on τε.

the historiographical genre in general.[215] However familiar, or expected in virtue of the genre, this is an implication that we attach to καί.

§135. We may also sense other types of implied meanings, and we may want to ascertain which enrichment καί conveys. One way to test this is to look for semantic or pragmatic asymmetrical signs, as for example, a change in tense, or the presence of other particles nearby. In particular, if καί—regardless of what punctuation mark precedes it,[216]—occurs in a "καί | x particle" pattern, we better understand its discourse function after detecting what complements the "x particle" clause. This complement may be another "x particle" clause that follows the first, either immediately or after other intervening clauses. Another asymmetrical sign is a pragmatic change in the source of the utterance (for example, καί μοι δοκεῖ).

§136. The latter asymmetrical feature relates to the discourse discontinuities I mention in §30. If καί co-occurs with linguistic elements that shift our attention to some new unit of the discourse, that καί introduces a transition. Thus, beyond monitoring occurrences of καί, we should always be monitoring the text for multi-act moves. Is any transition taking place? At which point in an episode does καί appear? Does καί occur within isolated word clusters?

§137. Finally, if καί follows a subordinating conjunction or is the first word of a main clause after a subclause (apodotic καί), we face discourse acts that are of equal weight, possibly expanding on preceding material or highlighting the ongoing piece of narration.

2.5 Conclusions

§138. This analysis of δέ, τε, and καί in Herodotus and Thucydides challenges two major dichotomous formulations in the scholarship, namely that particles work either as conjunctions or adverbs, and that particles either modify content or do not.[217]

§139. From examining δέ, τε, and καί in historiographical passages, I have found that the syntactic role of coordination can be associated with discourse meanings that

215 If we take into account Herodotus and Thucydides, the employment of καί for narrative progression is more regular in Thucydides than in Herodotus, partly because of the greater use of καί by the former, and because of the greater use of δέ by the latter (which echoes the epic use of δέ for subsequent narrative steps). In a brief survey of the linguistic constructions that ancient Greek historians use for storytelling, Dover focuses on the employment of καί (1997b:71-77). The scholar compares the frequency of "simple καί" across samples from Pherecydes, Herodotus, Thucydides, Plato, and Xenophon. Thucydides scores much higher than Herodotus. "(...) the difference is spectacular in respect of simple καί (...). It is clear that (...) Herodotus departed very markedly from the 'καί-style'" (p. 73 for the quotation).

216 IV.3.2 and IV.3.3 discuss how modern punctuation generally influences the segmentation of the text. The linking power of καί generates some reluctance, by modern editors, to put full stops before the particle. For instance, the *TLG* edition of Thucydides (Stuart Jones) includes only 77 καί after full stops.

217 Colleagues working on "conjunctive adverbs" challenge the first dichotomous formulation as well (see above §4).

are only implied. By "implied" I mean that the discourse meanings are not linguistically encoded but inferable from the co-text and context. Previous literature on δέ, τε, and καί in fact captures some implied meanings by applying adjectives such as "inceptive δέ" or "conclusive τε."[218] We can compare such implied meanings to sentential adverbs, which in English are defined as adverbs that do not contribute content but communicate attitudes towards content.[219] It is the association between the syntactic role of coordination and implied discourse meanings that suggests to me that dichotomies are insufficient for explaining the functioning of these particles.

§140. In line with contemporary studies on lexical items that in some modern languages are used as conjunctions but also as discourse markers, we propose to view each of the three particles as existing on a continuum. The continuum embraces several options exploited in historiography (and in other genres), ranging from the simplest *and*-coordination in content (e.g. τὰ ἐν Θεσσαλίῃ καὶ τὰ ἐν Ἀχαιίῃ, Herodotus 7.198.1) to discourse effects involving entire narrative sections (e.g. καὶ τὸ θέρος ἐτελεύτα, (t57) and (t58)). Those usages that barely correspond to "and" (e.g. δέ close to asyndeton, and "epic" τε) are integral to the picture. They show that in ancient Greek the same lexical items fulfill multiple functions in a variety of syntactic and semantic configurations. I have showed this multifunctionality on a methodological level. Throughout the chapter I have intentionally avoided comprehensive statistics about functions, but opted to analyze δέ across different syntactic constructions, and τε within its wide spectrum of cognitive and pragmatic implications.

§141. One of the goals in this chapter is to bridge a major theoretical gap by looking at the functioning of these particles on the smaller scale together with their functioning at a larger one—to consider, so to speak, how the micro-horizon of intra-sentence or intra-clause levels complements the macro-horizon. Quite often the particles in question serve discourse functions involving multi-clause and multi-sentence units. Furthermore, short phrases may anticipate topic frames that extend over several subsequent clauses. Methodologically I have pursued this goal by organizing the section on καί around pragmatic forces of the particle that are comparable across different scopes, from moves to acts.

§142. Overall the analysis has benefits for literary criticism. Attention is oriented to the pragmatic effectiveness of using certain particles at certain points of the discourse, which syntactic and semantic configurations may suggest but not entirely explain. Instances labeled superfluous or unclassifiable become *à propos*; they do make sense. We may find a reason behind such divergent translations as "for example," "just," "or," as well as behind untranslated καί. Further attention is devoted to what the brain finds convenient in producing and processing discourse successfully. It becomes apparent

[218] See above 2.2.3 and §78 respectively.

[219] See, e.g. Bach and Harnish 1979; Ifantidou-Trouki 1993 offers an updated discussion of sentential adverbs.

how δέ, τε and καί, like many other particles, are critical devices in facilitating these processes, for they convey what language is doing (metalinguistic meanings), and how narration proceeds (metanarrative meanings). This is why the forces of particles are seen to fit discourse acts and moves behind their phrasal, clausal, and sentential scope.

§143. Interim conclusions at the end of each section (IV.2.2.7; 2.3.8; 2.4.9) summarize specific findings on each of the three lexical items. Here I add a general note. On the one hand, the findings retrieve and substantiate input already provided in the literature; for example καί's potential to mean "and in particular," or the frequent occurrence in Herodotus and Thucydides of "sentential" τε. On the other hand, I posit entirely new readings. For instance, the recurrent pattern "καί/x δέ/x τε | x (other) particle" indicates a special discourse organization: the initial phrase is isolated from the rest and at the same time it projects its force over a number of upcoming clauses.[220] Another instance is τε's ability to evoke the sense of shared knowledge through its association of personal and place names.[221]

§144. On the methodological level, I find that combinations involving δέ, τε, καί, and other particles contribute to discourse articulation in ways as meaningful as the single items constituting them. This finding confirms that individual particles are semantically unstable and work together only with their co-text. A further methodological finding is that our understanding of the uses of these particles greatly profits from detaching ourselves from punctuation marks. Our inferences about the functions of δέ, τε, and καί should not depend on commas and full stops; rather, commas and full stops reflect, retrospectively, what δέ, τε, and καί among other words originally effected. It is more productive to compare uses of δέ, τε, and καί to intonation patterns in modern languages.[222]

	Il.	*Od.*	P	Ae	S	E	Ar	H	T
τε καί	343	213	65	81	73	103	79	866	343
καί τε (τ')	17	6	—	—	—	—	—	—	—
δέ τε (τ')	105	41	—	—	—	2	—	—	—
τε δέ (δ')	—	—	—	—	—	—	—	—	—
δὲ καί	86	61	42	80	11	71	27	411	388
καὶ δέ (δ')	16	14	—	—	—	—	—	—	—

Table 1: Absolute occurrences of δέ, τε, and καί combinations in our corpus

220 See (t10), (t20), (t38), (t41).

221 See §§65-69.

222 See above 2.3.7.

§145. Throughout this chapter I have set forth instances from other genres to indicate something of fundamental importance. The usages analyzed in the two *Histories* are common to several genres; at the same time Herodotus and Thucydides exploit basic functions to pursue communicative goals that are central to historiography, by adapting them quantitatively and qualitatively. Examples are the Herodotean preference for καὶ δή καί announcing the next macrotopic, and the Thucydidean preference for τε introducing separate statements.

§146. All in all, the functioning of *and*-coordination in the two masterpieces proves how fortunate we are: ancient Greek δέ, τε, and καί with their multifunctionality reveal a precision and a richness in language use that not only uncovers but also disentangles the complexity of "and.

IV.3

Discourse Segmentation

3.1 Introduction

§1. The present chapter focuses on how we segment Herodotean and Thucydidean discourse in reading, and on the relevance of particles to that. "We," "segment," and "discourse" require some glosses. "We" refers to the community reading the two *Histories* nowadays. This reading community does not apply a uniform practice in reading and/or teaching and/or researching those texts. However, the task we share of attempting to comprehend the texts does entail certain overarching aims and general constraints.

§2. Segmentation is a part of reading. While reading, we process stretches of text in a piecemeal progression. The size of such stretches may be bigger in the case of silent reading (as our eyes can span more words), and smaller in the case of reading aloud (eyes and ears focus on fewer words at a time), but the fundamental cognitive and intellectual experience is the same: we receive verbal input in pieces.[1] Usually written pages provide larger divisions of discourse (indentation, for example), and we may glance at them in a cursory manner as we start reading a clause; still, what we can follow word by word is a relatively small portion of discourse.[2] If we listen to stretches of text, segmentation happens in a more radical way, as the absence of written pages compels us to focus just on the verbal segments we receive sequentially.

§3. Finally, I take discourse as a comprehensive and dynamic notion that embraces various linguistic components of texts (morpho-lexical, syntactic, semantic, and pragmatic), as well as paralinguistic and extralinguistic components (punctuation, prosody, paragraphing, links to the contextual setting, short and long-term memory).[3] Furthermore, "discourse" evokes a distinctive feature of discourse analysis as a subfield

1 "... reading is not a simple matter of moving our eyes in a smooth, continuous motion along the lines of text. Our eyes move in a series of jumps, and reading takes place only when the eyes are still. Each time the eye lands on the line, it 'reads' an area of text to each side (and above and below) the landing point. In technical terms, at each 'fixation', we have a certain span of perception or 'eye-span'. ... Most of us can span three to five words at each fixation." (Kirkman 2006:9).

2 See e.g. Clark and Clark 1977:50-57.

3 Such a broad notion of discourse matches the view of discourse as the domain of language use (Du Bois 2003:11), and that of discourse as a process rather than a product (Widdowson 1979:71). See also I.1.4. I will take up this point again in 3.4. The term "paralinguistic" is glossed in §6.

of linguistics, that is, the consideration of discourse units, especially above the sentence level.[4] In light of that, segmentation encompasses micro and macro divisions, ranging from the way in which a vocative expression is set off to what made editors of the two *Histories* assign chapter numbers.

§4. Our piecemeal processing of discourse relies on several components that we make use of in order to segment texts. These components include the syntactic arrangements of words. We process signs of integration across words, and signs of boundaries between them. For instance, we associate a sense of completeness with main clauses, and we perceive syntactic integration in the constituents of a subclause. Likewise, we sense boundaries between list entries, and we isolate anacoluthic constructions from the surrounding co-text. All this is to say that we see syntactic characteristics of the text such as the presence of subordinating conjunctions, and the occurrence of finite or nonfinite verbs, as important cues in discourse segmentation.

§5. Further input comes from the spatial organization of the written text. If I visualize the *OCT* editions of Herodotus and Thucydides, my mind's eye recalls section and chapter numbers on the margins, and a larger space between words corresponding to the beginning of new sections. I also recall a series of commas, full stops, high stops, semicolons, and, from time to time, parentheses. Indentation is very sporadic. No capital letters, no exclamation points, no dashes occur.[5] On the larger scale, chapter and section numbers trigger the expectation that some more or less major boundary occurs—a topic shift, or a scene-shift, or a change of grammatical subject. As a matter of fact they affect paragraphing.[6] On the smaller scale, section numbers trigger expectations about discourse boundaries that are less strong than those of chapter numbers. Their lengths may vary, but the relation to main and subclauses tends to be constant: a section is made of multiple main and subclauses, supposedly showing some coherence. Sometimes sections coincide with *períodoi*,[7] especially in the editions of Thucydides, but this is not a rule. On the whole, visual divisions above the sentence level trigger certain expectations about discourse boundaries in the reader, and the visualization of written pages influences the way we come to grips with discourse segmentation.

§6. Interpretation of how texts divide into segments, then, depends on linguistic as well as paralinguistic signs. Paralinguistic signs support verbal expressions without being words, and have a meaning besides or beyond the words to which they are

4 In the 1970's and 80's the label for the study of intersentential relations was text linguistics (see e.g. Halliday and Hasan 1976; Kohonen and Enkvist 1978; Beaugrande and Dressler 1981).

5 More on the selection of punctuation marks in early printed editions in §19.

6 A seminal account of the meaning of paragraphs in discourse analysis is in Brown and Yule 1983:95-100. Paragraphing is genre-specific and it is often motivated by the occurrence of clause-initial adverbials that suggest the structure of discourse. Issues related to chapter and section numbers in print editions of the two *Histories* will be resumed in 3.7.

7 Throughout this chapter I will use the Greek transliteration of these terms, to distinguish them from the modern terms of punctuation marks (period, colon).

attached. In written code, generally speaking, paragraph boundaries, indentation, bold, italics, underline, and all punctuation marks are paralinguistic signs. For spoken code we can consider timbre, tone of voice, pace, and all the basic components of prosody—intonation, length, rhythm, and intensity.[8] Punctuation marks are particularly relevant to our processing of Greek texts (which lack features such as bold and italics). Punctuation is semiotically complex, and in fact it represents meaning components that are akin to particles. Therefore, punctuation marks deserve special consideration.

§7. The next sections discuss the main factors (modern as well as ancient) that contributed in the past, and contribute in the present, to determine the segmentation of ancient Greek texts, as well as some labels that have been attached to various units of discourse. Only in the light of those factors it is possible to establish matches and mismatches concerning the punctuating and segmenting roles of particles. The chapter, then, proposes a "holistic" principle of segmentation, which relies on two broad communicative notions, that is, "acts" and "moves."[9] Particles contribute to discourse segmentation by marking acts and moves together with other co-occurring features.

3.2 Punctuation Between Grammar and Prosody

§8. Let us start with contemporary conventions about the most standard signals of segmentation in written texts, that is, punctuation. For the purposes of the present chapter, I am going to single out a few points that account for conventional and cross-linguistic functions of punctuation marks. These points, in turn, will allow me to spell out some basic assumptions that modern readers either activate almost unconsciously, or tend to take for granted when approaching excerpts of ancient Greek prose.

§9. A recent monograph on the guiding functions of punctuation provides the following definition: "... punctuation is a nonverbal medium-dependent graphic feature that is transmitted via the visual channel and which, for the most part, communicates supplementary paralinguistic information."[10] Such a view stresses the nonverbal character of the signs, along with the nonverbal communication they effect. They are about words, but are not words per se (hence "para-linguistic"); they communicate—at a subsidiary level—interpretations about the flow of discourse[11] and its segments. With our eyes

8 Bolinger 1989:2.

9 See in particular II.2 and II.3 for working definitions of acts and moves respectively.

10 Patt 2013:252. The monograph focuses on the medium-dependency of punctuation, that is, the decisions taken by a language user as far as the presentation of verbal messages are concerned, either via writing or via speech (punctuation is thus taken in a broader sense, as it includes written and spoken realizations). Conversely, medium-independent decisions concern, according to the author, textual structures and syntactic arrangements (see Patt 2013:36-58).

11 Throughout the chapter I adopt "flow of discourse" after Bakker (1997b:74;134;140-141;148; 164), who in turn coins the phrase after the concept of "flow of consciousness" by Chafe (1994:5;54;70; in particular 30).

we naturally process this paralinguistic input together with the linguistic information, and the joint processing of the two types of information guides our comprehension of texts.

§10. But what, exactly, is the paralinguistic function of punctuation? That is to say, how does punctuation contribute to the meaning of words? The scholarly literature acknowledges a broad duality: some functions hinge on the general idea of revealing the grammatical structure, while some other functions hinge on the general idea of revealing elocution. Some works strongly favor what Skelton (1949:165) calls "the grammatical principle":

(t1)

> The work of punctuation is mainly to show, or hint at, the grammatical relation between words, phrases, clauses, and sentences.
>
> Fowler and Fowler 1906:233

(t2)

> On ultimate analysis, the divisibility of our speech or writing into paragraphs and sentences, clauses and individual words, is an intrinsic fact, inherent in thought itself; and our punctuation is not so much an imitation of our elocutionary devices as an independent attempt to represent this structure.
>
> Skelton 1949:6

Some other works state the function of clarifying syntax, but at the same time they take the elocutionary/rhetorical functions of punctuation on a level of complementarity:

(t3)

> Punctuation marks (...) do two jobs. One is *grammatical* and the other is *rhetorical*:
>
> *grammatical*: they show where the boundaries are meant to be between segments of larger statements, and how segments of text are meant to relate to one another;
>
> *rhetorical*: they show the emphasis or tone we want to give to a word or word-group.
>
> Kirkman 2006:5 (indentation in the text)

A similar view is expressed by Truss about two distinct functions of commas:

(t4)

> 1. To illuminate the grammar of a sentence; 2. To point up—rather in the manner of musical notation—such literary qualities as rhythm, direction, pitch, tone and flow.
>
> Truss 2003:70

An example of a grammatical "job" that punctuation marks might perform is when it is necessary to introduce a pause in order to make sense of a string of words. Consider

(t5)

> King Charles walked and talked half an hour after his head was cut off
>
> Skelton 1949:4

Unless we punctuate after "talked" ("King Charles walked and talked; half an hour after his head was cut off"), continuous reading would yield a paradoxical image. An example of the rhetorical "job" might involve the use of single quotation marks:

(t6)

> This is known as 'exact' replacement of ...
>
> Kirkman 2006:6

In some punctuating systems single quotation marks signpost a particular inflection of voice, which provides the word "exact" with the implied meaning "as they call it," or something equivalent to that.

§11. Even though both the grammatical and the elocutionary functions of punctuation nowadays tend to be seen as complementary and necessary, there is an area of significant imbalance that I would like to stress. The elocutionary side (often called "rhetorical"[12]) regards emphasis and prosodic qualities attached to words or word-groups. Elocution-based punctuation does not indicate the structure and the segmentation of

12 Deneau 1986 summarizes the literature that over centuries polarized the functions of punctuation in terms of grammar vs. rhetoric.

thoughts; rather, it conveys a "mode of speech."[13] Conversely, the grammatical side is explicitly related to text structure and segmentation. "Grammatical" punctuation shows where boundaries are, and how segments relate to one another (Kirkman, (t3)); it even represents "an independent attempt" (i.e. independent of elocution) to represent structure (Skelton, (t2)).

§12. Over the past decades studies on the prosodic values of punctuation have increased, which explore the relation of interdependence between discourse and intonation.[14] This is in contrast to the theoretical view expressed by the authors quoted thus far: the analysis of the prosodic qualities we attach to words is not confined to a more or less subjective "mode of speech" (Skelton) that hints at "literary qualities as rhythm, direction, pitch, tone and flow" (Truss, (t4)). Conversely, the emphasis on specific words reflects the informational status speakers assign to them.[15] As the next paragraphs will show, prosodic continuity and discontinuity directly convey the segmentation of discourse. Therefore, the duality in the functions of punctuation that I mentioned at the beginning of this discussion can be re-interpreted in terms of deep interlacing rather than opposition, and in terms of co-construction of boundaries, structure, and meaning.

§13. On this point Chafe 1988b is a salient article. It postulates that written language has its own prosody, albeit covert. Punctuation units (which are defined as "stretches of language between punctuation marks"[16]) reveal the prosody of the writer's inner voice. They do so in an approximate manner, as this example clarifies:

(t7)

1. Did you buy some artichokes?

2. What did you buy?

Chafe 1988b:403

[13] "[By elocutionary principle] I mean the conception of punctuation as representing or conforming to our mode of speech" (Skelton 1949:4). Such a principle "presents serious difficulties both in theory and in practice," as speech requires more symbols than the standard ones to render the speaker's inflection. Moreover, cross-cultural variation plays a role: "a correct mode of speech is by no means universal" (Skelton 1949:164).

[14] See e.g. Chafe 1988b; Scholes and Willis 1990; Borochovsky Bar-Aba 2003. A somehow precursory hint at the mingling of the elocutionary and grammatical functions of punctuation comes from Partridge (1953:6-7): "There have been two systems of punctuation: the rhetorical or dramatic or elocutionary (...) and the grammatical or constructional or logical (...). But to insist upon the dichotomy *dramatic-grammatical* would be both pedantic and inept. For much of the time, as is inevitable, the two coincide: a speaker tends to pause wherever either logic or grammar makes a pause; and even the most 'logical' or 'grammatical' of punctuators tends, when he is writing dialogue, to point what is clearly an elocutionary or dramatic pause (...)" (italics in the text).

[15] See e.g. II.5 §33-35; III.2 §§60-61; III.5 §§46-47; IV.4 §40 §44, n54, and n162 on γε being the equivalent of prosodic prominence attached to phrases with special informational status.

[16] Chafe 1988b:398.

The same question mark in these cases stands for two intonational realizations of questions that in fact are quite different: the intonation of the former question has a rising contour (the end being on a higher pitch than the start), whereas the intonation of the latter has a falling contour (the end being on a lower pitch than the start).[17] Punctuation units, Chafe shows, may correspond to "spokenlike" units imagined by oral readers (engaged in reading the written text aloud), or to a mix of "spokenlike" and "unspokenlike" units imagined by readers engaged in silent reading.[18] A series of experiments demonstrates that punctuation units in written styles tend to be longer than intonation units in spoken styles.[19] According to the author the reasons for this difference are two. First, "writers and (silent) readers are able to process larger chunks of information at a time;" second, "written language provides syntactic as well as punctuational clues to prosodic boundaries" (Chafe 1988b:424).

§14. Both points are very relevant to the present chapter. Chafe's first point ("writers and (silent) readers are able to process larger chunks of information at a time") holds true for writers and readers of texts that are meant to be read. In the case of many ancient Greek texts, however, the language was composed to be performed (in songs, on a stage, or through public delivery). The performance-constraint implies that listeners/spectators were supposed to receive smaller chunks of information at a time. This should constitute a caveat when we modern readers approach the modern punctuation of ancient Greek texts. His second point ("written language provides syntactic as well as punctuational clues to prosodic boundaries") is crucially relevant to discourse segmentation and the role of conjunctions, sentential adverbs, and particles in it. Conjunctions, for example, may signal prosodic breaks without being preceded by commas (Chafe 1988:415 and 419). Chafe's point about conjunctions is intuitively unchallenging; yet he suggests that in written language the syntactic articulation of thoughts helps in segmenting discourse whether or not punctuation marks stress syntax. There is a furher factor that determines punctuation in written language, Chafe continues. This factor is the inner voice of writers, whether it (deliberately) creates exceptionally short or exceptionally

17 Approximation can be seen also in the use of commas: the intonation contour may vary case by case, but overall commas stand for nonfalling pitches (think of the wording "comma intonation").

18 Silent reading is much less constrained in pace than reading aloud: a reader can choose to read fast or slowly according to a variety of purposes, which makes prosody less relevant. "In reading, (...) we are free of any tempo constraint that might be imposed by the producer of the language. We can follow whatever pace is comfortable, speeding up and slowing down as we wish" (Chafe 1988b:425n1 and 410 for the quote).

19 For Chafe's notion of intonation units see also II.2.1.1, and this chapter, §§71-72.

long units.[20] This is one of the reasons why linguists are developing more and more research on the relation between syntax, prosody, and discourse.[21]

§15. From the preceding discussion it emerges that syntactic arrangements of words and our individual voicing of texts jointly influence punctuation choices. Our research on ancient Greek particles confirms the latter point: while searching for functions of particles, it is more productive to consider the interlacing between grammatical and prosodic or elocutionary factors in discourse segmentation, rather than to split them (or, even more problematic, to see only grammar as structural). Particles show how grammar and prosody are integrated. Their position can tell us about prosodic boundaries and about discourse segmentation by complementing rather than contrasting syntactic information. Particles reveal grammar and elocution without a clear-cut division of labor.

3.3 Modern Punctuation of Ancient Greek Texts: Focus on Syntactic Hierarchy and on Periodic Styles

§16. In an article on the absence of punctuation at the end of speeches in Latin poetry, Feeney aligns with others in stressing the gap between the textual display ancient readers had at their disposal, and the modern layout of printed editions.[22] He points out the problem of punctuation, in particular, by reporting Heyworth's statement: "The punctuation of a classical text involves the imposition of modern conventions upon an alien environment."[23] Similarly, Denniston (1950:430) notes: "The punctuation and accentuation of our MSS are not to be trusted over-implicitly, and frequent changes should probably be made. Editors have been rather haphazard in this matter." Dover (1997b:27-28) quotes examples from Thucydides and Isaeus where modern punctuation differs across different editions; he concludes that the disagreement of editors is ultimately about the length of sentences, which is determined by colons, commas, and full stops. Sansone (1990:174) simply states: "(...) it is unscientific to assume that one can rely on the punctuation in a modern text of a classical author to provide evidence for

20 Agee's novel *A Death in the Family* provides an instance of exceptionally long units: "He has been dead all night while I was asleep and now it is morning and I am awake but he is still dead and he will stay right on being dead all afternoon and all night and all tomorrow while I am asleep again and wake up again and go to sleep again and he can't come back home again any more but I will see him once more before he is taken away." (Agee 1957:263-264; quoted in Chafe 1988:408). An instance of exceptionally short units is "Then" in the following excerpt from Sayle's collection of short stories *Barcelona Plates:* "(...) I wrote a script that was my best work so far. The producers loved the script, the money people came on board smooth as pie, a star attached their name, the film was a go go. *Then.* The producer, who'd just had a big hit by accident, tried to get clever. He didn't want (...)" (Sayle 2000:26; quoted in Hannay and Kroon 2005: 97-98; italics in the original).

21 See for example Couper-Kuhlen 1996, 2003; Couper-Kuhlen and Selting 1996; Selting 1996; Mycock 2011; Couper-Kuhlen and Thompson 2012; Dehé 2014.

22 Feeney 2011:45-46; 45n1 for *ad hoc* references.

23 Heyworth 2007:liii, quoted by Feeney (2011:45).

the stylistic characteristics of that author." In a critical edition of Plato's *Ion*, Rijksbaron (2007:68-69) acknowledges the shaky reliability of punctuation in printed editions of the dialogue (since 1578, the date of Estienne's edition); consequently, he warns the reader that in several points of his own edition he prefers to rely on the alternative punctuation offered by Byzantine manuscripts.[24]

§17. These remarks confirm that in modern editions of ancient Greek works punctuation is not a stable feature of the text. It is less original than the words,[25] and it is the result of editorial decisions taken at several stages. To some extent modern punctuation does reflect pre-print punctuation,[26] but correspondences are not one to one, quantitatively and qualitatively. In addition, modern punctuation lends itself to non-univocal interpretations; for example, opting for a semicolon instead of a full stop may be a decision made independent of syntactic and semantic reasons.[27] Moreover, translations only partly reflect the segmentation suggested by Greek words and by modern punctuation: however literal, they naturally adopt the punctuation habits of the target language, which adds to the instability in interpreting segments.[28]

§18. My argument focuses on particles, punctuation marks, and periodic style, but also on larger-scale divisions, specifically the relationship between particles and chapter or section numbers as signposts for indentation and paragraphing. I shall consider three major realities that presumably influence the modern punctuation and segmentation of ancient Greek works. The first is that the "covert prosody" of written texts (to recall Chafe's terminology) gives editors a range of choice in determining where and how to segment discourse. The editorial decisions based on the inferences of their readings may be independent of decisions about whether or not to reproduce the punctuation of earlier editions (see the previous section). The second reality is that we have inherited from early print books a set of punctuation marks that were established during advances in orthography made in this era (see the upcoming paragraphs in this section). The third reality is the presence of a parallel inheritance, namely the multifarious punctuation

24 Especially in the case of plays, doubts should be cast on punctuation in extant written editions, which may interfere with meaning quite substantially. In a chapter on punctuation in written redactions of Shakespearean plays, Crystal (2008:64-99) shows a great deal of variation, which influences not only the segmentation of lines, but also their syntactic interpretation.

25 The earliest ancient Greek literary manuscripts were written in capital letters, continuously (without word space), and usually without punctuation, accents, and breathings. Minuscule manuscripts (roughly starting from the first half of the 9th century) included punctuation, accents, and breathings more and more. On the prehistory of Greek accentuation, in particular, see Probert 2006.

26 More on this in IV.5.6.

27 See below §58 on the multifunctionality of punctuation marks (which mirrors the multifunctionality of particles). §§130-131 and 135 will consider how paralinguistic discrepancies found in the various editions of Herodotus and Thucydides reflect interpretive range.

28 In 3.10 and 3.11 I will often comment on matches and mismatches between segmentations provided by the Greek and by the English translations.

and division systems elaborated throughout centuries of manuscript transmission (see the next few sections). In other words, I see segmentation practices as resulting from the combination of these three aspects: processing syntactic and semantic information along with imagining the author's inner voice, mirroring previous print editions, and mirroring pre-print editions.

§19. Let us consider the second reality, that is, punctuation since the start of print editions. The very first appearance of a standard version of commas, colons, semicolons, and full stops (with the shape and the graphical relation to words we know and still use) date back to the Aldine edition of the treatise *De Aetna* of Pietro Bembo (1496). In a later sizable handbook on orthography (*Orthographiae ratio*, 1566), the section *Interpungendi ratio* by Aldus Manutius the Younger (1547-1597) describes, in no more than ten pages, the punctuation marks selected for printed texts: commas, semicolons, colons, full stops, question marks, and parentheses.[29] The main unit of segmentation is unequivocally the sentence: punctuation illuminates sentences otherwise obscure ("*equidem usu didici, obscuras saepe sententias, si recte distinguantur, illustrari*"); a single full stop means the end of a sentence ("*restat unicum punctum, quo sententia concluditur, ac terminatur*"); commas are applied to nouns and verbs rather than to whole or incomplete sentences ("[*virgula*]*: ea vero non integram sententiam, nec sententiae partes terminat, sed nomina, vel verba distinguit....*"[30] The set of punctuation marks selected by Manutius the Younger excludes exclamation markers and dashes, which are added at a later point.[31] This does not mean that the effects potentially signaled by exclamation marks and dashes were not considered in the Renaissance; it only means that the selected set of marks was felt sufficient for clarifying discourse segmentation.

§20. Chafe (1988b:401-402) stresses that 18th century handbooks privileged a "spokenlike" way of punctuating (in English), but that later works focused on grammatical conventions[32] (see also above, (t2)—(t4)). Along the same lines, I find that modern and contemporary editions of ancient Greek prose privilege the grammatical principle

[29] The print system of punctuating Greek texts (e.g. semicolons marked by high points, and question marks marked by semicolons) comes from the Greek types cut by Claude Garamont for Francis I of France between 1540 and 1550. It largely recalls analogous signs employed in medieval Byzantine manuscripts.

[30] Manutius 1566:787, 797, and 789 respectively.

[31] Let us consider for a moment how our reading of ancient Greek texts would have changed if the first editions in print had incorporated exclamation points as well (however sparingly). We would take the expression of emotions as an inherent part of the texts, even in genres that we overall associate with a composed style (such as historiography).

[32] Originally in 1762, Lowth writes: "Punctuation is the art of marking in writing the several pauses, or rests, between sentences, and the parts of sentences, (...) as they are expressed in a just and accurate pronunciation." (Lowth 1967[1762]:154; quoted in Chafe 1988:401). In 1985 Quirk, Greenbaum, Leech, and Svartvik write: "Punctuation practice is governed primarily by grammatical considerations and is related to grammatical distinctions." (Quirk, Greenbaum, Leech, and Svartvik 1985:1611; quoted in Chafe 1988b:401).

of punctuation over the elocutionary principle; at any rate, grammatical considerations are the decisive factor in punctuating texts. At some point (perhaps near the publication of 19th century grammars of ancient Greek) philology embraced a line of thinking that teaching practices of the time probably enhanced: punctuation clarifies the syntax of sentences. This was (and still is) an important service to readers of texts in dead languages, for different reasons: partly the lack of any spoken counterpart, partly the indirectness of indications about delivery in ancient times, make the task of comprehension more effortful. Therefore, scholars came to regard syntactic articulation as *the* substantial component of texts, which punctuation should partially illustrate and clarify.

§21. This view is related to the idea that in ancient Greek prose syntactic segmentation, and, in particular, hypotactical segmentation, is primary.[33] The function of the full stop punctuation mark at the end of periods illustrates this idea well.[34] Modern scholars have established a conceptual match between periods in the sense of *períodoi*, and periods in the sense of full stops. Modern and contemporary readings of ancient Greek prose take periods as *períodoi* (that is, complex sentences) bounded at each end by full stops; they are the grammatical and stylistic measure of complete segments in written discourse.[35] Decoding a prose text from full stop to full stop or *períodos* by *períodos* is the safest way to follow how discourse is segmented. Sentences and *períodoi* are so much seen as the building blocks of discourse that scholars count them for statistical or heuristic purposes. For example, Müller (1980:25) compares the length of sentences in large excerpts of Herodotus and Thucydides by counting the segments between full stops. Yaginuma (1995:133) considers the high word count of Thucydidean sentences and "the extraordinary size of his periods" as decisive factors supporting the idea that Thucydides wrote for readers rather than for listeners.[36]

§22. But what exactly makes a *períodos* complete, and divisions across periods the safest? An answer that would take into account the comprehensiveness of discourse would be less obvious than one would think, as the criteria for "completeness" and

33 Note that "grammar" in the title of this section refers to a traditional notion of grammar, that is, consisting of morphology and syntax. Recent linguistic works (e.g. Du Bois 2003; Hopper and Thompson 2008) question this notion and the idea that grammar rules pre-exist language use.

34 My upcoming discussion will focus on the syntactic and punctuation assumptions behind the rhetorical notion of "periodic style," that is to say, where the construction of several clauses is a part of formal speeches or formal writing. I refer to "period" as the equivalent of complex sentences, while "sentence" prototypically is the equivalent of a simple sentence, that is, a main clause + one dependent clause.

35 "The old stopping was frankly to guide the voice in reading aloud, while the modern is mainly to guide the mind in seeing through the grammatical construction." (Fowler and Fowler 1906:230). The relevance of *períodoi* to the articulation of texts certainly is not a point made just in modern times. See below, §39 for Aristotle's definition of *períodos*.

36 Willi (2010a:307) takes sentence length (in terms of number of words) as one of the test-criteria for recording differences among classical Greek oratory, historiography, Platonic dialogues, and Aristophanic dialogues.

"division" may differ.[37] What most interests me at this point is the answer provided by scholars of Herodotus and Thucydides (undoubtedly grounded on pre-modern literature on rhetoric). 19th and 20th century descriptions of the prose composition of the two historians include assessments about their periodic style. What makes a *períodos* a complete unit to those scholars is the syntactic articulation of thoughts—in particular, the way in which the mechanism of hypotaxis is exploited. What spans two consequent full stops is a construction of main and subordinate pieces that overall express cohesion and integratedness.[38] The more complex the arrangement of syntactic hierarchies within a *períodos*, the more elaborate is the periodic style. Periodic complexity means syntactic complexity.

§23. In addition to the criterion of syntactic complexity scholars apply a perfection scale, based on diachronic evolution, to assess *períodoi*: what is later and more complex is better; what is less complex and earlier is less good. Thucydides, according to Classen (1862:LXXIX) adopts a mature periodic style; the development is completed, and multi-clause periods are most common ("*Was (...) die Satzbildung betrifft, so ist zwar die Periode, welche sich durch Vorder-, Nach- und Zwischensätze gegliedert, bei Th.[ukydides] in vollständiger Ausbildung und geläufigstem Gebrauche*"). A few decades later Blass (1887:223-224) explicitly disagrees with Classen: Thucydides' work is ranked somewhere between the ancient "additive" and the later fully periodic style; Classen has overestimated it ("*Thukydides' Schreibart steht (...) in der Mitte zwischen der locker anfügenden alten und der späteren periodischen, und Classen behauptet viel zu viel, wenn er die gegliederte Periode dei Thukydides in vollständiger Ausbildung und geläufigstem Gebrauche sein lässt*").

§24. The sense of periodic perfection emerges from some converging ideas posited by Blass (1887) and by Müller (1980). When subclauses precede the main clause, Blass originally posits (1887:224), the resulting *períodos* is "ascending" ("*aufsteigend*") and perfect. Conversely, when the main clause comes first, and subclauses follow, the period is "descending" ("*absteigend*") and not perfect (or not even a proper period). The latter case instantiates "*die Art des Anreihens*" ("the stringing style," 1887:224).[39]

§25. About a century later, Müller retrieves Blass' notion and graphically represents the trend of perfect "ascending" *períodoi* as follows (Müller 1980:32):

[37] See §§38 and 40 for suggestions about intonational criteria. In fact, I shall argue, it is likely that ancient rhetors had in mind a comprehensive notion of completeness, which reached beyond hypotaxis.

[38] Raible (1992, 2001) analyzes tighter vs. looser clause linkage in terms of integration vs. aggregation. Subordination is commonly said to show integratedness, as sub- and main clauses are integrated with each other. Conversely, coordination and asyndetic clausal relations show un-integratedness. Contemporary studies tend to consider *degrees* of integratedness and of un-integratedness; see, for example König and Van der Auwera 1988 about conditional and concessive clauses in German and Dutch.

[39] The terminological link with Aristotle's "strung" diction (λέξις εἰρομένη) is immediate.

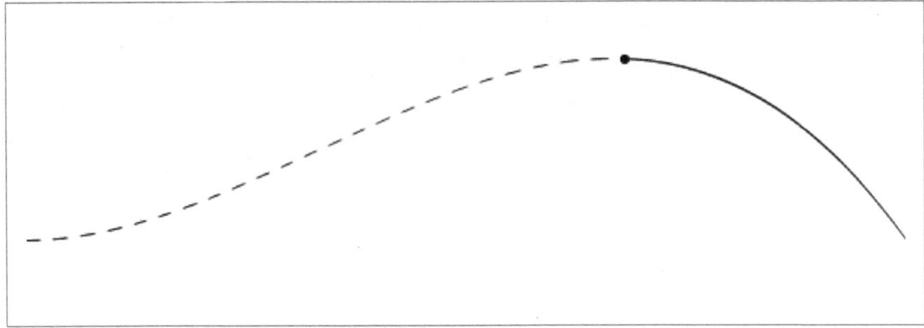

Figure 1: Müller's "arc of tension" (adapted)

Müller calls this "arc of tension" ("Spannungsbogen," 1980:32), which applies to the "perfect" configuration of *periodoi*. The subclauses that precede the main clause create an ascending trend that culminates in the crest, after which a shorter descending segment follows ("*Es entsteht ein ungleicher Spannungsbogen, der im vorderen, längeren und mehrgliedrigen Teil des Satzes allmählich ansteigt, in der Pause einen ruhenden Gipfelpunkt hat und im Schlußkolon*[40] *schnell abfällt*").[41] Müller sees Herodotus' style as an intermediate but still imperfect step towards a flawless periodic style.[42] Sometimes the shape of his *períodoi* is not a nice arc; in that case we find "*verunglückte Periode*" (1980:10).[43] He compares a fragment of Hecataeus, which he judges artless ("*kunstlos*"), not exciting ("*spannungslos*"), clumsy ("*holperig*"), and monotone ("*eintönig*,")[44] to Herodotus 1.8 (the beginning of Candaules' episode). He notes that Herodotus' harmony in the varied sequence

40 The term "*Schlußkolon*" ("end *kôlon*") is significant: in a later section I will point out that *kōlon* is commonly intended as "clause," even though ancient descriptions include phrases as well.

41 See below, §40 and n72 for a reading of this interpretation in intonational rather than hypotactical terms.

42 The same opinion is already expressed in Brouwer 1975. See also Dobson 1919:2.4. Demetrius (*On Style* 12) judged the diction of most of Herodotus' prose "separate/loose" (διῃρεμένη). On the alleged superiority of hypotaxis over parataxis see also IV.2 §7. In III.5 §§27-28 the hypotactic construction subclause + main clause is associated with calmness.

43 See 3.10.1 for a discourse analysis of Herodotus 1.174,103, where Müller sees unsuccessful/derailed/crashed periods (in German "*verunglückt*" literally means "having had an accident").

44 Müller 1980:6. Here is the text of Hecataeus' fragment in question (*Fragmenta* [Jacobi] 1a, 1, F frag. 15; see Athenaeus 2.35.AB): Ὀρεσθεὺς ὁ Δευκαλίωνος ἦλθεν εἰς Αἰτωλίαν ἐπὶ βασιλείαι, καὶ κύων αὐτοῦ στέλεχος ἔτεκε, καὶ ὃς ἐκέλευσεν αὐτὸ κατορυχθῆναι, καὶ ἐξ αὐτοῦ ἔφυ ἄμπελος πολυστάφυλος· διὸ καὶ τὸν αὐτοῦ παῖδα Φύτιον ἐκάλεσε. τούτου δ' Οἰνεὺς ἐγένετο, κληθεὶς ἀπὸ τῶν ἀμπέλων (οἱ γὰρ παλαιοί, φησιν, Ἕλληνες οἴνας ἐκάλουν τὰς ἀμπέλους)· Οἰνέως δ' ἐγένετο Αἰτωλός "Orestheus son of Deucalion went to Aetolia to assume kingship, and a female dog of his gave birth to a trunk, and he was the one who ordered the trunk to be sunk in the earth, and from it a vine rich in grapes grew up; this is why he also called his son 'the Planter.' Then from him Oineus was born, whose name comes from 'vine'—the ancients say that the Greeks called the vines *oínai*— Then from Oeneus Aetolus was born" (tr. AB).

of *kôla* replaces the abrupt row of *kôla* in Hecataeus ("*Die länger gewordenen Kola stehen nicht mehr abrupt nebeneinander, sondern sind schon viel harmonischer aneinandergefügt. Die Verknüpfungen sind abwechslungsreicher und komplizierter, sie klammern die Kola enger aneinander*" (1980:7).[45] Therefore, Herodotus' style constitutes an improvement in the use of "strung" diction ("*Zweifelsohne ist ein Fortschritt im Gebrauch der* λ. ε. [λέξις εἰρομένη] *zu erkennen*," 1980:7).

§26. Now let us turn to a textual example that illustrates how modern punctuation (at least in Thucydides) is used to clarify the syntax of *períodoi*.

(t8)

ὁπλίτας τε οὖν πολλούς μοι δοκεῖ χρῆναι ἡμᾶς ἄγειν καὶ ἡμῶν αὐτῶν καὶ τῶν ξυμμάχων, τῶν τε ὑπηκόων καὶ ἤν τινα ἐκ Πελοποννήσου δυνώμεθα ἢ πεῖσαι ἢ μισθῷ προσαγαγέσθαι, καὶ τοξότας πολλοὺς καὶ σφενδονήτας, ὅπως πρὸς τὸ ἐκείνων ἱππικὸν ἀντέχωσι, ναυσί τε καὶ πολὺ περιεῖναι, ἵνα καὶ τὰ ἐπιτήδεια ῥᾷον ἐσκομιζώμεθα, τὸν δὲ καὶ αὐτόθεν σῖτον ἐν ὁλκάσι, πυροὺς καὶ πεφρυγμένας κριθάς, ἄγειν, καὶ σιτοποιοὺς ἐκ τῶν μυλώνων πρὸς μέρος ἠναγκασμένους ἐμμίσθους, ἵνα, ἤν που ὑπὸ ἀπλοίας ἀπολαμβανώμεθα, ἔχῃ ἡ στρατιὰ τὰ ἐπιτήδεια (πολλὴ γὰρ οὖσα οὐ πάσης ἔσται πόλεως ὑποδέξασθαι), τά τε ἄλλα ὅσον δυνατὸν ἑτοιμάσασθαι, καὶ μὴ ἐπὶ ἑτέροις γίγνεσθαι, μάλιστα δὲ χρήματα αὐτόθεν ὡς πλεῖστα ἔχειν.

Thucydides 6.22

These then are what I consider the requirements: a considerable force of hoplites from Athens itself and our allies, both our own subjects and any we can persuade or pay to join us from the Peloponnese; a large number of archers and slingers to deal with the enemy cavalry; sufficient ships for overwhelming naval superiority, so there is no extra problem in bringing in supplies; merchant ships to transport the grain, wheat and rosted barley, we shall also need from home; master-bakers conscripted under hire in fair proportion from our mills, so that our forces will still have food if we are detained by adverse sailing conditions, as few cities will be able to cater for such a large army. Generlaly we must equip ourselves as completely as possible, and not leave anything dependent on others. In particular we need to have with us from here a very substantial sum of money ... (tr. Hammond)

This *períodos* (drawn from Stuart Jones' edition) is nearly coextensive with chapter 22—in fact this chapter has no internal sections. The speaker is Nicias, who explains all the

[45] On *kôla* in prose, see below 3.6.

equipment and the resources that are required in order to confront the Sicilian contingents. The length speaks for itself: the idea that Thucydides uses long periods depends on the fact that modern punctuation places full stops after a long series of subclauses and a main clause in between.[46] But this does not mean that Thucydides conceived the passage as one *períodos*, and that he "uses" or even prefers long *períodoi*.[47] When we face the *OCT* page of this excerpt, our eyes automatically glance through a large stretch of text spanning the initial chapter number to the full stop that concludes the first *períodos*. This reflexive action—perhaps along with Thucydides' reputation—makes us assume complexity even before we begin to decode words. But we also presume thematic coherence: we are confident that once main clauses are detected, the remaining parts will depend on them, and meaning will be accommodated according to the hierarchies established by syntax. Syntactic complexity is certainly there, and thematic coherence is undeniable. Nevertheless, to embrace such a sizable stretch of text as one periodic unit prevents us from appreciating the individual components in the order in which they are presented. The presumption of periodic unity obscures internal major boundaries signaled by particles; it blurs Thucydides' meticulous construction of discourse acts that illustrate Nicias' points. I refer the reader to the suggestions I make in the detailed analysis of this passage in IV.5.2. There I take particles, conjunctions, and other features as signposts for discourse acts whose syntactic ranking does not exhaust their pragmatic force. Such a pragmatic and rhetorical segmentation goes unnoticed if we exclusively orient our reading to answering questions such as "where is the main clause?" and "which subclauses/participles occur?".

§27. In conclusion: I took the example of *períodoi* to make a few general connections. First, I connect modern punctuation marks to the set of symbols derived from and used in pre-print and early print versions. Second, I connect grammatical principles to the elocutionary principles guiding punctuation. Third, I connect the way Greek texts are punctuated in modern editions to scholarly efforts to clarify grammatical structure. I show that scholarly appreciation of elaborate *períodoi* and qualitative judgments about periodic perfection have resulted in syntactic idealism. Finally and most important, I draw a connection between periodic complexity and hypotaxis. It emerges from all the connections I make that readerly segmentation is based on syntactic phenomena of subordination and coordination, as well as on the punctuation marks that are intended to clarify them. Let us see now how input from pre-print strategies of punctuation and from ancient notions of *períodos* enriches the perspective of discourse segmentation.

46 Perhaps there is a connection between the modern punctuation of the Greek, and Hammond's translation, which is ingeniously articulated into just three *periodoi* (while Jowett, for example, employs 4, and Hobbes 5).

47 Müller 1980 confirms that on average period length in Thucydides is greater than in Herodotus. The calculation is based on the number of *OCT* lines across two subsequent full stops.

3.4 Ancient Punctuation: Focus on Delivery

§28. Even though names of marks, graphic shapes, and conventions vary chronologically as well as geographically, it is commonly thought that before the first printed editions of classical texts, signs in Western punctuation mainly served performative needs—essentially where and how to pause, while reading aloud or performing.

(t9)

> For a millennium and a half, punctuation's purpose was to guide actors, chanters and readers-aloud through stretches of manuscript, indicating the pauses, accentuating matters of sense and sound, and leaving syntax mostly to look after itself.
>
> Truss 2003:72

Ong indicates that pre-print punctuation was based on performative criteria, and that clarifying syntax was secondary.[48] The ancient Greek habit of employing *scriptio* (or *scriptura*) *continua* (no word separation)—adopted by the Greeks from the oldest times, and by the Romans only in the 1st-2nd century CE, to imitate the Greek texts[49]—indicates the crucial role that aural decoding played in understanding writing.[50] In medieval times

48 "The oratorical considerations [...] are undoubtedly tied up to a degree with grammar and syntax. But in the case of all three punctuation marks which the early grammarians mention [*distinctiones*, which I introduce below], the clarification of the syntax is coincidental. The grammarians are interested primarily in the exigencies of breathing. It is convenient to place the breath pauses, and consequently the punctuation marks, where they will not interfere with the sense. But interest in both breathing and sense is quite independent of formal attention to grammatical structure." (Ong 1944:71). On the preeminence of performative criteria, see also Skelton 1949:163: "No one denies that our punctuation is elocutionary in origin. That is to say, it begins with the recognition that some of our elocutionary devices are a necessary part of speech, and must somehow be represented in writing also"; Parkes 1992:1-4; at 1: "in Antiquity the written word was regarded as a record of the spoken word, and texts were usually read aloud"; Feeney 2011:47-48: "The norm (...) would have been that it was up to the individual reader to mark up a text if he wanted to, relying on his own interpretation of what it meant and how it ran; in particular, the reader could use *distinctiones* or *punctūs* to signal places to pause or stop"; Patt 2013:71: "The different dots (like the structural word-spaces) can most probably be interpreted as guides for the reader: the punctuation marks should facilitate oral reading and declamation. By offering the reader an opportunity to breathe, they had a practical relevance and the different characters indicated the respective pause length."

49 In earlier times word division in Latin texts was the rule. Wingo (1972:16) defines the practice of *scriptio continua* as "one of the most astonishing cultural regressions of ancient history."

50 See Saenger (1997:11): "... oralization, which the ancients savored aesthetically, provided mnemonic compensation (through enhanced short-term aural recall) for the difficulty in gaining access to the meaning of unseparated text." Nagy (2009:421) comments on the practice of *scriptio continua* as follows: "... *scriptio continua* promoted the phonological realism of continuity in speaking or singing or reciting in ways that people really spoke and sang and recited."

the term denoting a group of signs "added in the classroom to guide the inexperienced reader in the correct pronunciation of text" was *prosodiae* (Saenger 1997:53). All this commentary attests to widespread belief that there is an inherent connection between the segmentation of discourse and the way in which a written text is realized with one's voice.[51]

§29. In a recent article, Vatri (2012) demonstrates that ancient Greek reading did not have to be oral for subjects to be able to decode *scriptio continua*.[52] In fact, the author shows, Thai readers—who read unspaced texts—visually process stretches of language "in the same way as in Western readers of spaced alphabetic scripts" (640). Vatri concludes that cues to decoding words and segmentation depend more on specific combinations of letters which readers recognize rather than on whether reading is silent or not. To this I would add that in light of what Chafe (1988b; see above §13) postulates, the segmentation of discourse is influenced by two phenomena: certain arrangements of words, including syntactic arrangements, and the covert (or inner) prosody of written language. By "written" I mean both "written to be read silently," and written transcriptions of performed language. They differ, of course, but the idea of prosodic imagery remains in either case, holding both for the implicit interaction of writer-reader as well as for the explicit interaction performer-listener. Thus, in my opinion, it is irrelevant whether silent reading was practiced or not at the time of *scriptio continua*. Discourse segmentation was applied to texts and processed in any case, in accordance with both word arrangements and inner prosody. I also add that a considerable amount of texts in archaic and classical Greece were designed to be publicly performed, which made the practice of reading aloud a necessary step.

§30. Among the ancient punctuation marks that are adopted in manuscripts of ancient Greek texts, I single out *paragraphḗ* (παραγραφή, later παράγραφος) and *stigmḗ* (στιγμή) or *distinctio*. *Paragraphḗ* is one of the oldest punctuation marks, and it corresponds to a stroke placed at the left margin of texts or near the start of a line. The word is first attested in Isocrates (*Antidosis* 59).[53] In manuscripts of plays a *paragraphḗ* may mark

And also: "the device of *scriptio continua* can be counted as yet another aspect of the overall accuracy and precision of the Greek writing system in representing the reality of Greek speech and song." Skelton (1949:164) offers a straightforward comment based on a general consideration of prosody: "It seems probable that the Greek scribes ran their words together, not merely for economy's sake, but because in speech we normally do so; for there are no more pauses in *bread and butter* than in *computation*." (italics in the text).

51 Parkes (1992:9; 15) and Feeney (2011:47-48) stress that up to the 6th century CE punctuation marks, however various in form and distribution, were not originated together with the text, but added at a later time, especially for scholastic purposes.

52 Vatri 2012 questions the main contention of Saenger 1997, which is that ancient reading was oral, and that word separation led to the development of silent reading.

53 The passage refers to reading aloud after some break: Ὤιμην μὲν οὖναὐτὸς δυνήσεσθαι διελθεῖν περὶ αὐτῶν· νῦν δέ με τὸ γῆρας ἐμποδίζει καὶ ποιεῖ προαπαγορεύειν. Ἵν' οὖν μὴ παντάπασιν ἐκλυθῶ πολλῶν ἔτι μοι λεκτέων ὄντων, ἀρξάμενος ἀπὸ τῆς παραγραφῆς ἀνάγνωθι τὰ περὶ τῆς

a change of speaker. In lyric texts it separates metrical groups of verses. The function in literary prose often is to signpost the end of sentences or sections, or to mark transitional points.[54] Johnson (1994:68) hypothesizes that such strokes were "practical aids to reading aloud," and were visually convenient whenever readers had to look back at the texts after possible breaks of any kind. For the purposes of the present chapter I observe that, on the one hand, a *paragraphḗ* can be compared to section and chapter numbers in modern editions of Herodotus and Thudydides.[55] On the other hand, its function in marking discontinuity in the source of utterances can be compared to modern quotation marks. In both cases *paragraphḗ* boundaries occur between units of discourse that are larger than simple sentences; this reflects a need (or a wish) to indicate segmentation on a larger scale than individual clauses and sentences.

§31. *Stigmaí* (later *distinctiones*) are dots placed at different heights to signal pauses. Higher, middle, and lower dots signal minor, medial, and major pauses respectively.[56] Pfeiffer (1968:177-180) remarks that the adoption of τελεία στιγμή, μέση στιγμή and ὑποστιγμή dates back to Aristophanes of Byzantium (3rd-2nd century BCE).[57] Medieval Byzantine manuscripts of the 9th to 10th century BCE still employ these different dots.[58] They show evidence, however, that the lowest dot (τελεία στιγμή, analogous to our full stop) does not always occur where we would put a full stop, and is, on average, relatively rare. As for middle-high dots (μέση στιγμή), it is often not clear which kind of boundary they stand for: sometimes they delimit segments in the middle of a clause,

ἡγεμονίας αὐτοῖς. "Now I thought that I should be able to go through these passages myself, but I find that my age hampers me and causes me to give out easily. So then, in order that I may not break down utterly while there are still many things which I must say, let the clerk begin at the place marked (ἀπὸ τῆς παραγραφῆς) and read the passage on the hegemony" (tr. Norlin).

54 Dalimier 2001:410 lists in the functions also the marking of statements external to the text ("parenthèse mentale"). In Byzantine manuscripts they frequently indicate the insertion of quotations.

55 See below 3.7 on modern paralinguistic segmentation beyond punctuation.

56 Parkes 1992:303-304. Chapter 4 of the *Art of Grammar* (τέχνη γραμματική) is titled περὶ στιγμῆς, and the text given in is: στιγμαί εἰσι τρεῖς· τελεία, μέση, ὑποστιγμή. † καὶ ἡ μὲν τελεία στιγμή ἐστι διανοίας ἀπηρτισμένης σημεῖον, μέση δὲ σημεῖον πνεύματος ἕνεκεν παραλαμβανόμενον, ὑποστιγμὴ δὲ διανοίας μηδέπω ἀπηρτισμένης ἀλλ' ἔτι ἐνδεούσης σημεῖον. Τίνι διαφέρει στιγμὴ ὑποστιγμῆς; Χρόνῳ· ἐν μὲν γὰρ τῇ στιγμῇ πολὺ τὸ διάστημα, ἐν δὲ τῇ ὑποστιγμῇ παντελῶς ὀλίγον. "Points are three: the final, the middle, and the inferior point. That is: the final point is a sign of a complete thought, the middle one signals that breath is taken, and the inferior point is sign of (a thought) not complete at all, but of (something) that is lacking. What is the difference between point and inferior point? It is a matter of time. At the moment of a point there is much interval, but for the inferior point (the interval) is absolutely little" (tr. AB). See the notes of Lallot (1997:91-92) on this chapter.

57 Blank 1983:52-53 argues that the tripartite system of *distinctiones* is late. Lamb 1914 mentions Aelius Donatus, (4th century CE) for this tripartition (cf. chapter "*de posituri*" in *Donati grammatici Urbis Romae Ars grammatica in Grammatici Latini*, ed. H. Keilii, Leipzig 1864:p. 372). Clemoes (1952:9) reports St. Isidore's (c. 560-636 CE) full description of the three types of dots.

58 Perria 1991:201.

which evidently do not coincide with clause boundaries.[59] Along similar lines Perria (1991:203-204) remarks that there is an extraordinarily rich spectrum of punctuation marks to be found in a particular collection of 9th century manuscripts. Besides στιγμαί, a few διαστολαί (similar to commas), and a few question marks, various strokes or "nails" (in the author's Italian text "chiodi") appear not only between main and subclauses but also after partitive constructions, or between subject and verb, or before and after parenthetical expressions. The author associates the abundance of these signs with the marking of vocal inflections and intonation.

§32. In spite of the relative scarcity of information about ancient punctuation theories, a particularly rich and old source stands out. This is the work of Nicanor, a Greek philologist who lived in the 1st century CE. He is one of the four commentators mentioned in the scholia of *Venetus A* of the *Iliad*, and was known as "the punctuator" (ὁ Στιγματίας).[60] His contribution is summarized and discussed in an article by David Blank, quoted above (n57). Blank suggests that the eight punctuation marks established by Nicanor (which I shall shortly introduce) are based on the Stoic distinction between complete and incomplete units of sense. What is strikingly relevant to the topics of this chapter, however, is that Nicanor connects the occurrence of different particles to different lengths of pauses, and therefore to different punctuation marks.

§33. According to Blank (1983:49-50), Nicanor's system of punctuation, devised for Homer, is as follows. Five types of *stigmaí* ("full stops" in Blank's translation) mark completeness (αὐτοτελεῖς λόγοι), while two *hypostigmaí* (corresponding to high dots) and one *hypodiastolḗ* (a kind of comma) mark incompleteness (ἐλλεῖπον). The five full stops indicate four to one moments of silence (χρόνοι) ranging from a stronger to a weaker degree of disconnection across two segments of discourse.[61] The deepest separation, which corresponds to a pause of four *chrónoi* (and corresponds, graphically, to a *teleía stigmḗ*), occurs between asyndetic clauses, and after vocative or exclamatory expressions. A less deep separation (three *chrónoi*, represented by a *hypoteleía stigmḗ*) is for segments

59 I base these observations on my own examination of the rich collection of photographs of manuscript pages that constitute the second volume of Harlfinger and Prato 1991, as well as the two manuscripts of Herodotus and Thucydides from which I transcribed the ancient punctuation of the four excerpts analyzed in IV.5.

60 The extant fragments of Nicanor's περὶ Ἰλιακῆς στιγμῆς are collected and commented upon by Friedländer (1850), those from Nicanor's περὶ Ὀδυσσειακῆς στιγμῆς by Carnuth (1875). See also Schmidt 1859:506-570. In addition, information about Nicanor's punctuation system comes from the scholia to Dionysius Thrax (*Scholia in Dionysii Thracis artem grammaticam*, by A. Hilgard, Leipzig 1901:24-28).

61 My report of Blank's summary of Nicanor's system uses the syntactically neutral term "segment," but note that Blank uses "sentences" throughout his entire description—even though at p. 62 he mentions "independent clauses" and then "clauses." The complex relation between Homeric meter, syntactic units, and phonological phrases is thoroughly discussed in Blankenborg 2015, a dissertation on performative pauses in the *Iliad* and the *Odyssey*.

introduced by δέ or by another *súndesmos*,[62] or as Nicanor puts it, τῶν ἰσοδυναμούντων τῷ δέ ("among those whose force is equal to that of δέ"), such as γάρ, ἀλλά, and αὐτάρ. Then comes a pause of two *chrónoi* (Nicanor's πρῶτη ἄνω στιγμή) for segments connected by correlatives, such as μέν ... δέ; ἤ ... ἤ; οὐκ ... ἀλλά. A pause of one *chrónos*, equivalent to a δεύτερα ἄνω στιγμή, separates segments introduced by καί. Finally, the τρίτη ἄνω στιγμή stands for one *chrónos* of pause preceding segments introduced by τε. All these full stops mark *lógoi* that are complete in themselves (αὐτοτελεῖς).

§34. The remaining marks separate incomplete segments; all of them correspond to one *chrónos* of pause. Two ὑποστιγμαί distinguish between "dramatic" vs. "undramatic" (ἐνυπόκριτος vs. ἀνυπόκριτος) renderings of segments, which remarkably evoke intonation patterns;[63] the "dramatic" ones separate protases from their subsequent apodoses, the "undramatic" isolate τὰ διὰ μέσου, parenthetical segments. Finally, the weakest disconnection is represented by a ὑποδιαστολή, which separates for the sake of clarity (πρὸς τὸ σαφέστερον διασταλτέον); it also separates relative pronouns from their antecedents, incomplete segments sharing a verbal argument, and complete segments sharing elements κατὰ κοινόν.

§35. Blank also records the dismissive attitude of nineteenth-century philologists towards the criteria of "the Punctuator" (1983:48, with nn. 5-8). One of the points on which Friedländer (first editor of the fragments of Nicanor's punctuation of the *Iliad*) "disagrees vehemently" with Nicanor concerns the relatively strong pause that Nicanor prescribes before καί and τε clauses.[64] Friedländer's characterization of Nicanor as articulating an excessively meticulous system of punctuation reveals an interesting discrepancy between the two men's attitudes toward the proper segmentation of language. A view of discourse that stresses the written aspect does not allow *and* segments to start after a full stop. However, they are acceptable from the perspective of an oral delivery, especially when "and" starts a new intonation unit, and coincides with the beginning of a separate discourse act or move.[65]

§36. On the whole, Nicanor's system confirms that punctuation marks and performative "instructions" were still deeply linked in the 1st century CE. The clearest sign of this intertwining seems to me the suggestion of a full stop (τελεία στιγμή, corresponding to the longest pause) after vocative and exclamatory expressions. From this I infer that

62 Ancient accounts of σύνδεσμοι are reported in I.2.5.2-5.3.

63 Blank specifies that "dramatic" refers to the "rise in pitch of the voice at the end of the protasis..., where no breath is permitted" (1983:50). Steinthal 1891:352 notes that the term ἐνυπόκριτος or ἐν ὑποκρίσει refers to the declamatory peak of a rise-and-fall intonation: "*weil beim Vortrage die Stimme bis zu dieser Stelle merklich steigt, und dann fällt; sie hat also besonders klare deklamatorische Bedeutung.*"

64 See Blank 1983:62 for the quotation, and for Friedländer's comment, "*adhuc nostro sensu freti Nicanoris supervacuam in distinguendo operositatem notavimus ...*" (1850:58).

65 On intonation units and acts, see II.2.1.1. On καί and τε introducing new acts or moves, see IV.2.3.3; 2.3.6; 2.4.4; 2.4.5; see also below §§111-112 about καί starting moves, and IV.5 §§14; 22; 44-45; 74 about τε starting moves.

Nicanor must have associated vocative and exclamatory expressions not only with separate but also with special intonational contours. Analogously, the term ἐνυπόκριτος ("dramatic"[66]) captures the prosodic relevance of a mark between a subclause and the related main clause.

§37. We should also note from the evidence of Nicanor that punctuation is seen as relating to a mix of lexical and syntactic clues emerging from texts, several of them being the conjunctions and adverbs that we call particles. At least for Nicanor, then, particles can determine the location of punctuation marks. We suppose that also in modern times particles can do that. There are differences, however: while in Nicanor the link is explicit and consistent, in printed editions the association is suggested implicitly and often inconsistently (let us think of full stops or commas before X δέ); also, Nicanor gives importance to the lexical item per se, whereas modern editors presumably combine the evidence of particles with their reconstruction of *períodoi* (e.g. καί preferably is not preceded by a full stop).

3.5 Ancient Segmentation: Units and Subunits Syntactically Unspecified

§38. The inquiry into the theoretical and diachronical complexity of these themes continues with the retrieval of a few ancient ideas related to discourse segmentation. The first are the ideas of completeness and incompleteness, which date back to the Stoics. According to Blank (1983:59-60) completion and incompletion are central to Stoic thoughts on grammar and rhetoric. They divide units of saying, or utterances, into two categories, one which they call λεκτά, are αὐτοτελῆ ("self-contained") if the expression is complete (ἀπαρτισμένην ἔχοντα τὴν ἐκφοράν), and the other ἐλλιπῆ if the expression is incomplete (ἀναπάρτιστον ἔχοντα τὴν ἐκφοράν).[67] Note that such ideas do not directly refer to a specific configuration of syntactic segments. If we think of intonational completion and incompletion, certain intonational profiles may match the delivery of certain syntactic units; but here there is no link between complete segments and specific syntactic segments, not even through intonation.

§39. Aristotle's definition of *períodos* does not clarify the syntactic status of what is λεκτά or ἐκφορά for the Stoics. Still, some English translations impose syntactic readings of the terms used by Aristotle.[68] The philosopher famously defines *períodos* as "a way of saying or diction (λέξις) that has a beginning and an end, and whose size is easy to take in

66 See above, n63; ὑπόκρισις in ancient grammarians means "delivery" (Dickey 2007:264).

67 This wording is attributed to Diocles of Magnesia, in Diogenes Laertius *Lives of philosophers* 7.63; an example of an incomplete λεκτόν is "Γράφει· ἐπιζητοῦμεν γάρ, τίς;" whereas a complete λεκτόν is "Γράφει Σωκράτης."

68 A significant example is Freese's translation for the Loeb edition (Freese 1939), where λέξις is regularly translated "sentence" and κῶλον "clause." In this section I use neutral terms (I render λέξις with "diction," and κῶλον with "segment").

at a glance" (λέγω δὲ περίοδον λέξιν ἔχουσαν ἀρχὴν καὶ τελευτὴν αὐτὴν καθ' αὑτὴν καὶ μέγεθος εὐσύνοπτον, *Rhetoric* 3.1409a). What primarily characterizes a λέξις that is not constructed from περίοδοι, but is εἰρομένη ("strung-on"), is the lack of τέλος.[69] Since the example he provides of λέξις εἰρομένη is a version of the incipit of Herodotus' *Histories*, which consists of a complete unit of sense ("This (is) the exposition of the investigation of Herodotus of Thurii"), the lack of τέλος must reside elsewhere. It is clear through his reference to round racetracks that Aristotle intends τέλος to mean "rounding out, fulfillment, coming full circle" rather than a linear end.[70] A few centuries later Cicero renders *períodos* as *ambitus verborum*.[71]

§40. This "circular" conceptualization of completeness was influenced by different practices in antiquity.[72] While commenting on the periodic style of Thucydides, Lamb (1914:105) explicitly connects the notion of *períodos* with one of them, that is, intonation. He writes: "in its widest and most literal sense it [period] merely means the rounding or circuit made by the rise and fall of the voice in anything beyond the simplest statement of fact; and this general meaning is fairly well given by the English word 'compass'." I align with Lamb. From the point of view of prosody, the starting and the concluding points of a *períodos* imply various inflections that the voice goes through between two similar prosodic moments.[73]

§41. Another important term in ancient discussion of discourse segmentation is κῶλον, "member."[74] Where do *kôla* come into the picture, in Aristotle's thoughts? In *Rhetoric* 3.1409b a *períodos* is said to be either "in *kôla*" or "simple" (περίοδος δὲ ἡ μὲν ἐν

69 [λέξις εἰρομένη] ἔστι δὲ ἀηδὴς διὰ τὸ ἄπειρον "[strung-on diction] is not pleasant, due to its lack of bounds" (*Rhetoric* 3.1409a).

70 On the etymological side, Waanders (1983:1) identifies for both the verb τελέω and the derived noun τέλος a basic reference to the idea of "achieving, realizing, carrying out, performing." On the ritual side, Nagy stresses the link between agonistic ordeals and existential ordeals; the τέλος of a hero's life represents the fulfillment of seasonality and equilibrium (2006:§107).

71 See also Cicero *De oratore* 3.51: old orators are not able to produce good periods (*circuitum et quasi orbem verborum conficere non possent*).

72 In an article on the metrical and the rhetorical definitions of *períodos*, Pace (2002:27) mentions several of them.

73 The "*Spannungsbogen*" ("arc of tension") Müller focuses on (see above, §25) may be re-defined in intonational terms as well. Contemporary studies in prosody do not explicitly discuss intonational curves over multi-clause stretches of text, but they consider something that is reminiscent conceptually. Over speeches or long turns in dialogue, speakers may apply special tones to mark several multi-clause units that work as paragraphs; they are called "paratones." The term "paratone" was coined by Fox (1973), and is used in Brown and Yule (1983:101) to indicate "speech paragraphs." Wennerstrom (2001, especially 100-114) discusses the complex relation between paratones (high, low, embedded) and topic structures. The notion overall conveys the idea that intonation can be used to embrace units of discourse exceeding single statements.

74 According to Robertson (1785:2) the *Suidas* records that the first author talking about *períodos* and *kôlon* is the Sophist Trasymachus (second part of the 5th century BCE). Throughout these paragraphs I will consider the ancient notion of *kôlon* in prose. Metrical *kôla* and metrical segmentation used in poetry represent a different topic; as my focus is on classical historiography, I will confine my inquiry to prose *kôla*.

κώλοις ἡ δ' ἀφελής). A λέξις "ἐν κώλοις" has to be complete, with distinct parts,[75] and easy to repeat in a single breath; it does not include division, but is a whole (ἔστιν δ' ἐν κώλοις μὲν λέξις ἡ τετελειωμένη τε καὶ διῃρημένη καὶ εὐανάπνευστος, μὴ ἐν τῇ διαιρέσει ... ἀλλ' ὅλη, *Rhetoric* 3.1409b).[76] In a later passage Aristotle further distinguishes diction-in-*kôla* into either one "with distinct parts" or "contrasting" (τῆς δὲ ἐν κώλοις λέξεως ἡ μὲν διῃρημένη ἐστὶν ἡ δὲ ἀντικειμένη, 1409b). To illustrate these two types, Aristotle adduces examples from Isocrates' *Panegyricus*, from which we can infer the syntactic status of the *kôla* he refers to. Interestingly, the quotations show a mix of main clauses, elliptical clauses, subclauses, participial and infinitive constructions, verbal phrases and noun phrases.[77] Aristotle sees the expression of contrast "in each of the two members," ἑκατέρῳ τῷ κώλῳ (ἀντικειμένη δὲ ἐν ᾗ ἑκατέρῳ τῷ κώλῳ ἢ πρὸς ἐναντίῳ ἐναντίον σύγκειται ἢ ταὐτὸ ἐπέζευκται τοῖς ἐναντίοις, 1409b-1410a), but "members" may be, for example, substantivized participles (see n77). Therefore, *kôla* are not only full clauses; the category must be syntactically inclusive rather than exclusive.

§42. Along the same lines, when Aristotle discusses παρίσωσις (assonance at the beginning of words) and παρομοίωσις (assonance at the end of words, or *homoiotéleuton*), the similarity of elements is considered across *kôla*: παρίσωσις δ' ἐὰν ἴσα τὰ κῶλα, παρομοίωσις δὲ ἐὰν ὅμοια τὰ ἔσχατα ἔχῃ ἑκάτερον τὸ κῶλον· (1410a). Freese (1939) translates, "equality of clauses is *parisôsis*; the similarity of the final syllables of each clause *paromoiôsis*. This must take place at the beginning or end of the clauses." However, taking *kôlon* as "clause" does not do justice to the Greek (or to Aristotle). The first example that is offered (of assonance at the beginning) Ἀγρὸν γὰρ ἔλαβεν ἀργὸν παρ' αὐτοῦ, "for he received from him land untilled" (Aristophanes *fr.* 649, reported in 1410a), where the assonance is between Ἀγρὸν and ἀργὸν within the same clause, and not across clauses. Analogously, the second example of assonance at the end is ἐν πλείσταις δὲ φροντίσι καὶ ἐν ἐλαχίσταις ἐλπίσιν (reported still in 1410a, and unattributed by scholars); again,

75 Freese 1939 (in the Loeb edition) writes "distinct in its parts" for διῃρημένη, literally "separated."

76 Cf. Dionysius of Halicarnassus, who states ἔστι δὴ τῆς συνθέσεως ἔργα τά τε ὀνόματα οἰκείως θεῖναι παρ' ἄλληλα καὶ τοῖς κώλοις ἀποδοῦναι τὴν προσήκουσαν ἁρμονίαν καὶ ταῖς περιόδοις διαλαβεῖν εὖ τὸν λόγον. (*De compositione verborum* 2.7,18-21). De Jonge (2008:185) translates the passage as follows: "the functions of composition are to place the words in a proper way beside each other and to give the clauses (κώλοις in Greek) the fitting harmony and to divide the discourse (λόγος) suitably into periods."

77 For example, the first quotation (Isocrates *Panegyricus* 1), which illustrates the "distinct" way, is a thought articulated in a main clause including two parallel (but not semantically contrasting) participial phrases (πολλάκις ἐθαύμασα τῶν τὰς πανηγύρεις συναγαγόντων καὶ τοὺς γυμνικοὺς ἀγῶνας καταστησάντων, "Several times I wondered at those who summoned the general assemblies and those who established the athletic games" (tr. AB). The second example illustrating the "contrasting" way is a ὥστε clause including two contrasted substantivized participles (ὥστε καὶ τοῖς χρημάτων δεομένοις καὶ τοῖς ἀπολαῦσαι βουλομένοις in Aristotle; nowadays the text established is ὥστε καὶ τοῖς χρημάτων δεομένοις καὶ τοῖς ἀπολαῦσαι τῶν ὑπαρχόντων ἐπιθυμοῦσιν ἀμφοτέροις ἁρμόττειν, "so that it fits both those who lack things, and those who wish to enjoy the things that are in their possession," *Panegyricus* 41 [tr. AB]).

the *homoiotéleuton* regards φροντίσι and ἐλπίσιν, which belong to different phrases, not to different clauses. Clauses are not the only syntactic construction Aristotle takes into account when he considers *kôla*. Finally, when Aristotle prescribes that *kôla* and *perídoi* should not be either too short or too long (δεῖ δὲ καὶ τὰ κῶλα καὶ τὰς περιόδους μήτε μυούρους εἶναι μήτε μακράς, 1409b), he uses for his criteria the rhythm of discourse and the listeners' convenience. His remark further supports the interpretation of *kôlon* as a unit that serves performative functions but is syntactically unspecified.

§43. Further important notes about *kôla* come from the author of *On Style* (περὶ ἑρμηνείας).[78] As Schenkeveld puts it (1964:30), for Demetrius "the existence of *kôla* is essential." The *kôlon* is the basic unit; already at the beginning of the treatise *kôlon* is defined as something that "aims at putting a thought together," (βούλεται διάνοιαν ἀπαρτίζειν, par. 2).[79] Its crucial function as a building block becomes clear when Demetrius compares *kôla* in prose to metrical units in poetry (par. 1). A *kôlon* is either a complete thought, or a complete part of a thought (par. 2).[80] Furthermore, Demetrius gives a name to short *kôla*, that is, κόμματα: ἡ δὲ τοιαύτη βραχύτης κατὰ τὴν σύνθεσιν κόμμα ὀνομάζεται ("such a brevity in composition is called *kómma*"; par. 9).[81] *Períodoi* are made of *kôla* and *kómmata*, but while *períodoi* depend on *kôla*, *kôla* exist independently of *períodoi*. What makes a mix of *kôla* and *kómmata* a *períodos*, then? Demetrius' definition of *períodos* is: ἔστιν γὰρ ἡ περίοδος σύστημα κώλων ἢ κομμάτων εὐκαταστρόφως πρὸς τὴν διάνοιαν τὴν ὑποκειμένην ἀπηρτισμένον ("the period is a system of *kôla* or *kómmata* that completes the underlying thought in a well-turned way," par. 10).[82] The shortest *períodos* is of two *kôla*, the largest is of four *kôla* (however, the size of *kôla* is not specified). The periodic style is called ἑρμηνεία κατεστραμμένη, the non-periodic style ἑρμηνεία

[78] There is still no consensus both about the date of the work and about which Demetrius is the author; see de Jonge 2009. The proposed dates span the 3rd century BCE to the 1st century CE. In this paragraph I will simply refer to Demetrius as the author.

[79] See also Morpurgo Tagliabue 1980:46-47; 47: "*I κῶλα per Demetrio sono unità semantiche*" ("for Demetrius *kôla* are semantic units"). For my discussion of Demetrius I am following the accounts of Schenkeveld (1964) and Morpurgo Tagliabue (1980).

[80] Interestingly, and by deliberately alluding to Aristotle's *Rhetoric*, Demetrius quotes the *incipit* of Herodotus as well, but to make a quite different point: while Aristotle was claiming that Ἡροδότου Θουρίου ἱστορίης ἀπόδεξις ἥδε has no τέλος, Demetrius says it does, as ἥδε allows the segment to come to an end.

[81] See also Dionysius of Halicarnassus *De compositione verborum* 26.8-9 ... πολλάκις δὲ καὶ εἰς κόμματα συνάγειν βραχύτερα κώλων ("[Elements that are] shorter than *kôla* often are brought together as *kómmata*").

[82] Cf. Dionysius of Halicarnassus *De compositione verborum* 16 ἡ τούτων [i.e. κώλων] ἁρμονία τὰς καλουμένας συμπληροῖ περίοδους "the concord of them [of *kôla*] bring the so-called *períodoi* to completion." However, in another passage the same Dionysius states that *kôla* and *kómmata* per se connote unperiodic discourse (ὁ ἑξῆς νοῦς ἀπερίοδος ἐν κώλοις τε καὶ κόμμασι λεγόμενος "the thought [expressed] in a row is unperiodic when it is uttered in *kôla* and *kómmata*," *De compositione verborum* 26. The latter passage contrasts with Demetrius' thoughts on the matter.

διηρημένη.[83] The latter is "loosened" as regards *kôla*: ἡ εἰς κῶλα λελυμένη, οὐ μάλα ἀλλήλοις συνηρτημένα "[the separating style] is loosened with respect to *kôla*, they are not quite linked to each other" (par. 12). All in all, Demetrius does not seem to offer definitions of *kôla* that associate them exclusively with clauses. "*Kómmata*" is introduced as a notion relative to *kôla*, but syntactic descriptions are absent. Note that if the term *kôlon* hints at parts of wholes, the etymology of *kómma* is straightforwardly related to segmentation: from κόπτω, κόμμα literally is something "cut off" (just as English "segment" comes from Latin *secare*, which also means "cut off").

§44. In the Roman era, Cicero provides further clues on ancient notions of *kôla* and *kómmata*; he calls them *membra* and *incisa* respectively. According to Schenkeveld Cicero belongs to the group of post-Aristotelean writers who couple period with rhythm rather than with a unifying thought (διάνοια). *Orator ad M. Brutum* 66-67 contains a remarkably extended section on the use, in forensic speeches, of *membra* and *incisa*, explicitly associated with *kôla* and *kómmata*. The *períodos* (*ambitus*) is said to consist of four members (*constat enim ille ambitus et plena comprehension e quattuor fere partibus, quae membra dicimus*),[84] which pleases ears (*auris impleat*) and is neither too short nor too long. These four members are similar to verses (in a spurious addition they are said to approximately correspond to an hexameter), and what links them are "bonds of continuation" (*quasi nodi apparent continuationis, quos in ambitu coniungimus*). Conversely, if we want to express ourselves member by member (*membratim volumus dicere*), we pause (*insistimus*). Examples of *incisa* (*kómmata*) quoted by Cicero are very short syntacticly independent but semantically correlated clauses (*missos faciant patronos* followed by *ipsi prodeant*; furthermore, *domus tibi deerat*? followed by *at habebas*), while examples of *membra* (*kôla*) are two interrogative clauses (*cur clandestinis consiliis nos oppugnant*? followed by *cur de perfugis nostris copias comparant contra nos*?).[85]

§45. Quintilian also uses the terms *incisum, membrum*, and *ambitus*.[86] He recalls that according to Cicero a period should encompass a single breath (*Institutio oratoria* 9.4.125).[87] St. Jerome (4th century CE) translates the Bible by using a system of punctuation that he

83 For an overview of the developments of these notions in other post-Aristotelean writers, see Schenkeveld 1964:31-33.

84 The specification that there are four members is reminiscent of Demetrius' definition (see above).

85 Bakker (1997b:140) remarks: "for Cicero there are pulmonary constraints on the flow of discourse, a physical necessity resulting in observable and expected breaks in the flow of speech in the performance and yielding a segmentation into relatively short units."

86 *At illa conexa series tris habet formas: incise, quae commata dicuntur; membra, quae kola, periodon quae est vel ambitus vel circumductum* (*Institutio Oratoria* 9.4.22).

87 Although Cicero himself adapts this thought by admitting: "It was failure or scantiness of breath that originated periodic structure and pauses between words; but now that this has once been discovered, it is so attractive that, even if a person were endowed with breath that never failed, we should not wish him to deliver an unbroken flow of words" (*De oratore* 3.46.181; translation by Robbins (1979:59)).

calls *per cola et commata*.[88] Still later in the *Etymologiae* of Isidorus of Sevilla (7th century CE) texts are divided into *períodoi, kôla* and *kómmata*, and there are indications of where one's voice should rest.[89] The distinction between *membrum* and *incisum* is kept also in Old English psalmody, where the period coincides with the verse, and each segment corresponds to a "breath-group."[90]

3.6 Modern Acknowledgment of Prose Colometry

§46. The evidence I have collected in the latter section has an interesting counterpart in modern studies on prose colometry. "Colometry" literally means "measurement in *kôla*"; the concept *per se* is neutral with respect to poetic meter and to prose.[91] Recall that for Demetrius *kôla* are in prose what meter is for poetry (*On Style*, par. 1; see above, §43). Dionysius of Halicarnassus in *De compositione verborum* devotes significant attention to the stylistic features that make prose poetic; those features primarily include word placement, rhythm, and sound. *Kôla* and *kómmata* are important units in this process.[92] In the 20th century Hellenists as well as Latinists have employed the notion of prose *kôla* in different types of discussions. I shall delineate some of them.

§47. Eduard Fraenkel was the first to contribute new ideas to the ancient notion of *kôla* in prose (1932, 1933).[93] His divisions into *kôla* (marked by vertical bars) are "retrospectively" inferred from postpositive elements (such as ἄν), which signal a boundary before the word they are phonologically attached to. This applies to participial phrases as well.[94] On the level of lexical cues, Fraenkel includes negative markers in the items that may indicate *kôlon* boundaries,[95] even though he does not specify how to distinguish between negations with phrasal scope and negations with clausal scope.

88 McDermott 1990:10. Robbins (1979:60) reports St. Jerome' original words, where the practice is compared to what "is customarily done with Demosthenes and Cicero" (*quod in Demosthene et Tullio solet fieri*). Interestingly, P. Oxy. 3891 including Thucydides 3.16-17 and dating back to the 2nd century CE, shows frequent gaps between groups of words, which Johnson (2004:83) identifies with *cola* and *commata*: "The text is at frequent intervals articulated by means of gaps (...). We are to recognize a system of demarcating *cola* and *commata*, intended no doubt to facilitate ἀνάγνωσις by marking the pauses."

89 Clemoes 1952:9.

90 See Clemoes 1952:3 and 10 (10 for the quotation).

91 According to the *New Oxford American Dictionary*, "prose" is a term first attested in the 14th century in old French. Etymologically it comes from *prosa oratio*, where *prosus* means "direct, straightforward" (from *prorsus*).

92 See De Jonge 2008:329-366 for the entire discussion of poetic prose; 183n46 and 184 with n48 for comments on *kôla* in Dionysius (which De Jonge consistently takes as "clauses"). See also *De compositione verborum* 26.136,9; *On the admirable style of Demosthenes* 39.213,1 and 43.227,4. Interestingly, De Jonge (2008:183n46) notes that the smallest segment Dionysius mentions is *kómma*, not (single) words.

93 See II.2 §§10-11.

94 See Wackernagel 1892, and the related discussion in II.2 §9.

95 See E. Fraenkel 1965:46, and II.2 n82.

§48. Robbins 1979 applies the notion of colometry in prose to analyze Cicero's *Third Oration Against Catilina*. He identifies periods of four *kôla* each, and each *kôlon* is comparable, in length, to a dactylic hexameter. *Kôla* are clauses or long phrases, whereas *kómmata* are short phrases or single adverbs, and even single conjunctions that connect two parts of a period (e.g. *ut*, 1979:58). The conclusion is a bold statement: "It is ... an injustice to classical prose writers to print them straight out, using only grammatical punctuation, in disregard of the carefully composed cola and periods. What a tremendous help it would be to students in learning and to teachers and scholars in explaining the classics if we were to write them out, in Saint Jerome's words, *per cola et commata*" (1979:62).

§49. In a pedagogically oriented article, Harrison (2007) proposes that students arrange Latin (and Greek) texts by indenting clauses and phrases on separate lines. She equates this practice with reading *per cola et commata,* thus assimilating *cola* to clauses and *commata* to phrases (2007:291). The segments thus obtained facilitate comprehension: "The line-divisions break the text into meaningful chunks and help students see which words do (and do not) go together" (2007:292). Such an approach is seen as "... opposed to more common translation methods, such as translating individual words, trying to intuit the sentence whole, or hunting and picking to reconstruct the sentence in English sentence form" (2007:293). The graphic representation of the segmentation Harrison devises is simple: "Main clauses generally begin flush left. Sub-units (e.g. long prepositional phrases) and subordinate clauses and their sub-units are indented. Parallel items, such as correlatives and compound phrases or clauses, are lined up under one another" (2007:294).

§50. Habinek (1985:127), building on E. Fraenkel's work, provides a useful list of units that serve as "rhythmical and rhetorical cola" in Latin texts (1985:128): "any weighted or expanded substantive, regardless of case; any weighted modifier, be it participial, adjectival, or adverbial in character; all prepositional phrases; phrases, such as infinitives, that substitute for substantives; and verb phrases." In addition, the author discusses single-word constituents (128-132); items in enumeration (132); brachylogy[96] (133); correlative constructions (134-135); and vocatives (135-136). Thus, Habinek's examination of *kôla* is based on various syntactic constructions; note that full clauses are hardly considered in his list.[97]

96 "Brachylogy is the consecutive repetition, usually asyndetical, of a grammatical construction with the omission ... of some item .... Because of the close grammatical parallelism and the dependent relationship between the two or more units in brachylogy, one might expect such units to cohere into a single colon" (Habinek 1985:133).

97 The scholar devotes a long chapter to pre-print punctuation of Latin texts (1985:42-88), and concludes that marks or spaces "regularly occur at the ends of certain grammatical constituents" (88); these grammatical constituents include the units identified by E. Fraenkel, and the units that I list above.

§51. Finally, Scheppers 2011 is a monograph entirely devoted to "the colon hypothesis" of the title. His basic hypothesis is twofold: as the author puts it, "the colon is the unit to which Greek word order rules ... are applicable," and "the colon is the elementary discourse unit, in other words: discourse *essentially* comes in *cola*" (17; italics in the text). Towards the beginning of the work (2011:15), Scheppers revises E. Fraenkel's *kôlon* typology and lists his own four categories of *kôla*: "autonomous verb clauses" (including "main finite clauses," "subordinate finite clauses," "participle clauses," and "infinitival clauses"); "parallel members" (such as οὔτε ... οὔτε ...); "syntactically non-integrated constituents" (such as parenthetical clauses); and finally, "fronted constituents" (including "topic noun phrases," "fronted prepositional phrases," "fronted markers," and "common grounds for complex structures"). He also suggests several specific criteria for identifying *kôlon* boundaries in his textual analyses of Lysias and Plato's excerpts. "Fronted negatives," for example, are one of them (243 and 258).[98]

§52. As Scheppers' monograph is sizable, and the majority of texts under examination are prose texts, this is a thorough contribution on Greek *kôla*. The scholar's application of his *kôlon* criteria in the textual analyses sometimes are questionable, and theoretical issues related to word order perhaps remain unsolved, but the fundamental idea is valuable in itself: if we posit the existence of *kôla* as segments of prose discourse, in accordance with the accounts (however general) of ancient scholars, an entire world of linguistic details emerge. Such details, which regular hypotactical analyses obscure, give us an enriched view of discourse segmentation, and can affect our comprehension of content.

3.7 Modern Segmentation Above the Sentence Level

§53. At least one more feature of modern readings of ancient Greek prose texts is influenced by earlier practices, besides modern punctuation and modern acknowledgment of prose colometry. This is the paralinguistic segmentation realized by chapter and section numbers, indentation, and extra space between words in the *OCT* editions.[99]

§54. Hemmerdinger (1981:54) tells us that Jungermann (1608) was the scholar who introduced chapter division (τρήματα *sive sectiones*) in Herodotus' *Histories*, whereas Hudson (1696) introduced chapter divisions in Thucydides.[100] With the exception of ms

98 Scheppers' use of the term "fronted" is not unambiguous. He defines fronting as "any phenomenon in which a constituent occurs to the left of the segment which constitutes the—somehow—'central' part of a clause, sentence, or similar construction" (2011:200).

99 The *TLG* online shows extra space unrelated to new numbers very rarely; also, new chapters consistently start a new line.

100 As for Herodotus, see also Nenci (1998:9), and West in Bowie 2007:30-32. For a useful summary of Thucydides' 28 print editions from the Aldine (1502) to Bekker's (1832-1846), see Arnold 1863:ix-xii. Book divisions are not directly relevant to this chapter, as they represent forms of macro-segmentation that depend less on the linguistic realization of the boundaries than

D of Herodotus (10th century), which, according to Hemminger (1981:54) shows a few traces of an ancient chapter division by means of Ionian numbers, medieval manuscripts do not include any such divisions. Therefore, our identification of loci in both works relies on a quite modern macro-segmentation of the texts. The criteria that brought scholars to divide chapters across centuries can generally be inferred by the texts themselves: different chapters straddle different settings or individual setting components,[101] different topics, or different (parts of) speeches. For section divisions uniform criteria are less easy to infer, as internal divisions within stretches of discourse that share the same communicative goals—moves, in our work—can be established on the basis of different assumptions. However, a crucial observation is that the texts display linguistic features from which more segmentation emerges than that suggested by numbers, or a different one.[102]

§55. In addition to chapter and section numbers, the *OCT* editions report two further paralinguistic signs: indentation and extra space between words. Both can co-occur with chapter and section numbers, but also occur independently. As for indentation, a sample of 11 chapters from book 1, 5, and 9 for Herodotus' *OCT* edition (Hude), and book 1, 5, and 8 from Thucydides' *OCT* (Stuart Jones) shows that no consistency (neither in form nor in content) underlies chapter starts that are indented and chapter starts that are not. Therefore some degree of arbitrariness has to be assumed, which we could at least lessen if we rely on actual linguistic features. In a very few cases indentation corresponds to section starts instead of chapter starts, and in one case it has no corresponding number.[103]

§56. As for extra space between words, the same sample of chapters gives a more interesting result: while chapter and section starts that are not indented are consistently marked by extra space between words (unless the new unit begins a new *OCT* line), there are uncountable extra spaces between words without any corresponding numbers, in both *Histories*.[104] The interest lies in the consistency behind this unnumbered

on the articulation of macro-content. On book divisions, see in particular Cagnazzi 1975 and her hypothesis of Herodotus' original division into 28 λόγοι; Bonner 1920 and Hemmerdinger 1955:15-19 for Thucydides.

101 I adopt Thorndyke's basic division of a story setting in place, time, and character(s). See later, §95.

102 Section 3.11 discusses in particular the linguistic features connected to moves and move boundaries.

103 In the whole second volume of *OCT*'s Thucydides, for example, see just 5.32.2; 5.39.2; 8.43.2; 8.103.2; 8.108.3. In the second volume of *OCT*'s Herodotus, Hude never indents at section starts. An exceptional case is to be found in Herodotus 9: before chapter 114 starts (with no indentation), a μέν sentence is indented with no corresponding section number. This overview of paralinguistic segmentation excludes the justification or the indentation of embedded texts from other sources, such as oracles, verses, and treaties texts: discourse discontinuity in those cases is consistent and signaled unequivocally.

104 Without consideration for justification purposes in print, clear extra spaces that do not accompany any number in the 33 chapters of Herodotus' sample are 44, and in the 33 chapters of Thucydides there are 33.

segmentation, which derives from the occurrence of particles and particle combinations. Extra spaces are found, for instance, before X γάρ and X μὲν δή segments. Even though there is no full coincidence between extra spaces in the *OCT* editions and extra spaces in the two old manuscripts I inspected, as far as the sample of chapters abovementioned are concerned,[105] I interpret all these extra spaces as recorded on the basis of a collation of pre-print editions.[106] The striking match between paralinguistic extra space between words and the linguistic features that in my reading start moves[107] confirms that particles and other co-occurrent features are crucial devices for discourse segmentation.

3.8 The Roles of Particles: Matches and Mismatches

§57. How should we assess the role of particles with respect to all the factors and views that I have delineated so far? First of all, particles constitute a device for marking discourse segmentation, but other linguistic devices may do the job as well, in combination with particles or independently: these are syntactic devices (e.g. hyperbata, subordinating conjunctions) or lexico-semantic devices (e.g. negations). Therefore, our interpretation of how to chunk ancient Greek discourse has to rely on multiple features. However, particles stand out, because of a quality that makes several of them similar to punctuation and other kinds of paralinguistic segmentation. This quality is the capacity of suggesting when and how discourse proceeds, or when and how discourse stops. A genitive absolute cannot do that, but δέ or μέν can.

§58. As far as the relationship between particles and modern punctuation is concerned, a few considerations are in order. According to Parkes (1992:1) the primary function of punctuation is "to resolve structural uncertainties in a text, and to signal nuances of semantic significance which might otherwise not be conveyed at all." This applies to particles as well. Punctuation and particles, in other words, both function as road signs. "Punctuation marks are the traffic signals of language: they tell us to slow down, notice this, take a detour, and stop" (Truss 2003:7). Likewise, as Denniston himself puts it (1954:xli-xlii), "The reader or listeners, when he has reached a certain point, meets a particle which looks back to the road he has traversed, and beckons him on in a certain direction."[108] The resonance between the metaphors is significant. Punctuation

[105] In general, in the manuscripts the insertion of punctuation marks automatically involves a visual gap between groups of words; here I take the pre-print extra spaces as always involving the occurrence of a puntucation mark.

[106] The modern editors' sensitivity to the Greek may also be considered a factor, even though the same sensitivity in fact does not bring editors to change section divisions whenever the Greek suggests major discontinuities elsewhere.

[107] On which see below §§62; 85; 110-111; 115; 121; 123; 125; 127; 129; 132; 152, and IV.5 28; 35; 46, 55-56; 66; 74; 79; 83; 92.

[108] For similar analogies in connection with particles and discourse markers in modern languages, see I.3 §§12 and 14.

and particles are both multifunctional. For example, the same graphic sign "comma" can be used to mark incompleteness of thoughts across contiguous segments in quite different ways, for example to join clauses, to set off list-entries, and to attach details.[109] Analogously, δέ in different constructions can signpost different relations across discourse segments.[110]

§59. However, it would be unfair to analogize particles to punctuation in modern editions of ancient Greek texts.[111] Particles represent more, and give more information, than modern punctuation does. Although they are subject to some variation in textual transmission, particles are more original than both modern punctuation and "posthumous" chapter and section divisions.[112] Furthermore, unlike punctuation marks, they are lexically differentiated, and frequently grouped in combinations. It is up to us modern readers to take on the challenge of grasping the hints that particles offer about segmenting and articulating discourse, by improving our sensitivity to their implications and to metacommunication.

§60. I do not deny that modern punctuation is a helpful tool for decoding ancient Greek texts. As I already noted, to some extent modern punctuation may even be inspired or motivated by the occurrence of particles, especially peninitial-position particles.[113] My point, however, is that full stops and commas do not simply aid our reading. On at least the visual and cognitive levels they signify much more. They paralinguistically suggest stronger and weaker discourse boundaries, and they shape the length of segments. Full stops cause us to presuppose that what occurs between them is a unit of some sort. Parentheses cause us to interpret the information contained within them as secondary information. The absence of exclamation marks causes us to assume that exclamatory acts are unlikely to occur. The list may continue. In other words, modern punctuation

[109] Among others, Truss (2003:83-90) offers a helpful overview of the multifarious functions of commas in English. A comma joins clauses, for example, as in "Sally was not paying any attention, her headache was worsening"; it marks list-entries, as in "Sally traveled to India, Bangladesh, and Nepal"; it marks the attachment of details, as in "Sally took one week off to go on vacation to Sardinia, Costa Rei" (examples are mine).

[110] See II.2.2.1; III.4 §34-38; IV.2.2.

[111] Duhoux (2006:532) rejects the hypothesis that ancient Greek particles worked, like modern punctuation marks, to identify word, phrase, and proposition boundaries because in ancient texts there was no word division. The decoding of Linear B confirms that it had word division; therefore, Duhoux concludes, the coexistence of particles and punctuation signs in ancient texts shows that particles do not compensate for the absence of graphical punctuation. My argument is different. First, particles do help in identifying at least proposition and phrase boundaries regardless of any presence of punctuation marks. Second, word division is different from punctuation; pre-print punctuation even increased once Greek texts included word space on a regular base (see above §31).

[112] See below §§98; 131; 134; 136-137 on mismatches between chapter beginnings and chapter endings across editions, and their relation to particle use.

[113] See II.2 §9. Dik insightfully calls modern punctuation marks placed in view of postpositive particles, indefinite markers and personal pronouns "punctuation after the fact" (1995:32).

marks suggest a *certain* reading of segments, units, and grammar, or a reading of them in a certain direction. This may or may not harmonize with what particles suggest. My analyses will show matches and mismatches between segments suggested by modern punctuation and segments suggested by particles. The mismatches comprise the more interesting evidence, as they motivate us to observe more closely what particles convey that modern punctuation cannot.

§61. A further comparison will be made between the occurrence of particles and chapter and section numbers as we find them in print editions. In those cases the discourse boundaries relate more to multiple sentences and multiple *períodoi*, in a word to segmentation on a larger scale. Also at this level matches and mismatches are observable. In some current editions we may even find indentations at chapter starts, and, as I already said earlier, extra spaces between words. But indentation does not consistently accompany chapter starts, and extra space between words does not accompany only section and chapter starts, which makes consistency hard to find.[114] However, extra spaces do almost consistently show a match with particles: as I will point out, extra spaces largely coincide with move boundaries signaled by particles and particle combinations. My general claim is that the occurrence of linguistic features, especially particles and particle combinations, is more reliable and more precise than modern segmentation also above the sentence level, at least in terms of lexical consistency and variation.

§62. Let us now briefly recall considerations about labels for segments. We have seen that the discussion of periodic styles in modern times privileges syntactic ranking (hypotaxis) and associated trends (subclauses following or preceding main clauses). The consideration of *kôla* and *kommata* in periods (*períodoi*) unfortunately is absent. Ancient views of segmentation, conversely, pay close attention to *kôla* and *kómmata* that represent smaller but no less relevant building blocks of discourse than *períodoi* (*kómmata*, in turn, represent smaller elements than *kôla*).

§63. The fact that the length and, most of all, the grammatical form of *kôla* and *kómmata* are left unspecified is, paradoxically, a very important cue. It means that no specific syntactic characterizations can be associated with them. Despite the tendency to translate *kôlon* as "clause," *kôla* do not necessarily coincide with clauses. Ancient punctuation practices (for all their diachronic and typological variety) signal the same: marks occur beyond clause boundaries. Both ancient segmentation and ancient punctuation apply a broader perspective than periodic or sentence-based articulation. Both consistently show that grammar and eloquence do not conflict. Modern studies in prose colometry recall and reinforce these ideas, which in ancient times were integral to the composition and interpretation of prose texts.

§64. Overall, ancient views about segmentation, pre-print punctuation, and the modern retrieval of the notion of prose colometry show that segmentation is inspired by

114 See above §§55-56, and the textual analyses below (3.10-3.11).

several phenomena of language production and language reception. Criteria and signs may differ. Priorities in establishing the criteria may change across time and reading (or teaching) habits. However, all these systems or frameworks start from words, from the linguistic material available. The distribution and the combination of linguistic features play a paramount role; although they may have been affected by textual transmission, they chronologically precede any ancient punctuation and paralinguistic marking. Now it is time to clarify how we can process language in order to infer discourse segmentation, where "discourse" is informed by syntax, semantics, and pragmatics.

3.9 The Holistic Principle of Discourse Segmentation

§65. In order to exemplify the perspective that is adopted in the textual analyses (see below 3.10-3.11, and IV.5.2-5), let us consider what the full stop in modern punctuation and the chapter number do in the following passage, drawn from the end of Thucydides' account of the plague that devastated Athens over the first years of the war (Book 2.47-54).

(t10)

ταῦτα μὲν τὰ κατὰ τὴν νόσον γενόμενα. [55] Οἱ δὲ Πελοποννήσιοι ...

Thucydides 2.54.5-55.1

This, then, was what happened during the disease.

The Peloponnesians ... (tr. AB)

The full stop invites us to consider ταῦτα μὲν ... and οἱ δὲ ... as quite separate segments. A further modern paralinguistic sign is the chapter number, which precedes οἱ δὲ Πελοποννήσιοι. It warns us that a major discourse boundary occurs. My point is that the language encodes this segmentation regardless of the presence of a full stop and a chapter number.

§66. Let me expand on how Thucydides' language provides all the information necessary for processing the two segments without the need of an intervening full stop. In order to understand this excerpt we need to process ταῦτα first. The pronoun refers to all the facts and events connected to "the disease," which we infer from τὰ κατὰ τὴν νόσον γενόμενα. Then we need to realize that what follows (οἱ δὲ Πελοποννήσιοι) introduces a totally different subject matter. How do we interpret the role of μέν and δέ in this context? The adjacent μέν and δέ clauses cannot be a manifestation of the μέν – δέ construction expressing semantic contrast. Rather, they juxtapose what the discourse is about: first "these (events)," and then "the Peloponnesians." On a larger scale, the μέν act rounds off a long section (the seven chapters that Thucydides devotes to the plague). At the same time it anticipates that the account will continue. This is the function that μέν performs in this utterance.[115] The δέ statement, conversely, opens a separate and new narrative section (starting with a new δέ segment). We may even "hear" the inner voice of the historian and imagine a specific intonation matching the μέν statement (resembling the tone of an interim conclusion[116]), and a different intonation matching the δέ statement (launching a new topical spin).

§67. We would not be able to comprehend how discourse is flowing[117] at this point in Thucydides' account if we did not process all this information, which regards the local co-text as well as a broader co-text and context. These steps sound natural; nonetheless, they require a combination of certain operations and skills: the activation of the short-term discourse memory (what was said in the previous units), anaphora processing (to retrieve a relevant referent for the pronoun), competence in syntax (to combine τά with γενόμενα, for example), competence in semantics (to connect "the disease" with the plague, for example), and encyclopedic and historiographical knowledge (to infer that anything to be said about the Peloponnesians at that point does not have the Athenians as its main subject). The full stop and the chapter number in modern editions adumbrate only a small part of this entire process.

§68. This chapter calls for paying attention to discourse as an organic whole made of several linguistic components. The approach we advocate implies a fundamental assumption: just as with any other kind of textual interpretation, interpretation of particles relies on Apollonius' and Heliodorus' idea that particles "co-signify" (συσσημαίνουσι) with other words.[118] The discourse analyses of Thucydides and Herodotus undertaken in the next part of the chapter and in IV.5 are based on a holistic principle. They consider the fundamental dimensions of language influencing each other (syntax, semantics, pragmatics), on local as well as global levels of discourse—that is, from phrases to paragraphs, from acts to genre.[119] Considering the pragmatic dimension, in particular, means taking account of the relation between language and dedicated communicative settings (or situations), and between co-text and paralinguistic context.

§69. We contend that this holistic view aligns with the equally holistic view of language that ancient rhetors expressed in several works. The pivotal concept for them was that of performance: for most of the genres and periods under discussion, written

115 Compare μέν in II.2 §52 (t16); III.5 §36 (t4); and below 3.11.4 about μὲν δή and μέν νυν. See also III.4 §28-30 about μέν used to hold the floor. μέν ... δέ in large-scale transitions and μέν conveying "more to follow" are already discussed in Bakker 1993b:302-303 and 299, respectively.

116 For a prosodic and perceptual analysis of nonfinal intonation in a modern language such as Italian, see for example Savino *et al.* 2006. About this value of μέν, see also below §140.

117 See above n11 on "the flow of discourse."

118 See I.2 §§61 and 83.

119 See I.1 §7; see also I.3§43 for the holistic view of grammar embraced in Construction Grammar (CxG).

compositions ended up as discourse embodied through speakers or singers—a type of discourse that was voiced and received aurally. This practice informed the description, by ancient writers, of forms, patterns, and stylistic rules of language.[120] We moderns have to content ourselves with only the written part of texts designed for performance.[121] However, words provide excellent clues on several sophisticated levels of communication. For example, they may reveal discourse segmentation, cognitive and/or syntactic projections, rhetorical figures, discourse patterns, phonological resonance, and context-dependent references.[122] Among the various components of literary language that help us detect all of this, particles stand out. They typically signal discourse procedures, communicative actions, and attitudes that reveal discourse strategies.

3.10 Herodotus' and Thucydides' Discourse Acts

§70. Two notions that we use in the light of this holistic principle are those of act and move.[123] Both reflect a discourse perspective that includes but also reaches beyond syntax and periodic divisions. Although classifications of act and move types are neither proposed nor wished for, acts and moves postulate a simple idea: people perform them to achieve discrete communicative goals and broader communicative goals respectively. In Herodotus and Thucydides, acts and moves are performed by the two authors; through authorial mimesis they are meant to be performed by speaking characters.

§71. Let us first concentrate on discourse acts, and on the role of particles in marking them As II.2 §§24-25 recalls, Bakker (1997b:146-155) compares hexametrical *kôla* in Homer to intonation units. While discussing Dionysius of Halicarnassus' view of sentences, Viljamaa (2003:173-176) also compares the ancient notion of prose *kôla* to the contemporary notion of intonation units. In his work on hyperbata, Markovic (2006:127) assumes the same.[124] Scheppers (2011:18-35) starts his investigation by illustrating the

[120] Aristotle himself focuses on the characteristics that make the *delivery* of different types of discourse appropriate and effective. In *Rhetoric* 3.1408a he lists strategies that make diction (λέξις) effective, among which is impassioning (συνομοπαθεῖ ὁ ἀκούων ἀεὶ τῷ παθητικῶς λέγοντι "the one who listens to someone talking in an impassionate way feels sympathetic," 1408a). 1409a is on the rhythm of prose (which I discussed above, in §42); 1411b-1413 highlights visualization among the clever features of a pointed saying (πρὸ ὀμμάτων ποιεῖν, "(talking by) setting things before the eyes"). Finally, in 1415a the introduction of a speech is compared to a prologue in poetry, and to a prelude in music. All of this suggests that effective prose composition mingles verbal and nonverbal powers of communication.

[121] On this point see also II.1 §§2-4 (about epic and lyric texts transmitted to us) and III.1.1 (about drama).

[122] This work examines aspects of these sophisticated levels of communication, including projection (II.2.4.1); discourse patterns (III.2), resonance (III.3), anaphoric choice (II.5), and, in this chapter, segmentation.

[123] For a thorough discussion of the theoretical bearing of the two notions, see II.2 and II.3.

[124] "I use the term colon to designate a syntactically, semantically, and rhythmically more or less complete segment of the sentence, i.e. the written equivalent of the intonation unit in spoken

centrality of intonation units, and shows that particles can mark *kôlon* boundaries. Certainly, particles may be compared to prosodic marking, and prosodic units may or may not coincide with syntactic boundaries. Nicanor indicates as much when he assigns longer and shorter pauses to stretches of text starting with certain particles (see above, §§33-34). To the extent that peninitial-position particles emphasize the group of words to which they are attached, they may signal prosodic boundaries and indicate *ad hoc* intonational contours—it is conceivable to think of a range of μέν clause intonational contours, δέ clause intonational contours, and so on. Goldstein's thorough research (2010, 2013b) on the prosodic relevance of the distribution of clitics in Classical Greek—including several particles—is a further landmark for us: it demonstrates that intonation has a crucial bearing on the construction of semantic and pragmatic meaning. In our terms, intonation has a crucial bearing on discourse segmentation.

§72. Our work intends to draw connections to studies in prose colometry as well as to research on intonation units/"intonational phrases" (Goldstein 2010:42). As our focus is on discourse strategies, we explore the discourse relevance of what is behind the idea of intonation unit/intonational phrase, rather than using the terms themselves. Likewise, we propose to consider what may be seen behind the term *kôlon*, rather than applying the term itself. Therefore, while constantly keeping in mind links between particles and prosody, on the one hand, and the links between particles and *kôla*, on the other, we call the basic segments of verbal communication discourse acts. Their value is more theoretical than philological—that is to say, the aim is not to reconstruct "original" discourse acts—what we identify throughout our volumes is *potential* discourse acts.[125] In modern languages discourse acts tend to be realized by intonation units in spoken varieties, and by punctuation units in written varieties.[126] They represent small steps, but these steps are strategic in that they let the speaker make points. They are acts because they perform communicative actions together with, and beyond the words uttered.[127]

§73. The following subsections will exemplify discourse segmentation in acts. Since their grammatical form is not what defines them, the analysis focuses on acts in continuous texts rather than on selected acts from different excerpts. In this way the very process of segmentation is in focus as well. The goal is to show how chunking discourse into acts changes the reading and the interpretation of the text, and how particles elucidate discourse acts. Given the relatively small scale of acts, comparisons will be made especially with modern as well as pre-print punctuation.

---

language." (Markovic 2006:127n1). Devine and Stephens' reading of hyperbata revolves around the notion of focal information rather than that of intonation: the basic idea is that " ... hyperbaton encodes focus in prose" (2000:33).

125 See II.2.1.1, and §23 for the idea of "potential discourse acts."

126 As Hannay and Kroon (2005) argue. See II.2 §20.

127 See II.2 §§21-22.

§74. Different is going to be the case of moves, that is, units typically made up of multiple acts. Comparisons in that case will include also paralinguistic segmentation above the sentence level. Also, the discussion of moves will require more general considerations, and special attention to the recurrence of particle combinations and other constructions. I remind the reader that chapter IV.5 blends the analysis of acts and that of moves, and clarifies the relation between them.

3.10.1 Segmenting an "unsuccessful" period in Herodotus

§75. Earlier in the chapter (§§ 24-25) I mentioned Müller's idea of successful periods, that is, syntactically complex wholes displaying a series of subclauses that culminate in a main clause. Müller adopts for these periods the notion, originally coined by Blass (1887), of "*aufsteigende Periode*" ("ascending period"). Discussing the periodic style of Herodotus, Müller suggests that the historian, in failing to sustain such "ascending periods," falls short of a perfection that later writes come to practice. The *Histories* of Herodotus from time to time includes what he calls "unsuccessful" ("*verunglückte*") periods. Müller lists some examples, among which is a passage from the episode of the Cnidians in book 1 (1.174.2-3). Müller is not the only scholar to noticed the peculiar way in which the narrative is articulated in that passage: How and Wells (1928:134) calls 174.3 "a model of confusion." This view is a longstanding one and seems to involve the issue of syntactic hierarchies: long before Müller and How and Wells, Bekker (whose edition of Herodotus dates back to 1845) decided to add a relative pronoun at the beginning of section 2, even though the reading is not attested in any manuscript.

§76. Let us first report the text as it appears in the *OCT* edition.[128] This way, we can begin by interpreting the excerpt according to its articulation in periods: from full stop to full stop, with intermediate commas, with section numbers as the only signals of higher level segmentation, and with an instance of indentation at the start of the chapter. Godley's translation directly follows, featuring in turn full stops and commas together with syntactic divisions appropriate to the flow of discourse in English.[129]

(t11)

[indent] [174] Οἱ μέν νυν Κᾶρες οὐδὲν λαμπρὸν ἔργον ἀποδεξάμενοι ἐδουλώθησαν ὑπὸ Ἁρπάγου, οὔτε αὐτοὶ οἱ Κᾶρες ἀποδεξάμενοι οὐδὲν οὔτε ὅσοι Ἑλλήνων ταύτην τὴν χώρην οἰκέουσι. [2] οἰκέουσι δὲ καὶ ἄλλοι καὶ Λακεδαιμονίων ἄποικοι Κνίδιοι, <οἳ>[130] τῆς χώρης τῆς σφετέρης τετραμμένης

[128] *OCT* to exemplify editorial choices for the sake of comparison

[129] For the sake of convenience, only Bekker's emendation is reported from the apparatus criticus of the *OCT* edition; the apparatus does not offer any further comments on the excerpt in question. The Greek of (t) reproduces Hude's text (*OCT*), except for the position of section numbers, which here appear right before the corresponding text, instead of in the margin.

[130] Bekker's addition (1845).

> ἐς πόντον, τὸ δὴ Τριόπιον καλέεται, ἀργμένης δὲ ἐκ τῆς Χερσονήσου τῆς Βυβασσίης, ἐούσης τε πάσης τῆς Κνιδίης πλὴν ὀλίγης περιρρόου [3] (τὰ μὲν γὰρ αὐτῆς πρὸς βορῆν ἄνεμον ὁ Κεραμεικὸς κόλπος ἀπέργει, τὰ δὲ πρὸς νότον ἡ κατὰ Σύμην τε καὶ Ῥόδον θάλασσα), τὸ ὦν δὴ ὀλίγον τοῦτο, ἐὸν ὅσον τε ἐπὶ πέντε στάδια, ὤρυσσον οἱ Κνίδιοι ἐν ὅσῳ Ἅρπαγος τὴν Ἰωνίην κατεστρέφετο, βουλόμενοι νῆσον τὴν χώρην ποιῆσαι.
>
> Herodotus 1.174.1-3
>
> Neither the Carians nor any Greeks who dwell in this country did any thing notable before they were all enslaved by Harpagus. (2.) Among those who inhabit it are certain Cnidians, colonists from Lacedaemon. Their country (it is called the Triopion) lies between the sea and that part of the peninsula which belongs to Bubassus, and all but a small part of the Cnidian territory is washed by the sea (3.) (for it is bounded on the north by the gulf of Ceramicus, and on the south by the sea off Syme and Rhodes). Now while Harpagus was conquering Ionia, the Cnidians dug a trench across this little space, which is about two-thirds of a mile wide, in order that their country might be an island. (tr. Godley)

Section 1 coincides with a period, with the people of Caria as the subject. The full stop occurs before οἰκέουσι δέ, where section 2 starts. The next full stop occurs only at the end of section 3; the subject of this second period is the Cnidians, one of the peoples of Caria. Overall this print edition segments the text into two periods including nine commas and a parenthesis (at the beginning of section 3). The punctuation yields a total of 13 complete and incomplete segments.

§77. Now, how would we process the content differently if we segment by discourse acts? Let us visualize the segmentation that results from using occurrences of particles, and features such as clauses, negations, and absolute constructions, to draw our boundaries.[131] The following translation attempts to reflect the sequence and the pace of acts.

(t12)

1. [indent] [174] Οἱ μέν νυν Κᾶρες
2. οὐδὲν λαμπρὸν ἔργον ἀποδεξάμενοι
3. ἐδουλώθησαν ὑπὸ Ἁρπάγου,
4. οὔτε αὐτοὶ οἱ Κᾶρες ἀποδεξάμενοι οὐδὲν
5. οὔτε ὅσοι Ἑλλήνων ταύτην τὴν χώρην οἰκέουσι.

131 See also IV.5 §6; act boundaries in Homer and Pindar II.2 §27 are identified on a slightly different basis.

6. (2) οἰκέουσι δὲ καὶ ἄλλοι καὶ Λακεδαιμονίων ἄποικοι Κνίδιοι,
7. <οἳ> τῆς χώρης τῆς σφετέρης τετραμμένης ἐς πόντον,
8. τὸ δὴ Τριόπιον καλέεται,
9. ἀργμένης δὲ ἐκ τῆς Χερσονήσου τῆς Βυβασσίης,
10. ἐούσης τε πάσης τῆς Κνιδίης πλὴν ὀλίγης περιρρόου
11. (3) (τὰ μὲν γὰρ αὐτῆς πρὸς βορέην ἄνεμον
12. ὁ Κεραμεικὸς κόλπος ἀπέργει,
13. τὰ δὲ πρὸς νότον
14. ἡ κατὰ Σύμην τε καὶ Ῥόδον θάλασσα),
15. τὸ ὦν δὴ ὀλίγον τοῦτο,
16. ἐὸν ὅσον τε ἐπὶ πέντε στάδια,
17. ὤρυσσον οἱ Κνίδιοι
18. ἐν ὅσῳ Ἅρπαγος τὴν Ἰωνίην κατεστρέφετο,
19. βουλόμενοι νῆσον τὴν χώρην ποιῆσαι.

So: the Carians, | as they did not do any splendid work, | they were enslaved by Harpagus. | They did not do anything, the Carians themselves, | and the Greeks that live in this region. | (2) Among other people living there are the Cnidians, colonists from Sparta. | Their region extends until the sea | —it is called Triopion—; | it adjoins the Chersonese of Bubassus. Except for a small part, it is entirely surrounded by the sea: | (3) on the one side, towards the Bora-wind, | the gulf of Ceramicus protects it; | on the other side, towards Notos, | the sea off Syme and Rhodes (protects it). | And so, that little part | —it is about five stades— | (is what) the Cnidians were digging, | at the time when Harpagus was conquering Ionia. | They wanted to make an island of their land. (tr. AB)

Each segment (which I number for convenience) represents a discourse act. For the sake of comparison, the modern punctuation of the *OCT* edition is retained (including the parenthesis at the beginning of section 3). Overall we obtain 19 discourse acts, 13 of which end with a modern punctuation mark. The 13 acts regularly coincide with dependent or independent clauses.[132] In the rest of the 6 cases our criteria were as follows: the negation οὐδέν separates act 2 from act 1 as οὔτε separates act 5 from 4. Two verbs belonging to two different clauses separate acts 2 and 3. The noun phrase ὁ Κεραμεικὸς κόλπος separates act 12 from 11 by analogy with the syntactically parallel noun phrase (with hyperbaton) ἡ κατὰ Σύμην τε καὶ Ῥόδον θάλασσα, which separates act 14 from 13. Acts 17

[132] The only exception is act 15, where the comma indicates that the intervening participial phrase ἐὸν ... στάδια, act 16, represents a temporary syntactic interruption to the clause.

and 18 are different clauses, even though no comma divides them. This brief survey of act boundaries shows how many different linguistic features contribute to identifying them.

§78. Every act is a strategic step in communication, regardless of whether or not it includes a verb form, and whether the verb form is finite or non-finite. Act divisions level out syntactic hierarchies, in fact: participial clauses stand on an equal footing with main clauses, just as vocatives stand equal to both. Hence the genitive absolute in act 7 is an act *per se*, just as 9 and 10 are. No relative pronoun is needed. Only modern readers who artificially impose a syntactic convergence of multiple clauses upon ὤρυσσον οἱ Κνίδιοι (act 17) would find the pronoun wanting, and still be left with a very imperfect period.

§79. Particles signal act divisions just as decisively as other linguistic features. Notice the act-peninitial position of δή in 8 and τε in 10.[133] τε in 10 marks also the coordination between two genitives absolute. Further act-peninitial particles are μὲν γάρ in 11 and ὦν δή in 15. They are combinations that introduce moves, as later paragraphs will clarify. As lexical markers, μὲν γάρ and ὦν δή are more precise segmenting devices than the parentheses, which are technically redundant; the former marks the opening of unframed discourse, while the latter conveys frame recall.[134] In fact, it is likely that these particles' occurrence was what originally motivated editors to insert the parentheses.[135] Finally, in act 1 the combination μέν νυν complements the priming function of the act as a whole (οἱ μέν νυν Κᾶρες): the Carians are cognitively "primed" as the focus of attention over the next few acts, and the μέν component announces projection.[136] Then a δέ act (act 6) shifts the attention to the Cnidians.

§80. Act divisions show how the pragmatic and cognitive gist of the passage unfolds in sequence. After the Carians have been dealt with in acts 1-5, the Cnidians come to the fore in act 6 as the next focus of attention—the pinning-down function of the construction καὶ ἄλλοι καί is notable.[137] Once this new focus has been established, acts 7 to 16 further narrow the focus with a series of geographical points that culminate in mention of a certain piece of land (τὸ ... ὀλίγον τοῦτο, act 15) that becomes the next crucial cognitive signpost. In fact, acts 15 and 16 together pave the way for the pivotal action of

133 See IV.4.5 for more elaborate discussion of the discourse functions of δή in Herodotus.

134 §108 in this chapter, as well as II.4 §§15-28, make it clear that γάρ may introduce unframed discourse. On μὲν δή occurring at moments of frame recall, see below §142.

135 Kerschensteiner (1964:29; 32-34; 48) captures the syntactic and stylistic essence of what she calls "*Parenthese*" ("parenthesis") in Herodotus beyond the sign in modern punctuation. A parenthetical sentence is the insertion of a main clause interrupting the grammatical nexus of clauses; it effects an addition ("*Ergänzung*") or an expansion ("*Erweiterung*") of the ongoing discourse; it represents a paratactic strategy to produce narrative interlacing of logical connections. Most parenthetical sentences in Herodotus start with γάρ.

136 More on μέν νυν in 3.11.4.

137 See IV.2 §§125-126, with (t68). The medieval manuscript shows a high dot before καὶ Λακεδαιμονίων.

the entire episode, ὤρυσσον οἱ Κνίδιοι ("the Cnidians were digging," 17).[138] Κνίδιοι is retrieved, and echoes Κνίδιοι in act 6. The syntactic prominence of ὤρυσσον οἱ Κνίδιοι as a main clause matches its cognitive prominence as the pivotal action. However, in the flow of discourse ὤρυσσον οἱ Κνίδιοι is not the climax of an imperfect period; rather, it is the device that Herodotus exploits to fix the image of "digging and digging."[139] For soon after ὤρυσσον οἱ Κνίδιοι appears another act, not quoted in (t12), that contains the same verb form ὤρυσσον (174.3). It is this repetition that fixes the image, and is instrumental to the narration of the wonder of the inexplicable wounds (introduced by καὶ δή, 174.4).[140]

§81. A more systematic comparison of modern punctuation, act segmentation, and medieval punctuation will be discussed in IV.5 using four longer excerpts. For now, let us complement these observations on 1.174.1-3 with the evidence from the oldest extant manuscript of Herodotus.[141] Several punctuation marks confirm the act boundaries of my interpretation. Those occurring in the manuscript where no modern punctuation marks appear are a comma separating acts 2 and 3; a high dot separating 4 and 5; a mid dot separating 11 and 12, and 13 and 14. No parenthesis occurs. Finally, there is no consistent match between high dots, mid dots, modern commas, and full stops.

§82. In summary, we see that the pragmatic organization of the piece fits the cognitive needs of listeners and readers well, even though the syntactic organization in main and subclauses in this passage is unsatisfactory to Müller, How and Wells, and Bekker. Particles help see the boundaries of discourse acts, and are more precise than modern punctuation in signaling the directions of discourse. Finally, a sample of pre-print punctuation on the passage reveals that medieval readers established boundaries equal to but also smaller than clauses. Also, the distribution of medieval punctuation marks does not necessarily coincide with the placement of modern commas and full stops. All of this confirms the non-absolute value of paralinguistic segmentation.

3.10.2 Segmenting a "descending" period in Thucydides

§83. Now let us consider a sample from Thucydides. In this case too we are dealing with a stretch of discourse that has been judged as ineffective. The passage 2.53.4, is from the chapters on the plague. It famously illustrates the shameless lack of respect for gods and human laws by the people affected by the desperate situation. Yaginuma (1995:137) calls this complex period "absteigend," "descending," referencing Blass 1887 (see above, §23): the main clause occurs at the very start, and is followed by a series of subclauses. Keep

[138] With this episode Herodotus sets out to explain why the Cnidians are unable to dig a trench to separate their peninsula from the mainland. The episode concludes by quoting a Delphic oracle: "Do not dig; if Zeus wanted, he could have made an island" (174.5).

[139] The choice of the imperfect may also contribute to this sense.

[140] On καὶ δή in Herodotus see IV.2 §100; on καί at narrative peaks, see IV.2.4.3.

[141] Manuscript A, Laurentianus 70,3 (10th century CE). The passage in question is on folio 44 verso.

in mind that this type of period is considered less felicitous than the ascending type, as the movement from independent to dependent elements is seen as lowering the tension. Blass assimilates this type of periods to parataxis. Yaginuma, moreover, points out that the passage proves that Thucydides wrote for readers instead of listeners: "several sentences are forcedly made into an 'absteigende Periode,' and so would be rather hard to follow in hearing" (1995:137).

§84. Let us first report the text, starting on a new line after every comma, to emphasize how we normally process the segmentation offered by print editions.

(t13)

[extra space] [4] θεῶν δὲ φόβος ἢ ἀνθρώπων νόμος οὐδεὶς ἀπεῖργε,

τὸ μὲν κρίνοντες ἐν ὁμοίῳ καὶ σέβειν καὶ μὴ ἐκ τοῦ πάντας ὁρᾶν ἐν ἴσῳ ἀπολλυμένους,

τῶν δὲ ἁμαρτημάτων οὐδεὶς ἐλπίζων μέχρι τοῦ δίκην γενέσθαι βιοὺς ἂν τὴν τιμωρίαν ἀντιδοῦναι,

πολὺ δὲ μείζω τὴν ἤδη κατεψηφισμένην σφῶν ἐπικρεμασθῆναι,

ἣν πρὶν ἐμπεσεῖν εἰκὸς εἶναι τοῦ βίου τι ἀπολαῦσαι.

Thucydides 2.53.4

No fear of god or human law was any constraint. Pious or impious made no difference in their view, when they could see all dying without distinction. As for offences against the law, no one expected to live long enough to be brought to justice and pay the penalty: they thought that a much heavier sentence had already been passed and was hanging over them, so they might as well have some enjoyment of life before it fell. (tr. Hammond)

My analysis of acts in Herodotus showed that some modern punctuation seems to reflect the occurrence of peninitial particles. This is clearly the case here: four out of five segments ending with modern punctuation marks start with μέν or δέ in peninitial position. Hammond's translation reflects this five-part division: the first two segments correspond to two simple sentences ("No fear of god or human law was any constraint." and "Pious or impious made no difference in their view, when they could see all dying without distinction."). The third segment extend to the colon ("As for offences against the law, no one expected to live long enough to be brought to justice and pay the penalty:"); the fourth and fifth are separated by a comma ("they thought that a much heavier sentence had already been passed and was hanging over them, so they might as well have some enjoyment of life before it fell."). The modern commas, however, have two adverse effects on interpretation that are not supported by the text. One is the implication that the sense remains incomplete through all the segments until the last. The other is the implication that punctuation marks are not warranted for any other boundary.

§85. The inadequacy of modern punctuation may be grasped by comparing it against the medieval punctuation found in an 11th century manuscript of Thucydides.[142] These marks are recorded in italics and curved brackets in the version of the passage I present below (t14), which represents my segmentation in acts. My translation in acts follows.

(t14)

1. [extra space] [4] θεῶν δὲ φόβος ἢ ἀνθρώπων νόμος
2. οὐδεὶς *{comma}* ἀπεῖργε, *{high dot}*
3. τὸ μὲν κρίνοντες
4. ἐν ὁμοίῳ καὶ σέβειν καὶ μὴ *{high dot}*
5. ἐκ τοῦ πάντας ὁρᾶν
6. ἐν ἴσῳ ἀπολλυμένους, *{high dot + extra space}*
7. τῶν δὲ ἁμαρτημάτων
8. οὐδεὶς ἐλπίζων
9. μέχρι τοῦ δίκην γενέσθαι
10. βιοὺς ἂν *{comma}*
11. τὴν τιμωρίαν ἀντιδοῦναι, *{high dot + extra space}*
12. πολὺ δὲ μείζω
13. τὴν ἤδη κατεψηφισμένην σφῶν ἐπικρεμασθῆναι, *{high dot}*
14. ἣν πρὶν ἐμπεσεῖν
15. εἰκὸς εἶναι
16. τοῦ βίου τι ἀπολαῦσαι. *{high dot}*

Fear of gods or law of mortals, | neither was a constraint. | First they were thinking | it is the same to be pious or not | —from seeing that everybody | was dying in the same way. | As for wrongdoings, | nobody was expecting | until the moment of the trial | to be alive | to pay the penalty. | Much more: | a sentence already passed was hanging over them; | before it fell | it was fair | to enjoy a bit of life. (tr. AB)

First the medieval punctuation. At 6 and 11 the high dot and extra space before the next word indicate a strong boundary, a reading that is not conveyed by the use of modern

142 Ms β M (British Museum 11727), 11th century CE; folio 43 verso + start 44 recto.

commas. The evidence of pre-print punctuation thus challenges the implication of incompleteness suggested by commas. As for the implication that no other intervening boundary requires punctuation, consider acts 2, 4, 7, and 10. The medieval comma in act 2 after οὐδείς probably suggests that οὐδείς grammatically and prosodically relates to φόβος as well as to νόμος. The high dot at the end of act 4 marks the boundary between the infinitive construction and the substantivized infinitive, which is a regular clause boundary. The comma at the end of act 10 is particularly interesting, as it reflects, as we will see, a specific discourse strategy.

§86. Several acts in my segmentation have no corresponding punctuation mark, either print or pre-print, at their end (see 1, 3, 5, 8, 9, 12, 14, 15). Most of the boundaries are clause boundaries (3/4; 5/6; 8/9; 14/15; 15/16); therefore, acts coincide with clauses. Mismatches between acts and clauses deserve *ad hoc* comments. But before entering into details it makes sense to illustrate the general difference between the interpretation deriving from a canonical segmentation and the interpretation resulting from the segmentation in acts.

§87. The discourse analysis I offer based on my segmentation does not challenge the syntactic articulation of the passage or the semantic prominence of the main clause that opens the period (θεῶν δὲ φόβος ἢ ἀνθρώπων νόμος οὐδεὶς ἀπεῖργε). Rather, it challenges the idea that "descending" syntax (main clause followed by a series of subclauses) reflects decreasing communicative interests. By looking instead at the passages' pragmatic articulation in acts, we see that there are significant intertextual connections that have been previously overlooked. The discourse acts turn out to be carefully sequenced and juxtaposed to convey the people's progressive introspection. Indeed, the acts that follow the main clause even reach a climax and denouement, totally in contrast to the view that the discourse "descends."

§88. Act 1 establishes the two parallel realms that constitute the subject of the upcoming discourse, fear of gods and human law. Act 2, which begins with οὐδείς,[143] negates both categories. The act-initial position of οὐδείς emphasizes the attitude of denial, renounciation, and failure that underlies other negative expressions in the Plague chapters.[144] Act 3, τὸ μὲν κρίνοντες, fulfills two pragmatic functions. τὸ μέν[145] projects a multiple-act stretch of discourse. The participle κρίνοντες introduces into the audience's minds the concrete image of a plurality of individuals thinking about and evaluating the situation. While it is remarkable, from a grammatical point of view, that the text should lack a pronoun to clarify who these individuals might be, in cognitive terms the omission

143 See above §47, §51. Further acts starting with negatives are commented in IV.5§§78-79; 82; 85.

144 See e.g. Thucydides 2.47.3-4 οὐ μέντοι τοσοῦτός γε λοιμὸς οὐδὲ φθορὰ οὕτως ἀνθρώπων οὐδαμοῦ ἐμνημονεύετο γενέσθαι. οὔτε γὰρ ἰατροὶ ἤρκουν τὸ πρῶτον θεραπεύοντες ἀγνοίᾳ, ἀλλ' αὐτοὶ μάλιστα ἔθνῃσκον ὅσῳ καὶ μάλιστα προσῇσαν, οὔτε ἄλλη ἀνθρωπεία τέχνη οὐδεμία; 2.51.2 ἕν τε οὐδὲ ἓν κατέστη ἴαμα.

145 Commentators agree on the adverbial meaning of the phrase: "on the one hand."

simply means that the referents are contextually accessible.[146] Acts 4 and 5 are variations of infinitive constructions: 4 is an infinitive clause and 5 features an infinitive as substantive.[147] Act 6 coincides with a participial phrase that alliterates with acts 4 and 5 (ἐν, ἐκ, ἐν).[148] Act 7 (τῶν δὲ ἁμαρτημάτων "of the wrongdoings")[149] has a crucial pragmatic and cognitive value that explains why it grammatically precedes the nouns it refers to. It is a δέ priming act that projects further acts on the topic "wrongdoings," that is, the topic exemplifying the lack of respect for law.[150] In act 8 (οὐδεὶς ἐλπίζων) οὐδείς resonates with the negation in act 2 (οὐδεὶς ἀπεῖργε); ἐλπίζων, a participle that refers to mental activity, resonates with κρίνοντες in act 3. Act 10 (βιοὺς ἄν) is a separate act because it is semantically ambivalent: it could be attached both to act 9 (μέχρι τοῦ δίκην γενέσθαι, "alive until the (moment of the) trial") and act 11 (τὴν τιμωρίαν ἀντιδοῦναι, "alive to pay the penalty").[151]

§89. Act 12 (πολὺ δὲ μείζω) begins the climax of the indirect thought,[152] and it features a discontinuity that the modern comma at the end of 11 obscures, but which the pre-print punctuation acknowledges (high dot and relatively large space before πολύ).[153] Rusten (1989:192) takes πολὺ δὲ μείζω to be dependent on ἐλπίζων (8), with an emphatic predicative position. Syntactically and semantically it may also depend on κρίνοντες (3). As for the noun that the comparative μείζω modifies, Rusten thinks it is τιμωρίαν to be connected to the subsequent κατεψηφισμένην ("pronounced against") in act 13;[154] Rhodes, on the other hand, (1988:103) reads πολὺ δὲ μείζω as a generic adverbial phrase: "people tended much more to think that a sentence already decided was hanging over them." Act 13, the longest in this excerpt (τὴν ἤδη κατεψηφισμένην σφῶν ἐπικρεμασθῆναι) represents the peak, because it expresses the impending doom from the internal point of view of the characters involved.[155] Finally, the denouement of the micropiece constituted by the reported thought ("before ruin fell, it was appropriate to enjoy a bit of life") features disentanglement on more levels. Semantically, clauses progress from the impending doom to some enjoyment, even though the chronological order

146 On the cognitive meaning of "zero-anaphora" see II.5 §15nn47-48. Rusten (1989:192) about κρίνοντες generally observes: "participles agree with the logical subject rather than the grammatical one."

147 The pre-print punctuation (high dot) after the end of act 4 (καὶ σέβειν καὶ μή) marks this syntactic (and presumably prosodic) boundary.

148 More on matches between discourse acts and sound effects below §89, and in IV.5 §§45; 83; 86.

149 With Poppo and Stahl 1875-1889, Vol. I, sect. 2:120-121, I read the genitive to work with both δίκην (9) and τιμωρίαν (11). Rusten 1989:192 argues that the genitive is fronted to give emphasis to "the errors," and takes τιμωρίαν as the only related noun.

150 Note that in the manuscript act 7 ends with a comma.

151 The pre-print comma after ἄν is compatible with this reading.

152 The representation of indirect thought in Herodotus and Thucydides is a salient topic of IV.4 in connection to voice and stance.

153 Exactly the same holds for the boundary between 6 and 7.

154 In line with Poppo and Stahl 1875-1889, Vol. I, sect. 2:120-121.

155 The combination of ἤδη and σφῶν suggests that; for ἤδη as a marker of stance, see IV.4.8.

of the moments is the opposite. Performatively, whereas acts 13 and 14 include more consonants, 15 and 16 employ more vowels—ἀπολαῦσαι alone includes two vowels and two diphthongs. It is as if the sequence of sounds reflects in performance the loosening of life—an ultimate form of empathy with the peoples' feelings.

§90. To sum up: act-segmentation brings attention to a number of syntactic, semantic, and prosodic details in this excerpt that directly contradicts the characterization of this *períodos* as hard to follow. One of these details is visible only after we take into account the discourse segmentation that I propose: 11 out of 16 acts end with verbs, and in particular two acts (11 and 16) end with 4-syllable verbs (ἀντιδοῦναι and ἀπολαῦσαι respectively).[156] In fact, act-analysis shows that there are more major discontinuities in this passage than previously acknowledged (see e.g. 7 and 12, given weak commas in modern punctuation), which challenges the interpretation of it as just one unit of discourse.[157] In addition, even though this excerpt fits the definition of "descending" *períodos* according to Blass, act-analysis reveals a progression from impersonal to personal elements of content that culminate in the vivid image of doom hanging over the heads of the people.

§91. In the segmentation discussed so far I have adopted a method of identifying acts based on particles and other linguistic features found *in situ*.[158] I have avoided general descriptions that attempt to use content to identify typical kinds of acts—such as "descriptive act," or "exhortative act." This is because we believe that there are no content-types that are independent of the actual stretches of discourse in which acts occur. The same holds for moves.

3.11 Herodotus' and Thucydides' Moves

§92. Moves are discourse units above the act level. They consist of either several acts that share the same overarching communicative goal, or one act that reveals a major discontinuity with what precedes it.[159]

§93. Just as in the case of acts, I study moves in situ instead of classifying content-types of moves in advance. A Herodotean judgment about whether a certain explanation of a phenomenon is credible or not can easily be described as a move whose point is to express an assessment. But the description of a plain before a battle can be interpreted as the initial part of a long narrative move, as well as a discrete move with a digressive character. In the pragmatic perspective we propose, we are not so much aiming at classifying fixed types of narrative actions, but rather at identifying what a move performs in its

156 More in IV.5 §112 on 4-syllable verbs in *clausulae*.

157 More in 3.11 on moves as discourse units above the act level.

158 See I.1 §7.

159 The concept of move is introduced in II.3.1. An example of a move that coincides with one act is quoted below n180.

communicative setting. For example, I do not view the abstract narrative task "description of a plain before a battle" as existing in some predetermined slot in historiographical discourse; the historian can choose to preface a battle narrative with whatever introductory information he considers essential to the ongoing discourse. This information may involve knowledge necessary for enabling the reader to follow the development of the battle; it may illuminate the conditions (striking or not, ominous or not) under which the battle takes place; it may build suspense; it may compete with images of the same plain known to the audience, etc. It is one or more of these *ad hoc* purposes that defines what the move does, that is, what its communicative goal is.

§94. From the actual linguistic realizations of moves, and especially from the occurrence of particles and other specific linguistic features, some general pragmatic characteristics of moves can be inferred nevertheless. The following paragraphs, which precede the textual analyses, outline them. Points are made about what distinguishes moves from acts, and how move boundaries can be detected. I also compare the term "move" to other labels that have been used for multi-sentence units.

§95. I started this section by saying that a move is a discourse unit made of more acts, or just one act that reveals a major discontinuity with what precedes it. This suggests that discontinuity is a decisive factor, whereas the number of acts—in other words, the move size—is less relevant. Discourse discontinuity is central to the identification of moves as well as acts; [160] if so, what makes the discontinuity across moves "major"? The relevant element that suggests a move start is some reorientation of the discourse.[161] Examples of reorientation include a change in subject, time, or place;[162] a change in verbal tense or mood; the occurrence of a postpositive particle with a projecting function; the occurrence of a performative verb (such as "I will explain"); and the occurrence of a marked demonstrative pronoun. All these features may appear alone, but more often they appear in combination.[163] Until the next reorientation, the discourse can be taken to unfold acts belonging to the same move. A one-act move results only from a combination of reorienting features.

§96. Moves are in part based on the cognitive idea of contextual frames.[164] Each move evokes, for the reader, a mental space that is the receptacle of items such as events, characters and arguments. The features that make events, characters, and arguments part of the same frame are what makes a move coherent. However, the term move adds to the cognitive idea of frame the interactional idea of communicative purpose. Often the

[160] In IV.2.2.6 I discuss forms of minor discontinuity, that is, discontinuity between different acts.

[161] Reorientation in Homer and Pindar is discussed in II2 §§68 and 70.

[162] I may say "change of setting," in line with Thorndyke (1977:80), who calls setting of stories the moment in which time, location and characters are established.

[163] This point further supports the claim that particles co-signify together with other elements of discourse, as noted by Apollonius Dyscolus (see above §68).

[164] See II.4 §12: a contextual frame is "a space in the mental representation of the discourse, which functions as a receptacle for specific characters, items, and events."

beginning of a move encodes its communicative purpose, more or less straightforwardly. For example, a speaker who switches, within his speech, from the communicative goal "persuading the audience to attack X" to the goal "listing the operations that are necessary to implement the attack" may underscore the different moves that he performs by using words or by inserting discourse acts that suggest to the addressees the respective overarching intentions.[165]

§97. Major discontinuities can be underscored not only linguistically but also paralinguistically. In modern writing and speech, moves can be detected also through paragraphs and paratones (speech paragraphs). The boundaries of paragraphs are marked visually by indentation; the boundaries of paratones are marked through intonational discontinuities by relatively higher or lower pitches, and by relatively longer pauses.[166] Those are the paralinguistic signs that accompany a major discourse discontinuity.

§98. From the seventeenth century onward (see §54), section and chapter numbers became the canonical paralinguistic segmentation of Herodotus' and Thucydides' *Histories* above the sentence level. However, sections or chapters do not always coincide with what pragmatically is a move. That is to say, segmentation numbers in modern editions sometimes do not match the occurrence of the linguistic discontinuities I mentioned earlier. This is why I associate moves directly with the occurrence of different linguistic features, including particles and particle combinations, which indicate discourse reorientation.[167]

§99. So far I established the following: discontinuity is more relevant than size, and it effects reorientation in the discourse; major discontinuities identify move starts, and are suggested by different linguistic features; paralinguistic means in modern texts are associated with major discontinuities (indentation, change of pitch, long pauses); for Herodotus and Thucydides, however, section and chapter numbers reflect them only partially. The next pragmatic characteristic concerns predictability. A couple of observations are in order.

§100. First, even though the exact size of a move cannot be predicted by its start, a relative sense of move length—that is to say, a move at least longer than one act—can be inferred from certain move starts. I refer to the acts that we call priming acts.[168] In Herodotus and Thucydides priming acts project several related acts, or at least more

[165] Later subsections and several comments in IV.5 will show instances of overaching goals of multi-act moves.

[166] See above, n73, for a definition of the term "paratone."

[167] In order to explain what he calls the "chunking of lager segments," Slings (2002:67-71) points out several features that Herodotus employs to mark POP moments of narration, that is, transitions from embedded material back to the main narrative thread. The terms "PUSH" and "POP" come originally from Polaniy and Scha (1983). My investigation follows the same methodological principle, which is to observe the linguistic features at disposal in the text; however, my analysis embraces more kinds of reorientation than transitions to and from embedded material.

[168] See II.2.5, and above 3.11.1.

than one. Therefore, from their occurrence we can predict that the move is going to be relatively long. Subsection 3.11.1 will discuss these particular move starts.

§101. The second observation concerns moves that are predictable because they are expected. They are expected due to genre conventions. Historiographers need or want to enact certain moves so that their discourse conforms to the genre. In that case moves are macro-moves: they are units of multiple moves that share a broad communicative goal, such as "providing a brief historical excursus about people X" or "narrating the reactions of X to the outcome of a battle."[169] Broad communicative goals are generally expected by modern readers[170] in the historiographical texts of Herodotus and Thucydides; these goals contribute to the recognition of the genre as such.

§102. Perhaps the clearest example of macro-moves in historiography is the insertion of speeches supposedly delivered by historical figures. Clarity about their boundaries comes from the linguistic codification of their beginning and end, and from their pragmatic consistency. Language can tell us that a speaker is going to take the floor by means of a set of possibilities. For instance, in the phrase ἔλεγε Ξέρξης τάδε (Herodotus 7.8) the name Xerxes and the *verbum dicendi* provide semantic clues, and the forward-looking pronoun provides a pragmatic clue; τάδε that tell us (without the aid of modern punctuation) to expect a direct speech by Xerxes. The speech forms a macro-move made up of several internal moves (each one in turn made up of several acts). Its end is signalled through ταῦτα εἴπας ἐπαύετο (7.8δ), with a symmetrical *verbum dicendi* and another pronoun that we now process as backward-looking. References to "I", "we", and "you" (singular or plural) through personal pronouns, verb forms, and vocatives provide the speech with pragmatic consistency.

§103. I prefer "macro-move" to two possibly parallel notions. One is the notion of episode. Episodes, which originally designated the parts between two choral songs in drama, are particularly at home in historiographical narratives. Their constitutive elements are a place, a time, and one or more characters.[171] Across episodes, at least one of these constitutive elements changes. However, while episodes can represent macro-moves, macro-moves include more than episodes: for instance, elaborated arguments

[169] Macro-move beginnings vary widely in their markings: they range from more to less elaborate discontinuities in Herodotus and Thucydides. The proems of both authors are marked elaborately; less so is the start of Thucydides' *Pentecontaetia* (1.89-118), Οἱ γὰρ Ἀθηναῖοι τρόπῳ τοιῷδε ἦλθον ἐπὶ τὰ πράγματα ἐν οἷς ηὐξήθησαν, which Hobbes translates: "Now the manner how the Athenians came to the administration of those affairs by which they so raised themselves was this." The two pragmatic elements of the latter macro-move beginning are γάρ and τοιῷδε.

[170] I refrain from assessments on the genre expectations of ancient audiences.

[171] See Van Dijk 1982:177: episodes are "coherent sequences of sentences of a discourse, linguistically marked for beginning and/or end, and further defined in terms of some kind of 'thematic unity'—for instance, in terms of identical participants, time, location or global event or action."

supporting a historical claim; ethnographic surveys regarding one people; speeches as well as accounts of indirect speeches; and several kinds of "digressions."[172]

§104. Another label used for general segments of written texts (of different size) is the term "discourse mode."[173] Scholars have classified discourse modes into the following subtypes: narration, description, reporting (that is, interrupting narration to report on the narrator's present, past, or future), and registering (that is, taking stock of the events being narrated). Each mode is viewed as characterized particularly by the use of certain tenses. Works such as Allan 2013 discuss text samples featuring overlaps between two modes, but the model in itself focuses on prototype-categories, on abstract types/styles of communication. In terms of discourse modes, Herodotus and Thucydides regularly blend narration and description, registering and description, reporting and narration. For the analysis of actual texts, I regard the concept of move as more neutral: by being not linked to a priori classifications of subtypes, it lets the reading of overarching communicative goals emerge from the 'local' arrangement of its constitutive discourse acts.

§105. In general macro-move boundaries are easier to infer than act and move boundaries, due to relatively straightforward semantic discontinuities and content closures (such as "and the winter ended" or "this is what he said").[174] The next subsections analyze co-signifying features by means of which move boundaries can be detected, which are less easy to process. The reason is that the features indicating move boundaries usually exceed semantic cues. The features analyzed constitute patterns, as they recur. This is why I privilege *ad hoc* passages over the examination of continuous excerpts—which I carried out in 3.10 for discourse acts. IV.5 complements this part by detecting moves in continuous texts.

§106. For each of the passages segmented and commented, I will indicate matches and mismatches with modern paralinguistic segmentation, that is, punctuation as well as chapter and section numbers, indentation, and extra space between words as they appear in the *OCT* editions.

[172] In putting "digressions" in quotes I align with De Jong (2004b:112), who argues that these passages are functional even though the term suggests that they are irrelevant. "Digressions" in Herodotus always help in understanding current, previous, and subsequent content. On digressions in Herodotus, see especially Cobet 1971 and De Jong 2002.

[173] Originally coined by Carola S. Smith (2003), and applied to classical literature especially in Adema 2007 and 2008, Kroon 2007 and 2012; see also Allan 2007, about "narrative mode" in Thucydides.

[174] For instance, one of the arguments of Cagnazzi 1975 in favor of Herodotus' original division in λόγοι is the recurrence of explicit mentions of transitions, endings, and beginnings concerning long narrative stretches (e.g. Herodotus 7.137.4 ἐπάνειμι δὲ ἐπὶ τὸν πρότερον λόγον; see below (t31)). About the uneasy task of detecting move ends in Homer and Pindar, see II.3 §3.

3.11.1 Move starts with priming acts

§107. I start the analysis of particles in moves by examining an understudied pattern: the use of particles in short acts that start moves. II.2 discusses short δέ acts in Homer that reorient the attention of performer and audience to a different setting or character. These are called "priming acts." Short δέ acts in Herodotus and Thucydides perform a similar priming function, but—perhaps not surprisingly, regarding the different genre—the spectrum of reorientation appears to be broader. For example, they may introduce new frames that include not only different individuals or a different spatio-temporal setting, but also a different scenario within an elaborate argument or debate. In this sense priming acts in Herodotus and Thucydides are closer to priming acts in drama.[175] The crucial point of commonality of all priming acts is projection: they foreshadow the unfolding of several elements, not just one. In other words, they introduce moves. They do so by constituting either the first act of a move, or a hinge act across two moves. Both Herodotus and Thucydides use them remarkably often.[176] A further characteristic is their shortness, which makes me compare them to *kómmata*, or short *kôla*.[177] The particles primarily involved in this pattern are γάρ, καί, and δέ.[178]

§108. Let us start with γάρ.[179] In genres where narratives are predominant (epic and historiography, within our corpus), γάρ can mark discourse discontinuity in several ways. γάρ segments can embed separate narratives, offer syntactically parenthetical thoughts, supply "external" elements that help comprehension, insert metanarrative comments, and expand on a piece of information previously mentioned. However short a γάρ segment may be, it always indicates a move boundary, because of the discontinuity it expresses.[180] In cognitive terms, γάρ lends itself particularly well to the marking of unframed discourse. This is suggested in II.4.2.1: for Homer and Pindar, instances of

175 See III.5 §§30-33; 43.

176 At 1.50.1 Thucydides employs this discourse strategy by letting the priming act be preceded by a further discourse act: Τῆς δὲ τροπῆς γενομένης | οἱ Κορίνθιοι | τὰ σκάφη μὲν οὐχ εἷλκον ἀναδούμενοι τῶν νεῶν ἃς καταδύσειαν, | πρὸς δὲ ...

177 See above, §§43-45; 48-49.

178 Sometimes also οὕτω δή and καὶ δή (the latter occurring only in Herodotus) work as independent acts that foreshadows a multi-act unit. See e.g. Herodotus 1.3.2 Οὕτω δὴ | ἁρπάσαντος αὐτοῦ Ἑλένην ...; 1.83.1 Οὕτω δὴ | οὗτοι μὲν συμφορὴν ποιησάμενοι μεγάλην ἐπέπαυντο; 3.3.3 οὕτω δή, | ἐπείτε ἀνδρώθη καὶ ἔσχε τὴν βασιληίην ...; Thucydides 4.73.4 οὕτω δὴ | τῷ μὲν Βρασίδᾳ αὐτῷ καὶ τοῖς ...; 4.75.1 οὕτω δὴ | ξυναγείραντες ἀπὸ τῶν ξυμμάχων στρατιὰν καὶ πλεύσαντες, | μάχῃ τε ...; 4.30.3 οὕτω δὴ | τούς τε Λακεδαιμονίους μᾶλλον κατιδὼν πλείους ὄντας, ... Instances of καὶ δή are reported in IV.2 §100 n153.

179 In this monograph γάρ is mainly discussed in II.3.2.2; II.4.2; III.2.2.4; III.3.3.1.5. An example of a γάρ priming act in drama is mentioned in III.5 §31; an example in Herodotus is mentioned in IV.5 §78.

180 An example of a γάρ act that is also a move (with no priming involved), is the famous authorial comment at the beginning of the Candaules episode (Χρόνου δὲ οὐ πολλοῦ διελθόντος, χρῆν γὰρ Κανδαύλῃ γενέσθαι κακῶς, ἔλεγε πρὸς τὸν Γύγην τοιάδε, Herodotus 1.81.1: "After not much time—Candaules was doomed to a bad end—he [Candaules] said to Gyges the following."

unframed discourse are storyworld information external to the frames of the ongoing narrative; the main narrator's intrusions into a character's feelings; and gnomic assessments contributing general views to particular events. The fact that parentheses in modern editions of Herodotus and Thucydides frequently bracket γάρ clauses is a further sign that the particle is compatible with discourse discontinuity. A linguistic feature that often accompanies γάρ moves is a tense shift;[181] especially at the beginning of "digressions,"[182] these shifts encode temporal discontinuity.

§109. In a short monograph on γάρ in Herodotus (*De* γάρ *particulae usu Herodoteo*, 1882) Broschmann remarks that γάρ may be used to "induce something new" (42), be it a new character, a new place, or a new event that is going to constitute the cause of a subsequent event. Broschmann's idea of new content is consistent with our view of unframed discourse and discontinuity. In several cases the sense of inducing something new conforms to the pragmatic goal of expanding, which in our terms means projecting multiple pieces of information. γάρ acts that introduce embedded narratives in both *Histories* can be full γάρ clauses.[183] In Herodotus ἦν γάρ clauses typically illustrate this function.[184] Short acts with γάρ simply amplify the discontinuity effect, because of their strong forward-oriented function.

§110. The form of a short act comprising γάρ (or other eligible particle) derives from the fact that the following segment begins in a manner consistent with act starts, typically a constituent followed by a postpositive particle. In the following example, μέν is the signal that marks the division after Σικελίας γάρ; other postpositive particles, and elements such as a negation or a subordinating conjunction, can initiate an act as well.[185]

181 See II.4 §28.

182 For the use of quotation marks for this term, see above n172.

183 See, e.g. Thucydides 1.34.2 and 3.54.2. On γάρ and embedded stories in Homer, see De Jong 1997, and the present work, II.3.2.2. On γάρ at the start of narrative expansions of a certain topic, see, besides this paragraph, n135 and n188. See also III.2 §§55-56.

184 Herodotus 1.8.1; 1.34.2; 1.73.4; 1.77.1; 1.91.5; 1.119.2; 1.126.1; 1.157.3; 1.207.7; 3.78.3; 4.80.4; 4.154.3; 5.111.1; 5.124.1; 6.23.3; 6.75.2; 6.87.1; 6.88.1; 6.102.1; 6.106.3; 6.109.2; 6.109.6; 6.136.2; 7.150.2; 7.168.1; 7.190.1; 7.206.2; 8.8.1; 8.65.5; 8.80.2; 8.102.3; 8.137.4. In Legrand (*TLG* edition), modern punctuation preceding ἦν γάρ clauses greatly varies: comma (10x); semicolon (8x); full stop (7x); parenthesis (5x); m-dash (2x).

185 E.g. Thucydides 1.9.4 || φαίνεται γὰρ | ναυσί τε πλείσταις αὐτὸς ἀφικόμενος καὶ Ἀρκάσι προσπαρασχών (postpositive particle); Herodotus 4.45.3 || Ἤδη γὰρ | Λιβύη μὲν ἐπὶ Λιβύης λέγεται ... (postpositive particle); Thucydides 1.10.2 || Λακεδαιμονίων γὰρ | εἰ ἡ πόλις ἐρημωθείη, ... (subordinating conjunction); Herodotus 3.16.6 || Λέγουσι γὰρ | ὡς πυθόμενος ἐκ μαντηίου ὁ Ἄμασις ... (subordinating conjunction) Thucydides 1.143.4 || οἱ μὲν γὰρ | οὐχ ἕξουσιν ἄλλην ἀντιλαβεῖν ἀμαχεί ... (negation); Herodotus 1.172.1 || τοῦτο γὰρ | οὐκ ἔχω ἀτρεκέως διακρῖναι, ... (negation).

(t15)[186]

[1] [indent] [τοῦ δ' αὐτοῦ χειμῶνος Ἀθηναῖοι ἐβούλοντο αὖθις μείζονι παρασκευῇ τῆς μετὰ Λάχητος καὶ Εὐρυμέδοντος ἐπὶ Σικελίαν πλεύσαντες καταστρέψασθαι, ... ἄπειροι οἱ πολλοὶ ὄντες τοῦ μεγέθους τῆς νήσου καὶ τῶν ἐνοικούντων τοῦ πλήθους καὶ Ἑλλήνων καὶ βαρβάρων ...] [2] [extra space] ||Σικελίας <u>γὰρ</u> | περίπλους μέν ἐστιν ὁλκάδι οὐ πολλῷ τινὶ ἔλασσον ἢ ὀκτὼ ἡμερῶν ...

Thucydides 6.1.1-2

[During the same winter the Athenians decided to cross the sea towards Sicily in order to bring it under control, by means of greater equipment than that under Laches and Eurymedon. ... Most of them had no idea of the size of the island and of the multitude of its inhabitants, both Greek and barbarian ...] About Sicily: circumnavigating it takes a merchant ship a bit less than eight days ... (tr. AB)

The long geo-political excursus on Sicily at the beginning of book 6 (6.1.2-5.3) starts with the short segment Σικελίας γάρ.[187] The oblique case of the noun "Sicily" confers an almost accidental character to the piece of information. Although morphology suggests a weak function, Σικελίας γάρ in fact has an important strategic and cognitive value: it primes a geopolitical reference to Sicily, and it foreshadows an expansion on it.[188] In this case the *OCT* paralinguistic segmentation (the full stop, number 2, the extra space between words) and my discourse segmentation match.

[186] Act boundaries are marked by one vertical bar, move boundaries by two. In the Greek I maintain the *OCT* paralinguistic segmentation by reporting numbers and the occurrence of extra space or indentation in square brackets. The text within the square brackets is not segmented.

[187] Thucydides' use of γάρ is quite frequent (1116 instances, against 1479 in Herodotus, which represents 0.7% of the total words in both cases). The high occurrence of "paratactic" γάρ is often cited in support of Herodotus' paratactic style; see, among others, Lamberts 1970, who explicitly talk about "die γάρ-Parataxe" (1970:136-140; 136 for the quotation). Along this line, Thucydides' style is more paratactic than the scholarship would lead us to believe.

[188] For an analogous pattern with γάρ in Herodotus, see 2.148.3-4: | ὁ δὲ δὴ λαβύρινθος καὶ τὰς πυραμίδας ὑπερβάλλει. || Τοῦ γὰρ | δυώδεκα μέν εἰσι αὐλαὶ κατάστεγοι, ἀντίπυλοι ἀλλήλῃσι, | ἓξ μὲν πρὸς βορέω, | ἓξ δὲ πρὸς νότον τετραμμέναι συνεχέες· "... this maze surpasses even the pyramids. It has twelve roofed courts with doors facing each other: six face north and six south, in two continuous lines, all within one outer wall" (tr. Godley). The first mention of the labyrinth—one of the most admired monuments of Egypt in antiquity—occurs towards the beginning of the chapter. After stating that words cannot describe it, and comparing it with other remarkable monuments, Herodotus starts a detailed report of the buildings constituting it. The linguistic pattern, again, is a short act whose pivotal word is γάρ. This γάρ act projects an expansion (or insertion) about the multiple components of "it" (τοῦ). The move goes on until the end of the chapter.

§111. καί represents the shortest possible of the projecting acts, as the following examples show.

(t16)

[4] [extra space] καὶ πάντων ὡς ἐπὶ τὸ πολὺ τοῖς αὐτοῖς χρωμένων | καὶ πανταχοῦ πολλῶν φαινομένων | μεγάλην τὴν ἔκπληξιν τοῖς ἐκ τῶν τριήρων Ἀθηναίοις παρεῖχε, | καὶ ἀφικόμενοι ἐς τὰς Ἀθήνας διεθρόησαν | ὡς χρήματα πολλὰ ἴδοιεν. [5] [extra space] || <u>καὶ</u> | οἱ <u>μὲν</u> | αὐτοί τε ἀπατηθέντες καὶ τοὺς ἄλλους τότε πείσαντες, | ἐπειδὴ διῆλθεν ὁ λόγος | ὅτι οὐκ εἴη ἐν τῇ Ἐγέστῃ τὰ χρήματα, | πολλὴν τὴν αἰτίαν εἶχον ὑπὸ τῶν στρατιωτῶν· || οἱ δὲ στρατηγοὶ πρὸς τὰ παρόντα ἐβουλεύοντο. [47.1] [indent] || καὶ | Νικίου <u>μὲν</u> ἦν γνώμη ...

Thucydides 6.46.4-47.1

And the fact that all those things [gold and silver objects] seemed to be used for the most part and everywhere produced great astonishment in the Athenians from the triremes, and once they reached Athens they spread the report about how many riches they saw. And so: the very individuals who had been deceived and had in turn persuaded others, when word spread that there was no money in Egesta, incurred great blame by the side of the soldiers. So, given the present situation, the leaders held a conference. And in particular: Nicias' opinion was ... (tr. AB)

This passage includes the peak and closure of the narrative about the Egestans' trick (6.46.3-5).[189] The Egestans were at war with the city of Selinous, and they had claimed that they had enough money to support the Athenians in their travel to Sicily to aid them against Selinous (6.6). In the second part of chapter 46, when the Athenians discover that no funds are forthcoming from Egesta, Thucydides retrospectively (οἱ δὲ Ἐγεσταῖοι ... ἐξετεχνήσαντο τότε, 46.3) narrates the trick that the Egestans had enacted in order to pretend to be wealthy. They had deceived the Athenian envoys by showing them many precious objects and offering dinner parties. At that moment the historian uses καί to introduce the turning point: the same envoys belatedly realize the truth, and the soldiers blame them. καί often introduces narrative peaks, especially in Thucydides.[190] Here, however, what is more relevant is the pattern of the short act: at the beginning of section 5, καί is followed by several acts (οἱ μὲν ...; ἐπειδὴ ...; ὅτι οὐκ ...; οἱ δὲ ...) which detail the unpleasant aftermath of a pleasant experience. The very same pattern occurs a few words later: || καὶ | Νικίου μέν helps us process the discourse as a general addition

[189] See especially Kallet 2001:27-31 on Thucydides' ability to judge while detailing the entire story of the Egestans' offer to the Athenians.

[190] See IV.2.4.3.

that introduces details on the situation (see καί, which starts a move) followed by a first element of the move (μέν accompanying the mention of Nicias' opinion). My translation attempts to render the force of these καί by means of enriched "ands," and by the colon ("And so:," "And in particular:"). Note that also in these two cases full stops, section number (46.5), extra spaces, and move starts coincide.

§112. A parallel example from Herodotus is of pragmatic as well as philological interest:

(t17)

[16.1] [extra space] Εἰ ὧν ἡμεῖς ὀρθῶς περὶ αὐτῶν γινώσκομεν, | Ἴωνες οὐκ εὖ φρονέουσι περὶ Αἰγύπτου. | Εἰ δὲ ὀρθή ἐστι ἡ γνώμη τῶν Ἰώνων, ... [17.1] [indent] || <u>Καὶ</u> | τὴν μὲν Ἰώνων γνώμην ἀπίεμεν, | ἡμεῖς δὲ ὧδέ κῃ περὶ τούτων λέγομεν, || Αἴγυπτον μὲν ...

Herodotus 2.16.1-17.1

Then, if we have the right knowledge of these things, it is the Ionians who do not think of Egypt appropriately. If the opinion of the Ionians is right, ... And now: we leave the opinion of the Ionians, and about these matters we relate the following. Egypt .... (tr. AB)

|| Καὶ | τὴν μὲν starts chapter 17—move start and chapter start overlap. Despite the fact that all manuscripts give καί, Reiske emended to κῃ, probably by analogy with the subsequent occurrence of ὧδέ κῃ. Perhaps the role of "and" at the beginning of a new chapter was not easy to explain. Lloyd (1989:247) remarks that "also" would be the appropriate translation, given that Herodotus here shares his opinion as he does elsewhere. Such an interpretation arises from the perception that καί in this case does not link conjuncts. I offer a pragmatic reading as an alternative. The καί in question works as an "and" pragmatically enriched—"and so," or "and now,"—which is intonationally isolated and stressed. The sense of continuity is expressed in relation to a relatively large portion of preceding discourse, not just to the preceding sentence. In fact, the Ionians' opinion occupies the entirety of chapters 15 and 16. The occurrence of μέν after καί (καί τὴν μὲν Ἰώνων) suggests an act boundary after καί. As one would expect, what begins in 17.1 is an account articulated in more than one segment and more than one move—see || Αἴγυπτον μὲν; in fact it continues for the rest of the chapter (17.1-17.6). Therefore, καί works as a short and separate act introducing a multi-act unit of discourse.

§113. The final two short acts have δέ in common.[191] The following examples show three aspects of priming acts particularly well.

[191] IV.2.2.5 already mentions the phenomenon.

(t18)

[3] [extra space] || τὸ δὲ πρὸ τοῦ ἡ ἀκρόπολις ἡ νῦν οὖσα πόλις ἦν, | καὶ τὸ ὑπ' αὐτὴν πρὸς νότον μάλιστα τετραμμένον. [4] [extra space] || <u>τεκμήριον δέ·</u> || τὰ γὰρ ἱερὰ ἐν αὐτῇ τῇ ἀκροπόλει ...

Thucydides 2.15.4

What now is the Acropolis earlier was a city, and also the part below, mostly towards the south. (Here is) the evidence: the temples on the Acropolis itself ... (tr. AB)

Following the usual pattern, τεκμήριον δέ is a short act separated from a segment containing γάρ, and consequently projects a multi-act sequence (15.4 to 15.6) consistent with a move. The sense of projection, however, additionally derives from the semantics of τεκμήριον, which in Thucydides has a methodological meaning as well: specifying evidence of a certain fact is a crucial component of the scientific inquiry by the historian. The first aspect, then, is the idea that priming acts project a move by means of all their components, syntactic, semantic, and pragmatic.[192]

§114. The second aspect is that priming acts are sometimes hinges between moves. In (t18) τεκμήριον δέ can be said to start a move but also to precede a γάρ move (note the Greek semicolon after δέ, which suggests a relatively strong boundary). Thus τεκμήριον δέ represents a hinge between the historical information conveyed through the previous acts, and the elucidation of the evidence supporting that information.

§115. The third aspect has to do with the reorientation of attention at narrative turning points. The next passage occurs at the climax of the Prexaspes episode (Herodotus 3.74-75).[193] The Magi have made Prexaspes their friend, and instruct him in the official speech he has to deliver in order to dispel suspicion from the Magi. In a stroke of narrative genius Herodotus reports this plan without describing Prexaspes' point of view at all, thereby allowing the tension of the moments preceding Prexaspes' delivery of his speech to have its full impact on the reader or listener. Then, when the time comes, Herodotus writes:

[192] A similar priming act is μαρτύριον δέ followed by Δήλου γάρ, "here is the proof; in Delos (...)," Thucydides 1.8.1 On the syntactic variety of δέ acts in the two *Histories* see IV.2.2.

[193] Further excerpts from this episode are analyzed below (t26), and in IV.4 (t30).

(t19)

[extra space] || Ὁ δὲ || τῶν μὲν δὴ ἐκεῖνοι προσεδέοντο αὐτοῦ, | τούτων μὲν ἑκὼν ἐπελήθετο, | ἀρξάμενος δὲ ...

Herodotus 3.75.1

But he, all the things that those men had asked of him, those he failed to recall, deliberately, and by starting ... (tr. AB)

ὁ δέ reorients both the historian's and the audience's attention so that it falls on Prexaspes, who has been silent thus far. The short act also begins a move that gradually unfolds everything in an elaborate speech, and reveals the truth in total contradiction to the Magi's expectations. This time there is a mismatch between moves and modern segmentation in sections and chapters. Ὁ δὲ || τῶν μὲν ... occurs between the beginning of chapter 75, about the Magi's order for Prexaspes to reach the top of the tower, and the beginning of section 2, about the start of Prexaspes' report. However, an extra space before Ὁ δὲ in the *OCT* edition does match my point about the move start.

§116. To sum up: all the examples I have given illustrate the same pattern: in certain co-texts particles indicate the occurrence of short acts. Content suggests a tight relation between these short acts and the multi-element units that follow. Except for the minimal case of short acts with καί, both the particle and the co-occurring word(s) foreshadow or project the subsequent elements. In the examined texts these co-occurring words can be pronouns (τοῦ, ὁ), names (Σικελίας), and nouns (τεκμήριον). This phenomenon is no less widespread in Thucydides than in Herodotus. Rather than judging it as a sign of spokenness from the perspective of syntactic incompleteness, we may regard it as a cognitively efficient means to guide the reader or hearer through the narrative.[194]

3.11.2 οὗτος forms at the end or start of moves

§117. An equally widespread phenomenon that is relevant to move boundaries concerns some usages of οὗτος in all its possible forms—adjective, pronoun, adverb. Herodotus provides copious evidence of that. Let us point out the context of this discourse strategy, first.

§118. Herodotus' style includes the ability to dovetail discrete pieces of narration by balancing given with new information.[195] Cooper (2002:2705) summarizes the various devices that the historian uses to form a bridge with given information by saying:

[194] For a theoretical discussion of priming acts vs. left dislocation, see De Kreij 2016. On the use of priming acts as a possible reflection of actors' calm attitude in speaking on stage, see III.5 §§30-33.

[195] See II.2 §17 about utterances balancing given and new info.

"endless new combinations of repeated proper noun, resumptive particle, resumptive participle, and demonstrative pronoun are taken up and recombined by our author."[196] This kind of dovetailing technique facilitates the processing of discourse: the reader or listener is taken by the hand in her efforts to keep track of relevant actions and participants as the narrative progresses. Perhaps this is one of the features that famously led Cicero to compare Herodotus' style to a calm river: *sine ullis salebris quasi sedatus amnis fluit*, "[he] flows like a calm river without any rapids," *Orator* 12.39; such is the flow of his discourse.

§119. In this section I will shed light on how demonstrative pronouns and "resumptive particles," to use Cooper's terms, contribute to the calm flow of discourse in Herodotus. I will also assess their presence in Thucydides. Even though the phenomenon is less notable there, my analysis offers some partial counterargument to longstanding judgments concerning the asperity of Thucydides' style, in particular the ancient opinion according to which his writing was δυσπαρακολούθητος, "hard to follow."[197]

§120. Recently, a group of Spanish scholars has begun to focus on the discourse functions of the adverb οὕτως in different genres (prose and poetry).[198] Ruiz Yamuza in particular explores the consecutive usages of οὕτως. When οὕτως appears at the end of argument or fables, the idea of consequence relates to the conclusion(s) to be drawn; for those cases the author coins the term "epimítico," "epimythic" (2012:228).[199] I take over the term and apply it to Herodotean and Thucydidean οὕτως and other οὗτος forms in acts or moves that wrap up historiographical accounts. "Epimythic" captures the metanrrative function of those forms: they are signposts for the conclusion(s) to be drawn once accounts are over.[200]

§121. This important role is played not only by the adverb οὕτως, but also by cognate pronominal and adjectival forms, especially the plural neuter form ταῦτα and the singular masculine nominative οὗτος.[201] The following examples show that different

[196] On this technique, see in particular Müller 1980:51-69.

[197] Dionysius of Halicarnassus *Letter to Gnaeus Pompeus* chapter 3. On ἀκολουθία, see also I.2 §§61-62. On asperity of style shared by Thucydides and Pindar, see in particular Hornblower 2004:355-360.

[198] Martínez Vázquez 2012 on οὕτως in Thucydides; Jiménez Delgado 2012 on οὕτως in various historiographical texts; Conti 2014 on οὕτως in Homer; Martínez Vázquez and Ruiz Yamuza 2011 on a scalar approach to οὕτως.

[199] Ruiz Yamuza's examples come from Aesop, Polybius, and Xenophon.

[200] Let me quote an example of epimythic οὗτως from my corpus: [extra space] || καὶ | ἡ μὲν ναυμαχία οὕτως ἐτελεύτα. || [35.1] [indent] "And the sea battle ended in this way," Thucydides 7.34.8. The battle in question is the sea battle fought by the Athenians against the Peloponnesians in the gulf of Corinth towards the beginning of the expedition to Sicily (7.34). The reader probably noted the καὶ | X μέν pattern as well. As we will see, the co-occurrence of μέν in this act is significant, as it anticipates that the narration is going to continue after this conclusion. Remarkably, while the chapter boundary is paralinguistically marked by new numbers, an extra space between words occurs before that point (see before καί), which matches my reading of καί as a move start.

[201] See E. Fraenkel (1965:26) about forms of οὗτος (or ὅδε) or the adverb οὕτως at summarizing points of prose.

οὗτος forms can contribute (together with other semantic and pragmatic features) an epimythic function by signaling the conclusion of accounts of different size.

(t20)

[4] [extra space] || <u>ταῦτα</u> ξυνθέμενοι διέλυσαν τὸν πόλεμον. [extra space] || <u>μετὰ δὲ ταῦτα</u> Κορίνθιοι ...

Thucydides 3.114.4

Having agreed on this they put the war to an end. After these [events], the Corinthians ... (tr. AB)

In this passage the grammatical subjects involved are the Acarnanians and the Amphilochians, who waged war with the Ambraciots. The referents of ταῦτα are the terms of the truce agreed upon by both parties. Since the account of these terms occupies several narrative acts (114.3-4), ταῦτα signals its end, together with the rest of the act's semantic content (ξυνθέμενοι, διέλυσαν, τὸν πόλεμον).[202] The act betweent the two extra spaces in the *OCT* edition (ταῦτα ξυνθέμενοι διέλυσαν τὸν πόλεμον) can be considered a separate move closing a multi-move section.

§122. The referent of the subsequent ταῦτα (μετὰ δὲ ταῦτα) is the whole of the events concerning the war between these parties. As frequently happens in historiography, μετὰ ταῦτα (with or without δέ[203]) is a hinge phrase indicating that what follows is a new account, which implies a resetting of the temporal frame at least (with individuals and place unaltered).[204] In the light of that, ταῦτα works as a dovetailing device looking backward to a discrete group of events, as well as forward to the upcoming change of frame. As such it can be considered to open a new move, which harmonizes with the location of section number [4] in the *OCT* edition. Let us examine a similar case in Herodotus:

[202] Ταῦτα performs this ultimately metanarrative function in countless Herodotean acts capping reported speeches; see e.g. Herodotus 1.110.1; 1.112.1; 2.19.1 Οὕτω σφι ταῦτα ἐχρήσθη "This was what [the oracle] declared to them." See also Thucydidean acts that summarize actions described in immediately previous discourse, e.g. 1.118.2 ταῦτα δὲ ξύμπαντα ὅσα ἔπραξαν οἱ Ἕλληνες πρός τε ἀλλήλους καὶ τὸν βάρβαρον ἐγένετο ἐν ἔτεσι πεντήκοντα μάλιστα μεταξὺ τῆς τε Ξέρξου ἀναχωρήσεως καὶ τῆς ἀρχῆς τοῦδε τοῦ πολέμου "The Greeks did all of these things—against each other and against foreigners—over fiftt years between the retreat of Xerxes and the beginning of this war"; 2.56.6 ταῦτα δὲ ποιήσαντες ἐπ' οἴκου ἀνεχώρησαν "After doing this [ravaging and devastating a few places], [the Athenians] returned home." Translations are mine.

[203] Especially on μετὰ δέ in Herodotus, see Jiménez Delgado 2013:47.

[204] In this sense the temporal phrase starts a new *kôlon*, in E. Fraenkel's terms ("*auch kurze adverbial Zeitbestimmungen können einen Antakt zu einem Kolon bilden*," 1965:45).

(t21)

[5] [extra space] || Οὗτός τε δὴ χρησμῳδέων προσεφέρετο, | καὶ | οἵ τε Πεισιστρατίδαι καὶ οἱ Ἀλευάδαι γνώμας ἀποδεικνύμενοι. [6.1]

Herodotus 7.6.5

So in the end he [king Xerxes] kept putting himself forward with oracles. And in addition, the Peisistratids as well as the Aleuades were delivering their opinions. (tr. AB)

In this passage Herodotus relates how Xerxes, finally persuaded by the oracles of Onomacritus, and by the advice of the Peisistratids and the Aleuades, decides to undertake the invasion of Greece. The king is the grammatical subject of the clauses preceding (t21), so there is no need to retrieve the referent with a demonstrative, especially in the nominative case, because the referent is already in focus.[205] What can justify, then, the use of a οὗτος form from a discourse perspective? The scene occurs at the end of chapter 6 in book 7. This means that at some point in the history of the segmentation of Herodotus' *Histories* editors felt that these clauses determined a chapter boundary. The boundary is conveyed at the linguistic level by οὗτός τε δή. Besides οὗτος, τε can be connected to the two historians' use of τε to achieve a coda-like effect in their texts.[206] In addition, δή regularly co-occurs with an epimythic οὗτος form (usually οὕτω δή and οὕτως ... δή) to close a major narrative step.[207]

§123. Not only can οὕτως fulfill an epimythic role; it can also trigger the start of the subsequent move. Here is an example:

(t22)

[2] [extra space] || τὸ μὲν οὖν μέγιστον μαρτύριον αὐτὸς εἶπεν, | ὅτι οἱ Ἴωνες αἰεί ποτε πολέμιοι τοῖς Δωριεῦσιν εἰσίν. [extra space] || ἔχει δὲ καὶ οὕτως· || ἡμεῖς γὰρ Ἴωνες ὄντες ...

Thucydides 6.82.2

Now: he himself mentioned the greatest evidence: that the Ionians from immemorial time are enemies of the Dorians. The situation is exactly this: we, by being Ionians ... (tr. AB)

205 For this cognitive terminology about the retrieval of referents in discourse, see II.5 §9.
206 See IV.2.3.4.
207 On τε δή see also below n222. On the term "epimythic," see above §120.

The speaker is the Athenian envoy Euphemus, who is trying to convince the Sicilians of Camarina to secede from Syracuse and join the Athenians (6.82-87). Let us focus on ἔχει δὲ καὶ οὕτως. οὕτως here does not look backward to a referent in the preceding text, but rather forward, to the entire argument constituted by the discourse acts that will follow. In other words οὕτως signals that a new move is about to occur, which will expand (note γάρ at its beginning[208]) on the point that Euphemus has just concisely made ("The Ionians from immemorial time are enemies of the Dorians"). Therefore οὕτως is a proleptic device. This function harmonizes with the idea that here ἔχει δὲ καὶ οὕτως is a hinge between the preceding and the following move. The extra space that precedes ἔχει (note that it does not coincide with any number) may reflect the discourse boundary occurring before the short hinge clause.

§124. Herodotus uses the masculine pronoun οὗτος in a similar way, that is, forward-oriented. Sometimes an individual who is going to play a major role in subsequent acts is recalled at the beginning by means of οὗτος, even when its referent, the proper name, appears as well.

(t23)

|| Ὀτάνης ἦν | Φαρνάσπεω μὲν παῖς, | γένεϊ δὲ καὶ χρήμασι ὅμοιος τῷ πρώτῳ Περσέων. || <u>Οὗτος</u> ὁ Ὀτάνης ...

Herodotus 3.68.1-2

Otanes was the son of Pharnaspes, and by ancestry and wealth he was akin to the Persian nobility. This Otanes ... (tr. AB)

During the account of the conspiracy of the seven Magi, Herodotus tells us that Otanes was the first to suspect that the "Smerdis" on the Persian throne was not the son of Cyrus. At that point he explains who Otanes was—note the priming act Ὀτάνης ἦν, preceding the acts that start with Φαρνάσπεω μὲν παῖς and γένεϊ δὲ. By means of οὗτος ὁ Ὀτάνης the historian begins a relatively long move (68.1-69.3) entirely devoted to Otanes' actions.[209] οὗτος, far from necessary from the perspective of anaphora resolution, becomes a device

208 See earlier (§§108-109), on γάρ at move starts.

209 The subsequent move starts at 69.4 with Otanes' daughter's implementation of the plan. It includes several οὗτος forms, which conveniently resume the preceding content: Ἀντιπέμπει πρὸς ταῦτα; ἢν ποιῇ ταῦτα; ὅμως μέντοι ποιήσειν ταῦτα; Ἡ μὲν δὴ ὑπεδέξατο ταῦτα (69.4-5).

for projecting the topical salience of the subsequent series of acts.[210] οὗτος opens a move whose point is to focus on Otanes.[211]

3.11.3 οὗτος forms + μέν; οὗτος forms + δή; act-peninitial δή

§125. Let us now briefly focus on a pattern that involves constructions with epimythic οὗτος forms accompanied by μέν. This pattern serves to round off multi-move units (that is, macro-moves). The most recurrent construction is ταῦτα μέν.[212]

(t24)

[extra space] || ταῦτα μὲν τὰ περὶ Πύλον γενόμενα. || [indent] [42] Τοῦ δ' αὐτοῦ θέρους ...

Thucydides 4.41.4-42.1

So, these were the facts about Pylos. In the same summer ... (tr. AB)

The account of the facts about Pylos occupies several chapters (4.2-6; 8-23; 26-41), alternating with episodes that occur elsewhere. The act, then, also constitutes a move that rounds off a quite extendend multi-move unit. The extra space before ταῦτα μέν matches, once again, my point about this being a move.

210 The narrative function of οὗτος that I have just described aligns with Bakker's idea (1999) that οὗτος in Homer works to convey vividness in accounts of past events: the Herodotean οὗτος that starts a long move indicates the narrator's cognitive and emotional involvement in recalling a specific individual. Lakoff (1974:347-348) reads some English usages of "this" with people as the referents in a very similar way.

211 Another clear example of this occurs at the beginning of the Candaules episode. Herodotus starts the move by saying Οὗτος δὴ ὦν ὁ Κανδαύλης ἠράσθη τῆς ἑωυτοῦ γυναικός (1.8.1), which not by chance occurs at the beginning of a new chapter. Further instances of the same function include: Οὗτος ὁ Δηιόκης, 1.96.2; Οὗτος ὁ Φάνης, 3.4.2; Οὗτος δὲ ὁ Μεγάβαζος, 4.144.1; Ἦν δὲ ὁ Θήρας οὗτος, 4.147.1. Herodotus uses the masculine form 239 times. Thucydides shows very different numbers: he uses οὗτος (nominative masculine singular) only 14 times, and in this way only at 2.29.2, ὁ δὲ Τήρης οὗτος. Otherwise the masculine form is employed in closures, just as ταῦτα is (see, for example, καὶ ὁ χειμὼν ἐτελεύτα οὗτος, 2.103.2; 8.60.3; ὅ τε χειμὼν ἐτελεύτα οὗτος, 3.25.2).

212 56 occurrences in Herodotus; 7 in Thucydides. In §65 above I commented on ταῦτα μέν in Thucydides 2.54.5 (end of chapter). The remaining 5 instances are 2.33.1 (start of chapter); 2.70.4 (penultimate clause of chapter 70, before the major closing about the second year of the war: καὶ [τὸ] δεύτερον ἔτος ἐτελεύτα τῷ πολέμῳ τῷδε ὃν Θουκυδίδης ξυνέγραψεν); 3.116.3 (penultimate clause of chapter 116, before καὶ ἕκτον ἔτος τῷ πολέμῳ ἐτελεύτα τῷδε ὃν Θουκυδίδης ξυνέγραψεν); 4.88.2, with οὖν (ταῦτα μὲν οὖν ἐν τῷ θέρει τούτῳ ἐγένετο); 7.87.6 (end of the Sicilian account).

§126. Further οὗτος forms are employed with μέν as well.[213] An exception is οὕτως, which usually does not co-occur with μέν.[214] The occurrence of οὗτος forms + μέν attests to the hinge function of acts between moves: while the demonstrative component looks back at previous discourse, μέν projects "more to come."

§127. Let us now turn to οὗτος forms accompanied by δή. This construction is also to be found at move transitions, and it occurs especially in Herodotus, where δή is exceptionally frequent.[215] In all these cases δή occurs in act-peninitial position.

(t25)

[extra space] || <u>Οὕτω δὴ</u> τὸ δεύτερον Ἰωνίη ἀπὸ Περσέων ἀπέστη. || [extra space] [105]

Herodotus 9.104

In this way Ionia revolted for the second time from the Persians. (tr. AB)

In this example οὕτω δή works as an epimythic closure device, to mark the end of a story.[216] Note the extra space before the οὕτω δή move.

§128. Further οὗτος forms are used in combination with δή to achieve similar communicative goals, for example to summarize a point, as in this case:

213 Already Oeltze mentions οὗτος forms employed with μέν and followed by δέ "in transitionibus" (1887:17). See, for example, in Thucydides τούτον (λόγον) at the start of 5.78 (and after direct speech); τούτῳ (τρόπῳ), clause initial at the end of 8.98; ἦν δὲ τοῦτο μὲν σχῆμα πολιτικόν, starting 8.89.3. At 5.111.1 τούτων μέν starts the dialogue between the Athenians and the Melians. In numerous cases τοῦτο μέν simply is the foil for a δέ counterpart.

214 It does in 8 cases, all in Thucydides, also involving the combinations μὲν οὖν and μὲν δή: 8.79.4 (μὲν οὕτως); 7.34.8; 1.110.4 (μὲν ... οὕτως); 2.13.6 and 1.93.8 (μὲν οὖν οὕτως); 2.101.6 and 5.60.4 (μὲν οὖν ... οὕτως); 2.4.8 (μὲν δὴ ... οὕτως). On the discursive functions of οὕτως in Thucydides, see Martínez Vázquez 2011. Thucydides uses οὕτως 75 times overall , and οὕτω 69. Herodotus uses οὕτως 25 times and οὕτω 491.

215 According to the *TLG* (Legrand's edition), Herodotus has 1,395 instances of δή (0.7%), against 201 in Thucydides (0.1%). See IV.4.5 and IV.4.6 for more on δή in the two *Histories*.

216 See also, e.g., Herodotus 1.3.2 Οὕτω δὴ ἁρπάσαντος αὐτοῦ Ἑλένην, τοῖσι Ἕλλησι δόξαι πρῶτον... "So, having him [Alexandros] abducted Helen, the Greeks first thought of... "; 6.32.1 Οὕτω δὴ τὸ τρίτον Ἴωνες κατεδουλώθησαν "So for the third time the Ionians were enslaved"; 9.28.1 Οὕτω δὴ ἔσχον οἱ Ἀθηναῖοι καὶ ὑπερεβάλοντο τοὺς Τεγεήτας "So the Athenians got [the command of wing at Plataea] over the Tegeans." All translations are mine. "Epimythic" is explained in §120. In Thucydides this word cluster appears only 13 times (against 108 in Herodotus): 1.131.1; 2.6.3; 12.4; 19.1; 70.1; 83.3; 3.98.1; 4.30.3; 73.4; 75.1; 5.16.1; 8.71.2; 99.1; often it marks a narrative turning point.

(t26)

[extra space] || Τοῖσι μάγοισι ἔδοξε | βουλευομένοισι Πρηξάσπεα φίλον προσθέσθαι, | ὅτι τε ἐπεπόνθεε πρὸς Καμβύσεω ἀνάρσια, | ὅς οἱ τὸν παῖδα τοξεύσας ἀπολωλέκεε, |καὶ διότι ..., | πρὸς δ' ἔτι ἐόντα ἐν αἴνῃ μεγίστῃ τὸν Πρηξάσπεα ἐν Πέρσῃσι. [extra space] [2] || Τούτων δή μιν εἵνεκεν | καλέσαντες φίλον προσεκτῶντο | πίστι τε λαβόντες καὶ ὁρκίοισι | ἦ μὲν ...

Herodotus 3.74.1-2

The Magi had resolved after consideration to make a friend of Prexaspes, because he had been wronged by Cambyses (who had killed his son with an arrow) and because ...; but besides this, because he was in great repute among the Persians. For these reasons they summoned him and tried to make him a friend, having bound him by tokens of good faith and oaths ... (tr. Godley)

"For these reasons" + δή is an example of Herodotean dovetailing. Actually the construction summarizes the reasons already given, but at the same time prefaces the narration of the subsequent action. In other words, each act that signals a move end simultaneously represents a new step in the discourse. Paralinguistic segmentation in this case acknowledges the major discontinuity; τούτων δή μιν εἵνεκεν starts section 2 of chapter 74.

§129. We can also interpret the function of δή without οὗτος forms, whenever it occurs in act-peninitial position and/or near temporal expressions.[217] The general discourse function we assign to act-peninitial δή in Herodotus is that of marking major steps in narrative progression—just as in Homer.[218] Already Apollonius Dyscolus associates δή to the sense of temporary conclusion, before starting something else.[219] Let us exemplify the role of δή at move transitions by considering how Herodotus marks the main steps in the (reported) narration of the encounter between the Nasamonians and the Pygmies:

(t27)

[6] | Διεξελθόντας δὲ χῶρον πολλὸν ψαμμώδεα καὶ ἐν πολλῇσι ἡμέρῃσι | ἰδεῖν δή κοτε δένδρεα ἐν πεδίῳ πεφυκότα, | καί σφεας προσελθόντας ἅπτεσθαι τοῦ ἐπεόντος ἐπὶ τῶν δενδρέων καρποῦ, | ἁπτομένοισι δέ σφι ἐπελθεῖν ἄνδρας μικρούς, μετρίων ἐλάσσονας ἀνδρῶν, | λαβόντας δὲ ἄγειν σφέας· | φωνῆς δὲ | οὔτε τι τῆς ἐκείνων τοὺς Νασαμῶνας γινώσκειν | οὔτε τοὺς ἄγοντας τῶν Νασαμώνων. [extra space] [7] || Ἄγειν τε δὴ αὐτοὺς δι' ἑλέων μεγίστων, | καὶ

217 On this function of δή especially in Herodotus, see IV.4.5.1.
218 See II.3.3.1.
219 See I.2 §§71 and 74.

> διεξελθόντας ταῦτα ἀπικέσθαι ἐς πόλιν | ἐν τῇ πάντας εἶναι τοῖσι ἄγουσι τὸ μέγαθος ἴσους, | χρῶμα δὲ μέλανας.
>
> Herodotus 2.32.6-7
>
> After this, they travelled over the desert, towards the west, and crossed a wide sandy region, until after many days they saw trees growing in a plain; when they came to these and were picking the fruit of the trees, they were met by little men of less than common stature, who took them and led them away. The Nasamonians did not know these men's language nor did the escort know the language of the Nasamonians. The men led them across great marshes, after crossing which they came to a city where all the people were of a stature like that of the guides, and black. (tr. Godley)

This excerpt fixes in our visual imagination two main events, the Nasamonians by the trees picking fruit, and then the Pygmies carrying away the Nasamonians. Both steps in Greek include δή and other significant co-occurring features. First, we find the construction δή κοτε, which recalls ὅτε δή in Homer.[220] Second, τε δή notably occurs after an unframed δέ act, the unframed information concerning the two people's mutual inability to understand each other.[221] τε δή retrieves the main frame of the account, and signals its end at the same time.[222] While the extra space and the start of section 7 do mark the move that starts with Ἄγειν τε δή, in the case of ἰδεῖν δή κοτε nothing on the paralinguistic level indicates any boundary (not even a modern comma). Yet, my interpretation of the moves that are relevant to major visual shifts springs from the two δή moments. All in all, unlike οὗτος forms + δή, which usually mark a move at the end of an account, δή without demonstrative pronouns can be found also at intermediate transitions of accounts. The most suitable combination fulfilling exactly this function is μὲν δή.

3.11.4 μὲν δή and μέν νυν in Herodotus

§130. Van Otterlo, H. Fränkel, and Immerwahr[223] are among the scholars who note that μέν and δέ can straddle two different accounts or themes, and mention μὲν δή and μέν νυν as variations of μέν in this function.[224] More specifically, they observe that μέν, μὲν

220 See II.3 §51.

221 For the notion of unframed discourse, see above §79.

222 Similar τε δή occur in Herodotus 7.217.1; 2.19.3; 2.32.7; 2.163. The combination is already mentioned in Klotz 1842:419. Hammer 1904:36 simply notices its relative frequency in Herodotus. Cooper (2002:2961-2962) doubts a clear function of the combination. τε can introduce the last item in a series by itself (IV.2 §78 with n124).

223 Van Otterlo 1944:171-172; H. Fränkel 1955:83; Immerwahr 1966: 58n39. See also Müller 1980:76-78.

224 Before them the phenomenon is observed by Hoogeveen 1769:672-685; Hartung 1832:263, 1833:16, 19, and 399-402; Bäumlein 1861:178-179; Denniston 1950:258-259 and 472-473

δή, and μέν νυν are often used to close or recapitulate a series of events, while δέ starts a new account or theme. In our terms this equals to saying that μὲν δή and μέν νυν often close macro-moves.

§131. Let me anticipate the main points of this subsection. μὲν δή and μέν νυν occur almost exclusively in Herodotus.[225] I take them to mark moves that end or start macro-moves. The fact that in print editions about one third of μὲν δή and μέν νυν moves either conclude or start chapters[226] matches with this idea.[227] The oscillation between end and start can be explained if we consider the discourse function of the same combinations while macro-moves are unfolding, that is, when they occur in the middle of a complex narrative (or speech). The μέν component in this respect is revealing, because of the metanarrative idea "more to come" underlying its use.

§132. Let us start the analyses with instances of μὲν δή and μέν νυν moves that summarize the events of sizable preceding discourse.

(t28)

[extra space] || Λυδοὶ <u>μὲν δὴ</u> ὑπὸ Πέρσῃσι ἐδεδούλωντο. || [extra space] [95] Ἐπιδίζηται δὲ δὴ τὸ ἐνθεῦτεν ἡμῖν ὁ λόγος ...

Herodotus 1.94.7

[originally writing in 1934].

225 According to the *TLG* edition online, μὲν δή occurs 391 times in Herodotus, against 9 in Thucydides; μέν νυν occurs 310 times in Herodotus and none in Thucydides (with the exception of just one μὲν νῦν, at 2.44.1 during Pericles' funeral oration). Thucydides uses μὲν οὖν instead (see below 3.11.5).

226 Out of 391 μὲν δή, 120 occur at the starting clause of a new chapter, and 50 occur in the closing clause of a chapter. The numbers for μέν νυν are not so different: 91 co-appear at the start, and 47 at the end of chapters. As for μὲν ὦν, the Ionic variant of μέν οὖν, 5 of the only 7 instances in Herodotus appear at chapter beginnings.

227 If we look at patterns of particle use across the highest level of discourse division in both *Histories*, which is book division, we see that almost all the books of both works start with a δέ act. The very beginnings of Herodotus 3 and 6 are an exception: interestingly, we find ἐπὶ τοῦτον δή and μέν νυν respectively; the former conforms to the pattern οὗτος forms + δή, which usually mark a move at the end of a macro-move, while the latter confirms the usage of μέν νυν at the beginning of macro-moves. The endings feature more variation. In Herodotus, the features employed correspond to those analyzed over the previous subsections: οὗτος (penultimate clause of book 1); ταῦτα μέν (penultimate clause of book 2); δὲ τούτου (penultimate clause of book 3); μὲν δή (last clause of book 4); δέ ταύτης (last period of book 5); οὕτω δή (last clause of book 6); ταῦτα μὲν δὴ οὕτω (last clause of book 7); μὲν ταῦτα (last clause of book 8); τε (last main clause of book 9). In Thucydides, only the end of book 7 is similar to what we find in Herodotus: ταῦτα μὲν τὰ περὶ Σικελίαν γενόμενα. All the other closures differ: we find καί (4 times), δέ (once), and γάρ (once). The occurrence of καί reflects the Thucydides' pervasive and multifunctional use of the particle. "Ands" at the end of accounts (resembling in function "and they lived happily ever after") are unquestionably part of his style; see IV.2 §§12 and 112.

> So, the Lydians were enslaved by the Persians. From this point on my discourse inquires ... (tr. AB)

(t29)

> || Νείλου <u>μέν νυν</u> πέρι τοσαῦτα εἰρήσθω. || [extra space] [35] Ἔρχομαι δὲ περὶ Αἰγύπτου μηκυνέων τὸν λόγον ...
>
> Herodotus 2.34.2

> About the Nile, it is enough to say this much. I am going to prolong the discourse about Egypt ... (tr. AB)

The μὲν δή and μέν νυν acts in the respective passages are discontinuous with respect to what precedes and follows, so they constitute moves.[228] Their role is fundamentally metanarrative; note that in both passages the subsequent δέ acts make metanarration explicit ("From this point on my discourse inquires ...," and "I am going to prolong the discourse about Egypt ..." respectively). In the case of (t28), the μὲν δή move concludes the account of the wars between Lydians and Persians, which starts at 1.46, and possibly even the entire Lydian account, which starts 46 chapters earlier (at 1.6). In the case of (t29) the μέν νυν move concludes the discussion of the Nile, which starts 24 chapters earlier (at 2.10). Note, by the way, the occurrence of τοσαῦτα in (t29), a variant of a οὗτος form. (t28) and (t29) close chapters in both Hude's (*OCT*) and Legrand's (*TLG*) editions. Also, in both editions full stops separate Λυδοὶ μὲν δή from Ἐπιδίζηται δέ. Additionally, the extra space before Λυδοὶ μὲν δή, which is unrelated to section numbers, paralleled by a rare indent in the *TLG* edition, match my reading of a move boundary. These moves frequently include οὗτος forms as well, and are usually followed by a δέ act whose content is totally different (as in (t28) and (t29).[229]

§133. Sometimes, in spite of the fact that modern segmentation at least partially acknowledges move boundaries,[230] modern punctuation obscures the closural force of

228 Besides the presence of significant pronouns and particles, also tense shifts across this kind of moves are frequent. See below (t30), (t33), (t37).

229 A further example, among many others, is Herodotus 1.5.3 [extra space] [5.3] Ταῦτα μέν νυν Πέρσαι τε καὶ Φοίνικες λέγουσι. || Ἐγὼ δὲ ... "This is what the Persians and the Phoenicians say. But I ...,". Even though this move is placed at the beginning of a chapter, the co-occurrence of μέν νυν, the verb λέγουσι, which evokes the activity of accounting, and the contrasting ἐγὼ δέ make this move a concluding one. A mismatch occurs between my interpretation of a move boundary before ἐγὼ δὲ and paralinguistic segmentation, which at that place only records a full stop. A parallel instance with μὲν δή is Herodotus 2.179, at the end of a section on the Egyptian city of Naucratis: Οὕτω μὲν δὴ Ναύκρατις ἐτετίμητο. || Ἀμφικτυόνων δέ ... "That is how much Naucratis was esteemed. The Amphictyons...."

230 See above, 3.7.

μὲν δή and μέν νυν moves. Here are two examples showing that a simple comma does not match the subject-closing function; a full stop would fit better the major discontinuity in the discourse.

(t30)

[extra space] [36] || Ὁ <u>μὲν δὴ</u> δίαιταν εἶχε ἐν Κροίσου, || ἐν δὲ τῷ αὐτῷ χρόνῳ τούτῳ ἐν τῷ Μυσίῳ Ὀλύμπῳ ὑὸς χρῆμα γίνεται μέγα· ...

Herodotus 1.36.1

So Adrastus lived in Croesus' house. About this same time a great monster of a boar appeared on the Mysian Olympus, ... (tr. Godley)

μὲν δή is a metanarrative sign that the encounter between Croesus and Adrastus is over, for the moment at least—Croesus has met him, talked with him, and decided to host him (1.35-36). What follows is a new frame, the beginning of the crucial account of the boar hunt, which will cause Adrastus to accidentally kill Croesus' son. The comma of print editions does not do justice to this discontinuity.[231]

§134. Similarly, in the following passage modern punctuation and segmentation only partially represent the frame shifts that occur after μέν νυν:

(t31)

[indent] || Ταῦτα *μέν νυν* πολλοῖσι ἔτεσι ὕστερον ἐγένετο τοῦ βασιλέος στόλου, || ἐπάνειμι δὲ ἐπὶ τὸν πρότερον λόγον. [138] || Ἡ δὲ στρατηλασίη ἡ βασιλέος | οὔνομα μὲν εἶχε ὡς ἐπ' Ἀθήνας ἐλαύνει, | κατίετο δὲ ἐς πᾶσαν τὴν Ἑλλάδα.

Herodotus 7.137.3-138.1

This, however, took place long after Xerxes' invasion of Greece, and I must get back to my story. [Indent] The purpose of Xerxes' expedition, which was directed nominally against Athens, was in fact the conquest of the whole of Greece. (tr. Marincola 2003)

Both the Greek edition and the translation capture paralinguistically one of the major discontinuities in the discourse: the new topic begun at ἡ δὲ στρατηλασίη ἡ βασιλέος. The new chapter number (138) in the Greek edition corresponds to the indentation in de Sélincourt and Marincola. However, there is another discontinuity besides this one.

[231] However, de Sélincourt's translation, for example, indents at this point. Godley simply divides the two segments with a full stop.

Prior to the chapter-break, features that co-occur with the first δέ signal a new move. The first-person ἐπάνειμι is a performative verb that explicitly encodes and projects the historian's narrative intervention. τὸν πρότερον λόγον ("the previous account") clarifies the nature of this intervention, which is to resume the preceding, interrupted narration of the invasion of Greece.[232] Overall, this first δέ's host clause constitutes a metanarrative move. It is likely that modern editions print a comma before ἐπάνειμι δὲ because editors construe μέν – δέ as a pair, which in Attic Greek can occur within the same thematic strand. But μέν νυν has a force different from μέν when it occurs alone: while single μέν is more flexible in function, μέν νυν always marks moves or even macro-moves. It is remarkable that in the *OCT* edition a very rare indentation occurs before ταῦτα μέν νυν, that is, an indentation that does not coincide with chapter starts.[233] Such a paralinguistic sign does fit the reading of a move boundary. The second major discontinuity occurs, as I have noted, at the chapter-break (with no indentation, by the way), where Herodotus shifts from metanarrative to actual narration; this second δέ act marks the beginning of a new macro-move.

§135. So far I have illustrated the appearance of μὲν δή and μέν νυν in moves that round off large units of discourse, and I have commented on two examples that show a mismatch between modern punctuation and move boundaries. Now two more examples follow, which illustrate mismatches directly on the level of chapter division. The discussion is central to the ambiguity of interpretation between ends and starts of relatively big discourse units.

§136. Let us consider the wording of a short move that in the *TLG* edition appears at the end of a chapter, whereas in the *OCT* edition it starts a new chapter:

(t32)

[extra space] || ἐσπεσόντες δὲ κατεστόρεσαν αὐτῶν ἑξακοσίους, | τοὺς δὲ λοιποὺς κατήραξαν | διώκοντες ἐς τὸν Κιθαιρῶνα· [extra space] [70] || οὗτοι <u>μὲν δὴ</u> ἐν οὐδενὶ λόγῳ ἀπώλοντο. || οἱ δὲ Πέρσαι καὶ ὁ ἄλλος ὅμιλος, ...

Herodotus 9.69.2-70.1

...in this attack they [the Thebans] trampled six hundred of them [Megarians and Phliasians], and pursued and drove the rest to Cithaeron. So these perished without anyone noticing. But when the Persians and the rest of the multitude... (tr. Godley)

232 This passage is part of Cagnazzi's evidence of Herodotus' original division of the *Histories* into λόγοι; see above n100 and n174.

233 See above, §55.

Legrand (*TLG* edition) places the utterance οὗτοι μὲν δὴ ἐν οὐδενὶ λόγῳ ἀπώλοντο at the end of chapter 69, whereas Hude (i.e. *OCT* edition, reported in (t32)) places it at the beginning of chapter 70.[234] The co-occurring elements that signal a major discourse discontinuity are the combination of a οὗτος form and μὲν δή. The comparison with other occurrences of οὗτος form and μὲν δή makes me align with Legrand rather than with Hude. Perhaps Hude did not want to separate μέν from δέ; however, in this case form and content clearly indicate a straddling of macro-moves, thematically and pragmatically.

§137. Legrand and Hude do agree on chapter segmentation in the following passage, but nevertheless the interpretation of an utterance *starting* a discourse unit can be challenged.

(t33)

[31][235] || πρῶτον <u>μὲν δὴ</u> λέγουσι Καμβύσῃ τῶν κακῶν ἄρξαι τοῦτο, || δεύτερα δὲ ἐξεργάσατο τὴν ἀδελφεὴν ἐπισπομένην ...

Herodotus 3.31.1

This, they say, was the first of Cambyses' evil acts; next, he destroyed his full sister, who had come with him ... (tr. Godley)

The "first of the evil acts" is Cambyses' order to kill his own brother Smerdis (3.30), whose murder has just been described. The οὗτος form τοῦτο in (t33) strengthens the backward-oriented discourse function of the act. In fact, the entire move resumes the preceding wording almost *verbatim*: 3.30 began with καὶ πρῶτα μὲν [τῶν κακῶν] ἐξεργάσατο τὸν ἀδελφεὸν Σμέρδιν, "First of all, he destroyed his brother Smerdis ...." πρῶτον μὲν δὴ λέγουσι Καμβύσῃ τῶν κακῶν ἄρξαι τοῦτο is therefore a standard case of a move that summarizes previous content. However, the same move also recalls the discourse structure of a list ("First ...; second ..."). The semantic clue "first ... second" influences the discourse segmentation so that the first evil occupies the first spot instead of the last in the organization of chapters. In other words, there are reasons to think of the move in question as concluding but at the same time starting a multi-act discourse unit. How can we make sense of this apparent variability in positioning?

§138. The answer lies in the appreciation of *intermediate* or hinge narrative steps. In (t32) οὗτοι μὲν δὴ ἐν οὐδενὶ λόγῳ ἀπώλοντο ("So these [Megarians and Phliasians] perished without anyone talking about it") in fact represents a step out of the account.

234 For similar discrepancies see 4.132; 186; 7.123; 8.114, where Legrand opts for the end and Hude for the start of the following chapter, and 8.104 and 6.115, where it happens vice versa: Hude opts for the end and Legrand for the start of the following chapter.

235 Here no extra space is recorded, as chapter 31 in the *OCT* edition starts a new line. See above §§54-55.

It resembles an aside, and most likely a non-neutral one.[236] Let us consider now a similar μέν νυν move that occurs at an intermediate point within a long account:

(t34)

[extra space] [5] || Τὰ μέν νυν ἱστορημένα δηλοῖ σαφέως παλαιὸν θεὸν Ἡρακλέα ἐόντα· [extra space] || καὶ | δοκέουσι δέ μοι ...

Herodotus 2.44.5

Therefore, what I have discovered by inquiry plainly shows that Heracles is an ancient god. And furthermore, I think ... (tr. Godley)

This passage occurs in the middle of Herodotus' account of the cult of Heracles in Egypt (2.42.3-45.3). We have here a straightforward metanarrative move: the historian explicitly tells us that he is stepping out of the host account. μέν νυν signals such a move.[237]

§139. These last two examples show a key feature of these combinations. When the host moves conclude or start macro-moves, as well as when they signal different moments within the same account, μὲν δή and μέν νυν convey two important metanarrative meanings at the same time. One is that the speaker is either stepping out of the narration to summarize the events described, or is stepping out to comment on some general aspect of the narrative.[238] Such overviews are mainly realized *a posteriori*—they follow the detailed account—but every now and then can also be found *a priori*. The other metanarrative meaning is that this stepping out is, on a larger scale, intermediate. μὲν δή and μέν νυν acts never coincide with the absolute final part of accounts. They do not represent the definitive end, but they do prepare the way for it.[239] There is always either

236 De Sélincourt translates ἐν οὐδενὶ λόγῳ as an evaluative comment attached to the independent clause by means of a m-dash: "—an inglorious end." Marincola notes: "Anti-Corinthian and anti-Megarian prejudice may ... be at work here" (de Sélincourt and Marincola 2003:679).

237 The fact that after the proem Herodotus starts with a Persian λόγος by means of μέν νυν is significant. The text says: [indent] || Ἡροδότου Θουρίου ἱστορίης ἀπόδεξις ἥδε, | ... τά τε ἄλλα καὶ δι' ἣν αἰτίην ἐπολέμησαν ἀλλήλοισι. [indent] [1] || Περσέων μέν νυν οἱ λόγιοι Φοίνικας αἰτίους φασὶ γενέσθαι τῆς διαφορῆς· || τούτους γάρ ... "This is the display of the inquiry of Herodotus of Halicarnassus, (...) including among others what was the cause of their waging war on each other. [1.1] The Persian learned men say that the Phoenicians were the cause of the dispute. These ...," Herodotus Proem, and 1.1 (tr. Godley). Bakker (2006:97) calls μέν νυν "discourse internal." The metanarrative function of the move resides in transitioning from the proem to the accountof the Persians by means of an intermediate "abstract" of the λόγος itself; it is only with the subsequent γάρ the discourse expands on it and unfolds its content.

238 The use of ἐγένετο, for example, exemplifies the generalizing component of summaries and comments: the act is about a process or episode that "was" or "happened" as a whole.

239 See Apollonius Dyscolus *On Conjunctions* 251,20 [δή] πολλάκις μετάβασιν λόγου ποιεῖται "[δή] often effects a transition of the discourse" in Dalimier 2001:186.

some further step that brings the account to a decisive close, or an entirely new account that begins immediately afterwards.

§140. The μέν component in these combinations gives a projecting function to these moves. It suggests that the speaker will go on with his discourse.[240] Earlier (§66) I associated this kind of μέν to modern nonfinal intonation at interim conclusions. As II.2 §52 reminds us, already Hoogeveen in the 18th century was pointing out μέν μεταβατικός ("transitional"), and even before him Devarius in the 16th century discussed μέν περιγραφικός, "summarizing."

§141. Because of their intermediate role, these segments possess an instability that can be witnessed in divergences among editorial decisions. To resolve the ambiguity, I suggest that we consider these intermediate steps as hinge moves. They differ both from what precedes and what follows them, and they reveal a discourse strategy affecting multiple acts (backward and forward), not just the local one that hosts the μὲν δή or μέν νυν.[241]

§142. Not infrequently μὲν δή and μέν νυν appear immediately after the report of direct speech.[242] In these cases too the two combinations indicate that the speaker is stepping out of the previous discourse (the words uttered by another speaker) in order to proceed with the narration in the third person. On other functionally analogous occasions, μὲν δή and μέν νυν signal what in II.4 §18 is presented as "frame recall:"[243] the moves hosting them retrieve a discourse thread, and the cognitive frame associated with it, after some interruption.[244]

240 The projecting function of μέν is argued in II.2.4.1 and III.2.2.7; on μέν at speech starts, see III.4 §55; III.4 §§28-30 discusses μέν as a floorholding device.

241 Often the metanarrative action that characterizes the stepping out is linguistically encoded. See (t31), (t35), and also, for example, Herodotus 2.117: Ὅμηρος μέν νυν καὶ τὰ Κύπρια ἔπεα χαιρέτω, "Let us take leave from Homer and the Cyprian epic"; 2.135.6: Ῥοδώπιος μέν νυν πέρι πέπαυμαι, "Let me stop talking about Rhodopis."

242 See, e.g., Herodotus 1.9.1; 101.1; 36.1; 36.3; 60.5; 63.1; 65.4; 116.3; 118.1; 155.2; 156.1 (μὲν δή). As for μέν νυν, see 4.133.3; 7.148.1; 8.126.1; 7.228.4 (after the quotation of the epigram for the Spartans); 1.5.3 (after reporting Persian and Phoenician accounts); 1.24.8 (after a report of what Corinthians and Lesbians say); 6.54.1 (after the report of the Greek genealogy of Spartan kings); 6.55.1 (after the historian's report on different accounts).

243 "Frame recall" matches the POP function that Slings identifies in the use of several linguistic items in Herodotus (see above n167).

244 μὲν δή occurs only nine times in Thucydides, much less than in Herodotus, but its discourse functions are the same in the two authors. Here is an instance of μὲν δή in the middle of an episode from Thucydides 1.45-46.1: | Τοιαύτῃ μὲν γνώμῃ οἱ Ἀθηναῖοι τοὺς Κερκυραίους προσεδέξαντο, | καὶ τῶν Κορινθίων ἀπελθόντων οὐ πολὺ ὕστερον δέκα ναῦς αὐτοῖς ἀπέστειλαν βοηθούς· | ἐστρατήγει δὲ ... | προεῖπον δὲ .... [46] || αἱ μὲν δὴ νῆες ἀφικνοῦνται ἐς τὴν Κέρκυραν, || οἱ δὲ Κορίνθιοι, | ἐπειδὴ αὐτοῖς παρεσκεύαστο, | ἔπλεον ἐπὶ τὴν Κέρκυραν ναυσὶ πεντήκοντα καὶ ἑκατόν .... With such thoughts in mind, the Athenians concluded an alliance with the Corcyraeans, and, shortly after the Corinthians had left, sent a squadron of ten ships to support Corcyra, under the command of .... Their instructions were .... [Indent] So these ships arrived at Corcyra, and when the Corinthians had completed their own preparations they sailed for Corcyra with a hundred and fifty ships (tr. Hammond). The information "the Athenians sent

§143. The last remarks concern slight differences in usage between the two combinations. In general, both μὲν δή and μέν νυν work as a cluster (that is, the forces of the two individual particles are combined), but they can also work as a combination keeping the forces of the two particles separate. The latter emerges when the δέ act that follows centers on an element of content that pairs with the element attached to the μὲν δή or μέν νυν segment.[245] However, while in Herodotus δή alone is not rare, νυν occurs without μέν only 14 times (against 310 μέν νυν).[246] From this datum I infer that μέν νυν works as a cluster more frequently than μὲν δή. Another slight difference in use is that μὲν δή can occur in acts that describe exciting or vivid moments of accounts, while μέν νυν does not.[247]

3.11.5 μὲν οὖν in Thucydides

§144. The combination μὲν οὖν appears more frequently in Thucydides than in Herodotus (85 occurrences against 7). *LSJ* (s.v. μέν) and Montanari (1329) take μέν νυν to be the Ionic variant of μὲν οὖν. The two combinations are similar in discourse function, from the usages I am going to comment.[248] Like μέν νυν, we find μὲν οὖν at closures together with οὗτος or τοιοῦτος/τοσαῦτος forms, immediately after the end of direct speech, and at the beginning of new accounts or at hinge points.[249] Unlike μέν νυν, in the *TLG* edition

ten ships to Corcyra" (δέκα ναῦς αὐτοῖς ἀπέστειλαν) is followed by multiple discourse acts giving details of the mission: the leader of the squadron, and the specific instructions. After this, the historian returns to the narration of the ships reaching Corcyra, with μὲν δή signaling this return.

245 E.g. Herodotus 1.116.3: Τὸν μὲν δὴ Ἀρτεμβάρεα πέμπει, τὸν δὲ Κῦρον ἦγον ἔσω οἱ θεράποντες κελεύσαντος τοῦ Ἀστυάγεος "So he sent Artembares away, and the attendants led Cyrus inside at Astyages' bidding," (tr. Godley). One possible reading of these segments would connect μέν and δέ, and take δή as a generic marker of a salient narrative step: "at that point (δή) what happened was that he [Astyages] sent Artembares away, and the attendants led Cyrus inside." An alternative reading is that μὲν δή seals the decision of Astyages in light of the preceding content, while τὸν δέ opens a different frame (and scene), with Cyrus alone at its center. In IV.5 I read μέν νυν as a cluster (§§ 56; 58), and as a combination (§§95-96). My examination of μὲν οὖν in Thucydides yields the same results: μὲν οὖν mostly work as a cluster, but sometimes content suggests a parallel between the constituents immediately attached to μέν and δέ.

246 All the occurrences of νυν are in direct speech. Notably, σύ νυν represents 9 of the 14 occurrences. A conversational value of νυν in drama is pointed out in III.4 §44.

247 For example, in Herodotus 3.78.2 the δή and μὲν δή acts contribute to the urgency of the scene. The scene is the fight between the Magi and the Persians who have just heard Prexaspes' accusation of the Magi: ὁ μὲν δὴ αὐτῶν φθάνει τὰ τόξα κατελόμενος, ὁ δὲ πρὸς τὴν αἰχμὴν ἐτράπετο. Ἐνθαῦτα δὴ συνέμισγον ἀλλήλοισι. Τῷ μὲν δὴ τὰ τόξα ἀναλαβόντι αὐτῶν, ἐόντων τε ἀγχοῦ τῶν πολεμίων καὶ προσκειμένων, "One rushed to take down a bow, the other went for a spear. Then the fighting started. The one that had caught up the bow found it was no use to him, as the antagonists were close and jostling one another" (tr. Godley). These instances of μὲν δή are reminiscent of the cluster καὶ δή, which in Herodotus may mark narrative peaks (as καί alone does); see IV.2.4.3 about καί at peaks, and IV.2 §§100-101 about καὶ δή.

248 Different is the range of functions of μὲν οὖν in drama; see III.2 §§82-83.

249 E.g. Thucydides 5.35.8 τὸ μὲν οὖν θέρος τοῦτο ἡσυχία ἦν καὶ ἔφοδοι παρ' ἀλλήλους "So for this summer there was peace and diplomacy between the two sides" (hinge point); 4.21.1 Οἱ μὲν οὖν

Thucydidean μὲν οὖν appears more frequently at the beginning of chapters and sections than at the end.[250]

§145. In order to illustrate the discourse functions of Thucydidean μὲν οὖν across different co-texts, let us look at four instances of μὲν οὖν within the same account, drawn from the narrative of the plague (2.47.3-54).

(t35)

| καὶ ἔθνῃσκον πολλῷ μᾶλλον ἤδη. [extra space] [3] || λεγέτω μὲν οὖν περὶ αὐτοῦ | ὡς ἕκαστος γιγνώσκει καὶ ἰατρὸς καὶ ἰδιώτης, | ἀφ' ὅτου εἰκὸς ἦν γενέσθαι αὐτό ...

Thucydides 2.48.2-3

And they died much more frequently, indeed.[251] Now, let a physician or someone in particular tell how each knew about it [the illness], from where it was likely to have come from ... (tr. AB)

(t36)

[extra space] || οἱ δὲ κύνες μᾶλλον αἴσθησιν παρεῖχον τοῦ ἀποβαίνοντος διὰ τὸ ξυνδιαιτᾶσθαι. [indent] [51.1] || Τὸ μὲν οὖν νόσημα, | πολλὰ καὶ ἄλλα παραλιπόντι ἀτοπίας, | ὡς ἑκάστῳ ἐτύγχανέ τι διαφερόντως ἑτέρῳ πρὸς ἕτερον γιγνόμενον, | τοιοῦτον ἦν ἐπὶ πᾶν τὴν ἰδέαν.

Thucydides 2.50.2-51.1

The dogs allowed more observation of the repercussion, because of their daily stay with humans. As for the illness, then, if one leaves aside the numerous and diverse aspects of weird particulars, which each one happened to experience differently from one another, this was the general idea on the whole. (tr. AB)

Λακεδαιμόνιοι τοσαῦτα εἶπον "Such and no more was the speech made by the Spartans" (after direct speech); 2.89.9 τούτων μὲν οὖν ἐγὼ ἕξω τὴν πρόνοιαν κατὰ τὸ δυνατόν "I shall bear all this in mind as best I can" (start of the last part of a speech by Phormio). All translations are by Hammond.

[250] It is found 20 times at chapter beginnings and 47 times at section beginnings, but only 6 times at chapter ends.

[251] On this and parallel instances of ἤδη, see IV.4.8.2 and 4.8.3.

(t37)

... φάσκοντες οἱ πρεσβύτεροι | πάλαι ᾄδεσθαι | 'ἥξει Δωριακὸς πόλεμος καὶ λοιμὸς ἅμ' αὐτῷ.' [extra space] [54.3] || ἐγένετο <u>μὲν οὖν</u> ἔρις τοῖς ἀνθρώποις | μὴ λοιμὸν ὠνομάσθαι ἐν τῷ ἔπει ὑπὸ τῶν παλαιῶν, | ἀλλὰ λιμόν, | ἐνίκησε δὲ ἐπὶ τοῦ παρόντος εἰκότως λοιμὸν εἰρῆσθαι ...

Thucydides 2.54.2-3

[they remembered that] old men used to say that in early times it was sung, "A Dorian war, and pestilence with it will come." Now, there was a dispute among people that in the verse the ancients did not mention "pestilence" but "famine." That they said "pestilence" won, as it can be expected given the present circumstances. (tr. AB)

(t38)

[extra space] [4] μνήμη δὲ ἐγένετο καὶ τοῦ Λακεδαιμονίων χρηστηρίου ... | καὶ αὐτὸς ἔφη ξυλλήψεσθαι. || [extra space] [5] περὶ <u>μὲν οὖν</u> τοῦ χρηστηρίου τὰ γιγνόμενα ᾔκαζον ὁμοῖα εἶναι· ἐσβεβληκότων δὲ τῶν Πελοποννησίων ἡ νόσος ἤρξατο εὐθύς ...

Thucydides 2.54.4-5

There was also recollection of an oracle for the Spartans ... and that he himself [the god] would be on their side. The events, then, seemed to fit the oracle: when the Peloponnesians invaded, the illness started right away ... (tr. AB)

Each of the μὲν οὖν segments occurs after a new section number, which reveals the editorial perception of a major discontinuity in discourse. In (t35) μὲν οὖν signals the beginning of a move introducing the opinion of doctors and individuals. The author for a moment steps back from the description of events: "Now, let us spend some words on how each doctor as well as individual knew about it [the illness] ..." In (t36) μὲν οὖν signals a move that pulls back from the details, even when they seem important (like the information about dogs), and offers an overarching and recapitulating assessment: "As for the illness, then, ... this was the general idea on the whole" (note the generic terms γιγνόμενον, ἐπὶ πᾶν). This use resembles several μέν νυν in Herodotus; τοιοῦτον echoes οὗτος forms. In (t37) μὲν οὖν indicates that a multi-act unit is ahead, which will deal with a new subject (ἐγένετο μὲν οὖν ἔρις), and which is related to the verse just reported. Therefore, μὲν οὖν in (t37) resembles that in (t35). In (t38) μὲν οὖν works as a hinge in a particularly clear way: it marks the ongoing move as resulting from the preceding account, and at the same time it introduces the notion of a comprehensive agreement between the events and the oracle (see the subsequent "The events, then, looked fitting the oracle").

§146. These instances of μὲν οὖν, then, have the same metanarrative meanings I identified for μέν νυν in Herodotus: μὲν οὖν, like μέν νυν, marks a stepping out from the preceding flow of narration, and it indicates an intermediate assessment or its beginning.[252]

3.12 Conclusions

§147. This chapter developed out of the following basic questions: how do particles contribute to the segmentation of discourse in Herodotus and Thucydides? What is their relationship to 'posthumous' punctuation, and to section/chapter divisions? What is their relationship to discourse boundaries, such as syntactic boundaries and prose-*kôla* boundaries?

§148. The initial sections consider main segmentation cues separately. The starting point is modern punctuation and the duality often discussed in literature, that is, the "grammatical" and the "rhetorical/elocutionary" functions of punctuation marks. Next comes the attention of modern scholars for periodic style and hypotactical articulation of texts. A further crucial aspect is represented by pre-print modalities of punctuating and ancient descriptions of textual segments, which reveal a fundamental focus on delivery, and leave syntactic definitions unspecified. Then the focus shifts to the retrieval of prose colometry in modern times. The final cues concern the paralinguistic segmentation above the sentence level that we find in *OCT* editions.

§149. A discussion of matches and mismatches concerning particles in relation to these segmentation cues follows. Particles work as road signs (a metaphor used for punctuation); they may provide directions about single acts as well as to multi-act units. The consideration of the deep interlacing between prosody and grammar, the complex inheritance of pre-print paralinguistic signs, and the richness of particles in frequency and lexical variation make us opt for a holistic principle for segmentation. This principle takes into account syntax, semantics, and pragmatics.[253]

§150. The textual analyses illustrate the adoption of this principle. The two fundamental elements of discourse segmentation are taken to be acts and moves. Acts and moves are strategic communicative steps that show a different degree of discontinuity

252 Denniston generally notes (1950:371) "from the second half of the fifth century, the transitional use of μὲν οὖν is very common." On μὲν οὖν as a cluster, see above n245.

253 A recent volume on discourse segmentation in Romance languages (Pons Bordería 2014) assesses, in a parallel way, the necessity of surpassing the limits of analyzing sentences, in spoken as well as written code. Labels attached to discourse units in the theoretical models presented include "act," "move," "frame," "nucleus," "enunciation," and "textual movement."

with what precedes and follows, and range in size from isolated phrases (priming acts) to macro-moves (expected by genre conventions). The general criteria used to identify act boundaries resemble those used to identify prose *kôla*. However, no content types of acts or moves are introduced. These segments are defined exclusively by the actual linguistic features that make them recognizable. So, patterns of co-occuring features lead us to identify, for instance, a γάρ move that in context X performs the communicative action Y; we do not deduce from γάρ that its host clause is a causal clause.

§151. Let me outline three general results emerging from the analyses. The first is that particles guide us to process discourse discontinuities on multiple levels. More specifically, particles, particle combinations, and other co-occurring linguistic features (such as οὗτος forms) signal discourse segmentation in a more authentic, more reliable, and more precise way than any kind of paralinguistic segmentation, old or recent.

§152. Sometimes the two communicative devices align—the paralinguistic one inspired by the linguistic one—but many other times there are mismatches. Mismatches should reorient our reading and make us privilege the linguistic over the (modern) paralinguistic signs. In fact, readers tend to infer the function of particles from (modern) paralinguistic segmentation, while actually it should be vice versa: the *ad hoc* function of particles should be stressed by means of *ad hoc* paralinguistic segmentation. For example, a modern comma that separates a μέν from a δέ construction might be totally inappropriate. If what co-occurs with that μέν and that δέ indicates a major discourse discontinuity, a full stop and an indent should be established between them. An exceptional match is constituted by the extra space between words that we find in the *OCT* editions, whose appearance seems to be especially guided by the presence of particles.

§153. The second general result is about two phenomena that particles reveal in the perspective of discourse segmentation, which no syntactic segmentation can show. The first relates to the idea of discourse hierarchy. Particles in priming acts that start moves have a superordinate role with respect to other particles that occur in subsequent acts. This superordinate role emerges from the fact that the priming acts pragmatically and semantically bind multiple segments that follow, in which other postpositive particles may occur. Such an organization of particle order reflects a discourse hierarchy.[254]

§154. The second phenomenon is the hinge function that especially particle combinations suggest in short moves between moves. What enables μὲν δή, μέν νυν moves (in Herodotus), and μὲν οὖν moves in Thucydides to work at the end of accounts but also at the beginning, and in the middle, is the following: most of the time the utterances that host those combinations represent intermediate closures either before a more comprehensive closure or before a parallel or contrasting move. For instance, they supply intermediate summaries, or they recall frames, or offer commentary on the ongoing

[254] This point is made also in IV.2 §§46 and 108 in connection to *and*-coordinating particles.

narrative. They work as hinge moves, which qualify as stepping out of the preceding discourse, while foreshadowing further progress.

§155. The third and final result concerns parallel and distinct usages—inferable from the passages under investigation—in a general comparison between the two historians' language. The parallel side is that acts in both authors emerge as comparably short segments. My analysis dismantles the idea that the size of periods in Thucydides is inherent in the historian's language use.

§156. The distinct side is related to moves. Herodotus employs οὗτος forms and combinations such as μὲν δή to signal move boundaries more generously than Thucydides. I believe this to be part of Herodotus' dovetailing technique,[255] which makes his flow of discourse as fluid as a river.[256]

§157. IV.5 complements these findings by merging the interpretation of acts and moves in situ, by drawing connections with other kinds of non-syntactic articulation (such as lexical resonance and sound effects), and by letting observations on coordination strategies (from IV.2) and on stance (from IV.4) converge in a unified discourse analysis.

255 See above §§ 118; 122; 128.
256 See above §118.

IV.4

Tracking Voice and Stance

4.1 Introduction

§1. Characters' speeches and deliberations are an indispensable part of Herodotus' and Thucydides' historiography; without these elements much of the *Histories'* essence would be lost. Regarding Thucydides, Dover (1988:74) characterizes most of his work as "a relation of what people did, said and thought." He goes on to say, "Delete the extensive and elaborate presentation of what they said, and the most striking of all the distinctive features of the work would be gone. Delete all reference to their thoughts, wishes, fears and the like, and the character of the narrative would be significantly changed." Herodotus shows a kind of subtlety about his characters' introspection that is different from but not inferior to Thucydides' method.

§2. Secondary literature acknowledges not only the importance but also the artistry of both historians' representation of speeches and thoughts. The present chapter addresses a neglected part of this artistry, namely the way in which the two historians use particles to represent their own and other people's voices and stances. A fundamental preface concerns commonalities and differences between the key notions selected for this purpose, that is, "voice" and "stance."

§3. "Voice" has been variously interpreted in linguistics and anthropology: it may refer to anything from *persona loquens* to the ideas of agency, self-representation, ethos, or identity.[1] In this chapter I consider voice across a discursive continuum ranging from fully reproduced speeches to summaries reporting the contents of an individual's speech. Behind the latter is the authorial voice, which needs to be taken into account as much as the characters' voice. I distinguish between explicit and implicit authorial statements, the former being characterized by "I" markers where the referent can only be the author.

§4. "Stance" is generally taken as a heading that encompasses evaluation, judgment, attitude, point of view, and perspective. The notion implies, on the one hand, agents

1 For a recent overview of literature, see Hewings 2012:187-188. Genette (1972:76; 225-267) takes voice as what in general denotes a relationship between verbal action and a person. Bal 2006 overviews the use of "voice" in narratology, and focuses on the ideological presuppositions of "voice" as a conceptual metaphor.

who express attitudes and evaluations, and on the other, objects of regard. Interactional linguistics, conversation analysis, corpus linguistics, discourse analysis, and sociocultural linguistics use the term "stancetaking" alongside "stance" because it conveys that stance results from an action that is situated and has an interactional character.[2] Throughout the chapter I refer to stance as the overall phenomenon of stancetaking; for the analyses I adopt the definition of stance by the linguist John Du Bois.

§5. The two concepts of voice and stance are decidedly linked, but also distinct. Voice encompasses all the expressions of a person's individuality, stance included. But what is voiced is not necessarily an act of stancetaking. At the same time stancetaking acts are not necessarily (represented as) uttered aloud. However, attributing stance to someone hints at the presence of at least an inner voice connected to the person in question, which is further connected to our auditory imagination of his/her words.[3] I assume that any expression of stance presupposes the existence of someone's voice—whether re-performed, echoed, or in the form of inner voice—whereas not all the manifestations of voice deal with stancetaking. Therefore, I take voice as a superordinate concept.

§6. Voice and stance are both indispensable for understanding the historiographical methods of Herodotus and Thucydides. Their narratives are driven by a concern with managing access to the voice and stance of political figures, groups of citizens, and prominent individuals. Not only does this approach enhance the vividness of the events being narrated and heighten the reader's sense of involvement in them, but it also allows the authors to detail the actors' points of view and personal styles, to illustrate their decisions and motives,[4] and to signpost crucial moments in the progress of the narrative.

§7. I focus on stance instead of "focalization" because stancetaking is a social activity. Speaking subjects take stance not in a vacuum but in a social environment, in front of or in relation to other subjects. The concept naturally leads to considerations of multiple subjects involved, and multiple vectors linking those subjects. Just as for the analysis of the source of and the relations between voices, the analysis of the source of and the relations between stancetakings is not an easy task. Stance directly involves personal attitudes, perceptions, calculations, and feelings, but it does not always manifest in a direct way. Unless explicit verbs of thinking or the like appear, attributing thoughts and considerations to characters or to the creators of the characters can be challenging.

2 See in particular Englebretson 2007, a collection of contributions on stancetaking in natural discourse across several languages.

3 On the auditory imagination that readers enact during silent reading in general, see Chafe 1988b:396-397, and IV.3 §§13-14. Mey 1999:127 posits that the "successful use of a voice in narration, in direct or in (free) discourse, is contingent upon its being used in an interactive situation, in a situation of *dialogue*" (italics in the text). He continues: "Given the fact that 'voices' in texts are born as a result of a dialogic cooperation between author and reader, we must ... look into the problem of how the voices, once born, are managed and guided in, and throughout, their textual lives."

4 Baragwanath 2008 is entirely devoted to the nexus of motivation and action in Herodotus.

In addition, literary texts play with the further level of interaction (real or imaginary) between authors and readers/listeners, which amplifies the possibilities for mirroring, juxtaposing, and manipulating the representation of stance. I choose stance because it indexes this complexity.

§8. A fundamental complexity regards "voice" too, if we acknowledge that multiple voices can be "heard" through the same utterance. Polyphony has wide and deep implications in literary texts. Rather than "polyphony" in the sense of interweaving several opinions and accounts (Herodotus' λόγοι) into one historiographical work, here I refer to the more specific sense of polyphony as delineated first by Voloshinov 1973 and Bakhtin 1981. The core idea is that a specific stretch of text can be designed to allow for multiple voices to utter it at the same time.[5] The blending of stancetakings by multiple subjects that I consider in this chapter relies on the possibility that expressions of multiple voices can overlap.

§9. In Herodotus and Thucydides, a wide spectrum of linguistic features can signal voice and stance. They range from obvious forms such as first person markers, deictic demonstratives and adverbs (τόδε, νῦν), evaluative expressions such as δοκεῖ μοι, the semantic cues of verbs of saying, thinking, considering, wondering, etc., the construction ὡς + participle, to less obvious forms, such as reflexives and indirect reflexive pronouns (αὑτός and σφ- + αὐτός forms),[6] comparatives, superlatives, and other scalar adjectives, the verb μέλλειν,[7] mood (e.g. oblique optative), and tense (e.g. imperfect vs. present).[8] Beyond lexical and syntactic cues, I include more large-scale cues given by narrative technique, such as the inclusion of direct and indirect speech, temporal manipulation, and even the amount of detail used in accounts of events.[9]

§10. In line with a major methodological point of our work,[10] particles signal voice and stance together with other features. Therefore, the best way to understand the contribution of particles to the representation of speech and thought is to observe

5 See below §18 on the "single vs. dual voice" debate concerning indirect speech.

6 The manuscript tradition indicates some uncertainty about breathing in αὑτόν forms, which adds to the complexity (on which see in particular Powell 1933 and 1934). The problem holds for Herodotus only minimally, as the reflexive pronoun he uses is ἑωυτόν; according to Powell (1933:210) the Herodotean manuscript tradition reports variation between reflexive and non-reflexive forms αὑτόν/αὐτόν only in 12 cases (out of 508 total occurrences of ἑωυτόν).

7 See e.g. Bakker 2005:99n13 "[in the *Iliad*] μέλλειν is frequently used in combination with the 'subjective' particle που ..., which underlines the necessarily 'subjective' nature of the verb: μέλλειν is the verbalization of what is evident to a consciousness." See also Basset 1979.

8 On verb forms that characterize indirect speech, see especially Rijksbaron 1984:53-58; 101-106; the author discusses also forms occurring after "verbs of perception and emotion" (55). I add the pragmatic nuances of presuppositions that characterize the constructions ὅτι + finite verb vs. accusative and infinitive, as in Huitink 2009. Huitink 2012 is entirely devoted to the interface between grammatical forms and communicative functions of reported discourse in Classical Greek.

9 On the latter point, see below §28.

10 See in particular I.1 §§17 and 18; I.4 §4, and the conclusions of individual chapters.

constructions and patterns that co-occur and co-signify with them, including all the features in the list given above.

§11. As Weydt points out about German particles (1969:60-66), there are particles that lend themselves very well to the expression of communicative intentions and subjective attitudes. Along these lines, Wakker 1997b explores the functions of "modal particles" in Herodotus and Thucydides—that is, particles signaling the speaker's or narrator's "attitude towards the proposition he is presenting" (Wakker 1997b:215). The current chapter develops themes touched upon in this article, as it discusses the same particles (ἄρα, δή, τοι, and ἦ μήν) in connection with direct and indirect speech, and investigates whose point of view is conveyed behind the use of ἄρα and δή. I complement and extend findings that Wakker acknowledges as "preliminary" (1997b:248), chiefly by establishing links with scholarly accounts of stance, by refining the question of who conveys stance, and by extending the analysis to include free indirect thoughts (that is, people's thoughts that are not introduced by reporting clauses).

§12. As in other chapters, I preface textual analyses with theoretical, methodological, and literary observations that guide the heuristics as well as the conclusions to be drawn. In the first part of the chapter (4.2, 4.3) I focus on "voice." 4.2 recalls general thoughts about casting others' voices in the two masterpieces, and about the authors' strategies to let their own voice emerge. Then, a few textual analyses (4.3) devote attention to particles and particle combinations that mark voice. τοι and γε in authorial statements are the core part of this analysis, together with ἦ μήν in indirect speech.

§13. In the second part (4.4) I introduce stance, the other core idea of the chapter, and apply its main features to study the language of Herodotus and Thucydides. I also explain why I adopt this framework instead of "focalization," and I add considerations about the stance of readers and the issue of Herodotean irony.

§14. The third part (4.5 to 4.9) includes analyses of multiple passages where particles play a role in marking explicit or implicit expressions of stance. In particular, I attempt to disentangle the complexity underlying several uses of δή in both authors (4.5, 4.6), in connection to people's sense of certainty. Further sections relate δῆθεν (4.7) and ἤδη (4.8) to stancetaking, through their links with δή. Finally (4.9), I argue that the use of ἄρα in the two *Histories* only partially relates to stance.

4.2 Tracking Voice

§15. As I said in §5, I take voice as a superordinate concept. Voice covers the representation of speech and thought in all its possible variants. Before discussing the role of particles in tracking someone's voice, let us recall first labels that are commonly used for the main variants, and then general considerations by recent scholarship on the representation of speech and thought in Herodotus and Thucydides.

§16. According to standard accounts, modern fiction employs "direct," "indirect," and "free indirect" ways to encode someone's speech and thought.[11] Direct forms are signaled by quotation marks; reporting clauses may precede as well ("she said," "she thought"). Direct thought differs from direct speech in that the reported words are not meant to represent words uttered aloud. Besides the lack of quotation marks, what makes speech and thought indirect is the occurrence of reporting clauses (this time explicitly present), and of backshift forms that replace the character's perspective with the narrator's (for example, from "Do I have to come now?" to "she wondered if she had to go at that very moment"). Free indirect forms, conversely, lack quotation marks and reporting clauses, and may show no backshifting.[12]

§17. Pascal (1977:8-9) sees "free indirect style" (after the original label "style indirect libre" in Bally 1912) as a hybrid form: it includes a mix of linguistic features that relate to the character as well as the narrator. An example is "He stopped. Was that the car he had seen here yesterday?" (Pascal 1977:8), where the question is formulated in such a way that it captures the immediacy usually associated with direct discourse, but at the same time retains the narrator's standpoint.

§18. Sanford and Emmott (2012:189) recall the two main readings of this hybrid status. On the one hand free indirect discourse can be interpreted as a variety of "single voice" (that is, the narrator's); on the other, it can be interpreted as a manifestation of "dual voice," that is, the mingling of the character's with the narrator's.[13] The "single/dual" debate is central to the topics of this chapter. I will consider indirect speech and

11 There are numerous variants in terminology and definitions in the scholarship. For example, Chafe (1994:247) distinguishes the following forms of represented speech and thought: "direct—verbatim indirect—indirect—elaborated referred-to—simple referred to." In landmark works on free indirect discourse (e.g. Banfield 1982 and Fludernik 1993) "discourse" covers both speech and thought. However, "indirect discourse" is not useful for Classical Greek historiography: while instances of free indirect thought may be identified or argued for, indirect speech is never free. The reconstruction of speeches in Herodotus and Thucydides had to meet specific genre expectations; for example, they are mostly public speeches, and in dialogic contexts short turns are avoided. In other words, direct speech in this genre does not encompass every kind of voiced utterance, but only those that are verisimilar enough in the local context, and instrumental to the accounts.

12 Sanford and Emmott specify that backshift is not always used. An example of partially "unbackshifted form" is the second sentence in the following excerpt: "She felt a little trembly in her chin and cheeks. What the hell was this?" (from T. Harris 1989, *The Silence of the Lambs*, London, p. 373; quoted after Sanford and Emmott 2012:188). "This" lends itself to both "backshifted" and "unbackshifted" interpretations, depending on the extent and the symbolic value of the proximity indicated by the pronoun. Fludernik 1993 discusses features of free indirect discourse extensively.

13 Pascal 1977 and Banfield 1982 are foundational works supporting the "dual voice" and the "single voice" interpretation respectively. The developments of the debate over the past decades exceed the purposes of this chapter. From a cognitive perspective, the notion of voice has been criticized (see especially Vandelanotte 2009:245-251). From the point of view of empirical studies on the "dual/single" ambiguity, Sanford and Emmott consider the current state still inconclusive (2012:189).

indirect thought "dual voice" devices. Some particles, in fact, seem to be used polyphonically, to mark the interplay between two voices.[14]

4.2.1 Speech and thought: A figured stage of voices

§19. Within classics, recent scholarship has had much to say about direct speech, indirect speech and thought, and explicit and implicit authorial statements in Herodotus and Thucydides. In this and the next subsections I bring the research done in classics in dialogue with the stylistic analyses that have been performed on modern texts.

§20. Dewald 1999 focuses on the "figured stage" that the initial narratives of the two *Histories* display by delving into the management of voices. In her view the historiographical discourse of both Herodotus and Thucydides is dialogic (Dewald 1999:247), but the two authors incorporate voices in different ways. From the beginning Herodotus reports the λόγοι of others and gives voice to their sources, in order to show how information has accumulated over time, and to warn his audience that accounts may be self-interested. The first chapters in Thucydides, conversely, focus on general processes that override individuality. It is not until later that Thucydides voices, with particular emphasis, the statements, fears, and thoughts of key persons and key groups, which he does as a way to embody political strategies and human tendencies.

§21. Dewald further finds that while Herodotus plays the role of the one who "gets told things and evaluates them from a distance" (1999:248), Thucydides provides an internal focus for political views that determine decisions and shape the world he wants to account for. Therefore in Thucydides the distance between author and character may collapse, which, as we will see, can be seen especially in the representation of thoughts.

§22. One of the devices employed to represent others' voices is direct speech, which can perform a number of historiographical functions in the two authors.[15] Speeches represent the most straightforward manifestation of someone's personality and opinion "there and then,"[16] whether they reconstruct the original words or are largely invented by the author.[17] As Tompkins states, Thucydidean speeches show "characters' discursive

14 Also the debate about polyphony developed considerably. For example, Nølke 2013 provides a thorough overview of French studies in linguistic polyphony (Bally, Genette, Ducrot, Anscombre), and proposes *ScaPoLine* ("la théorie SCAndinave de la POLyphonie LINguistiquE"), a new theory of polyphony that challenges the idea of the uniqueness of the speaking subject.

15 Hohti 1976, for example, divides Herodotus' speeches into "causative" and "non-causative" functions. Scardino 2012:75-84 analyzes the dramatic functions of indirect speeches in both authors.

16 Grethlein (2013b:99) sees speeches as "unmediated access to the past."

17 On the issue of authenticity of speeches in Thucydides, see in particular Hornblower 1987:45-72 and Rood 1998:46-48. Various aspects of Thucydidean speeches are discussed e.g. in De Romilly 1956, Hunter 1973, Stadter ed. 1973; Cogan 1981; Morrison 2006a; Scardino 2007:453-701; Pelling 2009. Morrison 1994 illustrates Thucydides' tendency to treat groups of citizens as analogous to individuals in terms of speech deliveries. The multiple meanings of speeches in Herodotus are

choices" that "reflect different styles of thought" (2013:463).[18] However, as several scholars point out, through the voice of others both historians manage to convey their own views about the complexity of certain situations, or else to mark aspects of a situation that deserve closer attention from the reader. Therefore, to the extent that direct speeches (or parts of them) represent implicit tokens of the authorial voice, they instantiate the "dual voice" modality. After all, access to the voice of each character or group comes from the voice of the author. What matters in terms of particle use in direct speech, as we shall see, is that particles can help implicitly stress either the author's disalignment with the speaking character's point of view, or his alignment with that character.

§23. Indirect speech is a more explicit "hybrid form."[19] The language employed may reflect different degrees of indirectness, from tenses, moods and pronouns that create the effect of direct speech, to backshifted forms and especially infinitive constructions, which underscore the distance from the reported voice.[20] The level of detail may vary as well: indirect speech is a "versatile mode of speech reporting" (Coulmas ed. 1986:5), which can range from faithful adaptations to summarizing paraphrases. Finally, and more crucially, using indirect speech allows the author to blur the boundaries between the thoughts of characters and his own thoughts.[21]

§24. Like indirect speech, which in both *Histories* is regularly introduced by reporting clauses, indirect thoughts of characters are regularly introduced by verbs of thinking, considering, pondering, etc.[22] The linguistic features included in the clauses attached to these verbs are of particular interest to me, as they can be securely attributed to the representation of others' thoughts—and therefore to the representation of the imagined voice potentially uttering them. In general, in my analyses I will assume that verbs denoting thinking and the like signal indirect thoughts just as reporting clauses signal indirect speech.

---

discussed e.g. in Solmsen 1943 and 1944; Waters 1966; Hohti 1976; Lang 1984b:18-36; Pelling 2006; De Bakker 2007; Schellenberg 2009.

18 Pavlou (2013:432-433) argues that even preambles to speeches (which she calls "attributive discourse") shed light on Thucydides' stance about the speech he is about to report.

19 Scardino 2012:69. Scardino 2012 discusses the linguistic, argumentative, and rhetorical characteristics of indirect speech in the two authors.

20 On the latter point see in particular Cooper 1974:76 on "intrusive infinitives" in Herodotus. Wakker (1997b:217-227) extensively analyses linguistic features that are used in indirect speech in both authors. They include inifinitive constructions, oblique optatives, and deictic shifts. The author makes it clear that in reported speech the wording is responsibility of the reporter, whereas the content or thinking expressed is to be attributed to the reported speaker (1997b:220). She concludes that there is a "sledding scale" between direct and indirect speech, "with at the one end minimal integration of the words reported into the matrix construction (i.e. "direct specch") and at the other end constructions in which the words reported are entirely nominalized, sometimes merely summarizing the speech reported."

21 On this point see especially the analysis of Thucydidean passages by Debnar 2013. See also below 4.6.3.

22 Lang 1995 collects a remarkable number of participles fulfilling this role in Thucydides.

§25. While the two historians do not seem to me to use free indirect speech (unlike modern fiction writers), they do employ the device of free indirect thought, the embedding of characters' considerations, descriptions, assessments in third-person narrative without a specific linguistic signal (such as "he thought").[23] In other words, the change of source is not necessarily marked by reporting clauses or participles. This is the difference in form from indirect thought. The features that become relevant in order to detect free indirect thought are pronouns, tense, and particles just as in the case of indirect thought.[24] In her discussion of "free indirect speech" in Herodotus and Thucydides, Wakker (1997b:224-227) also flags μέλλειν and indirect uses of reflexive pronouns to report the thoughts or words (she does not distinguish) of characters. In terms of voice, the "free" component does not change the fact that we can still "hear" the voice potentially uttering those indirect thoughts—especially if certain particles co-occur.

4.2.2 Authorial statements

§26. The most direct way for Herodotus and Thucydides to let their voice come to the fore is by inserting authorial statements explicitly. Such statements range from programmatic statements, where the two authors position themselves with respect to their predecessors or genre expectations, to *ad hoc* narratorial comments. In the latter case the speaking "I" evaluates beliefs or decisions, and aligns or, more typically, disaligns with sources of information or political exponents; in this sense, the author's voice expresses the author's stance.[25] The overt presence of the speaking "I" emerges more often in Herodotus than in Thucydides.[26] This is consistent with Thucydides' preference for using covert means to give voice to himself, by embedding it within his characters' thoughts.[27]

§27. Implicit authorial statements are utterances that, notwithstanding the absence of an explicit "I"-marker, are easily attributable to the author as the only possible source, due to their omniscient character. For example, De Jong (2004a:106) regards Herodotean prolepses about the end of a character's success (e.g. Herodotus 7.213 about Ephialtes) as implicit authorial statements. The author's evaluation of Ephialtes' lack of success is expressed in terms of omniscient knowledge about his future. In Thucydides, there is a

23 An example in English is given above, §17.

24 See §9 above, the list of linguistic features that help identifying a shift in the source of voice or thought.

25 De Bakker 2013 analyzes Thucydides' infrequent judgments about individual characters, and the function that these judgments fulfill.

26 While Herodotus' text abounds in "I" statements (with the variant of some "we," on which see in particular Dewald 2002), the explicit authorial statements by Thucydides are countable. See the list in Rood 2004:118, see also Lang et al. 2011:129-138. On Herodotus as "overt narrator," see in particular De Jong 2004a:102-105.

27 "The relative paucity of Thucydides' first-person appearances has led to the suspicion that Thucydides manipulates his narratorial stance so as to impose his judgment on narratees without their being aware of it" (Rood 2004:118, with a reference to Loraux 1986:149).

section where Pericles' advice to the Athenians is reported: as they approach war they should be confident in their resources and the income they receive from their allies. An inserted γάρ clause provides an external ("unframed") piece of information about the annual amount of money the Athenians would gather from the allies.[28] This information cannot be part of Pericles' advice; as Hornblower (1994:137) comments, "the focalizer is really Thucydides himself."

§28. However, especially in Thucydides the ways in which the authorial stance is conveyed in the two *Histories* exceed the modalities listed so far. Scholars find authorial stance implicitly revealed through different discourse strategies, ranging from local devices, such as the use of vicarious voices,[29] to global or large-scale devices, such as manipulation of time and space in narration, or artful juxtaposition of accounts across large blocks of text.[30] In the case of large-scale devices there is no inner voice to be recognized, as the author's stance is expressed through global strategies rather than in local instantiations (that is, actual identifiable words).

§29. The discussion outlined in the last subsections (4.2.1 and 4.2.2) invite a few conclusive considerations. The speech and thought of the people is a significant subject of interpretation in literary criticism. Also, Dewald's remarks connect the management of voices to the expression of points of view, epistemic and emotional states, and rational judgments. In other words, voice is presumed to be a vehicle for expressing stance. This is why in scholarship the analysis of voices mingles with the analysis of stance. Furthermore, the spots for the author's voice in the two *Histories* coincide with the moments in which the authors take stance. Nothwithstanding these convergences, it is important to keep in mind that tracking voice does not conceptually coincide with tracking stance. The next section shows that particles can help detect somone's voice, regardless of whether the voice in question is used to take stance about something or not.

[28] On "unframed discourse" see in particular II.4.2, with reference to γάρ.

[29] I have already discussed this strategy in the section on direct speech (see above, §22). Classical examples of vicarious voices are Solon for Herodotus, and Pericles for Thucydides; see e.g. Shapiro's study (1996) on Solon and Herodotus, and Edmunds (1975:7-88 and 209-212) on Pericles and Thucydides. Even though in both cases the vicarious voices should not be straightforwardly mapped onto those of the authors, it has been argued that the ideologies of the characters resonate significantly with the authors'. On Pericles' voice, for instance, Dewald comments: "Pericles is assigned the only focalized voice within the narrative that in force and scope resembles that of the Thucydides-narrator himself" (1999:243).

[30] Immerwahr 1966 was one of the first works highlighting the significance of narrative patterns as revealing of Herodotus' *Weltanschauung*. More recently, Rood 1998 examines Thucydides' use of narrative designs (including pace, displacements, and omissions) to convey specific views about history.

4.3 The Contribution of Particles to Marking Voice

§30. Particles are borderline words, hugging the fence between explicit and implicit communication. Their communicative meaning often relies more on what they imply than on what they directly say.[31] In a number of cases their most direct equivalent in English seems to be a certain intonation or gesture. As with intonation and gestures, their presence or absence makes a difference: the use of particles in certain contexts, and the avoidance of particles in other contexts, can reflect linguistic and literary habits that are worth examining.

§31. I expect the distribution of particles in narrative sections of Herodotus and Thucydides to be more interesting than their distribution in direct speech: narrative sections indeed feature a complex range of ways in which multiple voices and thoughts are represented. This is why in the following paragraphs I discuss a few particles and particle combinations that occur outside of direct speech while direct speech is their usual environment.

4.3.1 ἦ μήν in indirect speech

§32. The works of Scardino (2007; 2012) and De Bakker (2007) have shown that indirect speech in both *Histories* varies greatly depending on the author's intentions.[32] Despite the variation, a few features are generally constant: the occurrence of reporting clauses preceding indirect speech, and of reporting strategies within the speeches themselves, such as infinitive constructions.[33]

§33. ἦ μήν is one of the features that break the rules of backshift. As it is a formulaic combination that in Classical Greek occurs almost exclusively at the beginning of oaths, we would expect it to occur in direct speech. However, in Thucydides we find ἦ μήν in indirect speech as well, eight times.[34] Here is an example:

31 See I.1 §16.

32 See also above §23.

33 About backshift in general, see above §16.

34 Thucydides 4.88.1; 4.118.1; 5.38.1; 5.50.1; 6.72.5; 8.33.1; 8.75.2; 8.81.3. The only ἦ μήν in direct speech is in Thucydides 4.86.1. ἦ in Thucydides appears in direct speech in other combinations (5.100.1 ἦ που ἄρα; 1.142.3 ἦ που δή; 6.37.2 ἦ που γε δή), with the remarkable exception of ἦ που δή at 8.27.3, which is part of a reported speech by Phrinichus. Scardino (2012:86) observes that particles in indirect speech "display the emotional tension of the speaker." In Herodotus we find overall eight instances of ἦ μέν. Four of them appear at the beginning of reported oaths (3.74.2; 3.133.2; 4.154.3; 6.74.1—the latter in Hude's edition). One more instance is in an oath performed live by the queen of the Messagetae Tomyris at 1.212.3. The only other instance in direct speech concerns the terms of a pledge that Leotychides asks Hegesistratus to undertake (9.91.2). The remaining two instances are found at the start of a reported pledge by Babylonian men guaranteeing their intention to marry girls after buying them (1.196.3), and in the report of a speech by Hippias calling upon the same gods that Socles had invoked, assuring them that ἦ μήν the Corinthians would wish to have the Pisistratidae back (5.93.1). Wakker (1997b:216) quotes the

(t1)

οἱ δὲ Ἀκάνθιοι, πολλῶν λεχθέντων πρότερον ἐπ' ἀμφότερα, κρύφα διαψηφισάμενοι, διά τε τὸ ἐπαγωγὰ εἰπεῖν τὸν Βρασίδαν καὶ περὶ τοῦ καρποῦ φόβῳ ἔγνωσαν οἱ πλείους ἀφίστασθαι Ἀθηναίων, καὶ πιστώσαντες αὐτὸν τοῖς ὅρκοις οὓς τὰ τέλη τῶν Λακεδαιμονίων ὀμόσαντα αὐτὸν ἐξέπεμψαν, ἦ μὴν ἔσεσθαι ξυμμάχους αὐτονόμους οὓς ἂν προσαγάγηται, οὕτω δέχονται τὸν στρατόν.

Thucydides 4.88.1

The Acanthians debated long, with much said on either side, and then took a secret vote. Influenced both by the seduction of Brasidas' offer and by fear for their crop, they decided by a majority to secede from Athens. They made Brasidas pledge fidelity to the oaths sworn by the Spartan authorities when they sent him out, guaranteeing the autonomy of any people he brought over as allies, and with that pledge given they admitted his army. (tr. Hammond)

This is the only occurrence of ἦ μήν in indirect speech where Thucydides also records the original words, previously spoken by Brasidas during his speech to the Acanthians: αὐτός τε οὐκ ἐπὶ κακῷ, ἐπ' ἐλευθερώσει δὲ τῶν Ἑλλήνων παρελήλυθα, ὅρκοις τε Λακεδαιμονίων καταλαβὼν τὰ τέλη τοῖς μεγίστοις ἦ μὴν οὓς ἂν ἔγωγε προσαγάγωμαι ξυμμάχους ἔσεσθαι αὐτονόμους, ... (4.86.1). Brasidas' original words ἦ μὴν οὓς ἂν ἔγωγε προσαγάγωμαι ξυμμάχους ἔσεσθαι αὐτονόμους become ἦ μὴν ἔσεσθαι ξυμμάχους αὐτονόμους οὓς ἂν προσαγάγηται in a quite faithful repetition at the moment of the Acanthians' decision. ἦ μήν suggests that the Acanthians fully re-perform, rather than simply repeat or recall, the content of the oath. Through this touch of vividness Thucydides prepares the way for the judgment he later makes on the general attitude of the Acanthians (4.108.4), that they were moved by "blind wishes" rather than "sound forethought" to follow Brasidas.[35] In a recent article on oaths in the two historians, Lateiner (2012:157) records that Thucydides cites far more oaths than Herodotus (269 to 58), as he "has a penchant for narrating artfully evaded personal agreements, the pathology of personal oath."

Hippias example together with 1.212.3 (direct speech), and simply observes that ἦ μέν in indirect discourse is unproblematic. II.3.2.3 discusses ἦ at beginnings of embedded narratives in Homer; in these cases ἦ shares with the historiographical examples the function of marking the start of a performance.

35 Debnar 2001:189. Besides mentioning the eight instances of ἦ μήν in indirect speech, George (2009:162) remarks that μήν alone in Thucydides occurs six times in indirect speech, and five times passages that he labels "diaphonic" (1.3.3; 6.55.3, 2.97.6; 3.82.6; 7.75.6). About the latter, the scholar comments (2009:162) that μήν contributes to make the historian's observations "more explicitly personal."

4.3.2 τοι in Herodotus, in and beyond direct speech

§34. τοι occurs almost exclusively in direct speech, and *grosso modo* only in Herodotus.[36] The vast majority of them are datives of the second person pronoun, just as in Homer, and the act position can greatly vary. In nine cases τοι does not work as a second person pronoun. These instances always occur in act-peninitial position, together with other particles, and with εἰ or ἤν. Interestingly, all the co-texts and contexts suggest that the host discourse acts are part of persuasive assertions; the speakers' intent while uttering τοι seems to be to persuade their dialogic partners about something.[37] My general conclusion about τοι in Herodotus and Thucydides is that, whether it grammatically works as a "you" form or as a discourse particle, it retains a strong interactional connotation, in that it links the host act to an appeal to the dialogic partner ("I tell you" is one of the translations proposed[38]).

§35. One of the reasons why τοι occurs more often in Herodotean than in Thucydidean speeches may be that speeches in Herodotus are more dialogic. That is to say, they are arranged in dialogic sets, namely speeches that constitute dialogic turns, more than in Thucydides;[39] additionally, they involve more individuals talking to individuals, rather than collectives talking to collectives as in Thucydides.[40]

36 The *TLG* online records 185 occurrences for Herodotus (0.09% of total words), against 4 in Thucydides. Three Thucydidean instances occur in direct speech (by Pericles at 2.41.4; by Cleon at 3.40.4; by Nicias at 7.77.2), and one in a quotation from the *Homeric Hymn to Apollo* (3.104.4). On τοι in general, see, e.g. Denniston 1950:537; Ruijgh 1971:197-198; Sicking 1993:64; Wakker 1994:360-362; Wakker 1995:254-255. Wakker (1997b:228) states that τοι "expresses straighaway the speaker's attitude."

37 This finding aligns with the observations on the use of τοι in persuasive speeches in tragedy; see III.4.5.1. In Herodotus, at 3.3.3 (τοιγάρ τοι, ὦ μῆτερ, ...) the ten-year-old Cambyses assures his mother that he will turn Egypt upside down. At 3.29.2 (ἀτάρ τοι ὑμεῖς γε ...) adult Cambyses rebukes the Apis-priests; they cannot make a fool of him. At 3.145.3 (Ἀλλ' εἴ τοι σύ σφεας καταρρώδηκας) the crazy brother of Maeandrius wants to persuade Maeandrius to give him command of the soldiers if he (Maeandrius) is afraid of the Persians. At 5.39.2 (Εἴ τοι σὺ σεωυτοῦ μὴ προορᾷς) the Ephors strongly invite the former king of Sparta Anaxandrides to marry a woman that can bear him children, even if he does not take care of himself. At 8.57.2 the Athenian Mnesiphilus persuades Themistocles not to withdraw the fleet to the Isthmus but to remain in Salamis (Οὔ τοι ἄρα, ἢν ἀπάρωσι τὰς νέας ἀπὸ Σαλαμῖνος, περὶ οὐδεμιῆς ἔτι πατρίδος ναυμαχήσεις; "No; as a matter of fact, if they will withdraw the ships from Salamis, you will have a sea battle that is not in favour of a unified country"). On ἄρα and stance in Thucydides, see below §§171-172. Finally, at 8.65.5, after hearing Dicaeus' interpretation of the cloud of dust, Demaratus summons Dicaeus to keep silent, as a word on that by the Persian king would cost his head (Ἢν γάρ τοι ἐς βασιλέα ἀνενειχθῇ τὰ ἔπεα ταῦτα, ἀποβαλέεις τὴν κεφαλήν). The three remaining instances, Herodotus 2.120.3, 3.33.1, and 9.38.1 will be commented on below in §37 (with n44), as they do not occur in direct speech.

38 See Stephens 1837:49-50; Bäumlein 1861:236-239; Denniston 1950:537-542.

39 Lang 1984:21-36 and 100-130 for the identification of dialogues that Herodotus articulates in simpler to complex sets (pairs to decahexads).

40 See e.g. Lang 1984b:134-135 for individuals in Herodotus, and Morrison 1994 for collectives in Thucydides.

§36. In line with the dialogic nature of the single particle τοι, several particle combinations involving τοι in Herodotus' and Thucydides' works tend to occur in direct speeches. The only τοιγάρτοι (Thucydides 6.38.3) and two out of three τοιγάρ in Herodotus (3.3.3 and 8.114.2) are in direct speech; all five instances of τοίνυν in Thucydides, and 16 of 22 instances in Herodotus are in direct speech;[41] the same holds for 22 of 24 instances of καίτοι in Thucydides, and for 8 of 18 in Herodotus; all three instances of ἤτοι in Thucydides, and four of seven in Herodotus, are in direct speech.[42] Thus, a dialogic component in the use of τοι seems to affect the use of ἤτοι, τοίνυν, καίτοι (in Thucydides), and τοιγάρ. The sense of appeal to the dialogic partner in these combinations should complement the standard accounts of their function in the two *Histories*, which pay attention just to the disjunctive (ἤτοι) and the contrastive (καίτοι) relations between the constituents they link. By analogy, the tendency of μέντοι to be used much more frequently in non-direct speech (115 in non-direct speech vs. 28 in direct speech, as for Herodotus, and 69 vs. 11 in Thucydides) should invite scholars to explore the potential dialogism of the third-person utterances hosting μέντοι besides the concessive contribution of the particle (a cluster, in fact).[43]

§37. Let us now turn to τοι occurring in Herodotus' narrative sections, a fact which is unexpected in view of the particle's highly dialogic function. There are not many instances of this—three to be precise. For two of them both Legrand (*TLG* online) and Hude (*OCT*) give the same manuscript reading.[44] In 2.120.3, while expressing alignment with the Egyptian account about Helen, Herodotus argues the following: even if initially the Trojans wanted to risk their life to keep Helen (εἰ δέ τοι καὶ ἐν τοῖσι πρώτοισι χρόνοισι ταῦτα ἐγίνωσκον), in the end the disasters of war would have made them give her back to the Achaeans. In 3.33.1, while commenting on Cambyses' madness, the author argues that it would not be improbable that a physical illness would affect one's brain (οὔ νύν τοι ἀεικὲς οὐδὲν ἦν τοῦ σώματος νοῦσον μεγάλην νοσέοντος μηδὲ τὰς φρένας ὑγιαίνειν). In both contexts Herodotus provides persuasive arguments to defend other arguments

41 One of the Thucydidean instances is discussed below (§61 (t12)). The remaining instances are in Thucydides 3.45.4; 5.87.1; 5.89.1; 8.53.3. 6 of the Herodotean tokens occur in second position at the very beginning of the turn, which confirms the relevance of τοίνυν to dialogic arguments.

42 Two more ἤτοι occur in indirect speech (Herodotus 8.108.3 and 1.137.2).

43 E.g. George (2009:161) stresses that in Plato μέντοι quite often relates to dialogic, or at least diaphonic, contexts. See below n49 about "diaphony."

44 The third τοι not belonging to characters' direct speech is philologically controversial. At 9.38.1 Legrand reads Ὁ μέν τοι θάνατος ὁ Ἡγησιστράτου ὕστερον ἐγένετο τῶν Πλαταιικῶν ("The death of Hegesistratus, however, came later, after the events of Plataea"); manuscripts A, B, C, P, T, M, p and P and a give μέντοι. Hude, followed by Corcella (in Asheri et al. 2006:62), as well as Rosén (1989), conversely, read μέν νυν in line with manuscript d. In my view μέντοι (instead of μέν τοι, whose only attested occurrence in Herodotus is in direct speech, at 3.155.4) is as defensible as μέν νυν.

he has heard. It is as if by means of τοι he marks a contact (potential or real) with his audience, as he is engaged in the process of reasoning things through.[45]

§38. Herodotus, moreover, uses τοίνυν four times and καίτοι twice in accounts where the authorial "I" is explicitly present. At 1.57.3 τοίνυν occurs in a passage that delineates the contacts between Pelasgians and Athenians (1.57-58), which includes the first-person statements οὐκ ἔχω ἀτρεκέως εἰπεῖν (1.57.1), and ὡς ἐμοὶ καταφαίνεται εἶναι + ἔμοιγε δοκέει (1.58). At 2.15.2 τοίνυν not only appears a few words after ἐμοὶ δοκέει, but it starts a rare authorial question, which has a strong dialogic potential ("If, then, they [the Egyptians] once had no place to live in, why did they make such a business of the theory that they are the oldest race in the world?" [De Sélincourt and Marincola]). Also at 2.22.4 τοίνυν appears in an argument marked by an authorial question ("[If the Nile comes from melting snow] as it flows ... from a very hot into a cooler climate, how could it possibly originate in snow?")—see the "I" markers ἔγωγε οἶδα, and δοκέω (2.23). At 7.139 τοίνυν occurs in a famous argument that Herodotus makes, acknowledging the merits of Athens in the Persian war; the argument starts with a strong "I" deixis (see ἐξέργομαι γνώμην; μοι φαίνεται; οὐκ ἐπισχήσω). At 4.77.1 καίτοι introduces an alternative account introduced by "I (Herodotus) heard" (ἤκουσα); at 8.112.3 καίτοι continues Herodotus' insights on the people forced to give money to Themistocles, and is preceded by οὐχ ἔχω εἰπεῖν and δοκέω (8.112.2).[46]

§39. To recap, we have seen thus far that τοι has a dialogic nature in general; when it appears in authorial statements, τοι suggests a potential dialogic interaction with an imaginary (or real) audience.[47] Other explicit "I" markers (first person verbs and first person pronouns, both singular and plural[48]), which draw attention to the author's presence, also show signs of making possible appeals to the audience. The point of the connection is the emergence of the "I" that communicates the accounts, and therefore

45 II.5 §70 comments on a Homeric occurrence of τοι in narrator text (*Iliad* 10.316) that suggests a contact with the audience. The appeal to the audience and its understanding is what marks the combination καὶ γάρ τοι in Cooper's view (1998:1355).

46 μέντοι in Herodotus accompanies explicit authorial statements eleven times out of 115 total occurrences: see 1.139; 1.172; 2.63; 2.130; 4.46; 4.81; 4.155; 6.124; 8.8; 8.87; 8.128. In Thucydides this happens twice (3.113.6 μέντοι οἶδα; 8.87.4 ἐμοὶ μέντοι δοκεῖ).

47 De Jong (2004a:111) includes καίτοι and μέντοι in the list of devices that Herodotus uses to establish or underline a connection with the narratees.

48 First person pronouns often turn out to be syntactically redundant. On unnecessary (and therefore marked) nominatives, see II.2 §68.

signals the voice of the author.[49] Herodotus is more generous than Thucydides in potential appeals to the audience as well as in the use of overt "I" deixis.[50]

4.3.3 γε in authorial statements

§40. The relation between the explicit presence of the author and the particle γε is what I am going to discuss next. In general, γε's function is to reflect the speaker's personal involvement by emphasizing a certain element of the discourse. The emphasis provided by γε is comparable to English prosodic prominence attached to phrases with special informational status.[51] Therefore it causes no surprise to see that in both *Histories* γε appears more often times in direct speech than in the main narrative.[52] When it occurs in the main narrative, and in particular in explicitly authorial utterances, γε serves a

49 Kroon (1995:111-115) calls "diaphony" the ability of monological discourse to display "features of a communicative interaction, without having all formal characteristics of a dialogical discourse type" (112). She mentions first and second person pronouns, and metadiscursive expressions such as "I will tell you," "I think," "as you know" among the features that convey diaphony. On the authorial voice that conveys authorial stance, and on the relevance of μοι δοκεῖ to the stance triangle, see below 4.5.4; 4.6.2; §§62-63.

50 Self-referential expressions by Herodotus include οὐκ ἔχω εἰπεῖν (2.130.2; 6.124.2; οὐ μέντοι ἔχω γε εἰπεῖν at 8.87.3); ἡμεῖς ἴδμεν (4.46.2); γνώμη μοι ἀποδεδέχθω (8.8.3); ἀπέφαινόν μοι ἐς ὄψιν (4.81.4); ἀναβήσομαι (4.82.); δῆλά μοι ὧν γέγονε (2.146.2); δηλώσω (4.81.4); ἐγώ δ'ἔχω περὶ αὐτῶν γνώμην τήνδε (2.56.1); and the quite common ἐμοὶ δοκέει(ν), with slight variants: ἐμοὶ δοκέει(ν), 1.131.1; 2.4.1; 2.70.1; 2.77.3; 2.120.5; 2.124.4; 2.137.5; 3.5.1; 3.13.4; 3.45.3; 4.50.2; 4.87.2; 4.167.3; 6.95.2; 7.168.3; 8.30.2; 8.66.1; 9.113.2; μοι δοκέει, 1.152.2; 2.24.1; 2.49.3; 2.103.1; 3.38.5; 3.137.5; ἔμοιγε δοκέει(ν), 1.58.1; 2.53.3; δοκέει(ν) ἐμοί, 1.172.1; 2.56.1; 3.135.3; 5.67.1; 5.69.1; 6.30.1; 7.229.2; 8.22.3; 8.103.1; δοκέει μοι, 2.49.1; 2.98.2; δοκέει(ν) δέ μοι, 2.25.3; 2.42.5; 2.109.3; 2.116.1; 4.29.1; 4.198.1; 7.3.4; 7.173.4; 8.63.1; δοκέει δ'ἔμοιγε, 4.189.3; ἐμοὶ δὲ δοκέει, 6.84.3; ἐγὼ δοκέω, 4.155.1; ὡς ἐγὼ δοκέω, 2.63.3. This list does not include the instances uttered by characters. See above n26 for more on the disparity between authorial "I" statements in Herodotus and in Thucydides.

51 See II.5 §33-35; III.2 §§60-61; III.5 §§46-47; below §44 and n162. Powell (1938:65) records a few instances of καί ... γε in Herodotus, which he defines "climactic" (see 2.83.1; 2.111.4; 2.146.2; 2.155.1; 5.118.2; 6.56; 7.176.3); both particles mark a piece of information that is more salient than the preceding ones. For further discussion of γε in the *Histories* see IV.5 (§§20; 34; 62; 67-68; 73; 110). On γε as making the character on the stage more present as communicator, see III.2.2.5. On ὅ γε in Homer, see II.5.3.2.

52 This happens in 111 of 232 total occurrences of γε and γ' in Herodotus, and in 89 of 175 in Thucydides where either "I" or "you" markers co-occur with γε within three *TLG* lines. Several times γε in direct speech seems to contribute to strong emotional involvement, e.g. the expression of one's anger, as III.5 demonstrates about tragedy and comedy (see III.5.4.1, and §71). A clear example of this is at Herodotus 3.29.2, where Cambyses, furious at Apis' priests, strikes Apis' thigh and says: Ἄξιος μέν [γε] Αἰγυπτίων οὗτός γε ὁ θεός· ἀτάρ τοι ὑμεῖς γε οὐ χαίροντες γέλωτα ἐμὲ θήσεσθε. "That is a god worthy of the Egyptians. But for you, you shall suffer for making me your laughing-stock" (tr. Godley). A parallel example in Thucydides is a statement uttered by Gylippus and the Syracusan generals at 7.68.2 (whose first part I already commented at IV.2 §120 (t65) because of καί): ὡς δὲ ἐχθροὶ καὶ ἔχθιστοι, πάντες ἴστε, οἵ γε ἐπὶ τὴν ἡμετέραν ἦλθον δουλωσόμενοι: "It will be clear to all of you that the Athenians are not only enemies but the worst of enemies. They came against our country to enslave it."

parallel function, marking the author's voice and conveying a sense of his personal involvement in the statement being made. This is true even if γε's scope is limited to a noun phrase; the main thing to keep in mind is that the emphasis *per se* brings the author's presence to the foreground.

§41. The majority of occurrences is found in explicit authorial statements by Herodotus.[53] Let us focus here on an example of γε in an implicit authorial assertion:

(t2)

Τιμῶσι δὲ ἐκ πάντων τοὺς ἄγχιστα ἑωυτῶν οἰκέοντας μετά <u>γε</u> ἑωυτούς, δεύτερα δὲ τοὺς δευτέρους, ...

Herodotus 1.134.2

After themselves, of all people they [the Persians] honor those who live nearest them, [then they honor] second the second [people] nearest, ... (tr. AB)

No linguistic evidence confirms that Herodotus-the-historian is the source of this utterance; nevertheless the general and encyclopedic character of the content makes a different source unlikely. The roles of γε in this assertion are the following: γε marks the phrase μετὰ ἑωυτούς as recalling the immediately previous information (about the Persians honoring themselves by rank, in 1.134.1). It also possibly isolates the phrase as a separate discourse act and as a discrete intonation unit (|μετά γε ἑωυτούς |).[54] Finally, it indicates that the speaker narrows down the conditions under which the present claim (i.e. the Persians honor most of all the people closest to them) holds true.[55]

§42. In Thucydides 7 out of 39 (18%) first person authorial statements stress an element of discourse with γε.[56] Let us consider one of them, where γε has scope over an entire move rather than over just a phrase:[57]

[53] See Herodotus 1.49; 1.51.4; 1.60.3; 2.15.2; 2.49.2; 2.122.2; 4.32; 4.59.2; 5.118.2; 6.123.1; 7.139.1; 7.152.3.

[54] On γε being the equivalent of prosodic prominence attached to constituents, see e.g. Riemer 1823:366; Thiersch 1826:192-193; Hartung 1832:365; K. W. Krüger 1842:346; Denniston 1950:115; Humbert 1960:394-395; Menge 1914:245. As for this monograph, see below n162, and II.5 §33-35; III.2 §§60-61; III.4 §64; III.5 §§46-47, §§90-91.

[55] See Wakker 1994:308 "by using γε the speaker demarcates the applicability of his utterance." The "limitative" value of γε is pointed out in much earlier scholarship: see e.g. Hoogeveen 1769:219; Hartung 1832:364-365; Kühner 1835:398.

[56] See Thucydides 1.3.2; 2.54.3 (t3); 3.89.5; 7.86.5 (the famous evaluation of Nicias' undeserved misfortune, including a δή + superlative construction as well); 8.41.2; 8.87.4; 8.97.2.

[57] See e.g. Cauer 1914:74.

(t3)

οἱ γὰρ ἄνθρωποι πρὸς ἃ ἔπασχον τὴν μνήμην ἐποιοῦντο. ἢν δέ <u>γε</u> οἶμαί ποτε ἄλλος πόλεμος καταλάβῃ Δωρικὸς τοῦδε ὕστερος καὶ ξυμβῇ γενέσθαι λιμόν, κατὰ τὸ εἰκὸς οὕτως ᾄσονται.

Thucydides 2.54.3

Men accommodate their memories to their current experience. I imagine that if at some time another "Dorian war" comes after this one, with famine coinciding, the verse will in all likelihood be recited with that meaning. (tr. Hammond)

Thucydides makes a point about human psychology. Because memory is driven by experience, humans adapt verses to fit what they personally undergo; thus, it is probable that they would sing "The Dorian war will bring famine" if they were to undergo famine, as much as they had sung "The Dorian war will bring pestilence" after undergoing pestilence. δέ + γε + οἶμαι in the passage mark the upcoming move (made of four clauses: ἢν ... καταλάβῃ; ξυμβῇ; γενέσθαι λιμόν; ᾄσονται) as an authorial and authoritative supposition. δέ simply marks a discourse boundary after the gnomic sentence; οἶμαι deictically anchors the upcoming move in the voice of the author, and semantically qualifies the move as an opinion. Finally, γε draws attention to the upcoming content of the opinion as something worth remarking, for reasons that are contextually inferable.

§43. Within the account of the plague two more γε besides the one in (t3) accompany observations implicitly attributable by Thucydides (see 2.47.3 οὐ μέντοι τοσοῦτός γε λοιμὸς οὐδὲ φθορὰ οὕτως ἀνθρώπων οὐδαμοῦ ἐμνημονεύετο γενέσθαι, "but nowhere else was there recorded such virulence or so great a loss of life," and 2.49.8 τῶν γε ἀκρωτηρίων ἀντίληψις αὐτοῦ ἐπεσήμαινεν, "[symptoms] appeared when the disease took hold in their [the bodies'] extremities" [tr. Hammond]). In both cases the information stressed by γε is subjectively perceived as remarkable, and therefore indicates the speaker's (i.e. the author's) involvement—epistemic and emotional at the same time. These passages show that the marking of the author's voice, his epistemic and emotional involvement, and the expression of his opinion can coexist.[58] οἶμαι in (t3) makes the act of expressing an opinion explicit. In the tragedies and comedies under discussion in this work, γε is regularly found in acts of stancetaking about something.[59] On the whole, the

[58] Distinctions about these components are blurred especially when the combination γε δή appears (on which see n162).

[59] On γε in acts of stancetaking in drama, accompanied by high emotional arousal or not, see III.4 §§63-64 and III.5.4.2.

stress on some piece of information evokes someone's voice, both in authorial as well as in a character's utterance, and whether or not an act of stancetaking is attached to it.

§44. To sum up: γε in explicit authorial statements reflects the presence of the author as communicator, a human being with ideas and opinions, and puts his voice in the foreground.[60] γε can do the same in passages where the authorial voice is implicit, that is when first person markers are absent but the passage still seems to reflect the author's voice. Furthermore, the link that I see between γε and the speaker's voice is consistent with, and complements well, the numerous accounts in the scholarly literature that see γε as an equivalent of intonational prominence, especially exclamations (see n54). Therefore, its occurrence in indirect speech in Thucydides can be regarded as evoking the oral vividness of speech delivery.[61] Finally, γε marks someone's voice also when the stress on some element of discourse can be read as someone's opinion about something. Opinion and stance introduces us to the next section.

4.4 Tracking Stance

§45. Since someone's voice can be used, reported, echoed, or hinted at in order to convey rational activities such as judging, planning, and clarifying strategic intentions together with less rational activities such as having a certain feeling, and perceiving the surroundings in a certain way, then a more specific term than "voice" is needed. This term is stance. In this section I will draw ideas not just from a general/common meaning of stance, but from a specific study of stance presented by the linguist John Du Bois in 2007.

4.4.1 The stance triangle

§46. Du Bois defines stance as follows:

> (t4)
>
> Stance is a public act by a social actor, achieved dialogically through overt communicative means, of simultaneously evaluating objects, positioning subjects (self and others), and aligning with other subjects, with respect to any salient dimension of the sociocultural field.
>
> Du Bois 2007:163

60 This harmonizes with the findings in III.2 §60 and III.5 §45 about γε in drama, a major difference being that γε in Herodotus and Thucydides is much less frequent than in tragedy and comedy.

61 Thucydides 2.13.1; 4.27.3; 6.72.3; 7.48.4; 8.27.3 (2x). See IV.5 §20 on the passionate tone that Dover assigns to a γε passage in one of Nicias' speeches in book 6.

Stance is considered an act, that is, a dynamic attainment involving people and objects/states of affairs. Such an act is achieved through overt communication: people deliberately convey x about y to someone else, in linguistic, nonlinguistic, or both linguistic and nonlinguistic ways. The general act of taking stance for Du Bois consists of three components: evaluating, positioning, and aligning. Fundamental to structuring the act of stancetaking are the questions whose stance is conveyed, towards which object it is expressed, and whether it aligns or disaligns with others' stance.

§47. The following drawing illustrates the different components of stancetaking, and the dynamic relation between each of them, which Du Bois (2007:164) calls "vectors":

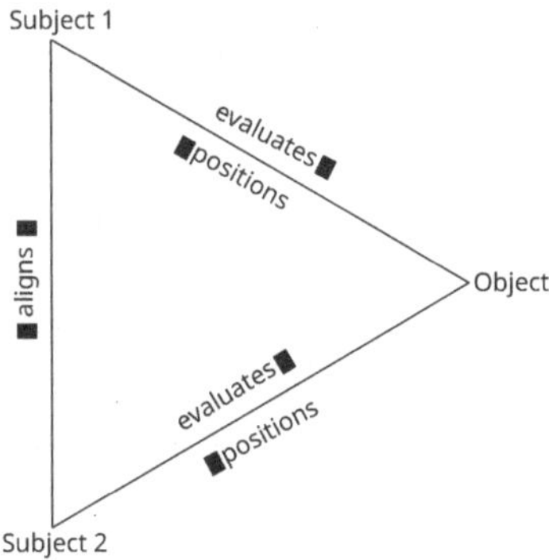

Figure 1: The stance triangle (Du Bois 2007:163)

Subject 1 takes stance by evaluating an object or state of affairs (evaluating vector). The same vector in the opposite direction is that of positioning: given a certain object or state of affairs, Subject 1 positions him- or herself with respect to it. The same bidirectional vectors work when another subject, Subject 2, takes stance about the same object or state of affairs—which may imply evaluating, positioning, or both. This is the second side of the stance triangle. Finally, someone's stance explicitly or implicitly relates to someone else's stance. The vector in this case (third side of the triangle) is a bidirectional relation of alignment (ranging from full alignment to full disalignment) between Subject 1 and Subject 2.

§48. What interests Du Bois and me in particular are the linguistic ways by which stancetaking is realized. Let us consider three utterances that exemplify the linguistic encoding of evaluating, positioning, and aligning. "I like this" instantiates the positioning of Subject 1 (the speaking "I") with respect to the object (the referent of the pronoun "this"). "That's nice" instantiates Subject 1's evaluating of the object identified by means of "that." Finally, "I agree" instantiates the alignment of Subject 1 with somebody else (Subject 2) about some matter (the latter two components remaining implicit).

§49. In his definition Du Bois characterizes these components as co-occurring ("a[n] ... act ... of simultaneously evaluating, ... positioning ... and aligning," see (t4) above). What does this mean? How can a subject simultaneously position herself, evaluate an object, and align with other people? The answer is provided in this next remark:

(t5)

> The stance triangle shows how a stance utterance that specifies only one of the three vectors can allow participants to draw inferences about the others.
>
> Du Bois 2007:164

Du Bois' point is that linguistic expressions of stance have both explicit and implicit aspects, and that receivers of these expressions are able to and do interpret on both levels at once. For example, if at a conference I judge an academic talk positively, and I take stance by explicitly evaluating the talk ("That was a great talk"), I also allow my colleagues to draw inferences about my alignment with the speaker as well as my own position with respect to the contents or the delivery (or both).

§50. In written communication language can be very shaded, as to the vectors of stance, depending on the degree of polysemy or implicitness that is intended or needed. Let us mention an example showing how complex it can be to track stance in language. The sign "*Dem lebendigen Geist*" ("To the lively mind/spirit") above the portal of the "New University" building of the University of Heidelberg can be interpreted as a public act of stance whose explicit linguistic component is just the dative case of "lively mind." The location of the dedication—the entrance of the University building—represents the nonlinguistic component of the meaning(s). The linguistic component has a little history of its own. The social actors who state "To the lively mind" are to be traced back to the 1920s. Later on further social actors change the adjective of the phrase: during the Nazi period the sign turns into "*Dem deutschen Geist*" ("To the German mind"). After the Second World War new actors decide to reinstate the previous dedication. The reinstated "To the lively mind," then, has complex and mainly implicit meanings. The physical and historical context loads the noun phrase with connotations that evoke quite precise political and philosophical opinions (whose ideological contents go beyond the purposes of this chapter), and yet leave them implicit. Only the individuals or groups who share the history of the dedication, its location, and the acknowledgment of its social/political/ideological value, can interpret the noun phrase as a public act of stance evoking specific evaluations, positions, and alignments.

§51. This brings us to the paramount characteristic of Du Bois' concept of stance: its social dimension. Stance is produced and understood within sociocultural frameworks. It indexes subjectivity and intersubjectivity, and it invokes sociocultural values. "[N]o stance stands alone" (Du Bois 2007:172).

4.4.2 Positioning, evaluating, and (dis)aligning in Herodotus and Thucydides

§52. In the case of Herodotus and Thucydides, the three vectors of positioning, evaluating and aligning are delineated within multiple sets of sociocultural frameworks. On the one hand the two *Histories* recreate subjective and intersubjective aspects of the characters' behavior. On the other the works reflect subjective and intersubjective aspects of the two historiographers' attitudes as well.[62] A crucial asymmetry, common to all third-person narration and all literary pieces, results. Internal characters are supposed to express only evaluation, positioning and alignment in relation to objects and subjects that are internal to the chronicles. The two authors, however, can represent not only evaluation, positioning, and alignment between characters, but they can also represent the same components in the vector "author—character(s)" and in the further vectors "author—contemporaries" and "author—predecessors" and "author—audience"—all of them deriving from the general vector "Subject 1—Subject 2" in the original model. These multifarious possibilities invite and enable a great deal of interpretative complexity from readers.[63]

§53. In order to prepare the ground for the analysis of particle use through the lens of stance theory, I will now quote some utterances from Herodotus and Thucydides that I regard as instances of evaluating, positioning, and aligning. In stancetaking, these three sub-acts occur simultaneously; however, I distinguish among the examples to better illustrate Du Bois' point, that in actual utterances one of the three components tends to be more explicit, while the remaining two are implicitly derived. For the sake of clarity I limit this selection to cases where stance is explicitly encoded. In the third part of the chapter I will offer a wider spectrum of instances, considering implicit vectors alongside further instances of explicit vectors.

§54. The purposes of this sampling are two. First, it establishes connections between the theoretical model of the stance triangle and representative linguistic features by means of which the three vectors are delineated in the two *Histories*. Second, it singles out features that directly co-occur with particles (which are further features to be taken into account), and are instrumental to the upcoming analysis of particles in stancetaking.

§55. The examples of features that mark stance in Herodotus and Thucydides start with linguistic markers of positioning, which include a variety of forms. In (t6), from

62 In the textual analyses I will focus on explicit authorial assessments—that is, assessments expressed by means of "I"-statements where the referent of "I" can only be the author—as well as implicit authorial statements identified as such by secondary literature. Therefore, I will assume that authors and narrators coincide: I am more interested in the expressions of subjectivity and intersubjectivity of the two authors than in establishing the narratological functions of the "I" in "I"-statements. See Rood 1998:10 "Readers of historical texts ... tend to identify author and narrator."

63 4.4.6 will resume and develop this crucial topic.

Thucydides, the speaker Nicias makes his position known through a combination of first-person markers (pronouns and first-person verbs) and nominative participles.

(t6)

ὅπερ ἐγὼ φοβούμενος, καὶ εἰδὼς πολλὰ μὲν ἡμᾶς δέον εὖ βουλεύσασθαι, ἔτι δὲ πλείω εὐτυχῆσαι ... ὅτι ἐλάχιστα τῇ τύχῃ παραδοὺς ἐμαυτὸν βούλομαι ἐκπλεῖν ...

Thucydides 6.23.3

... which fearing, and knowing that the business requires much good advice and more good fortune ..., I would so set forth as to commit myself to fortune as little as I may ... (tr. Hobbes)

Before the naval campaign to Sicily Nicias had initially expressed reluctance to undertake the expedition.[64] When, as seen in this speech, he finally changes his mind, Nicias clarifies his new position (βούλομαι ἐκπλεῖν) by couching it in terms of some cautious considerations: retaining some fear (φοβούμενος) about the undertaking, having awareness (εἰδώς) of the importance of good advice and fortune, and relying as little as possible on chance (ὅτι ἐλάχιστα ... παραδούς).

§56. In Herodotus several utterances on the Nile in book 2 provide especially good examples of authorial positioning. For instance:

(t7)

Πρόθυμος δὲ ἔα τάδε παρ' αὐτῶν πυθέσθαι, ὅ τι κατέρχεται μὲν ὁ Νεῖλος πληθύων ἀπὸ τροπέων τῶν θερινέων ἀρξάμενος ἐπ' ἑκατὸν ἡμέρας, ...

Herodotus 2.19.2

Yet I was anxious to learn from them why the Nile comes down with a rising flood for a hundred days from the summer solstice ... (tr. Godley)

Predicates are the crucial features (see the predicate nominal πρόθυμος ἔα + πυθέσθαι), as they convey the position of the speaking "I" (that is, eagerness to learn) concerning natural phenomena that look puzzling.

§57. Thucydides' positioning can be exemplified by this famous authorial statement that occurs towards the beginning of the account of the plague:

64 On Nicias' speaking style, and on the specific speech from which this excerpt is drawn, see IV.5.2.

(t8)

ἐγὼ δὲ οἷόν τε ἐγίγνετο λέξω ...

Thucydides 2.48.3

For my own part, I will tell what kind of thing happened. (tr. AB)

The author positions himself by characterizing his role as objective: he describes the actual course of events and adheres to actual facts.[65] This positioning is expressed in terms of disalignment with other people's position in relation to the object of inquiry (the plague), and the types of inquiry they have used. ἐγὼ δέ is a priming act (inferable from the subsequent postpositive τε) whose function is to foreground the first person pronoun.[66] ἐγώ is grammatically unnecessary but pragmatically and argumentatively crucial, as it makes explicit Thucydides' distance from the doctors and laymen (καὶ ἰατρὸς καὶ ἰδιώτης, 48.3) who have previously spoken about the event. Thucydides' type of inquiry is the central aspect of his positioning: he wishes to underscore the difference between his historiographical method and those of others, of speaking about the plague according to subjective perceptions and knowledge (λεγέτω μὲν οὖν περὶ αὐτοῦ ὡς ἕκαστος γιγνώσκει, 2.48.3[67]) versus speaking about what actually happened (οἷόν τε ἐγίγνετο λέξω, 2.48.3).

§58. The linguistic devices employed to express evaluation span a wider range of features than those used to mark positioning.[68] The following three excerpts offer a glimpse of this range. Let us consider first a stance act encoding evaluation by a character:

65 On this famous wording see in particular Repgen (1982) and Finley (1985:47-48, and 116n4), who comment on the German dictum "*wie es eigentlich gewesen*" ("how it actually was"), taken as a direct quotation of Thucydides 2.48.3 by the early nineteenth century historian Leopold Ranke. Stroud 1987 disaligns with Repgen and Finley, and takes οἷον as the accusative form of a neuter interrogative pronoun ("what") referring to αὐτό in the previous sentence, rather than an adverbial accusative of manner ("how"). He also reads τε as anticipating the καί that follows (ἐγὼ δὲ οἷόν τε ἐγίγνετο λέξω, καὶ ἀφ' ὧν ἄν τις σκοπῶν), and denies that τε has the emphatic function that Repgen sees. As II.4.5.2, III.2.2.3, and IV.2.3 point out, the copulative function of τε and a pragmatic enrichment need not be mutually exclusive.

66 On the notion of priming acts see II.2.5; instances of priming acts in Herodotus and Thucydides are discussed in IV.2 §§38-41 and 87; IV.3 §79, §88, §107, §§110-115; IV.5 §32, §46, §59, §63, §78.

67 μὲν οὖν in this act is commented on in IV.3 §145 (t35).

68 Throughout these sections I will use "evaluation" as a resultative noun related to the act of evaluating in Du Bois' sense. In literature, conversely, see e.g. notably Hunston and Thompson 2000, "evaluation" is taken as the equivalent of "stance," thus embracing what in Du Bois is "positioning" and "aligning" as well.

(t9)

Ἴσον ἐκεῖνο, ὦ βασιλεῦ, παρ' ἐμοὶ κέκριται, φρονέειν τε εὖ καὶ τῷ λέγοντι χρηστὰ ἐθέλειν πείθεσθαι·

Herodotus 7.16.α

O king, I judge it of equal worth whether a man is wise or is willing to obey good advice (tr. Godley)

With these diplomatic words Artabanus begins his response to a proposal that Xerxes had made concerning a disturbing dream of his. Xerxes had been advised in his sleep to invade Greece (7.12-14). Wishing to test the dream's veracity, he suggested that Artabanus should impersonate Xerxes before the two men go to sleep. If Artabanus in the guise of the king should experience the same terrifying dream as Xerxes had had, then Xerxes and all the Persians would have to trust the dream's suggestion. Artabanus' skepticism about both the invasion and the dream experiment makes him opt for starting with a gnomic statement; evoking a consolidated and common belief would probably make his perplexity more acceptable.[69] Indeed the *gnṓmē* ("being wise and being willing to be persuaded by those who say wise things are comparable qualities") potentially has multiple implications at this moment of the interaction between king and uncle.[70] The discourse act παρ' ἐμοὶ κέκριται, literally "it is judged by me," qualifies the *gnṓmē* as an act of stance explicitly.

§59. Herodotus also evaluates states of affairs in his own voice:

(t10)

χρῆν γὰρ Κανδαύλῃ γενέσθαι κακῶς

Herodotus 1.8.2

—of necessity, things for Candaules were evolving badly— (tr. AB)

Right at the beginning of the complicating action in the account of Gyges and Candaules, the author anticipates Candaules' doom.[71] Three linguistic features overall characterize

69 Scholarship acknowledges that gnomic statements are a typical trait of Artabanus' speech style; see, for example, Bischoff 1932:57-58; Shapiro 2000:101-103; Scardino 2007:182-183. In IV.5.5 I offer a discourse-oriented reading of Artabanus' speeches at 7.49 and 7.51.

70 One of them being that if the king listens to unwise people it means that he is not wise.

71 The Herodotean discourse act formed by the impersonal verb and the infinitive clause is hardly rendered in translation: Godley simply paraphrases "[Candaules], doomed to misfortune"; De Sélincourt and Marincola read "[the king], who was doomed to a bad end."

the utterance as evaluative. γάρ introduces pieces of information external to the account of sequential events,[72] thus suggesting discontinuity in the flow of discourse.[73] χρῆν echoes the historiographical motif of necessity, dear to Herodotus.[74] Finally, the adverb κακῶς is a typical example of an evaluative adverb, as it encodes subjective judgment.[75]

§60. The next instance, from Thucydides, includes evaluative adjectives, and it anticipates the relevance of δή in stancetaking.

(t11)

> κίνησις γὰρ αὕτη μεγίστη δὴ τοῖς Ἕλλησιν ἐγένετο καὶ μέρει τινὶ τῶν βαρβάρων, ὡς δὲ εἰπεῖν καὶ ἐπὶ πλεῖστον ἀνθρώπων.
>
> Thucydides 1.1.2
>
> For this was certainly the greatest commotion that ever happened among the Grecians, reaching also to part of the barbarians and, as a man may say, to most nations. (tr. Hobbes)

γάρ grants that the upcoming thought is associated with the preceding ones (see μέγαν τε ... καὶ ἀξιολογώτατον τῶν προγεγενημένω "[a war] big and most memorable if compared to the previous conflicts," 1.1). At the same time it marks a shift in the discourse, from a list of historiographical moves undertaken by the historian—ξυνέγραψε ... ἀρξάμενος ... καὶ ἐλπίσας ... τεκμαιρόμενος—to an authorial evaluation. Here Thucydides evaluates a general phenomenon that he calls κίνησις ("movement"[76]). μεγίστη δή is the core of the stancetaking act. μεγίστη encodes judgment in meaning (adjective "great") and form (superlative); δή, as I shall discuss in more detail later (4.6.2), intensifies μεγίστη in such a way as to mark the evaluation as one in whose certainty the author is personally invested.

72 See above §27, IV.3 §§108-109, and IV.5 §91. In my translation I render γάρ with an "em-dash," a punctuation mark that generally conveys discontinuity but also associative meaning.

73 The discourse act, in fact, occurs between a participial phrase and the main clause, both focusing on the complicating action: the Herodotean sequence of acts is the following: "Not so much time had passed" (Χρόνου δὲ οὐ πολλοῦ διελθόντος); "—of necessity, for Candaules things were evolving badly—" (χρῆν γὰρ Κανδαύλῃ γενέσθαι κακῶς); "he addressed Gyges with the following words" (ἔλεγε πρὸς τὸν Γύγην τοιάδε).

74 See in particular Munson 2001.

75 See De Jong 2013:255 on this as a metanarrative comment. In fact the discourse act, narratologically, works as a proleptic statement, even though the omniscient stance of Herodotus relies on the use of a finite past tense (χρῆν). A similar act occurs in Herodotus 9.109.2 (note, again, the imperfect): τῇ δὲ κακῶς γὰρ ἔδεε πανοικίῃ γενέσθαι "for she [the daughter of Masistes' wife] and all her house were doomed to evil."

76 On this occurrence of the term see in particular Rusten 2015.

§61. The final instances concern aligning and disaligning. Also in this case the relevant linguistic features cover a wide range, from negations to particles and the semantics of adverbs. In the fifth book of Thucydides (85-111), the Athenian envoys have a long exchange with the Melians, in the course of which it becomes necessary for them to express strong disalignment. In the speaking turn that precedes the discourse act in question, the Melians use a cautious litotes to point out that gods favor those who stand pious against unjust men (ὅμως δὲ πιστεύομεν τῇ μὲν τύχῃ ἐκ τοῦ θείου μὴ ἐλασσώσεσθαι, ὅτι ὅσιοι πρὸς οὐ δικαίους ἱστάμεθα, ... "Yet, as for fortune, we trust that our righteous stand against injustice will not disadvantage us in divine favour," 5.104 [tr. Hammond]). The Athenians retort:

(t12)

Τῆς μὲν τοίνυν πρὸς τὸ θεῖον εὐμενείας οὐδ' ἡμεῖς οἰόμεθα λελείψεσθαι·

Thucydides 5.105.1

Well, we do not think that we shall be short of divine favour either. (tr. Hammond)

Furley (2006:434n62) interprets τοίνυν here as marking the Athenians' reservations about the Melians' belief in gods: "the force of the particle τοίνυν might be cumbrously rendered: 'that goodwill of the gods *you refer to*' indicating that the Athenians do no set much store by it" (italics in the text). According to this reading, τοίνυν has scope over the phrase τῆς μὲν τοίνυν πρὸς τὸ θεῖον εὐμενείας. My examination of occurrences of τοίνυν in Thucydides, Herodotus, and other prose texts, however, has led to a different conclusion. I do not find, first, that the particle has scope over specific phrases; rather, it governs entire clauses and even multi-clause units of discourse. Second, it mostly occurs at the beginning of responses, to convey actual or potential disalignment with the previous speaker or between two parties that are facing each other.[77] Hammond's

[77] A particularly illuminating example outside of historiography is Andocides *On the Peace* 30: Συρακόσιοι δ' ὅτε ἦλθον ἡμῶν δεόμενοι, φιλότητα μὲν ἀντὶ διαφορᾶς ἐθέλοντες εἰρήνην δ' ἀντὶ πολέμου ποιεῖσθαι, τήν τε συμμαχίαν ἀποδεικνύντες ὅσῳ κρείττων ἡ σφετέρα εἴη τῆς Ἐγεσταίων καὶ Καταναίων, εἰ βουλοίμεθα πρὸς αὐτοὺς ποιεῖσθαι, ἡμεῖς τοίνυν εἱλόμεθα καὶ τότε πόλεμον μὲν ἀντὶ εἰρήνης, ... "Again, an urgent request came to us from Syracuse; she was ready to end our differences by a pact of friendship, to end war by peace; and she pointed out the advantages of an alliance with herself, if only we would consent to it, over those of the existing alliance with Segesta and Catana. But once more we chose war instead of peace, ..." (tr. Maidment). Here the speaking "I" uses τοίνυν to express his own disalignment with the Athenians ("we") about the eventual decision to attack Syracuse. The Athenians in this case are not only one of the parties involved but also the interlocutors. More about τοίνυν can be found above, in §36 and §38.

"Well, ..." his consistent method of rendering τοίνυν in Thucydides,[78] captures my interpretation well.[79]

§62. Now an example of alignment. In the passage below Herodotus aligns with Pindar on the importance of custom:

(t13)

καὶ ὀρθῶς μοι δοκέει Πίνδαρος ποιῆσαι, νόμον πάντων βασιλέα φήσας εἶναι.[80]

Herodotus 3.38.4

and it is, I think, rightly said in Pindar's poem that custom is lord of all. (tr. Godley)

This utterance seals a famous chapter in which Herodotus judges negatively Cambyses' disruptive attitude towards Egyptian customs, and asserts: "every human being has come to believe custom matters" (νενομίκασι τὰ περὶ τοὺς νόμους οἱ πάντες ἄνθρωποι, 3.38.2). The linguistic feature indexing alignment with Pindar is the adverb ὀρθῶς. The passage shows well that all three vectors of stance are actually represented: μοι δοκέει encodes the act of positioning and evaluating at the same time.[81]

§63. Finally, here is Thucydides disaligning with the Athenians about the fulfillment of an oracle. The excerpt is discussed also in IV.2 §109, (t55), as an instance of καί + the construction μοι δοκεῖ overall introducing a move.

78 On clause-initial "well" warning the interlocutor about a dispreferred (or thought to be dispreferred) reaction, see e.g. Aijmer 2013:40-41. See also III.4.4.2.

79 In addition to τοίνυν, a series of lexical choices create resonance with the previous words by the Melians, while the Athenians' opinion is opposed to that of the Melians: πρὸς τὸ θεῖον εὐμενείας (5.105.1) resonates with ἐκ τοῦ θείου and ὅσιοι (5.104); the "we" markers ἡμεῖς οἰόμεθα (5.105.1) resonate with πιστεύομεν and ἱστάμεθα (5.104); finally οὐδ'... λελείψεσθαι, in spite of the different scope of the negation, resonates with μὴ ἐλασσώσεσθαι. III.3 is entirely devoted to phonological, morphological, semantic, syntactic, and pragmatic phenomena of resonance in Classical drama. Resonance can often be employed in contexts of disagreement.

80 Plato in *Gorgias* 484b quotes this fragment from an otherwise unknown song of Pindar: νόμος ὁ πάντων βασιλεὺς θνατῶν τε καὶ ἀθανάτων. See Immerwahr 1966:319-322; Humphreys 1987:211-220; Evans:142-153.

81 See Rood 1998:246-248: the phrase "seem(s) to me" in general hedges authorial assessments. While in Herodotus it stresses "the subjectivity of hypothetical statements," or works to qualify superlatives, in Thucydides the phrase is employed more rarely and mostly "when he is re-creating past events." Rood agrees with Marincola (1989) that at 1.22.2 Thucydides' intention not to write "as it seemed to me" is not to set a polemical statement against Herodotus, but to assess its appropriateness in relation to the reconstruction of the past as opposed to the narration of contemporary history. In the present chapter the phrase μοι δοκέει/μοι δοκεῖ is considered in connection to the particle that often introduces it, that is, καί (see (t13), (t14)).

(t14)

καί μοι δοκεῖ τὸ μαντεῖον τοὐναντίον ξυμβῆναι ἢ προσεδέχοντο· οὐ γὰρ διὰ τὴν παράνομον ἐνοίκησιν αἱ ξυμφοραὶ γενέσθαι τῇ πόλει, ἀλλὰ διὰ τὸν πόλεμον ἡ ἀνάγκη τῆς οἰκήσεως ...

Thucydides 2.17.2

My view is that the oracle was fulfilled, but in the reverse of the general expectation. It was not the unlawful occupation which caused the disasters to the city, but the war which forced the occupation. (tr. Hammond)

The oracle in question had prohibited the occupancy of the Pelargikon, a sacred area of Athens. The Athenians held that the oracle was fulfilled in the sense that the people occupying the Pelargikon disregarded the oracle, which caused the disasters of the war. Against the Athenians Thucydides expresses a more rationalistic opinion. Yes, the oracle had been fulfilled, but on a different ground: the occupation of the Pelargikon was not the cause but the result of war. καί μοι δοκεῖ τὸ μαντεῖον τοὐναντίον ξυμβῆναι ἢ προσεδέχοντο includes all the linguistic ingredients of disalignment: the object of disalignment (the interpretation of the fulfillment of the oracle), the content of disalignment ("the contrary," τοὐναντίον), the disaligning subject (μοι), and the people with whom the speaking "I" disaligns (the unspecified third persons who have certain expectations, προσεδέχοντο).

4.4.3 Epistemic and emotional stance: Avoiding dichotomies

§64. Before moving on to the specifically literary implications of representing stance, we should take a moment to address one of the important ways in which stance has both a social and a cognitive dimension. Acts of stance reflect varying degrees of epistemicity and emotionality.[82] We probably would take "I don't believe you" as primarily an expression of epistemic stance, "That's horrible" as primarily an expression of emotional stance, and "I wish she were alive" as a mix of the two (conveying both the speaker's desire and state of knowledge).

§65. In line with Du Bois,[83] I shall not interest myself in establishing *a priori* classifications (distinguishing epistemic, emotional, and mixed expressions of stance), but

[82] See e.g. Ochs 1996 and Shoaps 2002 on affective stance; Kärkkäinen 2003 and Heritage and Raymond 2005 on epistemic stance. Conrad and Biber (2000:57) define epistemic stance in terms of "commenting on the certainty (or doubt), reliability, or limitations of a proposition, including comments on the source of information," whereas attitudinal stance refers to "conveying the speaker's attitudes, feelings, or value judgements."

[83] Du Bois 2007:144-145.

rather proceed by considering how epistemicity and emotionality co-exist in different degrees. In fact, Herodotus and Thucydides are capable of representing stance in terms that are epistemic and emotional at the same time. For example, Herodotus conveys the imperialistic calculation (epistemic stance) as well as the hyperbolic fever (emotional stance) of Xerxes when he forges the king's well-known statement, οὐ γὰρ δὴ χώρην γε οὐδεμίαν κατόψεται ἥλιος ὁμουρέουσαν τῇ ἡμετέρῃ, literally "the sun will not illuminate any land that will border ours," that is to say, "every land under the sun will be ours," 7.8.γ.2.[84] Thucydides' characterization of the Greeks' attitudes during the civil war, ἑτοῖμοι ἦσαν τὴν αὐτίκα φιλονικίαν ἐκπιμπλάναι ("[they] stood ready to satisfy their present lust for victory," 3.82.8), represents stance in a manner that has both epistemic and emotional components. The author captures the readiness of the Greeks as well as his own distaste for this attitude through his choice of the word φιλονικία, "lust for victory," (which in Thucydides always has a pathological connotation[85]), thus layering the Greek epistemic stance and his own emotional stance.

§66. This brings us to another, more subtle and more important way in which the boundaries in stance are blurred. To define *a priori* when an utterance reflects someone's stance and when it does not is intuitively problematic. According to Du Bois, stance is found when a social actor makes use of overt communicative means to perform a public act that refers to positioning, evaluating, and aligning. If just one of the vectors of the triangle is linguistically encoded, the contents of the other two may still be inferred. However, as the example "To the lively mind" suggests (see above §50), the directness of the linguistic encoding can be a problem: a certain linguistic form of an utterance can be perceived as an act of stance even though none of the most direct features occur (such as, for instance, an evaluative adverb, or a first-person verb positioning Subject 1, or an expression of disagreement).

§67. Let us mention a passage that shows the interlacing of narration, the author's emotional stance, and readers' emotional involvement. The tragic scene that Thucydides depicts towards the end of book 7, the slaughter of Athenians at the river Asinarus in Sicily (7.84), is dominated by clauses that lack evaluative adjectives and adverbs, typical markers of the author's stance. Yet the passage is commonly taken as a poignant description that arouses a great deal of emotion in readers. What seems *just* description or *just* narration actually conveys the author's emotional stance as well. The audience's emotional involvement derives from the author's careful combination of visual details

84 On Xerxes' "pride in his magnificence," and on Xerxes compared to Zeus, see Immerwahr 1966:177. On Xerxes depicted by Herodotus as a hybristic monarch, see especially Paduano 1978:78-82, and Nicolai 1998:18. Vannicelli (2017) discusses the elements of Xerxes' speech at 7.8 that mix imperialistic fever and oriental symbolism for absolute monarchy. Note the occurrence of δή, γε, and the double negation in this discourse act. As for historiographical occurrences of these features, see the later sections 4.5. and 4.6 about δή; see above §§40-44, and IV.5 §20, §34, §62, §67-68, §73 about γε; IV.5 §78 about double negation.

85 See Gomme *et al.* 1945-1981, vol. IV:407.

with his representation of selected Athenians' internal perceptions. All of this is designed to blur the boundaries between what is seen and what is felt, who is seeing things and who is feeling them. This is what makes the passage memorable.[86]

§68. Thus, stancetaking is best understood not as bound to certain types of discourse, such as descriptive or argumentative discourse, but either to linguistic features that in different contexts encode stance components, or to indirect cues to the emotional/epistemic involvement of author and audience. Thompson and Hunston (2000:6) claim that one of the main functions of evaluation (taken as equivalent to stance) is "to construct and maintain relations between the speaker or writer and hearer or reader."

§69. The next subsections complete the discussion about tracking stance by comparing the key notion to other notions used in literary criticism. The first, focalization, has a bearing on the idea of perception; the second and third (reader response and irony) focus on the relation between author and audience.

4.4.4 Stance vs. focalization

§70. Over the last couple of decades the narratological notion of "internal focalization"[87] has gained currency as an approach to studying the phenomenon of embedded thoughts, especially in Thucydides.[88] R. J. Allan (2013:379-380) equates "implicit embedded focalization" with "vicarious perception," "represented perception," and "free indirect perception," as no explicit verb of perception precedes it. Grethlein (2013:96, with n19) similarly

86 Hornblower (1991-2008, vol. III:733) "one of the most appallingly memorable chapters." In epic, for example, attention to visual details can have the narrative function of marking a peak or a complicating action by producing special emotional effects, such as horrifying readers who mentally reconstruct the scene. On the effectiveness of terrifying scenes in *Beowulf*, for example, see Renoir 1962. On the narrative and emotional functions of inserting visual details in Serbocroatian epic, see Bonifazi and Elmer 2016. On conversational storytelling as a regular locus for displaying affective stance, see Voutilainen *et al.* 2014. Günthner 2011 shows that speakers are able to index their affective stance in language on several grammatical levels, and by doing so they make the related events emotionally accessible to co-participants.

87 On the original concept of focalization, see Genette (1972:206-217; 206-207 for the quoted terms), who distinguishes between "*focalisation zéro*" ("zero focalization"; the narrator has unlimited access to the mind of characters), "*focalisation interne*" ("internal focalization"; the narrator's access is limited spatially), and "*focalisation externe*" ("external focalization"; the narrator can only be witness to characters). For Bal, instead, (1985:100-115) internal and external focalizations involve no access to the mind, but coincide with the intra- or extradiegetic locus of the focalizer. In general, the term is meant to clarify the distinction between the person who speaks (narratorial functions) and the person who perceives (focalizing functions). The first classicist to adopt the term "focalization" is Irene De Jong in her 1987 monograph *Narrators and Focalizers. The Presentation of the Story in the Iliad.*

88 See, for example, Connor 1985 about viewpoint; Hornblower 1994:134-135; Hornblower 1991-2008, vol. II:55-56 about Thucydides focalizing Brasidas through the eyes of various characters instead; Dewald 1999:244-248 (on Herodotean focalization as well); De Jong 2001:76-78; Zimmermann 2005; Scardino 2012:68-71; Allan 2013:378-381; Grethlein 2013b: 96-98; Fragoulaki 2013:129; 159. Focalization in Herodotus is discussed in Baragwanath 2008:41, 54, and 214n17.

equates "focalization" with "perception," noting that "focalisation ... is not limited to seeing, but embraces all senses as well as intellectual activities and emotional response."

§71. Rood (1998:11-14, and 294-296) points out the limits of the original definition of "focalization," if used to analyze texts: the distinction "who speaks" vs. "who perceives" is not always straightforward. Most of all, the focalizing role of the primary narrator has no fixed boundaries; he can choose to access the perspective of his characters to whatever degree serves his purposes. Considering focalization on the cognitive level would help, the scholar suggests (1998:12-13); the level of knowledge that is distinctive of a certain character vs. that of the narrator or the audience can be relevant to the recognition and the extent of focalization.

§72. The picture becomes even more complex if we take into account recent developments in cognitive studies. In the introduction of a monograph on viewpoint in language, the linguists Eve Sweetser and Barbara Dancygier argue for the human capability of multiple viewpoints on the the same scene.[89] While watching the same scene, two subjects can apprehend and simulate the viewpoint of their companion.[90] This suggests not only the sheer possibility to access another viewpoint, but also the capability of keeping into account multiple viewpoints at the same time, without necessarily being involved with only a single viewpoint at a time.

§73. One of the current debates about viewpoint and focalization in historiography focuses on how switches are encoded. How do we perceive, while reading, the shift from someone's eyes to others' eyes? And how do the historians' vantage points influence different focalizations and the language that they use to represent them?[91] I suggest that when contents concern more than one individual—which covers the vast majority of the two *Histories*—we may assume that the viewpoints represented can be multiple and coexisting. At least the viewpoint of the author always coexists with one more viewpoint that may be assigned to one of the characters. So, for example, the very same imperfect can convey aspects related to more people's perceptions instead of *either* X's *or* Y's. This observation leads to more general assessments about why I use stance instead of focalization.

89 "... we are not just capable of multiple viewpoints; we are in fact incapable of keeping to one single viewpoint of space, or of cognitive structure, when other humans are present" (Dancygier and Sweetser eds. 2012:2).

90 See, e.g. Jeannerod 2001 and Olsson and Nyberg 2011 on brain simulations of action; Addis *et al.* 2009 on episodic simulation of the past and the future.

91 For example, scholars have different views about whose perspective is adopted and when in Thucydides 2.84.1-3, which narrates how the Athenian general Phormio succeeds in trapping Peloponnesian ships in the gulf of Naupactus, while the Peloponnesians did not expect to get engaged in a sea battle. Just to mention one of the debated matters, Rijksbaron (2012:363-364) attributes imperfects to the primary narrator's viewpoint; conversely, Grethlein (2013b:95-96) associates the imperfects with the confusion of the ships, and agrees with Bakker (1997e) in interpreting the imperfect tense as an effort to render the events "as if they are seen on the spot."

§74. "Stance" shares with "focalization" the idea of revealing individual perception. Both notions also cover a wide range of cognitive activities, from sensory perception to emotional states. However, focalization has no social connotations, whereas the core idea of stance is that it is a social activity. The public character of speeches in historiography makes the concept of stance more suitable than focalization. One could object that stances conveyed in the form of thoughts are not public, but this is true only if the thoughts are viewed as private actions from within the time of the story. The thoughts become public when they enter the historical record, at which point they acquire accountability as factors that influenced political or military strategies. The stances taken by the historians themselves are public in this sense as well: their own explicit or implicit authorial statements presuppose reception by an audience.

§75. The concept of stance has some theoretical advantages over focalization. The analysis of the components of stance is socially oriented, which fits the public context of speeches as well as the strategic (if not directly political) value of people's thoughts in classical historiography. Also, the three basic components distinguished by Du Bois—evaluating, positioning, and aligning—provide more refined tools of analysis than what focalization offers. Herodotus' and Thucydides' language can orient the understanding of the receiver by emphasizing one of the three vectors—for example, by inserting adjectives that mark someone's act of evaluating something, or by inserting a particle that signals alignment or disalignment between the author and some of the characters. Most of all, focalization does not draw attention to the interplay of interactions between the subjects taking stance, and the multiple interpretive options that this interplay gives rise to. One of them is the relationship between author and audience.

4.4.5 Reader response: Eliciting the audience's stance

§76. The relationship between author and audience is worth dwelling on, as it is fundamental to interpreting stance in the two *Histories*. At an earlier point (§52) I refined the "Subject 1—Subject 2" vector in Du Bois' triangle by including several non-mutually exclusive variants, such as "author—character/group"; "author—contemporaries"; "author—predecessors"; "author—audience." The next two sections will bring these refinements to bear as I examine in more detail two aspects of vector: first, authorial strategies for eliciting readerly stance in both Herodotus and Thucydides, and second, the effect of Herodotean irony on interrelations between the author, audience, and character vectors.

§77. Let us first focus on the active role of the audience as subjects potentially involved in stancetaking.[92] Two recent reader response approaches have suggested that Herodotus and Thucydides actively call upon readers to formulate their own stance. In

[92] On the response by the *internal* audience of speeches in the two *Histories*, see, for example, Debnar 2001, and Lang et al. 2011:167-188, where the reactions to indirect speeches is analyzed

her 2008 monograph, Baragwanath suggests that Herodotus actively invites readers' individual deliberations and responses on matters. This does not mean that Herodotus does not offer explicit judgments; merely that he is keen to promote evaluative openness. He encourages readers to make inferences about the events he narrates, a narrative technique that tends to yield various or alternative readings. Consider for example the narration of Xerxes' dream in book 7. On the one hand the council scene preceding the dream yields a hybristic explanation of the attack from a Greek perspective. On the other hand the account of Xerxes' dream possibly reflects a Persian perspective and potentially yields a Persian explanation, as the dream is imbued with oriental motifs (2008:251). The insertion of the dream and all the details connected to it prompts the reader/listener to contemplate reasons from more than one side; it is a strategy of "enfranchising ... readers as capable judges" (Baragwanath 2008:20).

§78. The other reader response approach comes from Grethlein's perspective on the experiential quality of the narrative in Thucydides (see especially 2010:117-118, and 2013b:29-52). In brief, readers are invited to sense the events and feel the emotions from within the scenarios depicted: "Thucydides' readers experience the plot from the perspective of characters" (2010:280). Thucydides, Grethlein suggests, adopts strategies that make the past present and align the perception of readers with the perception of internal characters.[93] For example, the author maximizes the unpredictable character of events.[94] He blurs the temporal, spatial, sensorial, emotional distance between narrating subjects and narrated objects.[95] Finally, he indirectly invites readers to take stance about actual situations and alternative developments in events.[96] This last point is what makes Grethlein's approach similar to Baragwanath's: both scholars find that the narratives of the historians they respectively study unfold in ways that prompt readers to evaluate and take positions about circumstances and decisions.

§79. Both approaches suggest that Herodotus and Thucydides, albeit with different historiographical purposes, invite readers to observe the complexity of situations, to judge evidence, to reconstruct less immediately evident realities, to draw causal links, to test conjectures, to ponder possible resolutions—in a word, to be inquirers themselves.[97]

as well. Particle use, however, is not as relevant to this kind of response as it is to the response by external audience/readership.

93 See above §70 for Grethlein's understanding of "focalization" in terms of "perception."

94 On this point Grethlein aligns with Dunn: Thucydides employs a variety of techinques "that have the effect of trapping the reader, who is unable to attain a broader perspective, in the present" (Dunn 2007:132).

95 By evoking Plutarch's assessment that Thucydides makes his readers spectators (*De gloria Atheniensium* 347a), Grethlein stresses the experiential nature of using *enárgeia*, that is, vividness.

96 See Grethlein 2013b:109-111 about Thucydides and the openness of the past, the use of sideshadowing, and the opportunity—left to the reader—to compare speeches with what actually follows.

97 See, for example, Grethlein 2010:279 on the activity of reading as "an exercise in the art of reasoning and conjecturing."

These views stress that readers have an active role, especially when they respond to the authors' invitation to take stance.

§80. As we have seen, the two historians use different strategies to elicit audience's reactions. Herodotus provides direct and indirect authorial signs that call for the audience to make a judgment after the fact. These signs enable them to predict or to think about ultimate reasons and consequences *a posteriori.* Thucydides, too, involves his audience in a deeper understanding of historical events, but he chooses to make them experience history from the inside, on the spot as it were, and to produce empathic effects that bring the audience closer to characters.[98] In short, from a stance perspective we can say that Thucydides is interested in stressing possible alignments between characters and audience, whereas Herodotus is interested in stressing possible alignments between author and audience. I will retrieve this point while analyzing the discourse functions of δή and ἤδη.

4.4.6 Irony: The "author—audience" vector

§81. This subsection illustrates a pragmatic phenomenon that concerns the alignment between author and audience, and seems to occur primarily in Herodotus.[99] In her monograph on indirect discourse (1993), Fludernik makes an observation that pertains to an exquisitely Herodotean habit. She writes that the use of indirect discourse may yield ironic effects. The narrator may exploit the representation of other voices to stress the distance between his own and the character(s)' stance. Fludernik (1993:73-74) offers examples from English literature where indirect discourse and free indirect discourse are used as a "distancing device," especially if the narrator reports them "with obvious disagreement or sarcasm" (74).

§82. The irony conveyed by this distancing device results from the reader's ability to infer a gap between the author's knowledge or insight about something, and the characters'. This gap is suggested by the context in which the reported words appear. The clash of perspectives is not made explicit, but is left to the inferential abilities of the reader, who can choose how to react to it—for example by tittering, or by mentally recording that the author is hinting at some misunderstanding. This type of irony, then, is similar to dramatic irony: what characters say on the stage becomes incongruous with what the audience and the playwright know.

§83. Schellenberg 2009 comes to a similar conclusion. The article's central point is that Herodotus, by reporting a character's words or commenting on a character's

98 Emmott and Sanford (2012:216-218) refer to the notion of "participatory response," originally introduced by Allbritton and Gerrig (1991), to describe "reader reactions to situations being depicted in narratives" (216). These reactions include fears, hopes, and wishes for or against the characters.

99 4.6.4 raises the question of the extent of irony in Thucydides as far as the usages of δή are concerned.

speech, nudges his readers to notice a knowledge gap. In some situations the character's circumscribed perspective is shown to diverge from the broader perspective of author and readers. As Schellenberg (2009:131) puts it, Herodotus "insinuates himself among his readers by bringing them into a conspirational alliance against the speeches' ironic victims." The ironic effect is achieved when the readers feel amusement upon realizing that different readings of the text are designed for different audiences.[100]

§84. This irony is also noted by classicists who are engaged in defining certain Herodotean uses of δή. Cooper (2002:2939, emphasis original) states: "the proper meaning of δή is probably *clear as the light of day*. ... The ironic uses of δή are readily understood from this point of view. A word with the sense *clearly, obviously* may be encountered in almost any language with an ironic force, if the thought at hand is *not* actually very manifest and unquestionable." He also adds (2002:2940), "the ironic force of δή is so close to its proper nature that there is no way to confine its appearance to particular constructions."[101] Instances of "ironic" δή are discussed in 4.5.5; for now I merely wish to note that Herodotus' pervasive use of irony functions as a way of establishing a tighter relationship with his audience. In Du Boisian terms, this irony entails an implicit disalignment between author and character, and an implicit alignment between author and audience.[102]

4.5 δή in Herodotus: How It Connotes Voice and Stance

§85. δή is a particle by means of which we can track voice and, in particular, stance. Its contribution will be better understood if we begin with an overview of the basic characteristics of its occurrences. Herodotus is the best source, as δή is one of the most frequent

100 This take on irony resonates with Fowler's definition of the term in his dictionary of English originally published in 1926, cited by Schellenberg as well (2009:133n4): "Irony is a form of utterance that postulates a double audience, consisting of one party that hearing shall hear and shall not understand, and another party that, when more is meant than meets the ear, is aware both of that more and of the outsiders' incomprehension" (Fowler 1994:295).

101 See also Hartung (1832:282), who states that the sense of determination conveyed by δή sometimes is ironic ("*enthält bisweilen Ironie*"), and Schraut 1847:19. Denniston (1950:229-236) divides the ironic uses of δή according to seven different syntactic environments in which it occurs; "this use is so widespread that it demands separate treatment" (229). Long before Denniston, ironic meanings of δή were noticed by Stephanus 1572:966 (about Thucydides); Vigerus 1834 [1627]:501; Hoogeveen 1749:298 (about Lucian, and in combination with ὡς); Riemer 1823:425; Kühner 1835:388; Döderlein 1858:362 (about Homer); Thomas 1894; Smyth 1956:647.

102 I posit that a tighter relationship with listeners is easier to achieve and makes more sense than a tighter relationship with readers. Moreover, in the course of aural delivery, nonlinguistic features (such as facial gestures and intonation) could further render the ironic slant of some words.

particles in his work (1,395 instances overall, that is, 0.7% of the total words, according to the *TLG* online).[103]

§86. A general and significant fact regarding the Herodotean use of δή is that in at least 996 (71%) of these occurrences it is found in recurrent combinations, together with either other particles or other lexical items. The most frequent particle combinations are μὲν δή (393x), γὰρ δή (165x), καὶ δὴ καί (81x), δὲ δή (78x), ὦν δή (73x), δὴ ὦν (42x), and καὶ δή (51x). Constructions with other lexical items include ἐνθαῦτα δή (22x), ἔνθα δή (9x), τότε δή (8x), δή τοτε (7x), indefinite pronouns + δή (this being a set phrase known from Herodotus on[104]), and, most of all, οὗτος forms + δή (οὕτω δή, for example, recurs 109 times, but all the adjectival forms of the demonstrative should be included as well[105]). In all these constructions I take δή to be signifying together with the lexical item it accompanies.[106] Taking, then, this large proportion of occurrences into account, we see that δή does not appear alone so frequently. This fact helps explain why it is problematic to try to account for an independent and overarching value of δή.

§87. As we propose in all our analyses, approaching the study of a particle by starting from its co-text reveals how the particle works in discourse more clearly than if we make speculations about the particle in itself. A particle's multifunctionality emerges from its multiple co-texts.[107]

§88. δή appears in Herodotus much more frequently than in Thucydides: the difference is 1,395 vs. 201 occurrences, or 0.7% vs. 0.1% of the total words. This difference in number of occurrences, though noteworthy, is not as important as two macrophenomena. One phenomenon is that about two thirds of δή occurrences in Herodotus signal narrative progression,[108] or steps through which the author-narrator unfolds his accounts (see next section). Conversely, in Thucydides, δή occurrences that perform this function are significantly fewer (I count just 44 of 201 instances). The second phenomenon is that some Herodotean occurrences are those that scholars regard as an ironic use, a use that does not seem to have a clear parallel in Thucydides. Despite these differences, aspects of δή in Herodotus are essential for understanding δή in Thucydides; for this reason I will begin with Herodotus.[109]

103 See our frequency graphs (available online as I.5); Herodotus uses δή more than any other author in our corpus.

104 See Cooper 2002:2959, and Stephens 1837:64, about ὅσος δή.

105 See IV.3.11.3.

106 This does not imply that the different δή constructions work as clusters (on which, see I.1 §19); in δὲ δή for example the two particles work independently. The question of the scope of δή will be addressed in §100.

107 See Bybee 2010 and the framework of CxG (Construction Grammar), which stress a very similar point about learning and storing words in general. I.3.3.4 offers an overview of CxG.

108 E.g. in book 2, 100 of 155 occurrences relate to narrative progression.

109 The upcoming analysis is based on 407 occurrences of δή in Herodotus 1 and 2, and all the 201 occurrences found in Thucydides.

4.5.1 Voicing narrative progression

§89. Just as II.3.3.1 shows about Homer, δή in Herodotus frequently works to move forward narration by marking major steps in an account. In these cases δή does not function temporally,[110] to mark chronology, and pertain to content, but rather aids in the performance of discourse acts that advance narration. This discourse function is mainly fulfilled by the following δή constructions: μὲν δή, ὦν δή/δὴ ὦν, καὶ δὴ καί, καὶ δή, ἐνθαῦτα δή, ἔνθα δή, τότε δή, δή τοτε, οὗτος forms + δή, and δὲ δή.[111] The sense can be translated as follows: "then/so/as I said," when the construction is used to continue an account; "as I was saying," when the construction resumes the main thread of narration after embedded material (often after a reported speech);[112] "at that point," when the construction marks a narrative peak; "and so" when the host act of the construction wraps up an account.[113]

§90. In the combinations listed above the lexical items accompanied by δή would be able to fulfill the narrative functions I described by themselves. What δή adds in the combination is the marking of Herodotus' voice as narrator. This interpretation is based on two considerations. The first is that while very few δή occur in direct speech,[114] the remaining Herodotean δή occur in third-person narration, but have a strong bearing on the representation of the characters' voice and stance, as I will show. The second consideration is a comparison with δή in Homeric epic. II.3§54 establishes that across direct

[110] Scholars claiming the primarily temporal value of δή include Devarius (1588:63); Hoogeveen (1769:276); Hartung (1828 and 1832:223); Kühner (1835:386); Ellendt (1841:166); Döderlein (1858:363); Wetzell (1879:14-15); and Thomas (1894:85).

[111] I say "mainly" because sometimes, instead of the more usual δή constructions, we find δή alone performing this function in act-peninitial position. For example, after deciding to live and kill Candaules instead of being killed, Gyges asks Candaules' wife how to set on the king. Herodotus introduces Gyges' words by means of Ἐπειρώτα δὴ λέγων τάδε· "He inquired by saying:" (Herodotus 1.11.4). Wakker (1997b:241) also interprets this δή as a device that draws attention to what happens next, but she identifies a nuance that I do not see: her translation is "and so, you have to know, he asked."

[112] "As I said" and "As I was saying" are the ways in which I render what Wakker (1997b:241) and Van Ophuijsen (1993:141-148) call "anaphoric δή" used to continue a story.

[113] IV.3 §§127-143 offers several examples of this kind of δή, including discussion of μὲν δή and various particle combinations at different discourse transitions. Literature refers to the "recapitulating" or "resumptive" function of μὲν δή through e.g. Hartung (1832:262-263), Rieckher (1862:473-474), Denniston (1950:225), and Wakker (1997b:242: δή in combination with μέν is used to "round off a topic and prepare a topic switch").

[114] For books 1 the ratio is 17 out of 248 instances; for book 2, just 2 out of 159 instances. Even though this does not represent the average adequately—the earlier books have little direct speech in general (see Solmsen 1943:194)—the ratio of the last two books does not contradict the ratio of the first two: book 8 includes 5 δή in direct speech, out of 107 total occurrences, and book 9 shows 8 instances out of 111 total occurrences. Helpful tables recording the occurrence of character speeches in Herodotus are to be found in De Bakker 2007:183-237. Scardino estimates that direct speech in Herodotus occupies 18% of the work on average (2007:117), while direct speech in Thucydides occupies 20-25% (2007:453).

speech and narrator text, less than half of the instances mark narrative steps (even less in the *Iliad*). However, not only the main narrator uses this kind of δή, but also characters. Overall δή occurs more in direct speech than in narrator text.[115] The proportionally higher incidence of δή in direct speech in Homer thus sets a historical precedent for Herodotean usage, where δή in this discourse function is strongly associated with the presence of the speaker's voice, and in particular Herodotus the narrator's. This voice conveys no specific evaluation but just moderate involvement, a sort of investment (imbued with some amusement, I am tempted to add) in the process of unfolding his historiographical discourse.[116]

§91. A higher level of involvement may underly the narrator's use of καὶ δὴ καί and καὶ δή.[117] Both combinations have the effect of arousing interest in the reader, as they mark (thanks to the force of καί) the next piece of information as discursively salient. The narratorial voice participates in selecting the topic that follows (καὶ δὴ καί), or in singling out the visual or temporal detail (if not the narrative peak) that will serve as a focal point.

4.5.2 Perception of evidence

§92. I move on now to looking at δή in co-texts involving speech and perception. In those cases δή occurs mainly alone, and in different act positions.[118] Direct speech is linked with perception because both are instances of immediacy: the subject who speaks or perceives uses δή to convey his or her epistemic experience of evidentiality.[119] The subject can be

115 In II.4 §20 δή is interpreted as a sign of emotional convergence between performer and character, which is very relevant to our upcoming account of δή in stancetaking.

116 I already pointed out that authorial statements tend to coincide with acts of stancetaking. Marking narrative progression is different from making authorial statements; however, sharp distinctions between conveying just the voice and conveying voice + stance should be avoided. Some of the combinations that I mentioned above (§89) may be employed to introduce Herodotus' explicit stance about something rather than referring to the progress of events. An example is 1.58 πρὸς ὃ δὴ ὤν ἔμοιγε δοκέει οὐδέ τι Πελασγικὸν ἔθνος, ἐὸν βάρβαρον, οὐδαμὰ μεγάλως αὐξηθῆναι "Before that, I think, the Pelasgic stock nowhere increased much in number while it was of foreign speech" (tr. Godley).

117 For further discussion about these combinations, see IV.2 §§96-97 and 100-101, and in III.4 §§51-52.

118 At the end of the next subsection (see §100) I will recapitulate the act positions of δή.

119 See III.2 n181 for references (ranging from 1828 to 2019) indicating the main meaning of δή to be linked to something clear, evident, or obvious within and beyond Herodotus and Thucydides. Van Ophuijsen (1993:141 with n2) states, "the basic value of the particle relates to what is visible to the mind's eye as well as to the organ of sight," and gives French *voici, voilà* as the equivalent. Bakker observes: "[δή] conveys that the consciousness verbalized receives its input from the speaker's immediate environment, from what is perceptually clear and evident" (1997b:75). As I have already mentioned (§84), Cooper (2002:2939, emphasis original) affirms that "the proper meaning of δή is probably *clear as the light of day*." Wakker (1997b:238-241) aligns with Ruijgh 1971:646-647 in saying that δή signals "the importance and interest of the proposition

either a character or the author himself. Here is an example of δή in direct speech, which in Herodotus, I repeat, is not frequent at all:[120]

(t15)

Ἀλλ' εἴ τοι φίλον τοῦτο οὕτω γίνεσθαι, χρὴ <u>δὴ</u> τό γε ἐμὸν ὑπηρετέεσθαι ἐπιτηδέως.

Herodotus 1.108.5

So, if you like this to happen in this way, it is definitely my duty to obey scrupulously. (tr. AB)

This is how Harpagus concludes his reply to king Astyages, who has just ordered him to find and kill Cyrus, the newborn royal grandson. "It is definitely my duty to obey": δή is not only an apodotic particle that stresses the consequent character of the statement after the conditional clause, but it is also a marker of the clear perception that Harpagus expresses at that very moment: he realizes that he has no choice but to obey.[121] γε in τό γε ἐμόν contributes to stressing the individual sense of responsibility, and is a further marker of Harpagus' voice.

§93. The next example, conversely, comes from an observation by the author:

(t16)

ἔστι δὲ ἔσωθεν ἄλσος δενδρέων μεγίστων πεφυτευμένον περὶ νηὸν μέγαν, ἐν τῷ <u>δὴ</u> τὤγαλμα ἔνι·

Herodotus 2.138.3

... within is a grove of very tall trees growing around a great shrine where the image of the goddess is (tr. Godley)

Herodotus is describing the temple of the Egyptian goddess Bubastis, whom he takes as the equivalent of Greek Artemis (2.137.5). The moment of the report about the statue of the goddess in the shrine features δή; beyond general encyclopedic knowledge, here the

---

presented" (239). She consistently translates δή as "you must know." For her the meaning "obviously" is a later development of the orginal "look (how interesting)."

[120] For δή in direct speech see also Herodotus 1.115.3.

[121] The question of whether he is equally certain and committed to obeying Astyages in his heart is a different matter.

historian anchors the narration and the view of the statue to subjective and embodied perception.[122]

4.5.3 In indirect speech and indirect thought

§94. The point of the present subsection is to show how δή can contribute to signal indirect speech and indirect thought, and therefore can be taken as a marker of voice and stance. Instances encompass not only indirect speech preceded by reporting clauses, but also reported λόγοι marked by infinitive clauses, and, in addition, indirect thoughts, whether preceded by verbs of thinking, believing, and the like, or not.

§95. The lexical items that tend to co-occur with these δή are: γάρ, ἵνα, ὅπως, ὅτι + oblique optative, ὡς + participle,[123] superlatives,[124] and adjectives and adverbs indicating scalarity or extremes (such as πᾶς, πολύς forms, μάλιστα). Further important co-textual signs are those qualifying the communicative environment: "I" markers in a character's direct speech and in explicit authorial statements (which Herodotus generously employs); verbs of saying which introduce indirect speech (with various degrees of indirectness[125]); verbs of thinking, considering, meditating, intending; σφ- forms associated with αὐτός forms of pronouns.[126] These features do not always appear as δή's co-texts, but when they do, it is easier to interpret the particle.

§96. It may seem at first that the function of most of these δή is simply to help encode a character's act of evaluation. Keep in mind, however, that for Du Bois, evaluation occurs simultaneously with positioning and aligning. In this regard the work of Stephens and of Hartung is relevant: their separate assessments of δή have suggested

122 Book 2 is rich in parallels: see 2.32.6; 2.60.1; 2.68.1; 2.93.4; 2.96.5; 2.111.1; 2.155.2; 2.156.4. An authorial statement that uses δή in connection with perception occurs when Herodotus observes that the inhabitants of Busiris are beating themselves out of grief: Τύπτονται [μὲν] γὰρ δὴ μετὰ τὴν θυσίην πάντες καὶ πᾶσαι, μυριάδες κάρτα πολλαὶ ἀνθρώπων· τὸν δὲ τύπτονται, οὔ μοι ὅσιόν ἐστι λέγειν. "It is here that everybody—tens of thousands of men and women - when the sacrifice is over, beat their breast: in whose honor, however, I do not feel it is proper for me to say," 2.61.1 (tr. De Sélincourt and Marincola). Artabanus uses γάρ and δή at 7.16γ.1 to refer to a purely visual experience: φανήτω γὰρ δὴ καὶ ἐμοί, ὡς καὶ σοί, διακελευόμενον "let it [the dream] appear to me as well as to you, with its commands" (tr. De Sélincourt and Marincola).

123 Wakker (1997b:243-247) takes δή in causal and purpose constructions with ἵνα, ὅπως, ὅτι + oblique optative, and ὡς + participle as always expressing the viewpoint of the character involved in the cause or purpose in question. If the causal clause is introduced by ἅτε δή, conversely, then the viewpoint expressed is that of the narrator.

124 On δή accompanying superlatives, see Stephens 1837:63, Krüger 1846:347-348, and Denniston 1950:204-207. See also below 4.6.2, II.5 §68, and III.2 §74.

125 Scardino 2012:70.

126 While the fact that σφ- forms mark indirect reflexivity is generally accepted, the interpretation of αὐτός forms is not straightforward at all. For the editorial instability αὐτός/αὑτός in Thucydides, see in particular Powell 1934). The common reading of αὐτός as "plain" third person pronoun when it is not in attributive position can be challenged. Recent investigations into the pragmatic uses of αὐτός in Homer, for example, are found in Bonifazi 2012:134-155.

to us a way in which the particle is involved in connecting evaluation with positioning. According to Stephens, δή is one of the particles that in general indicate "the state of the speaker's mind"; in particular it may denote "determination of the judgment" and "determination of the will" (1837:57 and 58 respectively). In a slightly earlier publication, Hartung stated that with affirmative and negative particles δή expresses resoluteness and confidence ("*Entschiedenheit und zuversichtliche Behauptung,*" 1832:285). The force of δή described in these terms by Stephens and Hartung essentially concerns stancetaking. In contexts where δή and surrounding features do not advance stories or accounts of events, δή conveys positioning by expressing certainty, will, commitment, and confidence; at the same time these mental states convey evaluation: "X is certainly Y."[127]

§97. Some examples of characters' use of δή will help illustrate this point.

(t17)

Ἅρπαγος δὲ ἔφη, αὐτὸς γὰρ γράψαι, τὸ πρῆγμα ἑωυτοῦ <u>δὴ</u> δικαίως εἶναι.

Herodotus 1.129.2

"It was I," said the other, "who wrote the letter; the accomplishment of the work is rightly mine" (tr. Godley)

In spite of Godley's translation, the Greek reports Harpagus' words in the form of indirect speech (note ἔφη, and the infinitives γράψαι and εἶναι). At the same time αὐτός and ἑωυτοῦ point to the source of the utterance as the pivot. In this context δή broadly relates to Harpagus' voice, more specifically to Harpagus' determined assertion, and even more specifically to his evaluation of the assertion (δικαίως).[128]

§98. The next example is drawn from a point in a Persian λόγος when the Persians express an evaluation of the Greeks. The excerpt is a variant of indirect speech, where the reporting clause ("they say") refers to an articulated account instead of a single sentence.

(t18)

τὸ δὲ ἀπὸ τούτου Ἕλληνας <u>δὴ</u> μεγάλως αἰτίους γενέσθαι·

Herodotus 1.4.1

[127] See below §100 on the scope of δή as "certainly x," and II.3 §62 on the intensifying function of δή ("I feel/think very strongly that ...") in Homer. I consider these δή as reflecting stance that is somewhere between "epistemic" and "attitudinal" stance according to the definition of Conrad and Biber (see above, n82).

[128] A very similar analysis of δὴ γάρ is offered at II.4 §§19-20.

> But after this (the Persians say), the Greeks were very much to blame (tr. Godley)

"After this", as Herodotus will explain a bit later (1.4.3), refers to the fact that the Greeks raised a big army, invaded Asia, and destroyed the empire of Priam on account of a girl from Sparta. In this case the exact scope of δή is ambiguous or difficult to see: it is possible to associate δή either with the Greeks (Ἕλληνας δή), with the evaluating adverb (μεγάλως), or with the act Ἕλληνας δὴ μεγάλως αἰτίους γενέσθαι, whose initial boundary is suggested by δή in peninitial position.[129] Whatever δή actually qualifies, it signals that its associated piece of information bears the seal, as it were, of a specific voice (that of the Persians, in this case), and that the speaker's sense of certainty is driving its intensifying function.[130]

§99. Finally, an example of free indirect thought:

(t19)

> Οἱ δ' ἐκ τῆς αὐτῆς κώμης Μῆδοι ὁρῶντες αὐτοῦ τοὺς τρόπους δικαστήν μιν ἑωυτῶν αἱρέοντο· ὁ δὲ δή, οἷα μνώμενος ἀρχήν, ἰθύς τε καὶ δίκαιος ἦν.
>
> Herodotus 1.96.2

> Then the Medes of the same town, seeing his [Deioces'] behavior, chose him to be their judge, and he (for he coveted sovereign power) was honest and just. (tr. Godley)

In this passage the verb ὁρῶντες, on the local level, and the preceding content, on a more global level, enable us to interpret the evaluative description of Deioces as an example of free indirect thought. By preceding content we mean, on the one hand, the description of Deioces' righteousness towards the people (1.96.1), but on the other, Herodotus' preface to that account, which has a distinctly negative tone: "This Deioces, who had a lust for tyranny ..." (ἐρασθεὶς τυραννίδος). The difference between this prefatory assessment and the subsequent characterization of Deioces as "honest and just" is a sign that Herodotus evaluates Deioces differently from the Medes. δή, then, marks the assessment of this man as the Medes' own opinion, and only their own opinion—one, that is, from which Herodotus wishes to establish his authorial distance. Interpreted this way, δή serves an additional function, to stress the "author—audience" vector: we readers know from the

[129] δή also appears in indirect speech at 1.94.x; 1.96.2; 1.114.4 (also including γε); 2.13.3; 2.36.6; 2.42.2; 2.45; 2.116.2; 2.121.ε.2; 2.122.2; 2.126.1; 2.132.3; 2.134.1; 2.141.1; 2.141.2; 2.160.4; 2.177.1.

[130] Wakker offers a different reading (1997b:240): the Persians "call attention to this important proposition, and especially to its focus, ... 'the Greeks' by the use of *dḗ*." She translates δή "you must know."

omniscient narrator that Deioces had specific political interests, but the people could have not realized that.[131]

§100. Before turning to δή in authorial statements, let me summarize the question of its position and scope. The examples provided thus far show variability. Unlike δή in constructions that advance the narration of events, which consistently occur in act-peninitial position, and have scope over at least an entire discourse act, the δή that marks stance can occupy different positions and have different scopes. δή intensifying an adjective or adverb ("y is certainly/definitely/absolutely x"), has small scope and is mobile; conversely, if δή has bearing on an entire statement ("I am sure that x," "certainly x is the case"), δή has act scope, and it occurs in act-peninitial position (which typically happens in the γὰρ δή construction).[132]

4.5.4 In explicit and implicit authorial statements

§101. Authorial statements that explicitly or implicitly convey Herodotus' stance frequently feature a γάρ move including δή contiguous to γάρ. γάρ by itself has no specific link to voice or stance. However, one of its typical uses is to mark discontinuity by introducing unframed discourse,[133] as for example encyclopedic or cultural information necessary at a certain moment in an account, or explanations and illustrations of a piece of argument. Such stretches of text can be interpreted as authorial interventions in a number of cases.[134] To be sure, γάρ is not to be considered an "authorial" particle.[135] What γάρ does is to start a move that considers an aspect of something mentioned in the previous move, regardless of who performs either move; δή may mark that move as a point where some stancetaking is performed.

§102. In the following example γάρ and δή co-occur with the first person verb "I will say," the referent of the personal pronoun being Herodotus. In this case the historian is the performer of the preceding moves as well.

131 For δή in indirect thoughts preceded by reporting clauses or phrases, see 1.114.4; 2.17.3; 2.161.4; 2.172.2; 2.174.1. Further examples of the "author—audience" vector will be discussed later in 4.5.5 on "ironic δή."

132 The same conclusions are drawn in II.3 §64 with regard to δή in epic, and in III.2 §79 with regard to δή in tragedy and comedy.

133 For the term "unframed discourse," see II.4.2, and also above §27.

134 Hornblower (1994:134) remarks: "Sometimes γάρ introduces material whose focalizer is really Thucydides himself, the obvious example being that at 2.13.3, from the account of Athenian finances ostensibly taking the form of encouragement by Pericles." Of Herodotus Lang (1984b:154) remarks: "the ubiquity of *gar* in the *Histories* ... is evidence of the historian's readiness to explain." De Jong (2004a:110) takes γάρ clauses in narrator text as a device that provides "explanations to questions which the narrator assumes the narratees will have."

135 See below n148 about γὰρ δή uttered by characters.

(t20)

Οὐ γὰρ δὴ συμπεσεῖν γε φήσω τά τε ἐν Αἰγύπτῳ ποιεύμενα τῷ θεῷ καὶ τὰ ἐν τοῖσι Ἕλλησι·

Herodotus 2.49.2

... for I will not say that what is done in Egypt in connection with the god [Dionysus] and what is done among the Greeks originated independently (tr. Godley)

In an earlier clause the historian states (ἐγὼ μὲν νυν φημί) that Melampus was the one who introduced Dionysus to the Greeks, having learned about him in Egypt. γάρ and δή sustain this act of authorial positioning by starting an expansion: "this is why: 1. I won't say that the worship of Dionysus here and there coincides by chance (see (t20)); 2. I won't say that the Egyptians took these practices from the Greeks" (οὐ μὲν οὐδὲ φήσω, 2.49.3). γε stresses συμπεσεῖν, the coincidental occurrence of the worship of the same god in Egypt and Greece. It also signals, together with δή, the narratorial voice.[136]

§103. Here is an example of δή in an implicit authorial statement:

(t21)

Τούτου τοῦ ἔπεος Λυδοί τε καὶ οἱ βασιλέες αὐτῶν λόγον οὐδένα ἐποιεῦντο, πρὶν δὴ ἐπετελέσθη.

Herodotus 1.13.2

... an utterance to which the Lydians and their kings paid no regard until it was fulfilled. (tr. Godley)

No "I" marker occurs in this discourse segment, but only the omniscient author knows that the words of the oracle would have come true. De Jong (2013:257) quotes this very passage as an instance of prolepsis. In this case δή's contribution is to add to the semantic and temporal information "it was accomplished" (ἐπετελέσθη, aorist passive form) the speaker's (here the author's) commitment to its veracity.[137]

136 Among other instances of δή in explicit authorial statements, see in particular 1.58; 2.5.1; 2.11.1; 2.11.4; 2.49.1; 2.50.1; 2.120.2; 2.120.3; 2.150.2.

137 See also Herodotus 1.14.3; 1.25.2; 2.16.2 (also including γε); 2.22.1; 2.42.2; 2.46.2; 2.52.2; 2.104.4; 2.94.2 (also including γε and a superlative); 2.156.6; 2.164.2.

4.5.5 "Ironic" δή

§104. In the analysis of the Deioces passage earlier (§99, (t19)), I suggested that the certainty with which characters express their stance clashes with the author's stance. Some dubiousness is conveyed, and only indirectly—through additional information that lies elsewhere.[138] The analysis of (t19) exemplifies a general phenomenon that I had given a foretaste of earlier in the chapter (4.4.6), when I reviewed literature that labels these uses of δή as ironic. I now take up the topic again to develop it.

§105. Recall from §84 that δή, besides marking a character's determination or certainty, can suggest that the author disaligns with that character. The sense of irony is inferable from the awareness of a gap between, on the one hand, the consciousness of the internal characters as represented by the author, and on the other, the knowledge or perspective shared by the author with his audience, which creates a kind of alliance between them. Herodotus' audience is invited to react to the characters' stance by providing their own response (see above, 4.4.5). Herodotus often does not say directly that a character's perception is or will be proven to be a mistake, but he does use δή to hint at the potential divergence between the character's sense of certainty and his own scepticism. The presence of δή guides the reader to suspect the possibility of a mistake, first, and then to find the suspicion confirmed as the account proceeds—or, as in the case of Deioces, preceding information enables inference of present irony.

§106. Consider the following γάρ move including δή:

(t22)

Τὸ μέν νυν ἁρπάζειν γυναῖκας ἀνδρῶν ἀδίκων νομίζειν ἔργον εἶναι, τὸ δὲ ἁρπασθεισέων σπουδὴν ποιήσασθαι τιμωρέειν ἀνοήτων, τὸ δὲ μηδεμίαν ὤρην ἔχειν ἁρπασθεισέων σωφρόνων· δῆλα γὰρ <u>δὴ</u> ὅτι, εἰ μὴ αὐταὶ ἐβούλοντο, οὐκ ἂν ἡρπάζοντο.

Herodotus 1.4.2

Abducting young women, in their [= the Persians'] opinion, is not, indeed, a lawful act; but it is stupid after the event to make a fuss about avenging it. The

[138] "Dubiousness" is among the terms that Cooper uses to describe the main aspects of the irony suggested by δή, together with "inaccuracy" and "falsehood": "Especially in ὡς clauses the pretense is portrayed as bold, and the dubiousness is all the more perceptible." (2002:2939); "the dubiety ... relates to the unworthiness or inadequacy of the fact as a justification for the position taken up on this basis." (2002:2940); "With participles a suggestion of inaccuracy is the rule. ... δή ... after ὡς implies falsehood or want of the power to convince in the original thought or assertion restated" (2002:2940).

> only sensible thing is to take no notice; for it is obvious that no young woman allows herself to be abducted if she does not wish to be (tr. De Sélincourt and Marincola)

This sequence of discourse acts gives Herodotus' representation of the Persians' stance on abducting women. The thought "if women were not willing, they would not get abducted" sounds clear and obvious to them, but it does not mean that Herodotus endorses it. δή, or better to say, δῆλα γὰρ δὴ ὅτι, confines the certainty to the source of the thought (if not to the imagined voice), thus detaching it from authorial thought. The irony springs from the implicit discrepancy between the two views.

§107. Sometimes even a character can share in the irony usually confined to author and audience. Let us take for example a scene from the episode "Rhampsinitus and the thief" (2.121). Herodotus shares the thief's private intentions in advance. At the climactic point in the story, the thief finds that he must put his fellows out of action, so that he may enact his trick successfully. So, when his companions invite him to join a drinking party, he "lets himself be persuaded," as Marincola and De Sélincourt put it (2003 *ad loc.*). Here is Herodotus' Greek:

> (t23)
>
> τοὺς δὲ αὐτοῦ ὥσπερ εἶχον κατακλιθέντας πίνειν διανοέεσθαι καὶ ἐκεῖνον παραλαμβάνειν καὶ κελεύειν μετ' ἑωυτῶν μείναντα συμπίνειν. Τὸν δὲ πεισθῆναί τε <u>δὴ</u> καὶ καταμεῖναι·
>
> Herodotus 2.121δ.4
>
> ... they lay down there just as they were, disposed to drink, and included him and told him to stay and drink with them; and he consented and stayed. (tr. Godley)

δή, nestled within a series of infinitives that indicate the use of *oratio obliqua*, signals something subtle. After Herodotus relates how the thief's companions invited him to stay and drink, τὸν δὲ πεισθῆναί τε δὴ καὶ καταμεῖναι gives the thief's reaction: "he (said that he) would be persuaded indeed, and would stay." The medio-passive aorist infinitive form πεισθῆναι, and the δή, show that the words are to be identified with the thief's voice. This is where stance and irony come into play. The thief's official positioning (and official alignment with his fellows) is "yes, you convinced me," but author, audience, and the thief himself know that he had already decided to remain because he wanted his friends to get drunk and fall asleep. In this case three subjects align at the expense of other characters participating in the scene.[139]

§108. There are many other cases where δή suggests discrepancy in stance, with potentially ironic effects.[140] In general, through δή Herodotus may be found stressing the "author—audience" vector in the stance triangle. He implicitly warns the reader about some disalignment between his and the characters' stance, or, in complex scenes, between his and some of the characters' stance but not others'. In other words, he uses his character or characters' certainty as a foil to suggest that the reader should either distrust it outright or at least consider it critically.

4.5.6 Interim conclusion

§109. In Herodotus most instances of δή (which generally appear in combinations with other particles) mark narrative progression, that is, the voice of the author as narrator. δή in accompaniment with various linguistic features marks stance: this occurs when the host discourse act (or move) conveys either sensory perception, or positioning, evaluation, and alignment. More specifically, δή marks a sense of certainty or determination. This stancetaking manifests itself mainly through the modalities of indirect speech, indirect thought, and free indirect thought. The so-called ironic uses of δή are cases where the vector "alignment/disalignment" between author and audience is underlined. In particular, through δή Herodotus implicitly disengages himself from the certainty or determination of at least one of the characters involved in a certain situation. He warns his audience that some aspect(s) of the unfolding account are treacherous or erroneous, and therefore require careful judgment.

4.6 δή in Thucydides: Whose Stance?

§110. To understand the use of δή in Thucydides we must first consider it in relation to its most recurrent function in Herodotus, δή combinations that advance narrative. At an earlier point (§§89-90) I interpreted this preponderant function as a manifestation

139 Wakker (1997b:245n62) acknowledges that δή may have irony as one its side effects, but she disagrees on the idea that δή may describe, to use Denniston's words, "an ingenious stratagem or device" (1950:232); it is not the presence of δή that signals this, but rather the entire context. I point out that δή *per se* would not signal anything anyway, as it makes sense exclusively in context and with its co-text. Along the same lines, irony through δή is to be seen as an effect springing from an entire situation and from extralinguistic implications, which does not fit Wakker's prescriptive, rather than subjective, meaning of δή as "you must know."

140 See, e.g., 1.22.1; 1.80.4; 1.86.2; 2.134.1; 2.147.4; 8.76.2.

of Herodotus' voice as narrator. By narrative advance I meant either a scene-change accompanied by the introduction of turning points or facts, or the resumption of a narrative thread following some kind of interruption. In Thucydides the total number of δή occurrences is much smaller than in Herodotus (201 vs. 1,395 instances, i.e. 0.1% vs. 0.7% of total words); accordingly, we find far fewer δή constructions that advance narrative.[141] However, the proportion of οὕτω δή in Thucydides is about the same as in Herodotus (0.6% vs. 0.7% of the respective occurrences of δή).[142] In addition, δή combinations involving temporal markers[143] in Thucydides should include ἐπειδή as well, for the –δή component within the whole word (which functions as a temporal conjunction) corresponds to the pragmatic δή used for narrative progression. There are 236 instances of ἐπειδή in Thucydides (besides the instances of δή), or 0.15% of the word total; compare 46 in Herodotus, or 0.02% of the total. Taking all these numbers together then, we can say that while Thucydides employs δή to advance narrative far less often than Herodotus does, he nonetheless still does employ it to a noticeable degree.

§111. A far more important point of difference is Thucydides' use of δή in direct speech (which represents 26% of the total occurrences, that is, 54 of 201, against 5%, that is, 32 out of 625, in the Herodotean speeches of books 1, 2, 8, and 9). In general, it is worth exploring how δή marks someone's voice and stance through different degrees of directness in the representation of speech and thought. The next subsections delve into that.

4.6.1 Characters' stance in direct speech, indirect speech, and indirect thought

§112. Let us start with an instance of δή in direct speech. At 1.142.3 Pericles affirms that it is difficult (χαλεπόν) for a rival city to build fortresses in time of peace (ἐν εἰρήνῃ), and absolutely so (ἦ που δή) in a territory of enemies (ἐν πολεμίᾳ). At 6.37.2 Athenagoras, leader of the democratic party at Syracuse, doubts that the Athenians will succeed in the expedition, especially if the entire island is hostile to them (ἦ πού γε δὴ ἐν πάσῃ πολεμίᾳ Σικελίᾳ, "definitely, with all Sicily being an enemy territory").[144] From these examples

141 They include 12 τότε δή, 9 ἐνταῦθα/ἐντεῦθεν δή, 7 μὲν δή, 1 ὕστερον δή, 1 ὅτε δή, and 13 οὕτω δή (plus 5 more οὗτος forms). Overall, they constitute the 36% of δή combinations in Thucydides, against at least 71% in Herodotus (see above, §86). Neither καὶ δὴ καί nor καὶ δή ever occur; however, καί τι καί arguably fulfills a similar function to καὶ δὴ καί (see IV.2 §97). A particular construction used by Thucydides and not by Herodotus is δι' ὃ δὴ καί (1.128.1; 2.21.1; 2.42.1), meaning "this is why, in particular."

142 οὕτω δή in Thucydides marks narrative peaks at 1.131.1; 2.6.3; 2.12.4; 2.17.3; 2.19.1. τότε δή does the same at least at 2.84.3 and 8.92.2.

143 These include πρὶν δή (5x in Thucydides; 2x in Herodotus) and πρίν γε δή (2x in Thucydides; 5x in Herodotus). πρίν γε δή in Thucydides 1.132.5, 7.71.5 and in Herodotus 6.79.2, 9.22.2 marks narrative peaks.

144 The multi-functions of που (including the propositional reference to unspecified places—"somewhere") are thoroughly investigated in Koier 2013 within the framework of Construction Grammar (on which see I.3.3.4). Even though κου in Herodotus and που in Thucydides do not

we can infer that speakers use ἦ που + δή to reinforce their assessment—to express their own absolute certainty about it.[145] Further particles that immediately precede δή in direct speech besides ἦ που are μέν,[146] γε,[147] and γάρ.[148]

§113. Several δή discourse acts that encode someone's evaluation feature superlatives, comparatives, or adjectives such as "all." In these cases δή has scope over those words. Here is an example, again from direct speech:

(t24)

οὐ γὰρ δὴ πεφευγότες αὐτὰ ἐπὶ τὴν πλείστους <u>δὴ</u> βλάψασαν καταφρόνησιν κεχωρήκατε

Thucydides 1.122.4

For certainly you avoid them [stupidity, cowardice, indifference] not by imputing it to that which hath done most men hurt, contempt of the enemy (tr. Hobbes)

---

pose particular interpretive problems, I record here a couple of interesting data. First, the number of occurrences contradicts Denniston, who remarks (1950:491): "The tone of uncertainty, whether real or assumed, is ill-adapted to the precision of history .... There are a few examples in Thucydides." The *TLG* online actually includes 51 κου/που in Herodotus (48 κου and 3 που), against 49 που in Thucydides. Additional observations concern δήπου and δή κου. Two out of the four δήπου in Thucydides appear in a passage (8.87.4-5) where the historian expresses his "considerate opinion" on the Phoenician fleet (see Hornblower 1991-2008, vol. III:1004-1107); therefore the co-text relates to authorial stancetaking. As for Herodotus, conversely, only one δή κου out of five works as a cluster meaning "with no doubt"; in the remainder, κου works separately from δή.

145 In n34 I mentioned that at 8.27.3 ἦ που δή occurs in indirect speech.

146 μὲν δή is exceptionally uttered by characters in Thucydides 3.113.4 and 5.90.1. The passage in book 5 features ἦ μὲν δὴ νομιζομέν γε, with which the Melians react to the bold statement by the Athenians "in practical terms, the ones who dominate do what they can, and the ones who are weak assent" (δυνατὰ δὲ οἱ προύχοντες πράσσουσι καὶ οἱ ἀσθενεῖς ξυγχωροῦσιν, 5.89.1; tr. AB). ἦ marks the reaction as such (see III.2.2.10, where ἦ in drama is described as a marker of emotional involvement while speakers assess something or ask for confirmation about something). μὲν δή projects a move that is going to encompass several discourse acts. γε reinforces "we consider" and anticipates that the object of the consideration is going to be retrieved from something that the Athenians already mentioned (the idea of equal necessity, cf. 5.89.1 ἴσης ἀνάγκης). The thought is going to be: "we do believe that there is an advantage in preserving the idea of common good."

147 Thucydides 2.62.1; 4.92.4; 8.41.2; 6.37.2. Since the most interesting occurrences of γε δή are in authorial statements, I postpone our remarks on this combination to a later point (see n162).

148 Thucydides 1.81.6; 1.122.4; 2.40.3; 3.57.3; 3.66.2; 4.87.4; 5.111.3; 6.76.2; 6.77.1; 7.62.4. γὰρ δή in Thucydides is more frequently spoken by characters than in Herodotus (10 against 5 times); it consistently introduces associative facts that either look evident, or show the speaker's determination in stating something. See the upcoming (t24).

At the congress summoned by the Spartans in Sparta, the Corinthians want to solicit a vote for war. In this passage they warn the other Spartan allies that an attitude of disdain does not help to keep major shortcomings away (that is, stupidity, cowardice, and indifference). While expressing this opinion, introduced by γὰρ δή, they embed a second opinion, to which the second δή relates: disdain (καταφρόνησις) has harmed the greatest number of people. δή has scope over πλείστους (note the noun phrase τὴν πλείστους δὴ βλάψασαν καταφρόνησιν that surrounds it) and marks the certainty with which the Corinthians take this secondary stance.[149]

§114. Let us now consider δή in indirect speech. Thucydides is reporting the ruthless trick orchestrated by the oligarchs of Corcyra to eliminate the democrats of their own city. The Athenians are holding these democrats captive on an island.

(t25)

τῶν ἐν τῇ νήσῳ πείθουσί τινας ὀλίγους, ὑποπέμψαντες φίλους καὶ διδάξαντες ὡς κατ' εὔνοιαν <u>δὴ</u> λέγειν ὅτι κράτιστον αὐτοῖς εἴη ὡς τάχιστα ἀποδρᾶναι, πλοῖον δέ τι αὐτοὶ ἑτοιμάσειν· μέλλειν γὰρ <u>δὴ</u> τοὺς στρατηγοὺς τῶν Ἀθηναίων παραδώσειν αὐτοὺς τῷ δήμῳ τῶν Κερκυραίων.

Thucydides 4.46.5

They sent to the island friends of the captives, whom they instructed to tell them with seeming good-will that they had better escape as fast as they could, for the fact was that the Athenian generals were about to hand them over to the Corcyraean democracy; they would themselves provide a vessel. (tr. Jowett, adapted)

Through the two δή and the present tense of πείθουσί, λέγειν, and especially μέλλειν, Thucydides makes the voice and positioning of the oligarchs vividly audible. The second δή is suggestive of the tone that the false friends might take in direct speech, a usage reminiscent of Herodotus' "ironic" δή. This is a trick, and the friends' apparent

149 Further instances of δή in direct speech near superlatives or adjectives and pronouns indicating scalarity are Thucydides 1.33.2 ὀλίγοις δὴ ἅμάπαντα; 1.74.1 and 3.39.1 μάλιστα δή; 7.62.3 δὴ μάλιστα; 1.122.4 πλείστους δή; 2.64.3, 6.13.1, and 6.17.5 μεγίστ- δή; 2.64.3 πλείστων δή; 3.54.5 ὅτεπερ δὴ μέγιστος φόβος; 4.63.2 τὸ ξύμπαν τε δή; 5.113.1 πλεῖστον δή; 1.83.2 οὐδέν δὴ μᾶλλον; 2.64.1 πρᾶγμα μόνον δὴ τῶν πάντων ἐλπίδος κρεῖσσον γεγενημένον. At 1.84.2 δή near μᾶλλον contributes to signal that the speaker performs an act of stancetaking, especially positioning; the speaker, the king of Sparta Archidamus, conveys that they do not want to be persuaded by vexation: ἤν τις ἄρα ξὺν κατηγορίᾳ παροξύνῃ, οὐδὲν δὴ μᾶλλον ἀχθεσθέντες ἀνεπείσθημεν, "if anyone tries to provoke us with accusations, this is no more successful—we are not goaded into agreement" (tr. Hammond). At an earlier point of the same speech (1.81.6), Archidamus uses δή to convey the decisiveness with which he wishes to position himself and his people on their war expectations.

benevolence actually serves a ferocious intention; these δή amplify the gap in knowledge existing between the different groups of characters.[150]

§115. δή in the representation of indirect thoughts are easier to detect when δοκέω or another verb of thinking precedes the δή act.[151] The activity of thinking can also be entailed or alluded to through direct references to mental states or stances, as in this passage:

(t26)

Ἆγις δὲ αὐτοῖς ἑτοῖμος ἦν ἐκείνους μὲν μὴ λύειν δή τὰς Ἰσθμιάδας σπονδάς, ἑαυτοῦ δὲ τὸν στόλον ἴδιον ποιήσασθαι.

Thucydides 8.9.1

Agis was willing to let them [the Corinthians] observe the Isthmian truce, and to take on the expedition by himself. (tr. Hammond)

The mental state of the Spartan king Agis in this moment[152] is his willingness to procede with the expedition without the Corinthians. Tucker (1892, *ad loc.*) observes: "Agis is ambitious; he has been checked already in his fancy for acting alone, and he is quite ready to let the Corinthians stay at home and to take all the control upon himself. ... δή is ironical." The irony that Tucker probably alludes to resides in Agis' attitude: he pretends to allow the Corinthians to suspend military operations, but he is actually eager to act without them. Independently of whether δή implies that or not, Tucker indirectly confirms that the value of δή here is to be found in connection with someone's voice and stance (Agis' "sure!"), which does not emerge from Hammond's translation (*exempli gratia*).

150 More examples perhaps recalling the "irony" of some Herodotean δή are gathered in 4.6.4. A less complex co-text involving δή in indirect speech occurs at 4.23.1.

151 For example, in 8.87.1 we find the following description of Tissaphernes: βουλόμενος, ὡς ἐδόκει δή, ἀπολύεσθαι πρὸς αὐτοὺς τὰς διαβολάς, literally " ... resolved, as it seemed good to him, to dispel the suspicions against them ..." (tr. AB). The imperfect of δοκέω suggests that δή marks Tissaphernes' perception rather than Thucydides'. More examples of δή in reported thoughts are to be found at 2.24.1 and 4.40.1 (by the Athenians); 4.67.3 (by the Megarian cospirators) and 4.117.2 (by the Spartans, after guessing the thoughts of the Athenians); 6.24.2 (by the Athenians after Nicias' speech).

152 The Corinthians were supposed to sail together with the Spartans towards Chios, first, and then to Lesbos (8.8.2), but they were unwilling to move, because of the imminent Isthmian festival, which would impose a truce. On the religious scruples of the Corinthians, see Hornblower 1991-2008, vol. III:781-783.

4.6.2 Implicit authorial δή, especially with superlatives

§116. Earlier (§113) we have seen that characters may encode evaluations of an object or event by means of δή + superlatives or adjectives indicating extremes. When Thucydides himself evaluates, he uses δή largely with superlatives, especially μέγιστος.[153] Thucydides does not tend to show stance by using explicit authorial markers—he is much less generous than Herodotus in this respect—but his stance is inferrable from content: only the historian can assess the extent and magnitude of certain events in absolute terms.

(t27)

Καὶ ἡ μὲν μάχη τοιαύτη καὶ ὅτι ἐγγύτατα τούτων ἐγένετο, πλείστου δὴ χρόνου μεγίστη <u>δὴ</u> τῶν Ἑλληνικῶν καὶ ὑπὸ ἀξιολογωτάτων πόλεων ξυνελθοῦσα.

Thucydides 5.74.1

This, or something very close to it, is how this battle evolved. It was the largest battle that had been joined between major Greek cities for a very considerable time. (tr. Hammond)

This is a comment that Thucydides inserts towards the end of the account of the battle of Mantinea (5.64-75.3). There are four superlatives: ἐγγύτατα, πλείστου, μεγίστη, ἀξιολογωτάτων. They represent evaluative acts that reflect his historiographical stance. The second δή qualifies the core of his evaluation: Mantinea was the biggest battle between Greek cities. While the scope of this δή is technically small (μεγίστη δή), its co-occurrence with a superlative suffices to characterize the entire passage as an act of stancetaking.[154]

[153] δή + superlative is considered a "rather fixed combination" (Wakker 1997b:240n51). Scholars remarking that in earlier times include Hoogeveen 1769:290-295; Kühner 1835:389; Stephens 1837:63; Bäumlein 1861:102; Wetzell 1879:17; Kalinka 1890:194; Thomas 1894:101. About 8.1.2 κατάπληξις μεγίστη δή, echoed at 8.96.1 ἔκπληξις μεγίστη δή, Hornblower comments: "both times δή is a regular accompaniment of the superlative and indicates no doubt or irony" (1991-2008, vol. III:751). Besides (t27), see 1.1.2 κίνησις γὰρ αὕτη μεγίστη δή; 1.50.2 ναυμαχία γὰρ αὕτη ... μεγίστη δή; 2.31.2 στρατόπεδόν τε μέγιστον δὴ τοῦτο ἁθρόον Ἀθηναίων ἐγένετο; 3.113.6 πάθος γὰρ τοῦτο μιᾷ πόλει Ἑλληνίδι ἐν ἴσαις ἡμέραις μέγιστον δή; 7.75.7 μέγιστον γὰρ δὴ τὸ διάφορον τοῦτο; 8.1.2 and 8.96.1 ἔκπληξις μεγίστη δή; 8.41.2 ὃς αὐτοῖς ἔτυχε μέγιστός γε δὴ ὧν μεμνήμεθα γενόμενος. Further superlatives include γὰρ δή ... πρῶτος (1.93.4); βεβαιότατα δή (1.138.3); κράτιστος δή (1.138.3; πλεῖστον δή (2.97.3); πλεῖσται δή (3.10.5); δὴ πλεῖσται (3.17.4); βέλτιστοι δή (3.98.4); πλεῖστον δή (4.74.4); μάλιστα δή (4.108.3, 5.28.2 and 5.66.2); ἐπὶ πλεῖστον δή (6.54.5); πλεῖστα δή (7.56.4); πλεῖσται (7.70.4); ἥκιστα (7.86.5); παρ' ἐλάχιστον δή (8.76.4); ἐπικαιροτάτην δή (8.106.2). A few more superlatives are quoted in 4.6.3, as they relate to the blending of multiple voices. κατάπληξις μεγίστη δή (Thucydides 8.1.2) is commented on in IV.5 §38.

[154] I read πλείστου δὴ χρόνου as a conflation of a temporal expression and the historian's stance about the chronology of the battle.

§117. It goes without saying that Thucydidean authorial statements can include superlatives without δή as well; see, e.g. 8.87.4 (σαφέστατον); 1.138.6 (λαμπροτάτους). The absence of δή indicates that the host discourse act has no focal point in the personal involvement of the speaker while qualifying an object/person/event (which is what δή signals).

§118. Implicit authorial statements can also include δή without superlatives.[155] In the following passage Thucydidean usage aligns with constructions found in Homer and Herodotus.

(t28)

ἔτι πλέον κατεφρόνησαν καὶ ἠξίουν τοὺς στρατηγούς, οἷον <u>δὴ</u> ὄχλος φιλεῖ θαρσήσας ποιεῖν, ἄγειν σφᾶς ἐπὶ Κατάνην, ἐπειδὴ οὐκ ἐκεῖνοι ἐφ' ἑαυτοὺς ἔρχονται.

Thucydides 6.63.2

they [the Syracusans] took a yet more dismissive view of the Athenians, and—as the common people tend to do when their spirits are up—they insisted that their generals should let them out to Catana, since the Athenians were not coming against them. (tr. Hammond)

The parenthesis οἷον δὴ ὄχλος φιλεῖ θαρσήσας ποιεῖν, being of a gnomic character, draws attention to the authorial voice.[156] In particular, the construction οἷον δή[157] requires closer examination. To capture its tone correctly we must look to parallels in Homer and Herodotus. In Homer, οἷον δή starts exclamatory discourse acts.[158] In these cases οἷον δή is syntactically superfluous; its pragmatic value rests on conveying emotional involvement and giving an exclamatory tone to the content that follows.[159] Similarly, Herodotus

[155] See e.g. 7.44.1, where the relative clause coincides with an estimation that expresses scalarity: ἐν δὲ νυκτομαχίᾳ, ἣ μόνη δὴ στρατοπέδων μεγάλων ἔν γε τῷδε τῷ πολέμῳ ἐγένετο, "in a night battle—this was the only one fought between large armies in the whole of the war" (tr. Hammond). At 6.105.2 an authorial superlative is accompanied by ἤδη: καὶ τοῖς Λακεδαιμονίοις ἤδη εὐπροφάσιστον μᾶλλον τὴν αἰτίαν ἐς τοὺς Ἀθηναίους τοῦ ἀμύνεσθαι ἐποίησαν. "Thereby the Athenians at last gave the Lacedaemonians a right to complain of them and completely justified measures of retaliation" (tr. Jowett). On ἤδη and superlatives, see below §148.

[156] Hornblower (*ad loc.*) recalls that a similar gnomic content occurs without δή at 2.65.4 (ὅπερ φιλεῖ ὅμιλος ποιεῖν).

[157] οἷον δή is to be distinguished from the idiomatic ὅσος δή or ὅτις δή forms that convey approximation. See n104.

[158] See Cooper 2002:2941 on δή "in exclamations." Already the Homeric scholia established a link between δή and emotions; see I.2 §58.

[159] See *Iliad* 5.601; 13.633; 17.587; 21.57; *Odyssey* 1.32; 5.183; 11.429; 18.221; 20.393. For example, at *Odyssey* 5.183 Calypso comments on a speech that Odysseus just delivered: ἦ δὴ ἀλιτρός γ' ἐσσὶ

uses οἷα δή three times to convey the same emotionality. One of these instances deserves to be mentioned, as translations do not give it justice. Among the facts that Croesus—on the pyre—recalls about Solon is the time when Solon visited Sardis and made no account of all the prosperity he had seen there. The Greek is καὶ θεησάμενος πάντα τὸν ἑωυτοῦ ὄλβον ἀποφλαυρίσειε οἷα δὴ εἴπας (Herodotus 1.86.5). In Hude's edition οἷα δὴ εἴπας is put in parentheses; De Sélincourt and Marincola do not translate it, and Godley generically writes, "and [had] spoken as if he despised it." In light of the Homeric evidence, I read the segment as an independent exclamatory discourse act: "after seeing all the prosperity he would make no account of it—what a speech!"[160]

§119. Returning to Thucydides' οἷον δὴ ὄχλος φιλεῖ θαρσήσας ποιεῖν: instead of reading οἷον as the neuter form of a relative pronoun, the combination οἷον δή can be read as a construction syntactically non-integrated to the rest of the discourse. The entire utterance can be interpreted as an exclamatory authorial stance (thus reflecting emotional engagement) about mass psychology: "how the throng likes to get to action when the spirit is up!"[161] At 8.84.3 we find the only other Thucydidean parallel: τὸ δὲ πλῆθος τῶν στρατιωτῶν ὡς εἶδον, οἷα δὴ ναῦται, ὥρμησαν ἐκραγέντες ... ὥστε βάλλειν, which Hammonds translates: "At this the crowd of troops saw red, as sailors will, and surged forward to strike ..." I interpret οἷα δὴ ναῦται as an authorial comment with some exclamatory tone: "—sailors!—," implying "they were sailors (after all)!" or "as sailors typically do!"[162]

καὶ οὐκ ἀποφώλια εἰδώς, οἷον δὴ τὸν μῦθον ἐπεφράσθης ἀγορεῦσαι. "You definitely are a rogue, and what you know is not pointless; what a speech you devised to perform!" (tr. AB).

160 εἴπας is the participle aorist in the nominative case, unless we think of a "visionary" aorist, second person "what a speech!" (εἴπας being the epic/Ionic variant of Attic εἶπας). Two further occurences of οἷα δή in Herodotus share a similar function. At 1.122.1 the foster parents of Cyrus rejoice when they see him, as they were sure he had died; the text is μεγάλως ἀσπάζοντο οἷα δὴ ἐπιστάμενοι αὐτίκα τότε τελευτῆσαι, which I paraphrase as "they warmly welcomed him—they assumed that he had died then on the spot!" At 6.26.2 the Chians happen to be ruthlessly killed by Histiaeus: καὶ τῶν λοιπῶν Χίων, οἷα δὴ κεκακωμένων ἐκ τῆς ναυμαχίης, ὁ Ἱστιαῖος ἔχων ..., which I render: "and of the rest of the Chians—alas, they were already distressed by the seabattle!" I posit that the "already" component comes from the perfect tense of the participle, rather than from δή. At 3.129.3 οἷα δή is uncertain: both Hude and Legrand leave it in square brackets, as it is omitted in a few manuscripts: Τῇ δὲ δὴ ὀγδόῃ ἡμέρῃ ἔχοντί οἱ φλαύρως [οἷα δὴ] παρακούσας τις πρότερον ... ἐσαγγέλλει τῷ Δαρείῳ. "On the eighth day, when he [Darius] was doing poorly, someone who had heard ... told Darius of him" (tr. Godley). Indeed, this co-text does not resemble those in the other instances.

161 On the sociological connotations of ὄχλος in Thucydides, see in particular Hunter 1988.

162 I associate the relevance of intonation to occurrences of δή when γε δή also appears. In Thucydides, 7 of 10 instances of γε δή come from the author's voice; the remaining ones appear in direct speech. For example: ἔθνη γὰρ πλεῖστα δὴ ἐπὶ μίαν πόλιν ταύτην ξυνῆλθε, πλήν γε δὴ τοῦ ξύμπαντος λόγου τοῦ ἐν τῷδε τῷ πολέμῳ πρὸς τὴν Ἀθηναίων τε πόλιν καὶ Λακεδαιμονίων "The greatest number of nations, except the general roll of those which in this war adhered to Athens and Lacedaemon, were together at this one city," Thucydides 7.56.4 (tr. Hobbes). In Herodotus, 5 of 9 γε δή are uttered by the main narrator. Denniston (1950:246) links the combination γε δή in Herodotus and Thucydides to *a fortiori* statements. According to him, these statements are

4.6.3 When multiple voices share the same stance

§120. Stancetaking can include the manifestation—linguistic or nonlinguistic—of emotions. In this subsection I take up the emotional effect of stancetaking in situations where it is possible to infer an emotional alignment between Subject 1 and Subject 2. In some contexts Thucydides appears to suggest that he himself shares the same stance and its emotional load with some characters involved in the scene; in other words, the same stance is shared by multiple subjects and multiple voices.

§121. What is interesting in these cases is that such stancetaking acts bring to the reader's awareness the presence of separate voices speaking, as it were, in chorus. δή signals this potential polyphony. Thucydides uses δή in this polyphonic sense to conceal his authorial persona and to show emotional alignment with his characters.

(t29)

οἱ δὲ Λακεδαιμόνιοι καὶ οἱ ξύμμαχοι εἵποντο μὲν ὡς ἡγεῖτο διὰ τὸν νόμον, ἐν αἰτίᾳ δ' εἶχον κατ' ἀλλήλους πολλῇ τὸν Ἆγιν, νομίζοντες ἐν καλῷ παρατυχὸν σφίσι ξυμβαλεῖν καὶ πανταχόθεν αὐτῶν ἀποκεκλῃμένων καὶ ὑπὸ ἱππέων καὶ πεζῶν οὐδὲν δράσαντες ἄξιον τῆς παρασκευῆς ἀπιέναι. στρατόπεδον γὰρ <u>δὴ</u> τοῦτο κάλλιστον Ἑλληνικὸν τῶν μέχρι τοῦδε ξυνῆλθεν· ὤφθη δὲ μάλιστα ἕως ἔτι ἦν ἀθρόον ἐν Νεμέᾳ, ...

Thucydides 5.60.2-3

The Lacedaemonians and their allies followed Agis out of respect for the law, but they blamed him severely among themselves. For they believed that they had lost a glorious opportunity; their enemies had been surrounded on every side both by horse and foot; [3] and yet they were returning home having done nothing worthy of their great effort. No finer Hellenic army had ever up to that day been collected; its appearance was most striking at Nemea while the host was still one ... (tr. Jowett)

At the beginning of this passage Thucydides unambiguously reports the thoughts of Spartans and Argives (see νομίζοντες). But the stancetaking introduced by γὰρ δή has

conclusions that show even stronger evidence than what was previously adduced. Underlying this argumentative force is a more general pragmatic value: the combination (not a cluster) γε + δή allows the source of the utterance to come to the fore, and it marks an act of stance. Its force is equivalent to the prosodic emphasis that we may attach to a specific piece of information for whatever contextual purpose. Cobet (1876:483) reads irony behind some γε/γε δή in Demosthenes. I do not read irony in the two historians but rather the marking of narrative peaks (see above n143 about πρὶν γε δή). Irony with δή in Herodotus is independent of γε, and concerns selected occurrences, as we have seen.

a less clear source. The co-occurrence of the superlative κάλλιστον, with its sense of absolute judgment, suggests a moment of authorial stance; however, the lexical choice of κάλλιστον (which is usually uttered by a character in Thucydides),[163] may suggest the voice and stance of the Spartans and Argives as well.[164] The aorist ξυνῆλθεν could help to disambiguate if we assume that the internal viewpoint of characters is more likely to be expressed by imperfect forms.[165] However, even when imperfects occur in discourse acts that host δή, it is difficult to extract from the context whose stance in particular is communicated—especially if the scene has multiple participants, and if what is in question is just their stance.[166]

163 In 10 out of 12 cases the source of the utterance including the καλλιστ- form is a character (three times Brasidas; twice Hermocrates and Pericles; once Archidamus; one instance occurs in Xerxes' letter to Pausanias, and one in Phormio's thoughts about how to trap the Peloponnesian ships in the Gulf of Corinth). The eleventh occurrence is in narrator text ("beautiful suburbs," 2.34.5), and the twelfth is (t29). As for the referents of the adjective or pronoun, in 6 cases they have to do with attacks and military strategies in more or less general terms (1.129.3; 2.11.9; 2.84.3; 5.9.4; 6.33.3; 6.33.4). However, the specific referent "army" occurs only here. The connection to Sappho fr. 16.1-3 (Οἰ μὲν ἰππήων στρότον, οἰ δὲ πέσδων, οἰ δὲ νάων φαῖσ' ἐπὶ γᾶν μέλαιναν ἔμμεναι κάλλιστον) is inevitable for us modern readers. On κάλλος, καλός, and κάλλιστος as referring to something erotically attractive in ancient Greek literature, see Konstan 2015:49-61.

164 Hornblower (1991-2008, vol. III:157-158) notes that Stroud (1994:291) takes the passive form ὤφθη (at the end of the passage) as a sign of authorial autopsy, but he adds: "The autopsy idea is attractive but not certain, and no amount of emphatic language in Thucydides makes it so. As at 59.3 ..., Thucydides makes it hard to say how much is Spartan focalization and how much his own comment and opinion."

165 See e.g. Bakker 1997e; Grethlein 2013b:33.

166 Let us list here further instances of δή where I see Thucydides blurring his voice and stance, or in other words, where I infer his emotional alignment with characters. At 2.77.2 (πᾶσαν γὰρ δὴ ἰδέαν ἐπενόουν, εἴ πως σφίσιν ἄνευ δαπάνης καὶ πολιορκίας προσαχθείη, "they were now thinking of every possible means of securing control without the expense of a siege," tr. Hammond), the Peloponnesians' and Thucydides' thoughts seem to be blended. At 4.55.2 (ἔς τε τὰ πολεμικά, εἴπερ ποτέ, μάλιστα δὴ ὀκνηρότεροι ἐγένοντο, "in all military matters they [the Spartans] became yet more cautious than ever before," tr. Hammond) the Spartans' positioning seems to be joined with the author's. At 5.16.1 (πολλῷ δὴ μᾶλλον προυθυμοῦντο, "[Pleistoanax, son of Pausanias, and Nicias] became yet more enthusiastic for an end to the war," tr. Hammond) Thucydides seems to align with the two political leaders. At 5.50.4 (ὥστε πολλῷ δὴ μᾶλλον ἐπεφόβηντο πάντες καὶ ἐδόκει τι νέον ἔσεσθαι, "This greatly intensified the general anxiety, and it was thought that there would be a crisis," tr. Hammond) Thucydides seems to share the feelings of all the people attending the Olympic games. At 7.55.1 (οἱ μὲν Ἀθηναῖοι ἐν παντὶ δὴ ἀθυμίας ἦσαν, "The Athenians were in complete despair," tr. Hammond) Thucydides seems to share his stance with that of the Athenians. At 7.71.5 (πρίν γε δὴ οἱ Συρακόσιοι καὶ οἱ ξύμμαχοι ἐπὶ πολὺ ἀντισχούσης τῆς ναυμαχίας ἔτρεψάν τε τοὺς Ἀθηναίους, "until ... the Syracusans and their allies routed the Athenians," tr. Hammond) Thucydides seems to join perspective with the Syracusans at a narrative peak. Then, at the end of book 7 several acts including δή seem to convey the author's emotional alignment with the losing Athenians, e.g. 7.85.4 (πλεῖστος γὰρ δὴ φόνος οὗτος, "this was a most sizable slaughter," tr. AB).

Finally, there is an occurrence of δή + superlative that I find striking: it is found after the account of the spectacle enjoyed by the Athenians on the harbor at the outset of the Sicilian expedition. The Greek reads as follows: οἱ δὲ ξένοι καὶ ὁ ἄλλος ὄχλος κατὰ θέαν ἧκεν ὡς ἐπ'

§122. My reading complements the literary approaches that have focused on how Thucydides allows readers to enjoy thoughts and actions from within his narrative. Grethlein's reader response approach in particular suits my findings well. As I pointed out in §78, in his experiential model readers are invited to take stance more from following the *hic et nunc* of the narrative as it unfolds than from processing the author's *a posteriori* judgments.[167] Of course, Thucydides does make sweeping authorial statements several times in his history, but other times he conceals his stance by blending it with the characters'.

4.6.4 Any irony?

§123. A final question is whether there are Thucydidean instances of δή suggesting gaps in knowledge, the apprehension of which would result in readerly perception of irony. Our preceding discussion does not suggest that this would occur, perhaps with the exception of (t26) and (t25). Here I am going to mention a couple of passages that have aroused my interest; I invite the reader to adjudicate on those, and on the question in general.

§124. At 6.80.2 Hermocrates tries to convince the inhabitants of Camarina to join the Syracusan fight against Athens. At one point he says that aligning with the Syracusans would preserve the common interests of Sicily and keep the Athenians from making mistakes. The Greek of the last part is καὶ τοὺς Ἀθηναίους φίλους δὴ ὄντας μὴ ἐᾶσαι ἁμαρτεῖν. Earlier (79.1) Hermocrates had acknowledged Camarina's alliance with Athens and the help they had provided when the Athenians were in trouble. Here, perhaps, the δή indicates that while he acknowledges the evidence ("the Athenians, being your friends"), he also wishes to distance himself from aligning with the Camarinans' opinion: "you are sure that they are friends, but I am not so sure."[168]

§125. At 7.18.1 Thucydides' use of a ὅπως δή clause—very much like Herodotean ἵνα δή clauses—suggests that he is distancing himself from the characters. The author begins the chapter by saying that the Spartans were preparing their invasion of Attica

---

ἀξιόχρεων καὶ ἄπιστον διάνοιαν. παρασκευὴ γὰρ αὕτη πρώτη ἐκπλεύσασα μιᾶς πόλεως δυνάμει Ἑλληνικῇ πολυτελεστάτη δὴ καὶ εὐπρεπεστάτη τῶν ἐς ἐκεῖνον τὸν χρόνον ἐγένετο. "The foreigners and the rest of the crowd came there to witness for themselves a remarkable enterprise which would otherwise have seemed incredible. This first expeditionary force was indeed at that time the costliest and most magnificent Greek armadaever to sail from a single city," 6.31.1 (tr. Hammond). It is possible to interpret the passage as encompassing the joint view (in the literal sense of the word) of both Thucydides and the Athenians.

167 By studying the relation between imperfect tense and the characters' perspective in Thucydides, Bakker (E. J. Bakker 2007:118) comes to a similar conclusion: "the reader has become a witness who observes the events of the war in situ."

168 This reading is in line with Thucydides' introduction to this speech: Hermocrates' overall communicative intention by giving the speech was "to raise the prejudices of the people of Camarina against the Athenians beforehand" (ὁ Ἑρμοκράτης ... τῶν Καμαριναίων βουλόμενος προδιαβάλλειν τοὺς Ἀθηναίους ἔλεγε τοιάδε, 6.75.4).

ὅπως δὴ ἐσβολῆς γενομένης διακωλυθῇ, which Hammond translates "and imagined that an invasion would stop them." Without δή the ὅπως clause would simply convey the hope and intention of the Spartans. δή suggests that the Spartans were confident of their success, and the added nuance raises the suspicion of authorial disalignment. That Thucydides expresses skepticism here conforms with the general position he elsewhere expresses, *viz.* that the Athenians were at this point ready to escalate, rather than end, the conflict.[169]

§126. All things considered, the use of δή to exploit narrative potential for irony seems to me to characterize Herodotean practice more than it does Thucydides'. In any case I wish to underscore that such exploitation of irony does not merely function as a means for the historian to demonstrate his omniscient distance from the events he describes. It has consequences for the reader: the perception of irony triggers an act of evaluation, for the reader must, first, access the stance of the parties involved, and second, assess it against the situation described while getting critically engaged. This is the process that δῆθεν—which I will turn to in the subsequent section—particularly invites.

4.6.5 Interim conclusion

§127. Thucydides' use of δή resembles Herodotus' in that Thucydides also uses δή to advance narration and signal others' voices or thoughts, although he does so far less often than his predecessor does. His usage differs from Herodotus' in three major ways: he prefers to use δή to express authorial stance implicitly rather than explicitly; he uses δή in direct speech more frequently; and he favors the author's epistemic and emotional alignment with characters whenever, by means of δή, the source of the stance can ambiguously be attributed to the author as well as the characters.

4.7 Stance and Polyphony in the Use of δῆθεν

§128. Especially in Herodotus, δή's ironic potential lies in the author's ability to play with different characters' varying degrees of knowledge about things, as well as his deliberate efforts to underscore alignment between author and audience. The etymologically related δῆθεν[170] is a particle that amplifies this potential of δή. In spite of its relative

[169] This reading of mine harmonizes with Hornblower's comment: "δή indicates that this is presumed Syracusan and Corinthian thinking, but also that that thinking is precarious" (1991-2008, vol. III:572), and Wakker's remark (1997b:245): "By the retainment of the subjunctive, the purpose clause introduced by *hópōs* is explicitly characterized as presented from the perspective of the Lacedaemonians. But it is the narrator who, with *dḗ*, asks special attention for this purpose, which is not accomplished, as he will show later in the narrative."

[170] Following Schwyzer and Debrunner (1950:562) and Chantraine (*DELG*, s.v. δή), Beekes (2010:322) includes δῆθεν in "more or less fixed connections" of δή (δή + adverbial suffix -θεν).

infrequency in ancient Greek texts,[171] δῆθεν deserves special attention, as it has a quite complex communicative role.

§129. Powell (1938:85) says of δῆθεν in Herodotus: "implying falsity of speech or thought." Denniston uses a litotes to define δῆθεν (1950:264): "the nuance of pretense or unreality, and the ironical colour, which, though often present in δή, do not dominate that particle, are in δῆθεν but rarely absent."[172] Where does falsity come from in the text, and whose pretense is suggested? Most of all, what does the ironic color rest on?

§130. By analyzing the 13 occurrences of δῆθεν in Herodotus and the 5 in Thucydides, I noticed three consistencies: first, δῆθεν never appears in direct speech; second, it regularly involves someone's declaration of stance in situations where multiple characters or groups of characters are involved; finally, it regularly implies the author's disalignment with that stance. Here is an example from Herodotus:

(t30)

> Ταῦτα δὲ οὕτω ἐνετέλλοντο ὡς πιστοτάτου <u>δῆθεν</u> ἐόντος αὐτοῦ ἐν Πέρσῃσι, καὶ πολλάκις τε ἀποδεξαμένου γνώμην ὡς περιείη ὁ Κύρου Σμέρδις καὶ ἐξαρνησαμένου τὸν φόνον αὐτοῦ.
>
> Herodotus 3.74.3

> They gave him this charge, because they thought him to be the man most trusted by the Persians, and because he had often asserted that Cyrus' son Smerdis was alive, and had denied the murder. (tr. Godley)

The subjects of ἐνετέλλοντο are the Magi, who want to make the Persian nobleman Prexaspes their ally in order to enhance their political power against the royal family. According to the passage, they count on Prexaspes' excellent reputation among the

[171] Up to literature from the fourth century BCE, the *TLG* online records only 58 tokens of δῆθεν (13 in Herodotus, 12 in Aesopus; 7 in Euripides; 6 in the Corpus Hippocraticum; 5 in Thucydides; 2 in Aeschylus, Ctesias, Aeneas, and Callimachus; 1 in Sophocles, Xenophon, Plato, Aristotle, Xenocrates, Aratus, and Persaeus.

[172] See *Suidae Lexicon* s.v. δῆθεν (Adler 2004:36): ὡς δή φησι· τοῦτο δὲ προσποίησιν ἀληθείας ἔχει, δύναμιν δὲ ψεύδους. λαμβάνεται δὲ τὸ θεν ὡς παραπληρωματικόν "the δή says: "this has the pretension to truth, but the force of a lie. The θεν is taken as a filler." I thank José Miguel Jiménez Delgado for drawing my attention to this early definition. In modern times, before Denniston, Stephens retrieves the idea of a discrepancy between utterance and actual truth, and provides *ante litteram* a pragmatic interpretation of the use of the word: "... the speaker, by the use of δῆθεν, may apprize the audience how the matter really stands" (1837:9). Navarre 1904a:325-326 and Menge 1999 (1914): 246 qualify δῆθεν as often ironic. Navarre 1904a is a rare piece entirely devoted to the particle. The author interprets the semantic evolution of δῆθεν starting from a basic temporal sense ("from that moment on"), and evolving into different "logic meanings" ("significations logiques," 320), in this order: "therefore," "evidently," "consequently," "of course (ironically/sarcastically)," and "marking the assertion as false."

Persians, and on the fact that Prexaspes, king Cambyses' secret agent, and killer of Cambyses' brother Smerdis upon Cambyses' orders, had several times confirmed that Smerdis was still alive. The Magi instruct Prexaspes to publicly declare that the Smerdis on the throne is Cambyses' brother, thus reassuring the people that he is not an impostor, when in fact he is. The discourse act ὡς πιστοτάτου δῆθεν ἐόντος αὐτοῦ ἐν Πέρσῃσι opens a sequence of three genitive absolutes, which reiterate the Magi's motivations for this strategic move. Very similar reasons had already been expressed at 3.74.1, including the nobleman's good reputation (ἐόντα ἐν αἴνῃ μεγίστῃ τὸν Πρηξάσπεα ἐν Πέρσῃσι, "Prexaspes was highly respected among the Persians"). What does ὡς πιστοτάτου δῆθεν ἐόντος αὐτοῦ ἐν Πέρσῃσι add, then?

§131. Herodotus makes it apparent here that he is intruding into the Magi's thoughts, while at 74.1 he describes their motivations in a more objective way (note ὅτι). The linguistic markers of subjectivity in ὡς πιστοτάτου δῆθεν ἐόντος αὐτοῦ ἐν Πέρσῃσι are the construction ὡς + participle and δῆθεν.[173] δῆθεν's communicative role is to mark both the certainty with which the Magi evaluate Prexaspes' reliability, and Herodotus' disalignment at the same time. That is, Herodotus distances himself from the Magi's evaluation so that the full sense is, "I disassociate myself from their absolute certainty."[174] This narrative strategy allows Herodotus to call upon the reader to actively take stock of the certainty's subjective and epistemically limited nature. This intrusion into the Magi's subjective thoughts subtly adumbrates the subsequent account of Prexaspes' spectacular disregard of the Magi's expectations: he will announce the truth, and then will commit suicide.

§132. This use of δῆθεν is ironic in the sense that it reflects a double understanding, namely that of some of the internal characters, who are unaware of the actual outcome,[175] and that of the omniscient author who is about to prove that the Magi's understanding of the situation was in fact wrong. From a pragmatic perspective, δῆθεν signals the occurrence of not just a single voice or stance, but two: in the above example, the author's voice overlays and distances itself from the Magi's. Duality of voice is used to express duality of stance.

[173] Note the occurrence of the superlative as well, which resonates with the superlative at 74.1 ἐν αἴνῃ μεγίστῃ.

[174] See Navarre 1904a:326: δῆθεν marks that the uttered assertion is contrary to the reality, or at least "*qu'on ne la garantit pas, qu'on en laisse la responsabilité à l'intéressé*" ("one does not guarantee it, one leaves the responsibility up to the interested person").

[175] Readers may assume that Prexaspes disaligns with the Magi's evaluation as well; therefore, not all the characters involved are ultimately unaware of the actual outcome. However, Herodotus makes sure that readers do not know how Prexaspes receives the Magi's orders, and how he will react to the situation, thereby maintaining a high level of suspense. For this reason I do not claim that δῆθεν includes the disalignment of Prexaspes together with Herodotus': by means of δῆθεν the author establishes dialogue directly with readers, rather than with other co-participants in the story. De Jong (2004a:111) takes Herodotean δῆθεν as a way to draw the narratees' attention to the ongoing deceit.

§133. Also in the remaining twelve occurrences of δῆθεν in Herodotus the thoughts and actions marked by δῆθεν are meant to appear clear and logical, but actually turn out to be tricks or other acts of deception—in a word, pretenses. In all cases the reader is able to infer the falsity of these thoughts and actions by comparing them against the author's omniscient perspective.[176] This consistency of use permits a general conclusion: δῆθεν conveys polyphony; the particle's presence reveals a certain commitment on the author's part to giving voice to some characters' sense of clarity and certainty, while at the same time articulating his own disalignment.

§134. Let us now turn to an example from Thucydides:

(t31)

ἐν τούτῳ δ' οἱ Μαντινῆς καὶ οἷς ἔσπειστο πρόφασιν ἐπὶ λαχανισμὸν καὶ φρυγάνων ξυλλογὴν ἐξελθόντες ὑπαπῇσαν κατ' ὀλίγους, ἅμα ξυλλέγοντες ἐφ' ἃ ἐξῆλθον <u>δῆθεν</u>· προκεχωρηκότες δὲ ἤδη ἄπωθεν τῆς Ὄλπης θᾶσσον ἀπεχώρουν.

Thucydides 3.111.1

In the meantime, the Mantineans and such as had part in the truce, going out on pretence to gather potherbs and firewood, stole away by small numbers, and as they went, did indeed gather such things as they pretended to go forth for; but when they were gotten far from Olpae, they went faster away. (tr. Hobbes)

Thanks to a private truce between Demosthenes and the Mantinaeans (3.109) after a battle near Olpae (3.107-108), the Mantinaeans, joined by other Peloponnesian commanders,

176 At 1.59.4 δῆθεν marks a stratagem by Pisistratus; at 1.73.5 it marks the macabre pretense of animal flesh for human flesh; at 3.136.2 a trick by Democedes; at 6.1.1 a lie by Histiaeus; at 6.39.1 feigned ignorance about the murder of Cimon; at 7.211.3 a Spartan trick aimed at deceiving the Persians (De Sélincourt and Marincola *ad loc.* renders δῆθεν by translating "amongst the feints they employed was to ... pretend to be retreating in confusion"); at 8.5.1 Themistocles pretending to pass Eurybiades his own money; at 8.6.2 the Persians' deceptive plan to wait before attacking the Greeks at Artemisium; at 9.66.3 Artabazus making as if to do battle while the Persians start the retreat after Plataea; at 9.80.3 the helots' unawareness of selling gold to the Aeginetans as if it was brass; at 9.99.3 a Persians' trick to move the Milesians away on the pretext that they knew the area of Mycale.

At 6.138.4 δῆθεν exceptionally appears in a question that functions as indirect thought: the Pelasgians, worried about the dominance of the Attic mothers' children, wonder what they will do when they reach adulthood: τί δὴ ἀνδρωθέντες δῆθεν ποιήσουσι. The discrepancy in stance in this case is between the certainty with which the Pelasgians foresee the threat of the Attic boys, and Herodotus' disalignment with this line of thought, through δῆθεν. From δῆθεν the reader is warned against the characters' forecast, and is invited to judge the Pelasgians' decision to kill all those children and also the mothers as drastic, at the very least. Powell (1938:85) comments on δῆθεν in this passage: "perhaps merely emphatic."

are allowed to secretly escape. They pretend to seek forage and firewood, while actually making their way out of Olpae. As in the Herodotean example, δῆθεν accompanies a piece of information that has already been offered: πρόφασιν ... ξυλλογὴν ἐξελθόντες ("having gone out on pretense to gather material") is subsequently echoed by ξυλλέγοντες ἐφ' ἃ ἐξῆλθον ("having gathered the things they went out for"). In this case the pretense is made evident from the beginning (see πρόφασιν). What δῆθεν does is to make the entire discourse act ἅμα ξυλλέγοντες ἐφ' ἃ ἐξῆλθον δῆθεν ("gathering at the same time the things they went out for, sure") sound polyphonic: on the one hand we hear the voice of the Mantinaeans giving the ostensible version of their intentions; on the other we hear the voice of the author conveying that these intentions are fake.

§135. The account continues from the characters' perspective: the Mantinaeans go away faster (θᾶσσον ἀπεχώρουν); the Ambraciots, a further group of the Peloponnesian contingent, go out to forage too, and realize that the Mantineans are actually escaping (ὡς ἔγνωσαν ἀπιόντας, 3.111.2) at the point when they catch up with them (ὥρμησαν καὶ αὐτοὶ καὶ ἔθεον δρόμῳ, 3.111.2). Further attempts, assumptions, and uncertainty among different groups (allies as well as antagonists) follow, leading eventually to the killing of about two hundred Ambraciots (by the Acarnanians). The reader is thus invited to experience the different groups' thoughts and decisions in turn, following their sequential arrival on the scene.

§136. The remaining four occurrences of δῆθεν in Thucydides consistently signal the same kind of polyphony: characters' intentions and claims are presented as obvious even as the author evaluates them as treacherous.[177] This remarkable consistency further supports the conclusion we drew from Herodotean usage, that δῆθεν's function is to represent the characters' internal perspective alongside the author's external one. It achieves this function at the level of the act (that is, it has act scope). The characters express stance in the form of evaluation; the author, in the form of disalignment. His act of disalignment in turn activates the reader's ability to detect lies, deceptive maneuvers, and mistaken assumptions.

4.8 ἤδη as Stance Marker

§137. ἤδη is also etymologically related to δή.[178] ἤδη is more frequent than δῆθεν, especially in Thucydides (373 instances, against 136 in Herodotus, that is, 0.24% vs. 0.07% of total words), and unlike δῆθεν it occurs in direct speech as well. Despite its relation to δή,

177 At 1.92.1 the Spartans are said to propose a policy "for the common good δῆθεν"; at 127.1 the Spartans want to drive out a curse "to honor the gods δῆθεν"; at 3.68.1 the Spartans "deem worthy to rest from conflicts [with the Plataeans] δῆθεν"; at 4.99.1 the Boeotians do not want "to make truce with the Athenians δῆθεν." In these instances too I read the scope of δῆθεν as embracing the host discourse act.

178 Ellendt (1835:166-167) sees δή as diachronically derived from ἤδη, but the opposite trajectory (ἤδη derives from δή) is generally accepted.

ἤδη is not considered a particle—for example, Denniston does not include it—presumably because in canonical grammars it is classified as a temporal adverb that modifies the content of the host proposition, like ἔπειτα or πρότερον. However, recent literature shows that temporal adverbs such as πάλιν, ἔτι, and αὖτις relate to the ongoing discourse in a range of ways.[179] ἤδη shows a similar versatility that deserves careful analysis. Powell's *Lexicon to Herodotus*, for example, gives the word a puzzling combination of meanings. ἤδη has three main meanings: 1. "Of the past, contrasted w[ith] the pres[ent] ...; 2. Of the pres[ent] or fut[ure], contrasted w[ith] the past (...); 3. Logically, introd[ucing] a step in the argument" (Powell 1938:160). What makes ἤδη indicate contrast between past and present? Is this contrasting function totally absent from the "logical" function (number 3)? A discourse approach can resolve these questions. As we shall see, ἤδη's various meanings, which extend within and beyond the marking of time, in fact possess a common thread.

§138. In what follows, I will first contextualize the discussion by drawing from three bodies of scholarship on the topic: contemporary literature on phasal adverb, contemporary works on Latin *iam* and on ἤδη in Xenophon, and the work of nineteenth-century scholars on the relation between ἤδη and δή. I will then examine patterns of similarity in the co-texts that tend to occur with ἤδη and δή, and establish how far the two words share the function of revealing an individual's voice and stance. In the main, the uses of ἤδη generally resemble all the uses of δή I illustrated in sections 4.5 and 4.6. Their co-texts often follow the same pattern (e.g. marking narrative progression in act-initial position; marking the evaluating side of stance near scalar terms). These usages are observable in both *Histories*. A discourse function that is common to both lexical items and is particularly observable in Thucydides relates to the positioning and aligning vectors of stance. In direct or indirect speech, and in indirect thought, ἤδη gives voice to the characters positioning themselves as witnesses of the situation described. Thucydides may also use ἤδη to position himself in a similar fashion in implicit authorial statements. When ἤδη occurs in situations involving characters, it can blend the positioning of characters and that of the historian on the same situation, and it creates alignment. This may explain why Thucydides employs ἤδη three times as frequently as Herodotus. Finally, two further usages are illustrated with regard to both historiographical works: ἤδη expressing stance about time (typically when it is embedded in participial constructions), and a few cases where ἤδη means "now" propositionally, that is, when "now" modifies the propositional content of the host act.

§139. My inquiry benefits first of all from contemporary works on phasal adverbs, and on the so-called T (temporal) - A (aspectual)—M (modal) markers found in the Romance languages. Adverbs such as "still," "already," "not yet," and "no longer" in

[179] For studies that embrace a discourse perspective, see e.g. Revuelta Puigdollers 2006b on πάλιν; Wakker 2001 on ἔτι, Jiménez Delgado 2014 on αὖ and αὖθις, and Bonifazi 2012:263-273 on αὖτις.

English (and their counterparts in other Indoeuropean languages) are called "phasal adverbs." Phasal adverbs concern an "actual or potential transition between different phases of a state of affairs" (Hansen 2008:85). They have a semantic element that refers to "situation-external time" and are relational in nature; that is, they "relate the SoA [state of affairs] denoted by the host clause to a different SoA, which either precedes or follows it" (Hansen 2008:99). But they also refer to "situation-internal time" in that they "focus on specific internal stages of the SoA";[180] for instance, they are sometimes called "inchoative markers" and "continuative markers."[181]

§140. Some scholars take as core elements of phasal adverbs the inferences that the adverbs carry. Conventional inferential elements are what, for example, make us chuckle if we hear someone say: "John is still dead"; the utterance is not acceptable because of the conventional incompatibility of "still" with irreversible states. Other scholars stress the logico-semantic implications of phasal adverbs, which give rise to the notions of negative and positive polarity.[182] "Not yet" indicates positive polarity in that the orientation is towards a positive fulfillment of a phase, whereas "still not" indicates orientation towards a negative description of the situation. Still other scholars study their subjective use by speakers who give to the transitions between phases of events a context-dependent meaning.[183] Hansen in particular (2008:109) shows that in specific contexts the use of phasal adverbs can have a subjective connotation independent from (or even in contradiction with) logico-semantic considerations.[184] This brief theoretical outline introduces ἤδη as a lexical item that indicates phasality and may have a bearing on inchoation. Also, its meaning is not necessarily independent of the context of utterance.

§141. Studies in temporal-aspectual adverbs that in different Romance languages etymologically derive from Latin *iam* are also varied in their approaches and interpretations. These adverbs can be analyzed in light of their logico-semantic contribution to meaning, as well as in light of what they reveal of the speaker's attitudes or evaluations

180 "Situation-external" vs. "situation-internal" time is a distinction established by Comrie (1976:5); the former locates states of affairs with respect to other states of affairs or to the time of the utterance (typically expressed by tense), while the latter concerns the way in which states of affairs are temporally constituted *per se* (typically expressed by aspect).

181 E.g. Van der Auwera 1993 and 1998; Van Baar 1997. König 1991:157-162 discusses the focus particles that work as "phasal quantifiers" in different modern European languages; the author considers non-temporal scales as well (159).

182 E.g. Löbner 1989; Vandeweghe 1992. Polarity in linguistics refers to the relative orientation denoted by certain lexical items.

183 E.g. Michaelis 1996; Hansen 2008:171-172.

184 Let us suppose the following context and example, which I take from Hansen (2008:109): John and Peter agree to meet at some airport at 3pm on a certain day to leave for two different cities. Peter has to fly to Madrid at 4pm. Something causes John to reach the airport only at 4pm. John can utter "Peter is already on his way to Madrid" felicitously at 4pm even though the time of the utterance coincides with Peter's departure time, as the sense of "early" for John subjectively relates to his own delay, and not to the objective schedule of Peter's flight.

(therefore in terms of their pragmatic contribution to meaning).[185] Diachronic developments can widen the range of meanings too. For example, the level of pragmaticization (i.e. the process of shifting from propositional to non-propositional meanings) of these adverbs across time can be so high that in some languages they become interjections—as in the case of northern Italian *già*, which corresponds to "already," and can be used as a "confirmative particle" or an "interjectional form" in exclamative expressions such as *già!/eh già!, ah già,* and *di già!*.[186] Indirectly these studies warn us about the type of contribution to meaning that ἤδη as temporal-aspectual adverb can signal; a phasal adverb does not necessarily modify the propositional content of the host act.

§142. Kroon and Risselada (1998) interpret Latin *iam* in light of semantic as well as pragmatic considerations. By analyzing several co-texts of *iam*, they postulate that *iam*'s general function is evaluative ("an evaluative particle in all its occurrences"). The three components of its basic meaning are: polarity (affirmative polarity), phasality/scalarity ("*iam* indicates progress on a temporal or non-temporal scale"), and counter-presuppositional saliency ("*iam* focuses on the element in its scope as something which runs counter to a particular standard or expectation").[187] All the various uses depend on a combination of these three components. Kroon and Risselada's study illuminates one important aspect of this adverb in particular. Phasality, which typically concerns the handling of temporal phases (see above §§138-140), is combined with scalarity, which concerns scales other than the temporal one. This is why the two scholars assert that "*iam* indicates progress on a temporal or non-temporal scale." Kroon and Risselada in fact analyze *iam* together with comparatives, superlatives, and scalar terms such as "all" and "much," which do not necessarily pertain to the handling of time.[188]

§143. Partly inspired by this work, Wakker in 2002 published an article on ἤδη in Xenophon. ἤδη can also be explained through the notions of polarity, phasal scalarity, and denial of expectation, the author claims (2002:4).[189] In Xenophon ἤδη implies that a high point on a temporal or other scale has been reached (2002:6); therefore, in general

185 See e.g. Van der Auwera 1998 on propositional vs. context-dependent discursive functions of adverbs in a temporal-aspectual dimension; Bazzanella, Bosco, Calaresu, Garcea, Guil Povedano, Radulescu 2005 and 2007, and also Hansen and Strudsholm 2008 on the multiple uses of T (temporal)—A (aspectual)—M (modal) markers across Romance languages; Hansen 2002 and 2008 on French temporal-aspectual adverbs *déjà* "already" and *encore* "still"; Squartini 2013 "From TAM to discourse: The role of information status in Northern-Italian *già* 'already'," in Degand, Cornilie, and Pietrandrea eds. 2013:163-190.

186 See Squartini 2013:178: *già/eh già* are seen as "sheer confirmative particle[s]"; *ah già* marks "sudden remembrance"; 2013:175 *di già* is an "interjectional form restricted to a temporal-aspectual interpretation."

187 All the quotations are in Kroon and Risselada 1998:444.

188 Rosén (2009:360) agrees with Kroon and Risselada only partially: it should be added that *iam* can highlight also an entire sentence, besides single constituents.

189 Even though polarity is not relevant to our study of ἤδη in Herodotus and Thucydides, for the sake of clarity I note that Wakker (2002:13) reads ἤδη as indicating positive polarity (exactly like "already" in English), and ἔτι as indicating negative polarity (like "still" in English).

it works as an evaluative particle (2002:10). For the evaluation of temporal phases, one must take into account the tense that ἤδη accompanies, be it imperfect, aorist, present, or future. For the evaluation of non-temporal scales, the focus of ἤδη is a point in a scale, which is expressed by adjectives and adverbs such as "all/every," "much/more," or comparative and superlative forms (2002:7). By means of ἤδη the speaker evaluates the state of affairs linked to these adjectives or adverbs as occurring contrary to her expectations. The denial of expectation in the case of temporal scales concerns something that happens/has happened before the time expected.

§144. Some of the connections made in recent literature were anticipated by scholars in the nineteenth century. Heller, in a long article to Dunker (Heller 1853), for example, states that ἤδη is comparable with *déjà* (266), and that across its different uses, ἤδη concerns perceptions and expectations about time: the speaker perceives something that happens/has happened/will happen before he expected.[190] Heller (1853:257-258) therefore disagrees with Hartung's main conclusion, which sees "instantly," "in that very place"/"on the spot" as the fundamental meaning shared by ἤδη and δή.[191] Heller sees the origin of Hartung's reading in a passage from Aristotle's *Physics* (222b), which he quotes and criticizes (1853:258-259). Let us reproduce this passage, as it is salient both to Heller's objection and to the points I will make.

(t32)

τὸ δ' ἤδη τὸ ἐγγύς ἐστι τοῦ παρόντος νῦν ἀτόμου μέρος τοῦ μέλλοντος χρόνου (πότε βαδίζεις; ἤδη, ὅτι ἐγγὺς ὁ χρόνος ἐν ᾧ μέλλει), καὶ τοῦ παρεληλυθότος χρόνου τὸ μὴ πόρρω τοῦ νῦν (πότε βαδίζεις; ἤδη βεβάδικα). τὸ δὲ Ἴλιον φάναι ἤδη ἑαλωκέναι οὐ λέγομεν, ὅτι λίαν πόρρω τοῦ νῦν.

Aristotle *Physics* 222b

190 ... *non simpliciter* ἤδη *tempus praesenti coniunctum sive praeteritum sive futurum indicat, sed eius particulae propria vis est ea, ut significet, factum esse aliquid aut fieri aut futurum esse, antequam quis putet vel putaverit* "ἤδη does not simply indicate a time connected with the present, or the past, or the future, but its proper force is that of signifying that something happened, or is happening, or will happen before one believes/expects or has believed/expected" (Heller 1853:260) Later in his letter, Heller agrees with Hartung on one aspect by saying: *Bene Hartungius vidit, particulae* ἤδη *locum esse, ubi quae nondum evenerunt, cogitatione praecipiuntur: cuius usus ratio ... sponte apparet, quippe in eiusmodi sententiis quod fortasse futurum est, iam praesens et antequam quis expectaverit esse fingatur.* "Hartung sees right that the occurrence of ἤδη is where things that did not take place yet are perceived with the mind's thought: the reason of this use ... is clear in itself, for in sentences of this type what will possibly happen is pretended to be already present, and before one had expected" (Heller 1853:275; tr. AB).

191 See δή in ORPS (our online database) for Hartung's accounts and for the considerable amount of early literature on the relation between δή and ἤδη.

> 'Presently' or 'just' refers to the part of future time which is near the indivisible present 'now' ('When do you walk?' 'Presently,' because the time in which he is going to do so is near), and to the part of past time which is not far from the 'now' ('When do you walk?' 'I have just been walking'). But to say that Troy has just been taken-we do not say that, because it is too far from the 'now.' (tr. R. P. Hardie and R. K. Gaye, http://classics.mit.edu/Aristotle/physics.4.iv.html)

Heller's criticism is that Aristotle's explanation does not conform with the common use of ἤδη with tenses that are unrelated to the present, such as past and future. We will see, however, that what Aristotle says is not at all incompatible with the use of ἤδη with past and future tenses.[192]

4.8.1 Pragmatic relationship to δή

§145. Although nineteenth and early twentieth century scholarship shows attention for the relationship between ἤδη and δή, in more recent times this relationship is elided. A division of labors is more or less implicitly assumed: δή is a marker of either evidentiality or time, and ἤδη means "already" or "now." My research, however, aligns me with the approach of the earlier scholarship. As I will demonstrate in this subsection, ἤδη and δή show a significant overlap in scope, position, and function. Later subsections (4.8.2 and 4.8.3) will discuss a particular way in which ἤδη marks stance, especially in Thucydides, while 4.8.4 will single out usages that are not shared by δή (at least not in Herodotus and Thucydides). Let us start with the overlap in scope and position.

§146. ἤδη in act-initial and -peninitial position has scope over the entire act (see e.g. (t34), (t37)). If ἤδη occurs either after or before scalar terms such as comparatives, superlatives, πολύς and πᾶς forms, and semantically evaluative adjectives, the focus of ἤδη coincides with the scalar and the evaluative terms, as it does for δή as well. Another similarity with δή is that when scope is small—for example, over just one contiguous word—the act of stancetaking is considered to be the entire act hosting ἤδη and its focus.

§147. The most conspicuous overlap with δή is through the features that co-occur with ἤδη quite often. For example, we find οὗτος (and τοιοῦτος) forms contiguous with ἤδη at the beginning of acts that move the narration forward.[193] We also find ἤδη ὧν in Herodotus, which is reminiscent of δὴ ὧν and ὧν δή;[194] it not only occurs invariably in

[192] I may add that Aristotle's thought provides insights also into the use of past tenses with ἤδη; in fact, what distinguishes an acceptable from an unacceptable ἤδη utterance is not the specific past tense being used (the examples display a perfect in both cases), but the culturally-bound knowledge of events that are nearer or farther from "now," whatever moment "now" indicates.

[193] E.g. ἀπὸ ταύτης ἤδη ἐς αὐτόν τε τὸν Θερμαῖον κόλπον ἐγίνετο τῷ ναυτικῷ στρατῷ <ὁ> πλόος, Herodotus 7.123.3; καὶ οὕτως ἤδη κατὰ κράτος ἡ Ποτείδαια ἀμφοτέρωθεν ἐπολιορκεῖτο, Thucydides 1.64.3. See also Thucydides 1.118.1; 4.78.6; 5.38.1; 5.76.3; 6.48.1.

[194] See above, §§86 and 89. In Herodotus ἤδη ὧν occurs 12 times.

act-initial position, but it also constitutes a separate act, like καὶ δή.[195] Sometimes we find ἤδη δέ,[196] which is reminiscent of δὲ δή.[197] Similarly, ἐνταῦθα ἤδη (in Thucydides) and ἐνθεῦτεν ἤδη (in Herodotus) recall ἐνθαῦτα δή.[198] καὶ ἤδη—in the same use as the cluster καὶ δή—and καὶ τότε ἤδη, both introducing salient moments, occur only a few times.[199] In all these cases I take ἤδη to generally relate, on the pragmatic level, to the historian's voice in narrative progression, rather than to the marking of stance—in line with my reading of δή in parallel co-texts. The contiguity with γάρ (ἤδη γάρ or γὰρ ἤδη)[200] is different: sometimes the two lexical items overall introduce unframed discourse; some other times a γάρ move includes an act of stancetaking signaled by ἤδη.

§148. The features shared by ἤδη and δή that specifically relate to stance are comparatives (including μᾶλλον[201]), superlatives, πᾶς and πολύς forms,[202] and a few explicitly visual references. All of them can be found in direct and indirect speech, in indirect thought, and in Herodotean explicit authorial statements.[203] In these linguistic environments ἤδη reflects mainly the evaluating side of stance (even though positioning and alignment can be inferred as well, just as for δή). I draw a connection between these linguistic environments, and Wakker's definition of ἤδη as "evaluative particle" (see above, §143).

195 See, e.g. Herodotus 4.86.1 Ἤδη ὦν | ἐς μὲν Φᾶσιν ἀπὸ τοῦ στόματος .... The combination occurs also at 1.207.3; 1.209.4; 2.49.1; 2.144.1; 2.172.5; 3.155.4; 4.31.2; 4.100.2; 6.53.2; 7.184.3; 8.100.5. Powell (1938:160) sees especially in ἤδη ὦν, but also in ἤδη γάρ the function of introducing a logical step in an argument. More recently, in his commentary to Herodotus 8, Bowie (2007:191) remarks: "ἤδη ὦν, 'so then' combination often used by H[erodotus] to introduce a point that follows logically from what precedes." Probably Bowie has in mind Powell on this point (see above §137). On καὶ δή as a separate act, see IV.2 §100n153.

196 Herodotus 1.68.6; 2.175.5; 4.18.2; 7.35.1; 7.55.3; 9.14.1; 9.95.1; Thucydides 1.50.5; 1.95.1.

197 See above, §§86 and 89.

198 See Thucydides 4.35.2, 6.44.3, and 7.44.1 for ἐνταῦθα ἤδη; Herodotus 2.25.3; 2.181.4; 7.129.3; 7.225.2; 8.34.1; 9.102.2 for ἐνθεῦτεν ἤδη. At least on three occasions ἐνθεῦτεν ἤδη introduces a narrative peak in Herodotus: see 2.25.3 καὶ τὸ ἐνθεῦτεν ἤδη ὁμοίως; 7.225.2 ἐνθεῦτεν ἤδη ἑτεροιοῦτο τὸ νεῖκος, and 9.102.1 ἐνθεῦτεν ἤδη ἑτεροιοῦτο τὸ πρῆγμα; in all these cases the discourse act marks a significant change in the course of action.

199 See Herodotus 9.7.1 καὶ ἤδη ἐπάλξις ἐλάμβανε, and Thucydides 6.98.3 καὶ ἤδη ἀντιπαρατασσομένων ... τῶν Συρακοσίων στρατηγοὶ ... ἀνήγαγον. The remaining 8 instances of καὶ ἤδη in Thucydides are not act-initial, and they do not work as clusters. In Thucydides 7.59.1 we find καὶ τότε ἤδη πᾶσαι ἀμφοτέροις παρῆσαν καὶ οὐκέτι οὐδὲν οὐδετέροις ἐπῆλθεν to describe the two opposing sides at one of the climactic moments of the last battles in the Great Harbor in Syracuse.

200 Herodotus uses only ἤδη γάρ (resembling Homeric δὴ γάρ), and only twice (4.45.3 and 6.53.1); Thucydides, conversely, uses ἤδη γάρ at 2.77.4; 4.93.1, 4.130.6; 6.29.1; 7.2.2; 7.6.1; 7.44.3; 8.42.1; and γὰρ ἤδη at 1.51.2; 2.31.1; 2.63.2; 3.52.3; 3.90.2; 3.97.3; 7.31.5.

201 ἤδη and μᾶλλον co-occur in the same discourse act several times; see Thucydides 1.3.2, 2.94.4, 6.105.2, 7.57.9 (ἤδη ... μᾶλλον); 1.8.3, 1.8.4, 1.49.7, 2.48.3, 7.8.3, 7.37.1, 7.43.7, 8.71.3 (μᾶλλον ἤδη); 6.49.4, 6.59.2, 7.4.4 (ἤδη μᾶλλον). See also Herodotus 7.223.2 ἤδη πολλῷ μᾶλλον.

202 See *LSJ* s.v. ἤδη, our frequency graphs (available online as I.5) with superlatives, and with comparatives. See also Powell 1938:160.

203 The upcoming (t)s will display all of these features.

§149. Let us consider an example from direct speech in Thucydides.

(t33)

Καὶ ἐκ τῶν παρόντων, ὦ Ἀθηναῖοι καὶ ξύμμαχοι, ἐλπίδα χρὴ ἔχειν (ἤδη τινὲς καὶ ἐκ δεινοτέρων ἢ τοιῶνδε ἐσώθησαν) ...

Thucydides 7.77.1

Even in our present state, Athenians and allies, we must have hope. Before now men have reached safety from yet worse situations than this ... (tr. Hammond)

In the observation that starts with ἤδη Nicias expresses his view that in some unspecified past some people found safety from even worse situations. The fact that the verb is an aorist (ἐσώθησαν) does not necessarily mean that the focus of ἤδη is directly that past; it just reveals that the stance expressed by the speaker in the "now" of the utterance refers to a situation that took place in the past.[204] The scope of ἤδη extends to the entire act. Its position evokes ἦ δή at the beginning of turns of speaking.[205] The point of the act rests on δεινοτέρων, which is a comparative form suggesting scalarity. Evaluations go hand in hand with scalarity, as judgments can very well be made through points in scales denoting higher or lower degrees/extents of things.[206] ἤδη, therefore, expresses assurance while introducing the stancetaking act.[207]

204 See also, e.g., Herodotus 7.9α.2 Ἐπειρήθην δὲ καὶ αὐτὸς ἤδη ἐπελαύνων ἐπὶ τοὺς ἄνδρας τούτους ὑπὸ πατρὸς τοῦ σοῦ κελευσθείς "I myself have made trial of these men [the Greeks of Asia], when by your father's command I marched against them" (tr. Godley). ἤδη stresses Mardonius' own experience of the Greeks of Asia rather than the fact that this happened in the past. I observe that the scope of ἤδη in this act is over καὶ αὐτός.

205 See II.3 §§33-37 on reading act-initial ἤδη in Homer as ἦ δή. Below (§§155-156) I will mention a couple of passages where act-initial ἤδη seems to evoke the performance of ἦ δή *viva voce*.

206 For ἤδη accompanying the superlative form of an adjective in direct speech, see, e.g. Herodotus 1.30.2: at the beginning of the long exchange between Croesus and Solon, Croesus introduces his first question by prefacing it with a preliminary move: "we have heard a lot about you because of your wisdom and of your wanderings, how as one who loves learning you have traveled much of the world for the sake of seeing it." Then the actual question follows: νῦν ὦν ἐπειρέσθαι σε ἵμερος ἐπῆλθέ μοι εἴ τινα ἤδη πάντων εἶδες ὀλβιώτατον. "... so now I desire to ask you who is the most fortunate man you have seen" (tr. Godley). Neither "already" nor "now" can render what ἤδη does, for the word that immediately follows ἤδη is πάντων, which reflects non-temporal scalarity. Croesus is not interested in knowing at which moment in time Solon saw the happiest man, but, rather, in the greatest extent of Solon's knowledge and judgment. By means of intensifying πάντων ("the most blessed man out of everyone you have seen"), or ὀλβιώτατον ("THE most blessed man ever"), or πάντων εἶδες ὀλβιώτατον ("the most blessed man you have seen ever"), ἤδη marks Croesus' evaluating stance towards Solon's magnitude of wisdom.

207 For further examples of direct speech in Thucydides where ἤδη marks stance with no focus on time, see 1.69.5, with a πολύς form (πολλὰ ἡμᾶς ἤδη τοῖς ἁμαρτήμασιν αὐτῶν μᾶλλον ἢ τῇ ἀφ' ὑμῶν τιμωρίᾳ περιγεγενημένους); 1.80.1, again with a πολύς form (Καὶ αὐτὸς πολλῶν ἤδη

§150. A further commonality between ἤδη and δή that deals with stance concerns visual references (see above §93). These instances exclusively pertain to Herodotus' work. For these I take our cue from *LSJ*'s third main meaning of ἤδη: "of place." Herodotus in particular uses ἤδη to indicate the point from which geographical phenomena start or become visible.[208] I locate these instances within the larger frame of epistemic stance: through ἤδη the speaker assesses spatial locations and relations based on his own sensorial and intellectual activity. This point is the link to the next subsection.

4.8.2 Author's and characters' ἤδη to mark firsthand experience

§151. Both δή and ἤδη signal voice and stancetaking. While δή's particular contribution is to stress somebody's certainty or determination towards some state of affairs, ἤδη's particular contribution is to mark somebody's firsthand experience of something. I see the latter function at work, for example, in this explicit authorial statement by Herodotus:

πολέμων ἔμπειρός εἰμι); 1.42.2, with an evaluative adjective (καὶ οὐκ ἄξιον ἐπαρθέντας αὐτῷ φανερὰν ἔχθραν ἤδη καὶ οὐ μέλλουσαν πρὸς Κορινθίους κτήσασθαι); 3.48.2, again with an evaluative adjective (τάδε γὰρ ἔς τε τὸ μέλλον ἀγαθὰ καὶ τοῖς πολεμίοις ἤδη φοβερά); with comparative forms of πολύς (3.11.1 καὶ πρὸς τὸ πλέον ἤδη εἶκον τοῦ ἡμετέρου ἔτι μόνου ἀντισουμένου; 4.62.3 γνοὺς ὅτι πλείους ἤδη καὶ τιμωρίαις μετιόντες τοὺς ἀδικοῦντας); with a superlative form (6.34.9 τὸ δ' ἤδη τὰς μετὰ φόβου παρασκευὰς ἀσφαλεστάτας νομίσαντας; 6.84.2 καὶ ἐν τούτῳ προσήκετε ἤδη ἡμῖν τὰ μέγιστα; 7.66.2 καὶ ἀρχὴν τὴν ἤδη μεγίστην τῶν τε πρὶν Ἑλλήνων καὶ τῶν νῦν κεκτημένους); finally, see 1.82.3, where ἤδη relates to a verb expressing an opinion (καὶ ἴσως ὁρῶντες ἡμῶν ἤδη τήν τε παρασκευὴν καὶ τοὺς λόγους ...), and 3.37.1, where ἤδη relates to a personal assessment whose focus is on ἔγωγε (Πολλάκις μὲν ἤδη ἔγωγε καὶ ἄλλοτε ἔγνων δημοκρατίαν ὅτι ἀδύνατόν ἐστιν ἑτέρων ἄρχειν).

Further examples of direct speech in Herodotus where I read ἤδη marking stance with no direct focus on time are 3.53.4, with a πολύς form (Πολλοὶ δὲ ἤδη τὰ μητρώια διζήμενοι τὰ πατρώια ἀπέβαλον); 7.18.2, again with a πολύς form (Ἐγὼ μέν, ὦ βασιλεῦ, οἷα ἄνθρωπος ἰδὼν ἤδη πολλά τε καὶ μεγάλα πεσόντα πρήγματα ὑπὸ ἡσσόνων); 7.157.2, with an evaluative adjective (τοῦτο δὲ ἤδη δεινὸν γίνεται); 7.235.3, again with an evaluative adjective (καταδουλωθείσης δὲ τῆς ἄλλης Ἑλλάδος ἀσθενὲς ἤδη τὸ Λακωνικὸν μοῦνον λείπεται); 4.150.3, with a comparative form (Ἐγὼ μέν, ὦναξ, πρεσβύτερός τε ἤδη εἰμὶ καὶ βαρὺς ἀείρεσθαι); 4.134.2, with scope over the verb δοκέω (Ὡς ὦν οὕτω ἤδη δοκεόντων καὶ αὐτῷ μοι ἔχειν).

208 Examples include: the beginning of Egypt after Lake Serbonis (ἀπὸ ταύτης ἤδη Αἴγυπτος, 3.5.3); utter desert occupying the area northward of the territory of the Androphagi (Ἤδη δὲ κατύπερθε τούτων ἔρημός ἐστι ἐπὶ πολλόν, 4.18.3); the fact that Asia further east of India is inhabited (τὸ δὲ ἀπὸ ταύτης ἔρημος ἤδη τὸ πρὸς τὴν ἠῶ, 4.40.2); Libya adjoining Egypt (ἀπὸ γὰρ Αἰγύπτου Λιβύη ἤδη ἐκδέκεται, 4.41.1); ancient Scythia beginning from the Danube (Ἀπὸ Ἴστρου αὕτη ἤδη <ἡ> ἀκταίη Σκυθική ἐστι, 4.99.2). There is a connection to δή in contexts of visual perception; see e.g. Τὸν ἐγὼ ἤδη εἶδον λόγου μέζω (2.148.1), where the author indicates autopsy: he has seen the Egyptian monumental labyrinth himself.

(t34)

Ἤδη δὲ ἤκουσα καὶ ὕστατον διαβῆναι βασιλέα πάντων.

Herodotus 7.55.3

[I assert that] I also heard that the king crossed last of all. (tr. AB)

(t34) is about an alternative version of the sequence in which the Persian army and the service train crosses the Hellespont. The aorist form ἤκουσα[209] draws attention to the author's role as inquirer. By means of ἤδη Herodotus articulates personal confirmation or guarantee.[210] This use of ἤδη reminds us of δή voicing perceptions (see 4.5.2), where δή conveys immediacy through the experience of evidentiality.[211]

§152. Let us now quote a parallel from Thucydides' implicit authorial statements. The most unequivocal *locus* is the *incipit* of book 2:

(t35)

Ἄρχεται δὲ ὁ πόλεμος ἐνθένδε ἤδη Ἀθηναίων καὶ Πελοποννησίων καὶ τῶν ἑκατέροις ξυμμάχων.

Thucydides 2.1.1

From this point begins the war—here and now, I assert it—between the Athenians and the Peloponnesians and their respective allies. (tr. AB)

209 ἤδη accompanies ἤκουσα also at 4.77.1 Καίτοι τινὰ ἤδη ἤκουσα λόγον ἄλλον ὑπὸ Πελοποννησίων λεγόμενον; 7.35.1 Ἤδη δὲ ἤκουσα ὡς ...; 9.95.1 Ἤδη δὲ καὶ τόδε ἤκουσα ὡς .... See also 2.29.1 τὸ δ' ἀπὸ τούτου ἀκοῇ ἤδη ἱστορέων ....

210 Further explicit authorial statements including ἤδη occur at Herodotus 2.9.2 (ἤδη μοι καὶ πρότερον δεδήλωται); 6.53.2. ἤδη ὦν ὀρθῷ λόγῳ χρεωμένῳ μέχρι Περσέος ὀρθῶς εἴρηταί μοι; 1.207.3 Ἤδη ὦν ἐγὼ γνώμην ἔχω ...; 2.29.1 αὐτόπτης ἐλθών, τὸ δ' ἀπὸ τούτου ἀκοῇ ἤδη ἱστορέων. At 8.105.1 the co-occurrence of μέγιστος + πάντων makes the statement an explicit evaluation: Ἐκ τούτων δὴ τῶν Πηδασέων ὁ Ἑρμότιμος ἦν τῷ μεγίστη τίσις ἤδη ἀδικηθέντι ἐγένετο πάντων τῶν ἡμεῖς ἴδμεν "Hermotimus, who came from Pedasa, had achieved a fuller vengeance for wrong done to him than had any man whom we know." Further instances of ἤδη in unmistakable (if implicit) authorial statements occur, e.g., at 4.45.3 Ἤδη γὰρ Λιβύη μὲν ἐπὶ Λιβύης λέγεται ὑπὸ τῶν πολλῶν Ἑλλήνων ἔχειν τὸ οὔνομα γυναικὸς αὐτόχθονος "For Libya is said by most Greeks to be named after a native woman of that name"; 7.129.3 ἐπεὰν δὲ συμμιχθέωσι τάχιστα, ἐνθεῦτεν ἤδη ὁ Πηνειὸς τῷ οὐνόματι κατακρατέων ἀνωνύμους τοὺς ἄλλους εἶναι ποιέει "As soon as they are united, the name of the Peneus prevails, making the rest nameless." All translations are by Godley.

211 Besides ἤδη in Herodotean explicit statements, I counted 28 instances occurring in character speech (20%); ἤδη in Thucydides appears 69 times in character speech (18.4%).

In this excerpt the *hic et nunc* of the war is made to coincide with the *hic et nunc* of the proposition announcing it. Rather than contributing temporal content ("now"),[212] ἤδη has the pragmatic function of expressing the firsthand experience of the speaker, or the speaker's pretense of that. The present ἄρχεται contributes to the description of the beginning of the war as happening "now"; however, given the multifunctionality of the present tense, ἄρχεται alone is not strong enough to mark the discourse act as an act of the stance. ἤδη provides that reinforcement.[213] I interpret the relation of this use of ἤδη to stance in terms of the positioning vector: Thucydides positions himself with respect to the object 'spatio-temporal coordinates of events'; he places himself as witness of the beginning of the war. Likewise, any other speaker may use ἤδη to attest to his own immediate sensorial experience of something by positioning himself inside the narrated event as real or pretended participant.[214]

§153. ἤδη, it should be noted, retains the value of marking firsthand experience in all possible combinations of tense—all indicative tenses as well as the imperative present.[215]

212 More below §161 on ἤδη as "now."

213 At Thucydides 3.52.3 a short parenthetical γάρ move including ἤδη looks authorial: οἱ δέ (ἦσαν γὰρ ἤδη ἐν τῷ ἀσθενεστάτῳ) παρέδοσαν τὴν πόλιν "and they (for they were now at the weakest) delivered up the city" (tr. Hammond). "They" is the Plataeans, who were forced by circumstances to capitulate to the Peloponnesians. Note the presence of the superlative ἀσθενεστάτῳ, which connotes the act as an act of evaluating.

8.20.1 is a less straightforward passage: [καὶ ναύαρχος αὐτοῖς ἐκ Λακεδαίμονος Ἀστύοχος ἐπῆλθεν,] ᾧπερ ἐγίγνετο ἤδη πᾶσα ἡ ναυαρχία "[At which time there came also unto them from Lacedaemon for commander, Astyochus], who was now admiral of the whole navy" (tr. Hobbes). Hammond translates: "who was just now succeeding as overall admiral-in-chief." Neither translation takes into account that starting with Astyochus ναυαρχία as an institutional profession could have changed. In Smith et al. 1890, Smith s.v. *navarchus* clarifies: [S]omething more like an admiralty was needed when the new phase of the Peloponnesian War, after the campaigns at Syracuse, extended the sphere of Spartan naval enterprise. The expression in Thuc. 8.20 regarding Astyochus, ᾧπερ ἐγίγνετο ἤδη πᾶσα ἡ ναυαρχία perhaps indicates, by the use of the imperfect tense, that the office grew out of circumstances at that time." On the historical complexity of the institution of nauarchs, and on the same passage, see, more recently, Hornblower 1991-2008, vol. III: 806-807. Hornblower translates ἤδη "by this time." My analysis of ἤδη leads to an interpretation that harmonizes with Smith's suggestion. ᾧπερ ἐγίγνετο ἤδη πᾶσα ἡ ναυαρχία can be read as an implicit authorial discourse act that evaluates the "wholeness" (whatever that means) of the admiralty that started with Astyochus. At 1.22.1 ἤδη does occur within an explicit methodological statement by Thucydides, but the scope of ἤδη is the participial phrase ἐν αὐτῷ ἤδη ὄντες, which I connect to epistemic stance about time (see below, §160). Here the author adopts the *hic et nunc* of the political and military speakers.

214 This is how I explain the difference between, for example, the same genitive absolute with and without ἤδη, when the verb is in present tense. I read the contribution of ἤδη in τοῦ θέρους ἤδη τελευτῶντος (Thucydides 4.133.4), as opposed to τοῦ δ' αὐτοῦ θέρους τελευτῶντος (Thucydides 3.86.1) as follows: ἤδη marks someone's experience of the ending of summer from within the process (which can be linked to the inchoative interpretation "as summer was about to end"); conversely, if ἤδη does not occur, the end of summer is reported without any marker of participants experiencing it.

215 E.g. in Thucydides 7.77.6, the general Nicias, after a parenthetical γάρ move, invites the Athenian troops to consider themselves secure, if they reach some friendly territory of the Sicels; he uses

ἤδη enriches the semantic and contextual implications of the chosen tense—aspect, telicity, distance or nearness to the time of speaking—by anchoring that tense to a subjective act of stancetaking, which I express in terms of bearing witness to something.

§154. This use of ἤδη in implicit authorial statements mirrors, in my view, Thucydides' use of ἤδη to evoke the voice and to mark the stance of characters in indirect speech. Let us consider an example. At the end of his speech to the Spartans, Alcibiades explains what they can gain and what the Athenians can lose if Sparta fortifies Decelea, a village in northern Attica. Athens would lose revenues and tributes on many sides, including those from the allies, who would pay less attention to the Athenians once they see the Spartans' fighting power. Then comes this relative clause:

(t36)

οἳ τὰ παρ' ὑμῶν νομίσαντες <u>ἤδη</u> κατὰ κράτος πολεμεῖσθαι ὀλιγωρήσουσιν

Thucydides 6.91.7

... their allies, when they see that you are now carrying on the war in earnest, will not mind them. (tr. Jowett)

Alcibiades refers to an indirect thought by the Athenians' allies (νομίσαντες).[216] The following embedded infinitive construction begins with ἤδη (ἤδη κατὰ κράτος πολεμεῖσθαι). The allies are imagined as taking stance by evaluating the manner in which it is conducted (κατὰ κράτος πολεμεῖσθαι).[217] What ἤδη adds to this imagined evaluation is the allies' perceptual confirmation, their witnessing to the escalated warfare.

ἤδη and an imperative present: ἤδη νομίζετε ἐν τῷ ἐχυρῷ εἶναι.

216 Further instances of ἤδη preceded by semantic clues about thinking which feature forms of νομίζειν include Thucydides 4.115.3 νομίσαντες ταύτῃ ἑαλωκέναι ἤδη τὸ χωρίον; 4.128.3 νομίζοντες καὶ ἐν μεθορίοις εἶναι αὐτοὺς ἤδη καὶ διαπεφευγέναι; 4.129.2 ἀδύνατος ἤδη ἐνόμιζεν εἶναι διαβὰς τιμωρεῖν; 8.15.1 καὶ νομίσαντες μέγαν ἤδη καὶ σαφῆ τὸν κίνδυνον σφᾶς περιεστάναι. Forms of δοκεῖν occur in Herodotus 6.104.2 δοκέοντά τε εἶναι ἐν σωτηρίῃ ἤδη, ...; 3.153.2 and 3.154.1 ἐδόκεε εἶναι ἁλώσιμος ἤδη ἡ Βαβυλών, and Ὡς δέ οἱ ἐδόκεε μόρσιμον εἶναι ἤδη τῇ Βαβυλῶνι ἁλίσκεσθαι. Finally, more specific verbs recalling different mental activities include οἴομαι (Thucydides 8.92.7 οἵ τε γὰρ ἐν τῷ ἄστει ἤδη ᾤοντο τόν τε Πειραιᾶ κατειλῆφθαι καὶ τὸν ξυνειλημμένον τεθνάναι); καταγιγνώσκειν (Thucydides 7.51.1 ὡς καὶ αὐτῶν κατεγνωκότων ἤδη μηκέτι κρεισσόνων εἶναι σφῶν μήτε ταῖς ναυσὶ μήτε τῷ πεζῷ); ἐπιμελέσθαι (Thucydides 7.8.3 ὁ δὲ τὰ κατὰ τὸ στρατόπεδον διὰ φυλακῆς μᾶλλον ἤδη ἔχων ἢ δι' ἑκουσίων κινδύνων ἐπεμέλετο); and verbs of fear (Thucydides 4.28.2 δεδιὼς ἤδη καὶ οὐκ ἂν οἰόμενός οἱ αὐτὸν τολμῆσαι ὑποχωρῆσαι).

217 The occurrence of κατὰ κράτος significantly occurs also elsewhere near ἤδη; see Thucydides 1.64.3 καὶ οὕτως ἤδη κατὰ κράτος ἡ Ποτείδαια ἀμφοτέρωθεν ἐπολιορκεῖτο; 3.18.5 καὶ ἡ μὲν Μυτιλήνη κατὰ κράτος ἤδη ἀμφοτέρωθεν καὶ ἐκ γῆς καὶ ἐκ θαλάσσης εἴργετο; 5.116.3 καὶ κατὰ κράτος ἤδη πολιορκούμενοι; 8.1.2 καὶ τοὺς αὐτόθεν πολεμίους τότε δὴ καὶ διπλασίως πάντα

§155. I invite the reader to consider a performative aspect that I see behind these uses of ἤδη. With reference to (t36), ἤδη hints at an inner voice that we could "hear" if the thought would be uttered. It is as if Alcibiades would quote κατὰ κράτος πολεμεῖσθαι: "as soon as the allies think 'you are indeed fighting in earnest,' they will not mind." When ἤδη occurs in indirect speech, the hint at the speaking voice is straightforward. When it occurs in indirect thought (that is, preceded by reporting clauses or phrases such as "he thought"[218]) or in free indirect thought, the allusion to voice is only potential, but present nonetheless. The historians insert ἤδη to approximate the *hic et nunc* of the original speech or thought.[219] In this sense ἤδη resembles act-initial ἦ δή, and is a sign of

---

παρεσκευασμένους κατὰ κράτος ἤδη καὶ ἐκ γῆς καὶ ἐκ θαλάσσης ἐπικείσεσθαι (on which see IV.5 §41). See also κατ'ἀνάγκην ἤδη, Thucydides 8.2.3.

[218] ἤδη can also be found in discourse acts that are not preceded by clear reporting clauses or phrases but which still constitute someone's thought, calculation, supposition, or expectation. Linguistic features in these instances include *verba videndi* ("seeing" in the sense of "understanding" or "realizing"), and forms of μέλλειν that characterize the ongoing action as subjectively perceived. See Thucydides 2.90.4 ἰδόντες δὲ οἱ Πελοποννήσιοι κατὰ μίαν ἐπὶ κέρως παραπλέοντας καὶ ἤδη ὄντας ἐντὸς τοῦ κόλπου τε καὶ πρὸς τῇ γῇ, ὅπερ ἐβούλοντο μάλιστα, "The Peloponnesians, when they saw them sail in one long file, galley after galley, and that they were now in the gulf and by the shore (which they most desired) ..." (tr. Hobbes); Thucydides 7.4.4 προσεῖχέ τε ἤδη μᾶλλον τῷ κατὰ θάλασσαν πολέμῳ, ὁρῶν τὰ ἐκ τῆς γῆς σφίσιν ἤδη, ἐπειδὴ Γύλιππος ἧκεν, ἀνελπιστότερα ὄντα "And he [Nicias] was already beginning to concentrate more on the naval dimension of the war, as he could see that the arrival of Gylippus had now made the Athenians' prospects by land less encouraging" (tr. Hammond; note the occurrence of μᾶλλον and ἀνελπιστότερα); 7.69.2 καὶ ὁρῶν οἷος ὁ κίνδυνος καὶ ὡς ἐγγὺς ἤδη (note the evaluative adjective ἐγγὺς). See also Thucydides 6.31.1 ὡς ἤδη ἔμελλον μετὰ κινδύνων ἀλλήλους ἀπολιπεῖν lit. "as they were departing with dangers"; 6.96.1 καὶ μέλλοντας ἤδη ἐπὶ σφᾶς ἰέναι; 4.66.3 ῥᾷον δ' ἤδη ἔμελλον προσχωρήσειν τούτου γεγενημένου.

[219] The occurrences of ἤδη in indirect speech are introduced by verbs of saying, or by other verbs that either imply the use of voice, or signal a specific source of the account. Evidence from Herodotus is scarce: see 6.67.3 and 8.108.4 (reported speech depending on ἐκέλευε). Thucydides, on the other hand, offers plenty of examples. See 5.49.3 Ἠλεῖοι δὲ τὴν παρ' αὐτοῖς ἐκεχειρίαν ἤδη ἔφασαν εἶναι "The Eleans replied that the truce ... was already in force throughout Elis"; 7.49.3 [Nicias] ἔφη ... ἀλλ' ὅτι τάχιστα ἤδη ἐξανίστασθαι "they should move elsewhere now, as soon as possible"; 3.2.3 [Τενέδιοι γὰρ ὄντες αὐτοῖς διάφοροι καὶ Μηθυμναῖοι καὶ αὐτῶν Μυτιληναίων ... μηνυταὶ γίγνονται τοῖς Ἀθηναίοις ὅτι] ... καὶ εἰ μή τις προκαταλήψεται ἤδη, στερήσεσθαι αὐτοὺς Λέσβου "[But people from Tenedos (no friend of Lesbos), and Methymna, and some individuals from Mythilene itself ... reported to the Athenians that] ... if no pre-emptive action was taken immediately, Lesbos would be lost to Athens" (all tranlsations are by Hammond). Modern punctuation after Stuart and Jones has a comma after προκαταλήψεται; according to my reading ἤδη would make sense also as the beginning of the main clause (εἰ μή τις προκαταλήψεται, ἤδη στερήσεσθαι αὐτοὺς Λέσβου). See also 6.48.1 οὕτως ἤδη Συρακούσαις καὶ Σελινοῦντι ἐπιχειρεῖν (Alcibiades' reported speech); 6.49.4 τούς τε ἄλλους Σικελιώτας οὕτως ἤδη μᾶλλον καὶ ἐκείνοις οὐ ξυμμαχήσειν καὶ σφίσι προσιέναι καὶ οὐ διαμελλήσειν περισκοποῦντας ὁπότεροι κρατήσουσιν (Lamachus' reported speech); 8.91.2 and 8.92 6 (Teramene's reported speech). In Thucydides 8.27.4; 8.46.4; 4.115.5; and Herodotus 8.108.4 the reported speech including ἤδη is introduced by κελεύειν. In Herodotus 7.197.2 ἤδη is part of an account that Xerxes' guides tell to the king (7.197.1 ἔλεγόν οἱ ἐπιχώριον λόγον).

vividness that contrasts with the rules of backshift. Perhaps a similar performative allusion can be seen behind the uses of ἤδη to conclude discourse acts.[220]

4.8.3 Thucydides' blending of stances

§156. The next example features ἤδη in free indirect thought,[221] and it shows a further way to break rules of backshift. All the four ἤδη appearing in the account of the plague can be read as expressing the stance (whether about time or not) of the ill.[222] Here is one of them:

(t37)

ὅτι δὲ <u>ἤδη</u> τε ἡδὺ πανταχόθεν τε ἐς αὐτὸ κερδαλέον, τοῦτο καὶ καλὸν καὶ χρήσιμον κατέστη.

Thucydides 2.53.3

So,[223] definitely, what was enjoyable and in every way conducive to it[224] [to what was enjoyable], that became also honorable and useful. (tr. AB)

After introducing the general theme of lawlessness (2.53.1), the author points out people's indulgence of pleasures, as they felt inescapably near to death. "No one was prepared to persevere in what had once been thought the path of honour, as they could well be dead before that destination was reached" (2.53.2, tr. Hammond). (t37) immediately follows this consideration. The words further exemplify the general atmosphere of degradation and psychological distortion described at this point of the account, by introducing the idea of making a virtue of necessity. On closer inspection, actually, the

220 See for example Herodotus 8.49.1 ἡ γὰρ Ἀττικὴ ἀπεῖτο ἤδη, | τῶν δὲ λοιπέων πέρι προετίθεε; Thucydides 2.48.3 καὶ ἔθνῃσκον πολλῷ μᾶλλον ἤδη. | λεγέτω μὲν οὖν περὶ αὐτοῦ .... Unlike particles occurring at the end of priming acts (such as X δέ | ...) these ἤδη do not project further acts; they just give them a conclusion. In these cases ἤδη has scope either over the entire act, like ἤδη in initial or peninitial position, or it works as a kind of confirmatory tag-assessment ("it is/was really so"). Thucydides uses ἤδη in this usage more than Herodotus (38 to 9 instances). In our corpus only δῆθεν and ἄρα sometimes fulfill a similar function in a similar position.

221 For ἤδη occuring in discourse acts that report people's thoughts in Herodotus, see Herodotus 1.137.2 (stance of the Persians); 6.108.1 (stance of the Plataeans); 8.100.2 (embedded stance of the Athenians in Mardonius' speech).

222 Thucydides 2.51.6; 2.52.4; 2.53.3; 2.53.4.

223 ὅτι δέ is a rare combination that recalls "paratactic" ὥστε. It occurs also in Thucydides 3.104.5; 6.17.3; 6.55.1; 7.15.2. The presence of δέ suggests that a new act starts; no preceding verbs from which ὅτι might depend occur in the previous stretch of discourse. In Stuart and Jones' edition it consistently appears after a full stop. My translation attempts to capture the value of ὅτι δέ as an act initial discourse marker generally conveying continuation. Herodotus uses this combination 6 times.

224 "Conducive to it" after Rusten's translation (1989:192).

evaluative adjectives ἡδύ, κερδαλέον, καλόν, χρήσιμον, and the scalar adverb πανταχόθεν can be read as reporting directly the people's stance, ἤδη being a marker of that. It is also possible that the statement expresses Thucydides' point of view as well, and that ἤδη reflects the position of the author as witness. This would drive the general sense that in the account of the plague the author is emotionally aligned with the characters. In other words, ἤδη could mark polyphony or blending of perspectives involving the author and the characters.[225]

§157. Earlier in the chapter I suggested that δή, especially in Thucydides, can indicate the blending of the characters' stance and the author's stance (see 4.6.3). ἤδη can perform the same function: it can blend the way author and character(s) evaluate states of affairs,[226] or it can blend their positioning within situations. Such blending tends to occur when narration focuses on events (the most common kind of third person narration), not when Thucydides is explicitly commenting on them. The fact that Thucydides is evidently more interested than Herodotus in blending stances may explain why he uses ἤδη more often than his counterpart does (as I already noted, the frequency in Thucydides is 0.24% vs. 0.07% of total words in Herodotus; 373 vs. 136 instances respectively).

§158. Reading ἤδη as a sign of blended stance can change our interpretation of the text considerably. Consider the following passage, which represents the narrative peak of a complex episode involving two divisions of Athenians determined to attack a Peloponnesian garrison in Megara, and some Megarian collaborators of the Athenians. Thucydides explains a Megarian stratagem: there is a wagon that occasionally keeps the city's gates open at night; in this wagon they plan to hide a boat full of people ready to ambush the city.

225 For further ἤδη in discourse acts that seem to convey either the stance of someone in particular, or a blending of the characters' and the author's stances, see Thucydides 1.49.7; 4.128.3; 7.23.2; 7.24.3, 7.2.4; 7.43.7 (with μᾶλλον ἤδη); 7.70.8 (including a superlative form); 7.71.1 (including a comparative form); 7.73.1 (including a gnomic act). For an analysis of viewpoint and the theory of Conceptual Blending applied to Homeric passages, see Bonifazi 2018.

226 E.g. in Thucydides 7.84.3 ἤδη marks the blended stances of the Athenians and the author about the Syracusans making the crossing of river Asinarus difficult: καὶ οἱ πολέμιοι ἐπικείμενοι χαλεπὴν ἤδη τὴν διάβασιν ἐποίουν. At 1.57.2 once again the blended stance of the Athenians and the author is in question: οἵ τε γὰρ Κορίνθιοι φανερῶς ἤδη διάφοροι ἦσαν, "for the Corinthians were really patently hostile" (tr. AB). Herodotus uses this strategy as well, albeit not as frequently as Thucydides does. For instance, at Herodotus 9.118.1 ἤδη marks the blended stance of the author and the inhabitants of Sestos in the Chersonese: the latter are under siege, and the evaluation in question is about the desperate conditions of the besieged: Οἱ δὲ ἐν τῷ τείχεϊ ἐς πᾶν ἤδη κακοῦ ἀπιγμένοι ἦσαν, "Inside the town, the besieged were ... reduced to the direst extremity" (tr. De Sélincourt and Marincola). The imperfect tense tends to occur in such passages, which may reinforce the sense of internal perception; however, not only imperfects occur: e.g., at 7.55.1 Thucydides' third person narration reveals, through ἤδη, a blending of his own and the Syracusans' evaluative stance; note the perfect: Γεγενημένης δὲ τῆς νίκης τοῖς Συρακοσίοις λαμπρᾶς ἤδη καὶ τοῦ ναυτικοῦ, "As the victory for the Syracusans was really brilliant over the fleet as well ...." (tr. AB). I take "brilliant" from Hornblower's translation (1991-2008, vol. III:648).

(t38)

καὶ τότε πρὸς ταῖς πύλαις ἤδη ἦν ἡ ἅμαξα, καὶ ἀνοιχθεισῶν κατὰ τὸ εἰωθὸς ὡς τῷ ἀκατίῳ οἱ Ἀθηναῖοι ... ἰδόντες ἔθεον δρόμῳ ἐκ τῆς ἐνέδρας, βουλόμενοι φθάσαι πρὶν ξυγκλῃσθῆναι πάλιν τὰς πύλας καὶ ἕως ἔτι ἡ ἅμαξα ἐν αὐταῖς ἦν, κώλυμα οὖσα προσθεῖναι·

Thucydides 4.67.4

At this time that cart was at the gates, which were opened according to custom as for the boat. And the Athenians seeing it ..., arose from their ambush and ran with all speed to get in before the gates should be shut again (tr. Hobbes)

Hammond takes ἤδη as meaning "already" ("the wagon was already there"), but Hobbes focuses the attention on τότε. My reading is closer to Hobbes'. Rather than indicating that the wagon was "already" there, ἤδη together with καὶ τότε shifts the beginning of the episode's climactic moment into the *hic et nunc*,[227] pointing to the moment of the wagon's appearance at the gates. As soon as the Athenians see the wagon, they begin the attack.[228] ἤδη signals the convergence of the characters' and audience's viewpoints—the moment at which the audience perceives the wagon is one and the same as the characters'. ἤδη encodes experientiality, to recall Grethlein's terminology from §78.

§159. In §144 I quoted a passage from Aristotle's *Physics* commenting on the use of ἤδη. The philosopher finds that speakers of his time do not say (οὐ λέγομεν) Ἴλιον φάναι ἤδη ἑαλωκέναι, because the event is too far from νῦν. Now, in light of the excerpts we have seen, it is possible to reinterpret Aristotle's meaning to fit with the idea of ἤδη as a marker of firsthand experience, or, in other words, stancetaking by positioning oneself as participating in the "here and now" of the situation. ἤδη can be used when "now" is near, but not when "now" is far. In order to use ἤδη speakers should not perceive (or describe) a great distance between the time of the event and their own time. In a stance-based reading ἤδη can accompany the description of events that take place in a time far

227 See IV.2.4.3 on καί at narrative peaks in historiography, and II.3 §58 on δὴ τότε and καὶ τότε to mark narrative peaks in Homer.

228 The fact that I see this phenomenon more often in Thucydides than in Herodotus does not mean that Herodotus does not employ the same discourse strategy. Let us select two particularly vivid moments in the description of past events including ἤδη in Herodotus. At 1.85.4 Croesus' dumb son, terrified by the imminent killing of his father, *hic et nunc* starts speaking: μετὰ δὲ τοῦτο ἤδη ἐφώνεε τὸν πάντα χρόνον τῆς ζόης (commonly translated as "from that moment on"). At 7.219.1, in the Thermopylae account, Herodotus conveys the *hic et nunc* of the moment in which the Greeks realize that the Persians are near: "the third sign was the look-out men running from the hills ἤδη as day was breaking" (τρίτοι δὲ οἱ ἡμεροσκόποι καταδραμόντες ἀπὸ τῶν ἄκρων ἤδη διαφαινούσης ἡμέρης, tr. AB). The peculiar position of ἤδη between two participial phrases suggests a value that comprises both events.

from the "now" of the composition of the *Histories* only to the extent that it positions people in the *hic et nunc* of that past.[229]

4.8.4 Stance about time, and propositional "now"

§160. The next group of ἤδη appears with participial constructions largely involving past tense participles or present participles of εἰμί. In these cases ἤδη has scope over the whole construction, which works as a separate act (e.g. Ἐσκεδασμένου δὲ ἤδη τοῦ λόγου ἀνὰ τὴν πόλιν, Herodotus 4.14.2; τῶν ἐνθάδε ἤδη εἰρηκότων, Thucydides 2.35.1). In participial constructions ἤδη conveys epistemic stance (that is, stance concerning knowledge states), and exclusively about time.[230] ἤδη marks a subjective assessment about the time in which a state of affairs took place. Consider this passage from Herodotus:

(t39)

Τελμησσέες μέν νυν ταῦτα ὑπεκρίναντο Κροίσῳ <u>ἤδη</u> ἡλωκότι, οὐδέν κω εἰδότες τῶν ἦν περὶ Σάρδις τε καὶ αὐτὸν Κροῖσον

Herodotus 1.78.3

The Telmessians gave this answer when Croesus was already taken. They did not know yet anything about what happened in Sardis and about Croesus himself. (tr. AB)

The Telmessians were priests of Apollo Telmessus; Croesus had asked them to interpret the sudden appearance of snakes in Sardis. But before they could tell him the answer, Croesus was imprisoned by the Persians. ἤδη's meaning as "already" here signals the perception of an action that had taken place in the past (ἡλωκότι) from the perspective of the events 'there and then.' The Telmessians did not have access at the time to

229 Readers may wonder why the narrator/historiographer would not prefer to use νῦν instead of ἤδη. Three reasons can be adduced. First, accented νῦν tends to modify propositional content (think of "I'll write a message to the administration" vs. "I'll write a message to the administration now"). Second, ἤδη is richer than νῦν in meaning; it can convey stancetaking about states of affairs independently of time considerations (think of ἤδη κατὰ κράτος). Third, and more important, νῦν is a deictic marker; the moment referred to has to be inferred contextually, as for ἤδη, but this contextual dependency is explicit and straightforward. On the other hand, ἤδη retains the effect of immediacy, because it is not a deictic marker, and it concerns not only time. Most of all, with ἤδη the blending of other voices and stances remains implied without being imposed; ἤδη gives more flexibility in interpretation, and enhances polyphony. I do acknowledge that a very few times ἤδη in Thucydides works as propositional "now" (see §161); however, this is a variation in function that covers a minority of cases, and does not cancel the validity of the general point. ἤδη νῦν co-occur contiguously only in Herodotus 6.50.3 (at the beginning of direct speech).

230 Thucydides features these constructions at least 64 out of 373 times.

the information about Croesus' imprisonment (οὐδέν κω εἰδότες τῶν ἦν περὶ Σάρδις τε καὶ αὐτὸν Κροῖσον), but the author chooses to show commitment to the status of information in question from within the situation. "Already" reflects the author's epistemic stance about time.[231]

§161. Finally, I flag that in a few cases the interpretation of ἤδη may be that of a propositional meaning "now," which then modifies the semantic content.[232] For example, at 6.29.2 Thucydides reports Alcibiades' opinion: ἐπεμαρτύρετο μὴ ἀπόντος πέρι αὐτοῦ διαβολὰς ἀποδέχεσθαι, ἀλλ' ἤδη ἀποκτείνειν, εἰ ἀδικεῖ, ... "[Alcibiades] insisted that the Athenians should not credit attacks made on him [Alcibiades] in his absence, but if he really was a criminal, they should proceed to execute him there and then" (tr. Hammond). ἤδη corresponds to "there and then" in Hammond's translation, which is intended to clarify the time and the place of the hypothetical execution ("here and now" in the unbackshifted speech).

§162. An alternative interpretation could take ἤδη as having scope over an entire move introduced by ἀλλ(ά), and including act ἀποκτείνειν, the act εἰ ἀδικεῖ, and the subsequent act starting with ὅτι. This move would express Alcibiades' reported stance towards the Athenians' decisions: in unbackshifted speech he would express: "if I am really a criminal, then kill me!".[233] Both readings are defendable. The possible use of ἤδη to mark a propositional "now" or "here and now" simply reflects an aspect of multifunctionality that we stress also elsewhere in our work. The functions of ἤδη range from nonpropositional to propositional in a continuum.[234] What does not change is that the

231 Among many analogous instances in Thucydides, I mention a passage where the *hic et nunc* suggested by ἤδη in a participial phrase refers to the epistemic stance of Demosthenes and Eurymedon: ὁ δὲ Δημοσθένης καὶ Εὐρυμέδων, ἑτοίμης ἤδη τῆς στρατιᾶς οὔσης ἔκ τε τῆς Κερκύρας καὶ ἀπὸ τῆς ἠπείρου, ἐπεραιώθησαν ξυμπάσῃ τῇ στρατιᾷ τὸν Ἰόνιον ἐπ' ἄκραν Ἰαπυγίαν "Meanwhile Demosthenes and Eurymedon, their recruitment from Corcyra and the mainland now complete, took their whole armament across the Ionian gulf to the promontory of Iapygia," 7.33.3 (tr. Hammond).

232 Compare the discussion on ἤδη vs. νῦν in n229.

233 I read a propositional "now" behind ἤδη twice in direct speech: παυόμενοι λέγομεν ἤδη ὅτι οὐ Θηβαίοις παρέδομεν τὴν πόλιν (Thucydides 3.59.3); and μάθετε ἤδη (Thucydides 6.90.2 and 6.91.2). At 6.25.1 one of the Athenians asks Nicias to make a declaration about the contingent at vote: ἀλλ' ἐναντίον ἁπάντων ἤδη λέγειν ἥντινα αὐτῷ παρασκευὴν Ἀθηναῖοι ψηφίσωνται "but he should now declare in front of them all what forces he wanted the Athenians to vote him" (tr. Hammond). It would make sense to relate ἤδη to ἁπάντων, rather than to take it as "now" modifying the verb λέγειν. In Nicias' reply to this very request, conversely, a further ἤδη possibly refers to the *hic et nunc* of the situation in a propositional function (note the verb δοκεῖν, however evaluative): ὁ δὲ ἄκων μὲν εἶπεν ὅτι καὶ μετὰ τῶν ξυναρχόντων καθ' ἡσυχίαν μᾶλλον βουλεύσοιτο, ὅσα μέντοι ἤδη δοκεῖν αὐτῷ [τριήρεσι μὲν...] "Nicias was reluctant to reply, saying that he would prefer to have time to discuss the matter with his fellow commanders: but as far as he could see at present ...," 6.25.2 (tr. Hammond).

234 See I.3 §§11-12 and 54; IV.2 §3 on the continuum between propositional and non-propositional meanings of particles.

interpretation of propositional "now" springs from the understanding of the same kind of positioning by the speaker in the *hic et nunc* of the situation.

4.8.5 Interim conclusion

§163. The two *Histories* show that the uses of ἤδη significantly overlap with the uses of δή. Both lexical items are flexible in position and scope. Both occur in direct and indirect speech, indirect thought, and explicit and implicit authorial statements. They both have a bearing on the representation of people's voice and stance, including that of the authors themselves. The use of both lexical items with comparatives, superlatives, πᾶς and πολύς forms, and evaluative adjectives is a sign of their contribution to the expression of stance, be it perceptive, epistemic, emotional, or a combination thereof. An additional aspect common to δή is the link to visual perception; in some geographical observations by Herodotus ἤδη highlights the vision of space, in other words the *hic* more than the *nunc* of events. Finally, both δή and ἤδη are capable of indicating a blending of stances by different individuals.

§164. δή and ἤδη mark someone's stance by implying similar things, δή a sense of certainty or determination, and ἤδη personal guarantee (ἦ δή) or firsthand experience. ἤδη in particular shows that the speaker or perceiver is positioning himself *in* the situation described. When the focus of ἤδη is on actions expressed in participial constructions, then the stance shown relates exclusively to time. ἤδη is a marker of relativity from inside the world of events, regardless of whether this takes place in the past, the present, or the future. The blending of author's and character's respective stances creates an effect of immediacy, which is consistent with Aristotle's explanation of its meaning: ἤδη is used when the "now" is near. The fact that Thucydides uses ἤδη three times as often as Herodotus does may be connected to Thucydides' inclination towards blending perspectives.

4.9 ἄρα Between Discourse Cohesion and the Marking of Stance

§165. ἄρα does not occur often in Herodotus and Thucydides; there are only 66 and 40 instances respectively (0.03% and 0.02% of the total words). The particle's functions have been well explicated in landmark accounts that are surveyed elsewhere in this monograph.[235] I find, however, that Herodotus differs sharply from Thucydides in the way he uses ἄρα, and this finding contrasts with general expectations about the functions of ἄρα in prose. Because ἄρα has been labeled a "modal"/ "attitudinal particle,"[236] we

235 See II.4.3.2 and II.5.3.3.

236 A representative account in this direction is that of Wakker 1997b, which focuses on Herodotus and Thucydides. In a previous work on conditional clauses, Wakker devotes attention to the

expect it to relate almost exclusively to stance. More specifically, ἄρα in post-Homeric Greek is said to convey surprise,[237] mark information as interesting,[238] or express skepticism or disillusionment.[239] However, the picture that emerges from my investigation is quite different. The majority of instances in Herodotus do not relate to stance but rather to discourse cohesion. 41 of 66 instances show that Herodotus employs ἄρα in his own narration either to recall previous parts of the discourse or to recall embedded λόγοι. This pattern of usage is similar to the way ἄρα is used in the Homeric poems. Thucydides, for his part, inserts ἄρα in speeches or reports about others' speeches and thoughts most of the time (35 out of 40 instances). Thucydides uses the particle to show subjectivity. Rather than conveying surprise or disillusionment, ἄρα in Thucydides shows that the subjects are engaged in inferring possibilities[240] from actual situations or conceivable outcomes.

§166. It is useful to understand ἄρα in terms of three representative functions, which I will now illustrate through excerpts drawn from the two historians. As mentioned above, most of the Herodotean usages show that ἄρα possesses functions that extend beyond stance. Two subtypes may be distinguished. In a minority of Herodotean instances, and in all Thucydidean ἄρα, the particle does play a role in stance; I examine the special relation to stance in εἰ ἄρα + indicative or ἤν ἄρα + subjunctive constructions as the third function. All things considered, the significance of these findings on ἄρα may be viewed as the inverse of what I found on ἤδη: whereas ἤδη was found to relate to stance more than expected, ἄρα relates to it much less.

§167. 13 times in Herodotus ἄρα co-occurs with ὡς δέ in temporal or causal clauses that establish a change to a new setting or a new phase in an episode (ὡς δὲ ἄρα/ ὡς δ' ἄρα[241]). In these cases ἄρα has act scope, and its pragmatic function is to stress continuity with or logical consequentiality from preceding pieces of content.

(t40)

Οἱ δὲ Ἕλληνες, ὡς ἐν Πλαταιῇσι τὴν ληίην διείλοντο, ἔθαπτον τοὺς ἑωυτῶν χωρὶς ἕκαστοι. ... Ὡς δ' <u>ἄρα</u> ἔθαψαν τοὺς νεκροὺς ἐν Πλαταιῇσι οἱ Ἕλληνες, αὐτίκα ...

Herodotus 9.85.1, and 9.86.1

---

constructions εἰ/ἤν ἄρα (1994:343-350).

237 See e.g. Denniston 1950:35; Wakker 1994:345 ("signaling surprise" is taken as a characteristic use of ἄρα); Powell 1938:44 "w. reported sp., and acc. inf., implying surprise."

238 See, e.g. Hartung 1832:430; once again, Denniston 1950:32-33; Wakker 1997b:231.

239 See Denniston 1950:35 ("ἄρα expressing the surprise attendant upon disillusionment") and 38.

240 34 out of 40 instances feature εἰ or ἤν + ἄρα. This use appears in Herodotus 14 times, and it represents the only functional overlap across the two authors.

241 Herodotus 1.24.7; 1.27.1; 1.86.3; 1.111.5; 2.140.1; 3.134.1; 8.59.1; 8.94.2; 9.8.1; 9.19.3; 9.33.1; 9.86.1; 9.100.1. The same function applies to δ' ἄρα (without ὡς) at 1.111.1 and 2.141.3. The idiomatic construction εἰ μὴ ἄρα ("except") is considered separately (see Herodotus 4.32.1; 7.10.θ3).

> The Greeks, after dividing the booty in Plataea, buried their own fallen separately. ... As the Greeks buried the corpses in Plataea, immediately ... (tr. AB)

In (t40) I have included, along with the ἄρα act, a preceding stretch of text possessing the same content as the ἄρα act in order to show that ἄρα can retrieve that part of the discourse after some intervening details (9.85.2-3). This function directly echoes an exceedingly common Homeric usage, where ἄρα is used in announcing actions that naturally follow from preceding discourse (either directly preceding, or with intervening observations).[242]

§168. In these cases, therefore, ἄρα's value depends on previous parts of discourse rather than what follows. Sometimes, but not always, the main clause that follows ὡς δὲ ἄρα/ ὡς δ' ἄρα relates something remarkable, unexpected or simply exciting.[243] It is probably due to such instances that several scholars directly connect ἄρα to the feeling of interest. However, I take ἄρα's range to be limited to its host act (unlike γάρ, which can mark multi-act discourse units[244]).

§169. In the second representative function ἄρα does not relate to preceding discourse but to information that is external to the sequence of events. In other words, ἄρα can mark unframed discourse.[245] In these cases the author provides the audience with content that is independent of what characters know or are able to assume, in order to give his audience a comprehensive and cohesive picture of the situation.

242 See II.3 §§66 and II.5 §§51-62 on ἄρα as a marker of frame recall. Further instances in Herodotus occur at 9.19.3 ("once they arrived" at a place, the move being anticipated by the information "they continued their advance"); 9.8.1 ("after hearing that" following reported speech); 9.100.1 ("as they completed the preparations," after describing the preparations); 8.94.2 ("as they were fleeing" after mentioning a retreat); 9.33.1 ("when Mardonius' dispositions were complete," following the description of the dispositions); 8.59.1 ("as they gathered," after mentioning the decision to summon a conference). In 2.141.3 δ' ἄρα accompanies "while lamenting," after the mention of someone lamenting. At 8.135.1 ἄρα alone accompanies the narration of an action involving Mys, someone who had been introduced in a previous chapter (133). In a very few cases of εἰ/ἤν ἄρα clauses in Thucydides, ἄρα performs a similar function—overlapping with the marking of stance. For example, at 2.87.1 (εἴ τις ἄρα δι' αὐτὴν ὑμῶν φοβεῖται τὴν μέλλουσαν) ἄρα secures the connection to previous content (see φοβούμενοι, 2.86.5, and φοβουμένους, 2.86.6, both referring to the Peloponnesians).

243 E.g. at 8.59.1 people gather, and immediately afterwards Themistocles begins an unexpected and long speech; at 8.94.2 sailors flee, and immediately afterwards meet a mysterious ship; at 9.8.1 the ephors hear the message of the Athenians, and immediately afterwards decide to postpone their plans; at 8.135.1 the action involving Mys is the beginning of a real θῶμα (see 135.1 θῶμα μέγιστον); at 2.141.3 the person who complains in front of a god's shrine falls asleep all of a sudden, and has a dream.

244 See IV.3 §108; IV.5 §16, §19, §27, §39, §61, §68, §77, §§94-95.

245 On "unframed discourse" see II.4.2, and also above §27.

(t41)

ἡ δὲ Λάβδα ... εἰδυῖά τε οὐδὲν τῶν εἵνεκα ἐκεῖνοι ἀπικοίατο ... φέρουσα ἐνεχείρισε αὐτῶν ἑνί. Τοῖσι δὲ ἄρα ἐβεβούλευτο κατ' ὁδὸν τὸν πρῶτον αὐτῶν λαβόντα τὸ παιδίον προσουδίσαι. Ἐπείτε ὦν ἔδωκε φέρουσα ἡ Λάβδα, τὸν λαβόντα τῶν ἀνδρῶν θείῃ τύχῃ προσεγέλασε τὸ παιδίον, ...

Herodotus 5.92γ.2-3

Labda, ... knowing nothing of the purpose of their coming ... brought it [the baby] and placed it into the hands of one of them. Now they had planned on their way that the first of them who received the child should dash it to the ground. When, however, Labda brought and handed over the child, by divine chance it smiled at the man who took it. (tr. Godley)

In his long speech to the Spartans—designed to dissuade them from restoring Hippias—the Corinthian statesman Sosicles embeds a few narratives that illustrate the despotic behavior of Cypselus and Periander, former tyrants of Corinth. The passage in question is a climactic point in the story of baby Cypselus. The Bacchiadae, political leaders of Corinth, want to kill the baby to prevent the rise of his power in the future (which would be a threat for them). But when the men in charge of the murder reach the mother (Labda) and get the child, the child happens to smile to them, and they are unable to kill him. ἄρα occurs in a discourse act that inserts a piece of information that interrupts the chronological flow of the narrative, and yet is crucial to the understanding of the climax. In order to appreciate the unexpected outcome of the evil mission, the audience must know—and exactly at that moment—that the plan was to dash the baby to the ground. Tense discontinuity helps the audience process the temporal discontinuity: the verb of the δὲ ἄρα act is a pluperfect (ἐβεβούλευτο), while the preceding and following verbs are aorists (ἐνεχείρισε, ἔδωκε, προσεγέλασε).

§170. This and other ἄρα passages show a consistent pattern in which Herodotus attunes himself to the audience's need for contextual knowledge, by taking care to include external content necessary for following the narrative.[246] It is the external conditions of reception, then, that influence and motivate this use of ἄρα.[247] In these cases ἄρα

[246] See Herodotus 3.14.8; 3.70.1; 4.45.4; 4.64.3; 4.189.1; 4.205.1; 7.116.1; 7.152.3 (all of the ἄρα acts displaying tense discontinuity with both the preceding and the following act); 2.28.5; 2.58.1; 3.34.4; 8.8.1.

[247] I connect Herodotus' attention to the external conditions of reception to his use of ἄρα near *verba dicendi/sentiendi*, or expressions retrieving *ad hoc* λόγοι. In these passages ἄρα seems to indicate adherence to what was said or heard, which relate to occasional accounts external to those of Herodotus. This use well complements the idea that in Homer ἄρα metalinguistically indicates resonance with the discourse memory of epic (II.4.1). The Herodotean passages include 1.141.2 εἰπεῖν ἄρα αὐτὸν πρὸς τοὺς ἰχθῦς (the fable includes the words we report, which are uttered

stresses the "author—audience" vector not by aligning stance, but by giving attention to discourse cohesion.[248]

§171. The third and final function pertains to ἄρα in εἰ/ἤν discourse acts. Such occurrences make up 87% of the ἄρα found in Thucydides (35 of 40), and is found also in Herodotus, albeit less frequently. Except for four instances in the author's voice,[249] all are hypotheses voiced or thought by characters in direct speech, indirect speech, or indirect thought.[250] In general, hypotheses that are farther from real perceptions and closer to personal guesses take the form of ἤν ἄρα + subjunctive (against εἰ ἄρα +indicative). For example:

(t42)

Χρῆν μέν, ὦ ἄνδρες Βοιωτοί, μηδ' ἐς ἐπίνοιάν τινα ἡμῶν ἐλθεῖν τῶν ἀρχόντων ὡς οὐκ εἰκὸς Ἀθηναίοις, ἢν ἄρα μὴ ἐν τῇ Βοιωτίᾳ ἔτι καταλάβωμεν αὐτούς, διὰ μάχης ἐλθεῖν.

Thucydides 4.92.1

Men of Boeotia, no one among us generals should ever have allowed the thought to enter his mind that we ought not to fight with the Athenians, even although [*sic*] we may not overtake them on Boeotian soil. (tr. Jowett)

---

by a flute player addressing some fish; the infinitive depends on a *verbum dicendi* introducing a fable told to the Ionian messengers by Cyrus: ἔλεξέ σφι λόγον, 1.141.1). 2.28.5 εἰ ἄρα ταῦτα γενόμενα ἔλεγε; 3.34.3 Νῦν ἄρα μέ φασι Πέρσαι; 3.64.4 τὸ δὲ χρηστήριον ... ἐν Συρίῃ Ἀγβατάνοισι ἔλεγε ἄρα; 4.134.1 εἶπε ἄρα πρὸς τούς περ ἐώθεε; 7.17.1 εἶπε ἄρα τάδε; 8.111.2 ὡς κατὰ λόγον ἦσαν ἄρα αἱ Ἀθῆναι μεγάλαι τε καὶ εὐδαίμονες; 9.9.1 ἔλεγε ἄρα σφι τάδε; 7.152.3 ἐπεὶ καὶ ταῦτα λέγεται, ὡς ἄρα Ἀργεῖοι ἦσαν; 8.136.2 λεών τε πολλὸν ἄρα ἀκούων εἶναι καὶ ἄλκιμον; 9.8.1 Ὡς δὲ ἄρα ἤκουσαν οἱ ἔφοροι ταῦτα. Furthermore, at 1.111.5 the herdsman Mitridates reports ὡς ἄρα Μανδάνης τε εἴη παῖς ("that the baby was son of Mandanes") from the account he just heard from a servant (πυνθάνομαι τὸν πάντα λόγον, 111.5).

This use of ἄρα finds confirmation in Van den Besselaar's lexicographical study of ἄρα (1962:257-258): the scholar finds that one of ἄρα's functions in post-Homeric prose is to introduce others' words ("*em citações,*" "in quotations"), sometimes to stress their unacceptability, but sometimes with apparently neutral intentions.

248 In light of that I do not agree with Mulligan (2007), who considers the three instances of ἄρα in clauses that introduce direct speech (Herodotus 1.141.2; 4.134.1; 9.9.2), and connects the use of the particle to the character of the speech immediately following ("all three speeches ... are commanding, prompted by vivid evidence, and have an immediate effect on their audience," 2007:283).

249 Thucydides 3.82.7; 3.84.3; 6.24.4; 6.60.2.

250 For Thucydides the overall division is: 24 ἄρα in direct speech, 3 in indirect speech, 9 in indirect thought (36 out of 40 total instances); for Herodotus, we find 18 ἄρα in direct speech, 2 indirect speech, 5 indirect thought (25 out of 66 total instances).

The speaker is Pagondas, the only Boeotian commander to express the view that the Boeotians should join battle with the Athenians. At this point in time he does not know for certain that the Athenians have already left Boeotia, which in fact they had, as Thucydides informs his audience. Pagondas can only surmise that the Athenians are gone. ἄρα here marks Pagondas' supposition as a logical inference based on his state of knowledge; the particle functions as a signal of epistemic stance.[251]

§172. As a general rule, εἰ/ἤν ἄρα acts in Herodotus and Thucydides emphasize what is logically possible. The protasis does not always have to contain scenarios inferrable from facts known to speakers, as in the above example, but may even hypothesize extreme situations or unfortunate outcomes[252] (this gives rise to the translation of ἄρα as "even"). In other words, these ἄρα are subjectivized, and they are largely employed by characters in acts of epistemic stance. An emotional component may naturally accompany the epistemic one, but the extent and the type of emotion remains unspecified.

4.10 Conclusions

§173. This chapter investigates the way in which the two historians use particles to represent their own and other people's voices and stances. "Voice" is taken as a superordinate concept indicating the linguistic representation of any people's words (directly or indirectly conveyed) and any kind of thoughts. "Stance" is subsumed under "voice" as the linguistic representation of people's evaluating something, positioning oneself, and aligning or disaligning with others. The stance may be fully uttered, reported, or reproduced by the historian.

§174. "Stance" shares with "focalization" the idea of revealing individual perception, whether the character's or the main narrator's. However, I privilege "stance" over "focalization" because stancetaking is regarded as a social activity, whereas focalization has no social connotations. Du Bois' theoretical model of the stance triangle enables us to see the stancetaking subject in relation to objects as well as to other subjects. The identification of three vectors ("positioning," "evaluating," and "aligning") provides important interpretive guidance. They make us see connections between the different components of the triangle and the different linguistic features attached to their expressions. Also, they allow for adding variants, such as positioning oneself with respect to the object 'spatio-temporal coordinates of events,' and creating (dis)alignment between author and audience as further subjects involved.

251 Denniston (1950:37) approaches my reading: "ἄρα in a conditional protasis denotes that the hypothesis is one of which the possibility has only just been realized: 'if, after all'."

252 Van den Besselaar (1962:262) refers to εἰ/ἤν ἄρα hypotheses that are considered an "extreme case" ("caso-limite"). εἰ/ἤν ἄρα acts introduce outcomes that look unfortunate in the context of someone's speech or thought in Herodotus 3.45.4; 5.106.4; 7.9γ; 7.10θ.3; 7.149.1; 8.109.59.104.1; Thucydides 1.70.7; 1.84.2; 1.93.7; 1.140.1; 2.5.1; 3.56.5; 6.75.1.

§175. Sometimes particles signal voice regardless of whether the content represents a stancetaking act (see 4.3.1 and 4.3.2 about ἦ μήν and τοι; γε (4.3.3) represents a borderline case). δή and ἤδη that mark narrative progression especially in Herodotus further instantiate the presence of someone's voice. The bulk of the analysis, however, focuses on particles that signal stancetaking in direct and indirect speech, in indirect thoughts (whether free or not), and in explicit as well as implicit authorial statements. The temporal value that is traditionally assigned to δή and ἤδη is seen here as subsumed under their larger pragmatic value of stance markers.

§176. δή in Herodotus and in Thucydides frequently marks the evaluating side of stance, and lets positioning and aligning be inferred. The evaluating side concerns certainty or determination. A Herodotean characteristic of the use of δή, which in Thucydides is harder but not impossible to detect, involves irony. My reading of "ironic" δή points to the disalignment implicitly suggested between the stance of the author and the stance of some of the characters. A major difference in the usages of δή by the two historians is the following: Herodotus, on the one hand, tends to express authorial stance explicitly, and he usually makes it easy to attribute stance to his characters. Thucydides, on the other hand, prefers to be implicit about his own stance, and tends to blur the distinction between his own views and that of his characters.

§177. δῆθεν, etymological and semantic cognate of δή, occurs infrequently but makes a significant contribution to the issue of stance polyphony. The particle amplifies the ironic potential of δή by marking a clash in knowledge and stance that involves more participants. At once δῆθεν implies certainty, disassociation, pretense, and it blends at least two voices. Furthermore, its use activates the reader's ability to detect the complexity of some situations on multiple communicative levels.

§178. ἤδη, for its part, contributes especially to the positioning vector of the stance triangle: by underscoring somebody's firsthand experience of something, the speaker or perceiver positions himself with respect to the object 'spatio-temporal coordinates of events;' he places himself inside the narrated event as real or pretended participant. This is where the interpretation of propositional "now" springs from. Perhaps because of the sense of firsthand experience, no ἤδη in either masterpiece has ironic effects.

§179. Finally, the uses of ἄρα in Herodotus and Thucydides are less related to stance than what secondary literature suggests, and, within the marking of stance, the implied meanings have no direct connection to epistemic states such as skepticism, or emotions such as surprise. While ἄρα in Herodotus generally echoes Homeric narrative functions, ἄρα in Thucydides is almost exclusively attached to characters' logical inferences, that is, to epistemic stance concerning someone's reasoning and guessing about present or hypothetical situations.

§180. Beyond the analysis of the co-texts and contexts of δή, δῆθεν, ἤδη, and ἄρα in the two *Histories*, this chapter discusses four general methodological and interpretive points. First, we need to recognize the advantages of viewing particles and their functions in terms of a continuum. Disregarding *a priori* clear-cut distinctions between particles and adverbs enables readers to appreciate the continuity (and, to some extent, even the overlap) of δή and ἤδη in position and in discourse context. Likewise, distinguishing between "modal" and "connective" particles prevents readers from seeing the important role of ἄρα in connecting upcoming acts to preceding discourse. Finally, considering epistemic and emotional stance along a continuum helps readers see the contribution of both aspects to the expressions of subjectivity and of implicit alignment.

§181. Second, we need to examine indirect thought and free indirect thought more deeply than we have done thus far. Unlike indirect speech, which has received considerable attention in recent years, indirect thought in Herodotus and Thucydides is still understudied.[253] This chapter begins to close this gap by paying close attention to the way in which content that follows verbs like "thinking" "considering," "pondering," etc. is formulated. In addition, unlike free indirect speech, which in my view is not practised in the two *Histories*, free indirect thought does occur. Herodotus and Thucydides use the device not only as a way of accessing the mental states of their characters, but also to create interesting effects of both distance and alignment with those mental states.

§182. The third point is about alignment. For all the lexical items in focus, the communication of stance involves potentially several subjects. Some particle uses appear to reflect the author's metanarrative alignment with his audience. This has implications for Herodotean irony. Alignment can also occur between readers and characters: accordingly I offer a reading of experientiality in Thucydides. These observations enhance links between the interpretation of literary phenomena and the study of linguistic features. In addition, they pave the way for further interdisciplinary connections between literary criticism in Classics and cognitive studies (for example, on the human mind's natural ability to access multiple viewpoints in the same scene, as well as on the general phenomenon of conceptual blending).[254]

§183. My final point is related to the third. Several works stress that both historians are able to provide particularly vivid reports of a person's speech by breaking backshift rules—for example by keeping the tense that direct speech would have featured. Particles have a part to play in creating the effect of vividness: Wakker 1997b and George 2009 have already discussed ἦ μήν in indirect speech, and Scardino 2012 notices that particles reproduced in indirect speech recall the emotional tension of the speaker. This chapter establishes that, in addition to ἦ μήν in indirect speech, the occurrences of γε, δή, ἤδη and ἄρα in indirect speech, indirect thought, and free indirect thought signal

[253] A notable exception is Lang 1995, focusing on participles related to these verbs in Thucydides; however, Lang's aim is to show that historiography uses these participles to draw attention to the importance of characters' motivations; she does not interest herself in the linguistics of what comes after such participles.

[254] Relevant insights come especially from the multi-contribution volumes Schneider and Hartner 2012 (on blending and the study of narrative), and Dancygier and Sweetser eds. 2012 (on viewpoint in language).

the "presence" of a person's voice, or voice and stance. These usages represent further ways of breaking backshift rules, as third person narration breaks up in multiple strands attributable to multiple subjects. The present analysis reveals a third-person narration that is quite polyphonic. Voices and stances crowd the intricate world of Herodotus and Thucydides, so that, with proper attention to language, we may be witness to a truly "figured stage."

IV.5

Analysis of Four Excerpts

5.1 Introduction

§1. This chapter combines and exemplifies the main points made in IV.2, IV.3, and IV.4. Particles are observed in situ over relatively long passages, and their use is seen in relation to discourse segmentation, *and*-coordination strategies, and traces of peoples' voice and stance, all at once. The aim is to demonstrate how substantially the process of reading and comprehending the text changes if the aspects mentioned above are added to a more traditional analysis of sub- and main clauses.

§2. The four selected excerpts are representative of the major discourse settings of the two *Histories*, namely narrative sections and speeches. For the sake of comparison, they share some basic thematic affinities (two of them are accounts of reactions to major military enterprises, and two are "wise-advisor" speeches). Each of the four excerpts is thirty *OCT* lines long.

§3. The texts display modern punctuation as given in Stuart Jones' edition (*OCT* and *TLG* online) for Thucydides, and Hude's edition (*OCT*) for Herodotus (including extra spaces and indentation in square brackets), as well as the medieval punctuation from two important manuscripts (in italics within curved brackets).[1] Notes on philological aspects such as variants occur only when relevant to punctuation or to particles. Analogously, paleographical matters are not discussed; the sole purpose of including a sample of medieval punctuation is to remind us of one way in which pre-print texts were used over many centuries.

§4. The segmentation that I propose is in acts, small communicative steps of the discourse, and moves, multi-act units sharing an overarching communicative goal.[2] In

1 Ms β M (British Museum 11727), 11th century CE, for Thucydides, and Ms A (Laurentianus 70,3), 10th century CE, for Herodotus. Thanks are due to G. Liberman and to N. Wilson for help in retrieving the digitalized version online. The excerpts under examination (Thucydides 6.22-23 and 8.1) can be found on f. 163 recto and f. 217 verso respectively, in Ms β M; Herodotus 7.49 + 51, and 8.108-109.1 correspond to f. 277 recto-278 recto and f. 337 verso-338 recto respectively, in Ms A.

2 See II.2 about acts and II.3 about moves in general; IV.3.10 and IV.3.11 for illustrations of acts and moves in Herodotus and Thucydides.

the layout each line corresponds to an act, and each line space corresponds to a move boundary.

§5. My readings are not offered as objective descriptions, let alone as reconstructions of the original segmentation that Herodotus and Thucydides had in mind. Rather, they are interpretations of how discourse might be segmented if, on the one hand, we pay attention to several linguistic features of the language besides hypotactic segmentation, and, on the other hand, we take into account the ancient notions of *kôla* and *kómmata*, as well as the contemporary notion of the intonation unit.

§6. The upcoming analyses ultimately illustrate the holistic approach to discourse that we present throughout the work.[3] Boundaries are inferred on the basis of postpositive particles, participial constructions, parallel constructions, hyperbata, and negations, besides independent clauses and subclauses. As for particles, keys to segmentation are not only postpositive δέ and τε, but also καί, appearing in different constructions. Moreover, the occurrence of particles possibly evoking someone's voice and stancetaking (such as γε, δή, and ἤδη) help to single out parts of third-person narration that incorporate reported thoughts besides indirect speech. A further important key to segmentation is the lexical repetition of terms, which creates coherence within and across moves. Finally, verbs seem to frequently occupy act-final or move-final positions; even though this last remark calls for future research, the result per se is relevant to the purposes of the chapter.

§7. Comments in the next sections are made move by move (including a literal translation of my own), but the continuous texts are reported in the Appendix. General results and comparative data are all gathered in the conclusions.

5.2 Nicias' Warnings: Thucydides 6.22-23

§8. The first excerpt comes from the second speech of the Athenian general Nicias (6.20-23).[4] Nicias delivers this speech in Athens during the assembly debate over the proposal to invade Sicily (6.1-26). As the scholarly literature underscores,[5] Nicias embodies an attitude of stark caution and doubt towards the undertaking. He claims that the Athenians must possess a great contingent as well as military superiority in order to handle the high risks. Prior to the selected excerpt Nicias has explicitly suggested that the Athenians let the Sicilians live and settle their own affairs (6.13.1). He has also revealed his thoughts on the might of the Sicilian cities, their autonomy in food provision, and the considerable

3 See in particular I.1 §7 and IV.3.9.

4 Nicias' voice in Thucydides appears in the following passages: 6.9-14 and 6.20-23 (speeches in Athens); 6.25.2 (indirect discourse); 6.47 (indirect discourse); 6.68 (speech at Syracuse); 7.11-15 (letter to the Athenians); 7.48 (indirect discourse); 7.61-64 (speech before the battle in the harbor at Syracuse); 7.69.2 (indirect discourse); 7.77 (speech to the Athenian survivors).

5 See e.g. Westlake 1941 and 1968, Stahl 1973, Tompkins 1972, and Kohl 1977.

size of their fleets and cavalry (6.20). In light of these factors—Nicias warns his fellow citizens—careful plans should include a large force of infantry, and especially adequate equipment and supplies (6.21). In the present excerpt he substantiates and details these points. The final statements summarize his own view: Athens needs good planning and good luck, and therefore the best security is to maximize armament and minimize risks.

§9. In an attempt to define stylistic characterization in Thucydides, Tompkins (1972) analyzes Nicias' and Alcibiades' speeches as opposites both in content and style. While Alcibiades uses parataxis and presents his thoughts straightforwardly (especially by means of sentence-initial καί, 205), Nicias expresses possible complications in action, Tompkins believes, by means of syntactic complication, which results in a heavy use of hypotaxis and a preference for concessions. In a section discussing Nicias' "sentence complication" (184-204), Tompkins singles out semantic features that point to Nicias' conservative stance against adventurous enterprises: "concessions and reversals" (185) marked by the use of "still, yet, however, but"; several levels (or degrees) of subordination (185-188); impersonal verbs and abstract nouns (189-193). These features characterize, in Tompkins' view, Nicias' tendency to express concerns and reluctance.

§10. The analysis of particles, their immediate co-text, semantic input, syntactic contructions, and lexical repetition makes me divide the speech excerpt into 10 distinct moves. The communicative goals underlying them are the following: Nicias remarks that infantries are needed (acts 1-12); ships are needed as well, to carry supplies (13-20). He reminds his fellow citizens that cities cannot be in charge of (the supplies for) the army (21-22); total independence is needed as far as supplies are concerned (23-24). He warns about the necessity of money (25-28). He argues that military excellence in all departments is needed (29-35). Then he points out that founding new colonies requires exerting power from the very beginning (36-43). Even with fear and uncertainties, Nicias declares that he wants to set sail with an appropriate armament (44-52). He adds that only so there is success for the city and the army (53-55). Finally, he says he is willing to give up commanding in case someone else disagrees on these points (56-57).

§11. In the first discourse move (acts 1-12) Nicias details the requirements mentioned in the previous part of the speech (6.21). He starts with the infantries necessary for facing the enemies.

1. [*OCT* 22.1] [extra space] ὁπλίτας τε οὖν πολλούς
2. μοι δοκεῖ
3. χρῆναι ἡμᾶς ἄγειν *{mid dot}*
4. καὶ ἡμῶν αὐτῶν
5. καὶ τῶν ξυμμάχων, *{high or mid dot}*
6. τῶν τε ὑπηκόων *{mid dot}*
7. καὶ ἤν τινα ἐκ Πελοποννήσου δυνώμεθα
8. ἢ πεῖσαι

9. ἢ μισθῷ προσαγαγέσθαι,
10. καὶ τοξότας πολλοὺς
11. καὶ σφενδονήτας, *{mid dot}*
12. ὅπως πρὸς τὸ ἐκείνων ἱππικὸν ἀντέχωσι, *{high dot}*

And therefore numerous hoplites, it seems to me, we need to bring, both our own, and the allies'—the subjects', and whomever from the Peloponnese we may either convince or induce by payment. And numerous archers. And slingers. So that they can face the cavalry of those people.

οὖν marks the beginning of the move.[6] Together with οὖν, two more elements signal the structure of the unfolding argument, ὁπλίτας ... πολλούς, and τε. They have separate functions. ὁπλίτας ... πολλούς conveys the subject of the upcoming discourse acts. The adjective πολλούς adumbrates Nicias' rhetorical insistence on the large amount of resources the Athenians must provide. τε attached to the noun phrase projects a second conjunct introduced by καί—see act 10, καὶ τοξότας πολλούς, a symmetrical noun phrase including another accusative plural and the repetition of πολλούς.[7] In line with what we suggest about different genres, ὁπλίτας τε οὖν πολλούς is a priming act: it orients the attention of the audience to a discourse topic that projects at least beyond the following act.[8]

§12. μοι δοκεῖ in 2 is a crucial construction. I take it as an independent act surrounded by elements of a subclause depending on it. Most of all, μοι δοκεῖ projects not only the stancetaking character of the considerations that follow,[9] up to the mention of an alternative stancetaking (εἰ δέ τῳ ἄλλως δοκεῖ, act 56), but also a long series of infinitive constructions[10] that enhance cohesion among multiple moves. In fact, δοκεῖ's status as the only finite verb in an independent clause before νομίσατε, 28, is what persuaded editors to put the next full stop only before the sentence including νομίσατε.

§13. Apart from the central role of μοι δοκεῖ, the main component that shapes this specific move is the naming of the individual contingents (ὁπλίτας τε, 1; καὶ τοξότας, 10; καὶ σφενδονήτας, 11). Further articulation within this list is marked by parallel

6 See below §§64, 93, 97 on ὦν introducing moves in Herodotus. See also III.2 §§80-84 on οὖν in drama, with literature on οὖν in general. As for μέν οὖν in Thucydides, see IV.3.11.5.

7 See later in this excerpt (ναυσί περιεῖναι) πολύ in 13, (στρατιὰ) πολλή in 21, (χρήματα) πλεῖστα in 25. See also ἱππέων πολλῶν 6.21.1, and πολλοί ... ὁπλῖται 6.20.4.

8 See IV.2.2.5, §87, IV.3.11.1, and this chapter §§32, 42, 59, 63, 78, 103 on priming acts in Herodotus and Thucydides; II.2.5 on priming acts in Homeric and Pindaric poetry; III.5 §§30-33 on priming acts in drama.

9 On μοι δοκεῖ and other forms of explicit and implicit authorial statements in Herodotus and Thucydides, see IV.4 §38.

10 χρῆναι, 3; περιεῖναι, 13; ἄγειν, 16; ἑτοιμάσασθαι, 23; γίγνεσθαι, 24; ἔχειν, 25. Except for χρῆναι, 3, all of them occur before a pre-print dot, and at the end of the act. Conversely, ἄγειν, 3 depends on χρῆναι, 3; πεῖσαι, 8 and προσαγαγέσθαι, 9 depend on δυνώμεθα, 7; ὑποδέξασθαι, 22, depends on ἔσται, 22.

constructions introduced by καί ("from our own and from the allies," 4-5), by τε followed by καί ("[and within the allies] from our subject allies and from whomever..., 6-7[11]), and, finally, by ἤ ... ἤ ("...we may either convince or induce by payment," 8-9). A further component wraps the move up, the antagonistic connection established between "us" (ἡμᾶς, 3; ἡμῶν αὐτῶν, 4; δυνώμεθα, 7) and "those" (ἐκείνων, 12). Act 12 closes the first part of the argument by articulating the expected objective, that is, to oppose the enemy cavalry.

§14. The next move (13 to 20) conveys Nicias' speculation that ships will make it easier to transport supplies.

13. ναυσί τε καὶ πολὺ περιεῖναι, *{mid dot}*
14. ἵνα καὶ τὰ ἐπιτήδεια ῥᾷον ἐσκομιζώμεθα, *{high dot}*
15. τὸν δὲ καὶ αὐτόθεν σῖτον ἐν ὁλκάσι,
16. πυροὺς καὶ πεφρυγμένας κριθάς, ἄγειν, *{high dot}*
17. καὶ σιτοποιοὺς ἐκ τῶν μυλώνων πρὸς μέρος ἠναγκασμένους ἐμμίσθους, *{mid dot}*
18. ἵνα,
19. ἤν που ὑπὸ ἀπλοίας ἀπολαμβανώμεθα, *{mid or low dot}*
20. ἔχῃ ἡ στρατιὰ τὰ ἐπιτήδεια *{high dot}*

> And we need to be by far superior with ships, in order that we may also transport supplies more easily: the grain, (to be put) in trading vessels, also (should come) from here; (we need to bring) wheat and parched barley, and master-bakers conscripted and hired according to the portion of mills. In order that, in case at some point we are detained by impossibility to sail, the army may have supplies at its disposal.

Acts 13 and 14 connect infantry to naval army, and soldiers to supplies. The particle τε in ναυσί τε, 13, echoes ὁπλίτας τε, 1, and starts a new general entry ("we need ships as well").[12] This is an example of a mismatch between modern section division and move division: while the *OCT* text goes on with section 1, and it does not punctuate with any full stop, ναυσί τε, 13, establishes the new discourse topic. Indeed, τε in Herodotus and in Thucydides often signals the beginning of a new move.[13]

[11] The subclause in 7 is a clausal variant of a noun phrase, which Thucydides writes quite frequently.

[12] The lack of grammatical symmetry makes it clear that τε καί in 13 are not to be processed together; the occurrence of the scalar term πολύ suggests that καί's role is to intensify that term.

[13] See IV.2 §§85-87, and below §§22, 40, 44-45, 74. See also Bonifazi 2015:258 for a Pindaric example. Redondo Moyano 1995 (1995:205-206) notes that in Herondas τε can connect a sequence of sentences. I thank Tom Recht, UC Berkeley, for sharing his thoughts about this type of τε, and thoughts about an analogous employment of Latin *-que* in Sallust.

§15. Some grammatical elements of this second move resonate with elements of the first. For example, the subordinating conjunction ἵνα, 14, echoes the necessary anticipation of plans in 12 (with ὅπως and the subjunctive), and the first person plural verb ἐσκομιζώμεθα, 14, resonates with δυνώμεθα, 7. In 14 the theme "supplies" is introduced (τὰ ἐπιτήδεια), which forms the subject matter of the following acts (15 to 20). Later, ἵνα and a first person plural subjunctive are repeated (see 18 and 19[14]); furthermore, the close of the move is sealed by the repetition of ἐπιτήδεια, 20. All these lexical repetitions help stressing the thematic importance of the elements referred to, and at the same time have the organizational function of framing the piece of discourse devoted to them.

§16. The next move consists of just two acts. It is a γάρ move that illustrates the necessity for autonomy on the part of the military forces.

21. (πολλὴ γὰρ οὖσα
22. οὐ πάσης ἔσται πόλεως ὑποδέξασθαι), *{mid dot}*

For, if the army is sizable, not every city will be able to accommodate it.

Syntactically, this is an independent period, and it forms a complete thought.[15] Because it is followed by a further infinitive construction dependent on μοι δοκεῖ (i.e. ἑτοιμάσασθαι, 23), the unit works as a discrete whole embedded within the larger discourse. Its syntactic autonomy is what presumably led editors of printed editions to encapsulate the thought in a parenthesis. The eleventh-century-manuscript that I checked (British Museum 11727) has no parenthesis, but only a high dot and a middle dot framing the unit. The dots do not imply the interpretation of the move as secondary to the main argumentative line—an effect that parentheses do have. In a discourse perspective, the particle γάρ together with the shift of tense in ἔσται, 22 (the previous finite verb is ἔχῃ, 20), are more precise than a dot, and less loaded than a parenthesis: they indicate that the upcoming piece has to be processed as a thought that is associated but also discontinuous with respect to the preceding discourse.[16] The discontinuity in tense expressed by ἔσται, 22, foreshadows οἷοί τε ἐσόμεθα, 33, and Nicias' further remarks about the future decisions to take.

14 I read που, 19, as a propositional reference to an unspecified point in time or place, given the semantic clues provided by ὑπὸ ἀπλοίας ἀπολαμβανώμεθα. On the different constructions that allow us to disambiguate the propositional vs. nonpropositional functions of που, see Koier 2013.

15 Note that the participial phrase in the nominative is anacoluthic, which I regard as a sign of pragmatic relevance: the phrase retrieves the coreferential nominative ἡ στρατιὰ, 20, and establishes "the army" as the ultimate agent (the army cannot count on any city being able to provide them with food).

16 See II.3.2.2 and II.4.2 on γάρ starting moves, and introducing "unframed discourse" in Homer. On tense discontinuity co-occurring with γάρ moves, see II.4 §§16, 21, 28 about epic and lyric, and IV.3 §108 about historiography.

§17. The next move (23-24) concludes the topic of the supplies by reinforcing the point about autonomy.

23. τά τε ἄλλα ὅσον δυνατὸν ἑτοιμάσασθαι, *{mid dot}*
24. καὶ μὴ ἐπὶ ἑτέροις γίγνεσθαι, *{mid dot}*

> And as for the rest of the supplies, (it is necessary that) they be ready as much as possible, which is to say, they should not be provided thanks to others.

The subject matter here is "the remaining supplies" to be prepared in addition to those already mentioned. τε in τά τε ἄλλα, 23, resumes the discourse about τὰ ἐπιτήδεια, 20, after the γάρ move. Its pragmatic function here resembles that of τε in ναυσί τε, 13; in both cases it marks a link between parallel constituents that are separated by different linguistic material (see IV.2 §83). καί in 24 does not simply answer τε; rather, while marking an addition it corrects the immediately preceding utterance by putting it in more precise terms: καὶ μὴ ἐπὶ ἑτέροις γίγνεσθαι means, "that is to say, (it seems to me that supplies should) not be provided thanks to others."[17]

§18. The subject matter of the next move is χρήματα, "money."

25. μάλιστα δὲ χρήματα αὐτόθεν ὡς πλεῖστα ἔχειν. *{high dot}*
26. [extra space] τὰ δὲ παρ' Ἐγεσταίων,
27. ἃ λέγεται ἐκεῖ ἑτοῖμα, *{high dot}*
28. νομίσατε καὶ λόγῳ ἂν μάλιστα ἑτοῖμα εἶναι. *{high or mid dot}*

> Most of all, we must have money from here, as much as we can (get). As for the money from the Egestans, the amount that is said to be ready there, please consider it to be mostly ready, but just in words.

The δέ act in 25 qualifies it as a new, separate act. A lexical item occurs twice, at the beginning and at the end of the move, μάλιστα (25 and 28), albeit in different act positions and with different scope.[18] This move is divided into two parts. The first (25), introduced by δέ, makes the point about financial autonomy. The second part also starts with δέ, and it expands on the same topic (see τά, 26, retrieving χρήματα). Overall it works as a warning, introduced as if almost incidentally, about the alleged reality of the Egestan contribution (later revealed in chapter 46 of book 6). In light of this reading, the full stop posited by editors after ἔχειν, 25, is questionable. On the local level it would make

17 On καί implying better approximation, see IV.2 §104 and III.2 §36.

18 μάλιστα near δέ has scope over the entire act, whereas the second μάλιστα intensifies ἑτοῖμα. Lexical repetition is recognized as a relevant device; see below §111, and also §§26, 28, 35, 39, 74, 84.

sense, if we take it to mark the boundary that δέ indicates. On the global level, however, it happens to be an exceptional full stop after a considerable amount of discourse, and therefore it represents a major pause—the immediately preceding full stop in the *OCT* edition is to be found at the end of 21.2, that is, before act 1. This segmentation based on hypotaxis obscures the coeherence and the thematic connection between the two thoughts about money.[19]

§19. The next move starts with γάρ; the overarching communicative goal is to illustrate and expand on the crucial point of the capabilities of Athenian resources alone.

29. [*OCT* 23.1] [extra space] ἢν γὰρ αὐτοὶ ἔλθωμεν ἐνθένδε *{mid or low dot}*
30. μὴ ἀντίπαλον μόνον παρασκευασάμενοι, *{high dot}*
31. πλήν γε πρὸς τὸ μάχιμον αὐτῶν, τὸ ὁπλιτικόν, *{high dot}*
32. ἀλλὰ καὶ ὑπερβάλλοντες τοῖς πᾶσι, *{mid dot}*
33. μόλις οὕτως οἷοί τε ἐσόμεθα *{high dot}*
34. τῶν μὲν *{low dot or comma}* κρατεῖν, *{high dot}*
35. τὰ δὲ *{low dot or comma}* καὶ διασῶσαι. *{high dot}*

If, for the sake of illustration, we depart just by ourselves from here, having prepared not just a "match"[20]—except, mind you, against their real fighters, the hoplites—but indeed excelling in all departments, we will scarcely in this way be able to rule over what we wish to rule over, and even to save what we wish to save.

The move coincides with the next *períodos*, and it corresponds to chapter section 23.1. However, the individual discourse acts (29 to 35) do not coincide with syntactic clauses, and their ranking is not to be considered in terms of "main" vs. "subordinate." Here I have identified acts based on the occurrence of particles, negations, and a οὗτος form.[21]

§20. The result is a series of segments whose individual syntactic shapes vary significantly. The first act establishes the subject matter: "if we depart from here with our own force"; the subordinate clause ἢν ... ἔλθωμεν forming it, strategically sets up the hypothetical scenario Nicias intends to comment on. Act 32 answers act 30 in construction and syntactic parallelism (μὴ ... παρασκευασάμενοι, 30; ἀλλὰ ... ὑπερβάλλοντες, 32).

[19] The *OCT* edition does report an extra space between words before τὰ δὲ παρ' Ἐγεσταίων, which does not match any section numbers (on this phenomenon see IV.3 §56). In this case it is hard to tell whether the modern full stop is motivated by the extra space, provided that the latter already appears in Byzantine manuscripts, or the extra space in the *OCT* edition is motivated by the full stop at the end of a supposedly very long period.

[20] The quotation marks reflect my reading of a quasi-quotation of the term ἀντίπαλον from Alcibiades' words at 6.17.8 ὑπόλοιπον γὰρ ἡμῖν ἐστὶν ἀντίπαλον ναυτικόν ("for we still have a naval match left," tr. AB).

[21] On the relevance of οὗτος forms in discourse segmentation, see IV.3.11.2 and 3.11.3.

Both are participial phrases; they frame act 31, where the particle γε gives emphasis to the encapsulated act. Let us focus on the discourse function that the encapsulated act performs. πλήν γε πρὸς τὸ μάχιμον αὐτῶν, τὸ ὁπλιτικόν led Dover (1954-1955:8) to imagine "a tone of warning and an admonitory gesture" accompanying πλήν γε, and "vehement emphasis and a change from admonition to a more menacing tone" accompanying τὸ μάχιμον. He paraphrases the content of segments 29-32 as follows: "if we go to Sicily after ourselves raising at Athens a force not simply (as has been proposed) a match for the Siceliots (as it is called by the proposers)—only, mind you, it isn't a match for that element in their forces which really does the fighting, their hoplites—but (as I would propose) superior in all arms, ..." From this reading I infer that the speaker, while uttering πλήν, τὸ μάχιμον, and τὸ ὁπλιτικόν implies meanings that are hinted at, and left unsaid. γε is a most apt particle to do that.[22] In this case γε has scope over the entire noun phrase (πλήν γε πρὸς τὸ μάχιμον αὐτῶν, τὸ ὁπλιτικόν, 32).[23] Perhaps Nicias intends to implicitly contrast his opinion about the necessity of a superior force in all respects with Alcibiades' confidence that the naval superiority of Athens is enough to grant success.[24] The effect on the pragmatic level is the stress on the act including γε. Dover concludes his analysis by saying: "Just as we have not really read a Greek orator's speech until we have heard in our imagination the sound of the speaker's voice and seen his gesticulation, so a Thucydidean speech requires us to recreate in our own minds as much as possible of the visual and auditory images that were in the author's mind when he wrote it" (1954-1955:8). It is significant that Dover associates this comment with the occurrence of πλήν γε; our joint analyses in this monograph show, in concurrence with Dover's observation, that γε is frequently connected to the speaker's voice and a sense of liveliness.[25]

§21. The discourse act in 33 is characterized by the "wrapping up" use of the demonstrative adverb οὕτως,[26] by the negatively-oriented adverb μόλις, and by the future tense of ἐσόμεθα: "We will scarcely in this way be able to ...". The condition expressed at 29-32 is hard to fulfill; but even if it is fulfilled, it will result (that is Nicias' prediction behind the future tense) in goals difficult to achieve: to rule what Athens wishes to conquer, and to save what Athens wishes to save. In the manuscript a low dot or comma (it is difficult to tell which sign it is precisely) occurs after both τῶν μέν, 34 and τὰ δέ, 35. These are paralinguistic signs that suggest a performative pause. Such a pause would enhance the

22 See II.5 §41; III.3.3.1.1; III.5 §§47, 60, and 63.

23 This is my interpretation of the scope of γε in the remaining two Thucydidean instances of πλήν γε as well (2.34.5 and 7.56.4).

24 See Thucydides 6.18.5 [Alcibiades speaking] "Our ability to stay if successful, or to return if not, will be secured to us by our navy, as we shall be superior at sea to all the Sicilians put together" (tr. Crawley and Strassler, in Strassler 1996:372).

25 See IV.4 §§40-44 and here below §§62, 67-68, 73 on γε as a sign of someone's voice in assertions and opinions in historiography. See below §34, and III.5 §§45-58 on γε in acts of stancetaking that are often emotionally loaded, and in acts expressing high arousal.

26 See IV.3 §§120-121.

sense of the twofold difficulty that Athens faces, which Nicias goes on to elaborate in the two acts formed by the two infinitive constructions.

§22. A future tense also closes the next move, made up of acts 36 to 43 (ἕξουσιν, 43), which again coincide with a *períodos* and a chapter section.

36. [*OCT* 23.2] [extra space] πόλιν τε νομίσαι χρὴ
37. ἐν ἀλλοφύλοις καὶ πολεμίοις οἰκιοῦντας ἰέναι, *{mid dot}*
38. οὓς πρέπει τῇ πρώτῃ ἡμέρᾳ
39. ᾗ ἂν κατάσχωσιν *{low dot}*
40. εὐθὺς κρατεῖν τῆς γῆς, *{high dot}*
41. ἢ εἰδέναι ὅτι,
42. ἢν σφάλλωνται, *{low dot or comma}*
43. πάντα πολέμια ἕξουσιν. *{light high dot}*

And finally, we need to consider those who go to found a city as a colony as (being) among strangers, even enemies. It is fitting that on the very first day on which they occupy it, they immediately rule over the land. Or, (it is good that) they are aware that, if they fail, they will gain an environment utterly hostile.

Rhetorically this move represents the climax and final point of the argument; τε is the particle that introduces it (analogous τε occur in 13 and 23). Lexically and syntactically the move illustrate Nicias' stylistic preferences: hypotactic "complications" (see the relative-conditional clause ᾗ ἂν κατάσχωσιν, 39, and the hypothetical clause ἢν σφάλλωνται, 42); and references to cautious pondering (νομίσαι, 36; εἰδέναι, 41). On the one hand he refrains from being direct (see the impersonal verbs χρή, 36, and πρέπει, 38, and references to abstract individuals—"they" instead of "those of us"). On the other hand, he depicts potentialities as certainties, dangers as actual facts ("founding a city among strangers, even enemies," 37; "if they fail, they will gain an environment utterly hostile," 42-43). Overall, the move conjures up the risky situation of conquering a potentially hostile territory.

§23. The next move focuses on Nicias' own deliberation, which opens the very last part of his speech (6.23.3). In ring-composition fashion, the move is framed by first person markers (here we see ἐγώ, 44, and ἐμαυτὸν βούλομαι, 51), recalling μοι δοκεῖ, 2.[27]

44. [*OCT* 23.3] [extra space] ὅπερ ἐγὼ φοβούμενος,
45. καὶ εἰδὼς *{mid dot}*
46. πολλὰ μὲν ἡμᾶς δέον εὖ βουλεύσασθαι, *{mid dot}*
47. ἔτι δὲ πλείω εὐτυχῆσαι *{mid dot}*

27 See also later acts: ἡγοῦμαι, 54; παρίημι, 57.

48. (χαλεπὸν δὲ
49. ἀνθρώπους ὄντας),
50. ὅτι ἐλάχιστα τῇ τύχῃ παραδοὺς
51. ἐμαυτὸν βούλομαι ἐκπλεῖν, *{high dot}*
52. παρασκευῇ δὲ *{mid dot}* ἀπὸ τῶν εἰκότων ἀσφαλὴς ἐκπλεῦσαι. *{high dot}*

Even though I have this fear, and I know, on the one hand, that we need to deliberate many things well, and on the other, that we need good luck even more, which is difficult [to get], as we are human beings, still, by keeping to the minimum my exposure to fortune, I wish to set out myself, and for us to set sail safely with an armament that is apt to the situation.

As we saw with previous stretches of discourse, the force of each act within a move is obscured if we aim at finding periodic perfection—that is, if we read impatiently, so to speak, through the text from the beginning of 23.1 by assuming that the information given is secondary or subsidiary, until we reach the main clause (ἐμαυτὸν βούλομαι ἐκπλεῖν, 51). To read in this manner would be to miss the strategic sequence of the acts that precede the main clause, as well as the pragmatic force conveyed.

§24. The concessive flavor of ὅπερ (44), combined with the possibly concessive nuance of the participles φοβούμενος, 44, and εἰδώς, 45, reflects Nicias' cautious internal state: he fears, he is aware, and yet he decides to sail. A further element of hesitation concerns his confidence in τύχη: he knows that more than good counsel, they need good luck (ἔτι δὲ πλείω εὐτυχῆσαι, 47). At the same time, he does not want to be exposed to τύχη (ὅτι ἐλάχιστα τῇ τύχῃ παραδούς, 50).[28] What makes the two utterances logically harmonious instead of contradictory is the idea expressed through acts 48 and 49 (χαλεπὸν δὲ | ἀνθρώπους ὄντας), which I am going to focus on next.

§25. Modern editors put χαλεπὸν δὲ ἀνθρώπους ὄντας in parentheses, which leave the impression that the thought is incidental or superfluous. Hornblower (1991-2008, vol. III:359) on the contrary rightly argues that the content of this parenthesis is actually an important argumentative step: "The 'parenthesis' is nothing of the sort, but an organic element in a characteristically paratactic and jerky sequence: 'we shall need the help of fortune; but that is something hard for mortals to be sure of; so I would rather, after all, trust as little as possible to fortune'. That is to say, there is an understood accusative absolute ὄν, thus: χαλεπὸν δὲ ὂν ἀνθρώπους ὄντας." The first of the two acts is a syntactically elliptical statement commenting on 47: "we need good luck even more—that's difficult, though." The second act is also a grammatically elliptical segment: "as we are human beings." Parentheses are paralinguistic additions that, while clarifying syntactic

[28] See Hornblower 1991-2008, vol. III:359 on the complex relationship between Nicias and the idea of fortune.

embeddedness, constitute an interpretive filter as well, in that they imply the communication of secondary information. In this case it is essential to follow the individual discourse steps as Thucydides conjoins them, as Hornblower suggests. In the Greek, the particle δέ at 48 suffices to signal the beginning of a discrete discourse act; so, no parentheses are necessary.[29]

§26. ἐκπλεῦσαι at the end of 52 has puzzled Poppo and Stahl (1875-1889, Vol. III, Sect. 1:61), who hypothesize that it is a spurious addition (mainly because of the lexical repetition ἐκπλεῖν, 51, and ἐκπλεῦσαι, 52), and put ἐκπλεῦσαι in square brackets. The odd variation in tense between the two verbs also puzzled Dover (1965:34): "The semantics of verbal aspect in Greek prose literature have not yet been investigated with sufficient care to provide an objective explanation of the change of aspect here." I read the act containing ἐκπλεῦσαι as different in force from the preceding act, and I take the variation of tense in ἐκπλεῦσαι as one of the signs. Even though in syntactic terms the two infinitives are equally dependent on βούλομαι, the first infinitive clause (with ἐκπλεῖν) may be interpreted as a declaration ("I decide that I set sail"), while the second clause (with ἐκπλεῦσαι), act 52, may be interpreted as an exhortation or strong wish ("I wish that we set sail with an appropriate armament"). Several elements are in favor of this reading. The juxtaposition ἐμαυτόν - παρασκευῇ marks the distinction between the personal participation in setting sail, and the decisive element on which a successful participation depends, namely the armament.[30] The particle δέ suggests a different act altogether, rather than a link between two equal elements (given by the content of the two infinitives). The lexical repetition of the same verb ultimately emphasizes the difference in aspect, which contributes to the idea of acts with different illocutionary forces. Finally, a very similar wording right after the end of Nicias' speech matches the interpretation of the general's *intention*, however resolute, to set sail safely, rather than an effective decision taken on behalf of all: ὁ μὲν Νικίας τοσαῦτα εἶπε νομίζων τοὺς Ἀθηναίους τῷ πλήθει τῶν πραγμάτων ἢ ἀποτρέψειν ἤ, εἰ ἀναγκάζοιτο στρατεύεσθαι, μάλιστ' <ἂν> οὕτως ἀσφαλῶς ἐκπλεῦσαι ("Nicias said such things thinking that either he would dissuade the Athenians with the argument of the magnitude of matters, or, if he was forced to do the expedition, they would set sail in this absolutely safe way," 6.24.1 [tr. AB]).[31]

§27. For the fifth time in this excerpt (after 13, 21, 23, and 25), particles and other co-occurring features make me see a new move start that does not coincide with modern section division:

29 IV.2.2 discusses different syntactic constructions where δέ invariably marks the beginning of a new discourse act.

30 The term παρασκευή in general is dear to war historians, but here it is not retrieved from previous mention in this speech (the earliest occurrence of the noun is at 6.21.2, which precedes our excerpt).

31 Instead of the adverb ἀσφαλῶς, act 52 displays ἀσφαλής, which I take as accusative masculine plural form of the adjective. Nicias uses "we" several times in the excerpt under examination (see 3, 7, 14, 19, 29, 33, 46), and he does that also in the following move.

53. ταῦτα γὰρ
54. τῇ τε ξυμπάσῃ πόλει βεβαιότατα ἡγοῦμαι *{high dot}*
55. καὶ ἡμῖν τοῖς στρατευσομένοις σωτήρια. *{high dot}*

These conditions are what I think form the best security for the city, and salvation for us combatants.

Acts 53-55 represent a recap move signalled by an "epimythic" οὗτος[32] form and the particle γάρ. The referent of ταῦτα must be all the suggestions that Nicias expressed during the speech he is about to close. The function of γάρ is to insert the final general assessment (see ἡγοῦμαι) by the speaker.[33] τε in 54 and καί in 55 mark the two parallel components of the assessment. The act in 54 specifies the benefits for the city; the act in 55 the benefits for the soldiers.

§28. The final acts mention the possibility of another opinion and of another command.

56. [extra space] εἰ δέ τῳ ἄλλως δοκεῖ, *{mid or low dot}*
57. παρίημι αὐτῷ τὴν ἀρχήν. *{high dot}*

If anyone has a different opinion, I offer to resign the command to him.

In this case the extra space preceding εἰ δέ in the *OCT* edition matches my pragmatic reading of 56 and 57 as a separate move. τῳ ... δοκεῖ is the key feature, as it thematically juxtaposes the opinion of someone else to Nicias'—see μοι δοκεῖ at 2. The move boundary is even greater if we consider that 56 and 57 constitute the counterpart of a multi-move unit starting with μοι δοκεῖ. Ring-composition by means of lexical repetition is also at work here.

§29. All comparative results are gathered in 5.6, at the end of the four analyses. Here I just conclude by relating this analysis on the whole to Tompkins' idea that Nicias is a master of "sentence complication." The suggested articulation of the text in moves and acts shows that Nicias as a speaker is capable of expressing his thoughts by using a variety of means in addition to syntactic complexity. Each small step seems shaped in such a way to facilitate comprehension rather than to complicate it.

[32] See IV.3 §120-121. "Epimythic," borrowed from Ruiz Yamuza and originally applied just to the adverb οὕτως, captures the metanarrative function of signposting the conclusion(s) to be drawn once narrative accounts are over.

[33] Here the superlative form βεβαιότατα is explicitly linked to the stance taken by the speaking "I". For discussion of superlative forms in connection with someone's stance, see IV.4.6.2.

5.3 Reactions After the Sicilian Expedition: Thucydides 8.1

§30. *A priori* Hellenists may be inclined to think that, however structurally complex Thucydidean speeches are in general, speakers nonetheless tend to present information in rather small segments. Therefore an act division such as the one presented in the previous section may not surprise, after all—it would simply reflect the character of spoken discourse. Now, let us see if the size of acts and moves in 8.1, a narrative section, is different with respect to 6.22-23. Book 8 starts with the reactions of the Athenians to the news of the devastating defeat in Sicily. Just as many other chapters, chapter 1 weaves together multifarious facts, feelings, decisions, and courses of action with the kind of exemplary elegance that has caused modern readers to observe in Thucydidean style the sharpness of the author's mind.[34]

§31. I divide the chapter into 12 moves. The overarching communicative goals I infer, in brief, are the following: the historian stresses the disbelief of the Athenians, as the news spreads (acts 1-6). Then he focuses on the Athenians grudging against those who voted for the expedition (7-9). He enacts a close-up on the Athenians' anger towards seers (10-13). Then he comes to the highest point of the description of feelings: distress and consternation are pervasive (14-16). Afterwards he expands on the deep sense of deprival (17-22), and on the lack of hope for survival (23-26). The historian moves on to detailing the fears of threats and attacks (27-35). At that point his access to the mind of the Athenians shifts to the "nevertheless" components of their thoughts: it is necessary to act (36-44); thrift and measures have to be managed wisely (45-49). Thucydides concludes that the Athenians are ready to act (50-52), and immediately (53-55). At that point he wraps up the account of the entire summer (56).

§32. By means of the first move, Thucydides reports the announcement of the defeat, and he depicts the Athenians' disbelief of the surviving soldiers even before mentioning their disbelief of the messengers.

1. [*OCT* 1.1] [indent] ἐς δὲ τὰς Ἀθήνας
2. ἐπειδὴ ἠγγέλθη,
3. ἐπὶ πολὺ μὲν ἠπίστουν *{high dot}*
4. καὶ τοῖς πάνυ τῶν στρατιωτῶν ἐξ αὐτοῦ τοῦ ἔργου διαπεφευγόσι
5. καὶ σαφῶς ἀγγέλλουσι, *{comma or low dot}*
6. μὴ οὕτω γε ἄγαν πανσυδὶ διεφθάρθαι· *{high dot}*

In Athens: when it was announced, (first of all) for a long time they did not trust either those of the very soldiers who had escaped after the event

34 "The mind and style of a serious writer are connected with each other like the stem and leaves of a tree" (Lamb 1914:85, on Thucydides' intellect).

itself, or those who announced it with no ambiguity; they could not believe that (the Athenian army) had been destroyed SO utterly.

In order to illustrate the importance of act 1, we need to consider the closure of book 7. Hornblower (1991-2008, vol. III:749) remarks that what straddles books 7 and 8 is a μέν ... δέ construction. [35] The text is: ταῦτα μὲν τὰ περὶ Σικελίαν γενόμενα. [*OCT* 8.1] ἐς δὲ τὰς Ἀθήνας ... "These were the accounts about Sicily. In Athens..." The combination of μέν and a οὗτος form within such co-texts indicates that a section is rounded off but more is to come—which in several modern languages can be rendered by means of a nonfinal intonation contour. The δέ act that follows suggests a major shift in subject and setting, from the expedition in Sicily to the reactions and consequences in Athens. It is a priming act: it is short and lacks predicates, but it nevertheless performs a crucial cognitive and pragmatic re-orientation. Now the historian moves to Athens, a post-Sicily Athens. The act primes the geographical/physical setting of the upcoming account.

§33. The move goes on with a short and simple subclause (ἐπειδὴ ἠγγέλθη, 2), which establishes the temporal setting complementing the spatial one. The ἀγγελία, the public and formal announcement of the defeat, works as the (only) relevant chronological reference. In act 3, μέν (following the entire phrase ἐπὶ πολύ) marks the beginning of the account of reactions, and therefore projects several components.[36] The co-occurrence of ἠπίστουν with μέν—a verb form whose subjects (the Athenians in general) are so much in focus that they are not even mentioned[37]—triggers the expectation that some other action (or, better, reaction) by the same subjects will follow.

§34. 4 and 5 are separate acts marked by syntactic parallelism (καί + participle in dative); despite its apparent length, 4 forms just one act because of the bundling effect of the hyperbaton τοῖς ... διαπεφευγόσι. γε in act 6 works to retrieve implicit information[38] and signal emotional involvement at the same time. The retrieval, in this case complemented by the anaphoric marker οὕτω, concerns the content of the announcement, which ἐπειδὴ ἠγγέλθη, 2, leaves implicit. The emotional involvement partly resides in the stress given to οὕτω: capital letters for "so" in my translation render the probable prosodic prominence of οὕτω γε (compare the way "SO" in English would signal the speaker's emotional involvement as well). The presence of γε tells us also that a voice

35 See IV.3 §§66-67 and n227 on μέν ... δέ straddling settings, chapters and even books.

36 On μέν marking pragmatic projection, see especially II.2 §§46-62; see also III.4 §§33 and 55, and §§28-30 (the latter on floor-holding μέν).

37 Thucydides frequently uses these verb forms where the third person plural is not encoded by a disambiguating reference, but is left to the readers' cognitive reconstruction of the scene. An instance of that is commented in IV.3 §88 (κρίνοντες). The notions of referents "accessible" in the speaker's mind are discussed in II.5 §§7-9.

38 See IV.4 §41, II.5 §42, III.4 §63, and III.5 §60. For more on γε, see above §20 with n25.

is represented here; the emotional involvement may ambiguously be that of Athenians blending with that of the historian.[39]

§35. The next move focuses on a different emotional state: the initial distrustful attitude gives way to shocked acknowledgment, as the truth comes to be accepted.

7. [extra space] ἐπειδὴ δὲ ἔγνωσαν,
8. χαλεποὶ μὲν ἦσαν τοῖς ξυμπροθυμηθεῖσι τῶν ῥητόρων τὸν ἔκπλουν, *{high dot}*
9. ὥσπερ οὐκ αὐτοὶ ψηφισάμενοι, *{high dot}*

When they realized (that this was the case), they first had a hostile attitude towards those, among the orators, who contributed to the desire to depart—as if they themselves did not vote for it.

The *OCT* extra space before ἐπειδή at 7 does not accompany a section number, and may have been decided on the basis of the editors' perception of a major boundary in the discourse—or, otherwise, the acknowledgement that medieval scribes put such an extra space in the manuscript. My reading is that a move boundary occurs, indeed, and lexical repetition, once again, comes into play. Just as ἐπειδή in 2 provides the temporal setting for the first move, ἐπειδή in 7 provides the temporal setting for the second move. All the manuscripts, except for B, give ἐπειδή τε instead of ἐπειδὴ δέ, which is interesting. Poppo explicitly says that τε does not make sense here, because it does not answer μέν.[40] However, τε may be fully justifiable, if we think of the Thucydidean usage of τε at discourse transitions.[41] In addition, the sense of contrast that can be inferred from the act (between the moment of the announcement, at 2, and the moment of the actual acknowledgment of the announcement, at 7) does not depend on δέ in itself, but it depends on the semantic co-text (from act 2 on).[42] As for μέν in χαλεποὶ μὲν ἦσαν, 8, it marks the first element of several, in keeping with the function of μέν in 3 and (later) μέν in 17.

§36. The escalation in Thucydides' report about the emotional arousal goes on with a "close-up" involving the same unspecified Athenians, this time directly angry at vaticinators, seers, and those practicing divination.

10. ὠργίζοντο δὲ
11. καὶ τοῖς χρησμολόγοις τε καὶ μάντεσι *{mid dot}*
12. καὶ ὁπόσοι τι τότε αὐτοὺς θειάσαντες *{comma}* ἐπήλπισαν

39 See IV.4.3.3 on γε and voice, and below §38 on the blending of stances.

40 "*etsi interdum* μέν *et* τε *inter se respondent, hic non videtur ferri posse*" (Poppo and Stahl 1866-1883, Vol. IV, Sect. 2:8).

41 See above §14 with n13.

42 See IV.2 §§ 3 and 27. In III.5 §§38-41 the whole texts of δέ acts following μέν acts are said to express semantic contrast—not the particle δέ per se.

13. ὡς λήψονται Σικελίαν. *{high dot}*

> They developed anger towards both vaticinators and seers, and as many as encouraged, by offering divination to them, the hope that they would conquer Sicily.

Modern editors presumably put a comma (instead of a full stop) after ψηφισάμενοι, 9 (see the end of the previous move) because they assume that χαλεποὶ μὲν ἦσαν, 8 and ὠργίζοντο δέ, 10, reflect a thematically related μέν ... δέ construction. However, the syntactic symmetry provided by the two verb forms in the indicative, and the semantic affinity (negative feelings towards somebody) is not as important as the asymmetry Thucydides conveys. ὠργίζοντο δέ expresses a climax, and δέ, far from hinting at a contrast, simply introduces a new act and a new move. I note that τε καί in 11 stresses the "common knowledge" connection that links the two professional categories of vaticinators and seers.[43]

§37. Starting from act 6 the historian not only pretends, as he usually does, to have access to the internal states of characters, but he also directly presents in third-person the thoughts of the Athenians. In other words, the account of reactions shifts to an indirect thought modality. The use of αὐτός is revealing (see αὐτοί, 9; αὐτούς, 12; and, later, αὐτούς, 15)[44]: the subjects around whom facts and feelings occur are the Athenians (in direct speech it would be "we ourselves"), but the narration keeps being in the third person. The overarching effect is a blending of voices: the narrator's and the characters'.[45]

§38. The climactic moment of the description is reached when the historian changes the grammatical subject (from individuals to concepts), and employs comprehensive terms to generalize and deepen the pervasiveness of the Athenians' internal states.

14. [*OCT* 1.2] [extra space] πάντα δὲ πανταχόθεν
15. αὐτοὺς ἐλύπει τε καὶ περιειστήκει ἐπὶ τῷ γεγενημένῳ *{mid dot}*
16. φόβος τε καὶ κατάπληξις μεγίστη δή. *{high or mid dot}*

> Everything everywhere was distressing them, and turned out for the worse after what had happened. (Their) fear and consternation were truly considerable.

The feelings that predominate among the citizens are distress (see ἐλύπει, 15), fear and consternation (φόβος τε καὶ κατάπληξις, 16). The act in 16 is quite emphatically different and separate from the preceding. It contains μεγίστη δή, a feature that is explored

[43] See IV.2 §68 about shared encyclopedic/common knowledge in phrases linked by τε καί in Herodotus and Thucydides.

[44] On αὐτός as a marker of indirect reflexivity in Homeric epic, see Bonifazi 2012:145-149.

[45] More thoughts on voices and stances blended in Thucydides can be found in IV.4.6.3 and 4.8.3.

more closely in IV.4 §116 (concerning the two *Histories*). In a pragmatic perspective, the construction δή + superlative relates to voice and stance. δή signals not only the speaker's voice but also her communicative actions of stancetaking. The speaker positions herself with respect to that reality ("I feel strongly about X"), and at the same time evaluates that reality ("X is really Y"). A fascinating aspect of δή marking someone's voice and stance in Thucydides is the potential polyphony, namely the potential blending of more voices through the same utterance—which I already advanced for acts 9-12, independently of the use of δή. In act 16 the voice and stance could be the despairing Athenians' or the historian's. I advance that Thucydides may deliberately leave the reference ambiguous, possibly to stress—in an indirect form—some sense of sharedness or empathy.

§39. A quite elaborate γάρ move follows, which expands on the emotional atmosphere established in 14-16.

17. ἅμα μὲν γὰρ στερόμενοι *{high dot}*
18. καὶ ἰδίᾳ ἕκαστος καὶ ἡ πόλις
19. ὁπλιτῶν τε πολλῶν καὶ ἱππέων
20. καὶ ἡλικίας
21. οἵαν οὐχ ἑτέραν ἑώρων ὑπάρχουσαν *{comma}*
22. ἐβαρύνοντο· *{high dot}*

23. ἅμα δὲ ναῦς οὐχ ὁρῶντες ἐν τοῖς νεωσοίκοις ἱκανὰς *{high dot}*
24. οὐδὲ χρήματα ἐν τῷ κοινῷ *{high or mid dot}*
25. οὐδ' ὑπηρεσίας ταῖς ναυσὶν *{comma}*
26. ἀνέλπιστοι ἦσαν ἐν τῷ παρόντι σωθήσεσθαι, *{mid or low dot}*

> [Let me illustrate:] At once they felt deprived both as individuals, in their private sphere, and as a city. (Deprived) of numerous hoplites and horsemen, and youth, the kind that they could not see others replacing. They had a heavy heart.
>
> At the same time, they did not see the ships in the boathouses to be sufficient, nor the financial resources available to the community, nor crew for the ships. They did not expect in the present circumstances to survive.

γάρ in fact introduces two moves, starting with ἅμα μέν, 17, and ἅμα δέ, 23 respectively (see the space in between, and the indentation in my translation). In Thucydides ἅμα not infrequently forms a construction with μέν or δέ; the construction works as a discourse marker introducing facts or states that co-occur with each other.[46] In this passage strong lexical and semantic parallelisms across the ἅμα μέν and the ἅμα δέ units reinforce

[46] See Thucydides 2.20.4; 3.115.4; 4.103.5; 4.130.5; 4.132.2; 5.7.1; 7.68.1; 7.84.2; 8.47.1.

this idea of co-occurrence: participles referring to the generic "they," the Athenians (στερόμενοι, 17; ὁρῶντες, 23), and negative or privative concepts (στερόμενοι, 17; οὐχ, 21; οὐχ, 23; οὐδέ, 24; οὐδ'(έ), 25; ἀνέλπιστοι, 26). In view of this, μέν and δέ serve, together with ἅμα, to index the desolation of a people towards a parallel sense of lack of means, namely at the present and for the future. In these two parallel units the only particles occurring except for μέν and δέ are καί and τε. The repetition of καί gives rise to an accumulation effect[47]: καὶ ἕκαστος, 18; καὶ ἡ πόλις, 18; καὶ ἡλικίας, 20; see also its negative counterpart οὐδὲ (οὐδὲ χρήματα, 24; οὐδ' ὑπηρεσίας, 25). τε signals a construction of two conjuncts (ὁπλιτῶν τε πολλῶν καὶ ἱππέων, 19), which along with ἡλικίας, 20, grammatically depend on στερόμενοι, 17, and semantically instantiate what "the city" means to the Athenians. Something particularly striking in these moves is the strategic placement and the length of verbal forms. ἐβαρύνοντο, 22 is an act in itself; the relatively high number of syllables forming it iconically mirrors the heaviness of the semantic meaning ("they had a heavy heart"), and possibly of its utterance. Symmetrically, at the end of the ἅμα δέ move, ἀνέλπιστοι ἦσαν, 26, concludes the picture of the hopeless atmosphere in Athens. Act 26 is masterfully filled with verb forms: ἀνέλπιστοι ἦσαν ἐν τῷ παρόντι σωθήσεσθαι.[48]

§40. The modern comma after σωθήσεσθαι does not sufficiently convey the strength of what I see as a move boundary: act 27 (below) begins a new phase of the account of reactions and thoughts about threats and further attacks from enemies, which constitutes a separate discourse unit.

27. τούς τε ἀπὸ τῆς Σικελίας πολεμίους *{comma}*
28. εὐθὺς σφίσιν ἐνόμιζον
29. τῷ ναυτικῷ ἐπὶ τὸν Πειραιᾶ πλευσεῖσθαι,
30. ἄλλως τε καὶ τοσοῦτον κρατήσαντας, *{mid dot}*
31. καὶ τοὺς αὐτόθεν πολεμίους
32. τότε δὴ καὶ διπλασίως πάντα παρεσκευασμένους *{high or mid dot}*
33. κατὰ κράτος ἤδη
34. καὶ ἐκ γῆς καὶ ἐκ θαλάσσης ἐπικείσεσθαι, *{high or mid dot}*
35. καὶ τοὺς ξυμμάχους σφῶν μετ' αὐτῶν ἀποστάντας. *{high dot}*

And the enemies from Sicily, they [the Athenians] thought, could directly sail with their navy against the Piraeus, especially after winning in such a crushing way. And the enemies from their own area, right at that moment could have clearly gained everything twofold, certainly by force: they could arrive both by land and by sea. And their allies, after seceding from (the Athenians) themselves[, they would join those people].

47 On the accumulation effect of numerous subsequent καί, see IV.2 §132.

48 More remarks on the position of verbs will follow in 5.6.

The hyperbaton that frames act 27 (τούς ... πολεμίους), and the occurrence of τε—which at this point is unsurprising at the beginning of moves—introduce a very different subject, that is, the threatening thought of the enemies, of their possible move directly against the Piraeus. ἄλλως τε καί in 30 signals the climax of this thought: "especially after such a victory."[49] καί in 31 (καὶ τοὺς αὐτόθεν πολεμίους) answers τε in 27 (τούς τε ἀπὸ τῆς Σικελίας πολεμίους). The two conjuncts, then, span more than one act (27-30, and 31-34); the content refers to the Sicilian enemies and the "local" enemies.[50] In act 35 καί introduces the final "entry" of potentially threatening people, namely the newfound allies of the Greek enemies.

§41. τότε δή in 32 links the situation described (the possession of twice as many resources as those at the enemies' disposal) to the very moment of the thought of the Athenians about it.[51] I draw a pragmatic connection between δή in 32 and ἤδη in 33 (κατὰ κράτος ἤδη). The two lexical items introduce two acts that express a subjective perception of evidence as well as certainty by the Athenians (see "clearly" and "certainly" in my translation).[52] Once again, Thucydides uses a third-person description of the thoughts of the Athenians (see ἐνόμιζον, 28), but he then manages to blur the distance between his own and the Athenian's cognition in representing the content of the thoughts. As for κατὰ κράτος ἤδη, 33, I see it as an independent act because its content can be referred to both 32 and 34: by force the enemies would gain double resources; by force they would attack by land and sea.

§42. By means of the next move Thucydides illustrates the resilient attitude of the Athenians.[53]

36. [*OCT* 1.3] [extra space] ὅμως δὲ
37. ὡς ἐκ τῶν ὑπαρχόντων ἐδόκει χρῆναι
38. μὴ ἐνδιδόναι, *{mid dot}*
39. ἀλλὰ παρασκευάζεσθαι
40. καὶ ναυτικόν,
41. ὅθεν ἂν δύνωνται ξύλα ξυμπορισαμένους,
42. καὶ χρήματα,
43. καὶ τὰ τῶν ξυμμάχων ἐς ἀσφάλειαν ποιεῖσθαι, *{mid dot}*
44. καὶ μάλιστα τὴν Εὔβοιαν, *{mid dot}*

Nevertheless, the opinion was that, given the circumstances, it was necessary not to give in, but to prepare (the following): a fleet, after purchasing

49 IV.2 §§122-132 focus on καί marking a climactic point in discourse.

50 αὐτόθεν literally means "from here." Thucydides maintains the Athenians' point of view (see above §37 about αὐτός).

51 Compare the value of δή τότε in Homer in II.3 §58.

52 On ἤδη, see IV.4.8; on ἤδη + κατὰ κράτος, see especially §154.

53 With reference to the passage, Hornblower (1991-2008, vol. III:752) comments: "This resilience is astonishing."

> timber wherever they could; money; and making the relationships with the allies stable, in particular Euboea.

In this act division ὅμως δέ, 36, is separate from ὡς ἐκ ..., 37, because the latter belongs to the infinitive subclause. ὅμως δέ is in fact a powerful act in itself: the construction suggests that the argument will take a totally different direction. Because it activates a new frame, this very short act works as a priming act. The new frame is not spatial or temporal, but rather argumentative: it includes the series of decisions that the Athenians take in spite of all their misgivings and feelings of despair that Thucydides has carefully depicted up to now.[54] In content, ὅμως δέ starts a unit that embraces acts 36 to 49, which coincides with a long *períodos* identified by modern punctuation. However, I sub-divide the move into two: 36-44, and 45-49.

§43. ἐδόκει in 37 projects multiple entries illustrating what seemed to the Athenians to be the right course of action. μὴ ἐνδιδόναι and ἀλλὰ παρασκευάζεσθαι, 38-39, represent a further "abstract," that is, an anticipated summary of the Athenians' opinion. The two acts are syntactically parallel and semantically opposite: not to give in, but to get ready. What follows is a list of the three kinds of preparations chosen, plus a specification regarding the third type of preparation, stabilizing relationships with allies. καί links these preparations (καὶ ναυτικόν, 40; καὶ χρήματα, 42; καὶ τὰ τῶν ξυμμάχων ἐς ἀσφάλειαν ποιεῖσθαι, 43); at the same time, the parallel repetition of καί makes them discrete. The last καί, however (44), introduces a different kind of information, namely a detail concerning one of the allies.[55]

§44. Starting at 45 below, the historian narrates about a different set of decisions by the Athenians; they want to take some political measures regarding the city itself.

45. τῶν τε κατὰ τὴν πόλιν τι ἐς εὐτέλειαν σωφρονίσαι, *{mid dot}*
46. καὶ ἀρχήν τινα πρεσβυτέρων ἀνδρῶν ἑλέσθαι, *{mid dot}*
47. οἵτινες περὶ τῶν παρόντων
48. ὡς ἂν καιρὸς ᾖ
49. προβουλεύσουσιν. *{high dot}*

> Also, (the opinion was) to be wise on the matter of thrift within the city,[56] and to elect a board of elders, who, on appropriate occasions, should take counsel on measures beforehand.

[54] The major discourse boundary is fully acknowledged on the paralinguistic level by the start of a new section, the extra space, and Hammond's indentation in his translation (2009:415).

[55] On καί pinning concepts down, and introducing examples or instantiations, see IV.2 §§102-105 and III.2 §36; see also §17 in this chapter.

[56] *Ex silentio* κατὰ τὴν πόλιν, 45, must refer to Athens.

In 50 τε signals a move boundary, in line with several preceding cases (see 1, 13, 23, and 36 in excerpt 1; 27, here, and 50 in this excerpt). The last verb form, προβουλεύσουσιν, coincides with the last act of the move, in line with ἐβαρύνοντο, 22.[57]

§45. The next move (50-52) also starts with τε:

50. [*OCT* 4] πάντα τε πρὸς τὸ παραχρῆμα περιδεές, *{mid dot}*
51. ὅπερ φιλεῖ δῆμος ποιεῖν, *{high dot}*
52. ἑτοῖμοι ἦσαν εὐτακτεῖν. *{mid dot}*

Against the fear of the moment in everything—the δῆμος likes to do this—they were ready to be orderly.

This time Thucydides adds a closing and comprehensive (see πάντα, 50) note about the Athenians. He seems to start zooming out from the details of their thoughts. Act 51 is syntactically a subclause, but in content it is the key utterance of the move: "which the δῆμος likes to do." Poetic flourishes surrounding the clause both help set the statement off rhetorically and underline its solemn character: note, first, the strong alliteration in the two framing utterances (in 50 through the repetition of initial π, in 52 through the ε/η sound); and the assonance across 51 and 52 (of the diphthong ει in φιλεῖ and ποιεῖν in 51, and εὐτακτεῖν in 52).

§46. Acts 53-55 exemplify the statement made in the previous move:

53. [extra space] καὶ
54. ὡς ἔδοξεν αὐτοῖς, *{high dot}*
55. καὶ ἐποίουν ταῦτα, *{high dot}*

And so, what seemed fit to them, they enacted.

καί in 53 signals the start of a new move, and the extra space in *OCT* seems to acknowledge that. It stands alone before the subclause of 54 because it projects multiple acts, and therefore works as a priming act. The second καί in 55 is an "apodotic" καί that has clausal scope and marks an immediate correspondence between thoughts and actions.[58] The zooming out from thoughts results in the shift to action.

§47. The last move (and act) of this excerpt, which opens with a further καί, is a coda that completes Thucydides' zooming out.

56. καὶ τὸ θέρος ἐτελεύτα. *{high dot}*

And so, the summer ended.

57 For an overview of the relevance of verb positions to the segmentation in acts, see later, §112.

58 See IV.2 §§113 and 137 on apodotic καί, and IV.3 §§111-112 on καί as a priming act.

The conjunct that καί links to τὸ θέρος ἐτελεύτα is the entire Thucydidean account of that particular summer (the nineteenth since the start of the war; it occupies chapters 19 to 87 of book 7, and the current chapter of book 8). The statement functions as a formulaic closure of a substantial stretch of text, and as such presents itself as a unit with more independence than modern punctuation gives it credit for (see the modern comma after ταῦτα, 55). Conversely, in his English translation Hammond (2009:415) indents, which harmonizes with what a discourse analysis suggests.[59]

§48. All in all, the number of acts and moves across these two first excerpts is similar: the speech includes 57 acts and 10 moves; the narrator text 56 acts and 12 moves. Both stretches of text allow the audience to chunk discourse in manageable units, regardless of hypotaxis and the complexity of the content.

5.4 Reactions After Salamis: Herodotus 8.108-109.1

§49. The next excerpt is thematically similar to the passage just analyzed. Just as Thucydides 8.1 narrates the reactions of the Athenians after the devastating news of the defeat in Sicily, Herodotus 8.108.1 narrates the reaction of the Greeks, this time to the successful battle at Salamis against the Persians. The Herodotean account, like the Thucydidean one, displays a narrative style typical of the historian, masterfully combining thoughts and actions, events and words into a harmonious whole.[60]

§50. I have chosen to juxtapose similar sections from the two authors so that we may be able to compare their styles at the level of discourse segmentation. Conventional wisdom might lead us to expect Herodotean narrative to be divisible into more (i.e. smaller) segments than Thucydides', for example, or to give evidence of more extensive use of parataxis. As the analysis will show, neither of these two expectations is met.[61]

§51. The excerpt is divided into 18 moves, by means of which Herodotus points out the following: the Greeks expect the Persian ships to be at Phalerum (1-6); they get ready to chase them (7-8); as they do not see them, they move towards Andros (9-11). They have an assembly in Andros (12-13). The historian zooms in on Themistocles, who expresses his opinion (14-18). Then Eurybiades takes the floor (19-21). Herodotus presents Eurybiades' idea in short (22-23). The first point is that it is problematic if Xerxes

59 See IV.2.4.5, where the same passage is commented on (t58). On the imperfect tense of the last clause, see Bakker 1997e:31.

60 Earlier at n34 I quoted Lamb's comparison between the stem and leaves of a tree, and the mind and style of a serious writer (Thucydides, in that case). The masterful description I am going on to comment involves the same deep connection between mind and style, and stem and leaves, for Herodotus no less than for Thucydides.

61 Once again, the continuous text is reported in the final Appendix. A general paleographical note concerns the medieval punctuation of the manuscript Laurentianus A. I observed that most of the commas are lighter in color than dots; in addition, the same light color appears in all the accents written on words (or rather, groups of words, as individual words are not always spaced). This coloring may be a sign of a different, possibly later, hand.

is forced to stay in Greece (24-27); either if he keeps things quiet (28-33); or if he takes initiatives (34-39). In the latter case, Eurybiades remarks, the Persians would steal the nourishment of the Greeks (40-41). Eurybiades thinks that Xerxes actually will not stay (42-45). It is better to let him go (46-47); it is better that the battle goes on in Persia (48-49). The other generals agree with Eurybiades (50). Themistocles realizes his low chance of convincing the Greeks to sail (51-54). But he also realizes that he could count on the Athenians (55-58). So, he starts a speech (59).

§52. Here is the text of the first move:

1. [*OCT* 108.1] [extra space] ὡς δὲ ἡμέρη ἐγίνετο, *{comma}*
2. ὁρῶντες οἱ Ἕλληνες κατὰ χώρην μένοντα τὸν στρατὸν τὸν πεζὸν *{comma}*
3. ἤλπιζον καὶ τὰς νέας εἶναι περὶ Φάληρον, *{mid dot}*
4. ἐδόκεόν τε ναυμαχήσειν σφέας *{mid dot}*
5. παραρτέοντό τε
6. ὡς ἀλεξησόμενοι. *{mid dot}*

> When dawn arrived, the Greeks could see that the land army was still in the area. They were expecting that the ships as well would be at Phalerum. They were of the opinion that they would have another sea battle, and so they prepared to defend themselves.

From a discourse perspective temporal or causal clauses accompanied by δέ often provide new starting points for subsequent action.[62] Accordingly, this δέ marks the beginning of a new act that is also the beginning of a move that extends beyond the temporal or causal clause and embraces segments 1 to 6. At the same time, act 1 provides the setting for the entire account of the day after the battle, chapters 108 to 112. It also resumes the narrative thread: after the account of the battle, which ends at chapter 96, Herodotus shifts to narrating events on the Persian side, recounting Xerxes' decision to retreat and leave Mardonius in charge of a new campaign (chapters 97 to 107). Acts 1 and 2 (ὡς δὲ ἡμέρη ἐγίνετο | ὁρῶντες οἱ Ἕλληνες κατὰ χώρην μένοντα τὸν στρατὸν τὸν πεζόν) play the cognitive role of reorienting the audience's attention to the Greek side of the battlefield, not differently from act 1 in the Thucydidean excerpt above (ἐς δὲ τὰς Ἀθήνας, 8.1.1).

§53. Act 2 (ὁρῶντες οἱ Ἕλληνες κατὰ χώρην μένοντα τὸν στρατὸν τὸν πεζὸν) actually narrows the field of vision in the audience's mind's eye by orienting it through the vision of the Greeks: the Greeks see that the Persian land army is still there, at Phalerum. The participle ὁρῶντες instantiates a strategy very common in historiography, that

[62] See e.g. Bakker 1991. On "preposed" temporal clauses in Homer, see II.3§56.

of providing "participial preludes" (the use of participles to encode introductions to actions).[63]

§54. I read what follows as a subtle articulation of the Greeks' reaction, step by step, and, from the perspective of Herodotus' narration, act by act. Acts 3 to 5 all start with an imperfect verb (ἤλπιζον, 3, ἐδόκεον, 4, and παραρτέοντο, 5). However, the symmetry is interwoven with a different type of design, embracing the verbs starting 2 to 5: "observing—expecting," 2-3, on the one hand, and "expressing a view—preparing," 4-5, on the other. Particles suggest a further link, which distinguish acts 1-3 from acts 4-6. ἐδόκεόν τε ναυμαχήσειν σφέας, 4, and παραρτέοντό τε, 5, display a bisyndetic construction of τε with clausal scope. This construction separates 4 from 3, it stresses a particularly tight link between the two conjuncts,[64] and makes acts 4-6 a whole. A further feature that makes 4-6 cohere is the double use of future tense (ναυμαχήσειν, 4, and ἀλεξησόμενοι, 6). A full stop after Φάληρον, 3, would reflect the relevance of the bisyndetic construction to discourse segmentation. The comma of modern editions, however, invites a continuous reading that obscures the distinction between observation and its practical consequences. The final construction ὡς + future participle confirms Herodotus' access to the internal stance of the Greeks in line with the preceding acts.

§55. An extra space in the *OCT* not accompanying a section or chapter number matches my reading of a move boundary between 6 and 7.

7. [extra space] ἐπεὶ δὲ ἐπύθοντο τὰς νέας οἰχωκυίας, *{low dot + light comma}*
6. αὐτίκα μετὰ ταῦτα ἐδόκεε ἐπιδιώκειν. *{high dot}*

When they learned that the ships were gone, they immediately opted for chasing them.

Act 7 contains a construction parallel to act 1, a temporal clause with δέ. This is the clue that a new move is being established: just as the previous one did, the same construction here provides a new contextual frame for a new action.[65] Now, the focus is on the decision to chase the Persian ships, which constitutes the next step in reasoning after the initial defensive thought (acts 1-6). This decision, in turn, establishes the ground for a series of subsequent narrative steps, made up of an account of the chasing trip and events that occur along the way (acts 7-11), and a debate taking place in Andros (intermediate stop on the way to the Hellespont, acts 12-13).

§56. The next move boundary in my reading once more coincides with the paralinguistic suggestion given by an extra space between words in the *OCT* edition.

63 With reference to Thucydides, see Lang 1995:48; 49 for the quotation.

64 See IV.2 §§63 and 68 on τε in bisyndetic constructions in both historians.

65 For the cognitive notion of contextual frame, see II.4 §12.

9. [extra space] τὸν μέν νυν ναυτικὸν τὸν Ξέρξεω στρατὸν
10. οὐκ ἐπεῖδον
11. διώξαντες μέχρι Ἄνδρου,

Now, the naval part of Xerxes army, [this] they did not see, although they were making chase as far as Andros.

It it tempting to think that the extra space is connected to the occurrence of μέν νυν, 9. As IV.3.11.4 has shown, this combination often occurs either at the beginning or at the end of episodes. In this case μέν νυν may indicate the end of the Greeks' speculations, or alternatively, mark the beginning of the Greeks' realization that they had made an incorrect assumption. This beginning puts upfront the fundamental object of the Greeks' considerations thus far, the Persians' ships, to which the denial of their expectation follows. I read τὸν ... ναυτικὸν τὸν Ξέρξεω στρατόν as a separate act that isolates a grammatical object preceding the verb it depends on (ἐπεῖδον), and οὐκ ἐπεῖδον, 10, as a further discourse act stressing the negative outcome. Acts 10 and 11 in fact close the scenario opened by ὁρῶντες, 2, τὸν στρατόν, 2 (even though at 2 it refers to the land army), and τὰς νέας, 3. The particles and the semantic design of these acts make me see a separate move, rather than the first part of a μέν ... δέ construction (see δέ in 12 here below) with νυν working as a distinct discourse marker.[66] Accordingly, the modern comma at 11 could be replaced by a full stop.

§57. In 11 and 12 "Andros" is repeated, which makes more sense if 11 and 12 are taken as belonging to two different moves.

12. ἐς δὲ τὴν Ἄνδρον ἀπικόμενοι
13. ἐβουλεύοντο. *{high dot}*

So, once they reached Andros, they held a consultation.

The length of the verb form and the imperfect of ἐβουλεύοντο suggest an iconic rendering of what could have been a long consultation.[67]

§58. The next move indicates a shift from collective ideas and actions to the individual proposal of Themistocles. Once again, μέν νυν performs the segmenting function.

14. [*OCT* 108.2] Θεμιστοκλέης μέν νυν γνώμην ἀπεδείκνυτο *{light comma}*
15. διὰ νήσων τραπομένους
16. καὶ ἐπιδιώξαντας τὰς νέας *{mid or low dot + light comma}*
17. πλέειν ἰθέως ἐπὶ τὸν Ἑλλήσποντον

[66] An instance of νυν working separately from μέν in μέν νυν is commented in §95.
[67] See above §39 about ἐβαρύνοντο in Thucydides 8.1.2.

18. λύσοντας τὰς γεφύρας· *{high dot}*

> Now, Themistocles expressed the opinion that, while carrying on through the islands, and pursuing the [Persian] ships, they could sail directly to the Hellespont, in order to destroy the bridges.

"Themistocles" semantically provides a new entry—an individual emerging from an unspecified group of Greek soldiers. μέν νυν tells us that something distinct from the preceding discourse is going to start. The semantic juxtaposition that the historian inserts later by mentioning a second individual and "the opposite opinion" (Εὐρυβιάδης δὲ τὴν ἐναντίην ταύτῃ γνώμην ἐτίθετο, 19-20) makes the two characters the salient figures and dialectical voices of the moment.[68] To be sure, μέν (even within the combination μέν νυν) and δέ do not imply the semantic juxtaposition. They just tell us to process the content in terms of two aspects of a larger whole; it is the surrounding components that make the two aspects semantically symmetrical and opposing.[69]

§59. The next move, actually, anticipates something asymmetrical in the juxtaposition, on the pragmatic and cognitive level:

19. Εὐρυβιάδης δὲ *{comma}*
20. τὴν ἐναντίην ταύτῃ γνώμην ἐτίθετο, *{high dot}*
21. λέγων ὡς

> But Eurybiades proposed the opposite opinion to that, by saying the following.

The medieval comma after Εὐρυβιάδης δέ suggests a possible performative pause or intonational break in line with the prosodic treatment of Εὐρυβιάδης δέ as a "first position"-constituent.[70] I read the phrase as a priming act, even though syntactically it is fully integrated into the main clause of which it is the grammatical subject (see 20). The point is that the historian re-orients the audience's attention to Eurybiades, to expand on the latter's opinion. The key to that is λέγων ὡς, 21, a metanarrative act introducing Eurybiades' relatively long speech (indirectly reported). The occurrence of εἰ immediately afterwards, and the function of ὡς following "saying"—i.e. to signpost the upcoming reported speech—suggests an act boundary between ὡς and εἰ. On the whole

68 Herodotus uses a chiastic structure that includes semantic repetition to underscore the diametrically opposed views of the two leaders: "the Greeks should sail to the Hellespont to break the bridges" (17-18, Themistocles), vs. "if they break the bridges that is the greatest harm" (22-23, Eurybiades).

69 See III.5 §§37-43 on pragmatic and semantic differences in μέν ... δέ constructions.

70 See Fraser 2001:140-141; see also II.2 §§12-16. Blankenborg 2015 identifies in the whole constituted by peninitial particles and their preceding words a sign of what he calls "audible punctuation."

this move anticipates Herodotus' asymmetrical way of reporting Eurybiades' opinion. If we consider the account up to now, 19-21 represent a further step in a progressive zooming in on a specific moment of the reactions after Salamis (collective thoughts and actions—assembly—general opinion of Themistocles—reported words by Eurybiades).

§60. Acts 22-48 constitute Herodotus' summary of Eurybiades' words. I subdivide the unit into five moves. The first represents a summary of Eurybiades' ultimate point, which the subsequent γάρ move illustrates in detail.[71]

22. εἰ λύσουσι τὰς σχεδίας, *{comma}*
23. τοῦτ' ἂν μέγιστον πάντων σφεῖς κακὸν τὴν Ἑλλάδα ἐργασαίατο.

If they destroy the bridges of boats, this would do to Greece the greatest harm of all.

Before I introduce the γάρ move that follows, I highlight a mismatch between the act and move-based segmentation that is under consideration here, and the modern full stops occurring at the end of 13 and, here, at the end of 23. These two full stops make 14-23 a whole. The resulting periodic unit (Θεμιστοκλέης μέν νυν ..., 14; the semicolon at 18; Εὐρυβιάδης δέ ..., 19; the full stop at 23) embraces Themistocles' idea (14-18) and the very beginning of Eurybiades' idea (19-23). I believe this segmentation is largely inspired not only by the sequence of sub- and main clauses, but also by the semantic juxtaposition "Themistocles—Eurybiades." The act and move-based segmentation suggests something quite different. It follows the flow of discourse beyond hypotaxis, and beyond the presupposition that μέν and δέ must always signal semantic symmetry and opposition. The flow of discourse indicates two separate moves that end before 23: 14-18 presents Themistocles' idea, and 19-21 *projects the account* of Eurybiades' idea. Then, a major discourse boundary is conveyed by λέγων ὡς, 21, in spite of the suspended hypotaxis and the modern comma. Act 21 introduces the whole of Eurybiades' reported words, which spans acts 22-48.

§61. The next move is quite elaborate; it illustrates what is likely to happen if the Greeks break the bridge and Xerxes remains in Europe. γάρ is the pragmatic signal that the illustration is going to take place. Further moves within the γάρ move can be identified as well. I present here the entire illustration of Eurybiades' argument (24-41) with a space indicating what I read as further move boundaries in between (see the corresponding indentations in my translation).

24. [*OCT* 108.3] [extra space] εἰ γὰρ ἀναγκασθείη
25. ἀπολαμφθεὶς
26. ὁ Πέρσης μένειν ἐν τῇ Εὐρώπῃ, *{comma}*

71 See above §43 and II.3 §14 on narrative abstracts preceding the elaborated version of an account.

27. πειρῷτο ἂν ἡσυχίην μὴ ἄγειν, *{high dot}*

28. ὡς
29. ἄγοντι μέν οἱ ἡσυχίην *{low dot}*
30. οὔτε τι προχωρέειν
31. οἷόν τε ἔσται τῶν πρηγμάτων *{mid dot}*
32. οὔτε τις κομιδὴ τὸ ὀπίσω φανήσεται, *{high dot}*
33. λιμῷ τέ οἱ ἡ στρατιὴ διαφθερέεται, *{high dot}*

34. ἐπιχειρέοντι δὲ αὐτῷ καὶ ἔργου ἐχομένῳ *{mid dot + comma}*
35. πάντα τὰ κατὰ τὴν Εὐρώπην
36. οἷά τε ἔσται προσχωρῆσαι
37. κατὰ πόλις τε καὶ κατὰ ἔθνεα, *{light comma}*
38. ἤτοι ἁλισκομένων γε
39. ἢ πρὸ τούτου ὁμολογεόντων· *{high dot}*

40. τροφήν τε ἕξειν σφέας
41. τὸν ἐπέτειον αἰεὶ τὸν τῶν Ἑλλήνων καρπόν. *{high dot}*

For if the Persian [king] should be forced, once he is away, to remain in Europe, he would attempt not to keep things quiet.

Because, if he keeps quiet, on the one hand, he will not be able to advance his affairs. And no way of coming back will appear, and the army will be devastated by famine.

If, on the other hand, he takes the initiative and keeps at his work, every place in Europe will be able to go over to him, city by city and people by people, either as they are being subdued, or as they agree to support him.

And so they will have food, the ever-yearly fruit of the Greeks.

The acts in this passage are easily identified through syntactic and pragmatic boundaries, mainly due to parallelism and repetition.[72] ὡς in 28 is isolated as it is followed by a μέν act, and thus projects multiple segments that articulate the causal link it expresses.[73]

72 Bowie (2007:197), who lists the parallel clauses included in this part of Eurybiades' indirect speech by indenting them, comments: "its relative clarity and plainness suit a Spartan."

73 See above, §46, and IV.3 §§111-112 on καί constituting an act on its own. Denniston (1950:371) notes about structures involving a μέν and δέ component: "Normally μέν and δέ stand second in their respective clauses, and everything between the last stop and the word preceding μέν applies to the whole μέν ... δέ complex. (Strictly speaking, one should say, not 'clause' but 'word group', which does not necessarily coincide with punctuation.)"

The sequence οὔτε, 30, οὔτε, 32, and τε, 33, lists the consequences that Xerxes will experience if he remains inactive (ἄγοντι μέν οἱ ἡσυχίην, 29). Conversely, the τε in 31 and 36 belong to the idiomatic phrase οἷός τε εἰμί.

§62. Acts 35-39 unfold what 34 projects, that is, what could happen in case Xerxes becomes active (ἐπιχειρέοντι δὲ αὐτῷ καὶ ἔργου ἐχομένῳ, which parallels ἄγοντι μέν οἱ ἡσυχίην, 29). It is noteworthy that also in this case the sense of juxtaposition rests on the semantic opposition given by the co-texts of μέν and δέ, rather than by the bare μέν and δέ. τε καί in 37 signals a shared knowledge-based association of items (κατὰ πόλις τε καὶ κατὰ ἔθνεα). γε at the end of 38 may be seen as corresponding to an intonational mark distinguishing the first from the second conjunct.[74] It also evokes Eurybiades' voice, as if the historian's report is about to break the rules of indirect discourse and let the actually uttered words emerge, or pretend to do that.[75] Finally, the τε in act 40 (τροφήν τε ἕξειν ...) has scope over 40 and 41: the content and the size of the last sub-move makes me assimilate this τε to those serving to close an argument (IV.2.3.4).

§63. The next acts (42 to 45) comprise a move starting with ἀλλά followed by γάρ:

42. [*OCT* 108.4] [extra space] ἀλλὰ
43. δοκέειν γὰρ
44. νικηθέντα τῇ ναυμαχίῃ *{comma}*
45. οὐ μενέειν ἐν τῇ Εὐρώπῃ τὸν Πέρσην· *{high dot}*

> Instead, [Eurybiades] thinks that, having been defeated in the sea battle, the Persian will not remain in Europe.

γάρ marks the unfolding of the ἀλλά move; at the same time, its peninitial position isolates ἀλλά, and makes ἀλλά a priming act in itself (like several καί in Thucydides). ἀλλά decidedly re-orients the discourse by signaling a substantial replacement of all the hypotheses outlined in the previous segments. In fact, acts 43 to 47 articulate the precisely opposite scenario: οὐ μενέειν ἐν τῇ Εὐρώπῃ τὸν Πέρσην, 45 vs. ὁ Πέρσης μένειν ἐν τῇ Εὐρώπῃ, 26.

§64. A ὦν move follows:

46. ἐατέον ὦν εἶναι φεύγειν,
47. ἐς ὃ ἔλθῃ φεύγων ἐς τὴν ἑωυτοῦ· *{high dot}*

[74] Compare Herodotus 1.120.1 ἤτοι ἑκόντος γε ἢ ἀέκοντος; Thucydides 2.40.2 ἤτοι κρίνομέν γε ἢ ἐνθυμούμεθα ὀρθῶς τὰ πράγματα; 6.34.2 ἤτοι κρύφα γε ἢ φανερῶς; 6.40.1 ἤτοι μαθόντες γε ἢ μεταγνόντες.

[75] See IV.4 §23 on hybrid forms of indirect discourse, and §§32-33, 114-115, 155 on particles marking someone's voice in indirect speech. See IV.4.3.3 on γε and the author's voice in the two *Histories*.

> Therefore he has to be allowed to escape, until the moment he arrives, in the course of his flight, at his own land.

ὦν tells us that the upcoming thought follows from the previous one: Xerxes won't stay quietly; therefore, let him go.[76]

§65. With the final move Herodotus begins to step out of the reported speech:

48. τὸ ἐνθεῦτεν δὲ περὶ τῆς ἐκείνου ποιέεσθαι ἤδη τὸν ἀγῶνα
49. ἐκέλευε. *{high dot}*

> He recommended that, at that point, the contest definitely be conducted about HIS land.

The historian in 48 still allows the audience to hear Eurybiades' voice through use of expressions such as the temporal marker τὸ ἐνθεῦτεν—which anchors the report to the moment of the speech—the distancing/dismissive tone of ἐκεῖνος for Xerxes, and the assenting force of ἤδη in his stancetaking.[77] Then (49) he inserts ἐκέλευε, which is the pivotal word of the stepping out, as it occurs after a series of elliptical infinitives. Therefore, I take ἐκέλευε as a separate act.[78]

§66. The next move takes Herodotus definitively out of the reported speech, as the opening οὗτος form indicates.[79]

50. [extra space] ταύτης δὲ εἴχοντο τῆς γνώμης καὶ Πελοποννησίων τῶν ἄλλων οἱ στρατηγοί. *{high dot}*

> With this opinion they agreed too, the rest of the Peloponnesian generals.

Note the extra space in the *OCT* edition. As in other occasions,[80] there is a match between this paralinguistic segmentation and my reading of a move boundary. The next move boundary is suggested by even more linguistic features:

51. [*OCT* 109.1] [extra space] ὡς δὲ ἔμαθε ὅτι
52. οὐ πείσει τούς γε πολλοὺς πλέειν ἐς τὸν Ἑλλήσποντον
53. ὁ Θεμιστοκλέης, *{comma}*
54. μεταβαλὼν πρὸς τοὺς Ἀθηναίους *{mid dot}*

[76] About further ὦν moves in Herodotus, see below §§93 and 97; see also above n6.

[77] On ἤδη in indirect speech, see IV.4 §§138, 154-155, and n219, where I cite this very passage. On κεῖνος in blame contexts in Pindar, see Bonifazi 2004c:292-294, and Bonifazi 2012:60-62.

[78] Also, it is a 4-syllable verb, a detail that I will resume in the conclusions of the chapter.

[79] On οὗτος forms after the conclusion of direct speech, see in particular Bakker 1999:11-14.

[80] See §§28, 35, 46, 55, 56, 79, 83, 92; see also IV.3 §§85, 110, 115, 125, 127, 132, 152, and n104.

> When he perceived that he would not persuade the MAJORITY to sail toward the Hellespont, Themistocles, turning to the Athenians[81] ...

A new moment of the scene is established by a temporal clause with δέ, ὡς δὲ ἔμαθε, 51. The construction resonates with similar frame-setting clauses used earlier (see ὡς δὲ ἡμέρη ἐγίνετο, 1, and ἐπεὶ δὲ ἐπύθοντο, 7). In addition, the focus turns away from the reaction of a group of listeners, the Peloponnesian generals in segment 51, to the reaction of an individual, who responds by taking action. The role of ὅτι at the end of act 51 is comparable to the role of ὡς at the end of 21: ὅτι signposts the upcoming content of Themistocles' understanding. I take ὁ Θεμιστοκλέης, 53, as a separate act because of its position within the part of the account that turns the attention back to Themistocles: he is the subject of all the clauses in 51, 52, 54, and, below 59.

§67. γε in 54 puts prosodic emphasis on τοὺς πολλούς in such a manner as to suggest that Themistocles, though realizing that he cannot persuade the majority, still hopes to persuade some of them. The capital letters in my translation are an attempt to render that emphasis. Because γε's scope in this case is over a πολύ form, the particle works as a scalar quantifier, generating what we would call a scalar implicature:[82] "the majority" evokes a quantitative alternative either "upwards" in the direction of everyone or "downwards" (as here) in the direction of a minority.[83] Combined with the future tense (πείσει, 52), the γε here seems to signpost not only Themistocles' mental state as he prepares to deliver his speech of response, but also his voice. The whole act 52 stands out as a reproduction of the general's immediate words, as if Herodotus could present his thought re-uttered.[84]

§68. I divide the remaining text into two moves, which here below are combined for the sake of convenience:

55. (οὗτοι γὰρ μάλιστα ἐκπεφευγότων περιημέκτεον, *{comma}*
56. ὁρμέατό τε ἐς τὸν Ἑλλήσποντον πλέειν
57. καὶ ἐπὶ σφέων αὐτῶν βαλόμενοι,
58. εἰ ὦλλοι μὴ βουλοίατο) *{mid dot}*

59. ἔλεγέ σφι τάδε· *{mid dot}*

[81] Asheri and Vannicelli in Asheri et al. (2003:307) remark that μεταβάλλω in Herodotus also means: "to change one's mind." Accordingly, they propose the double reading "having turned to the Athenians" or "having changed his mind towards the Athenians."

[82] The notion of "scalar implicature" comes originally from the pragmatic account of Grice 1975. The notion of "scalar quantifier upper bounded" when it implies "but not all" and "lower bounded" when it implies "at least" was first introduced by Horn 1972. Overall the literature attests to the necessity of combining semantics and pragmatics in defining the processing of scalar terms.

[83] On γε marking an implied contrast, see above §20 with n22.

[84] See IV.4 §§33 and 155 on the reperformance of someone's words within indirect speech.

> For these men [the Athenians] were angry, as they [the Persians] had escaped, and they pressed for sailing to the Hellespont. And attacking on their own,[85] even if the rest should not want to.
>
> He spoke as follows ...

γάρ in 55 indicates that Herodotus is about to expand on why Themistocles turns to the Athenians. Editors put this γάρ move in a parenthesis. In a hypotactically-based segmentation it is fundamental to signal the occurrence of syntactic non-integratedness; here, the parenthesis signals that the participle μεταβαλών in 54 is temporarily separated from "its" main clause, ἔλεγέ σφι τάδε, 59. However, as I have noted before,[86] the paralinguistic sign of parenthesis suggests that its enclosed contents have minor or peripheral status in the discourse. Not differently from earlier examples, segments 55-58 prove the contrary. οὗτοι, 55, is a non-neutral retrieval of referents. On the one hand it resembles the Herodotean use of οὗτος forms for individuals at the beginning of moves.[87] On the other, it retrospectively clarifies Themistocles' mental calculation when he assessed τούς γε πολλούς in 50: knowing that the Athenians were already angry and determined to set sail, Themistocles thinks he can count on them. That is, the prosodic emphasis in 52 makes the suggestion—later confirmed by οὗτοι in 55—that Themistocles hopes to convince, if not the entire majority, at least the Athenians, who make up part of the majority constituted by Athenians and Peloponnesians.[88] Thus γε, especially as a negation precedes it, signposts a contrastive thought that is left unsaid: "not the majority γε" implies "but perhaps some of them." Taken all together, the thought expressed in 55-58 is not minor or peripheral but crucial, and it is crucial at the place where it occurs—that is, after Themistocles turns his gaze, so to speak, to the Athenians, but before he actually begins to speak, at which point he specifically addresses his comments to them.

§69. The end of the excerpt coincides with ἔλεγέ σφι τάδε, 59. This act has the fundamental segmenting role of announcing the direct speech that follows (109.2-4).

5.5 Artabanus' Warnings: Herodotus 7.49 and 51

§70. Xerxes' uncle Artabanus is commonly regarded as one of the "tragic warners" in Herodotus along with Solon, Croesus, and Amasis. The role they all play is "to foreshadow what is going to happen and help the reader notice the blindness of the rulers who did

85 The phrase "attacking on their own" is borrowed from Bowie (2007:198).

86 See above §§16 and 25.

87 See below, n117. About οὗτος as non-neutral retrieval of referents, see above n21, §§27 and 32.

88 This interpretation aligns with Bowie's comment about the passage: "The stage is here set for the subsequent increasing separation of Athenians and Peloponnesians" (2007:198).

not pay attention to them."[89] Artabanus plays a major role in Xerxes' deliberations about whether or not to attack Greece. He contributes thoughts on the gods' jealousy (7.10), initially objects to Xerxes' assumptions about dreams (7.16), but changes his mind after having the same dream that Xerxes had (18.2-3). Later, he meditates on the uncertainty of human success (7.46), and at 7.47.2 divulges to Xerxes his dread about two factors that are greatly hostile to the king. His final speeches take place in chapters 49, where he expands on these two factors, and in 51, with his final warning on the Ionians. Xerxes's final reaction is harsh: "you are most mistaken" (σφάλλεαι ... δὴ μάλιστα, 52.1). The king repudiates his uncle and sends him back to Susa (53.1).

§71. Artabanus' warning speeches have many parallels with Nicias' speech in Thucydides, and their similar motifs have been discussed by Scardino (2007:720-722). The main difference, Scardino argues (2007:721), is that while Nicias focuses on concrete problems and practical details, Artabanus abstracts philosophy and wisdom from historical events.[90] Not by chance are chapters 49 and 51 rich in *gnômai*.[91]

§72. The verbal exchange between the king and his uncle occupies chapters 46 to 51, and is quite elaborate. Lang (1984a:34) considers the ten extended turns that occur in these chapters one of the "most impressive and most patterned dialogues in the whole work." Overall, Xerxes and Artabanus share the same number of turns (five to five). 7.49 and 51 (30 *OCT* lines on the whole) represent the final turns by Artabanus within this highly dialogic section. Even though the interruption of chapter 50 (the king's final turn) makes the excerpt(s) less ideal for the comparative purposes of IV.5, Artabanus' moves are actually quite consistent: while reinterpreting the king's points in his own terms (see later, §88), in chapter 51 Artabanus fundamentally prolongs his warnings.

§73. I divide Herodotus 7.49 in 11 moves conveying these major points: in general, no blame is to be addressed about the Persian army and ships (1-5); still, land and sea are worrisome (6-11); sea is hostile (12-18); several harbors would be needed (19-22); but that is not the case (23-24); circumstances rule over human beings (25-27); land is the second element (28-30); land is hostile too (32-37); people think that no success is enough (38-39); more territory would mean more trouble (40-43); a man that is ἄριστος

89 Saïd 2002:122. On Artabanus as "wise adviser" see Immerwahr 1954:37-40; Solmsen compares him to Solon (1982:85), but also to Croesus (1974:88-89). Pelling (1991) compares him to Thucydidean Archidamus.

90 His "commentaries on the downfall of greatness" (especially in 7.46) are "a way of building an ethical framework around the events of the *Histories*, of giving a larger meaning to the events it records" (Romm 1998:63).

91 Scardino 2007:182-183. Shapiro (2000:103) notes: "Artabanus' *gnômai* consistently advocate the importance of careful planning in an uncertain world." Bischoff 1932:57-58 already commented on the gnomic style of the Persian adviser. Herodotus' account of Artabanus' lapse in judgment, when he allows himself to be persuaded by Xerxes about the veridicity of the dream, shows an ironic slant; see Christ 2013:246. Solmsen (1974:92) comments: "That Artabanus despite his balanced and superior judgement succumbs to the daemon and accepts his indications as true is the height of irony."

has to show sense of fear and boldness (44-49). The first move (Artabanus asserting that no blame is to be addressed about Persian army and ships, in general) corresponds to acts 1-5.

1. [*OCT* 7.49.1] Ὦ βασιλεῦ, *{mid dot}*
2. οὔτε στρατὸν τοῦτον,
3. ὅστις γε σύνεσιν ἔχει,
4. μέμφοιτ' ἂν *{comma}*
5. οὔτε τῶν νεῶν τὸ πλῆθος· *{high dot}*

My king, neither this army nor the plethora of ships would ANYONE OF SENSE find dissatisfying.

After the initial act, the formal address to the king,[92] the first point of the argument is constructed by means of litotes (see οὔτε, 2 and οὔτε, 5). Instead of expressing direct approval, Artabanus stresses that the Persian army and navy can draw no complaint. Act 3 (ὅστις γε σύνεσιν ἔχει) closely resembles ἥτις γε σώφρων (Euripides, *Medea* 1369, discussed in III.3 §79). In both passages γε marks an element of the discourse that stands out because of some intended contrastive implications. In Artabanus' reasoning, "whoever has sound judgment would not blame ...," suggests that there could exist one who is not so intelligent.[93] γε works like prosodic stress in English and other modern languages (see the capital letters in my translation); I see it as a reflection of the speaker's voice.[94]

§74. The next move enacts a shift of attention to two crucial elements of Artabanus' argument that he mentioned at an earlier point (7.47.2; see below): land and sea.

6. ἥν τε πλεῦνας συλλέξῃς, *{comma}*
7. τὰ δύο τοι
8. ἁ λέγω *{mid dot}*
9. πολλῷ ἔτι πολεμιώτερα γίνεται. *{high dot}*
10. [extra space] τὰ δέ δύο ταῦτα ἐστὶ
11. γῆ τε καὶ θάλασσα. *{high dot}*

[92] On vocatives as separate discourse acts, see II.2§10-11 with n22 (about Fraenkel 1965); II.2§§77-78; II.3§70; III.5 §§30, 67-68; IV.2 §31; IV.3 §36 (about Nicanor's punctuation in relation to vocatives). In his *Lexicon* (s.v. βασιλεύς), Powell 1938 records 57 "My king" vocatives, eleven of which are not preceded by the vocative particle ὦ.

[93] There might be some irony in the fact that Artabanus utters these words to Xerxes; Artabanus' previous judgments of the king's experience with dreams, combined with Xerxes' own judgments in general about the expedition, do not indicate the conclusions of the king as those of an individual "of sense." On the irony cast by means of the episode of the dreams, see in particular Christ 2013.

[94] See above, §§20 and 34.

> In case you gather more, let me tell you: the two elements that I am speaking of are much more hostile. The two elements are these: land and sea.

The move is divided into two parts: 6-9 and 10-11. Both parts center on the notion "two things" (τὰ δύο, 7; τὰ δέ δύο, 10). As for the move start, both Hude in the *OCT* and Legrand in the *TLG* online have τε, even though the "a" manuscripts (including Laurentianus 70,3) and "P" (Codex Parisinus 1633) have δέ. The *and*-coordination structure of the passage (οὔτε, 2, οὔτε, 5, τε, 6, and, later, οὔτε, 12) and the regular occurrence of τε at move starts[95] fully support Hude and Legrand's choice.[96] δέ in act 10 opens the second part of the move by simply marking a new step. The modern full stop after γίνεται, 9, matches the discourse perspective: the speaker stops before making a new and short statement by means of which he names the two elements, "land and sea." However, the extra space between words notwithstanding, I do not see 10-11 as an independent move, because of the strong thematic coherence provided by the lexical repetition δύο - δύο.

§75. Back to act 7, τοι deserves special consideration, especially since Artabanus uses it seven times in chapter 49 (see also acts 24, 29—again with δύο— 33, 34, 35, 40, and also 19 by means of καίτοι). As I say in IV.4.3.2, in Herodotus τοι oscillates between the reference to "you" and the interactional usage. Ultimately its use has a crucial interpersonal and argumentative function: it marks the exclusivity of the face-to-face interaction (see the translation "let me tell you,"[97]), and it generally suggests a persuasive intention by the speaker. We may say that τοι characterizes the move pragmatically, just as "the two things" characterizes the move semantically.

§76. In fact τὰ δύο τοι, 7, constitutes a crucial independent act. It retrieves the topic of the two "most hostile" elements anticipated in a previous speech and left unexplained. At 7.47.2 Artabanus' words are ὁρέων τοι δύο τὰ μέγιστα πάντων ἐόντα πολεμιώτατα ("as I see it, let me tell you, two greatest things are the greatest enemies of all"). Those words are retrieved in chapter 49 by means of τοι, 7, δύο, 7 and 10—and later in 29—and πολεμιώτερα, 9). Essentially τὰ δύο τοι establishes the subject matter of what follows. The verb λέγω in 8 semantically and pragmatically stresses the ongoing discourse being performed by Artabanus.

§77. The next move, a γάρ move, explains why Artabanus thinks of the sea as a great enemy.

12. [*OCT* 49.2] [extra space] οὔτε γὰρ τῆς θαλάσσης
13. ἔστι λιμὴν τοσοῦτος οὐδαμόθι,

[95] See above §§14, §22, §40, §§44-45.

[96] No further τε occurs in the remaining part of chapter 49, except for τε καί, 10, which marks the two conjuncts "land and sea" as an association derived from widespread knowledge (see IV.2 §68).

[97] Compare III.4 §58 and quoted literature.

14. ὡς ἐγὼ εἰκάζω, *{comma}*
15. ὅστις
16. ἐγειρομένου χειμῶνος
17. δεξάμενός σευ τοῦτο τὸ ναυτικὸν
18. φερέγγυος ἔσται διασῶσαι τὰς νέας.[98] *{mid dot}*

For, regarding the sea, nowhere is there a harbor large enough, as I personally estimate, that when a storm arises, after receiving this fleet, will be able to save the ships.

οὔτε γάρ in 12 has a double significance. First, οὔτε resonates with οὔτε, 2, and οὔτε, 5, and it progresses the series of thematic additions by means of τε (a big army, many ships, gathering more, and now a large harbor). Second, however different the scope and the syntactic functions of the two particles may be, τε near γάρ in Herodotus can accompany the presentation of knowledge shared beyond the context of the ongoing narrative or speech.[99] In cognitive terms οὔτε γάρ in 12 introduces "unframed discourse"[100] about harbors that can (cannot, in this case) receive a fleet adequately.

§78. Even though οὔτε γὰρ τῆς θαλάσσης ἔστι λιμὴν τοσοῦτος οὐδαμόθι is syntactically unified, my pragmatic and cognitive reading divides it into two distinct acts. Beyond syntax, οὔτε γὰρ τῆς θαλάσσης, 12, is a priming act establishing "the sea" as the subject to which Artabanus wants to draw Xerxes' attention;[101] the subject is going to be articulated in several acts. I take the double negation (οὔτε, 12, οὐδαμόθι, 13) and the existential use of ἔστι as further suggestions about an act boundary between 12 and 13.[102]

§79. Acts 19-22 constitute a καίτοι move, whose purpose is to adjust the previous statement by adding further details.[103]

19. [extra space] καίτοι
20. οὐκὶ ἕνα αὐτὸν δεῖ εἶναι [τὸν λιμένα],[104] *{mid dot + light comma}*
21. ἀλλὰ παρὰ πᾶσαν τὴν ἤπειρον
22. παρ' ἣν δὴ κομίζεαι. *{high dot}*

Actually, there should be not just one [harbor], but [many of them] all along the coast that you travel by.

98 Here Legrand puts a high dot instead of a full stop.

99 See IV.2 §59.

100 See II.4 §§11-14.

101 See IV.3 §110 about a further example of a priming act involving a noun in an oblique case.

102 See II.3 §49 with n154, and III.4 §68 about ἔστι + nominative constructions.

103 See IV.4 §§36 and 38 for more information about καίτοι in Herodotus.

104 The manuscripts report τὸν λιμένα, but Krüger proposed to remove it (see the *apparatus criticus* of the *OCT* edition, vol. II, p. 166).

The extra space not accompanying any new section number in this case matches a reading that gives pragmatic importance to καίτοι. Because of its overarching function, and because of its position before the negative marker οὐκί, καίτοι represents an act in itself. ἀλλά in 21 "answers" the negation οὐκί in 19 by introducing a replacement on the semantic level ("not X but Y").[105] δή in 22 occurs in act-peninitial position after the constituent παρ' ἥν. In the light of its co-text and context, the particle marks a piece of information that is interactionally evident: from the preceding discourse it is obvious to speaker and addressee that the need of multiple harbors refers to a piecemeal coastal navigation.[106]

§80. The next move is an ὦν δή move: in this case δή has a different role, namely in combination with ὦν it marks the next major step in discourse. ὦν's contribution is to project a logically consequent step.[107]

23. [*OCT* 49.3] [extra space] οὐκ ὦν δὴ
24. ἐόντων τοι λιμένων ὑποδεξίων, *{comma}*

This is clearly not the case—mind you—that there are capacious harbors.

Translations tend to mingle the two acts in one coherent clause (e.g. De Sélincourt and Marincola write, "But there is not a single one," 2003:434). However, the pace of speech according to the two acts is different: "That is not the case—mind you, that there are capacious harbors." The act boundary is given, in my view, by the genitive absolute construction, which makes 24 a separate act. τοι turns out to be in act-peninitial position.[108]

§81. Under the influence of hypotactic principles, translations tend to link the genitive absolute above, "that there are capacious harbors" (οὐκ ὦν δὴ ἐόντων τοι λιμένων ὑποδεξίων, 24) to the immediately following finite verb μάθε, 25 (see below). The rationale is that a secondary clause such as ἐόντων ... ὑποδεξίων cannot stand alone, but needs to be attached to an independent finite verb—hence the comma after ὑποδεξίων. If we conversely segment the text on the pragmatic basis of acts and moves, the result is that 25-27 can be seen as a distinct move:

25 μάθε ὅτι
26. αἱ συμφοραὶ τῶν ἀνθρώπων ἄρχουσι
27. καὶ οὐκὶ ὤνθρωποι τῶν συμφορέων. *{mid dot}*

105 See III.2 §66.

106 This reading is inspired by the analysis of the distribution of δή in drama (III.2.2.8).

107 See IV.3 §79 and IV.4 §§86, 89 on the combination ὦν δή.

108 "Mind you" in my translation renders the strong interactional character of τοι. The pragmatics of the discourse marker "mind you" in English is especially explored in Bell 2009.

Learn: 'circumstances rule over human beings,' and not 'human beings [rule over] circumstances.'

The goal of Artabanus' move is to let the king learn from proverbial wisdom. While 23 and 24 negate the existence of capacious harbors, 25-27 generalize Artabanus' point: actual circumstances can be more decisive than human determination. As argued in II.3 (§§50, 68, 70, 74), Pindaric beginnings that lack syndetic items tend to encode major discourse transitions. Here the imperative form μάθε is discontinuous enough, especially if we consider that it conveys an authoritative instruction given by a king's uncle to the king himself.[109] Furthermore, as III.4.5.3 shows, dialogic turns in drama that start with no connective items do usually encode a connection with the context or co-text in other ways (for example by means of an anaphoric οὗτος form, or an appeal to the "you" interlocutor). This seems to be what happens here as well, even if we deal with a move within the same speech rather than a new turn in drama (which does not necessarily coincide with a new move).

§82. In a discourse perspective, a salient element in segments 26 and 27 is οὐκί, 27, as it introduces what in pragmatics is called a metalinguistic negation. A metalinguistic negation is when an entire utterance is negated, and not just the individual element(s) in it.[110] Or as Miestamo (2009:221) puts it, "metalinguistic negations are objections to utterances." With his utterance Artabanus attempts a radical alteration of thought; he instructs Xerxes that the saying "circumstances control human beings" means (see καί, "that is to say") that the reverse "human beings control circumstances" does not hold true. The translation offered here takes the role of ὅτι to be the equivalent of a colon, the paralinguistic sign that we use to introduce a quotation or direct speech.[111]

§83. The next move starts with an extra space in *OCT* that seems to acknowledge the force of καὶ δή at move starts.

28. [extra space] καὶ δὴ
29. τῶν δύο τοι
30. τοῦ ἑτέρου εἰρημένου *{comma}*
31. τὸ ἕτερον ἔρχομαι ἐρέων. *{high dot}*

[109] Stahl (2012:146) about this passage comments: "here the adviser turns stern instructor."

[110] An example in English is "Around here we don't like coffee—we love it" (Horn 1989:382). The second assertion replaces the first wholesale: the speaker's fervor for coffee necessarily invalidates the tepidity of the initial statement.

[111] Compare the instances of ὅτι introducing direct speech in the two *Histories*: e.g. Herodotus 2.115.4 λέγων ὅτι· "Ἐγὼ εἰ μὴ περὶ πολλοῦ ἡγεόμην ..."; Thucydides 1.137.4 ἐδήλου δὲ ἡ γραφὴ ὅτι 'Θεμιστοκλῆς ἥκω παρὰ σέ ...; 2.12.3 τοσόνδε εἰπὼν ἐπορεύετο ὅτι 'ἥδε ἡ ἡμέρα τοῖς Ἕλλησι μεγάλων κακῶν ἄρξει.'; 1.51.2 (without modern quotation marks) πρίν τινες ἰδόντες εἶπον ὅτι νῆες ἐκεῖναι ἐπιπλέουσιν. Further instances of ὅτι before an act boundary include e.g. Herodotus 6.137.1 πλὴν τὰ λεγόμενα, ὅτι | Ἑκαταῖος μὲν ὁ Ἡγησάνδρου ἔφησε; Thucydides 1.87.4 εἶπον ὅτι | σφίσι μὲν ...; 1.91.4 εἶπεν ὅτι | ἡ μὲν πόλις .... See above, the discussion about λέγων ὡς | (§59).

> Now look: of the two elements I was mentioning, now that I have spoken about the former, I am going to tell about the latter.

καὶ δή works as a cluster, and constitutes an act in itself.[112] Its function is to focus the hearer or interlocutor's attention on something in particular, and at that particular moment of the discourse—hence the translation "now look." I read the position of τοι in 29 to be peninitial after the constituent τῶν δύο. The assonance and alliteration in segments 30-31 (ἑτέρου εἰρημένου + ἕτερον ἔρχομαι ἐρέων), the lexical insistence on forms of the same *verbum dicendi* and on ἕτερος forms, and the explicit performative verbs ἔρχομαι ἐρέων add prominence to the move that Artabanus is about to perform.

§84. Overall, acts 28-31 represent an elaborate introduction to the topic "land," second cardinal entry of the speech, and subject of the next move (32-37).

32. [*OCT* 49.4] [extra space] γῆ δὴ πολεμίη
33. τῇδέ τοι κατίσταται· *{high dot}*
34. εἰ θέλει τοι μηδὲν ἀντίξοον καταστῆναι, *{comma}*
35. τοσούτῳ τοι γίνεται πολεμιωτέρη
36. ὅσῳ ἂν προβαίνῃς ἑκαστέρω,
37. τὸ πρόσω αἰεὶ κλεπτόμενος·

> Land is hostile, really. Here is how it has become [hostile], I tell you: if it wants no obstacle to stand before you, it becomes more hostile the further and further you advance, always blindfolded as to what lies ahead.[113]

Modern editions make the beginning of section 4 of chapter 49 coincide with γῆ δὴ πολεμίη. My discourse analysis backs this reading up: after the elaborate announcement about the second hostile element that Xerxes should take into account, Artabanus opens a new move by uttering γῆ δὴ πολεμίη, 32, a communicative step that is relevant for three reasons. First, the speaker includes the explicit mention of the element (γῆ); second, he reconnects the main point to previous discourse (πολεμίη recalls πολεμιώτερα at 9 and πολεμιώτατα, 47.2); third, he uses δή to openly mark γῆ ... πολεμίη as his own stance: he thinks that yes, definitely, land is hostile.[114] In the remainder, lexical repetition reinforces the idea (see πολεμιωτέρη, 35) and the pragmatic intention to persuade the king (see τοι repeated in 33, 34, and 35).

§85. In line with the gnomic conclusion of the argument about sea, Artabanus concludes the argument about land with another *gnṓmē*:

[112] Further instances of καὶ δή in Herodotus are commented upon in IV.2 §100 and IV.3 §80. On καὶ δή in other genres, see III.4 §§51-52 and IV.2 §101 and n156.

[113] How and Wells *ad loc.* see the potentially twofold meaning of κλεπτόμενος as a passive form ("blindfold") and as a middle form ("stealing").

[114] More on δή in stancetaking acts both in speeches and in narrative sections in IV.4.5 and 4.6.

38. εὐπρηξίης δέ[115]
39. οὐκ ἔστι ἀνθρώποισι οὐδεμία πληθώρη. *{mid dot}*

Of success, human beings have no satisfaction whatsoever.

The word order of this statement suggests a possible segmentation in two acts. Let us recall οὔτε γὰρ τῆς θαλάσσης | ἔστι λιμὴν τοσοῦτος οὐδαμόθι, 12-13. εὐπρηξίης δέ gives cognitive prominence to the topic of the statement, that is, success (as in 12 "the sea" does). Of the 13 remaining instances of οὐκ ἔστι in Herodotus, nine can be read as act-initial.[116] The reinforcement of the negation through οὐδεμία within the same act occurs also at 8.118.3, also in direct speech: Δέσποτα, οὐκ ἔστι οὐδεμία [*sc.* σωτηρίη] "Sire, there is none [no rescue is possible]."

§86. After closing the parallel arguments on sea and land, Artabanus tries to persuade his interlocutor by making a point on a major risk involving territorial expansion in general.

40. [*OCT* 49.5] [extra space] καὶ δή τοι,
41. ὡς οὐδενὸς ἐναντιουμένου,
42. λέγω
43. τὴν χώρην πλεῦνα ἐν πλέονι χρόνῳ γινομένην λιμὸν τέξεσθαι. *{mid dot}*

Now look, I tell you, if no one opposes you, I say that a territory made larger over a larger period of time will engender famine.

In this new move we find a further καὶ δή (cf. 29), a further τοι (cf. 7, 24, 29, 33, 34, 35), and a further λέγω (cf. 8; cf. also ἐγὼ εἰκάζω, 14, and ἔρχομαι ἐρέων, 31). These features strengthen the direct, attentive, and authoritative tone adopted by Artabanus. In act 43 word order and alliterative as well as assonantal patterns add rhetorical force to the message (τὴν χώρην πλεῦνα ἐν πλέονι χρόνῳ).

§87. Artabanus' last move consists in revealing two fundamental qualities that a man excelling over the others (ἀνὴρ ... ἄριστος, with indirect reference to Xerxes) should demonstrate.

44. Ἀνὴρ δὲ
45. οὕτω ἂν εἴη ἄριστος, *{comma}*
46. εἰ
47. βουλευόμενος μὲν ἀρρωδέοι, *{light comma}*

[115] Legrand, conversely, accepts γάρ, as given in the group of manuscripts "a" and in manuscript P. See II.4.2.2 on γάρ introducing *gnômai* in Pindar.

[116] Herodotus 2.120.3; 2.149.4; 3.62.3; 3.155.2; 7.10.α; 7.102.2; 7.197.2; 8.65.2; 8.118.3.

48. πᾶν ἐπιλεγόμενος πείσεσθαι χρῆμα, *{mid dot}*
49. ἐν δὲ τῷ ἔργῳ θρασὺς εἴη. *{high dot}*

A man like this would be best: if, on the one hand, he should make decisions with a sense of fear, taking into account every event to be endured, and, on the other hand, if he should be bold in action.

This last move mixes features of *gnômai* with wishes: general terms (ἀνήρ, 44), and general states (πᾶν ... χρῆμα, 48; τῷ ἔργῳ, 49) are combined with desirable states (ἄριστος, 45; θρασύς, 49), and a conditional period framing the whole. Particles, subordinating conjunctions, and adverbial pronouns signpost almost each argumentative act. οὕτω projects a longer exposition.[117] εἰ appears alone as it starts the expression of a multiple condition, articulated by μέν, 47, and δέ, 49. The hyperbaton πᾶν ... χρῆμα makes for 48 as an individual act.

§88. In his reply to this speech (chapter 50), Xerxes points out that taking risks and running into trouble is better than fearing everything. Great gains require great risks (μεγάλα γὰρ πρήγματα μεγάλοισι κινδύνοισι ἐθέλει καταιρέεσθαι, 50.3). So, he continues, they will conquer all Europe and will come back home safely (καταστρεψάμενοι πᾶσαν τὴν Εὐρώπην νοστήσομεν ὀπίσω, 50.3). Artabanus' tactic in responding to Xerxes is to summarize the king's views by offering an account in his own terms (see, for example, ἀρρωδέειν, below in 2, which reminds us of ἀρρωδέοι, act 47 of chapter 49).

§89. Chapter 51 can be divided into 8 moves, with the following communicative goals: to invite Xerxes to follow his counsel (1-3); to motivate more warnings as more facts deserve attention (4); to recall Cyrus' conquest of Ionia except for Athens, the mother state (5-6); to suggest that it is not a good idea to put the Ionians against Athens (7-9); to reassure that the Persians can be successful without the Ionians (10-11); to state that the Ionians rightly would turn out to act disadvantageously for the Persians (12-15); to further illustrate the disadvantages (16-19); finally, to recall that end points are not necessarily as clear as beginning points (20-22).

§90. By means of the opening move, Artabanus insists that the king should accept his advice.

1. [*OCT* 51.1] Ὦ βασιλεῦ, *{mid dot}*

2. ἐπείτε ἀρρωδέειν οὐδὲν ἐᾷς πρῆγμα, *{comma}*
3. σὺ δέ μεο συμβουλίην ἔνδεξαι· *{high dot}*

My king, since you allow that having fear is not an issue, be the one who receives my counsel.

117 I see an analogy with οὗτος used by Herodotus to introduce topical figures (IV.3 §§121-124).

The boundaries in these three acts fully coincide with medieval interpunction and modern punctuation. It is not by chance that after the vocative particle ὦ, 1, a subordinating conjunction (ἐπείτε, 2) and a postpositive particle (δέ, 3) occur at each beginning; they signpost the start of discourse acts, however syntactically diverse. δέ in 3 is an instance of "apodotic" δέ.[118] Even though it has no syntactic function, on the pragmatic level the particle marks a discourse discontinuity between the act motivating Artabanus' further advice (2) and the authoritative act of recommending Xerxes to accept his counsel.

§91. The following move strategically motivates the need for further counsel, by means of a call for fair proportion: a longer series of facts requires a longer series of statements.

4. ἀναγκαίως γὰρ ἔχει περὶ πολλῶν πρηγμάτων πλεῦνα λόγον ἐκτεῖναι. *{high dot}*
For of necessity can a longer talk be prolonged to cover a longer series of facts.

γάρ and ἔχει in 4 encode the marking of unframed discourse through the associative force of γάρ, and the comprehensiveness of the present tense. The statement sounds gnomic, in line with some of Artabanus' previous moves (acts 26-27, 38-39, and 44-49 in chapter 49). Note in addition the alliteration of "p" through περὶ πολλῶν πρηγμάτων πλεῦνα. It is as if Artabanus exploits general wisdom to back up his will to extend the warnings. The proposed act-based segmentation enhances what could be a deliberate pun by Herodotus: exactly when Artabanus points out the necessity of more words, he delivers a particularly long segment, ending with ἐκτεῖναι, "stretching out."

§92. The start of the next move is asyndetic:

5. [extra space] Κῦρος ὁ Καμβύσεω Ἰωνίην πᾶσαν πλὴν Ἀθηνέων κατεστρέψατο
6. δασμοφόρον εἶναι Πέρσῃσι. *{high dot}*

Cyrus, son of Cambyses, conquered all Ionia except for Athens, so that it is tributary to the Persians.

The formal method of referring to Xerxes' grandfather Cyrus, by giving his proper name together with the patronymic, enables Artabanus to strategically place his whole statement in a broader, countrywide perspective, while at the same time calling on the

[118] On apodotic δέ, see IV.2.2.4. Macan (1908, vol. I:72) calls this δέ *in apodosi* "especially remarkable ... as a) the subject is the same as that of the *protasis*, b) the phrase is imperative."

admonitory power of historical precedent.[119] The extra space in the *OCT* (without section number) matches my reading of a move boundary. By means of this asyndetic statement Artabanus starts a series of considerations centered on the Ionians, the subject of his last elaborate argument. Therefore, retrospectively I interpret acts 5-6 as conveying a major transition in the discourse.[120]

§93. Artabanus' considerations about the Ionians start with an ὦν move: it is not good to ask the Ionians to assist in the conquest of Athens, their mother city:

7. [*OCT* 51.2] τούτους ὦν τοὺς ἄνδρας
8. συμβουλεύω τοι
9. μηδεμιῇ μηχανῇ ἄγειν ἐπὶ τοὺς πατέρας· *{high dot}*

Therefore these men, I suggest, you do not lead against their fathers by any contrivance.

ὦν in 7 suggests to the audience that they process the content of the move as a logical consequence to the previous utterance. τούτους ... τοὺς ἄνδρας is an anaphoric expression; the referents (the Ionians) are to be mentally retrieved on the basis of the preceding phrase Ἰωνίην πᾶσαν, 5.[121] τοι at 8 conveys the speaker's persuasive intention, and is a further marker of the move as a whole (see the performative verb συμβουλεύω "I advise," which recalls previous analogous verbs such as λέγω, and 8, ἐγὼ εἰκάζω, 14, and ἔρχομαι ἐρέων, 31).

§94. The following καὶ γάρ does not work as a cluster. γάρ signposts the new move as supporting the advice provided, whereas καί simply intensifies ἄνευ τούτων ("even without them").[122]

10. καὶ γὰρ ἄνευ τούτων
11. οἷοί τέ εἶμεν τῶν ἐχθρῶν κατυπέρτεροι γίνεσθαι. *{high dot}*

For even without them we can prevail over our enemies.

Although τε belongs to the idiomatic phrase οἷός τε εἰμί, it serves as a postpositive word that indicates an intonational and discoursive boundary before its preceding word (οἷοί in this case). This makes for 11 as a separate act.

§95. The following is an extended γάρ move.

119 On later historical confirmation of some of Artabanus' arguments against Xerxes' blind predictions, see in particular Stahl 2012:146-149.

120 See above §81 about asyndetic acts.

121 See above n37.

122 For a similar discussion of καὶ γάρ, see II.3 §§31-32.

12. Ἦ γάρ σφεας,
13. ἢν ἕπωνται,
14. δεῖ ἀδικωτάτους γίνεσθαι καταδουλουμένους τὴν μητρόπολιν, *{mid dot}*
15. ἢ δικαιοτάτους *{comma}* συνελευθεροῦντας.[123] *{high dot}*

16. [*OCT* 51.3] ἀδικώτατοι μέν νυν γινόμενοι *{comma}*
17. οὐδὲν κέρδος μέγα ἡμῖν προσβάλλουσι, *{high dot}*
18. δικαιότατοι δὲ γινόμενοι *{comma}*
19. οἷοί τε δηλήσασθαι μεγάλως τὴν σὴν στρατιὴν γίνονται.

> For either, if they follow us, they must become most unrighteous by enslaving their mother state, or they must become most righteous by contributing to her liberation.
>
> Now, if they become most unrighteous they do not provide any significant profit to us, while if they become most righteous they become capable of greatly damaging your army.

γάρ in 12 introduces an expansion of the point, "it is not a good idea to pit the Ionians against their fathers (i.e. the Athenians)." σφεας, near γάρ, grants referent and topic continuity. The move in turn consists of two parallel expansion-moves. The first illustrates equally unfortunate scenarios: "If the Ionians were to enslave their mother state on behalf of us, this would be unrighteous for them and for Athens; if they would liberate their mother state on behalf of Athens, this would be inconvenient for us" (13-15). The second expansion spells out the negative consequences: "neither behavior would be advantageous for the Persians: we would have either no profit, or—directly—damage" (16-19). Alongside γάρ, 12, and νυν, 16, the semantically antithetical terms "most unrighteous" vs. "most righteous" (ἀδικότατος vs. δικότατος) determine the structure of these expansions, where each term is used twice (ἤ ... ἀδικωτάτους, 14, ἢ δικαιοτάτους, 15;[124] ἀδικώτατοι μέν, 16; δικαιότατοι δέ, 18). In the light of this semantic structure, I do not see νυν in 16 as part of a μέν νυν cluster, but, rather, as a particle introducing the second expansion.[125]

123 Here Legrand inserts a high dot (Greek semicolon) instead of a full stop.

124 Perhaps the medieval comma between ἢ δικαιοτάτους and συνελευθεροῦντας in 7 was meant to highlight both the symmetry with ἀδικωτάτους, 14, as well as the syntactically ellipitical value of the following participle (συνελευθεροῦντας).

125 Powell (1938:234) recalls a minority of occurrences of νυν in Herodotus outside the combination μέν νυν; 14 instances are labelled "introducing command or exhortation," and one instance "introducing speech"; all of them can be seen as move starters, in our terms. As for the cluster μέν νυν, see IV.3 §§130-132, §§134-135, §§138-143, and above §§56 and 58.

§96. Overall, there is a discrepancy between this discourse analysis and the modern indication of discourse boundaries. Section numbers 2 and 3 are located near τούτους ὦν τοὺς ἄνδρας and ἀδικώτατοι μέν νυν respectively; they suggest that major transitions occur first between "Cyrus did not conquer Athens" and "no Ionians against the Athenians", and, second, between "righteousness and unrighteousness of the Ionians" and "bad effects of both the righteousness and the unrighteousness of the Ionians." Attention to particles and to other co-textual elements indicates a different articulation. The major boundary occurs at 5-6 with the asyndetic start "Cyrus ...". Then the consequent thought ("ὦν no Ionians against the Athenians," 7-9) is illustrated through two γάρ moves ("we can win wthout them," 10-11, and "both their righteousness and unrighteousness would be detrimental for us," 12-19; the latter being split into two parts).

§97. In line with previous argumentative closures, Artabanus inserts at this point a final gnomic thought.

20. ἐς θυμὸν ὦν βάλεο καὶ τὸ παλαιὸν ἔπος

21. ὡς εὖ εἴρηται, *{high dot}*
22. τὸ μὴ ἅμα ἀρχῇ πᾶν τέλος καταφαίνεσθαι. *{high dot}*

Therefore, lay in your heart also the old saying, as it is well put: not together with the beginning is the end made clear.

For the third time a stern instruction to listen to the old uncle occurs (see the imperative βάλεο, 20, which reminds us of μάθε (act 25 in chapter 49), and ἔνδεξαι, 3 earlier in this chapter). ὦν marks the move as a thought that naturally follows from the preceding discourse. Actually this conclusive thought rounds off all of Artabanus' conversational turns in chapters 46 to 51.[126] What makes it sound like an overarching consideration by the wise warner is the double meaning of the saying. Act 22 literally means: "the end is not made all clear together with the beginning" (τὸ μὴ ἅμα ἀρχῇ πᾶν τέλος καταφαίνεσθαι). However, the word sequence highlights ἀρχῇ πᾶν τέλος as the core part of the message, which seems to allude to the end of Xerxes' reign.[127] The strategically inserted subclause ὡς εὖ εἴρηται (21) stresses the clever formulation.[128]

126 See above §72 on the exceptionally long exchange between these two interlocutors.

127 This type of message harmonizes with Artabanus' pre-eminent mode of speech in Solmsen's terms (1974:92), that is, the expression of "balanced and superior judgement."

128 *Pace* Macan (1908, vol. I:150), who takes ἔπος εὖ εἰρημένον as "almost a Herodotean formula." εὖ in Herodotus occurs only once more in combination with the same verb (Μεγακρέοντος ἀνδρὸς Ἀβδηρίτεω ἔπος εὖ εἰρημένον ἐγένετο, ὃς ..., 7.120.1). Also in this passage the formulation of a character (someone from Abdera called Megacreon), is clever enough to convey possibly two ambiguous messages by means of the same wording.

5.6 Conclusions

§98. Let us first compare some data across the four excerpts.

	sections	*períodoi*	moves	clauses	acts
1. (T. speech)	4	7	10	59	47
2. (T. narr.)	4	6	12	39	56
3. (H. narr.)	5	8[129]	18	58	59
4. (H. speech)	8 [5+3]	15 [9+6]	19 [11+8]	52 [33+19]	71 [49+22]

Table 1

Table 1 assumes that sections are identified via numbers, *períodoi* are identified by full stops, and clauses include main clauses, subclauses with finite verbs, and participial clauses. A qualitative difference should be stressed concerning clauses vs. acts in general: while infinitives often fall in the same act together with the verb they depend on, several acts include no verb form at all.

§99. In terms of large-scale segmentation (sections, *períodoi* and moves), the Herodotean speech, excerpt 1, consistently shows higher numbers, roughly doubling those of Thucydides' speech, excerpt 4 (8 vs. 4 sections; 15 vs. 7 *períodoi*; 19 vs. 10 moves). There is a convergence in the perception of a more segmented discourse in excerpt 4 as opposed to the less segmented discourse in excerpt 1. However, while the Herodotean excerpts (3 and 4) significantly differ in number of *períodoi* (8 vs. 15), the number of moves is comparable (18 vs. 19). This suggests that from a pragmatic perspective major discourse boundaries are found equally often in narrator text and in speech, at least in the two excerpts under examination. This invites us to consider that a holistic discourse approach can capture discontinuities that modern punctuation and its focus on hypotaxis ignores.

§100. Admittedly, most full stops coincide with move ends. Also, all section numbers coincide with move starts. However, the reading in moves only partially coincides with the *OCT* segmentation provided by section numbers and by full stops wrapping up *períodoi*. For example, in excerpt 1 the (modern) very long period almost overlapping with Thucydides 6.22—which, I repeat, in Stuart and Jones' edition has no internal sections—is here divided into five distinct moves. Moreover, in spite of the modern full stop closing the supposedly long period at the end of 25, I see thematic continuation between 25 and 28. Further evidence of mismatch between my discourse segmentation

129 The eighth period actually ends with a semicolon after ἔλεγέ σφι τάδε (Herodotus 8.109.1); however, the boundary between narrator text and direct speech makes for periodic completeness.

and section divisions concerns γάρ in all the excerpts. γάρ is a move starter, just as in the other 'monological' texts of our corpus (Homer and Pindar). However, only in Thucydides 23.1 (excerpt 1), Herodotus 108.3 (excerpt 3), and Herodotus 7.49.2 (excerpt 4) does a new section number co-occur with the act hosting γάρ (against 10 γάρ moves).

§101. In terms of small-scale segmentation, the similar number of acts across the first three excerpts is representative of a finding that I believe to be general and crucial. In both authors the flow of discourse proceeds by steps that are relatively short. Not only do syntactic boundaries, particles, and particle combinations contribute to that, but also repetitions and various kinds of parallelism.

§102. The division of the Herodotean speech in 71 acts reaffirms the possibility of chunking discourse in small steps. The remarkable difference between acts and clauses in excerpts 3 and 4 (71 acts and 52 clauses in the Herodotean speech, vs. 59 acts and 58 clauses in the Herodotean narrator text) consolidates the idea that several act boundaries can be found on the sub-clausal level.

§103. The segmentation in acts produces the effect of evening out syntactic hierarchies; therefore, it enhances the importance of single communicative steps whose syntactic form may suggest a subsidiary status. Priming acts constitute a particularly good case in point: they are short and syntactically dependent on what follows; still, they have an important pragmatic and cognitive function (e.g. ὁπλίτας τε οὖν πολλούς, 1 in excerpt 1; ἐς δὲ τὰς Ἀθήνας, 1, and ὅμως δέ, 36, in excerpt 2; Εὐρυβιάδης δέ, 19, in excerpt 3; οὔτε γὰρ τῆς θαλάσσης, 12, in excerpt 4, chapter 49).

§104. Independently of whether they have a priming function or not, some of the acts that I identified are very short (e.g. in excerpt 3: 13, 25, 42, 49—one word; 5, 6, 10, 19, 21, 43, 53—two words; 15, 24, 30, 38, 44, 59—three words). I draw a potential link between them, the *kómmata* mentioned by ancient writers (see IV.3 §§43-45, 46, 48-49), and Fraenkel's *Kurzkola* (II.2 §14). The medieval punctuation sometimes indicates boundaries between very short stretches of text as well—invariably, phrases.[130] However partial this result is, it suggests that our canonical segmentation in subclauses and main clauses is not the only way to see how discourse progresses. A holistic approach lets the role of particles and other features emerge together with the canonical segmentation.

§105. As for matches and mismatches with modern commas, full stops, and with medieval punctuation, two simple results emerge. First, more than once medieval punctuation in the manuscript appears at the end of what I read as an act, whereas no modern punctuation is inserted (see 3, 6, 20, 29, 33, 39, 45, 54 in excerpt 1; 3, 11, 12, 15, 17, 21, 23, 24, 25, 27, 32 in excerpt 2; 2, 4, 14, 16, 19, 29, 31, 34, 44, 54, 58 in excerpt 3; 8, 30 in chapter

130 See τῶν τε ὑπηκόων, 6, between two mid dots, and τὰ δέ, 35, between a high and a low dot, in excerpt 1; ἐβαρύνοντο, 22, between a comma and a high dot in excerpt 2; Εὐρυβιάδης δέ, 19, between a high dot and a comma in excerpt 3; Ὦ βασιλεῦ, 1 between a high dot and a mid dot in excerpt 4 (chapter 51).

49, and 16 and 18 in chapter 51 in excerpt 4). In far fewer cases modern punctuation appears where there is no medieval sign (see 9, 15, 18, 26, 41, 44, and 49 in excerpt 1; 2, 7, 29, 40, 41, 42 in excerpt 2; 11, 46, and 57 in excerpt 3). This suggests that medieval punctuation matches the division in acts more than modern punctuation does, at least in three excerpts—excerpt 4 (Artabanus) is different: at 2, 3, 13, 36, 37, 40, 41 in chapter 49, and 12, 13 in chapter 51, modern punctuation appears where there is no medieval sign.

§106. Second, there is no clear correspondence between modern full stops and medieval high dots, and between modern commas and medieval mid dots: high dots are equally present when full stops and commas occur; and modern commas may equally correspond to mid as well as to high dots. This means that the modern indication of weaker and stronger boundaries is not directly related to the occurrence of specific medieval signs.

§107. Let me now comment on the use of δέ, τε, and καί in relation to discourse segmentation. In excerpt 1 the eight occurrences of δέ (see the beginning of acts 15, 25, 26, 35, 47, 48, 52, 56) and their surrounding text indicate a variety of ways in which the δέ act is discrete—only at 56 does the act mark a semantic opposition. Conversely, in the two narrator texts (excerpts 2 and 3) all δέ occur at move starts.

§108. As for τε, the most important result is that it can introduce entire moves, especially in Thucydides (see 1, 13, 23, 36 in excerpt 1; 27, 45, 50, in excerpt 2; see also 40 in excerpt 3, and 6 in excerpt 4, chapter 49). In these instances τε follows a term that represents the topic of the next few acts. Almost all the occurrences of τε καί are between noun phrases that are combined on the basis of broadly known semantic frames (τοῖς χρησμολόγοις τε καὶ μάντεσι, 11; φόβος τε καὶ κατάπληξις, 16 in excerpt 2; κατὰ πόλις τε καὶ κατὰ ἔθνεα, 37 in excerpt 3; γῆ τε καὶ θάλασσα, 11 in excerpt 4, chapter 49).

§109. In line with the general frequencies of καί in the two *Histories* (see our frequency graphs [available online as I.5]) the Thucydidean excerpts include 42 instances, while the Herodotean excerpts include only 10. Several discourse acts start with καί linking conjuncts (with or without particular enrichments); in excerpt 2 this happens 17 times out of 25 total occurrences. Conversely, καί intensifying one constituent has a mobile position within the act (see, e.g. 13, 14, 15, 28, 32, 35, 37 in excerpt 1). It is noteworthy that καί in Thucydides' narrator text is more frequent than in Thucydides' speech (25 against 17 tokens).

§110. Some particles are not cues to segmentation, but, rather, markers of someone's voice or voice and stance in specific acts. γε (πλήν γε πρὸς τὸ μάχιμον αὐτῶν, τὸ ὁπλιτικόν, 31, in excerpt 1; μὴ οὕτω γε ἄγαν πανσυδὶ διεφθάρθαι, 6, in excerpt 2; ἤτοι ἁλισκομένων γε, 38, and οὐ πείσει τούς γε πολλοὺς πλέειν ἐς τὸν Ἑλλήσποντον, 52, in excerpt 3; ὅστις γε σύνεσιν ἔχει, 3 in excerpt 4, chapter 49) signposts vocal liveliness and emphasis on meanings left unsaid. δή (φόβος τε καὶ κατάπληξις μεγίστη δή, 16, in excerpt 2; γῆ δὴ πολεμίη, 32, and παρ' ἣν δὴ κομίζεαι, 22, in excerpt 4, chapter 49) conveys someone's certainty or the evident character of something. Finally, ἤδη (κατὰ κράτος ἤδη, 33, in excerpt 2; τὸ ἐνθεῦτεν δὲ περὶ τῆς ἐκείνου ποιέεσθαι ἤδη τὸν ἀγῶνα, 46, in excerpt 3) reflects a sense of confidence as if characters express their stance *viva voce*.

§111. While particles and particle combinations often relate to move boundaries, an important element contributing to shaping moves is lexical repetition. I have pointed out several repetitions of terms that contribute to thematic and pragmatic coherence. With respect to the broader phenomenon of resonance, which includes multifarious reuses of verbal features across different turns of speaking (see III.3), here we deal with a monologic reuse of words. Further research into the relation between lexical repetition and morphological similarity, on the one hand, and our way of processing the sequence/order of linguistic elements, on the other, could lead to significant results.[131] For the moment I flag three aspects of lexical repetition that make it relevant to segmentation. First, it exemplifies a way in which discourse segmentation goes beyond hypotactic divisions. Second, in spite of Thucydides' fondness for linguistic variation, the historian offers evidence of lexical repetition at strategic moments of the articulation of the discourse (see e.g. πολλούς, 1 and 10, τὰ ἐπιτήδεια, 14 and 20, ἐκπλεῖν and ἐκπλεῦσαι, 51-52, in excerpt 1; ἐπειδή, 2 and 7, in excerpt 2). Third, the power of lexical repetition does not emerge as much in our silent reading as it does if the text is read aloud. This harmonizes with the idea of "audible" strategies of segmentation, namely the possible link between particles and particular intonational contours, and, more importantly, the potential match between discourse acts and intonation units.

§112. The final point concerns the position of verbs. In his monograph on Thucydides' narration, Lamb observes (1914:250-254) that verb forms frequently occur at the end of sentences in the form of *clausulae* (often they are four-syllable verbs). According to the discourse segmentation that I propose, the narrator-text excerpts (2 and 3, thus not only in Thucydides but also in Herodotus) do display verb forms that seem to fit a performative closure: ἐβαρύνοντο, 22, and προβουλεύσουσιν, 49, in excerpt 2; ἐβουλεύοντο, 13, and ἐκέλευε, 49, in excerpt 3. In Thucydides' excerpts moves mostly end with verbs (9 out of 12 times, and 7 out of 10, respectively). I would take this point further: act division reveals this tendency on an even smaller scale. Verb forms are predominant at the end of acts, at least in narrator text. Besides individual occurrences, let me point out six times in succession (ἠγγέλθη, 2; ἠπίστουν, 3; διαπεφευγόσι, 4; ἀγγέλλουσι, 5; διεφθάρθαι, 6; ἔγνωσαν, 7) and later five times in succession in excerpt 2 (σωφρονίσαι, 45; ἑλέσθαι, 46; παρόντων, 47; ᾖ, 48; προβουλεύσουσιν, 49); four times in succession (περιημέκτεον, 55; πλέειν, 56; βαλόμενοι, 57; βουλοίατο, 58) in Herodotus' narrator text (excerpt 3). This speech excerpt shows that too: three times in succession, for example, in chapter 49 (λέγω, 8; γίνεται, 9; ἐστί, 10) and four in chapter 51 (γινόμενοι, 16; προσβάλλουσι, 17; γινόμενοι, 18; γίνονται, 19). These data are far too little to make general claims. However,

131 Du Bois' notion of "dialogic syntax" (2014) centers exactly on that, and it is considered to work in dialogic as well as monologic texts.

especially for Thucydides, my limited results not only corroborate general findings about SOV clauses in ancient Greek,[132] but also suggest that verb position might be one of the features shaping discourse acts.

§113. To sum up: this analysis shows that the discourse seen act by act and move by move is segmented *much more* than, and often *differently* from, what a modern hypotactic analysis yields. The main advantage of this kind of segmentation is the slower pace of reading it institutes, which allows a number of phenomena to be appreciated below and above the level of the clause. It also lets the occurrence and the role of particles and particle combinations emerge. Together with different co-occurring words, particles mark moves with overarching communicative goals, individual acts, the speaker's and narrator's voice and stance, and various coordination strategies.

5.7 Appendix: The Continuous Texts Divided into Acts and Moves

Excerpt 1: Thucydides 6.22-23

1. [*OCT* 22.1] [extra space] ὁπλίτας τε οὖν πολλούς
2. μοι δοκεῖ
3. χρῆναι ἡμᾶς ἄγειν *{mid dot}*
4. καὶ ἡμῶν αὐτῶν
5. καὶ τῶν ξυμμάχων, *{high or mid dot}*
6. τῶν τε ὑπηκόων *{mid dot}*
7. καὶ ἤν τινα ἐκ Πελοποννήσου δυνώμεθα
8 ἢ πεῖσαι
9. ἢ μισθῷ προσαγαγέσθαι,
10. καὶ τοξότας πολλοὺς
11. καὶ σφενδονήτας, *{mid dot}*
12. ὅπως πρὸς τὸ ἐκείνων ἱππικὸν ἀντέχωσι, *{high dot}*

13. ναυσί τε καὶ πολὺ περιεῖναι, *{mid dot}*
14. ἵνα καὶ τὰ ἐπιτήδεια ῥᾷον ἐσκομιζώμεθα, *{high dot}*
15. τὸν δὲ καὶ αὐτόθεν σῖτον ἐν ὁλκάσι,
16. πυροὺς καὶ πεφρυγμένας κριθάς, ἄγειν, *{high dot}*
17. καὶ σιτοποιοὺς ἐκ τῶν μυλώνων πρὸς μέρος ἠναγκασμένους ἐμμίσθους, *{mid dot}*
18. ἵνα,
19. ἤν που ὑπὸ ἀπλοίας ἀπολαμβανώμεθα, *{mid or low dot}*

[132] See e.g. A. Taylor 1994.

20. ἔχῃ ἡ στρατιὰ τὰ ἐπιτήδεια_*{high dot}*

21. (πολλὴ γὰρ οὖσα
22. οὐ πάσης ἔσται πόλεως ὑποδέξασθαι), *{mid dot}*

23. τά τε ἄλλα ὅσον δυνατὸν ἑτοιμάσασθαι, *{mid dot}*
24. καὶ μὴ ἐπὶ ἑτέροις γίγνεσθαι, *{mid dot}*

25. μάλιστα δὲ χρήματα αὐτόθεν ὡς πλεῖστα ἔχειν. *{high dot}*
26. [extra space] τὰ δὲ παρ' Ἐγεσταίων,
27. ἃ λέγεται ἐκεῖ ἑτοῖμα, *{high dot}*
28. νομίσατε καὶ λόγῳ ἂν μάλιστα ἑτοῖμα εἶναι. *{high or mid dot}*

29. [*OCT* 23.1] [extra space] ἢν γὰρ αὐτοὶ ἔλθωμεν ἐνθένδε *{mid or low dot}*
30. μὴ ἀντίπαλον μόνον παρασκευασάμενοι, *{high dot}*
31. πλήν γε πρὸς τὸ μάχιμον αὐτῶν, τὸ ὁπλιτικόν, *{high dot}*
32. ἀλλὰ καὶ ὑπερβάλλοντες τοῖς πᾶσι, *{mid dot}*
33. μόλις οὕτως οἷοί τε ἐσόμεθα *{high dot}*
34. τῶν μὲν *{low dot or comma}* κρατεῖν, *{high dot}*
35. τὰ δὲ *{low dot or comma}* καὶ διασῶσαι. *{high dot}*

36. [*OCT* 23.2] [extra space] πόλιν τε νομίσαι χρὴ
37. ἐν ἀλλοφύλοις καὶ πολεμίοις οἰκιοῦντας ἰέναι, *{mid dot}*
38. οὓς πρέπει τῇ πρώτῃ ἡμέρᾳ
39. ᾗ ἂν κατάσχωσιν *{low dot}*
40. εὐθὺς κρατεῖν τῆς γῆς, *{high dot}*
41. ἢ εἰδέναι ὅτι,
42 ἢν σφάλλωνται, *{low dot or comma}*
43. πάντα πολέμια ἕξουσιν. *{light high dot}*

44. [*OCT* 23.3] [extra space] ὅπερ ἐγὼ φοβούμενος,
45. καὶ εἰδὼς *{mid dot}*
46. πολλὰ μὲν ἡμᾶς δέον εὖ βουλεύσασθαι, *{mid dot}*
47. ἔτι δὲ πλείω εὐτυχῆσαι *{mid dot}*
48. (χαλεπὸν δὲ
49. ἀνθρώπους ὄντας),
50. ὅτι ἐλάχιστα τῇ τύχῃ παραδοὺς
51. ἐμαυτὸν βούλομαι ἐκπλεῖν, *{high dot}*

52. παρασκευῇ δὲ *{mid dot}* ἀπὸ τῶν εἰκότων ἀσφαλὴς ἐκπλεῦσαι. *{high dot}*

53. ταῦτα γὰρ
54. τῇ τε ξυμπάσῃ πόλει βεβαιότατα ἡγοῦμαι *{high dot}*
55. καὶ ἡμῖν τοῖς στρατευσομένοις σωτήρια. *{high dot}*

56. [extra space] εἰ δέ τῳ ἄλλως δοκεῖ, *{mid or low dot}*
57. παρίημι αὐτῷ τὴν ἀρχήν._*{high dot}*

Excerpt 2: Thucydides 8.1

1. [*OCT* 1.1] [indent] ἐς δὲ τὰς Ἀθήνας
2. ἐπειδὴ ἠγγέλθη,
3. ἐπὶ πολὺ μὲν ἠπίστουν *{high dot}*
4. καὶ τοῖς πάνυ τῶν στρατιωτῶν ἐξ αὐτοῦ τοῦ ἔργου διαπεφευγόσι
5. καὶ σαφῶς ἀγγέλλουσι, *{comma or low dot}*
6. μὴ οὕτω γε ἄγαν πανσυδὶ διεφθάρθαι· *{high dot}*

7. [extra space] ἐπειδὴ δὲ ἔγνωσαν,
8. χαλεποὶ μὲν ἦσαν τοῖς ξυμπροθυμηθεῖσι τῶν ῥητόρων τὸν ἔκπλουν, *{high dot}*
9. ὥσπερ οὐκ αὐτοὶ ψηφισάμενοι, *{high dot}*

10. ὠργίζοντο δὲ
11. καὶ τοῖς χρησμολόγοις τε καὶ μάντεσι *{mid dot}*
12. καὶ ὁπόσοι τι τότε αὐτοὺς θειάσαντες *{comma}* ἐπήλπισαν
13. ὡς λήψονται Σικελίαν. *{high dot}*

14. [*OCT* 1.2] [extra space] πάντα δὲ πανταχόθεν
15. αὐτοὺς ἐλύπει τε καὶ περιειστήκει ἐπὶ τῷ γεγενημένῳ *{mid dot}*
16. φόβος τε καὶ κατάπληξις μεγίστη δή. *{high or mid dot}*

17. ἅμα μὲν γὰρ στερόμενοι *{high dot}*
18. καὶ ἰδίᾳ ἕκαστος καὶ ἡ πόλις
19. ὁπλιτῶν τε πολλῶν καὶ ἱππέων
20. καὶ ἡλικίας
21. οἵαν οὐχ ἑτέραν ἑώρων ὑπάρχουσαν *{comma}*
22. ἐβαρύνοντο· *{high dot}*

23. ἅμα δὲ ναῦς οὐχ ὁρῶντες ἐν τοῖς νεωσοίκοις ἱκανὰς *{high dot}*
24. οὐδὲ χρήματα ἐν τῷ κοινῷ *{high or mid dot}*
25. οὐδ' ὑπηρεσίας ταῖς ναυσὶν *{comma}*
26. ἀνέλπιστοι ἦσαν ἐν τῷ παρόντι σωθήσεσθαι, *{mid or low dot}*

27. τούς τε ἀπὸ τῆς Σικελίας πολεμίους *{comma}*
28. εὐθὺς σφίσιν ἐνόμιζον
29. τῷ ναυτικῷ ἐπὶ τὸν Πειραιᾶ πλευσεῖσθαι,
30. ἄλλως τε καὶ τοσοῦτον κρατήσαντας, *{mid dot}*
31. καὶ τοὺς αὐτόθεν πολεμίους
32. τότε δὴ καὶ διπλασίως πάντα παρεσκευασμένους *{high or mid dot}*
33. κατὰ κράτος ἤδη
34. καὶ ἐκ γῆς καὶ ἐκ θαλάσσης ἐπικείσεσθαι, *{high or mid dot}*
35. καὶ τοὺς ξυμμάχους σφῶν μετ' αὐτῶν ἀποστάντας. *{high dot}*

36. [*OCT* 1.3] [extra space] ὅμως δὲ
37. ὡς ἐκ τῶν ὑπαρχόντων ἐδόκει χρῆναι
38. μὴ ἐνδιδόναι, *{mid dot}*
39. ἀλλὰ παρασκευάζεσθαι
40. καὶ ναυτικόν,
41. ὅθεν ἂν δύνωνται ξύλα ξυμπορισαμένους,
42. καὶ χρήματα,
43. καὶ τὰ τῶν ξυμμάχων ἐς ἀσφάλειαν ποιεῖσθαι, *{mid dot}*
44. καὶ μάλιστα τὴν Εὔβοιαν, *{mid dot}*

45. τῶν τε κατὰ τὴν πόλιν τι ἐς εὐτέλειαν σωφρονίσαι, *{mid dot}*
46. καὶ ἀρχήν τινα πρεσβυτέρων ἀνδρῶν ἑλέσθαι, *{mid dot}*
47. οἵτινες περὶ τῶν παρόντων
48. ὡς ἂν καιρὸς ᾖ
49. προβουλεύσουσιν. *{high dot}*

50. [*OCT* 4] πάντα τε πρὸς τὸ παραχρῆμα περιδεές, *{mid dot}*
51. ὅπερ φιλεῖ δῆμος ποιεῖν, *{high dot}*
52. ἑτοῖμοι ἦσαν εὐτακτεῖν. *{mid dot}*

53. [extra space] καὶ
54. ὡς ἔδοξεν αὐτοῖς, *{high dot}*
55. καὶ ἐποίουν ταῦτα, *{high dot}*

56. καὶ τὸ θέρος ἐτελεύτα. *{high dot}*

Excerpt 3: Herodotus 8.108-109.1

1. [*OCT* 108.1] [extra space] ὡς δὲ ἡμέρη ἐγίνετο, *{comma}*
2. ὁρῶντες οἱ Ἕλληνες κατὰ χώρην μένοντα τὸν στρατὸν τὸν πεζὸν *{comma}*
3. ἤλπιζον καὶ τὰς νέας εἶναι περὶ Φάληρον, *{mid dot}*
4. ἐδόκεόν τε ναυμαχήσειν σφέας *{mid dot}*
5. παραρτέοντό τε
6. ὡς ἀλεξησόμενοι. *{mid dot}*

7. [extra space] ἐπεὶ δὲ ἐπύθοντο τὰς νέας οἰχωκυίας, *{low dot + light comma}*
8. αὐτίκα μετὰ ταῦτα ἐδόκεε ἐπιδιώκειν. *{high dot}*

9. [extra space] τὸν μέν νυν ναυτικὸν τὸν Ξέρξεω στρατὸν
10. οὐκ ἐπεῖδον
11. διώξαντες μέχρι Ἄνδρου,

12. ἐς δὲ τὴν Ἄνδρον ἀπικόμενοι
13. ἐβουλεύοντο. *{high dot}*

14. [*OCT* 108.2] Θεμιστοκλέης μέν νυν γνώμην ἀπεδείκνυτο *{light comma}*
15. διὰ νήσων τραπομένους
16. καὶ ἐπιδιώξαντας τὰς νέας *{mid or low dot + light comma}*
17. πλέειν ἰθέως ἐπὶ τὸν Ἑλλήσποντον
18. λύσοντας τὰς γεφύρας· *{high dot}*

19. Εὐρυβιάδης δὲ *{comma}*
20. τὴν ἐναντίην ταύτῃ γνώμην ἐτίθετο, *{high dot}*
21. λέγων ὡς

22. εἰ λύσουσι τὰς σχεδίας, *{comma}*
23. τοῦτ᾽ ἂν μέγιστον πάντων σφεῖς κακὸν τὴν Ἑλλάδα ἐργασαίατο.

24. [*OCT* 108.3] [extra space] εἰ γὰρ ἀναγκασθείη
25. ἀπολαμφθεὶς
26. ὁ Πέρσης μένειν ἐν τῇ Εὐρώπῃ, *{comma}*
27. πειρῷτο ἂν ἡσυχίην μὴ ἄγειν, *{high dot}*

28. ὡς
29. ἄγοντι μέν οἱ ἡσυχίην *{low dot}*
30. οὔτε τι προχωρέειν
31. οἷόν τε ἔσται τῶν πρηγμάτων *{mid dot}*
32. οὔτε τις κομιδὴ τὸ ὀπίσω φανήσεται, *{high dot}*
33. λιμῷ τέ οἱ ἡ στρατιὴ διαφθερέεται, *{high dot}*

34. ἐπιχειρέοντι δὲ αὐτῷ καὶ ἔργου ἐχομένῳ *{mid dot + comma}*
35. πάντα τὰ κατὰ τὴν Εὐρώπην
36. οἷά τε ἔσται προσχωρῆσαι
37. κατὰ πόλις τε καὶ κατὰ ἔθνεα, *{light comma}*
38. ἤτοι ἁλισκομένων γε
39. ἢ πρὸ τούτου ὁμολογεόντων· *{high dot}*

40. τροφήν τε ἕξειν σφέας
41. τὸν ἐπέτειον αἰεὶ τὸν τῶν Ἑλλήνων καρπόν. *{high dot}*

42. [*OCT* 108.4] [extra space] ἀλλὰ
43. δοκέειν γὰρ
44. νικηθέντα τῇ ναυμαχίῃ *{comma}*
45. οὐ μενέειν ἐν τῇ Εὐρώπῃ τὸν Πέρσην· *{high dot}*

46. ἐατέον ὦν εἶναι φεύγειν,
47. ἐς ὃ ἔλθῃ φεύγων ἐς τὴν ἑωυτοῦ· *{high dot}*

48. τὸ ἐνθεῦτεν δὲ περὶ τῆς ἐκείνου ποιέεσθαι ἤδη τὸν ἀγῶνα
49. ἐκέλευε. *{high dot}*

50. [extra space] ταύτης δὲ εἴχοντο τῆς γνώμης καὶ Πελοποννησίων τῶν ἄλλων οἱ στρατηγοί. *{high dot}*

51. [*OCT* 109.1] [extra space] ὡς δὲ ἔμαθε ὅτι
52. οὐ πείσει τούς γε πολλοὺς πλέειν ἐς τὸν Ἑλλήσποντον
53. ὁ Θεμιστοκλέης, *{comma}*
54. μεταβαλὼν πρὸς τοὺς Ἀθηναίους *{mid dot}*

55. (οὗτοι γὰρ μάλιστα ἐκπεφευγότων περιημέκτεον, *{comma}*
56. ὁρμέατό τε ἐς τὸν Ἑλλήσποντον πλέειν
57. καὶ ἐπὶ σφέων αὐτῶν βαλόμενοι,
58. εἰ ὦλλοι μὴ βουλοίατο) *{mid dot}*

59. ἔλεγέ σφι τάδε· *{mid dot}*

Excerpt 4: Herodotus 7.49 and 51

1. [*OCT* 7.49.1] Ὦ βασιλεῦ, *{mid dot}*
2. οὔτε στρατὸν τοῦτον,
3. ὅστις γε σύνεσιν ἔχει,
4. μέμφοιτ' ἂν *{comma}*
5. οὔτε τῶν νεῶν τὸ πλῆθος· *{high dot}*

6. ἤν τε πλεῦνας συλλέξῃς, *{comma}*
7. τὰ δύο τοι
8. τὰ λέγω *{mid dot}*
9. πολλῷ ἔτι πολεμιώτερα γίνεται. *{high dot}*
10. [extra space] τὰ δέ δύο ταῦτα ἐστὶ
11. γῆ τε καὶ θάλασσα. *{high dot}*

12. [*OCT* 49.2] [extra space] οὔτε γὰρ τῆς θαλάσσης
13. ἔστι λιμὴν τοσοῦτος οὐδαμόθι,
14. ὡς ἐγὼ εἰκάζω, *{comma}*
15. ὅστις
16. ἐγειρομένου χειμῶνος
17. δεξάμενός σευ τοῦτο τὸ ναυτικὸν
18. φερέγγυος ἔσται διασῶσαι τὰς νέας.[133] *{mid dot}*

19. [extra space] καίτοι
20. οὐκὶ ἕνα αὐτὸν δεῖ εἶναι [τὸν λιμένα],[134] *{mid dot + light comma}*
21. ἀλλὰ παρὰ πᾶσαν τὴν ἤπειρον
22. παρ' ἣν δὴ κομίζεαι. *{high dot}*

23. [*OCT* 49.3] [extra space] οὐκ ὦν δὴ
24. ἐόντων τοι λιμένων ὑποδεξίων, *{comma}*

25. μάθε ὅτι
26. αἱ συμφοραὶ τῶν ἀνθρώπων ἄρχουσι
27. καὶ οὐκὶ ὤνθρωποι τῶν συμφορέων. *{mid dot}*

[133] Here Legrand puts a high dot instead of a full stop.

[134] The manuscripts report τὸν λιμένα, but Krüger proposed to remove it (see the *apparatus criticus* of the *OCT* edition, vol. II, p. 166).

28. [extra space] καὶ δὴ
29. τῶν δύο τοι
30. τοῦ ἑτέρου εἰρημένου *{comma}*
31. τὸ ἕτερον ἔρχομαι ἐρέων. *{high dot}*

32. [*OCT* 49.4] [extra space] γῆ δὴ πολεμίη
33. τῇδέ τοι κατίσταται· *{high dot}*
34. εἰ θέλει τοι μηδὲν ἀντίξοον καταστῆναι, *{comma}*
35. τοσούτῳ τοι γίνεται πολεμιωτέρη
36. ὅσῳ ἂν προβαίνῃς ἑκαστέρω,
37. τὸ πρόσω αἰεὶ κλεπτόμενος·

38. εὐπρηξίης δέ[135]
39. οὐκ ἔστι ἀνθρώποισι οὐδεμία πληθώρη. *{mid dot}*

40. [*OCT* 49.5] [extra space] καὶ δή τοι,
41. ὡς οὐδενὸς ἐναντιουμένου,
42. λέγω
43. τὴν χώρην πλεῦνα ἐν πλέονι χρόνῳ γινομένην λιμὸν τέξεσθαι. *{mid dot}*

44. Ἀνὴρ δὲ
45. οὕτω ἂν εἴη ἄριστος, *{comma}*
46. εἰ
47. βουλευόμενος μὲν ἀρρωδέοι, *{light comma}*
48. πᾶν ἐπιλεγόμενος πείσεσθαι χρῆμα, *{mid dot}*
49. ἐν δὲ τῷ ἔργῳ θρασὺς εἴη. *{high dot}*

[7.50]

1. [*OCT* 51.1] Ὦ βασιλεῦ, *{mid dot}*
2. ἐπείτε ἀρρωδέειν οὐδὲν ἐᾷς πρῆγμα, *{comma}*
3. σὺ δέ μεο συμβουλίην ἔνδεξαι· *{high dot}*

4. ἀναγκαίως γὰρ ἔχει περὶ πολλῶν πρηγμάτων πλεῦνα λόγον ἐκτεῖναι. *{high dot}*

135 Legrand, conversely, accepts γάρ, as given in the group of manuscripts “a” and in manuscript P.

5. [extra space] Κῦρος ὁ Καμβύσεω Ἰωνίην πᾶσαν πλὴν Ἀθηνέων κατεστρέψατο
6. δασμοφόρον εἶναι Πέρσῃσι. *{high dot}*

7. [*OCT* 51.2] τούτους ὦν τοὺς ἄνδρας
8. συμβουλεύω τοι
9. μηδεμιῇ μηχανῇ ἄγειν ἐπὶ τοὺς πατέρας· *{high dot}*

10. καὶ γὰρ ἄνευ τούτων
11. οἷοί τέ εἰμεν τῶν ἐχθρῶν κατυπέρτεροι γίνεσθαι. *{high dot}*

12. Ἢ γάρ σφεας,
13. ἢν ἕπωνται,
14. δεῖ ἀδικωτάτους γίνεσθαι καταδουλουμένους τὴν μητρόπολιν, *{mid dot}*
15. ἢ δικαιοτάτους *{comma}* συνελευθεροῦντας.[136] *{high dot}*

16. [*OCT* 51.3] ἀδικώτατοι μέν νυν γινόμενοι *{comma}*
17. οὐδὲν κέρδος μέγα ἡμῖν προσβάλλουσι, *{high dot}*
18. δικαιότατοι δὲ γινόμενοι *{comma}*
19. οἷοί τε δηλήσασθαι μεγάλως τὴν σὴν στρατιὴν γίνονται.

20. ἐς θυμὸν ὦν βάλεο καὶ τὸ παλαιὸν ἔπος
21. ὡς εὖ εἴρηται, *{high dot}*
22. τὸ μὴ ἅμα ἀρχῇ πᾶν τέλος καταφαίνεσθαι. *{high dot}*

[136] Here Legrand inserts a high dot (Greek semicolon) instead of a full stop.

Bibliography

(Anonymous). 1824. *Lexicon Thucydidaeum: A Dictionary in Greek and English, of the Words, Phrases, and Principal Idioms, Contained in the History of the Peloponnesian War of Thucydides*. London. https://archive.org/details/lexiconthucydida00lond.

Abbott, T. K. 1890. "On δή after Relatives in Plato." *Hermathena* 7:44–45.

Abraham, W., ed. 1991. *Discourse Particles across Languages*. Berlin.

———. 1991. *Discourse Particles: Descriptive and Theoretical Investigations on the Logical, Syntactic and Pragmatic Properties of Discourse Particles in German*. Amsterdam.

Addis, D. R., L. Pan, M.-A. Vu, N. Laiser, and D. L. Schacter. 2009. "Constructive Episodic Simulation of the Future and the Past: Distinct Subsystems of a Core Brain Network Mediate Imagining and Remembering." *Neuropsychologia* 47:2222–2238.

Adema, S. M. 2007. "Discourse Modes and Bases in Vergil's *Aeneid*." In *The Language of Literature. Linguistic Approaches to Classical Texts*, ed. R. J. Allan, and M. Buijs, 42–64. Leiden.

———. 2008. *Discourse Modes and Bases. The Use of Tenses in Vergil's Aeneid*. Amsterdam.

Adler, A. 2004. *Lexicographi graeci I.2: Suidae Lexicon*. Munich.

Aftosmis, J. 2010. Paradigm and Discourse in Archaic Greek Poetry. PhD diss., University of California, Berkeley.

Agha, A. 2001. "Register." In *Key Terms in Language and Culture*, ed. A. Duranti, 212–215. Malden, MA.

Ahrens, H. L. 1845. *De crasi et aphaeresi cum corollario emendationum babrianarum*. Stolberg. http://books.google.de/books?id=-lzFAAAAMAAJ&hl=de&pg=PA8%23v=onepage&q&f=false.

———. 1859. "Ein Beitrag zur Etymologie der griechischen Zahlwörter." *Zeitschrift für vergleichende Sprachforschung auf dem Gebiete des Deutschen, Griechischen und Lateinischen* 8:329–361. http://www.jstor.org/stable/40845338?seq=29.

Aijmer, K. 2002. *English Discourse Particles: Evidence from a Corpus*. Amsterdam.

———. 2009. "The Pragmatic Marker *well*: A Text Study." In *Coherence and Cohesion in Spoken and Written Discourse*, ed. O. Dontcheva-Navratilova and R. Povolná, 4–29. Newcastle.

———. 2013. *Understanding Pragmatic Markers: A Variational Pragmatic Approach*. Edinburgh.

Aijmer, K., A. Foolen, and A.-M. Simon-Vandenbergen. 2006. "Pragmatic Markers in Translation: A Methodological Proposal." In Fischer 2006:101–114. Amsterdam.

Aijmer, K., and A.-M. Simon-Vandenbergen. 2003. "The Discourse Particle *well* and Its Equivalents in Swedish and Dutch." *Linguistics* 41:1123–1161.

———. 2004. "A Model and a Methodology for the Study of Pragmatic Markers: The Semantic Field of Expectation." *Journal of Pragmatics* 36:1781–1805.

———. 2011. "Pragmatic Markers." In *Discursive Pragmatics*, ed. J. Zienkowski, J.-O. Östman, and J. Verschueren, 223–427. Amsterdam.

Alberti, G. B. 1959. "L'uso delle particelle nella formula di correlazione πρῶτον... ἔπειτα." *Maia* 11:44–62.

Allan, R. J. 2007. "Sense and Sentence Complexity: Sentence Structure, Sentence Connection, and Tense-Aspect as Indicators of Narrative Mode in Thucydides' Histories." In *The Language of Literature: Linguistic Approaches to Classical Texts*, ed. R. J. Allan, and M. Buijs, 93–121. Leiden.

———. 2009. "Towards a Typology of the Narrative Modes in Ancient Greek: Text Types and Narrative Structure in Euripidean Messenger Speeches." In Bakker and Wakker 2009:171–203. Leiden.

———. 2011. "The Historical Present in Thucydides: Capturing the Case of αἱρεῖ and λαμβάνει." In *The Historical Present in Thucydides: Semantics and Narrative Function*, ed. J. Lallot, A. Rijksbaron, B. Jacquinod, and M. Buijs, 37–63. Leiden.

———. 2013. "History as Presence: Time, Tense and Narrative Modes in Thucydides." In *Thucydides Between History and Literature*, ed. A. Tsakmakis, and M. Tamiolaki, 371–390. Berlin.

———. 2017. "Ancient Greek Adversative Particles in Contrast." In Denizot and Spevak 2017:273–301.

Allan, W. 2000. "Euripides and the Sophists: Society and the Theatre of War." In *Euripides and Tragic Theatre in the Late Fifth Century*, ed. M. J. Cropp, 145–156. Champaign, IL.

———. 2001. *Euripides. The Children of Heracles*. Warminster.

Allbritton, D. W., and R. J. Gerrig. 1991. "Participatory Responses in Text Understanding." *Journal of Memory and Language* 30:603–626.

Allen, D. S. 2003. "Angry Bees, Wasps, and Jurors: The Symbolic Politics of ὀργή in Athens." In *Ancient Anger: Perspectives from Homer to Galen*, ed. S. Braund and G. W. Most, 76–98. New York.

Allen, T. W. 1931. *Homer. Iliad*. 2 vols. Oxford.

Allen, W. S. 1973. *Accent and Rhythm: Prosodic Features of Latin and Greek. A Study of Theory and Reconstruction*. Cambridge.

Altenberg, B. 2010. "Conclusive English *then* and Swedish *då*: A Corpus-Based Contrastive Study." *Languages in Contrast* 10:102–123.

Altenmüller, E., S. Schmidt, and E. Zimmermann. 2013. "A Cross-Taxa Concept of Emotion in Acoustic Communication: An Ethological Perspective." In Altenmüller, Schmidt, and Zimmermann 2013:339–355. Oxford.

———, ed. 2013. *The Evolution of Emotional Communication: From Sounds in Nonhuman Mammals to Speech and Music in Man*. Oxford.

Ameka, F. 1992. "Interjections: The Universal yet Neglected Part of Speech." *Journal of Pragmatics* 18:101–118.

Andersen, G. 1998. "The Pragmatic Marker *like* from a Relevance-Theoretic Perspective." In Jucker and Ziv 1998:147–170. Amsterdam.

———. 2001. *Pragmatic Markers and Sociolinguistic Variation: A Relevance-Theoretic Approach to the Language of Adolescents*. Amsterdam.

Andersen, G., and T. Fretheim, eds. 2000. *Pragmatic Markers and Propositional Attitude*. Amsterdam.

Ángeles Durán López, M. de los. 2000. "Las partículas griegas y las funciones de comunicación." *Revista Española de Lingüística* 30:45–76.

Antonopoulou, E., and K. Nikiforidou. 2011. "Construction Grammar and Conventional Discourse: A Construction-Based Approach to Discoursal Incongruity." *Journal of Pragmatics* 43:2594–2609.

Archakis, A. 2001. "On Discourse Markers: Evidence from Modem Greek." *Journal of Pragmatics* 33:1235–1261.

Arend, W. 1933. *Die typische Szenen bei Homer*. Berlin.

Argaman, O. 2010. "Linguistic Markers and Emotional Intensity." *Journal of Psycholinguistic Research* 39:89–99.

Ariel, M. 1988. "Referring and Accessibility." *Journal of Linguistics* 24:65–87.

———. 1990. *Accessing Noun Phrase Antecedents*. London.

———. 1991. "The Function of Accessibility in a Theory of Grammar." *Journal of Pragmatics* 16:443–463.

———. 1996. "Referring Expressions and the +/- Coreference Distinction." In *Reference and Referent Accessibility*, ed. J. K. Gundel and T. Fretheim, 13–25. Amsterdam.

———. 2008. *Pragmatics and Grammar*. Cambridge.

———. 2010. *Defining Pragmatics*. Cambridge.

———. 2012. "Relational and Independent *and* Conjunctions." *Lingua* 122:1692–1715.

———. 2014. "*Or* Constructions: Monosemy versus Polysemy." In *Competing Motivations*, ed. B. Mac Whinney, A. Malchukov, and E. A. Moravcsik, 333–347. Oxford.

Arnim, H. von. 1912. *Sprachliche Forschungen zur Chronologie der platonischen Dialoge*. Vienna.

Arnold, M. B. 1961. *Emotion and Personality*. Vol. 1: *Psychological Aspects*. London.

Arnold, T. 1863. *The History of the Peloponnesian War by Thucydides*. 6th ed. Oxford.

Arnold, T. K. 1881. *A Practical Introduction to Greek Prose Composition*. Part 2: "The Particles." London.

Asheri, D. 1988. "Introduzione generale" In *Erodoto. Le storie*. Libro I: *La Lidia e la Persia*, ed. D. Asheri and V. Antelami, ix-lxix. Milan.

Asheri, D., A. B. Lloyd, and A. Corcella. 2007. *A Commentary on Herodotus Books I-IV*. Oxford.

Asheri, D., P. Vannicelli, A. Corcella, and A. Fraschetti. 2003. *Erodoto. Le storie*. Libro VIII: *La vittoria di Temistocle*. Milan.

———. 2006. *Erodoto. Le storie*. Libro IX: *La battaglia di Platea*. Milan.

Ast, F. 1835. *Lexicon Platonicum*. Leipzig.

Athanassaki, L. 2012. "Recreating the Emotional Experience of Contest and Victory Celebrations: Spectators and Celebrants in Pindar's *Epinicians*." In *Approaches to Archaic Greek Poetry*, ed. X. Riu and J. Portulas, 173-219. Messina.

Auer, P. 1992. "Introduction: John Gumperz' Approach to Contextualization." In *The Contextualization of Language*, ed. P. Auer and A. Di Luzio, 1–37. Amsterdam.

———. 2000. "Pre- and Post-Positioning of *wenn*-Clauses in Spoken and Written German." In *Cause - Condition - Concession - Contrast: Cognitive and Discourse Perspectives*, ed. E. Couper-Kuhlen and B. Kortmann, 173–204. Berlin.

———. 2002. "Projection in Interaction and Projection in Grammar." *Interaction and Linguistic Structures* 33:1–39.

———. 2005. "Projection in Interaction and Projection in Grammar." *Text. Interdisciplinary Journal for the Study of Discourse* 25:7–36.

———. 2009a. "On-Line Syntax: Thoughts on the Temporality of Spoken Language." *Language Sciences* 31:1–13.

———. 2009b. "Projection and Minimalistic Syntax in Interaction." *Discourse Processes* 46:180–205.

Auer, P., E. Couper-Kuhlen, and F. Müller. 1999. *Language in Time: The Rhythm and Tempo of Spoken Interaction*. New York.

Auer, P., and A. Di Luzio, eds. 1992. *The Contextualization of Language*. Amsterdam.

Auer, P., and Y. Maschler. 2013. "Discourse or Grammar? VS Patterns in Spoken Hebrew and Spoken German Narratives." *Language Sciences* 37:147–181.

Auer, P., and S. Pfänder, eds. 2011. *Constructions: Emerging and Emergent*. Berlin.

Auffarth, C. 2007. "Ritual, Performanz, Theater: Die Religion der Athener in Aristophanes' Komödien." In *Literatur und Religion 1: Wege zu einer mythisch-rituellen Poetik bei den Griechen*, ed. A. F. Bierl, R. Lämmle, and K. Wesselmann, 387–414. Berlin.

Ausfeld, C. 1903. "De Graecorum precationibus quaestiones." *Jahrbuch Für Klassische Philologie, Supplementum* 28:503–547.

Austin, J. L. 1962. *How to Do Things with Words*. Cambridge, MA.

Austin, N. 1966. "The Function of Digressions in the *Iliad*." *Greek, Roman, and Byzantine Studies* 7:295–312.

Auwera, J. van der. 1993. "'Already' and 'Still': Beyond Duality." *Linguistics and Philosophy* 16:613–653.

———. 1998. *Adverbial Constructions in the Languages of Europe*. Berlin.

Auwera, J. van der, and V. A. Plungian. 1998. "Modality's Semantic Map." *Linguistic Typology* 2:79–124.

Ax, W. 1982. "Aristarch und die 'Grammatik.'" *Glotta* 60:96–109.

———. 1991. "Sprache als Gegenstand der alexandrinischen und pergamenischen Philologie." In *Geschichte der Sprachtheorie. Bd. 2: Sprachtheorien der abendländischen Antike*, ed. P. Schmitter, 275–301. Tübingen.

Baar, T. van. 1997. *Phasal Polarity*. Amsterdam.

Bach, K. 1994. "Conversational Implicature." *Mind & Language* 9:124–162.

Bach, K., and R. M. Harnish. 1979. *Linguistic Communication and Speech Acts*. Cambridge, MA.

Bader, F. 1973. "Lat. *nempe, porceo* et les fonctions des particules pronominales." *Bulletin de la Société de Linguistique* 68:27–75.

Baechle, N. 2007. *Metrical Constraint and the Interpretation of Style in the Tragic Trimeter*. Lanham, MD.

Bain, D. 1977. *Actors and Audience: A Study of Asides and Related Conventions in Greek Drama*. Oxford.

Baker, C. L. 1995. "Contrast, Discourse Prominence, and Intensification, with Special Reference to Locally Free Reflexives in British English." *Language* 71:63–101.

Bakhtin, M. M. 1981 [1934]. *The Dialogic Imagination: Four Essays by M. M. Bakhtin*. Austin.

Bakker, E. J. 1986. "*Hosper* en *eiper*: Een aspect van Attische conversatie." *Lampas* 19:142–158.

———. 1988. *Linguistics and Formulas in Homer: Scalarity and the Description of the Particle 'per.'* Amsterdam.

———. 1990a. "Homeric Discourse and Enjambement: A Cognitive Approach." *Transactions of the American Philological Association* 120:1–21.

———. 1990b. "Homerus als orale poëzie: De recente ontwikkelingen." *Lampas* 23:384–405.

———. 1991. "Foregrounding and Indirect Discourse: Temporal Subclauses in a Herodotean Short Story." *Journal of Pragmatics* 16:225–247.

———. 1993a. "Activation and Preservation: The Interdependence of Text and Performance in an Oral Tradition." *Oral Tradition* 8:5–20.

———. 1993b. "Boundaries, Topics and the Structure of Discourse. An Investigation of the Ancient Greek Particle *de*." *Studies in Language* 17:275–311.

———. 1993c. "Concession and Identification. The Diachronic Development of the Particle 'per'." In *Miscellanea Linguistica Graeco-Latina*, ed. L. Isebaert, 1-17. Namur.

———. 1993d. "Discourse and Performance: Involvement, Visualization and 'Presence' in Homeric Poetry." *Classical Antiquity* 12:1–29.

———. 1995. "Noun-Epithet Formulas, Milman Parry, and the Grammar of Poetry." In *Homeric Questions*, ed. J. P. Crielaard, 97–125. Amsterdam.

———. 1997a. "Introduction." In *Grammar as Interpretation. Greek Literature in Its Linguistic Contexts*, ed. E. J. Bakker, 1–6. Leiden.

———. 1997b. *Poetry in Speech: Orality and Homeric Discourse*. Ithaca, NY.

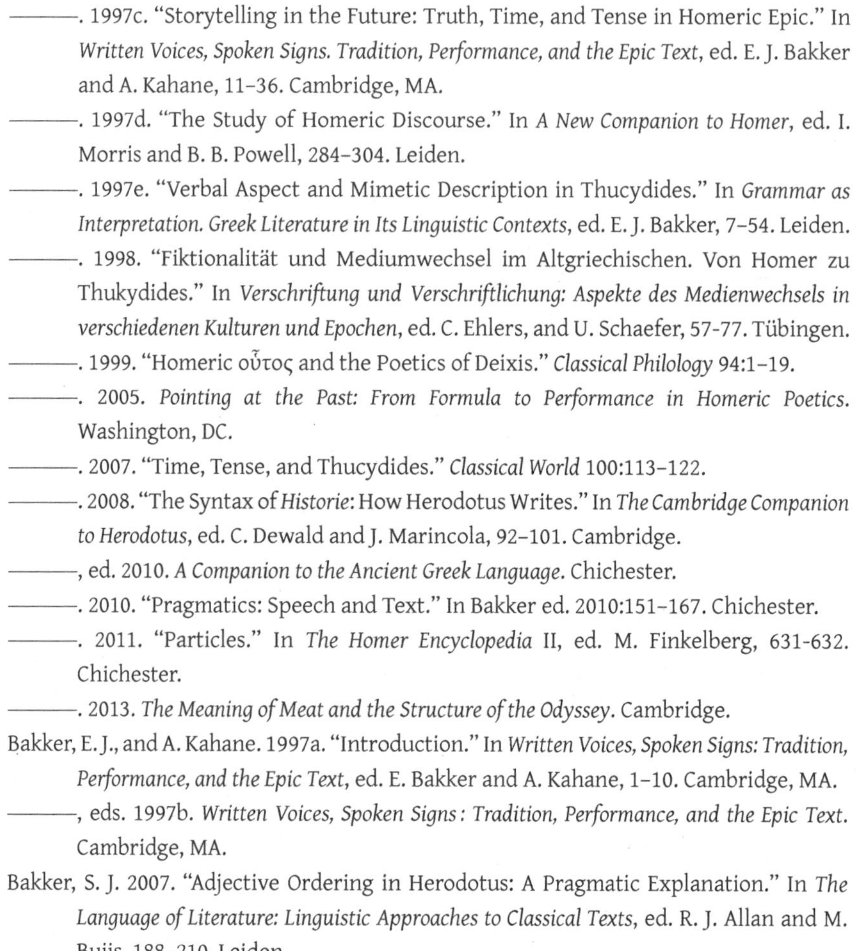

———. 1997c. "Storytelling in the Future: Truth, Time, and Tense in Homeric Epic." In *Written Voices, Spoken Signs. Tradition, Performance, and the Epic Text*, ed. E. J. Bakker and A. Kahane, 11–36. Cambridge, MA.

———. 1997d. "The Study of Homeric Discourse." In *A New Companion to Homer*, ed. I. Morris and B. B. Powell, 284–304. Leiden.

———. 1997e. "Verbal Aspect and Mimetic Description in Thucydides." In *Grammar as Interpretation. Greek Literature in Its Linguistic Contexts*, ed. E. J. Bakker, 7–54. Leiden.

———. 1998. "Fiktionalität und Mediumwechsel im Altgriechischen. Von Homer zu Thukydides." In *Verschriftung und Verschriftlichung: Aspekte des Medienwechsels in verschiedenen Kulturen und Epochen*, ed. C. Ehlers, and U. Schaefer, 57-77. Tübingen.

———. 1999. "Homeric οὗτος and the Poetics of Deixis." *Classical Philology* 94:1–19.

———. 2005. *Pointing at the Past: From Formula to Performance in Homeric Poetics.* Washington, DC.

———. 2007. "Time, Tense, and Thucydides." *Classical World* 100:113–122.

———. 2008. "The Syntax of *Historie*: How Herodotus Writes." In *The Cambridge Companion to Herodotus*, ed. C. Dewald and J. Marincola, 92–101. Cambridge.

———, ed. 2010. *A Companion to the Ancient Greek Language*. Chichester.

———. 2010. "Pragmatics: Speech and Text." In Bakker ed. 2010:151–167. Chichester.

———. 2011. "Particles." In *The Homer Encyclopedia* II, ed. M. Finkelberg, 631-632. Chichester.

———. 2013. *The Meaning of Meat and the Structure of the Odyssey*. Cambridge.

Bakker, E. J., and A. Kahane. 1997a. "Introduction." In *Written Voices, Spoken Signs: Tradition, Performance, and the Epic Text*, ed. E. Bakker and A. Kahane, 1–10. Cambridge, MA.

———, eds. 1997b. *Written Voices, Spoken Signs : Tradition, Performance, and the Epic Text.* Cambridge, MA.

Bakker, S. J. 2007. "Adjective Ordering in Herodotus: A Pragmatic Explanation." In *The Language of Literature: Linguistic Approaches to Classical Texts*, ed. R. J. Allan and M. Buijs, 188–210. Leiden.

———. 2009. "On the Curious Combination of the Particles ΓΑΡ and ΟΥΝ." In Bakker and Wakker 2009:41–61. Leiden.

Bakker, S. J., and G. C. Wakker, eds. 2009. *Discourse Cohesion in Ancient Greek*. Leiden.

Bakker, M. P. de. 2007. Speech and Authority in Herodotus' *Histories*. PhD diss., University of Amsterdam.

———. 2013. "Character Judgements in the *Histories*: Their Function and Distribution." In *Thucydides between History and Literature*, ed. A. Tsakmakis and M. Tamiolaki, 23–40. Berlin.

Bal, M. 1985. *Narratology: Introduction to the Theory of Narratology*. Toronto.

———. 2006. "Narrativity and Voice." In *Encyclopedia of Language and Linguistics*, ed. E. K. Brown and A. Anderson, 477-482. 2nd ed. Oxford.

Balassidis, C. 1979. "'Περὶ τοῦ 'οὐ μὴν ἀλλά', 'οὐ μέντοι ἀλλά', 'οὐ γὰρ ἀλλά'." *Athenaion* 7:221–227.

Bally, C. 1912. "Le style indirect libre en Français moderne." *Germanisch-Romanische Monatsschrift* 4:549–556; 597–606.

Bamberg, M. G. W, ed. 1997. *Oral Versions of Personal Experience: Three Decades of Narrative Analysis*. Mahwah, NJ.

Bamberg, M. G. W., and V. Marchman. 1991. "Binding and Unfolding: Towards the Linguistic Construction of Narrative Discourse." *Discourse Processes* 14:277–305.

Banfield, A. 1982. *Unspeakable Sentences: Narration and Representation in the Language of Fiction*. London.

Bara, B. G. 2010. *Cognitive Pragmatics: The Mental Processes of Communication*. Cambridge, MA.

Baragwanath, E. 2008. *Motivation and Narrative in Herodotus*. Oxford.

Bari, M. F. Di. 2010. "ὅδ' ἐκεῖνος: Aristofane, Cavalieri 1331, Nuvole 1167." *Lexis* 28:329-342.

Barlow, S. A. 1971. *The Imagery of Euripides: A Study in the Dramatic Use of Pictorial Language*. Bristol.

———. 1996. *Euripides. Heracles*. Warminster.

Barner, W. 1967. *Neuere Alkaios-Papyri aus Oxyrhynchos*. Hildesheim.

Barnes, H. R. 1986. "The Colometric Structure of Homeric Hexameter." *Greek, Roman, and Byzantine Studies* 27:125–150.

Baron, C. 1890. *Le pronom relatif et la conjonction en grec*. Paris.

Barrett, J. 2002. *Staged Narrative. Poetics and the Messenger in Greek Tragedy*. Berkeley.

Barrett, L. F., and J. A. Russell. 2009. "Circumplex Models." In *The Oxford Companion to Emotion and the Affective Sciences*, ed. D. Sander and K. R. Scherer, 85–88. Oxford.

Barrett, W. S. 1964. *Euripides. Hippolytus*. Oxford.

———. 2007. "A Detail of Tragic Usage: The Application to Persons of Verbal Nouns in -μα." In *Greek Lyric, Tragedy, and Textual Criticism: Collected Papers*, ed. M. L. West, 351-367. Oxford.

Barron, A. 2014. "Variational Pragmatics." In *The Encyclopedia of Applied Linguistics online*, ed. C. A. Chapelle, https://onlinelibrary.wiley.com/doi/abs/10.1002/9781405198431.wbeal1429.

Barth-Weingarten, D. 2012. "Of Ens 'n' Ands: Observations on the Phonetic Make-up of a Coordinator and Its Uses in Talk-in-Interaction." *Language and Speech* 55:35–56.

Barth-Weingarten, D., E. Reber, and M. Selting, eds. 2010. *Prosody in Interaction*. Amsterdam.

Barthes, R. 1957. *Mythologies*. Paris.

———. 1977. *Poétique du récit*. Paris.

Basile, N. 1998. *Sintassi storica del greco antico*. Bari.

Basset, L. 1979. *Les emplois périphrastiques du verbe grec μέλλειν: Étude de linguistique grecque et essai de linguistique générale*. Lyon.

———. 1988. "Valeurs et emplois de la particule dite modale en grec ancien." In *In the Footsteps of Raphael Kühner*, ed. H. A. Mulder, A. Rijksbaron, and G. C. Wakker, 27–37. Amsterdam.

———. 1989. *La syntaxe de l'imaginaire: Étude de modes et des négations dans l'Iliade et l'Odyssée*. Lyon.

———. 1997. "ἀλλ' ἐξόλοισθ' αὐτῶι κοαξ. Réexamen des emplois de ἀλλά à la lumière de l'enonciation dans *Les Grenouilles* d'Aristophane." In Rijksbaron 1997:75–99. Amsterdam.

Battezzato, L. 2005. "Lyric." In *A Companion to Greek Tragedy*, ed. J. Gregory, 149–166. Oxford.

Battezzato, L., and M. A. Rodda. 2018. "Particelle e asindeto nel greco classico." *Glotta* 94:3–37.

Bauer, W., and N. Wecklein. 1894. *Des Euripides Medea*. Munich.

Bäumlein, W. von. 1846. *Untersuchungen über die griechischen Modi und die Partikeln kén und án*. Heilbronn.

———. 1859. "Zu der Lehre von den Partikeln κέν und ἄν." *Jahrbücher Für Classische Philologie* 5:1–10.

———. 1861. *Untersuchungen über griechische Partikeln*. Stuttgart.

———. 1863. "Griechische Syntax (Jahresbericht)." *Philologus* 19:282–307.

Bay, S. M. 2009. "The Deferment of Postpositive Particles in Documentary Papyri." *Bulletin of the American Society of Papyrologists* 46:75–79.

Bazzanella, C. 1990. "Phatic Connectives as Interactional Cues in Contemporary Spoken Italian." *Journal of Pragmatics* 14:629–647.

———. 1995. "I segnali discorsivi." In *Grande Grammatica Italiana di Consultazione* III, ed. L. Renzi, G. Salvi, and A. Cardinaletti, 225–257. Bologna.

———. 1999. "Corrispondenze funzionali di 'well' in italiano: Analisi di un testo letterario e problemi generali." In *Linguistica testuale comparativa. In memoriam Maria-Elisabeth Conte*, ed. G. Skytte and F. Sabatini, 99–110. Copenhagen.

———. 2003. "Dal latino *ante* all'italiano *anzi*: La 'deriva modale.'" In *Colloquia absentium. Studi sulla comunicazione epistolare in Cicerone*, ed. A. Garcea, 123–140. Turin.

———. 2004. "Emotions, Language, and Context." In *Emotion in Dialogic Interaction: Advances in the Complex*, ed. E. Weigand, 55–72. Amsterdam.

———. 2006. "Discourse Markers in Italian: Towards a 'Compositional' Meaning." In Fischer 2006:449–464. Amsterdam and Boston.

Bazzanella, C., and C. Bosco. 2005. "Corpus Linguistics and the Modal Shift: Pragmatic Markers and the Case of *allora*." In *Romance Corpus Linguistics: Corpora and Historical Linguistics*, ed. C. D. Pusch, J. Kabatek, and W. Raible, 443–453. Tübingen.

Bazzanella, C., C. Bosco, E. Calaresu, A. Garcea, P. Guil Povedano, and A. Radulescu. 2005. "Dal latino 'iam' agli esiti nelle lingue romanze: verso una configurazione pragmatica complessiva." *Cuadernos de filologia italiana* 12:49–82.

Bazzanella, C., C. Bosco, A. Garcea, B. Gili Fivela, J. Miecznikowski, and F. Tini Brunozzi. 2007. "Italian *allora*, French *alors*: Functions, Convergences and Divergences." *Catalan Journal of Linguistics* 6:9–30.

Bazzanella, C., and L. Morra. 2000. "Discourse Markers and the Indeterminacy of Translation." In *Argomenti per una linguistica della traduzione*, ed. I. Korzen, and C. Marello, 149–157. Alessandria.

Beaman, K. 1984. "Coordination and Subordination Revisited: Syntactic Complexity in Spoken and Written Narrative Discourse." In *Coherence in Spoken and Written Discourse*, ed. D. Tannen, 12:45–80. Norwood, NJ.

Beaugrande, R. de, and W. U. Dressler. 1981. *Introduction to Text Linguistics*. London.

Bechtel, F. 1921. *Die griechischen Dialekte*. Berlin.

Beck, D. 2005. *Homeric Conversation*. Washington, DC.

———. 2009. "Speech Act Types, Conversational Exchange, and the Speech Representational Spectrum in Homer." In *Narratology and Interpretation: The Content of Narrative Form in Ancient Literature*, ed. A. Rengakos and J. Grethlein, 137–151. Berlin.

———. 2012. *Speech Presentation in Homeric Epic*. Austin.

Beck, I. 1971. *Die Ringkomposition bei Herodot und ihre Bedeutung für die Beweistechnik*. Hildesheim.

Bednarek, M. 2009. "Emotion Talk and Emotional Talk: Cognitive and Discursive Perspectives." In *Language and Social Cognition: Expression of the Social Mind*, ed. H. Pishwa, 395–432. Berlin.

Beeching, K. 2002. *Gender, Politeness and Pragmatic Particles in French*. Amsterdam.

Beekes, R. 2010. *Etymological Dictionary of Greek*. 2 vols. Leiden.

Béguelin, M.-J. 2010. "Noyaux prédicatifs juxtaposés." In *La parataxe: Entre dépendance et intégration*, ed. M.-J. Béguelin, M. Avanzi, and G. Corminboeuf, 3–33. Bern.

Bekker, I. 1845. *Herodoti De bello persico libri novem*. Berlin.

———. 1863. *Homerische Blätter* I. Bonn.

Bell, D. M. 1998. "Cancellative Discourse Markers: A Core/Periphery Approach." *Pragmatics* 8:515–541.

———. 2009. "Mind You." *Journal of Pragmatics* 41:915–920.

Belli, G. 1987. "Aristotele e Posidonio sul significato del 'syndesmos.'" *Aevum* 61:105–107.

Benfey, T. 1839-1842. *Griechisches Wurzellexikon* I. Berlin. https://www.digitale-sammlungen.de/de/view/bsb10584794?page=5.

Benedetto, V. di. 1958. "Dionisio Trace e la Techne a lui attribuita." *Annali Classe di Lettere e Filosofia della Scuola Normale Superiore di Pisa* 27:169–210.

———. 1959. "Dionisio Trace e la Techne a lui attribuita (continuazione e fine)." *Annali della Scuola Normale Superiore di Pisa. Classe di Lettere e Filosofia* 28:87–118.

———. 1973. "La Techne spuria." *Annali della Scuola Normale Superiore di Pisa. Classe di Lettere e Filosofia* 3:797–814.

———. 1990. "At the Origins of Greek Grammar." *Glotta* 60:19–39.

Bennekom, R. van. 1975. "The Definitions of ΣΥΝΔΕΣΜΟΣ and ΑΡΘΡΟΝ in Aristotle, 'Poetics' Ch. 20." *Mnemosyne* 28:399–411.

Bentein, K. 2015. "Particle-usage in Documentary Papyri (I–IV AD): An Integrated, Sociolinguistically-informed Approach." *Greek, Roman and Byzantine Studies* 55:721–753.

Berettoni, P. 1969. "Ricerche sulla frase interrogativa in greco antico." *Annali della Scuola Normale Superiore di Pisa* 38:39–97.

Bergaigne, A. 1877. *De coniunctivi et optativi in indoeuropaeis linguis informatione et vi antiquissima*. Paris.

Bergen, G. van, R. van Gijn, L. Hogeweg, and S. Lestrade. 2011. "Discourse Marking and the Subtle Art of Mind-Reading: The Case of Dutch *eigenlijk*." *Journal of Pragmatics* 43:3877–3892.

Berrendonner, A. 1990. "Pour une macro-syntaxe." *Travaux de Linguistique* 21:25–36.

Berrendonner, A., and M.-J. Reichler-Béguelin. 1995. "Accords associatifs." In *Référence, inférence: l'anaphore associative*, ed. G. Kleiber and C. Schnedecker, 21–42. Montpellier.

Bertrand, N. 2010. L'ordre des mots chez Homère: structure informationnelle, localisation et progression du récit. PhD diss., University of Lille.

Bertuccelli Papi, M. 2009. "Implicitness." In *Key Notions for Pragmatics*, ed. J. Verschueren and J.-O. Östman, 139–162. Amsterdam.

Besselaar, J. J. van den. 1958. "As Partículas Gregas." *Boletim de Estudos Clássicos* 2:117–130.

———. 1962. "Estudo Lexicográfico do Particula ἄρα." *Boletim de Estudos Clássicos* 5:221–265.

Besslich, S. 1966. *Schweigen-verschweigen-übergehen: die Darstellung des Unausgesprochenen in der Odyssee*. Heidelberg.

Bestgen, Y., and W. Vonk. 1995. "The Role of Temporal Segmentation Markers in Discourse Processing." *Discourse Processes* 19:385–406.

Bétant, É. A. A. 1843. *Lexicon Thucydideum*. Geneva.

Beye, C. R. 1964. "Homeric Battle Narrative and Catalogues." *Harvard Studies in Classical Philology* 68:345–373.

Biber, D. 1988. *Variation across Speech and Writing*. Cambridge.

———. 1994. "An Analytical Framework for Register Studies." In *Sociolinguistic Perspectives on Register*, ed. D. Biber and E. Finegan, 31–56. New York.

———. 1995. *Dimensions of Register Variation: A Cross-Linguistic Comparison*. Cambridge.

———. 2006. *University Language: A Corpus-Based Study of Spoken and Written Registers*. Amsterdam.

———. 2010. "Corpus-Based and Corpus-Driven Analyses of Language Variation and Use." In *The Oxford Handbook of Linguistic Analysis*, ed. B. Heine and H. Narrog, 159–191. Oxford.

Biber, D., S. Conrad, and R. Reppen. 1998. *Corpus Linguistics: Investigating Language Structure and Use*. Cambridge.

Bierl, A. F. 2001. *Der Chor in der alten Komödie: Ritual und Performativität*. Munich.

Bierl, A. F., F. Graf, and J. Latacz, eds. 2013. *Homers Ilias: Gesamtkommentar*. Basel.

Biraud, M. 2010. *Les interjections du théâtre grec antique: Étude sémantique et pragmatique*. Louvain-la-Neuve.

Birkler, W. 1867. *Die oratorischen Transitions- und Argumentations-Phrasen τί δέ; τί δέ δή; τί οὖν; τί δαί; τί δῆτα;*. Ehingen and Tübingen.

Bischoff, H. 1932. *Der Warner bei Herodot*. Leipzig.

Bjorkman, B. M. 2010. "Towards a Unified Asymmetric Semantics for *and*." *On Linguistic Interfaces* II:1-13.

Blake, N. F. 1996. *Essays on Shakespeare's Language: 1st series*. Misterton.

Blakemore, D. 1987. *Semantic Constraints on Relevance*. Oxford.

———. 1988. "So as a Constraint on Relevance." In *Mental Representations: The Interface between Language and Reality*, ed. R. M. Kempson, 183–195. Cambridge.

———. 1989. "Denial and Contrast: A Relevance Theoretic Analysis of *but*." *Linguistics and Philosophy* 12:15–37.

———. 1992. *Understanding Utterances: An Introduction to Pragmatics*. Oxford.

———. 2000. "Indicators and Procedures: *nevertheless* and *but*." *Journal of Linguistics* 36:463–486.

———. 2002. *Relevance and Linguistic Meaning : The Semantics and Pragmatics of Discourse Markers*. Cambridge.

Blakemore, D., and R. Carston. 2005. "The Pragmatics of Sentential Coordination with *and*." *Lingua* 115:569–589.

Blank, D. 1983. "Remarks on Nicanor, the Stoics, and the Ancient Theory of Punctuation." *Glotta* 61:48–67.

Blank, D. L. 1982. *Ancient Philosophy and Grammar: The Syntax of Apollonius Dyscolus*. Chico, CA.

Blankenborg, R. 2015. Audible Punctuation: Performative Pause in Homeric Prosody. PhD diss., University of Nijmegen.

Blass, F. 1887. *Die Attische Beredsamkeit: Von Gorgias bis zu Lysias* I. 2nd ed. Leipzig.

———. 1906. *Aeschylos' Choephoren*. Halle.

Blass, R. 1990. *Relevance Relations in Discourse: A Study with Special Reference to Sissala*. Cambridge.

Bloch, A. 1955. "Was bedeutet das 'epische' τε?" *Museum Helveticum* 12:145–153.

Block, E. 1982. "The Narrator Speaks: Apostrophe in Homer and Vergil." *Transactions of the American Philological Association* 112:7–22.

Blomqvist, J. 1969. *Greek Particles in Hellenistic Prose*. Lund.

———. 1974. "Juxtaposed τε καί in Post-Classical Prose." *Hermes* 102:170–178.

———. 1979. *Das sogenannte KAI adversativum. Zur Semantik einer griechischen Partikel.* Uppsala.

———. 1981. "On Adversative Coordination in Ancient Greek and as a Universal Linguistic Phenomenon." *Acta Societatis Linguisticae Upsaliensis. Nova Series* 3:57–70.

———. 1995. "ἀλλά… μήν, ἀλλά… μέντοι, and Atticistic Particle Usage." *Eranos* 93:3–23.

Bloomfield, M. 1885. "Four Etymological Notes." *American Journal of Philology* 6:44–46.

Blühdorn, H. 2008. "Subordination and Coordination in Syntax, Semantics and Discourse: Evidence from the Study of Connectives." In *"Subordination" versus "Coordination" in Sentence and Text: A Cross-Linguistic Perspective*, ed. C. Fabricius-Hansen and W. Ramm, 59–85. Amsterdam.

Boas, H. C., ed. 2010. *Contrastive Studies in Construction Grammar*. Amsterdam.

Bodin, L., and P. Mazon. 1919 [1902]. *Extraits d'Aristophane et de Ménandre*. Paris.

Boegehold, A. L. 1999. *When a Gesture Was Expected: A Selection of Examples from Archaic and Classical Greek Literature*. Princeton.

Bois, J. W. du. 2003. "Argument Structure: Grammar in Use." In *Preferred Argument Structure: Grammar as Architecture for Function*, ed. J. W. Du Bois, L. E. Kumpf, and W. J. Ashby, 11–60. Amsterdam.

———. 2007. "The Stance Triangle." In *Stancetaking in Discourse: Subjectivity, Evaluation, Interaction*, ed. R. Englebretson, 139–182. Amsterdam.

———. 2010 [2001]. "Towards a Dialogic Syntax." Unpublished paper.

———. 2011. "Co-Opting Intersubjectivity: Dialogic Rhetoric of the Self." In *The Rhetorical Emergence of Culture*, ed. C. Meyer and F. Girke, 52–83. New York.

———. 2014. "Towards a Dialogic Syntax." *Cognitive Linguistics* 25:359–410.

Bois, J. W. du, and R. Giora. 2014. "From Cognitive-Functional Linguistics to Dialogic Syntax." *Cognitive Linguistics* 25:351–357.

Bois, J. W. du, and E. Kärkkäinen. 2012. "Taking a Stance on Emotion: Affect, Sequence, and Intersubjectivity in Dialogic Interaction." *Text & Talk* 32:433–451.

Boisacq, E. 1916. *Dictionnaire étymologique de la langue grecque*. Paris.

Bolden, G. B. 2006. "Little Words That Matter: Discourse Markers 'So' and 'Oh' and the Doing of Other-Attentiveness in Social Interaction." *Journal of Communication* 56:661–688.

———. 2008. "Reopening Russian Conversations: The Discourse Particle '-to' and the Negotiation of Interpersonal Accountability in Closings." *Human Communication Research* 34:99–136.

———. 2009. "Implementing Incipient Actions: The Discourse Marker 'so' in English Conversation." *Journal of Pragmatics* 41:974–998.

Bolinger, D. 1989. *Intonation and Its Uses*. Stanford.

Bolkestein, A. M. 1996. "Free but Not Arbitrary: 'Emotive' Word Order in Latin?" In *On Latin: Linguistic and Literary Studies in Honour of Harm Pinkster*, ed. R. Risselada, J. R. de Jong, and A. M. Bolkestein, 7–24. Amsterdam.

Bollack, J. 1990. *L'Oedipe Roi de Sophocle*. Lille.

Bolling, G. M. 1902. "καίτοι with the Participle." *American Journal of Philology* 23:319–321.

———. 1929. "The Meaning of που in Homer." *Language* 5:100–105.

———. 1935. "Review of Denniston, *The Greek Particles*." *Language* 11:260–262.

———. 1960. "Description of ἐπεί Syntax in Homer." *Glotta* 38:18–38.

Bolly, C., and L. Degand. 2013. "Have You Seen What I Mean? From Verbal Constructions to Discourse Markers." *Journal of Historical Pragmatics* 14:210–235.

Bond, G. W. 1981. *Euripides. Heracles*. Oxford.

Bonifazi, A. 2001. *Mescolare un cratere di canti: pragmatica della poesia epinicia in Pindaro*. Alessandria.

———. 2004a. "Communication in Pindar's Deictic Acts." *Arethusa* 37:391–414.

———. 2004b. "Relative Pronouns and Memory: Pindar beyond Syntax." *Harvard Studies in Classical Philology* 102:41–68.

———. 2004c. "Κεῖνος in Pindar: Between Grammar and Poetic Intention." *Classical Philology* 99:283–299.

———. 2008. "Memory and Visualization in Homeric Discourse Markers." In *Orality, Literacy, Memory in the Ancient Greek and Roman World*, ed. E. A. Mackay, 35–64. Leiden.

———. 2009. "The Pragmatic Meanings of Some Discourse Markers in Homer." In *Pragmatische Kategorien: Form, Funktion und Diachronie*, ed. E. Rieken and P. Widmer, 29–36. Wiesbaden.

———. 2010. "Anaphoric Pronouns αὐτός and κεῖνος in Homer: A Cognitive-Pragmatic Approach." In *La Morfologia del Greco tra Tipologia e Diacronia*, ed. Pierluigi Cuzzolin, G. F. Nieddu, G. Paulis, and I. Putzu, 97–114. Pavia.

———. 2012. *Homer's Versicolored Fabric: The Evocative Power of Ancient Greek Epic Word-Making*. Washington, DC.

———. 2015. "Problematizing Syndetic Coordination: Ancient Greek 'and' from Homer to Aristophanes." In *Perspectives on Historical Syntax*, ed. C. Viti, 251–269. Amsterdam.

———. 2018. "Embedded focalization and free indirect speech in Homer as viewpoint blending." In *Homer in Performance: Rhapsodes, Narrators, and Characters*, ed. J. Ready and C. Tsagalis, 230-254. Austin.

———. 2019. "Autos and the Center-Periphery Image Schema." In *Towards a Cognitive Classical Linguistics: The Embodied Basis of Constructions in Greek and Latin*, ed. W. M. Short and E. Mocciaro, 126-148. Berlin.

Bonifazi, A., and D. F. Elmer. 2012a. "Composing Lines, Performing Acts: Clauses, Discourse Acts, and Melodic Units in a South Slavic Epic Song." In *Orality, Literacy and Performance in the Ancient World*, ed. E. Minchin, 89–109. Leiden.

———. 2012b. "The Meaning of Melody: Remarks on the Performance-Based Analysis of Bosniac Epic Song." In *Child's Children: Ballad Study and Its Legacies*, ed. J. Harris and B. Hillers, 293–309. Trier.

———. 2016. "Visuality in Bosniac and Homeric Epic." *Classics@* 14. Washington, DC. https://chs.harvard.edu/classics14-bonifazi-and-elmer/

Bonitz, H. 1854. *Beiträge zur Erklärung des Thukydides*. Vienna.

———. 1867. "Über den Gebrauch von τε γάρ bei Aristoteles." *Zeitschrift für die österreichischen Gymnasien* 18:672–682.

———. 1870. *Index aristotelicus*. Berlin.

Bonner, R. J. 1920. "The Book Divisions of Thucydides." *Classical Philology* 15:73–82.

Boogaart, R. 2009. "Semantics and Pragmatics in Construction Grammar: The Case of Modal Verbs." In *Contexts and Constructions*, ed. A. Bergs and G. Diewald, 213–241. Amsterdam.

Bopp, F. 1833. *Vergleichende Grammatik des Sanskrit, Zend, Griechischen, Lateinischen, Litthauischen, Gothischen und Deutschen*. Berlin.

Borochovsky Bar-Aba, E. 2003. "Punctuation Marks: Procedural and Conceptual Uses." *Journal of Pragmatics* 35:1031–1048.

Bothe, F. H. 1829. *Aristophanis Aves*. Leipzig.

Bouma, G., P. Hendriks, and J. Hoeksema. 2007. "Focus Particles inside Prepositional Phrases: A Comparison of Dutch, English, and German." *Journal of Comparative Germanic Linguistics* 10:1–24.

Bornemann, E., and E. Risch. 1978. *Griechische Grammatik*. 2nd ed. Frankfurt and Berlin.

Bower, A. R. 1997. "Deliberative Action Constructs: Reference and Evaluation in Narrative." In *Toward a Social Science of Language* II, ed. G. R. Guy, C. Feagin, D. Schiffrin, and J. Baugh, 57–76. Amsterdam.

Bower, G. H., J. B. Black, and T. J. Turner. 1979. "Scripts in Memory for Text." *Cognitive Psychology* 11:177–220.

Bowie, A. M. 2007. *Herodotus. Histories. Book VIII*. Cambridge Greek and Latin Classics. Cambridge.

———. 2013. *Homer. Odyssey, Books XIII and XIV*. Cambridge.

Brandt, P. 1898. *De particularum subiunctivarum apud Pindarum usu*. Leipzig.

Brandt, W. 1908. *Griechische Temporalpartikeln vornehmlich im ionischen und dorischen Dialekt*. Göttingen.

Brannan, R. 2008. "The Discourse Function of ἀλλά in Non-Negative Contexts." Presentation at the Evangelical Theological Society's 60th National Meeting, Providence, RI, November 19-21.

Braswell, B. K. 1988. *A Commentary on the Fourth Pythian Ode of Pindar*. Berlin.

Breitenbach, L. 1841. "Über die Partikeln οὔκουν und οὐκοῦν." *Zeitschrift für Altertumswissenschaft* 8:105–112.

Bremond, C. 1973. *Logique du récit*. Paris.

Brewster, C. 1992. "Discourse and Relevance: The Case of Modern Greek *lipon*." In *Studies in Greek Linguistics: Proceedings of the 12th Annual Meeting of the Department of

Linguistics, Faculty of Philosophy, Aristotle University of Thessaloniki, 18–20 April 1991, ed. G. Beloudes, 357-375. Thessaloniki.

Bright, W., ed. 1966. *Sociolinguistics: Proceedings of the UCLA Sociolinguistics Conference, Los Angeles, May 1964*. The Hague.

Brinkmann, A. 1913. "Lückenbüsser (μέντοι γε, καίτοι γε)." *Rheinisches Museum* 68:320.

Brinton, L. J. 1990. "The Development of Discourse Markers in English." In *Historical Linguistics and Philology*, ed. J. Fisiak, 45–71. Berlin.

———. 1996. *Pragmatic Markers in English: Grammaticalization and Discourse Functions*. Berlin.

———. 2006. "Pathways in the Development of Pragmatic Markers in English." In *The Handbook of the History of English*, ed. A. van Kemenade and B. Los, 307–334. Malden, MA.

Brisard, F., J.-O. Östman, and J. Verschueren, eds. 2009. *Grammar, Meaning and Pragmatics*. Amsterdam.

Briz, A., and M. Estellés. 2010. "On the Relationship between Attenuation, Discourse Particles and Position." In *New Approaches to Hedging*, ed. G. Kaltenböck, W. Mihatsch, and S. Schneider, 289–304. Bingley.

Broadhead, H. D. 1960. *Aeschylus. Persae*. Cambridge.

Brock, R. 2003. "Authorial Voice and Narrative Management in Herodotus." In *Herodotus and His World*, ed. R. Derow and P. Parker, 3–16. Oxford.

Brody, J. 1987. "Particles Borrowed from Spanish as Discourse Markers in Mayan Languages." *Anthropological Linguistics* 29:507–521.

Bromig, G. 1879. *De asyndeti natura et apud Aeschylum usu*. Münster.

Broschmann, M. 1882. *De γάρ particulae usu herodoteo*. Leipzig.

Brouwer, S. 1975. *Een studie over enige archaïsche elementen in de stijl van Herodotus*. Utrecht.

Brown, G., and G. Yule. 1983. *Discourse Analysis*. Cambridge.

Brown, H. P. 2006. "Addressing Agamemnon: A Pilot Study of Politeness and Pragmatics in the *Iliad*." *Transactions of the American Philological Association* 136:1–46.

Brown, P., and S. Levinson. 1978. "Universals in Language Usage: Politeness Phenomena." In *Questions and Politeness: Strategies in Social Interaction*, ed. E. N. Goody, 56–311. Cambridge.

Brownson, C. L. 1922. *Xenophon. Anabasis*. London.

Brownson, C. L. 1980. *Xenophon. Anabasis*. Cambridge, MA.

Brugmann, K. 1883. "Über ἄρα, ἄρ, ῥα und Litauisch *ir*." *Sitzungsberichte der Gesellschaft der Wissenschaft zu Leipzig* 1-2:37–70.

———. 1897. *Grundriss der vergleichenden Grammatik der indogermanischen Sprachen: Vergleichende Laut-, Stammbildungs- und Flexionslehre*. 2nd ed. Straßburg.

———. 1904. *Die Demonstrativpronomina der indogermanischen Sprachen: eine bedeutungsgeschichtliche Untersuchung*. Leipzig.

Brugmann, K., and B. Delbrück. 1900. *Grundriss der vergleichenden Grammatik der indogermanischen Sprachen*. Stuttgart.

Brugmann, K., and A. Thumb. 1913. *Griechische Grammatik*. Munich.

Bruijnen, S., and S. Sudhoff. 2013. "Wir müssen sowieso erst herausfinden, was das überhaupt bedeutet. Die Partikeln *sowieso* und *überhaupt* im Deutschen und Niederländischen." *Germanistische Mitteilungen* 39:79–104.

Buchwald, O. 1865. *De interrogativarum ἦ et οὔκουν particularum apud graecos poetas tragicos usu*. Breslau.

Buck, C. D. 1955. *The Greek Dialects*. 3rd ed. Chicago.

Budelmann, F. 1998. "Review of S. Pfeiffer-Petersen, *Konfliktstichomythien bei Sophokles: Funktion und Gestaltung*." *The Classical Review*, n.s. 48:5–7.

———. 2000. *The Language of Sophocles: Communality, Communication, and Involvement*. Cambridge.

Budelmann, F., and P. E. Easterling. 2010. "Reading Minds in Greek Tragedy." *Greece & Rome* 57:289–303.

Budé, G. 1556 [1529]. *Commentarii linguae graecae*. Paris. https://play.google.com/store/books/details?id=AVCflAobFkkC&rdid=book-AVCflAobFkkC&rdot=1.

Buffing, P. 2011. "'Ik heb het wel gezegd dat je beter bij mij kon blijven!' [On Character Changes in Euripides' Medea as Reflected in Her Language Use.]." Unpublished paper. Amsterdam.

Bühler, K. 1965. *Sprachtheorie*. 2nd ed. Jena.

Buijs, M. 2005. *Clause Combining in Ancient Greek Narrative Discourse. The Distribution of Subclauses and Participial Clauses in Xenophon's Hellenica and Anabasis*. Leiden.

———. 2007. "Aspectual Differences and Narrative Technique: Xenophon's *Hellenica & Agesilaus*." In *The Language of Literature: Linguistic Approaches to Classical Texts*, ed. R. J. Allan and M. Buijs, 122–153. Leiden.

Bundy, E. L. 1962. *Studia pindarica*. Berkeley.

Burguière, P. 1960. *Histoire de l'infinitif en grec*. Paris.

Burkert, W. 1972. *Homo necans: Interpretationen altgriechischer Opferriten und Mythen*. Berlin.

Burton, R. W. B. 1962. *Pindar's Pythian Odes: Essays in Interpretation*. Oxford.

———. 1980. *The Chorus in Sophocles' Tragedies*. Oxford.

Bury, J. B. 1890. *The Nemean Odes of Pindar*. London.

———. 1892a. *The Isthmian Odes of Pindar*. London.

———. 1892b. "μέν... τε. Appendix A." In *Isthmian Odes of Pindar*, ed. J. B. Bury, 153–161. London.

Bury, R. G. 1926. *Plato. Laws*. London.

Buttmann, P. 1825. "εὖτε, ἦὖτε, δεῦτε." In *Lexilogus, oder Beiträge zur griechischen Wort-Erklärung, hauptsächlich für Homer und Hesiod* II, 227–233. Berlin.

———. 1841. "Excursus XII: De particula δέ in apodosi." In *Demosthenis oratio in Midiam: Cum annotatione critica et exegetica*, 153-164. 3rd ed. Berlin.

Buxton, R. G. A. 1982. *Persuasion in Greek Tragedy*. Cambridge.

Bybee, J. L. 2010. "Chunking and Degrees of Autonomy." In *Language, Usage and Cognition*, ed. J. L. Bybee, 33–56. Cambridge.

Bybee, J. L. 2010. *Language, Usage and Cognition*. Cambridge.

Bybee, J. L., and P. J. Hopper, eds. 2001. *Frequency and the Emergence of Linguistic Structure*. Amsterdam.

Byron, P. A., and D. K. Heeman. 1998. "Discourse Marker Use in Task-Oriented Spoken Dialog." *Technical Report* 664:1–28.

Bywater, I. 1892. "Apodotic δέ." In *Nicomachean Ethics, 34*. Oxford.

Caffi, C. 2006. "Pragmatic Presupposition." In *Encyclopedia of Language and Linguistics*, ed. E. K. Brown and A. Anderson, 17–25. 2nd ed. Amsterdam.

———. 2010. "Weakening or Strengthening? A Case of Enantiosemy in Plato's *Gorgias*." In *New Approaches to Hedging*, ed. G. Kaltenböck, W. Mihatsch, and S. Schneider, 181–202. Bingley.

Caffi, C., and R. W. Janney. 1994. "Toward a Pragmatics of Emotive Communication." *Journal of Pragmatics* 22:325–373.

Cagnazzi, S. 1975. "Tavola dei 28 *logoi* di Erodoto." *Hermes* 103:385–423.

Cairns, D. L. 2003. "Ethics, Ethology, Terminology: Iliadic Anger and the Cross-Cultural Study of Emotion." In *Ancient Anger: Perspectives from Homer to Galen*, ed. S. Braund and G. W. Most, 11–49. Cambridge.

———. 2008. "Look Both Ways: Studying Emotion in Ancient Greek." *Critical Quarterly* 50:43–62.

Cairns, F. 2011. "Money and the Poet: The First Stasimon of Pindar *Isthmian 2*." *Mnemosyne* 64:21–36.

Calame, C. 1985. "L'impact du passage de l'oral à l'écrit sur l'énoncé de l'énonciation dans la littérature de la Grèce archaïque." In *Oralità: Cultura, letteratura, discorso. Atti del convegno internazionale (Urbino 21-25 Luglio 1980)*, ed. B. Gentili and G. Paioni, 101–118. Rome.

———. 2009. "Fra racconto eroico e poesia rituale: Il soggetto poetico che canta il mito (Pindaro, *Olimpica* 6)." *Quaderni Urbinati di Cultura Classica* 92:11–26.

———. 2013. "Choral Polyphony and the Ritual Functions of Tragic Songs." In *Choral Mediations in Greek Tragedy*, ed. R. Gagné and M. Govers Hopman, 35–58. Cambridge.

Callipo, M. 2011. *Dionisio Trace e la tradizione grammaticale*. Rome.

Callow, K. 1992. "The Disappearing 'de' in 1 Corinthians." In *Linguistics and New Testament Interpretation*, ed. D. A. Black, 183–193. Nashville.

Campbell, L. 1867. "The Sophist and Statesman of Plato. General Introduction." In *The Sophistes and Politicus of Plato*, i-xc. Oxford.

———. 1894. *Plato's Republic* II. Oxford.

Canakis, C. 1995. KAI: The Story of a Conjunction. PhD diss., University of Chicago.

Capelle, C. 1877. "γάρ (Review of Pfudel and Sernatinger)." *Philologus* 36:700–710.

Carbaugh, D. 2005. *Cultures in Conversation*. London.

Carey, C. 1991. "The Victory Ode in Performance: The Case for the Chorus." *Classical Philology* 86:192–200.

Carnuth, O. 1875. *Nicanoris Peri odysseiakīs stigmīs reliquiae emendatiores*. Berlin.

Carston, R. 2002. *Thoughts and Utterances: The Pragmatics of Explicit Communication*. Oxford.

Carston, R., and S. Uchida. 1998. *Relevance Theory: Applications and Implications*. Amsterdam.

Carter, D. M. 2007. *The Politics of Greek Tragedy*. Exeter.

Caspers, C. 2010. "The Pragmatic Function and Textual Status of Euripidean οὔ που and ἦ που." *Classical Quarterly* 60:327–344.

Cauer, P. 1889. "Zur homerischen Interpunktion." *Rheinisches Museum* 44:347–368.

———. 1914. *Die Kunst des Übersetzens*. 5th ed. Berlin.

Cavallin, A. 1941. "(τὸ) λοιπόν. Eine bedeutungsgeschichtliche Untersuchung." *Eranos* 39:121–144.

Cavallo, G., ed. 2008. *Hellenistic Bookhands*. Berlin.

Celle, A., and R. Huart. 2007. "Connectives as Discourse Landmarks: Introduction." In *Connectives as Discourse Landmarks*, ed. A. Celle and R. Huart, 1–11. Amsterdam.

Cesare, A.-M. De. 2010. "On the Focusing Function of Focusing Adverbs: A Discussion Based on Italian Data." *Linguistik Online* 44: https://bop.unibe.ch/linguistik-online/article/view/406/643.

Chafe, W. L. 1976. "Givenness, Contrastiveness, Definiteness, Subjects, Topics, and Point of View." In *Subject and Topic*, ed. C. N. Li, 25–55. New York.

———. 1979. "The Flow of Thought and the Flow of Language." In *Syntax and Semantics. Vol. 12: Discourse and Syntax*, ed. T. Givón, 159–181. New York.

———, ed. 1980. *The Pear Stories: Cognitive, Cultural, and Linguistic Aspects of Narrative Production*. Norwood, NJ.

———. 1982. "Integration and Involvement In Speaking, Writing, and Oral Literature." In *Spoken and Written Language*, ed. D. Tannen, 35–53. Norwood, NJ.

———. 1985. "Speaking, Writing, and Prescriptivism." In *Georgetown University Round Table*, ed. D. Schiffrin, 95–103. Cambridge.

———. 1987. "Cognitive Constraints on Information Flow." In *Coherence and Grounding in Discourse*, ed. R. S. Tomlin, 21–51. Amsterdam.

———. 1988a. "Linking Intonation Units in Spoken English." In *Clause Combining in Grammar and Discourse*, ed. J. Haiman and S. A. Thompson, 1–27. Amsterdam.

———. 1988b. "Punctuation and the Prosody of Written Language." *Written Communication* 5:395–426.

———. 1994. *Discourse, Consciousness, and Time: The Flow and Displacement of Conscious Experience in Speaking and Writing*. Chicago.

———. 1997. "The Interplay of Syntax and Prosody in the Expression of Thoughts." *Proceedings of the Annual Meeting of the Berkeley Linguistics Society* 23:389–401.

———. 2001. "The Analysis of Discourse Flow." In *The Handbook of Discourse Analysis*, ed. H. E. Hamilton, D. Tannen, and D. Schiffrin, 671–687. Oxford.

Chanet, A.-M. 1979. "Ἕως et πρίν en grec classique." *Revue des Études Grecques* 92:166–207.

———. 1990. "Négation sur parataxe et structures apparentées en grec : Comment se construit l'interprétation globale." *L'information Grammaticale* 46:28–33.

Chang, M.-H., and H.-Y. Su. 2012. "To Mark or Not to Mark the Cause, That Is the Question: Causal Marking in Taiwanese Conversation." *Journal of Pragmatics* 44:1743–1763.

Chaniotis, A., ed. 2012. *Sources and methods for the study of emotions in the Greek world*. Stuttgart.

Chaniotis, A., and P. Ducrey, eds. 2013. *Unveiling Emotions II: Emotions in Greece and Rome: Texts, Images, Material Culture*. Stuttgart.

Chantraine, P. 1927. *Histoire du parfait grec*. Paris.

———. 1933. *La formation des noms en grec ancien*. Paris.

———. 1942. *Grammaire homérique*. Vol. 1: *Morphologie*. Paris.

———. 1953a. *Grammaire homérique*. Vol. 2: *Syntaxe*. Paris.

———. 1953b. "Remarques sur certaines particules homériques & la structure de la phrase complexe et la parataxe." In *Grammaire homérique* II, 340–364. Paris.

———. 1956. *Études sur le vocabulaire grec*. Paris.

———. 1961. *Morphologie historique du grec*. Paris.

———. 2009. *Dictionnaire étymologique de la langue grecque: Histoire des mots*. Ed. J. Taillardat, O. Masson, and J.-L. Perpillou. Revised edition. Paris.

Chapman, R. W. 1911. "ἀλλά… μέν." *The Classical Review* 25:204–205.

Chomsky, N. 1965. *Aspects of the Theory of Syntax*. Cambridge, MA.

Chomsky, N., and J. A. McGilvray. 2012. *The Science of Language*. Cambridge.

Christ, M. R. 2013. "Herodotean Kings and Historical Inquiry." In *Herodotus* I, ed. R. Vignolo Munson, 212–250. Oxford.

Christ, W. von. 1880. "Der Gebrauch der griechischen Partikel τε mit besonderer bezugnahme auf Homer." In *Sitzungsberichte der Königliche Bayerische Akademie der Wissenschaften*, 25–76. https://publikationen.badw.de/de/007459045/pdf/CC%20BY.

Christidis, A. P. 1987. "On the Interplay of Deixis and Anaphora in the History of Greek: Ancient Greek ἦν, ἵνα, Modern Greek νά, να." *Minos* 20-22:97–111.

Christodoulidou, M. 2011. "Lexical Markers within the University Lecture." *Novitas-ROYAL (Research on Youth and Language)* 5:143–160.

Clark, H. H. 1996. *Using Language*. Cambridge.

Clark, H. H., and E. V. Clark. 1977. *Psychology and Language: An Introduction to Psycholinguistics*. New York.

Clark, H. H., and C. R. Marshall. 1981. "Definite Reference and Mutual Knowledge." In *Elements of Discourse Understanding*, ed. I. Sag, A. K. Joshi, and B. Webber, 10–63. Cambridge.

Clark, M. 1997. *Out of Line: Homeric Composition beyond the Hexameter*. Lanham, MD.

Clarke, M. 2010. "Semantics and Vocabulary." In Bakker 2010:120–133. Chichester.

Classen, J. 1854. *Beobachtungen über den homerischen Sprachgebrauch.* Frankfurt.

———. 1859. "[Review of Ameis' edition of Homer's *Odyssey*]." *Neue Jahrbücher für Philologie und Pädagogik* 79:306.

———. 1862. *Thukydides* I. Berlin.

———. 1879. *Beobachtungen über den homerischen Sprachgebrauch.* 2nd ed. Frankfurt.

Classen, J., and J. Steup. 1892–1922. *Thukydides. Erklärt von J. Classen.* 3rd ed. 8 vols. Berlin.

Clayman, S. E. 2013. "Turn-Constructional Units and the Transition-Relevance Place." In *The Handbook of Conversation Analysis*, ed. J. Sidnell and T. Stivers, 150–166. Malden, MA.

Cleef, F. L. van. 1895. *Index Antiphonteus.* Ithaca, NY.

Clemoes, P. 1952. *Liturgical Influence on Punctuation in Late Old English and Early Middle English Manuscripts.* Cambridge.

Cobet, C. G. 1856. *Novae lectiones.* Leiden.

———. 1873. *Variae lectiones.* Leiden.

———. 1875. "Homerica." *Mnemosyne* 3:359–373.

———. 1876. *Miscellanea critica quibus continentur observationes criticae in scriptores praesertim Homerum et Demosthenem.* Leiden.

Cobet, J. 1971. "Herodots Exkurse und die Frage der Einheit seines Werkes." *Historia* 17:171–176.

Cogan, M. 1981. *The Human Thing: The Speeches and Principles of Thucydides' History.* Chicago.

Cohen, E. 2007. "Discourse Markers: Cotext and Context Sensitivity." *Proceedings of the Israeli Linguistic Society* 16:v – xxiii.

Cohen, G. L. 1988. "Origin of the Greek Particle *de*." In *Pursuit of Linguistic Insight*, ed. G. L. Cohen, 135–136. Rolla.

Cohn, L. 1882. "μέντοι." *Hermes* 17:645–647.

Cole, T. 1987. "1 + 1 = 3: Studies in Pindar's Arithmetic." *American Journal of Philology* 108:553–568.

———. 1988. *Epiploke: Rhythmical Continuity and Poetic Structure in Greek Lyric Verse.* Cambridge, MA.

Cole Babbitt, F. 1901. "The Use of μή in Questions." *Harvard Studies in Classical Philology* 12:307–317.

Collard, C. 2005. "Colloquial Language in Tragedy: A Supplement to the Work of P. T. Stevens." *The Classical Quarterly* 55:350–386.

———. 2007. "On Stichomythia." In *Tragedy, Euripides and Euripideans: Selected Papers*, ed. C. Collard, 16–30. Bristol.

Collinge, N. E. 1988. "Thoughts on the Pragmatics of Ancient Greek." *Proceedings of the Cambridge Philological Society* 214:1–13.

Collins, C. 1991. *The Poetics of the Mind's Eye: Literature and the Psychology of Imagination.* Philadelphia.

Collins, D. 2004. *Master of the Game: Competition and Performance in Greek Poetry*. Washington, DC.

Collitz, H. 1895. "The Etymology of ἄρα and μάψ." *Transactions of the American Philological Association* 26:xxxix – xl. http://www.jstor.org/stable/2935698?seq=39.

Comrie, B. 1976. *Aspect*. Cambridge.

———. 1985. *Tense*. Cambridge.

Conacher, D. J. 1998. *Euripides and the Sophists*. London.

Connor, W. R. 1984. *Thucydides*. Princeton.

———. 1985. "Narrative Discourse in Thucydides." In *The Greek Historians: Literature and History. Papers Presented to A. E. Raubitschek*, ed. M. H. Jameson, 1–17. Stanford.

Conrad, S., and D. Biber. 2000. "Adverbial Marking of Stance in Speech and Writing." In *Evaluation in Text: Authorial Stance and the Construction of Discourse*, ed. S. Hunston and G. Thompson, 56–73. New York.

———, eds. 2001. *Variation in English: Multi-Dimensional Studies*. Harlow.

Considine, P. 1966. "Some Homeric Terms for Anger." *Acta Classica: Proceedings of the Classical Association of South Africa* 9:15–25.

Conte, M. E. 1999. *Condizioni di coerenza*. Alessandria.

Conti, L. 2014. "El espectro funcional de οὕτω(ς) en los poemas homéricos." *Emerita* 82:25–49.

Cook, A. 1992. "Particles, Qualification, Ordering, Style, Irony and Meaning in Plato's Dialogues." *Quaderni Urbinati di Cultura Classica* 40:111–126.

Cook-Gumperz, J., and J. J. Gumperz. 1976. "Context in Children's Speech." In *Papers on Language and Context*, ed. J. Cook-Gumperz and J. J. Gumperz, 1–26. Berkeley.

Cooper, G. L., III. 1974. "Intrusive Oblique Infinitives in Herodotus." *Transactions of the American Philological Association* 104:23–76.

———, after K. W. Krüger. 1998. *Greek Syntax: Attic Greek Prose Syntax* II. Ann Arbor.

———, after K. W. Krüger. 2002. *Greek Syntax: Early Greek Poetic and Herodotean Syntax* IV. Ann Arbor.

Copeland, J. E. 1997. "On the Tarahumara Particle *pa*: An Optional Mode of Delimiting Information Segments." In *The Twenty-Third LACUS Forum 1996*, ed. A. Melby, 313–324. Chapel Hill.

Cornish, F. 1999. *Anaphora, Discourse, and Understanding*. Oxford.

———. 2002. "Anaphora: Lexico-Textual Structure, or Means for Utterance Integration within a Discourse? A Critique of the Functional-Grammar Account." *Linguistics* 40:469–493.

———. 2005. "Degrees of Indirectness: Two Types of Implicit Referents and Their Retrieval via Unaccented Pronouns." In *Anaphora Processing: Linguistic, Cognitive and Computational Modelling*, ed. A. Branco, T. McEnery, and R. Mitkov, 199–220. Amsterdam.

Corrigan, R., E. A. Moravcsik, H. Ouali, and K. Wheatley, eds. 2009. *Formulaic Language. Vol. 1: Distribution and Historical Change*. Amsterdam and Philadelphia.

Corssen, W. 1863. *Kritische Beiträge zur lateinischen Formenlehre*. Leipzig.

Corum, C. 1975. "Basques, Particles, and Babytalk: A Case for Pragmatics." In *Proceedings of the First Annual Meeting of the Berkeley Linguistics Society* 1975:90–99.

Coseriu, E. 1980. "Partikeln und Sprachtypus. Zur strukturell-funktionellen Fragestellung in der Sprachtypologie." In *Wege zur universalien Forschung. Beiträge zum 60. Geburtstag von Hansjakob Seiler*, ed. C. Brettschneider and G. Lehmann, 199–206. Tübingen.

Coulmas, F., ed. 1986. *Direct and Indirect Speech*. Berlin.

Coulon, V, ed. 1958. *Aristophane. Les Oiseaux, Lysistrata*. Trans. H. van Daele. Paris.

Coulon, V., and P. J. de La Combe. 2012. *Aristophane. Les Grenouilles*. Paris.

Couper-Kuhlen, E. 1988. "On the Temporal Interpretation of Postposed *when*-Clauses in Narrative Discourse." In *Papers in Language and Mediaeval Studies Presented to Alfred Schopf*, ed. R. Matthews and F. Schmole-Rostowsky, 353–372. Frankfurt.

———. 1996. "Intonation and Clause Combining in Discourse: The Case of *because*." *Pragmatics* 6:389–426.

———. 2003. "Intonation and Discourse: Current Views from Within." In *The Handbook of Discourse Analysis*, ed. H. E. Hamilton, D. Schiffrin, and D. Tannen, 13–34. Oxford.

———. 2005. "Prosodic Cues of Discourse Units." In *Encyclopedia of Language and Linguistics*, ed. E. K. Brown and A. H. Anderson, 178-182. 2nd ed. Oxford.

Couper-Kuhlen, E., and B. Kortmann, eds. 2000. *Cause, Condition, Concession, Contrast: Cognitive and Discourse Perspectives*. Berlin.

Couper-Kuhlen, E., and M. Selting, eds. 1996. *Prosody and Conversation*. Cambridge.

———. 2001. "Introducing Interactional Linguistics." In *Studies in Interactional Linguistics*, ed. M. Selting and E. Couper-Kuhlen, 1–22. Amsterdam.

Couper-Kuhlen, E., and S. A. Thompson. 2012. "The Grammar of pro-Repeat Responses to Informings in English Conversation." Presentation at Left/Right-Asymmetries in Conversational Language, FRIAS, Freiburg, May 16–17.

Crespo, E. 1997. "Sintaxis de los elementos de relación en griego clásico." In *Actas del IX Congreso Español de Estudios Clásicos* II, ed. F. R. Adrados and A. Martínez Díez, 3–42. Madrid.

———. 2009. "Conjunctive Adverbs in Ancient Greek." In *Early European Languages in the Eyes of Modern Linguistics*, ed. K. Loudová and M. Žáková, 111–20. Brno.

———. 2017. "A Unitary Account of the Meaning of *kaí*." In Denizot and Spevak 2017:257–272.

Crespo, E., J. de la Villa, and A. R. Revuelta. 2006. *Word Classes and Related Topics in Ancient Greek: Proceedings of the Conference on "Greek Syntax and Word Classes" held in Madrid on 18-21 June 2003*. Louvain-la-Neuve.

Cristofaro, S. 2003. *Subordination*. Oxford.

Croft, W. 2001. *Radical Construction Grammar: Syntactic Theory in Typological Perspective.* Oxford.

Croft, W., and D. A. Cruse. 2004. *Cognitive Linguistics.* Cambridge.

Cruttenden, A. 1997. *Intonation.* Cambridge.

Crystal, D. 2008. *"Think on My Words": Exploring Shakespeare's Language.* Cambridge.

Csapo, E. 2002. "Kallippides on the Floor-Sweepings: The Limits of Realism in Classical Acting and Performance Styles." In *Greek and Roman Actors: Aspects of an Ancient Profession*, ed. P. Easterling and E. Hall, 127–147. Cambridge.

Cuenca, M.-J. 2000. "Defining the Indefinable? Interjections." *Syntaxis* 3:29–44.

———. 2006. "Interjections and Pragmatic Errors in Dubbing." *Meta: Journal des traducteurs/Meta: Translators' Journal* 51:20–35.

Cuenca, M.-J., and M.-J. Marín. 2009. "Co-Occurrence of Discourse Markers in Catalan and Spanish Oral Narrative." *Journal of Pragmatics* 41:899–914.

Culy, C. 1997. "Logophoric Pronouns and Point of View." *Linguistics* 35:845–860.

Curtius, G. 1873. *Grundzüge der griechischen Etymologie.* 4th ed. Leipzig.

Cutting, J. 2008. *Pragmatics and Discourse: A Resource Book for Students.* 2nd ed. London.

Cuypers, M. P. 2004. "Apollonius of Rhodes." In *Narrators, Narratees, and Narratives in Ancient Greek Literature*, ed. I. J. F. de Jong, R. Nünlist, and A. Bowie, 43–62. Leiden.

———. 2005. "Interactional Particles and Narrative Voice in Apollonius and Homer." In *Beginning from Apollo: Studies in Apollonius Rhodius and the Argonautic Tradition*, ed. M. P. Cuypers, and M. A. Harder, 35–69. Leuven-La-Neuve.

Daiute, C., and K. A. Nelson. 1997. "Making Sense of the Sense-making Function of Narrative Evaluation." *Journal of Narrative and Life History* 7:207–215.

Dalimier, C. 2001. *Apollonius Dyscole. Traité des conjonctions. Introduction, texte, traduction et commentaire.* Paris.

Dancygier, B. 2012. *The Language of Stories: A Cognitive Approach.* Cambridge.

Dancygier, B., and E. Sweetser. 2000. "Constructions with *if*, *since*, and *because*: Causality, Epistemic Stance, and Clause Order." In *Cause, Condition, Concession, Contrast*, ed. B. Kortmann and E. Couper-Kuhlen, 111–142. Berlin.

———, eds. 2012. *Viewpoint in Language: A Multimodal Perspective.* Cambridge.

Danek, G. 1988. *Studien zur Dolonie.* Vienna.

Daneš, F. 1990. "On the Stylistic Relevance of the Choice of Anaphoric Expressions." *Rivista di Linguistica* 2:121–139.

Dascal, M., and T. Katriel. 1977. "Between Semantics and Pragmatics: Two Types of 'but'—Hebrew 'aval' and 'ela.'" *Theoretical Linguistics* 4:143–171.

Davidse, K., L. Vandelanotte, and H. Cuyckens, eds. 2010. *Subjectification, Intersubjectification and Grammaticalization.* Berlin.

Davies, M. 1988. "Monody, Choral Lyric, and the Tyranny of the Handbook." *Classical Quarterly* 38:52–64.

———. 1991. *Sophocles. Trachiniae.* Oxford.

Dawe, R. D. 2006 [1982]. *Sophocles. Oedipus Rex*. Cambridge.

Debnar, P. 2001. *Speaking the Same Language: Speech and Audience in Thucydides' Spartan Debate*. Ann Arbor.

———. 2013. "Blurring the Boundaries of Speech: Thucydides and Indirect Discourse." In *Thucydides Between History and Literature*, ed. A. Tsakmakis and M. Tamiolaki, 271–286. Berlin.

Dedaić, M. N., and M. Mišković-Luković. 2010. *South Slavic Discourse Particles*. Amsterdam.

Defour, T. 2008. "The Speaker's Voice: A Diachronic Study on the Use of Well and Now as Pragmatic Markers." *English Text Construction* 1:62–82.

Degand, L., B. Cornillie, and P. Pietrandrea, eds. 2013. *Discourse Markers and Modal Particles: Categorization and Description*. Amsterdam.

———. 2013. "Modal Particles and Discourse Markers: Two Sides of the Same Coin?" In Degand, Cornillie, and Pietrandrea 2013:1–18. Amsterdam.

Degand, L., and A.-M. Simon-Vandenbergen, eds. 2011. *Grammaticalization, Pragmaticalization, and (Inter)subjectification: Methodological Issues in the Study of Discourse Markers*. Berlin.

Dehé, N. 2014. *Parentheticals in Spoken English: The Syntax-Prosody Relation*. Cambridge.

Delbrück, B. 1893. *Vergleichende Syntax der indogermanischen Sprachen*. Straßburg.

Delogu, F. 2009. "Presupposition." In *Key Notions for Pragmatics*, ed. J. Verschueren and J.-A. Östman, 195-207. Amsterdam.

Deneau, D. P. 1986. "Pointing Theory and Some Victorian Practices." *Yearbook of Research in English and American Literature* 4:97–134.

Denis, D. 2015. The Development of Pragmatic Markers in Canadian English. Ph.D diss., University of Toronto.

Denizot, C., and O. Spevak, eds. 2017. *Pragmatic Approaches to Latin and Ancient Greek*. Amsterdam and Philadelphia.

Denniston, J. D. 1929. "Four Notes on Greek Particles." *Classical Review* 43:118–119.

———. 1930. "Notes on the Greek Particles." *Classical Review* 44:213–215.

———. 1950. *The Greek Particles*. 2nd ed. Oxford.

———. 1952. *Greek Prose Style*. Oxford.

Denniston, J. D., and D. L. Page, eds. 1957. *Aeschylus. Agamemnon*. Oxford.

Deppermann, A., R. Fiehler, and T. Spranz-Fogasy. 2006. *Grammatik und Interaktion. Untersuchungen zum Zusammenhang von grammatischen Strukturen und Gesprächsprozessen*. Radolfzell.

Des Places, E. 1929. *Étude sur quelques particules de liaison chez Platon*. Paris.

———. 1947. *Le pronom chez Pindare*. Paris.

Detienne, M. 1981. *L'invention de la mythologie*. Paris.

Devarius, M. 1588. *Liber de graecae linguae particulis*. Rome. https://reader.digitale-sammlungen.de/de/fs1/object/display/bsb10163896_00001.html.

Devarius, M., and R. Klotz. 1835–1842. *Matthaei Devarii liber de Graecae linguae particulis.* Leipzig.

Devine, A. M., and L. D. Stephens. 1994. *The Prosody of Greek Speech.* New York.

———. 2000. *Discontinuous Syntax : Hyperbaton in Greek.* New York .

Dewald, C. 1999. "The Figured Stage: Focalizing the Initial Narratives of Herodotus and Thucydides." In *Contextualizing Classics: Ideology, Performance, Dialogue: Essays in Honor of John J. Peradotto*, ed. T. M. Falkner, N. Felson, and D. Konstan, 221–252. Lanham, MD.

———. 2002. "I Didn't Give You My Own Genealogy: Herodotus and the Authorial Persona." In *Brill's Companion to Herodotus*, ed. E. J. Bakker, I. J. F de Jong, and H. van Wees, 267–289. Leiden.

Dewald, C., and J. Marincola, eds. 2006. *The Cambridge Companion to Herodotus.* Cambridge.

Dér, C. I., and A. Markó. 2010. "A Pilot Study of Hungarian Discourse Markers." *Language and Speech* 53:135–180.

Dickey, E. 1996. *Greek Forms of Address: From Herodotus to Lucian.* Oxford.

———. 2007. *Ancient Greek Scholarship.* Oxford.

Diels, H., and W. Kranz. 1951–1952. *Die Fragmente der Vorsokratiker: griechisch und deutsch.* 3 vols. Berlin.

Diessel, H. 1999. *Demonstratives: Form, Function, and Grammaticalization.* Amsterdam.

Diewald, G. 1999. "Die dialogische Bedeutungskomponente von Modalpartikeln." In *Dialogue Analysis and the Mass Media*, ed. B. Naumann, 187–199. Tübingen.

———. 2008. "Die Funktion 'idiomatischer' Konstruktionen bei Grammatikalisierungsprozessen—Illustriert am Beispiel der Modalpartikel *ruhig*." In *Konstruktionsgrammatik*. Vol. 2: *Von der Konstruktion zur Grammatik*, ed. K. Fischer and A. Stefanowitsch, 33–57. Tübingen.

Diggle, J. 1984. *Euripidis fabulae. Cyclops, Alcestis, Medea, Heraclidae, Hippolytus, Andromacha, Hecuba.* Oxford.

———. 1994. *Euripidis fabulae. Helena, Phoenissae, Orestes, Bacchae, Iphigenia Aulidensis, Rhesus.* Oxford.

Dijk, T. van. 1979. "Pragmatic Connectives." *Journal of Pragmatics* 3:447–56.

———. 1982. "Episodes as Units of Discourse Analysis." In *Analyzing Discourse: Text and Talk*, ed. D. Tannen, 177–195. Washington, DC.

Dik, H. 1995. *Word Order in Ancient Greek: A Pragmatic Account of Word Order Variation in Herodotus.* Amsterdam.

———. 2007. *Word Order in Greek Tragic Dialogue.* Oxford.

Dik, S. C. 1968. *Coordination.* Amsterdam.

———. 1978. *Functional Grammar.* Amsterdam.

———. 1989. *The Theory of Functional Grammar.* Dordrecht.

Dikken, M. den, ed. 2013. *The Cambridge Handbook of Generative Syntax.* Cambridge.

Dillon, M. 1995. "By Gods, Tongues, and Dogs: The Use of Oaths in Aristophanic Comedy." *Greece and Rome* 42:135–151.

Dimock, G. E. 1952. "'ἀλλά in Lysias and Plato's *Phaedrus*." *American Journal of Philology* 73:381–396.

Dindorf, G. 1870. *Lexicon Sophocleum*. Leipzig.

Dindorf, W. 1873. *Lexicon Aeschyleum*. Leipzig.

Dinsmore, J. 1987. "Mental Spaces from a Functional Perspective." *Cognitive Science* 11:1–21.

Dittenberger, W. 1881. "Sprachliche Kriterien für die Chronologie der platonischen Dialoge." *Hermes* 16:321–345.

Dittmar, N. 2010. "Register." In *Variation and Change: Pragmatic Perspectives*, ed. M. Fried, J.-O. Östman, and J. Verschueren, 221–233. Amsterdam.

Dobrov, G. 1988. "The Syntax of Coreference in Greek." *Classical Philology* 83:275–288.

Dobson, J. F. 1919. *The Greek Orators*. London.

Dodds, E. R. 1960 [1944]. *Euripides. Bacchae*. Oxford.

Döderlein, L. 1850. *Homerisches Glossarium*. Erlangen.

———. 1858. *Homerica particula* γάρ *nusquam refertur ad insequentem sententiam*. Erlangen.

Dontcheva-Navratilova, O., and R. Povolná, eds. 2009. *Coherence and Cohesion in Spoken and Written Discourse*. Newcastle.

Doron, E. 1994. "The Discourse Function of Appositives." In *Proceedings of the Ninth Annual Conference of the Israel Association for Theoretical Linguistics and of the Workshop on Discourse*, ed. R. Buchalla and A. Mitwoch, 53–65. Jerusalem.

Dover, K. J. 1954–1955. "Problems in Thucydides VI and VII." *Proceedings of the Cambridge Philological Society* 183:4–11.

———. 1960. *Greek Word Order*. Cambridge.

———. 1965. *Thucydides. Book VI*. Oxford.

———. 1968. *Aristophanes. Clouds*. Oxford.

———. 1972. *Aristophanic comedy*. Berkeley.

———. 1987a. "Language and Character in Aristophanes." In *Greek and the Greeks: Collected Papers*. Vol. 1: *Language, Poetry, Drama*, 237–248. Oxford.

———. 1987b. "Some Types of Abnormal Word-Order in Attic Comedy." In *Greek and the Greeks: Collected Papers*. Vol. 1. *Language, Poetry, Drama*, 43–66. Oxford.

———. 1987c. "The Style of Aristophanes." In *Greek and the Greeks: Collected Papers*. Vol. 1: *Language, Poetry, Drama*, 224–236. Oxford.

———. 1988. *Greek and the Greeks: Collected Papers*. Vol. 2: *The Greeks and Their Legacy: Prose Literature, History, Society, Transmission, Influence*. Oxford.

———. 1993. *Aristophanes. Frogs*. Oxford.

———. 1997a. *The Evolution of Greek Prose Style*. Oxford.

———. 1997b. "Units of Utterance." In *The Evolution of Greek Prose Style*, 26–40. Oxford.

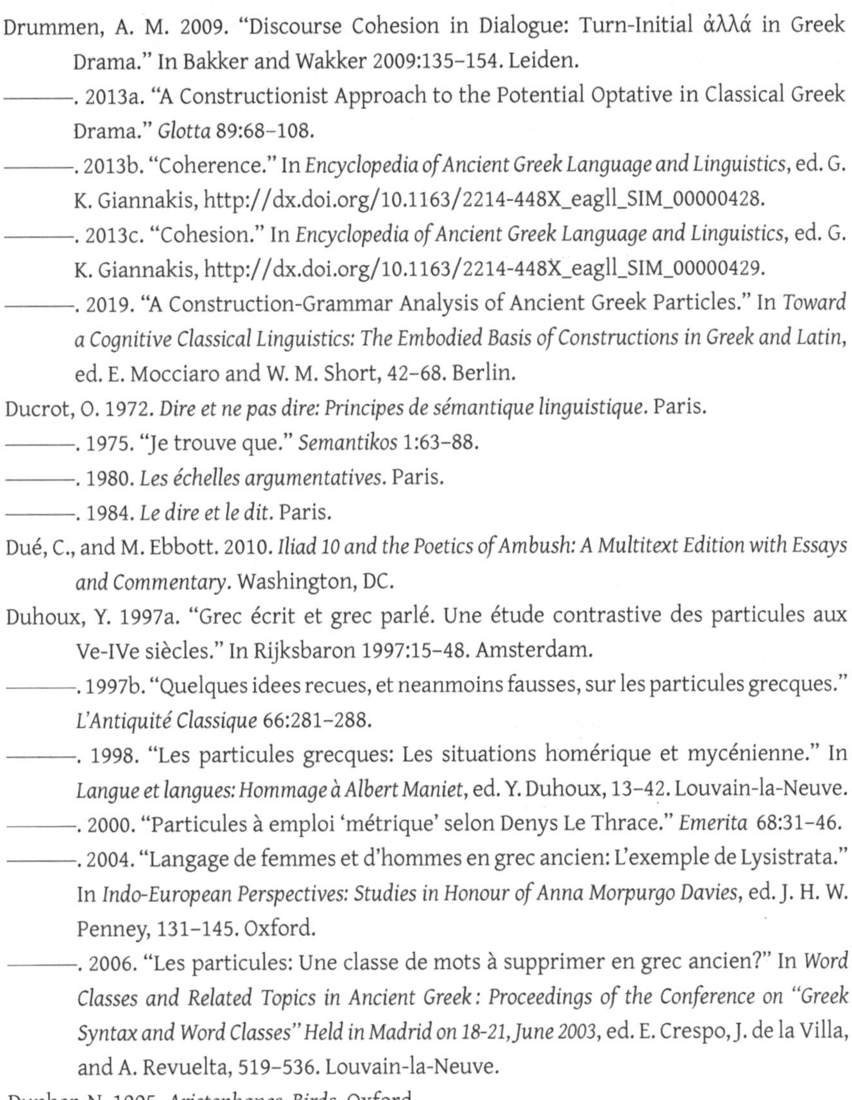

Drummen, A. M. 2009. "Discourse Cohesion in Dialogue: Turn-Initial ἀλλά in Greek Drama." In Bakker and Wakker 2009:135–154. Leiden.

———. 2013a. "A Constructionist Approach to the Potential Optative in Classical Greek Drama." *Glotta* 89:68–108.

———. 2013b. "Coherence." In *Encyclopedia of Ancient Greek Language and Linguistics*, ed. G. K. Giannakis, http://dx.doi.org/10.1163/2214-448X_eagll_SIM_00000428.

———. 2013c. "Cohesion." In *Encyclopedia of Ancient Greek Language and Linguistics*, ed. G. K. Giannakis, http://dx.doi.org/10.1163/2214-448X_eagll_SIM_00000429.

———. 2019. "A Construction-Grammar Analysis of Ancient Greek Particles." In *Toward a Cognitive Classical Linguistics: The Embodied Basis of Constructions in Greek and Latin*, ed. E. Mocciaro and W. M. Short, 42–68. Berlin.

Ducrot, O. 1972. *Dire et ne pas dire: Principes de sémantique linguistique*. Paris.

———. 1975. "Je trouve que." *Semantikos* 1:63–88.

———. 1980. *Les échelles argumentatives*. Paris.

———. 1984. *Le dire et le dit*. Paris.

Dué, C., and M. Ebbott. 2010. *Iliad 10 and the Poetics of Ambush: A Multitext Edition with Essays and Commentary*. Washington, DC.

Duhoux, Y. 1997a. "Grec écrit et grec parlé. Une étude contrastive des particules aux Ve-IVe siècles." In Rijksbaron 1997:15–48. Amsterdam.

———. 1997b. "Quelques idees recues, et neanmoins fausses, sur les particules grecques." *L'Antiquité Classique* 66:281–288.

———. 1998. "Les particules grecques: Les situations homérique et mycénienne." In *Langue et langues: Hommage à Albert Maniet*, ed. Y. Duhoux, 13–42. Louvain-la-Neuve.

———. 2000. "Particules à emploi 'métrique' selon Denys Le Thrace." *Emerita* 68:31–46.

———. 2004. "Langage de femmes et d'hommes en grec ancien: L'exemple de Lysistrata." In *Indo-European Perspectives: Studies in Honour of Anna Morpurgo Davies*, ed. J. H. W. Penney, 131–145. Oxford.

———. 2006. "Les particules: Une classe de mots à supprimer en grec ancien?" In *Word Classes and Related Topics in Ancient Greek: Proceedings of the Conference on "Greek Syntax and Word Classes" Held in Madrid on 18-21, June 2003*, ed. E. Crespo, J. de la Villa, and A. Revuelta, 519–536. Louvain-la-Neuve.

Dunbar, N. 1995. *Aristophanes. Birds*. Oxford.

Dunkel, G. 1990. "J. Wackernagel und die idg. Partikel **so, *ke, *kem* und **an*." In *Sprachwissenschaft und Philologie. Jacob Wackernagel und die Indogermanistik heute*, ed. H. Eichner, and E. Rix, 100–130. Wiesbaden.

———. 1992. "Die Grammatik der Partikeln." In *Rekonstruktion und relative Chronologie*, ed. R. Beekes, A. Lubotsky, and J. Weitenberg, 153–177. Innsbruck.

Dunn, F. M. 2007. *Present Shock in Late Fifth-Century Greece*. Ann Arbor.

Düntzer, H. 1872. "Über *au, aute, autis, authis*." In *Homerische Abhandlungen*, ed. by H. Düntzer, 579–592. Leipzig.

Dupont-Roc, R., and J. Lallot. 1980. *Aristote. La Poétique. Texte, traduction, notes*. Paris.

Durling, R. J. 1988. "Some Particles and Particle Clusters in Galen." *Glotta* 66:183–189.

———. 1995. "*Atar oun kai* in Galen and His Predecessors." *Glotta* 73:76.

Dynel, M. 2011. "Stranger than Fiction? A Few Methodological Notes on Linguistic Research in Film Discourse." *Brno Studies in English* 37:41–61.

Earp, F. R. 1944. *The Style of Sophocles*. Cambridge.

———. 1948. *The Style of Aeschylus*. Cambridge.

Ebel, H. 1856. "Zur griechischen Lautlehre." *Zeitschrift für Vergleichende Sprachforschung* 5:61–68. http://books.google.com/books?id=RAMHX0xGKgQC&pg=PA61%23v=onepage&q&f=false.

Ebeling, H. 1880-1885. *Lexicon Homericum*. 2 vols. Leipzig.

Eberhard, E. 1889. "Die Partikel καί im homerischen Verse." *Zeitschrift für die österreichischen Gymnasien* 40:581–599.

Ebhardt, K. 1866. *Der rhetorische Schluß und seine Anwendung in den Schriften der Griechen und Römer*. Weilburg.

———. 1877. *Die sprachlichen Formen mit welchen die Glieder des Schlusses im Griechischen und Lateinischen eingeführt werden*. Weilburg.

———. 1880. *Der rhetorische Schluss : 2 Abhandlungen*. Weilburg.

Eco, U. 1990. "Presuppositions." In *The Limits of Interpretation*, ed. U. Eco, 222–262. Bloomington.

Edmunds, L. 1975. *Chance and Intelligence in Thucydides*. Cambridge, MA.

———. 1992. "The Blame of Karkinos: Theorizing Theatrical Space." In *Antike Dramentheorien und ihre Rezeption*, ed. B. Zimmermann, 214–239. Stuttgart.

———. 2008. "Deixis in Ancient Greek and in Latin Literature: Historical Introduction and State of the Question." *Philologia Antiqua* 1:67–98.

Edwards, M. W. 1966. "Some Features of Homeric Craftsmanship." *Transactions of the American Philological Association* 97:115–179.

———. 1991. *The Iliad: A Commentary* V. Cambridge.

———. 2002. *Sound, Sense, and Rhythm: Listening to Greek and Latin Poetry*. Princeton.

Ehlich, K. 1982. "Anaphora and Deixis: Same, Similar, or Different?" In *Speech, Place, and Action*, ed. R. J. Jarvella and W. Klein, 315–338. Chichester, New York, Brisbane, Toronto, and Singapore.

Eichholz, D. E. 1952. "A Curious Use of μέν." *Classical Review* 2:144–145.

Ellendt, F. 1835. 2 vols. *Lexicon Sophocleum*. Vol. 2: https://archive.org/details/lexiconsophocle01ellegoog.

Elliott, A. 1969. *Euripides. Medea*. London.

Elmsley, P. 1821. *Euripides. Bakchai*. Oxford.

Emde Boas, E. van. 2010. Linguistic Studies in Euripides' *Electra*. PhD diss., University of Oxford.

———. 2017a. "Analyzing Agamemnon: Conversation Analysis and Particles in Greek Tragic Dialogue." *Classical Philology* 112:411–434.

———. 2017b. *Language and character in Euripides' Electra. Linguistic studies in Euripides' Electra*. Oxford.

Emde Boas, E. van, A. Rijksbaron, L. Huitink, M. de Bakker. 2019. *The Cambridge Grammar of Classical Greek*. Cambridge.

Emmott, C. 1997. *Narrative Comprehension*. Oxford.

Enfield, N. J. 2006. "Social Consequences of Common Ground." In *Roots of Human Sociality: Culture, Cognition and Interaction*, ed. N. J. Enfield, and S. C. Levinson, 399–430. Oxford.

———. 2013. *Relationship Thinking: Agency, Enchrony, and Human Sociality*. Oxford.

Enfield, N. J., and S. H. Levinson. 2006. *Roots of Human Society. Culture, Cognition and Interaction*. Oxford.

Englebretson, R. 2007. *Stancetaking in Discourse: Subjectivity, Evaluation, Interaction*. Amsterdam.

Erbse, H. 1980. "Zur normativen Grammatik der Alexandriner." *Glotta* 58:236–258.

Erman, B. 2001. "Pragmatic Markers Revisited with a Focus on *you know* in Adult and Adolescent Talk." *Journal of Pragmatics* 33:1337–1359.

Erp Taalman Kip, A. M. van. 1997. "*H gar* in Questions." In Rijksbaron 1997:151–156. Amsterdam.

———. 2009. "*Kai mên, kai dê* and *êdê* in Tragedy and Comedy." In Bakker and Wakker 2009:111–133. Leiden.

Ervin-Tripp, S. M. 1969. "Sociolinguistics." *Advances in Experimental Social Psychology* 4:91–165.

Essen, M. H. N. von. 1887. *Index Thucydideus*. Berlin.

Estienne, H. 1572a. *Thesaurus Graecae Linguae* I. Paris. https://books.google.de/books?id=IXFpAAAAcAAJ&printsec=frontcover&source=gbs_ge_summary_r&cad=0#v=onepage&q&f=false.

———. 1572b. *Thesaurus Graecae Linguae* II. Paris. https://books.google.de/books?id=wH9lAAAAcAAJ&printsec=frontcover#v=onepage&q&f=false.

———. 1572c. *Thesaurus Graecae Linguae* III. Paris. https://books.google.de/books?id=lruWDlp8xVwC&pg=PA1&source=gbs_selected_pages&cad=2#v=onepage&q&f=false.

———. 1572d. *Thesaurus Graecae Linguae* IV. Paris. https://books.google.de/books?id=FIBlAAAAcAAJ&pg=PA31&source=gbs_selected_pages&cad=2#v=onepage&q&f=false

———. n.d. *Thesaurus Graecae Linguae*. Appendix. Paris.

Eucken, R. C. 1866. *De Aristotelis dicendi ratione*. Pars I: *Observationes de particularum usu*. Gottingen.

Evans, J. A. S. 1965. "Despotes Nomos." *Athenaeum* 43:142–153.

Fabricius-Hansen, C. 1983. "Wieder ein *wieder*? Zur Semantik von *wieder*." In *Meaning, Use and Interpretation of Language*, ed. A. von Bäuerle, R. Schwarze, and C. Stechow, 97–120. Berlin.

Fairbanks, B. G. 2009. Ojibwe Discourse Markers. PhD diss., University of Minnesota.

Fairclough, H. R. 1906. "A Study of ἆρα in Plato." *Proceedings of the American Philological Association* 37:xlvi.

Falco, V. de. 1950. *Sophocles. Aiace*. Naples.

Farrar, F. W. 1867. *A Brief Greek Syntax and Hints on Greek Accidence*. London.

Feeney, D. 2011. "*Hic finis fandi*: On the Absence of Punctuation for the Endings (and Beginnings) of Speeches in Latin Poetic Texts." *Materiali e discussioni per l'analisi dei testi classici* 66:45–91.

Fehling, D. 1956. "Varro und die grammatische Lehre von der Analogie und der Flexion." *Glotta* 35:214–270.

———. 1957. "Varro und die grammatische Lehre von der Analogie und der Flexion (2. Teil)." *Glotta* 36:48–100.

———. 1979. "Review of Siebenborn 1976." *Gnomon* 51:488–490.

Feldman, J. A. 2006. *From Molecule to Metaphor: A Neural Theory of Language*. Cambride, MA.

Feldman, J. A., E. Dodge, and J. Bryant. 2010. "Embodied Construction Grammar." In *The Oxford Handbook of Linguistic Analysis*, ed. B. Heine and H. Narrog, 111–137. Oxford.

Felson, Nancy. 1999. "Vicarious Transport in Pindar's *Pythian* Four." *Harvard Studies in Classical Philology* 99:1–31.

———. 2004. "The Poetics of Deixis in Pindar's Pythian IX." In *The Poetics of Deixis in Alcman, Pindar, and Other Lyric*, ed. N. Felson, 365–89. Special issue, *Arethusa* 37.3. Baltimore.

———, ed. 2004. *The Poetics of Deixis in Alcman, Pindar, and Other Lyric*. Special issue, *Arethusa* 37.3. Baltimore.

Feng, G. 2010. *A Theory of Conventional Implicature and Pragmatic Markers in Chinese*. Bingley.

Ferguson, C. A. 1994. "Dialect, Register, and Genre: Working Assumptions about Conventionalization." In *Sociolinguistic Perspectives on Register*, ed. D. Biber and E. Finegan, 15–30. New York.

Ferrara, K. W. 1997. "Form and Function of the Discourse Marker *anyway*: Implications for Discourse Analysis." *Linguistics* 35:343–378.

Ferrari, A., L. Cignetti, A.-M. De Cesare, L. Lala, M. Mandelli, C. Ricci, and E. Roggia. 2008. *L' interfaccia lingua-testo: Natura e funzioni dell' articolazione informativa dell' enunciato*. Alessandria.

Ferreira, F., and B. Swets. 2002. "How Incremental Is Language Production? Evidence from the Production of Utterances Requiring the Computation of Arithmetic Sums." *Journal of Memory and Language* 46:57–84.

Ferretti, T. R., M. Kutas, and K. McRae. 2007. "Verb Aspect and the Activation of Event Knowledge." *Journal of Experimental Psychology: Learning, Memory and Cognition* 33:182–196.

Fielder, G. E. 2008. "Bulgarian Adversative Connectives: Conjunctions or Discourse Markers?" In *Crosslinguistic Studies of Clause Combining: The Multifunctionality of Conjunctions*, ed. R. Laury, 79–97. Amsterdam.

———. 2010. "*Ama*, a Bulgarian Adversative Connective." In *South Slavic Discourse Particles*, ed. M. N. Dedaić and M. Mišković-Luković, 23–44. Amsterdam.

Fillmore, C. J. 1973. "May We Come In?" *Semiotica* 9:97–116.

———. 1976. "The Need for Frame Semantics within Linguistics." *Statistical Methods in Linguistics* 12:5–29.

———. 1982. "Toward a Descriptive Framework for Spatial Deixis." In *Speech, Place, and Action*, ed. R. J. Jarvella and W. Klein, 31–59. Chichester.

Fillmore, C. J., and C. Baker. 2010. "A Frames Approach to Semantic Analysis." In *The Oxford Handbook of Linguistic Analysis*, ed. B. Heine and H. Narrog, 313–339. Oxford.

Fillmore, C. J., P. Kay, and M. C. O'Connor. 1988. "Regularity and Idiomaticity in Grammatical Constructions: The Case of Let Alone." *Language* 64:501–538.

Fina, A. de, and A. Georgakopoulou. 2012. *Analyzing Narrative*. Cambridge.

Finglass, P. J. 2011. *Sophocles. Ajax*. Cambridge.

Finkelberg, M. 1990. "A Creative Oral Poet and the Muse." *American Journal of Philology* 111:293–303.

———, ed. 2011. *The Homer Encyclopedia*. 3 vols. Oxford.

Finley, J. H. 1939. "The Origins of Thucydides' Style." *Harvard Studies in Classical Philology* 50:35–84.

Finley, M. I. 1985. *Ancient History : Evidence and Models*. London.

Finnegan, R. 2011. *Why Do We Quote? The Culture and History of Quotation*. Cambridge.

Firth, A. 2009. "Ethnomethodology." In *The Pragmatics of Interaction*, ed. S. d'Hondt, J.-O. Östman, and J. Verschueren, 66–78. Amsterdam.

Fischer, K. 2000. "Discourse Particles, Turn-Taking, and the Semantics-Pragmatics Interface." *Revue de Sémantique et Pragmatique* 8:111–137.

———. 2006a. "Frames, Constructions, and Invariant Meanings: The Functional Polysemy of Discourse Particles." In Fischer 2006:427–447. Amsterdam.

———. 2006b. "Towards an Understanding of the Spectrum of Approaches to Discourse Particles: Introduction to the Volume." In Fischer 2006:1–19. Amsterdam.

———, ed. 2006. *Approaches to Discourse Particles*. Amsterdam.

———. 2010. "Beyond the Sentence: Constructions, Frames and Spoken Interaction." *Constructions and Frames* 2:185–207.

Fischer, K., and M. Alm. 2013. "A Radical Construction Grammar Perspective on the Modal Particle-Discourse Particle Distinction." In *Discourse Markers and Modal Particles:*

Categorization and Description, ed. L. Degand, B. Cornillie, and P. Pietrandrea, 47–88. Amsterdam.

Fishman, J. A. 1966. "Language Maintenance and Language Short as a Field of Inquiry." In *Language Loyalty in the United States*, ed. J. A. Fishman, M. E. Haugen Einar Warshauer, R. G. Hayden, J. E. Hofman, V. C. Nahirny, 32–70. The Hague.

———. 1970. *Sociolinguistics: A Brief Introduction*. Rowley, MA.

Fisiak, J, ed. 1990. *Historical Linguistics and Philology*. Berlin.

Flacelière, R. 1970. *Euripide. Medée*. Paris.

Fleischman, S. 1986. "Evaluation in Narrative: The Present Tense in Medieval 'Performed Stories.'" *Yale French Studies* 70:199–251.

———. 1990. *Tense and Narrativity: From Medieval Performance to Modern Fiction*. Austin.

———. 1997. "The 'Labovian Model' Revisited With Special Consideration of Literary Narrative." *Journal of Narrative and Life History* 7:159–168.

Fleischman, S., and M. Yaguello. 2004. "Discourse Markers across Languages: Evidence from English and French." In *Discourse Across Languages and Cultures*, ed. C. L. Moder and A. Martinovic-Zic, 129–147. Amsterdam.

Fletcher, J. 2012. *Performing Oaths in Classical Greek Drama*. Cambridge.

Flothuis, M. H. 1929. *Die Partikel in Wörtern, Redensarten und Sätzen. Eine idiomatische Darstellung*. Groningen.

Fludernik, M. 1993. *The Fictions of Language and the Languages of Fiction: The Linguistic Representation of Speech and Consciousness*. London.

———. 1995. "Middle English *þo* and Other Narrative Discourse Markers." In *Historical Pragmatics*, ed. A. H. Jucker, 359–392. Amsterdam.

———. 1996. *Towards a "Natural" Narratology*. London.

———. 2000. "Narrative Discourse Markers in Malory's *Morte D'Arthur*." *Journal of Historical Pragmatics* 1:231–262.

Foley, H. P. 1999. "Modern Performance and Adaptation of Greek Tragedy." *Transactions of the American Philological Association* 129:1–12.

———. 2003. "Choral Identity in Greek Tragedy." *Classical Philology* 98:1–30.

Foley, J. M. 1990. *Traditional Oral Epic: The Odyssey, Beowulf, and the Serbo-Croatian Return Song*. Berkeley.

———. 1995. *The Singer of Tales in Performance*. Bloomington.

Foolen, A. 1991. "Polyfunctionality and the Semantics of Adversative Conjunctions." *Multilingua* 10:79–92.

———. 1993. *De betekenis van partikels: Een dokumentatie van de stand van het onderzoek, met bijzondere aandacht voor maar*. Nijmegen.

———. 1994. "A Pragmatic Analysis of Norwegian Modal Particles." *Lingua: International Review of General Linguistics* 93:301–312.

———. 1996. "Pragmatic Particles." In *Handbook of Pragmatics*, ed. J.Verschueren, J.-O. Östman, J. Blommaert, and C. Bulcaen, 1–24. Amsterdam.

———. 2006. "Polysemy Patterns in Contrast: The Case of Dutch 'Toch' and German 'Doch.'" In *Pragmatic Markers in Contrast*, ed. K. Aijmer, and A.-M. Simon-Vandenbergen, 59–72. Oxford.

———. 2012. "The Relevance of Emotion for Language and Linguistics." In *Moving Ourselves, Moving Others: Motion and Emotion in Intersubjectivity, Consciousness and Language*, ed. A. Foolen, U. M. Lüdtke, T. P. Racine, and J. Zlatev, 349–368. Amsterdam.

Forbes, K. 1958. "The Relations of the Particle ἄν with κε(ν), κα, καν." *Glotta* 37:179–182.

Ford, A. 1997. "The Inland Ship: Problems in the Performance and Reception of Homeric Epic." In *Written Voices, Spoken Signs: Tradition, Performance, and the Epic Text*, ed. A. Kahane and E. J. Bakker, 138–166. Cambridge, MA.

Ford, C. E., B. A. Fox, and S. A. Thompson, eds. 2002. *The Language of Turn and Sequence.* Oxford.

Forman, L. L. 1897. *Index Andocideus, Lycurgeus, Dinarcheus*. Oxford.

Fowler, H. N., and W. R. M. Lamb. 1914. *Plato. Euthyphro, Apology, Crito, Phaedo, Phaedrus.* Cambridge, MA.

Fowler, H. W. 1994. *A Dictionary of Modern English Usage*. Ware.

Fowler, H. W., and F. G. Fowler. 1906. *The King's English*. Oxford.

Fox, A. 1973. "Tone-Sequences in English." *Archivum Linguisticum* 4:17–26.

Fox, B. A. 1983. "The Discourse Function of the Participle in Ancient Greek." In *Discourse Perspectives on Syntax*, ed. F. Klein-Andreu, 23–41. New York.

———. 1987. *Discourse Structure and Anaphora. Written and conversational English.* Cambridge.

Fox Tree, J. E. 2006. "Placing *like* in Telling Stories." *Discourse Studies* 8:723–743.

Fraenkel, E. 1932. "Kolon und Satz I. Beobachtungen zur Gliederung des antiken Satzes." *Nachrichten der Göttinger Gesellschaft der Wissenschaften, Philosophisch-Historische Klasse*, 197–213.

———. 1933. "Kolon und Satz II. Beobachtungen zur Gliederung des Antiken Satzes." *Nachrichten der Göttinger Gesellschaft der Wissenschaften, Philosophisch-Historische Klasse*, 319–354.

———. 1950. *Aeschylus. Agamemnon*. Oxford.

———. 1964. *Kleine Beiträge zur klassischen Philologie* I. Rome.

———. 1965. *Noch einmal Kolon und Satz*. Munich.

———. 1977. *Due seminari romani di Eduard Fraenkel: Aiace e Filottete di Sofocle*. With a premise of L. E. Rossi. Rome.

Fragoulaki, M. 2013. *Kinship in Thucydides: Intercommunal Ties and Historical Narrative.* Oxford.

Franke, F. 1833. *De usu particularum* οὐδέ *et* οὔτε *(= De particulis negantibus linguae graecae commentatio II)*. Rinteln.

Fränkel, H. 1921. *Die homerischen Gleichnisse*. Göttingen.

———. 1925. "Griechische Wörter: (4) περ." *Glotta* 14:6–13.

———. 1926. "Der kallimachische und der homerische Hexameter." *Göttinger Nachrichten* 2:197–229.

———. 1955. *Wege und Formen frühgriechen Denkens: Literarische und philosophiegeschichtliche Studien*. Munich.

Fränkel, J. J. 1947. "A Question in Connection with Greek Particles." *Mnemosyne* 13:183–201.

Frascarelli, M. 2007. "Subjects, Topics and the Interpretation of Referential pro." *Natural Language & Linguistic Theory* 25:691–734.

Fraser, Bruce. 1988. "Types of English Discourse Markers." *Acta Linguistica Hungarica* 38:19–33.

———. 1990. "An Approach to Discourse Markers." *Journal of Pragmatics* 14:383–395.

———. 1996. "Pragmatic Markers." *Pragmatics* 6:167–190.

———. 1999. "What Are Discourse Markers?" *Journal of Pragmatics* 31:931–952.

———. 2009. "Topic Orientation Markers." *Journal of Pragmatics* 41:892–898.

Fraser, Bruce (UK). 2001. "The Clause Start in Ancient Greek: Focus and the Second Position." *Glotta* 77:138–177.

Fraser, B., and M. Malamud-Makowski. 1996. "English and Spanish Contrastive Discourse Markers." *Language Sciences* 18:863–881.

Frazer, R. M. 1981. "Corrective HTOI in Homer and Hesiod." *Mnemosyne* 34:265–271.

Frede, M. 1977. "The Origins of Traditional Grammar." In *Historical and Philosophical Dimensions of Logic, Methodology and Philosophy of Science*, ed. R. E. Butts and J. Hintikka, 51–79. Dordrecht.

Frederking, A. 1882. "Sprachliche Kriterien für die Chronologie der platonischen Dialoge." *Jahrbuch für Klassische Philologie* 125:534–541.

Freese, J. H. 1939. *Aristotle, with and English translation: the "Art" of rhetoric*. London.

Frege, G. 1892. "Sinn und Bedeutung." *Zeitschrift für Philosophie und Philosophische Kritik* 100:25–50.

Fried, M. 2009a. "Construction Grammar as a Tool for Diachronic Analysis." *Constructions and Frames* 1:262–291.

———. 2009b. "Word Order." In *Grammar, Meaning and Pragmatics*, ed. F. Brisard, J.-O. Östman, and J. Verschueren, 289–300. Amsterdam.

———. 2010. "Constructions and Frames as Interpretive Clues." *Belgian Journal of Linguistics* 24:83–102.

Fried, M., and J.-O. Östman. 2004. "Construction Grammar: A Thumbnail Sketch." In *Construction Grammar in a Cross-Language Perspective*, ed. M. Fried and J.-O. Östman, 11–86. Amsterdam.

———. 2005. "Construction Grammar and Spoken Language: The Case of Pragmatic Particles." *Journal of Pragmatics* 37:1752–1778.

Friedländer, L. 1850. *Nicanoris peri Iliakēs stigmēs reliquiae emendatiores*. Königsberg.

———. 1859a. "Dissertationis de vocabulis homericis quae in alterutro carmine non inveniuntur." *Neue Jahrbücher für Philologie und Pedagogik* 79:801–835.

———. 1859b. "Analecta Homerica." Third supplement to *Jahrbuch für Klassische Philologie*: 457–484. Leipzig.

Friis Johansen, H., and E. W. Whittle. 1980. *Aeschylus. The Suppliants*. Copenhagen.

Frisk, H. 1946. "ΜΗΝΙΣ. Zur Geschichte eines Begriffes." *Eranos* 44:28–40.

———. 1972. *Griechisches etymologisches Wörterbuch*. Heidelberg.

Fritsch, E. A. 1856. *Vergleichende Bearbeitung der griechischen und lateinischen Partikeln*. Giessen.

———. 1859. *Nam, enim, etenim, ἄρα, γάρ*. Wetzlar.

Fritzsche, F. 1897. *De particulae οὐδέ usu Sophocleo*. Rostock.

Frohberger, H. 1860. "Miscellen (δέ without preceding μέν)." *Philology* 15:342.

Fuami, S. 2009. "*Well* in Shakespeare: Discourse, Collocation and Text." *The Online Proceedings of the Annual Conference of the Poetics and Linguistics Association (PALA)*.

Fuchs, A. 1993. *Remarks on Deixis*. Heidelberg.

Fuhr, K. 1878. "Excurse zu den attischen Rednern (τε... καί: τε... τε: οὐ μέντοι: οὐ μήν)." *Rheinisches Museum* 33:578–599. www.rhm.uni-koeln.de/033/Fuhr2.pdf.

Führer, R. 2010. "τε." In *Lexikon des frühgriechischen Epos* IV, ed. B. Snell and H. J. Mette, 342–343. Göttingen.

Fujii, S. 2000. "Incipient Decategorization of MONO and Grammaticalization of Speaker Attitude in Japanese Discourse." In Andersen and Fretheim 2000:85–118. Amsterdam.

Fulkerson, Laurel. 2013. *No Regrets: Remorse in Classical Antiquity*. Oxford.

Funkhaenel, K. H. 1847. "ὁ δέ, Etc., without Preceding μέν." *Zeitschrift für Altertumswissenschaften* 5:1075–1079.

Furley, W. D. 2006. "Thucydides and Religion." In *Brill's Companion to Thucydides*, ed. A. Rengakos and A. Tsakmakis, 415–438. Leiden.

Furman, R., and A. Özyürek. 2007. "Development of Interactional Discourse Markers: Insights from Turkish Children's and Adults' Oral Narratives." *Journal of Pragmatics* 39:1742–1757.

Gährken, B. 1950. *Die Partikel γάρ*. Münster.

Gaines, P. 2011. "The Multifunctionality of Discourse Operator *okay*: Evidence from a Police Interview." *Journal of Pragmatics* 43:3291–3315.

Gardner, R. 2005. "Conversation Analysis." In *The Handbook of Applied Linguistics*, ed. A. Davies and C. Elder, 262-284. Malden, MA.

Garfinkel, H. 1967. *Studies in Ethnomethodology*. Cambridge.

Garvie, A. F. 1986. *Aeschylus. Choephori*. Oxford.

———. 1994. *Homer, Odyssey Books VI-VIII*. Cambridge.

———. 1998. *Sophocles. Ajax*. Warminster.

Garzya, A. 1953. *Euripides. Andromacha*. Leipzig.

Gebauer, G. 1877. *De hypotacticis et paratacticis argumenti ex contrario formis quae reperiuntur apud oratores Atticos*. Zwickau.

Geluykens, R. 1992. *From Discourse Process to Grammatical Construction: On Left-Dislocation in English*. Amsterdam.

Gelzer, T. 1960. *Der epirrhematische Agon bei Aristophanes*. Munich.

Genette, G. 1972. *Figures 3*. Paris.

Gentili, B, ed. 2013. *Pindaro. Le Olimpiche*. Rome.

Gentili, B., P. Angeli Bernardini, E. Cingano, and P. Giannini. 1995. *Le Pitiche*. Rome.

Gentili, B., and L. Lomiento. 2003. *Metrica e ritmica: Storia delle forme poetiche nella Grecia Antica*. Milan.

Gentili, B., and F. Perusino. 1999. *Colometria antica dei testi poetici Greci* I. Pisa.

Georgakopoulou, A. 1995. "Narrative Organisation and Contextual Constraints: The Case of Modern Greek Storytelling." *Journal of Narrative and Life History* 5:161–189.

———. 1997. *Narrative Performances: A Study of Modern Greek Storytelling*. Amsterdam.

———. 2007. *Small Stories, Interaction and Identities*. Studies in Narrative 8. Amsterdam.

Georgakopoulou, A., and D. Goutsos. 1996. "Connectives as Discourse Markers in Greek." *Studies in Greek Linguistics* 16:411–422.

———. 1998. "Conjunctions versus Discourse Markers in Greek: The Interaction of Frequency, Position, and Functions in Context." *Linguistics* 36:887–917.

George, C. H. 2005. *Expressions of Agency in Ancient Greek*. Cambridge.

———. 2009. "Greek Particles: Just a Literary Phenomenon?" In *Discourse Cohesion in Ancient Greek*, ed. S. J. Bakker and G. C. Wakker, 155–169. Leiden.

Gerber, D. E. 1982. *Pindar's Olympian One: A Commentary*. Toronto.

———. 2002. *A Commentary on Pindar Olympian Nine*. Stuttgart.

Gerö, E. C. 2000. "The Usage of *an* and *ke* in Ancient Greek: Towards a Unified Description." *Glotta* 76:177–191.

Gerolemou, M. 2011. *Bad Women, Mad Women*. Classica Monacensia 40. Tübingen.

Gildersleeve, B. L. 1882. "Studies in Pindaric Syntax II. On AN and KEN in Pindar." *American Journal of Philology* 3:446–455.

———. 1885. *Pindar. The Olympian and Pythian Odes*. London.

Gildersleeve, B. L., and P. Stork. 1980. *Syntax of Classical Greek from Homer to Demosthenes*. Groningen.

Giora, R. 1990. "On the So-called Evaluative Material in Informative Texts." *Text* 10:299–319.

———. "'A Good Arab Is Not a Dead Arab—a Racist Incitement': On the Accessibility of Negated Concepts." In *Explorations in Pragmatics: Linguistic, Cognitive and Intercultural Aspects*, ed. I. Kecskes and L. R. Horn, 129–162. Berlin.

Giora, R., and N. Balaban. 2001. "Lexical Access in Text Production: On the Role of Salience in Metaphor Resonance." In *Text Representation*, ed. T. Sanders, J. Schilperoord, and W. Spooren, 111–124. Amsterdam.

Givón, T., ed. 1983. *Topic Continuity in Discourse: A Quantitative Cross-language Study.* Amsterdam.

———. 1984. *Syntax: A Functional-Typological Introduction* I. Amsterdam.

———. 1987. "Beyond Foreground and Background." In *Coherence and Grounding in Discourse*, ed. R. S. Tomlin, 175–188. Amsterdam.

———, ed. 1997. *Conversation: Cognitive, Communicative and Social Perspectives.* Amsterdam.

———. 2005. *Context as Other Minds: The Pragmatics of Sociality, Cognition and Communication.* Amsterdam.

Glück, H. 1993. *Metzler Lexikon Sprache.* Stuttgart.

Gobbo, F. del. 2003. Appositives at the Interface. PhD diss., University of California, Irvine.

Godley, A. D. 1920–1925. *Herodotus.* 4 vols. Cambridge, MA.

Goffman, E. 1959. *The Presentation of Self in Everyday Life.* Harmondsworth.

———. 1974. *Frame Analysis: An Essay on the Organization of Experience.* Boston.

Goldberg, A. 1995. *Constructions. A Construction Grammar Approach to Argument Structure.* Chicago.

———. 2006. *Constructions at Work.* Oxford.

Goldhill, S. 2000. "Greek Drama and Political Theory." In *The Cambridge History of Greek and Roman Political Thought*, ed. C. Rowe and M. Schofield, 60–88. Cambridge.

———. 2012. *Sophocles and the Language of Tragedy.* Oxford.

Goldstein, D. M. 2010. Wackernagel's Law in Fifth-Century Greek. PhD diss., University of California, Berkeley.

———. 2019. "Language Change and Linguistic Theory: The Case of Archaic Indo-European Conjunction." *Transactions of the Philological Society* 117:1-34.

———. 2012. "Iterated Modal Marking and Polarity Focus in Ancient Greek." *Transactions of the Philological Society* 110:1–25.

———. 2013a. "The Synchrony and Diachrony of a Scalar Coordinator: Latin *nedum* 'let alone.'" *Indo-European Linguistics* 1:68–106.

———. 2013b. "Wackernagel's Law and the Fall of the Lydian Empire." *Transactions of the American Philological Association* 143:323–346.

———. 2016. *Classical Greek Syntax: Wackernagel's Law in Herodotus.* Leiden.

Gomme, A. W., A. Andrewes, and K. J. Dover. 1945–1981. *A Historical Commentary on Thucydides.* 5 vols. Oxford.

Gomperz, Theodor. 1883. *Herodoteische Studien.* Vienna.

Gonda, J. 1954. "The History and Original Function of the Indo-European Particle *kue*, Especially in Greek and Latin." *Mnemosyne* 7:177–214; 265–296.

———. 1956. *The Character of the Indo-European Moods.* Wiesbaden.

———. 1957. "The Original Value of Gr. *-de.*" *Mnemosyne* 10:97–102.

———. 1963. "Review of Moorhouse, Studies in the Greek Negatives." *Mnemosyne* 16:289–293.

Gonzaga, M. 1926. "Paratactic *Kai* in the New Testament" *Classical Journal* 21:580–586.

González Merino, J. I. 1981. "Las partículas en Menandro." *Estudios Clásicos* 25:163–184.

González, M. 2004. *Pragmatic Markers in Oral Narrative: The Case of English and Catalan.* Amsterdam.

Goodwin, C. 1996. "Transparent Vision." In *Interaction and Grammar*, ed. E. Ochs, E. A. Schegloff, and S. A. Thompson, 370–404. Cambridge.

Goodwin, W. W. 1889. *Syntax of the Moods and Tenses of the Greek Verb Rewritten and Enlarged.* London.

Goody, E. N. 1995. *Social Intelligence and Interaction: Expressions and Implications of the Social Bias in Human Intelligence.* Cambridge.

Goutsos, D. 1997. *Modeling Discourse Topic: Sequential Relations and Strategies in Expository Text.* Norwood, NJ.

Grafström, C. A. 1865. *De usu particulae ἄρα apud Homerum.* Uppsala.

Grassmann, H. 1877. "Ursprung der Präpositionen im Indogermanischen." *Zeitschrift für vergleichende Sprachforschung* 23:559–579.

Graves, C. E. 1911. *Aristophanes. The Clouds.* Cambridge.

Graziosi, B., and J. Haubold. 2010. *Homer. Iliad Book VI.* Cambridge.

Green, E. L. 1901. "περ in Thucydides, Xenophon, and the Attic Orators." *Proceedings of the American Philological Association* 32:135-136.

Green, G. M. 1996. *Pragmatics and Natural Language Understanding.* 2nd ed. Mahwah.

Greenwood, E. 2006. *Thucydides and the Shaping of History.* London.

Grégoire, A. 1930. "Notes sur la place occupée par les particules γε et δέ dans la versification homérique." In *Serta leodiensia, ad celebrandam patriæ libertatem iam centesimvm annvm recvperatam composvervnt philologi leodienses*, 159–176. Liège.

Grethlein, J. 2003. *Asyl und Athen: Die Konstruktion kollektiver Identität in der griechischen Tragödie.* Stuttgart.

———. 2007. "The Hermeneutics and Poetics of Memory in Aeschylus's *Persae*." *Arethusa* 40:363–396.

———. 2010. *The Greeks and Their Past: Poetry, Oratory and History in the Fifth Century BCE.* Cambridge.

———. 2013a. "Choral Intertemporality in the Oresteia." In *Choral Mediations in Greek Tragedy*, ed. R. Gagné and M. Govers Hopman, 78–99. Cambridge.

———. 2013b. *Experience and Teleology in Ancient Historiography: Futures Past from Herodotus to Augustine.* Cambridge.

———. 2013c. "The Present of the Past in Thucydides." In *Thucydides Between History and Literature*, ed. A. Tsakmakis and M. Tamiolaki, 91–118. Berlin.

Grethlein, J., and A. Rengakos, eds. 2009. *Narratology and Interpretation: The Content of Narrative Form in Ancient Literature.* Berlin.

Grice, H. P. 1957. "Meaning." *Philosophical Review* 66:377–388.

———. 1961. "The Causal Theory of Perception." Supplementary volume, *Proceedings of the Aristotelian Society* 35:121–152.

———. 1975. "Logic and Conversation." In *Syntax and Semantics*. Vol. 3: *Speech Acts*, ed. P. Cole and J. L. Morgan, 41–58. New York.

———. 1981. "Presupposition and Conversational Implicature." In *Radical Pragmatics*, ed. P. Cole, 183–198. New York.

———. 1989. *Studies in the Way of Words*. Cambridge, MA.

Griffith, M. 1999. *Sophocles. Antigone*. Cambridge.

———. 2001. "Antigone and Her Sister(s): Embodying Women in Greek Tragedy." In *Making Silence Speak: Women's Voices in Greek Literature and Society*, ed. A. P. M. H. Lardinois and L. McClure, 117–136. Princeton.

Grimm, J. 1962. "Die Partikel *ara* im frühen griechischen Epos." *Glotta* 40:3–41.

Groeneboom, P. 1930. *Aeschylus' Persae*. Groningen.

———. 1938. *Aeschylus' Zeven Tegen Thebe*. Groningen.

———. 1949. *Aeschylus' Choephori*. Groningen.

———. 1952. *Aeschylus' Eumenides*. Groningen.

———. 1966 [1944]. *Aeschylus' Agamemnon*. Amsterdam.

Groningen, B. A. van. 1937. *Paratactische Compositie in de Oudste Grieksche Literatuur*. Amsterdam.

———. 1958. *La composition littéraire archaïque grecque: Procédés et réalisations*. Amsterdam.

Grosheide, F. W. 1915. "Kai Gar in het Nieuwe Testament." *Theologische Studien* 33:108–110.

Gross, A. 1905. "Sprachgebrauch in der Stichomythie." In *Die Stichomythie in der griechischen Tragoedie und Komoedie*, 82–94. Berlin.

Grosse, E. 1858. *Quaest. gramm. de part. Graec. specimen. I. De particulis copulativis τε et καί apud Pindarum*. Aschersleben.

Grosz, B. J., and C. L. Sidner. 1986. "Attention, Intentions, and the Structure of Discourse." *Computational Linguistics* 12:175–204.

Gruber, W. E. 1986. *Comic Theaters: Studies in Performance and Audience Response*. Athens, GA.

Grundy, P. 2000. *Doing Pragmatics*. London.

Guiraud, C. 1962. *La phrase nominale en grec d'Homère à Euripide*. Paris.

Gumbrecht, H. U. 2003. *Die Macht der Philologie: über einen verborgenen Impuls im wissenschaftlichen Umgang mit Texten*. Frankfurt.

Gumperz, J. J. 1982. *Discourse Strategies*. Cambridge.

Gundel, J. K. 2010. "Reference and Accessibility from a Givenness Hierarchy Perspective." *International Review of Pragmatics* 2:148–168.

Gundel, J. K., and T. Fretheim. 2002. *Information Structure*. Amsterdam.

Gundel, J. K., N. Hedberg, and R. Zacharski. 1993. "Cognitive Status and the Form of Referring Expressions in Discourse." *Language* 69:274–307.

———. 2012. "Underspecification of Cognitive Status in Reference Production: Some Empirical Predictions." *Topics in Cognitive Science* 4:249–268.

Günthner, S. 2008. "Projektorkonstruktionen im Gespräch: Pseudoclefts, 'Die Sache ist-' Konstruktionen und Extrapositionen mit 'es'." *Gesprächsforschung* 9:86–114.

———. 2011. "Between Emergence and Sedimentation: Projecting Constructions in German Interactions." In *Constructions: Emerging and Emergent*, ed. P. Auer and S. Pfänder, 156-185. Berlin.

———. 2012. "Eine interaktionale Perspektive auf Wortarten: das Beispiel 'und zwar.'" In *Nicht-flektierende Wortarten*, ed. B. Rothstein, 14-47. Berlin and New York.

Günthner, S., W. Imo, and J. Bücker. 2014. *Grammar and Dialogism: Sequential, Syntactic, and Prosodic Patterns between Emergence and Sedimentation*. Linguistik - Impulse & Tendenzen 61. Berlin.

Gusmani, R. 1967. "Zwei Kyprische Konjunktionen." *Glotta* 45:19–25.

Guy, G. R., C. Feagin, D. Schiffrin, and J. Baugh, eds. 1997. *Towards a Social Science of Language: Papers in Honor of William Labov*. Amsterdam.

Haacke, A. 1857. *Quaestionum Homericarum capita duo*. Vol. 1: *De particula ἄρα*. Nordhausen.

Habinek, T. N. 1985. *The Colometry of Latin Prose*. Classical Studies 25. Berkeley.

Haddington, P. 2004. "Stance Taking in News Interviews." *SKY Journal of Linguistics* 17:101–142.

Hadley, W. S. 1889. *The Hippolytus of Euripides*. Cambridge.

Haegeman, L. 1993. "The Interpretation of the Particle *da* in West Flemish." *Lingua* 90:111–128.

Hafez, O. M. 1991. "Turn-Taking in Egyptian Arabic: Spontaneous Speech vs. Drama Dialogue." *Journal of Pragmatics* 15:59–81.

Haiman, J., and S. A. Thompson, eds. 1988. *Clause Combining in Grammar and Discourse*. Amsterdam.

Hainsworth, B. 1993. *The Iliad: A Commentary* IV. Cambridge.

Hajdú, I. 1989. *Über die Stellung der Enklitika und Quasi-Enklitika bei Pindar und Bakchylides*. Lund.

Hajnal, I. 2004. "*E-ke-qe* oder *e-ke*?—Mündlichkeit und Schriftlichkeit in den Mykenischen Palastarchiven." In *Analecta homini universali dicata. Arbeiten zur Indogermanistik, Linguistik, Philologie, Politik, Musik und Dichtung. Festschrift für Oswald Panagl zum 65. Geburtstag*, ed. T. Krisch, T. Lindner, U. Müller, 233–251. Stuttgart.

Hakulinen, A. 1998. "The Use of Finnish *nyt* as a Discourse Particle." In Jucker and Ziv 1998:83–96. Amsterdam.

———. 2001. "On Some Uses of the Discourse Particle 'kyl(lä)' in Finnish Conversation." In *Studies in Interactional Linguistics*, ed. M. Selting and E. Couper-Kuhlen, 171–198. Amsterdam.

Hall, E. 1996. *Aeschylus. Persians*. Warminster.

Hall, E., and A. Wrigley, eds. 2007. *Aristophanes in Performance, 421 BC-AD 2007: Peace, Birds and Frogs*. London.

Halla-aho, H., and P. Kruschwitz. 2010. "Colloquial and Literary Language in Early Roman Tragedy." In *Colloquial and Literary Latin*, ed. E. Dickey and A. Chahoud, 133–159. Cambridge.

Halleran, M. R. 1995. *Euripides. Hippolytus*. Warminster.

Halliday, M. A. K. 1967. "Notes on Transitivity and Theme in English, Part 2." *Journal of Linguistics* 3:199–244.

———. 1978. *Language as Social Semiotic: The Social Interpretation of Language and Meaning*. London.

———. 1985. *An Introduction to Functional Grammar*. Oxford.

Halliday, M. A. K., and R. Hasan. 1976. *Cohesion in English*. London.

Hammer, B. 1904. *De τε particulae usu Herodoteo, Thucydideo, Xenophonteo*. Leipzig.

Hammond, M. 2009. *Thucydides. The Peloponnesian War*. Translated by M. Hammond with an Introduction and Notes by P. J. Rhodes. Oxford.

Han, D. 2011. "Utterance Production and Interpretation: A Discourse-Pragmatic Study on Pragmatic Markers in English Public Speeches." *Journal of Pragmatics* 43:2776–2794.

Hancock, J. L. 1917. *Studies in Stichomythia*. Chicago.

Hand, F. 1824. *De particulis Graecis dissertatio secunda. De particula τε cum aliis vocabulis coniuncta*. Jena.

Hanks, W. F. 1989. "Text and Textuality." *Annual Review of Anthropology* 18:95–127.

———. 1993. "Metalanguage and Pragmatics of Deixis." In *Reflexive Language: Reported Speech and Metapragmatics*, ed. J. A. Lucy, 122–157. Cambridge.

Hannay, M., and C. H. M. Kroon. 2005. "Acts and the Relationship between Discourse and Grammar." *Functions of Language* 12:87–124.

Hansen, M.-B. M. 1996. "*Eh bien*: Marker of Comparison and Contrast." In *Content, Expression and Structure: Studies in Danish Functional Grammar*, ed. E. Engberg-Pedersen, M. Fortescue, P. Harder, L. Heltoft, and L. Falster Jakobsen, 315–342. Amsterdam.

———. 1997. "*Alors* and *Donc* in Spoken French: A Reanalysis." *Journal of Pragmatics* 28:153–187.

———. 1998a. *The Function of Discourse Particles: A Study with Special Reference to Spoken Standard French*. Amsterdam.

———. 1998b. "The Semantic Status of Discourse Markers." *Lingua* 104:235–260.

———. 2002. "From Aspectuality to Discourse Marking: The Case of French *déjà*' and *encore*." *Belgian Journal of Linguistics* 16:23–51.

———. 2008. *Particles at the Semantics/Pragmatics Interface: Synchronic and Diachronic Issues. A Study with Special Reference to the French Phasal Adverbs*. Amsterdam.

Hansen, M.-B. M., and E. Strudsholm. 2008. "The Semantics of Particles: Advantages of a Contrastive and Panchronic Approach: A Study of the Polysemy of French *déjà* and Italian *già*." *Linguistics* 46:471–505.

Hansen, W. F. 2002. *Ariadne's Thread : A Guide to International Tales Found in Classical Literature*. Ithaca.

Harder, P. 1996. *Functional Semantics: A Theory of Meaning, Structure and Tense in English*. Berlin.

Harlfinger, D., and G. Prato, eds. 1991. *Paleografia e codicologia greca. Atti del II colloquio internazionale*. Alessandria.

Harrison, R. R. 2007. "A Structural Arrangement of Text to Facilitate Reading." *The Classical Journal* 102:291–303.

Harry, J. E. 1902. "Indicative Questions with μή and ἆρα μή." *Bulletin, University of Cincinnati* 7:427-434. [reprinted from *Studies in Honor of B. L. Gildersleeve*, 1902, Baltimore]

Hartel, W. von. 1874. "Homerische Studien II." *Sitzungsberichte der Akademie der Wissenschaften in Wien, Philosophisch-Historische Klasse* 76:329–376.

Hartung, J. A. 1828. *Commentatio de particulis δή et ἤδη*. Erlangen.

———. 1832-1833. *Lehre von den Partikeln der griechischen Sprache*. Erlangen.

Haslam, M. W. 2013. "New Readings at *Iliad* 4.511 and 512?" *Zeitschrift für Papyrologie und Epigraphik* 184:1–3.

Havelock, E. A. 1963. *Preface to Plato*. Oxford.

Havet, L. 1923. "Notes critiques sur Eschyle. Enquête sur τε et δέ dans les tragédies d'Eschyle étrangères à l'Orestie." *Revue de Philologie* 47:108–140.

Haviland, J. B. 2007. "Person Reference in Tzotzil Gossip: Referring Dupliciter." In *Person Reference in Interaction: Linguistic, Cultural, and Social Perspectives*, ed. N. J. Enfield and T. Stivers, 226–252. Cambridge.

Hawkins, J. 1977. "The Pragmatics of Definiteness." *Linguistische Berichte* 47:1–27.

Hayashi, M. 2013. "Turn Allocation and Turn Sharing." In *The Handbook of Conversation Analysis*, ed. J. Sidnell and T. Stivers, 167–190. Malden, MA.

Heath, M. 1988. "Receiving the *Kômos*, the Context and Performance of Epinician." *American Journal of Philology* 109:180–195.

Heine, B. 2013. "On Discourse Markers: Grammaticalization, Pragmaticalization, or Something Else?" *Linguistics* 51:1205–1247.

Heinemann, T. 2008. "Questions of Accountability: Yes-no Interrogatives that are Unanswerable." *Discourse Studies* 10:55–71.

Heinze, H. 1878. "Griechisches τε... καί." *Wissenschaftliche Monatsblätter* 6:150–151.

Held, G. 1992. "Politeness in Linguistic Research." In *Politeness in Language: Studies in Its History, Theory and Practice*, ed. R. J. Watts, S. Ide, and K. Ehlich, 131–153. Berlin.

———. 2003. *Partikeln und Höflichkeit*. Frankfurt.

Hell, J. G. van, L. Verhoeven, M. Tak, and M. van Oosterhout. 2005. "To Take a Stance: A Developmental Study of the Use of Pronouns and Passives in Spoken and Written Narrative and Expository Texts in Dutch." *Journal of Pragmatics* 37:239–273.

Heller, H. 1853. "Epistola ad Max. Dunkerum de particulis ἤδη et δή." *Philologus* 8:254–308.

Heller, J. C. 1858. "De Particula ἄρα." *Philologus* 13:68–121.

Hellwig, A. 1974. "Zur Funktion und Bedeutung der griechischen Partikeln." *Glotta* 52:145–171.

Hemmerdinger, B. 1955. *Essai sur l'histoire du texte de Thucydide*. Collection d'études anciennes. Paris.

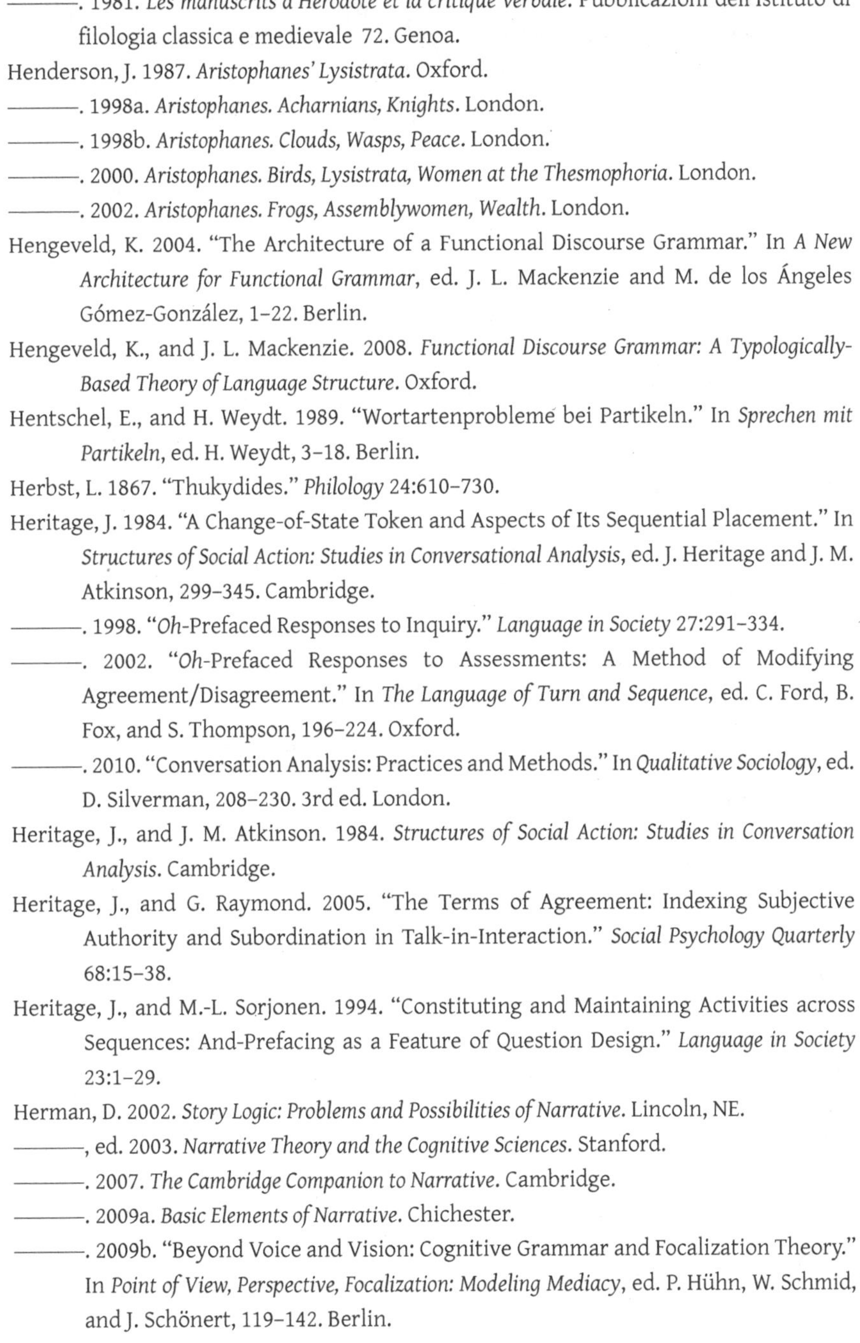

———. 1981. *Les manuscrits d'Hérodote et la critique verbale*. Pubblicazioni dell'Istituto di filologia classica e medievale 72. Genoa.

Henderson, J. 1987. *Aristophanes' Lysistrata*. Oxford.

———. 1998a. *Aristophanes. Acharnians, Knights*. London.

———. 1998b. *Aristophanes. Clouds, Wasps, Peace*. London.

———. 2000. *Aristophanes. Birds, Lysistrata, Women at the Thesmophoria*. London.

———. 2002. *Aristophanes. Frogs, Assemblywomen, Wealth*. London.

Hengeveld, K. 2004. "The Architecture of a Functional Discourse Grammar." In *A New Architecture for Functional Grammar*, ed. J. L. Mackenzie and M. de los Ángeles Gómez-González, 1–22. Berlin.

Hengeveld, K., and J. L. Mackenzie. 2008. *Functional Discourse Grammar: A Typologically-Based Theory of Language Structure*. Oxford.

Hentschel, E., and H. Weydt. 1989. "Wortartenprobleme bei Partikeln." In *Sprechen mit Partikeln*, ed. H. Weydt, 3–18. Berlin.

Herbst, L. 1867. "Thukydides." *Philology* 24:610–730.

Heritage, J. 1984. "A Change-of-State Token and Aspects of Its Sequential Placement." In *Structures of Social Action: Studies in Conversational Analysis*, ed. J. Heritage and J. M. Atkinson, 299–345. Cambridge.

———. 1998. "*Oh*-Prefaced Responses to Inquiry." *Language in Society* 27:291–334.

———. 2002. "*Oh*-Prefaced Responses to Assessments: A Method of Modifying Agreement/Disagreement." In *The Language of Turn and Sequence*, ed. C. Ford, B. Fox, and S. Thompson, 196–224. Oxford.

———. 2010. "Conversation Analysis: Practices and Methods." In *Qualitative Sociology*, ed. D. Silverman, 208–230. 3rd ed. London.

Heritage, J., and J. M. Atkinson. 1984. *Structures of Social Action: Studies in Conversation Analysis*. Cambridge.

Heritage, J., and G. Raymond. 2005. "The Terms of Agreement: Indexing Subjective Authority and Subordination in Talk-in-Interaction." *Social Psychology Quarterly* 68:15–38.

Heritage, J., and M.-L. Sorjonen. 1994. "Constituting and Maintaining Activities across Sequences: And-Prefacing as a Feature of Question Design." *Language in Society* 23:1–29.

Herman, D. 2002. *Story Logic: Problems and Possibilities of Narrative*. Lincoln, NE.

———, ed. 2003. *Narrative Theory and the Cognitive Sciences*. Stanford.

———. 2007. *The Cambridge Companion to Narrative*. Cambridge.

———. 2009a. *Basic Elements of Narrative*. Chichester.

———. 2009b. "Beyond Voice and Vision: Cognitive Grammar and Focalization Theory." In *Point of View, Perspective, Focalization: Modeling Mediacy*, ed. P. Hühn, W. Schmid, and J. Schönert, 119–142. Berlin.

———. 2010. "Directions in Cognitive Narratology: Triangulating Stories, Media, and the Mind." In *Postclassical Narratology: Approaches and Analyses*, ed. J. Alber and M. Fludernik, 137–162. Columbus.

———. 2011. *The Emergence of Mind : Representations of Consciousness in Narrative Discourse in English*. Lincoln, NE.

Hermann, E. 1912. *Griechische Forschungen I. Die Nebensätze in den griechischen Dialektinschriften*. Leipzig.

Hermann, G. 1799. *Aristophanis Nubes cum scholiis*. Leipzig.

Hermann, J. G. J. 1823. *Euripidis Bacchae*. Leipzig.

———. 1825. *Sophocles. Oedipus Coloneus*. 1st ed. Leipzig.

———. 1831. *Libri IV de particula ἄν*. Leipzig.

———. 1852. *Aeschyli Tragoediae*. Leipzig.

Herwerden, H. van. 1866. *Sophoclis Oedipus Rex*. Utrecht.

———. 1902. *Lexicon Graecum suppletorium et dialecticum*. Leiden.

Hesk, J. 2003. *Sophocles. Ajax*. London.

———. 2006. "Homeric Flyting and How to Read It: Performance and Intratext in *Iliad* 20.83-109 and 20.178-258." *Ramus* 35:4–28.

———. 2007. "Combative Capping in Aristophanic Comedy." *Cambridge Classical Journal* 53:124–160.

Hewings, A. 2012. "Stance and Voice in Academic Discourse across Channels." In *Stance and Voice in Written Academic Genres*, ed. K. Hyland and C. Sancho Guinda, 187–201. Basingstoke.

Heyworth, S. J. 2007. *Sexti Properti elegos: critico apparatu instructos*. Oxford.

Hickie, W. J. 1853. *The Comedies of Aristophanes*. London.

Hilgard, A., ed. 1901. *Grammatici Graeci I.3: Scholia in Dionysii Thracis Artem Grammaticam*. Grammatici Graeci I.3. Leipzig.

Hiller, E. 1886. "Die Partikel ῥα." *Hermes* 21:563–569.

Hilton, J. 1997. "The Role of Discourse and Lexical Meaning in the Grammaticalisation of Temporal Particles in Latin." *Glotta* 74:198–210.

Hinrichs, G. 1875. *De Homericae Elocutionis Vestigiis Aeolicis: Dissertatio Inauguralis Philologica*. Jena.

Hirschberg, J. 2006. "Pragmatics and Intonation." In *The Handbook of Pragmatics*, ed. L. R. Horn and G. Ward, 515–537. Malden, MA.

Hobbes, T. 1723. *The History of the Grecian War: In Eight Books; Written by Thucydides; Faithfully Translated from the Original by Thomas Hobbes of Malmsbury; With Maps Describing the Country*. 2 vols. 3rd ed. London.

Hoefer, H. 1882. *De particulis Platonicis capita selecta*. Bonn.

Hoekstra, A. 1965. *Homeric Modifications of Formulaic Prototypes*. Amsterdam.

Hoey, M. 1979. *Signalling in Discourse*. Birmingham.

Hoffmann, K. 1967. *Der Injunktiv im Veda*. Heidelberg.

Hoffmann, T., and G. Trousdale, eds. 2013. *The Oxford Handbook of Construction Grammar.* Oxford.

Hoffmann, V. 1880. *De Particularum Nonnullarum apud Herodotum Usu*. Halle.

———.1884. *Über den Gebrauch der Partikel ὦν bei Herodot*. Piła.

Hogan, P. C. 2010. "Fictions and Feelings: On the Place of Literature in the Study of Emotion." *Emotion Review* 2:184–195.

———. 2011. *What Literature Teaches Us about Emotion*. Cambridge.

Hogeweg, L. 2009a. "The Meaning and Interpretation of the Dutch Particle *wel*." *Journal of Pragmatics* 41:519–539.

———. 2009b. "What's So Unreal about the Past? Past Tense and Counterfactuals." In *Studies on English Modality: In Honour of Frank Palmer*, ed. A. Tsangalidis and R. Facchinetti, 181–208. Bern.

———. 2009c. *Word in Process. On the Interpretation, Acquisition, and Production of Words.* Nijmegen.

Hohti, P. 1976. *The Interrelation of Speech and Action in the Histories of Herodotus*. Helsinki.

Hölker, K. 1990. "Französisch: Partikelforschung." In *Lexikon Der Romanistischen Linguistik* V-1, 77–88. Tübingen.

Hollmann, W. B. 2013. "Constructions in Cognitive Sociolinguistics." In *The Oxford Handbook of Construction Grammar*, ed. T. Hoffmann and G. Trousdale. Oxford Handbooks Online.

Holmes, D. H. 1895. *Index Lysiacus*. Bonn.

Holmes, J. 1986. "Functions of *you know* in Women's and Men's Speech." *Language in Society* 15:1–22.

Holmes, N. 2011. "Interrogative *nam* in Early Latin." *Mnemosyne* 65:203–218.

Hoogeveen, H. 1769. *Doctrina Particularum Linguae Graecae*. [Vol. 1: https://play.google.com/books/reader?id=Hu1MAAAAcAAJ&hl=en&pg=GBS.PP3; Vol. 2: https://books.google.de/books?id=Ve1MAAAAcAAJ&printsec=frontcover&hl=de#v=onepage&q&f=false]. Leiden.

Hopper, P J. 1979. "Aspect and Foregrounding in Discourse." In *Syntax and Semantics*. Vol. 12. *Discourse and Syntax*, ed. T. Givón, 213–41. New York.

———. 1988. "Emergent Grammar and the A Priori Grammar Postulate." In *Linguistics in Context: Connecting Observation and Understanding : Lectures from the 1985 LSA/TESOL and NEH Institutes*, ed. D. Tannen, 117–134. Norwood, NJ.

———. 2004. "The Openness of Grammatical Constructions." In *Proceedings from the Annual Meeting of the Chicago Linguistic Society* 40:153–175.

———. 2011. "Emergent Grammar and Temporality in Interactional Linguistics." In *Constructions: Emerging and Emergent*, ed. P. Auer and S. Pfänder, 22–45. Berlin.

Hopper, P. J., and S. A. Thompson. 1984. "The Discourse Basis for Lexical Categories in Universal Grammar." *Language* 60:703–752.

———. 2008. "Projectability and Clause Combining in Interaction." In *Crosslinguistic Studies of Clause Combining*, ed. R. Laury, 99–123. Amsterdam.
Hopper, P. J., and E. Closs Traugott. 2003. *Grammaticalization*. 2nd ed. Cambridge.
Horie, P. I., and S. Iwasaki. 1996. "Register and Pragmatic Particles in Thai Conversation." In *Pan-Asiatic linguistics: Proceedings of the Fourth International Symposium on Languages and Linguistics, January 8-10*, ed. S. Premsrirat Iam Thongdee et al., 1197–1205. Bangkok.
Horn, L. R. 1972. On the Semantic Properties of Logical Operators in English. PhD diss., University of California, Los Angeles.
———. 1989. *A Natural History of Negation*. 2nd ed. Stanford.
Horn, L. R., and G. L. Ward, eds. 2006. *The Handbook of Pragmatics*. Malden, MA.
Horn, W. 1926. *Quaestiones ad Xenophontis elocutionem pertinentes*. Halle.
Hornblower, S. 1987. *Thucydides*. London.
———. 1991–1998. *A Commentary on Thucydides*. 3 vols. Oxford.
———. 1994. "Narratology and Narrative Techniques in Thucydides." In *Greek Historiography*, ed. S. Hornblower, 131–166. Oxford.
Horrocks, G. 1997. "Bibliography." In *Greek: A History of the Language and Its Speakers*, 366–380. London.
How, W. W., and J. Wells. 1928. *A Commentary on Herodotus, with Introduction and Appendixes*. Oxford.
Huang, Y. 1991. "A Neo-Gricean Pragmatic Theory of Anaphora." *Journal of Linguistics* 27:301–335.
———. 2006. "Anaphora, Cataphora, Exophora, Logophoricity." In *Encyclopedia of Language and Linguistics*, 2nd ed. Amsterdam.
———. 2007. *Pragmatics*. Oxford.
———. 2010. "Neo-Gricean Pragmatic Theory of Conversational Implicature." In *The Oxford Handbook of Linguistic Analysis*, ed. B. Heine and H. Narrog, 607–631. Oxford.
Huart, P. 1968. *Le vocabulaire de l'analyse psychologique dans l'oeuvre de Thucydide*. Paris.
Hübner, E. 1883. *Grundriss zu Vorlesungen über die griechische Syntax*. Berlin.
Hude, K. 1901. "Über γάρ in appositiven Ausdrücken." *Hermes* 36:313–315.
———. 1904. "Über γάρ in appositiven Ausdrücken." *Hermes* 39:476–477.
Hudson, J. 1696. *Thoukudidou peri tou peloponnēsiakou polemou biblia oktō. Thucydidis de bello peloponnesiaco libri octo*. Oxford.
Huitink, L. 2009. "Pragmatic Presupposition and Complementation in Ancient Greek." In *Discourse Cohesion in Ancient Greek*, ed. G. C. Wakker S. J. Bakker, 21–40. Leiden.
———. 2012. Reported Discourse in Classical Greek: Grammatical Form and Communicative Function. PhD diss., University of Oxford.
Humbert, J. 1960. *Syntaxe grecque*. 3rd ed. Paris.
Hummel, P. 1993. *La syntaxe de Pindare*. Louvain.
Humphreys, M. W. 1897. "Notes on Greek Grammar." *Classical Review* 11:138–141.

Humphreys, S. 1987. "Law, Custom and Culture in Herodotus." *Arethusa* 20:211–220.

Hunston, S., and G. Thompson. 2000. *Evaluation in Text: Authorial Stance and the Construction of Discourse*. Oxford.

Hunter, V. 1973. *Thucydides: The Artful Reporter*. Toronto.

———. 1988. "Thucydides and the Sociology of the Crowd." *The Classical Journal* 84:17–30.

Hutchinson, G. O. 1985. *Aeschylus. Septem Contra Thebas*. Oxford.

Hymes, D. 1977. "Discovering Oral Performance and Measured Verse in American Indian Narrative." *New Literary History* 8:431–457.

———. 1997. "On Communicative Competence." In *Linguistic Anthropology: A Reader*, ed. A. Duranti, 53–73. 2nd ed. Cambridge.

Hymes, D., R. Bauman, and J. Sherzer. 1989. "Ways of Speaking." In *Explorations in the Ethnography of Speaking*, 433–451. 2nd ed. Cambridge.

Ifantidou, E. 2000. "Procedural Encoding of Explicatures by the Modern Greek Particle *taha*." In Andersen and Fretheim 2000:119–143.

———. 2001. *Evidentials and Relevance*. Amsterdam.

Ifantidou-Trouki, E. 1993. "Sentential Adverbs and Relevance." *Lingua* 90:69–90.

Immerwahr, H. R. 1954. "Historical Action in Herodotus." *Transactions of the American Philological Association* 85:16–45.

———. 1966. *Form and Thought in Herodotus*. American Philological Association Monograph 23. Cleveland.

Imo, W. 2005. "A Construction Grammar Approach to the Phrase 'I mean' in Spoken English." *InLiSt - Interaction and Linguistic Structures* 42: http://kops.uni-konstanz.de/bitstream/handle/123456789/3791/InLiSt42.pdf?sequence=1&isAllowed=y.

———. 2007. *Construction Grammar und Gesprochene-Sprache-Forschung*. Reihe Germanistische Linguistik 275. Tübingen.

———. 2008. "Individuelle Konstrukte oder Vorboten einer neuen Konstruktion? Stellungsvarianten der Modalpartikel *halt* im Vor- und Nachfeld." In *Konstruktionsgrammatik II: Von der Konstruktion zur Grammatik*, ed. A. Stefanowitsch and K. Fischer, 135–156. Tübingen.

———. 2013. *Sprache in Interaktion: Analysemethoden und Untersuchungsfelder*. Berlin.

Ingalls, W. B. 1979. "Formular Density in the Similes of the *Iliad*." *Transactions of the American Philological Association* 109:87–109.

Inglese, G. 2018. "Connectives and Discourse Markers in Ancient Greek: The Diachrony of *atár* from Homeric Greek to Classical Attic." *Journal of Greek Linguistics* 18:93–123.

Ingria, R. 2005. "Grammatical Formatives in a Generative Lexical Theory: The Case of Modern Greek και." *Journal of Greek Linguistics* 6:61–101.

Ireland, S. 1974. "Stichomythia in Aeschylus: The Dramatic Role of Syntax and Connecting Particles." *Hermes* 102:509–524.

Irigoin, J. 1953. *Recherches sur les mètres de la lyrique chorale grecque*. Paris.

Irmscher, J. 1950. *Götterzorn bei Homer*. Leipzig.

Italie, G. 1953. *Aeschylus. Perzen*. Leiden.

———. 1955. *Index Aeschyleus*. Leiden.

Itani, R. 1993. "The Japanese Sentence-Final Particle *ka*: A Relevance-Theoretic Approach." *Lingua* 90:129–147.

Itsumi, K. 2009. *Pindaric Metre: The "Other Half."* Oxford.

Izutsu, K., and M. N. Izutsu. 2013. "From Discourse Markers to Modal/Final Particles: What the Position Reveals about the Continuum." In *Discourse Markers and Modal Particles: Categorization and Description*, ed. L. Degand, B. Cornillie, and P. Pietrandrea, 217–236. Amsterdam.

Jääskeläinen, A. 2013. Todisteena äänen kuva. Suomen kielen imitatiivikonstruktiot [Imitations of sounds as evidence: the constructions of imitatives in the Finnish language]. PhD diss., University of Helsinki.

Jacquinod, B. 1997. "Sur le rôle pragmatique de *kaitoi*." In Rijksbaron 1997:131–149. Amsterdam.

Jahn, C. F. 1847. *Grammaticorum Graecorum de coniunctibus doctrina*. Greifswald.

Janko, R. M. 1992. *The Iliad: A Commentary* IV. Cambridge.

Jannaris, A. N. 1897. *An Historical Greek Grammar*. London.

Jeannerod, M. 2001. "Neural Simulation of Action: A Unifying Mechanism for Motor Cognition." *Neuroimage* 14:103–109.

Jebb, R. C. 1888. *Sophocles. Antigone*. Cambridge.

———. 2004 [1892]. *Sophocles. Plays: Trachiniae*. Ed. P. E. Easterling and B. Goward. London.

———. 2004 [1893]. *Sophocles. Plays: Oedipus Tyrannus*. Ed. P. E. Easterling and J. S. Rusten. London.

———. 2004 [1896]. *Sophocles. Plays: Ajax*. Ed. P. E. Easterling and P. Wilson. London.

Jefferson, G. 1983. "Notes on a Systematic Deployment of the Acknowledgement Tokens 'yeah' and 'mmhm.'" *Tilburg Papers in Language and Literature* 30:1–18.

Jespersen, O. 1933. "Monosyllabism in English." In *Linguistica: Selected Papers in English, French and German*, 384–408. Copenhagen.

Jiménez Delgado, J. M. 2012. "οὕτως recapitulativo en Heródoto." In *Lingüística XL. El Lingüista Del Siglo XXI*, ed. A. Cabedo Nebot and P. Infante Ríos, 133–140. Madrid.

———. 2013. "Adverbios temporales como conectores con valor consecutivo en griego antiguo." *Cuadernos de Filología Clásica. Estudios Griegos e Indoeuropeos* 23:31–52.

———. 2013. "Καὶ μάλα: Estructurus de focalización y polaridad positiva." *Veleia* 30:249–258.

———. 2014. "Adverbios, partículas y marcadores del discurso: αὖ y αὖθις en los historiadores griegos." *Emerita* 82:223–247.

Johnson, W. A. 1994. "The Function of the Paragraphus in Greek Literary Prose Texts." *Zeitschrift für Papyrologie und Epigraphik* 100:65–68.

———. 2004. *Bookrolls and Scribes in Oxyrhynchus*. Studies in Book and Print Culture. Toronto.

Johnstone, B. 2002. *Discourse Analysis*. Malden, MA.

Jones, W. H. S. 1910. "καὶ οὐ, ἀλλ' οὐ, οὐδέ." *Classical Review* 24:51.

Jong, I. J. F. de. 1987. *Narrators and Focalizers: The Presentation of the Story in the Iliad*. Amsterdam.

———. 1991. *Narrative in Drama: The Art of the Euripidean Messenger-Speech*. Leiden.

———. 1997. "*Gar* Introducing Embedded Narratives." In Rijksbaron 1997:175–85. Amsterdam.

———. 2001a. *A Narratological Commentary on the Odyssey*. Cambridge.

———. 2001b. "The Origins of Figural Narration in Antiquity." In *New Perspectives on Narrative Perspective*, ed. W. van Peer and S. Chatman, 67–81. New York.

———. 2004a. "Herodotus." In *Narrators, Narratees, and Narratives in Ancient Greek Literature*, ed. I. J. F. de Jong, R. Nünlist, and A. M. Bowie, 101-114. Leiden.

———. 2004b. *Narrators and Focalizers*. 2nd ed. London.

———. 2007. "Sophocles' *Trachiniae* 1–48, Euripidean Prologues, and Their Audiences." In *The Language of Literature: Linguistic Approaches to Classical Texts*, ed. R. J. Allan, M. Buijs, A. Rijksbaron, and I. J. F. de Jong, 7–28. Leiden.

———, ed. 2007. *Time in Ancient Greek Narrative*. Leiden.

———. 2009. "Metalepsis in Ancient Greek Literature." In *Narratology and Interpretation: The Content of Narrative Form in Ancient Literature*, ed. A. Rengakos and J. Grethlein, 87–115. Berlin.

———. 2012. *Homer. Iliad, Book XXII*. Cambridge.

———, ed. 2012. *Space in Ancient Greek Literature: Studies in Ancient Greek Narrative*. Leiden.

———. 2013. "Narratological Aspects of the Histories of Herodotus." In *Herodotus and the Narrative of the Past*, ed. R. Vignolo Munson, 253–291. New York.

———. 2014. *Narratology and Classics: A Practical Guide*. Oxford.

Jong, I. J. F. de., R. Nünlist, and A. Bowie, eds. 2004. *Narrators, Narratees, and Narratives in Ancient Greek Literature: Studies in Ancient Greek Narrative*. Leiden).

Jong, I. J. F. de., and J. P. Sullivan, eds. 1994. *Modern Critical Theory and Classical Literature*. Leiden.

Jonge, C. C. de. 2008. *Between Grammar and Rhetoric: Dionysius of Halicarnassus on Language, Linguistics and Literature*. Leiden.

———. 2009. "Review of Marini, N., ed., 2007, *Demetrio, Lo Stile. Pleiadi 4*." *Bryn Mawr Classical Review* 2009.08.12. http://bmcr.brynmawr.edu/2009/2009-08-12.html.

———. 2015. "Grammatical Theory and Rhetorical Teaching." In *Brill's Companion to Ancient Scholarship*, ed. F. Montanari and A. Rengakos, 979–1011. Leiden.

Jonker, D.-E. 2014. "Oh, Well, You Know, Do Not You? Socio-Historical Discourse Analysis of Jane Austen's Fictional Works." MA thesis, Leiden University.

Joost, A. 1895. "Beobachtungen über den Partikelgebrauch Lucians." In *Festschrift zum fünfzigjährigen Doctorjubiläum Ludwig Friedländer*, ed. H. Baumgart, 163–182. Leipzig.

Jowett, B. 1881. *Thucydides*. 2 vols. Oxford.

Jucker, A. H. 1993. "The Discourse Marker *well*: A Relevance-Theoretical Account." *Journal of Pragmatics* 19:435–452.

———, ed. 1995. *Historical Pragmatics*. Pragmatics and Beyond New Series 35. Amsterdam.

———. 1997. "The Discourse Marker *well* in the History of English." *English Language and Linguistics* 1:91–110.

———. 2002. "Discourse Markers in Early Modern English." In *Alternative Histories of English*, ed. R. Watts and P. Trudgill, 210–230. London.

———. 2010. "Historical Pragmatics." In *Variation and Change: Pragmatic Perspectives*, ed. M. Fried, J.-O. Östman, and J. Verschueren, 110–122. Amsterdam.

Jucker, A. H., and Y. Ziv, eds. 1998. *Discourse Markers: Descriptions and Theory*. Amsterdam.

———. 1998. "Discourse Markers: Introduction." In Jucker and Ziv 1998:1–12. Amsterdam.

Jung, V. 1991. *Thukydides und die Dichtung*. Frankfurt.

Jungermann, G. 1608. [*Hērodotou Halikarnassēos Historiōn logoi 9, epigraphomenoi Mousai. Tou autou exegēsis peri tēs Homerou biotēs.*] = *Herodoti Halicarnassei Historiarum libri IX, IX Musarum nominibus inscripti. Eiusdem narratio de vita Homeri*. Editio adornata opera & studio Gothofredi Jungermani. Frankfurt.

Jurk, J. 1900. *Ramenta Hippocratea*. Berlin.

Juslin, P. N. 2013. "Vocal Affect Expression: Problems and Promises." In *The Evolution of Emotional Communication: From Sounds in Nonhuman Mammals to Speech and Music in Man*, ed. E. Altenmüller, S. Schmidt, and E. Zimmermann, 252–273. Oxford.

Kachru, B. B., S. Saporta, R. B. Lees, Y. Malkiel, and A. Pietrangeli, eds. 1973. *Issues in Linguistics: Papers in Honor of Henry and Renée Kahane*. Urbana.

Kahane, A. 1994. *The Interpretation of Order: A Study in the Poetics of Homeric Repetition*. Oxford.

Kakridis, P. I. 1974. *Aristophanous. Ornithes*. Athens.

Kalinka, E. 1890. "De usu coniunctionum quarundam apud scriptores Atticos antiquissimos." In *Dissertationes Philologae Vindobonenses*, 145–212. Vienna.

Kallenberg, H. 1886. "Herodot (Jahresberichte des philologischen Vereins zu Berlin)." *Zeitschrift für das Gymnasialwesen* 40:294–328.

———. 1897. "Herodot." *Zeitschrift für das Gymnasialwesen* 51:167–222.

———. 1913. "Ὅτι und ὡς bei Plato als Hilfsmittel zur Bestimming der Zeitfolge seiner Schriften." *Rheinisches Museum für Philologie* 68:465–476.

Kallet, L. 2001. *Money and the Corrosion of Power in Thucydides: The Sicilian Expedition and Its Aftermath*. Berkeley.

Kambylis, A. 1964. *Anredeformen bei Pindar*. Athens.

Kamerbeek, J. C. 1953. *Sophocles: Ajax*. Leiden.

———. 1959. *Sophocles. Trachiniae*. Leiden.

———. 1967. *Sophocles. Oedipus Tyrannus*. Leiden.

———. 1978. *Sophocles. Antigone*. Leiden.

Kannicht, R. 1969. *Euripides. Helena. Herausgegeben und erklärt von Richard Kannicht.* Heidelberg.

Kapatsinski, V. 2010. "Frequency of Use Leads to Automaticity of Production: Evidence from Repair in Conversation." *Language and Speech* 53:71–105.

Kärkkäinen, E. 2003. *Epistemic Stance in English Conversation: A Description of Its Interactional Functions, with a Focus on "I think."* Amsterdam.

Karttunen, L. 1974. "Presupposition and Linguistic Context." *Theoretical Linguistics* 1:181–194.

Karttunen, L., and S. Peters. 1979. "Conventional Implicature." In *Syntax and Semantics.* Vol. 11: *Presuppositions*, ed. C. Oh and D. Dineen, 1–56. New York.

Kaster, R. A. 2005. *Emotion, Restraint, and Community in Ancient Rome.* Classical Culture and Society. Oxford.

Katsures, A. G. 1975. *Linguistic and Stylistic Characterization: Tragedy and Menander.* Ioannina.

Katz, J. T. 2007. "The Epic Adventures of an Unknown Particle." In *Greek and Latin from an Indo-European Perspective*, ed. C. H. George, 65–79. Cambridge.

Kayser, W. C. 1862. "Der Text der homerischen Gedichte. Jahresbericht." *Philologus* 18:647–704.

Keelhoff, J. 1892. "εἰ δ' οὖν peut-il être synonyme de εἰ δὲ μή?" *Revue de l'instruction publique en Belgique* 35:161–176.

Keevallik, L. 2008. "Conjunction and Sequenced Actions: The Estonian Complementizer and Evidential Particle *et.*" In *Crosslinguistic Studies of Clause Combining: The Multifunctionality of Conjunctions*, ed. R. Laury, 125–152. Amsterdam.

Keil, H. 1857–1880. *Grammatici Latini.* 8 vols. Leipzig.

Kemp, A. 1987. "The *Téchnē Grammatikḗ* of Dionysius Thrax." In *The History of Linguistics in the Classical Period*, ed. D. J. J. D. Taylor, 169–189. Amsterdam.

Kent, A. 2012. "Compliance, Resistance and Incipient Compliance When Responding to Directives." *Discourse Studies* 14:711–730.

Kerschensteiner, J. 1964. "Zum Gebrauch der Parenthese bei Herodot." *Münchener Studien zur Sprachwissenschaft* 17:29–50.

Keysar, B., D. J. Barr, J. A. Balin, and T. S. Paek. 1998. "Definite Reference and Mutual Knowledge: Process Models of Common Ground in Comprehension." *Journal of Memory and Language* 39:1–20.

Kienpointner, M., ed. 1999. *Ideologies of Politeness.* Special issue, *Pragmatics* 9.

Kim, H. 2004. "*Really* as a Free-Standing TCU in English Conversation." *Language Research* 40:861–883.

King, B. 1992. "On the Meaning of Empty Words." *Semiotica* 89:257–265.

Kirk, G. S., B. Hainsworth, M. W. Edwards, R. Janko, and N. Richardson. 1993. *The Iliad : A Commentary.* Cambridge.

Kirk, G. S. M. 1985. *The Iliad: A Commentary* I. Cambridge.

Kirkman, J. 2006. *Punctuation Matters: Advice on Punctuation for Scientific and Technical Writing*. 4th ed. London.

Kirsner, R. S., and V. J. van Heuven. 1999. "How Dutch Final Particles Constrain the Construal of Utterances: Experiment and Etymology." In *Discourse Studies in Cognitive Linguistics*, ed. K. van Hoek, A. A. Kibrik, and L. Noordman, 165–183. Amsterdam.

Klapproth, D. M. 2004. *Narrative as Social Practice: Anglo-Western and Australian Aboriginal Oral Traditions*. Berlin.

Klein, J. S. 1988. "Homeric Greek *au*: A Synchronic, Diachronic, and Comparative Study." *Historische Sprachforschung* 101:249–288.

———. 1992. "Some Indo-European Systems of Conjunction: Rigveda, Old Persian, Homer." *Harvard Studies in Classical Philology* 94:1–51.

Kloss, G. 2001. *Erscheinungsformen komischen Sprechens bei Aristophanes*. Berlin.

Klotz, R. 1835. *Matthaei Devarii liber de Graecae linguae particulis: Reinholdi Klotz adnotationes continens* I. Leipzig. https://archive.org/details/matthaeidevarii01unkngoog.

———. 1842. *Matthaei Devarii liber de Graecae linguae particulis: Reinholdi Klotz adnotationes continens* II. Leipzig. www.mdz-nbn-resolving.de/urn/resolver.pl?urn=urn:nbn:de:bvb:12-bsb10584881-0.

Knight, W. F. J. 1938. "Review of Denniston, *The Greek Particles*." *American Journal of Philology* 59:490–494.

Kock, T. 1864. *Aristophanes. Die Vögel*. Berlin.

Kohl, W. 1977. *Die Redetrias vor der sizilischen Expedition : (Thukydides 6, 9-23)*. Beiträge zur klassischen Philologie 91. Meisenheim am Glan.

Köhnken, A. 2006. *Darstellungsziele und Erzählstrategien in antiken Texten*. Berlin.

Kohonen, V., and N. E. Enkvist. 1978. *Text Linguistics, Cognitive Learning and Language Teaching*. Turku.

Koier, E. 2013. *Interpreting Particles in Dead and Living Languages: A Construction Grammar Approach to the Semantics of Dutch ergens and Ancient Greek pou*. Utrecht.

Koike, D. A. 1996. "Functions of the Adverbial *ya* in Spanish Narrative Discourse." *Journal of Pragmatics* 25:267–279.

Koktová, E. 1986. *Sentence Adverbials in a Functional Description*. Amsterdam.

König, E. 1991. *The Meaning of Focus Particles*. London.

König, E., and J. van der Auwera. 1988. "Clause Integration in German and Dutch Conditionals, Concessive Conditionals, and Concessives." In *Clause Combining in Grammar and Discourse*, ed. J. Haiman and S. A. Thompson, 101–133. Amsterdam.

Konopka, A. E., and S. Brown-Schmidt. 2014. "Message Encoding." In *The Oxford Handbook of Language Production*, ed. M. A. Goldrick, 3–20. Oxford.

Konstan, D. 2001. *Pity Transformed*. London.

———. 2006. *The Emotions of the Ancient Greeks: Studies in Aristotle and Classical Literature*. Toronto.

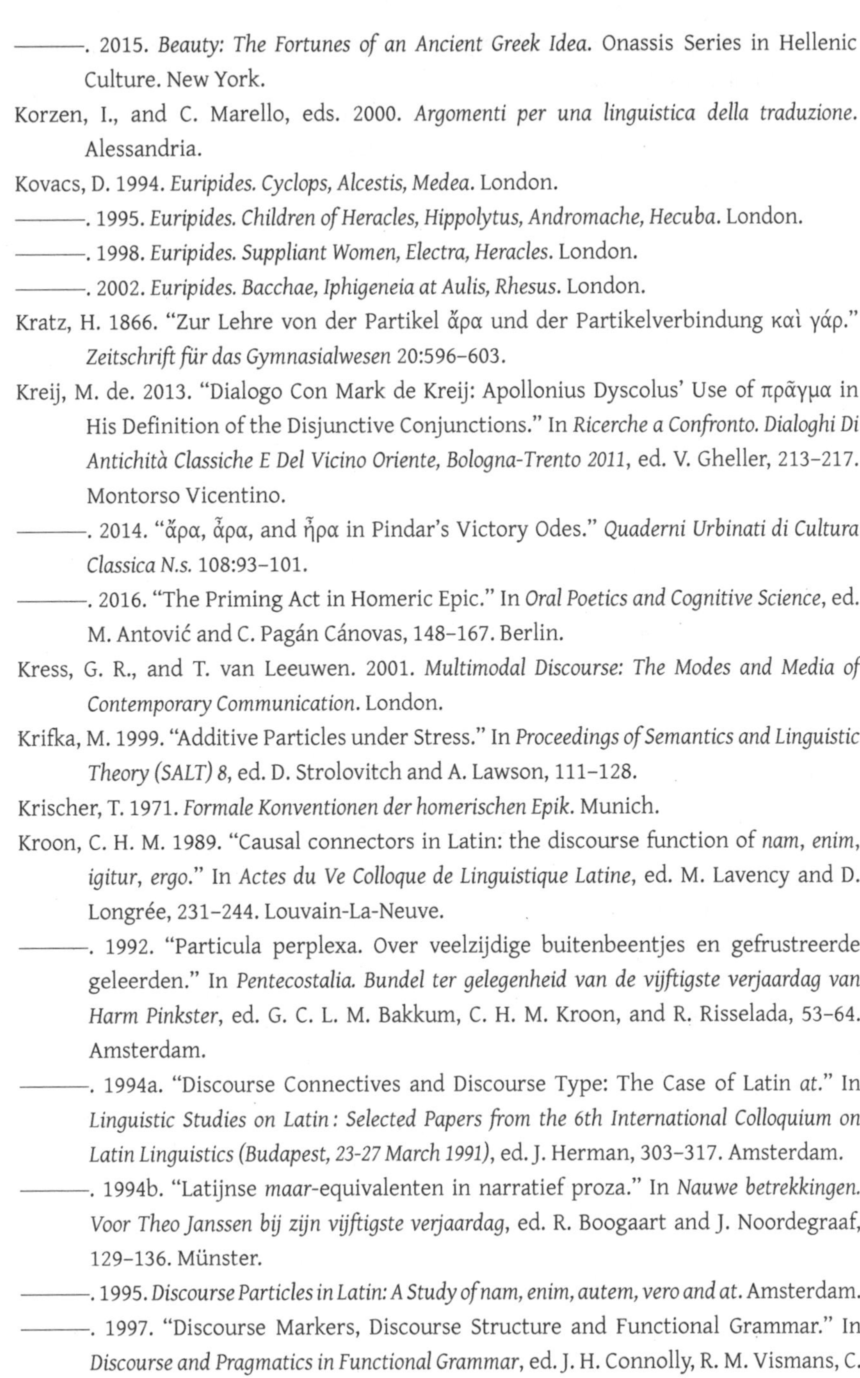

———. 2015. *Beauty: The Fortunes of an Ancient Greek Idea.* Onassis Series in Hellenic Culture. New York.

Korzen, I., and C. Marello, eds. 2000. *Argomenti per una linguistica della traduzione.* Alessandria.

Kovacs, D. 1994. *Euripides. Cyclops, Alcestis, Medea.* London.

———. 1995. *Euripides. Children of Heracles, Hippolytus, Andromache, Hecuba.* London.

———. 1998. *Euripides. Suppliant Women, Electra, Heracles.* London.

———. 2002. *Euripides. Bacchae, Iphigeneia at Aulis, Rhesus.* London.

Kratz, H. 1866. "Zur Lehre von der Partikel ἄρα und der Partikelverbindung καὶ γάρ." *Zeitschrift für das Gymnasialwesen* 20:596–603.

Kreij, M. de. 2013. "Dialogo Con Mark de Kreij: Apollonius Dyscolus' Use of πρᾶγμα in His Definition of the Disjunctive Conjunctions." In *Ricerche a Confronto. Dialoghi Di Antichità Classiche E Del Vicino Oriente, Bologna-Trento 2011*, ed. V. Gheller, 213–217. Montorso Vicentino.

———. 2014. "ἄρα, ἆρα, and ἦρα in Pindar's Victory Odes." *Quaderni Urbinati di Cultura Classica N.s.* 108:93–101.

———. 2016. "The Priming Act in Homeric Epic." In *Oral Poetics and Cognitive Science*, ed. M. Antović and C. Pagán Cánovas, 148–167. Berlin.

Kress, G. R., and T. van Leeuwen. 2001. *Multimodal Discourse: The Modes and Media of Contemporary Communication.* London.

Krifka, M. 1999. "Additive Particles under Stress." In *Proceedings of Semantics and Linguistic Theory (SALT) 8*, ed. D. Strolovitch and A. Lawson, 111–128.

Krischer, T. 1971. *Formale Konventionen der homerischen Epik.* Munich.

Kroon, C. H. M. 1989. "Causal connectors in Latin: the discourse function of *nam, enim, igitur, ergo.*" In *Actes du Ve Colloque de Linguistique Latine*, ed. M. Lavency and D. Longrée, 231–244. Louvain-La-Neuve.

———. 1992. "Particula perplexa. Over veelzijdige buitenbeentjes en gefrustreerde geleerden." In *Pentecostalia. Bundel ter gelegenheid van de vijftigste verjaardag van Harm Pinkster*, ed. G. C. L. M. Bakkum, C. H. M. Kroon, and R. Risselada, 53–64. Amsterdam.

———. 1994a. "Discourse Connectives and Discourse Type: The Case of Latin *at.*" In *Linguistic Studies on Latin : Selected Papers from the 6th International Colloquium on Latin Linguistics (Budapest, 23-27 March 1991)*, ed. J. Herman, 303–317. Amsterdam.

———. 1994b. "Latijnse *maar*-equivalenten in narratief proza." In *Nauwe betrekkingen. Voor Theo Janssen bij zijn vijftigste verjaardag*, ed. R. Boogaart and J. Noordegraaf, 129–136. Münster.

———. 1995. *Discourse Particles in Latin: A Study of* nam, enim, autem, vero *and* at. Amsterdam.

———. 1997. "Discourse Markers, Discourse Structure and Functional Grammar." In *Discourse and Pragmatics in Functional Grammar*, ed. J. H. Connolly, R. M. Vismans, C. S. Butler, and R. A. Gatward, 17–32. New York.

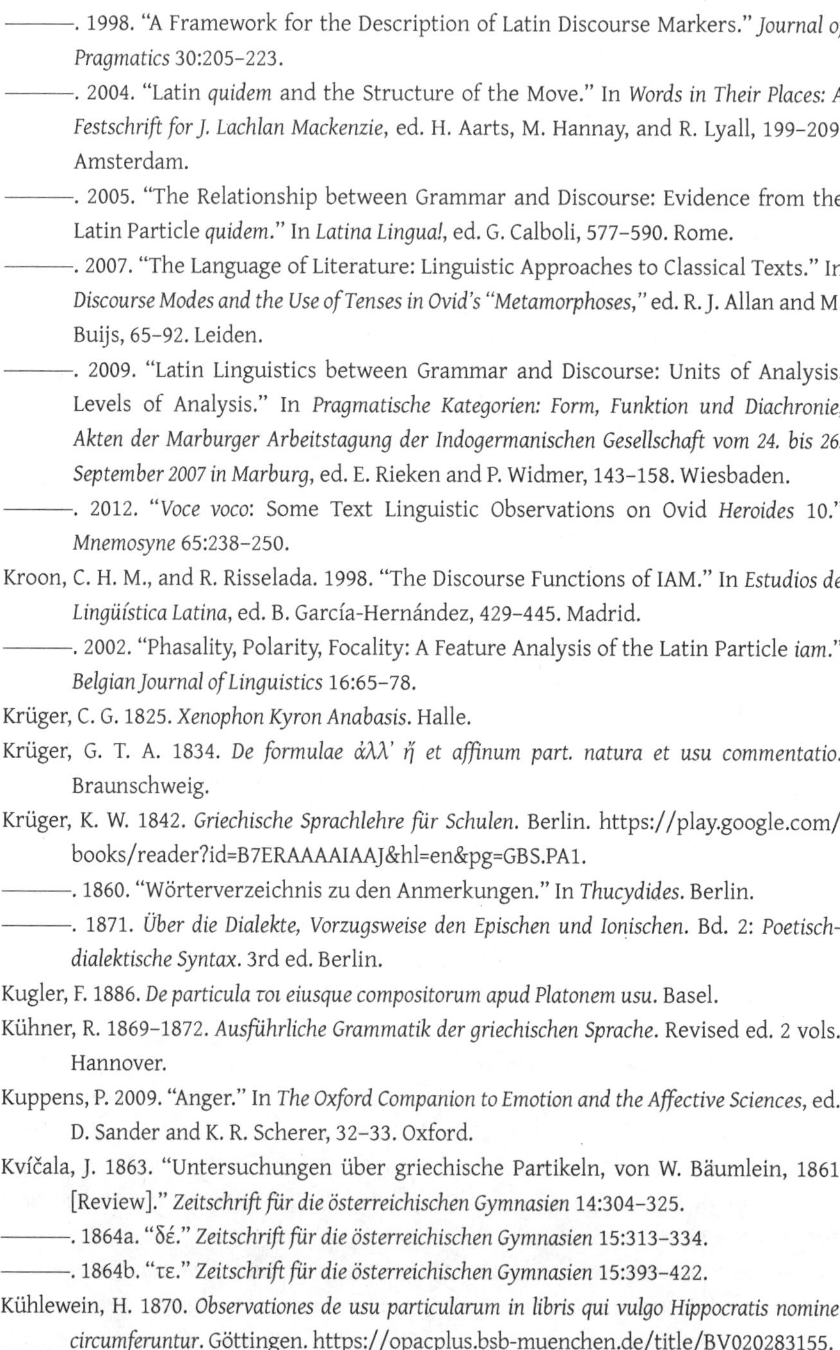

———. 1998. "A Framework for the Description of Latin Discourse Markers." *Journal of Pragmatics* 30:205–223.

———. 2004. "Latin *quidem* and the Structure of the Move." In *Words in Their Places: A Festschrift for J. Lachlan Mackenzie*, ed. H. Aarts, M. Hannay, and R. Lyall, 199–209. Amsterdam.

———. 2005. "The Relationship between Grammar and Discourse: Evidence from the Latin Particle *quidem*." In *Latina Lingua!*, ed. G. Calboli, 577–590. Rome.

———. 2007. "The Language of Literature: Linguistic Approaches to Classical Texts." In *Discourse Modes and the Use of Tenses in Ovid's "Metamorphoses,"* ed. R. J. Allan and M. Buijs, 65–92. Leiden.

———. 2009. "Latin Linguistics between Grammar and Discourse: Units of Analysis, Levels of Analysis." In *Pragmatische Kategorien: Form, Funktion und Diachronie; Akten der Marburger Arbeitstagung der Indogermanischen Gesellschaft vom 24. bis 26. September 2007 in Marburg*, ed. E. Rieken and P. Widmer, 143–158. Wiesbaden.

———. 2012. "*Voce voco*: Some Text Linguistic Observations on Ovid *Heroides* 10." *Mnemosyne* 65:238–250.

Kroon, C. H. M., and R. Risselada. 1998. "The Discourse Functions of IAM." In *Estudios de Lingüística Latina*, ed. B. García-Hernández, 429–445. Madrid.

———. 2002. "Phasality, Polarity, Focality: A Feature Analysis of the Latin Particle *iam*." *Belgian Journal of Linguistics* 16:65–78.

Krüger, C. G. 1825. *Xenophon Kyron Anabasis*. Halle.

Krüger, G. T. A. 1834. *De formulae ἀλλ' ἤ et affinum part. natura et usu commentatio*. Braunschweig.

Krüger, K. W. 1842. *Griechische Sprachlehre für Schulen*. Berlin. https://play.google.com/books/reader?id=B7ERAAAAIAAJ&hl=en&pg=GBS.PA1.

———. 1860. "Wörterverzeichnis zu den Anmerkungen." In *Thucydides*. Berlin.

———. 1871. *Über die Dialekte, Vorzugsweise den Epischen und Ionischen*. Bd. 2: *Poetisch-dialektische Syntax*. 3rd ed. Berlin.

Kugler, F. 1886. *De particula τοι eiusque compositorum apud Platonem usu*. Basel.

Kühner, R. 1869–1872. *Ausführliche Grammatik der griechischen Sprache*. Revised ed. 2 vols. Hannover.

Kuppens, P. 2009. "Anger." In *The Oxford Companion to Emotion and the Affective Sciences*, ed. D. Sander and K. R. Scherer, 32–33. Oxford.

Kvíčala, J. 1863. "Untersuchungen über griechische Partikeln, von W. Bäumlein, 1861 [Review]." *Zeitschrift für die österreichischen Gymnasien* 14:304–325.

———. 1864a. "δέ." *Zeitschrift für die österreichischen Gymnasien* 15:313–334.

———. 1864b. "τε." *Zeitschrift für die österreichischen Gymnasien* 15:393–422.

Kühlewein, H. 1870. *Observationes de usu particularum in libris qui vulgo Hippocratis nomine circumferuntur*. Göttingen. https://opacplus.bsb-muenchen.de/title/BV020283155.

Kühner, R. 1835. *Ausführliche Grammatik der griechischen Sprache*. Bd. 2: *Syntaxe*. Hannover.

Kühner, R., and B. Gerth. 1955. *Ausführliche Grammatik der griechischen Sprache*. 2 vols. 4th ed. Hannover.

Labéy, D. 1950. *Manuel des particules grecques*. Paris.

Labov, W. 1972. *Language in the Inner City*. Philadelphia.

Labov, W., and J. Waletzky. 1967. "Narrative Analysis." In *Essays on the Verbal and Visual Arts*, ed. J. Helm, 12–44. Seattle.

Lakoff, R. T. 1971. "If's, And's and But's About Conjunction." In *Studies in Linguistic Semantics*, ed. C. J. Fillmore and D. T. Langendoen, 115–150. New York.

———. 1973. "Questionable Answers and Answerable Questions." In *Issues in Linguistics: Papers in Honor of Henry and Renée Kahane*, ed. Y. Malkiel, S. Saporta, A. Pietrangeli, R. B. Lees, and B. B. Kachru, 453–467. Urbana.

———. 1974. "Remarks on This and That." *Chicago Linguistic Society* 10:345–356.

———. 2003. "Nine Ways of Looking at Apologies: The Necessity for Interdisciplinary Theory and Method in Discourse Analysis." In *The Handbook of Discourse Analysis*, ed. H. E. Hamilton, D. Tannen, and D. Schiffrin, 199–214. Oxford.

Lallot, J. 1997. *Apollonius Dyscole. De la construction (syntaxe)*. Paris.

———. 1998. *La Grammaire de Denys le Thrace*. Paris.

———. 1999. "Philologie et grammaire à Alexandrie." In *Actes Du XXXIe congrès international de l'Association des Professeurs de Langues Anciennes de l'Enseignement Supérieur*, ed. L. Basset and F. Biville, 41–49. Lyon.

Lallot, J., A. Rijksbaron, B. Jacquinod, and M. Buijs, ed. 2011. *The Historical Present in Thucydides: Semantics and Narrative*. Leiden.

Lam, P. W.Y. 2010. "Discourse Particles in Corpus Data and Textbooks: The Case of *well*." *Applied Linguistics* 31:260–281.

Lamari, A. A. 2013. "Making Meaning: Cross-references and Their Interpretation in Thucydides' Sicilian Narrative." In *Thucydides Between History and Literature*, ed. A. Tsakmakis and M. Tamiolaki, 287–308. Berlin.

Lamb, W. R. M. 1914. *Clio Enthroned : A Study in Prose-Form in Thucydides*. Cambridge.

———. 1930. *Lysias*. London.

———. 1967. *Plato*. 7 vols. London.

Lambert, F. 2003. "Le 'Balancement' en *men/de* en grec classique." In *Ordre et distinction dans la langue et le discours: Actes du colloque international de Metz (18, 19, 20 Mars 1999)*, ed. B. Combettes, C. Schnedecker, A. Theissen, and J. Lengert, 270–285. Paris.

———. 2006. "Emplois et valeurs de *toinun*: Aux frontières de la syntaxe." In *Word Classes and Related Topics in Ancient Greek : Proceedings of the Conference on "Greek Syntax and Word Classes" Held in Madrid on 18-21, June 2003*, ed. E. Crespo, J. de la Villa, and A. R. Revuelta, 537–556. Louvain-la-Neuve.

Lamberts, E. 1970. *Studien zur Parataxe bei Herodot*. Wien.

Lamers, H., and A. Rademaker. 2007. "Talking About Myself: A Pragmatic Approach to the Use of Aspect Forms in Lysias 12.4-19." *Classical Quarterly* 57:458–476.

Lammert, R. 1874. *De pronominibus relativis Homericis: Cap. III. De pronominibus relativis cum τε particula coniunctis*. Leipzig.

Lan, B. le. 2007. "Orchestrating Conversation: The Multifunctionality of *well* and *you know* in the Joint Construction of a Verbal Interaction." In *Connectives as Discourse Landmarks*, ed. A. Celle and R. Huart, 103–116. Amsterdam.

Lancelot, C. 1664. *Le jardin des racines grecques, mises en vers françois, avec un traité des prépositions et autres particules indéclinables, et un recueil alphabétique des mots françois tirés de la langue grecque, soit par allusion, soit par étymologie. Nouvelle édition, revue, corrigée exactement et augmentée*. 2nd ed. Paris.

Lancker Sidtis, D. van. 2008. "The Relation of Human Language to Human Emotion." In *Handbook of the Neuroscience of Language*, ed. B. Stemmer and H. A. Whitaker, 199–207. Amsterdam.

Landau, B., and R. Jackendoff. 1993. "What and Where in Spatial Language and Spatial Cognition." *Behavioral and Brain Sciences* 16:217–238.

Landreth, M. C. 1978. "The Position of the Particles AN and KE(N) in Pindar." *Eranos* 76:13–18.

Lang, E. 1977. *Semantik der koordinativen Verknüpfung*. Berlin.

Lang, M. L. 1984a. *Herodotean Narrative and Discourse*. Cambridge, MA.

———. 1984b. "Unreal Conditions in Homeric Narrative." *Greek, Roman, and Byzantine Studies* 30:5–26.

———. 1995. "Participial Motivation in Thucydides." *Mnemosyne* 48:48–65.

Lang, M. L., J. S. Rusten, and R. Hamilton. 2011. *Thucydidean Narrative and Discourse*. Ann Arbor, MI.

Langacker, R. W. 1987. *Foundations of Cognitive Grammar*. Vol. 1: *Theoretical Prerequisites*. Stanford.

———. 1990. *Concept, Image, and Symbol*. Cognitive Linguistics Research 1. Berlin.

———. 2001. "Discourse in Cognitive Grammar." *Cognitive Linguistics* 12:143–188.

———. 2005. "Integration, Grammaticization, and Constructional Meaning." In *Grammatical Constructions: Back to the Roots*, ed. M. Fried and H. C. Boas, 157–189. Amsterdam.

———. 2008. *Cognitive Grammar*. Oxford.

———. 2010. "Cognitive Grammar." In *The Oxford Handbook of Linguistic Analysis*, ed. B. Heine and H. Narrog, 87–109. Oxford.

Lange, L. 1873. "Der homerische Gebrauch der Partikel εἰ I-II." *Abhandlungen der philologisch-historischen Classe der Koeniglich Saechsischen Gesellschaft der Wissenschaften*, 309–566.

Langslow, D. R. 2000. "Latin Discourse Particles, 'Medical Latin' and 'Classical Latin.'" *Mnemosyne* 53:537–560.

Lardinois, A. P. M. H. 1996. "Who Sang Sappho's Songs?" In *Reading Sappho: Contemporary Approaches*, ed. E. Greene, 150–172. Berkeley.

———. 2006. "The Polysemy of Gnomic Expressions and Ajax' Deception Speech." In *Sophocles and the Greek Language*, ed. I. J. F. de Jong and A. Rijksbaron, 213–223. Leiden.

Larsen, I. 1991a. "Boundary Features." *Notes on Translation* 5:48–54.

———. 1991b. "Notes on the Function of γάρ, οὖν, μέν, δέ, καί and τε in the Greek New Testament." *Notes on Translation* 5:35–47.

———. 1991c. "Quotations and Speech Introducers in Narrative Texts." *Notes on Translation* 5:55–60.

———. 1991d. "Word Order and Relative Prominence in New Testament Greek." *Notes on Translation* 5:29–34.

Latacz, J. 1977. *Kampfparänese, Kampfdarstellung und Kampfwirklichkeit in der "Ilias", bei Kallinos und Tyrtaios*. Zetemata 66. Munich.

Lateiner, D. 2012. "Oaths: Theory and Practice in the Histories of Herodotus and Thucydides." In *Thucydides and Herodotus*, ed. E. Foster and D. Lateiner, 154–184. Oxford.

Lattimore, R. 1967. *The Odyssey of Homer*. London.

Lattmann, H. 1919. "Negation, Indefinitum, Intensivum und gr. μή." *Zeitschrift für vergleichende Sprachforschung auf dem Gebiete der Indogermanischen Sprachen* 49:92–111.

Lauer, S. 1959. *Zur Wortstellung bei Pindar*. Winterthur.

Laury, R. 2005. "Dialogic Syntax and the Emergence of Topics in Interaction – an Initial Exploration." *Tranel (Travaux Neuchâtelois de Linguistique)* 41:165–189.

———, ed. 2008. *Crosslinguistic Studies of Clause Combining*. Typological Studies in Language 80. Amsterdam.

Laury, R., and E.-L. Seppänen. 2008. "Clause Combining, Interaction, Evidentially, Participation Structure, and the Conjunction-Particle Continuum: The Finnish *että*." In *Crosslinguistic Studies of Clause Combining: The Multifunctionality of Conjunctions*, ed. R. Laury, 153–178. Amsterdam.

Law, V., and I. Sluiter, eds. 1995. *Dionysius Thrax and the Téchnē Grammatikḗ*. The Henry Sweet Society Studies in the History of Linguistics 1. Münster.

Leaf, W. 1900. *The Iliad: Books 1-12*. 2nd ed. London.

———. 1902. *The Iliad: Books 13-24*. 2nd ed. London.

Lee, D. J. N. 1967. "The Modal Particles *an, ke(n), ka*." *American Journal of Philology* 88:45–56.

Lee, D. Y. W. 2001. "Genres, Registers, Text Types, Domains, and Styles: Clarifying the Concepts and Navigating a Path through the BNC Jungle." *Language Learning and Technology* 5:37–72.

Lee-Goldman, R. 2011. "*No* as a Discourse Marker." *Journal of Pragmatics* 43:2627–2649.

Leech, G. N. 1983. *Principles of Pragmatics*. London.

Leeuwen, J. van. 1896. *Aristophanis Ranae*. Leiden.

———. 1898. *Aristophanis Nubes*. Leiden.

———. 1900. *Aristophanis Equites*. Leiden.

———. 1901. *Aristophanis Acharnenses*. Leiden.

———. 1902. *Aristophanis Aves*. Leiden.

———. 1903. *Aristophanis Lysistrata*. Leiden.

Lefkowitz, M. R. 1988. "Who Sang Pindar's Victory Odes?" *American Journal of Philology* 109:1–11.

———. 1991. *First-Person Fictions: Pindar's Poetic "I."* Oxford.

———. 1995. "The First Person in Pindar Reconsidered—Again." *Bulletin of the Institute of Classical Studies* 40:139–150.

Lehiste, I., and P. Ivic. 1986. *Word and Sentence Prosody in Serbocroatian*. Cambridge, MA.

Lehmann, C. 1977. "A Universal about Conditional Sentences." In *Linguistica Generalia I. Studies in Linguistic Typology*, ed. M. Romportl, 231–241. Prague.

———. 1988. "Towards a Typology of Clause Linkage." In *Clause Combining in Grammar and Discourse*, ed. J. Haiman and S. A. Thompson, 181–225. Amsterdam.

Leino, J., and J.-O. Östman. 2005. "Constructions and Variability." In *Grammatical Constructions: Back to the Roots*, ed. M. Fried and H. C. Boas, 191–213. Amsterdam.

Lenk, U. 1997. "Discourse Markers." In *Handbook of Pragmatics*, ed. J. Verschueren, J.-O. Östman, J. Blommaert, and C. Bulcaen, 1–17. Amsterdam.

———. 1998. *Marking Discourse Coherence: Functions of Discourse Markers in Spoken English*. Tübingen.

Leumann, M. 1949. "Μέν und μήν, δέ und δή." *Museum Helveticum* 6:85–89.

Levet, J. P. 1988. "Recherches sur le verbe 'HMI." *Ediston logodeipnon, Logopédies. Mélanges de philologie et de linguistique grecques offerts à Jean Taillardat*, 155–169.

Levin, S. 1979. "The Connective Particles in Classical Greek Discourse." *CUNY Forum Papers in Linguistics, V-VI: Proceedings of the 9th Annual Meeting of the Northeast Linguistics Society*, 1.52–58. Flushing, NY.

Levinsohn, S. H. 1987. *Textual Connections in Acts*. Atlanta.

Levinson, S. C. 1983. *Pragmatics*. Cambridge.

———. 1987. "Minimization and Conversational Inference." In *The Pragmatic Perspective*, ed. J. Verschueren and M. Bertucelli-Papi, 61–129. London.

———. 2006. "On the Human 'Interactional Engine.'" In *Roots of Human Sociality: Culture, Cognition and Interaction*, ed. N. J. Enfield and S. C. Levinson, 39–69. Oxford.

———. 2013. "Action Formation and Ascription." In *The Handbook of Conversation Analysis*, ed. J. Sidnell and T. Stivers, 103–130. Malden, MA.

Levi-Strauss, C. 1960. "L'analyse morphologique des contes russes." *International Journal of Slavic Linguistics and Poetics* 3:122–149.

Lewis, D. M. 2011. "A Discourse-Constructional Approach to the Emergence of Discourse Markers in English." *Linguistics* 49:415–443.

Liberman, G. 2004. *Pindarus. Pythiques*. Paris.

Liberman, M., and J. Pierrehumbert. 1984. "Intonational Invariance under Changes in Pitch Range and Length." In *Language Sound Structure*, ed. M. Aronoff, R. T. Oehrle, F. Kelley, and B. Wilker Stephens, 157–233. Cambridge, MA.

Liddell, H. G., R. Scott, and H. S. Jones. 1940. *A Greek-English Lexicon*. 9th ed. Oxford.

Liddicoat, A. J. 2007. *An Introduction to Conversation Analysis*. London.

Linell, P. 1998. *Approaching Dialogue: Talk, Interaction and Contexts in Dialogical Perspectives*. Amsterdam.

———. 2007. "Dialogicality in Languages, Minds and Brains: Is There a Convergence between Dialogism and Neuro-Biology?" *Language Sciences* 29:605–620.

———. 2009. "Grammatical Constructions in Dialogue." In *Contexts and Constructions*, ed. A. Bergs and G. Diewald, 97–110. Amsterdam.

Linke, K. 1977. *Die Fragmente des Grammatikers Dionysios Thrax*. Berlin.

Linke, R. 1873. *De particulae δέ significatione affirmativa apud Sophoclem*. Halle.

Liuzzo, P. M. 2012. "Παραπλήσιον ζωγράφων. Breve storia del confronto metodologico di storiografia e pittura." *Clamm Magazine*. www.clammmag.com/παραπλησιον-ζωγραφων-parte-i.

Ljungdahl, S. 1871. *De transeundi generibus quibus utitur Isocrates*. Uppsala.

Lloyd, A. B. 1989. *Erodoto. Le storie*. Libro II: *L'Egitto*. Milan.

Lloyd, M. 1994. *Euripides. Andromache*. Warminster.

———. 2004. "The Politeness of Achilles: Off-Record Conversation Strategies in Homer and the Meaning of 'Kertomia.'" *Journal of Hellenic Studies* 124:75–89.

Lloyd-Jones, H. 1997 [1994]. *Sophocles. Ajax, Electra, Oedipus Tyrannus*. London.

———. 1998 [1994]. *Sophocles. Antigone, The Women of Trachis, Philoctetes, Oedipus at Colonus*. London.

Lloyd-Jones, H., and N. G. Wilson. 1990. *Sophoclis Fabulae*. Oxford.

Löbner, S. 1989. "German *schon - erst - noch*: An Integrated Analysis." *Linguistics and Philosophy* 12:167–212.

Lohmann, D. 1970. *Die Komposition der Reden in der Ilias*. Berlin.

Longacre, R. E. 1974. "Narrative versus Other Discourse Genres." In *Advances in Tagmemics*, ed. R. M. Brend, 357–376. Amsterdam.

———. 1985. "Discourse Peak as a Zone of Turbulence." In *Beyond the Sentence*, ed. J. Wirth, 81–92. Ann Arbor, MI.

———. 1989. "Two Hypotheses Regarding Text Generation and Analysis." *Discourse Processes* 12:413–460.

———. 1990. *Storyline Concerns and Word Order Typology in East and West Africa*. Los Angeles.

———. 1995. "Left Shifts in Strongly VSO Languages." In *Word Order in Discourse*, ed. P. Downing and M. P. Noonan, 331–354. Amsterdam.

———. 1996. *The Grammar of Discourse*. 2nd ed. New York.

Lopes, R. 2008. "As partículas gregas: *gar*." *Boletim de Estudos Clássicos (Coímbra)* 49:27–33.

López Eire, A. 1996. *La Lengua Coloquial de La Comedia Aristofánica*. Murcia.

Loraux, N. 1986. *The Invention of Athens: The Funeral Oration in the Classical City*. Cambridge, MA.

Lord, A. B. 1951. "Composition by Theme in Homer and Southslavic Epos." *Transactions and Proceedings of the American Philological Association* 82:71–80.

———. 1960. "The Theme." In *The Singer of Tales*, 68–98. Cambridge, MA.

———. 1981. "Memory, Fixity, and Genre in Oral Traditional Poetries." In *Oral Traditional Literature: A Festschrift for Albert Bates Lord*, ed. J. M. Foley, 451–461. Columbus.

———. 2000. *The Singer of Tales*. 2nd ed. Cambridge, MA.

Lorimer, W. L. 1934. "Magnum de particulis opus." *Classical Review* 48:221–223.

———. 1935. "Review of Denniston's *Greek Particles*." *Classical Review* 49:12–14.

Louden, B. 1993. "Pivotal Contrafactuals in Homer." *Classical Antiquity* 12:181–198.

Louviot, E. 2013. "Transitions from Direct Speech to Narration in Old English Poetry." *Neophilologus* 97:383–393.

Louwerse, M. M., and H. H. Mitchell. 2003. "Towards a Taxonomy of a Set of Discourse Markers in Dialog: A Theoretical and Computational Linguistic Account." *Discourse Processes* 35:199–239.

Lowe, J. C. B. 1973. "Γ'ἄρα, γ'ἆρα and τἄρα." *Glotta* 51:34–64.

Lowth, R. 1762. *A Short Introduction to English Grammar. With Critical Notes*. London.

———. 1999. "Why German 'schon' and 'noch' Are Still Duals: A Reply to Van der Auwera." *Linguistics and Philosophy* 22:45–107.

Lucci, J. 2012. "Sophocles the Comedian: Wordplay, Unequal Status, and Humor in Sophoclean Tragedy." Presentation at CAMWS 108th Annual Meeting, Baton Rouge, LA, March 28–31.

Ludlow, P. 2011. *The Philosophy of Generative Linguistics*. Oxford.

Ludwig, T. 1882. *De enuntiatorum interrogativorum apud Aristophanem usu*. Königsberg.

Lühr, R. 2010. "Partikeln in indogermanischen Sprachen." *Linguistik Online* 44:131–157.

Luke, K. K. 1990. *Utterance Particles in Cantonese Conversation*. Amsterdam.

Lundon, J. 2011. "Homeric Commentaries." In *Ancient Scholarship and Grammar: Archetypes, Concepts and Contexts*, ed. S. Matthaios, F. Montanari, and A. Rengakos. Berlin.

Luraghi, S. 2007. "The Discourse Function of *gar*: Some Reflections." Presentation at the 6th International Colloquium on Ancient Greek Linguistics, University of Groningen, June 27–29.

Luraghi, S., and G. Celano. 2012. "Connectives and Discourse Structure: Between Foreground and Background." Presentation at the conference "Discourse Markers in Corpus Languages," Vitoria-Gasteiz, November 28–30.

Luraghi, S., and E. Sausa. 2015. "Hate and Anger, Love and Desire: The Construal of Emotions in Homeric Greek." In *Historical Linguistics 2013: Selected Papers from the 21st International Conference on Historical Linguistics, Oslo, Norway, 5-9 August 2013*, ed. D. T. T. Haug, 233–256. Amsterdam.

Lutoslawski, W. 1897. "The Style of Plato." In *The Origin and Growth of Plato's Logic*, ed. W. Lutoslawski. London.

Lüttel, V. 1981. *Kas und kai. Dialektale und chronologische Probleme im Zusammenhang mit Dissimilation und Apokope*. Göttingen.

Lutzky, U. 2012. *Discourse Markers in Early Modern English*. Amsterdam.

Lutzky, U., and J. Demmen. 2013. "*Pray* in Early Modern English Drama." *Journal of Historical Pragmatics* 14:263–284.

Lyons, J. 1977. *Semantics*. Cambridge.

———. 1982. "Deixis and Subjectivity: Loquor, Ergo Sum?" In *Speech, Place, and Action*, ed. R. J. Jarvella and W. Klein, 101–124. Chichester.

Macan, R. W. 1908. *Herodotus : The Seventh, Eighth, and Ninth Books*. 2 vols. London.

MacDowell, D. M. 1971. *Aristophanes. Wasps*. Oxford.

Mackay, E. A. 2001. "The Frontal Face and 'You.' Narrative Disjunction in Early Greek Poetry and Painting." *Acta Classica: Proceedings of the Classical Association of South Africa* 44:5–34.

Mackie, H. S. 2003. *Graceful Errors: Pindar and the Performance of Praise*. Ann Arbor, MI.

Magister, T. 1832. *Ecloga vocum Atticarum*. Ed. F. Ritschl. Halle.

Maidment, K. J. 1953. *Minor Attic Orators in Two Volumes*. Vol. 1: *Antiphon ; Andocides*. London.

Malicki, C. 1907. *De palin particula*. Greifswald.

Mann, W. C., and S. A. Thompson. 1987. "Rhetorical Structure Theory: A Framework for the Analysis of Texts." *Papers in Pragmatics* 1:79–105.

Manutius, A. the Younger. 1566. *Orthographiae Ratio*. Venice. https://www.digitale-sammlungen.de/de/view/bsb11280798?page=5.

Margerie, H. 2010. "On the Rise of (inter)subjective Meaning in the Grammaticalization of *kind of/kinda*." In *Subjectification, Intersubjectification and Grammaticalization*, ed. K. Davidse, L. Vandelanotte, and H. Cuyckens, 315–346. Berlin.

Marincola, J. 1989. "Thucydides 1.22.2." *Classical Philology* 84:216–223.

Marincola, J., and A. De Sélincourt. 2003. *Herodotus. The Histories*. London.

Markantonatos, G. A. 1986. *Sophokleous Oidipous Tyrannos*. Athens.

Markovic, D. 2006. "Hyperbaton in the Greek Literary Sentence." *Greek, Roman, and Byzantine Studies* 46:127–146.

Marmaridou, S. S. A. 2000. *Pragmatic Meaning and Cognition*. Amsterdam.

Marold, C. 1881. *Über die gotischen Konjunktionen, welche οὖν und γάρ vertreten*. Königsberg.

Martin, R. P. 1989. *The Language of Heroes: Speech and Performance in the "Iliad."* Ithaca.

———. 1997. "Similes and Performance." In *Written Voices, Spoken Signs*, ed. A. Kahane and E. J. Bakker, 138–166. Cambridge, MA.

———. 2000. "Wrapping Homer Up: Cohesion, Discourse and Deviation in the *Iliad*." In *Intratextuality: Greek and Roman Textual Relations*, ed. A. Sharrock and H. Morales, 43–65. Oxford.

Martín López, M. I. 1993. "La función discursiva de la partícula griega *de*." *Habis* 24:219–234.

Martínez Vázquez, R. 2011. "Οὕτως como adverbio conjuntivo e ordenación en la lengua de Tucídides." Presented at the XL Simposio y III Congreso de la Sociedad Española de Lingüística, Lingüística XL. "El lingüista ante el siglo XXI," Madrid, February 7–10.

Martínez Vázquez, R., and E. Ruiz Yamuza. 2011. "Una pproximación escalar al empleo de adverbio como adjunto y conjunto: οὕτως." *Habis* 42:315–336.

Martino, F. de, and O. Vox. 1996. *Lirica Greca*. Vol. 1. Bari.

Maschler, Y. 1998. "*Rotse lishmoa keta*? 'Wanna Hear Something Weird/Funny (Lit. "a Segment")'? The Discourse Markers Segmenting Isreali Hebrew Talk-in-Interaction." In Jucker and Ziv 1998:13–59. Amsterdam.

———. 2003. "The Discourse Marker *nu*: Israeli Hebrew Impatience in Interaction." *Text* 23:89–128.

———. 2009. *Metalanguage in Interaction: Hebrew Discourse Markers*. Amsterdam.

Masini, F., and P. Pietrandrea. 2010. "Magari." *Cognitive Linguistics* 21:75–121.

Masinyana, A.-M. S. O. 2013. "*Ke* in Utterances: Uses and Functions of the Xhosa Discourse Marker *ke*." MA thesis, University of Cape Town.

Mastromarco, G., and P. Totaro. 2006. *Commedie di Aristofane* II. Turin.

Mastronarde, D. J. 1979. *Contact and Discontinuity: Some Conventions of Speech and Action on the Greek Tragic Stage*. Berkeley.

———. 2000. "Euripidean Tragedy and Genre: The Terminology and Its Problems." In *Euripides and Tragic Theatre in the Late Fifth Century*, ed. M. J. Cropp, 23–39. Champaign, IL.

———. 2002. *Euripides. Medea*. Cambridge.

Matsumoto, Y. 2010. "Interactional Frames and Grammatical Descriptions: The Case of Japanese Noun-Modifying Constructions." *Constructions and Frames* 2:135–157.

Matthaios, S. 1999. *Untersuchungen zur Grammatik Aristarchs: Texte und Interpretation zur Wortartenlehre*. Göttingen.

———. 2001. "Das Wortartensystem der Alexandriner: Skizze seiner Entwicklungsgeschichte und Nachwirkung." *Göttinger Beiträge zur Sprachwissenschaft* 5:65–94.

———. 2002. "Neue Perspektiven für die Historiographie der antiken Grammatik: Das Wortartensystem der Alexandriner." In *Grammatical Theory and Philosophy of Language in Antiquity*, ed. P. Swiggers and A. Wouters, 161–220. Leuven.

———. 2003. "Trypho aus Alexandria: Der erste Syntaxtheoretiker vor Apollonios Dyskolos?" In *Syntax in Antiquity*, ed. P. A. Swiggers and A. Wouters, 97–132. Leuven.

Matthaios, S., F. Montanari, and A. Rengakos, eds. 2011. *Ancient Scholarship and Grammar: Archetypes, Concepts and Contexts*. Trends in Classics. Supplementary Volumes 8. Berlin.

Matthiae, A. 1825. *Ausführliche griechische Grammatik*. 2nd ed. Leipzig.

Matthiae, A., K. Matthiae, and B. Matthiae. 1841. *Lexicon Euripideum*. Leipzig.

Matthiae, K. 1845. *Beitrag zur Lehre von den griechischen Partikeln ge, ara, men, de, an*. Quedlinburg.

Matthiessen, C. M. I. M., and S. A. Thompson. 1988. "The Structure of Discourse and 'Subordination.'" In *Clause Combining in Grammar and Discourse*, ed. J. Haiman and S. A. Thompson, 275–329. Amsterdam.

Mazeland, H. 2012. "NOU als discourse marker in het taalgebruik van kleuters [NOU as a Discourse Marker in Talk-in-Interaction of Pre-School Children]." In *Gesprekken in het onderwijs: Bijdragen over onderzoek naar interactie en leren voor Jan Berenst*, ed. K. de Glopper, M. Gosen, and J. Kruiningen, 39–71. Delft.

Mazeland, H., and M. Huiskes. 2001. "Dutch *but* as a Sequential Conjunction: Its Use as a Resumption Marker." In *Studies in Interactional Linguistics*, ed. M. Selting and E. Couper-Kuhlen, 141–170. Amsterdam.

Mazeland, H., and L. Plug. 2010. "Doing Confirmation with *ja/nee hoor*: Sequential and Prosodic Characteristics of a Dutch Discourse Particle." In *Prosody in Interaction*, ed. D. Barth-Weingarten, E. Reber, and M. Selting, 161–187. Amsterdam.

McDermott, J. 1990. *Punctuation for Now*. London.

McDonald, M. 1992. *Ancient Sun, Modern Light: Greek Drama on the Modern Stage*. New York.

———. 2007. "Rhetoric and Tragedy: Weapons of Mass Persuasion." In *A Companion to Greek Rhetoric*, ed. I. Worthington, 473–489. Oxford.

McHoul, A. W. 1987. "An Initial Investigation of the Usability of Fictional Conversation for Doing Conversation Analysis." *Semiotica* 67:83–103.

Meineck, P. 2011. "The Neuroscience of the Tragic Mask." *Arion: A Journal of Humanities and the Classics* 19:113–158.

———. 2013. "'The Thorniest Problem and the Greatest Opportunity': Directors on Directing the Greek Chorus." In *Choral Mediations in Greek Tragedy*, ed. M. Govers Hopman and R. Gagné, 352–383. Cambridge.

Meisterhans, K. 1900. *Grammatik der attischen Inschriften*. Berlin.

Menge, H. 1999 [1914]. *Repetitorium des griechischen Syntax*. Ed. A. Thierfelder and J. Wiesner. 10th ed. Darmstadt.

Menrad, J. 1913. "Homerica. (1) τε im Nachsatz? (2) δέ mit Ellipse des Verbums?" *Bayerische Blätter für das Gymnasial-Schulwesen* 49:232–235.

Mette, A. 1979. "ἀλλά." In *Lexikon des frühgriechischen Epos* I, ed. B. Snell and H. J. Mette, 505–535. Göttingen.

Metzger, F. 1880. *Pindars Siegeslieder*. Leipzig.

Meurman-Solin, A. 2012. "The Connectives *and*, *for*, *but*, and *only* as Clause and Discourse Type Indicators in 16th- and 17th-Century Epistolary Prose." In *Information Structure and Syntactic Change in the History of English*, ed. A. Meurman-Solin, M. J. López-Couso, and B. Los, 164–196. Oxford Studies in the History of English 2. Oxford.

Mey, J. L. 1999. *When Voices Clash: A Study in Literary Pragmatics*. Berlin.

———. 2001. *Pragmatics: An Introduction*. 2nd ed. Malden, MA.

Meyer, H. 1933. Hymnische Stilelemente in der frühgriechischen Dichtung. PhD diss., Cologne.

Meyer, L. 1866. "Über die anlautende Consonantenverbindung ϝϱ (vr) in der homerischen Sprache." *Zeitschrift für vergleichende Sprachforschung* 15:1–42.

Michaelis, L. A. 1996. "On the Use and Meaning of *already*." *Linguistics and Philosophy* 19:477–502.

———. 2010. "Sign-Based Construction Grammar." In *The Oxford Handbook of Linguistic Analysis*, ed. B. Heine and H. Narrog, 139–158. Oxford.

Miestamo, M. 2009. "Negation." In *Grammar, Meaning and Pragmatics*, ed. F. Brisard, J.-O. Östman, and J. Verschueren, 208–229. Amsterdam.

Miller, J., and R. Weinert. 1995. "The Function of *like* in Dialogue." *Journal of Pragmatics* 23:365–393.

Minard, A. 1937. *Deux relatifs homériques*. Paris.

Minchin, E. 1992. "Scripts and Themes: Cognitive Research and the Homeric Epic." *Classical Antiquity* 11:229–241.

———. 2001. *Homer and the Resources of Memory: Some Applications of Cognitive Theory to the Iliad and the Odyssey*. Oxford.

———. 2007. *Homeric Voices: Discourse, Memory, Gender*. Oxford.

———. 2008. "Spatial Memory and the Composition of the *Iliad*." In *Orality, Literacy, Memory in the Ancient Greek and Roman World*, ed. E. A. Mackay, 9–34. Leiden.

Misener, G. 1904. *The Meaning of γάρ*. Baltimore.

———. 1908. "The εἰ γάρ Wishes." *Classical Philology* 3:137–144.

———. 1937. "Review of Denniston, *The Greek Particles*." *Classical Philology* 32:176–178.

———. 1955. "Review of Denniston, *The Greek Particles*, 2nd Edition." *Classical Philology* 50:51.

Mišković-Luković, M. 2009. "Is There a Chance that I Might Kinda Sort of Take You Out to Dinner? The Role of the Pragmatic Particles *kind of* and *sort of* in Utterance Interpretation." *Journal of Pragmatics* 41:602–625.

———. 2010. "Markers of Conceptual Adjustment: Serbian *baš* and *kao*." In *South Slavic Discourse Particles*, ed. M. N. Dedaić and M. Mišković-Luković, 65–89. Amsterdam.

Mišković-Luković, M., and M. N. Dedaić. 2010. "South Slavic Discourse Particles: Introduction." In *South Slavic Discourse Particles*, ed. M. N. Dedaić and M. Mišković-Luković, 1–22. Amsterdam.

———. 2012. "The Discourse Marker *odnosno* at the ICTY: A Case of Disputed Translation in War Crime Trials." *Journal of Pragmatics* 44:1355–1377.

Mithun, M. 1988. "The Grammaticization of Coordination." In *Clause Combining in Grammar and Discourse*, ed. J. Haiman and S. A. Thompson, 333–359. Amsterdam.

Molinelli, P. 2008. "Tra oralità e scrittura: *rogo* nelle lettere private in Latino." In *Diachronica et synchronica: Studi in onore di Anna Giacalone Ramat*, ed. R. Lazzeroni, E. Banfi, G. Bernini, M. Chini, and G. Marotta, 365–378. Pisa.

———. 2010. "From Verbs to Interactional Discourse Markers: The Pragmaticalization of Latin *rogo, quaeso*." In *Papers on Grammar* XI, ed. G. Calboli and P. Cuzzolin, 181–192. Rome.

Molinos Tejada, M. T. 1992. "La Particule modale *ka* dans la litterature dorienne." *Revue Des Études Grecques* 105.502–503:328–348.

Möllering, M. 2001. "Teaching German Modal Particles: A Corpus-Based Approach." *Language Learning & Technology* 5:130–151.

Monro, D. B. 1882a. *A Grammar of the Homeric Dialect*. Oxford.

———. 1882b. "τε in Homer." *Transactions of the Oxford Philological Society* 1882:14–15.

Montanari, F. 2005. *Vocabolario della lingua greca*. 2nd ed. Turin.

Monteil, P. 1963. *La phrase relative en grec ancien: Sa formation, son développement, sa structure des origines à la fin du 5. siècle a. C.* Paris.

Montes de Oca Vega, M. 2004. "In iqualtica yectica ygratia: los marcadores del discurso como estrategia para evangelizar." In *De historiografía lingüística e historia de las lenguas*, ed. I. Guzmán Betancourt, P. Maníes, and A. H. de León-Portilla, 107–123. Mexico City.

Moore, C. 2006. "The Use of *videlicet* in Early Modern Slander Depositions: A Case of Genre-Specific Grammaticalization." *Journal of Historical Pragmatics* 7:245–263.

Moorhouse, A. C. 1952. "Observations on Epic ἀλλά." *Classical Quarterly* 2:100–104.

———. 1959. *Studies in the Greek Negatives*. Cardiff.

———. 1982. *The Syntax of Sophocles*. Leiden.

Morpurgo Davies, A. 1997. "Particles in Greek Epigraphical Texts: The Case of Arcadian." In Rijksbaron 1997:49–73. Amsterdam.

Morpurgo Tagliabue, G. 1980. *Demetrio: Dello stile*. Rome.

Morrison, J. V. 1994. "A Key *Topos* in Thucydides: The Comparison of Cities and Individuals." *American Journal of Philology* 155:525–541.

———. 2006a. "Interaction of Speech and Narrative in Thucydides." In *Brill's Companion to Thucydides*, ed. A. Rengakos and A. Tsakmakis, 251–277. Leiden.

———. 2006b. *Reading Thucydides*. Columbus.

Mortillaro, M., M. Mehu, and K. R. Scherer. 2013. "The Evolutionary Origin of Multimodal Synchronization and Emotional Expression." In *The Evolution of Emotional Communication: From Sounds in Nonhuman Mammals to Speech and Music in Man*, ed. E. Altenmüller, S. Schmidt, and E. Zimmermann, 3–25. Oxford.

Mosblech, P. W. 1838. "Einiges über die Partikel τε." *Zeitschrift für die Alterthumswissenschaft* 5:948–950.

Mossman, J. 2011. *Euripides. Medea*. Oxford.

Most, G. W. 1993. "Hesiod and the Textualization of Personal Temporality." In *La componente autobiografica nella poesia greca e latina fra realtà e artificio letterario*, ed. G. Arrighetti and F. Montanari, 73–92. Pisa.

Moulton, C. 1977. *Similes in the Homeric Poems*. Göttingen.

Muchnová, D. 1993. "Les propositions causales en *epei*." *Graecolatina Pragensia* 14:89–96.

———. 2000. "*Epei* en tant que particule dans les phrases autonomes." *Graecolatina Pragensia* 18:119–136.

———. 2003. "*Epei* homérique: sémantique, syntaxe, pragmatique." *Gaia* 7:105–116.

———. 2004. "Les emplois paratactiques de *hos*." *Graecolatina Pragensia* 20:121–131.

———. 2006. "Entre conjonction et particule: Le cas de *epei*." In *Word Classes and Related Topics in Ancient Greek: Proceedings of the Conference on "Greek Syntax and Word Classes" Held in Madrid on 18-21, June 2003*, ed. E. Crespo, J. de la Villa, and A. R. Revuelta Puigdollers, 557–570. Louvain-la-Neuve.

———. 2007. "À propos des interprétations pragmatiques de ὅτι causal chez Homère." *Acta Universitatis Carolinae Philologica— Graecolatina Pragensia* 22:85–102.

———. 2009. "*Epei* Clauses in Narrative Discourse in Ancient Greek." In *Early European Languages in the Eyes of Modern Linguistics*, ed. K. Loudová and M. Žáková, 229–240. Brno.

———. 2011. *Entre conjonction, connecteur et particule: Le cas de ἐπεί en grec ancien; Étude syntaxique, sémantique et pragmatique*. Prague.

Mueller, F. 1910. *Quaestiones grammaticae de γάρ particulisque adversativis enuntiata eorumque membra coniungentibus*. Göttingen.

Mueller, M. 2011. "The Politics of Gesture in Sophocles' Antigone." *Classical Quarterly* 61:412–425.

———. 2015. *Objects as Actors: Props and the Poetics of Performance in Greek Tragedy*. Chicago.

Muellner, L. C. 1990. "The Simile of the Cranes and Pygmies: A Study of Homeric Metaphor." *Harvard Studies in Classical Philology* 93:59–101.

———. 1996. *The Anger of Achilles: Mēnis in Greek Epic*. Cornell.

Mühll, P. von der. 1946. *Homer. Odyssey*. Basel.

Müller, D. 1980. *Satzbau, Satzgliederung und Satzverbindung in der Prosa Herodots*. Meisenheim am Glan.

Müller, F. 1927. *Stilistische Untersuchung der Epinomis des Philippos von Opus*. Gräfenhainichen.

Müller, W. 1874. *De Theophrasti dicendi ratione. Pars prima. Observationes de particularum usu*. Göttingen.

Mulligan, B. 2007. "ἄρα Introducing Direct Speech in Herodotus." *Mnemosyne* 60:281–284.

Munson, R. V. 2001. "Ananke in Herodotus." *Journal of Hellenic Studies* 121:30–50.

———. 2013. *Herodotus*. 2 vols. Oxford.

Munteanu, D. L. 2011. "Comic Emotions: Shamelessness and Envy (Schadenfreude); Moderate Emotion." In *Emotion, Genre and Gender in Classical Antiquity*, ed. D. L. Munteanu, 89–112. London.

———. 2012. *Tragic Pathos: Pity and Fear in Greek Philosophy and Tragedy*. Cambridge.

Murphy, C. T. 1938. "Aristophanes and the Art of Rhetoric." *Harvard Studies in Classical Philology* 49:69–113.

Murray, A. T., and G. E. Dimock. 1995. *Homer. Odyssey*. 2nd ed. Cambridge, MA.

Murray, A. T., and W. F. Wyatt. 1999. *Homer. Iliad*. 2nd ed. 2 vols. Cambridge, MA.

Murray, G. 1955 [1937]. *Aeschyli septem quae supersunt tragoediae*. Oxford.

Musurillo, H. 1970. "Particles in the Prometheus Bound." *Classical Philology* 65:175–177.

Mutzbauer, C. 1884–1886. *Der Homerische Gebrauch der Partikel μέν*. 2 vols. Cologne.

Mycock, L. 2010. "Prominence in Hungarian: The Prosody-syntax Connection." *Transactions of the Philological Society* 108:265–297.

Myhill, J., and J. Hibiya. 1988. "The Discourse Function of Clause-Chaining." In *Clause Combining in Grammar and Discourse*, ed. J. Haiman and S. A. Thompson, 361–398. Amsterdam.

Naber, S. A. 1855. "Homerica." *Mnemosyne* 4:193–217.

Nachmansson, E. 1920. *Beiträge zur Kenntnis der altgriechischen Volkssprache*. Uppsala.

Naeke, A. F. 1842. *De ἠδέ et ἰδέ particulis apud Homerum*. Bonn.

Nägelsbach, C. F. 1830. *Commentatio de particula γε usu Homerico*. Nürnberg.

———. 1834. *Anmerkungen zur Ilias*. Nürnberg. https://www.digitale-sammlungen.de/de/view/bsb10234415?page=8.

Nagler, M. N. 1974. *Spontaneity and Tradition: A Study in the Oral Art of Homer*. Berkeley.

Nagy, G. N. 1979. *The Best of the Achaeans: Concepts of the Hero in Ancient Greek Poetry*. Baltimore.

———. 1990. *Pindar's Homer. The Lyric Possession of the Epic Past*. Baltimore.

———. 1995. "Transformations of Choral Lyric Traditions in the Context of Athenian State Theater." *Arion* 3:41–55.

———. 1996. *Poetry as Performance: Homer and Beyond*. Cambridge.

———. 1999. "Epic as Genre." In *Epic Traditions in the Contemporary World: The Poetics of Community*, ed. M. Beissinger, J. Tylus, and S. Wofford, 21–32. Berkeley.

———. 2006. *The Epic Hero*. 2nd online ed. Washington, DC. http://nrs.harvard.edu/urn-3:hlnc.essay:Nagy.The_Epic_Hero.2005.

———. 2009. "Performance and Text in Ancient Greece." In *Performances and Texts: Oxford Handbook of Hellenic Studies*, ed. G. Boys-Stones, B. Graziosi, and P. Vasunia, 417–431. Oxford.

Naiden, F. S. 2012. "Blessèd Are the Parasites." In *Greek and Roman Animal Sacrifice: Ancient Victims, Modern Observers*, ed. C. A. Faraone and F. S. Naiden, 55–83. Cambridge.

———. 2013. *Smoke Signals for the Gods: Ancient Greek Sacrifice from the Archaic Through Roman Periods*. Oxford.

Nauck, A. 1879. "Kritische Bemerkungen." *Bulletin de l'académie impériale des sciences de St.-Petersbourg* 25:409–479.

Navarre, O. 1900. *Essai sur la rhétorique grecque avant Aristote*. Paris.

———. 1904a. "Études sur les particules greques: δῆθεν." *Revue des études anciennes* 6:320–328.

———. 1904b. "Études sur les particules greques: ἤδη." *Revue des études anciennes* 6:77–98.

———. 1905. "Études sur les particules greques: τοίνυν." *Revue des études anciennes* 7:125–30.

———. 1908. "Études sur les particules greques: οὖν." *Revue des études anciennes* 10:293–335.

———. 1932. "La particule greque ΔΗ." *Melanges Glotz* 2:667–679.

Neil, R. A. 1901. "The Particle γε (Appendix I)." In *The Knights of Aristophanes*, 185–201. Cambridge.

Neitzel, H. 1975. *Homer-Rezeption bei Hesiod*. Bonn.

Nenci, G., ed. 1998. *Erodoto. Le storie*. Libro VI: *La battaglia di Maratona*. Milan.

Nesselrath, H.-G. 1992. *Ungeschehenes Geschehen: "Beinahe-Episoden" im griechischen und römischen Epos von Homer bis zur Spätantike*. Stuttgart.

Nicolai, R. 2001. "Thucydides' Archaeology: Between Epic and Oral Traditions." In *The Historian's Craft in the Age of Herodotus*, ed. N. Luraghi, 263–285. Oxford.

Nikiforidou, K. 2009. "Constructional Analysis." In *Grammar, Meaning and Pragmatics*, ed. F. Brisard, J.-O. Östman, and J. Verschueren, 16–32. Amsterdam.

———. 2010. "Viewpoint and Construction Grammar: The Case of Past + Now." *Language and Literature* 19:265–284.

Nimis, S. A. 1987. *Narrative Semiotics in the Epic Tradition: The Simile*. Bloomington.

Noh, E.-J. 2000. *Metarepresentation: A Relevance-Theory Approach*. Amsterdam.

Nølke, H. 2013. "La Polyphonie Linguistique." *Lalies* 33:7–76.

Nordgren, L. 2012. The Greek Interjections: Studies on the Syntax, Semantics and Pragmatics of the Interjections in Fifth-Century Drama. PhD diss., Stockholm University.

———. 2015. *Greek Interjections: Syntax, Semantics and Pragmatics*. Berlin.

Norlin, G. 1980–1986. *Isocrates*. 3 vols. Cambride, MA.

Norrick, N. R. 2000. *Conversational Narrative*. Amsterdam.

———. 2001. "Discourse Markers in Oral Narrative." *Journal of Pragmatics* 33:849–878.

———. 2009a. "Interjections as Pragmatic Markers." *Journal of Pragmatics* 41:866–91.

———. 2009b. "Pragmatic Markers: Introduction." *Journal of Pragmatics* 41:863–865.

Nugent, T. 1773. "The Third Part of the Greek Primitives, Which Treats of the Undeclinable Particles." In *The Primitives of the Greek Tongue. Containing a Complete Collection of All the Roots or Primitives Words, Together with the Most Considerable Derivatives of the Greek Language*, 312–30. London.

Nünlist, R., and I. J. F. de Jong, eds. 2007. *Time in Ancient Greek Literature*. Leiden.

Nuolijärvi, P., and L. Tiittula. 2011. "Irony in Political Television Debates." *Journal of Pragmatics* 43:572–87.

Ochs, E. 1996. "Linguistic Resources for Socializing Humanity." In *Rethinking Linguistic Relativity*, ed. J. J. Gumperz and S. C. Levinson, 407–437. Cambridge.

Ochs, E., E. A. Schegloff, and S. A. Thompson, eds. 1996. *Interaction and Grammar*. Cambridge.

Ochs Keenan, E., and B. Schieffelin. 1976. "Foregrounding Referents: A Reconsideration of Left-Dislocation in Discourse." *Proceedings of the Annual Meeting of the Berkeley Linguistics Society* 2:240–257.

Oeltze, O. 1887. *De Particularum μέν et δέ apud Thucydidem Usu*. Halle am Saale. https://play.google.com/books/reader?id=1RJAAAAAYAAJ&hl=en&pg=GBS.PA5.

Oguse, A. 1968. "Sur Les Concessives à Principale Négative." *Revue de Philologie, de Littérature et de Histoire Anciennes* 42:262–284.

Öhman, A. 2009. "Fear." In *The Oxford Companion to Emotion and the Affective Sciences*, ed. D. Sander and K.R. Scherer, 182–183. Oxford.

Olson, S. D. 1998. *Aristophanes. Peace*. Oxford.

———. 2002. *Aristophanes. Acharnians*. Oxford.

Olsson, C.-J., and L. Nyberg. 2011. "Brain Simulation of Action May Be Grounded in Physical Experience." *Neurocase* 17:501–505. https://www.tandfonline.com/doi/abs/10.1080/13554794.2010.547504?journalCode=nncs20.

O'Neill, E. 1938. *Aristophanes. Women at the Thesmophoria*. New York.

Ong, W. J. 1944. "Historical Backgrounds of Elizabethan and Jacobean Punctuation Theory." *Publications of the Modern Language Association of America* 59:349–360.

———. 1984. "Orality, Literacy, and Medieval Textualization." *New Literary History* 16:1–12.

Onodera, N. O. 2004. *Japanese Discourse Markers: Synchronic and Diachronic Discourse Analysis*. Amsterdam.

———. 2011. "The Grammaticalization of Discourse Markers." In *The Oxford Handbook of Grammaticalization*, ed. H. Narrog and B. Heine, 614–624. Oxford.

Ophuijsen, J. M. van. 1993. "*Oun, Ara, Dh, Toinun*: The Linguistic Articulation of Arguments in Plato's *Phaedo*." In Van Ophuijsen and Sicking 1993:67–164.

Ophuijsen, J. M. van, and C. M. J. Sicking. 1993. *Two Studies in Attic Particle Usage: Lysias and Plato*. Leiden.

Ophuijsen, J. M. van, and P. Stork. 1999. *Linguistics into Interpretation: Speeches of War in Herodotus VII 5 & 8-18*. Leiden.

Oranje, H. 1984. *Euripides' Bacchae: The Play and Its Audience*. Leiden.

Oreal, E. 1997. "Sur la fonction argumentative de quelques particules Grecques." *Lalies* 17:229–249.

Orlandini, A. 1994. "'Si non eo die, at postridie': une analyse pragmatique du connecteur Latin *at*." *Lalies* 14:159–175.

———. 1995. "De la connexion: une analyse pragmatique des connecteurs Latins *atqui* et *immo*." *Lalies* 15:259–269.

———. 1999. "de la connexion: une analyse pragmatique des connecteurs Latins *autem* et *ceterum*." *Indogermanische Forschungen* 104:142–163.

Orlandini, A., and P. Poccetti. 2007. "Les opérateurs de coordination et les connecteurs en Latin et dans d'autres langues de la Méditerranée ancienne." In *La Coordination. Rivages Linguistiques*, ed. A. Rousseau, L. Begioni, and N. Quayle, 189–224. Rennes.

———. 2009. "Corrélation, coordination et comparaison en Latin et dans les langues Italiques." *Langages* 174:53–66.

Oropeza-Escobar, M. 2011. *Represented Discourse, Resonance and Stance in Joking Interaction in Mexican Spanish*. Amsterdam.

Ortolá Guixot, A. F. 2001. "The Use of the Modal Particle *an* in Thucydides' Speeches." *Quaderns de Filologia. Estudis Lingüístics* 6:175–196.

Osborne, R. 1993. "Women and Sacrifice in Classical Greece." *The Classical Quarterly* 43:392–405.

Östman, J.-O. 1991. "On the Language-Internal Interaction of Prosody and Pragmatic Particles." In *Levels of Linguistic Adaptation*, ed. J. Verschueren, 203–221. Amsterdam.

———. 1995. "Pragmatic Particles Twenty Years after." In *Organization in Discourse. Proceedings from the Turku Conference*, ed. B. Wårvik, S.-K. Tanskanen, and R. Hiltunen, 14:95–108. Turku.

———. 1999. "Coherence through Understanding through Discourse Patterns: Focus on News Reports." In *Coherence in Spoken and Written Discourse*, ed. W. Bublitz, U. Lenk, and E. Ventola, 77–100. Amsterdam.

———. 2005. "Construction Discourse: A Prolegomenon." In *Construction Grammars: Cognitive Grounding and Theoretical Extensions*, ed. J.-O. Östman and M. Fried, 121–144. Amsterdam.

Östman, J.-O., and M. Fried. 2004. "Historical and Intellectual Background of Construction Grammar." In *Construction Grammar in a Cross-Language Perspective*, ed. M. Fried and J.-O. Östman, 1–10. Amsterdam.

Östman, J.-O., and G. Trousdale. 2013. "Dialects, Discourse, and Construction Grammar." In *The Oxford Handbook of Construction Grammar*, ed. T. Hoffmann and G. Trousdale. Oxford.

Östman, J.-O., and T. Virtanen. 1999. "Theme, Comment, and Newness as Figures in Information Structure." In *Discourse Studies in Cognitive Linguistics: Selected Papers from the 5th International Cognitive Linguistics Conference, Amsterdam, July 1997*, ed. K. van Hoek, A. A. Kibrik, and L. Noordman, 91–110. Amsterdam.

Ostrowiecki, H. 1994. "Limites du dialogue. Breve étude de la particule *oun* dans le Menon." *Revue de philologie, de littérature et d'histoire anciennes* 68:171–185.

Ostwald, M. 2009. *Language and History in Ancient Greek Culture*. Philadelphia.

Otterlo, W. A. A. van. 1944. *Untersuchungen über Begriff, Anwendung und Entstehung der griechischen Ringkomposition*. Amsterdam.

Ottsen, P. G. 1847. *De rerum inventione ac dispositione, quae est in Lysiae atque Antiphontis orationibus*. Flensburg.

Owren, M. J., M. Philipp, E. Vanman, N. Trivedi, A. Schulman, and J.-A. Bachorowski. 2013. "Understanding Spontaneous Human Laughter: The Role of Voicing in Inducing Positive Emotion." In *The Evolution of Emotional Communication: From Sounds in Nonhuman Mammals to Speech and Music in Man*, ed. E. Altenmüller, S. Schmidt, and E. Zimmermann, 175–190. Oxford.

Pace, G. 2002. "Il Termine Periodos Nella Dottrina Metrica E Ritmica Antica." *Quaderni Urbinati di Cultura Classica* 71:25–46.

Pagani, L. 2011. "Pioneers of Grammar: Hellenistic Scholarship and the Study of Language." In *From Scholars to Scholia: Chapters in the History of Ancient Greek Scholarship*, ed. F. Montanari and L. Pagani, 17–64. Berlin.

Page, D. L. 1938. *Euripides. Medea*. Oxford.

———. 1972. *Aeschyli septem quae supersunt tragoedias*. Oxford.

Paley, F. A. 1881. *A Short Treatise on the Greek Particles and Their Combinations According to Attic Usage*. Cambridge. http://archive.org/stream/shorttreatiseong00palerich.

Palmer, L. R. 1980. *The Greek Language*. London.

Pander Maat, H. L. W. 2001. "Unstressed en/and as a Marker of Joint Relevance." In *Text Representation: Linguistic and Psycholinguistic Aspects*, ed. T. Sanders and W. Spooren, 197–230. Amsterdam.

Páez Martínez, M. 2012. "Bibliography about Greek Particles (1935-2010)." *Syntaktika* 42:3–43.

Parkes, M. B. 1992. *Pause and Effect. An Introduction to the History of Punctuation in the West*. Aldershot.

Parry, M. 1936. "On Typical Scenes in Homer." *Classical Philology* 31:404–407.

———. 1971. *The Making of Homeric Verse: The Collected Papers of Milman Parry*. Ed. A. Parry. Oxford.

Partee, B. H., and H. L. W. Hendriks. 1997. "Montague Grammar." In *Handbook of Logic and Language*, ed. J. van Benthem and A. ter Meulen, 5–91. Amsterdam.

Partridge, E. 1953. *You Have a Point There: A Guide to Punctuation and Its Allies*. London.

Pascal, R. 1977. *The Dual Voice: Free Indirect Speech and Its Functioning in the Nineteenth-Century European Novel*. Manchester.

Passot, F. 2007. "A Because B so A: Circularity and Discourse Progression in Conversational English." In *Connectives as Discourse Landmarks*, ed. A. Celle and R. Huart, 117–134. Amsterdam.

Passow, F. 1841–1857. *Handwörterbuch der griechischen Sprache*. 5th ed. Leipzig.

Patt, S. 2013. *Punctuation as a Means of Medium-Dependent Presentation Structure in English: Exploring the Guide Functions of Punctuation*. Tübingen.

Patten, G. 2009. *Pindar's Metaphors: A Study in Rhetoric and Meaning*. Heidelberg.

Pavlou, M. 2013. "Attributive Discourse in the Speeches in Thucydides." In *Thucydides Between History and Literature*, ed. A. Tsakmakis and M. Tamiolaki, 409–434. Berlin.

Pawley, A., and F. Hodgetts Syder. 2000. "The One-Clause-at-a-Time Hypothesis." In *Perspectives on Fluency*, ed. H. Riggenbach, 163–199. Ann Arbor, MI.

Pearson, A. C. 1917. "Index to the Tragedies and Fragments [of Sophocles]." In *The Fragments of Sophocles* III, ed. A. C. Pearson. Cambridge.

Pearson, A. C., ed. 1903. *The Helena of Euripides*. Cambridge.

Pecorella, G. B. 1962. *ΤΕΧΝΗ ΓΡΑΜΜΑΤΙΚΗ. Testo critico e commento*. Bologna.

Pedley, J. Griffiths, ed. 1972. *Ancient literary sources on Sardis*. Cambridge, MA.

Peile, T. W. 1839. "Note on τε." In *Agamemnon*, ed. T. W. Peile, 378–394.

Pekarek Doehler, S. 2011a. "Clause-Combining and the Sequencing of Actions: Projector Constructions in French Talk-in-Interaction." In *Subordination in Conversation: A Cross-Linguistic Perspective*, ed. R. Laury and R. Suzuki, 103–148. Amsterdam.

———. 2011b. "Emergent Grammar for All Practical Purposes: The on-Line Formating of Dislocated Constructions in French Conversation." In *Constructions: Emerging and Emergent*, ed. S. Pfänder and P. Auer, 46–88. Berlin.

Pelliccia, H. 1987. "Pindarus Homericus: *Pythian* 3.1-80." *Harvard Studies in Classical Philology* 91:39–63.

———. 1989. "Pindar, *Nemean* 7.31-36 and the Syntax of Aetiology." *Harvard Studies in Classical Philology* 92:71–101.

———. 1998. "The Transposition of Aeschylus, Agamemnon 1203-1204 and the Uses of *môn*." In *Mir Curad: Studies in Honor of Calvert Watkins*, ed. J. H. Jasanoff, 561–572. Innsbruck.

Pelling, C. 1991. "Thucydides' Archidamus and Herodotus' Artabanus." In *Georgica: Greek Studies in Honour of George Cawkwell*, ed. M. Flower and M. Toher, 120-142. London.

———. 2005. "Tragedy, Rhetoric, and Performance Culture." In *A Companion to Greek Tragedy*, ed. J. Gregory, 83–102. Oxford.

———. 2006. "Speech and Narrative in the Histories." In *The Cambridge Companion to Herodotus*, ed. C. Dewald and J. Marincola, 103–121. Cambridge.

———. 2009. "Thucydides' Speeches." In *Thucydides: Oxford Readings in Classical Texts*, ed. J. S. Rusten, 176–187. Oxford.

Pennebaker, J. W. 2011. *The Secret Life of Pronouns: What Our Words Say about Us*. New York.

Perdicoyianni-Paléologue, H. 2002. "The Interjections in Greek Tragedy." *Quaderni Urbinati di Cultura Classica* 70:49–88.

Pernée, L. 1987. "Deux Exemples Pour Illustrer La Nécessité d'une Traduction élaborée en Grec Ancien." *Les Études Classiques* 55:121–135.

Perpillou, J. L. 1978. "Débuts de phrase en Grec méridional archaique." In *Etrennes de septantaine. Travaux de linguistique et de grammaire comparée offerts à Michel Lejeune*, 179–181. Paris.

Perria, L. 1991. "L'interpunzione nei manoscritti della 'collezione filosofica'." In *Paleografia e codicologia greca. Atti del II colloquio internazionale*, eds. D. Harlfinger and G. Prato, 199–209. Alessandria.

Person, R. F. 2009. "'Oh' in Shakespeare: A Conversation Analytic Approach." *Journal of Historical Pragmatics* 10:84–107.

Persson, P. 1886. *Studia Etymologica*. Uppsala.

Pfeiffer, R. 1968. *History of Classical Scholarship*. Oxford.

Pfeiffer-Petersen, S. 1996. *Konfliktstichomythien bei Sophokles: Funktion und Gestaltung*. Wiesbaden.

Pfeijffer, I. L. 1999. *Three Aeginetan Odes of Pindar: A Commentary on Nemean V, Nemean III, and Pythian VIII*. Leiden.

Pfudel, E. 1871. *Beiträge zur Syntax der Causalsätze bei Homer*. Liegnitz.

Philippi, J. 2008. *Einführung in die generative Grammatik*. Göttingen.

Pickering, M. J., and S. Garrod. 2006. "Alignment as the Basis for Successful Communication." *Research on Language and Computation* 4:203–228.

Pickering, P. E. 1999. *Verbal Repetition in Greek Tragedy*. London.

———. 2000a. "Repetitions and Their Removal by the Copyists of Greek Tragedy." *Greek, Roman, and Byzantine Studies* 41:123–139.

———. 2000b. "Verbal Repetition in Prometheus and Greek Tragedy Generally." *Bulletin of the Institute of Classical Studies* 44:81–101.

———. 2003. "Did the Greek Ear Detect 'Careless' Verbal Repetitions?" *The Classical Quarterly* 53:490–499.

Pickering, P. E., and M. J. Pickering. 2002. "Do Real People Talk Like Electra and Orestes?—Repetition in Dialogue: Tragedy Compared with Natural Speech." Presentation at the Joint Classical Association and Classical Association of Scotland Annual Conference, Edinburgh, April 4–7.

Piderit, K. W. 1854. "[Review of Classen 1854]." *Neue Jahrbücher für Philologie und Pädagogik* 70:69–78.

Pinborg, J. 1975. "Classical Antiquity: Greece." In *Current Trends in Linguistics*. Vol. 13: *Historiography of Linguistics*, ed. T.A. Sebeok, 1:69–126. The Hague.

Pinkster, H. 1972. *On Latin Adverbs*. Amsterdam.

———. 2010. "The Use of Quia and Quoniam in Cicero, Seneca, and Tertullian." In *Studies in Classical Linguistics in Honor of Philip Baldi*, ed. B. R. Page and A. D. Rubin, 81–96. Leiden.

Platnauer, M. 1964. *Aristophanes: Peace*. Oxford.

Platt, A. 1911. "Plato, *Republic*, 614 B." *The Classical Review* 25:13–14.

Pokorny, J. 1959. *Indogermanisches Etymologisches Wörterbuch*. Bern.

Polanyi, L. 1988. "A Formal Model of the Structure of Discourse." *Journal of Pragmatics* 12:601–638.

Polanyi, L., and R. J. H. Scha. 1983. "The Syntax of Discourse." *Text* 3:261–270.

Polo Arrondo, J. F. 2007. "De la subordinación al discurso: Un ejemplo en Griego antiguo." *Interlingüística* 17:827–836.

———. 2011. "A New Approach to Subordination in Ancient Greek: The Case of πλήν." Presentation at the Linguistics and Classical Languages Conference, Rome, Febrary 17–19.

Pomerantz, A. 1984. "Agreeing and Disagreeing with Assessments: Some Features of Preferred/Dispreferred Turn Shapes." In *Structures of Social Action*, ed. J. M. Atkinson and J. Heritage, 57–101. Cambridge.

Pons Bordería, S. 2014. *Discourse Segmentation in Romance Languages*. Amsterdam.

Pons Bordería, S., and M. Estellés Arguedas. 2009. "Expressing Digression Linguistically: Do Digressive Markers Exist?" *Journal of Pragmatics* 41:921–936.

Pontani, F. M. 1951. *Eschilo. I Persiani*. Rome.

Poppo, E. F., and J. M. Stahl. 1875–1889. *Thucydidis de bello Peloponnesiaco Libri Octo*. 3rd ed. Leipzig.

Posner, R. 1980. "Semantics and Pragmatics of Sentence Connectives in Natural Language." In *Speech Act Theory and Pragmatics*, ed. J. R. Searle, F. Kiefer, and M. Bierwisch, 169–203. Dordrecht.

Pott, A. F. 1836. *Etymologische Forschungen auf dem Gebiete der indo-germanischen Sprachen*. Halle.

Powell, J. E. 1933. "Studies on the Greek Reflexive-Herodotus." *The Classical Quarterly* 27:208–221.

———. 1934. "Studies on the Greek Reflexive—Thucydides." *Classical Quarterly* 28:159–174.

———. 1938. *A Lexicon to Herodotus*. Cambridge.

Powers, M. 2014. *Athenian Tragedy in Performance: A Guide to Contemporary Studies and Historical Debates*. Iowa City.

Praetorius, F. 1873. *Der homerische Gebrauch von ē (ēe) in Fragesätzen*. Kassel.

Preacher, K.J. 2001. *Calculation for the Chi-Square Test: An Interactive Calculation Tool for Chi-Square Tests of Goodness of Fit and Independence [computer Software]*. http://www.quantpsy.org/chisq/chisq.htm.

Preuss, S. 1892. *Index Demosthenicus*. Leipzig.

———. 1896. *Index Aeschineus*. Leipzig.

———. 1904. *Index Isocrateus*. Leipzig.

Prince, E. F. 1981. "Towards a Taxonomy of given and New Information." In *Radical Pragmatics*, ed. P. Cole, 223–256. New York.

Prince, G. 1997. "Narratology and Narratological Analysis." *Journal of Narrative and Life History* 7:39–44.

Privitera, G. A. 1982. *Pindaro. Le Istmiche*. Milan.

Probert, Ph. 2006. *Ancient Greek Accentuation: Synchronic Patterns, Frequency Effects, and Prehistory*. Oxford.

———. 2015. *Early Greek Relative Clauses*. Oxford.

Propp, V. Ja., and L. Scott, trans. 1958. *Morphology of the Folktale*. Bloomington.

Provenza, A. 2013. "Madness and Bestialization in Euripides' Heracles." *The Classical Quarterly* n.s. 63:68–93.

Pucci, P. 2007. "Euripides and Aristophanes: What Does Tragedy Teach?" In *Visualizing the Tragic: Drama, Myth, and Ritual in Greek Art and Literature*, ed. C. Kraus, S. Goldhill, H. P. Foley, and J. Elsner, 105–126. Oxford.

Purves, A. C. 2010. *Space and Time in Ancient Greek Narrative*. Cambridge.

Quaglio, P. 2009. *Television Dialogue: The Sitcom Friends vs. Natural Conversation*. Amsterdam.

Quirk, R., S. Greenbaum, G. Leech, and J. Svartvik. 1985. *A Comprehensive Grammar of the English Language*. London.

Race, W. H. 1989. "Elements of Style in Pindaric Break-Offs." *American Journal of Philology* 110:189–209.

———. 1997. *Pindar. Victory Odes and Fragments*. Cambridge, MA.

———. 2000. "Explanatory de-Clauses in the *Iliad*." *The Classical Journal* 95:205–227.

———. 2002. "Framing Hyperbata in Pindar's *Odes*." *The Classical Journal* 98:21–33.

Räder, H. 1953. *Ein Problem in griechischer Syntax. Die Verbindung der Partikel* an *mit Futurum*. Copenhagen.

Radermacher, L. 1902. "Drei Deutungen. III δέ?" *Rheinisches Museum* 57:480.

———. 1908. "ὡς, ὁμοίως und Verwandtes." *Rheinisches Museum* 63:312–313.

———. 1928. "Bemerkungen zur Sprache des Sophokles." *Wiener Studien* 46:130–132.

Raeburn, D., and O. R. H. Thomas. 2011. *The Agamemnon of Aeschylus*. Oxford.

Raible, W. 1992. *Junktion. Eine Dimension der Sprache und ihre Realisierungsformen zwischen Aggregation und Integration*. Heidelberg.

———. 2001. "Linking Clauses." In *Language Typology and Language Universals*, ed. M. Haspelmath, E. König, W. Österreicher, and W. Raible, 590–617. Berlin.

Ramsay, W. M. 1898. "καί meaning *or*." *The Classical Review* 12:337–341.

Rassow, J. 1889. "De collocatione particularum τε, καί, οὔτε, οὐδέ in fabulis Euripideis: Analecta Euripidea, Pars II." In *Jahresbericht über das städtische Gymnasium und das mit Demselben verbundene Realprogymnasium zu Greifswald*. Greifswald.

Raymond, G. 2004. "Prompting Action: The Stand-Alone *so* in Ordinary Conversation." *Research on Language and Social Interaction* 37:185–218.

Ready, J. L. 2011. *Character, Narrator, and Simile in the Iliad*. Cambridge.

Redeker, G. 1990. "Ideational and Pragmatic Markers of Discourse Structure." *Journal of Pragmatics* 14:367–381.

———. 1991. "Linguistic Markers of Discourse Structure: Review of Discourse Markers by D. Schiffrin." *Linguistics* 29:1139–1172.

———. 2006. "Discourse Markers as Attentional Cues at Discourse Transitions." In Fischer 2006:339–358.

Redondo, J. 1989. "De nuevo sobre la cuestión de las partículas Griegas." *Actas del VII congreso Español de estudios clásicos I, Madrid*, 261–266. Madrid.

Redondo Moyano, E. 1993. "El repertorio de las partículas en Griego antiguo." *Veleia* 10:221–226.

———. 1995. *Estudio sintáctico de las partículas en el período Helenístico*. Amsterdam.

Rehdantz, C. 1866. *Index to Demosthenes, Philippics*. Leipzig.

Reinhold, H. 1894. "Index." In *Hyperidis orationes sex, cum ceterarum fragmentis*, ed. F. Blass. Leipzig.

Reisenzein, R. 1994. "Pleasure-Arousal Theory and the Intensity of Emotions." *Journal of Personality and Social Psychology* 67:525–539.

Reisig, K. C. 1823. *Commentarii in Sophoclis Oedipum Coloneum*. Jena.

Renoir, A. 1962. "Point of View and Design for Terror in Beowulf." *Neuphilologische Mitteilungen* 63:154–167.

Repgen, K. 1982. "Über Rankes Diktum von 1824." *Historisches Jahrbuch* 102:439–449.

Revelle, W., and K. R. Scherer. 2009. "Personality (and Emotion)." In *The Oxford Companion to Emotion and the Affective Sciences*, ed. D. Sander and K. R. Scherer, 304–305. Oxford.

Revermann, M. 2006a. *Comic Business: Theatricality, Dramatic Technique, and Performance Contexts of Aristophanic Comedy*. Oxford.

———. 2006b. "The Competence of Theatre Audiences in Fifth- and Fourth-Century Athens." *Journal of Hellenic Studies* 126:99–124.

Revuelta Puigdollers, A. R. 1996. *Estudio de las partículas Griegas αὖ, αὖτε, αὖθις, ἄψ, πάλιν y ὀπίσω en Griego antiguo*. Madrid.

———. 1998. "Focusing Particles in Latin. Some Remarks." In *Estudios de lingüística Latina: actas del IX coloquio internacional de lingüística Latina* II, ed. B. García-Hernández, 689–704. Madrid.

———. 2000. "Parallel Focus Particles, Especially in Ancient Greek." In *Cien años de investigación semántica: de Michel Bréal a la actualidad: actas del congreso internacional de semántica; Universidad de La Laguna 27-31 de octubre de 1997*, ed. M. Martínez Hernández, 1175–1190. Madrid.

———. 2006a. "Los Adverbios en Griego Antiguo. Las Partículas." In *Sintaxis Griega*, ed. D. Jiménez López. Liceus E-Excellence. El Portal de las Humanidades.

———. 2006b. "Word Classes, Functions and Syntactic Level: The Case of Palin." In *Word Classes and Related Topics in Ancient Greek: Proceedings of the Conference on "Greek Syntax and Word Classes" held in Madrid on 18-21, June 2003*, ed. E. Crespo, J. de la Villa, and A. R. Revuelta Puigdollers, 455–470. Louvain-la-Neuve.

———. 2009a. "Particles and Discourse Cohesion in Ancient Greek." In *Proceedings of the 8th International Conference on Greek Linguistics, August 30th–September 2nd, 2007*, ed. G. K. Giannakis, M. Baltazani, G. I. Xidopoulos, and T. Tsagalidis, 394–405. Ioannina.

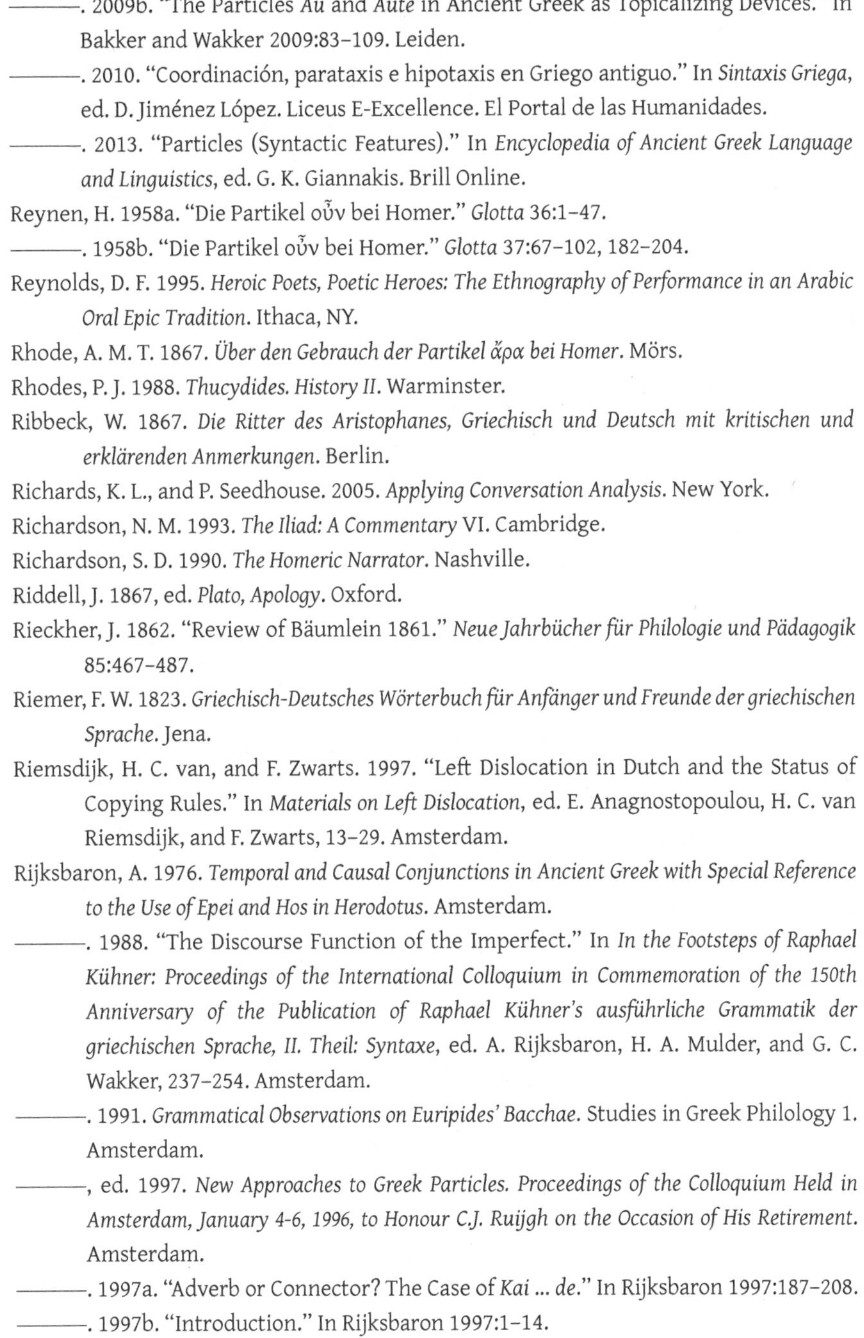

———. 2009b. "The Particles *Au* and *Aute* in Ancient Greek as Topicalizing Devices." In Bakker and Wakker 2009:83–109. Leiden.

———. 2010. "Coordinación, parataxis e hipotaxis en Griego antiguo." In *Sintaxis Griega*, ed. D. Jiménez López. Liceus E-Excellence. El Portal de las Humanidades.

———. 2013. "Particles (Syntactic Features)." In *Encyclopedia of Ancient Greek Language and Linguistics*, ed. G. K. Giannakis. Brill Online.

Reynen, H. 1958a. "Die Partikel οὖν bei Homer." *Glotta* 36:1–47.

———. 1958b. "Die Partikel οὖν bei Homer." *Glotta* 37:67–102, 182–204.

Reynolds, D. F. 1995. *Heroic Poets, Poetic Heroes: The Ethnography of Performance in an Arabic Oral Epic Tradition*. Ithaca, NY.

Rhode, A. M. T. 1867. *Über den Gebrauch der Partikel ἄρα bei Homer*. Mörs.

Rhodes, P. J. 1988. *Thucydides. History II*. Warminster.

Ribbeck, W. 1867. *Die Ritter des Aristophanes, Griechisch und Deutsch mit kritischen und erklärenden Anmerkungen*. Berlin.

Richards, K. L., and P. Seedhouse. 2005. *Applying Conversation Analysis*. New York.

Richardson, N. M. 1993. *The Iliad: A Commentary* VI. Cambridge.

Richardson, S. D. 1990. *The Homeric Narrator*. Nashville.

Riddell, J. 1867, ed. *Plato, Apology*. Oxford.

Rieckher, J. 1862. "Review of Bäumlein 1861." *Neue Jahrbücher für Philologie und Pädagogik* 85:467–487.

Riemer, F. W. 1823. *Griechisch-Deutsches Wörterbuch für Anfänger und Freunde der griechischen Sprache*. Jena.

Riemsdijk, H. C. van, and F. Zwarts. 1997. "Left Dislocation in Dutch and the Status of Copying Rules." In *Materials on Left Dislocation*, ed. E. Anagnostopoulou, H. C. van Riemsdijk, and F. Zwarts, 13–29. Amsterdam.

Rijksbaron, A. 1976. *Temporal and Causal Conjunctions in Ancient Greek with Special Reference to the Use of Epei and Hos in Herodotus*. Amsterdam.

———. 1988. "The Discourse Function of the Imperfect." In *In the Footsteps of Raphael Kühner: Proceedings of the International Colloquium in Commemoration of the 150th Anniversary of the Publication of Raphael Kühner's ausführliche Grammatik der griechischen Sprache, II. Theil: Syntaxe*, ed. A. Rijksbaron, H. A. Mulder, and G. C. Wakker, 237–254. Amsterdam.

———. 1991. *Grammatical Observations on Euripides' Bacchae*. Studies in Greek Philology 1. Amsterdam.

———, ed. 1997. *New Approaches to Greek Particles. Proceedings of the Colloquium Held in Amsterdam, January 4-6, 1996, to Honour C.J. Ruijgh on the Occasion of His Retirement*. Amsterdam.

———. 1997a. "Adverb or Connector? The Case of *Kai ... de*." In Rijksbaron 1997:187–208.

———. 1997b. "Introduction." In Rijksbaron 1997:1–14.

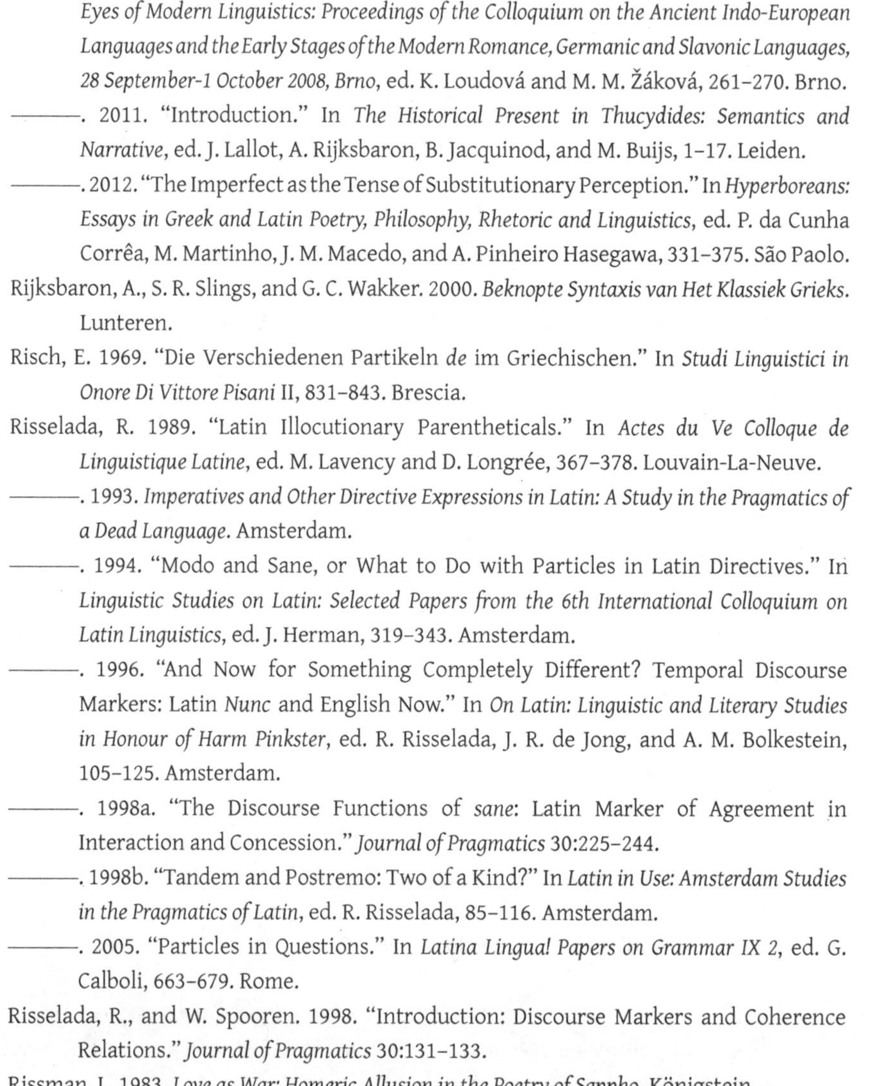

———. 2002 [1984]. *The Syntax and Semantics of the Verb in Classical Greek: An Introduction*. 3rd ed. Amsterdam.

———. 2007. *Plato, Ion, or On the Iliad*. Leiden.

———. 2009. "Negatives in Questions (and Answers): The Case of '*Oukoun* (...) *Ou*'. Or: Does Ancient Greek Have a Word for 'no'?" In *Early European Languages in the Eyes of Modern Linguistics: Proceedings of the Colloquium on the Ancient Indo-European Languages and the Early Stages of the Modern Romance, Germanic and Slavonic Languages, 28 September-1 October 2008, Brno*, ed. K. Loudová and M. M. Žáková, 261–270. Brno.

———. 2011. "Introduction." In *The Historical Present in Thucydides: Semantics and Narrative*, ed. J. Lallot, A. Rijksbaron, B. Jacquinod, and M. Buijs, 1–17. Leiden.

———. 2012. "The Imperfect as the Tense of Substitutionary Perception." In *Hyperboreans: Essays in Greek and Latin Poetry, Philosophy, Rhetoric and Linguistics*, ed. P. da Cunha Corrêa, M. Martinho, J. M. Macedo, and A. Pinheiro Hasegawa, 331–375. São Paolo.

Rijksbaron, A., S. R. Slings, and G. C. Wakker. 2000. *Beknopte Syntaxis van Het Klassiek Grieks*. Lunteren.

Risch, E. 1969. "Die Verschiedenen Partikeln *de* im Griechischen." In *Studi Linguistici in Onore Di Vittore Pisani* II, 831–843. Brescia.

Risselada, R. 1989. "Latin Illocutionary Parentheticals." In *Actes du Ve Colloque de Linguistique Latine*, ed. M. Lavency and D. Longrée, 367–378. Louvain-La-Neuve.

———. 1993. *Imperatives and Other Directive Expressions in Latin: A Study in the Pragmatics of a Dead Language*. Amsterdam.

———. 1994. "Modo and Sane, or What to Do with Particles in Latin Directives." In *Linguistic Studies on Latin: Selected Papers from the 6th International Colloquium on Latin Linguistics*, ed. J. Herman, 319–343. Amsterdam.

———. 1996. "And Now for Something Completely Different? Temporal Discourse Markers: Latin *Nunc* and English Now." In *On Latin: Linguistic and Literary Studies in Honour of Harm Pinkster*, ed. R. Risselada, J. R. de Jong, and A. M. Bolkestein, 105–125. Amsterdam.

———. 1998a. "The Discourse Functions of *sane*: Latin Marker of Agreement in Interaction and Concession." *Journal of Pragmatics* 30:225–244.

———. 1998b. "Tandem and Postremo: Two of a Kind?" In *Latin in Use: Amsterdam Studies in the Pragmatics of Latin*, ed. R. Risselada, 85–116. Amsterdam.

———. 2005. "Particles in Questions." In *Latina Lingua! Papers on Grammar IX 2*, ed. G. Calboli, 663–679. Rome.

Risselada, R., and W. Spooren. 1998. "Introduction: Discourse Markers and Coherence Relations." *Journal of Pragmatics* 30:131–133.

Rissman, L. 1983. *Love as War: Homeric Allusion in the Poetry of Sappho*. Königstein.

Ritter, C. 1888. *Untersuchungen über Plato: Die Echtheit und Chronologie der platonischen Schriften*. Stuttgart.

———. 1921. "Review of Platonic Literature." *Bursian's Jahresbericht* 187:1–227.

Ritter, F. 1870. *Sophokles' König Oidipus*. Leipzig.

Robbins, C. J. 1979. "A Colometric Arrangement of Cicero." *The Classical Journal* 75:57–62.

Robertson, J. 1785. *An Essay on Punctuation*. London.

Robins, R. H. A. 1995. "The Authenticity of the *Téchnē*: The Status Quaestionis." In Law and Sluiter 1995:13–26.

Robinson, D. 2006. *Introducing Performative Pragmatics*. New York.

Romm, J. S. 1998. *Herodotus*. New Haven.

Romilly, J. de. 1956. *The Mind of Thucydides*. Ithaca, NY and London.

———. 1974. *Eschyle: Les Perses*. Paris.

Rood, T. 1998. *Thucydides: Narrative and Explanation*. Oxford.

———. 2004. "Thucydides." In *Narrators, Narratees, and Narratives in Ancient Greek Literature*, ed. I. J. F. de Jong, R. Nünlist, and A. M. Bowie, 115–128. Leiden.

Rosén, H. B. 1987-1989. *Herodotus. Historiae*. 2 vols. Leipzig.

———. 1989. "On the Use and Function of Sentential Particles in Classical Latin." In *Actes du Ve colloque de linguistique Latine, Louvain-La-Neuve/Borzée 1989*, ed. M. Lavency and D. Longrée, 391–402. Louvain-la-Neuve.

———. 1993. "Demum: A Message-Articulating Particle." In *Florilegium historiographiae linguisticae. Études d'historiographie de la linguistique et de grammaire comparée à la mémoire de Maurice Leroy*, ed. J. de Clercq and P. Desmet, 173–184. Louvain-la-Neuve.

———. 1999. *Latine loqui: Trends and Directions in the Crystallization of Classical Latin*. München.

———. 2002. "Complementarity within the Pool of Cohesion Devices?" In *Theory and Description in Latin Linguistics: Selected Papers from the XIth International Colloquium on Latin Linguistics, Amsterdam, June 24 - 29, 2001*, ed. A. M. Bolkestein, C. H. M. Kroon, H. Pinkster, H. W. Kemmelink, and R. Risselada, 333–346. Amsterdam.

———. 2003. "*Immo*—Its Atypical Use in Petronius." In *Petroniana. Gedenkschrift Für Hubert Petersmann*, ed. J. Herman and H. Rosén, 167–181. Heidelberg.

———. 2007. "On Particles and Otiose Emendations: Epitactic Sed." In *L' Art de la Philologie: Mélanges en L'honneur de Leena Löfstedt*, ed. J. Härmä and M. Ursin, 177–184. Helsinki.

———. 2009. "Coherence, Sentence Modification, and Sentence-Part Modification—The Contribution of Particles." In *New Perspectives on Historical Latin Syntax*. Vol. 1: *Syntax of the Sentence*, ed. P. Baldi and P. Cuzzolin, 317–442. Berlin.

Rosenberg, E. 1874a. "Die Partikel τοίνυν in der attischen Dekas." *Neue Jahrbücher für Philologie und Pädagogik* 109 (=*Jahrbücher für klassische Philologie* 20):109–121.

———. 1874b. "Die Partikel τοίνυν." *Philologus* 33:560.

Rosenthal, W. 1894. *De Antiphontis in Particularum Usu Proprietate*. Berlin.

Rösler, W. 1983. "Über Deixis und einige Aspekte mündlichen und schriftlichen Stils in antiker Lyrik." *Würzburger Jahrbücher für die Altertumswissenschaft* 9:7–28.

Rost, V. C. F., ed. 1836. *Novum Lexicon Graecum Ex Christiani Tobiae Dammii Lexico Homerico-Pindarico*. Leipzig.

———. 1859. *Über Ableitung, Bedeutung und Gebrauch der Partikel οὖν*. Gotha.

Rothkopf, E. Z., D. G. Fisher, and M. J. Billington. 1982. "Effects of Spatial Context during Acquisition on the Recall of Attributive Information." *Journal of Experimental Psychology: Learning, Memory, and Cognition* 8:126–138.

Rouchota, V. 1998. "Procedural Meaning and Parenthetical Discourse Markers." In Jucker and Ziv 1998:97–126.

Rouchota, V., and A. H. Jucker, eds. 1998. *Current Issues in Relevance Theory*. Amsterdam.

Roulet, E. 1981. "Échanges, interventions et actes de langage dans la structure de la conservation." *Études de linguistique appliquée* 44:7–39.

———. 1984. "Speech Acts, Discourse Structure, and Pragmatic Connectives." *Journal of Pragmatics* 8:31–47.

———. 1995. *Geneva School. Handbook of Pragmatics: Manual*. John Benjamins online.

———. 1997. "A Modular Approach to Discourse Structures." *Pragmatics* 7:125–46.

———. 2006. "The Description of Text Relation Markers in the Geneva Model of Discourse Organization." In Fischer 2006:115–131.

Roulet, E., A. Auchlin, J. Moeschler, C. Rubattel, and M. Schelling. 1985. *L'articulation du Discours en Francais Contemporain*. Bern.

Roulet, E., L. Fillietaz, and A. Grobet. 2001. *Un modèle et un instrument d'analyse de l'organisation du discours*. Frankfurt am Main.

Roussel, L. 1960. *Eschyle. Les Perses*. Montpellier.

Rubin, D. C. 1995. *Memory in Oral Traditions: The Cognitive Psychology of Epic, Ballads, and Counting-out Rhymes*. Oxford.

Ruffell, I. 2008. "Audience and Emotion in the Reception of Greek Drama." In *Performance, Iconography, Reception: Studies in Honour of Oliver Taplin*, ed. M. Revermann and P. Wilson, 37–58. Oxford.

Rühlemann, C. 2013. *Narrative in English Conversation*. Cambridge.

Ruijgh, C. J. 1957. *L'élément Achéen Dans La Langue épique*. Assen.

———. 1967. *Études Sur La Grammaire et Le Vocabulaire Du Grec Mycénien*. Amsterdam.

———. 1971. *Autour de "TE Epique": Études Sur La Syntaxe Grecque*. Amsterdam.

———. 1981. "L'emploi de HTOI Chez Homere et Hesiode." *Mnemosyne* 34:272–287.

———. 1985a. "Le Mycénien et Homère." In *Proceedings of the Mycenaean Colloquium of the VIIIth Congress of the International Federations of the Societies of Classical Studies (Dublin, 27. August-1st September 1984)*, ed. A. Morpurgo Davies and Y. Duhoux, 143–190. Louvain-la-Neuve.

———. 1985b. "L'emploi 'Inceptif' du Thème du Présent du Verbe Grec." *Mnemosyne* 38:1–61.

———. 1990. "La Place des Enclitiques dans L'orde des Mots chez Homère après la Loi de Wackernagel." In *Sprachwissenschaft und Philologie. Jacob Wackernagel und die Indogermanistik heute*, ed. E. Eichner and H. Rix, 213–233. Wiesbaden.

———. 1992. "L'emploi le plus ancien et les emplois plus récents de la particule κε/ἄν." In *La langue et les textes en Grec ancien: actes du colloque Pierre Chantraine (Grenoble, 5-8 Septembre 1989)*, ed. F. Létoublon, 75–84. Amsterdam.

———. 1995. "D'Homère aux origines proto-mycéniennes de la tradition épique." In *Homeric Questions*, ed. J. P. Crielaard, 1–96. Amsterdam.

———. 2006. "The Use of the Demonstratives ὅδε, οὗτος and (ἐ)κεῖνος in Sophocles." In *Sophocles and the Greek Language: Aspects of Diction, Syntax and Pragmatics*, ed. I. J. F. de Jong and A. Rijksbaron, 151–162. Leiden.

Ruiz Yamuza, E. 2000. "Objective and Subjective Modality Satellites in Ancient Greek: *Tacha* and *Isoos*." *Glotta* 76:237–248.

———. 2012. "Los Matices de la Consecuencia: Ejemplificación con οὕτως." In *Lingüística XL. El lingüista del siglo XXI*, ed. A. Cabedo Nebot and P. Infante Ríos, 225–232. Madrid.

Rumpel, J. 1883. *Lexicon Pindaricum*. Leipzig.

Runge, S. E. 2007. "Teaching Them What NOT to Do: The Nuances of Negation in the Greek New Testament." Presentation at the Evangelical Theological Society Annual Meeting, San Diego, CA, November 13–16.

Ruppenhofer, J., and L. A. Michaelis. 2010. "A Constructional Account of Genre-Based Argument Omissions." *Constructions and Frames* 2:158–184.

Russell, J. A. 1980. "A Circumplex Model of Affect." *Journal of Personality and Social Psychology* 39:1161–1178.

Rusten, J. S. 1989. *Thucydides. The Peloponnesian War, Book II*. Cambridge.

———. 2015. "Kinesis in Thucydides' Preface." In *Kinesis: Essays for Donald Lateiner on the Ancient Depiction of Gesture, Motion, and Emotion*, ed. C. Clark, E. Foster, and J. P. Hallett. Ann Arbor.

Rutherford, R. B. 2010. "The Greek of Athenian Tragedy." In Bakker 2010:441–454.

———. 2012. *Greek Tragic Style: Form, Language and Interpretation*. Cambridge.

Ryan, M.-L. 1980. "Fiction, Non-Factuals, and the Principle of Minimal Departure." *Poetics* 9:403–422.

———. 1991. *Possible Worlds, Artificial Intelligence, and Narrative Theory*. Bloomington.

———. 2003. "Cognitive Maps and the Construction of Narrative Space." In *Narrative Theory and the Cognitive Sciences*, ed. D. Herman, 214–242. Stanford.

———. 2007. "Toward a Definition of Narrative." In *The Cambridge Companion to Narrative*, ed. D. Herman, 22–35. Cambridge.

Saayman, F. 1990. "Conjunctions in Classical Greek Syntax." *Acta Classica: Proceedings of the Classical Association of South Africa* 33:91–102.

Sacks, H. 1995. *Lectures on Conversation*. Oxford.

Sacks, H., E. A. Schegloff, and G. Jefferson. 1974. "A Simplest Systematics for the Organization of Turn-Taking for Conversation." *Language* 50:696–735.

Saenger, P. H. 1997. *Space between Words: The Origins of Silent Reading*. Stanford.

Saeve, H. 1864. *Quaestiones de dicendi usu Thucydidis. I. De vi et usu particulae γάρ.* Uppsala.
Sagawe, K. 1893. *δέ Im Nachsatz bei Herodot.* Breslau.
Saïd, S. 2002. "Herodotus and Tragedy." In *Brill's Companion to Herodotus*, ed. E. J. Bakker, I. J. F. de Jong, and H. van Wees. Leiden.
Sakita, T. 2006. "Parallelism in Conversation: Resonance, Schematization, and Extension from the Perspective of Dialogic Syntax and Cognitive Linguistics." *Pragmatics & Cognition* 14:467–500.
Salmon, W. 2010. "Double Subjects and Verbal Demonstrations." *Journal of Pragmatics* 42:3431–3443.
Sambre, P. 2010. "Framing from Grammar to Application." *Belgian Journal of Linguistics* 24:1–15.
Sampson, J. 1997. "'Genre,' 'Style' and 'Register'. Sources of Confusion?" *Revue Belge de philologie et d'histoire* 73:699–708.
Sanders, E. 2013. "Sexual Jealousy and Eros in Euripides' *Medea*." In Sanders et al. 2013:41–58.
———. 2014. *Envy and Jealousy in Classical Athens: A Socio-Psychological Approach.* Oxford.
Sanders, E., C. Thumiger, C. Carey, and N. J. Lowe, eds. 2013. *Erôs in Ancient Greece.* Oxford.
Sanford, A. J., and C. Emmott. 2012. *Mind, Brain and Narrative.* Cambridge.
Sanford, A. J., and S.C. Garrod. 1998. "The Role of Scenario Mapping in Text Comprehension." *Discourse Processes* 26:159–190.
Sanmartí Boncompte, F. 1951. *La particula modal ἄν-κε.* Barcelona.
Sansone, D. 1990. "The Computer and the *Historia Augusta*: A Note on Marriot." *Journal of Roman Studies* 80:174–177.
Savino, M., M. Griceb, B. Gili Fivelac, and G. Marottad. 2006. "Intonational Cues to Discourse Structure in Bari and Pisa Italian: Perceptual Evidence." In *Atti Del convegno internazionale speech prosody 2006*, 144–147. Dresden.
Sbisà, M. 1999. "Presuppositions, Implicature and Context in Text Understanding." In *Modeling and Using Context. Second International and Interdisciplinary Conference Context '99*, ed. P. Bouquet, L. Serafini, P. Brézillon, M. Benerecetti, and F. Castellani, 324–338. Trento.
Scardino, C. 2007. *Gestaltung und Funktion der Reden bei Herodot und Thukydides/the Composition and Function of Speeches in Herodotus and Thucydides.* Berlin.
———. 2012. "Indirect Discourse in Herodotus and Thucydides." In *Herodotus and Thucydides*, ed. D. Lateiner and E. Foster, 67–96. Oxford.
Schadewaldt, W. 1938. *Iliasstudien.* Abhandlungen der philologisoh-historisohen Klasse der Sächsischen Akademie der Wissenschaften, Bd. 43. Nr. 6. Leipzig.
Schäfer, H. 1877. *De Nonnullarum Particularum apud Antiphontem Usu.* Göttingen.
Schank, R. C. 1995. *Tell Me a Story: Narrative and Intelligence.* Evanston.
Schank, R. C., and R. P. Abelson. 1977. *Scripts, Plans, Goals, and Understanding: An Inquiry into Human Knowledge Structures.* Hillsdale.

Schegloff, E. A. 1967. *The First Five Seconds: The Order of Conversational Openings*. Berkeley.

———. 1968. "Sequencing in Conversational Openings." *American Anthropologist* 70:1075–1095.

———. 1984. "On Some Gestures' Relation to Talk." In *Structures of Social Action*, ed. J. M. Atkinson and J. Heritage, 266–298. Cambridge.

———. 1987. "Recycled Turn Beginnings: A Precise Repair Mechanism in Conversation's Turn-Taking Organization." In *Talk and Social Organisation*, ed. G. Button and J. R. E. Lee, 70–85. Clevedon.

———. 1996. "Turn Organization: One Intersection of Grammar and Interaction." In Ochs et al. 1996:52–133. Cambridge.

———. 2001. "Discourse as an Interactional Achievement III: The Omnirelevance of Action." In *The Handbook of Discourse Analysis*, ed. D. Schiffrin, D. Tannen, and H. E. Hamilton, 229–249. Malden, MA.

———. 2006. "Interaction: The Infrastructure for Social Institutions, the Natural Ecological Niche for Language, and the Arena in Which Culture Is Enacted." In *Roots of Human Sociality: Culture, Cognition and Interaction*, ed. N. J. Enfield and S. C. Levinson, 70–96. Oxford.

———. 2007. *Sequence Organization in Interaction. A Primer in Conversation Analysis I.* Cambridge.

Schegloff, E. A., E. Ochs, and S. A. Thompson. 1996. "Introduction." In Ochs et al. 1996:1-51.

Schein, S. L. 2013. *Sophocles. Philoctetes*. Cambridge.

Schellenberg, R. S. 2009. "'They Spoke the Truest of Words': Irony in the Speeches of Herodotus's *Histories*." *Arethusa* 42:131–150.

Schenkeveld, D. M. 1964. *Studies in Demetrius On Style*. Amsterdam.

———. 1982. "Studies in the History of Ancient Linguistics I: ΣΥΝΔΕΣΜΟΙ ΥΠΟΘΕΤΙΚΟΙ AND Ο ΕΑΝ ΕΠΙΖΕΥΚΤΙΚΟΣ." *Mnemosyne* 35:248–268.

———. 1983. "Linguistic Theories in the Rhetorical Works of Dionysius of Halicarnassus." *Glotta* 61:67–94.

———. 1988. "From Particula to Particle—The Genesis of a Class of Words." In *L'héritage des Grammairiens Latins de l'Antiquité Aux Lumières : Actes Du Colloque de Chantilly 2-4 Septembre 1987*, ed. I. Rosier-Catach, 81–93. Paris.

———. 1994. "Scholarship and Grammar." In *La philologie Grecque à l'époque Hellénistique et Romaine*, ed. F. Montanari, 263–301. Geneva.

———. 1995. "The Linguistic Contents of Dionysius' Παραγγέλματα." In Law and Sluiter 1995:41–53.

Schepe, K. 1878. *De transitionis formulis quibus oratores Attici praeter Isocratem, Aeschinem, Demosthenemque utuntur*. Bückeburg.

Scheppers, F. 2011. *The Colon Hypothesis: Word Order, Discourse Segmentation and Discourse Coherence in Ancient Greek*. Brussels.

Schiffrin, D. 1987. *Discourse Markers*. Cambridge.

———. 1990. "Between Text and Context: Deixis, Anaphora, and the Meaning of *Then*." *Text* 10:245–270.

———. 1992. "Anaphoric *Then*: Aspectual Textual, and Epistemic Meaning." *Linguistics* 30:753–792.

———. 1994. *Approaches to Discourse*. Oxford.

———. 2006. "Discourse Marker Research and Theory: Revisiting *and*." In Fischer 2006:315–338. Amsterdam.

Schiffrin, D., A. De Fina, and A. Nylund, eds. 2010. *Telling Stories*. Washington, DC.

Schiffrin, D., D. Tannen, and H. E. Hamilton. 2008. *The Handbook of Discourse Analysis*. Malden, MA.

Schironi, F. 2010. "Technical Languages: Science and Medicine." In Bakker 2010:338–353.

Schleppegrell, M. 1990. "Paratactic 'Because.'" *Journal of Pragmatics* 16:291–306.

Schmerling, S. F. 1975. "Asymmetric Conjunction and Rules of Conversation." In Cole and Morgan 1975:211–231.

Schmid, C. 1905. *Homerische Studien I*. Landau

Schmidt, K. T. H. L. 1891. *De usu part. τε earumque quae cum τοι compositae sunt apud oratores Atticos*. Rostock.

Schmidt, K. E. A. 1859. *Beiträge zur Geschichte der Grammatik des Griechischen und des Lateinischen*. Halle.

Schneider, E. 1885. *Quaestionum Hippocratearum specimen*. Bonn.

Schneider, K. P., and A. Barron, eds. 2008. *Variational Pragmatics: A Focus on Regional Varieties in Pluricentric Languages*. Amsterdam.

Schneider, R., and M. Hartner. 2012. *Blending and the Study of Narrative: Approaches and Applications*. Narratologia 34. Berlin.

Schneidewin, F. W., and A. Nauck. 1861. *Sophocles. König Oedipus*. Berlin.

Schnyder, B. 1995. *Angst in Szene gesetzt: zur Darstellung der Emotionen auf der Bühne des Aischylos*. Tübingen.

Scholes, B. J, and R. J. Willis. 1990. "Prosodic and Syntactic Functions of Punctuation: A Contribution to the Study of Orality and Literacy." *Interchange* 21:13–20.

Schömann, G. F. 1831. *Isaei Orationes XI*. Grieswald.

———. 1862. *Die Lehre von den Redetheilen nach den Alten*. Berlin. https://books.google.lu/books?id=LmhCAAAAMAAJ&printsec=frontcover&hl=de#v=onepage&q&f=false.

Schonack, W. 1908. *Curae Hippocrateae*. Berlin.

Schöner, W. 1989. *Aristophanes. Die elf erhaltenen Komödien*. Vienna.

———. 1862. *Die Lehre von den Redetheilen nach den alten dargestellt und beurtheilt*. Berlin.

Schourup, L. 1982. *Common Discourse Particles in English: 'like', 'well', 'y'know'*. New York.

———. 1999. "Discourse Markers." *Lingua* 107:227–265.

———. 2011. "The Discourse Marker Now: A Relevance-Theoretic Approach." *Journal of Pragmatics* 43:2110–2129.

Schraut, J. 1847. *Die Griechischen Partikeln im Zusammenhange mit den ältesten Stämmen der Sprache.* Bd. 1: *μέν und δέ.* Neuss.

———. 1848. *Die Griechischen Partikeln im Zusammenhange mit den ältesten Stämmen der Sprache.* Bd. 2: *ἄν und κέν*. Neuss.

———. 1849. *Die Griechischen Partikeln im Zusammenhange mit den ältesten Stämmen der Sprache.* Bd. 3: *γέ, ἄρα, γάρ*. Neuss.

———. 1857. *Über die Bedeutung der Partikel γάρ in den scheinbar vorgeschobenen Sätzen.* Rastatt.

Schrickx, J. G. 2009. "Namque als Variante von Nam?" *Mnemosyne* 62:250–271.

———. 2010. "Die Partikel Nempe Diskurspragmatisch Neu Betrachtet." In *Latin Linguistics Today. Akten des 15. internationalen Kolloquiums zur lateinischen Linguistik Innsbruck, 4.-9. April 2009*, ed. P. Anreiter and M. Kienpointner, 613–624. Innsbruck.

———. 2011. *Lateinische Epistemische Partikeln: Nempe, Quippe, Scilicet, Videlicet Und Nimirum*. Leiden.

———. 2014. "Latin Commitment-Markers: *Scilicet* and *Videlicet*." In *Certainty—Uncertainty—and the Attitudinal Space in between*, ed. S. Cantarini, W. Abraham, and E. Leiss 285–296. Studies in Language Companion Series 165. Amsterdam and Philadelphia.

Schröder, O. 1927. *Aristophanes. Die Vögel. Erklärt von Theodor Kock. Neue Bearbeitung.* 4th ed. Berlin.

Schuren, L. 2015. *Shared Storytelling in Euripidean Stichomythia*. Leiden.

Schütz, Christian G. 1806 [1782]. *Henrici Hoogeveen Doctrina particularum Graecarum. Recensuit breviavit et auxit C. G. Schütz.* 2nd ed. Leipzig.

Schwarz-Friesel, M. 2013. *Sprache und Emotion*. 2nd ed. Tübingen.

Schweighaeuser, J. 1824. *Lexicon Herodoteum*. Strasbourg. Vol 2 available at https://www.digitale-sammlungen.de/de/view/bsb10236167?page=6 [1840 edition available at: https://archive.org/details/lexiconherodote03schwgoog/page/n14/mode/2up?view=theater.]

Schwyzer, E., and A. Debrunner. 1950. *Griechische Grammatik.* Bd. 2: *Syntax*. Munich.

Scodel, R. 2000. "Verbal Performance and Euripidean Rhetoric." In *Euripides and Tragic Theatre in the Late Fifth Century*, ed. M. J. Cropp, 129–144. Champaign.

———. 2012. "ἦ and Theory of Mind in the *Iliad*." In *Homer, gedeutet durch ein großes Lexikon: Akten des Hamburger Kolloquiums vom 6.-8. Oktober 2010 zum Abschluss des Lexikons des Frühgriechischen Epos*, ed. M. Meier-Brügger, 319–334. Berlin.

Scott, M., and C. Tribble. 2006. *Textual Patterns: Key Words and Corpus Analysis in Language Education*. Amsterdam.

Scott, W. C. 1974. *The Oral Nature of the Homeric Simile*. Leiden.

———. 2005. "The Patterning of the Similes in Book 2 of the *Iliad*." In *Approaches to Homer: Ancient and Modern.*, ed. R. J. Rabel, 21–54. Swansea.

———. 2009. *The Artistry of the Homeric Simile*. Hanover, NH.

Seaford, R. 1996. *Euripides. Bacchae*. Warminster.

Seager, J. 1829. *Hoogeveen's Greek Particles. Abridged and Translated into English*. London.

Searle, J. R. 1969. *Speech Acts*. Cambridge.

———. 1975. "Indirect Speech Acts." In Cole and Morgan 1975:59–82.

———. 1979. "A Taxonomy of Illocutionary Acts." In *Expression and Meaning: Studies in the Theory of Speech Acts*, 1–29. Cambridge.

Segal, C. 1986. *Pindar's Mythmaking: The Fourth Pythian Ode*. Princeton.

Segal, E. M., J. F. Duchan, and P. J. Scott. 1991. "The Role of Interclausal Connectives in Narrative Structuring: Evidence From Adults' Interpretations of Simple Stories." *Discourse Processes* 14:27–54.

Seiler, H. 1950. *Die Primären Griechischen Steigerungsformen*. Hamburg.

Seiler, J. 1908. "Wie 'gewinnen wir Homer die Art ab'?" *Zeitschrift für das Gymnasialwesen* 62:161–181.

Sekali, M. 2007. "'He's a Cop but He Isn't a Bastard'. An Enunciative Approach to Some Pragmatic Effects of the Coordinator *but*." In *Connectives as Discourse Landmarks*, ed. A. Celle and E. Huart, 155–175. Amsterdam.

Selkirk, E. O. 1984. *Phonology and Syntax: The Relation between Sound and Structure*. Cambridge, MA.

Selting, M. 1994. "Emphatic Speech Style—with Special Focus on the Prosodic Signalling of Heightened Emotive Involvement in Conversation." *Journal of Pragmatics* 22:375–408.

———. 1996. "On the Interplay of Syntax and Prosody in the Constitution of Turn-Constructional Units and Turns in Conversation." *Pragmatics* 6:357–388.

Selting, M., and E. Couper-Kuhlen, eds. 2001. *Studies in Interactional Linguistics*. Amsterdam.

Sens, A. 2000. "The Particle *Htoi* in Apollonian Narrative." In *Apollonius Rhodius*, ed. M. A. Harder, R. F. Regtuit, and G. C. Wakker, 173–193. Leuven.

Sernatinger, B. 1874. *De particula γάρ, partes I et II*. Rastatt.

Shalev, D. 2001. "Illocutionary Clauses Accompanying Questions in Greek Drama and Platonic Dialogue." *Mnemosyne* 54:531–561.

Shapiro, S. O. 1996. "Herodotus and Solon." *Classical Antiquity* 15:348–364.

———. 2000. "Proverbial Wisdom in Herodotus." *Transactions of the American Philological Association* 130:89–118.

Sherzer, J. 1982. "Poetic Structuring of Kuna Discourse: The Line." *Language in Society* 11:371–390.

Shipp, G. P. 1972. *Studies in the Language of Homer*. 2nd ed. Cambridge.

Shoaps, R. A. 2002. "'Pray Earnestly': The Textual Reconstruction of Personal Involvement in Pentecostal Prayer and Song." *Journal of Linguistic Anthropology* 12:34–71.

Shorey, P. 1907. "The Force of καίτοι." *The Classical Journal* 3:27–30.

———. 1919. "On δέ γε in Retort." *Classical Philology* 14:165–174.

———. 1926. “Statistics of Style in the Seventh Platonic Epistle (δ' οὖν).” *Classical Philology* 21:258.

———. 1928. “The Pathos and Humor of *Au*.” *Classical Philology* 23:285–287.

———. 1933. “On the *Erotikos* of Lysias in Plato’s *Phaedrus*.” *Classical Philology* 28:131–132.

Sicking, C. M. J. 1986. “Griekse Partikels: Definitie en Classificatie.” *Lampas* 19:125–141.

———. 1991. “The Distribution of Aorist and Present Tense Stem Forms in Greek, Especially in the Imperative.” *Glotta* 69:14–43, 154–170.

———. 1993. “Devices for Text Articulation in Lysias I and XII.” In Van Ophuijsen and Sicking 1993:1–66.

———. 1996a. “Aspect Choice: Time Reference or Discourse Function?” In *Two Studies in the Semantics of the Verb in Classical Greek*, ed. C. M. J. Sicking and P. Stork, 1–118. Leiden.

———. 1996b. “Partikels in Vragen bij Plato.” *Lampas* 29:446–463.

———. 1997. “Particles in Questions in Plato.” In Rijksbaron 1997:157–174.

Sideras, A. 1971. *Aeschylus Homericus: Untersuchungen zu den Homerismen der aischyleischen Sprache*. Göttingen.

Sidnell, J. 2007. “Comparative Studies in Conversation Analysis.” *Annual Review of Anthropology* 36:229–244.

———. 2010. *Conversation Analysis: An Introduction*. Malden, MA.

Sidnell, J., and N. J. Enfield. 2012. “Language Diversity and Social Action: A Third Locus of Linguistic Relativity.” *Current Anthropology* 53:302–333.

Siebenborn, E. 1976. *Die Lehre von der Sprachrichtigkeit und ihren Kriterien: Studien zur antiken normativen Grammatik*. Amsterdam.

Sier, K. 1988. *Die lyrischen Partien des Choephoren des Aischylos*. Stuttgart.

Silk, M. S. 1998. “Style, Voice and Authority in the Choruses of Greek Drama.” *Der Chor im antiken und modernen Drama*, ed. P. Riemer and B. Zimmermann, 1–26. Stuttgart.

———. 2010. “The Language of Greek Lyric Poetry.” In Bakker 2010:424–440.

Sinclair, J. M., and R. M. Coulthard. 1975. *Towards an Analysis of Discourse: The English Used by Teachers and Pupils*. London.

Skelton, R. 1949. *Modern English Punctuation*. London.

Sköries, U. 1998. “Features of a Blame Type Using *and*: An Analysis of an Example.” *Journal of Pragmatics* 30:49–58.

———. 1999. *Bedeutung und Funktion von and Als Dialogische Instruktion*. Frankfurt am Main.

Slater, N. W. 2002. *Spectator Politics: Metatheatre and Performance in Aristophanes*. Philadelphia.

Slater, W. J. 1969. *Lexicon to Pindar*. Berlin.

———. 1983. “Lyric Narrative: Structure and Principle.” *Classical Antiquity* 2:117–132.

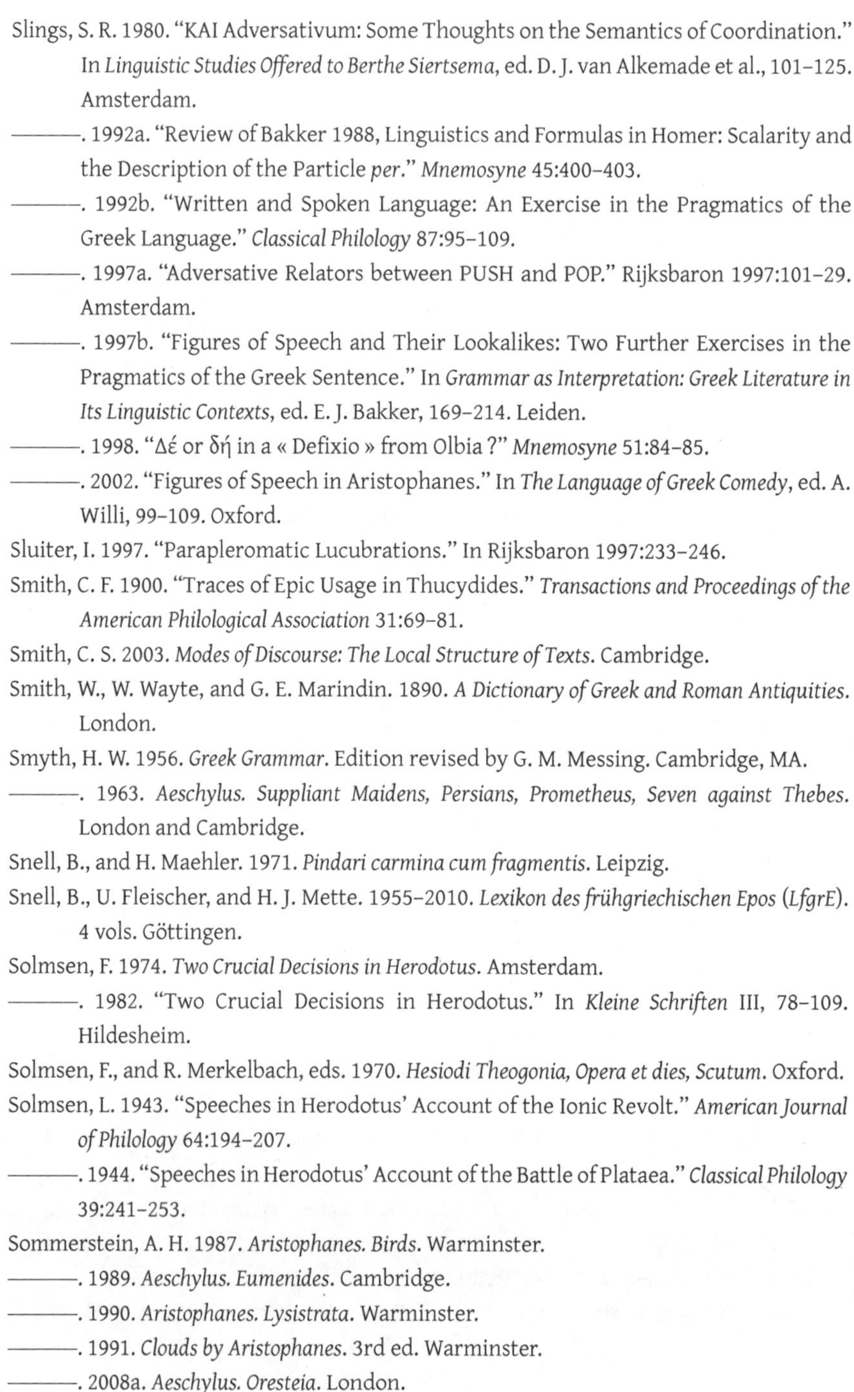

Slings, S. R. 1980. "KAI Adversativum: Some Thoughts on the Semantics of Coordination." In *Linguistic Studies Offered to Berthe Siertsema*, ed. D. J. van Alkemade et al., 101–125. Amsterdam.

———. 1992a. "Review of Bakker 1988, Linguistics and Formulas in Homer: Scalarity and the Description of the Particle *per*." *Mnemosyne* 45:400–403.

———. 1992b. "Written and Spoken Language: An Exercise in the Pragmatics of the Greek Language." *Classical Philology* 87:95–109.

———. 1997a. "Adversative Relators between PUSH and POP." Rijksbaron 1997:101–29. Amsterdam.

———. 1997b. "Figures of Speech and Their Lookalikes: Two Further Exercises in the Pragmatics of the Greek Sentence." In *Grammar as Interpretation: Greek Literature in Its Linguistic Contexts*, ed. E. J. Bakker, 169–214. Leiden.

———. 1998. "Δέ or δή in a « Defixio » from Olbia ?" *Mnemosyne* 51:84–85.

———. 2002. "Figures of Speech in Aristophanes." In *The Language of Greek Comedy*, ed. A. Willi, 99–109. Oxford.

Sluiter, I. 1997. "Parapleromatic Lucubrations." In Rijksbaron 1997:233–246.

Smith, C. F. 1900. "Traces of Epic Usage in Thucydides." *Transactions and Proceedings of the American Philological Association* 31:69–81.

Smith, C. S. 2003. *Modes of Discourse: The Local Structure of Texts*. Cambridge.

Smith, W., W. Wayte, and G. E. Marindin. 1890. *A Dictionary of Greek and Roman Antiquities*. London.

Smyth, H. W. 1956. *Greek Grammar*. Edition revised by G. M. Messing. Cambridge, MA.

———. 1963. *Aeschylus. Suppliant Maidens, Persians, Prometheus, Seven against Thebes*. London and Cambridge.

Snell, B., and H. Maehler. 1971. *Pindari carmina cum fragmentis*. Leipzig.

Snell, B., U. Fleischer, and H. J. Mette. 1955–2010. *Lexikon des frühgriechischen Epos* (*LfgrE*). 4 vols. Göttingen.

Solmsen, F. 1974. *Two Crucial Decisions in Herodotus*. Amsterdam.

———. 1982. "Two Crucial Decisions in Herodotus." In *Kleine Schriften* III, 78–109. Hildesheim.

Solmsen, F., and R. Merkelbach, eds. 1970. *Hesiodi Theogonia, Opera et dies, Scutum*. Oxford.

Solmsen, L. 1943. "Speeches in Herodotus' Account of the Ionic Revolt." *American Journal of Philology* 64:194–207.

———. 1944. "Speeches in Herodotus' Account of the Battle of Plataea." *Classical Philology* 39:241–253.

Sommerstein, A. H. 1987. *Aristophanes. Birds*. Warminster.

———. 1989. *Aeschylus. Eumenides*. Cambridge.

———. 1990. *Aristophanes. Lysistrata*. Warminster.

———. 1991. *Clouds by Aristophanes*. 3rd ed. Warminster.

———. 2008a. *Aeschylus. Oresteia*. London.

———. 2008b. *Aeschylus. Persians, Seven against Thebes, Suppliants, Prometheus Bound.* London.

———. 2010. *Aeschylean Tragedy*. Bristol.

Sorjonen, M.-L. 2001. *Responding in Conversation: A Study of Response Particles in Finnish.* Amsterdam.

Spencer-Datey, H. 2000. *Culturally Speaking: Managing Rapport Through Talk Across Cultures.* London.

Spengel, L. 1862. "τε in Antiphon." *Rheinisches Museum* 17:166–169.

Sperber, D., and D. Wilson. 1995 [1986]. *Relevance: Communication and Cognition*. 2nd ed. Oxford.

Spitzner, F. 1832. *Homeri Ilias*. Göttingen.

Sobolewski, S. 1893 "οὐδέ and καὶ οὐ." *Russische Philologische Rundschau* 2:48.

Squartini, M. 2013. "From TAM to Discourse: The Role of Information Status in North-Western Italian Già 'already.'" In *Discourse Markers and Modal Particles: Categorization and Description*, ed. L. Degand, B. Cornillie, and P. Pietrandrea, 163–190. Amsterdam.

Stadter, P. A., ed. 1973. *The Speeches in Thucydides*. Chapel Hill.

Stahl, H.-P. 1973. "Speeches and Course of Events in Book Six and Seven of Thucydides." In Stadter 1973:60-77.

———. 2012. "Herodotus and Thucydides on Blind Decisions Preceding Military Action." In *Thucydides and Herodotus*, ed. E. Foster and D. Lateiner. Oxford.

Stahl, J. M. 1902. "Über Eine Besondere Bedeutung von γάρ." *Rheinisches Museum* 52:1–7.

———. 1907. *Kritisch-Historische Syntax des griechischen Verbums der klassischen Zeit.* Heidelberg.

Stainton, R. J. 1994. "Using Non-Sentences: An Application of Relevance Theory." *Pragmatics & Cognition* 2:269–284.

Stalnaker, R. C. 1974. "Pragmatic Presupposition." In *Semantics and Philosophy*, ed. M. K. Muniz and P. K. Unger, 197–213. New York.

Stanford, W. B. 1958. *Aristophanes. The Frogs*. London.

———. 1963. *Sophocles. Ajax*. London.

———. 1983. *Greek Tragedy and the Emotions*. London.

Starkie, W. J. M. 1911. *Aristophanes. The Clouds*. London.

Steen, G. 2005. "Basic Discourse Acts: Toward a Psychological Theory of Discourse Segmentation." In *Cognitive Linguistics. Internal Dynamics and Interdisciplinary Interaction*, ed. F. J. Ruiz de Mendoza Ibáñez and M. S. Peña Cervel, 283–312. Berlin.

Steen, G. A. H. van. 2000. *Venom in Verse: Aristophanes in Modern Greece*. Princeton.

Stein, H. 1884. *Herodoti Historiae*. Bern.

Steiner, D. 2010. *Homer, Odyssey Books XVII-XVIII*. Cambridge.

Steinthal, H. 1863. *Geschichte der Sprachwissenschaft bei den Griechen und Römern: Mit besonderer Rücksicht auf die Logik*. Cambridge. https://play.google.com/books/reader?id=6gYJAAAAQAAJ&hl=en&pg=GBS.PA1.

Stenström, A.-B. 1994. *An Introduction to Spoken Interaction*. London.

———. 1998. "From Sentence to Discourse: Cos (because) in Teenage Talk." In Jucker and Ziv 1998:127–146.

Stephens, E. 1837. *A Treatise on the Greek Expletive Particles*. Oxford.

Stevens, P. T. 1971. *Euripides. Andromache*. Oxford.

———. 1976. *Colloquial Expressions in Euripides*. Wiesbaden.

Stinton, T. C. W. 1977. "Pause and Period in the Lyrics of Greek Tragedy." *The Classical Quarterly* 27:27–66.

Stivers, T., N. J. Enfield, and S. C. Levinson. 2007. "Person Reference in Interaction." In *Person Reference in Interaction: Linguistic, Cultural, and Social Perspectives*, ed. N. J. Enfield and T. Stivers, 1–20. Cambridge.

Stoddard, K. 2004. *The Narrative Voice in the Theogony of Hesiod*. Leiden.

Strassler, R. B. 1996. *The Landmark Thucydides*. With the translation of R. Crawley. New York.

Strauss Clay, J. 1983. *The Wrath of Athena: Gods and Men in the Odyssey*. Princeton.

———. 2011. *Homer's Trojan Theater: Space, Vision, and Memory in the Iliad*. Cambridge.

Streeck, J. 1995. "On Projection." In *Social Intelligence and Interaction: Expressions and Implications of the Social Bias in Human Intelligence*, ed. E. N. Goody, 87–110. Cambridge.

———. 2009. "Forward-Gesturing." *Discourse Processes* 46:161–179.

Streeck, J., and J. S. Jordan. 2009. "Projection and Anticipation: The Forward-Looking Nature of Embodied Communication." *Discourse Processes* 46:93–102.

Stroud, R. S. 1987. "'Wie es eigentlich gewesen' and Thucydides 2.48. 3." *Hermes* 115:379–382.

———. 1994. "Thucydides and Corinth." *Chiron* 24:267–304.

Sturm, J. 1882. *Geschichtliche Entwickelung der Constructionen mit ΠΡΙΝ*. Würzburg.

Sturz, F. W. 1801–1804. *Lexicon Xenophonteum*. 4 vols. Leipzig.

Vol. 1: https://play.google.com/store/books/details?id=hR0TAAAAQAAJ&rdid=book-hR0TAAAAQAAJ&rdot=1;

Vol. 2: https://www.digitale-sammlungen.de/de/view/bsb10238720?page=7;

Vol. 3: https://archive.org/details/lexiconxenophon00sturgoog/page/n6/mode/2up;

Vol. 4: https://play.google.com/store/books/details/Friedrich_Wilhelm_Sturz_Lexicon_Xenophonteum?id=9B0TAAAAQAAJ.

Stürmer, F. 1912. "Über die Partikel δή bei Homer." *Berliner Philologische Wochenschrift* 32:1844–1845.

Stvan, L. S. 2006. "Diachronic Change in the Discourse Markers Why and Say in American English." In *Corpus Linguistics*, ed. A. M. Hornero Corsico, M. J. Luzón, and S. Murillo Ornat, 61–76. Bern.

Sudhoff, S. 2012. "Fokuspartikelinventare des Niederländischen und Deutschen." In *Nicht-flektierende Wortarten*, ed. B. Rothstein, 203–223. Berlin.

Svartvik, J. 1980. "Well in Conversation." In *Studies in English Linguistics for Randolph Quirk*, ed. Greenbaum S., G. N. Leech, and J. Svartvik, 167–177. London.

Swan, T. 1988. *Sentence Adverbials in English: A Synchronic and Diachronic Investigation*. Oslo.

Sweetser, E. 1990. *From Etymology to Pragmatics. Metaphorical and Cultural Aspects of Semantic Structure*. Cambridge.

Swift, L. A. 2010. *The Hidden Chorus: Echoes of Genre in Tragic Lyric*. Oxford.

Swiggers, P., and A. Wouters, eds. 2002. *Grammatical Theory and Philosophy of Language in Antiquity*. Leuven.

———, eds. 2003. *Syntax in Antiquity*. Leuven.

Tabachovitz, D. 1943. *Études sur le Grec de la basse époque*. Uppsala.

———. 1951. *Homerische εἰ-Sätze: eine sprachpsychologische Studie*. Lund.

Taboada, M. 2004. *Building Coherence and Cohesion: Task-Oriented Dialogue in English and Spanish*. Amsterdam.

———. 2006. "Discourse Markers as Signals (or Not) of Rhetorical Relations." *Journal of Pragmatics* 38:567–592.

Takahara, P. O. 1998. "Pragmatic Functions of the English Discourse Marker Anyway and Its Corresponding Contrastive Japanese Discourse Markers." In Jucker and Ziv 1998:327–351.

Takanashi, H. 2011. "Complementary Stylistic Resonance in Japanese Play Framing." *Pragmatics* 21:231–264.

Talmy, L. 1995. "Narrative Structure in a Cognitive Framework." In *Deixis in Narrative: A Cognitive Science Perspective*, ed. J. F. Duchan, G. A. Bruder, and L. E. Hewitt, 421–460. Hillsdale, NJ.

Tannen, D. 1984. *Conversational Style: Analyzing Talk among Friends*. Norwood.

Tannen, D., and C. Kakava. 1992. "Power and Solidarity in Modern Greek Conversation: Disagreeing to Agree." *Journal of Modern Greek Studies* 10:11–34.

Tanskanen, S. K. 2006. *Collaborating towards Coherence: Lexical Cohesion in English Discourse*. Amsterdam.

Taplin, O. 1977. "Did Greek Dramatists Write Stage Instructions?" *Proceedings of the Cambridge Philological Society* 23:121–132.

———. 1978. *Greek Tragedy in Action*. London.

———. 1986. "Fifth-Century Tragedy and Comedy: A Synkrisis." *Journal of Hellenic Studies* 106:163–174.

———. 1989. *The Stagecraft of Aeschylus: The Dramatic Use of Exits and Entrances in Greek Tragedy*. Oxford.

Tarriño Ruiz, E. 2009. "Adverbios Y Partículas." In *Sintaxis Del Latín Clásico*, ed. J. M. Baños, 349–374. Madrid.

Tate, J. 1956. "Review: Greek Particles." *The Classical Review* n.s. 6:125–126.

Taylor, A. 1994. "The Change from SOV to SVO in Ancient Greek." *Language Variation and Change* 6:1–37.

———. 1996. "A Prosodic Account of Clitic Position in Ancient Greek." In *Approaching Second: Second Position Clitics and Related Phenomena*, ed. A. L. Halpern and A. M. Zwicky, 477–503. Stanford.

Taylor, D. J. 1987. "Rethinking the History of Language Science in Classical Antiquity." In *The History of Linguistics in the Classical Period*, ed. D. J. Taylor, 1–16. Amsterdam.

———, ed. 1987. *The History of Linguistics in the Classical Period*. Amsterdam.

Terry, R. B. 1995. *A Discourse Analysis of First Corinthians*. Dallas.

Teuffel, W. S., and N. Wecklein. 1901. *Aeschylos' Perser*. Leipzig.

Theodoropoulou, M. 2012. "The Emotion Seeks to Be Expressed: Thoughts from a Linguist's Point of View." In Chaniotis 2012:433–468. Stuttgart.

Thesleff, H. 1954. *Studies on Intensification in Early and Classical Greek*. Leipzig.

Thiel, H. van. 1996. *Homeri Ilias*. Hildesheim.

Thiemann, C. 1881. "Über den Gebrauch der Partikel δή und ihre Bedeutung bei Homer." *Zeitschrift für das Gymnasialwesen* 35:530–534.

Thiersch, F. 1826. *Griechische Grammatik vorzüglich des homerischen Dialektes*. 3rd ed. Leipzig.

———. 1852. "Disquisitiones de analogiae Graecae capitibus minus cognitis I." *Abhandlungen der Philosophisch-Philologischen Classe der königlich bayerischen Akademie der Wissenschaften* 6:377–454.

———. 1855. "Disquisitiones analogiae Graecae capitibus minus cognitis II." *Abhandlungen der Philosophisch-Philologischen Classe der königlich bayerischen Akademie der Wissenschaften* 7:309–388.

Thomas, F. W. 1894. "ἤδη and δή in Homer." *Journal of Philology* 23:81–115.

Thomas, J. 1995. *Meaning in Interaction*. London.

Thompson, S. A. 1983. "Grammar and Discourse: The English Detached Participial Clause." In *Discourse Perspectives on Syntax*, ed. F. Klein-Andreu, 43–65. New York.

Thompson, S. A., and W. C. Mann. 1988. "Rhetorical Structure Theory: Toward a Functional Theory of Text Organization." *Text* 8:243–281.

Thorndyke, P. W. 1977. "Cognitive Structures in Comprehension and Memory of Narrative Discourse." *Cognitive Psychology* 9:77–110.

Thrall, M. E. 1962. *Greek Particles in the New Testament: Linguistic and Exegetical Studies*. Leiden.

Thumb, A., and E. Kieckers. 1932. *Handbuch der griechischen Dialekte*. 2nd ed. Heidelberg.

Thumiger, C. 2013. "Mad Eros and Eroticized Madness in Tragedy." In Sanders et al. 2013:27–40.

Thummer, E. 1969. *Pindar. Die Isthmischen Gedichte*. Heidelberg.

Thyresson, I. L. 1977. *The Particles in Epicurus*. Lund.

Tichy, E. 2015. "*Ilias* Diachronica Eta–*Ilias* Diachronica Pi (*Iliad* 7 to 16)." FreiDok—University of Freiburg. https://www.freidok.uni-freiburg.de/pers/15752.

Titrud, K. 1991. "The Overlooked Καί in the Greek New Testament." *Notes on Translation* 5:1–28.

Todd, O. J. 1932. *Index Aristophaneus*. Cambridge, MA.

Todorov, T., W. Empson, J. Cohen, F. Rigolot, and G. Genette. 1979. *Sémantique de La Poésie*. Paris.

Tofilski, L. 2002. "Modality in Pindar's Odes: Study of Pragmatic-Systematic Functions of ἄν/κε(ν) Particle with the Optative in the Main Clause in Greek." *Eos* 89:353–360.

Tomlin, R. S. 1997. "Mapping Conceptual Representations into Linguistic Representations: The Role of Attention in Grammar." In *Language and Conceptualization*, ed. E. Pederson and J. Nuyts, 162–189. Cambridge.

Tompkins, D. P. 1972. "Stylistic Characterization in Thucydides: Nicias and Alcibiades." *Yale Classical Studies* 22:181–214.

———. 2013. "The Language of Pericles." In *Thucydides Between History and Literature*, ed. A. Tsakmakis and M. Tamiolaki, 447–464. Berlin.

Torck, D. M. F. 1996. *Aspects de la Causalité Discursive en Français Oral Contemporain*. PhD diss., VU University Amsterdam.

Tournier, E. 1833. "Sur la signification de quelques particules Grecques." *Revue de Philologie* 7:33–44, 133–139.

Traglia, A., ed. 1974. *Marcus Terentius Varro. Opere*. Turin.

Traugott, E. Closs. 1986. "On the Origins of 'AND' and 'BUT' Connectives in English." *Studies in Language* 10:137–150.

———. 2007. "Discussion Article: Discourse Markers, Modal Particles, and Contrastive Analysis, Synchronic and Diachronic." *Catalan Journal of Linguistics* 6:139–157.

Traugott, E. Closs., and R. B. Dasher. 2002. *Regularity in Semantic Change*. Cambridge.

Traugott, E. Closs., and G. Trousdale. 2013. *Constructionalization and Constructional Changes*. Oxford.

Trenkner, S. 1960. *Le Style καί dans le Récit Attique Oral*. Assen.

Truckenbrodt, H. 2004. "Zur Strukturbedeutung von Interrogativsätzen." *Linguistische Berichte* 199:313–350.

Truss, L. 2003. *Eats, Shoots & Leaves: The Zero Tolerance Approach to Punctuation*. London.

Tsagalis, C. 2010. "The Dynamic Hypertext: Lists and Catalogues in the Homeric Epics." *Trends in Classics* 2:323–347.

———. 2012. *From Listeners to Viewers: Space in the Iliad*. Cambridge, MA.

Tsakmakis, A. 2010. "On the Meaning and Uses of γε in Comic Conversation." In *Παραχορήγημα* II, ed. G. M. Sifakis and S. Tsitsiridis, 345–359.

Tucker, T. G. 1906. *The Frogs of Aristophanes*. London.

———. 1908. *Aeschylus. The Seven against Thebes*. Cambridge.

Turner, F., and E. Pöppel. 1983. "The Neural Lyre: Poetic Meter, the Brain, and Time." *Poetry* 142:277–307.

Turner, M. 1996. *The Literary Mind*. New York.

Txurruka, I. G. 2003. "The Natural Language Conjunction *and*." *Linguistics and Philosophy* 26:255–285.

Urgelles-Coll, M. 2010. *The Syntax and Semantics of Discourse Markers*. London.

Usener, H. 1878. "Grammatische Bemerkungen. VII δὴ ἄν." *Neue Jahrbücher für Philologie und Pädagogik* 48:66–67.

Uthoff, H. 1884. *Quaestiones Hippocrateae*. Marburg.

Vahlen, J. 1885. "Appositional γάρ." In *Aristotelis de Arte Poetica Liber: tertiis curis recognovit et adnotatione critica auxit*, ed. J. Vahlen, 99–102. 3rd ed. Leipzig.

Valdmets, A. 2013. "Modal Particles, Discourse Markers, and Adverbs with Lt-Suffix in Estonian." In *Discourse Markers and Modal Particles: Categorization and Description*, ed. L. Degand, B. Cornillie, and P. Pietrandrea, 107–132. Amsterdam.

Vandelanotte, L. 2009. *Speech and Thought Representation in English: A Cognitive-Functional Approach*. Berlin.

Vandeweghe, W. 1992. *Perspektivische evaluatie in het Nederlands. De partikels van de AL/NOG/PAS-groep*. Ghent.

Vannicelli, P. 2017. *Erodoto. Le Storie. Libro VII*. Milan.

Vara, J. 1974. "Huella de H Procedente de S en la *Iliada*, y el Origen de la Épica." *Emerita: boletín de linguística y filología clásica* 42:287–304.

Vatri, A. 2012. "The Physiology of Ancient Greek Reading." *The Classical Quarterly* 62:633–647.

Venneman, T. 1975. "Topic, Sentence Accent, and Ellipsis: A Proposal for Their Formal Treatment." In *Formal Semantics of Natural Language*, ed. E.L. Keenan, 313–328. Cambridge.

Verdenius, W. J. 1947. "Notes on the Presocratics." *Mnemosyne*, ser. 3, 13:271–289.

———. 1955. "Notes on Hippocrates 'Airs Waters Places.'" *Mnemosyne*, ser. 4, 8:14–18.

———. 1956. "Review of Denniston 1954." *Mnemosyne* 9:248–252.

———. 1974. "Inceptive δέ again." *Mnemosyne* 27:173–174.

———. 1975. "Adversative καί Again." *Mnemosyne* 28:188–190.

———. 1982. "Pindar's Second *Isthmian Ode*: A Commentary." *Mnemosyne* 35:1–37.

Verdenius, W. J., and J. H. Waszink. 1946. *Aristotle on Coming-to-Be and Passing-away: Some Aomments*. Leiden.

Verhagen, A. 2005. *Constructions of Intersubjectivity: Discourse, Syntax and Cognition*. Oxford.

Vermeule, E. 1979. *Aspects of Death in Early Greek Art and Poetry*. Berkeley.

Vernant, J.-P., and P. E. Vidal-Naquet. 1986. *Mythe et Tragédie en Grèce Ancienne*. Paris.

Verrall, A. W. 1881. *The Medea of Euripides*. London.

Verschueren, J. 1999. *Understanding Pragmatics*. London.

Vidal-Naquet, P. E., and A. Szegedy-Maszak. 1986. "Land and Sacrifice in the *Odyssey*: A Study of Religious and Mythical Meanings." In *The Black Hunter: Forms of Thought and Forms of Society in the Greek World*, 15–38. Baltimore.

Viger, F. 1752 [1627]. *De Praecipuis Graecae Dictionis Idiotismis Liber*. Leiden. https://books.google.co.uk/books?id=pw5ZAAAAcAAJ&pg=PA7&lpg=PA7&dq=vigerus+idiotismis+1627&source=bl&ots=kmuzoTxmg3&sig=2-7XnvTGdVf3YGdsXOmE_GRTnU&hl=en&sa=X&ei=fKSzVPb0E4j3O_7pgNAD&ved=0CEYQ6AEwBw#v=onepage&q=vigerus%20idiotismis%201627&f=false.

———. 1834. *De Praecipuis Graecae Dictionis Idiotismis Liber cum Animadversionibus H. Hoogevenii, et I.c. Zeunii. Ed. et Annotationes Addidit G. Hermannus*. 4th ed. Leipzig.

Viljamaa, T. 2003. "Colon and Comma. Dionysius of Halicarnassus on the Sentence Structure." Swiggers and Wouters 2003:163–178.

Villa, J. de la. 2000. "La subordinación en griego antiguo: análisis y perspectivas." In *Actas del X Congreso Español de Estudios Clásicos* I, ed. E. Crespo and M. J. Barrios, 117–165. Madrid.

Visconti, J. 2009. "From 'Textual' to 'Interpersonal': On the Diachrony of the Italian Particle Mica." *Journal of Pragmatics* 41:937–950.

Visser, E. 1987. *Homerische Versifikationstechnik: Versuch einer Rekonstruktion*. Frankfurt.

Visvardi, E. 2015. *Emotion in Action: Thucydides and the Tragic Chorus*. Leiden.

Viti, C. 2006. "And in the Early Indo-European Languages." *Archivio Glottologico Italiano* 91:129–165.

———. 2008. "The Meanings of Coordination in the Early Indo-European Languages." *Revue de Sémantique et Pragmatique* 24:35–64.

Voloshinov, V. N. 1973 [1929]. *Marxism and the Philosophy of Language*. New York.

Voutilainen, L., P. Henttonen, M. Kahri, M. Kivioja, N. Ravaja, and M. Sams. 2014. "Affective Stance, Ambivalence, and Psychophysiological Responses during Conversational Storytelling." *Journal of Pragmatics* 68:1–24.

Waanders, F. M. J. 1983. *The History of Telos and Teleō in Ancient Greek*. Amsterdam.

———. 1997. "Particulars of Some Proto-Indo-European Particles." In Rijksbaron 1997:269–274.

Wace, A. J. B., and F. H. H. Stubbings. 1962. *A Companion to Homer*. London.

Wackernagel, J. 1892. "Über ein Gesetz der indogermanischen Wortstellung." *Indogermanische Forschungen* 1:333–436.

———. 1893. *Beiträge zur Lehre vom griechischen Akzent*. Basel.

———. 1895. "Miszellen zur griechischen Grammatik." *Zeitschrift für vergleichende Sprachforschung* 33:1-62.

———. 1916. "Sprachliche Untersuchungen zu Homer." *Glotta* 7:161–319.

———. 1920. *Vorlesungen über Syntax: Mit besonderer berücksichtigung von Griechisch, Lateinisch und Deutsch*. Basel.

Wähdel, H. 1869. *Über Bedeutung und Gebrauch der Partikel οὖν beim Aristophanes*. Stralsund.

Wakker, G. C. 1994. *Conditions and Conditionals: An Investigation of Ancient Greek*. Amsterdam.

———. 1995. "'Welaan dan dus nu.' Partikels in Sophocles." *Lampas* 28:250–270.

———. 1996. "The Discourse Function of Particles. Some Observations on the Use of *man/mhn* in Theocritus." In *Hellenistica Groningana*. Bd. 2: *Theocritus*, ed. M.A. Harder, R.F. Regtuit, and G.C. Wakker, 247–63. Groningen.

———. 1997a. "Emphasis and Affirmation: Some Aspects of μην in Tragedy." In Rijksbaron 1997:209–231.

———. 1997b. "Modal Particles and Different Points of View in Herodotus and Thucydides." In *Grammar as Interpretation. Greek Literature in Its Linguistic Contexts*, ed. E. J. Bakker, 215–250. Leiden.

———. 2001. "Le problème d'ἔτι μέν avec Aoriste." *Syntaktika* 22:1–14.

———. 2002. "Une première description de ἤδη chez Xénophon." *Syntaktika* 23:1-14.

———. 2009a. *Daarom dan dus. Kleine woorden, grote effecten*. Groningen.

———. 2009b. "'Well I Will Now Present My Arguments.' Discourse Cohesion Marked by *Oun* and *Toinun* in Lysias." In Bakker and Wakker 2009:63–81.

Wälchli, B. 2005. *Co-Compounds and Natural Coordination*. Oxford.

Walker, A. D. 1993. "Enargeia and the Spectator in Greek Historiography." *Transactions of the American Philological Association* 123:353–377.

Walrod, M. 2006. "The Marker is the Message: The Influence of Discourse Markers and Particles on Textual Meaning." Presented at the Tenth International Conference on Austronesian Linguistics (10ICAL). Palawan, January 17–20.

Walsh, T. R. 2005. *Fighting Words and Feuding Words: Anger and the Homeric Poems*. Lanham, MD.

Waring, H. Z. 2003. "'Also' as a Discourse Marker: Its Use in Disjunctive and Disaffiliative Environments." *Discourse Studies* 5:415–436.

Waters, K. H. 1966. "The Purpose of Dramatisation in Herodotos." *Historia* 15:157–171.

Wathelet, P. 1964. "Mycénien et grec d'Homère, 2: La particule καί." *L'antiquité Classique* 33:10–44.

———. 1997. "Les particules *ke(n)* et *an* dans les formules de l'épopée Homérique." In Rijksbaron 1997:247–268.

Watkins, C. 1977. "À propos de ΜΗΝΙΣ." *Bulletin de la société de linguistique de Paris* 72:187–209.

Watts, R. J. 1989. "Taking the Pitcher to the Well." *Journal of Pragmatics* 18:203–231.

Weber, H. 1864. *Die dorische Partikel Ka: Ein Beitrag zu der Lehre von den griechischen Dialekten*. Halle.

———. 1884. "γάρ." *Philologische Rundschau* 4:1078.

Wecklein, N. 1885. *Ausgewählte Tragödien des Euripides*. Bd. 4: *Hippolytos*. Leipzig.

———. 1902. *Aeschylus. Die Schutzflehenden*. Leipzig.

———. 1903. *Euripides. Bakchen*. 2nd ed. Leipzig.

Wehr, J. 1869. *Quaestiones Aristophaneae. Pars I, De Particularum Nonnullarum Usu*. Göttingen.

Wells, J. B. 2009. *Pindar's Verbal Art: An Ethnographic Study of Epinician Style*. Washington, DC.

Wennerstrom, A. K. 2001. *The Music of Everyday Speech: Prosody and Discourse Analysis*. Oxford.

Wentzel, E. 1847. *Über den Gebrauch der Partikel τε bei Homer*. Glogau.

Werkhofer, K. T. 1992. "Traditional and Modern Views: The Social Constitution and the Power of Politeness." In *Politeness in Language: Studies in Its History, Theory and Practice*, ed. R. J. Watts, S. Ide, and K. Ehlich, 155–199. Berlin.

Werres, J. 1936. *Die Beteuerungsformeln in der attischen Komödie*. Bonn.

West, M. L. 1966. *Hesiod. Theogony*. Oxford.

———. 1990. "Colloquialisms and Naïve Style in Aeschylus." In *Owls to Athens: Essays on Classical Subjects Presented to Sir Kenneth Dover*, ed. E. M. Craik, 3–12. Oxford.

———. 1999. *Homeri Ilias*. 2 vols. Berlin.

Westlake, H. D. 1941. "Nicias in Thucydides." *Classical Quarterly* 35:58–65.

———. 1968. *Individuals in Thucydides*. Cambridge.

Wetzell, C. 1879. *Beiträge zu dem Gebrauche einiger Partikeln bei Antiphon*. Frankfurt am Main.

Weydt, H. 1969. *Abtönungspartikel: Die deutschen Modalwörter und ihre französischen Entsprechungen*. Bad Homburg.

———. 1979. *Die Partikeln der deutschen Sprache*. Berlin.

———. 1983. *Partikeln und Interaktion*. Tübingen.

———, ed. 1989. *Sprechen mit Partikeln*. Berlin.

Weydt, H., and K.-H. Ehlers. 1987. *Partikel-Bibliographie Internationale Sprachenforschung zu Partikeln und Interjektionen*. Frankfurt.

Widdowson, H. G. 1979. "Rules and Procedures in Discourse Analysis." In *The Development of Conversation and Discourse*, ed. T. Myers, 61–71. Edinburgh.

———. 1995. "Discourse Analysis: A Critical View." *Language and Literature* 4:157–172.

Wierzbicka, A. 1986a. "A Semantic Metalanguage for the Description and Comparison of Illocutionary Meanings." *Journal of Pragmatics* 10:67–107.

———. 1986b. "Introduction." *Journal of Pragmatics* 10:519–534.

———. 1992. "The Semantics of Interjection." *Journal of Pragmatics* 18:159–192.

———. 1999. *Emotions Across Languages and Cultures: Diversity and Universals*. Cambridge.

———. 2006. *English: Meaning and Culture*. Oxford.

———. 2010. *Experience, Evidence, and Sense: The Hidden Cultural Legacy of English*. Oxford.

Wiesner, J. 1999. "Appendix: ausführliche Darstellung der koordinierenden und nuancierenden Partikeln." In *Repetitorium des griechischen Syntax*, ed. H. Menge, 247–364. 10th ed. Darmstadt.

Wilamowitz-Moellendorff, U. von. 1895. *Euripides. Herakles*. 2nd ed. Berlin.

———. 1927. *Aristophanes. Lysistrate*. Berlin.

Wiles, D. 2007. *Mask and Performance in Greek Tragedy: From Ancient Festival to Modern Experimentation*. Cambridge.

———. 2008. "The Poetics of the Mask in Old Comedy." In *Performance, Iconography, Reception: Studies in Honour of Oliver Taplin*, ed. M. Revermann and P. Wilson, 374–392. Oxford.

Wilkins, J. 1993. *Euripides, Heraclidae*. Oxford.

Willi, A. 2003. "Sophistic Innovations." In *The Languages of Aristophanes: Aspects of Linguistic Variation in Classical Attic Greek*, 118–156. Oxford.

———. 2010a. "Register Variation." In Bakker 2010:297–310.

———. 2010b. "The Language of Old Comedy." In *Brill's Companion to the Study of Greek Comedy*, ed. G. W. Dobrov, 471–510. Leiden.

———. 2017. "Register Variation and Tense/Aspect/Mood Categories in Ancient Greek: Problems and Perspectives." In *Variation and Change in Ancient Greek Tense, Aspect and Modality*, ed. K. Bentein, M. Janse, and J. Soltic, 261–286. Leiden.

Willmott, J. C. 2007. *The Moods of Homeric Greek*. Cambridge.

———. 2009. "Modality of English Conditional Sentences: The Evidence of Ancient Greek." In *Studies on English Modality*, ed. R. Facchinetti and A. Tsangalidis, 209–228.

———. 2011. "*Outis* and What He Can Tell Us About Negation in Homeric Greek." In *Ratio et Res Ipsa: Classical Essays Presented by Former Pupils to James Diggle on His Retirement*, ed. P. Millett, S. P. Oakley, and R. J. E. Thompson, 63–80. Cambridge.

Willms, L. 2014. *Transgression, Tragik und Metatheater: Versuch einer Neuinterpretation des antiken Dramas*. Tübingen.

Wills, J. 1993. "Homeric Particle Order." *Historische Sprachforschung* 106:61–81.

Wilson, J. C. 1909. "On the Use of ἀλλ' ἤ in Aristotle." *Classical Quarterly* 3:121–124.

Wilson, D., and D. Sperber. 1992. "On verbal irony." *Lingua* 87:53–76.

———. 2004. "Relevance Theory." In *Handbook of Pragmatics*, ed. G. Ward and L. R. Horn, 607–632. Oxford.

———. 2012a. "Linguistic Form and Relevance." In *Meaning and Relevance*, 149–168. Cambridge.

———. 2012b. *Meaning and Relevance*. Cambridge.

Wilson, N. G. 2007. *Aristophanes. Fabulae*. Oxford.

———. 2012. *Meaning and Relevance*. Cambridge.

Winer, G. B. 1867. *Grammatik des neutestamentischen Sprachidioms*. 7th ed. Leipzig.

Wingo, E. O. 1972. *Latin Punctuation in the Classical Age*. The Hague.

Winograd, E., and V. E. Church. 1988. "Role of Spatial Location in Learning Face-Name Associations." *Memory & Cognition* 16:1–7.

Winter, K. 2014. *Artificia mali. Das Böse als Kunstwerk in Senecas Rachetragödien*. Heidelberg.

Wittgenstein, L. 1953. *Philosofische Untersuchungen*. Oxford.

Wolferen, A. J. van. 2003. "Vertelde en gespeelde wereld: taalkundige notities bij de openingen van Euripides' tragedies." PhD diss., VU University Amsterdam.

Worman, N. 1999. "The Ties That Bind: Transformations of Costume and Connection in Euripides' *Heracles*." *Ramus: Critical Studies in Greek and Roman Literature* 28:89–107.

———. 2012. "Oedipus Abuser: *Ge* and Insult in the Exchange with Teiresias (OT 316-462)." Presentation at *Word Play: Ancient Greek Drama and the Role of Particles*, Heidelberg, November 16–18.

———. n.d. "Deixis and the Demarcation of Violent Characters in Greek Tragedy."

Wouden, T. van der, and A. Foolen. 2015. "Dutch Particles in the Right Periphery." *Final Particles*, ed. S. Hancil, A. Haselow, and M. Post, 221–247. Berlin. Published online in 2011 at Tonvanderwouden.nl: https://pure.knaw.nl/ws/files/1663443/fipa_2011_06.pdf.

Wouk, F. 2001. "Solidarity in Indonesian Conversation: The Discourse Marker Ya." *Journal of Pragmatics* 33:171–191.

Wouters, A. 1979. *The Grammatical Papyri from Graeco-Roman Egypt: Contributions to the Study of the "Ars Grammatica" in Antiquity*. Brussels.

———. 1995. "The Grammatical Papyri and the *Techne Grammatike* of Dionysius Thrax." In Law and Sluiter 1995:95–109.

Wray, A., and M. Perkins. 2000. "The Functions of Formulaic Language: An Integrated Model." *Language & Communication* 20:1–28.

Wright, M. 2013. "Tragedy and quotation: between performance and textuality." Paper presented at the Classical Association Annual Meeting, Department of Classics, University of Reading, 3–6 April 2013.

Xanthou, M. 2007. "Το ασύνδετο στους επινίκους του Πινδάρου και του Βακχυλίδη: η διερεύνηση της λειτουργίας του ως ρητορικού και αφηγηματικού τρόπου." PhD diss., Aristotle University of Thessaloniki.

Yaginuma, S. 1995. "Did Thucydides Write for Readers or Hearers?" In *The Passionate Intellect*, ed. L. Ayres, 131–142. London.

Yang, L. C. 2006. "Integrating Prosodic and Contextual Cues in the Interpretation of Discourse Markers." In Fischer 2006:265–298.

Yilmaz, E. 2004. *A Pragmatic Analysis of Turkish Discourse Particles: YANİ, İŞTE, and ŞEY*. Ankara.

Young, D. 1974. *Aeschylus. The Oresteia*. Norman.

Yus, F. 2010. "Relevance Theory." In *The Oxford Handbook of Linguistic Analysis*, ed. B. Heine and H. Narrog, 679–701. Oxford.

Zakowski, S. 2014. "Inference and metarepresentation: Ancient Greek ἦ που as a constraint on higher-level explicatures." *Journal of Pragmatics* 74:109–128.

———. 2017. From coherence to procedures: a relevance-theoretic approach to the discourse markers δέ, γάρ and οὖν in Basil the Great's *Hexaemeron*, Gregory of Nazianzus's *Invectives Against Julian* and Heliodorus's *Aethiopica*. PhD diss., Ghent University.

Zanetto, G., and D. Del Corno. 1987. *Aristofane. Gli Uccelli* [text and commentary by Zanetto, Italian translation by Del Corno]. Milan.

Zeevat, H., and K. Jasinskaja. 2007. "'And' as an Additive Particle." In *Language, Representation and Reasoning: Memorial Volume to Isabel Gómez Txurruka*, ed. M. Aurnague, K. Korta, and J. M. Larrazabal, 315–340. Vitoria-Gasteiz.

Zima, E., G. Brône, K. Feyaerts, and P. Sambre. 2008. "Resonance Activation in Interactional Parliamentary Discourse." In *Linearisation and Segmentation in Discourse: Multidisciplinary Approaches to Discourse 2008 (MAD 08), Feb 20-23 2008, Lysebu, Oslo*, ed. W. Ramm and C. Fabricius-Hansen, 137–147. Oslo.

Zimmermann, E. 2005. *Focalization in Thucydides' Sicilian Expedition*. PhD diss., University of North Carolina, Chapel Hill.

Zoran, G. 1984. "Towards a Theory of Space in Narrative." *Poetics Today* 5:309–335.

Zwicky, A. M. 1985. "Clitics and Particles." *Language* 61:283–305.

Zycha, J. 1885. "Der Gebrauch von ἐπεί, ἐπείπερ, ἐπειδή, ἐπειδήπερ." *Wiener Studien* 7:82–115.

PARTICLE INDEX

Particle Index

See also the Table of Contents for sections and subsections including individual particles and particle combinations in the titles.

Index of Subjects

Index Locorum